KU-333-575

WOLVERHAMPTON LIBRARIES
FOR REFERENCE ONLY

X400 000020 1832

NOTABLE TWENTIETH-CENTURY SCIENTISTS

NOTABLE TWENTIETH-CENTURY SCIENTISTS

VOLUME 2 F-K

Emily J. McMurray, Editor

Jane Kelly Kosek and Roger M. Valade III, Associate Editors

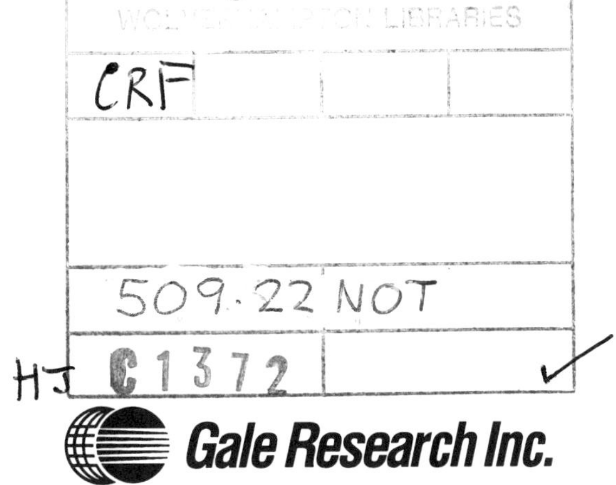

Gale Research Inc.

An International Thomson Publishing Company

NEW YORK • LONDON • BONN • BOSTON • DETROIT • MADRID
MELBOURNE • MEXICO CITY • PARIS • SINGAPORE • TOKYO
TORONTO • WASHINGTON • ALBANY NY • BELMONT CA • CINCINNATI OH

Editor
Emily J. McMurray

Production Editor
Donna Olendorf

Associate Editors
Joanna Brod
Pamela S. Dear
Kathleen J. Edgar
Marie Ellavich
David M. Galens
Jeff Hill
Denise E. Kasinec
Thomas F. McMahon
Jane Kelly Kosek
Mark F. Mikula
Mary L. Onorato
Scot Peacock
Terrie M. Rooney
Deborah A. Stanley
Aarti Dhawan Stephens
Brandon Trenz
Roger M. Valade III
Polly A. Vedder
Thomas Wiloch

Assistant Editors
John Jorgenson
Margaret Mazurkiewicz
Geri J. Speace
Linda Tidrick
Kathleen Wilson

Senior Editor
James G. Lesniak

Picture Permissions Supervisor
Margaret A. Chamberlain

Picture Permissions Assistant
Susan Brohman

Front Matter Design
Paul Lewon

Art Director
Cynthia Baldwin

Cover Design
Mark Howell

While every effort has been made to ensure the reliability of the information presented in this publication, Gale Research Inc. does not guarantee the accuracy of the data contained herein. Gale accepts no payment for listing; and inclusion in the publication of any organization, agency, institution, publication, service, or individual does not imply endorsement of the editors or publisher. Errors brought to the attention of the publisher and verified to the satisfaction of the publisher will be corrected in future editions.

™ This book is printed on acid-free paper that meets the minimum requirements of American National Standard for Information Sciences—Permanence Paper for Printed Library Materials, ANSI Z39.48-1984.

This publication is a creative work copyrighted by Gale Research Inc. and fully protected by all applicable copyright laws, as well as by misappropriation, trade secret, unfair competition, and other applicable laws. The authors and editors of this work have added value to the underlying factual material herein through one or more of the following: unique and original selection, coordination, expression, arrangement, and classification of the information.

Gale Research Inc. will vigorously defend all of its rights in this publication.

Copyright © 1995
Gale Research Inc.
835 Penobscot Building
Detroit, MI 48226-4094

All rights reserved including the right of reproduction in whole or in part in any form.

ISBN 0-8103-9181-3 (Set)
ISBN 0-8103-9183-X (Volume 2)

Printed in the United States of America.
Published simultaneously in the United Kingdom by Gale Research International Limited
(An affiliated company of Gale Research Inc.)

I(T)P™ Gale Research Inc., an International Thomson Publishing Company.
ITP logo is a trademark under license.

Library of Congress Cataloging-in-Publication Data

Notable twentieth century scientists / Emily J. McMurray, editor.
p. cm.
Includes bibliographical references and index
ISBN 0-8103-9181-3 (set)
1. Scientists—Biography—Dictionaries. 2. Engineers-
-Biography—Dictionaries. I. McMurray, Emily J., 1959- .
Q141.N73 1995
509.2′2—dc20
[B] 94-5263
CIP

10 9 8 7 6 5 4 3 2 1

Contents

Introduction

Over the past several years, Gale Research Inc. has received numerous requests from librarians for a source providing biographies of scientists. *Notable Twentieth-Century Scientists* has been designed specifically to fill that niche. The four-volume set provides students, educators, librarians, researchers, and general readers with an affordable and comprehensive source of biographical information on approximately 1,300 scientists active in this century in all of the natural, physical, and applied sciences, including the traditionally studied subjects of astronomy, biology, botany, chemistry, earth science, mathematics, medicine, physics, technology, and zoology, as well as the more recently established and as yet sparsely covered fields of computer science, ecology, engineering, and environmental science. International in scope, *Notable Twentieth-Century Scientists* coverage ranges from the well-known scientific giants of the early century to contemporary scientists working at the cutting edge of discovery and knowledge.

Superior Coverage of Women, Minority and Non-Western Scientists

Addressing the growing interest in and demand for biographical information on women, minority and non-Western scientists, *Notable Twentieth-Century Scientists* also seeks to bring to light the achievements of more than 225 women scientists, almost 150 Asian American, African American, Hispanic American, and Native American scientists, and nearly 75 scientists from countries outside North America and Western Europe. The scarcity of published information on scientists representing these groups became evident during the compilation of this volume; as a result, information for many of the sketches on these listees has been obtained through telephone interviews and correspondence with the scientists themselves or with their universities, companies, laboratories, or families.

Though we have made every attempt to include key figures, we make no claim to having isolated the "most notable" women, minority, or non-Western scientists—an impossible goal. We are pleased that the majority of the biographies we wanted to feature are included; however, time constraints, space limitations, and research and interview availability prevented us from listing more scientists deserving of inclusion. Our hope is that in presenting these entries, we are providing a basis for future research on the lives and contributions of these important and historically marginalized segments of the scientific community.

Inclusion Criteria

A preliminary list of scientists was compiled from a wide variety of sources, including established reference works such as the *Dictionary of Scientific Biography,* history of science indexes, science periodicals, awards lists, and suggestions from organizations and associations. The advisory board, made up of librarians, academics, and individuals from scientific associations, evaluated the names and made suggestions for inclusion. Final selection of names to include was made by the editors on the basis of the following criteria:

- Discoveries, inventions, overall contributions, influence, and/or impact on scientific progress in the twentieth century
- Receipt of a major science award; all Nobel Prize winners in Physics, Chemistry, and Physiology or Medicine are found here, as are selected recipients of numerous other awards, including the Fields Medal (mathematics), Albert Lasker awards (medicine), the Tyler Prize (environmental science), the National Medal of Science, and the National Medal of Technology
- Involvement or influence in education, organizational leadership, or public policy
- Familiarity to the general public
- Notable "first" achievements, including degrees earned, positions held, or organizations founded; several listees involved in the first space flights are also included

Entries Provide Easy Access to Information

Entries are arranged alphabetically by surname. The typical *Notable Twentieth-Century Scientists* entry provides the following information:

- **Entry head**—offers an at-a-glance information: name, birth/death dates, nationality and primary field(s) of specialization.

- **Biographical essay**—ranges from 400 to 2500 words and provides basic biographical information [including date and place of birth, parents names and occupations, name(s) of spouse(s) and children, educational background and degrees earned, career positions, awards and honors earned] and scientific ~~endeavors and achievements~~ explained in prose accessible to high school students and readers without a scientific background. Intratextual headings within the essays highlight the significant events in the listee's life and career, allowing readers to find information they seek quickly and easily. In addition, **bold-faced** names in entries direct readers to entries on scientists' colleagues, predecessors, or contemporaries also found in *Notable Twentieth-Century Scientists.*

- **Selected Writings** by the Scientist section—lists representative publications, including important papers, textbooks, research works, autobiographies, lectures, etc.

- **Sources** section—provides citations of biographies, interviews, periodicals, obituaries, and other sources about the listee for readers seeking additional information.

Indexes Provide Numerous Points of Access

In addition to the complete list of scientists found at the beginning of each volume, readers seeking the names of additional individuals of a given country, heritage, gender, or profession can consult the following indexes at the end of volume 4 for additional listings:

- **Field of Specialization Index**—groups listees according to the scientific fields to which they have contributed
- **Gender Index**—provides lists of the women and men covered
- **Nationality/Ethnicity Index**—arranges listees by country of birth and/or citizenship and/or ethnic heritage
- Comprehensive **Subject Index**—provides volume and page references for scientists and scientific terms used in the text. Includes cross references.

Photos

Individuals in *Notable Twentieth-Century Scientists* come to life in the 394 photos of the scientists.

Acknowledgments

The editors would like to thank, in addition to the advisory board, the following individuals for their assistance with various aspects of the production of *Notable Twentieth-Century Scientists*: Bruce Seely, Secretary of the Society for the History of Technology and Professor at Michigan Technological University, Houghton, Michigan for his assistance in identifying notable engineers; Nancy Anderson, librarian at University of Illinois at Urbana Champaign Mathematics Library for assistance with mathematicians; Arthur Norberg, former director of the Charles Babbage Institute Center for the History of Information Processing at the University of Minnesota, Minneapolis, for assistance with computer scientists; and Kathleen Prestwidge for much assistance in identifying and providing information about minority and women scientists. Special acknowledgment is also due to Jim Kamp and Roger Valade for their technical assistance and to Denise Kasinec for her administrative assistance in the preparation of these volumes.

Advisory Board

Russell Aiuto
Senior Project Officer, Council of Independent Colleges
Former Director of the Scope, Sequence and Coordination of Secondary School
Science program, National Science Teachers Association
Washington, DC

Stephen G. Brush
Professor, Department of History and Institute for
Physical Science & Technology
University of Maryland, College Park

Nancy Bard
Head Reference Librarian,
Thomas Jefferson High School for Science and Technology
Alexandria, Virginia

James E. Bobick
Head, Science and Technology Department
The Carnegie Library of Pittsburgh
Pittsburgh, Pennsylvania

Michael J. Boersma
Science Exhibit Developer, Museum of Science and Industry
Chicago, Illinois

Catherine Jay Didion
Executive Director, Association for Women in Science
Washington, DC

Kathleen J. Prestwidge
Professor Emerita, Bronx Community College
Flushing, New York

Lewis Pyenson
Professeur titulaire, Department of History, University of Montreal
Quebec, Canada

Robin N. Sinn
Head Reference Librarian, Academy of Natural Science
Philadelphia, Pennsylvania

John Sweeney
Head of Science and Technology Information Service
British Library Science Reference and Information Service
London, England

Contributors

Russell Aiuto, Ethan E. Allen, Julie Anderson, Olga K. Anderson, Denise Adams Arnold, Nancy E. Bard, Dorothy Barnhouse, Jeffery Bass, Matthew A. Bille, Maurice Bleifeld, Michael Boersma, Barbara A. Branca, Hovey Brock, Valerie Brown, Leonard C. Bruno, Raymond E. Bullock, Marjorie Burgess, Gerard J. Buskes, Joseph Cain, Jill Carpenter, Dennis W. Cheek, Kim A. Cheek, Tom Chen, Miyoko Chu, Jane Stewart Cook, Kelly Otter Cooper, G. Scott Crawford, Tom Crawford, Karin Deck, Margaret DiCanio, Mindi Dickstein, Rowan L. Dordick, John Henry Dreyfuss, Thomas Drucker, Kala Dwarakanath, Marianne Fedunkiw, Martin R. Feldman, Eliseo Fernandez, George A. Ferrance, Jerome P. Ferrance, William T. Fletcher, David N. Ford, Karyn Hede George, Chris Hables Gray, Loretta Hall, Betsy Hanson, Robert M. Hawthorne, Jr., Elizabeth Henry, T. A. Heppenheimer, Frank Hertle, J. D. Hunley, Roger Jaffe, Jessica Jahiel, Jeanne Spriter James, J. Sydney Jones, D. George Joseph, Mark J. Kaiser, Lee Katterman, Sandra Katzman, Janet Kieffer Kelley, Evelyn B. Kelly, Karen S. Kelly, James Klockow, Susan E. Kolmer, Geeta Kothari, Jennifer Kramer, Marc Kusinitz, Roger D. Launius, Penelope Lawbaugh, Benedict A. Leerburger, Jeanne M. Lesinski, Linda Lewin, John E. Little, Pamela O. Long, C. D. Lord, Laura Mangan-Grenier, Gail B. C. Marsella, Liz Marshall, Renee D. Mastrocco, Patricia M. McAdams, William M. McBride, Mike McClure, Avril McDonald, Christopher McGrail, Kimberlyn McGrail, Donald J. McGraw, William J. McPeak, Carla Mecoli-Kamp, Leslie Mertz, Robert Messer, Philip Metcalfe, Fei Fei Wang Metzler, George A. Milite, Carol L. Moberg, Sally M. Moite, Patrick Moore, Paula M. Morin, M. C. Nagel, Margo Nash, Laura Newman, David E. Newton, F. C. Nicholson, Joan Oleck, Donna Olshansky, Nicholas Pease, Daniel Pendick, David Petechuk, Tom K. Phares, Devera Pine, Karl Preuss, Rayma Prince, Barbara J. Proujan, Amy M. Punke, Lewis Pyenson, Susan Sheets Pyenson, Jeff Raines, Mary Raum, Leslie Reinherz, Jordan P. Richman, Vita Richman, Francis Rogers, Terrie M. Romano, Daniel Rooney, Shari Rudavsky, Kathy Sammis, Karen Sands, Neeraja Sankaran, Joel Schwarz, Philip Duhan Segal, Alan R. Shepherd, Joel Simon, Michael Sims, Julian A. Smith, Linda Wasmer Smith, Lawrence Souder, Dorothy Spencer, John Spizzirri, David Sprinkle, Darwin H. Stapleton, Sharon F. Suer, Maureen L. Tan, Peter H. Taylor, Melinda Jardon Thach, Sebastian Thaler, R. F. Trimble, Cynthia Washam, Wallace Mack White, C. A. Williams, Katherine Williams, Nicholas S. Williamson, Philip K. Wilson, Rodolfo A. Windhausen, Karen Wilhelm, Karen Withem, Alexandra Witze, Cathleen M. Zucco.

Photo Credits

Photographs appearing in *Notable Twentieth-Century Scientists* were received from the following sources:

AP/Wide World Photos: **pp. 1, 31, 36, 38, 45, 48, 75, 98, 108, 112, 129, 150, 166, 169, 172, 174, 186, 192, 195, 198, 202, 203, 207, 211, 219, 221, 231, 234, 241, 278, 285, 295, 297, 299, 310, 313, 315, 321, 322, 326, 331, 341, 344, 348, 358, 373, 377, 388, 390, 397, 401, 402, 414, 417, 424, 434, 437, 441, 456, 476, 481, 484, 496, 503, 507, 516, 518, 529, 539, 541, 544, 550, 556, 565, 568, 573, 597, 613, 624, 628, 649, 657, 660, 668, 671, 675, 685, 702, 707, 709, 713, 722, 725, 744, 746, 756, 761, 763, 768, 771, 774, 778, 803, 806, 833, 835, 842, 853, 855, 877, 885, 890, 900, 932, 939, 949, 951, 959, 970, 986, 990, 1023, 1045, 1057, 1060, 1062, 1084, 1090, 1125, 1134, 1137, 1160, 1163, 1172, 1184, 1185, 1188, 1191, 1202, 1203, 1206, 1211, 1216, 1219, 1234, 1236, 1240, 1246, 1253, 1261, 1271, 1281, 1284, 1313, 1339, 1346, 1354, 1357, 1386, 1392, 1405, 1410, 1414, 1420, 1429, 1436, 1444, 1455, 1465, 1475, 1483, 1493, 1499, 1507, 1513, 1516, 1525, 1536, 1549, 1568, 1573, 1591, 1600, 1618, 1643, 1654, 1666, 1678, 1680, 1683, 1714, 1720, 1724, 1733, 1741, 1751, 1762, 1767, 1777, 1781, 1800, 1802, 1803, 1808, 1818, 1832, 1849, 1865, 1877, 1891, 1894, 1898, 1908, 1917, 1961, 1970, 1975, 2005, 2016, 2029, 2034, 2039, 2041, 2049, 2064, 2072, 2101, 2106, 2112, 2122, 2125, 2128, 2153, 2158, 2161, 2168, 2170, 2176, 2200, 2208, 2227, 2236, 2245, 2266, 2273, 2302, 2305;** The Bettmann Archive: **pp. 12, 426, 739, 925, 1037;** Courtesy of Keiiti Aki: **p. 14;** UPI/Bettmann: **pp. 58, 511, 546, 583, 751, 945, 1003, 1016;** Courtesy of Francisco Jose Ayala: **p. 80;** UPI/Bettmann Newsphotos: **pp. 83;** Archive Photos: **pp. 102, 523, 1040, 1210, 1769, 1990, 2132, 2276;** Courtesy of George Keith Batchelor: **pp. 124;** Photograph by Ingbert Gruttner, Courtesy of Arnold Beckman: **pp. 131;** Courtesy of Robert Arbuckle Berner: **p. 160;** Courtesy of Yvonne Brill: **p. 255;** Courtesy of Lester Brown: **p. 266;** Courtesy of Glenn W. Burton: **p. 283;** Courtesy of John R. Cairns: **p. 291;** The Granger Collection, New York: **pp. 304, 469, 652, 655, 1050, 1086, 1168, 1480, 1588, 1754, 1796, 2019, 2054;** New York University Medical Center Archives: **p. 355;** Courtesy of Stanley N. Cohen: **p. 379;** Courtesy of Rita R. Colwell: **p. 386;** Courtesy of Francisco Dallmeier: **p. 445;** Courtesy of Michael Ellis DeBakey: **p. 466;** Courtesy of Dennis Jack: **p. 489;** Courtesy of Nance K. Dicciani: **p. 495;** Courtesy of Theodor O. Diener: **p. 499;** Courtesy of Edsgar Dijkstra: **p. 501;** Archive/DPA: **pp. 513, 839, 1958;** Courtesy of Mildred Dresselhaus: **p. 521;** Courtesy of Cecile Hoover Edwards: **p. 559;** Courtesy of Helen T. Edwards: **p. 561;** Courtesy of the estate of Philo T. Farnsworth: **p. 609;** Courtesy of Lloyd Ferguson: **p. 622;** Courtesy of Solomon Fuller: **p. 710;** Courtesy of William Gates: **p. 733;** Courtesy of Adele Jean Goldberg: **p. 781;** Courtesy of Mary L. Good: **p. 796;** © Michael K. Nichols/Magnum Photos: **p. 798;** Courtesy of Govindjee: **p. 809;** Courtesy of Evelyn Granville: **p. 812;** Photograph by Washington University Photographic Services, Courtesy of Viktor Hamburger: **p. 851;** Courtesy of Wesley L. Harris, Sr.: **p. 868;** Courtesy of William Hewlett: **p. 918;** Photograph by Bradford Bachrach, Courtesy of Gladys Hobby: **p. 935;** Archive/Express Newspapers: **pp. 937, 961;** Courtesy of Phillip G. Hubbard: **p. 967;** Courtesy of Russell Hulse: **p. 978;** Courtesy of Keiichi Itakura: **p. 998;** Courtesy of Frank B. Jewett: **p. 1021;** Courtesy of Barbara Crawford Johnson: **p. 1026;** Courtesy of Marvin M. Johnson: **p. 1032;** Courtesy of Harold S. Johnston: **p. 1036;** Courtesy of Yuet Wai Kan: **p. 1056;** Courtesy of Motoo Kimura: **p. 1097;** Courtesy of Georges Köhler: **p. 1117;** Courtesy of Thomas E. Kurtz: **p. 1147;** Courtesy of Raymond Kurzweil: **p. 1149;** Mary Evans Picture Library: **pp. 1178, 1462, 1637, 1829, 2027, 2119, 2138, 2250;** The Granger Collection: **p. 1197, 1640, 1737;** Courtesy of Susan E. Leeman: **p. 1213;** Courtesy of Carroll Leevy: **p. 1214;** © Leonard Freed/Magnum Photos: **p. 1222;** Courtesy of Aldo Leopold: **p. 1226;** Courtesy of Julian H. Lewis: **p. 1239;** Courtesy of Irene D. Long: **p. 1270;** © Dennis Stock/Magnum Photos: **p. 1277;** Courtesy of Stanford University Visual Services: **p. 1350;** Courtesy of Evangelia Micheli-Tzanakou: **p. 1370;** Courtesy of Elizabeth and James Miller: **p. 1376;** Courtesy of Stanley L. Miller: **p. 1379;** Courtesy of Beatrice Mintz: **p. 1394;** Courtesy of Russell Mittermeier: **p. 1397;** Courtesy of Robert N. Noyce: **p. 1491;** Courtesy of NASA: **p. 1497;** Courtesy of David Packard: **p. 1523;** Courtesy of Jennie Patrick: **p. 1535;** Brown Brothers, Sterling, Pa.: **pp. 1542, 1708, 1871, 1998,**

2193, 2213, 2222; © Bruce Davidson/Magnum Photos: **p. 1545;** Courtesy of Irene C. Peden: **p. 1559;** Courtesy of the estate of Edith Peterson: **p. 1578;** Photo by Charles Harrington/Cornell University Photography, Courtesy of David Pimentel: **p. 1583;** Courtesy of Al Qöyawayma: **p. 1627;** Courtesy of Elsa Reichmanis: **p. 1661;** Courtesy of Juan C. Romero: **p. 1707;** Courtesy of Mary Ross: **p. 1711;** Courtesy of Stanley Runcorn: **p. 1727;** Archive/Nordick: **p. 1730;** Courtesy of Carl Sagan: **p. 1758;** Courtesy of Pedro A. Sanchez: **p. 1774;** Courtesy of Brookhaven National Laboratory: **p. 1785;** Photograph by Burgdorf Fotografi, Courtesy of Mogens Schou: **p. 1792;** Courtesy of Mary M. Shaw: **p. 1823;** Courtesy of Isadore M. Singer: **p. 1852;** Courtesy of Michael Smith: **p. 1868;** Courtesy of Chauncey Starr: **p. 1904;** Courtesy of Walter S. Sutton: **p. 1950;** Photograph by Robert P. Matthews, Courtesy of Joseph Taylor, Jr.: **p. 1980;** Courtesy of Stuart Taylor: **p. 1984;** Courtesy of Edward Teller: **p. 1987;** Topham/The Imageworks: **p. 2002;** Courtesy of Sheila E. Widnall: **p. 2184;** Courtesy of Richard Wilstatter: **p. 2219;** Photograph by John Sholtis, Courtesy of Norton Zinder: **p. 2297.**

Entry List

Branson, Herman
Brattain, Walter Houser
Braun, Karl Ferdinand
Breit, Gregory
Brenner, Sydney
Bressani, Ricardo
Bridgman, Percy Williams
Brill, Yvonne Claeys
Bronk, Detlev Wulf
Brønsted, Johannes Nicolaus
Brooks, Ronald E.
Brouwer, Luitzen Egbertus Jan
Brown, Herbert C.
Brown, Lester R.
Brown, Michael S.
Brown, Rachel Fuller
Browne, Marjorie Lee
Bucher, Walter Herman
Buchner, Eduard
Bullard, Edward
Bundy, Robert F.
Burbidge, E. Margaret
Burbidge, Geoffrey
Burnet, Frank Macfarlane
Burton, Glenn W.
Bush, Vannevar
Butenandt, Adolf

Cairns, Jr., John
Calderón, Alberto P.
Caldicott, Helen
Callender, Clive O.
Calvin, Melvin
Cambra, Jessie G.
Canady, Alexa I.
Cannon, Annie Jump
Cantor, Georg
Cardona, Manuel
Cardozo, W. Warrick
Cardús, David
Carlson, Chester
Carothers, Wallace Hume
Carrel, Alexis
Carrier, Willis
Carruthers, George R.
Carson, Benjamin S.
Carson, Rachel
Carver, George Washington
Castro, George
Cech, Thomas R.
Chadwick, James
Chain, Ernst Boris
Chamberlain, Owen
Chamberlin, Thomas Chrowder
Chance, Britton
Chandrasekhar, Subrahmanyan
Chang, Min-Chueh
Chargaff, Erwin
Charpak, Georges
Chaudhari, Praveen
Cherenkov, Pavel A.
Chestnut, Harold
Chew, Geoffrey Foucar
Child, Charles Manning
Chinn, May Edward
Cho, Alfred Y.
Chu, Paul Ching-Wu
Church, Alonzo
Clarke, Edith
Claude, Albert
Claude, Georges
Clay, Jacob
Clay-Jolles, Tettje Clasina
Cloud, Preston
Cobb, Jewel Plummer
Cobb, William Montague
Cockcroft, John D.
Cohen, Paul
Cohen, Stanley
Cohen, Stanley N.
Cohn, Mildred
Cohn, Zanvil
Colmenares, Margarita
Colwell, Rita R.
Commoner, Barry
Compton, Arthur Holly
Conway, Lynn Ann
Conwell, Esther Marly
Cooke, Lloyd M.
Coolidge, William D.
Cooper, Leon
Corey, Elias James
Cori, Carl Ferdinand
Cori, Gerty T.
Cormack, Allan M.
Cornforth, John
Coulomb, Jean
Courant, Richard
Cournand, André F.
Cousteau, Jacques
Cowings, Patricia S.
Cox, Elbert Frank
Cox, Geraldine V.
Cox, Gertrude Mary
Cram, Donald J.
Cray, Seymour
Crick, Francis
Cronin, James W.
Crosby, Elizabeth Caroline
Crosthwait Jr., David Nelson
Curie, Marie
Curie, Pierre

Dale, Henry Hallett
Dalén, Nils
Dallmeier, Francisco
Dalrymple, G. Brent
Daly, Marie M.
Daly, Reginald Aldworth
Dam, Henrik
Daniels, Walter T.
Dantzig, George Bernard
Darden, Christine
Dart, Raymond A.
Dausset, Jean
Davis, Margaret B.
Davis, Marguerite
Davis, Jr., Raymond
Davisson, Clinton
DeBakey, Michael Ellis
de Broglie, Louis Victor
Debye, Peter
de Duvé, Christian
de Forest, Lee
de Gennes, Pierre-Gilles
Dehmelt, Hans
Deisenhofer, Johann
Delbrück, Max
Deligné, Pierre
Dennis, Jack B.
de Sitter, Willem
d'Hérelle, Félix
Diaz, Henry F.
Dicciani, Nance K.
Diels, Otto
Diener, Theodor Otto
Dijkstra, Edsger W.
Dirac, Paul
Djerassi, Carl
Dobzhansky, Theodosius
Doisy, Edward A.
Dole, Vincent P.
Domagk, Gerhard
Donaldson, Simon
Douglas, Donald W.
Draper, Charles Stark
Dresselhaus, Mildred S.
Drew, Charles R.
Drucker, Daniel Charles
Dubois, Eugène
Dubos, René
Dulbecco, Renato
Durand, William F.
Durrell, Gerald
du Vigneaud, Vincent
Dyson, Freeman J.

Earle, Sylvia A.
Eccles, John C.
Eckert, J. Presper
Eddington, Arthur Stanley
Edelman, Gerald M.
Edgerton, Harold
Edinger, Tilly

Edison, Thomas Alva
Edwards, Cecile Hoover
Edwards, Helen T.
Ehrenfest, Paul
Ehrenfest-Afanaseva, Tatiana
Ehrlich, Paul
Ehrlich, Paul R.
Eigen, Manfred
Eijkman, Christiaan
Einstein, Albert
Einthoven, Willem
Eisner, Thomas
Eldredge, Niles
Elion, Gertrude Belle
El-Sayed, Mostafa Amr
Elton, Charles
Emerson, Gladys Anderson
Enders, John F.
Engler, Adolph Gustav Heinrich
Enskog, David
Erlanger, Joseph
Ernst, Richard R.
Esaki, Leo
Esau, Katherine
Estrin, Thelma
Euler, Ulf von
Euler-Chelpin, Hans von
Evans, Alice
Evans, James C.

F

Faber, Sandra M.
Farnsworth, Philo T.
Farquhar, Marilyn G.
Farr, Wanda K.
Fauci, Anthony S.
Favaloro, René Geronimo
Fedoroff, Nina V.
Feigenbaum, Edward A.
Feigenbaum, Mitchell
Fell, Honor Bridget
Ferguson, Lloyd N.
Fermi, Enrico
Fersman, Aleksandr Evgenievich
Feynman, Richard P.
Fibiger, Johannes
Fieser, Louis
Fieser, Mary Peters
Fischer, Edmond H.
Fischer, Emil
Fischer, Ernst Otto
Fischer, Hans
Fisher, Elizabeth F.
Fisher, Ronald A.
Fitch, Val Logsdon
Fitzroy, Nancy D.
Fleming, Alexander
Fleming, John Ambrose
Flexner, Simon
Florey, Howard Walter
Flory, Paul
Flügge-Lotz, Irmgard
Fokker, Anthony H. G.
Forbush, Scott Ellsworth
Ford, Henry
Forrester, Jay W.
Forssmann, Werner
Fossey, Dian
Fowler, William A.
Fox, Sidney W.
Fraenkel, Abraham Adolf
Fraenkel-Conrat, Heinz
Franck, James
Frank, Il'ya
Franklin, Rosalind Elsie
Fraser-Reid, Bertram Oliver
Fréchet, Maurice
Freedman, Michael H.
Frenkel, Yakov Ilyich
Friedman, Jerome
Friedmann, Aleksandr A.
Friend, Charlotte
Frisch, Karl von
Frisch, Otto Robert
Fujita, Tetsuya Theodore
Fukui, Kenichi
Fuller, Solomon

Gabor, Dennis
Gadgil, Madhav
Gadgil, Sulochana
Gagarin, Yuri A.
Gajdusek, D. Carleton
Gallo, Robert C.
Gamow, George
Gardner, Julia Anna
Garrod, Archibald
Gasser, Herbert Spencer
Gates, Bill
Gates, Jr., Sylvester James
Gaviola, Enrique
Gayle, Helene Doris
Geiger, Hans
Geiringer, Hilda
Geller, Margaret Joan
Gell-Mann, Murray
Ghiorso, Albert
Giacconi, Riccardo
Giaever, Ivar
Giauque, William F.
Gibbs, William Francis
Giblett, Eloise R.
Gilbert, Walter
Gilbreth, Frank
Gilbreth, Lillian
Glaser, Donald
Glashow, Sheldon Lee
Glenn, Jr., John H.
Goddard, Robert H.
Gödel, Kurt Friedrich
Goeppert-Mayer, Maria
Goethals, George W.
Gold, Thomas
Goldberg, Adele
Goldmark, Peter Carl
Goldring, Winifred
Goldschmidt, Richard B.
Goldschmidt, Victor
Goldstein, Avram
Goldstein, Joseph L.
Golgi, Camillo
Good, Mary L.
Goodall, Jane
Goudsmit, Samuel A.
Gould, Stephen Jay
Gourdine, Meredith Charles
Gourneau, Dwight
Govindjee
Granit, Ragnar Arthur
Granville, Evelyn Boyd
Greatbatch, Wilson
Greenewalt, Crawford H.
Griffith, Frederick
Grignard, François Auguste Victor
Gross, Carol
Grothendieck, Alexander
Groves, Leslie Richard
Guillaume, Charles-Edouard
Guillemin, Roger
Gullstrand, Allvar
Gutenberg, Beno
Guth, Alan
Gutierrez, Orlando A.

Haagen-Smit, A. J.
Haber, Fritz
Hadamard, Jacques
Hahn, Otto
Haldane, John Burdon Sanderson
Hale, George Ellery
Hall, Lloyd Augustus
Hamburger, Viktor
Hamilton, Alice
Hanafusa, Hidesaburo
Hannah, Marc R.
Hansen, James
Harden, Arthur
Hardy, Alister C.
Hardy, Godfrey Harold
Hardy, Harriet
Harmon, E'lise F.
Harris, Cyril
Harris, Wesley L.
Hartline, Haldan Keffer
Hassel, Odd

Lancefield, Rebecca Craighill
Land, Edwin H.
Landau, Lev Davidovich
Landsberg, Helmut E.
Landsteiner, Karl
Langevin, Paul
Langmuir, Irving
Latimer, Lewis H.
Lattes, C. M. G.
Laub, Jakob Johann
Laue, Max von
Lauterbur, Paul C.
Laveran, Alphonse
Lawless, Theodore K.
Lawrence, Ernest Orlando
Leakey, Louis
Leakey, Mary
Leakey, Richard E.
Leavitt, Henrietta
Le Beau, Désirée
Lebesgue, Henri
Le Cadet, Georges
Leder, Philip
Lederberg, Joshua
Lederman, Leon Max
Lee, Raphael C.
Lee, Tsung-Dao
Lee, Yuan T.
Leeman, Susan E.
Leevy, Carroll
Leffall, Jr., LaSalle D.
Lehmann, Inge
Lehn, Jean-Marie
Leloir, Luis F.
Lemaître, Georges
Lenard, Philipp E. A. von
Leopold, Aldo
Leopold, Estella Bergere
Leopold, Luna
Lester, Jr., William Alexander
Levi-Civita, Tullio
Levi-Montalcini, Rita
Lewis, Gilbert Newton
Lewis, Julian Herman
Lewis, Warren K.
Li, Ching Chun
Li, Choh Hao
Libby, Willard F.
Liepmann, Hans Wolfgang
Lillie, Frank Rattray
Lim, Robert K. S.
Lin, Chia-Chiao
Lipmann, Fritz
Lippmann, Gabriel
Lipscomb, Jr., William Nunn
Little, Arthur D.
Lizhi, Fang
Lloyd, Ruth Smith
Loeb, Jacques
Loewi, Otto
Logan, Myra A.
London, Fritz
Long, Irene D.
Lonsdale, Kathleen
Lord Rayleigh
See Strutt, John William
Lorentz, Hendrik Antoon
Lorenz, Edward N.
Lorenz, Konrad
Lovelock, James E.
Luria, Salvador Edward
Lwoff, André
Lynen, Feodor
Lynk, Miles Vandahurst

Maathai, Wangari
MacArthur, Robert H.
Macdonald, Eleanor Josephine
MacDonald, Gordon
MacGill, Elsie Gregory
Mac Lane, Saunders
MacLeod, Colin Munro
Macleod, John James Rickard
Maillart, Robert
Maiman, Theodore
Maloney, Arnold Hamilton
Mandelbrot, Benoit B.
Mandel'shtam, Leonid Isaakovich
Manton, Sidnie Milana
Marchbanks, Jr., Vance H.
Marconi, Guglielmo
Marcus, Rudolph A.
Margulis, Gregori Aleksandrovitch
Margulis, Lynn
Marie-Victorin, Frère
Markov, Andrei Andreevich
Martin, A. J. P.
Massevitch, Alla G.
Massey, Walter E.
Massie, Samuel P.
Masters, William Howell
Matthews, Alva T.
Matuyama, Motonori
Mauchly, John William
Maunder, Annie Russell
Maury, Antonia
Maury, Carlotta Joaquina
Maynard Smith, John
Mayr, Ernst
McAfee, Walter S.
McCarthy, John
McCarty, Maclyn
McClintock, Barbara
McCollum, Elmer Verner
McConnell, Harden
McMillan, Edwin M.
Medawar, Peter Brian
Meitner, Lise
Mendenhall, Dorothy Reed
Merrifield, R. Bruce
Meselson, Matthew
Metchnikoff, Élie
Meyerhof, Otto
Michel, Hartmut
Micheli-Tzanakou, Evangelia
Michelson, Albert
Midgley, Jr., Thomas
Miller, Elizabeth C. and James A.
Miller, Stanley Lloyd
Millikan, Robert A.
Milne, Edward Arthur
Milnor, John
Milstein, César
Minkowski, Hermann
Minkowski, Rudolph
Minot, George Richards
Minsky, Marvin
Mintz, Beatrice
Mitchell, Peter D.
Mittermeier, Russell
Mohorovičić, Andrija
Moissan, Henri
Molina, Mario
Moniz, Egas
Monod, Jacques Lucien
Montagnier, Luc
Moore, Charlotte E.
Moore, Raymond Cecil
Moore, Ruth
Moore, Stanford
Morawetz, Cathleen Synge
Morgan, Arthur E.
Morgan, Garrett A.
Morgan, Thomas Hunt
Mori, Shigefumi
Morley, Edward Williams
Morrison, Philip
Moseley, Henry Gwyn Jeffreys
Mössbauer, Rudolf
Mott, Nevill Francis
Mottelson, Ben R.
Moulton, Forest Ray
Muller, Hermann Joseph
Müller, K. Alex
Müller, Paul
Mulliken, Robert S.
Mullis, Kary
Munk, Walter
Murphy, William P.
Murray, Joseph E.

N

Nabrit, Samuel Milton
Nagata, Takesi
Nambu, Yoichiro
Nathans, Daniel
Natta, Giulio
Neal, Homer Alfred
Néel, Louis

Chronology of Scientific Advancement

1895 Scottish physicist *C. T. R. Wilson* invents the cloud chamber

French physicist *Jean Baptiste Perrin* confirms the nature of cathode rays

1896 American agricultural chemist *George Washington Carver* begins work at the Tuskegee Institute

1897 English physicist *J. J. Thomson* discovers the electron

1898 Polish-born French radiation chemist *Marie Curie* and French physicist *Pierre Curie* discover polonium and radium

1900 German physicist *Max Planck* develops Planck's Constant

1901 Austrian American immunologist *Karl Landsteiner* discovers A, B, and O blood types

German geneticist *Wilhelm Weinberg* outlines the "difference method" in his first important paper on heredity

1902 English geneticist *William Bateson* translates Austrian botanist Gregor Mendel's work

1903 Polish-born French radiation chemist *Marie Curie* becomes the first woman to be awarded the Nobel Prize

German chemist *Otto Diels* isolates molecular structure of cholesterol

1904 English electrical engineer *John Ambrose Fleming* develops the Fleming Valve

Russian physiologist *Ivan Petrovich Pavlov* receives the Nobel Prize for digestion research

1905 German-born American physicist *Albert Einstein* publishes the theory of relativity

German chemist *Fritz Haber* publishes *Thermodynamics of Technical Gas Reactions*

German chemist *Walther Nernst*'s research leads to the Third Law of Thermodynamics

1906 Danish physical chemist *Johannes Nicolaus Brønsted* publishes his first paper on affinity

English neurophysiologist *Charles Scott Sherrington* publishes *The Integrative Action of the Nervous System*

1907 Prussian-born American physicist *Albert Michelson* becomes the first American to receive the Nobel Prize for physics

1908 American astrophysicist *George Ellery Hale* discovers magnetic fields in sunspots

1909 German bacteriologist and immunologist *Paul Ehrlich* discovers a cure for syphilis

American engineer and inventor *Charles Franklin Kettering* successfully tests the first prototype of the electric automobile starter

1910 English American mathematician *Alfred North Whitehead* and English mathematician and philosopher *Bertrand Russell* publish the first volume of *Principia Mathematica*

American engineer and inventor *Lee De Forest* attempts the first live broadcast of radio

New Zealand-born English physicist *Ernest Rutherford* postulates the modern concept of the atom

1911 English mathematician *Godfrey Harold Hardy* begins his collaboration with J. E. Littlewood

Polish-born French radiation chemist *Marie Curie* becomes the first scientist to win a second Nobel Prize

1912 Danish physicist *Niels Bohr* develops a new theory of atomic structure

Austrian physicist *Victor Hess* discovers cosmic rays

English biochemist *Frederick Gowland Hopkins* publishes a groundbreaking work illustrating the nutritional importance of vitamins

German physicist *Max von Laue* discovers X-ray diffraction

Austrian physicist *Lise Meitner* becomes the first woman professor in Germany

German meteorologist and geophysicist *Alfred Wegener* proposes the theory of continental drift

1913 German bacteriologist and immunologist *Paul Ehrlich* gives an address explaining the future of chemotherapy

English physicist *Henry Gwyn Jeffreys Moseley* discovers atomic number

French physicist *Jean Baptiste Perrin* verifies German-born American physicist *Albert Einstein*'s calculations of Brownian Motion

American astronomer and astrophysicist *Henry Norris Russell* publishes Hertzsprung-Russell diagram

Russian-born American aeronautical engineer *Igor I. Sikorsky* designs *Ilya Mourometz* bomber

German chemist *Richard Willstätter* and Arthur Stoll publish their first studies of chlorophyll

American geneticist *A. H. Sturtevant* develops gene mapping

1916 American chemist and physicist *Irving Langmuir* receives a patent for an energy-efficient, longer-lasting tungsten filament light bulb

American geneticist and embryologist *Thomas Hunt Morgan* publishes *A Critique of the Theory of Evolution*

German theoretical physicist *Arnold Sommerfeld* reworks Danish physicist *Niels Bohr*'s atomic theory

American anatomist *Florence Rena Sabin* publishes *The Origin and Development of the Lymphatic System*

1918 Danish physical chemist *Johannes Nicolaus Brønsted* publishes his thirteenth paper on affinity

1919 New Zealand-born English physicist *Ernest Rutherford* determines that alpha particles can split atoms

1920 American astronomer *Harlow Shapley* convinces the scientific community that the Milky Way is much larger than originally thought and the Earth's solar system is not its center

1921 Canadian physiologist *Frederick G. Banting* and Canadian physiologist *Charles Herbert Best* discover insulin

1923 Danish physical chemist *Johannes Nicolaus Brønsted* redefines acids and bases

English astronomer *Arthur Stanley Eddington* publishes *Mathematical Theory of Relativity*

American astronomer *Edwin Hubble* confirms the existence of galaxies outside the Milky Way

American physicist *Robert A. Millikan* begins his study of cosmic rays

1924 French theoretical physicist *Louis Victor de Broglie* publishes findings on wave mechanics

English astronomer *Arthur Stanley Eddington* determines the mass-luminosity law

1925 German-born American physicist *James Franck* and German physicist *Gustav Hertz* prove Danish physicist *Niels Bohr*'s theory of the quantum atom

Italian-born American physicist *Enrico Fermi* publishes a paper explaining Austro-Hungarian-born Swiss physicist *Wolfgang Pauli*'s exclusion principle

English statistician and geneticist *Ronald A. Fisher* publishes *Statistical Methods for Research Workers*

1926 German-born English physicist *Max Born* explains the wave function

American physicist and rocket pioneer *Robert H. Goddard* launches the first liquid-propellant rocket

American geneticist *Hermann Joseph Muller* confirms that X rays greatly increase the mutation rate in *Drosophila*

Austrian physicist *Erwin Schrödinger* publishes his wave equation

1927 American physicist *Arthur Holly Compton* receives the Nobel Prize for X-ray research

English physiologist *Henry Hallett Dale* identifies the chemical mediator involved in the transmission of nerve impulses

German chemist *Otto Diels* develops a successful dehydrogenating process

German physicist *Werner Karl Heisenberg* develops the Uncertainty Principle

Belgian astronomer *Georges Lemaître* formulates the big bang theory

Hungarian American mathematical physicist *Eugene Paul Wigner* develops the law of the conservation of parity

American astronomer *Edwin Hubble* puts together the theory of the expanding universe, or Hubble's Law

1928 German chemist *Otto Diels* and German chemist *Kurt Alder* develop the Diels-Alder Reaction

Scottish bacteriologist *Alexander Fleming* discovers penicillin

Austro-Hungarian-born German physicist *Hermann Oberth* publishes a book explaining the basic principles of space flight

Indian physicist *C. V. Raman* discovers the Raman Effect

1929 American physicist *Robert Van de Graaff* constructs the first working model of his particle accelerator

Danish astronomer *Ejnar Hertzsprung* receives the Gold Medal Award for calculating the first intergalactic distance

Norwegian American chemist *Lars Onsager* develops the Law of Reciprocal Relations

German-born American mathematician *Hermann Weyl* develops a mathematical theory for the neutrino

Russian-born American physicist and engineer *Vladimir Zworykin* files his first patent for color television

1930 English statistician and geneticist *Ronald A. Fisher* publishes *The Genetical Theory of Natural Selection*

Austrian-born American mathematician *Kurt Friedrich Gödel* proves the incompleteness theorem

Austro-Hungarian-born Swiss physicist *Wolfgang Pauli* proposes the existence of the neutrino

1931 American engineer *Vannevar Bush* develops the differential analyzer with colleagues

American chemist *Wallace Hume Carothers* founds the synthetic rubber manufacturing industry with his research

South African-born American virologist *Max Theiler*'s research leads to the production of the first yellow-fever vaccine

German biochemist *Otto Warburg* establishes the Kaiser Wilhelm Institute for Cell Physiology

1932 English atomic physicist *John Cockcroft* and Irish experimental physicist *Ernest Walton* split the atom

American physicist *Carl David Anderson* discovers the positron

English-born Indian physiologist and geneticist *John Burdon Sanderson Haldane* publishes *The Causes of Evolution*

American physicist *Ernest Orlando Lawrence* develops the cyclotron and disintegrates a lithium nucleus

1933 Canadian-born American biologist and bacteriologist *Oswald Theodore Avery* identifies DNA as the basis of heredity

English physicist *Paul Adrien Maurice Dirac* wins the Nobel Prize for his work on the wave equation

Italian-born American physicist *Enrico Fermi* proposes his beta decay theory

German inventor *Felix Wankel* successfully operates the first internal combustion, rotary engine

1934 French nuclear physicist *Frédéric Joliot-Curie* and French chemist and physicist *Irène Joliot-Curie* discover artificial radioactivity

American inventor *Edwin H. Land* develops a commercial method to polarize light

New Zealand-born English physicist *Ernest Rutherford* achieves the first fusion reaction

American chemist and physicist *Harold Urey* receives the Nobel Prize in chemistry for his discovery of deuterium, or heavy hydrogen

1935 American seismologist *Charles F. Richter* and German American seismologist *Beno Gutenberg* develop the Richter(-Gutenberg) Scale

English physicist *James Chadwick* receives the Nobel Prize for the discovery of the neutron

1936 German experimental physicist *Hans Geiger* perfects the Geiger-Mueller Counter

Russian biochemist *Aleksandr Ivanovich Oparin* publishes his origin of life theory

English mathematician *Alan Turing* publishes a paper detailing a machine that would serve as a model for the first working computer

1937 Russian-born American biologist *Theodosius Dobzhansky* writes *Genetics and the Origin of Species*

Australian English pathologist *Howard Walter Florey* discovers the growth potential of polymeric chains

German-born English biochemist *Hans Adolf Krebs* identifies the workings of the Krebs Cycle

Hungarian American biochemist and molecular biologist *Albert Szent-Gyorgyi* receives the Nobel Prize for isolating vitamin C

1938 German chemist *Otto Hahn*, Austrian physicist *Lise Meitner*, and German chemist *Fritz Strassmann* discover nuclear fission

American physicist *Carl David Anderson* discovers the meson

1939 Swiss-born American physicist *Felix Bloch* measures the neutron's magnetic movement

American chemist *Wallace Hume Carothers* founds the synthetic fiber industry with his research

French-born American microbiologist and ecologist *René Dubos* discovers tyrothricin

American chemist *Linus Pauling* develops the theory of complimentarity

Russian-born American aeronautical engineer *Igor I. Sikorsky* flies the first single-rotor helicopter

1940 American physicist and inventor *Chester Carlson* receives a patent for his photocopying method

English experimental physicist *George Paget Thomson* forms the Maud Committee

1941 German-born English biochemist *Ernst Boris Chain* and Australian English pathologist *Howard Walter Florey* isolate penicillin

German-born American physicist *Hans Bethe* develops the Bethe Coupler

American biochemist *Fritz Lipmann* publishes "Metabolic Generation and Utilization of Phosphate Bond Energy"

1942 Hungarian American physicist and biophysicist *Leo Szilard* and Italian-born American physicist *Enrico Fermi* set up the first nuclear chain reaction

German-born American biologist *Ernst Mayr* proposes the theory of geographic speciation

American physicist *J. Robert Oppenheimer* becomes the director of the Manhattan Project

1943 German-born American molecular biologist *Max Delbrück* and Italian-born American molecular biologist *Salvador Edward Luria* publish a milestone paper regarded as the beginning of bacterial genetics

English physicist *James Chadwick* leads the British contingent of the Manhattan Project

French oceanographer *Jacques-Yves Cousteau* patents the Aqualung

Italian-born American molecular biologist *Salvador Edward Luria* devises the fluctuation test

1944 German American rocket engineer *Wernher Von Braun* fires the first fully operational V-2 rocket

Austrian-born American biochemist *Erwin Chargaff* discovers the genetic role of DNA

American nuclear chemist *Glenn T. Seaborg* successfully isolates large amounts of plutonium and develops the actinide concept

American paleontologist *George Gaylord Simpson* publishes *Tempo and Mode in Evolution*

Russian-born American microbiologist *Selman Waksman* develops streptomycin

1945 English physicist *James Chadwick* witnesses the first atomic bomb test

American biochemist *Fritz Lipmann* discovers coenzyme A

Hungarian American mathematician *Johann Von Neumann* publishes a report containing the first written description of the stored-program concept

American chemist *Linus Pauling* determines the cause of sickle-cell anemia

Austrian physicist *Erwin Schrödinger* publishes *What Is Life?*

1946 American geneticist *Joshua Lederberg* and American biochemist *Edward Lawrie Tatum* show that bacteria may reproduce sexually

English zoologist *Julian Huxley* becomes the first director-general of UNESCO

1947 French oceanographer *Jacques-Yves Cousteau* breaks the free diving record using his Aqualung

Hungarian-born English physicist *Dennis Gabor* discovers holography

American inventor *Edwin H. Land* demonstrates the first instant camera

American mathematician *Norbert Wiener* creates the study of cybernetics

1948 American physicist *John Bardeen* develops the transistor

American chemist *Melvin Calvin* begins research on photosynthesis

Russian-born American physicist *George Gamow* publishes "Alpha-Beta-Gamma" paper

American zoologist and sex researcher *Alfred Kinsey* publishes *Sexual Behavior in the Human Male*

American biochemist *Wendell Meredith Stanley*

receives Presidential Certificate of Merit for developing an influenza vaccine

Swedish chemist *Arne Tiselius* receives the Nobel Prize for research in electrophoresis

1949 Hungarian-born American physicist *Edward Teller* begins developing the hydrogen bomb

American astronomer *Fred Lawrence Whipple* suggests the "dirty snowball" comet model

1950 American geneticist *Barbara McClintock* publishes the discovery of genetic transposition

1951 American chemist *Katharine Burr Blodgett* receives the Garvan Medal for women chemists

American biologist *Gregory Goodwin Pincus* begins work on the antifertility steroid the "pill"

Dutch-born English zoologist and ethologist *Nikolaas Tinbergen* publishes *The Study of Instinct*

1952 German-born American astronomer *Walter Baade* presents new measurements of the universe

French-born American microbiologist and ecologist *René Dubos* publishes a book linking tuberculosis with certain environmental conditions

American microbiologist *Alfred Day Hershey* conducts the "Blender Experiment" to demonstrate that DNA is the genetic material of life

Italian-born American molecular biologist *Salvador Edward Luria* discovers the phenomenon known as restriction and modification

American microbiologist *Jonas Salk* develops the first polio vaccine

English chemist *Alexander Todd* establishes the structure of flavin adenine dinucleotide (FAD)

1953 Russian theoretical physicist *Andrei Sakharov* and Russian physicist *Igor Tamm* develop the first Soviet hydrogen bomb

English molecular biologist *Francis Crick* and American molecular biologist *James D. Watson* develop the Watson-Crick model of DNA

English molecular biologist *Rosalind Elsie Franklin* provides evidence of DNA's double-helical structure

American physicist *Murray Gell-Mann* publishes a paper explaining the strangeness principle

American zoologist and sex researcher *Alfred Kinsey* publishes *Sexual Behavior in the Human Female*

French microbiologist *André Lwoff* proposes that "inducible lysogenic bacteria" can test cancerous and noncancerous cell activity

English biologist *Peter Brian Medawar* proves acquired immunological tolerance

American chemist *Stanley Lloyd Miller* publishes "A Production of Amino Acids under Possible Primitive Earth Conditions"

Austrian-born English crystallographer and biochemist *Max Perutz* develops method of isomorphous replacement

1955 English chemist *Alexander Todd* and English chemist and crystallographer *Dorothy Crowfoot Hodgkin* determine the structure of vitamin B12

American biochemist *Sidney W. Fox* begins identifying properties of microspheres

American microbiologist *Jonas Salk*'s polio vaccine pronounced safe and ninety-percent effective

English biochemist *Frederick Sanger* determines the total structure of the insulin molecule

1956 American biochemist *Stanley Cohen* extracts NGF from a mouse tumor

American experimental physicist *Leon Max Lederman* helps discover the "long-lived neutral kaon"

1957 American biochemist *Arthur Kornberg* and Spanish biochemist *Severo Ochoa* use DNA polymerase to synthesize DNA molecules

1958 American physicist *James Van Allen* discovers Van Allen radiation belts

American geneticist *George Wells Beadle* receives the Nobel Prize for the One Gene, One Enzyme Theory

American population biologist *Paul R. Ehrlich* makes his first statement regarding the problem of overpopulation

German physicist *Rudolf Mössbauer* discovers recoilless gamma ray release

1959 American computer scientist *Grace Hopper* develops the COBOL computer language

German physicist *Rudolf Mössbauer* uses the Mössbauer Effect to test the theory of relativity

1960 English physicist and biochemist *John Kendrew* and Austrian-born English crystallographer and biochemist *Max Perutz* formulate the first three-dimensional structure of the protein myoglobin

American Chemist *Willard F. Libby* receives the Nobel Prize for his development of radiocarbon dating

Russian-born American virologist *Albert Sabin*'s oral polio vaccine is approved for manufacture in the United States

1961 French biologists *François Jacob* and *Jacques Monod* discover messenger ribonucleic acid (mRNA)

American chemist *Melvin Calvin* receives the Nobel Prize in his chemistry for research on photosynthesis

American biochemist *Marshall Warren Nirenberg* cracks the genetic code

1962 American marine biologist *Rachel Carson* publishes *Silent Spring*

Russian theoretical physicist *Lev Davidovich Landau* receives the Nobel Prize for his research into theories of condensed matter

Hungarian-born American physicist *Edward Teller* becomes the first advocate of an "active defense system" to shoot down enemy missiles

New Zealand-born English biophysicist *Maurice Hugh Frederick Wilkins* shows the helical structure of RNA

1963 German American physicist *Maria Goeppert-Mayer* becomes the first woman to receive the Nobel Prize for theoretical physics

American chemist *Linus Pauling* becomes the only person to receive two unshared Nobel Prizes

1964 American psychobiologist *Roger W. Sperry* publishes the findings of his split-brain studies

1965 American geneticist *A. H. Sturtevant* publishes *The History of Genetics*

1967 English astrophysicist *Antony Hewish* and Irish astronomer *Jocelyn Susan Bell Burnell* discover pulsars

South African heart surgeon *Christiaan Neethling Barnard* performs the first human heart transplant

American primatologist *Dian Fossey* establishes a permanent research camp in Rwanda

1968 American physicist *Luis Alvarez* wins the Nobel Prize for his bubble chamber work

1969 American astronaut *Neil Armstrong* becomes the first man to walk on the moon

1970 Indian-born American biochemist *Har Gobind Khorana* synthesizes the first artificial DNA

American biologist *Lynn Margulis* publishes *Origins of Life*

1971 English ethologist *Jane Goodall* publishes *In the Shadow of Man*

1972 American evolutionary biologist *Stephen Jay Gould* and American paleontologist *Niles*

Eldredge introduce the concept of punctuated equilibrium

American physicist *John Bardeen* develops the BCS theory of superconductivity

American inventor *Edwin H. Land* reveals the first instant color camera

1973 American radio engineer *Karl Jansky* receives the honor of having the Jansky unit adopted as the unit of measure of radiowave intensity

Austrian zoologist and ethologist *Konrad Lorenz* receives the Nobel Prize for his behavioral research

American biochemist and geneticist *Maxine Singer* warns the public of gene-splicing risks

1974 English astrophysicist *Antony Hewish* receives the first Nobel Prize awarded to an astrophysicist

1975 French oceanographer *Jacques-Yves Cousteau* sees his Cousteau Society membership reach 120,000

American zoologist *Edward O. Wilson* publishes *Sociobiology: The New Synthesis*

1976 American computer engineer *Seymour Cray* introduces the CRAY-1 supercomputer

1977 Russian-born Belgian chemist *Ilya Prigogine* receives the Nobel Prize in chemistry for his work on nonequilibrium thermodynamics

1980 American biochemist *Paul Berg* receives the Nobel Prize for the biochemistry of nucleic acids

1981 American virologist *Robert C. Gallo* develops a blood test for the AIDS virus and discovers human T-cell leukemia virus

1982 American astronaut and physicist *Sally Ride* becomes the first American woman in space

1983 Indian-born American astrophysicist and applied mathematician *Subrahmanyan Chandrasekhar* receives the Nobel Prize for research on aged stars

American primatologist *Dian Fossey* publishes *Gorillas in the Mist*

French virologist *Luc Montagnier* discovers the human immunodeficiency virus (HIV)

American astronomer and exobiologist *Carl Sagan* publishes an article with others suggesting the possibility of a "nuclear winter"

1986 American physicist *Richard P. Feynman* explains why the space shuttle *Challenger* exploded

1987 Chinese American physicist *Paul Ching-Wu Chu* leads a team that discovers a method for higher temperature superconductivity

1987 American molecular biologist *Walter Gilbert* begins the human genome project to map DNA

1988 English theoretical physicist *Stephen Hawking* publishes *A Brief History of Time: From the Big Bang to Black Holes*

English pharmacologist *James Black* receives the Nobel Prize for his heart and ulcer medication work

1989 German-born American physicist *Hans Dehmelt* and German physicist *Wolfgang Paul* share the Nobel Prize for devising ion traps

1990 American physicists *Jerome Friedman, Henry W. Kendall,* and *Richard E. Taylor* are awarded the Nobel Prize for confirming the existence of quarks

American surgeon *Joseph E. Murray* receives the Nobel Prize for performing the first human kidney transplant

1991 German physician and cell physiologist *Bert Sakmann* and German biophysicist *Erwin Neher*

are awarded the Nobel Prize for inventing the patch clamp technique

English biochemist *Richard J. Roberts* and American biologist *Phillip A. Sharp* share the Nobel Prize for their research on DNA structure

American astrophysicists *Russell A. Hulse* and *Joseph H. Taylor, Jr.* receive the Nobel Prize for their work on binary pulsars

NOTABLE TWENTIETH-CENTURY SCIENTISTS

Sandra M. Faber

1944-

American astronomer

Sandra M. Faber, an astronomer and professor at the Lick Observatory of the University of California, Santa Cruz, has made significant contributions to the big bang theory, a model of cosmic evolution which states that the universe was created in a giant explosion of a super-dense nucleus of matter some fifteen billion years ago. Faber's work in defining and developing theories of the evolution of galaxies has resulted in a number of discoveries relating to this model of the universe, including the Faber-Jackson relation. In 1984, working with theoretical physicists George Blumenthal and Joel Primack at Santa Cruz, Faber further hypothesized that the universe was now composed largely of cold, dark matter, rather than the hot, neutrino-based matter scientists had earlier supposed. In 1990, working with a group of six other astronomers, Faber participated in identifying the great attractor, a concentration of matter whose gravitational pull on galaxies as distant as 150-million light years away seems to defy previously accepted laws of expansion.

Faber was born Sandra Moore in Boston on December 28, 1944, the only child of Donald Edwin and Elizabeth Mackenzie (Borwick) Moore. Her father was an insurance executive with an interest in science; her mother was a homemaker with an interest in medicine. Raised in the Midwest, Faber gained an interest in astronomy through star gazing with her father. In an interview with Alan Lightman and Roberta Brawer in *Origins,* she observed: "I was born when my mother was 42 and my father was [43]. . . . Their education came from the beginning of this century rather than the middle of the century, as it would have had the age gap been more normal." As a result, Faber found herself influenced by early twentieth-century scientific literature, including James Jeans' *The Stars in Their Courses* and Hoyle's *Frontiers of Astronomy,* which espoused the steady-state theory, in which the universe has neither a beginning or an end. Although Faber ceased subscribing to the theory as an adult, the intellectual experiences of her youth left her left a strong influence on her.

Faber attended Swarthmore College in Pennsylvania and obtained her bachelor's degree in physics in 1966. While at Swarthmore, she met Andrew Leigh Faber, whom she married on June 9, 1967. They have two daughters, Robin Leigh and Holly Ilena. Faber's mentor at Swarthmore was Sarah Lee Lippincott, an astronomer who was not a member of the university faculty. Observing that Lippincott's career had been limited by the lack of a Ph.D., Faber became determined to obtain one for herself.

Faber attended Harvard University, where she completed a Ph.D. in astronomy in 1972. Further graduate work was affected by the fact that Faber's husband took a position at the Naval Research Laboratory in Washington, DC. To continue her research there, Faber obtained an office at the lab among astronomers who were "doing things like measuring the temperature of Venus and studying water masers," she reported in *Origins.* A year-and-a-half later, she was offered a residency at the Department of Terrestrial Magnetism, where she worked alongside astronomers **Vera Cooper Rubin** and Kent Ford.

Research Leads to Faber-Jackson Relation

When she completed her doctoral thesis, a study of elliptical galaxies, Faber accepted a position as assistant professor and astronomer at the Lick Observatory at the University of California, Santa Cruz. Her early work at Lick led her to study further the formation, structure and evolution of galaxies, and postulate that the outer regions of certain small galaxies had been stripped away by massive companion galaxies. In 1975 she developed, with graduate student Robert Jackson, the Faber-Jackson relation. This was the first of many galactic "sealing laws" and related the size of elliptical galaxies to the internal orbital speeds of their component stars. It was later developed into an important formula used to calculate distances between galaxies.

In 1977 Faber was promoted to associate professor and astronomer at Lick, and made full professor in 1979. That same year, with colleague John Gallagher, she wrote a review concluding that galaxies are surrounded by enormous pockets of invisible matter, an idea that led Faber and her colleagues to predict that the galaxies themselves had been formed from this invisible matter. This resulted in the 1984 theory of dark matter, which suggested that invisible, or dark, matter is cold and lightless, a series of weakly interacting particles that eventually cluster together to form galaxies.

WOLVERHAMPTON PUBLIC LIBRARIES

In the early 1980s Faber collaborated with six other astronomers in the Seven Samurai project to measure the distances and velocities of elliptical galaxies, those collections of stars arranged in an elliptical pattern that seemingly have no internal structure. The project led to the 1990 discovery of the great attractor, a concentrated "galaxy of clumped galaxies" and matter which exerts a steady gravitational pull on an area of space approximately 100 million light years across, which includes our own Milky Way. The astronomers have also identified over 250 galaxies of two types, spiral and elliptical, that are moving toward the great attractor at an average rate of 400 miles per second. Some believe that the existence of the great attractor has weakened proof of the big bang theory and that it contradicts Faber's own theory of dark matter. But Faber believes the discovery will not make the older theory obsolete. On the contrary, her latest theory proposes that dark matter consists of two new particles, one of which is massive, the other which is light. A computer model of this theory shows that such a mix of matter would, in fact, predict such clumping.

In 1985 Faber was presented the Dannie Heineman Prize for astrophysics by the American Astronomical Society and the American Institute for Physics, in recognition of "her spirited observational approach" and for her insights into and advancement of "the theory of galaxy evolution." The following year she received an honorary doctorate of science from Swarthmore College, and is one of the few women to have been extended membership in the National Academy of Sciences. In 1990 she helped establish the Keck Observatory on the summit of Mauna Kea in Hawaii, where she is co-chair of the science committee. She is also a member of the wide-field camera design team for the Hubble Space Telescope.

"I think of myself now in terms of the ancient Greeks," she stated in *Origins:* "What they saw in the universe was the sun, the planets, and the earth. And they might have said, 'Well, why is the earth the way it is, or why is the sun the way it is?' . . . The earth is the way it is because we happen to be on it. This is the old anthropic way of answering cosmological questions. I really think that we will probably find that our universe is the way it is to some extent just because we're in it."

SELECTED WRITINGS BY FABER:

Books

(Editor) *Near Normal Galaxies: From the Planck Time to the Present: The Eighth Santa Cruz Summer Workshop in Astronomy and Astrophysics, July 21 -August 1, 1986, Lick Observatory,* Springer-Verlag, 1987.

Periodicals

"Variations in Spectral-Energy Distributions and Absorption-Line Strengths Among Elliptical Galaxies," *Astrophysical Journal,* No. 179, 1973, p. 731.

"Ten-Color Intermediate-Band Photometry of Stars," *Astronomy and Astrophysics Supplement,* No. 10, 1973, p. 201.

(With Robert E. Jackson), "Velocity Dispersions and Mass-to-Light Ratios for Elliptical Galaxies," *Astrophysical Journal,* No. 204, 1976, p. 668.

SOURCES:

Books

Lightman, A. and Brawer, R., "Interview with Sandra Faber," *Origins,* Harvard University Press, 1990, pp. 324–40.

Pasachoff, J., "Interview with Sandra Faber," *Journey Through the Universe,* Saunders, 1992.

Periodicals

Bagne, Paul, "Interview with Sandra Faber," *Omni,* July, 1990, pp. 62–92.

"Faber Receives Heineman Prize for Work in Astrophysics," *Physics Today,* March, 1986, p. 119.

Hilts, Philip J., "Far Out In Space, A Giant Discovery," *New York Times,* January 12, 1990, p. 22.

Wilford, John Noble, "Astronomers Say Proof of Black Hole Theory is Almost Within Their Grasp," *New York Times,* January 17, 1992, p. 17.

Wilford, John Noble, "Star Clusters Astonish Astronomers," *New York Times,* January 21, 1992, p. 6.

—Sketch by Mindi Dickstein

Philo T. Farnsworth
1906-1971
American inventor

On the statue erected in his honor in the U. S. Capitol Statuary Hall, Philo T. Farnsworth is called the Father of Television. He was the first person to propose that pictures could be televised

Philo T. Farnsworth

electronically, which he did when he was 14 years old. By the time he was 21, Farnsworth had proved his ideas by televising the world's first electronically-produced image. From the day he sketched out for his high school chemistry teacher his ideas for harnessing electricity to transmit images, until his death in 1971, Farnsworth amassed a portfolio of over 100 television-related patents, some of which are still in use today.

Farnsworth was born in Indian Creek, Utah, on August 19, 1906. The first of five children born to Serena Bastian and Lewis Edwin Farnsworth, he was named after his grandfather, Philo Taylor Farnsworth I, the leader of the Mormon pioneers who settled that area of southwestern Utah. Although there was no electricity where he lived, Farnsworth learned as much as he could about it from his father and from technical and radio magazines. Lewis Farnsworth was a farmer and regaled his son with technical discussions about the telephone, gramophone, locomotives, and anything else the younger Farnsworth was curious about. When the family moved to a farm in Idaho with its own power plant, he poked and probed and mastered the lighting system and was soon put in charge of maintaining it. It had never run so smoothly. Farnsworth was adept at inventing gadgets even before he went to high school, and he won a national invention contest when he was 13 years old.

Dreaming of Television

In 1920, he read that some inventors were attempting to transmit visual images by mechanical means. For the next two years, he worked on an electronic alternative that he was convinced would be faster and better; he came up with the basic design for an apparatus in 1922. Farnsworth discussed his ideas and showed sketches of the apparatus to his high school chemistry teacher Justin Tolman. Little did they know that this discussion would later be critical in settling a patent dispute between Farnsworth and his competitor at the Radio Corporation of America (RCA), **Vladimir Zworykin**.

Farnsworth took physics courses by correspondence from the University of Utah and later enrolled at Brigham Young University. He was largely self-taught but so impressed two of his chemistry professors at BYU with his ideas about television that they gave him the run of the chemistry and glass labs to start work on his theories.

In 1924, Farnsworth's father died and he was left with the responsibility of supporting the family. After a short time in the navy, he moved to Salt Lake City to work as a canvasser for the Community Chest. There Farnsworth made friends with George Everson, the businessman who was organizing the fundraising effort, and his associate Leslie Gorrell. Farnsworth told Everson and Gorrell about his ideas for a television, and they invested $6,000 in his venture. With additional backing from a group of bankers in San Francisco, Farnsworth was given a research lab and a year to prove his concepts.

Building the First Television System

Farnsworth was married to his college sweetheart Elma Pem Gardner on May 27, 1926, and the next day they left for California, where Farnsworth would set up his lab in San Francisco. With assistance from his wife, Elma, better known as Pem, and her brother Cliff, Farnsworth designed and built all the components—from the vacuum transmitter tubes to the image scanner and the receiver—that made up his first television system. The key invention was his Image Dissector camera, which scanned relatively slowly in one direction and relatively quickly in the opposite direction, making possible much greater scanning speeds than had been achieved earlier. All television receivers use this basic system of scanning.

On September 7, 1927, three weeks before the deadline, Farnsworth gathered his friends and engineering colleagues in a room adjoining the lab and amazed them with the first two-dimensional image ever transmitted by television—the image of his wife and assistant, Pem. His backers continued their support for a year and in September 1928, the first television system was unveiled to the world. In 1929, some of the bankers who invested in the research formed a company called Television Laboratories Inc., of which Farnsworth was named vice president and director of research.

The Challenge of the Marketplace

At the same time, RCA began aggressively competing with Farnsworth for control of the emerging television market and challenged the patent on his invention. With the testimony of Farnsworth's high school teacher, Justin Tollman, it was determined that Farnsworth had indeed documented his ideas one year before RCA's Vladimir Zworykin. This was but the first of many challenges from RCA, but in the end the corporate giant was forced to work out a cross-licensing arrangement with Farnsworth.

The victor in dozens of legal challenges by RCA, Farnsworth eventually licensed his television patents to the growing industry and let others refine and develop his basic inventions. His patents were first licensed in Germany and Great Britain, and only later did the Federal Communications Commission allocate broadcast channels in the United States. During his early years in San Francisco, Farnsworth did other important work as well. He made the first cold cathode-ray tube, the first simple electron microscope, and a means for using radio waves to sense direction—an innovation now known as radar. He received more than 300 patents worldwide during his career.

Farnsworth eventually set up his own company, which boomed during World War II with government contracts to develop electronic surveillance and other equipment. The Farnsworth Radio and Television Corp. took a downturn after the war and was sold to the International Telephone and Telegraph Company (ITT) in 1949. Farnsworth remained with the company for some time as a research consultant. Late in his life he turned his attention to the field of atomic energy. Farnsworth died of emphysema on March 11, 1971, in Holladay, a suburb of Salt Lake City.

For his pioneering work, Farnsworth received the First Gold Medal awarded by the National Television Broadcasters Association in 1944. During his lifetime he also was presented with honorary doctorates in science from Indiana Technical College (1951) and Brigham Young University (1968). Posthumously, the inventor was remembered with a twenty-cent stamp with his likeness, issued in 1983, and his induction into the National Inventors Hall of Fame in 1984. The Philo T. Farnsworth Memorial Museum was dedicated in his honor in Rigby, Idaho, in 1988.

SOURCES:

Books

Dedication of the Statue of Philo T. Farnsworth, Proceedings in the U.S. Capitol Rotunda, U.S. Government Printing Office, 1990.

Everson, George, *The Story of Television: The Life of Philo T. Farnsworth,* Norton, 1949.

Farnsworth, Elma, *Distant Vision: Romance and Discovery on an Invisible Frontier,* Pemberlykent, 1990.

Periodicals

May, Dennis, "Philo T. Farnsworth: The Father of Television," *BYU Today,* May 1989, pp. 33–36.

—Sketch by Olga Anderson

Marilyn G. Farquhar
1928-
American cell biologist and experimental pathologist

Marilyn G. Farquhar was a influential cell biologist who struggled from humble beginnings to leave an indelible impression on her field. Farquhar greatly advanced scientific knowledge of the mechanisms of renal disease and protein trafficking within cells. She published numerous papers and received various honors in her career, such as election by her peers to the National Academy of Sciences.

Marilyn Gist Farquhar was born July 11, 1928, in Tulare, California, the second of Brooks DeWitt and Alta Gertrude Green Gist's two children. A pediatrician friend of Alta's was an early catalyst for Farquhar's interest in medicine and biology. Farquhar grew up in Tulare and completed her early schooling there. She attended a country school from grades one through four and completed her elementary education at Wilson School in Tulare. She later went to Tulare Union High School, where her interest in biology was further sparked by an inspiring science teacher.

Although few of Farquhar's high school classmates attended college, her parents saw to it that she would not miss the opportunity. She attended the University of California at Berkeley, where she received an A.B. in zoology in 1949. In 1951 she entered her first marriage, which produced two sons,

Bruce and Douglas. At the University of California at San Francisco (UCSF) Farquhar received an M.A. in 1953 and a Ph.D. in 1955. Her first project at UCSF was to begin the operation of one of the first electron microscopes in the Bay Area. That project led directly to the subject of her Ph.D. dissertation, which was electron microscopy of secretory processes in the front part of the pituitary gland.

Farquhar did her postdoctoral work at Rockefeller University with the Nobel Prize-winning biologist **George Palade**, whom she eventually married on June 7, 1970. After her postdoctoral work she returned to UCSF and took a post as an assistant research pathologist. She researched cellular and molecular mechanisms of renal disease (disease involving the kidneys and their surroundings) and the secretory processes of various systems including the liver and pancreas. Farquhar considered her work in these two areas to be her most important contributions to her field.

After eight years with UCSF as a researcher and teacher, Farquhar became a professor of cell biology and pathologist at Yale University's medical school in 1973. She became Sterling Professor of Cell Biology there in 1987, and in the same year she was awarded the Wilson Medal of the America Society of Cell Biology for her work on secretion and membrane trafficking. Farquhar also received the Homer Smith Award of the American Society of Nephrology for her study of the cellular and molecular mechanisms of renal disease in 1987. The next year, 1988, she was honored for career achievements in her field by election to the prestigious National Academy of Sciences. Farquhar returned to California in 1990 to be professor of pathology at the medical school of the University of California in San Diego.

Farquhar is a passionate lover of nature and music. She is especially fond of the chamber and orchestral works of J. S. Bach, Ludwig van Beethoven, Johannes Brahms, and Franz Schubert. She and Palade have often taken long walks on Del Mar beach in California. They have also vacationed in Colorado, hiking in the mountains and attending classical music festivals there.

SOURCES:

Farquhar, Marilyn G., interview with John Henry Dreyfuss conducted March 1, 1994.

—Sketch by John Henry Dreyfuss

Wanda K. Farr
1895-
American biochemist

Wanda K. Farr solved a major scientific mystery in botany by showing that the substance cellulose, an important compound found in all plants, is made by tiny, cellular structures called plastids. The discovery was all the more notable because the process of cellulose synthesis had been obscured by the very techniques that previous researchers were using to study the phenomenon under the microscope.

Farr was born Wanda Margarite Kirkbride in New Matamoras, Ohio, on January 9, 1895, the daughter of C. Fred and Clara M. Kirkbride. Although Farr's father died of tuberculosis when she was a child, her budding interest in living things was nurtured by her great-grandfather, Samuel Richardson, who was a prominent local physician. Farr had initially decided to attend medical school, but her family insisted she not become a doctor, fearing she too would be exposed to tuberculosis. Farr enrolled at Ohio University in Athens, where she received her B.S. in botany in 1915. She did graduate work in botany at Columbia University, earning her M.S. in 1918. It was there she met her future husband, Clifford Harrison Farr, who was completing work for a Ph.D. in botany.

When Clifford went to the Agricultural and Mechanical College of Texas to teach plant physiology, Farr accepted a position as instructor of botany at Kansas State College in 1917 to be closer to him. After they were married, the young couple moved to Washington, where Clifford Farr worked at the Department of Agriculture during World War I. Here, their son Robert was born, and Farr completed her research for her master's degree from Columbia.

After the war, they moved back to Texas A & M and then to Iowa in 1919, where Clifford became a faculty member of the University of Iowa's botany department. There, the two botanists continued to pursue their research on root hair cells—the tiny, fine hairs on plant roots that absorb water and nutrients from the soil. In 1925 Clifford accepted a position at Washington University in St. Louis, and the couple again moved. It was there, in February, 1928, that her husband died from a long-standing heart condition. Farr was later remarried to E. C. Faulwetter.

Begins Research on Cotton

After her husband's death, Farr abandoned her plan to return to Columbia to finish her doctorate and she remained at Washington University to teach her late husband's classes. She also became a research assistant at the Barnard Skin and Cancer Clinic in St. Louis from 1926 to 1927, where she learned new techniques for growing animal cells in culture dishes. After the school year ended, the Bache Fund of the National Academy of Sciences awarded her a grant to continue her studies of root hairs. Her work led in 1928 to a position with the U.S. Department of Agriculture working as a cotton technologist at the Boyce Thompson Institute, which was at that time located in Yonkers, New York.

The cotton industry was eager to learn more about cotton so it could train their employees to be better judges of the quality of this crop. Farr's work centered on the origin of cellulose, which makes up most of the cell walls of cotton fibrils and provides its form and stiffness. Though she and her coworkers studied the chemical content and other characteristics of the fibrils, they were confounded—as were scientists before them—by the origin of cellulose. Researchers knew that sugar was made in tiny structures called plastids, which capture the sun's energy during the process of photosynthesis. Molecules of cellulose, however, seemed to spring into existence fully formed within the cytoplasm of cells.

The problem, Farr discovered, was that plastids seemed to disappear into the cytoplasm when mounted in water for study under the microscope. Normally, light waves refract or bend when traveling from one medium, such as air, into another medium, such as water. (This refraction of light waves is what makes a spoon placed into a glass of water seem to bend.) The cellulose plastids, however, do not do this; rather, light passes directly through them, and they are rendered indistinguishable from the liquid medium. When these plastids fill with cellulose, the pressure within the structures makes them explode, spilling the cellulose molecules into the cytoplasm, where they are then visible. Thus, when viewed through a microscope, these molecules appear to arise suddenly, fully formed.

In 1936, during her studies of cotton cellulose, Farr was appointed Director of the Cellulose Laboratory of the Chemical Foundation at the Boyce Thompson Institute, and she later worked for the American Cyanamide Company (1940–43) and the Celanese Corporation of America (1943–54). In 1954 she was the twelfth annual Marie Curie lecturer at Pennsylvania State University. In 1956 she established her own laboratory, the Farr Cytochemistry Lab, in Nyack, New York. She also taught botany and cytochemistry at the University of Maine from 1957 to 1960, later serving as an occasional lecturer. At the time, she was one of the few women to become director of a research laboratory.

In a 1940 *New York Times* article about Farr, she was described as "versatile, chic, vivacious, [and] as modern as tomorrow." Her versatility included using her knowledge of cellulose to analyze the sheets from a 3,500-year-old Egyptian tomb for New York's Metropolitan Museum of Art to determine if they were made of cotton or linen (she determined they were linen). Among the organizations Farr belonged to were the American Association for the Advancement of Science; the American Chemical Society; the New York Academy of Science; the Royal Microscope Club (London); the American Institute of Chemists; Phi Beta Kappa; Sigma Xi; and Sigma Delta Epsilon.

SELECTED WRITINGS BY FARR:

Periodicals

(With S. H. Eckerson) "Formation of Cellulose Membranes by Microscopic Particles of Uniform Size in Linear Arrangement," *Contributions of the Boyce Thompson Institute,* Volume 6, 1934, p. 189.

"Microscopical and Microchemical Analysis of Material of Plant Origin from Ancient Tombs," *American Journal of Botany,* Volume 31, 1944, p. 9.

SOURCES:

Books

Yost, Edna, *American Women of Science,* Frederick A. Stokes Company, 1943.

Periodicals

"Cellulose Explained," *Time,* November 25, 1935, p. 54.

"Cellulose Factory Located in Plants," *New York Times,* December 27, 1939, p. 10.

"Challenging Approach to Study Brings Rewards to Scientist," *New York Times,* January 14, 1940, section 2, p. 8.

—*Sketch by Marc Kusinitz*

Anthony S. Fauci
1940-
American immunologist

Early in his career, Anthony S. Fauci carried out both basic and clinical research in immunology and infectious diseases. Since 1981, Fauci's research has been focused on the mechanisms of the human

Anthony S. Fauci

immunodeficiency virus (HIV), which causes acquired immunodeficiency syndrome (AIDS). His work has lead to breakthroughs in understanding the virus's progress, especially during the latency period between infection and full-blown AIDS. As director of both the National Institute of Allergy and Infectious Diseases (NIAID) and the Office of AIDS Research at the National Institutes of Health (NIH), Fauci is involved with much of the AIDS research performed in the United States and is responsible for supervising the investigation of the disease mechanism and the development of vaccines and drug therapy.

Anthony Stephen Fauci was born on December 24, 1940, in Brooklyn, New York, to Stephen A. Fauci, a pharmacist, and Eugenia A. Fauci, a homemaker. He attended a Jesuit high school in Manhattan and had a successful academic and athletic career there. After high school, Fauci entered Holy Cross College in Worcester, Massachusetts, as a premedical student, graduating with a B.A. in 1962. He then attended Cornell University Medical School, from which he received his medical degree in 1966 and where he completed both his internship and residency.

Begins work at NIAID

In 1968, Fauci became a clinical associate in the Laboratory of Clinical Investigation of NIAID, one of the eleven institutes that comprise the NIH. Except for one year spent at the New York Hospital Cornell Medical Center as chief resident, he has remained at the NIH throughout his career. His earliest studies focused on the functioning of the human immune system and how infectious diseases impact the system. As a senior staff fellow at NIAID, Fauci and two other researchers delineated the mechanism of Wegener's granulomatosis, a relatively rare and fatal immune disease involving the inflammation of blood vessels and organs. By 1971, Fauci had developed a drug regimen for Wegener's granulomatosis that is ninety-five percent effective. He also found cures for lymphomatoid granulomatosis and polyarteritis nodosa, two other immune diseases.

In 1972, Fauci became a senior investigator at NIAID and two years later he was named head of the Clinical Physiology Section. In 1977, Fauci was appointed deputy clinical director of NIAID. Fauci shifted the focus of the Laboratory of Clinical Infection at NIAID towards investigating the nature of AIDS in the early 1980s. It was his lab that demonstrated the type of defect that occurs in the T4 helper cells (the immune cells) and enables AIDS to be fatal. Fauci also orchestrated early therapeutic techniques, including bone-marrow transplants, in an attempt to save AIDS patients. In 1984, Fauci became the director of NIAID, and the following year the coordinator of all AIDS research at NIH. He has worked not only against the disease but also against governmental indifference to AIDS, winning larger and larger budgets for AIDS research. When the Office of AIDS Research at NIH was founded in 1988, Fauci was made director; he also decided to remain the director of NIAID. He and his research teams have developed a three-fold battle plan against AIDS: researching the mechanism of HIV, developing and testing drug therapies, and creating an AIDS vaccine.

In 1993, Fauci and his team at NIH disproved the theory that HIV remains dormant for approximately ten years after the initial infection, showing instead that the virus attacks the lymph nodes and reproduces itself in white blood cells known as CD4 cells. This discovery could lead to new and radical approaches in the early treatment of HIV-positive patients. Earlier discoveries that Fauci and his lab are responsible for include the 1987 finding that a protein substance known as cytokine may be responsible for triggering full-blown AIDS and the realization that the macrophage, a type of immune system cell, is the virus's means of transmission. Fauci demonstrated that HIV actually hides from the body's immune system in these macrophages and is thus more easily transmitted. In an interview with Dennis L. Breo published in the *Journal of the American Medical Association,* Fauci summed up his research to date: "We've learned that AIDS is a multiphasic, multifactorial disease of overlapping phases, progressing from infection to viral replication to chronic smoldering disease to profound depression of the immune system."

In drug therapy work, Fauci and his laboratory have run hundreds of clinical tests on medications such as azidothymidine (AZT), and Fauci has pushed for the early use of such drugs by terminally ill AIDS patients. Though no truly effective antiviral drug yet exists, drug therapies have been developed that can prolong the life of AIDS victims. Potential AIDS vaccines are still being investigated, a process complicated by the difficulty of finding willing research volunteers and the fact that animals do not develop AIDS as humans do, which further limits available research subjects. No viable vaccine is expected before the year 2000.

Fauci married Christine Grady, a clinical nurse and medical ethicist, in 1985. They have three daughters: Jennifer, Megan, and Alison. Fauci is an avid jogger, a former marathon runner, and enjoys fishing. Widely recognized for his research, he is the recipient of numerous prizes and awards, including a 1979 Arthur S. Flemming Award, the 1984 U.S. Public Health Service Distinguished Service Medal, the 1989 National Medical Research Award from the National Health Council, and the 1992 Dr. Nathan Davis Award for Outstanding Public Service from the American Medical Association. Fauci is also a fellow of the American Academy of Arts and Sciences and holds a number of honorary degrees. He is the author or coauthor of over 800 scientific articles and has edited several medical textbooks.

SELECTED WRITINGS BY FAUCI:

Periodicals

(With others) "Effect of Cyclophosphamide upon the Immune Response in Wegener's Granulomatosis," *New England Journal of Medicine,* Volume 285, 1971, pp. 1493–1496.

"The Revolution in Clinical Immunology," *Journal of the American Medical Association,* Volume 246, 1981, pp. 2567–2572.

"The Acquired Immune Deficiency Syndrome (AIDS)—The Ever Broadening Clinical Spectrum," *Journal of the American Medical Association,* Volume 249, 1983, pp. 2375–2376.

SOURCES:

Books

Current Biography Yearbook, 1988, H. W. Wilson, 1989, pp. 153–156.

Periodicals

Breo, Dennis L., "The US Race to 'Cure' AIDS—At '4' on a Scale of Ten, Says Dr. Fauci," *Journal of the American Medical Association,* June 9, 1993, pp. 2898–2900.

Hilts, Philip J., "AIDS Advocates Are Angry at U.S. But Its Research Chief Wins Respect," *New York Times,* September 4, 1990, p. A14.

Russell, Cristine, "Anthony S. Fauci: A Hard-Driving Leader of the Lab War on AIDS," *Washington Post,* November 3, 1986, pp. A12-A13.

Other

Fauci, Anthony S., interview with J. Sydney Jones conducted December 27, 1993.

—Sketch by J. Sydney Jones

René Geronimo Favaloro
1923-
Argentine surgeon

One of the pioneers of bypass heart surgery, in which a vein from the patient's leg is substituted for a damaged artery at the heart, René Geronimo Favaloro also established one of Latin America's leading medical teaching facilities, the Institute of Cardiology and Cardiovascular Surgery in Buenos Aires, Argentina.

Favaloro was born in La Plata, Argentina, to Ida Y. Raffaelli, a dressmaker, and Juan B. Favaloro, a carpenter. He attended the National College and Medical School at the University of La Plata, receiving his M.D. in 1949. His internship, residency and first staff position were at the Instituto General San Martin in La Plata, and he took a postgraduate course at Rawson Hospital in Buenos Aires. After twelve years practicing medicine in the remote Pampas of Argentina, he visited the Cleveland Clinic in 1961, curious about the latest techniques in myocardial revascularization (increasing a restricted blood supply to the heart). The *Cleveland Plain Dealer* recounted a story that the visiting professional—tall, dark, handsome and quite imposing but speaking little English—walked into a doctor's office at the Clinic and said softly, "I want to work here."

Helps Pioneer Coronary Bypass Surgery

Attempts at revascularization began before World War II with little success. Donald R. Effler, head of the thoracic and cardiovascular department at the Clinic, said in his introduction to Favaloro's book, *Surgical Treatment of Coronary Arteriosclerosis,* that he believed the primary reason for this lack of success was inadequate diagnosis; treatments were largely based on clinical assumptions. In 1957, Dr. F. Mason Sones, Jr., of the Cleveland Clinic was searching for a simple diagnostic tool to accurately identify coronary arterial disease. He developed angiography, in which dye is inserted via catheter into the arteries, exposing on X rays the exact location of blockages. The technique also enabled much finer diagnostic evaluations, allowing the individual needs of each patient to be identified, a relatively accurate prognosis predicted, and the appropriate therapy undertaken. The tool became the major determinant in selecting candidates for bypass surgery.

When Favaloro joined the thoracic and cardiovascular team at the Clinic as an observer in 1962, revascularization was still tenuous. Two techniques were being used: the pericardial patch graft, in which the wall of a blocked artery is opened and "patched" with part of a leg vein in an attempt to increase the size of the artery; and the mammary artery implant, in which one end of the mammary artery in the chest is inserted into the wall of the left ventricle, supplying the ventricle with blood to be pumped into the vessels. Favaloro's observations went far beyond the operating room, however. He plunged into all the documentation he could find on revascularization. In his now famous 1967 bypass operation, he inserted one end of the saphenous vein, removed from the patient's leg, into the aorta, the large artery above the heart. The other end he inserted into an artery below the obstruction, fully restoring the blood flow.

Although the first to perform a full bypass at the Clinic, Favaloro was not the first to use the procedure. David Sabiston, Jr., of Duke University in North Carolina unsuccessfully performed the first known human bypass in 1962. The first successful bypass was by H. Edward Garrett in 1964. Both operations were used in emergency situations. Neither doctor considered or developed the procedure as a standard treatment, nor did they publish documentation on the procedure for almost 10 years.

Favaloro approached the procedure from an entirely different perspective. His research convinced him the procedure would be effective in treating certain types of heart disease. He planned his first bypass, fully intending to adopt it as a standard procedure for appropriate candidates, and published a paper on it in 1968. The *New York Times* quotes Lawrence H. Cohn, chair of the Cardiac Surgery Committee of the American College of Cardiology as saying, "Favaloro was the first to recognize the importance of this technique and develop it."

Over the years, the coronary bypass has been refined and improved. Some critics declare it "overused," causing many patients to pay for unnecessary surgery. However, the procedure lasts longer than more recent treatments, such as angioplasty (inserting a tiny balloon into the restricted artery via catheter and inflating the balloon to compress plaque against the artery wall), and remains the most important treatment for coronary arteriosclerosis.

By 1970, Favaloro and the cardiovascular team at the Clinic had performed more than one thousand bypass operations, of which almost a quarter were multiple bypasses, with the death rate an astonishingly low 4.2%. In 1971, at the height of his surgical career, Favaloro left the Clinic, returned to Buenos Aires, and established the Favaloro Foundation to teach bypass surgery. In 1992, after twenty years of dedication and hard work, Favaloro's lifelong dream was fulfilled with the completion of his 10-story, $55 million Institute of Cardiology and Cardiovascular Surgery, one of the finest medical teaching institutes in Latin America. By then, his programs had trained more than 300 heart surgeons, half of whom are Latin American, and his team had performed thousands of by-pass operations.

Favaloro is married to Maria A. Delgado. He is a member of the Medical Society of La Plata and the Societe Internationale de Chirurgie. He was elected a fellow of the American College of Surgeons in 1967, which also made him an honorary fellow in 1990. He has also served in the Army of the Republic of Argentina as a lieutenant.

Considered a hero by both his medical colleagues and the people of his nation—who frequently suggest him as a presidential candidate—the surgeon who, contrary to the norms of society, turned his back on fame and fortune both at the beginning and the height of his career, described himself in an interview with the *Cleveland Plain Dealer* as "still a simple, country doctor."

SELECTED WRITINGS BY FAVALORO:

Books

Surgical Treatment of Coronary Arteriosclerosis, Williams & Wilkins, 1970.

Do You Know San Martin?, [Buenos Aires], 1986.

The Challenging Dream of Heart Surgery: From the Pampas to Cleveland, Little, Brown, 1994.

SOURCES:

Periodicals

Cleveland Clinic Foundation Fellow, Volume 1, number 4, 1983, pp. 1, 4.

Cleveland Clinic Newsletter, October, 1967, p. 1; July, 1971, p. 3.
Cleveland Plain Dealer, September 11, 1987; November 8, 1992.
New York Times, August 18, 1992.

—*Sketch by David Petechuk*

Nina V. Fedoroff
1942-
American molecular biologist

Nina V. Fedoroff is most widely recognized for her successful duplication and genetic analysis of the transposable elements in maize (corn), first identified by American geneticist **Barbara McClintock**. Fedoroff and her students demonstrated that it was possible to use maize transposable elements to clone maize genes, which paved the way for further developments in gene cloning.

Fedoroff was born on April 9, 1942, in Cleveland, Ohio, a child of Russian immigrants who escaped the anarchy of Russian upheaval in the early 1900s. She counted among her ancestors nobles, scientists, clerics, and diplomats under the Russian czars. Her mother, Olga S. (Snegireff) Fedoroff, became a Russian instructor and translator for the United States Air Force Language School. Fedoroff's father, Vsevolod N. Fedoroff, was employed as an engineer for the Carrier Corporation. In 1959, Fedoroff married Joseph Hacker, with whom she had a daughter, Natasha, a year later. They divorced in 1962. In 1966, Fedoroff married Patrick Gaganidze, and gave birth to their son, Kyr, in 1972. Fedoroff and Gaganidze were divorced in 1978. In 1990, Fedoroff married Michael Broyles.

Fedoroff's academic interests surfaced at an early age. At age 16, she took college history courses and taught music. She took her state high school exams on her own and graduated first in her class. Married and a young mother, Fedoroff entered Syracuse University and began her studies with the aid of a scholarship. While studying at the university, Fedoroff earned tuition and living expenses by working as a freelance flutist, a music teacher, and a Russian-English translator for the Air Force Language School, eventually becoming the assistant manager of the Translation Bureau at Biological Abstracts. In 1966, she graduated summa cum laude from Syracuse, was voted salutatorian, and was elected to Phi Beta Kappa.

For a time, Fedoroff considered becoming a professional musician and was hired as a flutist by the Syracuse Symphony Orchestra. While playing chamber music one afternoon in the late 1960s, Fedoroff met **James D. Watson**, who had won the 1962 Nobel Prize with **Francis Crick** for their work on the structure of deoxyribonucleic acid (DNA). Deciding that she could not devote sufficient time to a career in music, Fedoroff returned to school, intent upon becoming a physician. She was thus introduced to laboratory work and came to the conclusion that "doing experiments was more absorbing and interesting than anything I'd ever done before," as she stated in correspondence to Mary Raum. Fedoroff was awarded a National Science Foundation Undergraduate Summer Research Award and spent three months at Woods Hole Marine Biological Laboratory in Massachusetts. Regarding her experience at Woods Hole, Fedoroff commented: "I was exposed to many new techniques and new concepts—after that summer, there was no doubt in my mind that I wanted to do experiments for the rest of my life, a decision I have never regretted."

After receiving a National Science Foundation Grant for graduate work, Fedoroff began studying at Rockefeller University. She graduated with a Ph.D. in 1972 and was elected to the scientific honor society Sigma Xi. The University of California, Los Angeles (UCLA), hired Fedoroff in a temporary capacity as an acting assistant professor. Fedoroff taught classes and conducted research on nuclear ribonucleic acid (RNA) from 1972 to 1974. Shortly thereafter, she was awarded postdoctoral fellowships from the prestigious Damon Runyon-Walter Winchell Cancer Research Fund and the National Institutes of Health.

Meets McClintock

In the early 1970s, as Fedoroff concluded her postdoctoral work, she presented a lecture at the Cold Spring Harbor Laboratory. The laboratory, just outside New York City, was a landmark where emergent ideas in molecular biology circulated among conclaves of scientists during annual summer conventions. This was the site of the evolution of the "Phage Group," which met there from 1940 to 1952, a gathering of bacterial research scientists that demonstrated that bacteriophages, very simple organisms weighing one billionth of a gram, manifested the same basic genetic phenomena as did most complex higher organisms. The ability of bacteriophages to reproduce rapidly made them an indispensable study mechanism to laboratory biologists. Fedoroff, who had at one point studied bacteriophages, encountered McClintock, who would later win a Nobel Prize for her discovery of mobile genes in the chromosomes of corn. Fedoroff's meeting with McClintock changed the direction of her scientific pursuits; Fedoroff was so intrigued by McClintock's ideas that she studied

McClintock's complicated writings on corn chromosomes and educated herself on the subject.

Fedoroff left UCLA and joined the Department of Embryology at the Carnegie Institution of Washington, where, by 1978, she was placed in a permanent position as a staff scientist. Her laboratory work based on McClintock's research then began in earnest. She commented: "There were times when I wanted to give up, especially in my first summer of 5 AM to 2 AM days in the field doing maize genetics." In conjunction with her scientific work, Johns Hopkins University hired Fedoroff as a full professor in the department of biology.

Studies Bacteriophages and Maize

Fedoroff's scientific pursuits included studies in molecular biology, biochemistry, and biology. In 1972, she had studied the replication of viruses that destroy bacteria in her research on the replicase of bacteriophage f2. Bacteriophages are bacterial viral parasites composed of proteins and DNA that reproduce rapidly. In Fedoroff's studies, bacteria were replicated and transformed into active biological agents when they were given access to a bacterial host cell. Fedoroff was responsible for the first full sequencing of a 5S ribosomal RNA gene. The work was important because Fedoroff created a "map" or "guide" of the sub-elements of a genetic material found in all cells and many viruses. In addition, her studies shed light upon ribosomes, the principal sites of protein synthesis in cells.

Although successful in her work on bacteriophages and sequencing, Fedoroff stated that her "most significant scientific achievement has been the cloning and molecular genetic analysis of maize transposable elements." Transposable elements, also known as "jumping genes," were of interest because of their ability to move to new positions on the chromosome. Little research had been done in this area on plants when Fedoroff undertook her project. Fedoroff noted: "The work done in my laboratory has contributed substantially to the development of the entire field of plant molecular biology." Along with her students, and in collaboration with J. Schell of Cologne, Germany, Fedoroff discovered that these transposable elements were mobile in plants other than maize. The system of cloning was very rapidly picked up by the molecular biology community, and, according to Fedoroff, "[paved] the way for using the maize transposable elements to mark and clone genes in other plants." She continued: "Our molecular genetic investigations of maize transposable elements has led to the elucidation of a completely novel epigenetic regulatory mechanism . . . [and the identification of] the first regulatory protein that can interact with an epigenetically silent gene and reactivate it."

The aspects of Fedoroff's work that she finds most intriguing are the study of molecular bases of plant development, gene expression, and interactions between cellular and genetic processes. Fedoroff stated: "I am especially interested in the mechanisms that underlie a plant's commitment to a different part of its growth cycle or to altering its physiological state in response to cues from the environment." Fedoroff contributed to the field through the training of students in plant biology. Serving as a Phi Beta Kappa Visiting Scholar from 1984 to 1985, she traveled to a number of universities and gave lectures, met with classes, and held informal meetings with students. She has been very active in recombinant DNA and genetic engineering controversies. By lecturing, writing popular and technical pieces, and appearing in television documentaries and on radio talk shows, Fedoroff has been able to extend her ideas to a general audience.

Fedoroff is a member of the American Academy of Arts and Sciences and the National Academy of Sciences. A prolific writer who has published more than seventy-eight scientific works and numerous non-technical pieces, Fedoroff has also served as an editor, reviewer, and translator. Fedoroff's personal concerns about the various practical uses of molecular biology have led her to debate the idea of introducing genetically engineered organisms into the environment. Fedoroff has promoted scientific exchange between scientists from the former Soviet Union and Western scientists by founding and directing the International Science Foundation. In 1991, Fedoroff rejoined the Syracuse Symphony as a guest flutist, and her hobbies include cooking, gardening, skiing, and playing tennis. The New York Academy of Sciences named Fedoroff an outstanding contemporary American woman scientist in 1992.

SELECTED WRITINGS BY FEDOROFF:

Books

(With D. Botstein) *The Dynamic Genome: Barbara McClintock's Ideas in the Century of Genetics,* Cold Spring Harbor Press, 1992.

Periodicals

"Transposable Genetic Elements in Maize, "*Scientific American,* Volume 250, 1984, pp. 84–98.

"Maize Transposable Elements," *Perspectives in Biology and Medicine,* Volume 35, 1991, pp. 2–19.

SOURCES:

Fedoroff, Nina V., correspondence with Mary Raum, January 18, 1994.

—*Sketch by Mary Raum*

Edward A. Feigenbaum
1936-
American computer scientist

A pioneer in the field of artificial intelligence, Edward A. Feigenbaum took a slightly different approach to his work than some of his colleagues. While much of the focus on artificial intelligence involved efforts to mimic human behavior, Feigenbaum shifted his focus to improving computer performance, regardless of how it compared to human functioning.

Feigenbaum was born January 20, 1936, in Weehawken, New Jersey, the son of Fred J. and Sara Feigenbaum. He attended the Carnegie Institute of Technology, where he earned his B.S. in electrical engineering in 1956. While an undergraduate Feigenbaum acquired an interest in the Logic Theorist program, which was at the forefront of the artificial intelligence field. Developed by Carnegie faculty members **Herb Simon** and **Allen Newell**, Logic Theorist was a computer program that focused on the problem-solving process. Accepted into the Graduate School of Industrial Administration at Carnegie, Feigenbaum found it "a spectacular intellectual environment." Commenting in Pamela McCorduck's book *Machines Who Think,* Feigenbaum explained that "it wasn't just a question of a high level of innovation being tolerated. A high level of innovation was absolutely necessary for your survival there. . . . And it was quite clear that the most significant things in computer science were taking shape there right under our noses."

In 1959 Feigenbaum became a Fulbright fellow at the National Physical Laboratory near London; then in 1960, he earned his Ph.D. in industrial administration from Carnegie for research relating to cognitive psychology. This research project, called EPAM (Elementary Perceiver and Memorizer), was designed to use the computer to model the rote learning of nonsense syllables. Besides being of value to psychologists, EPAM interested other academics because of a mechanism called a discrimination net (which provided a relatively simple and flexible way of recognizing and storing information through the process of association).

Serving first as an assistant, and then as an associate professor of business administration at the University of California at Berkeley through the early 1960s, Feigenbaum was next appointed an associate professor of computer science and director of the Computer Center at Stanford University in 1965. He shifted gears that year, however, dropping EPAM and his work in psychology to focus on projects which aimed to improve computer performance regardless of the computer's relationship to human behavior.

Feigenbaum, along with Bruce Buchanan and **Joshua Lederberg**, began work on DENDRAL, a system developed to analyze unidentified chemical compounds by accepting data from a mass spectrograph (which photographs charged particles that have been separated into a spectrum) and a nuclear magnetic resonance (NMR) spectrometer. DENDRAL used this information to produce a topological model of the molecular structure of the compounds and to draw conclusions about the compounds. In working with chemists on this project, Feigenbaum came to recognize the tremendous amount of specialized information humans required to perform the kind of analysis DENDRAL was being designed to execute. In order to generate good hypotheses that would prove useful to a chemist, the project required developing a large data base of this information from which the computer could draw and make procedural decisions. The program was used by chemists at a number of universities and industrial laboratories.

As a result of the DENDRAL project, Feigenbaum and his colleagues made some important observations. They observed that the knowledge of a human expert often includes some educated guesswork based on past experience. Much of this experiential knowledge is privy to the expert simply because he or she is unable to adequately explain it and is, perhaps, unaware of it. Through careful observation, however, that knowledge can be brought to the surface. These observations led to the existence of the knowledge engineer, a person who works to identify the expert's knowledge and organize it into a format that can be used in a computer program. Feigenbaum's work in the applications of artificial intelligence led to the creation of the Stanford Heuristic Programming Project.

While teaching at Berkeley, Feigenbaum and colleague Julian Feldman tried to develop interest in artificial intelligence by offering a course in the computer modeling of thought. In *Machines Who Think,* Pamela McCorduck records Feigenbaum's recollections of what went into getting that course off the ground: "In order to get it into the curriculum in the business school, it being a rather bizarre subject for business schools, we enlisted the aid of Herb Simon and his Social Science Research Council Committee on Computer Simulation of Cognitive Processes. They gave us a few thousand dollars to buy our way into the curriculum by giving this money to the dean of the business school to let us teach this course. . . . It attracted a wide variety of students from different parts of the university, ranging from things like neurophysiology all the way through economics, physics, math, business; almost anyone you could imagine dropped into that course." Feigenbaum and Feldman found it difficult to gather materials for the class because resources were scattered in a wide variety of academic areas. As a result, they put together a book themselves featuring selected articles on artificial intelligence. *Computers and Thought,* published in 1963, was quite successful and was translated into Japanese, Russian, and many European languages. In 1975, Feigenbaum married H. Penny Nii (he has four children, Janet Denise, Carol Leonora, Sheri Bryant, and Karin Bryant). A year later Feigenbaum was named chair of the Computer Science Department at Stanford. Besides his academic activities, he also helped to found a knowledge engineering company called Teknowledge—the first company to commercially develop and market expert systems—and IntelliGenetics, a firm that markets expert computer systems for use in gene splicing.

SELECTED WRITINGS BY FEIGENBAUM:

Books

(With Julian Feldman) *Computers and Thought: A Collection of Articles,* McGraw, 1963.

(With Avron Barr) *The Handbook of Artificial Intelligence,* HeurisTech Press, 1981.

(With Pamela McCorduck) *The Fifth Generation: Artificial Intelligence and Japan's Computer Challenge to the World,* Addison-Wesley, 1983, revised edition, New American Library, 1984.

(With Pamela McCorduck and H. Penny Nii) *The Rise of the Expert Company: How Visionary Companies Are Using Artificial Intelligence to Achieve Higher Productivity and Profits,* Times Books, 1988.

SOURCES:

Books

McCorduck, Pamela, *Machines Who Think,* Freeman, 1979, pp. 274–288.

Mishkoff, Henry C., *Understanding Artificial Intelligence,* Sams, 1985, p. 49.

Periodicals

Kenner, Hugh, "Putting Mike in a Box," *Byte,* September, 1989, pp. 400–402.

—*Sketch by Daniel Rooney*

Mitchell Feigenbaum
1944-
American physicist

Mitchell Feigenbaum is one of the creators of the discipline cutting across mathematics, physics, and computer science known as chaos theory. Feigenbaum came across one of the essential ideas of the theory in the course of casual observation but then pursued it with tenacity. His persistence paid off when he was able to determine certain universal features of a wide variety of processes, and his name has become attached to a particular universal value. An interdisciplinary area like chaos theory could scarcely have come into existence without Feigenbaum's ability to be fascinated by what others would either not have noticed or else have relegated to the level of an inconvenience.

Mitchell Jay Feigenbaum was born on December 19, 1944, in Philadelphia, but his family moved soon thereafter to Brooklyn, where his father worked for the Port of New York and his mother taught in the public schools. Feigenbaum had an early interest in explaining physical phenomena at Samuel J. Tilden High School. After graduation he proceeded to the City College of New York for an undergraduate degree in electrical engineering, because electrical engineers were considered highly employable. He received his bachelor's degree in 1964 and moved to the Massachusetts Institute of Technology to pursue a doctorate in particle physics.

After receiving his Ph.D. in 1970, Feigenbaum took positions at Cornell University and Virginia Polytechnic Institute with disappointing results. He was not prolific in publishing, and the problems on which he was working did not attract a sympathetic group of colleagues. Fortunately he was brought in as a junior researcher at Los Alamos National Laboratory at a time when there was a general housecleaning. The atmosphere at Los Alamos offered Feigenbaum the time and the audience for some of his personal interests and investigations.

Tackles Nonlinear Functions

Feigenbaum was particularly interested in nonlinear phenomena. Most of the machinery that had been developed in physics and in mathematical physics was applicable to the linear case, where there is a proportion between input and output. The most common technique for dealing with nonlinear processes was to approximate them by a linear process and hope that the difference between the linear and nonlinear cases was small. This seemed to Feigenbaum to be the height of wishful thinking, and he was curious about what might happen if nonlinear phenomena were tackled head-on.

While there seemed to be little hope of attacking nonlinearity directly with the tools then available, Feigenbaum could at least take advantage of the computing power available in the mid–1970s and look at what happened to nonlinear functions as the output from one application of the function was fed in as the input for the next application. What he noted was that one could start with two numbers so close to one another as to be indistinguishable and by repeated application of the same simple but not linear function end up with numbers very far apart. This was a striking piece of evidence against the intuitive feeling that if you start with close numbers and do the same thing to both, the results will also be close. While the intuition seems to hold for linear functions, nonlinear functions lead to entirely different outcomes. However, experience with lengthy sequences of nonlinear functions had not been accumulated before Feigenbaum began investigating the problem.

Feigenbaum credits the mathematician **Stephen Smale** with having given him a push toward understanding what he had observed. Smale had observed that even quadratic functions, the next simplest ones after linear functions, still raised unsolved theoretical problems. As a result, Feigenbaum was strengthened in his conviction that what he had noticed in his computations was anything but the result of his ignorance. What he proceeded to observe was that some of the same phenomena that occur for quadratic functions in Smale's observation recur for more complicated nonlinear functions. After a period of intense computation, Feigenbaum developed a mathematical model to account for his conclusion and was ready to publish his findings. The results of Feigenbaum's intense labors were surprising in light of the variety of nonlinear functions. What Feigenbaum had apparently discovered was that the rate at which values either tended to diverge or to fall into nearby classes was independent of the particular function with which one started. In other words, although it had been expected that nonlinear functions would be much harder to analyze than linear functions, there appeared to be respects in which they were more like one another than linear functions were.

Chaos Theory

It was not true that the Feigenbaum results applied equally to all nonlinear functions, but they described broad classes. The rate to which the value converged was called the Feigenbaum constant, not because he was the first to notice the convergence in a particular case, but because he was the first to observe the universality of the phenomenon. One name that has been applied to the area created by Feigenbaum is "chaos theory", a name that has proved confusing, as the point of the theory is that even this apparent irregularity can be analyzed as part of a more regular phenomenon. Chaos theory describes and analyzes apparent, not true chaos. A more general name would be "complexity theory", as it has been argued that what Feigenbaum showed is that the details of a function are not important in what it does to points if the function is repeated often enough. Not far from Los Alamos, the Santa Fe Institute was created to study complexity across disciplinary boundaries.

Feigenbaum returned to Cornell University in 1982. In 1986, he accepted an appointment as professor of mathematics and physics at Rockefeller University in New York City, where he still remains. Since the early 1980s, when his work on chaos theory propelled him to national fame, he has also been a visiting scholar at a variety of institutions. Further recognition has come in the form of awards. Feigenbaum received a MacArthur Foundation award in 1984 and a Wolf Foundation prize in physics in 1986. However, there has been considerable opposition to his work as well. On occasion, leading academic journals have not accepted his work for publication, as it does not fit the categories of experimental physics or theoretical mathematics that they recognize. Mathematicians have pointed out that a rigorous proof of Feigenbaum's observations was only supplied in 1979 by a mathematician. Even colleagues working in chaos theory have taken issue with the novelty of Feigenbaum's work. An acrimonious quarrel between Feigenbaum and the mathematician **Benoit B. Mandelbrot** has developed, both claiming paternity of chaos theory.

SELECTED WRITINGS BY FEIGENBAUM:

Periodicals

"Quantitative Universality for a Class of Nonlinear Transformations," *Journal of Statistical Physics,* 1978, pp. 25–52.

"Universal Behavior in Nonlinear Systems," *Physica,* 1983, pp. 16–39.

SOURCES:

Books

Gleick, James, *Chaos,* Penguin, 1988.

Gulick, Denny, *Encounters with Chaos,* McGraw-Hill, 1992.

Waldrop, M. Mitchell, *Complexity,* Simon & Schuster, 1992.

—*Sketch by Thomas Drucker*

Honor Bridget Fell
1900-1986
English biologist

Honor Bridget Fell was a pioneer in the study of bone and cartilage development. Her work, conducted over a period of more than sixty years, allowed scientists to study bone growth and the effects of vitamins and other substances on embryonic development.

Fell was born to Colonel William and Alice Pickersgill-Cunliffe Fell in Fowthorpe, Yorkshire, on May 22, 1900, the youngest of nine children. As a child, she showed a keen interest in nature, particularly animals. Among her pets were several ferrets, one of whom she brought to her sister's wedding. In school, she developed an interest in biology. She received her bachelor of science degree in 1922 and her Ph.D. in 1924 from Edinburgh University.

While doing her doctoral research, Fell met the pathologist T. S. P. Strangeways, who specialized in rheumatology. He was then working on projects involving tissue culture, a technique that had been brought to England from the United States after World War I. Strangeways was impressed with Fell's ability and enthusiasm, and invited her to join the staff of the Strangeways Research Hospital. After obtaining a grant from Britain's Medical Research Council, Fell joined Strangeways as the pathologist's assistant in 1923.

Work on Bone Formation

During the next few years, Fell studied chick embryos and examined their cartilage and bone structures. Her work with Strangeways pioneered the use of organ culture techniques; her own work on bone formation, published in 1925, is still considered a primary reference. After Strangeways' death in 1926, Fell took charge of the hospital temporarily until being formally appointed director in 1929. Considering both her age (twenty-nine) and sex, this was no small accomplishment.

Fell remained as director of Strangeways for the next forty-one years. During that time she and her colleagues continued to study bone formation, primarily *in vitro* (artificial environment) development. Around 1950 she began studying the effects of vitamin A on bones. She identified the processes by which vitamin A depletes cellular material critical to bones and cartilage. She also examined the effects of such substances as hydrocortisone on bones and cartilage.

During her years at Strangeways, Fell had to deal with a financial situation she referred to as "something of a nightmare;" in its early years Strangeways relied on private donations. Later, foundation grants from such organizations as the Rockefeller Foundation helped ease the strain somewhat. Fell, quoted in *Developmental Biology,* said that often she would have to enact "stringent and often unpopular economies" to make ends meet, but she still managed to maintain a supportive atmosphere in which scientists were encouraged to do their best work.

Fell retired from Strangeways in 1970, remaining active in scientific study for the rest of her life. Shortly after her retirement, she was invited to work at the Division of Immunology of the Department of Pathology at the University of Cambridge. During this time she was able to devote her full attention to research on bones and cartilage. Her work at this time helped lead to the discovery of the immune response regulator interleukin–1. In 1979, Fell returned to Strangeways, where she conducted research on collagen degradation in synovial tissue.

In 1952 Fell was named a fellow of the Royal Society and, in 1955, a fellow of Girton College. In 1963, she was named Dame Commander of the British Empire. Other honors included degrees from Harvard University, Cambridge University, and Smith College. Fell was known as a dedicated scientist who believed strongly in assisting other scientists and providing intellectual and moral support. In her spare time, travel was one of her primary interests. But her devotion to science was always paramount, and it kept her in the lab until two weeks before her death on April 22, 1986.

SELECTED WRITINGS BY FELL:

Books

"The Strangeways Research Laboratory and Cellular Interactions," in Dingle and Gordon, editors, *Cellular Interactions.* Elsevier/North-Holland, 1981.

Periodicals

"The Histogenesis of Cartilage and Bone in the Long Bones of the Embryonic Fowl," *Journal of Morphological Physiology,* Volume 40, 1925, pp. 417–439.

SOURCES:

Periodicals

Poole, A. Robin and Arnold I. Caplan, "An Appreciation: Dame Honor Bridget Fell F.R.S."

Developmental Biology, Volume 122, 1987, pp. 297–299.

—*Sketch by George A. Milite*

Lloyd N. Ferguson
1918-
American chemist

Lloyd N. Ferguson

After a long and distinguished career as a chemist and educator at the California State University, Los Angeles, Lloyd N. Ferguson achieved emeritus status in 1986. In addition to teaching, Ferguson conducted important research on the relationship between the chemistry of organic compounds and properties such as odor and taste, alicycles (organic compounds with unusual molecular structures), and cancer chemotherapy during his years at California State. Despite all these accomplishments, Ferguson considers his efforts to encourage minority youth to pursue careers in science as one of his more significant contributions through the years. An active educator and writer, Ferguson has published six textbooks and numerous pedagogical articles, and he is the recipient of several awards, including the Distinguished Teaching award of the Manufacturing Chemists Association in 1974, the American Chemical Society award in chemical education in 1978, and the Outstanding Teaching award from the National Organization of Black Chemists in 1979.

Lloyd Noel Ferguson was born in Oakland, California, on February 9, 1918, the son of Noel Swithin and Gwendolyn Louise (Johnson) Ferguson. He studied chemistry at the University of California at Berkeley, receiving his Bachelor of Science degree, with honors, in 1940 and his doctorate in 1943. Additionally, at intervals between 1941 and 1944, Ferguson worked on National Defense research projects, and he was assistant professor at the Agricultural and Technical College at Greensboro, North Carolina, during 1944–45. He married Charlotte Olivia Welch on January 2, 1944; they have two sons and a daughter.

Studies the Chemistry of Aroma and Taste

In 1945, two years after receiving his doctorate, Ferguson joined the faculty of Howard University in Washington, D.C., becoming a full professor in 1955 and chairing the chemistry department from 1958 to 1965. Ferguson's research during this period included studies of the chemical properties of aromatic molecules; in particular, he investigated halogenation, the complex mechanisms by which aromatic molecules combine with a halogen. Ferguson also studied the molecular components and biochemical processes of taste—research that is valuable, as Ferguson argued in his 1958 article titled "The Physicochemical Aspects of the Sense of Taste," in gaining a fuller understanding "about the ways chemicals stimulate biological activity." Exploring one aspect of such research, Ferguson investigated whether a chemical compound's structural configuration has an effect on its taste by measuring the absorption of sweet and nonsweet compounds by various surfaces. Ferguson wrote three of his textbooks as a professor at Howard University: *Electron Structures of Organic Molecules, Textbook of Organic Chemistry,* and *The Modern Structural Theory of Organic Chemistry.* In 1953, Ferguson was awarded a Guggenheim fellowship, which took him to the Carlsberg Laboratory in Copenhagen, Denmark. Between 1961 and 1962 he was a National Science Foundation fellow at the Swiss Federal Institute of Technology in Zurich, Switzerland.

Studies Alicycles and Chemotherapy

In 1965 Ferguson joined the faculty at California State University in Los Angeles as professor of chemistry; he then chaired the chemistry department from 1968–71. During this period, Ferguson's areas of research included the chemistry of alicycles. In his

1969 article "Alicyclic Chemistry: The Playground for Organic Chemists," Ferguson describes alicycles as providing "ideal systems for measuring electrical and magnetic interaction between nonbonded atoms and for studying the [structural] and mechanistic aspects of organic reactions," and as supplying "models for elucidating the chemistry of natural products such as steroids, alkalids, vitamins, carbohydrates, [and] antibiotics."

In 1970, Ferguson received an honorary doctorate of science degree from Howard University. He published three additional textbooks during the following decade: *Organic Chemistry: A Science and an Art, Highlights of Alicyclic Chemistry,* both volume 1 and 2, and *Organic Molecular Structure.* Along with his national teaching and educational awards, Ferguson received Outstanding Professor awards from California State University in 1974 and 1981. Ferguson's interest in cancer chemotherapy is reflected by his service on the chemotherapy advisory committee of the National Cancer Institute from 1972–75 and by articles such as "Cancer: How Can Chemists Help?" In 1973 Ferguson was appointed to the United States national committee to the International Union of Pure and Applied Chemistry (IUPAC) for three years. He also served on the National Sea Grant Review Panel from 1978–81 and was affiliated with the National Institute of Environmental Health Sciences from 1979–83. In 1986, Ferguson retired as emeritus professor of chemistry at California State University.

Ferguson is a member of the American Chemical Society, the National Cancer Institute, the American Association for the Advancement of Science, and the Royal Chemical Society, among other professional and scientific bodies. Ferguson accepted a post as visiting professor at the University of Nairobi in Kenya during 1971–1972. In 1976, he was awarded the Distinguished American Medallion from the American Foundation for Negro Affairs. In 1984–85, Ferguson taught at Bennett College in Greensboro, North Carolina, as a United Negro College Fund scholar-at-large. He has helped establish both the National Organization of Black Chemists and Engineers (1989) and the American Chemical Society's SEED (Support of the Educationally and Economically Disadvantaged) program.

SELECTED WRITINGS BY FERGUSON:

Books

Electron Structures of Organic Molecules, Prentice-Hall, 1952.

The Modern Structural Theory of Organic Chemistry, Prentice-Hall, 1963.

Organic Chemistry: A Science and an Art, Willard Grant, 1972.

Highlights of Alicyclic Chemistry, 2 volumes, Franklin, 1973–77.

Organic Molecular Structure, Willard Grant, 1974.

Periodicals

(With Gerald E. K. Branch) "Absorption Spectra of Some Linear Conjugated Systems," *Journal of the American Chemical Society,* September, 1944, pp. 1467–75.

(With Albert Y. Garner) "Aromatic Compound and Complex Formation," *Journal of the American Chemical Society,* February 20, 1954, pp. 1167–69.

"The Physicochemical Aspects of the Sense of Taste," *Journal of Chemical Education,* September, 1958, pp. 437–44.

"Alicyclic Chemistry: The Playground for Organic Chemists," *Journal of Chemical Education,* July, 1969, pp. 404–12.

"Cancer: How Can Chemists Help?," *Journal of Chemical Education,* November, 1975, pp. 689–94.

"Bio-Organic Mechanisms II: Chemoreception," *Journal of Chemical Education,* June, 1981, pp. 456–61.

—*Sketch by M. C. Nagel*

Enrico Fermi
1901-1954
Italian-born American physicist

Enrico Fermi's fame rests on accomplishments in the fields of both theoretical and experimental physics. At the age of 25, he developed a statistical method for describing the behavior of a cloud of electrons that later came to be known as Fermi-Dirac statistics. In combination with another system of mathematics, Bose-Einstein statistics, it provides a method for analyzing any system of discrete particles, such as photons, electrons, or neutrons. Fermi also devised an explanation for the process of beta decay, an event in which an atomic nucleus emits an electron and changes into a new nucleus. Fermi's major experimental contributions involved the study of nuclear changes brought about as a result of neutron bombardment of nuclei. This field of research eventually led to Fermi's participation in the Manhattan Project, during which the first controlled fission reactions were carried out. For his work on neutron bombardment, Fermi was awarded the 1938 Nobel Prize for Physics.

Enrico Fermi

Fermi was born in Rome on September 29, 1901. His father, Alberto Fermi, was employed by the Italian state railway system, while his mother, Ida de Gattis, had been a school teacher before her marriage. The Fermis had two other children, a son, Giulio, and a daughter, Maria. Giulio died when Enrico was 14 with apparently traumatic effects on the younger brother. Fortunately, Enrico soon made the acquaintance of a young man, Enrico Persico, who was to become his best friend and a close professional colleague for the rest of his life.

Obtains His Early Education in Italy and Northern Europe

Fermi exhibited unusual intellectual talents at an early age. He did well in school but also read a great deal on his own. A friend of his father, Adolfo Amidei, assumed some responsibility for Fermi's intellectual development, arranging to have books on mathematics and physics given to him in the proper sequence. According to his friend and colleague, **Emilio Segrè**, Fermi knew as much classical physics by the time he graduated from high school as did the typical university graduate student. That knowledge had come not only from books, but also from experiments designed and carried out by Fermi and Persico.

In November, 1918, Fermi applied for a scholarship at the Reale Scuola Normale in Pisa. His entrance essay dealt with the mathematics and physics of vibrating reeds and convinced the examiners that he was a candidate of unusual promise. Four years later, Fermi was granted his doctorate in physics, *magna cum laude,* from Pisa. His thesis dealt with experiments he had conducted using X rays.

Since the scientific community was not then well developed in Italy, Fermi set out for Northern Europe to continue his studies. He spent seven months with **Max Born** at the University of Göttingen and then returned to Rome. He taught mathematics for one year in Rome before traveling north again, this time to the University of Leiden. There he studied with the great Dutch physicist **Paul Ehrenfest** and became close friends with **Samuel A. Goudsmit** and **George Uhlenbeck**, both of whom later emigrated to the United States.

Fermi returned to Italy in 1925, hoping to be appointed to a chair in mathematical physics. When this opportunity was offered to another man instead, Fermi accepted a teaching position at the University of Florence. During his first year at Florence, Fermi wrote a paper that was to establish his name among physicists almost immediately. The paper dealt with an application of **Wolfgang Pauli**'s Exclusion principles, discovered earlier the same year, to the atoms in a gas. Pauli's Exclusion principles restrict the possible location of electrons. Fermi postulated that the same rules developed by Pauli for electrons might also be applied to the atoms in a gas. The mathematical system he invented, later developed independently by **Paul Dirac**, has become known as Fermi-Dirac statistics.

This accomplishment came about at a propitious time for Fermi. In Rome, Orso Mario Corbino had just begun a campaign to revitalize Italian science, which had been in a long period of decline. Corbino, as both chairman of the physics department at the University of Rome and a powerful figure in the Italian government, obtained authorization to create a new chair of theoretical physics at Rome, a position that he immediately offered to Fermi. In 1926, Fermi left Florence to assume his new position in Corbino's department. Over the next half dozen years, Corbino's dreams were realized as a number of first class physicists and young students were attracted to Rome.

Great Discoveries Made in Theoretical and Experimental Physics

During that period, Fermi and his colleagues concentrated on the latest developments in atomic theory. Along with many other chemists and physicists, they were working out the implications of quantum and wave mechanics, relativity, and uncertainty to atomic theory. By the turn of the decade, however, many of those problems had been solved, and Fermi began to look elsewhere for challenges. He, like many others, settled on the atomic nucleus as a new focus of research.

One of the first problems to which he turned was beta decay. Beta decay is the process by which a neutron in an atomic nucleus breaks apart into a proton and electron. The electron is then emitted from the nucleus as a beta particle. The mechanics of beta decay appeared to violate known physical principles and were, therefore, the subject of intense study in the early 1930s. Wolfgang Pauli had suggested, for example, that the apparent violation of conservation laws observed during beta decay could be explained by assuming the existence of a tiny, essentially massless particle, also released during the event. Fermi was later to name that particle the *neutrino* ("little neutron"). In 1933, Fermi proposed a theory for beta decay. He said that the event occurs because a neutron moves from a state of higher energy to one of lower energy as it undergoes conversion to a proton and electron. To explain the process by which this occurs, Fermi postulated the existence of a new kind of force, a force now known as the *weak force.*

Fermi's interest in the nucleus also prompted him to return to the laboratory and to design a number of experiments in this field. An important factor motivating this research was the recent discovery of artificial radioactivity by **Irène Joliot-Curie** and her husband, **Frédéric Joliot-Curie**. The Joliot-Curies had found that bombarding stable isotopes with alpha particles would convert the original isotopes into unstable, radioactive forms. Fermi reasoned that this type of experiment might be even more effective if neutrons, rather than alpha particles, were used as the "bullets." Neutrons have no electrical charge and are, therefore, not repelled by either the negatively charged electrons or the positively charged nuclei in an atom.

Beginning in 1934, Fermi and his colleagues systematically submitted one element after another to bombardment by neutrons. Progress was slow until a key discovery was made. In contrast to previous expectations, it turned out that slow neutrons—neutrons that have been slowed by passing through substances containing hydrogen—are more effective in bringing about nuclear changes than are fast neutrons. After revising his experimental procedure based on this discovery, Fermi had greater success. Over a period of months, he was able to show that 37 of the 63 elements he studied could be converted to radioactive forms by neutron bombardment.

The element among all others that especially intrigued Fermi was uranium. He knew that one reaction that could reasonably be expected as the result of neutron bombardment of uranium was the production of a new element with an atomic number one greater than that of uranium. But no such element exists naturally. So, the successful bombardment of uranium with neutrons might well result in the formation of the first synthetic element.

When this experiment was actually performed, the results were ambiguous. Fermi did not feel that he had enough evidence to announce the preparation of a new element. His sponsor, Corbino, had no such reluctance, however. Motivated by a desire to exalt the "new Italian science," Corbino reported that Fermi had indeed discovered element #93 and suggested that it be named *italium.*

In fact, Fermi did not recognize the revolutionary nature of his experimental results. Bombardment of uranium with neutrons had resulted not in a simple nuclear transformation, but in nuclear fission, a process during which the uranium atom is split, unleashing tremendous amounts of energy. The true nature of this reaction was later elucidated by **Lise Meitner** and **Otto Robert Frisch**.

As the 1930s came to a close, Fermi's future became more uncertain. Fascist influences were growing not only in Hitler's Germany, but also in Mussolini's Italy. These political changes troubled Fermi in a number of ways. For one thing, they threatened the nature of his scientific work since political factors now determined what was "correct" research and what was not. In addition, Fermi's family felt threatened since his wife was Jewish and subject, therefore, to the dangers of state-enforced anti-Semitism.

Defection to the West Marks the Beginning of New Life

Fortunately, a solution for his dilemma presented itself in November of 1938 when Fermi was informed that he had won the Nobel Prize for physics. The award had been given for his research on the bombardment of elements by slow neutrons. The Fermis and a few friends decided that their trip to Stockholm to accept the prize would be a one-way passage. After the ceremony, he would defect to the West. On January 2, 1939, he arrived in the United States and assumed a new post as professor of physics at Columbia University.

The timing of Fermi's arrival in the United States was indeed fortuitous. At almost the same time, **Niels Bohr** was delivering to American physicists news of the discovery of nuclear fission by **Otto Hahn** and **Fritz Strassmann** in Germany. The significance of this discovery was immediately apparent to Fermi and his colleagues. A movement was soon under way to inform the U.S. government of the political and military implications of the Hahn-Strassmann discovery. That movement culminated in the famous August 2, 1939 letter to President Franklin D. Roosevelt, written by **Leo Szilard** and signed by **Albert Einstein**, that discussed the importance of nuclear research.

Fermi's immediate future was now laid out for him. He became involved in the Manhattan Project to determine whether a controlled nuclear chain reaction was possible and, if so, how it could be used in the construction of a nuclear weapon. Although his initial work was carried out at Columbia, Fermi eventually moved to the University of Chicago. He began work there in April, 1942, with a team of the nation's finest physicists attempting to produce the world's first sustained nuclear fission reaction.

That effort came to a successful conclusion under the squash courts at the university on December 2, 1942. At 3:21 p.m., instruments indicated that a self-sustaining chain reaction was taking place in the world's first atomic "pile," a primitive nuclear reactor. The message sent to Washington confirming this event stated, "The Italian navigator has landed in the New World." In response to that message, James Conant, director of the project, asked, "Are the natives friendly?" indicating that the team was ready to go ahead with further research. The reply from Fermi's team was, "Yes, very friendly," and the race to build a bomb was on its way.

For the next two years, Fermi continued his research on nuclear fission at the Argonne National Laboratory outside of Chicago. Towards the end of that work, on July 11, 1944, Fermi and his wife became naturalized citizens of the United States. A few weeks later, Fermi left for Hanford, Washington, where he briefly assisted in the design and construction of a new plutonium processing plant. In September, he moved on to Los Alamos, New Mexico, where final assembly of the first nuclear weapons was to occur. There Fermi was placed in charge of his own special division (the F division) whose job it was to solve special problems as they arose during bomb construction.

After the first successful tests at Los Alamos, on July 16, 1945, and after the bombs were dropped on Japan a month later, Fermi concluded his work with the Manhattan Project. He returned to the University of Chicago, where he became Charles H. Swift Distinguished Service Professor of Physics and a member of the newly created Institute for Nuclear Studies. He remained at Chicago for the rest of his life, a period during which he received many honorary degrees and other awards. Included among the former were honorary doctorates from Washington University, Yale, and Harvard. He also received the Civilian Medal of Merit in 1946 for his work on the Manhattan Project, the Franklin Medal from the Franklin Institute in 1947, and the Transenter Medal from the University of Liége in Belgium in 1947.

Fermi's health began to fail in 1954, and exploratory surgery showed that he had stomach cancer. He refused to give up his work, however, and continued his research almost until he died, in his sleep, on November 30, 1954. He was buried in Chicago. Shortly after his death, he was posthumously awarded the first Enrico Fermi Award, given by the U.S. Atomic Energy Commission. Since his death, Fermi has received additional honors, including the naming of element #100, *fermium,* after him and the choice of the unit *fermimeter* for nuclear dimensions.

In addition to his great mental genius, Fermi was a highly-respected and well-loved person. His long-time colleague, Segrè, has written of Fermi's special pleasure in working with younger colleagues, a tendency that helped maintain his own youthful spirit.

SELECTED WRITINGS BY FERMI:

Books

Fisica per i Licei, N. Zanichelli (Bologna), 1929.

Introduzione all Fisica Atomica, N. Zanichelli, 1929.

Molecole e Cristalli, N. Zanichelli, 1934.

Thermodynamics, Prentice-Hall, 1937.

Fisica per Istituti Tecnici Commerciali, N. Zanichelli, 1938.

Nuclear Physics, University of Chicago Press, 1950.

Elementary Particles, Yale University Press, 1951.

SOURCES:

Books

Allison, Samuel K., "Enrico Fermi," *Biographical Memoirs,* Volume 30, National Academy of Sciences, 1957, pp. 124–155.

Fermi, Laura, *Atoms in the Family: My Life with Enrico Fermi,* University of Chicago Press, 1954.

Garraty, John, editor, *Dictionary of American Biography,* Supplement 5, Scribner's, 1955, pp. 219–221.

Gillispie, Charles Coulson, editor, *Dictionary of Scientific Biography,* Volume 4, Scribner, 1975, pp. 576–583.

Jaffe, Bernard, *Men of Science in America,* Simon and Schuster, 1958.

McGraw-Hill Modern Men of Science, Volume 1, McGraw-Hill, 1984, pp. 168–169.

Segrè, Emilio, *Enrico Fermi, Physicist,* University of Chicago Press, 1970.

—Sketch by David E. Newton

Aleksandr Evgenievich Fersman 1883-1945

Russian geochemist

Aleksandr Evgenievich Fersman was a Russian geochemist and mineralogist. He made major contributions to Russian geology, both in theory and exploration, advancing scientific understanding of crystallography and the distribution of elements in the earth's crust, as well as founding a popular scientific journal and writing biographical sketches of eminent scientists. He was known as a synthesist of ideas from different subdisciplines.

Fersman was born on November 8, 1883 in St. Petersburg to a family that valued both art and science. His father, Evgeny Aleksandrovich Fersman, was an architect; his mother, Maria Eduardovna Kessler, a pianist and painter. Fersman's maternal uncle, A. E. Kessler, had studied chemistry under Russian chemist Aleksandr Mikhailovich Butlerov.

At the family's summer estate in the Crimea, Fersman first discovered minerals and began to collect them. When his mother became ill, the family traveled to Karlovy Vary (Carlsbad) in Czechoslovakia. There the young Fersman explored abandoned mines and added to his collection of crystals and druses (crystal-lined rocks).

Studies the Properties of Crystals

Fersman graduated from the Odessa Classical Gymnasium in 1901 with a gold medal and entered Novorossisk University. He found the mineralogy course so dull that he decided to study art history instead. He was dissuaded by family friends (the chemist A. I. Gorbov and others) who encouraged him to delve into molecular chemistry. He subsequently studied physical chemistry with B. P. Veynberg, who had been a student of Russian chemist Dmitri Ivanovich Mendeleev. Veynberg taught Fersman about the properties of crystals.

The Fersman family moved to Moscow in 1903 because Aleksandr's father became commander of the First Moscow Cadet Corps. Fersman transferred to Moscow University, where his interest in the structure of crystals continued. Studying with mineralogist **V. I. Vernadsky**, he became an expert in goniometry (calculation of angles in crystal) and published seven scientific papers on crystallography and mineralogy as a student. When Fersman graduated in 1907, Vernadsky encouraged him to become a professor.

By 1908 Fersman was doing postgraduate work with **Victor Goldschmidt** at Heidelberg University in Germany. Goldschmidt sent him on a tour of western Europe to examine the most interesting examples of natural diamond crystals in the hands of the region's jewelers. This work formed the basis of an important monograph on diamond crystallography Fersman and Goldschmidt published in 1911.

While a student in Heidelberg, Fersman also visited French mineralogist François Lacroix's laboratory in Paris and encountered pegmatites for the first time during a trip to some islands in the Elbe River that were strewn with the rocks. Pegmatites are granitic rocks that often contain rare elements such as uranium, tungsten, and tantalum. Fersman was to devote years to their study later in his career.

Begins Teaching Career

In 1912 Fersman returned to Russia, where he began his administrative and teaching career. He became curator of mineralogy at the Russian Academy of Science's Geological Museum. He would be elected to the Academy and become the museum's director in 1919. During this period Fersman also taught geochemistry at Shanyavsky University and helped found *Priroda,* a popular scientific journal to which he contributed throughout his life.

Fersman participated in an Academy of Science project to catalogue Russia's natural resources starting in 1915, traveling to all of Russia's far-flung regions to assess mineral deposits. After the Russian Revolution, Lenin consulted Fersman for advice on exploiting the country's mineral resources. During World War I Fersman consulted with the military, advising on strategic matters involving geology, as he was also to do in World War II.

In the early 1920s, Fersman devoted himself to one of geochemistry's major theoretical questions: the distribution of the chemical elements in the earth's crust. Fersman worked out the percentages for most of the elements and proposed that these quantities be called "clarkes" in honor of Frank W. Clarke, an American chemist who had pioneered their study. Clarkes had traditionally been expressed in terms of weight percentages; Fersman calculated them in terms of atomic percentages. His work showed different reasons for the terrestrial and cosmic distribution of the elements. He was very interested in the ways in which elements are combined and redistributed in the earth's crust. He coined the term "technogenesis" for the role of humans in this process, concentrating some elements and dispersing others through extraction and industrial activities.

Over the next twenty years, Fersman was responsible for a reassessment of the U.S.S.R.'s mineral resources. There were many areas, such as Soviet Central Asia and Siberia, which were thought to be resource-poor. Fersman showed otherwise, traveling from the Khibiny Mountains north of the Arctic

Circle near Finland to the Karakum Desert north of Iran. He found rich deposits of apatite (a phosphorus-bearing mineral useful in fertilizers) in the former and a lode of elemental sulfur in the latter.

Fersman was acutely aware of the history of his profession and of science in general, passing on to his students his respect for his predecessors, especially Mendeleev and Vernadsky. He wrote many biographical sketches of distinguished scientists and published a number of popular works on mineral collecting. He was active in the Academy of Science of the U.S.S.R., serving in five different administrative posts, and received a number of honors, including the Lenin Prize. He died in the Soviet Georgian city of Sochi on May 20, 1945.

SELECTED WRITINGS BY FERSMAN:

Books

Pegmatity ("Pegmatites"), [Leningrad], 1911.
(With Victor Goldschmidt) *Der Diamant* (monograph), [Heidelberg], 1911.
Geokhimia Rossii ("Geochemistry of Russia"), [Petrograd], 1922.

SOURCES:

Books

Dictionary of Scientific Biography, Volume 4, Scribner, 1970.
Grigoriev, D. P., and I. I. Shafranovsky, *Vydayushchiesya russkie mineralogi* ("Distinguished Russian Mineralogists"), [Moscow/Leningrad], 1949, pp. 196–233.
Pisarzhevsky, O., *Fersman,* [Moscow], 1959.

—*Sketch by Valerie Brown*

Richard P. Feynman
1918-1988
American physicist

Richard P. Feynman

Richard P. Feynman made significant advances in the understanding of superfluidity, weak nuclear interactions, and quarks, and shared the Nobel Prize for physics in 1965 for his contributions to the theory of quantum electrodynamics. In early 1986, Feynman served on the presidential commission that investigated the space shuttle *Challenger* incident, demonstrating to the nation that defective O-rings reacted too slowly to hot gases in cold temperatures, causing the shuttle to explode.

Richard Phillips Feynman was born in New York City on May 11, 1918, to Melville Arthur and Lucille Phillips Feynman. His father worked a number of jobs, but spent most of his years as a sales manager for a uniform manufacturer. Feynman had a younger sister, Joan. A brother, Henry, died in infancy. His youth was spent reading assorted mathematics books and the *Encyclopaedia Britannica,* as well as conducting experiments and fixing radios. As a student, Feynman excelled in math and science. He participated in the physics club and, as head of his high school's algebra team, placed first in the New York City math team competition when he was a senior. He was so adept at mathematics that his high school geometry teacher let Feynman teach the class.

Feynman applied to Columbia University but was not accepted, in part because he lacked in other subjects what he made up for in math and science. Accepted by the Massachusetts Institute of Technology (MIT), he enrolled as a mathematics major in 1936 but became disillusioned with its prospect as a viable career. He eventually leap-frogged from electrical engineering to physics, wherein he became fascinated with nuclear physics, a field that had only just begun to flourish after the discovery of the neutron in 1932. When MIT gave a graduate course on nuclear physics in the spring of 1938, Feynman jumped at the chance to take it, even though he was only a junior. At MIT, he was distinguished by several of his professors as one of the best students they had had in years. When he was a senior, he competed in the nation's most prestigious mathematics contest, the Putnam competition. As James Gleick wrote in *Genius: The Life and Science of Richard Feynman,* "One of Feynman's fraternity brothers was surprised to see him return home while the examination was still going on. Feynman learned later that the scorers had been astounded by the gap between his result and the next four." Feynman's senior thesis, "Forces and Stresses in Molecules," caused a stir among MIT's physics faculty because it presented a much simpler way to calculate the electrostatic force in a solid crystal. He received his bachelor's degree in physics from MIT in 1939 and later published a shorter version of his thesis in *Physical Review.*

Feynman's admittance to Princeton's graduate school was almost hampered by the fact that he was Jewish. Though, unlike many institutions of the time, Princeton did not set a quota on the number of Jews they admitted, they were reluctant to accept very many because they were not easily placed among American industries strongly prejudiced against them. Also, Feynman's test scores in history, literature, and the fine arts were very weak. Nonetheless, he was accepted to graduate studies at Princeton in 1939 and became the teaching assistant for American physicist **John Archibald Wheeler**, who coined the term "black hole." In February, 1941, Feynman gave his first professional presentation at the physics department seminar. In attendance were some of the most notable figures of early twentieth-century physics, including Swiss-born American physicist **Wolfgang Pauli**, Hungarian American mathematical physicist **Eugene Wigner**, and Hungarian American mathematician **John von Neumann**; American physicist **Albert Einstein** was also present. Feynman was so scared that he later remembered little of his presentation.

In anticipation of war, America began recruiting physicists in a push to develop instrumentation and weaponry that would eventually change the face of war forever. In the spring of 1941, Feynman turned down a long-awaited job offer from Bell Laboratories, opting instead to spend that summer working at the Frankford Arsenal in Philadelphia. Returning to Princeton, he was pulled into the Manhattan Project by American physicist **Robert Wilson**. Like many major universities and development companies throughout the United States, Princeton was employed in the effort to isolate the lighter, or radioactive, isotopes of uranium. Wilson sought Feynman's help in calculating the speed at which uranium atoms of varying weight would separate in the magnetic field produced by Wilson's isotron, or isotope separator. While working on this problem, Feynman completed his dissertation on "The Principle of Least Action in Quantum Mechanics," and received his Ph.D. in theoretical physics in June of 1942. Shortly after graduation, Feynman married his high school sweetheart, Arline Greenbaum, who had been diagnosed with tuberculosis a year earlier. After a short wedding on Staten Island, which neither family attended, Feynman drove his wife to a charity hospital in New Jersey.

Integral in Building the Atomic Bomb

In 1942, Wilson's isotron was shut down so isolation efforts could be concentrated on Berkeley's seemingly more productive Calutron. Early in 1943, American physicist **J. Robert Oppenheimer** recruited Feynman and other members of the Princeton team to develop the atomic bomb in the secluded desert surroundings of Los Alamos, New Mexico. On March 28, Feynman and Arline boarded a train for Albuquerque, where Oppenheimer had arranged for Arline to stay in a sanitarium. Feynman would hitchhike or borrow a car to visit his wife on many weekends. At Los Alamos, Feynman worked with some of the world's top physicists and mathematicians, including Oppenheimer, American physicist **Edward Teller**, and von Neumann. One of the most important of these colleagues was group leader and future Nobel Prize-winner **Hans Bethe**, a nuclear physicist and professor from Cornell University. While at Los Alamos, Feynman worked on computing how fast neutrons would diffuse through a critical mass of uranium or plutonium as it approached the reaction that leads to a nuclear explosion. He also developed calculating techniques to do many of the complex mathematical computations involved in designing a nuclear bomb, and he determined the limits of how many radioactive materials could be stored together safely without starting an explosive chain reaction. Tuberculosis wasted Arline Feynman away. She died on June 16, 1945. A month later to the day, at 5:30 in the morning, her husband stood twenty miles from the steel tower that held the first atomic bomb and watched it explode. Less than a month later, Hiroshima and Nagasaki were bombed, and Japan surrendered, ending World War II.

Plugs Holes in the Theory of Quantum Electrodynamics

Feynman left Los Alamos in October of 1945 and, at Bethe's invitation, accepted a position as associate professor of physics at Cornell. Feynman began to think more about problems in the theory of quantum electrodynamics, problems that he had worked on while at MIT and Princeton, and even sporadically at Los Alamos. Quantum electrodynamics is the study of electromagnetic radiation and how electrically-charged particles, such as atoms and their electrons, interact. It also investigates what happens when electrons, positrons, and photons collide with each other. The main principles of quantum electrodynamics had been formulated in the mid 1920s by English physicist **Paul Dirac**, German physicist **Werner Heisenberg**, and Pauli. Although quantum electrodynamics explained how light could be made of waves and particles, problems in the theory soon developed. The chief problems were the need for electrons to have infinite masses and infinite electric charges so that other aspects of the theory would work. American physicist **Willis E. Lamb** also demonstrated, in a discovery known as "the Lamb shift," that the hydrogen atom gave off energy levels that were not predicted by earlier theories.

Feynman was inspired one day in the Cornell cafeteria. He noticed a student spinning a cafeteria plate in the air. As the plate spun around, it wobbled, though the two motions were not synchronized. Thus a mathematical description of the motion of the plate had to account for two motions. Feynman's computations concerning such motions further advanced previous theories of quantum electrodynamics by eliminating the need for the idea of infinity and explaining the Lamb shift. His theory also made quantum electrodynamics vastly more accurate in predicting subatomic events. Subsequent experiments have confirmed the great accuracy of Feynman's reformulation of quantum electrodynamics. He also introduced a graphic aid that came to be known as a "Feynman diagram," which shows how subatomic particles, represented by arrows and lines, interact through space and time. Feynman's diagrams were simple, elegant, and powerful expressions of fundamental subatomic actions. They were also very popular; by the early 1950s, Feynman's diagrams began to appear frequently in academic articles about quantum electrodynamics.

Two other physicists were also reformulating quantum electrodynamics. American physicist **Julian Schwinger** was no stranger to Feynman; both hailed from New York and were the same age. Japanese physicist **Sin-Itiro Tomonaga** had developed his theories by 1943, but was unable to publish them in the West until after the War. Both men had independently developed different mathematical approaches that led to results similar to Feynman's. The three men shared the Nobel Prize for physics in 1965. In 1950, Feynman left Cornell for the California Institute of Technology near Los Angeles. The offer included an immediate sabbatical year which he spent in Brazil, performing sambas as a musician while theorizing the role of mesons—fundamental particles made up of a quark and an antiquark—in the cohesion of the atomic nucleus. When he returned in June of 1952, he married Mary Louise Bell, whom he divorced four years later. In 1954, Feynman became the third person to win the Albert Einstein Award, after American mathematician **Kurt Gödel** and Schwinger.

Contributes to Knowledge of Quarks

While at Cal Tech, Feynman worked on a variety of other problems. One of these was a theory of superfluidity, which he developed to explain why liquid helium behaves in such strange ways (e.g., defying gravity, losing heat instead of gaining it when it flows). An interest in the weak nuclear force, that is, the force that makes the process of radioactive decay possible, led Feynman and American physicist **Murray Gell-Mann** to the supposition that the emission of beta-particles from radioactive nuclei acts as the chief agitator in the decay process. As Gleick explained, Feynman also contributed to "a theory of partons, hypothetical hard particles inside the atom's nucleus, that helped produce the modern understanding of quarks." Quarks are paired elementary particles, one of which has a charge of ⅔, and the other, −⅓. In 1973, Feynman received the Niels Bohr International Gold Medal.

In 1958, Feynman met Gweneth Howarth while in Switzerland. Gweneth, a domestic servant, turned down Feynman's first offer to come to the United States and work for him as a maid. After his long-distance pursuit of her by mail, she was finally won over and arrived in California in the summer of 1959. They were married on September 24, 1960. Their first child, Carl, was born in 1962. They adopted a daughter, Michelle, six years later. In October, 1978, Feynman was diagnosed with myxoid liposarcoma, a rare cancer that affects the soft tissues of the body. The tumor from the cancer weighed six pounds and was located in the back of his abdomen, where it had destroyed his left kidney. His long-term chances were not good: less than fifty percent of patients survived for five years, and the chances for lasting ten years were close to zero.

Explains Why the Shuttle Exploded

The space ship *Challenger* exploded above Cape Kennedy in Florida on January 28, 1986. NASA's acting chief administrator, William R. Graham, asked Feynman to serve on the presidential commission that would investigate the accident. Graham's wife had suggested Feynman because she remembered some of his lectures. The appointment to the commission was not well timed, as Feynman had been recently diagnosed with a second rare form of bone cancer, Waldenström's macroglobulinemia. When the presidential commission began its public hearings on the accident in early February, 1986, the discussion quickly turned toward the effects of cold temperatures on O-rings. These rubber rings seal the joints of the solid rocket boosters on either side of the large external tank that holds the liquid oxygen and hydrogen fuel for the shuttle. Feynman demonstrated to the public the cause of the disaster. He bent a piece of O-ring in a clamp and immersed it in a glass of ice water, then released the piece of O-ring from the clamp to reveal how slowly it regained its original shape when it was cold. Feynman thus showed that the slow reaction time of the O-ring had allowed hot gases to escape, erode the O-ring, and burn a hole in the side of the right solid rocket booster, ultimately causing the destruction of the spacecraft and the deaths of the seven astronauts.

In Appendix F to the commission's final report, "Personal Observations on the Reliability of the Shuttle," Feynman contended that the managers of the NASA shuttle project came up with wildly unreasonable numbers to show that the spacecraft would be safe. He concluded the report with these words: "For a successful technology, reality must take precedence over public relations, for nature cannot be fooled." Feynman, diagnosed with yet another cancerous abdominal tumor in October, 1987, died of complications on February 15, 1988.

SELECTED WRITINGS BY FEYNMAN:

Books

Quantum Electrodynamics, W. A. Benjamin, 1961.

(With R. Leighton and Matthew Sands) *The Feynman Lectures on Physics,* Addison-Wesley Publishing Co., 1963–65.

The Character of Physical Law, MIT Press, 1965.

Photon-Hadron Interactions, W. A. Benjamin, 1972.

QED: The Strange Theory of Light and Matter, Princeton University Press, 1985.

(With Ralph Leighton) *Surely You're Joking, Mr. Feynman!: Adventures of a Curious Character* (memoirs), Norton, 1985.

(With Leighton) *What Do You Care What Other People Think?: Further Adventures of a Curious Character* (memoirs), Norton, 1988.

Periodicals

"The Theory of Positrons," *Physical Review,* Volume 76, 1949, p. 749.

"Atomic Theory of Liquid Helium Near Absolute Zero," *Physical Review,* Volume 91, 1953, p. 1301.

(With Murray Gell-Mann) "Theory of the Fermi Interaction," *Physical Review,* Volume 109, 1958, p. 193.

SOURCES:

Books

Gleick, James, *Genius: The Life and Science of Richard Feynman,* Pantheon, 1992.

Periodicals

"Richard P. Feynman," *Scientific American,* June, 1988, pp. 38, 42.

—Sketch by Patrick Moore

Johannes Fibiger
1867-1928
Danish pathologist and bacteriologist

Johannes Fibiger was a Danish bacteriologist whose early work on childhood diphtheria and tuberculosis demonstrated the vital role medical research could play in controlling diseases that threatened public health. In 1926, Fibiger received the Nobel Prize in physiology or medicine for demonstrating how cancer-like tissues could be induced experimentally in the laboratory.

Johannes Andreas Grib Fibiger was born on April 23, 1867, in the Danish village of Silkeborg. His father, Christian Fibiger, was a district physician; his mother, Elfride Muller, was a writer and the daughter of a Danish politician. When Fibiger was three, his father died and the family moved to Copenhagen, where he attended the University of Copenhagen at age sixteen and studied medicine, biology, and zoology. After earning his medical degree in 1890, he undertook several years of medical apprenticeship in various hospitals and with the Danish army. In 1891, he married Mathilde Fibiger, a distant cousin and physician's daughter, with whom he had two children.

It was while working as an assistant in a bacteriological laboratory at the University of Copenhagen that Fibiger was persuaded to undertake doctoral work on diphtheria, a virulent childhood disease that caused its victims to suffocate. Fibiger discovered better methods of growing diphtheria bacteria in the laboratory and demonstrated that there were two distinct forms of the bacillus, an important step in identifying carriers of the disease who frequently displayed no symptoms. At the turn of the century, diphtheria was a major public health problem, and epidemics were frequent in Denmark and throughout the rest of the developed world. Fibiger produced an experimental serum against the disease and carefully monitored the results of an inoculation program. In 1897, the International Medical Congress published his report, a model of its kind, which brought Fibiger international attention and confirmed the effectiveness of the serum. The young scientist had received his Ph.D. only two years earlier. Fibiger later came to regard his work on diphtheria as his highest scientific achievement.

In 1900, at age thirty-three, he joined the faculty of the Institute of Pathological Anatomy, one of a number of young professors hired by the University of Copenhagen. He was also appointed director of the institute and launched a successful program to construct a modern research facility for pathology and anatomy. Within its walls, Fibiger and another faculty member, C. O. Jenson, conducted research on tuberculosis in cattle and humans. Flying in the face of popular opinion, they demonstrated that humans could contract tuberculosis from infected cattle, especially by drinking their milk. Supported by the research of other investigators in Europe, these findings led to the passage of strict regulations governing the sale of raw milk, resulting in fewer adolescent deaths due to tuberculosis.

Seeks to Produce Cancer in the Laboratory

Fibiger's experiments on tubercular rats led him to the discovery for which he won the Nobel Prize. Performing a series of routine dissections in 1907, he discovered abscesses that appeared to be cancerous in the stomach lining of three wild rats. Microscopic examination revealed that the abscesses contained the larvae of a minute parasitic worm or nematode.

By the early 1900s, scientists had ample observational data suggesting that environmental irritants such as soot and harsh chemicals produced cancer in chimney sweeps and chemical workers. Many scientists thought that chronic irritation from mechanical or chemical agents was the basis of all cancer, but no one had yet succeeded in turning normal cells into cancerous cells under laboratory conditions.

Working on the hypothesis that the parasites produced a chemical toxin that induced cancer of the stomach, Fibiger undertook an ambitious research program. He trapped and examined more than a thousand wild rats, feeding them worm larvae, and even injecting them with the parasite, all without result. Surmising that the larvae was not passed from rat to rat but through an intermediate host, he traced the parasite to a rare species of cockroach found near a Copenhagen sugar refinery. By feeding healthy rats a diet of white bread and cockroaches, Fibiger finally succeeded in producing stomach abscesses in more than a hundred animals. For the first time, a researcher had induced what at the time was thought to be cancer in a laboratory setting. Fibiger reported his achievement in the *Journal of Cancer Research* and was awarded the 1926 Nobel Prize in medicine or physiology for his discovery of *Spiroptera carcinoma,* the parasitic worm that he thought had produced the cancer. Yet, in his acceptance speech, Fibiger expressed doubt that parasites played any great role in gastric cancer in humans.

Later investigators would find a number of weaknesses in Fibiger's research. Like most scientists of the period, Fibiger had not thought to check his findings against a control group of rats fed on a diet of only white bread. Nor was it easy to reproduce Fibiger's findings in other laboratories due to the lack of a standard strain of laboratory rats in the 1920s; Fibiger's animals had all been caught in the wild. Other investigators expressed doubt that the abscesses described by Fibiger were truly cancerous. There was some evidence that the abscesses might have been caused by a diet deficient in vitamin A. Nonetheless, the lasting effect of Fibiger's prize-winning discovery—later refuted by other researchers—was the great impetus it gave to other investigators to pursue laboratory research on the causes of cancer.

Fibiger abandoned parasitology after World War I to follow the work of two Japanese scientists who induced skin cancer in rabbits by painting their ears with coal tar. Conducting his own experiments by painting the backs of rats with the irritant, Fibiger reported two valuable insights: that cancer did not occur with the same frequency in all species or even within the same species, and that individual predisposition played an important role in susceptibility to cancer. At the time of his death, he was working with two colleagues on a vaccine for cancer, hoping to demonstrate that inoculating laboratory animals with matter drawn from malignant tumors would induce immunity to the disease.

During his long career as director of the Institute of Pathological Anatomy at the University of Copenhagen, Fibiger divided his time between research and teaching. He was a generous colleague who was widely respected for his meticulous laboratory methods. He published seventy-nine scientific papers and served as secretary and then president of the Danish Medical Society, and as president of the Danish Cancer Commission. He was co-editor and founder of *Acta Pathologica et Microbiologica Scandinavica.* In 1927, he was awarded the Nordhoff-Jung Cancer Prize.

On January 30, 1928, less than two years after delivering his Nobel Prize speech, Johannes Fibiger died in Copenhagen of a massive heart attack. He was sixty years old and had recently learned that he had colon cancer.

SELECTED WRITINGS BY FIBIGER:

Books

(With Fridtjof Bang), *Experimental Production of Tar Cancer in White Mice,* Host and Son, 1921.

Periodicals

"On Spiroptera Carcinomata and Their Relation to True Malignant Tumors; With Some Remarks on Cancer Age," *Journal of Cancer Research,* Volume 3, 1919, pp. 367–87.

SOURCES:

Books

Fox, Daniel M., editor, *Nobel Laureates in Medicine or Physiology: A Biographical Dictionary,* Garland Publishing, 1990, pp. 177–81.

Magill, Frank N., editor, *The Nobel Prize Winners: Psychology or Medicine,* Volume 1, Salem Press, pp. 267–74.

Oberling, Charles, *The Riddle of Cancer,* Yale University Press, 1952.

Secher, Knud, *The Danish Cancer Researcher Johannes Fibiger,* H. K. Lewis & Company Ltd., 1947.

Sourkes, Theodore L., *Nobel Prize Winners in Medicine and Physiology, 1901–1965,* Abelard-Schuman, 1966, pp. 123–27.

Periodicals

Annals of Internal Medicine, May 1, 1992, pp. 765–69.

—*Sketch by Philip Metcalfe*

Louis F. Fieser
1899-1977
American organic chemist

Louis F. Fieser was a renowned educator, researcher, and author. In addition to writing numerous research papers, reference books, and textbooks, he developed methods of synthesizing various compounds including an antimalarial drug, vitamin K, and carcinogenic (or cancer-causing) chemicals for use in medical research. He also invented napalm, and he played a key role in developing the drug cortisone for treating arthritis. Among the many awards he received for his contributions was the American Chemical Society's Award in Chemical Education, which recognized his thirty years of innovative and inspiring teaching at Harvard University.

Louis Frederick Fieser was born on April 7, 1899, in Columbus, Ohio, to Louis Frederick and Martha Victoria (Kershaw) Fieser. The younger Fieser earned an A.B. degree from Williams College in 1920, and went on to earn a Ph.D. in chemistry from Harvard in 1924. The following year he spent in Frankfurt, Germany, and at Oxford University in England doing postgraduate work with a Harvard travel fellowship. On his return to the United States in 1925, he accepted a teaching position at Bryn Mawr College. Initially leery of teaching at an all-women's college, his expectation of intellectually inferior students proved groundless, and he remained there until 1930. It was here that he met a chemistry student named Mary Peters, whom he married in 1932. **Mary Peters Fieser** would collaborate with him on numerous research projects, as well as many books.

Louis F. Fieser joined the chemistry department at Harvard in 1930 as assistant professor. There he became known for his well-organized, entertaining, and imaginative lectures, and especially for his ability to inspire interest in laboratory work. In 1939, he became the Sheldon Emery Professor of Organic Chemistry. He retained this post until 1968, and after his retirement devoted his time to writing, lecturing, and performing laboratory research.

Synthesizes Vitamin K

One of Fieser's most famous accomplishments was developing a method of synthesizing vitamin K, a blood coagulant, in the laboratory. During the 1930s, biochemist **Henrik Dam** of Copenhagen discovered that a substance (later called "Koagulations-Vitamin") found in certain green plants, especially alfalfa, prevented hemorrhages. Although other researchers succeeded in isolating the vitamin, the amount available from natural sources was too small to be of practical use. As Fieser explained in a 1939 lecture he gave to the Boylston Chemical Club at Harvard (as quoted in *Science*), the work of his research team "culminated in the establishment of the structure by a synthesis . . . which has the merit of providing a practical method for the production of the pure material in quantity." Vitamin K also proved useful in prenatal care and for other therapeutic anti-hemorrhagic purposes.

Fieser headed a chemistry research team at Harvard that investigated a number of other important topics in the field of chemistry. During the 1930s, he conducted research on the chemical causes of cancer and developed methods of synthesizing various carcinogens (cancer-causing agents) for use in medical research. During World War II, the Japanese invasion of the East Indies blocked the Allies, including the United States, from access to most of the world supply of quinine, a major antimalarial medicine. As part of his work on the chemistry of quinones in general, Fieser investigated the use of naphthoquinones as a substitute. His research team eventually synthesized the drug lapinone, which proved to be effective against malaria.

Wins Gratitude and Condemnation for Invention of Napalm

One of Fieser's most controversial accomplishments was also invented during wartime. In 1941, the

National Defense Research Committee contracted with Fieser to develop napalm, the jellied gasoline substance used in bombs and flame-throwers. Fieser and his research team also discovered a civilian use for napalm—it was an effective crabgrass killer, as it burned away crabgrass seeds without harming grass roots needed for lawns. But it was the military application that received the most attention. During and after World War II, Fieser received letters from many who credited the invention with saving thousands of American lives. But during the Vietnam Conflict, public reaction to napalm was quite different. Many criticized it as an immoral weapon whose use was intended to harm Vietnamese civilians. Fieser again received letters about his invention, this time critical of him and his work. He maintained, however, that he felt no guilt about inventing napalm. He believed scientists could not be held responsible for how other people used their discoveries. "You don't know what's coming," he said in an interview reported in the *New York Times.* "That wasn't my business. . . . I was working on a technical problem that was considered pressing." In *Time,* he maintained that he would "do it again, if called upon, in defense of the country."

In contrast to his work on napalm, public reaction to Fieser's contributions to the development of synthetic cortisone was consistently positive. Cortisone, one of the hormones secreted by the cortex (outer layer) of the adrenal glands, was found to be useful in treating rheumatoid arthritis and related diseases. Other researchers had discovered most of the necessary steps in synthesizing cortisone. In 1951, Fieser played a key role in the completion of this process by his discovery of a missing portion of the cortisone molecule.

Fieser was elected to the National Academy of Sciences in 1940. For his work on cancer, Fieser was awarded the Katherine Berkan Judd Prize from Memorial Hospital in 1941. In addition to the award from the American Chemical Society, he received the Manufacturing Chemists' Association Award in 1959 and the Norris Award, also in 1959, for his teaching skills. He later served on the Surgeon General's Advisory Committee on Smoking and Health that issued the 1964 report linking cigarette smoking with cancer.

A prolific writer, Fieser published over 300 research papers, and he wrote or co-wrote numerous chemistry textbooks and reference books with his wife, Mary Peters Fieser. Although he avoided making any public comments about the Vietnam War despite the controversy over napalm, he did take an active role in trying to reduce hostilities in another part of the world. In 1967, he joined four other scientists in initiating a public statement, addressed to U.S. President Lyndon B. Johnson and signed by eighty prominent Americans, urging the United States to pursue a peace settlement in the Middle East between Israel and the Arab countries. Fieser died in Cambridge on July 25, 1977, at age seventy-eight.

SELECTED WRITINGS BY FIESER:

Books

(With Mary Peters Fieser) *Organic Chemistry,* Wiley, 1944.

Introduction to Organic Chemistry, Heath, 1946.

(With Mary Peters Fieser) *Reagents for Organic Synthesis,* Volumes 1–8, Wiley, 1967.

Periodicals

"The Synthesis of Vitamin K," *Science,* January 12, 1940, pp. 31–36.

"Some Aspects of the Chemistry and Biochemistry of Cholesterol," *Science,* May 21, 1954, pp. 710–716.

"Steroids," *Scientific American,* January, 1955, pp. 52–60.

SOURCES:

Books

Modern Men of Science, McGraw Hill, 1968, pp. 153–156.

Periodicals

Journal of Chemical Education, March, 1985, pp. 186–191.

New York Times, September 16, 1944, p. 22; September 21, 1946, p. 21; September 19, 1967, p. 2; December 27, 1967, p. 8; July 27, 1977, p. B2.

Time, January 5, 1968, pp. 66–67.

—Sketch by Donna Olshansky

Mary Peters Fieser
1909-
American organic chemist

Mary Peters Fieser's substantial contributions to the field of organic chemistry include her work on the Harvard research team headed by her husband, **Louis Fieser**, and her authorship of numerous key texts and reference books in the field. She was involved in numerous important areas, including the synthesis of vitamin K, the development of an antimalarial drug, and the synthesis of cortisone and carcinogenic chemicals for medical research. For her research, publications, and skill in teaching chemistry students how to write, she was awarded the prestigious Garvan Medal in 1971.

Fieser was born in 1909 in Atchison, Kansas, to Robert Peters, an English professor, and Julia (Clutz) Peters, a bookstore owner and manager. Her father accepted a position at what is now Carnegie-Mellon University, and Fieser grew up in Harrisburg, Pennsylvania. Her family believed strongly in educational and professional achievement for women: Fieser's mother did graduate work in English, and her sister, Ruth, became a mathematics professor; her grandmother, who had educated her seven children herself at home until they were college age, impressed upon Fieser the importance of using her education constructively.

After attending a private girls' school, Fieser went to Bryn Mawr College, where she earned a B.A. in chemistry in 1930. There, she met her future husband, **Louis Fieser**, who was a chemistry instructor at the college. She enjoyed his courses, finding his emphasis on experimental rather than theoretical chemistry to be especially interesting. When Louis left Bryn Mawr in 1930 to teach at Harvard, she went with him. There, she performed chemistry research in his laboratory while earning a master's degree in organic chemistry, which she received in 1936.

When the couple married in 1932, Fieser continued her professional association with her husband on his research team. This arrangement benefited Fieser enormously in her professional career, because bias against women in the field of chemistry very strong at that time. For instance, her analytical chemistry professor at Harvard, Gregory Paul Baxter, refused to allow her to perform her experiments in the laboratory with the rest of the class. Instead, Fieser had to perform experiments in the deserted basement of another building, with little or no supervision. Once married, however, she was free to conduct research on her husband's team unhampered. As she commented during an interview with the *Journal of Chemical Education,* there were too many obstacles to an academic career in chemistry as a single woman, but after she was married, "I could do as much chemistry as I wanted, and it didn't matter what Professor Baxter thought of me."

Contributes to Vitamin K Synthesis

As part of Louis Fieser's research team, Mary Fieser helped develop a practical method of obtaining substantial amounts of vitamin K. The antihemorrhagic properties of vitamin K had been discovered during the 1930s by **Henrik Dam** in Copenhagen. Researchers had discovered this vitamin in green plants and especially in dried alfalfa, but the amount available from these sources was too small to be of practical use in medical therapy. The Fieser research group developed a method of synthesizing large amounts of vitamin K in a short period of time. The vitamin's blood-clotting characteristic has proved useful in prenatal therapy and other therapeutic purposes as well.

The Fiesers also focused on the use of naphthoquinones as antimalarial drugs. Quinine was one of the standard drugs used to treat malaria. When Japan invaded the East Indies during World War II, most of the world's supply of quinine became inaccessible to the Allies. The Fieser research team undertook a study of naphthoquinones as an alternative treatment. The Fiesers' research focused on isolating and identifying intermediate compounds along the reaction pathway. Their work ultimately contributed to the synthesis of the antimalarial drug lapinone.

Fieser worked on numerous other projects, including studies of the chemical causes of cancer. She helped develop methods of synthesizing various carcinogenic chemicals for use in medical research. She also played an important role in one of the Fiesers' more well-known projects: their contribution to the synthesis of cortisone, a steroid hormone used in the treatment of rheumatoid arthritis.

Publishes Major Textbooks and Reference Works

Fieser was highly regarded by her colleagues for her skill as a research chemist. Harvard chemist William von Doering is quoted in the *Journal of Chemical Education* as saying that she was "a very gifted experimentalist" and an "active, influential part of the team." In addition to her research, Fieser wrote or cowrote with her husband a dozen chemistry texts and reference books, beginning in 1944 with the best-selling textbook *Organic Chemistry.* One of their most widely used publications, *Reagents for Organic Synthesis,* was the first reference work of its kind for researchers in organic chemistry. It was the result of a comprehensive, international review of organic chemistry literature from which Mary Fieser culled the results of studies in chemical synthesis.

Fieser's books were especially noteworthy because of her expert writing skills—an unusual ability for a chemist at that time. Fieser attempted to improve the quality of writing in her field by publishing *Style Guide for Chemists.* She and her husband, also a skilled writer, often argued at length over minor stylistic issues, such as the placement of a comma. These differences over writing style prompted Fieser's sister, Ruth, to suggest that their by-line "Fieser and Fieser" be changed to "Fieser versus Fieser."

In 1971, Fieser was awarded the Garvan Medal for her research contributions, her writing, and her skill in teaching chemistry students how to write. The Garvan Medal was established to "honor an American woman for distinguished service in chemistry." Her colleagues also noted that the awards her husband received were due at least in part to her efforts in the laboratory. In her leisure time, Fieser enjoyed indulging her strong competitive streak by organizing games for her husband's research group after work hours and setting up contests in ping-pong, badminton, and horseshoes for the graduate students. She and her husband owned many cats, including one named in honor of their work on synthesizing vitamin K. Their cats' photographs were used in their published work and came to be their trademark.

SELECTED WRITINGS BY FIESER:

Books

(With Louis Fieser) *Organic Chemistry,* Wiley, 1944.

(With L. Fieser) *Style Guide for Chemists,* Reinhold, 1959.

(With L. Fieser) *Reagents for Organic Synthesis,* Volumes 1–16, Wiley, 1967.

SOURCES:

Books

O'Neill, Lois Decker, editor, *The Women's Book of World Records and Achievements,* Doubleday, 1979, p. 168.

Periodicals

"Mary Fieser: Garvan Medal," *Chemical & Engineering News,* December 14, 1970, p. 64.

Pramer, Stacey, "Mary Fieser: A Transitional Figure in the History of Women," *Journal of Chemical Education,* March, 1985, pp. 186–191.

—Sketch by Donna Olshansky

Edmond H. Fischer
1920-
Chinese-born American biochemist

Edmond H. Fischer was the joint recipient with his longtime associate, **Edwin Krebs**, of the Nobel Prize in Physiology or Medicine in 1992 for discoveries dealing with reversible protein phosphorylation as a biological regulatory mechanism. Responsible for a wide range of basic processes, including cell growth and differentiation, regulation of genes, and muscle contraction, protein phosphorylation is now the subject of one in every twenty papers published in biology journals. Application of Fischer and Krebs's work to medicine has elucidated mechanisms of diseases such as cancer and diabetes, and has yielded drugs that inhibit the body's rejection of transplanted organs. The recognition accorded Fischer and Krebs, who began a collaboration at the University of Washington in Seattle in the early 1950s, was hailed within the scientific community as long overdue.

Edmond H. Fischer was born on April 6, 1920, in Shanghai, China. His father, Oscar Fischer, had come to China from Vienna, Austria, after earning degrees in business and law. Fischer's mother, Renée Tapernoux Fischer, was born in France. She had come to Shanghai with her family after first arriving in Hanoi, where her father was a journalist for a Swiss publication. In Shanghai, Fischer's grandfather founded the first French newspaper published in China and helped to establish a French language school that Fischer attended.

At the age of seven, Fischer was sent, along with two older brothers, to a Swiss boarding school near Lake Geneva. One of his brothers studied engineering at the Swiss Federal Polytechnical Institute in Zurich and the other went to Oxford to study law. While he was in high school, Fischer developed a lifelong friendship with Wilfried Haudenschild, whose inventiveness and unusual ideas impressed him. The two decided that one would be a scientist and the other a physician, so that together they would cure all the ills of the world. Fischer was also influenced in his youth by classical music and for a time entertained the idea of becoming a professional musician. Instead he decided to become a scientist.

After entering the School of Chemistry at the University of Geneva at the start of World War II, Fischer was able to earn a degree in biology and another in chemistry. He received his doctorate at Geneva in 1947 and worked at the university on research until 1953. American universities at the time afforded more opportunities in the new field of biochemistry, and Fischer soon found himself in the United States. His first position was at the California Institute of Technology, where he was given a post-doctoral fellowship. Fischer was amazed that wherever he went in the United States he was offered a job. In Europe, research positions in his field were next to impossible to obtain.

Invitation to Seattle Leads to Collaboration

Hans Neurath, chair of the department of biochemistry at the University of Washington, invited Fischer to Seattle. On his first visit he found the scenery reminiscent of Switzerland and accepted Neurath's offer of an assistant professorship at the new medical school at the university. Thus began a long association with Edwin Krebs. Krebs had worked in the laboratory of **Carl Ferdinand Cori** and **Gerty T. Cori** in St. Louis on the enzyme phosphorylase in the late 1940s (enzymes are proteins that encourage or inhibit chemical reactions). The Coris won the Nobel Prize in 1947 for their isolation of phosphorylase, showing its existence in active and inactive form. Fischer had worked on a plant version of the same enzyme while he was in Switzerland.

In the mid–1950s Fischer and Krebs set out to determine what controlled the protein's activity. Their experiments centered on muscle contraction. A resting muscle needs energy (stored as glycogen in the body) in order to contract, and phosphorylase frees glucose from glycogen for use by the muscle. Fischer and Krebs discovered that an enzyme they called protein kinase was responsible for adding a phosphate group from the compound ATP (adenosine triphosphate, the cell's energy store) to phosphorylase, which activated the enzyme. In a reverse reaction, an enzyme called protein phosphatase removed the phosphate, turning phosphorylase off. Protein kinases are present in all cells and are critical for many phases of cell activity, including metabolism, respiration, protein synthesis, and response to stress.

Research Opens Field to Important Discoveries

By the 1970s biochemical research in the area that Fischer and Krebs opened up was so extensive that 5 percent of papers in biology journals dealt with protein phosphorylation. Between 1 and 5 percent of the genetic code may be concerned with protein kinases and phosphatases. Science has made connections that show the role of protein kinases in diseases, including cancer, diabetes, and muscular dystrophy. Fischer and Krebs have also been able to demonstrate in their research how the immune system is activated. They showed how a surface protein starts a chain reaction that recruits lymphocytes to fight infection.

In the field of organ transplants, drugs that influence phosphorylation prevent rejection of the transplants by the body's immune system. The drug cyclosporin has been developed and is widely used to prevent the rejection of liver, kidney, or pancreatic transplants in human beings. Cyclosporin and another drug, FK–506, inhibit protein phosphatase, thereby preventing the rejection of tissues in organ transplant operations. Irregular protein kinase activity can cause abnormal cell growth leading to tumors and cancer. Philip Cohen, a colleague from the University of Dundee, comments in a *New Scientist* interview that protein kinases and phosphatases "will be the major drug targets of the 21st century."

Edmond H. Fischer has received many honors for his scientific research over the course of his long career. Notable, besides the Nobel Prize, are his election to the American Academy of Arts and Sciences in 1972 and his winning of the Werner Medal from the Swiss Chemical Society as early as 1952. Fischer has been married twice. His first wife, Nelly Gagnaux, died in 1961. He had two sons, François and Henri, with her. In 1963, he married Beverly Bullock, a native Californian. Besides his accomplishment in classical piano, Fischer also enjoys painting, piloting a plane, and mountaineering. Along with his colleague, Krebs, Fischer annually joins research groups in retreats at the University of Washington Park Forest Conference Center in the foothills of the Cascade Mountains. There they review their latest findings and lay plans for their future research, which they continue in the role of emeritus professors at the University of Washington. Philip Cohen, commenting on the nature of their collaboration in *New Scientist,* said, "They complement each other. Fischer has lots of brilliant ideas; Krebs has the judgment to know which of the ideas are worth following."

SELECTED WRITINGS BY FISCHER:

Periodicals

(With E. G. Krebs) "The Phosphorylase *b* and *a* Converting Enzyme of Rabbit Skeletal Muscle," *Biochimica Biophysica Acta,* Volume 20, 1956, pp. 150–157.

(With E. G. Krebs and A. B. Kent) "The Muscle Phosphorylase *b* Kinase Reaction," *Journal of Biological Chemistry,* Volume 231, 1959, pp. 1698–1704.

Proceedings of the National Academy of Sciences, USA, 1988, pp. 7182–7186, 1989, pp. 5257–5261.

(With N. F. Zander, D. E. Cool, C. D. Diltz, and others) "Suppression of V-FMS-Induced Transformation by Overexpression of a Truncated T-Cell Protein Tyrosine Phosphatase," *Oncogene,* Volume 8, 1993, pp. 1175–1182.

SOURCES:

Periodicals

Altman, Lawrence K., "Americans Win Nobel for Clues to Cell Signals," *New York Times,* October 13, 1992, p. C3.

Baum, Rudy, and Stu Borman, "Marcus Wins Chemistry Nobel; Two Biochemists Take Medicine Prize," *Chemical and Engineering News,* October 19, 1992, pp. 6–7.

Brown, Phyllida, "Protein Manipulators 'Stumble' on Nobel Prize," *New Scientist,* October 17, 1992, p. 7.

Marx, Jean, "U.S. Researchers Gather a Bumper Crop of Laurels," *Science,* October 23, 1992, pp. 542–543.

Neurath, Hans, "Edmond H. Fischer and Edwin G. Krebs: 1992 Nobel Laureates in Physiology or Medicine," *Advances in Protein Phosphatases,* Volume 7, 1993, pp. 1–8.

Other

Fischer, Edmond H., Nobel lecture, Karolinska Institutet, December 8, 1992.

Press release, Karolinska Institutet, October 12, 1992.

—*Sketch by Vita Richman*

Emil Fischer
1852-1919
German chemist

Emil Fischer was a professor of chemistry for forty years who also served as director of the German chemical industries during World War I. Fischer's research on important organic substances such as sugars, enzymes, and proteins, built the foundation for modern biochemistry. He was the scientist who initially described the action of enzymes as a lock and key mechanism where the structure of an enzyme fits exactly into the molecule with which it reacts to "unlock" a biochemical reaction. In 1902 he received the Nobel Prize in chemistry for his laboratory synthesis of sugars and purine, a substance found naturally in all deoxyribonucleic acid (DNA). Fischer was dedicated to academic research and was among the first scientists in the world to promote substantial industrial as well as governmental support for university laboratories.

Emil Hermann Fischer was born on October 9, 1852 in Euskirchen, Germany, near Bonn and Cologne. With five older sisters, he was the only son of Laurenz Fischer and Julie Poensgen Fischer. His father was a successful businessman who started as a grocer, then added a wool spinning mill and a brewery as he prospered. Fischer described his youth as happy in his unfinished autobiography, *Aus meinem Leben* (Out of my Life). Fischer was a brilliant student, graduating in 1869 at the top of his class from the Gymnasium (high school) of Bonn. After graduation, Fischer tried working in business with an uncle, but he was much more interested in building a laboratory. He entered the University of Bonn in the spring of 1871.

Follows a Master Chemist to a Lifelong Career

After less than a year at the University of Bonn, Fischer transferred to Strasbourg where he studied under the noted chemist, **Adolf von Baeyer**. Fischer's creativity flourished in the academic atmosphere of Strasbourg; he especially noted in his autobiography the accessibility of his professors, and the opportunities to travel and visit other chemical laboratories. For his doctorate Fischer did research on fluorescein, a coal tar dye that shows a fine yellow-green fluorescence in solution, and is used to trace water through systems. Fischer's researches into coal, coal tar, and the synthesis of organic chemicals, did much to build the German dye industry. Dyes manufactured in Germany soon captured the world market.

Expands Research

Fischer received his doctoral degree in 1874 from Strasbourg, but he continued his research on coal tar dyes with a cousin, Otto Philipp Fischer, until 1878. Ultimately he acquired a number of patents for industrially useful chemicals. In 1875 Fischer was invited to follow Baeyer to the University of Munich where Fischer became associate professor of analytical chemistry in 1879. His researches included the discovery of a new compound, phenylhydrazine, a chemical he later used extensively in research on sugars. By 1878 he figured out the chemical formula for phenylhydrazine, and this discovery stimulated other researches leading to the development of such synthetic drugs as novocaine. In 1881 Fischer began investigations into a new field, purine chemistry (part of a group of nucleic acids), identifying three amino acids and synthesizing many more. This research resulted in many more advances in the German drug industry.

Fischer left in 1882 to accept the position of professor of chemistry at the University of Erlangen, near Nuremberg. At Erlangen, Fischer continued his work on purines and began to study carbohydrates in 1884. His subsequent work with phenylhydrazine in an unventilated laboratory caused him to suffer the effects of phenylhydrazine poisoning which attacks the kidney, liver, and respiratory system. Fischer had, from an early age, periodically suffered from stomach disorders; the added contamination to phenylhydrazine made him extremely ill. Upon his recovery in 1885 he accepted a chair in Würzburg, where, he wrote in his autobiography, "gaiety and humor flourished." In 1888 Fischer married Agnes Gerlach. They had three sons before she died in 1895. While Fischer was at Würzburg he was honored with a Bavarian medal.

Berlin Brings World Recognition and a Nobel Prize

In 1892 Fischer accepted the position of professor in charge of the chemistry department at the University of Berlin, the most prestigious position for an academic chemist in Germany at that time. He was offered full freedom in the construction of a new building at the chemical institute of Berlin, and his subsequent design of a well-ventilated laboratory became a model for university laboratories all over the world. In addition, his teaching methods led to the formation of small groups of students involved in basic scientific research. With the help of his cooperative teams of students, and fellow researchers from many countries, he designed a careful plan for each research project. As the work progressed he always looked for deviations from the expected results. Each unusual occurrence was researched systematically to its conclusion. This strategy permanently influenced both graduate education in chemistry and the expectations of universities for research and publication from their professors worldwide.

Fischer's researches into sugar and purines had proven especially successful. He synthesized about one hundred and thirty purines, which included caffeine, theophylline (used in the preparation of the motion sickness drug Dramamine), and uric acid. In addition, after studying the three-dimensional shapes of sugar molecules, Fischer synthesized glucose as well as about thirty other sugars. By 1899 Fischer finished most of his work on sugars and purines and began research on proteins and enzymes in an effort to identify their chemical nature. Fischer was elected to membership in the Academy of Sciences, and, in 1902, he received the Nobel Prize "for his synthesis in the groups of sugars and purine," as quoted by Eduard Farber in *Nobel Prize Winners in Chemistry.* In 1909 he received the Helmholtz Medal for his work on sugar and protein chemistry.

Fischer believed in basic research. Determined to keep the preeminent position of world leader in chemical research for Germany, a position he did much to create, he gathered support from industry, government, and other scientists to establish a number of research institutes—the Kaiser Wilhelm Society for the Advancement of Sciences, the Kaiser Wilhelm Institute for Chemistry in Berlin-Dahlem, and the Kaiser Wilhelm Institute for Coal Research in Mulheim-Ruhr. Fischer was interested in research in every branch of chemistry. As director of the University of Berlin laboratories he started a radiochemistry laboratory where, years after his death, scientists **Otto Hahn** and **Lise Meitner** worked on research that led to the fission of uranium and the ultimate development of the atomic bomb.

Makes Major Contribution to German War Effort

World War I took Fischer away from most of his experimental investigations as he redirected his research concentrations toward the war effort. Besides being the leading chemist in Germany, he had long worked closely with industry and government. The British blockade would have brought the defeat of Germany by 1915 had Fischer and his colleagues not succeeded in using the resources they had to synthesize much of what they could no longer get on the world market. He led the development of synthetic saltpeter (potassium nitrate) and nitric acid, both used in the manufacture of explosives. As food became in short supply he coordinated research and production of synthetic fertilizers. Fischer directed research to replace diminishing supplies of camphor (used to stabilize gunpowder) and pyrites which supplied sulfur for explosives.

Before World War I scientists had enjoyed the freedom to travel and communicate with other scientists regardless of political differences and skirmishes between their respective countries. However, World War I brought a change. Scientists became national resources. Fischer ended his long friendship with British chemist, Sir **William Ramsay**, also a Nobel laureate. But research alone could not win the war, and not all of Fischer's projects were successful. It was obvious to Fischer that Germany would be defeated. In an effort to organize the rebuilding of chemical research and industry in Germany to gain back the leadership it had before the war, Fischer and a friend made plans to form the German Society for the Advancement of Chemical Instruction.

The war years were personally tragic for Fischer. He lost his two younger sons, which left him depressed, and he was suffering from cancer. Emil Fischer died in Berlin, July 15, 1919. Some reports say he died of cancer, most say it was suicide. His remaining son, Hermann Otto Laurenz Fischer (1888–1960) went on to become a Professor of Biochemistry at the University of California in Berkeley. On October 9, 1952, Fischer's son dedicated the Emil Fischer Library at the University of California which is the repository of the collected works of Fischer, including the manuscript for his autobiography, research files, and Fischer's correspondences in World War I.

SELECTED WRITINGS BY FISCHER:

Books

Aus meinem leben (autobiography; title means "Out of my Life;" also known as "Remembrances of Life"), Julius Springer [Berlin], 1921.

Nobel Lectures. Chemistry 1901–1921, [Amsterdam-New York], 1966, pp.

Other

Emil Fischer Papers (a collection of correspondence, papers, and research notes) Emil Fischer Library, University of California, Berkeley. 21–35.

SOURCES:

Books

Farber, Eduard, *Nobel Prize Winners in Chemistry,* Henry Schuman, 1953, pp. 7–11.

Farber, Eduard, editor, *Great Chemists,* Interscience, 1961, pp. 981–95.

Periodicals

Carroll, Felix A., "Emil Fischer and the German Universities," *Journal of Chemical Education,* February, 1979, pp. 107–108.

Kauffman, George, "Emil Fischer: His Role in Wilhelmian German Industry, Scientific Institutions, and Government," *Journal of Chemical Education,* June, 1984, pp. 504–505.

Millar, Margaret, et al., "Chemists as Autobiographers: The 19th Century," *Journal of Chemical Education,* April, 1985, pp. 279–81.

—Sketch by M. C. Nagel

Ernst Otto Fischer
1918-
German inorganic chemist

The field of organometallic chemistry—the study of compounds of metal and carbon—is tremendously important not only to an understanding of such basic structures as the B vitamins, but also to the chemical industry as a whole. The growth of plastics as well as the refining of petroleum hydrocarbons all involve at some stage the metal-to-carbon bond which is at the heart of organometallic chemistry, and Ernst Otto Fischer has played a crucial role in the pioneering of this science. Co-recipient of the 1973 Nobel Prize in chemistry for his X-ray analysis of the structure of a particular iron-to-carbon bond in so-called "sandwich compounds," Fischer, working with members of his research laboratory in Munich, was also on the cutting edge of transition-metal research, synthesizing totally new classes of compounds.

Fischer was born on November 10, 1918, in the Munich suburb of Solln. The third child of Valentine Danzer Fischer and Karl Tobias Fischer, a physics professor at Munich's Technische Hochschule, Fischer attended the Theresien Gymnasium (high school), graduating in 1937. Following this, Fischer spent two years compulsory service in the German army, a stint which was extended with the outbreak of World War II in 1939. In between serving in Poland, France, and Russia, Fischer was able, in the winter of 1941–42, to begin his studies in chemistry at the Technische Hochschule in Munich. Captured by the Americans, he was held in a prisoner of war camp until repatriation in the fall of 1945. He renewed his chemistry studies in Munich in 1946, studying under Walter Hieber, well known for his early work on combining metals with molecules of carbon and oxygen, or metal-carbonyl chemistry. Fischer earned his Ph.D. degree in 1952 for research on carbon-to-nickel bonds; his course was well set by this time for a career in the new field of organometallic chemistry.

Confirms Surprising New Metal-Carbon Structure

After earning his doctorate, Fischer stayed on at the Technische Hochschule, working as an assistant researcher. He and his first research students were drawn to a puzzling compound reported by the chemists T. Kealy and P. Pauson. In an attempt to link two cyclopentadiene—five-carbon—rings together, these scientists discovered an unknown compound which they believed involved an iron atom linked between two consecutive longitudinal rings of carbon. The intervening iron atom seemed to join with a carbon atom on each of the rings. That such metal-to-carbon bonds exist was not the surprising thing. In fact, such unstable bonds are necessary for catalytic processing of such compounds. What was interesting about this compound (initially called dicyclopentadienyl iron) was that it was not unstable at all. It was in fact highly stable both thermally and chemically. Such stability made no sense to Fischer given the nature of the proposed structure of the compound, and he theorized that it was in fact an entirely new sort of molecular complex. An English chemist, **Geoffrey Wilkinson**, soon proposed an alternate structure to the compound (now renamed ferrocene): He described ferrocene as made up of an atom of iron sandwiched between two parallel rings, one on top of the other rather than in a line on the same plane. Thus the iron formed bonds not just with a single atom on each ring, but with all of the atoms and also with the electrons *within* the rings, accounting for its stability. From this description came the term "sandwich compounds." Meanwhile, Fischer and his research team, including W. Pfab, carried out meticulous X-ray crystallography on ferrocene, elucidating the compound's structure, and proving Wilkinson's theory correct. The examination and discovery of the structure of ferrocene was a watershed event in the field of organometallic chemistry, spawning a new generation of inorganic chemists.

Continued Studies in Sandwich Compounds Wins Nobel

From ferrocene, Fischer and his team went on to determine the structure of, as well as synthesize, other transition metals—those substances at a stage in between metal and organic—especially dibenzenechromium, an aromatic hydrocarbon. Such substances are termed aromatic not because of smell, but because of structure: They are hydrocarbons in closed rings which are capable of uniting with other atom groups. Fischer showed dibenzenechromium to be another sandwich compound with two rings of benzene joined by an atom of chromium in between. This bit of research earned him world-wide renown in scientific circles, as the neutral chromium molecule and neutral benzene molecules had been thought to be uncombinable. Fischer's rise in academia parallelled the swift advance of his research: by 1954 he was an assistant professor at the Technische Hochschule; by 1957, a full professor at the University of Munich; and in 1964 he came back to the Technische Hochschule—by now called the Technische Universität or Technical University—as director of the Institute for Inorganic Chemistry, replacing the retiring director and his former mentor, Professor Hieber. Fischer's laboratory, equipped with all the latest equipment for spectrographic and structural analysis, soon became a center for worldwide organometallic research, and Fischer, whose talents at lecturing were equal to those in research, soon became the leading spokesperson for the new study. He also began lecturing around the world, and spent two visiting professorships in the United States in 1971 and 1973.

In 1973 Fischer was awarded the Nobel Prize, sharing it with the English Wilkinson for their "pioneering work, performed independently, on the chemistry of the organometallic, so-called sandwich compounds." At about this same time, Fischer and his team at Munich's Technical University were successfully synthesizing both the first carbene complexes and carbyne complexes—carbon atoms triply joined to metal atoms—which heralded an entirely new class of metal complexes of a transitional sort and spurred research in the field.

In addition to the Nobel, Fischer—a life-long bachelor—has also won the Göttingen Academy Prize in 1957 and the Alfred Stock Memorial Prize of the Society of German Chemists in 1959, as well as honorary membership in the American Academy of Arts and Sciences and full membership in the German Academy of Scientists. Among the many commercial and industrial spin-offs of his work is the creation of catalysts employed in the drug industry and also in oil refining, leading to the manufacture of fuels with low lead content.

SELECTED WRITINGS BY FISCHER:

Books

(With H. Werner) *Metal (pi)-Complexes,* Elsevier, 1966.

(With Karl Heinz Dotz and others) *Transition Metal Carbene Complexes,* Verlag Chemie, 1983.

Periodicals

"The Nomenclature of Metal Compounds Containing Two Cyclopentadienyl Rings," *Zeitzschrift für Naturforschung,* Volume 9b, 1954, pp. 619–620.

"New Results on Aromatic Metal Carbonyls," *Journal of Inorganic and Nuclear Chemistry,* Volume 8, 1958, pp. 268–272.

"Transition Metal Carbonyl Carbene Complexes," *Pure and Applied Chemistry,* Volume 30, 1972, pp. 353–372.

SOURCES:

Books

A Biographical Encyclopedia of Scientists, Facts on File, 1981, Volume 1, pp. 264–265.

Hinduja Foundation Encyclopedia of Nobel Laureates 1901–1987, Konark Publishers, 1988, pp. 486–487.

Periodicals

Seyferth, Dietmar, and Alan Davison, "The 1973 Nobel Prize for Chemistry," *Science,* November 16, 1973, pp. 699–701.

—Sketch by J. Sydney Jones

Hans Fischer
1881-1945
German chemist

Hans Fischer was a medically-minded chemist who won the Nobel Prize for chemistry for his pioneering investigations into the chemical structure of pyrroles, molecular compounds which give the specific color to many important biological substances, including blood, bile, and the leaves of plants. Building on the foundations laid by his predecessors and colleagues, many of them from Fischer's homeland of Germany, he spearheaded a series of investigations lasting more than two decades that led to the synthesis of hemoglobin, bilirubin, and (more than 25 years after his death) chlorophyll. During the course of his investigations, Fischer developed and oversaw an extremely productive microanalytical approach to studying chemical compounds, especially the pigments that occur in nature. By overseeing specific laboratory procedures conducted simultaneously by several labs, Fischer was able to conduct more than 60,000 microanalyses of chemical substances. In 1930, he won the Nobel Prize, primarily for his work in elucidating the structure of and synthesizing the blood pigment hemin.

Fischer was born at Höchst am Main in Germany on July 27, 1881, to Eugen Fischer, a dye chemist, and Anna Herdegen Fischer. Through his father's work as laboratory director at the Kalle Dye works, Fischer developed an early interest in the chemical nature of pigments, or coloring matter. Interested in both chemistry and medicine, Fischer received his doctorate in chemistry in 1904 from the University of Marburgh and his M.D. in 1908 from the University of Munich. After working on chemical structure of peptides and sugars with **Emil Fischer** (no relation) in Berlin, Fischer went to the Physiological Institute in Munich, where he first began his study (under Freidrich von Müller) of pigments, an area that was to become the overriding focus of his scientific pursuits. Fischer's dual expertise in chemistry and medicine led him to become chair of medical chemistry at the University of Innsbruch in 1916. Although he published his first notable scientific paper (on the subject of bilirubin, or bile pigment) in 1915, his research efforts soon came to a standstill due to World War I and the following years of reconstruction after Germany's defeat. Fischer's ill health also impeded his research efforts. He contracted tuberculosis when he was 20 years of age and had a kidney removed in 1917 due to complications from the disease.

Lays Groundwork for Nobel Prize-winning Discovery

In 1921, Fischer's investigation of pigments began in earnest as he accepted an appointment as director of the Institute für Anoreganische Chemise at the Technische Hochschule, or Technical University, in Munich. It was there that Fischer would conduct his groundbreaking research into pyrrole chemistry for nearly a quarter of a century. Fischer immediately reinitiated his studies of bile pigments and organized a number of specialized laboratories to simultaneously conduct the specific tasks needed to determine their chemical structures. Using a process known as Gattermann aldehyde synthesis to systematically prepare the numerous compounds needed for pyrrole derivatives, Fischer organized teams of microanalysts, sometimes referred to as "Gattermann cooks." He also set up specific laboratories to work on individual segments of a chemical problem, such as making calorimetric determinations and developing X-ray diagrams. By segmenting the work, Fischer's laboratory turned out more new chemical compounds than any laboratory that had preceded it.

Fischer's first major advance was the discovery of porphyrin synthesis in 1926. Porphyrins are made up of pyrroles joined in a chemical ring and are the pigments that appear throughout nature. The accepted view in chemistry prior to Fischer's work was that a single basic porphyrin structure was the primary component for all pigments occurring in nature. Fischer began to unravel the fundamental chemical structure of the porphin (the nucleic core of porphyrins), which had been proposed by W. Küster in 1912. This accomplishment led to the discovery of specific molecular structures of individual porphyrin groups that make up certain pigments. Specifically, Fischer had found that porphyrins are made up of four pyrrole nuclei bound by methane groups into a ring structure. This led to the creation of porphyrin in a laboratory setting. With the ability to synthesize porphyrin, Fischer and his colleagues were able to further determine thousands of specific porphyrin structures. In *Great Chemists,* **Heinrich Wieland**, an organic chemist, describes Fischer's attempt to synthesize porphyrins. "Fischer began to put the pyrrole segments together in mosaiclike arrangements and then to weld together, by brilliant synthetic procedures, the semimolecules of the pyrrometheenes produced in this manner." Fischer soon recognized that porphyrins differed primarily through the components that made up the rings. He also discovered that bilirubin was derived from hemin and identified it as a porphyrin.

In 1929, Fischer successfully synthesized hemin, showing that its ring had a center atom of iron. Fischer received the Nobel Prize in chemistry in 1930 for his synthesis of hemin, which is one of two components of hemoglobin, the red respiratory protein of erythrocytes (red blood cells or corpuscles). During the Nobel Prize ceremonies, Fischer was also noted for his demonstration that hemin is related to chlorophyll, the light absorbing, green plant pigment. In 1944, Fischer finally worked out the chemical structure of and synthesized the pigment bilirubin, which he had first begun investigating during World War I. Over the years, Fischer's laboratory had synthesized approximately 130 porphyrins. He also conducted in-depth studies of the specific structure of chlorophyll and published 129 papers on the topic. He successfully identified chlorophyll's pyrrole rings, which had a center of magnesium rather than iron like hemin's pyrrole rings. The synthesis of chlorophyll, while based largely on Fischer's work, was not accomplished until 1960, 15 years after his death.

Obsession with Work Leads to Suicide

Fischer was a dedicated scientist who had few outside interests. He was also secretive and seldom discussed his work with other scientists outside of his laboratory. Fischer's lack of outside interests extended to politics as well. Although he privately expressed concern over the rise of dictator Adolf Hitler and Nazi Germany, he chose not to speak out publicly. In 1935, Fischer married Wiltrud Haufe. Despite being three decades older than his bride, Fischer was a happily married man and once confided to Wieland, who was a personal friend, that his wife had greatly enriched his life.

Despite Fischer's dedication to his work, which some colleagues called obsessive, he did enjoy taking long motoring vacations in his car. His other love was the outdoors. Although he constantly battled the debilitating effects of tuberculosis, Fischer was an expert skier, accomplished hiker, and an avid mountain climber, a passion he shared with his father until an accident claimed the elder Fischer's life. Germany's involvement in World War II added to Fischer's woes. Because of supply restrictions and frequent bombing raids made by Allied forces, his work was seriously restricted. When a bombing run destroyed Fischer's institute, the scientist gave in to despair. In 1945, Fischer committed suicide, despondent over what he viewed as the destruction of his life's work.

Although he was able to organize large scientific efforts and had an intuitive feel for the chemical structures involved in the field of pyrrole chemistry, Fischer was not noted for his ability to clearly write or lecture on such topics. Despite this fact, he published the definitive work on pyrrole chemistry in three volumes, *Die Chemie des Pyrrols,* which has remained a standard text on the subject. In addition to the Nobel Prize, Fischer received the Leibig Memorial Medal in 1929 and the Davy Medal in 1936. He also received an honorary degree from Harvard University in 1935.

SELECTED WRITINGS BY FISCHER:

Books

(With Hans Orth) *Die Chemie des Pyrrols,* three volumes, Akademische Verlags-gesellschaft, 1934–1940.

Periodicals

"Hemin und Porphyrine," *Verhandlungen der deutschen Gesellschaft für innere Medizin,* Volume 45, 1933, pp. 7–27.

SOURCES:

Books

Gillispie, Charles Coulston, editor, *Dictionary of Scientific Biography,* Volume 15, supplement 1, Scribner, 1978, pp. 157–58.

Wasson, Tyler, editor, *Nobel Prize Winners,* H. W. Wilson, 1987, pp. 325–26.

Wieland, Heinrich, profile of Fischer in *Great Chemists,* edited by Eduard Farber, Interscience, 1961, pp. 1527–33.

Periodicals

Nature, October 11, 1947, pp. 494–95.

—*Sketch by David Petechuk*

Elizabeth F. Fisher
1873-1941
American geologist

Elizabeth F. Fisher was one of the first women field geologists in the United States. A professor at Wellesley College for thirty-two years, she taught geology, geography, and resource conservation. In 1918, Fisher helped locate oil wells in Texas as the first female geologist hired by an oil company.

Fisher was born in Boston, Massachusetts, on November 26, 1873, to Charles and Sarah Cushing Fisher. In 1894, while still a student at the Massachusetts Institute of Technology, she began teaching courses in geology and geography at Wellesley College; in 1896 she earned her S.B. degree from MIT. The next year, she traveled to Russia with the International Geological Congress; during her four-month stay, she and other foreign geologists visited the famous oil wells of Baku on the shores of the Caspian Sea.

She was an instructor at Wellesley College until 1906, when she was made an associate professor of geology and mineralogy there. In 1909, she became professor and head of the department of geology and geography. She also taught extension courses at Harvard and Radcliffe. In her lectures, Fisher addressed agricultural issues such as soil erosion and fertilization, as well as water supply and water power, advocating the reclamation of deserts and swamplands for agricultural use. Fisher's main research interests were river terraces, shorelines, and natural resource conservation. When World War I caused shortages of fuels and metals, Fisher also advocated the economic efficiency of mining. She wrote a textbook for junior high schools on natural resources; the book, *Resources and Industries of the United States,* described the position of the United States in world commerce and the natural and economic factors that stimulated its industrial growth. It also emphasized the dependence of the industries on natural resources and the critical need for conservation.

Hired to Scout Oil Fields

During a nationwide oil shortage in 1918, an oil company in Kansas hired Fisher to help locate oil wells in their north central Texas fields. She was the first woman sent out by an oil company to do such a survey. In 1926, Fisher became professor emeritus at Wellesley College. After her retirement she participated in a geographical survey of coastal Florida. On the shores of the twenty-seven-mile-wide Lake Okeechobee, she noted that drainage canals had lowered the level of the lake by about four feet. She is quoted in a Wellesley College news release as saying that "This uncovered about 80,000 acres of the richest muck land one would care to see; land so rich that weeds were growing ten feet high." She described the farmers growing radishes there that were as big as beets, and she calculated that further drainage of the lake could add nearly one million acres of arable land, on which Florida farmers might raise all the nation's sugar.

After her retirement, Fisher filled out a Wellesley College questionnaire, now preserved in the Wellesley College Archives. She noted her travels to national parks in Alaska in 1900 and a trip she took with twelve geology students to camp and ride horseback in Glacier National Park in 1919. At the bottom of the questionnaire, which Fisher filled out by hand, she had written, "At present I am studying and getting well." She died on April 25, 1941, in Los Angeles, California, after what the Wellesley College Office of Publicity described as a long illness. Fisher was a fellow of the American Association for the Advancement of Science and the American Geographical Society. She was also an active member of the Appalachian Mountain Club and the Boston Society of Natural History.

SELECTED WRITINGS BY FISHER:

Books

Resources and Industries of the United States, Ginn & Co., 1919.

SOURCES:

Books

Who Was Who in America, Marquis, 1973.

Periodicals

"Conservation Work by Professor Elizabeth Fisher," *Wellesley Alumnae Quarterly,* January, 1919.

"Elizabeth Fisher, Geologist, Dies," *The Boston Herald,* May 2, 1941.

Other

"Wellesley Geologist, on Survey of Florida Everglades, Finds Fountain of Eternal Sweetness in Reclaimed Land," news release, Wellesley College Archives.

Wellesley College Questionnaire for Faculty and Officers of Administration, Wellesley College Archives.

—Sketch by Miyoko Chu

Ronald A. Fisher
1890-1962
English statistician and geneticist

Sir Ronald A. Fisher was a prominent mathematician who formalized and extended the field of statistics and revolutionized the concept of experimental design. He worked for fourteen years as a research statistician and later held professorships in genetics, another field to which he made significant contributions. He wrote some three hundred papers and seven books throughout his prodigious career.

The son of George Fisher, a partner in a fine arts auction firm, Ronald Aylmer Fisher was born on February 17, 1890, in the north London suburb of East Finchley. The youngest of seven children, Fisher was a precocious child. In her biography, *R. A. Fisher: The Life of a Scientist,* Fisher's daughter Joan Fisher Box describes an incident that occurred when the scientist was about three years old: he engaged his nurse in a breakfast-table conversation about the successive halving of the number two; after she answered the first three questions of his series, he concluded that "half of a sixteenth must be a thirty-toof."

During his school years at Stanmore Park and Harrow schools, Fisher developed a facility for visualizing complex geometrical relationships in his mind. Because of his poor eyesight, he was not allowed to read or write under artificial light, so he often listened to lectures without taking notes and solved problems mentally. This ability later proved fruitful, when his geometrical interpretation of statistics led him to new results.

In 1909, Fisher earned a scholarship to attend Gonville and Caius College in Cambridge, where he concentrated on mathematics and theoretical physics, while also pursuing interests in biometry and genetics. As an undergraduate, he published his first scholarly paper, discussing an absolute criterion for fitting frequency curves. Following his graduation in 1912, he continued his studies for another year, investigating statistical mechanics, quantum theory, and the theory of errors.

During his first six years out of college, he searched for an occupation that would suit him, even working briefly as a farm laborer in Canada. Primarily, however, he worked as a statistician for the Mercantile and General Investment Company in London (1913–15) and as a public school teacher (1915–19). Although he was unhappy and apparently ineffective as a teacher, he was nonetheless recognized as a brilliant thinker who had some difficulty explaining his ideas to others. In 1917, he married Ruth Eileen Guinness, the daughter of a doctor; they had eight children and eventually separated.

Even though his jobs did not support research opportunities, Fisher published several notable papers. One of his earliest accomplishments in statistics (published in 1915) was to establish, in mathematical terms, an exact method of sample measurement in statistics. A child of the upper class, he also wrote two papers on eugenics, the science of improving the human race through selective mating. His concern that the—as he thought—less talented lower classes produced offspring at a faster rate than the—in his mind—more capable upper classes influenced his personal choice to have a large family. This was, in addition to being jingoistic, a risk on his part considering his own genetic shortcomings regarding his poor vision, a trait he could have engendered to several large generations of Fishers. His 1918 paper on Gregor Mendel's theory of inherited characteristics laid the foundation for his later work on the statistical analysis of variance.

Establishes Renowned Statistical Research Center

His growing reputation as a mathematician brought Fisher two promising job offers in 1919. One, from the noted statistician **Karl Pearson** (with whom he developed a lifelong feud), was to work at the Galton Laboratory in London's University College under Pearson's close supervision. Recognizing a better opportunity to conduct his own research, Fisher accepted a second offer from Sir John Russell at the Rothamsted Experimental Station, about twenty-five miles north of London. Established in 1843, this agricultural research laboratory had accumulated a sixty-six-year backlog of statistical data; it would be Fisher's job to analyze this material. For the next fourteen years, Fisher took advantage of the huge data resources at Rothamsted to derive new analysis techniques as well as agricultural results. On the theoretical side, he formulated the analysis of variance. Now a fundamental tool of statistical analysis, it isolates the effects of several variables in an experiment, showing what contribution each made to the results. Subsequently, he advocated factorial experimentation, in which several factors are varied simultaneously, rather than varying one factor at a time. This approach not only speeds results by gathering information on the effects of several factors, but it also accounts for the possibility that the effect of a factor may be influenced by interaction with other factors.

In another innovation of experimental design, Fisher advocated the random arrangement of samples receiving different treatments. Traditional agricultural experiments arranged samples according to elaborate placement schemes on checkerboard plots to avoid bias from extraneous factors such as variations in soil and exposure to weather. Fisher showed that assigning these positions randomly, rather than according to a systematic pattern, facilitated statistical analysis of the results. His 1925 textbook *Statistical Methods for Research Workers* is considered a landmark work in this field, although it is so difficult to read that, as Fisher's friend and colleague M. G. Kendall wrote in *Studies in the History of Statistics and Probability,* "Somebody once said that no student should attempt to read it unless he had read it before."

During the course of his career, Fisher's theoretical work also included improvements to different tests of statistical significance. He refined the Helmert-Pearson chi-square test (including the addition of degrees of freedom) and the t-distribution test, also developing what would eventually be called the F-distribution test after Fisher himself. He introduced the concept of the null hypothesis to designate random processes. Deviations from the null hypothesis indicate significant correlations in statistical samples. Fisher developed procedures for determining when results deviate from the null hypothesis sufficiently to justify an assumption that correlations are significant. He derived the distributions of numerous statistical functions, including partial and multiple correlation coefficients and the regression coefficient in analyses of covariance. Covariance is a term used to describe samples in which statistical results are influenced by different factors. Regression analysis allows the statistician to screen out the effect of all factors other than the one whose significance is being tested. In his 1922 paper "On the Mathematical Foundations of Theoretical Statistics," he analyzed and formalized existing knowledge in the field. Fisher became a Fellow of the Royal Society in 1929. That same year he published a paper on sampling moments that would provide the foundation for future development of that topic. During the 1930s, he wrote several substantial papers on the logic of inductive inference, building on earlier work on the maximum likelihood estimate.

Employs Statistical Methods in Genetics Research

In the agrarian setting of Rothamsted, Fisher also pursued his interest in genetics by breeding various animals such as mice, snails, and poultry, even in his own home. He applied his mathematical prowess to Mendel's work on inheritance, resulting in the 1930 publication of *The Genetical Theory of Natural Selection.* In it, he showed that Mendelian selection always favors the dominance of beneficial genes and concluded that Mendel's results were mathematically compatible with **Charles Darwin**'s theory of natural selection. His work solidified the growing consensus among theorists of evolution that the Darwinian model, favoring selection over genetic mutation as the explanation for evolutionary change, best fit the available data. Fisher left Rothamsted in 1933 to occupy the Galton Chair of Eugenics at University College, a position he held until 1943. In 1935, he established a blood-typing department in the Galton Laboratory, which developed important information on the inheritance of rhesus blood groups. That same year, he published *Design of Experiments,* another landmark text in statistical science. The following year, he published his first presentation on discriminant analysis, an approach to statistical samples in which several factors influence outcomes that is now used in such areas as weather forecasting, medical research, and educational testing. During a 1936 summer lectureship at Iowa State College's agricultural research center at Ames (where he had also taught during the summer of 1931), Fisher established contacts that helped popularize his techniques among American educators and psychologists, as well as agriculturalists.

In 1943, he joined Cambridge University as Balfour Professor of Genetics. He was knighted in 1952 and served as president of the Royal Society from 1952 until 1954. Both the Royal Society and the Royal Statistical Society awarded him several prestigious medals during his tenure at the University of Cambridge. He formally retired in 1957, but continued working until a successor was found in 1959. In 1950, Fisher published *Contributions to Mathematical Statistics,* an annotated collection of forty-three of his most significant papers, many of which had originally appeared in rather obscure journals. During the late 1950s, he wrote several articles criticizing the presumption of a cause-and-effect relationship between smoking and cancer based only on the establishment of a correlation between them. When he left Cambridge in 1959, he moved to Adelaide, Australia, to join several of his former students as a statistical researcher for the Commonwealth Scientific and Industrial Research Organization. He died on July 29, 1962, as a result of an embolism following an intestinal disorder.

SELECTED WRITINGS BY FISHER:

Books

The Genetical Theory of Natural Selection, Clarendon (London), 1930, 2nd edition, Dover (New York), 1958.

Design of Experiments, [London], 1935, 7th edition, Oliver and Boyd (Edinburgh), 1960.

Contributions to Mathematical Statistics, Wiley, 1950.

Statistical Methods for Research Workers, Hafner, 1973.

The Design of Experiments, Revised 8th edition, Hafner, 1974.

Statistical Methods, Experimental Design, and Scientific Inference, Oxford University Press, 1990.

Periodicals

"On the Mathematical Foundations of Theoretical Statistics," *Philosophical Transactions of the Royal Society,* Volume 222A, 1922, pp. 309–68.

"Has Mendel's Work Been Rediscovered?," *Annals of Science,* Volume 1, 1936, pp. 115–37.

SOURCES:

Books

Box, Joan Fisher, *R. A. Fisher: The Life of a Scientist,* Wiley, 1985.

Fienberg, Stephen E., *R. A. Fisher, An Appreciation,* Springer-Verlag, 1990.
Gillespie, Charles Coulston, editor, *Dictionary of Scientific Biography,* Volume 5, Scribner, 1974, pp. 7–11.
Pearson, E. S. and M. G. Kendall, editors, *Studies in the History of Statistics and Probability,* Hafner Press, 1970, pp. 439–53.
Tankard, James W., *The Statistical Pioneers,* Schenkman, 1984, pp. 111–33.

—Sketch by Loretta Hall

Val Logsdon Fitch
1923-
American physicist

Val Logsdon Fitch has worked at the frontiers of particle physics for the better part of forty years, making discoveries about atomic structure and conservation. In the 1950s, he collaborated with **James Rainwater** at Columbia University to study the properties of mu-mesic atoms (muonic atoms). Mu-mesic atoms are those in which mu-mesons (muons) rather than electrons orbit the nucleus. The Fitch-Rainwater studies produced new and startling information about the size of the atomic nucleus. In the early 1960s, Fitch and **James W. Cronin**, then at Princeton University, tackled another intriguing problem in particle physics, the K-meson. One consequence of this line of research was the discovery that the combination of charge conjugation and parity, designated as CP, is not conserved in certain reactions involving K-mesons. Fitch and Cronin were awarded the 1980 Nobel Prize for their discovery. Except for a single year at Columbia, Fitch has spent all of his academic career at Princeton University.

Val Logsdon Fitch was born to Fred B. and Frances M. (Logsdon) Fitch on March 10, 1923, on a cattle ranch near Merriman, Nebraska, a short distance from the South Dakota border. In his Nobel Prize lecture, Fitch observed how improbable it was that one should "begin life on a cattle ranch (in Cherry County, Nebraska), and then to appear in Stockholm to receive the Nobel Prize in physics." After an injury to the elder Fitch on the ranch, the family moved to nearby Gordon, Nebraska, where Fitch attended public primary and secondary schools. After graduation, he joined the U.S. Army.

War Research Stimulates an Interest in Physics

In 1943, Fitch was assigned to the Special Engineering Detachment located in Los Alamos, New Mexico, the research center of the Manhattan Project. In that assignment, he had contact with some of the world's greatest physicists who were working on the design of the atomic bomb. Originally interested in chemistry, Fitch changed his career plans to physics as a result of his wartime experiences.

After his discharge, Fitch enrolled in Montreal's McGill University and earned his bachelor of science degree in electrical engineering two years later. He then went to Columbia to begin his doctoral research on the study of mu-mesic atoms under Nobel laureate Leo James Rainwater. Discovered in 1935 by Carl Anderson, the mu-meson is now known to be a type of lepton, a particle similar to the ordinary electron, but more than two hundred times as heavy.

At Columbia, Fitch investigated the possibility of an atomic structure consisting of a nucleus and mu-mesons rather than a nucleus and ordinary electrons. It was already known that such atoms could be manufactured when a mu-meson is captured by an atom and incorporated into its structure. Under the right circumstances, the mu-meson falls to the K energy level of the atom, the energy level nearest the nucleus. There, it travels in an orbital much closer to the nucleus than does the ordinary electron.

In fact, the size of the mu-meson's K orbital is determined by the size of the nucleus itself. In Fitch's research, he found that the meson travels so closely to the nucleus that it actually passes through the nucleus more than half of the time. The orbital diameter calculated by Fitch allowed him to estimate the size of the lead nucleus used in the experiment, a size that turned out to be much smaller than previously had been estimated.

Particle Research Continues at Princeton

Fitch's mu-mesic atom studies earned him a Ph.D. in physics in 1954. He then accepted a position at Princeton University, where he rose to the rank of professor in 1960. He also became chair of the department in 1976 and, in the same year, was appointed Cyrus Fogg Brackett Professor of Physics. Fitch continued his research on particle physics at Princeton and, in the mid-1960s, became involved in another project with revolutionary consequences.

This undertaking involved a study of the phenomenon known as CP symmetry. The history behind the problem dates to 1956 when **Tsung-Dao Lee** and **Chen Ning Yang** announced the hypothesis that parity ("left-handedness" vs. "right-handedness") might not be conserved in certain types of nuclear reactions. Confirmation of that hypothesis by **Chien-Shiung Wu** and her colleagues at Columbia startled the world of physics. It meant that classical laws of conservation (as of mass, energy, charge, momentum, etc.) might not be inviolate after all.

In 1964, Fitch collaborated with Princeton University researcher James Cronin in a series of experiments that addressed that question of CP invariance, although rather indirectly. The experiments were an attempt to understand the decay scheme of a particle known as the neutral K-meson, K^0. As an accidental by-product of this research, Fitch and Cronin observed a number of reactions (about one in five hundred) in which CP symmetry was violated.

Their discovery was significant because it suggested yet another possible level of invariance, one in which parity, charge conjugation and time (CPT) are conserved in nuclear changes. Consequently, a violation of time symmetry (time-reversal) would be implied, and with it greater insight into the origins of the universe. The possibility of early universe production of common matter surpassing anti-matter motivates a large field of research in particle physics. In addition to the 1980 Nobel Prize for physics for this research, Fitch has also been given the 1968 Research Corporation Award, the 1968 Ernest Orlando Lawrence Award, and the 1976 John Price Wetherill Medal of the Franklin Institute.

Fitch was married to the former Elise Cunningham in 1949. They had two sons, John Craig and Alan Peter. After his first wife's death in 1972, Fitch married a second time, to Daisy Harper Sharp, on August 14, 1976. He describes his hobbies as growing bonsai trees, listening to classical music, hiking, jogging, and camping, and conservation.

SELECTED WRITINGS BY FITCH:

Periodicals

(With C. A. Quarles) "The K(+) Decay Probability," *Physical Review B,* Volume 140, 1965, p. 1088.

"Experiments on Time-Reversal Invariance," *Nuclear Particle Physics Annual,* Volume 1, 1967, pp. 117–180.

SOURCES:

Books

McGraw-Hill Modern Scientists and Engineers, Volume 1, McGraw-Hill, 1980, pp. 377–378.

Periodicals

"Fitch and Cronin Share Nobel Prize for CP Violation," *Physics Today,* December, 1980, pp. 17–19.

Robinson, Arthur L., "1980 Nobel Prize in Physics to Cronin and Fitch," *Science,* November 7, 1980, pp. 619–621.

—Sketch by David E. Newton

Nancy D. Fitzroy
1927-
American engineer

Nancy D. Fitzroy's career has resulted in several inventions and patents in thermal engineering. Her career encompasses over four decades of research in the private sector and includes research in the properties of materials, heat transfer, and fluid flow. She received the Society of Women Engineers Achievement Award in 1972.

Born October 5, 1927, in Pittsfield, Massachusetts, Nancy Deloye Fitzroy studied at Rensselaer Polytechnic Institute in Troy, New York, receiving a bachelor of science degree in chemical engineering there in 1949. She began her professional career with Knolls Atomic Power Laboratory, where she was assistant engineer from 1950 to 1952, and during that time, in 1951, she married. She next served as development engineer for the Hermes Missile Project for one year, then moved to General Engineering Laboratory, where she was development engineer for the next ten years.

In 1963 Fitzroy accepted a post as heat transfer engineer with Advanced Technological Laboratories, which she held until 1965, when she joined the company's Research and Development Center as a consultant on heat transfer. She later served in various managerial posts there until 1987, when she became an independent consultant. During the 1960s Fitzroy was also a lecturer in the advanced engineering course given by General Electric, and in the early 1970s she served as research committee adviser to the National Science Foundation.

During her career, Fitzroy researched a variety of subjects dealing with electronics and temperatures. She was one of the first to study heat transfer surfaces in nuclear-reactor cores, and she holds a patent in the area of cooling of integrated circuits. Fitzroy invented a thermal chip that is used to measure temperatures in such circuits (integrated circuits incorporate various electronic components on a single piece of silicon without need for wires). She also developed a thermal protection system for hardened radar antennae which was utilized in the U.S. defense early warning system.

In addition, Fitzroy is the author of a book on heat transfer and fluid flow for General Electric.

Fitzroy's career has also included serving as president of the American Society of Mechanical Engineers from 1985 to 1987, and she holds memberships in the National Society of Professional Engineers and the American Institute of Chemical Engineers. Her contributions have earned her honors such as the Demers Medal of the Rensselaer Polytechnic Institute in 1975, the Centennial Medallion of the American Society of Mechanical Engineers in 1980, and an achievement award from the Federation of Professional Women in 1984. While she has enjoyed recognition for her work, Fitzroy advises aspiring engineers not to expect "lots of glamour." She has quipped, "I'm a hard working engineer, but it took something silly like flying [a] helicopter to get invited to the White House for tea." A licensed airplane and helicopter pilot, Fitzroy also enjoys sailing.

SOURCES:

Fitzroy, Nancy Deloye, address at Society of Women Engineers and Engineering Foundation Conference, August 19–24, 1973.

—Sketch by Karen Withem

Alexander Fleming
1881-1955
Scottish bacteriologist

Alexander Fleming

Scottish bacteriologist Alexander Fleming is best known for his 1928 discovery of the bacteria-fighting antibiotic penicillin, widely regarded as one of the greatest medical discoveries of the twentieth century. Before penicillin, the few drugs that were available to fight bacterial disease were inefficient and highly toxic to the human body. Fleming's discovery won him the 1945 Nobel Prize for medicine jointly with **Ernst Chain** and Baron **Howard W. Florey**.

Fleming's life was simple. He was born in a farmhouse in Lochfield, Ayrshire, Scotland, on August 6, 1881, the third of four children by Hugh Fleming, a farmer, and his second wife, Grace (Morton) Fleming. He had two stepbrothers and two stepsisters from Hugh Fleming's first marriage. His father died when Fleming was seven and his mother and oldest stepbrother, Thomas, were left to manage the farm.

The natural intelligence Fleming possessed became evident even though his early education was basic. He first attended a tiny local school, then a larger moorland school in Dorval, walking a total of eight miles a day to attend class; these long walks through natural surroundings may have sparked Fleming's interest in living inhabitants and also helped hone his critical observation skills. At age twelve Fleming transferred to the Kilmarnock Academy, a school that had high standards but limited resources. He stayed at the Academy only one year. Throughout his early and later education, Fleming, who greatly enjoyed competition, always scored at or near the top of his class, apparently without much effort.

When Fleming turned thirteen he moved to London to join his brother John and stepbrother Thomas, a physician who practiced ophthalmology. Upon arriving, Fleming attended classes at Regent Street Polytechnic for two years to prepare for a career in business. At sixteen, after completing his course work, he secured a position as a clerk in a shipping company. Fleming joined the London Scottish Regiment in 1900 and, though he never served in battle, he remained associated with his unit until 1914.

In 1901, at twenty years of age, Fleming inherited 250 pounds, a large sum at that time. Following Thomas's advice, Fleming decided to study medicine and, not surprisingly, scored at the top of the national medical school entrance exam. Fleming chose to study at St. Mary's Medical School, which was within walking distance of his London home. When he entered St. Mary's in 1901, Fleming began what would become a nearly continuous fifty-four-year relationship with that institution. As a student, he won many class prizes for his high test scores, including a scholarship in his first year that paid for his entire tuition.

After successfully completing his medical school studies in 1906, Fleming qualified for a position as a doctor that same year. Though he decided to continue his education, pursuing an M.B. and B.S. at London University, he concurrently accepted a job at St. Mary's as a junior assistant, working in the research laboratory of noted pathology professor Sir **Almroth Edward Wright**—initially only as a temporary means of support. In 1908 Fleming earned his degrees with honors, receiving the London University Gold Medal. The next year, while still working full-time for Wright, he passed the Fellowship of the Royal College of Surgeons exam, thus enabling him to pursue a career in surgery. However, Fleming decided to stay in laboratory research, which he felt to be a more exciting and less arduous career path. In Fleming's time, scientists knew of the natural defense capabilities of the human body, and the direction in research was to augment or stimulate the body's own immune system to help fight bacterial disease. Fleming's research reflected this trend, focusing mainly on the prevention and treatment of bacterial infection. He was at the forefront of his area of expertise; Fleming received some of the initial samples of one of the first antibacterial agents, Salvarsan, an arsenical agent developed by **Paul Ehrlich** for use in the treatment of syphilis. Fleming quickly became an expert in the administration of Salvarsan and also conducted experiments with this drug; he found that, while it was effective in destroying the bacteria that caused syphilis, Salvarsan produced a number of toxic side effects. Despite the imperfection of Salvarsan, Fleming maintained a belief that a safe and effective antibacterial substance could be found.

Studies Antiseptics During World War I

Interrupting his research at St. Mary's temporarily, Fleming served as a captain in the British Royal Army Medical Corps during World War I. Stationed in Boulogne, France, he worked in a wound research laboratory under the command of Professor Wright. Together they researched the efficacy of antiseptics on wound infections, an accepted treatment at that time. Fleming found that antiseptics did more harm than good because they not only failed to kill all of the bacteria but also destroyed protective white blood cells (the body's natural defense mechanism) thereby allowing infection to spread more rapidly.

In 1919, after the war ended, Fleming resumed his research at St. Mary's, studying antibacterial mechanisms. He was particularly motivated to find an effective yet safe antibacterial substance after witnessing the horrible suffering caused by bacterial infections during the war. Fleming remained convinced that an ideal bacteria-fighting agent could be found that would destroy the invading bacteria yet not harm the body's own white blood cell defenses.

Around 1921, Fleming fortuitously discovered his first antibacterial agent. He had cultured a sample of his own nasal mucosa during a bout with the common cold. While studying the plate, Fleming noticed that the nasal mucus had dissolved a bacterial colony that had contaminated the plate. The bacteriolytic component of the mucus was named "lysozyme." Later, with the aid of colleague V. D. Allison, Fleming discovered that lysozyme, an enzyme, was present in a number of substances including human blood serum, tears, and saliva, as well as egg whites and turnip juice. Though lysozyme was safe to human tissue, however, it had no effect on disease-producing bacteria, and was thus of little medical use. Nevertheless, Fleming continued his search for an effective yet non-toxic antibacterial substance.

Fleming's Discovery of Penicillin

In 1928 Fleming discovered, also serendipitously, his second and more famous antibacterial substance: penicillin. However, many highly coincidental factors needed to come together before the discovery of this wonder drug was even possible. One of the main factors that led to the discovery of penicillin was Fleming's own untidy habits. Instead of the normal practice of promptly discarding bacterial culture plates, Fleming held onto his plates far beyond their usefulness. Before finally disposing of the plates, though, he would examine each one to note any interesting developments. On one particular plate he noticed that a strange mold contaminant had inhibited the growth of the disease-causing bacteria *Staphylococcus aureus* that had been cultured on the plate.

The circumstances that led to this mold's growth on Fleming's culture plate were almost astronomically improbable. First, the mold itself, later identified as *Penicillium notatum,* was a very rare organism; the only reason it was floating near Fleming's lab in the first place was because a scientist on the floor below was studying the mold's effect on asthma sufferers. This was not enough though: in order for the mold to display its anti-bacterial properties, it needed to grow *before* the bacteria grew. For that to occur, conditions had to be first cold (for the mold) then warm (for the bacteria). As luck would have it, Fleming took a week's vacation, during which time London experienced first a cold spell, then later a warm spell. As the bacteria grew, it flourished everywhere except for an empty zone around the already-growing mold; hence the inhibitory effect of the mold could be easily observed. The combined effect of all of the above factors led to Fleming's discovery of the world's first safe and effective antibiotic. Fleming isolated the *Penicillium* mold for further investigation, and named the particular component of the mold responsible for killing bacteria "penicillin."

Not being very adept at writing or speaking, Fleming was unable to effectively communicate the potential importance of his discovery. His colleagues had little interest because they thought it was merely another type of lysozyme, from a mold rather than mucus. Fleming could not clearly express the critical difference between lysozyme and penicillin—that penicillin, unlike the former bacteriolytic agent, could inhibit disease-producing bacteria.

Though Fleming's own major research with penicillin lasted less than a year, it revealed that it was effective in killing some disease-producing bacteria yet was non-toxic to white blood cells and living tissue. Fleming also tested penicillin superficially by applying it to wounds, but was discouraged with the mixed results. And while he thought it might be a useful as an injection for wounds, he never actually took the next logical step of injecting the drug into infected areas. He subsequently made only a few fleeting and unenthusiastic references to penicillin in later papers and lectures; for example, he mentioned in one work that penicillin seemed to be a better dressing for septic wounds than other, stronger chemicals. After his initial research, Fleming used penicillin mainly as a laboratory convenience for keeping his vaccine cultures free of certain bacteria. He did give the substance to several colleagues in other laboratories, presumably for further research, but never focused much attention beyond that on the drug.

Fleming's quick dismissal of penicillin was probably due to the fact that the drug did not remain in the blood system very long, and was an unstable and hard to purify substance. Fleming, not being a chemist, was unable to stabilize or adequately concentrate the penicillin component himself. The instability of penicillin may have discouraged Fleming from believing that it had the potential to be an effective antibacterial agent. However, whether or not Fleming actually realized the enormous therapeutic powers of penicillin cannot be conclusively determined from his writings.

For twelve years after its initial discovery, the life-saving potential of penicillin remained untapped. In 1940, two Oxford University chemistry scientists, Ernst Chain and Howard Florey, were fortuitously led to Fleming's article on penicillin during a literature search on antibacterial agents. They were able to isolate and purify penicillin and then later test the drug systemically in clinical trials with wondrous success, confirming penicillin's antibiotic qualities.

By 1942, the therapeutic power of penicillin was clearly established. Today penicillin is still successfully used in the treatment of many bacterial diseases, including pneumonia, strep throat, scarlet fever, gonorrhea, and impetigo. Moreover, its discovery led to the development of additional antibiotics that have proven useful in destroying a broad spectrum of pathogenic bacteria. Unfortunately, the overuse and/or misuse of antibiotics has allowed certain bacteria to develop resistance to some common antibiotics, including penicillin. As such, the need continues for the development of newer—and in most cases stronger—antibiotics.

Career Recognized with Nobel Prize

After news of the discovery of penicillin spread, Fleming began receiving most of the recognition and fame for its discovery—due in no small part to the dramatic story surrounding his improbable discovery of the drug. Fleming was knighted in 1944, and in 1945, along with Florey and Chain, received the Nobel Prize in medicine. Fleming subsequently acquired 25 honorary degrees, 26 medals, 18 prizes, 13 decorations, and honorary membership in 89 scientific academies and societies.

He worked continuously at St. Mary's, being promoted to Assistant Director of the Inoculation Department in 1921, later known as the Institute of Pathology and Research; this department was renamed in 1948 as the Wright-Fleming Institute. In addition, he held a post as a bacteriology professor at London University from 1928 until his retirement from teaching in 1948. Fleming married Irish nurse Sarah Marion McElroy in 1915; in 1924 the couple had their only child, Robert, who, like his father, became a physician. Fleming's health deteriorated after Sarah's death in 1949. In 1953 his health improved somewhat after he married Amalia Coutsouris-Voureka, a bacteriologist and former student. On March 11, 1955, just over two months after his retirement, Fleming died of a heart attack at his home in London, England. Interestingly, though his death was sudden and unexpected, Fleming had expressed his desire to be cremated just days earlier. His ashes are interred at St. Paul's Cathedral in London.

SELECTED WRITINGS BY FLEMING:

Books

(With G. F. Petrie) *Recent Advances in Serum and Vaccine Therapy,* Churchill, 1934.

Periodicals

(With L. Colebrook) "On the Use of Salvarsan in Treatment of Syphilis," *Lancet,* Volume 1, 1911, pp. 1631–1634.

"Lysozyme: A Bacteriolytic Ferment Found Normally in Tissues and Secretions," *Lancet,* Volume 1, 1929, pp. 217–220.

"On the Antibacterial Action of Cultures of a Penicillium, with Special Reference to Their Use in the Isolation of B. influenzae," *British Journal of Experimental Pathology,* Volume 10, 1929, pp. 226–236.

SOURCES:

Books

Biographical Dictionary of Scientists: Biologists, Bedrick Books, 1983, pp 46–47.

Dictionary of Scientific Biography, Scribner, 1972, pp. 28–31.

Great Events from History II, Volume 2: *1910–1931,* Salem Press, 1991, pp. 873–77.

MacFarlane, Gwyn, *Alexander Fleming, the Man and the Myth,* Harvard University Press, 1984.

Nobel Prize Winners, H. W. Wilson, 1987, pp. 329–31.

World of Scientific Discovery, Gale, 1994, p. 248.

—*Sketch by Carla Mecoli-Kamp*

John Ambrose Fleming
1849-1945
English electrical engineer

John Ambrose Fleming

John Ambrose Fleming was a pioneering engineer who made numerous contributions both to the theoretical aspects and practical applications of electricity. Fleming played an important role in the development of lighting, heating, and radio and, as a consultant in private industry, was a proponent of their widespread conventional use. Fleming's most wide ranging practical contribution to the field of electrical engineering was the development of the thermionic (or radio) valve, which acts as a rectifier for high frequency currency, permitting the current to flow in only one direction. Also known as the Fleming valve or diode, this precursor to the transistor revolutionized the infant field of radio as it became an essential part of nearly every radio transmitter and receiver for more than three decades, it was an important component of early televisions and computers as well. Fleming was also an accomplished educator who helped train a trailblazing cadre of electrical engineers.

Born in Lancaster, England, on November 29, 1849, Fleming was the eldest of seven children born to James Fleming, a minister, and the daughter of John Bazley White, a pioneer in the manufacturing of Portland cement. In 1854, Fleming's family moved to London, where his father became minister of the Kentish Town Congregational Chapel. Fleming's aptitude for science and mechanics was evident early in his life as he excelled in geometrical drawing at a private school for boys. When he was eleven, he had already set up his own workshop, where he spent his time building model engines and ships rather than playing with other children. In 1863, he entered the University College School in London. Despite his lack of aptitude for the required Latin courses (he was at the bottom of his class), Fleming excelled in mathematics and passed the London matriculation at the age of 17.

In 1867, Fleming entered University College to study physics and mathematics. Unfortunately, as one of seven children, he received little financial support from his family; within a year, he was forced to leave school and go to work. He first took a position with a Dublin shipbuilding firm, believing that he could gain some practical experience, but left after only a few months when he quickly grew bored with tracing drawings. He next worked as a clerk for a firm on the London Stock Exchange. Although far from his area of interest, this job, which he held for two years, provided ample free time during the evenings to study. He received his bachelor of science degree in 1870 from University College, graduating as one of the two top students in his class.

After a year and a half as the science master at Rossall School, Fleming had saved enough money to continue his scientific education. He returned to London to attend the Royal School of Mines in South Kensington, where he studied advanced chemistry under Edward Frankland and Frederick Guthrie. By 1874, Fleming had assumed teaching duties in the school's Advanced Chemical Laboratories. Although his career seemed to be heading in the direction of chemistry, his attention turned to physics as he worked with Guthrie on experiments in electrically charged bodies, such as an iron ball. This early work in the ability of certain elements to store or discharge negative and positive charges laid some of the groundwork for Fleming's later work on his radio valve. Guthrie also presented Fleming with the opportunity to present the first scientific paper to the newly formed Physical Society of London. Fleming's discussion, published in the *Proceedings of the Society of London,* focused on the contact theory of the galvanic cell.

But Fleming's education was to be interrupted once more by the need for money; in 1884, he became science master at Cheltenham College, where he incorporated hands-on experimentation by the students into his teaching approach. By 1877 Fleming was able to return to his studies, enrolling at St. John's College in Cambridge. (He received extra financial support for winning the school's entrance exhibition.) Before returning to college, Fleming had become interested in the work of James Clerk Maxwell, who had written the groundbreaking two-volume book *Electricity and Magnetism.* After spending the first six months at St. John's in an intensive study of mathematics, Fleming began his study of electricity and mathematics under Maxwell at the school's Cavendish Laboratory. Devoted to his studies, Fleming spent little time socializing, even going so far as to move off the college's campus where he felt he could spend more time studying without being interrupted by the social aspects of college life.

During his studies at the Cavendish Laboratory, Fleming worked on improving the Carey-Foster Bridge, a method for measuring the difference between two nearly equal resistances in electrical conduction. Fleming's improvement made the measuring device faster and more accurate and was called Fleming's banjo by Maxwell because of the measuring wire's circular shape.

Serves as Consultant to Electrical Power Industry

After receiving his Doctor of Science degree in 1880, Fleming became a lecturer in applied mechanics in St. John's new engineering laboratories and was elected a fellow of the college in 1883. By this time, Fleming had begun acting as a consultant for private industry, including the Edison Telephone and Electric Light Companies, the Swan Lamp Factory, and the London National Company. In his capacity as an adviser to these burgeoning electrical companies, Fleming was a primary contributor to the development of electrical generator stations and distribution networks. With both the Swan and Edison companies, Fleming lent his expertise to photometry (the measurement of electric light intensity) and was largely responsible for the large-bulb incandescent lamp with an aged filament as the light source. Fleming was also asked by a number of towns in England to be an adviser for the development of municipal electric lighting systems. In 1899, he was hired by the Marconi Wireless Telegraph Company, where he worked as a scientific adviser and helped design the Poldhu Power Station in Cornwall, England. This station, the largest wireless station in England, was the source of the first transatlantic wireless telegraph transmission. Although the message was simple (the Morse Code equivalent of the letter S, which is three dots), it marked the beginning of intercontinental wireless communication. Fleming maintained his association with the Marconi company for thirty years, making many marked improvements in early radio devices. Overall, his consulting work resulted in many new methods and instruments for measuring high-frequency currents and for new designs of transformers.

Makes Major Advance in Radio Communications

Fleming's most important contribution to electrical engineering was in the field of the radio telegraph and the telephone. Although he developed the 2-electrode, or Fleming valve in 1904, he laid the foundation for this discovery many years earlier when, in 1884, **Thomas Alva Edison** announced his discovery of the Edison effect, which described the escape of electrons or ions from a heated solid or liquid. Fleming repeated Edison's experiments in 1899 using both direct and alternating currents, but he found little practical use for the discovery. But in 1904, while searching for a more efficient and reliable detector of weak electrical currents, he had what he described as a "sudden very happy thought," as noted in a biography by J. T. MacGregor-Morris in *Notes and Records of the Royal Society.* Fleming's inspiration was to make a new lamp, or tube, that would have a hot filament and an insulated plate sealed inside a high vacuum tube. Further experimentation showed that the tube's sensitivity to extremely weak currents alternating at very high frequencies made it a major advance in radio technology.

Fleming dubbed his radio tube a thermionic valve because it acted much like a check valve that allows fluids to pass in only one direction. Essentially, the valve worked by utilizing a cathode that was kept hot, thus causing electrons to evaporate into the vacuum tube. The second electrode, called the anode, remained cool to prevent the evaporation of electrons from it. When an alternating current was applied, the electrical currents flowed in one direction. This discovery revolutionized radio science by providing the first truly reliable method to measure high-frequency radio waves. Two years later, **Lee de Forest** took Fleming's diode valve and added a third electrode, thus effectively separating the high-frequency circuit from that of the filament, making amplification possible.

Although the Fleming valve was eventually replaced by the transistor, it remained an important component of radios for nearly three decades and was also used in the early days of computers and television. Fleming himself helped support the infant technology of television by becoming president of the Television Society of London, which published a monthly journal and sponsored readings of new papers on the subject.

Fleming's long and productive scientific career spanned several decades. Despite increasing deafness, which began in middle age, he continued to work in his field, using an assistant to take notes at the lectures he attended to keep up-to-date on the latest advances in the field of electrical engineering. He gave his last presentation to the Physical Society in 1939, 65 years after presenting the society's inaugural address in 1874. His awards were numerous and included the Hughes Medal in 1910, the Faraday Medal of the Institution of Electrical Engineers in 1928, and the Gold Medal of the Institute of Radio Engineers in 1933. He was knighted in 1929.

In addition to his scientific research, Fleming was also an accomplished educator and, as professor of electrical technology at University College for 41 years, he helped train a new group of engineers that would help advance electrical engineering to new heights. He retired in 1936 and was appointed an emeritus professor.

Despite his teaching, research, and consultation duties, Fleming maintained many outside interests, including mountain climbing and painting in watercolors. He was also an avid amateur photographer, having made his own first camera in his workshop when he was only a teenager. Fleming's first wife, Clara Ripley, died in 1917. He married Olive Franks in 1933. Fleming died on April 18, 1945, at the age of 95.

SELECTED WRITINGS BY FLEMING:

Books

The Alternate Current Transformer, The Electrician Printing and Publishing Company (London), 1901.

Principles of Electric Wave Telegraphy, [London], 1906.

Memories of a Scientific Life, 1934.

Periodicals

"On the New Contact Theory of the Galvanic Cell," *Proceedings Physical Society of London,* March 21, 1874.

SOURCES:

Books

Biographical Dictionary of Scientists: Engineers and Inventors, Peter Bedrick Books, 1986, pp. 64–65.

Concise Dictionary of Scientific Biography, Scribner, 1981, pp. 32–33.

MacGregor-Morris, J. T., "Sir Ambrose Fleming," *Notes and Records of the Royal Society of London,* 1945, pp. 141–144.

Periodicals

"Sir Ambrose Fleming, F.R.S.," *Nature,* June 2, 1945, pp. 662–663.

—*Sketch by David Petechuk*

Simon Flexner
1863-1946
American pathologist and bacteriologist

Simon Flexner pioneered in field investigations where infectious diseases were potentially epidemic. He discovered the Flexner bacillus, the cause of a common form of dysentery, and the Flexner serum for treating meningitis. His research expertise was already legend when he was selected as the organizing director of the Rockefeller Institute for Medical Research in New York City. For thirty-five years he cultivated the spirit and guided the work of the new institute, while implementing John D. Rocke-

Simon Flexner

feller's vision of bringing medicine into the realm of science.

Flexner, the fourth of nine children, was born in Louisville, Kentucky, on March 25, 1863, to Jewish immigrants. His father, Morris, emigrated from Bavaria, first to Strasbourg, France, where he taught school, then eventually to Louisville. He became a peddler and eventually a wholesale merchant of dry goods. Flexner's mother, Esther Abraham, grew up in Alsace and was a dressmaker in Paris before immigrating with her sister to live with relatives in Louisville.

Illness Transforms the Wayward Youth

When Morris Flexner's business failed in 1873, the future of his nine children seemed bleak. Young Simon failed to finish sixth grade and his delinquent behavior prompted his father to arrange a tour of the town jail, where, he warned, Simon might end up if he did not change his ways. Young Flexner drifted from one menial job to another until he fell victim to typhoid fever at the age of sixteen. But his near-fatal illness transformed him into a self-directed student of science. He began work as a drugstore apprentice while he earned a degree and a medal for excellence at the Louisville College of Pharmacy.

Flexner then taught himself to use a microscope while tending to prescriptions in his brother Jacob's pharmacy. Without books or teachers, he mastered the basics of histology and pathology as he examined tissue specimens given to him by doctors who patronized the store. Flexner found his calling when he realized that his observations on patients' tissues could aid physicians in their diagnoses of diseases. So, at 26, Flexner earned his medical degree at the University of Louisville, a two-year medical school, although this rudimentary education provided no opportunities to perform either physical examinations or laboratory studies. A year later, after publishing two papers based on his microscopic observations, Flexner was sent to Johns Hopkins University by his younger brother Abraham, a recent graduate of the school.

Develops Expertise in Infectious Diseases

In Baltimore, Flexner joined other young physicians studying pathology under William Henry Welch, a chief architect of scientific medicine in the United States. During the next thirteen years Flexner studied many pathological problems, advancing from Welch's personal assistant to full professor. He became familiar with a wide range of infectious diseases and left behind a harvest of original reports.

In 1893, Johns Hopkins, at the behest of the Maryland Board of Health, sent Flexner to diagnose an epidemic of cerebrospinal meningitis raging among Cumberland coal miners. Tracking the dying men to their cabins on precipitous hillsides to conduct autopsies and collect tissues samples, Flexner quickly determined that the disease was caused by a diplococcus bacteria. In another case, he led an 1899 commission from Johns Hopkins to study the diseases in the Philippines just after the Spanish-American War. While learning about epidemics of typhoid fever, malaria, dengue, leprosy, and tuberculosis, Flexner made a thorough investigation of dysentery. He succeeded in isolating the bacillus that causes a prevalent form of the disease, an organism now known as the Flexner bacillus. Upon his return to the States, he became professor of Pathology at the University of Pennsylvania. Two years later, the federal government sent Flexner to investigate an epidemic in San Francisco's Chinatown and, within a month, he had confirmed original suspicions that the disease was bubonic plague.

Selected as the First Director of the Rockefeller Institute

At the turn of the century, no medical research centers existed in the United States comparable to the Pasteur, Koch, Pavlov, and Kitasato institutes of Europe and Japan. Most American laboratories were only for instructing students and were primitively equipped. A pioneering effort to correct this situation came in 1901 with the founding of the Rockefeller Institute for Medical Research, created through an endowment by John D. Rockefeller. A year later, its board, headed by William Welch, chose Flexner to head the new institute, one devoted to investigations into human disease. He relinquished his professorship in Pennsylvania to pursue that for which there was no assurance of permanence or success.

For over thirty years, Flexner gave the Institute its unique scientific direction. His special genius resided in his respect for individuality and his understanding of the scientific temperament. Although his career had been concerned with pathology of infectious diseases, he established a broad scientific scope and pressed for the application of biochemistry and the physical sciences to studies of human biology.

Flexner brought together a distinguished group of scientists, including **Hideyo Noguchi**, his protegee from Pennsylvania, S. J. Meltzer, Phoebus Aaron Theodor Levene, **Alexis Carrel**, **Jacques Loeb**, **Karl Landsteiner**, Eugene Opie, Rufus Cole, and **Peyton Rous**. Attracted by the promise of unlimited experimental freedom and the finest available laboratory equipment, plus an independent endowment from Rockefeller to finance their work, these researchers came from all over the world. John D. Rockefeller's experiment in scientific philanthropy, under Flexner's leadership, created one of the world's greatest biomedical research institutions.

In 1906, soon after the institute's laboratories opened, an epidemic of cerebrospinal meningitis enveloped New York City. Flexner quickly furthered the institute's new mission by developing an antimeningococcus serum from the blood of inoculated horses. Injected directly into the spinal canal of the victims, the serum reduced fatalities by fifty percent. Flexner continued to supervise the manufacture of thousands of bottles a year, and the Flexner serum remained the best therapy for meningitis until the emergence of sulfa drugs in the 1930s. Four years later, poliomyelitis was epidemic in New York. Flexner and his assistants proved its viral origins and postulated one mode of transmission, but they found no cure. However, because Flexner showed how to transfer the virus from one monkey to another, he enabled scientists in the 1950s to maintain a pool of the virus for use in successful polio vaccines.

In 1903, Flexner married Helen Whitall Thomas, author of the autobiographical memoir *Quaker Childhood.* Her father, a physician and leading aristocrat in Baltimore, was instrumental in the founding of both Johns Hopkins Medical School and Bryn Mawr College. Helen, whose older sister was president of Bryn Mawr, was teaching English there when she first met Simon Flexner. Their first year of marriage was spent in Europe, where Flexner scouted for scientists to recruit to the Rockefeller Institute, and studied biochemistry in the Berlin laboratory of **Emil Fischer**. The Flexners had two sons, William Welch, a physicist, and James Thomas, an author of American history, biography, and art. Two of Flexner's own brothers were noted intellectuals. Bernard was a well known lawyer, and Abraham, author of the 1910 report that reformed American medical education, was director of the Institute for Advanced Study at Princeton.

Although Rockefeller Institute's welfare was uppermost in his mind, Flexner undertook other activities on behalf of medical education, research, and public health. A charter trustee of the Rockefeller Foundation, he contributed to the establishment of National Research Council fellowships and to the founding of the Peking Union Medical College. When Welch relinquished all interest in *The Journal of Experimental Medicine* in 1902, Flexner moved it to the Rockefeller, where he served as editor from 1905 until his death in 1946.

Still at the height of his powers, Flexner relinquished his duties as director in 1935 and spent ten good years in retirement. As Eastman Professor at Oxford University in 1937, he wrote *The Evolution and Organization of the University Clinic.* Later, he and his son James wrote a biography of William Welch, chronicling the history of medical science in America. During his long career, Flexner published several hundred scientific papers and essays. His contributions were rewarded with honorary degrees from eighteen universities and membership in numerous scientific societies. He was elected a member of the National Academy of Sciences (1908), the American Philosophical Society (1901), and the Royal Society of London (1919). On his eightieth birthday, an editorial in *The New York Times* called Flexner a guiding genius of American medical science, noting that "a man of this scientific caliber belongs to the world." He died three years later on May 2, 1946, in New York City, of a coronary occlusion following an operation.

SELECTED WRITINGS BY FLEXNER:

Books

(With L. E. Holt) *Bacteriological and Clinical Studies of the Diarrheal Diseases of Infancy with Reference to the Bacillus Dysenteriae (Shiga),* Rockefeller Institute for Medical Research, 1904.

(With J. W. Jobling) "Serum Treatment of Epidemic Cerebro-spinal Meningitis," *Journal of Experimental Medicine,* 1908, Volume 10, pp. 141–203.

(With son, James T. Flexner) *William Henry Welch and the Heroic Age of American Medicine,* Viking, 1941.

SOURCES:

Books

Corner, G. W., *History of the Rockefeller Institute,* Rockefeller University Press, 1965.

Paul, John R., *A History of Poliomyelitis,* Yale University Press, 1971, pp. 107–25.

Thomas, J. T., *An American Saga: The Story of Helen Thomas and Simon Flexner,* Little, Brown, 1984.

Periodicals

Hospital Practice, April 15, 1988, pp. 213–66.

Obituary Notices of Fellows of the Royal Society of London, 1948–1949, Volume 6, pp. 409–45.

—*Sketch by Carol L. Moberg*

Howard Walter Florey
1898-1968
Australian English pathologist

Howard Walter Florey

The work of Howard Walter Florey gave the world one of its most valuable disease-fighting drugs—penicillin. **Alexander Fleming** discovered, in 1929, the mold that produced an antibacterial substance, but was unable to isolate it. Nearly a decade later, Florey and his colleague, biochemist **Ernst Chain**, set out to isolate the active ingredient in Fleming's mold and then conduct the clinical tests that demonstrated penicillin's remarkable therapeutic value. Florey and Chain reported the initial success of their clinical trials in 1940, and the drug's value was quickly recognized. In 1945, Florey shared the Nobel Prize in medicine or physiology with Fleming and Chain.

Howard Walter Florey was born on September 24, 1898, in Adelaide, Australia. He was one of three children and the only son born to Joseph Florey, a boot manufacturer, and Bertha Mary Wadham Florey, Joseph's second wife. Howard also had two half sisters by his father's first wife, Charlotte Ames. Florey expressed an interest in science early in life. Rather than follow his father's career path, he decided to pursue a degree in medicine. Scholarships afforded him an education at St. Peter's Collegiate School and Adelaide University, the latter of which awarded him a Bachelor of Science degree in 1921. An impressive academic career earned Florey a Rhodes scholarship to Oxford University in England. There he enrolled in Magdalen College in January 1922. His academic prowess continued at Oxford, where he became an excellent student of physiology under the tutelage of renowned neurophysiologist Sir **Charles Scott Sherrington**. Placing first in his class in the physiology examination, he was appointed to a teaching position by Sherrington in 1923.

Florey's education continued at Cambridge University as a John Lucas Walker Student. Already fortunate enough to have learned under a master such as Sherrington, he now came under the influence of Sir **Frederick Gowland Hopkins**, who taught Florey the importance of studying biochemical reactions in cells. A Rockefeller Traveling Scholarship sent Florey to the United States in 1925, to work with physiologist Alfred Newton Richards at the University of Pennsylvania, a collaboration that would later prove beneficial to Florey's own research. On his return to England and Cambridge in 1926, Florey received a research fellowship in pathology at London Hospital. That same year, he married Mary Ethel Hayter Reed, an Australian whom he'd met during medical school at Adelaide University. Howard and Ethel Florey had two children, Charles and Paquita.

Pioneers New Approach in Pathology

Florey received his Ph.D. from Cambridge in 1927, and remained there as Huddersfield Lecturer in Special Pathology. Equipped with a firm background in physiology, he was now in a position to pursue experimental research using an approach new to the field of pathology. Instead of describing diseased tissues and organs, Florey applied physiologic concepts to the study of healthy biological systems as a means of better recognizing the nature of disease. It was during this period in which Florey first became familiar with the work of Alexander Fleming. His own work on mucus secretion led him to investigate the intestine's resistance to bacterial infection. As he became more engrossed in antibacterial substances, Florey came across Fleming's report of 1921 describing the enzyme lysozyme, which possessed antibacterial properties. The enzyme, found in the tears, nasal secretions, and saliva of humans, piqued Florey's interest, and convinced him that collaboration with a chemist would benefit his research. His work with lysozyme showed that extracts from natural substances, such as plants, fungi and certain types of bacteria, had the ability to destroy harmful bacteria.

Florey left Cambridge in 1931 to become professor of pathology at the University of Sheffield, returning to Oxford in 1935 as director of the new Sir William Dunn School of Pathology. There, at the recommendation of Hopkins, his productive collaboration began with the German biochemist Ernst Chain. Florey remained interested in antibacterial substances even as he expanded his research projects into new areas, such as cancer studies. During the mid 1930s, sulfonamides, or "sulfa" drugs, had been introduced as clinically effective against streptococcal infections, an announcement which boosted Florey's interest in the field. At Florey's suggestion, Chain undertook biochemical studies of lysozyme. He read much of the scientific literature on antibacterial substances, including Fleming's 1929 report on the antibacterial properties of a substance extracted from a Penicillium mold, which he called penicillin. Chain discovered that lysozyme acted against certain bacteria by catalyzing the breakdown of polysaccharides in them, and thought that penicillin might also be an enzyme with the ability to disrupt some bacterial component. Chain and Florey began to study this hypothesis, with Chain concentrating on isolating and characterizing the "enzyme," and Florey studying its biological properties.

Convinced of Penicillin's Clinical Value

To his surprise, Chain discovered that penicillin was not a protein, therefore it could not be an enzyme. His challenge now was to determine the chemical nature of penicillin, made all the more difficult because it was so unstable in the laboratory. It was, in part, for this very reason that Fleming eventually abandoned a focused pursuit of the active ingredient in Penicillium mold. Eventually, work by Chain and others led to a protocol for keeping penicillin stable in solution. By the end of 1938, Florey began to seek funds to support more vigorous research into penicillin. He was becoming convinced that this antibacterial substance could have great practical clinical value. Florey was successful in obtaining two major grants, one from the Medical Research Council in England, the other from the Rockefeller Foundation in the United States.

By March of 1940, Chain had finally isolated about one hundred milligrams of penicillin from broth cultures. Employing a freeze-drying technique, he extracted the yellowish-brown powder in a form that was yet only ten percent pure. It was non-toxic when injected into mice and retained antibacterial properties against many different pathogens. In May of 1940, Florey conducted an important experiment to test this promising new drug. He infected eight mice with lethal doses of streptococci bacteria, then treated four of them with penicillin. The following day, the four untreated mice were dead, while three of the four mice treated with penicillin had survived. Though one of the mice that had been given a smaller dose died two days later, Florey showed that penicillin had excellent prospects, and began additional tests. In 1941, enough penicillin had been produced to run the first clinical trial on humans. Patients suffering from severe staphylococcal and streptococcal infections recovered at a remarkable rate, bearing out the earlier success of the drugs in animals. At the outset of World War II, however, the facilities needed to produce large quantities of penicillin were not available. Florey went to the United States where, with the help of his former colleague, Alfred Richards, he was able to arrange for a U.S. government lab to begin large-scale penicillin production. By 1943, penicillin was being used to treat infections suffered by wounded soldiers on the battlefront.

Recognition for Florey's work came quickly. In 1942, he was elected a fellow in the prestigious British scientific organization, the Royal Society, even before the importance of penicillin was fully realized. Two years later, Florey was knighted. In 1945, Florey, Chain and Fleming shared the Nobel Prize in medicine or physiology for the discovery of penicillin (although Florey and Fleming had some disagreement over who "discovered" the valuable drug).

Penicillin prevents bacteria from synthesizing intact cell walls. Without the rigid, protective cell wall, a bacterium usually bursts and dies. Penicillin does not kill "resting" bacteria, only prevents their proliferation. Penicillin is active against many of the "gram positive" and a few "gram negative" bacteria. (The gram negative/positive designation refers to a staining technique used in identification of microbes.) Penicillin has been used in the treatment of pneumonia, meningitis, many throat and ear infections, Scarlet Fever, endocarditis (heart infection), gonorrhea, and syphilis.

Australian Scientists Woo Florey

Following his work with penicillin, Florey retained an interest in antibacterial substances, including the cephalosporins, a group of drugs that produced effects similar to penicillin. He also returned to his study of capillaries which he had begun under Sherrington, but would now be aided by the recently developed electron microscope. Florey remained interested in Australia, as well. In 1944, the prime minister of Australia asked Florey to conduct a review of the country's medical research. During his trip, Florey found laboratories and research facilities to be far below the quality one would have expected of a "civilized community." The trip also inspired efforts to establish graduate-level research programs at the Australian National University. For a while, it looked as if Florey might even return to Australia to head a new medical institute at the University. That never occurred, although Florey did do much to help plan the institute and recruit scientists to it. During the late 1940s and 1950s, Florey made trips almost every year to Australia to provide consultation to the new Australian National University, to which he was appointed Chancellor in 1965.

Florey's stature as a scientist earned him many honors in addition to the Nobel Prize. In 1960, he became president of the Royal Society, a position he held until 1965. Tapping his experience as an administrator, Florey invigorated this prestigious scientific organization by boosting its membership and increasing its role in society. In 1962, he was elected Provost of Queen's College, Oxford University, the first scientist to hold that position. He accepted the presidency of the British Family Planning Association in 1965, and used the post to promote more research on contraception and the legalization of abortion. That same year, he was granted a peerage, becoming Baron Florey of Adelaide and Marston. When Florey's wife, Mary Ethel, died in 1966, he married Margaret Jennings, a colleague and assistant for some 30 years, in a quiet ceremony the following year. Florey died of a heart attack on February 21, 1968.

SELECTED WRITINGS BY FLOREY:

Books

(With Ernst Chain), *Antibiotics: A Survey of Penicillin, Streptomycin, and Other Antimicrobial Substances from Fungi, Actinomycetes, Bacteria and Plants,* Oxford University Press, 1949.

Periodicals

(With Chain, and others), "Penicillin As a Chemotherapeutic Agent," *Lancet,* Volume 2, 1940, pp. 226–228.

SOURCES:

Books

Bickel, Lennard, *Rise Up to Life: A Biography of Howard Walter Florey Who Gave Penicillin to the World,* Angus and Robertson Ltd., 1972.

Williams, Trevor, *Howard Florey: Penicillin and After,* Oxford University Press, 1984.

—Sketch by Lee Katterman

Paul Flory
1910-1985
American chemist

Paul Flory is widely recognized as the founder of the science of polymers. The Nobel Prize in chemistry he received in 1974 was awarded not for any single specific discovery, but, more generally, "for his fundamental achievements, both theoretical and experimental, in the physical chemistry of macromolecules." That statement accurately reflects the wide-ranging character of Flory's career. He worked in both industrial and academic institutions and was interested equally in the theory of macromolecules and in the practical applications of that theory.

Paul John Flory was born in Sterling, Illinois, on June 19, 1910. His parents were Ezra Flory, a clergyman and educator, and Martha (Brumbaugh) Flory, a former school teacher. Ezra and Martha's ancestors were German, but they had resided in the United States for six generations. Both the Flory and the Brumbaugh families had always been farmers, and Paul's parents were the first in their line ever to have attended college.

After graduation from Elgin High School, Flory enrolled at his mother's alma mater, Manchester College, in North Manchester, Indiana. The college was small, with an enrollment of only 600. He earned his bachelor's degree in only three years, at least partly because the college "hadn't much more than three years to offer at the time," as he was quoted as having said by Richard J. Seltzer in *Chemical and Engineering News.* An important influence on Flory at Manchester was chemistry professor Carl W. Holl. Holl apparently convinced Flory to pursue a graduate program in chemistry. In June of 1931, therefore, Flory entered Ohio State University and, in spite of an inadequate background in mathematics and chemistry, earned his master's degree in organic chemistry in less than three months. He then began work

Paul Flory

immediately on a doctorate, but switched to the field of physical chemistry. He completed his research on the photochemistry of nitric oxide and was granted his Ph.D. in 1934.

Chance Assignment Leads to Polymers

Flory's doctoral advisor, Herrick L. Johnston, tried to convince him to stay on at Ohio State after graduation. Instead, however, he accepted a job at the chemical giant, Du Pont, as a research chemist. There he was assigned to a research team headed by **Wallace H. Carothers**, who was later to invent the process for making nylon and neoprene. Flory's opportunity to study polymers was ironic in that, prior to this job, he knew next to nothing about the subject. Having almost *any* job during the depths of the Great Depression was fortunate, and Flory was the envy of many classmates at Ohio State for having received the Du Pont offer.

Flory's work on the Carothers team placed him at the leading edge of chemical research. Chemists had only recently begun to unravel the structure of macromolecules, very large molecules with hundreds or thousands of atoms, and then to understand their relationship to polymers, molecules that have chemically combined to become a single, larger molecule. The study of polymers was even more difficult than that of macromolecules because, while the latter are very large in size, they have definite chemical compositions that are always the same for any one substance. Polymers, on the other hand, have variable size and composition. For example, polyethylene, a common polymer, can consist of anywhere from a few hundred to many thousands of the same basic unit (monomer), arranged always in a straight chain or with cross links between chains.

With his background in both organic and physical chemistry, Flory was the logical person to be assigned the responsibility of learning more about the physical structure of polymer molecules. That task was made more difficult by the variability of size and shape from one polymer molecule to another—even among those of the same substance. Flory's solution to this problem was to make use of statistical mechanics to average out the properties of different molecules. That technique had already been applied to polymers by the Swiss chemical physicist Werner Kuhn and two Austrian scientists, Herman Mark and Eugene Guth. But Flory really developed the method to its highest point in his research at Du Pont.

During his four years at Du Pont, Flory made a number of advances in the understanding of polymer structure and reactions. He made the rather surprising discovery, for example, that the rate at which polymers react chemically is not affected by the size of the molecules of which they are made. In 1937, he discovered that a growing polymeric chain is able to terminate its own growth and start a new chain by reacting with other molecules that are present in the reaction, such as those of the solvent. While working at Du Pont, Flory met and, on March 7, 1936, married Emily Catherine Tabor. The Florys had two daughters, Susan and Melinda, and a son, Paul John, Jr. Flory's work at Du Pont came to an unexpected halt when, during one of his periodic bouts of depression, Carothers committed suicide in 1937. Although deeply affected by the tragedy, Flory stayed on for another year before resigning to accept a job as research associate with the Basic Science Research Laboratory at the University of Cincinnati. His most important achievement there was the development of a theory that explains the process of gelation, which involves cross-linking in polymers to form a gel-like substance.

Wartime Need Prompts New Discoveries

Flory's stay at the University of Cincinnati was relatively brief. Shortly after World War II began, he accepted an offer from the Esso (now Exxon) Laboratories of the Standard Oil Development Company to do research on rubber. It was apparent to many American chemists and government officials that the spread of war to the Pacific would imperil, if not totally cut off, the United States' supply of natural rubber. A massive crash program was initiated, therefore, to develop synthetic substitutes for natural rubber. Flory's approach was to learn enough information about the nature of rubber molecules to be able to predict in advance which synthetic products were likely to be good candidates as synthetic substitutes ("elastomers"). One result of this research was the discovery of a method by which the structure of polymers can be studied. Flory found that when polymers are immersed in a solvent, they tend to expand in such a way that, at some point, their molecular structure is relatively easy to observe.

In 1943, Flory was offered an opportunity to become the leader of a small team doing basic research on rubber at the Goodyear Tire and Rubber Company in Akron, Ohio. He accepted that offer and remained at Goodyear until 1948. One of his discoveries there was that irregularities in the molecular structure of rubber can significantly affect the tensile strength of the material.

In 1948, Flory was invited by **Peter Debye**, the chair of Cornell University's department of chemistry, to give the prestigious George Fisher Baker Lectures in Chemistry. Cornell and Flory were obviously well pleased with each other as a result of this experience, and when Debye offered him a regular appointment in the chemistry department beginning in the fall of 1948, Flory accepted—according to Maurice Morton in *Rubber Chemistry and Technology*—"without hesitation." The Baker Lectures he presented were compiled and published by Cornell University Press in 1953 as *Principles of Polymer Chemistry.* Flory continued his studies of polymers at Cornell and made two useful discoveries. One was that for each polymer solution there is some temperature at which the molecular structure of the polymer is most easily studied. Flory called that temperature the theta point, although it is now more widely known as the Flory temperature. Flory also refined a method developed earlier by the German chemist Hermann Staudinger to discover the configuration of polymer molecules using viscosity. Finally, in 1956, he published one of the first papers ever written on the subject of liquid crystals, a material ubiquitous in today's world, but one that was not to be developed in practice until more than a decade after Flory's paper was published.

In 1957, Flory became executive director of research at the Mellon Institute of Industrial Research in Pittsburgh. His charge at Mellon was to create and develop a program of basic research, a focus that had been absent from that institution, where applied research and development had always been of primary importance. The job was a demanding one involving the supervision of more than a hundred fellowships. Eventually, Flory realized that he disliked administrative work and was making little progress in refocusing Mellon on basic research. Thus, when offered the opportunity in 1961, he resigned from Mellon to accept a post at the department of chemistry at Stanford University. Five years later, he was appointed Stanford's first J. G. Jackson-C. J. Wood Professor of Chemistry. When he retired from Stanford in 1975, he was named J. G. Jackson-C. J. Wood Professor Emeritus. In 1974, a year before his official retirement, Flory won three of the highest awards given for chemistry—the National Medal of Science, the American Chemical Society's Priestley Medal, and the Nobel Prize in chemistry. These awards capped a career in which, as Seltzer pointed out, Flory had "won almost every major award in science and chemistry."

Flory's influence on the chemical profession extended far beyond his own research work. He was widely respected as an outstanding teacher who thoroughly enjoyed working with his graduate students. A number of his students later went on to take important positions in academic institutions and industrial organizations around the nation. His influence was also felt as a result of his two books, *Principles of Polymer Chemistry,* published in 1953, and *Statistical Mechanics of Chain Molecules,* published in 1969. Leo Mandelkern, a professor of chemistry at Florida State University, is quoted by Seltzer as referring to the former work as "the bible" in its field, while the latter has been translated into both Russian and Japanese.

Supports Human Rights as Nobel Prize Winner

Flory was also active in the political arena, especially after his retirement in 1975. He and his wife decided to use the prestige of the Nobel Prize to work in support of human rights, especially in the former Soviet Union and throughout Eastern Europe. He served on the Committee on Human Rights of the National Academy of Sciences from 1979 to 1984 and was a delegate to the 1980 Scientific Forum in Hamburg, at which the topic of human rights was discussed. As quoted by Seltzer, Morris Pripstein, chair of Scientists for Sakharov, Orlov, and Scharansky, described Flory as "very passionate on human rights. . . . You could always count on him." At one point, Flory offered himself to the Soviet government as a hostage if it would allow Soviet scientist Andrei Sakharov's wife, Yelena Bonner, to come to the West for medical treatment. The Soviets declined the offer, but eventually did allow Bonner to receive the necessary treatment in Italy and the United States.

Flory led an active life with a special interest in swimming and golf. In the words of Ken A. Dill, professor of chemistry at the University of California, San Francisco, as quoted by Seltzer, Flory was "a warm and compassionate human being. He had a sense of life, a sense of humor, and a playful spirit. He was interested in, and cared deeply about, those around him. He did everything with a passion; he didn't do anything half way." Flory died on September 8, 1985, while working at his weekend home in

Big Sur, California. According to Seltzer, at Flory's memorial service in Stanford, James Economy, chair of the American Chemical Society's division of polymer chemistry, expressed the view that Flory was "fortunate to depart from us while still at his peak, not having to suffer the vicissitudes of old age, and leaving us with a sharply etched memory of one of the major scientific contributors of the twentieth century."

SELECTED WRITINGS BY FLORY:

Books

Principles of Polymer Chemistry, Cornell, 1953.

Statistical Mechanics of Chain Molecules, Interscience, 1969.

Selected Works of Paul J. Flory (three volumes), Stanford University Press, 1985.

SOURCES:

Periodicals

Morton, Maurice, "Paul John Flory, 1910–1985, part I: The Physical Chemistry of Polymer Synthesis," *Rubber Chemistry and Technology,* May-June, 1987, pp. G47-G57.

Seltzer, Richard J., "Paul Flory: A Giant Who Excelled in Many Roles," *Chemical and Engineering News,* December 23, 1985, pp. 27–30.

—Sketch by David E. Newton

Irmgard Flügge-Lotz
1903-1974
German-born American engineer

Irmgard Flügge-Lotz conducted pioneering studies of aircraft wing lift distribution, making significant contributions to modern aeronautic design. She became an advisor to the National Aeronautics and Space Administration (NASA), as well as to German and French research institutes. During an era when few women engaged in engineering as an occupation, she became Stanford University's first female professor in its College of Engineering.

The eldest daughter of a journalist, Irmgard Flügge-Lotz was born on July 16, 1903, in Hameln, Germany. Her interest in engineering began during her childhood as members of her mother's family worked in the construction business. Flügge-Lotz became intrigued with the science as she visited various family building sites. In her teens she took on much responsibility in providing for her family. Her father, Oskar Lotz, had left his newspaper job when he was drafted into the German Army during World War I. To assist with family finances, Flügge-Lotz began tutoring fellow students. She continued to work after her father returned from the war in ill health.

Upon graduation from high school, she opted to further her education in applied mathematics and engineering. After six years of classwork, she received the German equivalent of a Ph.D. in engineering from the Technical University of Hanover. The topic of her dissertation concerned the mathematical theory of circular cylinders and heat conduction.

Wins Supervisory Position

Despite her advanced degree, Flügge-Lotz had difficulty finding a level of employment that was on par with her education. Her first professional position reflected the limited opportunities available to women in engineering during that time. Obtaining a job with the Aerodynamische Veruchsanstalt (AVA) research institute in Gottingen, she was to spend half of her time as a cataloguer.

Perceptions of Flügge-Lotz's abilities changed dramatically when she applied herself to a problem which had daunted two leading aerodynamicists, including the director of the institute. A decade earlier, one of her colleagues had developed an equation for his theory about the lift distribution of an airplane wing. However, the equation was not successful consistently. When Flügge-Lotz tackled the problem, she solved the equation for the general case. Continuing to work with the equation, she developed it so that it had widespread practical applications. Her brief career as a cataloguer ended as she was named supervisor of a group of engineers who researched theoretical aerodynamics within the AVA.

While in this position, she deciphered a method of calculating the lift distribution on aircraft wings known as the "Lotz-method"—a technique that is still in use today. She issued her findings for publication. Continuing to delve into wing theory, she added to the knowledge of the effects of control surfaces, propeller slipstream, and wind-tunnel wall interference.

The course of Flügge-Lotz's career changed in 1938 when she married Wilhelm Flügge, a civil engineer. The husband and wife team began work at Berlin's Deutsche Versuchsanstalt für Luftfahrt (DVL), a German agency similar to the U.S. government's NASA. Beginning work as a consultant in flight and aerodynamics, Flügge-Lotz conducted groundbreaking research in automatic control theory, especially pertaining to on-off controls. Subsequently, these controls, being reliable and inexpensive to build, came into widespread use.

By 1944 the Flügges had relocated to the small town of Saulgau, continuing work for the DVL there. After Germany's loss of World War II, the Flügges joined the staff of French National Office for Aeronautical Research, called ONERA, in Paris. Flügge-Lotz headed a research group in theoretical aerodynamics, continuing her studies of automatic control theory. In 1948 the Flügges left Paris to join the staff at Stanford University in California.

Creates Seminar for Students

Her husband obtained work as a professor at the university, while Flügge-Lotz began as a lecturer. She was prohibited from a similar position due to nepotism regulations. She found time to further her research and established graduate coursework in mathematical hydro- and aerodynamics. She also designed a weekly seminar in fluid mechanics. The course was attended by Stanford students as well as by young engineers from the National Advisory Committee for Aeronautics—NASA's predecessor. The seminar has continued to serve as an important arena for faculty and students of varying specializations to share their findings.

Flügge-Lotz was not offered a full professorship until 1960. Her promotion occurred after she attended the First Congress of the International Federation of Automatic Control in Moscow as the only female delegate from the United States. Upon her return from that congress, she was named professor of aeronautics and astronautics as well as of engineering mechanics. She was the first woman to achieve such status at Stanford.

During her tenure at Stanford, Flügge-Lotz used computers in the development of aerodynamic theory. Working with her students, she helped solved numerous problems in compressible boundary-layer theory. The results of her automatic control research were published in book form as *Discontinuous Automatic Control* and *Discontinuous and Optimal Control.*

Of the numerous awards and honors she received during her career were the Society of Women Engineers Achievement Award in 1970. She was also the first female chosen by the American Institute of Aeronautics and Astronautics (AIAA) to deliver the prestigious annual von Karman Lecture in 1971. The AIAA also elected her as its first woman fellow.

Flügge-Lotz retired from teaching in 1968. She maintained her research activities, however, studying heat transfer and the control of satellites. She died on May 22, 1974.

SELECTED WRITINGS BY FLÜGGE-LOTZ:

Books

Discontinuous Automatic Control, Princeton University Press, 1953.

Discontinous and Optimal Control, McGraw-Hill, 1958.

Periodicals

(With A. F. Johnson) "Laminar Compressible Boundary Layer Along a Curved, Insulated Surface," *Journal of the Aeronautical Sciences,* Volume 22, 1955, pp. 445–454.

(With M. D. Maltz) "Attitude Stabilization Using a Contactor Control System with a Linear Switching Criterion," *Automatica,* Volume 2, 1963, pp. 255–274.

(With T. K. Fannelöp) "Viscous Hypersonic Flow over Simple Blunt Bodies: Comparison of the Second-order Theory with Experimental Results," Journal de Mécanique, Volume 5, 1966, pp. 69–100.

(With Jose L. Garcia Almuzara) "Minimum Time Control of a Nonlinear System," *Journal of Differential Equations,* Volume 4, 1968, pp. 12–39.

(With T. A. Reyhner) "The Interaction of a Shock Wave with a Laminar Boundary Layer," *International Journal of Nonlinear Mechanics,* Volume 3, 1968, pp. 173–199.

—Sketch by Karen Wilhelm

Anthony H. G. Fokker
1890-1939
Dutch aircraft designer and manufacturer

The name Anthony H. G. Fokker is best known in association with Fokker aircraft. During World War I, Fokker became the preeminent designer of German aircraft—after failing to sell his aviation concepts to the Italian and French governments. Probably most disconcerting from the Allies' point of view was that Fokker, designing for German air fighting forces, invented a method for firing machine gun bullets between a plane's propeller blades, eliminating possible propeller damage. This innovation revolutionized aviation warfare and German pilots used Fokker's invention with deadly results. After World War I, Fokker based his operations in his native Netherlands, continuing to adapt and improve his manufacture of airplanes. His post-war achievements included the design and construction of several planes that went on to break aviation records for speed and distance.

Anton Herman Gerard Fokker was born April 6, 1890, in Kediri, Java, in the Netherlands East Indies. His father, Anthony G. Fokker, owned a coffee plantation there, but he retired and took his family to the Netherlands when his son "Tony"—as his colleagues later knew him—was six years old. The youngster did poorly in school and his father despaired of ever seeing his son amount to anything. Fokker wrote later in the opening pages of his autobiography, *The Flying Dutchman,* that his classes were boring and his teachers stupid. He acquired an early interest in mechanical engineering and then aviation and flying. When aviation pioneers the Wright brothers made their demonstration tour of Europe early in the century, Fokker's enthusiasm for flying dramatically increased—despite active discouragement from his father.

Achieves Fame in Germany

In search of a flight education, Fokker left his parents' home in Haarlem, Netherlands, and located a school for automotive engineers near Mainz, Germany, that also offered courses in aviation engineering. Fokker's two attempts to build an airplane at the school ended in failure. The young Dutchman then joined with a German officer who was willing to bankroll Fokker's plans. Fokker's first successful airplane lacked the ailerons (movable stabilizing flaps on the trailing edge of the wings) characteristic of most aircraft then and since and instead relied on tilted wing tips for stability. It was an innovative design but proved too unstable for anything other than straight flights; the plane had poor maneuverability. Over the weeks after his first flight late in December 1910, however, Fokker continued to make improvements, including the eventual addition of ailerons. On May 16, 1911, Fokker flew his airplane across the Rhine river from near Wiesbaden to the aero club in Mainz, where he passed the flying exam and received his pilot's license. Flushed with this success, Fokker began to give demonstration flights and gradually built up a reputation that spread as far as the German capital of Berlin, and he even gave a flying demonstration in Russia in 1912. Among his distinctive flight achievements at this time, Fokker became the first pilot to execute an upside down loop in midair.

Fokker's reputation as a flier and innovative designer was a mixed blessing, for at the start of World War I the German government pressed Fokker into service designing aircraft for the aviation division of its armed forces. Before the war, Fokker had tried to sell his ideas to the French and Italians, but they had shown little interest. During his wartime stay in Germany, Fokker designed some forty models of aircraft, some of which were made famous by German flying ace Baron Manfred von Richthofen, who, late in the war, flew a Fokker-designed D.VII. Some regarded this airplane as the deadliest of the war.

Perhaps more dramatic than his aircraft designs, however, was Fokker's invention of a synchronized firing mechanism for plane-mounted machine guns that allowed the weapons to fire through the rotating blades of a propeller. French pilots had already mounted a machine gun on the nose of their pusher-type Farman aircraft, so called because the propeller was situated at the rear and "pushed" the aircraft; this design allowed clear shooting from the front but limited the flight performance of the plane. Machine guns could be mounted on aircraft with front-mounted propellers, but their effectiveness was limited because they could not shoot straight ahead—in another effort to protect the propeller, the guns could only shoot to the side. Then the French put heavy, metal deflectors on their propeller blades and mounted a machine gun behind them. This was unsatisfactory, however, because the bullets could still damage the propellers. Moreover, splinters of metal from bullets ricocheting off the propeller blades endangered the pilot.

German aviation officers, who had become aware of this French innovation, approached Fokker, who solved the problem within a few days. His solution was to attach a small knob to the propeller, which struck a cam connected to the hammer of the machine gun. When the device was engaged, the rotating propeller fired the gun at the precise moment that a space between the blades opened. Although the invention did not work perfectly the first time, Fokker was able to perfect his invention in a (long) day's work. Of particular concern was that there be plenty of space between the rotating propeller blades and the bullet as it passed between them. When put into combat situations, Fokker's invention transformed the airplane into a deadly weapon. Unfortunately for Germany, air warfare was still a small part of a country's overall might, and the allied nations combined forces defeated Germany in 1918.

After its loss in the war, Germany was submerged in chaos and uncertainty. To protect himself and his business, the now-famous Fokker smuggled himself and his airplanes out of Germany. Back in the Netherlands, Fokker continued to design airplanes and soon became the preeminent designer and manufacturer of commercial aircraft in the world. In recognition of Fokker's achievement, Queen Wilhelmina awarded him with two medals, the Ridder der Oranje Nassau Orde and the Gouden Medialle Voor Voortvarenheid en Vernunft. These honors came in addition to two similar awards he had received in

Germany in recognition of his aid to that country's war effort.

Aircraft Sought in America

After the war, American aviation enthusiast Brigadier General Billy Mitchell persuaded the U.S. Army to purchase several of Fokker's D.40 fighter monoplanes for experimental purposes. Over a three-year period the Army and Navy purchased additional aircraft from Fokker's plant in the Netherlands, with sales amounting to $750,000. One of these aircraft was the soon-to-be historic T-2. In May, 1923, lieutenants Oakley G. Kelly and John A. Macready piloted a Fokker Transport T-2 in the first nonstop flight across the American continent.

The Army wished to continue dealing with Fokker but was faced with a "buy American" sentiment that prevailed after World War I. Fokker therefore established the Fokker Aircraft Corporation at Habrouck Heights, New Jersey. Soon thereafter, in 1925, Admiral Richard E. Byrd, purchased the first of Fokker's tri-motors, an airplane design employing three separate motors and propellors. Fokker had designed the airplane in the United States and cabled the plans to his Netherlands plant. Workers there rushed to build the airplane and ship it to the United States to compete in (and win) the first Ford Reliability Tour in 1925. Byrd christened the airplane the *Josephine Ford* and flew it on his historic flight over the North Pole in 1926.

Byrd flew a similar Fokker named the *America* (with larger wings designed to carry heavier loads) across the Atlantic in 1927, in the wake of Charles Lindbergh's famous pioneering flight. Meanwhile, two Army lieutenants, L. J. Maitland and A. F. Hegenberger, flew a Fokker tri-motor from California to Hawaii, establishing the world record for flying over water. Wing commander Charles Kingsford-Smith broke that record three years later by circumnavigating the world in a Fokker tri-motor that was the sister ship to Admiral Byrd's airplane. In January 1929 a Fokker tri-motor named the *Question Mark* set an air-refueling (in which a plane is refueled while airborne to allow continuous flying) record of 150 hours. The success and fame of Fokker's tri-motor airplane caused automaker **Henry Ford**, who had also taken to building airplanes, to create his own version, the Ford tri-motor.

In 1929 Fokker Aircraft Corporation became a subsidiary of General Motors (GM). Later in the year Fokker disagreed with GM management over the design of aircraft and left Fokker Aircraft, which was then renamed General Aviation Corporation. The company moved to California in 1934 to become North American Aviation, a forerunner of North American Rockwell. After achieving nearly twenty years of fame and success with his airplane designs, Fokker seemed to lose interest in flying and turned his attention to designing boats. His first marriage ended in divorce. His second wife died in 1929 after less than a year of marriage. Fokker himself died a decade later in New York City, on December 23, 1939, evidently of pneumococcal meningitis. As for Fokker's firm in the Netherlands, it survived him and found its niche as a small but successful manufacturer of short-haul aircraft such as the Fokker 100, which went into service in the 1980s.

SELECTED WRITINGS BY FOKKER:

Books

Flying Dutchman: The Life of Anthony Fokker, Holt, 1931, reprinted, Arno Press, 1972.

SOURCES:

Books

Casey, Louis S., *The First Nonstop Coast-to-Coast Flight and the Historic T–2 Airplane,* Smithsonian Institution, 1964.

Swanborough, Gordon and Peter M. Bowers, *United States Military Aircraft since 1909,* Putnam, 1989.

Periodicals

"A. H. G. Fokker Dies; Airplane Designer," *New York Times,* December 24, 1939.

Embree, George, "The Flying Dutchman," *Dun's Review,* May 1968, pp. 78–85.

"Fokker Flies High by Aiming Low," *Business Week,* February 5, 1966, pp. 74–77.

Gould, Bruce, "Winged Terror," *American Magazine,* April 1931, pp. 20–21, 98-106.

Martin, Robert E., "Tony Fokker: Wizard of Flight," *Popular Science Monthly,* May 1931, pp. 29–36, 123–24.

Martin, Robert E., "Tony Fokker and the World War," *Popular Science Monthly,* June 1931, pp. 24–26, 148.

Martin, Robert E., "Tony Fokker Captures America," *Popular Science Monthly,* July 1931, pp. 38–40, 131–32.

"Q.E.D.," *Time,* July 4, 1938, p. 32.

"Transition," *Newsweek,* January 1, 1940, p. 40.

"Up from the Ashes," *Forbes,* June 1, 1971, pp. 40–47.

—Sketch by Karl Preuss

Scott Ellsworth Forbush
1904-1984
American geophysicist

A pioneer in the study of cosmic-ray intensities, Scott Ellsworth Forbush was an important contributor to geophysical knowledge. His 1937 discovery, which found that the intensity of cosmic rays decreases after solar flares, was named the Forbush effect in his honor. The investigations Forbush conducted into geomagnetic phenomena brought him international recognition from his peers in the scientific community.

Forbush was born in Hudson, Ohio, on April 10, 1904. Attending Ohio's Case School of Applied Science, he graduated in 1925 with a B.S. degree in physics. Forbush was then a graduate student at Ohio State University for only two quarters before joining the National Bureau of Standards, where he remained until 1927. Accepting an appointment in Washington, D.C., at the Carnegie Institution's Department of Terrestrial Magnetism, Forbush worked for the organization until his retirement in 1969.

The Carnegie Institution soon sent Forbush to the Magnetic Observatory in Huancayo, Peru. His field work here was primarily concerned with geomagnetic research, the study of magnetic phenomena in their relation to the earth. He remained in Huancayo for two years, then departed to serve on the *Carnegie,* a research ship operated by the institution. While anchored a mile offshore of Apia, Samoa, on November 19, 1929, an explosion ripped through the aft of the vessel and the ship sank. Forbush survived without serious injury and returned to the observatory at Huancayo, where he was named observer in charge, a position he held until 1931.

At this point, Forbush was granted a year's leave of absence from the Carnegie Institution in order to attend Johns Hopkins University as a graduate student in physics and mathematics. During this period, he also did additional graduate work at George Washington University, the National Bureau of Standards, and the United States Department of Agriculture.

In 1932, the Carnegie Institution initiated plans to establish a worldwide network of ionization chambers in order to continuously record cosmic radiation. The project was led by **Arthur Holly Compton** and **Robert A. Millikan**, and called for the use of five separate geomagnetic observatories around the world: the Cheltenham Magnetic Observatory in Maryland; the National Astronomical Observatory in Teolayucan, Mexico; the Christchurch Magnetic Observatory in New Zealand; the Godhaven Magnetic Observatory in Greenland; and the Huancayo Magnetic Observatory. By 1935, seven meters had been constructed and tested, and in 1937 Forbush was chosen to head the project. Five of the meters were permanently installed in the different observatories and recording had begun by 1938; the two remaining meters were used for special investigations, typically latitude surveys in the Atlantic and Pacific oceans.

Discovers a Variation in Cosmic Ray Intensity

In 1937, Forbush discovered that a worldwide decrease in the intensity of cosmic rays occurred during some magnetic storms. This became known as the Forbush decrease or effect. Initially it was believed that this effect was the result of the influence of the equatorial ring current (ERC) on the trajectories of cosmic-rays. This conclusion was reached due to the similarities in the variations of cosmic-ray intensity, both during the storm and when compared to the geomagnetic field produced by the ERC. It was not until 1957 that the true causes of this effect were understood. John Simpson made use of detectors installed on a satellite and clearly demonstrated that the reduction in the intensity of the cosmic-rays occurred inside the plasma cloud coming from the sun. Simpson observed that the magnitude of the cosmic-ray intensity was essentially the same from the observatories on earth as it was at a distance of 47,835 kilometers from the earth, and he argued that it was the magnetic fields in these clouds rather than the ERC that caused this effect.

During World War II, Forbush served with the Naval Ordnance Laboratory as head of the analysis section and was also involved in operations research with the Navy Department. He returned to scientific research and made another important discovery in 1946. He found that during some large eruptions in the gaseous envelope of the sun, there appeared a solar flare effect. A solar flare is an increase in cosmic-ray intensity due to the ejection of protons by the sun during the eruptions. On November 19, 1949, three of the Carnegie's ionization chambers recorded a solar-flare event. Climax, Colorado recorded an increase of cosmic-ray intensity of two hundred percent while Cheltenham, Maryland reported an increase of forty-five percent—Huancayo did not detect any increase due to its close proximity to the ERC. Forbush, along with M. Schein and T. B. Stinchcomb, demonstrated that the solar-flare effect was due to nucleonic components. They predicted that a nucleonic detector could have recorded an increase in cosmic-ray intensity ten times greater than the meters in use at the observatories. Their prediction was later supported by a recording registered on a neutron detector in Manchester, England, during the same event on November 19.

In 1957, Forbush became head of the analytical and statistical geophysics section at the Carnegie Institution's department of terrestrial magnetism. The University of San Marcos in Lima, Peru, made him an honorary professor in 1959. Working with Mateo Casaverde, Forbush wrote *The Equatorial Electrojet in Peru,* which was published in 1961. That same year Forbush was the recipient of the Sir Charles Chree Medal from the Institute of Physics and the Physical Society in London, England. His election to the National Academy of Sciences followed in 1962. The Case Institute of Technology awarded Forbush with an honorary doctorate in 1962. He was next recognized by the American Geophysical Union, which gave him their John A. Fleming Award in 1965.

Forbush was a man of exceptionally high standards. He took great exception to sloppiness, particularly in the treatment of statistical data. A man of many talents, Forbush often accompanied his wife, an accomplished pianist, on the cello. He continued his research into cosmic-ray variations up until his death. He had keen analytical insights, as well as an ability to devise statistical methods to apply to geomagnetic results which allowed him to discover new phenomena and provide support for the controversial results of others. Forbush died on April 4, 1984, just six days shy of his eightieth birthday.

SELECTED WRITINGS BY FORBUSH:

Books

(With Mateo Casaverde) *Equatorial Electrojet in Peru,* Carnegie Institution of Washington, 1961.

SOURCES:

Books

Green, Jay, editor, *McGraw-Hill Modern Scientists and Engineers,* Volume I, McGraw-Hill, 1980.

Periodicals

Jonathan, Will, "The Solar Weather Man," *Saturday Review,* March 3, 1962, pp. 46–47.

Pomerantz, Martin, "Scott Ellsworth Forbush," *Physics Today,* October, 1984, p. 111.

—*Sketch by Chris McGrail*

Henry Ford
1863-1947
American industrialist and inventor

Henry Ford, mechanic, inventor, industrialist, and social activist, launched the era of the automobile, and in doing so provided the tools necessary for the mass production of consumer goods. The founder of the Ford Motor Company, Ford is associated with the creation of the assembly line, an industrial innovation that allowed cars—and later a variety of manufactured goods—to be produced quickly and efficiently. In realizing his goal of making inexpensive, high-quality automobiles available to the ordinary person, Ford was integral in bringing about the modern, consumer age.

Henry Ford was born in Springwells, Michigan (now part of Dearborn), on July 30, 1863, the first child of William and Mary Litogot Ford. The Fords were prosperous farmers with some ninety-one acres under cultivation. Though Ford's father expected his eldest son to follow in his footsteps, young Henry was never interested in the demanding life of a farmer on the mid-nineteenth-century frontier. Instead he decided to leave the farm and make his living as a mechanic. At the age of sixteen, with only seven years of formal education, Ford left his parent's farm to seek his fortune in nearby Detroit. Over the course of the next five decades, he would become the wealthiest man in America.

Ford had shown a mechanical inclination at an early age. He had tinkered with the farm machinery he had been charged to operate and he had invented a number of labor-saving devices to ease his farm chores. With these mechanical abilities, he quickly found a position in Detroit as an apprentice at the James Flowers and Brothers Machine Shop, a small company that was busily manufacturing valves and fire hydrants for the rapidly-growing city. While working for the Flowers Brothers, Ford earned a meager salary of two dollars and fifty cents a week—a dollar a week less than his rent in a Detroit boarding house. To supplement his income he took a night job repairing clocks and watches—no small sacrifice considering his day job required twelve hours of labor a day, six days a week.

Ford, however, was forward-looking and determined to become a wealthy man. He saw his position with the Flowers Brothers as only the first step in a career. Nine months later, he left the machine shop in order to work for the Detroit Dry Dock Company. His new wage was fifty-cents a week less, but he felt the experience he would get working on steam engines at the dry dock company would be more valuable to

Henry Ford

him in the long term. By the time he was twenty, Ford was a traveling "engine expert" for the Westinghouse company. His job took him all across southern Michigan repairing Westinghouse traction engines, which were self-propelled threshing machines. It was during these travels that he gained his first exposure to a new machine, the internal combustion engine.

Begins Work on a Horseless Carriage

Ford had taken up residence in Dearborn in 1882 when he took his job as a traveling engineer with Westinghouse. In 1888, he married Clara Bryant, quit his traveling job, and settled down on a farm in Dearborn. Ford did not find farming any more attractive as a young husband in his twenties than he had as a teenager. He spent most of his time over the next three years tinkering with machinery. It was during this period that Ford built his first internal combustion engine, a two-cylinder device he used to power a bicycle.

In 1891, convinced that electricity was the key to building an effective mechanical vehicle, Ford took a position as a night engineer with **Thomas Alva Edison**'s Detroit Illuminating company. Two years later, he had risen to chief engineer, and was earning an impressive salary of $100 per month. With this new wage Ford was able to support both his family—his only child, Edsel, was born in 1893—and his experiments with the "horseless carriage."

Working mainly at night (and using most of his family's disposable income in the process) Ford began developing his first horseless carriage soon after he was hired at Detroit Illuminating. He tested his prototype engine Christmas Eve, 1893, in the family kitchen. He clamped his invention to the kitchen sink, provided a spark with household current, and fed gasoline to the engine's cylinders by dribbling it in from a tea cup. It took Ford two and a half years to refine this crude engine and to design and build the vehicle that it would power. But finally, in June 1896, the Ford Quadricycle was ready to be tested on the cobblestone roads of old Detroit. Although it was not the first gasoline-powered car—the Duryea brothers had built one in Springfield, Massachusetts, three years previously and Gottlieb Daimler had demonstrated his horseless carriage at least six years before—the Quadricycle caused something of a sensation in Detroit. In addition, it displayed many of the properties that were to become hallmarks of Ford automobiles; it was light, inexpensive, utilitarian, easy to repair, and reliable.

The Ford Racers

On August 5, 1899, with the backing of William Murphy, a wealthy Detroit businessman, Ford founded the Detroit Automobile Company. While this—Ford's first business venture—was an economic failure, the company gave Ford the chance to concentrate all of his energies on designing and building automobiles. During this period his understanding of the automobile and the automobile manufacturing process grew immeasurably. Soon after the Detroit Automobile Company failed, Ford developed a four-cylinder, twenty-six horsepower racing engine and mounted it on his company's last prototype chassis. The crucial test of the new car came on October 10, 1901, in a ten-mile race just outside of Detroit. Ford matched his vehicle against what was then the world's fastest automobile, a car designed and driven by Alexander Winton. In an exciting race, Ford's first as a driver, he caught and passed the much more experienced Winton in the eighth lap on the one-mile oval and went on to win by a quarter mile.

The publicity from this important victory allowed Ford to raise more money for his second and third automobile-making ventures, the Henry Ford Company (later renamed Cadillac) and the Ford Motor Company, formed in 1903. Although the new companies were founded to build automobiles for the public, Ford instead became obsessed with building race cars, which he felt provided excellent free publicity as well as a practical laboratory for refining his ideas. He built two racers, the Arrow and the 999, that were to set several world records. One of his most memorable publicity stunts, however, involved plowing a four mile course on the frozen surface of Lake St. Clair northeast of Detroit. Slipping and sliding on the cinder-covered ice, Ford set a new world's record, covering one mile in 36 seconds (100 miles per hour) on January 9, 1904, with the new Ford Motor Company's Model B. The resulting publicity helped the company to sell 1700 cars in 1904, for a total of more than one million dollars. After two failed attempts, Henry Ford had launched a hugely successful car company.

Ford's Vision of a Car for the Common Man

Prior to 1908, the horseless carriage was typically considered a rich person's toy. Most automobiles then being manufactured were built for wealthy individuals, who would be able to hire someone to both drive and, when necessary, repair the vehicle. Ford's vision was different. He saw the automobile as the tool that would end the dreary isolation of the American farmer, and that would allow the inhabitants of the teeming urban slums to move to the outskirts of the great cities where there was plenty of room for new housing developments but no transportation to the factories. To do this, Ford knew the automobile must be priced within the range of the common man, it would have to be reliable, and it would require interchangeable and inexpensive replacement parts.

In 1906, the Ford Motor Company came out with the Model N, a $600 dollar runabout, and on October 1, 1908, the Model T. The Model T was exactly the car Ford had dreamed about, a lightweight, inexpensive, reliable automobile, priced to be available to the common man. In its first year, Ford sold 8000 Model Ts. Over the course of the next three years Model T sales increased dramatically with 18,000 sold in 1909, 34,000 in 1910, and 78,000 in 1911. In 1916, the year of its greatest production, 730,000 of the automobiles were sold. By 1922, Ford was the richest man in America. And, unlike most of his wealthy contemporaries, Ford was greatly appreciated by many Americans.

Ford and Mass Production

Ford is often credited with inventing the moving assembly line, a system for carrying an item that is being manufactured past a series of stationary workers who each assemble a particular portion of the finished product. Ford made the first industrial application of the idea, and the result revolutionized manufacturing, making our modern consumer society possible. (Without the moving assembly line, televisions, medical products, home computers and many other goods we take for granted would be prohibitively expensive for most people.) It should be noted, however, that the moving assembly line was probably the invention of dozens of Ford production supervisors in addition to Ford—who undoubtedly contributed to its development and who certainly approved of the idea and rewarded the persons responsible for perfecting it. Using this method Ford was able to realize his vision of the Model T as a mass-produced consumer item designed for the common man. The Ford Motor Company built fifteen million Model Ts between 1908 and 1927, an impossible feat in the days prior to the advent of interchangeable parts and the moving assembly line. The addition of a conveyor belt that carried preassembled parts to the point in the factory where they were to be bolted onto the Model T chassis allowed the process of automobile mass production to reach full fruition.

Ford as a Social Activist

Ford's deeply-held belief in his duty (as a wealthy man) to work for the common good led him to share the benefits of mass production with both the people who bought his automobiles and with the workers who made them. After the second year of production, Ford either dropped the price or enhanced the features of the Model T every year, carrying out his stated goal of increasing the Model T's value annually. The price of the Model T, initially $850 in 1908, dropped to as low as $260 in 1924, while the quality of the car itself had been much improved. In January, 1914, Ford decided to share the success of the Model T with his workers. He doubled the pay of the average worker in the Ford plants from $2.50 to $5.00 a day and cut the work day from nine hours to eight. While reviled by his fellow industrialists, this move was wildly popular with his workers. Ford saw his action not only the right thing to do, but also as a good economic decision. In one move he drastically reduced the turnover of his workers, raised employee morale, and created a new class of industrial workers who could afford to buy Ford automobiles. Ford regarded low wages as "the cutting of buying power and the curtailment of the home market." And by increasing his workers' salaries, he forced his fellow industrialists to pay their workers more, putting the Model T Ford within their economic reach as well.

Ford was also far ahead of his time in employing the physically challenged. He felt, given a chance to work, the blind and the deaf would work much harder than other workers. In addition, he believed in hiring former criminals, thereby providing them with an alternative to a life of crime.

Ford had less success with his other humanitarian goals. In 1915 he financed and sailed on the "Peace" ship, his ill-fated attempt to end the European war before America was drawn into it. According to Ford, war was nonproductive and something that should not be indulged in no matter how badly a nation's "honor" had been sullied. But at that time the theory of war was widely credited as a "manly contest of arms," and Ford was ridiculed for his views. The *Chicago Tribune* labeled him an anarchist and an ignorant idealist. Ford sued for libel and won, but was awarded only six cents in damages.

Ford's final years were ones of decline. By 1920 he had bought out the other shareholders in the Ford Motor Company and was solely in charge. He ignored the advice of his subordinates, chased away many of his best executives, and by 1927, the last year of the production of the Model T, his company had been eclipsed by General Motors. His last years were marred by scandals, the worst of which was his financing of a vehemently anti-Semitic magazine. In 1933 he defied President Roosevelt by refusing to take part in the National Recovery Act, and in 1937 and 1941, Ford Motor Company was rocked by violent strikes. Ford suffered a stroke in 1938. His only son, Edsel, died of cancer in 1943, another terrible blow. Ford himself died on April 7, 1947, leaving a legacy that includes the concept of mass production and the moving assembly line, his car company—the second largest in the world, with more than a hundred billion dollars in yearly sales—and the Ford Foundation, which he dedicated to the purpose of "advancing human welfare."

SELECTED WRITINGS BY FORD:

Books

(With Samuel Crowther) *My Life and Work,* Doubleday, 1922.

(With Samuel Crowther) *Today and Tomorrow,* Doubleday, 1926.

(With Samuel Crowther) *Moving Forward,* Doubleday, 1931.

SOURCES:

Books

Bennett, Harry and Paul Marcus, *Ford: We Never Called Him Henry,* TOR, 1951.

Nevins, Allan and F. E. Hill, *Ford: The Times, the Man, the Company,* 3 volumes, Scribners, 1954.

Rae, John B., editor, *Great Lives Observed: Henry Ford,* edited by John B. Rae, Prentice-Hall, 1969.

Wik, Reynold M., *Henry Ford and Grass-roots America,* University of Michigan Press, 1972.

—Sketch by Jeff Raines

Jay W. Forrester
1918-
American computer scientist and electrical engineer

One of the most important names in computer evolution is Jay W. Forrester. In August of 1949, the U.S.S.R. exploded an atomic weapon. That event had a profound impact on Forrester, even though he was nowhere near the explosion, and was neither a member of the military nor a government official. At the time, Forrester was working in the Electrical Engineering Department at Massachusetts Institute of Technology (MIT), and the atomic explosion caused the United States Navy to take a second look at the Whirlwind computer he had developed. As a result, the Whirlwind became the prototype for a defense system that would last into the 1980s, and Forrester would become recognized as a primary player in the development of the computer.

Jay Wright Forrester was born in Nebraska on July 14, 1918, and raised on a cattle ranch belonging to his parents, Marmaduke M. and Ethel Pearl (Wright) Forrester. Forrester took an interest in electricity at an early age. While still in high school, he created a wind-driven, twelve-volt electrical system using old automobile parts. The system brought electricity to the family's cattle ranch for the first time. Following graduation from high school in 1935, Forrester enrolled at the University of Nebraska as an electrical engineering major. Four years later, he graduated at the top of his class.

In the summer of 1939, Forrester became a graduate student at MIT. He also began working as a research assistant in MIT's High Voltage Laboratory. The following year, he went to work in the new Servomechanisms Laboratory, a part of the electrical engineering department. In the early 1940s, Forrester worked to develop electric and hydraulic servomechanisms for gun mounts and radar.

Heads Up Whirlwind Project for MIT and the U.S. Navy

By 1944, Forrester was thinking of leaving the Servomechanisms Laboratory in order to start his own business. In an effort to keep Forrester from leaving, Gordon Brown, the director of the laboratory, offered Forrester his choice of several projects. Forrester agreed to tackle a project sponsored by the United States Navy. The project involved building an aircraft stability and control analyzer (ASCA) that could be used in the testing of new aerodynamic designs. This would allow the navy to test the effects

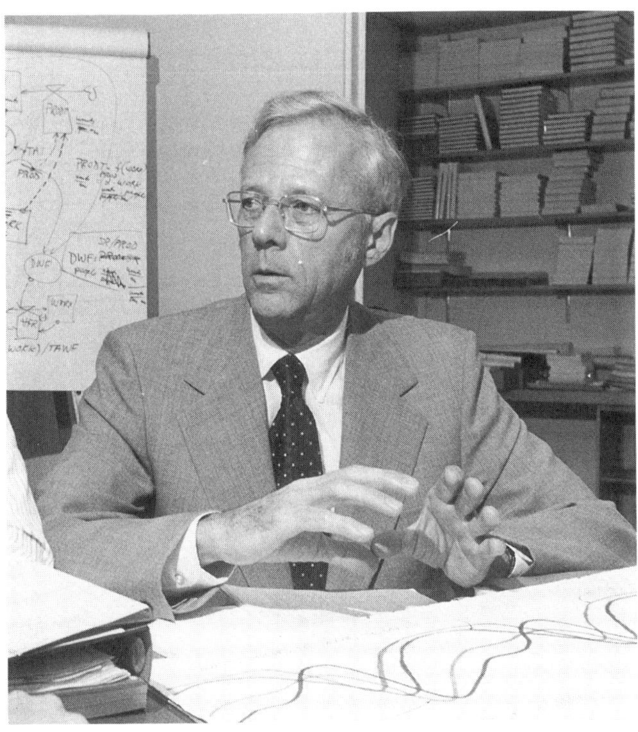

Jay W. Forrester

of design changes to an aircraft. Specifically, the project called for the building of an analog computer that would simulate an aircraft's performance. The navy wanted this simulator to respond to pilot responses to a situation in real time, meaning the computer would react to a pilot's response as quickly as an actual aircraft.

By the spring of 1945, Forrester concluded that an analog computer could not be programmed to respond in real time—it was too slow. Perry Crawford, of the Special Devices Center of the Navy, suggested that Forrester look into digital computing as an alternative. Forrester investigated this possibility, speaking with experts from Harvard University and the University of Pennsylvania. He concluded that digital computing provided the best potential for achieving real time simulation, so in 1946 he convinced Brown to establish a digital computer development program at the Servomechanisms Laboratory. With the conversion from an analog to a digital computer, the ASCA project became known as Whirlwind. Forrester became director of the new Digital Computer Laboratory. That same year, he completed his M.S. degree and married Susan Swett; eventually they would have three children, Judith, Nathan, and Ned.

By 1947, Forrester and his team were developing the Whirlwind, modeling it after a general-purpose parallel computer. In 1948, they built the frame on a twenty-five thousand square foot area. Forrester's next barrier in the project involved the thousands of vacuum tubes that went into the machine. Because a vacuum tube had a life expectancy of only about five hundred hours, the computer was continually blowing tubes, causing the Whirlwind to shut down frequently. Realizing that something had to be done to reduce the number of shut-downs, Forrester directed his attention to the vacuum tubes. He discovered that by using a silicon-free cathode material, he could eliminate the loss of cathode emissions, thereby prolonging the life of the tube. Indeed, Forrester's discovery extended the life of a typical vacuum tube from five hundred hours to five hundred thousand hours. Next, Forrester installed a system in Whirlwind to automatically check for components that showed early indications of failure. This allowed Whirlwind operators to repair or replace a component before an error occurred.

Invents Magnetic Core Computer Memory

Having progressed beyond the vacuum tube problem, Forrester and his team were able to get the Whirlwind up and running—in real time. While this represented a great success, the Whirlwind was still subject to shut-downs. The storage tubes, like the vacuum tubes before Forrester's improvements, had a short life span. The tubes were also limiting in that the computer could not run programs that required a great deal of memory. What's more, the tubes were expensive. All of these problems added up to a memory system that was too undependable, too limiting, and too expensive. Forrester's resolution of this problem would dictate the way computer memory was designed for years to come.

At that time, computer memory operated either on a dependable but slow, one-dimensional mercury delay line, or on a two-dimensional Williams Tube that was faster but not very dependable. Forrester tried to improve upon these options by developing a cathode-ray tube memory that was constantly charged by electrons. A deflected beam could change and read the charge. This device, called the MIT Storage Tube, provided effective memory, but again proved far too costly to be of practical use. Forrester then started thinking about a three-dimensional memory system, but struggled in trying to come up with the right material for creating it.

In 1949, Forrester read an advertisement for Deltamax, a material developed by the Germans during World War II to build magnetic amplifiers in tanks. Thinking this might provide an answer to the memory problem, Forrester ordered some Deltamax and began testing. Creating small rings made from the Deltamax, Forrester was able to run a current through the rings, magnetizing them in a north or south direction. This reversing of current could be used in the Whirlwind to change from one binary state to another. The rings, while effective, proved again to be too slow to meet the performance needs of the

Whirlwind. Forrester would eventually replace the Deltamax with magnetic ferrite cores in conjunction with a wire grid to achieve a successful, three-dimensional, magnetic core memory system.

It was at about that time that the U.S.S.R. exploded an atomic weapon that led to a renewed interest in the Whirlwind. By 1949, the navy was losing interest and confidence in the Whirlwind project. The atomic explosion, however, sent a message to President Truman and the U.S. military that computers would soon be required as a first line of national defense. Intelligence reports on the incident suggested that the Soviets now had the ability to launch an atomic weapon at the United States, and the Whirlwind became the military's best hope for developing an air defense system that could detect and snuff out an atomic bomb. Forrester was put in charge of implementing Whirlwind as the heart of a new defense system. The system, called SAGE (Semi-Automatic Ground Environment), began testing in 1951. The completed Whirlwind would be able to identify unfriendly aircraft and direct interceptors to cut them off.

By 1953, SAGE could monitor forty-eight aircraft simultaneously. That year, the magnetic core memory was added to the Whirlwind. The switch from tubes to magnetic core memory doubled the speed of the Whirlwind, while providing a very reliable system at a lower cost. It was Forrester's magnetic core memory that would set the trend for the development of increasingly faster and more reliable computers. In 1954, Forrester's achievements were recognized by his home state alma mater, the University of Nebraska, with the awarding of an honorary Ph.D.

Creates Field of System Dynamics

Forrester left the SAGE program in 1956. By that time, the system was running fairly smoothly, and Forrester felt his presence was no longer necessary to ensure the project's success. Forrester made a major career shift by accepting an offer to become a professor at MIT's new Sloan School of Management. Forrester's ability to link his expertise in engineering and computers with his new work at the Sloan School would gain him wide recognition in a new field—system dynamics. The SAGE system, meanwhile, would be ready for implementation in 1958. SAGE would provide an air defense system that would last into the 1980s.

At the Sloan School, Forrester used his engineering background to identify similarities between a policy in an organization, and a transfer function in an engineering device. This similarity suggested to Forrester that it was possible to construct mathematical models of the policy structure of an organization. Concluding, however, that such mathematical models would be far too complicated to work with, he directed his focus to using experimental and empirical approaches to study the policy structure of an organization. This work broke new ground in the management field. Drawing on his computer background, Forrester used computer simulations to analyze the behavior of social systems and to determine the implications of models. His approach became known as "system dynamics." Forrester is now recognized as the creator of the field of system dynamics. System dynamics would eventually be applied to a variety of topics including tax policies, inflation, policy design, energy, unemployment, urban and world growth, stagnation, and other areas.

The release of Forrester's book *Industrial Dynamics* in 1961 brought widespread attention to his approach to organizational structures. His 1968 work, *Principles of Systems,* was designed as a textbook on system dynamics. Also in 1968, Forrester was presented the Inventor of the Year Award from George Washington University. In 1969, Forrester's title, *Urban Dynamics,* was published. The narrative focuses on the application of system dynamics to the growth and stagnation of cities. That same year, Forrester was awarded an honorary Ph.D. from Boston University, and the Valdemar Poulsen Gold Medal from the Danish Academy of Technical Sciences. Two years later, Forrester received an honorary Ph.D. from Newark College.

In 1971, Forrester's *World Dynamics* was released. In this book, Forrester applied principles of system dynamics to those factors affecting world equilibrium. Forrester suggests that industrialization may represent a greater problem for the earth than overpopulation. Forrester identified pollution, crowding, and depletion of resources as factors endangering the earth's equilibrium. The next year Forrester was named a Germeshausen Professor at MIT. He was also recipient of the Systems, Man, and Cybernetics Society Award for Outstanding Accomplishment. Union College awarded him an honorary Ph.D. in 1973.

In 1974, Forrester was given the Howard N. Potts Award from the Franklin Institute as well as another honorary Ph.D. from the University of Notre Dame. The 1975 release of *Collected Papers of Jay W. Forrester* provided a chronological look at the evolution of system dynamics through a series of papers written by Forrester between 1958 and 1972. Forrester's work was recognized globally, as indicated by his being given an honorary Ph.D. from the University of Manheim, Germany, in 1979. That year, he was also named to the National Inventors Hall of Fame.

SELECTED WRITINGS BY FORRESTER:

Books

Industrial Dynamics, MIT Press, 1961.

Principles of Systems, Wright-Allen Press, 1968.
Urban Dynamics, MIT Press, 1969.
World Dynamics, Wright-Allen Press, 1971.
Collected Papers of Jay W. Forrester, Wright-Allen Press, 1975.

SOURCES:

Books

Slater, Robert, *Portraits in Silicon,* MIT Press, 1987, pp. 91–99.

—*Sketch by Daniel Rooney*

Werner Forssmann
1904-1979
German physician

Werner Forssmann, a surgeon and urologist, was relatively unknown in his native Germany when he won the Nobel Prize in 1956 for his work in heart catheterization. His ground-breaking experiment had been done almost three decades earlier, and when he received word of the award—after a morning of surgery during which he had operated on three patients with kidney disease—he commented, as quoted in *Mayo Clinic Proceedings,* "I feel like a village parson who has just learned that he has been made bishop."

Werner Theodor Otto Forssmann was born on August 29, 1904, in Berlin, the only child of Julius Forssmann, a lawyer employed by a life insurance company, and Emmy Hindenberg. Forssmann's father died in World War I while young Forssmann was still a student in the Askanische Gymnasium, a school emphasizing a humanistic approach to education. His mother worked as an office clerk and his grandmother took over the role of running the household. Forssmann's uncle, a doctor just outside of Berlin, became an influential force in his nephew's life, ultimately convincing Forssmann to pursue a career in medicine. In 1922, after graduating from the Gymnasium, Forssmann entered the Friedrich Wilhelm University in Berlin, passing the state examination in 1928. Forssmann's doctoral thesis on the effects of concentrated liver on pernicious anemia, a blood deficiency, marked the way for his later experiments. Together with a small group of fellow students, Forssmann experimented on himself, taking large doses of liver concentrate daily and demonstrating its healthful effects on blood. After receiving his doctor's diploma in early 1929 and being frustrated in his efforts to obtain a post as an internist, Forssmann worked for a short time in a private women's clinic in Spandau. Then, through family connections, he secured an internship at the August Viktoria Home in Eberswalde, a small town northeast of Berlin.

Seeks Cardiac Diagnostic Tool

Training as a surgeon, Forssmann nevertheless gave thought to an earlier passion of his, one inspired by a teacher he encountered in medical school: heart diagnosis. He was dissatisfied with the inaccuracy and uncertainty of diagnostic techniques such as percussion, auscultation, X ray, and even electrocardiography. He became convinced that there was an internal diagnostic method that would not involve major risks, trigger automatic reflex actions, or disturb the balance of pressure in the thorax. As early as the mid-nineteenth century, there had been a procedure known as cardiac catheterization in animal experiments. Doctors had performed the procedure in the late nineteenth century to determine blood pressure in the right and left chambers of the heart. Some of these procedures employed the use of a catheter inserted through the jugular vein of a horse. Forssmann believed that he could do this on humans through a vein at the elbow traditionally used for intravenous injections. His research on cadavers supported his idea, and by the summer of 1929 Forssmann approached his supervisor, Dr. Richard Schneider, with a plan to catheterize his own heart with a ureteric catheter. Schneider, however, would not allow such a dangerous experiment in his hospital.

Undaunted, Forssmann set out to convince a surgical nurse in his section of his experiment's feasibility so he could gain access to the sterilized instruments he needed. Eventually, the nurse agreed to aid him, even agreeing to be the first subject. Forssmann, however, had no intention of experimenting on anyone but himself initially. He gave himself a local anesthetic in the left elbow and then made an incision. Once he had opened his vein, he inserted the catheter about a foot up his arm and had the nurse accompany him to the X-ray lab. There, Forssmann stood behind a fluoroscope screen with a mirror placed so that he could see the image of the catheter, which he pushed up until it was in the right ventricle of his heart. Then he calmly ordered that photographs be made of this momentous achievement.

The results of this experiment were published in a short paper in the prestigious *Klinische Wochenschrift* and won Forssmann a position at the Charité Hospital in Berlin. But the reception to his article by other physicians was cool and his superior at the Charité did not approve of his unorthodox techniques, so Forssmann was soon back in Eberswalde. He continued his experiments for the next two years, during which time he proved that the insertion of a catheter in the heart was painless and caused no damage to the blood vessels. He also pioneered techniques for measuring pressure inside the heart and for injecting opaque material for X-ray studies of the heart. Still, his work was reviled by most physicians, who called it unethical and considered his experiments stunts. By 1931, Forssmann, discouraged by the response to his work, gave up experimental medicine. He returned to the Charité Hospital in Berlin and soon moved on to the Mainz City Hospital. It was there, in 1932, that he met the woman who would become his wife, Dr. Elsbet Engel, a resident in internal medicine. Though their marriage was happy and fruitful (they would have six children together), it also necessitated another change of hospitals for Forssmann, for it was against the hospital's policy for a married couple to work together. Forssmann trained as a urologist in Berlin at the Rudolph Virchow Hospital, then took a position as a surgeon and urologist at the City Hospital of Dresden-Friedrichstadt for two years. Later, he became a senior surgeon at the Robert Koch Hospital in Berlin. His colleagues considered him a fine surgeon.

Fame Comes Late in Life

During World War II, Forssmann served as an army surgeon, surviving six years spent in Germany, Norway, Russia, and in a prisoner of war (POW) camp. Back in Germany after the War, he practiced as a country doctor in the Black Forest village of Wambach for three years before returning to the practice of urology in 1950 at Bad Kreuznach. It was only after the war that Forssmann discovered that others had continued working with his cardiac catheterization experiment of 1929. The most notable implementation was by two Americans, **Dickinson Woodruff Richards, Jr.**, and **André F. Cournand,** who developed it into a tool for diagnosis and research. In 1954, Forssmann received the Leibniz Medal from the German Academy of Science in Berlin, yet he was refused a professorship at the University of Mainz. He had resigned himself to being a little-known doctor in Bad Kreuznach when, on October 18, 1956, he was notified that he had won, along with Richards and Cournand, the Nobel Prize for Physiology or Medicine for his contribution to the knowledge of heart catheterization and pathological changes in the circulatory system.

The Nobel Prize finally earned Forssmann renown and respect; in *Clinical Cardiology,* H. W. Heiss called him "one of the great fathers of cardiology." In 1958, he became the chief of the surgical division of the Evangelical Hospital of Düsseldorf, and ten years later he was awarded the gold medal of the Society of Surgical Medicine of Ferrara. After he retired, Forssmann spent his time in the Black Forest, where he enjoyed the outdoors and nature. He died of a heart attack in Schopfheim, West Germany, on June 1, 1979.

SELECTED WRITINGS BY FORSSMANN:

Books

Experiments on Myself: Memoirs of a Surgeon in Germany (originally published in Germany by Droste Verlag GmbH, Düsseldorf, 1972), translated by Hilary Davies with a preface by André Cournand, St. Martin's, 1974.

Periodicals

"Die Sondierung des rechten Herzens," *Klinische Wochenschrift,* Volume 45, 1929, pp. 2085–2087, reprinted as "Catheterization of the Right Heart," *Classics of Cardiology,* Volume 3, 1983, pp. 352–355.

SOURCES:

Books

Comroe, Julius H., Jr., *Exploring the Heart: Discoveries in Heart Disease and High Blood Pressure,* Norton, 1983.

Johnson, Steven L., *The History of Cardiac Surgery, 1896–1955,* Johns Hopkins University Press, 1972.

Nobel Laureates in Medicine or Physiology: A Biographical Dictionary, Garland Publishing, 1990.

Periodicals

Heiss, H. W., "Werner Forssmann: A German Problem with the Nobel Prize," *Clinical Cardiology,* July, 1992, pp. 547–549.

New York Times, June 7, 1979.

Steckelberg, James M., Ronald E. Vlietstra, Jurgen Ludwig, and Ruth J. Mann, "Werner Forssmann (1904–1979) and His Unusual Success Story," *Mayo Clinic Proceedings,* November, 1979, pp. 746–748.

—Sketch by J. Sydney Jones

Dian Fossey
1932-1985
American primatologist

Dian Fossey is remembered by her fellow scientists as the world's foremost authority on mountain gorillas. But to the millions of wildlife conservationists who came to know Fossey through her articles and book, she will always be remembered as a martyr. Throughout the nearly 20 years she spent studying mountain gorillas in central Africa, the American primatologist tenaciously fought the poachers and bounty hunters who threatened to wipe out the endangered primates. She was brutally murdered at her research center in 1985 by what many believe was a vengeful poacher.

Fossey's dream of living in the wilds of Africa dates back to her lonely childhood in San Francisco. She was born in 1932, the only child of George, an insurance agent, and Kitty, a fashion model, (Kidd) Fossey. The Fosseys divorced when Dian was 6 years old. A year later, Kitty married a wealthy building contractor named Richard Price. Price was a strict disciplinarian who showed little affection for his stepdaughter. Although Fossey loved animals, she was allowed to have only a goldfish. When it died, she cried for a week.

Fossey began her college education at the University of California at Davis in the preveterinary medicine program. She excelled in writing and botany, she failed chemistry and physics. After two years, she transferred to San Jose State University, where she earned a bachelor of arts degree in occupational therapy in 1954. While in college, Fossey became a prize-winning equestrian. Her love of horses in 1955 drew her from California to Kentucky, where she directed the occupational therapy department at the Kosair Crippled Children's Hospital in Louisville.

Book Inspires Career Choice

Fossey's interest in Africa's gorillas was aroused through primatologist **George Schaller**'s 1963 book, *The Mountain Gorilla: Ecology and Behavior.* Through Schaller's book, Fossey became acquainted with the largest and rarest of three subspecies of gorillas, *Gorilla gorilla beringei.* She learned that these giant apes make their home in the mountainous forests of Rwanda, Zaire and Uganda. Males grow up to six feet tall and weigh 400 pounds or more. Their arms span up to eight feet. The smaller females weigh about 200 pounds.

Schaller's book inspired Fossey to travel to Africa to see the mountain gorillas in their homeland.

Dian Fossey

Against her family's advice, she took out a three-year bank loan for $8,000 to finance the seven-week safari. While in Africa, Fossey met the celebrated paleoanthropologist **Louis Leakey,** who had encouraged **Jane Goodall** in her research of chimpanzees in Tanzania. Leakey was impressed by Fossey's plans to visit the mountain gorillas.

Those plans were nearly destroyed when she shattered her ankle on a fossil dig with Leakey. But just two weeks later, she hobbled on a walking stick up a mountain in the Congo (now Zaire) to her first encounter with the great apes. The sight of six gorillas set the course for her future. "I left Kabara (gorilla site) with reluctance but with never a doubt that I would, somehow, return to learn more about the gorillas of the misted mountains," Fossey wrote in her book, *Gorillas in the Mist.*

Her opportunity came three years later, when Leakey was visiting Louisville on a lecture tour. Fossey urged him to hire her to study the mountain gorillas. He agreed, if she would first undergo a preemptive appendectomy. Six weeks later, he told her the operation was unnecessary; he had only been testing her resolve. But it was too late. Fossey had already had her appendix removed.

The L.S.B. Leakey and the Wilkie Brothers foundations funded her research, along with the National Geographic Society. Fossey began her career in Africa with a brief visit to Jane Goodall in

Tanzania to learn the best methods for studying primates and collecting data.

She set up camp early in 1967 at the Kabara meadow in Zaire's Parc National des Virungas, where Schaller had conducted his pioneering research on mountain gorillas a few years earlier. The site was ideal for Fossey's research. Because Zaire's park system protected them against human intrusion, the gorillas showed little fear of Fossey's presence. Unfortunately, civil war in Zaire forced Fossey to abandon the site six months after she arrived.

She established her permanent research site September 24, 1967, on the slopes of the Virunga Mountains in the tiny country of Rwanda. She called it the Karisoke Research Centre, named after the neighboring Karisimbi and Visoke mountains in the Parc National des Volcans. Although Karisoke was just five miles from the first site, Fossey found a marked difference in Rwanda's gorillas. They had been harassed so often by poachers and cattle grazers that they initially rejected all her attempts to make contact.

Theoretically, the great apes were protected from such intrusion within the park. But the government of the impoverished, densely populated country failed to enforce the park rules. Native Batusi herdsmen used the park to trap antelope and buffalo, sometimes inadvertently snaring a gorilla. Most trapped gorillas escaped, but not without seriously mutilated limbs that sometimes led to gangrene and death. Poachers who caught gorillas could earn up to $200,000 for one by selling the skeleton to a university and the hands to tourists. From the start, Fossey's mission was to protect the endangered gorillas from extinction—indirectly, by researching and writing about them, and directly, by destroying traps and chastising poachers.

Fossey focused her studies on some 51 gorillas in four family groups. Each group was dominated by a sexually mature silverback, named for the characteristic gray hair on its back. Younger, bachelor males served as guards for the silverback's harem and their juvenile offspring.

Experiences Historic Touch with Gorilla

When Fossey began observing the reclusive gorillas, she followed the advice of earlier scientists by concealing herself and watching from a distance. But she soon realized that the only way she would be able to observe their behavior as closely as she wanted was by "habituating" the gorillas to her presence. She did so by mimicking their sounds and behavior. She learned to imitate their belches that signal contentment, their barks of curiosity and a dozen other sounds. To convince them she was their kind, Fossey pretended to munch on the foliage that made up their diet. Her tactics worked. One day early in 1970, Fossey made history when a gorilla she called Peanuts reached out and touched her hand. Fossey called it her most rewarding moment with the gorillas.

She endeared laymen to Peanuts and the other gorillas she studied through her articles in National Geographic magazine. The apes became almost human through her descriptions of their nurturing and playing. Her early articles dispelled the myth that gorillas are vicious. In her 1971 *National Geographic* article she described the giant beasts as ranking among "the gentlest animals, and the shiest." In later articles, Fossey acknowledged a dark side to the gorillas. Six of 38 infants born during a 13-year-period were victims of infanticide. She speculated the practice was a silverback's means of perpetuating his own lineage by killing another male's offspring so he could mate with the victim's mother.

Three years into her study, Fossey realized she would need a doctoral degree to continue receiving support for Karisoke. She temporarily left Africa to enroll at Cambridge University, where she earned her Ph.D. in zoology in 1974. In 1977, Fossey suffered a tragedy that would permanently alter her mission at Karisoke. Digit, a young male she had grown to love, was slaughtered by poachers. Walter Cronkite focused national attention on the gorillas' plight when he reported Digit's death on the CBS Evening News. Interest in gorilla conservation surged. Fossey took advantage of that interest by establishing the Digit Fund, a non-profit organization to raise money for anti-poaching patrols and equipment.

But the money wasn't enough to save the gorillas from poachers. Six months later, a silverback and his mate from one of Fossey's study groups were shot and killed defending their three-year-old son, who had been shot in the shoulder. The juvenile later died from his wounds. It was rumored that the gorilla deaths caused Fossey to suffer a nervous breakdown, although she denied it. What is clear is that the deaths prompted her to step up her fight against the Batusi poachers by terrorizing them and raiding their villages. "She did everything short of murdering those poachers," Mary Smith, senior assistant editor at National Geographic, told contributor Cynthia Washam in an interview. A serious calcium deficiency that causes bones to snap and teeth to rot forced Fossey to leave Africa in 1980. She spent her three-year sojourn as a visiting associate professor at Cornell University. Fossey completed her book, *Gorillas in the Mist,* during her stint at Cornell. It was published in 1983. Although some scientists criticized the book for its abundance of anecdotes and lack of scientific discussion, lay readers and reviewers received it warmly.

When Fossey returned to Karisoke in 1983, her scientific research was virtually abandoned. Funding had run dry. She was operating Karisoke with her own savings. "In the end, she became more of an animal activist than a scientist," Smith said. "Science kind of went out the window."

Brutal Murder Remains a Mystery

On Dec. 27, 1985, Fossey, 54, was found murdered in her bedroom at Karisoke, her skull split diagonally from her forehead to the corner of her mouth. Her murder remains a mystery that has prompted much speculation. Rwandan authorities jointly charged American research assistant Wayne McGuire, who discovered Fossey's body, and Emmanuel Rwelekana, a Rwandan tracker Fossey had fired several months earlier. McGuire maintains his innocence. At the urging of U.S. authorities, he left Rwanda before the charges against him were made public. He was convicted in absentia and sentenced to die before a firing squad if he ever returns to Rwanda.

Farley Mowat, the Canadian author of Fossey's biography, *Woman in the Mists,* believes McGuire was a scapegoat. He had no motive for killing her, Mowat wrote, and the evidence against him appeared contrived. Rwelekana's story will never be known. He was found dead after apparently hanging himself a few weeks after he was charged with the murder. Smith, and others, believe Fossey's death came at the hands of a vengeful poacher. "I feel she was killed by a poacher," Smith said. "It definitely wasn't any mysterious plot."

Fossey's final resting place is at Karisoke, surrounded by the remains of Digit and more than a dozen other gorillas she had buried. Her legacy lives on in the Virungas, as her followers have taken up her battle to protect the endangered mountain gorillas. The Dian Fossey Gorilla Fund, formerly the Digit Fund, finances scientific research at Karisoke and employs camp staff, trackers and anti-poaching patrols.

The Rwanda government, which for years had ignored Fossey's pleas to protect its mountain gorillas, on September 27, 1990, recognized her scientific achievement with the Ordre (sic) National des Grandes Lacs, the highest award it has ever given a foreigner. Gorillas in Rwanda are still threatened by cattle ranchers and hunters squeezing in on their habitat. According to the Colorado-based Dian Fossey Gorilla Fund, by the early 1990s, fewer than 650 mountain gorillas remained in Rwanda, Zaire and Uganda. The Virunga Mountains is home to about 320 of them. Smith is among those convinced that the number would be much smaller if not for Fossey's 18 years of dedication to save the great apes. "Her conservation efforts stand above everything else (she accomplished at Karisoke)," Smith said. "She singlehandedly saved the mountain gorillas."

SELECTED WRITINGS BY FOSSEY:

Books

Gorillas in the Mist, Houghton Mifflin Company, 1983.

Periodicals

"Making Friends With Mountain Gorillas," *National Geographic,* January, 1970, pp. 48–67.

"More Years With Mountain Gorillas," *National Geographic,* October, 1971, pp. 574–585.

"The Imperiled Mountain Gorilla," *National Geographic,* April 1981, pp. 501–522.

SOURCES:

Books

Current Biography Yearbook, H.W. Wilson Company, 1985, pp. 121–123.

Hayes, Harold T.P., *The Dark Romance of Dian Fossey,* Simon and Schuster, 1990.

Mowat, Farley, *Woman in the Mists,* Warner Books, 1987.

Schoumatoff, Alex, *African Madness,* Alfred A. Knopf, 1988, pp. 5–42.

Periodicals

Brower, Montgomery, "The Strange Death of Dian Fossey," *People,* February 17, 1986, pp. 46–54.

Hayes, Harold, "The Dark Romance of Dian Fossey," *Life,* November, 1986, pp. 64–70.

New Yorker, January 27, 1986, pp. 26–27.

Other

Smith, Mary, interview with Cynthia Washam conducted July 23, 1993.

—Sketch by Cynthia Washam

William A. Fowler
1911-
American physicist

William A. Fowler is noted for his theories dealing with how stars produce heat and light based on his explanations of the synthesis of chemical elements in the universe. Fowler received the 1983

Nobel Prize in physics in recognition of "his theoretical and experimental studies of the nuclear reactions of important in the formation of the chemical elements in the universe." His contributions have been of benefit to the fields of astronomy, astrophysics, cosmology, and geophysics in addition to nuclear physics.

Fowler was born on August 9, 1911, in Pittsburgh, Pennsylvania, to John MacLeod, an accountant, and Jennie Summers (Watson) Fowler. The Fowlers had two other children, Arthur Watson, born in 1913, and Nelda, born in 1919. When William was two years old, his family moved to Lima, Ohio, where he attended Horace Mann Grade School and Central High School. At Central, Fowler was president of the senior class, a varsity football and baseball player, and valedictorian of the graduating class of 1929.

Fowler received his bachelor's degree from Ohio State University in 1933 and his Ph.D. in nuclear physics at the Kellogg Radiation Laboratory at the California Institute of Technology (Cal Tech) in 1936. Immediately, he was offered a job as research fellow at Kellogg and then, over the next forty-five years, was promoted from assistant to full professor. He retired from the California Institute of Technology in 1982 and was named emeritus professor of physics.

Fowler entered Ohio State University in the fall of 1929 intending to major in ceramic engineering. Two years later, however, he switched to engineering physics, a field in which would earn his bachelor of science. Although he had to work throughout his college years in order to support himself, Fowler was able to record the highest grade point average in his graduating class.

Begins Nuclear Research at Cal Tech

Upon graduation from Ohio State, Fowler decided to enter the California Institute of Technology for his graduate work. There, he was assigned to assist the director of the W. K. Kellogg Radiation Laboratory, C. C. Lauritsen, whom Fowler credits as being the greatest influence in his life, according to an article in *Physics Today*. For his doctoral dissertation, Fowler studied the production of radioactive isotopes as the result of bombarding light elements with protons and deuterons. He was granted his Ph.D. in physics *summa cum laude* in 1936.

Lauritsen was well satisfied with the work of the young Fowler and asked him to stay on as a research fellow in nuclear physics. Three years later, Fowler began his climb up the academic ladder with an appointment as assistant professor at Cal Tech and then, in 1942, with a promotion to associate professor. At this point, World War II interrupted the normal research taking place at Cal Tech. Lauritsen and Fowler were assigned to work in Washington, D.C., on the development of proximity fuses for bombs, shells, and rockets. Later in the war, Fowler became involved in the development of the atomic bomb. For his wartime contributions, Fowler was given the U.S. Government Medal for Merit in 1948.

Explains the Origins of the Elements

Scientists have long been intrigued by the question of how the chemical elements are formed in the universe. A major revelation took place in 1939 when physicist **Hans Albrecht Bethe** at Cornell University and **Carl F. Von Weizsäcker** at the University of Berlin proposed a mechanism by which hydrogen is converted into helium in a star. The CN cycle (for the carbon and nitrogen involved in the process) not only explained the conversion of hydrogen to helium, but also showed how energy is released in the process.

The question remained, however, as to how elements heavier than helium can burn, and thus be formed in a star. At one point, **George Gamow** had suggested a simple and reasonable explanation. The capture of a neutron by one atom could result in the formation of a new atom one atomic number greater than the original. But the problem with Gamow's hypothesis was that it could not be confirmed experimentally. Researchers at Kellogg had demonstrated that no stable mass of 5 or 8 could exist. With these gaps, Gamow's theory became untenable.

By the early 1950s, Fowler had become convinced that the production of heavier elements can take place through the fusion of helium atoms. By 1954, the details of that process were becoming clear. Fowler spent the 1954–55 academic year at Cambridge University working with the eminent astrophysicist **Fred Hoyle** and the husband and wife team of **Geoffrey Burbidge** and **Margaret Burbidge**. Together the four researchers identified a process by which helium can be converted to carbon, carbon to iron, and eventually iron to the heavier elements (by neutron capture).

In 1975, Fowler, Hoyle, and the Burbridges published one of the classic papers of modern science, "Synthesis of the Elements in Stars," which often referred to the authors' initials as B_2FH. The ideas presented in the paper were the basis for the Nobel Prize committee's decision to award a share of the 1983 physics prize (along with **Subrahmanyan Chandrasekhar**) to Fowler.

The mechanisms by which elements are formed in the universe continued to dominate Fowler's research agenda for another two decades. Working often with Hoyle, he developed hypotheses about the formation of elements in bodies other than stars, such as the recently discovered radio galaxies. He also became increasingly interested in the study of neutrinos and other astronomical phenomena.

Fowler has long been in great demand as a lecturer and visiting scholar. He has been a Fulbright lecturer and Guggenheim Fellow at the University of Cambridge twice, in 1954–55 and again in 1961–62, and also at St. John's College in the latter visit, and has lectured at the University of Washington, the Massachusetts Institute of Technology, and the Institute of Theoretical Astronomy at Cambridge. He has received honorary doctorates from the University of Chicago, Ohio State University, Denison University, Arizona State University, the University of Liège, and the Observatorie de Paris.

Fowler was married to the former Ardiane Foy Olmsted on August 24, 1940. They have two daughters, Mary Emily and Martha Summers. Fowler's colleague Bethe, writing in *Science,* described him as "full of humor and cheerfulness," and noted that Fowler's most outstanding characteristic is that "he loves people."

SELECTED WRITINGS BY FOWLER:

Books

(With Fred Hoyle) *Nucleosynthesis in Massive Stars and Supernovae,* University of Chicago Press, 1965.

Nuclear Astrophysics, American Philosophical Society, 1967.

Periodicals

(With Fred Hoyle and Geoffrey and Margaret Burbridge) "Synthesis of the Elements in Stars," *Review of Modern Physics,* Volume 92, 1957, pp. 547–650.

SOURCES:

Books

McGraw-Hill Modern Scientists and Engineers, Volume 10, McGraw-Hill, 1980, pp. 388–390.

Periodicals

Bethe, Hans. A., "The 1983 Nobel Prize in Physics," *Science,* November 25, 1983, pp. 881–883.

"Nobel Prize to Chandrasekhar and Fowler for Astrophysics," *Physics Today,* January, 1984, pp. 17–20.

—*Sketch by David E. Newton*

Sidney W. Fox
1912-
American biochemist

The biochemist Sidney W. Fox is best known for his research on thermal polymerization. Polymerization is a chemical process by which molecules of different elements are combined into more complex structures. Fox has studied such polymerization processes under conditions similar to those thought to have reigned on earth before the advent of life. His work, though highly controversial, may shed light on the chemistry of the origins of life.

Sidney Walter Fox was born in Los Angeles, California, on March 24, 1912, to Jacob and Louise (Burmon) Fox. His lifetime of interest in the principles of life began at the age of twelve, reading biology texts in San Diego's Balboa Park, where he spent his summers with his father. It was this early exposure, he would later recall, that inspired him to take up the study of chemistry. He enrolled at the University of Southern California at Los Angeles and received a bachelor's degree in 1933. Following his graduation, Fox traveled to New York to work in the laboratory of Max Bergmann—one of the world's leading authorities in the new field of biochemistry—at the Rockefeller Institute.

In 1935, Fox returned to California to continue his education with the thermodynamics expert Hugh M. Huffman, then at the California Institute of Technology. Fox presented his Ph.D. thesis on thermal data in the urea cycle in 1940. He then worked briefly at Cutter Labs and as a researcher at the University of Michigan in 1941, before again returning to California to take a position at F. E. Booth & Co., to work on a process of extracting vitamin A from shark's oil. When that project ended in 1943, Fox returned to pure research while teaching protein chemistry at Iowa State College, where he remained until 1955. First at Iowa State's Institute for Atomic Research and later at the university's Agricultural Experimental Station, studying the genetics of corn, Fox pursued research that would gradually lead him into the study of life's origins. He became head of the Agricultural Station in 1949.

The Primordial Soup

By this time, the theories of Russian chemist **Aleksandr Ivanovich Oparin** on the chemistry of the origins of life were beginning to replace the theory of spontaneous generation. Oparin pictured an inhospitable early Earth. Its air and young seas composed primarily of ammonia and such carbon-containing (organic) compounds as methane, it would nevertheless be the perfect crucible for the origin of life. Still, while all the separate components abounded, there would be little tendency for them to combine, forming the more complex molecules of living matter. The difficulty Oparin faced was to find the source of energy needed to drive the reactions that would turn this primordial soup into the building blocks of life.

In 1953, **Stanley Lloyd Miller**, then a graduate student at the University of Chicago, tested Oparin's theory. In a sealed flask, he combined the elements Oparin had suggested and then supplied what he considered a reasonable form of energy, electricity, as might have come from lightning striking the ancient seas. What formed was a variety of the most critical organic particles in life today in a thick, organic ooze coating the vessel's walls. Although the experiment was a success of sorts, the organic compounds thus created were highly unstable. How could these fragile structures survive in such a harsh climate long enough to evolve into life's vastly complex organic systems?

In the early 1950s, Fox began his research struggling with these issues. He found that when nearly dry mixtures of pre-organic chemicals were heated, long protein-like molecules called polymers were readily formed. He also noted that if these polymers were then exposed to water—as could happen in a case as simple as a rain shower washing a small volcanic pool—they themselves would break down into the very amino acids that are the building blocks of proteins.

In testing his theory, Fox, almost by accident, hit upon an astounding finding, providing not only a possible solution to the problem of stability but also perhaps offering an explanation of how cells could have arisen. While washing out test tubes in which amino acids had been cooked, a milky residue formed. At first Fox couldn't account for the layer, but, while on a lecture tour in 1959, an idea came to him. Telephoning his lab assistant, Jean Kendrick, he suggested she look for something resembling bacteria. She did find something similar. A large number of small bubbles, uniform in size, that Fox would come to call proteinoid microspheres, filled the samples. Oparin had earlier proposed that cell-like structures might have been the mechanism early life employed to concentrate organic materials. He had noted that certain chemicals form clumps when surrounded by water and showed that these structures, which he called coacervate droplets, mimicked some of the functions of living cells.

The crucial difference that separated Fox's work from Oparin's was its starting point. While Oparin began with assumptions he could not prove, including the presence of an already organic molecule, methane, in the original matrix, Fox needed to assume little. Fox stressed that he chose conditions for his experiments that were similar to what would actually have existed at the time of primordial synthesis. His experiments had revealed fundamental, empirical, and repeatable evidence that early precursors to cells may have formed as a natural by-product of thermal polymerization. The next phase was to discover what properties these proto-cells exhibited.

The Universal Ancestor

Assuming the directorship of Florida State University's Oceanographic Institute in 1955, Fox began the process of identifying the properties of the microspheres. Avoiding all presuppositions as to what life must have been like when it began, he could not easily narrow the search. The work, laborious and time consuming, eventually uncovered more than twenty unique properties that were essential aspects of life.

Early on Fox noted that the microspheres had a semi-permeable double membrane that allowed only certain materials to enter while holding others outside. This may have allowed the cells to accumulate just the right mixture of chemicals to develop life's increasingly complex systems. And they proved to be remarkably stable, some remaining intact for up to six years. The stability combined with semi-permeability led to another interesting possibility. If a microsphere survived long enough, using its membrane to grow in size, and, instead of bursting like a soap bubble, divided into two new microspheres both with a similar mix inside, these two new microspheres might in turn grow and divide. In other words, they may have developed an early form of reproduction, one of life's universal attributes. Fox did indeed note that his microspheres were capable of this behavior, budding like yeast. And, while this form of reproduction was primitive in relation to today's cellular reproduction, which makes use of DNA, it may have been just such a pathway that led to the development of DNA itself. Working with Allen Vegotsky at Florida State and Joseph Johnson of the Massachusetts Institute of Technology, Fox was able to provide some experimental evidence of this. The team noted that a key intermediate of modern nucleic acid, ureidosuccinic acid, was formed under conditions no more remarkable than those found at hot springs in America's national parks.

Speaking to the American Association for the Advancement of Science during a 1959 plenary session in Chicago, Fox discussed his theory of the origins of life. Publicity from the talk caught the eye of one of the government's newest and best funded research programs, the National Aeronautics and Space Administration (NASA). The public's fascination with NASA helped change the attitude then prevalent toward research into the origin of life, bringing studies once considered too radical to even be considered into the mainstream. In 1961, NASA created the Institute for Space Biosciences with Fox as director. With ample resources, Fox's investigation of the properties of the microspheres widened.

In 1963 Fox moved to the University of Miami, where he would remain until 1989, continuing to investigate the microspheres. While there he took up an entirely new direction in his research, studying a property of the microspheres that he daringly speculated might be a precursor of mental functioning. Having long known the microspheres to be composed of a double membrane, it was not until Fox exposed them to sunlight that he discovered their electrical properties. They exhibited an electrical gradient remarkably similar to that of neurons, or brain cells. Working with Aristotel Pappelis at SIUC, he discovered that the bubbles could even react to the external environment by adapting their charges. This behavior was so similar to the function of the neuron that it led him to announce in 1991 that the "mind is there from the very beginning—not the mind in the sense we take it but rather the fundamental principle that separates organic matter—and brain tissue in particular—from all other matter, the ability to discriminate."

In August 1993, Fox joined the faculty at the University of South Alabama as distinguished research scientist, where he continues his research at the Coastal Research and Development Institute. A member of many national and international organizations, Fox has three sons: Jack Lawrence, Ronald Forrest, and Thomas Oren. He has been the recipient of many honors and awards, including the Honors Medal and a citation as Outstanding Scientist of Florida, given by the Florida Academy of Science in 1968; the Texas Christian University's Distinguished Scientist of the Year Award (1968); and the Iddles Award (1973).

SELECTED WRITINGS BY FOX:

Books

(Editor with K. Dose, G. A. Deborin and T. E. Pavlovskaya) *The Origins of Life and Evolutionary Biochemistry,* Plenum Press, 1974.

The Emergence of Life: Darwinian Evolution from the Inside, Basic Books, 1988.

Periodicals

"Evolution of Protein Molecules and Thermal Synthesis of Biochemical Substances," *American Scientist,* Volume 44, 1956, pp. 347–59.

"Origin of Life," *Science,* February 1958, pp. 346–47.

"How Did Life Begin?" *Science,* July 1960, pp. 200–08.

"Origins of Biological Information and the Genetic Code," *Molecular & Cellular Biochemistry,* April 1974, pp. 129–42.

SOURCES:

Books

Biological Science, edited by W. T. Keeton and J. L. Gould, Norton, 1986, pp. 998–1006.

Other

Fox, Sidney W., interviews with Nicholas S. Williamson, September-October 1993.

—*Sketch by Nicholas S. Williamson*

Abraham Adolf Fraenkel
1891-1965
German-born Israeli mathematician

Abraham Adolf Fraenkel was a set theorist who participated in the development of modern logic. He is best known for his work on Ernst Zermelo's set theory and the introduction of "Urelements," which **Wolfgang Pauli** used to formulate the exclusion principle in quantum physics. Fraenkel's prose was clear and easy to read, and the accessibility of his writings only added to his influence. He began teaching in Jerusalem on sabbatical in 1929 and left Germany permanently in 1933, after Adolph Hitler was elected chancellor. He spent the rest of his life in Israel.

Born in Munich on February 17, 1891, Fraenkel's orthodox Jewish heritage had a strong influence on him from his youngest days. His great-grandfather, B. H. Auerbach-Halberstadt, had been widely known for his rabbinical teachings, and Fraenkel's parents, Sigmund and Charlotte (Neuburger) Fraenkel, made sure that the young boy was reading Hebrew by the age of five. Brought up in a literate family that placed such a strong emphasis on education, Fraenkel advanced quickly in his studies; he attended the universities of Munich, Marburg, and Berlin, and he earned his doctorate from the University of Breslau in 1914 at the age of twenty-three. During World War I, Fraenkel served as a sergeant in the German medical corps, also working with the meteorological service. Beginning in 1916, he accepted a position as privatdocent, an unsalaried lecturer at the University of Marburg, where he began his most important research. He married Malkah Wilhemina Prins on March 28, 1920; they would have four children.

Provides Crucial Definitions for Set Theory

Fraenkel had long been interested in the work of Ernst Zermelo, who in the early years of the century had published his innovative and controversial work on set theory. Specifically, Zermelo had conjectured that, given any set of numbers, a single element could be selected and that definite properties of that element could be determined; this was known as the axiom of choice, but the problem was that Zermelo offered little proof for much of his theory, insisting that mathematics could only progress if certain axioms were simply accepted. This radical notion was unacceptable to many of those working in mathematics. Though some, like **Jacques Hadamard**, agreed to accept Zermelo's theory until a better way could be found, **Jules Henri Poincaré** and other mathematicians fought adamantly against it.

Instead of accepting or rejecting the theory outright, Fraenkel searched for ways to put Zermelo's work on a firmer foundation. Zermelo's theory already worked well in the case of finite sets. But for infinite sets, his assumptions were more questionable. What Fraenkel did was substitute a notion of function for Zermelo's idea of determining a definite property of an item in a set. By doing so, he not only clarified much of Zermelo's set theory but rid the theory of its dependence on the axiom of choice, which had been one of the most controversial elements of the work.

Fraenkel's findings on set theory appeared initially in two separate works: a popular 1919 introductory textbook and a 1922 research article determining the independence of the axiom of choice. This latter work included as part of the proof a newly-defined term, Ur-elements—infinite and distinct pairs of objects which do not in themselves define a set. Although some mathematicians at the time questioned the validity of these Ur-elements, the physicist **Wolfgang Pauli** used them in his proof of the exclusion principle just three years later.

With these investigations, Fraenkel was propelled to the forefront of set-theory research. Over the course of the next several years, he published numerous articles on the subject while continuing to teach. He had been promoted to assistant professor at the University of Marburg in 1922, and in 1928 he accepted a full professorship at the University of Kiel. Although grateful for his position at Kiel, Fraenkel took a leave of absence in 1929 to become a visiting professor at the Hebrew University in Jerusalem. He taught at the Hebrew University for two years, but after a disagreement with the administration there he returned to Kiel.

When Fraenkel returned to Germany in 1931, the country was troubled. Racked by a brutal economic depression and the punishing conditions inflicted by the Treaty of Versailles, the country had become increasingly intolerant. Although Fraenkel's position at Kiel seemed assured, he could not ignore the growing power of the Nazi party. In January of 1933, Adolf Hitler became chancellor, and a month later Fraenkel and his family left Germany. They went to Amsterdam, and after watching events unfold from there for two months, Fraenkel decided that the situation in his native country would not soon improve. He sent in his resignation to the University of Kiel in April of 1933, and the Hebrew University welcomed him back as a full professor despite their earlier disagreement. Fraenkel would never again live in Germany.

The experience of having to leave his homeland because of his religion marked Fraenkel for the rest of his life. Although he continued to publish texts on set theory over the course of his career, the focus of his research shifted. He became increasingly interested in the study of modern logic and the specific contributions Jewish scientists and mathematicians had made to their fields. Fraenkel had begun his work as a historian of Jewish mathematicians in 1930 and 1932, when he had written two long articles on the career of **Georg Cantor**, the founder of set theory, who was half Jewish. Cantor was then of interest to Fraenkel more due to the nature of his research than his ethnic background, however, and it was not until after he settled permanently into his position at the Hebrew University that he began a wider investigation of Jewish mathematicians and scientists. In the field of logic, Fraenkel investigated the natural numbers, describing them in terms of modern ideas of logic and reasoning. While he underscored the need for continuity in consideration of the number line, he was also interested in opposing arguments. After a discussion with **Albert Einstein**, who suggested the possibility that the atomistic conception of the number line might one day take precedence over continuity in mathematics, Fraenkel wrote an article explaining these views of the intuitionists, as they were known. He remained ultimately unconvinced, however, primarily because he considered mathematical continuity necessary to the foundation of modern calculus.

In 1958, Fraenkel published his last major work, *Foundations of Set Theory,* a textbook which served to summarize his work in this field. A year later, he retired from his teaching position at the Hebrew University. In celebration of his seventieth birthday in 1961, several members of the mathematical community assembled a collection of essays and research articles related to Fraenkel's work. Mathematicians from many countries contributed to the collection, *Essays on the Foundation of Mathematics,* but Fraenkel never saw it in its final form. He died in Jerusalem on October 15, 1965, just months before the book's publication.

SELECTED WRITINGS BY FRAENKEL:

Books

Abstract Set Theory, North-Holland, 1953.

Integers and the Theory of Numbers, Scripta Mathematica, 1955.
Foundations of Set Theory, North-Holland, 1958.
Extension of the Number Concept, Scripta Mathematica, 1964.

Periodicals

"Recent Controversies about the Foundations of Mathematics," *Scripta Mathematica,* Volume 13, 1947, pp. 17–36.
"The Intuitionistic Revolution in Mathematics and Logic," *Bulletin of the Research Council of Israel,* Volume 3, 1954, pp. 283–289.
"Jewish Mathematics and Astronomy," *Scripta Mathematica,* Volume 25, 1960, pp. 33–47.

SOURCES:

Books

Biographical Encyclopedia of the World, Institute for Research in Biography, 1940, p. 201.
Gillespie, Charles Coulson, editor, *Dictionary of Scientific Biography,* Volume 5, Scribner, 1972, pp. 107–109.
Hayden, Seymour and John F. Kennison, *Zermelo-Fraenkel Set Theory,* C. E. Merrill, 1968.
Pinl, Max, and Lux Furtmüller, *Mathematicians Under Hitler,* Secker and Warberg, 1973, pp. 161–162.
Temple, George, *100 Years of Mathematics,* Springer-Verlag, 1981, pp. 263–264.

—Sketch by Karen Sands

Heinz Fraenkel-Conrat
1910-
German-born American biochemist

Heinz Fraenkel-Conrat is an internationally known German-born biochemist who became a naturalized citizen of the United States. The majority of his research, and the studies for which he is best known, were conducted at the University of Berkeley, California. Fraenkel-Conrat's research helped advance the study of viruses. He determined that under certain conditions, a virus could be separated into its component parts. These studies revealed both the virus's infective agent and its method of replication. Fraenkel-Conrat's research inspired numerous studies of viruses, which proved useful in the explanation of molecular biological processes such as replication and mutation.

Heinz Ludwig Fraenkel-Conrat was born July 29, 1910, in Breslau, Germany—now Wroclaw, Poland—to Ludwig Fraenkel, a gynecologist who was famous for his discoveries concerning mammalian ovulation, and Lili Conrat Fraenkel. Fraenkel-Conrat was educated at schools in Munich, Vienna, Geneva, and at the University of Breslau, the latter from which he received his M.D. in 1933. He left Germany when Adolf Hitler and his Nazi party came into power. In 1936, Fraenkel-Conrat obtained his Ph.D. in biochemistry from the University of Edinburgh in Scotland, for studies on ergot alkaloids and thiamine. Alter this, he came to the United States and studied a type of enzyme at the Rockefeller Institute for Medical Research in New York. He unexpectedly discovered that enzymes formed peptide bonds, which, in turn, form the building blocks of proteins. Fraenkel-Conrat next joined his brother-in-law, K. H. Slotta, as a research associate at the Instituto Butantan at Sao Paulo, Brazil, where he began to study the components of snake venoms. The work resulted in the isolation of a protein from rattlesnake venom that acted as a neurotoxic and also destroyed red blood cells.

Fraenkel-Conrat left Brazil and returned to the United States, becoming a naturalized citizen in 1941. He became a member of the H. M. Evans Institute of Experimental Biology at the Berkeley Campus of the University of California in 1938. For more than ten years, his research involved purifying hormones, particularly follicle-stimulating hormones, and studying how structural changes effected hormonal activity. Some of this work was carried out at the Western Regional Research Laboratory of the U.S. Department of Agriculture, where he worked from 1938 to 1942, first as an associate chemist and then later as a chemist. His work at this time also focused on modifying protein groups. Fraenkel-Conrat and his coworkers documented how modifying a protein's structure changed its function. Several of their techniques were later used by others studying proteins.

Examines Viral Make-up and Properties of RNA

Fraenkel-Conrat joined the virus laboratory of the University of California, Berkeley, in 1952. In 1960, using techniques similar to those in his protein work, he and his collaborators were able to determine the complete amino acid sequence—consisting of 158 amino acid residues—of the tobacco mosaic virus, making it the biggest protein of known structure at the time. Several years before Fraenkel-Conrat's virus research, scientists had determined that viruses contained a protein shell and nucleic acid; the latter was believed to carry the virus's genetic information.

From his studies of protein structure, Fraenkel-Conrat began further studies with the tobacco mosaic virus. He developed techniques that enabled him to gently separate the protein material from the nucleic acid, in the form of ribonucleic acid (RNA), without seriously damaging either part. He then recombined the protein and nucleic acid. If both molecules were intact, the particles rejoined and were once more infective.

Fraenkel-Conrat's subsequent research proved to be his most distinguished work. Continuing his experiments, he showed that when the two substances were separated, the protein coat had no infective properties but the ribonucleic acid still was somewhat infective. Subsequent studies showed that the protein shell was needed to get the nucleic acid, which carried the virus's genetic material, into a host cell. Once inside the cell, the nucleic acid took over the host cell's own genetic material, deoxyribonucleic acid (DNA), and began reproducing itself, making not only more infective nucleic acid but compatible protein coatings as well. This study provided definitive proof that RNA can act like DNA as the genetic blueprint for cell reproduction. Fraenkel-Conrat continued to study RNA and, along with B. Singer and other colleagues, developed new methods for stabilizing the acid for better structural studies.

From 1952 until 1958, Fraenkel-Conrat was a professor of virology at the University of California, Berkeley; he later became a professor of molecular biology. In 1968, his research emphasis concentrated on how RNA was translated in viruses and how viruses replicated this material. Since 1982, when he retired, he has been emeritus professor of molecular biology. For his contributions to the field of molecular biology, he was honored by a Lasker Award and received the first California Scientist of the Year Award in 1958. He was also a member of the National Academy of Sciences. After retiring, his interests remained with the field of virology and he wrote a number of virology texts. For close to ten years, Fraenkel-Conrat was also one of the editors of, and a contributor to, the journal *Comprehensive Virology,* starting in 1973.

Fraenkel-Conrat married Jane Operman on July 15, 1938. They had two children, Richard and Charles. His second marriage, on June 1, 1964, was to Beatrice Brandon Singer, who worked with him in his laboratory. He made his retirement home in California, where he occasionally involved himself in research.

SELECTED WRITINGS BY FRAENKEL-CONRAT:

Books

Design and Function at the Threshold of Life: The Viruses, Academic Press, 1962.

(With Paul C. Kimball and Jay A. Levy) *Virology,* 2nd edition, Prentice-Hall, 1988.

Periodicals

(With Robley C. Williams) "Reconstitution of Tobacco Mosaic Virus from Its Inactive Protein and Nucleic Acid," *Proceedings of the National Academy of Sciences,* October, 1955, pp. 690–98.

"Rebuilding a Virus," *Scientific American,* June, 1956, pp. 42–47.

"Virus Reconstitution and the Proof of the Existence of Genomic RNA," *Bioessays,* July, 1990, pp. 351–52.

SOURCES:

Books

McGraw-Hill Modern Scientists and Engineers, McGraw-Hill, 1980, pp. 390–91.

—*Sketch by Barbara J. Proujan*

James Franck
1882-1964
German-born American physicist

James Franck was a physicist whose experimental work with atoms and electrons proved **Niels Bohr**'s theory that atoms are quantized—that they transmit and absorb energy in discrete quantities or packages. Along with collaborator **Gustav Hertz**, he was awarded the 1925 Nobel Prize in physics. Franck was also known for his outspoken opposition to the use of the atomic bomb, which he helped develop during World War II.

Franck was born in Hamburg, Germany, on August 26, 1882, to Jacob Franck, a German Jewish banker, and Rebecka Nachum Drucker. Although Jacob Franck was deeply religious—he observed Jewish holidays with fasting and chanting—his spiritual devotion did not, on the whole, pass on to James, who would later declare science and nature as his true love and religion. He attended school at the Wilhelm Gymnasium in Hamburg before enrolling at the University of Heidelberg. Franck's father wanted him to study law and economics with the hope that his son would take over the family business. Out of a sense of duty, Franck complied, but after attending law lec-

James Franck

tures for a short time, he determined to follow his own path and enrolled in the faculty of chemistry.

Heidelberg was where Franck met **Max Born,** the German physicist with whom he formed his closest friendship. After two terms studying chemistry, Franck enrolled in the doctoral program at the University of Berlin. Under the influence of its physics professor, **Emil Warburg**, he became interested in physics and switched fields. He began a study to determine the mobility of ions using a method invented by Cambridge physicist **Ernest Rutherford**.

After graduating with a D.Phil. in 1906, Franck continued to pursue the same lines of research, exploring the forces between electrons and atoms at the physics faculty of the University of Frankfurt-on-Maïn. He returned to Berlin in 1908 to become an assistant to Professor Heinrich Rubens. There, Franck began collaborating with the German physicist Gustav Hertz on a series of experiments that would provide direct proof of Bohr's theoretical model of atomic structure, demonstrate the quantized energy transfer from kinetic, or moving, energy to light energy, and establish both of their reputations.

Bohr had postulated that an atom's nucleus, or core, is surrounded by "orbits" of negatively charged electrons. Bohr theorized that these orbits revolve around the nucleus at set distances known as shells. The number of electrons and, thus, the number of shells vary according to the type of atom. Atoms ranking high on the periodic table of elements contain more electrons than simple elements such as hydrogen, which has just one proton and one electron. These extra electrons are contained in extra shells, according to a definite pattern. The first shell contains two electrons; the second, eight; the third, eighteen; the fourth; thirty-two; and fifth, fifty, and so on. As soon as the first shell is full, electrons begin to fill up the second shell, then the third, up to the last shell.

In their natural, unexcited state, the electrons try to stay as close to the nucleus as possible, that is, in an inner shell. Bohr suggested that electrons would jump from one shell to another if energy were applied to them. The distance they would jump would depend on the amount of energy supplied; when the energy source were withdrawn, they would fall back to their original position. The energy emitted by electrons falling back in toward the nucleus would be exactly equivalent to that absorbed by them when jumping to an outer shell. Most importantly, atoms receiving energy could not absorb just any amount but only the specific amount they would need to make a leap. Thus, Bohr spoke of the atom as being "quantized."

Experimentally Proves Bohr's Theory of the Quantum Atom

Franck and Hertz did not set out to prove Bohr's theory. In fact, they were not even familiar with his work at the time they were carrying out their experiments. Rather, they were interested in measuring the energy needed to ionize atoms of mercury. To this end, they bombarded atoms of mercury vapor with electrons moving at controlled speeds. Below a certain speed, the electrons would bounce off the atoms with perfect elasticity, indicating that the electrons did not possess sufficient energy to ionize the mercury atom, that is, to transfer enough energy to the mercury to enable *its* electrons to jump from one atomic shell into another. Above a certain speed, Franck and Hertz discovered that resonance occurred. At this point, energy was transferred from the electrons to the atoms, causing the mercury gas to glow. They found that energy had been transferred from the electrons to the atoms in discrete amounts. The energy value of the light emitted from the ionized atoms was equivalent to the energy given to them by the electrons. This experiment proved that the quantized energy had changed from the kinetic energy of the moving electrons to the electromagnetic energy given off by the glowing mercury. It also provided direct experimental evidence for Bohr's theory of the quantized atom, a crucial step in the development of twentieth-century physics.

This experiment was also significant because it led to the realization that the light spectrum of an atom holds the key to its atomic structure. The discontinuous bands of light in an atomic spectrum, each representing a particular energy level, correspond to the range of possible jumps that an excited electron could make as it drops from the outer shells, where the absorption of energy had sent it, back to its original inner shell.

Decorated with Iron Cross for War Service

Franck's work was unexpectedly interrupted with the outbreak of the First World War. He signed up and became an officer. He served through 1918, working with a group of physicists who prepared and later directed chemical warfare. Franck received the Iron Cross for his valor; he also received a serious leg injury, which almost claimed his life. Returning to academia in 1918, he was named as the head of the physics division at the Kaiser Wilhelm Institute for Physical Chemistry, later renamed the Max Planck Institute. There, Franck pursued his work on electron impact measurements. It was also at the institute that he met Niels Bohr, with whom he developed a lasting friendship. Franck always regarded Bohr as a physicist second to none and consulted him regularly. "I never felt . . . such hero worship as [I did] to[ward] Bohr," he said in an interview excerpted in *Redirecting Science: Niels Bohr, Philanthropy, and the Rise of Nuclear Physics.*

In 1920, with the influence of Born, Franck was appointed professor and director of the Second Physical Institute of the University of Göttingen. The friendship between Franck and Born blossomed into a close working relationship, with Franck the experimenter complementing Born the theorist. During their twelve years at Göttingen, the pair used one another as sounding boards for their ideas, discoveries, and publications, although they collaborated on only a few joint papers. The only contention between them was Franck's habit of holding frequent consultations with Bohr, a practice that tended to slow down their work. More than sixty letters between Franck and Born have survived from the 1920s.

In the spring of 1921, at Bohr's invitation, Franck paid a visit to Copenhagen in time for the March opening of Bohr's Institute of Theoretical Physics. By now, his reputation preceded him and his visit made front page news in Denmark. His meeting with the Swedish physicist Oskar Klein and Norwegian Svein Rosseland convinced him to continue his experimental work on Bohr's theories.

Back at the University of Göttingen a couple of months later, Franck concentrated on building a research facility of international repute. He afforded his students considerable academic freedom. Scientific discussions between teacher and pupils would occur as often during a walk or bicycle ride as in the laboratory. The standards for admission to his school were extremely high but once accepted, a student was assured of his unwavering support and friendship, both professionally and personally.

Franck continued to investigate collisions between atoms, the formation and disassociation of molecules, fluorescence, and chemical processes. In 1925, building on three previously unconnected theories, he published a paper dealing with the elementary processes of photochemical reactions. In it he set out the connection between electron transition and the motion of nuclei, and described a general rule for vibrational energy distribution. This rule was later expressed by the American physicist Edward U. Condon in terms of quantum mechanics (a mathematical interpretation of particle structures and interactions) and became known as the Franck-Condon principle, which is applied to a large number of chemical and spectroscopic phenomena. In 1926 Franck published a book summarizing his work in this area.

Also in 1926, Franck traveled to Sweden to accept the 1925 Nobel Prize in physics, awarded jointly to him and Hertz for their experiments proving Bohr's atomic theory. He returned to Göttingen to begin his next project, the study of photosynthesis, but had no sooner begun his experiments when Adolf Hitler's arrival on the German political stage changed his life.

Resigns from Göttingen to Protest Anti-Semitism

When Hitler's anti-Semitic Nazi regime took control of Germany, a new law was declared that barred Jews from the civil service, excepting those who had served in the First World War. Although Franck's position was secure, he could not in good conscience continue to work for a regime dedicated to racism, so on April 17, 1933, he sent letters to the minister of education and to the rector of the university, announcing his resignation and decrying the government's discriminatory policy. Hoping to remain in Germany, Franck searched for another position. Two possibilities presented themselves, one being the chair of physics at the University of Berlin, which would shortly be open. Though it was a position Franck would have coveted under other circumstances, it would have meant working for the government. The other possibility was the directorship of the Kaiser Wilhelm Institute for Physical Chemistry, a position that retiring director **Fritz Haber** hoped Franck would accept. Internal problems in the institute, however, prevented Franck from assuming this post as well. Franck decided to accept a visiting lectureship at the Johns Hopkins University in America. After the three month period of that position he returned to Göttingen to contemplate his uncertain future. Tentative offers were made from universities in the United States, but they did not promise the permanency Franck was seeking. He decided to accept an offer from Bohr for a year's work at his Institute of Theoretical Physics.

Franck arrived in Copenhagen in April 1934, and, with his assistant Hilde Levi, set to studying the fluorescence of green plants, an extension of his previous work studying energy exchanges in complex molecular systems. Under Bohr's direction, he also began administering experimental nuclear research at the Institute. He was frustrated by poor facilities and slow coworkers and, as stated in *Redirecting Science,* wrote of this period: "My nuclear physics exhausts itself at present in work which is just about to be completed when someone else publishes it in *Nature.*" Working with a master theorist such as Bohr also proved difficult for Franck. "Bohr's genius was so superior. And one cannot help that one would get so strong inferiority complexes in the presence of such a genius that one becomes sterile," he later said in an interview quoted in *Redirecting Science.* After being used to having his own laboratory and students, it was hard for Franck to get used to working in Bohr's shadow.

Emigrates to United States

The combination of numerous frustrations spurred Franck to accept an offer to settle in the United States. In late 1935, he became a professor at Johns Hopkins University, where he spent three years before moving to the University of Chicago to fill its chair of physical chemistry. With the help of the Samuel Fels Fund, a laboratory dedicated to research into photosynthesis was built, which Franck directed until his retirement in 1949, though he continued to work there for many years subsequently. He became an American citizen in the early 1940s.

When the Second World War broke out, Franck played a leading role in the Manhattan Project, the American government-sponsored atomic bomb project. Like the other German scientists on the team, he was driven by a desire to beat Hitler to the production of a nuclear weapon. But he firmly believed that the bomb should be used as a mode of deterrence, not as a means of aggression. When the U.S. finally developed the bomb and subsequently deployed it against the Japanese, Franck was a harsh critic.

In 1942, a crisis struck in Franck's private life with the death of his wife, Ingrid Josephson, who had been sick for many years. He coped with the loss by immersing himself in his work. He chaired a committee of scientists charged with exploring the social and political implications of detonating an atom bomb. That committee's findings, titled the Franck Report, was submitted to the U.S. Secretary of War, Henry Stimson, in 1945, and warned the United States Government against the use of the bomb as a military weapon. The report also speculated on the dangers of embarking upon an arms race and also urged the U.S. to restrict nuclear testing to areas where human life would not be endangered. The Franck Report has been seen as a testament to Franck's integrity, conviction, and sense of scientific responsibility.

With the end of the war, Franck returned to his post at the University of Chicago where he continued his work with photosynthesis. He was particularly curious as to how plants are able to transform visible light into a form of energy that they use for sustenance and growth. He began experiments on the emanation of electromagnetic radiation of chlorophyll, a key ingredient in the photosynthesis process. Happy to be back at work, Franck experienced joy in his personal life as well. In 1946, he married Hertha Sponer, a professor of physics at Duke University in North Carolina, whom Franck knew from Göttingen and Berlin. They had two daughters, Dagmar and Elizabeth.

Franck was honored with numerous awards during his long career. In addition to the Nobel Prize, he was awarded the highest honor of the German Physical Society, the Max Planck Medal in 1953. Two years later, he received the Rumford Medal of the American Academy of Arts and Sciences. He became a foreign member of the Royal Society of London in 1964 and a member of the U.S. National Academy of Sciences.

During a visit in 1964 to Göttingen, the city where he had spent his most productive years and which had made him an honorary citizen in 1953, Franck died suddenly on May 21. He was eighty-three. He was remembered by his colleagues as a brilliant experimentalist, a dedicated scientist, and a kind and generous man.

SELECTED WRITINGS BY FRANCK:

Books

(With P. Jordan) *Anregung von Quantensprungen durch Stosse,* J. Springer, 1926.

Photosynthesis in Plants, Iowa State College Press, 1949.

SOURCES:

Books

Aaserud, Finn, *Redirecting Science: Niels Bohr, Philanthropy and the Rise of Nuclear Physics,* Cambridge University Press, 1990.

Biographical Memoirs of the Royal Society, Volume 11, Royal Society (London), 1965, pp. 53–74.

Born, Max, *My Life: Recollections of a Nobel Laureate,* Scribner's, 1975.

Cline, Barbara Lovett, *Men Who Made a New Physics,* University of Chicago Press, 1987, p. 108.

Levitan, Tina, *The Laureates: Jewish Winners of the Nobel Prize,* Twayne, 1960, p. 74.

Segre, Emilo, *From X-rays to Quarks,* W. H. Freeman and Co., 1980, p. 137.

Weber, Robert L., *Pioneers of Science: Nobel Prize Winners in Physics,* Institute of Physics, 1980, p. 75.

Periodicals

Bulletin of the Atomic Scientists, October, 1964, pp. 16–20.

Other

Correspondence between Franck and Bohr is available on microfilm as part of the Bohr General Correspondence in the Niels Bohr Library of American Physics in New York.

"The James Franck Papers," Joseph Regenstein Library, University of Chicago.

Kuhn, Thomas S., six sessions of interviews with Franck, July, 9–14, 1962, housed at the Archive for the History of Quantum Physics, microfilm 35, section 2 (available at the American Philosophical Society, Philadelphia, and the Niels Bohr Library of the American Institute of Physics, New York).

—Sketch by Avril McDonald

Il'ya Frank
1908-1990
Russian physicist

In 1936–37 Il'ya Frank, in collaboration with Igor Tamm, developed a theoretical explanation for the optical phenomenon known as Cherenkov radiation—radiation that is emitted when a charged particle travels faster than the speed of light. For this theory, the two scientists received a number of awards, including three Stalin Prizes, an Order of Lenin, and the Vavilov Gold Medal. They also shared the 1958 Nobel Prize in physics with Pavel Cherenkov for their work on the subject.

Il'ya Mikaylovich Frank was born on October 23, 1908, in Leningrad. He was the second son of Mikhail Luydvigovic Frank, a professor of mathematics, and Yelizaveta Mikhailovna Gratsianova Frank, a physician. Frank earned his bachelor's degree in physics from Moscow State University in 1930. Frank's specialization at Moscow State University was photoluminescence of solutions—substances that emit light without an external source acting upon them. He began his career at the State Optical Institute in Leningrad (now St. Petersburg), where he undertook a study of light-induced chemical reactions. His work at this time, according to *Nobel Prize Winners,* was characterized by "procedural elegance, originality, and thorough analysis of experimental data." It resulted in his being granted a doctorate in physical and mathematical sciences in 1935.

Following his graduation, Frank was invited by S. I. Vavilov, his former teacher at Moscow State University, to become a member of the newly established **P. N. Lebedev Institute** in Moscow where he remained for the rest of his academic career. Shortly thereafter, a colleague at the Lebedev Institute, **Pavel Cherenkov** discovered an intriguing new optical phenomenon whereby the passage of gamma rays through water resulted in the formation of a blue glow. The phenomenon was eventually named Cherenkov radiation in his honor. Cherenkov was not able, however, to explain how or why the phenomenon occurred.

Faster than the Speed of Light

In 1936, in an effort to develop a theoretical explanation for Cherenkov effect, Frank initiated research with a colleague at the Institute, **Igor Tamm**. Their hypothesis centered on the movement of charged particles at velocities greater than the speed of light. Though a fundamental law of physics says that nothing can travel faster than the speed of light *in a vacuum,* it is possible for the speed of an object to be greater than the speed of light in another medium.

Frank and Tamm found that when an electron travels through a substance at a velocity greater than the speed of light, it emits energy in the form of Cherenkov radiation. The phenomenon has often been compared to a sonic boom or to the water waves generated by a sailing ship. Frank and Tamm were able to predict a number of phenomena that should accompany the release of Cherenkov radiation, all of which were soon confirmed experimentally.

Sharing the Nobel Prize

Frank and Tamm's theory was soon applied to the invention of the Cherenkov detector. The Cherenkov detector is a device made of glass or some other transparent material through which rapidly moving particles pass, which allows the resulting Cherenkov radiation to be analyzed photoelectrically. This analysis determines particle properties such as charge and velocity. Cherenkov detectors have become important devices for the study of particles produced in accelerators such as the cyclotron, a device that accelerates particles to great speeds in a circular pattern. For their work on the Cherenkov effect and its implications, Frank, Tamm, and Cherenkov shared the Nobel Prize for physics in 1958; they were the first Russians to be awarded the honor.

Apart from his research on Cherenkov radiation, which he continued as late as the 1980s, Frank was also involved in the study of nuclear phenomena for many years. During World War II, like other physicists, he researched nuclear processes related to the development of nuclear weapons and power plants. At the conclusion of the war, Frank was appointed director of the Lebedev Institute's Laboratory of the Atomic Nucleus, a position he held until his death on June 22, 1990. In 1944, Frank was concurrently appointed professor of physics at Moscow State University, where he was also made director of the Laboratory of Radioactive Radiation. After leaving the latter post in 1956, he oversaw the creation of the Laboratory of Neutron Physics at Dubna, a research center north of Moscow. The laboratory soon became an important center for the study of the neutron. Frank married Ella Abramovna Beilikhis, a historian, in 1937. Their only child, Alexander, is also a physicist employed at the Dubna neutron research center.

SELECTED WRITINGS BY FRANK:

Periodicals

(With Igor Tamm) "Coherent Visible Radiation of Fast Electrons Passing through Matter," *Compt. Rend. Acad. Sci. URSS,* 14 (1937), pp. 109–114.

"A New Type of Nuclear Reaction (The Splitting of Uranium and Thorium Nuclei under the Influence of Neutrons)," *Priroda,* 9 (1939), pp. 20–27.

SOURCES:

Books

A Biographical Encyclopedia of Scientists, Volume 1, Facts on File, 1981, pp. 280–281.

McGraw-Hill Modern Men of Science, Volume 1, McGraw, 1984, p. 182.

McGraw-Hill Modern Scientists and Engineers, Volume 1, McGraw, 1980, p. 393.

Nobel Prize Winners, H. W. Wilson, 1987, pp. 344–346.

Weber, Robert L., *Pioneers of Science: Nobel Prize Winners in Physics,* American Institute of Physics, 1980, pp. 171–172.

—Sketch by David E. Newton

Rosalind Elsie Franklin
1920-1958
English molecular biologist

The story of a great scientific discovery usually involves a combination of inspiration, hard work, and serendipity. While all these ingredients play a part in the discovery of DNA, the relationships between the four individuals who pieced together the double-helix model of the master molecule provides a subplot tainted by controversy. At the center of this quartet stands British geneticist Rosalind Franklin, who made key contributions to studies of the structures of coals and viruses, in addition to providing the scientific evidence upon which **James Watson** and **Francis Crick** based their double-helix model. Compounding the irony that Franklin died four years before Watson, Crick and **Maurice Wilkins** shared the Nobel Prize for this discovery (the Nobel Committee honors only living scientists), is James Watson's characterization of Franklin in his personal chronicle of the search for the double-helix as a competitive, stubborn, unfeminine scientist. Despite his account, Franklin has been depicted elsewhere as a devoted, hard-working scientist who suffered from her colleagues' reluctance to treat her with respect.

Franklin was born in London on July 25, 1920, to a family with long-standing Jewish roots. Her parents, who were both under the age of twenty-five when she was born, were avowed socialists. Ellis Franklin devoted his life to fulfilling his socialist ideals by teaching at the Working Men's College, while his wife, Muriel Waley Franklin, cared for their family, in which Rosalind was the second of five children and the first daughter. From an early age, Franklin excelled at science. She attended St. Paul's Girls' School, one of the few educational institutions that offered physics and chemistry to female students. A foundation scholar at the school, Rosalind decided at the age of fifteen to pursue a career in science, despite her father's exhortations to consider social work. In 1938, Franklin enrolled at Newnham College, Cambridge, the second youngest student in her class.

She graduated from Cambridge in 1941 with a high second degree and accepted a research scholarship at Newnham to study gas-phase chromatography with future Nobel Prize winner **Ronald G. W. Norrish**. Finding Norrish difficult to work with, she quit graduate school the following year to accept a job as assistant research officer with the British Coal Utilization Research Association (CURA). At CURA, she applied the physical chemistry experience she had garnered at Cambridge to studies concerning the microstructures of coals, using helium as a measurement unit. From 1942 to 1946, she authored five papers, three of them as sole author, and submitted her thesis to Cambridge. Franklin moved to Paris in 1947 to take a job with the Laboratoire Central des Services Chimiques de l'Etat. There she became fluent in French and, under the tutelage of Jacques Mering, learned the technique known as X-ray diffraction. Using this technique, Franklin was able to describe in exacting detail the structure of carbon and the changes that occur when carbon is heated to form graphite. In 1951, she left Paris for an opportunity to try her new skills on biological substances. As a member of Sir John T. Randall's Medical Research Council at King's College, London, Franklin was charged with the task of setting up an X-ray diffraction unit in the laboratory to produce diffraction pictures of DNA.

Begins Work on Structure of DNA

Eager to apply Franklin's X-ray diffraction skills to the problem of DNA structure, Randall had lured her to his lab with a Turner Newall Research Fellowship and the promise that she would be working on one of the more pressing research problems of the era—puzzling out the structure and function of DNA. When she arrived in Randall's research unit, she started working with a student, Raymond Gosling, who had been attempting to capture pictures of the elusive DNA. No stranger to the sexism rife in science at that time, Franklin made no apologies for the fact she was a woman. Maurice Wilkins, already well ensconced in the lab and working on the same problem as Franklin, took a disliking to her the first time they met. Franklin's biographers have difficulty ascertaining exactly why Wilkins and Franklin did not find common ground. Anne Sayre has suggested that the discomfort might have stemmed from the fact that Wilkins, only four years older than Franklin, may have misinterpreted her presence in his lab as a subordinate, whereas she considered herself an equal. Their mutual dislike of one another was not helped by the fact that the staff dining room was open only to the male faculty. In addition, she was the only Jew on staff. But the animosity between the two did not detract Franklin from her work, and shortly after arriving at King's, she started X-raying DNA fibres that Wilkins had obtained from a Swiss investigator.

Within a few months of joining Randall's team, Franklin gave a talk describing preliminary pictures she had obtained of the DNA as it transformed from a crystalline form, or A pattern, to a wet form, or B pattern, through an increase in relative humidity. The pictures showed, she suggested, that phosphate groups might lie outside the molecule. In the audience that November day sat James Watson, a twenty-four-year-old American who was also working on unraveling the molecular structure of DNA. Working with Francis Crick at Cambridge, Watson was even more disinclined than Wilkins to like and respect Franklin. Compounding his dislike for her was Franklin's refusal to set aside hard crystallographic data in favor of model building. Perhaps for that reason, Franklin remained publicly scornful of the notion gradually gaining adherents that perhaps the DNA molecule had a helical structure. In her unpublished reports, however, she suggested the probability that the B form of DNA exhibited such a structure, as did, perhaps, the A form. Throughout the spring of 1952, she continued studying the A form, which seemed to produce more readable X-ray photographs. This presumed legibility proved deceptive, however, because the A form does not show the double-helical structure as clearly as the B form.

Research Provides Evidence of DNA's Double-Helical Structure

In the late spring of 1952, Franklin travelled to Yugoslavia for a month, where she visited coal research labs. When she returned, she and Gosling continued to investigate the A form, to no avail. In January 1953, she started model building, but could think of no structure that would accommodate all of the evidence she had gleaned from her diffraction pictures. She ruled out single and multi-stranded helices in favor of a figure-eight configuration. Meanwhile, Watson and Crick were engaged in their own model building, hastened by the fear that the American scientist **Linus Pauling** was nearing a discovery of his own. Although Watson had not befriended Franklin in the past two years, he had grown quite close to Wilkins. In *The Double-helix,* Watson recalls how Wilkins showed him the DNA diffraction pictures Franklin had amassed (without her permission), and immediately he saw the evidence he needed to prove the helical structure of DNA. Watson returned to Crick in Cambridge and the two began writing what would become one of the best-known scientific papers of the century: "A Structure for Deoxyribose Nucleic Acid." Franklin and Gosling, who had been working on a paper of their own, quickly revised it so that it could appear along with the Watson and Crick paper. Although it is unclear how close Franklin was to a similar discovery—in part because of the misleading A form—unpublished drafts of her paper reveal that she had deduced the sugar-phosphate backbone of the helix before Watson and Crick's model was made public.

On April 25, 1953, Watson and Crick published their article in the British science journal *Nature,* along with a corroborative article by Franklin and Gosling providing essential evidence for the double-helix theory. In July of 1953, she and Gosling published another paper in *Nature* that offered "evidence for a 2-chain helix in the crystalline structure of sodium deoxyribonucleate." But Franklin's interest in the world of DNA research had already begun to wane by the spring of 1953. Despite all the excitement surrounding the double-helical structure, she had decided to move on to a lab that she hoped would offer a more congenial working environment. When she informed Randall of her intention to leave King's College for J. D. Bernal's unit at Birkbeck College, he made it clear that the DNA project was to stay in his lab. Although Gosling had been warned against further associating with Franklin, they continued to meet in private and finish their DNA work. She also continued to work on coal, but devoted the bulk of her efforts to applying crystallographic techniques to uncover the structure of the tobacco mosaic virus (TMV).

Franklin did, in fact, find the Birkbeck lab more to her liking, even though she complained to some of her friends that Bernal, a strong Marxist, attempted to foist his political views on anyone who would listen. In comparison to the situation at King's College, however, she found this bearable. She did not even complain about her lab situation. At Birkbeck she worked in a small lab on the fifth floor while her X-ray equipment sat in the basement. Because there was no elevator in the building, she made frequent treks up and down the stairs. The roof leaked, and she had to set up pots and pans to catch the water. But Franklin didn't mind adversity. In fact, she told friends she preferred the challenge it presented, whether at work or even while travelling. She loved to travel and once journeyed to Israel in the steerage of a slow boat sheerly for the adventure of it. She said she preferred to travel with little money "because then you need your wits," an attitude that stood her in good stead in 1955 when the Birkbeck lost its backing from the Agricultural Research Council, in part, Franklin thought, because they did not approve of a project headed by a woman. Franklin successfully sought funding from another government source—the U.S. Public Health Service. The year after Franklin began at Birkbeck, the South African scientist **Aaron Klug** joined the laboratory. By 1956, Franklin had obtained some of the best pictures of the crystallographic structure of the TMV and, along with her colleagues, disproved the then-standard notion that TMV was a solid cylinder with RNA in the middle and protein subunits on the outside. While Franklin confirmed that the protein units did lay on the outside, she also showed that the cylinder was hollow, and that the RNA lay embedded among the protein units. Later, she initiated work that would support her hypothesis that the RNA in the TMV was single-stranded.

Franklin spent the summer of 1956 in California with two American scientists, learning from them techniques by which to grow viruses. Upon returning to England, Franklin fell ill, and friends began to suspect she was in pain a great deal of the time. That fall, she was operated on for cancer and, the following year, she had a second operation, neither of which stopped either her work or the disease. Franklin knew she was dying, but did not let that impede her progress. She began working on the polio virus, even though people warned her it was dangerous and highly contagious. She died of cancer at the age of 37 on April 16, 1958. Four years later, Watson, Crick, and Wilkins won the Nobel Prize in medicine or physiology, and Watson penned his potboiler account of the discovery of DNA. Although he vilifies her throughout his account, he tones down his earlier depiction of her as the mad, feminist scientist in an epilogue: "Since my initial impressions of her, both scientific and personal (as recorded in the early pages of this book), were often wrong, I want to say something here about her achievements." He continues that he and Crick "both came to appreciate greatly her personal honesty and generosity, realizing years too late the struggles that the intelligent woman faces to be accepted by a scientific world which often regards women as mere diversions from serious thinking."

SELECTED WRITINGS BY FRANKLIN:

Periodicals

"Evidence for 2-Chain Helix in Crystalline Structure of Sodium Deoxyribonucleate," *Nature,* Volume 172, 1953, pp. 156–57.

(With Aaron Klug) "Order-Disorder Transitions in Structures Containing Helical Molecules," *Discussions of the Faraday Society,* Volume 25, 1958, pp. 104–10.

SOURCES:

Books

Judson, Horace Freeland, *The Eighth Day of Creation: Makers of the Revolution in Biology,* Simon and Schuster, 1980.

Sayre, Anne, *Rosalind Franklin and DNA,* Norton, 1975.

Watson, James D., *The Double-Helix: A Personal Account of the Discovery of the Structure of DNA,* Norton, 1980.

Periodicals

Klug, A., "Rosalind Franklin and the Discovery of the Structure of DNA," *Nature,* 219, 1968.

—*Sketch by Shari Rudavsky*

Bertram Oliver Fraser-Reid
1934-
Jamaican Canadian chemist

Bert Fraser-Reid is a distinguished researcher in organic synthesis and sugar chemistry. In 1966, at the University of Waterloo in Ontario, he developed a process to make synthetic pheromones, the chemical attractants produced naturally by insects and other species. For this discovery, he received the Merck, Sharpe and Dohme Award for outstanding contribution to organic chemistry in Canada in 1977. At Duke University in Durham, North Carolina, Fraser-Reid has conducted groundbreaking research on the synthesis of organic compounds from simple sugars. In addition, he has led a research team that developed a unique process to combine simple sugars into oligosaccharides, complex sugars composed of two or more monosaccharides. This process, as Fraser-Reid indicated in *Black Enterprise,* "may have some potential to facilitate the development of a cure for AIDS." A *Black Enterprise* writer speculates that Fraser-Reid's research may ultimately earn him a Nobel Prize in chemistry, for which he has already been nominated.

Bertram Oliver Fraser-Reid, who has dual Jamaican and Canadian citizenship, was born on February 23, 1934, in Coleyville, Jamaica, to William Benjamin Reid and Laura Maria Fraser. Fraser-Reid was working as a teacher when, at the age of twenty-two, he became interested in chemistry. This led him to Queen's University in Kingston, Ontario, Canada, where he earned his B.S. degree in 1959 and his M.S. degree in 1961. Fraser-Reid married Lillian Lawryniuk on December 21, 1963; they have two children, Andrea and Terry. Fraser-Reid received his doctorate in chemistry from the University of Alberta in 1964. From 1964 to 1966, he held a postdoctoral fellowship at the Imperial College of the University of London.

Achieves Synthesis of Pheromones

In 1966, Fraser-Reid joined the faculty of the University of Waterloo, where he remained until 1980. During this period, he was able to effect the organic synthesis (the preparation of complex organic structures from simpler compounds) of pheromones, which social insects emit to transmit messages about food sources, the presence of predators, and reproductive behavior. The Canadian Forestry Service was subsequently able to control insect populations that were damaging timber by using synthetic pheromones to disrupt the insect's mating cycles; relying on synthetic pheromones allowed the Forestry Service to discontinue their use of DDT, the controversial insecticide now banned throughout much of the world. Since glucose (a form of sugar) was the basis for Fraser-Reid's synthetic pheromones, the larger implication of his achievement is that sugars can be used in place of petroleum for industrial applications of organic synthesis—a discovery with potentially global economic ramifications in terms of the manufacture of plastics and pharmaceuticals.

Fraser-Reid was a professor of chemistry at the University of Maryland from 1980 to 1982. He joined the faculty of Duke University in 1982, becoming the James B. Duke professor of chemistry in 1985. Commenting on his experiences as an educator, Fraser-Reid told *Black Enterprise,* "It never ceases to amaze me how young impressionable minds can mature into competent scientists." He encourages all students, and especially black students at Duke, to consider careers in science and engineering. Nonetheless, he is quoted in *Science* as regretting that "The black students in my classes are first and foremost Americans, and over the past 15 to 20 years Americans have not been going into science and engineering."

Accomplishes Synthesis of Oligosaccharides

During his tenure at Duke, Fraser-Reid's research turned to the biochemistry of oligosaccharides, which his team of researchers have been able to synthesize from simple sugars. As Fraser-Reid noted in *Black Enterprise,* oligosaccharides are "among the most important biological regulators in nature ... They regulate the whole immune system." Oligosaccharides are involved in the biological functioning of the antigenic substances found in the blood, which are complex carbohydrates capable of stimulating an immune response. Thus, advances in the understanding of oligosaccharides and in oligosaccharide synthesis promise to play an important role in the medical battle against AIDS.

Fraser-Reid was named Senior Distinguished U.S. Scientist by the Alexander von Humboldt Foundation in 1989. In 1990, he received both a Jamaican National Foundation Award and the American

Chemical Society Claude S. Hudson Award in Carbohydrate Chemistry. In 1991, he received the National Organization of Black Chemists and Chemical Engineers' Percy Julian Award. In 1993, he served as chair of the Gordon Conference on Carbohydrates. Fraser-Reid was also awarded the 1995 Haworth Memorial Medal and Lectureship of the Royal Society of Chemistry. His professional memberships include the Chemical Institute of Canada, the American Chemical Society, the American Institute of Chemistry, and the British Chemical Society. He also serves as consultant to Blackside Films on minorities in science. An accomplished organist, Fraser-Reid has performed at recitals internationally.

SELECTED WRITINGS BY FRASER-REID:

Periodicals

(With Robert C. Anderson) "Synthesis of Bis-g-lactones from 'Diacetone Glucose,'" *Journal of Organic Chemistry,* November 29, 1985, pp. 4781–4786.

(With Joseph Barchi, Jr. and Ramin Faghih) "Avermectin Chemistry," *Journal of Organic Chemistry,* February 19, 1988, pp. 923–925.

(With Jarosz Slawomir) "Synthesis of Higher Sugars Via Allytin Derivatives of Simple Monosaccharides," *Journal of Organic Chemistry,* August 18, 1989, pp. 4011–4013.

"Novel Carbohydrate Transformations Discovered En Route to Natural Products," *Pure and Applied Chemistry,* Volume 61, number 7, 1989, pp. 1243–1256.

(With Uko E. Udodong and C. Srinivas Rao) "n-Pentenyl Glycosides in the Efficient Assembly of the Blood Group Substance B Tetrasaccharide," *Tetrahedron,* Volume 48, number 23, 1992, pp. 4713–4724.

SOURCES:

Periodicals

"Driven by Sugar," *Black Enterprise,* February, 1990, p. 86.

"Science at Duke in Black and White," *Science,* May 13, 1988, p. 877.

—Sketch by M. C. Nagel

Maurice Fréchet
1878-1973
French mathematician

Maurice Fréchet was one of the creators of the twentieth-century discipline of topology, which deals with the properties of geometric configurations; his research added a new degree of abstractness to the mathematical advances of the previous generation. He profited from a rich mathematical environment during his studies and in turn passed on a wealth of ideas to his students over a long career. Some of the mathematicians who had learned their skills before Fréchet's work appeared could not help wondering whether there were advantages to the new degree of generality in his work. The answer lay in the fruitfulness of the methods of Fréchet for addressing problems whose solution included concrete problems of long standing.

René Maurice Fréchet was born on the 10th of September in 1878 in Maligny, a small town in provincial France, where his father Jacques directed an orphanage. Soon after Fréchet's birth the family moved to Paris, much to his advantage in terms of mathematical environment. His mother Zoé was responsible for a boardinghouse for foreigners, which early put Fréchet in contact with a cosmopolitan community. This may be reflected in his subsequent hospitality toward students and collaborators from all over the world. At his lycée (high school), he was singularly fortunate in learning mathematics from **Jacques Hadamard**, already a mathematician of distinction who would shortly thereafter provide a proof of a central result of number theory called the prime number theorem. Fréchet's talents blossomed under Hadamard's encouragement and he was well prepared to enter the École Normale Supérieure, the great French scientific university, in 1900. Hadamard was not the only mathematical influence on the young Fréchet. After graduating from the École Normale, he began to work with mathematician **Émile Borel**, who was only seven years older than Fréchet but who had started his career so early that he may have seemed to belong to an earlier generation. Fréchet collaborated with Borel on the publication of a series of the latter's lectures and continued to be involved with the publishing of the so-called Borel collection for Gauthier-Villars. Even though Borel's role in the collection was primarily an editor's, he also wrote all the volumes to begin with, the first exception being one written by Fréchet. In turn, Fréchet undertook the editing of a series on general analysis published by Hermann (the other great mathematical publisher in Paris) and undertook the writing of several of the volumes as well.

Fréchet wrote his thesis under Hadamard, who had returned to Paris, and then followed Hadamard in teaching at the level of the lycée for a few years. His marriage in 1908 to Suzanne Carrive produced four children, whom he supported with professorships outside of Paris until 1928. He was officially connected with the University at Poitiers from 1910 to 1918, but World War I took him out of mathematics and into the less familiar surroundings of working as an interpreter with the British army, where his early exposure to different languages was of help. After his return from military service, he was head of the Institute of Mathematics at the University of Strasbourg, still a provincial appointment. It was not until 1928 that he was called to the University of Paris.

Proposes Revolutionary Variations of Topology Theory

One of the reasons for the delay in the recognition of Fréchet's work by the French academic establishment was its revolutionary character. The notions of set theory as introduced by the German mathematician **Georg Cantor** in the previous century were slowly winning converts, although there were differences of opinion about which axioms ought to be accepted. What Fréchet did in his thesis and in the most influential of his subsequent work was to bring the ideas of general set theory to bear on questions of the new discipline of topology, the generalization of geometry that had been given a good deal of prominence in French mathematics by the work of **Jules Henri Poincaré**. The questions that Poincaré had raised were new, but they were in the context of classical mathematics, centered on space with standard Cartesian coordinates (those points commonly expressed as located along x, y, and z axes), although perhaps in more than three dimensions.

This much of a revolution the mathematical community had come to accept, but Fréchet's thesis pushed the level of abstractness to new heights. Rather than looking just at sets of points in Cartesian space, he was prepared to handle sets of points in arbitrary spaces—so-called abstract spaces. The important tool that he used to handle such sets was a distance function. The ordinary distance function for sets of points with Cartesian coordinates (x, y) comes from the Pythagorean theorem and involves taking the square root of the sums of the squares of the differences in each coordinate. Since in abstract spaces there weren't necessarily any coordinates to assign to points, the distance function had to be more general and governed by some of the principles that applied to the Cartesian version.

The advantage of the new approach of Fréchet was that complicated algebraic expressions could be replaced by general considerations about distance. Spaces with a distance function were called metric spaces and proved to be the setting for expressing many of the results hitherto considered limited to spaces with real numbers as coordinates. Having once introduced these ideas into topology, Fréchet proceeded to look at calculus in metric spaces, an area that became known as functional analysis. Again, the basis for progress on long-standing problems was the avoidance of the complicated calculations that had bedeviled earlier work and the application of general notions from topology instead. Fréchet extended the notions of derivatives and integrals from standard calculus so that they could be used in the setting of a metric space; in addition, he introduced new types of functions called functionals, which took real numbers as values but could operate on the points of abstract spaces. Much of his work from his thesis onward was summarized in *Les espaces abstraits,* published in 1926.

Fréchet taught at the University of Paris until 1949, and a good deal of his time there was spent on questions of probability. Just as general questions about calculus could be asked in the setting of abstract metric spaces, so the techniques of probability could be moved there as well. The application of probability to continuous quantities, as opposed to discrete quantities that took only a finite number of values, had always been dependent on calculus, and Fréchet's results showed that the extension to the abstract setting could be fruitful as well. As with functional analysis in general, the more one could move away from messy computations, the more one could hope that the idea behind a proof could be visible.

Another possible reason for Fréchet's move into probability was the hope that a more concrete area would make the techniques of abstract spaces more palatable to the part of the mathematical community uneasy about getting too far from applications. If so, the efforts proved largely unavailing, at least in France, although the level of abstractness introduced by Fréchet was one of the inspirations for the Polish mathematical school between World Wars I and II. It is perhaps indicative of the relative opinions of his work that Fréchet was elected to the Polish Academy of Sciences in 1929 but not to the French Academy of Sciences until 1956. He was recognized as a member of the Legion of Honor, and some accumulation of praise could hardly be avoided as he lived into his nineties. He died in Paris on the 4th of June in 1973, having earned belated recognition of his role in bringing mathematics into the twentieth century on the wings of abstractness.

SELECTED WRITINGS BY FRÉCHET:

Books

Les espaces abstraits, Gauthier-Villars, 1926.
L'arithmétique de l'infini, Hermann, 1934.

(With Ky Fan) *Initiation to Combinatorial Topology,* translated by Howard M. Eves, Prindle, Weber, & Schmidt, 1967.

SOURCES:

Books

Bell, E. T., *The Development of Mathematics,* 2nd edition, McGraw-Hill, 1945.
Dictionary of Scientific Biography, Volume 17, Scribner, 1990, pp. 309–311.
Temple, George, *100 Years of Mathematics,* Springer-Verlag, 1981.
Young, Laurence, *Mathematicians and Their Times,* North-Holland, 1981.

—Sketch by Thomas Drucker

Michael H. Freedman
1951-
American mathematician

Michael H. Freedman has been recognized by the American Mathematical Society, the International Congress of Mathematicians, the United States government, and the MacArthur Foundation for his research breakthroughs in topology, a branch of mathematics that deals with the properties of geometric objects rather than their sizes and shapes. Freedman's work has been fundamental in making progress with some of the most difficult problems in four-dimensional geometry and topology. He is perhaps best known for his proof of the four-dimensional Poincaré conjecture, a problem dating from 1904.

Michael Hartley Freedman was born in Los Angeles on April 21, 1951, to Benedict Freedman and Nancy Mars Freedman. Freedman began his post-secondary education with a year at the Berkeley campus of the University of California in 1968. He then transferred to Princeton University where he received his Ph.D. under William Browder four years later. After his graduation in 1973, he took a position for two years as a lecturer in the Department of Mathematics at the University of California, Berkeley. He spent the following year at the Institute for Advanced Study in Princeton. Then he returned to California, this time to the University of California, San Diego (UCSD) campus, where he quickly progressed through the ranks of assistant professor, associate professor, and full professor. In 1985 Freedman was appointed by UCSD as the first to professor to hold the newly endowed Charles Lee Powell chair of mathematics.

Freedman Solves the Simply Connected Surgery Problem

Throughout the twentieth century, mathematicians have made progress in understanding geometric objects in terms of associated algebraic operations. In particular, topologists have tried to use algebra to classify multi-dimensional surfaces, which they call manifolds. Objects such as spheres can exist in several dimensions: To envision a six-dimensional sphere, imagine a baseball, and add to its usual three dimensions measures for its age, color, and weight.

In 1904, French mathematician **Jules Henri Poincaré** designed a system to classify manifolds. He imagined a loop of string wrapped around a surface and determined how far the loop could be shrunk. On a sphere, the loop could be shrunk to a single point. On a torus, or doughnut-like shape, a loop encircling the hole can't shrink smaller than the circumference of the hole. Thus, a sphere and a torus belong to different groups.

Three-dimensional manifolds pose special classification problems because they can be stretched in many different ways. Poincaré devised a series of tests and asked his colleagues to prove that any three-dimensional manifold, no matter how distorted, could be classified as a sphere if it meets the tests. The statement of this problem evolved over the years, but not until 1961 did **Stephen Smale** give the first proof of the Poincaré conjecture for some dimensions. Smale and other topologists followed algebraic guidelines in cutting the manifold apart and sewing it back together as a sphere, a technique known as surgery. Manifolds of dimension three and four do not have as much "room" for maneuvering. Thus, the necessary surgery is much more difficult and the four-dimensional Poincaré conjecture remained unsolved for another two decades.

Finally, after seven years of work, Freedman solved the surgery problem for simply connected four-dimensional manifolds. In 1982 he published his solution in the paper "The Topology of Four-Dimensional Manifolds." This paper gives a complete classification of all simply connected, four-dimensional manifolds in terms of two numbers. In the course of proving this theorem, Freedman exhibited several new four-dimensional manifolds, including the first examples of such manifolds that do not support a coordinate system for calculus. These results, along with nearly fifty papers on the structure and classification of three- and four-dimensional manifolds, resolved many fundamental issues concerning manifolds in this dimension range.

In 1984 Freedman received a five-year MacArthur Foundation Fellowship to foster further accomplishment. That same year he was elected to the National Academy of Sciences, and the next year to the American Academy of Arts and Sciences. In 1986 he received the Fields Medal, an award in mathematics comparable to the Nobel Prize. Also in 1986 the American Mathematical Society awarded the Veblen Prize to Freedman for his work in four-dimensional topology. In his response to this award, Freedman explained the importance of interplay among the various branches and applications of mathematics. He stated, "Mathematics is not so much a collection of different subjects as a way of thinking. As such, it may be applied to any branch of knowledge. I want to applaud the efforts now being make by mathematicians to publish ideas on education, energy, economics, defense, and world peace. Experience inside mathematics shows that it isn't necessary to be an old hand in an area to make a contribution." He added, "Outside mathematics the situation is less clear, but I can't help feeling that there, too, it is a mistake to leave important issues entirely to the experts."

Freedman and Leslie Blair Howland were married on September 18, 1983, and they have two children, Hartley and Whitney. The couple also have a son, Benedict, from a previous marriage. Freedman is an accomplished rock climber, having made a solo climb of the northeast ridge of Mount Williamson in 1970 and receiving recognition as the Great Western boulder climbing champion in 1979.

SELECTED WRITINGS BY FREEDMAN:

Books

(With Feng Luo) *Selected Applications of Geometry to Low Dimensional Topology,* American Mathematical Society University Lecture Series 1, 1990.

Periodicals

"The Topology of Four-Dimensional Manifolds," *Journal of Differential Geometry,* Volume 17, 1982, pp. 357–454.

SOURCES:

Periodicals

Bylinsky, Gene, "America's Hot Young Scientists," *Fortune,* October 8, 1990, pp. 56–70.

"Michael H. Freedman Awarded 1986 Veblen Prize," *Notices of the American Mathematical Society,* March 1986, pp. 227–228.

Milnor, John, "The Work of Michael Freedman," *Notices of the American Mathematical Society,* November, 1986, pp. 901–902.

—Sketch by Robert Messer

Yakov Ilyich Frenkel
1894-1954
Russian physicist

Yakov Ilyich Frenkel, who grew up in a nineteenth-century Russia ruled by czars, became a founder of the twentieth-century atomic theory of solids and gave his name to phenomena now known as Frenkel excitons and Frenkel defects.

Frenkel was born in Rostov, Russia, on February 10, 1894, and showed an early interest in music and painting. However, he developed a passion for mathematics and physics, and wrote his first independent paper on mathematics in 1911, when he was seventeen. The paper described what Frenkel thought was a new kind of calculus. Instead, it turned out to be a calculus already in existence, known as finite differences. He matriculated at the physics and mathematics faculty of St. Petersburg University in 1913, graduating three years later with honors. In 1918 he taught at Tavrida University in Simferopol, in Ukraine, returning to Petrograd (Leningrad) three years later to work at the Physico-Technical Institute, which was directed by a friend and colleague, A. F. Joffe. Frenkel remained at the institute for the rest of his life, while also teaching theoretical physics at Leningrad Polytechnic Institute.

The early years of Frenkel's career were an important time in the elucidation of atomic structure by physicists. In 1913 the great Danish physicist **Neils Bohr** proposed his new model of the atom. Formerly, the atom was conceived to be a tiny, positively charged heavy nucleus surrounded by negatively charged electrons spinning around the nucleus at arbitrary distances. Bohr revised this model, based on the so-called spectral series of hydrogen—the sequence of wavelengths that characterize the light emitted by energized atoms and that can be used to identify specific atoms. In Bohr's new model, electrons of all atoms are restricted to orbits with discrete energy levels around a nucleus of protons and neutrons; these energy levels are associated with characteristic wavelengths for each atom. According to this theory, a photon or "particle" of light is released when an electron moves from an outer orbit or higher-energy level to an inner orbit or lower-energy level. Building on Bohr's work, Frenkel proposed in 1916 that there exists on the surface of metals a double electric layer. This idea led to the first evaluations of surface tensions of metals, that is, the forces acting on the surface, and of contact potentials—the work needed between any two points to move a unit charge from one point to the other. This concept has applications in the study of semiconductors (materials that are neither good conductors nor good insulators), and must be taken into account in any analysis of physical electronics experiments.

Eight years later, Frenkel expanded on the virial theory, which explains the behavior of gases that do not behave in a mathematically simple ("ideal") manner, to demonstrate that when metal condenses from a vapor, the valence electrons (those responsible for chemical bonds) migrate at a rate equal to that of intra-atomic motion. Throughout the late 1920s and into the 1930s, Frenkel contributed greatly to the understanding of metallic behavior and helped to describe high-density stars. In 1930 he and J. G. Dorfman clarified the concept of single-domain ferromagnetic particles, that is, ferromagnetic particles with a single set of oppositely directed fields emanating from them.

Frenkel also studied thermal motion and its relation to the structure of crystals. In 1926 he showed that the normal, orderly arrangement of atoms in a crystal can sometimes contain a defect caused when an atom or ion is removed from its position and placed at an interstitial position—a location equidistant from three other atoms or ions. This defect, in which a misplaced atom or ion and a corresponding vacancy occur, migrates throughout the crystal, and is called a Frenkel defect. In 1930 and 1931 Frenkel studied the absorption of light in solid dielectrics (materials that are electrical insulators or in which an electric field can be contained with minimum loss of strength) and semiconductors, and showed that when light is absorbed an excitation state can arise in the absence of ionization of the materials' atoms or molecules. This state, which has properties of a quasi particle and can be thought of as an electron and a hole in a bound state, Frenkel called an exciton. He also described another type of excitation generated by light in solid material that is associated with a free electron and a free hole and is called a Frenkel exciton.

Breaking with traditional thought concerning the close relationship of liquid and gaseous states, Frenkel established an analogy between liquids and solids. Using this concept he constructed a theory of diffusion and viscosity, and in 1945 developed his theory of the liquid state in a monograph called *The Kinetic Theory of Liquids.* This monograph earned him his country's State Prize in 1947. In 1937 and 1938 he published with his colleague T. A. Kontorova the first theoretical demonstration that in distortion-free crystal lattices particle motion is still possible. This movement, which leads to a gradual displacement of rows of atoms, explains the plastic deformation of crystals. Frenkel's research extended to electrodynamics, electron theory, investigations of atomic nuclei, and problems of meteorology and geophysics. Between 1944 and 1949 he proposed a theory of atmospheric electrification in which he was able to link the electrification of clouds with the existence of electric fields in cloudless atmosphere.

Frenkel was elected an associated member of the Academy of Sciences of the U.S.S.R. in 1929, following which he traveled to the United States, where he lectured at the University of Minnesota from 1930 to 1931. In 1932, E. L. Hill of the University of Minnesota published a new theory of light based on Frenkel's work. Hill described light as not being an independent element in the universe, but rather the result of excitement of atoms. Frenkel died in Leningrad on January 23, 1954.

SELECTED WRITINGS BY FRENKEL:

Books

Wave Mechanics: Elementary Theory, Clarendon, 1932.

Wave Mechanics: Advanced General Theory, Clarendon, 1934.

Kinetic Theory of Liquids, Clarendon, 1946.

SOURCES:

Books

Concise Dictionary of Scientific Biography, Scribner, 1981.

Gillispie, Charles Coulson, editor, *Dictionary of Scientific Biography,* Volume 5, Scribner, 1972.

Magill, Frank N., *Magill's Survey of Science: Physical Science,* Salem Press, Volume 5, 1992, pp. 2235–2237.

Periodicals

New York Times, March 8, 1932, p. 25.

—Sketch by Marc Kusinitz

Jerome Friedman
1930-
American physicist

Jerome Friedman shared the 1990 Nobel Prize for physics with physicists **Henry Kendall** and **Richard Taylor** for the trio's research leading to the discovery of quarks—supercharged subatomic particles found in protons and neutrons. Friedman had originally become interested in atomic research while at Stanford University, where he worked with physicist Robert Hofstadter on his studies of the atomic nucleus. This research went on until 1960, when Friedman left Stanford to join the physics faculty of the Massachusetts Institute of Technology (MIT); Kendall and Taylor joined Friedman at MIT in the early 1960s. Originally, the three scientists intended to merely extend Hofstadter's original findings; instead, they made a discovery once described by a colleague as "one of the pivotal contributions to physics in this century."

Friedman was born in Chicago on March 28, 1930, the younger of two sons of Selig and Lillian Warsaw Friedman. Selig Friedman had immigrated to the United States in 1913; he later became the owner of a sewing machine repair business. Friedman's early interests revolved around art and music, but he redirected his energies after a chance encounter with Albert Einstein's book *Relativity.* Even though he was offered a scholarship to the Art Institute of Chicago, Friedman decided to pursue this new interest in science by studying physics at the University of Chicago in the late 1940s. While at the university, he had the opportunity to work on projects with physicists **Enrico Fermi** and Valentine Telegdi. Remaining at the University of Chicago for the bulk of his studies, Friedman received his bachelor's degree in physics in 1950, his master's degree in 1953, and his doctorate in 1956.

The focus of Friedman's research—nuclear physics—was determined early in his academic career. While still at Chicago, Friedman carried out studies on the "weak force," which explains changes such as beta, or organic particle, decay. He chose to continue in this field when he left school in late 1956 to accept an appointment as research associate at Stanford University's High Energy Physics Laboratory. **Robert Hofstadter**—winner of 1961 Nobel Prize in physics for his research on the structure of protons and neutrons—was director of the laboratory. Hofstadter's work during the 1950s constituted the latest in physicists' efforts to define the smallest building blocks of matter. When scientist John Dalton first announced his atomic theory in 1808, he indicated that atoms constituted these basic components. Near the end of the nineteenth century, Sir **Joseph John Thomson** showed Dalton's hypothesis was incorrect by identifying electrons. Two decades later, physicist **Ernest Rutherford** discovered the atomic nucleus and a second subatomic particle, the proton. In 1932, Rutherford's student **James Chadwick** discovered a third particle, the neutron.

For some time, the belief that atoms consisted of three fundamental particles—proton, neutron, and electron—appeared to explain much observed phenomena. The invention of particle accelerators in the 1930s, however, soon invalidated this view. First dozens, and later hundreds, of new elementary particles were discovered as the by-products of these "atom smashers," which sped subatomic fragments toward atoms at high velocities. Upon being struck, the atoms would break and their fragmentary contents could be studied. In 1964, physicist **Murray Gell-Mann** postulated that some of these tiny fragments—which he named quarks—were the smallest components of all "fundamental" particles. The problem was that no one had ever observed a quark (indeed, many physicists thought that the concept was no more than a mathematical construction for bringing order to particle physics). Hofstadter's research provided the first hint that quarks might actually have measureable physical properties. He bombarded atomic nuclei with the high-powered electron beams of the Stanford Linear Accelerator (SLA) and found evidence for structure *within* protons and neutrons. From the way electron beams were scattered by nucleons (protons and neutrons), Hofstadter concluded that these particles were not discreet points, but "fuzzy little balls" which probably had a more detailed structure as yet undetectable in his research.

It was into this research setting that Friedman came in 1957. He disagreed with researchers who felt that Hofstadter's work was essentially complete. Friedman's stance was supported by two factors. First, improvements in the SLA vastly increased the ability of its electron beam to penetrate the atomic nucleus, allowing researchers a clearer look at protons and neutrons. Secondly, a suggestion by theoretical physicist James Bjorken prompted Friedman, Henry Kendall and Richard Taylor to look more closely at the nature of inelastic collisions (in which nucleons are actually blown apart) rather than at elastic collisions (in which electrons are scattered by nucleons, which then remain intact). In following up on Bjorken's suggestion, Friedman, Kendall, and Taylor found that their data strongly suggested the existence of tiny points of matter within nucleons which could be identified by their tendency to deflect electrons during inelastic scattering. This confirmation of the existence of quarks and gluons (the matter that holds quarks together) not only gave scientists a more complete picture of atomic structure, it also validated the theories advanced by Gell-Mann and Hofstadter.

Over the course of his career in physics, Friedman has held a number of academic posts. He rose from researcher to professor at MIT in 1960; he also served as director of MIT's Laboratory of Nuclear Science from 1980 to 1983 and as head of its physics department from 1983 to 1988. In addition to his academic research, Friedman has been involved in many administrative and political endeavors in the scientific community (he has, for example, served as a member of the Department of Energy's High Energy Advisory Panel and as chairman of the Science Policy Committee for the construction of the Superconducting Super Collider). Along with the Nobel Prize, Friedman and his associates also received the 1989 W. K. H. Panofsky Prize from the American Physical Society. In 1956, Friedman married the former Tania Letesky-Baranovsky, with whom he has four children: Ellena, Joel, Martin, and Sandra.

SELECTED WRITINGS BY FRIEDMAN:

Periodicals

(With Henry Kendall and Richard Taylor) "Observed Behavior of Highly Inelastic Electron-Proton Scattering," *Physical Review Letters,* Number 27, 1969, p. 935.

SOURCES:

Books

Magill, Frank N., editor, *Great Events from History,* Volume 2, Salem Press, 1991, pp. 1871–1875.

Periodicals

"APS Presents a Host of Awards at Spring Meeting in Baltimore," *Physics Today,* June 1989, pp. 95–96.

Lindley, David, "Quark-Hunters Are Rewarded," *Nature,* October 25, 1990, p. 698.

Lubkin, Gloria B., "Friedman, Kendall and Taylor Win Nobel Prize for First Quark Evidence," *Physics Today,* January, 1991, pp. 17–20.

Sutton, Christine, "Nobel Trophy for the Hunters of the Quark," *New Scientist,* October 27, 1990, p. 14.

Waldrop, M. Mitchell, "Physics Nobel Honors the Discovery of Quarks," *Science,* October 26, 1990, pp. 508–509.

—*Sketch by David E. Newton*

Aleksandr A. Friedmann
1888-1925
Russian mathematician and astrophysicist

Aleksandr A. Friedmann is best known for his application of **Albert Einstein**'s general theory of relativity to the field of astronomy. By developing a mathematical model of the universe according to Einstein's theory, he depicted the universe in a state of expansion. This model, which became known as the Friedmann model or Friedmann universe, laid the foundation for future discussions of the "big bang" theory of modern astronomy.

Aleksandr Aleksandrovich Friedmann was born in St. Petersburg, Russia, on June 29, 1888 to Aleksandr Friedmann, a musical composer, and Ludmila (Vojácek) Friedmann, the daughter of the Czech composer, Hynek Vojácek. He graduated from the Second St. Petersburg Gymnasium in 1906, having already published his first paper, a work examining Bernoulli's numbers, in 1905. He then entered St. Petersburg University where he studied mathematics. Friedmann graduated from the university in 1910; in 1914, while studying meteorology at the Pavlovsk Aerological Observatory, he received a master's degree in pure and applied mathematics from the University of St. Petersburg.

Between 1914 and 1917 Friedmann served as pilot and navigator in the air corps, where he tested bombing procedures and helped compose a set of ballistic tables. According to a biographical sketch in *Soviet Physics Uspekhi,* Friedmann was so "entranced" with air that, in order to thoroughly understand air and aerological phenomena, he had to "plunge himself into it." Thus, frequently throughout the rest of his life, Friedmann often went up in dirigibles and balloons.

Friedmann held his first academic post, teaching theoretical mechanics, at Perm University in 1918. Two years later, he moved to Petrograd where he lectured in hydrodynamics. His research in theoretical meteorology and hydromechanics was well received, and he remains known as a central figure in the development of theories of atmospheric vortices, wind gusts, and vertical air fluxes. In addition, hc studied the causes of atmospheric temperature inversions and examined the theories on atmospheric turbulence. In a 1922 publication, an *Experiment in the Hydromechanics of Compressible Liquids,* Friedmann outlined his theory of the vertical motion in a liquid, and he described the mobility of a compressed liquid at different pressures. This work formed the foundation of theoretical meteorology, a field which later evolved into the hydrodynamic studies of pressure waves, storms centers, and radiant heat exchange as used in long-range weather forecasting.

Friedmann was a conscientious, self-critical, and hard-working scientist. He readily praised his subordinates in the presence of others and lavished compliments upon colleagues who made interesting discoveries. Finding regular working hours much too short, Friedmann would gather his students together in his apartment each morning to discuss particular problems and concerns.

Identifies Einstein's "Biggest Blunder"

While in Petrograd, Friedmann developed close working ties with a number of physicists and mathematicians, and he began to study seriously the theory of relativity. He simplified Albert Einstein's theory in a 1923 physics text, *The World as Space and Time.* The model of the universe which Einstein developed in 1917 described a static, invariable, universe. In this model, Einstein introduced a "cosmological constant" to account for the universe not collapsing upon itself due to the force of gravity. This antigravity constant was, like gravity, a value Einstein believed to be uniformly present throughout the universe. In a 1922 article, "On the Curvature of Space," Friedmann presented his own cosmological theory; he argued that a static, nonevolving, and nonexpanding universe was inconsistent with the general theory of relativity. He discarded Einstein's cosmological constant and mathematically proved that the universe was dynamic and free to expand or contract merely through the force of gravity. Einstein replied, claiming that Friedmann's solution contained a mathematical error which reduced his theory to a static universe as well. After lengthy personal deliberation with Einstein, Friedmann convinced him of the mathematical soundness of a dynamic universe. Einstein retracted the cosmological constant from his field equations for general relativity and later claimed that inserting this constant had been the "biggest blunder" of his life.

Friedmann's solution has become a standard cosmological model. Friedmann models or Friedmann universes are cosmological models which assume a homogeneity of the distribution of matter in space and an isotropy or equivalency in the expansion or contraction of the universe accountable only by gravity. Friedmann's mathematical theory of the expanding universe laid the groundwork for later observational astronomical and cosmological accounts of the "big bang" theory. Friedmann contracted typhoid fever, and on September 16, 1925, he died at the age of thirty-seven. In recognition of his many scientific endeavors, he was posthumously awarded the Lenin Prize. According to the account in *Soviet Physics Uspekhi,* a colleague claimed Friedmann had "the lofty soul of a student of the eternal problems of creation and the noble nature of a priest of pure knowledge."

SELECTED WRITINGS BY FRIEDMANN:

Books

Opyt gidromekhaniki szhimaemoy zhidkosti ("Experiment in the Hydromechanics of Compressible Liquids"), [Petrograd], 1922.

(with V.K. Fredericks) *Mir kak prostranstvo i vremya* ("The World as Space and Time"), [Petrograd], 1923; second edition, [Moscow], 1965.

Periodicals

"Uber die Krummung des Raumes" ("On the Curvature of Space"), *Zeitschrift fur Physik,* 1922, pp. 377–386.

"O dvizhenii szhimaemoy zhidkosti" ("On the Motion of a Compressible Liquid"), *Izvestiya gidrologicheskogo instituta,* 1923, pp. 21–28.

"O krivizne prostranstva" ("On the Curvature of Space"), *Zhurnal Russkago fiziko-khimicheskago obshchestva,* 1924, pp. 59–68.

SOURCES:

Books

Gillispie, Charles Coulson, editor, *Dictionary of Scientific Biography,* Scribner, Volume 5, 1972, pp. 187–189.

Overbye, Dennis, *Lonely Hearts of the Cosmos: The Story of the Scientific Quest for the Secret of the Universe,* HarperCollins, 1991.

Periodicals

Odenwald, Sten, "Einstein's Fudge Factor," *Sky & Telescope,* April, 1991, pp. 362–366.

Polubarinova-Kochina, P. Y., "Aleksandr Aleksandrovich Friedmann (On the seventy-fifth anniversary of his birth)," *Soviet Physics Uspekhi,* January-February, 1964, pp. 467–472.

—Sketch by Philip K. Wilson

Charlotte Friend
1921-1987
American microbiologist

As the first scientist to discover a direct link between viruses and cancer, Charlotte Friend made important breakthroughs in cancer research, particularly that on leukemia. She was successful in immunizing mice against leukemia and also in pointing a way toward new methods of treating the disease. Because of Friend's work, medical researchers developed a greater understanding of cancer and how it can be fought.

Friend was born on March 11, 1921, in New York City to Russian immigrants. Her father died of endocarditis (heart inflammation) when Charlotte was three, a factor that may have influenced her early decision to enter the medical field; at age ten she wrote a school composition entitled, "Why I Want to Become a Bacteriologist." Her mother's job as a pharmacist also exposed Friend to medicine. After graduating from Hunter College in 1944, she immediately enlisted in the U.S. Navy during World War II, rising to the rank of lieutenant junior grade.

After the war, Friend entered graduate school at Yale University, obtaining her Ph.D. in bacteriology in 1950. Soon afterward, she was hired by the Sloan-Kettering Institute for Cancer Research, and in 1952 became an associate professor in microbiology at Cornell University, which had just set up a joint program with the institute. During that time Friend because interested in cancer, particularly leukemia, a cancer of blood-forming organs that is a leading killer of children. Her research on the cause of this disease led her to believe that, contrary to the prevailing medical opinion, leukemia is caused by a virus. To confirm her theory, Friend took samples of leukemia tissue from mice and, after putting the material through a filter to remove cells, injected it into healthy mice. These animals developed leukemia, indicating that the cause of the disease was a substance smaller than a cell. Using an electron microscope, Friend was able to discover and photograph the virus she believed responsible for leukemia.

However, when Friend presented her findings at the April, 1956, annual meeting of the American Association for Cancer Research, she was denounced by many other researchers, who refused to believe that a virus was responsible for leukemia. Over the next year support for Friend's theory mounted, first as Dr. Jacob Furth declared that his experiments had confirmed the existence of such a virus in mice with leukemia. Even more importantly, Friend was successful in vaccinating mice against leukemia by injecting a weakened form of the virus (now called the "Friend virus") into healthy mice, so they could develop antibodies to fight off the normal virus. Friend's presentation of a paper on this vaccine at the cancer research association's 1957 meeting succeeded in laying to rest the skepticism that had greeted her the previous year.

In 1962, Friend was honored with the Alfred P. Sloan Award for Cancer Research and another award from the American Cancer Society for her work. The next year she became a member of the New York Academy of Sciences, an organization that has members from all fifty states and more than eighty countries. In 1966 Friend left Sloan-Kettering to become a professor and director at the Center for Experimental Cell Biology at the newly formed medical school of New York's Mount Sinai Hospital. During this time she continued her research on leukemia, and in 1972 she announced the discovery of a method of altering a leukemia mouse cell in a test tube so that it would no longer multiply. Through chemical treatment, the malignant red blood cell could be made to produce hemoglobin, as do normal cells.

Although the virus responsible for leukemia in mice has been discovered, there is no confirmation that a virus causes leukemia in humans. Likewise, her treatment for malignant red blood cells has limited application, because it will not work outside of test tubes. Nonetheless, Friend had pointed out a possible cause of cancer and developed a first step toward fighting leukemia (and possibly other cancers) by targeting specific cells.

In 1976, Friend was elected president of the American Association for Cancer Research, the same organization whose members had so strongly criticized her twenty years earlier. Two years later, she was chosen the first woman president of the New York Academy of Sciences. Friend was long active in supporting other women scientists and in speaking out on women's issues. During her later years, she expressed concern over the tendency to emphasize patient care over basic research, feeling that without sufficient funding for research, new breakthroughs in patient care would be impossible. Friend died on January 13, 1987, of lymphoma.

SELECTED WRITINGS BY FRIEND:

Periodicals

"Cell-Free Transmission in Adult Swiss Mice of a Disease Having the Characteristic of Leukemia," *Journal of Experimental Medicine,* Volume 105, 1957, pp. 307–318.

"Immunological Relationships of a Filterable Agent Causing a Leukemia in Adult Mice," *Journal of Experimental Medicine,* Volume 10, 1959, pp. 217–221.

(With J. G. Holland, William Scher, and Toru Sato) "Hemoglobin Synthesis in Murine Virus-Induced Leukemia Cells In-Vitro: Stimulation of Erythroid Differentiation by Dimethyl Sulfoxide," *Proceedings of National Academy of Sciences,* Volume 68, pp. 378–382.

SOURCES:

Books

Beattie, Edward, *Towards the Conquest of Cancer,* Crown Publishing, 1988.

Marget, Madeline, *Life's Blood,* Simon & Schuster, 1992.

Noble, Iris, *Contemporary Women Scientists,* Julian Messner, 1979.

Periodicals

Diamond, Leila, and Sandra Wolman, "Viral Oncogenesis and Cell Differentiation: The Contributions of Charlotte Friend," *Annals of the New York Academy of Sciences,* Volume 567, August 4, 1989.

Papers of Charlotte Friend, Mount Sinai Medical Center, 1993.

Schmeck, Harold M., Jr., "Charlotte Friend Dies at 65; Researched Cancer Viruses," *New York Times,* January 16, 1987.

"Science Academy Installs First Female President," *Newsday,* December 9, 1977.

Thomas, Emy, "Cancer Award Honors Woman," *New York World-Telegram and Sun,* May 9, 1962.

—*Sketch by Francis Rogers*

Karl von Frisch
1886-1982
Austrian zoologist

Karl von Frisch

Karl von Frisch won the Nobel Prize in 1973 for his pioneering work in the field of animal physiology and behavior. Frisch was a leading researcher in the study of insect behavior, and his studies proved that fish have acute hearing and that bees communicate effectively through a ritual dance. Frisch's discoveries and subsequent Nobel Prize were also significant because this was the first major acknowledgement of advances made in the study of ethology.

Frisch was born in Vienna in 1886 into a family dedicated to science. His father, Anton Ritter von Frisch, was a physician, and his mother, Marie Exner, came from a long line of distinguished scientists and scholars. From his earliest years, Frisch was exposed to the natural world, in large part due to a country house that his family retreated to every summer. There, the young Frisch spent his time collecting various species of animals. "Even before I went to school," he wrote in his autobiography, *A Biologist Remembers,* "I had a little zoo in my room." But Frisch was not simply a collector; he was also a keen observer. "I discovered that miraculous worlds may reveal themselves to a patient observer where the casual passer-by sees nothing at all," he said in his autobiography. A few early observations—most notably that the sea animals he collected in an aquarium in his room waved their tentacles when he turned on the lights—piqued an interest in the sensory systems of animals that would last his lifetime.

By the time Frisch reached college age, it was clear that his interests were focused on zoology. Nevertheless, his father thought medicine a more practical field than zoology, and in 1905 Frisch enrolled as a student of medicine at the University of Vienna. Medical school, Frisch later wrote, proved invaluable in providing a background in histology, anatomy and human physiology. He studied with his uncle, Sigmund Exner, who was a renowned physiologist and lecturer at the university. Though Exner taught human physiology, he encouraged his nephew to pursue his interest in animals by aiding him in a research project on the position of pigments in the compound eyes of certain beetles, butterflies and crustaceans. According to Frisch, his uncle's openness toward the study of animals in a course limited to human physiology was unheard of at the time. Comparing the physiology of humans and animals would only later be seen as so invaluable that it was made into a separate discipline. In the middle of his third year as a medical student, Frisch found himself increasingly frustrated by the "medical character" of the curriculum. He finally decided to drop his medical studies to pursue the field of ethology, or the study of animal behavior. He transferred to the Zoological Institute at the University of Munich, where he studied under Richard von Hertwig. He continued to cultivate the interests he had developed under his uncle's leadership, researching light perception and color changes in minnows. It was at this time that he discovered minnows had an area on the forehead filled with sensory cells—a "third, very primitive eye," he called it in *A Biologist Remembers.* This explained why blind minnows reacted to light by changing color in the same way as minnows with sight. Frisch wrote his doctoral thesis on this subject and received his degree in 1910.

Challenges Scientific Community

Frisch also began to question the common assumption of the time that fish and all invertebrates were color blind. He successfully trained minnows to respond to colored objects, proving that they could perceive color. These findings, however, were not kindly received by members of the scientific community, and Frisch's most notable opponent was Karl von Hess, the director of Munich Eye Clinic. The debate arose partly because of the theoretical connection between Frisch and the views of the famous naturalist Charles Darwin. Frisch believed in Darwinism, which theorized that the survival of certain species of animals depended on the development of their senses. Frisch hypothesized that animal behavior, rather than simply being a fixed mechanism, had an "adaptive biological significance," assumptions that were still a source of disagreement among scientists at the time. Despite the arguments about his research, Frisch was offered a teaching job at the University of Munich in 1921.

While teaching at the University of Munich, Frisch continued to study color perception in animals on vacations spent at his family's summer home. Having proved that color-blindness in fish was a fallacy, he turned to prove the same for bees. He conjectured that the adaptive purpose of the bright coloration of flowers was to guide bees to nectar. The bees, in turn, aided the flowers through pollination. That bees would be color-blind seemed untenable to Frisch. To test his hypothesis, he used research strategies similar to the ones he had used with fish. He conditioned their behavior by placing drops of sugar water on squares of blue-colored cardboard. He then placed these blue squares among plain gray squares. Eventually, he placed blue squares without sugar water among the gray squares. He found that the bees continued to go to the blue squares for their food, proving that they could differentiate color.

In 1914 Frisch's research was interrupted by the outbreak of World War I. He was excused from military duty because of poor eyesight but accepted a plea from his brother, who was a physician, to volunteer at a Red Cross hospital in dire need of help. His background in medical school qualified him to establish a bacteriologic laboratory at the hospital, enabling rapid diagnosis of diseases such as cholera, dysentery and typhoid. While at the hospital, he met a nurse, Margarethe Mohr, whom he married in 1917. Eventually they had three daughters and a son.

Meanwhile his research on bees continued to deepen. During the war, he would take a few weeks' leave from the hospital every summer, returning to his country house to research the bees. As the war came to an end, his work at the hospital lessened and his students returned to the Zoological Institute. After a 4-year hiatus, he began teaching again and in January 1919 became an assistant professor.

Discovers the "Dance of the Bees"

Eventually Frisch became interested in scout bees—those that left the hive to explore a region for food. He set out dishes of sugar water and observed their behavior. When the dish was empty a scout bee occasionally came to the dish. When the food dish was full the scout would return in a matter of minutes with a whole company of bees. "It was clear to me that the bee community possessed an excellent intelligence function," Frisch wrote in his autobiography, "but how it functioned I did not know."

In the spring of 1919 Frisch developed a glass cage in which he placed a single honeycomb that could be observed from all sides. Through continuous observation and experimentation, Frisch concluded that scout bees, who foraged for food for the whole honeycomb, conveyed this information to the other bees by performing a kind of dance on the honeycomb. This dance excited the forager bees, who then flew directly to the food. In retrospect, Frisch called his first discovery of the bees' dance "the most far-reaching observation of my life." It would be another 20 years before Frisch fully understood the complexity of this dance.

In the fall of 1921, Frisch was appointed professor of zoology and director of the Zoologic Institute at Rostock University and began investigating whether fish could hear. The physiology of fish indicated that they could not. They did not have any of the characteristics thought to be necessary for the sense of hearing, like ear lobes, auditory canals, middle ears, or a cochlea in the inner ear, which was thought to be the center of hearing in humans. Frisch used his proven methods of behavior conditioning to test hearing in fish. He whistled to blind catfish before feeding them. Eventually he whistled but did not feed them and the catfish continued to respond. The answer seemed simple—or, as one skeptical scientist put it, "There is no doubt. The fish comes when you whistle." Frisch eventually refined his early research in this area with the help of his students and discovered other facts that supported his initial findings.

In 1925 Frisch began working at the Zoological Institute of the University of Munich. However, during World War II, the Zoological Institute at the University was destroyed, and Frisch spent those years in his country home and at the University of Graz. In 1950 he returned to Munich to rebuild the Institute as its director. During this time, he wrote many books for the general public as well as for the scientific community. Frisch retired in 1958 and died in 1982.

The Nobel Prize

About his life's work, Frisch wrote philosophically in *A Biologist Remembers:* "The layman may wonder why a biologist is content to devote 50 years of his life to the study of bees and minnows without ever branching out into research on, say, elephants, or at any rate the lice of elephants or the fleas of moles. The answer to any such question must be that every single species of the animal kingdom challenges us with all, or nearly all, the mysteries of life."

This attitude was shared by the Nobel committee, who rewarded him with the prize in medicine and physiology in 1973. The prize, which Frisch shared with two other animal behaviorists, **Konrad Lorenz** and **Nikolaas Tinbergen**, was a departure for the Nobel Committee. Never before had there been such public recognition of the interactive study of animals and humans. In an article in *Science* magazine regarding the Nobel Prize, Frisch was praised for teaching the world that "human behavior [is not] something . . . outside nature" but something that is "subject to the principles that mold the biology, adaptability and the survival of other organisms."

SELECTED WRITINGS BY FRISCH:

Books

Bees: Their Vision, Chemical Senses, and Language, Cornell University Press, 1950.

The Dancing Bees: An Account of the Life and Senses of the Honey Bee, Methuen, 1954, Harcourt, 1955.

Ten Little Housemates, translation by Margaret D. Senft, Pergamon, 1960.

Man and the Living World, Harcourt, 1963.

A Biologist Remembers, translation by Lisbeth Gombrich, Pergamon, 1967.

SOURCES:

Books

Current Biography, H. W. Wilson, February, 1974.

Periodicals

New York Times, October 12, 1973.

Science, November 2, 1973, pp. 464–466.

—Sketch by Dorothy Barnhouse

Otto Robert Frisch
1904-1979
Austrian-born English experimental physicist and inventor

Otto Robert Frisch was an Austrian experimental physicist, noted for his contribution to the development of atomic physics. He was one of the first to realize the possibility of separating uranium isotopes and using the resultant uranium–235 to manufacture the atom bomb. He also played an important role in the development of the American atomic bomb.

Frisch was born in Vienna on October 1, 1904, to Justinian Frisch and Auguste Meitner. His mother was an accomplished pianist, composer, and conductor, though she largely retired from music when she married. Frisch's aunt, on his mother's side, was the renowned atomic physicist, **Lise Meitner**. Justinian Frisch, who had a doctorate in law and a love of art, held a variety of jobs before settling down to a career, variously, as a technical advisor to a publishing company, a publisher, and a printer. During World War II, he spent time in a concentration camp.

Frisch's love of mathematics, kindled by his father, was obvious from an early age. In 1914, at the age of ten, he was sent to the local high school, where he distinguished himself not just in math and science, but also in languages and art. In 1922, Frisch entered the University of Vienna, taking physics as his major and math as his minor. For his doctoral thesis, he prepared a paper on the discoloration of rock salt by cathode rays. Frisch graduated in 1926 with a D.Phil. at the age of twenty-two.

He first joined a company that manufactured X-ray dosimeters. After a year, he was offered a job in Berlin in the optics division of the Physikalisch Technische Reischsanstalt (PTR), a government-run laboratory, under Dr. Carl Müller, an inventor. Together they worked on developing a new unit of brightness to replace the candle power. During this period, Frisch attended weekly lectures at the University of Berlin, where he met some of the great physicists of the day, including Max Planck and Albert Einstein. In his third year at PTR, he worked part-time in the University of Berlin's physics department under the direction of Professor Peter Pringsheim, whom he helped to design an instrument to detect mercury vapors in the air.

He left PTR in 1930 to become an assistant to **Professor Otto Stern,** the Nobel Prize-winning experimental physicist, at the University of Hamburg. There his duties were to take measurements and help design the equipment used in their research into molecular beams. In one of their experiments, they proved that beams of atoms or molecules, like beams of electrons, behave like waves. Frisch also published the results of his own research into the particle-like characteristics of light.

With the rise to power of Hitler, Frisch, with his Jewish background, was ousted from the university and forced to leave Germany for England in 1933. With the help of Stern, he managed to secure a grant from the newly established Academic Assistance Council, which enabled him to work under **Patrick Blackett** at Birkbeck College, London. Blackett put Frisch to work finding the gamma rays thought to be emitted by the mutual annihilation of positrons and electrons. Unfortunately, he was beaten to it by two French scientists. He then turned to the construction of a cloud chamber that would be sensitive to particles passing through it for over a second and allow them to be photographed. Although technically successful, it never caught on as a research tool, and Frisch quickly turned his attention to the emerging science of artificial radioactivity. Discovered in 1933 by the husband and wife team of **Frédéric Joliot-Curie** and **Irène Joliot-Curie,** artificial radioactivity seemed to occur when the nucleus of a stable aluminum atom was bombarded with alpha particles, that is, helium nuclei traveling at several thousand miles a second. Frisch built a machine that could detect the emission of very short-lived particles or rays, and within days, was able to detect radioactive emissions from phosphorous and sodium.

When Frisch's year in London was up, Danish physicist **Niels Bohr** invited him to join the Institute of Theoretical Physics in Copenhagen. Here he was introduced to many of the day's great scientists, some of whom he captured in the pen and ink drawings he was so fond of producing. Frisch also enjoyed playing the violin and the piano, and was particularly fond of chamber music. He was a keen tennis player and mountaineer.

Initially, he continued the work he had begun in London with Blackett, discovering two more radioactive isotopes. Then he moved into the study of neutrons. With the Czech physicist George Placzek, he measured the absorption of neutrons shot at slow speed through gold, cadmium, boron, and other elements. For the thick layers of gold they needed for their experiment, the two scientists used several Nobel Prize medals that some of Bohr's German friends had left with him for safe keeping! They demonstrated that gold and cadmium have a strong preference for capturing neutrons of well-defined low energy, confirming Bohr's theory of the compound nucleus.

Explains Nuclear Fission

In 1938, Frisch played an important in explaining the results of an experiment by the German scientists **Otto Hahn** and **Fritz Strassmann**. In bombarding the nucleus of uranium with slow moving neutrons, they discovered that a substance was emitted that seemed to be an isotope of barium, but could not explain their results. It was Frisch, together with his aunt, Lise Meitner, who accounted for their findings, and experimentally proved that the uranium nucleus had cleaved into two halves. Frisch was the first to use the term "fission" to describe the process. Nephew and aunt cooperated on follow-up experiments in Copenhagen on the byproducts of fission, demonstrating the variety of half-lives possessed by various radioactive substances. Frisch was also kept busy designing parts for a cyclotron, a spiral particle accelerator.

In 1939, Frisch's research was once again interrupted by Hitler, this time with the invasion of Denmark. At the invitation of the Australian physicist Marcus Oliphant, he accepted a post as auxiliary lecturer at the University of Birmingham, where he continued his research into nuclear fission. Because of the war and the secrecy surrounding his work, he was unable to publish his important discovery of spontaneous nuclear fission and the credit for that finding went to two Russian physicists. He was credited, though, with the idea of separating uranium isotopes to produce pure uranium–235, the substance used to start nuclear chain reactions. The results of his experiments were sent to the British government and led to the founding of the Maud Committee, a group charged with investigating the possibility of Britain developing nuclear explosives. Ironically, Frisch was invited to serve as a technical advisor to its subcommittee even though he was officially a German.

Limited by the war work that was going on in Birmingham, Frisch moved to Liverpool in August of 1940 to continue his experiments under **James Chadwick**. Here he supervised the building of a machine used to measure the isotopic composition of uranium by examination of its alpha ray spectrum. Called a pulse height analyzer or kicksorter, it was later refined and is now a standard instrument in nuclear physics labs.

Joins American A-Bomb Project

Frisch became a English citizen in 1943 so that he could accept an invitation to join the American atomic bomb project under the direction of **J. Robert Oppenheimer** at Los Alamos in the New Mexican desert. He mainly developed equipment for the project, but also served as group leader of the famous "dragon experiment," which was a sort of dry run of a nuclear explosion. Frisch designed "the guillotine," the apparatus used to carry out the test, and was also engaged in experiments carried out near the first explosive site.

After the war ended in 1945, Frisch joined the Atomic Energy Research Establishment in Harwell, England, as a division leader with the grade of Deputy Chief Scientific Officer. The following year, he was awarded the Order of the British Empire by the Queen. In 1947, Frisch was offered the Jacksonian Professorship at the University of Cambridge, where he was in charge of the nuclear physics department of the Cavendish Laboratory. He became fully integrated into the British physics establishment in 1948 when he was elected a fellow of the Royal Society. In 1951, Frisch married Ulla Blau, an Austrian-born graphic artist, with whom he had a son, Tony—who delighted his father by becoming a physicist—and a daughter, Monica.

One of Frisch's most important achievements at Cambridge was his invention of the "Sweepnik" nuclear measuring device for measuring the tracks of charged particles as they pass through the liquid of a bubble chamber. The prototype was so successful that a company, Laserscan Ltd., was set up to manufacture them. Frisch was named chairman, a position he held until his death. After his retirement from Cambridge in 1972 at the age of sixty-seven, Frisch continued working for the firm. Frisch was almost seventy-five when he died on September 22, 1979, from injuries received in a fall.

SELECTED WRITINGS BY FRISCH:

Books

Meet the Atom: A Popular Guide to the Modern Physics, A. A. Wynn, 1947.

Atomic Physics Today, Basic Books, 1961.

Working with Atoms, Brockhampton Press, 1965.

The Nature of Matter, Thames & Hudson, 1973.

What Little I Remember, Cambridge University Press, 1979.

SOURCES:

Periodicals

Peirls, Sir Rudolf, "Otto Robert Frisch," *Proceedings of the Royal Society,* Volume 27, 1981, pp. 283–306.

—*Sketch by Avril McDonald*

Tetsuya Theodore Fujita
1920-
Japanese-born American meteorologist

In 1974, Tetsuya Theodore Fujita became the first scientist to identify microburst wind shear, a particularly intense and isolated form of wind shear later blamed for several devastating airline accidents in the 1980s. The development of Doppler radar allowed Fujita to track and explain the microburst phenomenon, which in the 1990s is far better understood and avoided by aviators. Fujita also lent his name to the "F Scale" he developed to measure the strength of tornadoes by analyzing the damage they cause on the ground.

Fujita was born in Kitakyushu City, Japan, on October 23, 1920, to Tomojiro, a schoolteacher, and Yoshie (Kanesue) Fujita. Fujita showed an early aptitude for science and obtained the equivalent of a bachelor's degree in mechanical engineering from the Meji College of Technology in 1943. It was while he was working as an assistant professor of physics at Meji that U.S. forces dropped the atom bomb on the Japanese cities of Hiroshima and Nagasaki. Fujita visited the ruins three weeks after the bombings. By measuring the scorch marks on bamboo vases in a cemetery in Nagasaki, Fujita was able to show that only one bomb had been dropped. Surveying the damage in Hiroshima, Fujita calculated how high above the ground the bombs had exploded in order to create their unique starburst patterns, which would become important to his later work.

Leaving Meji College in 1949, Fujita became an assistant professor at Kyushu Institute of Technology

Tetsuya Theodore Fujita

while pursuing his Ph.D. in atmospheric science at Tokyo University. Like others involved in atmospheric science, he had read the published articles of Horace R. Byers of the University of Chicago, who had conducted groundbreaking research on thunderstorms in 1946 and 1947. Fujita translated two of his own articles on the same subject into English and sent them to Byers. Byers was impressed with Fujita's work and the two men began a correspondence. In 1953, the year Fujita received his doctorate, Byers extended an invitation to the Japanese scientist to work at the University of Chicago as a visiting research associate.

Fujita worked at the University as a senior meteorologist until 1962, when he became an associate professor. For two years beginning in 1961, he was the director of the Mesometeorological Research Project, and in 1964 Fujita became the director of the Satellite and Mesometeorology Research Project. Fujita was made a full professor in 1965 and has held the Charles E. Merriam Distinguished Service Professorship since 1989 on an active basis and on an emeritus basis since 1991. He became a naturalized U.S. citizen in 1968 and adopted the first name Theodore for use in the United States. He married Sumiko Yamamo in June, 1969, and has a son, Kazuya, from his first marriage.

Creates F Scale

Since the mid-1960s, Fujita and his graduate students had done extensive aerial surveys of tornadoes. Fujita claims to have logged over 40,000 miles flying in small planes under the worst of weather conditions. In the late 1960s, Fujita developed his tornado "F Scale." Traditionally, meteorologists had listed only the total number of tornadoes that occurred, having no objective way to measure storm strength. Fujita constructed a system of measurement that correlates ground damage to windspeed. His six point system operates on an F-0 to F-5 scale and is similar to the Richter scale used to measure the strength of earthquakes.

Fujita did not actually witness a tornado until June 12, 1982, so the mainstay of his work was research on the aftermath of tornadoes. While at the National Center for Atmospheric Research in Denver, Colorado, Fujita spotted a tornado in the region early and collected some of the best data on the phenomenon ever.

Introduces Concept of Microbursts

In 1974, Fujita began analyzing the phenomenon of microbursts. Flying over the devastation wrought by a tornado, he noticed patterns of damage similar to those he had witnessed in Hiroshima and Nagasaki. "If something comes down from the sky and hits the ground it will spread out; it will produce the same kind of outburst effect that was in the back of my mind, from 1945 to 1974," Fujita explained in *The Weather Book: An Easy to Understand Guide to the U.S.A.'s Weather.* Meteorologists knew by the mid-1970s that severe storms produce downdrafts, but they assumed those downdrafts lost most of their force before they hit the ground and therefore did not cause much damage, so the phenomenon was largely ignored. Encouraged by Byers, Fujita coined the term "downburst" and began research to prove his thesis that downdraft is a significant weather phenomenon. Aided by the National Center for Atmospheric Research, he set up a project near Chicago that detected 52 downbursts in 42 days.

Fujita was eventually able to show that downdrafts cause so-called wind shear, a sudden and dramatic change in wind velocity, which causes damage on the ground and is a particular hazard in aviation, especially to planes taking off, landing, or flying low. Windspeeds up to F-3 are common for downbursts (higher F Scale readings usually indicate tornadoes). Fujita has commented that a lot of damage attributed to tornadoes in the past has really been the work of downbursts. "After I pointed out the existence of downbursts, the number of tornadoes listed in the United States decreased for a number of years," Fujita noted in *The Weather Book.*

Fujita's research finally gained national attention in the 1980s. Wind shear caused by downdraft was cited as a contributing factor in the July, 1982, crash of a Pan American 727 in New Orleans, Louisiana, which killed 154 people. During that event, the airliner was observed sinking back to the ground shortly after takeoff—the apparent result of wind shear. Another accident occurred in August, 1985, when Delta Flight 191 crashed at Dallas-Ft. Worth Airport, killing 133 people. Again wind shear was suspected to be the immediate cause of the catastrophe.

Air safety has improved dramatically because of Fujita's work, which led to the development of Doppler radar. Doppler radar is so sensitive it actually picks up particles of debris in the air that are as fine as dust. Movements of these particles are tracked to measure shifts in wind velocity. "This is particularly important in being able to detect the precursor events for severe weather," Frank Lepore, public affairs officer for the National Weather Service, told Joan Oleck in an interview. By 1996, the Weather Service and U.S. Air Force together will have installed 137 Doppler systems, essentially blanketing the continental United States. Harking back to the airline accidents of the 1980s, Lepore noted "a reduction in those incidents today because there is Doppler radar available. By being able to measure the internal velocity of air moving inside a storm system, [aviators] can see rising and falling volumes of air. . . . They're now getting 20- and 25-minute warning on the systems that cause tornadoes."

Since 1988, Fujita has directed the Wind Research Lab at the University of Chicago. Among his many awards have been the 1989 Medaille de Vermeil from the French National Academy of Air and Science for identifying microbursts; the 1990 Fujiwara Award Medal from the Meteorological Society of Japan for his research on mesometeorology; the 1991 Order of the Sacred Treasure, Gold and Silver Star from the Government of Japan for his tornado and microburst work; and the 1992 Transportation Cultural Award from the Japanese Government for his contributions to air safety.

SELECTED WRITINGS BY FUJITA:

Books

The Downburst: Microburst and Macroburst, Report of Projects NIMROD and JAWS, University of Chicago Satellite and Mesometeorology Research Project, Department of the Geophysical Sciences, 1985.

DFW Microburst on August 2, 1985, University of Chicago Satellite and Mesometeorology Research Project, Department of the Geophysical Sciences, 1986.

U.S. Tornadoes, Part I, 70-Year Statistics, University of Chicago Satellite and Mesometeorology Research Project, Department of the Geophysical Sciences, 1987.

SOURCES:

Books

Williams, Jack, *The Weather Book: An Easy to Understand Guide to the U.S.A.'s Weather,* Vintage Books, 1992, pp. 122–23.

Periodicals

Frank, James, "Mr. Tornado," *Chicago Tribune,* May 10, 1990.

McClellan, J. Mac, "Technicalities: Tracking the Elusive Wind Shear," *Flying,* October, 1982, pp. 22–23.

McKean, Kevin, "Solving the Mystery of Wind Shear," *Discover,* September 1982, pp. 78–81.

Taubes, Gary, "Ted Fujita: On the Tornado's Tail," *Discover,* May, 1983, pp. 48–53.

Other

Lepore, Frank, interview with Joan Oleck conducted on September 30, 1993.

—*Sketch by Joan Oleck*

Kenichi Fukui
1918-
Japanese engineer and theoretical chemist

Kenichi Fukui is a theoretical chemist whose career has been devoted to explaining the nature of chemical reactions. His work is distinguished from that of other chemists by its mathematical structure, and he has made a major contribution to bridging the gap between quantum theory, a mathematical theory of the behavior of molecules and atoms, and practical chemistry. He has made it easier both to understand and predict the course of chemical reactions, and he shared the 1981 Nobel Prize in chemistry with **Roald Hoffmann** for his achievements.

Fukui was born October 4, 1918, in Nara on the island of Honshu, Japan. He was the eldest of three sons born to Chie and Ryokichi Fukui. His father was a merchant and factory manager who played a major role in shaping his son's career; he persuaded Fukui to study chemistry. Fukui had no interest in chemistry during high school, and he later described his father's persuasiveness as the "most decisive occurrence in my educational career." He enrolled at the Department of Industrial Chemistry at Kyoto Imperial

Kenichi Fukui

University, and he has remained associated with that university ever since. Fukui graduated from the university in 1941, and he spent most of World War II at a fuel laboratory, performing research on the chemistry of synthetic fuel.

Fukui returned to Kyoto University in 1945, when he was named assistant professor. He received his Ph.D. in engineering in 1948 and was elevated to a full professorship in physical chemistry in 1951. At the beginning of his career, his research interests ranged broadly through the areas of chemical reaction theory, quantum chemistry, and physical chemistry. But during the 1950s, Fukui began theorizing about the role of electron orbitals in molecular reactions. Molecules are groups of atoms held together by electron bonds. Electrons circle the nuclei in what are called orbitals, similar to the orbit of planets around the sun in our solar system. Whenever molecules react with one another, at least one of these electron bonds is broken and altered, forming a new bond and thus changing the molecular structure. At the time Fukui began his work, scientists understood this process only when one bond was changed; the more complex reactions, however, were not understood at all.

Theories Increase Understanding of Chemical Reactions

During the 1950s, Fukui theorized that the significant elements of this interaction occurred in the highest occupied molecular orbital of one molecule (HOMO) and the lowest unoccupied molecular orbital of another (LUMO). Fukui named these "frontier orbitals." The HOMO has high energy and is willing to lose an electron, and the LUMO has low energy and is thus willing to accept an electron. The resulting bond, according to Fukui, is at an energy level between the two starting points. Over the next decade, Fukui developed and tested his theory using complex mathematical formulas, and he attempted to use it to predict the process of molecular interaction and bonding.

Fukui continued to break new ground in theoretical chemistry through the 1960s. Other chemists began research on these same problems during this period, but Fukui's work was largely neglected. His use of advanced mathematics made his theories difficult for most chemists to understand, and his articles were published in journals that were not widely read in the United States and Europe. In an interview quoted in the *New York Times,* Fukui also attributed some of his obscurity to resistance from Japanese colleagues: "The Japanese are very conservative when it comes to new theory. But once you get appreciated in the United States or Europe, then after that the appreciation spreads back to Japan."

Two of the chemists who had been working independently of Fukui were Roald Hoffmann of Cornell University and **Robert B. Woodward** of Harvard, and in 1965 they came to conclusions that were similar to his, though they had arrived there along a different path. Staying away from complex math, these two developed a formula almost as simple as a pictorial representation. Taken together, the work of Fukui and the American team enabled research scientists to predict how reactions would occur and to understand many complexities never before explained. These formulae answered questions about why some reactions between molecules occurred quickly and others slowly, as well as why certain molecules reacted better with some molecules than with others. They removed much of guesswork from this area of chemistry research.

For the advancements in knowledge their work had brought, Fukui and Hoffmann were jointly awarded the 1981 Nobel Prize in chemistry. Woodward, who would probably also have shared in the prize, had died two years before. Fukui was one of the first Japanese to receive the Nobel Prize in any field, and the very first in the area of chemistry. Since winning the Nobel Prize, Fukui has remained at Kyoto University, and he is still active in his field. He has continued his research on chemical reactions and has expanded his formula to predict the interaction of three or more molecules.

Fukui was elected senior foreign scientist of the American National Science Foundation in 1970. In 1973, he participated in the United States-Japan

Eminent Scientist Exchange Program. In 1978 and 1979, he was vice-president of the Chemical Society in Japan, and he served as their president from 1983 to 1984. In 1980, he was made a foreign member of the National Academy of Sciences, and in 1982 he was named President of the Kyoto University of Industrial Arts and Textile Fibers. He is a member of the International Academy of Quantum Molecular Science, the European Academy of Arts, Sciences, and Humanities, and the American Academy of Arts and Sciences.

Fukui was married in 1947 to Tomoe Horie. They have one son and one daughter. In his spare time Fukui enjoys walking, fishing, and golf.

SELECTED WRITINGS BY FUKUI:

Books

Theory of Orientation and Stereoselection, Springer-Verlag, 1975.

SOURCES:

Books

Nobel Prize Winners, H. W. Wilson, 1987.

Periodicals

Boffey, Philip M., "2 Share Nobel in chemistry; 3 Win in Physics," *New York Times,* October 20, 1981, p. A1.

"Chemistry Prize to Fukui and Hoffmann," *Physics Today,* December, 1981, pp. 20–22.

Streitwieser, Andrew Jr., "The 1981 Nobel in Chemistry," *Science,* November 6, 1981, pp. 627–629.

—*Sketch by Kimberlyn McGrail*

Solomon Fuller
1872-1953
Liberian-born American neurologist and psychiatrist

Solomon Fuller, the first black psychiatrist in the United States, played a key role in the development of psychiatry in the 1900s. Known for his research on dementia, Fuller helped make the United

Solomon Fuller

States the leader in psychiatry that it is today. In addition, as a professor at Boston University School of Medicine for more than 30 years, Fuller helped train the next generation of psychiatrists.

Solomon Carter Fuller was born on August 11, 1872 in Monrovia, Liberia. His family, however, had American roots; his grandfather, John Lewis Fuller, had been a slave in Virginia who had been able to buy his freedom and move his family to Liberia. Solomon's father, also named Solomon, was a coffee planter and an official in the Liberian government. His mother, Anna Ursala James, whose parents were physicians and missionaries, set up a school to teach Carter and other area children. Fuller's early education also included six years—from age 10 to 16—at the College Preparatory School of Monrovia.

In 1889, at the age of 17, Fuller left Liberia to attend Livingstone College in North Carolina. He graduated in 1893, began studying medicine at Long Island College Hospital, and later transferred to Boston University School of Medicine. Fuller received his M.D. degree in 1897. Upon graduation, Fuller accepted a position as intern and official helper in the pathology lab at Westborough State Hospital in Massachusetts. After two years he was promoted to pathologist, a position in which he remained for 22 years. Fuller was also a consultant to the hospital for an additional 23 years.

At the same time that he was beginning his career in medicine, Fuller also became a member of the medical faculty at Boston University School of Medicine. He taught at BUSM for 34 years, becoming, in turn, an instructor, lecturer, associate professor, and emeritus professor of neurology.

Focus on Mental Illness

According to Robert H. Sharpley in George E. Gifford, Jr.'s *Psychoanalysis, Psychotherapy, and the New England Medical Scene, 1844–1944,* Fuller's decision to pursue a career in neurology and psychiatry was influenced by a lecture at the American Medico-Psychological Association given by neurologist S. Weir Mitchell. According to Sharpley, Mitchell, in his lecture, criticized hospitals for not studying mental illness. In addition, he called for hospitals to study both the pathology and psychology of their patients. Fuller followed Mitchell's advice by collecting and analyzing data on patients with various mental disorders, Sharpley says. To further his knowledge, in 1900 Fuller took advanced courses at the Carnegie Laboratory in New York. He then went to Europe in 1904, studying under Emil Kraepelin and Alois Alzheimer, professors at the University of Munich's psychiatric clinic. Once back in the United States, Fuller continued his work at Westborough and BUSM. Fuller became known for his work on Alzheimer's disease, a degenerative neurological disorder in which memory, judgment, and the ability to reason progressively deteriorate. He also focused his research on the organic causes of disorders such as schizophrenia and manic-depressive psychosis (now called bipolar disorder). Finally, Fuller practiced psychiatry, which he continued past his retirement.

Fuller helped develop the neuropsychiatric unit at the Veterans Administration Hospital in Tuskegee, Alabama, personally training the doctors who went on to head the department. According to Sharpley, Fuller's knowledge of the venereal disease, syphilis later helped these doctors diagnose syphilis in black World War II veterans who had been misdiagnosed with behavioral disorders.

In 1909 Fuller married Meta Vaux Warrick, a sculptor who had at one point studied under Rodin. Fuller and his wife had three sons. In his personal life, Fuller enjoyed photography, gardening, and book binding. Though he became blind in his later years, by all reports he continued to work, seeing patients and reading via "talking books." Fuller died on January 16, 1953. Though Fuller hated being called "an excellent black psychiatrist," he is remembered to this day both for his work and for his pioneering role as the first black psychiatrist. The mental health facility at Boston University is now officially known as the Dr. Solomon Carter Fuller Mental Health Center. And in 1972, the American Psychiatric Association and the Black Psychiatrists of America established the Solomon Carter Fuller Institute.

SELECTED WRITINGS BY FULLER:

Periodicals

"Four Cases of Pernicious Anemia among Insane Subjects," *New England Medical Gazette,* 1901.

"Neurofibrils in Manic Depressive Insanity," *Manic-Depressive Symposium,* New England Society of Psychiatry, 1910.

SOURCES:

Books

"Solomon Carter Fuller," by Robert H. Sharpley, in *Psychoanalysis, Psychotherapy, and the New England Medical Scene, 1844–1944,* edited by George E. Gifford, Jr., Science History Publications/USA, 1978, pp. 181–195.

Periodicals

Boston Globe, June 8, 1971, p. C2.

"Solomon Carter Fuller, 1872–1953," by Montague W. Cobb, *Journal of the National Medical Association,* September, 1954, pp. 370–372.

"Solomon Carter Fuller," by Owen J. McNamara, *Centerscope,* winter, 1976, pp. 26–30.

—Sketch by Devera Pine

Dennis Gabor
1900-1979
Hungarian-born English physicist

Dennis Gabor

Dennis Gabor is best known for inventing and developing holography, which earned him the Nobel Prize in physics in 1971. Early in his career, Gabor built a crude prototype of the electron microscope, but did not pursue its development, and his regret over not continuing his work on this idea lasted throughout his lifetime. The discovery of holography was Gabor's triumph, though he could not have realized at the time the widespread application it has today. Among Gabor's other achievements was the quartz mercury lamp.

Dennis Gabor, the oldest of three sons, was born on June 5, 1900, in Budapest, Hungary. His mother, Ady Jacobvits, was a former actress. His father, Berthold, grandson of Russian-Jewish immigrants, ultimately became the director of the Hungarian General Coal Mines. Although Gabor's family became Lutherans in 1918, religion appeared to play a minor role in his life. He maintained his church affiliation through his adult years but characterized himself as a "benevolent agnostic."

Gabor showed an early interest in science. By age fifteen he and his younger brother George were replicating experiments they read about in science journals in their homemade laboratory. After being called up for military service in the Austro-Hungarian army in 1918, Dennis Gabor joined the Officers Training Corps and trained in artillery and horsemanship. He served briefly in Italy before World War I ended. Following the war he entered the Budapest Technical University in 1918 for a four-year course in mechanical engineering. His third year was interrupted, however, when he was once again called up for military service. Since he was opposed to serving in the military for what he felt was a reactionary monarchy, he left the country and went to Berlin.

Begins Professional Scientific Investigations

Gabor studied at the Technische Hochschule in Berlin, where he earned his diploma in 1924; he received his doctorate in engineering from the same institution in 1927. His doctoral dissertation involved the measure of lightning-induced fast surges in high-voltage power lines. To measure these surges, Gabor developed a cathode-ray oscilloscope with a fast response. (An oscilloscope temporarily displays in a visible wave form the variations in a fluctuating electrical quantity.) Rather than using a coil of wire in the form of a long cylinder to carry the current (a selenoid) common at the time, Gabor chose a short, iron-encased coil. This was done to confine the magnetic field within the shorter area of the coil and prevent it from being influenced by stray magnetic fields. In this device, Gabor had the crude forerunner for the magnetic lens of an electron microscope. Gabor chose not to pursue this work, however, a choice he came to regret. He later told physicist **Leo Szilard** that, although he felt he had the expertise necessary at the time to build the electron microscope, he lost interest in electrons after finishing his doctoral work.

Later, Gabor would describe his years in Berlin as some of the happiest of his life. He frequently went to the University of Berlin to hear lectures by the renowned scientists of the day, including **Max Planck**, **Walther Nernst**, and Max von Laue. He attended a seminar conducted by **Albert Einstein** and enjoyed the company of many other future expatriate Hungarians who would flee Hitler's Germany, including Szilard, who was instrumental in convincing the U.S. government to develop the atomic bomb. When Gabor completed his doctorate in 1927, he secured a position in the physics lab of Siemens and Halske in Siemensstadt, Germany. His most notable achievement there was the invention of the quartz mercury lamp. His contract was terminated within weeks of Adolf Hitler's ascent to power in 1933.

Gabor then returned to Hungary, where he worked on the development of the plasma lamp, a new kind of fluorescent lamp. He was unable to sell the patent there but was able to work out an inventor's agreement with British Thomson-Houston Company (BTH) to work on the lamp in England. Gabor traveled to Rugby, England, and began his long association with BTH in 1934. He worked on his lamp until 1937, and was appointed to the permanent staff that year despite the fact that his efforts on the plasma lamp proved unsuccessful. From 1937 to 1948 he worked in the area of electron optics, which involves directing and focusing beams of electrons. On August 8, 1936, Gabor married Marjorie Louise Butler, a fellow employee of BTH. The Gabors had no children.

As a non-British citizen, Gabor initially was not permitted to have anything to do with the war effort during World War II. Ultimately, he was granted special status, which meant that a special research hut was built for him outside the high security area at BTH. He was not privy to any of the classified research being conducted there during the war. Indeed the only journal he was able to receive regularly was *Nature.* Because Gabor was unaware of the development of radar by fellow British scientists and its successful employment in the war against the Axis powers, he spent much of his wartime working on a system to detect airplanes by the heat of their engines. The war years also brought personal sadness to Gabor. His parents had visited him in 1938, but he could not persuade them to stay in England. They returned to Hungary shortly before Hitler invaded Poland. Then in 1942 his father, who had greatly influenced him, passed away.

Discovers Holography

After the war Gabor again turned his attention to the electron microscope. Bothered by his earlier failure to develop the instrument, he was determined to make a comeback in the field. His goal was to be able to "see" individual atoms. During this time period the resolution power of the electron microscope was limited by a technical barrier caused by the electron lens then in use. At a certain level of magnification, the lens distorted the image, and some information was lost.

Gabor's idea, which came to him while he was sitting on a bench at a tennis club in London in 1947, was to take an electron picture, distorted by problems with the lens, but one that could be corrected by optical means utilizing light. His theory was expressed in papers published that year in which he first coined the term "hologram" (Greek for "completely written"). In practical terms, Gabor's idea found only limited use as an electron-optical technique. Its implications for beams of light, however, awaited only the invention of the laser.

During these postwar years Gabor seriously considered accepting one of the many offers he received to come to the United States, feeling he lacked support at BTH for his work. His naturalization as a British citizen in 1946 was one of several factors that guaranteed he would remain in England. Gabor finally did leave BTH in 1949, when he accepted a position as a reader in electron physics at the Imperial College of Science and Technology of the University of London (a reader is the equivalent of an associate professor in an American university). Although for a time Gabor continued to entertain the possibility of moving to the United States, a number of highly skilled postgraduate students at Imperial College allowed him to work on many of his ideas. He and his students built a number of devices, including a flat television tube, a Wilson cloud chamber, and an analog computer. In 1958 he was appointed professor of applied electron physics.

During the same time period, Associated Electrical Industries, the parent company of BTH, had begun work in 1950 on a holographic electron microscope. While not directly involved in the day-to-day operations of the project, Gabor was closely involved as a consultant. By 1953 a system had been built, but the images were no better than those from other methods. In addition to random disturbances in the pictures, there were two images instead of one. No further work was done on the project, and in 1955 it was permanently shut down. Gabor was bitterly disappointed.

Nobel Prize Brings Recognition

The invention of the laser in 1960 sparked renewed interest in holography (the process of making or using holograms), since a constant narrow light source where all waves were in phase was now available to experimenters. In that same year, Emmett N. Leith and Juris Upatnieks from the Willow Run Laboratory at the University of Michigan replicated Gabor's earlier experiments and were able to eliminate the second image that had so consistently plagued Gabor as he worked on the holographic electron microscope. The first laser holograms in 1962 ensured Gabor's reputation.

In 1967, Gabor retired from Imperial College, but remained a professor emeritus and research fellow while serving as a part-time consultant for CBS Laboratories in Stamford, Connecticut. He also found time to continue his own research. He was able to show the application of holography to computer data processing, where it has been particularly useful in data compression. Additionally, he was in great demand as a speaker on the subject of holography. He received his highest honor in December of 1971, when he was awarded the Nobel Prize in physics for his work in holography. His Nobel lecture was illustrative of the issues that dominated his concerns in later years, namely the role of science and technology in society.

In the 1960s Gabor saw much that contributed to his belief in the irrationality of human behavior. He opposed both the Vietnam War and the space program. His first book on the subject, *Inventing the Future,* published in 1963, outlined his belief in the need for scientists and engineers to develop socially useful inventions. This book and its sequel, *The Mature Society,* published in 1972, are surprisingly optimistic in their outlook, given Gabor's own pessimism. He was highly influenced by novelist and critic Aldous Huxley and the British eugenicists, believing that scientific progress and enlightenment would enable humanity to move toward a socially engineered society free of the failures that have plagued human societies throughout history.

After Gabor was awarded the Nobel Prize, Lawrence Bartell of the University of Michigan set out to develop a holographic electron microscope by forming images of electron clouds in gas-phase atoms. He shared his work with Gabor in April of 1974, and Gabor immediately began designing his own holographic electron microscope. In the summer of that year, however, Gabor suffered a stroke that left him unable to read or write. Despite this he was able to maintain contact with his colleagues. He even was able to visit the Museum of Holography in New York City when it opened in 1977. He died in a London nursing home in February of 1979.

Gabor was the author of numerous works, with translations in many European languages. He was the recipient of many awards and an honored member of scientific societies around the world. The legacy of his pioneering efforts in holography is evident in science and everyday life—from medicine to computing, mapmaking, photography, and supermarket checkouts. Futurists predict that three-dimensional holographic images will play an even larger role in conveying visual information and providing entertainment.

SELECTED WRITINGS BY GABOR:

Books

The Electron Microscope, Hulton Press, 1945, Chemical Publishing Co., 1948.

Inventing the Future, Secker & Warburg, 1963, Knopf, 1964.

Innovations: Scientific, Technological, and Social, Oxford University Press, 1970.

Mature Society, Secker & Warburg, 1972. *Proper Priorities of Science and Technology,* University of Southampton Press, 1972.

Periodicals

"A New Microscopic Principle," *Nature,* May 15, 1948, pp. 777–778.

"Microscopy by Reconstructed Wave-Fronts," *Proceedings of the Royal Society,* Volume A197, 1949, p. 454.

"Microscopy by Reconstructed Wave Fronts: II," *Proceedings of the Royal Society,* Volume B64, 1951, p. 244.

SOURCES:

Books

Contemporary Authors, Volume 17–20R, Gale, 1976, p. 266.

Wasson, Tyler, editor, *Nobel Prize Winners,* H. W. Wilson, 1987, pp. 358-361.

—*Sketch by Dennis W. Cheek and Kim A. Cheek*

Madhav Gadgil
1942-
Indian ecologist

Madhav Gadgil is a noted ecologist and co-author of a text on the ecological history of India. His fields of expertise involve the effects of biology and human behavior on the environment, and include conservation and theoretical population biology. He has practical experience in conservation and environmental planning and was awarded the Padma Shri by the President of India for his professional efforts.

Gadgil was born May 24, 1942, in Pune, India, near Bombay. His father, Dhananjaya Gadgil, was an economist and his mother, Pramila Kale, was a housewife. Gadgil is the youngest of four children with two brothers and a sister; one brother, Purushottam, is also a scientist, working as a plant pathologist at the New Zealand Forest Research Institute. Gadgil received the first part of his education in India. He completed a zoology major for his bachelor's degree at Poona University in 1963. He then studied at Bombay University in India, where he received his Masters of Science in zoology in 1965. For his doctorate he went to Harvard University in the United States. He completed his studies in biology and received his Ph.D. in 1969.

His first academic positions were as a research fellow in applied mathematics and then as a lecturer in biology at Harvard. Then in 1971 he returned to India as a scientific officer at the Maharashtra Association for Cultivation of Science in Pune, a position which he held until 1973. He then moved on to become first Assistant, then Associate, and finally full Professor at the Centre for Theoretical Studies, Indian Institute of Science, Bangalore, India. He was appointed Associate Professor in 1975 and full Professor in 1981, a position which he still holds.

He also spent a decade, beginning in 1982, as Chairman of the Centre for Ecological Sciences at the Indian Institute of Sciences. During this period he took the opportunity to return briefly to the United States—he spent the Spring of 1991 at Stanford University in California as the Visiting Professor of Human Biology. Since 1990 he has also been honorary professor at the Jawaharlal Nehru Centre for Advanced Scientific Research. From 1991 to 1994 he was ASTRA Professor in Biological Sciences at the Indian Institute of Science in Bangalore.

In addition to being a Fellow of the Indian National Science Academy (since 1983) and the Indian Academy of Sciences (since 1979), Gadgil has been a Foreign Associate of the U.S. National Academy of Sciences since 1991. His extensive conservation and environmental planning experience outside academia includes serving as a member of the Karnataka State Board for Wildlife for six years (1976–82), a member of the Scientific Advisory Panel for Biosphere Reserves, MAB/UNESCO (1985–87), and a member of the Biodiversity Coordination Committee, IUBS-SCOPE-UNESCO, since 1991. He was also Chairman of the Fuelwood and Fodder study Group, Planning Commission, for the Government of India (1987–88) and Section Co-ordinator of the Global Biodiversity Assessment, UNEP 1993.

His experience in science and technology planning and organization includes being a member of the Scientific Advisory Council to the Prime Minister of India, from 1986 to 1989. Gadgil's work also extends into the private sector—he has been a member of the Board of Directors of NEPA Mills, a public sector paper mill in Nepanagar province of India, since 1990. Gadgil is a coauthor of "Life Historical Consequences of Natural Selection," an article published in 1970 which is considered to be a citation classic. He also wrote, with R. Guha, *This Fissured Land: An Ecological History of India;* this book was published in 1992. In addition, Gadgil has authored or coauthored more than 100 research papers and almost 100 popular articles in three Indian languages and English.

Received Award from India's President

For his work, Gadgil has received recognition in both his home country and others. For example, Gadgil was awarded the Padma Shri by the President of India in 1981. This is one of four national awards given by the president of India every year for distinguished service to the country in one of a number of subjects. He was also the 1986 recipient of the Shanti Swarup Bhatnagar Award for Biological Sciences in 1986. Outside India, he was given the PEW Scholars Award in Conservation and the Environment in 1993. PEW is administered by the University of Michigan, Ann Arbor on behalf of the PEW Charitable Trust.

In an interview with Marianne Fedunkiw, Gadgil said his current research delves into four areas: conservation biology, human ecology, ecological history, and theoretical population biology. His interest in science began early. "I was very interested in natural history since childhood," he told Fedunkiw. "I like figuring things out and science seemed like the most interesting work to get into."

Beyond natural history, Gadgil's hobbies include hiking, and reading classical literature in Sanskrit. Gadgil is married to atmospheric scientist **Sulochana Phatak Gadgil** and they have two children, a daughter, Gauri, and a son, Siddhartha. Gadgil and his wife met while undergraduates at Poona University and married in 1965, just before both travelled to Harvard University.

SELECTED WRITINGS BY GADGIL:

Books

(With R. Guha) *This Fissured Land: An Ecological History of India,* Oxford University Press, 1992.

Periodicals

(With W. H. Bossert) "Life Historical Consequences of Natural Selection," *American Naturalist,* Volume 104, 1970, pp. 1–24.

(With Volume D. Vartak) "Sacred Groves of Western Ghats of India," *Economic Botany,* Volume 30, 1977, pp. 152–160.

(With F. Berkes and C. Folke) "Indigenous Knowledge for Biodiversity Conservation," *Ambio,* Volume 22, issue 2–3, 1993, pp. 151–156.

SOURCES:

Gadgil, Madhav, interview with Marianne Fedunkiw conducted by telephone, fax and E-mail, May 5 and 11, 1994.

—Sketch by Marianne Fedunkiw

Sulochana Gadgil
1944-
Indian atmospheric scientist

Sulochana Gadgil, an Indian scientist, is best known for her work on monsoon climate variability and dynamics. The monsoon, a seasonal wind that often brings severe storms to Asia, can have a profound effect on life in India. Gadgil's investigations into this phenomenon include the monsoon's rainfall patterns, climate changes, and effects on the area's agriculture.

Sulochana Phatak Gadgil was born June 7, 1944, in Pune, India, just southeast of Bombay. Her father, Veshwant Phatak, was a physician and her mother, the former Indumati Kanhere, was a homemaker. She was the third of four girls; two of Gadgil's sisters followed their father into medicine. Gadgil completed both her Bachelor of Science (1963) and her Masters of Science (1965) degrees at Poona University in India. Her first degree major was chemistry; she then switched to applied mathematics for her M.Sc. She then travelled to the United States, where she completed her Ph.D., also in applied mathematics, at Harvard University in 1970. When asked by interviewer Marianne Fedunkiw how her studies in mathematics led to meteorological studies, Gadgil replied that it "provided a strong background in fluid dynamics. My Ph.D. thesis in applied mathematics at Harvard was under the committee on oceanography and dealt with the dynamics of the gulf stream." Her first position after receiving her doctorate was a one-year appointment as a research fellow at the Massachusetts Institute of Technology in Cambridge. In 1971 she returned to Pune, India, as Pool Officer in the Council of Scientific and Industrial Research of the Indian Institute of Tropical Meteorology, a position she held until 1973. Since then she has been a professor at the Indian Institute of Science in Bangalore, India, rising from assistant professor to associate professor in 1981, then to full professor in 1986. Gadgil has also served as Chairman of the Centre for Atmospheric Sciences at the Indian Institute of Science since 1989.

Gadgil married ecologist **Madhav Gadgil** in 1965. They were born in the same city and knew each other as undergraduates at Poona University. They married just before travelling to Harvard University for their doctoral studies, Sulochana in applied mathematics and Madhav in biology. They have two children, a daughter, Gauri, who studies anthropology and a son, Siddhartha, who, like his mother, is a student of mathematics. When she is not working, Gadgil enjoys birdwatching and listening to Indian classical music.

In addition to being a fellow of the Indian Academy of Science and a member of the Indian Meteorological Society, Gadgil serves on the advisory committee of the National Centre for Medium Range Weather Forecasts. For five years, from 1989 to 1993, she served on a committee on Climate Change and Oceans; she has also contributed to a committee on Space Sciences for the government of India, as well as a joint Scientific Committee of World Climate Research Programme.

Her research interests include tropical atmospheric and oceanic circulations, rainfall patterns in monsoonal Asia, monsoon climate variability and dynamics, and climate and agriculture. Gadgil is the author of more than 40 scientific articles on atmospheric and oceanic circulations, climatology and theoretical population biology. For her work, she was recognized with the University Grants Commission of India Career Award in 1980 and, two years later, with the B. N. Desai Award of the India Meteorological Society, for her monsoon research. When asked by Fedunkiw why she became a scientist, Gadgil replied, "Because I enjoy thinking about how the world works."

SELECTED WRITINGS BY GADGIL:

Periodicals

(With D. R. Sikka) "On the Maximum Cloud Zone and ITCZ over the Longitudes during the Southwest Monsoon," *Monthly Weather Review,* Volume 108, 1978, pp. 1122–1135.

(With N. Volume Joshi) "Climatic Clusters of the Indian Region," *Journal of Climatology,* Volume 3, 1983, pp. 47–63.

(With P. Volume Joseph and N. Volume Joshi) "Ocean-atmosphere Coupling over Monsoon Regions," *Nature,* Volume 312, 1984, pp. 141–143.

SOURCES:

Gadgil, Sulochana, interview with Marianne Fedunkiw conducted by fax and E-mail, May 5 and 11, 1994.

—Sketch by Marianne Fedunkiw

Yuri A. Gagarin
1934-1968
Russian cosmonaut

Yuri A. Gagarin was the first human in space. In 1961, this boyish-looking Soviet cosmonaut captured the attention of the world with his short flight around the Earth. "He invited us all into space," American astronaut **Neil Armstrong** said of him, as quoted in *Aviation Week and Space Technology*. Gagarin died in 1968 when the jet that he was flying crashed, as he was preparing to return to space.

The third of four children, Yuri Alekseevich Gagarin was born on a collective farm in Klushino, U.S.S.R., on March 9, 1934. His father, Aleksey Ivanovich Gagarin, was a carpenter on the farm and his mother, Anna, a dairymaid. Gagarin grew up helping them with their work. Neither of his parents had much formal education, but they encouraged him in his schooling. During World War II, the family was evicted from their home by invading German troops, and Gagarin's older brother and sister were taken prisoner for slave labor, though they later escaped.

After the war, Gagarin went to vocational school in Moscow, originally intending to become a foundry worker, and then he moved on to the Saratov Industrial Technical School. He was still learning to be a foundryperson, although his favorite subjects were physics and mathematics. In 1955, during his fourth and final year of school, he joined a local flying club. His first flight as a passenger, he later wrote in *Road to the Stars,* "gave meaning to my whole life." He quickly mastered flying, consumed by a new determination to become a fighter pilot. He joined the Soviet Air Force after graduation. The launch of Sputnik—the first artificial satellite sent into space—occurred on October 4, 1957, while he pursued his military and flight training. He graduated with honors that same year and married medical student Valentina Ivanova Goryacheva. They would have two children, a daughter and a son.

Gagarin volunteered for service in the Northern Air Fleet and joined the Communist Party. He followed closely news of other Sputnik launches; although there had been no official announcement, Gagarin guessed that preparations for manned flights would soon begin and he volunteered for cosmonaut duty. Gagarin completed the required weeks of physical examinations and testing in 1960, just before his twenty-sixth birthday. He was then told that he had been made a member of the first group of twelve cosmonauts. The assignment was a secret, and he was forbidden to tell even his wife until his family had settled into the new space-program complex called Zvezdniy Gorodok (Star Town), forty miles from Moscow. An outgoing, natural leader, the stocky, smiling Gagarin stood out even among his well-qualified peers. **Sergei Korolyov**, the head of the Soviet space program and chief designer of its vehicles, thought Gagarin had the makings of a first-rate scientist and engineer, as well as being an excellent pilot. In March of 1961, Korolyov approved the selection of Gagarin to ride Vostok I into orbit.

Makes First Human Flight Into Space

Senior Lieutenant Gagarin made history on April 12, 1961, when a converted ballistic missile propelled his Vostok capsule into Earth orbit from the remote Baikonur Cosmodrome. "Off we go!" the cosmonaut exclaimed. The Vostok was controlled automatically, and Gagarin spent his time reporting observations of the Earth and his own condition. He performed such tasks as writing and tapping out a message on a telegraph key, thus establishing that a human being's coordination remained intact even while weightless in space. Proving that people could work in space, he also ate and drank to verify that the body would take nourishment in weightlessness. He commented repeatedly on the beauty of the Earth from space and on how pleasant weightlessness felt.

Gagarin rode his spacecraft for 108 minutes, ejecting from the spherical reentry module after the craft reentered the atmosphere just short of one complete orbit. Ejection was standard procedure for all Vostok pilots, although Gagarin dutifully supported the official fiction that he had remained in his craft all the way to the ground—a requirement for international certification of the flight as a record. Cosmonaut and capsule landed safely near the banks of the Volga River.

After doctors proclaimed him unaffected by his flight, Gagarin was presented to the public as an international hero. He received an instant promotion to the rank of major and made appearances around the world. He was named a Hero of the Soviet Union and a Hero of Socialist Labor, and he became an honorary citizen of fourteen cities in six countries. He received the Tsiolkovsky Gold Medal of the Soviet Academy of Sciences, the Gold Medal of the British Interplanetary Society, and two awards from the International Aeronautical Federation. The flight had many implications for international affairs: American leaders extended cautious congratulations and redoubled their own efforts in the space race, while the Soviet media proclaimed that Gagarin's success showed the strength of socialism.

Gagarin became commander of the cosmonaut team. In 1964 he was made deputy director of the cosmonaut training center at the space program headquarters complex—where he oversaw the selection and training of the first women cosmonauts. He served as capsule communicator—the link between cosmonauts and ground controllers—for four later space flights in the Vostok and Voskhod programs. At various times during this period, he also held political duties; he chaired the Soviet-Cuban Friendship Society and served on the Council of the Union and the Supreme Soviet Council of Nationalities.

Gagarin always wanted to venture back to space, and in 1966 he was returned to active status to serve as the backup cosmonaut to Vladimir Komarov for the first flight of the new Soyuz spacecraft. When the Soyuz 1 mission ended and Komarov died due to a parachute malfunction, Gagarin was assigned to command the upcoming Soyuz 3. But Gagarin himself did not live to fly the Soyuz 3 mission. On March 27, 1968, he took off for a routine proficiency flight in a two-seat MiG–15 trainer. He and his flight instructor became engaged in low-level maneuvers with two other jets. Gagarin's plane crossed close behind another jet and was caught in its vortex; he lost control and the jet crashed into the tundra at high speed, killing both occupants instantly.

Gagarin was given a hero's funeral. The Cosmonaut Training Center was renamed in his honor, as were his former hometown, a space tracking ship, and a lunar crater. His wife continued to work as a biomedical laboratory assistant at Zvezdniy Gorodok, and Gagarin's office there was preserved as a museum; a huge statue of him was erected in Moscow. His book *Survival in Space* was published posthumously. Written with space-program physician Vladimir Lebedev, the work outlines Gagarin's views on the problems and requirements for successful long-term space flights. On April 12, 1991, thirty years after Gagarin's flight, his cosmonaut successors, along with eighteen American astronauts, gathered at Baikonur to salute his achievements.

SELECTED WRITINGS BY GAGARIN:

Books

Road to the Stars, translated by G. Hanna and D. Myshne, Foreign Languages Publishing House, 1962.

(With Vladimir Lebedev) *Survival in Space,* translated by Gabriella Azrael, Bantam Books, 1969.

SOURCES:

Books

Hooper, Gordon R., *The Soviet Cosmonaut Team,* GRH Publications, 1986.

Oberg, James E., *Red Star in Orbit,* Random House, 1981.

Periodicals

Aviation Week and Space Technology, April 8, 1991, p. 7.

—*Sketch by Matthew A. Bille*

D. Carleton Gajdusek
1923-
American microbiologist and virologist

A biomedical scientist, D. Carleton Gajdusek is credited with the identification of slow virus infection in humans. He discovered this disease while studying an isolated population in New Guinea that practiced cannibalism. For his discovery, Gajdusek was awarded the Nobel Prize in physiology or medicine in 1976.

Daniel Carleton Gajdusek was the elder of two sons of a Slovakian-born butcher, Karl Gajdusek, and Ottilia Dobrozscky Gajdusek, whose parents had come to the United States from Hungary. He was born on September 9, 1923 in Yonkers, New York. His father's family was one of tradesmen and farmers, contributing to Gajdusek's appreciation of laughter and conversation; his mother's American-born and educated siblings spurred Gajdusek's interest in academics. His aunt, Irene Dobrozscky, was an entomologist at the Boyce Thompson Institute for Plant Research in Yonkers, through whom Gajdusek met Dr. William J. Youden, a chemist and mathematician who later tutored him. He frequented New York City's museums, especially the Metropolitan Museum of Art and the Museum of Natural History. His scientific aspirations and appetite for knowledge were created in large part by his aunt and his mother, who read to him from Plutarch, Homer, and Virgil before he learned to read on his own.

At age ten, one of his favorite books was *The Microbe Hunters* by Paul de Kruif, which inspired him to stencil the names of twelve microbiologists on the steps which led to his attic chemistry lab. By the time he was thirteen he was working at the Boyce Thompson Institute under Dr. John Arthur, synthesizing commercial weed killer. He graduated from the University of Rochester with a B.S. in biophysics at age nineteen and went on to Harvard University Medical school where he graduated three years later. He lived and worked at Children's Hospital, Boston, during most of medical school, and took a pediatric mission in postwar Germany after his internship and residencies in pediatrics. Interested in children, he undertook pediatric specialty training at Columbia University and Harvard. His postdoctoral studies included fellowships in physical chemistry, virology and immunology at the California Institute of Technology, where he was senior fellow in physical chemistry from 1948–49; Harvard, where he did virus research from 1949–52 on a fellowship from the National Foundation for Infantile Paralysis, and at the Institut Pasteur in Iran and the Hull Institute in Melbourne. He began to work as chief of the Study of Child Growth, Development and Behavior and Disease Patterns in Primitive Cultures at the National Institutes of Health, which eventually became the Slow, Latent and Temperate Infections laboratory and the Central Nervous Systems Studies laboratory in the National Institute of Neurological and Communicative Disorders and Strokes.

It was during Gajdusek's tour of military service at the Walter Reed Army Institute of Research in 1952 and 1953 in Washington, DC, under Dr. Joseph Smadel that he first studied viral and rickettsial diseases. Smadel recognized his talents, and taught him methods of laboratory and field research as well as how to synthesize and present scientific data. From 1954–55 he studied rabies, plague, arbovirus infections, scurvy and the other epidemic diseases of Iran, Afghanistan, and Turkey at the Institut Pasteur in Tehran. These studies of epidemic diseases in isolated populations were of profound interest to him. He felt that they could provide information about the development of the nervous system and its related learning and behavioral patterns.

Travels to New Guinea

With this in mind, Gajdusek visited populations in South America, New Britain, the Micronesian and Melanesian islands, and other exotic places. His postdoctoral fellowship in 1955 as an investigator in virus genetics and immunology with **Frank Macfarlane Burnet** at the Walter and Eliza Hull Institute of Medical research in Melbourne, led him to Australia repeatedly. There, a public health physician, Dr. Vincent Zigas, had just returned from a remote area in New Guinea. Zigas alerted him to a strange and fatal degenerative neurological disease of the Fore, a tribe of 35,000 who lived in the eastern highlands of New Guinea in 160 villages. The Fore exhibited a stone-age culture, and committed cannibalism as part of a funeral rite for close relatives. The Fore referred to the strange disease as "kuru," meaning shakes or tremors. Kuru killed around one percent of those Fore who practiced cannibalism. Throughout the next year Gajdusek and Zigas acquainted themselves with the Fore, during which time over 200 people died of the disease. Since women and children were particularly susceptible, a number of the communities had all but vanished. The symptoms of kuru indicated that it was clearly a neurological disease; shaking followed by loss of muscle control and coordination, then a general motor weakness making walking impossible. The condition degenerated into a loss of ability to stand, and then to sit up, with dementia, or brain deterioration, preceding death. The course of kuru from the onset of tremors, to its final stages lasted roughly a year. When Gajdusek's group studied the brains of the kuru victims, they found trauma in the gray matter, along with the displacement of neurons, the granular cells which constitute the fundamental, functional units of nervous tissue; hypertrophy and proliferation of astrocytes, or star-shaped cells of supporting tissue; damage to parts of Purkinje cells, nerve cells; and the presence of starchy plaques. They concluded that kuru was a disease which altered degeneratively the very structure of brain tissue. At first Gajdusek considered an inherited, genetic cause of kuru; the population was an isolated one, and a defective gene pool would have explained the absence of any outward signs of infection, such as fever or inflammation. Additionally, his attempts to grow the disease in lab cultures or transmit it to animals using traditional inoculation methods were unsuccessful.

Identifies Kuru as Slow Virus in Humans

An American veterinary neuropathologist who worked for the National Institute of Health, William Hadlow, read a professional report that Gajdusek and Zigas published on kuru in 1959. Hadlow, investigating a viral disease in sheep called scrapie, in Comton, England, noticed a resemblance between the two afflictions. It was he who suggested that kuru, like scrapie, may have been caused by a virus requiring a long incubation period, which explained why the inoculation technique associated with a short-term virus used by Gajdusek failed to transmit the kuru disease in animals. Hadlow's observation of striking similarities in brain tissue affected by scrapie and kuru aided Gajdusek's search for the transmissible agent. The high rate of kuru among women and children—principle participants in cannibalistic rituals involving brains and organs of dead kuru victims—and substantiation of transmissibility of scrapie by Icelandic veterinarian Bjorn Sigurdsson, supported the theory of a slow virus transmitted by consumption of human tissue.

Gajdusek's investigative work with kuru offered possibilities regarding other degenerative human diseases of the brain, as several of them were classified as slow virus infections. Perhaps the most famous of these was the presenile dementia Creutzfeldt-Jakob disease, or CJD. Gajdusek's and Gibbs' study of CJD showed that a chronic, deteriorate human brain disease occurring worldwide—and not just in an isolated population as in the case of kuru—resulted from a slow virus infection.

Work with Kuru and Other Diseases Leads to Nobel Prize

Gajdusek was co-recipient of the Nobel Prize in physiology or medicine in 1976 for his studies of kuru and other neurological diseases which led to the identification of slow virus in humans. He is the author and editor of monographs and has written a considerable number of reports for journals of research. His roles as virologist, microbiologist and true anthropologist have led to fundamental change in microbiology and neurology. Although a bachelor, he has adopted and educated many New Guinean boys whose subsequent return to New Guinea contributes to an educated class. He continues to head the Laboratory of Central Nervous System Studies at the National Institutes of Health in Bethesda, Maryland.

SELECTED WRITINGS BY GAJDUSEK:

Books

Kuru: Early Letters and Field Notes from the Collection of D. Carleton Gajdusek, edited by D. Carleton Gajdusek and Judith Farquar, Raven Press, 1981.

SOURCES:

Books

Eron, Carol, *The Virus That Ate Cannibals,* Macmillan, 1981.

Les Prix Nobel en 1976, Norstedt and Soner, 1976.

Periodicals

Marsh, Richard F., "The 1976 Nobel Prize for Physiology or Medicine," *Science,* November 26, 1976, pp. 928–929.

Mims, Cedric, "Antipodean . . . ," *Nature,* October 28, 1976.

Tower, Donald B., "D. Carleton Gajdusek, MD—Nobel Laureate in Medicine for 1976," *Archives of Neurology,* April, 1977, pp. 205–208.

—Sketch by Janet Kieffer Kelley

Robert C. Gallo
1937-
American virologist

Robert C. Gallo, one of the best-known biomedical researchers in the United States, is considered the codiscoverer, along with **Luc Montagnier** at the Pasteur Institute, of the human immunodeficiency virus (HIV). Gallo established that the virus causes acquired immunodeficiency syndrome (AIDS), something which Montagnier had not been able to do, and he developed the blood test for HIV, which remains a central tool in efforts to control the disease. Gallo also discovered the human T-cell leukemia virus (HTLV) and the human T-cell growth factor interleukin–2.

Gallo's initial work on the isolation and identification of the AIDS virus has been the subject of a number of allegations, resulting in a lengthy investigation and official charges of scientific misconduct which were overturned on appeal. Although he has now been exonerated, the ferocity of the controversy has tended to obscure the importance of his contributions both to AIDS research and biomedical research in general. As Malcolm Gladwell observed in 1990 in the *Washington Post:* "Gallo is easily one of the country's most famous scientists, frequently mentioned as a Nobel Prize contender, and a man whose research publications were cited by other researchers publishing their own work during the last decade more often than those of any other scientist in the world."

Gallo was born in Waterbury, Connecticut, on March 23, 1937, to Francis Anton and Louise Mary (Ciancuilli) Gallo. He grew up in the house that his Italian grandparents bought after they came to the United States. His father worked long hours at the welding company which he owned. The dominant memory of Gallo's youth was of the illness and death of his only sibling, Judy, from childhood leukemia. The disease brought Gallo into contact with the nonfamily member who most influenced his life, Dr. Marcus Cox, the pathologist who diagnosed her disease in 1948. During his senior year in high school, an injury kept Gallo off the high school basketball team and forced him to think about his future. He began to spend time with Cox, visiting him at the hospital, even assisting in postmortem examinations. When Gallo entered college, he knew he wanted a career in biomedical research.

Gallo attended Providence College, where he majored in biology, graduating with a bachelor's degree in 1959. He continued his schooling at Jefferson Medical College in Philadelphia, where he got an introduction to medical research. In 1961 he worked

Robert C. Gallo

as a summer research fellow in Alan Erslev's laboratory at Jefferson. His work studying the pathology of oxygen deprivation in coal miners led to his first scientific publication in 1962, while he was still a medical student.

In 1961 Gallo married Mary Jane Hayes, a woman he knew from his hometown whom he had begun dating in his first year of college. Together they had two children. Gallo graduated from medical school in 1963; on the advice of Erslev, he went to the University of Chicago because it had a reputation as a major center for blood-cell biology, Gallo's research interest. From 1963 to 1965 he did research on the biosynthesis of hemoglobin, the protein that carries oxygen in the blood.

Treats Cancer Patients

In 1965 Gallo was appointed to the position of clinical associate at the National Institutes of Health (NIH) in Bethesda, Maryland. He spent much of his first year at NIH caring for cancer patients. Despite the often depressing work environment, he observed some early successes at treating cancer patients with chemotherapy. Children were being cured of the very form of childhood leukemia that killed his sister almost twenty years before. In 1966, Gallo was appointed to his first full-time research position, as an associate of Seymour Perry, who was head of the medicine department. Perry was studying how white blood cells grow in various forms of leukemia. In his laboratory Gallo studied the enzymes involved in the synthesis of the components of deoxyribonucleic acid (DNA), the carrier of genetic information.

The expansion of the NIH and the passage of the National Cancer Act in 1971 led to the creation of the Laboratory of Tumor Cell Biology at the National Cancer Institute (NCI), a part of the NIH. Gallo was appointed head of the new laboratory. He had become intrigued with the possibility that certain kinds of cancer had viral origins, and he set up his new laboratory to study human retroviruses. Retroviruses are types of viruses which possess the ability to penetrate other cells and splice their own genetic material into the genes of their hosts, eventually taking over all of their reproductive functions. At the time Gallo began his work, retroviruses had been found in animals; the question was whether they existed in humans. His research involved efforts to isolate a virus from victims of certain kinds of leukemia, and he and his colleagues were able to view a retrovirus through electron microscopes. In 1975, Gallo and Robert E. Gallagher announced that they had discovered a human leukemia virus, but other laboratories were unable to replicate their results. Scientists to whom they had sent samples for independent confirmation had found two different retroviruses not from humans, but from animals. The samples had been contaminated by viruses from a monkey or a chimp and the idea that a virus could cause cancer was publicly ridiculed.

Despite the humiliation Gallo suffered and the damage this premature announcement did to his reputation, he continued his efforts to isolate a human retrovirus. He turned his attention to T-cells, white blood cells which are an important part of the body's immune system, and developed a substance called T-cell growth factor (later called interleukin-2), which would sustain them outside the human body. The importance of this growth factor was that it enabled Gallo and his team to sustain cancerous T-cells long enough to discover whether a retrovirus existed within them. These techniques allowed Gallo and his team to isolate a previously unknown virus from a leukemia patient. He named the virus human T-cell leukemia virus, or HTLV, and he published this finding in *Science* in 1981. This time his findings were confirmed, and as Michael Specter noted in the *New York Review of Books,* Gallo was "transformed from a loser to a star."

Develops Blood Test for the AIDS Virus

It was Gallo's experience with viral research that made him so important in the effort to identify the cause of AIDS, after that disease had first been characterized by doctors in the United States. In further studies of HTLV, Gallo had established that it could be transmitted by breast-feeding, sexual intercourse, and blood transfusions. He also observed that the incidence of cancers caused by this virus was concentrated in Africa and the Caribbean. HTLV had these and other characteristics in common with what was then known about AIDS, and Gallo was one of the first scientists to hypothesize that the disease was caused by a virus. In 1982, the National Cancer Institute formed an AIDS task force with Gallo as its head. In this capacity he made available to the scientific community the research methods he had developed for HTLV, and among those whom he provided with some early technical assistance was **Luc Montagnier** at the Pasteur Institute in Paris.

Gallo tried throughout 1983 to get the AIDS virus to grow in culture, using the same growth factor that had worked in growing HTLV, but he was not successful. Finally, a member of Gallo's group named Mikulas Popovic developed a method to grow the virus in a line of T-cells. The method consisted, in effect, of mixing samples from various patients into a kind of a cocktail, using perhaps ten different strains of the virus at a time, so there was a higher chance that one would survive. This innovation allowed the virus to be studied, and observing the similarities to the retroviruses he had previously discovered, Gallo called it HTLV–3. In 1984, he and his colleagues published their findings in *Science.* Gallo and the other scientists in his laboratory were able to establish that this virus caused AIDS, and they developed a blood test for the virus. In a 1993 issue of *New York Times Magazine,* Nicholas Wade writes: "After twelve grim years, Gallo's blood test is still the only weapon of real value that scientists have yet managed to devise against this baffling disease."

Allegations Overshadow Scientific Accomplishments

Almost a year before Gallo announced his findings, Montagnier at the Pasteur Institute had identified a virus he called LAV, though he was not able to prove that it caused AIDS. The two laboratories were cooperating with each other in the race to find the cause of AIDS and several samples of this virus had been sent to Gallo at the National Cancer Institute. The controversy which would embroil the American scientist's career for almost the next decade began when the United States government denied the French scientists a patent for the AIDS test and awarded one to his team instead. The Pasteur Institute believed their contribution was not recognized in this decision, and they challenged it in court. Gallo did not deny that they had preceded him in isolating the virus, but he argued that it was proof of the causal relationship and the development of the blood test which were most important, and he maintained that these advances had been accomplished using a virus which had been independently isolated in his laboratory.

This first stage of the controversy ended in a legal settlement that was highly unusual for the scientific community: Gallo and Montagnier agreed out of court to share equal credit for their discovery. This settlement followed a review of records from Gallo's laboratory and rested on the assumption that the virus Gallo had discovered was different from the one Montagnier had sent him. An international committee renamed the virus HIV, and in what Specter calls "the first such negotiated history of a scientific enterprise ever published," the American and French groups published an agreement about their contributions in *Nature* in 1987. In 1988, Gallo and Montagnier jointly related the story of the discoveries in *Scientific American.*

Questions about the isolation of the AIDS virus were revived in 1989 by a long article in the *Chicago Tribune.* The journalist, a Pulitzer Prize winner named John Crewdson, had spent three years investigating Gallo's laboratory, making over one hundred requests under the Freedom of Information Act. He directly questioned Gallo's integrity and implied he had stolen Montagnier's virus. The controversy intensified when it was established that the LAV virus which the French had isolated and the HTLV–3 virus were virtually identical. The genetic sequencing in the two were in fact so close that some believed they actually came from the same AIDS patient, and Gallo was accused of simply renaming the virus Montagnier had sent him. Gallo's claim to have independently isolated the virus was further damaged when it was discovered that in the 1984 *Science* article announcing his discovery of HTLV–3 he had accidently published a photograph of Montagnier's virus.

Finding of Scientic Misconduct Reversed on Appeal

In 1990, pressure from a congressional committee forced the NIH to undertake an investigation. In the *Washington Post,* Malcolm Gladwell observed of this inquiry: "No other investigation has taken so long, dealt with a scientific discovery of such importance or directly implicated so distinguished a researcher." The NIH investigation found Popovic guilty of scientific misconduct but Gallo guilty only of misjudgment. A committee of scientists which oversaw the investigation was strongly critical of these conclusions, and the group expressed concern that Popovic had been assigned more than a fair share of the blame. In June 1992, the NIH investigation was superseded by the Office of Research Integrity (ORI) at the Department of Health and Human Services, and in December of that year ORI found both Gallo and Popovic guilty of scientific misconduct. Based largely on a single sentence in the 1984 *Science* article that described the isolation of the virus, the ORI report found Gallo guilty of misconduct for "falsely reporting that LAV had not been transmitted to a permanently growing cell line." This decision renewed the legal threat from the Pasteur Institute, whose lawyers moved to claim all the back royalties from the AIDS blood test, which then amounted to approximately $20 million.

Gallo strongly objected to the findings of the ORI, pointing to the fact that the finding of misconduct turned on a single sentence in a single paper. Other scientists objected to the panel's priorities, believing that the charge of misconduct concerned a misrepresentation of a relatively minor issue which did not negate the scientific validity of Gallo's conclusions. Lawyers representing both Gallo and Popovic brought their cases before an appeals board at the Department of Health and Human Services. Popovic's case was heard first, and in December 1993 the board announced that he had been cleared of all charges. As quoted in *Time,* the panel declared: "One might anticipate ... after all the sound and fury, there would be at least a residue of palpable wrongdoing. This is not the case." The ORI immediately withdrew all charges against Gallo for lack of proof.

According to *Time,* in December 1993 Gallo considered himself "completely vindicated" of all the allegations that had been made against him. He has established that before 1984 his laboratory had succeeded in isolating other strains of the virus which were not similar to LAV. Many scientists now believe that the problem was simply one of contamination, a mistake which may have been a consequence of the intense pressure for results in many laboratories during the early years of the AIDS epidemic. It has been hypothesized that the LAV sample from the Pasteur Institute contaminated the mixture of AIDS viruses which Popovic concocted to find one strain that would survive in culture; it is believed that this strain was strong enough to survive and be identified by Gallo and Popovic for a second time.

In 1990, when the controversy was still at its height, Gallo published a book about his career called *Virus Hunting,* which seemed intended to refute the charges against him, particularly the *Tribune* article by Crewdson. Gallo made many of the claims that were later supported by the appeals board, and in the *New York Times Book Review,* Natalie Angier called him "a formidable gladiator who firmly believes in the importance of his scientific contributions." Angier wrote of the book: "His description of the key experiments in 1983 and 1984 that led to the final isolation of the AIDS virus are intelligent and persuasive, particularly to a reader who was heard the other side of the story. Although the reviews of *Virus Hunting* were not entirely sympathetic, many felt the controversy was misplaced. A number of reviewers commented on how this controversy had virtually paralyzed one of the most important AIDS research laboratories in the world. In the *Washington Post,* J. D. Robinson observed that "thousands of hours and untold psychic energy which could have been devoted to seeking a cure for AIDS have been spent responding to inquiries and accusations."

The many allegations and the long series of investigations have distracted many people from the accomplishments of a man whose name appears on hundreds of scientific papers and who has won most major awards in biomedical research except the Nobel Prize. Gallo has actually received the coveted Albert Lasker Award twice, once in 1982 for his work on the viral origins of cancer, and again in 1986 for his research on AIDS. He has also been awarded the American Cancer Society Medal of Honor in 1983, the Lucy Wortham Prize from the Society for Surgical Oncology in 1984, the Armand Hammer Cancer Research Award in 1985, and the Gairdner Foundation International Award for Biomedical Research in 1987. He has received eleven honorary degrees.

SELECTED WRITINGS BY GALLO:

Books

Virus Hunting: AIDS, Cancer and the Human Retrovirus, HarperCollins, 1991.

Periodicals

"The First Human Retrovirus," *Scientific American,* December, 1986, pp. 88–99.

"The AIDS Virus," *Scientific American,* January, 1987, pp. 46–57.

(With Luc Montagnier) "The Chronology of AIDS Research," *Nature,* April, 1987, pp. 435–436.

(With Luc Montagnier) "AIDS in 1988," *Scientific American,* October, 1988, pp. 40–49.

"My Life Stalking AIDS," *Discover,* October, 1989, pp. 31–34.

SOURCES:

Periodicals

Angier, Natalie, review of "Virus Hunting," *New York Times Book Review,* March 24, 1991, p. 3.

Cohen, Jon, "HHS: Gallo Guilty of Misconduct," *Science,* Volume 259, January 1993, pp. 168–170.

Gladwell, Malcolm, "At NIH, an Unprecedented Ethics Investigation," *The Washington Post,* August 17, 1990, p. A8.

Gorman, Christine, "Victory at Last for a Beseiged Virus Hunter," *Time,* November 22, 1993, p. 61.

Greenberg, Dan, "Washington Perspective: Misconduct Finding in the Gallo Case," *The Lancet,* Volume 339, January 16, 1993, pp. 166–167.

Ostrom, Neenyah, "Robert Gallo Found Guilty of Scientific Misconduct," *Christopher Street,* Febuary 15, 1993, pp. 13–16.

Robinson, J. D., "Key Player Chronicles Fascinating Search for AIDS Viruses," *The Washington Post,* April 22, 1991, p. F1.

Specter, Michael, "The Case of Dr. Gallo," *New York Review of Books,* August 15, 1991, pp. 49–52.

Wade, Nicholas, "Method and Madness: The Vindication of Robert Gallo," *New York Times Magazine,* December 26, 1993, p. 12.

—*Sketch by Karyn Hede George*

George Gamow
1904-1968
Russian-born American physicist

George Gamow

George Gamow was a celebrated physicist best known for his work dealing with the origins of the universe. Gamow also made important contributions to the unraveling of the genetic code in molecular biology. In addition to his research, Gamow was a great popularizer of physics and astronomy, particularly in his books dealing with a fictional character by the name of "Mr. Tompkins." Born in Russia, Gamow was trained in physics at the University of Leningrad shortly after the Russian Revolution, and his earliest important work on the theory of alpha decay of radioactive nuclei was carried out at the University of Göttingen in the late 1920s. As the political situation in his homeland gradually became more difficult, he decided to defect to the United States, and in 1933 became a professor at George Washington University.

Educates Himself in Mathematics and Science

George Gamow was born in Odessa, Russia, on March 4, 1904, the son of Anthony M. Gamow and Alexandra (Lebedinzeva) Gamow. Both of his parents were teachers, his father an instructor of Russian language and literature. Gamow's grandfather had been a general in the Russian army. Gamow was a precocious boy who taught himself mathematics and science. While his classmates were working their way through conventional school subjects, Gamow was teaching himself differential equations and the theory of relativity. Formal schooling was difficult at the time because of revolutionary battles, but Gamow eventually graduated from Odessa Normal in 1920.

As one of his earliest research projects, Gamow attempted to find out if communion bread from the local church was really different from ordinary bread by examining it under a microscope. He became fascinated with optics and astronomy in 1917 when his father gave him a telescope for his thirteenth birthday. In 1922, Gamow entered Novorossysky University in Odessa, planning to major in mathematics. He felt dissatisfied with his instruction there, however, at least partly because he was better educated than were some of his teachers. A year later, therefore, Gamow transferred from Novorossysky to the University of Petrograd (later, the University of Leningrad).

Gamow's tenure at Petrograd also seems not to have been very satisfying. He has been quoted by George Greenstein in *American Scholar* as having later stated, "I was around the university, I was not in the university." Part of the problem was that he was passing courses, but generally not going to classes. His advisor assigned him a research problem in optics, but Gamow did not seem to be very interested in the work. In 1928, therefore, when given the opportunity to spend a summer at the University of Göttingen, he eagerly accepted. Most of his biographers say that Gamow was awarded his Ph.D. by Petrograd in 1928.

But Greenstein, a colleague who interviewed him later in life, tells a different story. "He lost interest in his Ph.D. thesis research," Greenstein writes, "and sent the University of Leningrad his work on radioactivity instead. It seems that they never got around to awarding him a degree."

Quantum Mechanics Is Applied to Radioactivity

The "work on radioactivity" mentioned by Greenstein was Gamow's first major scientific accomplishment. While at Göttingen, he read about **Ernest Rutherford**'s failed efforts to bombard an atom's nucleus with alpha, or positively charged, particles. Gamow decided to see if quantum theory, about which he had only recently learned, would explain Rutherford's results. He eventually developed a theory that involved the process of "tunneling." Tunneling is a mechanism by which particles are able to break through (actually, to "tunnel under") a potential energy barrier that would, under classical laws of physics, appear to prevent their passage. The American physicists Edward Uhler Condon and Ronald Gurney were reaching the same conclusion at almost the same time.

News of Gamow's work soon spread throughout the physics community, and he was invited by **Niels Bohr** to become a Carlsberg fellow at his Institute for Theoretical Physics in Copenhagen from 1928 to 1929. There Gamow continued his research on nuclear phenomena and also began to study the physics of stars' interiors. After a brief trip home in the summer of 1929, Gamow was on the road again, this time to Cambridge as a Rockefeller fellow. At the Cavendish Laboratories at Cambridge, he worked with Rutherford, the preeminent nuclear scholar in the world, for a year. There Gamow's primary achievement was the calculation of the energy needed to split an atomic nucleus using protons, the positively charged element of the nucleus. Within a few months, **John Douglas Cockroft** and **Ernest Walton** had begun the design of a machine—the world's first particle accelerator—to put Gamow's results into practical use.

At the conclusion of his year at the Cavendish Laboratories, Gamow was invited by Bohr to return to Copenhagen for a second year. His time there was to be devoted primarily to research on a quantum theory of the nucleus, a subject on which he had been asked to give a paper for the 1931 International Congress on Nuclear Physics in Rome. Gamow's return to the Soviet Union in 1931 was significant for two reasons. First, he married Loubov Wochminzewa. Second, he found a dramatically altered political climate, one in which foreign travel was much more closely supervised than it had ever been in his lifetime. In fact, the government told Gamow that he would not be permitted to attend the Rome conference. That decision convinced Gamow that he did not want to remain in the Soviet Union. Although he accepted an appointment as professor of physics at the University of Leningrad, he began devising a scheme to escape from the Soviet Union. The secret plans made by Gamow and his wife over the next two years read, according to Greenstein, "like a paperback thriller written by someone in an ironical frame of mind." The one actual attempt they made to flee to Finland was thwarted, however, by weather conditions, and they were forced to return to Leningrad.

Solvay Conference Provides Opportunity for Escape

As it turned out, the Soviet government solved Gamow's problem for him when, in the fall of 1933, it ordered him to attend the International Solvay Congress in Brussels and provided him and his wife with the visas and tickets needed to make the trip. When the Gamows left Leningrad in later 1933 for Brussels, they knew they would not be returning. At the conclusion of the Solvay conference, therefore, the Gamows set their sights on the West. Gamow visited the Pierre Curie Institute in Paris, the Cavendish Laboratories, and Bohr's Institute for two months each before accepting a summer (1934) teaching assignment at the University of Michigan. The following year, he became professor of physics at George Washington University in Washington, D.C., a post he held until 1956, and he became a U.S. citizen in 1940. His earliest work at George Washington was carried out in conjunction with **Edward Teller,** a Hungarian physicist who had also defected to the United States. Together, the two worked out a theoretical explanation for the process by which a radioactive nucleus emits a beta particle, or high-speed electron. The theory became known as the Gamow-Teller Selection Rule. During World War II, Gamow was assigned to the U. S. Navy Bureau of Ordinance where he worked in the division of high explosives. After the war, he worked on the theory of war games for the U.S. Army and eventually became involved in research on the hydrogen bomb with Teller.

Gamow also began to focus on a new field, astrophysics. He decided to investigate the physical, chemical, and nuclear changes that might have occurred during the first few moments of the universe's creation. Gamow developed a theory that described the formation of the light elements, hydrogen and helium, but he did not see how heavier elements could have been produced as a result of the universe's beginnings. Eventually he concluded that these elements must have been formed much later in the history of the universe, in the center of stars. Over the years, Gamow developed mathematical formulations that described how this process of heavy element formation might have taken place. One of his most important papers on the subject of astrophysics was the now famous Alpha-Beta-Gamma paper that appeared in the April 1, 1948 issue of *Physical Review.* The paper's name is derived from the last names of its three authors, Ralph Alpher, **Hans Bethe,** and Gamow. It summarizes the hypothesized changes that took place during the first few moments following the big bang.

After 1953, Gamow began work on an entirely new subject, the young field of molecular biology. The impetus for this change of direction was the discovery by **James Watson** and **Francis Crick** of the structure of the deoxyribonucleic acid (DNA) molecule. An inherent question posed by that discovery was how the genetic information stored in DNA molecules could be used by cells in the manufacture of proteins. Gamow hypothesized the existence of a genetic "code" consisting of the four nitrogen bases found in a DNA molecule. A combination of three successive bases, Gamow suggested, might code for a specific amino acid. The arrangement of bases in a DNA molecule, therefore, could carry instructions for a sequence of amino acids, that is, for a protein molecule. Although the details of Gamow's analysis were not correct, his hypothesis of the genetic code was.

Ends Associations with George Washington University and Wife

In 1956, Gamow ended two long-term relationships, one with George Washington University and the other with his wife of 25 years, Loubov. He moved to Boulder, Colorado, where he became professor of physics at the University of Colorado. Two years later, he was married to Barbara Perkins. Gamow had long been interested in writing about science for the layperson, and his first effort along these lines described a tiny universe only five miles wide. No American publisher was interested in the story, but it was eventually accepted by C. P. Snow, editor of the British science magazine *Discovery.* The "toy universe" stories were later collected in Gamow's popular book, *Mr. Tompkins in Wonderland,* and then extended in a second book, *Mr. Tompkins Explores the Atom.*

The "Mr. Tompkins" of these stories is a bank teller who tends to fall asleep while listening to his father-in-law's lectures on physics. In his dreams, Mr. Tompkins is able to reinterpret those lectures in a more understandable setting, as readers of the books might. In other works, Gamow presented somewhat more serious descriptions of scientific ideas that were still easily accessible to most readers. Among these were *The Birth and Death of the Sun,* in 1940, *Biography of the Earth,* in 1941, and *The Creation of the Universe,* in 1952. Gamow's popular texts earned him the Kalinga Prize from the United Nations Educational, Scientific, and Cultural Organization (UNESCO) in 1956.

Gamow was tall, blonde-haired, and blue-eyed, and was renowned for his sense of humor. Greenstein has described him as "exuberant, jovial, rough, and friendly," with qualities of "playfulness and inventiveness, and a resolute refusal to be trapped within a ponderous consistency." He held a special passion for magic and loved to regale his friends with the tricks he had mastered. Gamow had a lifelong habit of consuming large quantities of alcohol, and though he rarely—if ever—lost control because of his drinking, alcohol may ultimately have led to his early death at the age of sixty-four. During the last few years of his life, he was constantly ill and finally died in Boulder on August 19, 1968.

SELECTED WRITINGS BY GAMOW:

Books

The Constitution of Atomic Nuclei and Radioactivity, Clarendon, 1931, second edition published as *Structure of Atomic Nuclei and Nuclear Transformations,* 1937, third edition, written with C. L. Critchfield, published as *Theory of Atomic Nucleus and Nuclear Energy Sources,* 1949.

Mr. Tompkins in Wonderland; or, Stories of c, G, and h, Cambridge University Press, 1939, Macmillan, 1941.

The Birth and Death of the Sun: Stellar Evolution and Subatomic Energy, Viking, 1940.

Biography of the Earth: Its Past, Present, and Future, Viking, 1941.

Mr. Tompkins Explores the Atom, Macmillan, 1944.

The Creation of the Universe, Viking, 1952.

My World Line: An Informal Autobiography, Viking, 1970.

Periodicals

(With R. Alpher and H. Bethe), "The Origin of Chemical Elements" *Physical Review,* April 1, 1948, pp. 803–804.

"History of the Universe," *Science,* number 158, 1967, pp. 766–769.

SOURCES:

Books

Abbott, David, *The Biographical Dictionary of Scientists (Physicists),* P. Bedrich, 1984, pp. 71–72.

Current Biography, H. W. Wilson, 1951.

Daintith, John, et al., *A Biographical Encyclopedia of Scientists,* Volume 1, Facts on File, 1981, pp. 299–300.
Gillispie, Charles Coulson, editor, *Dictionary of Scientific Biography,* Volume 5, Scribner's, 1975, pp. 271–273.
McGraw-Hill Modern Men of Science, Volume 1, McGraw-Hill, 1984, pp. 185–186.
McGraw-Hill Modern Scientists and Engineers, McGraw-Hill, 1980, pp. 419–420.

Periodicals

Greenstein, George, "The Magician," *American Scholar,* winter, 1990, pp. 118–125.

—*Sketch by David E. Newton*

Julia Anna Gardner
1882-1960
American geologist and stratigraphic paleontologist

Julia Anna Gardner's work as a stratigraphic paleontologist was an important addition to the study of geology, especially throughout the Western Hemisphere. Stratigraphy is concerned with the geographical origin, composition, disposition, and succession of sedimentary rock or earth. In the early 1900s, Gardner began a study of mollusks found in strata that dated back to Mesozoic and Cenozoic eras. Her study of mollusks was to continue throughout her career, and contributed to national and international advancements in both paleontology and geology. In addition, her work made substantial contributions to the area of economic geology, most notably in the petroleum sector. Petroleum geologists were able to use her stratigraphic data when searching for oil deposits, particularly in Texas and the southern rim of the Caribbean.

Born in Chamberlain, South Dakota, on January 26, 1882, Gardner was the only child of Charles Henry Gardner and Julia M. (Brackett) Gardner. Her mother was a teacher, originally from Dixon, Illinois. Her father, a physician, died when she was four months old. When Gardner was thirteen years old, she and her mother returned to Dixon. They later moved to North Adams, Massachusetts, where she attended Drury Academy. An inheritance from her grandmother allowed her to enter Bryn Mawr College in 1901, where she studied geology and paleontology. She graduated in 1905 and taught at the elementary-school level before returning to Bryn Mawr to receive a master's degree in 1907. She began doctoral studies at Johns Hopkins that same year, receiving her Ph.D. in 1911. Her dissertation was titled *On Certain Families of Gasteropoda from the Miocene and Pliocene of Virginia and North Carolina.*

Becomes Affiliated with the United States Geological Survey

Gardner was to teach from time to time at Johns Hopkins University, but for most of her career she worked for the United States Geological Survey (USGS). The USGS was involved with strata mapping projects throughout the United States, Mexico, and the Caribbean area. She began field work with them in 1908, while pursuing her doctoral degree. In 1914, she investigated the taxonomy of Oligocene mollusks found in northern and western Florida. When World War I began, her desire to help alleviate the suffering brought on by the war led her to serve as a Red Cross volunteer in France. After the war was over, she remained in France with the American Friends Service Committee until 1920.

She then returned to the United States, where she was hired by the USGS to work on a geologic mapping project on the lower Rio Grande. It was while working on this project that she was made associate geologist and then geologist. During this period, Gardner also spent time in Europe promoting the exchange of ideas and geological data with European colleagues. With the outbreak of World War II, she joined the military geology unit of the USGS. By analyzing maps and aerial photographs, this unit supplied the United States with strategic and tactical information concerning the movements of the Japanese military. At the end of the war, Gardner was sent to Japan to map the West Pacific islands. While there, she also was able to extend her knowledge of the island's fossils through a study of the area's animal life. Gardner retired in 1952. She received a Distinguished Service Award from the Interior Department for her work with the USGS. That same year, she served as president of the Paleontological Society, and in 1953, was elected a vice president of the Geological Society of America. Even though retired, Gardner continued to do contract work for the USGS for several years. In 1954, she was involved in writing, along with L. R. Cox, the gastropod volume for a book entitled *Treatise on Invertebrate Paleontology,* when she suffered cerebral paralysis and was unable to continue her work. Her condition grew progressively worse over the years, and on November 15, 1960, she died of a stroke at her home in Bethesda, Maryland.

SELECTED WRITINGS BY GARDNER:

Books

The Molluscan Fauna of the Alum Bluff Group of Florida, U.S. Government Printing Office (Washington, DC), 1926–1950.

On Certain Families of Gasteropoda from the Miocene and Pliocene of Virginia and North Carolina, U.S. Government Printing Office (Washington, DC), 1943–1948.

Mollusca of the Tertiary Formations of Northeastern Mexico, [New York], 1945.

SOURCES:

Books

Notable American Women, the Modern Period, edited by Barbara Sicherman and Carol Hurd Green, Belknap Press (Cambridge, MA), 1980, pp. 260–262.

—*Sketch by Jane Stewart Cook*

Archibald Garrod
1857-1936
English physician and chemist

Archibald Garrod was a physician whose innovative work in clinical medicine and chemistry led him to discover a new class of human disease based on hereditary factors. A pioneer in biochemistry, Garrod stressed the chemical uniqueness of each person. For his work on inborn errors of metabolism, Garrod was elected to the Royal Society and received a knighthood.

Archibald Edward Garrod was born in London on November 25, 1857, the fourth and youngest son of Sir Alfred Baring Garrod and Elisabeth Ann Colchester. Garrod's father, a distinguished professor of medicine at University College in London, was the first physician to note the presence of uric acid in patients suffering from gout. In later years, Garrod would cite his father's discovery as the first quantitative biochemical investigation performed on living humans.

As a child, Garrod demonstrated an early talent for illustration and a lasting interest in color. He studied physical geography at Marlborough and astronomy at Oxford, where he graduated with first-class honors in natural science. Deciding to follow in his father's footsteps, Garrod began the study of medicine at St. Bartholomew's Hospital in London. He received a number of scholarships and spent a year attending medical clinics in Vienna, resulting in the publication of a book on the laryngoscope, a device used to examine the interior of the throat. A tall, handsome man, Garrod became a skilled clinician whose reassuring manner enabled him to gather detailed medical histories from his patients. In 1884, Garrod joined the staff of St. Bartholomew's Hospital, but promotion was slow and for nearly three decades he had ample time to pursue his interest in chemistry and disease. He wrote a number of papers on joint disorders, his father's specialty, pointing out the difference between rheumatism and rheumatoid arthritis as diseases.

Work in Chemistry Leads to Discovery of Genetic Disease

Garrod's interest in joint disease led him to study the chemistry of pigments in urine. While working as a visiting physician at the Great Osmond Street Hospital for Sick Children, he examined a three-month old boy, Thomas P., whose urine was stained a deep reddish-brown. Garrod's diagnosis was alkaptonuria, which is caused by an abnormal build-up of homogentisic acid, or alkapton. In a normal person, the acid is broken down through a series of chemical reactions into carbon dioxide and water. But in rare cases, the metabolic process is interrupted and the acid is excreted in the urine, where it turns black on contact with the air. According to the germ theory of disease, which had transformed the study of medicine in Garrod's time, alkaptonuria was thought to be a bacterial infection of the intestine. The disorder was almost always diagnosed in infancy, lasted throughout life and was thought to be contagious. Garrod's training in physical science, however, led him to investigate the disease as a series of chemical reactions. He reviewed 31 cases of alkaptonuria from his own practice and from the medical literature, and presented his findings to the Royal Medical and Chirurgical (Surgical) Society of London in 1899. Alkaptonuria, he noted, although rare, tended to appear among children of healthy parents. It was not contagious and seemed to be a harmless error in metabolism.

When a third child with alkaptonuria was born to the parents of Thomas P., Garrod suspected that something more than mere chance was involved. When he learned that Thomas P.'s parents were blood relations—their mothers were sisters—he inquired into the backgrounds of other families with one or more children with alkaptonuria. In every instance, their parents were also first cousins. It was while walking home from the hospital one afternoon that

Garrod conceived of the possibility that alkaptonuria might be a disease caused by heredity (genetics). Gregor Mendel's work on the principles of heredity, newly discovered in England, offered a simple explanation. The mating of first cousins apparently created conditions under which a rare, recessive Mendelian factor (or gene) appeared in the offspring. Garrod's classic paper on alkaptonuria was published in *Lancet* in 1902.

Garrod went on to study other metabolic disorders, including the pigment disorders porphyria, the cause of George III's madness, and albinism. Like alkaptonurics, albinos tended to be children of parents who were first cousins. In a series of lectures delivered before the Royal College of Physicians in 1908, Garrod described such disorders as "inborn errors of metabolism." In each instance, he claimed, a genetic factor caused a deficiency in a certain enzyme which led to a premature block in the chemistry of normal metabolism. In his book, *Inborn Errors of Metabolism* (1909), Garrod described an important new class of diseases which were genetic, not bacteriological in origin.

In recognition of his contributions to science, Garrod was made a fellow of the Royal Society in 1910, and was knighted in 1918. He spent World War I in the Army Medical Service on the island of Malta as consulting physician to the British forces in the Mediterranean. Two of his sons were killed in combat, a third died of the Spanish influenza following the armistice.

After the War, Garrod returned briefly to St. Bartholomew's, but was soon summoned to Oxford to become Regius Professor of Medicine. In his lectures, Garrod urged students to think of disease in terms of biochemistry. Clinicians, he argued, were uniquely placed to observe anomalies of nature which they could then investigate in the laboratory. In his later writings, Garrod hypothesized that there might be a molecular (genetic) basis for all variations in life functions, including physical appearance, susceptibility to disease, even behavior.

Garrod retired in 1927. He and his wife, Laura Elizabeth, whom he married in 1886, moved to Cambridge to be near their daughter, Dorothy, a noted archaeologist and teacher at Newnham College. Archibald Edward Garrod died at home on March 28, 1936. He was 78.

The significance of Garrod's contribution to the science of genetics was not appreciated in his lifetime; he was an elderly physician when most young geneticists were botanists and zoologists. It was not until the 1940s that Garrod's pathbreaking work in human genetics was rediscovered and applied to gene theory.

SELECTED WRITINGS BY GARROD:

Books

Inborn Errors of Metabolism, Hodder & Stoughton, 1909.

The Debt of Science to Medicine, Clarendon Press, 1924.

Periodicals

"The Incidence of Alkaptonuria: A Study of Chemical Individuality," *Lancet,* Volume 2, 1902, pp. 1616–20.

SOURCES:

Books

Dictionary of Scientific Biography, Volume 17, p. 333–36.

Harris, H., introduction to *Garrod's Inborn Errors of Metabolism,* Oxford University Press, 1963, pp. vii-xi.

Periodicals

The American Journal of Human Genetics, July 1, 1992, pp. 216–19.

Times (London), March 30, 1936, p. 14B.

—*Sketch by Philip Metcalfe*

Herbert Spencer Gasser
1888-1963
American neurophysiologist and physician

During a life devoted to the medical sciences, Herbert Spencer Gasser mastered the fields of physiology, electronics, optics, photography, applied mathematics, and pharmacology. His studies with **Joseph Erlanger** on nerve properties, using new techniques to measure the weak electrical currents of nerve fibers, were rewarded with a Nobel Prize in 1944. This work opened an era of research on pathways of the nervous system and has led to a better understanding of the mechanisms of pain and reflex actions. Gasser's career as scholar, professor, and experimenter culminated in 1935, when he became the second scientific director of the Rockefeller Institute for Medical Research in New York City.

Herbert Gasser was born in Platteville, Wisconsin, on July 5, 1888. His mother, Jane Griswold, who descended from an early Connecticut family, was a teacher trained in Wisconsin's first State Normal School in Platteville. Gasser's father, Herman, was born in the Tyrol and came to the United States as a boy. Herman was a self-educated man who eventually qualified in medicine and became a country doctor. His scholarly interests in debates on evolution during his day led him to name the first of his three children after British philosopher Herbert Spencer. Reading was the most important amusement for young Herbert and his siblings, Mary and Harold. Gasser was also adept at handicrafts, and proved it by setting up a shop to make furniture. His efforts to learn photographic techniques using a simple box Kodak camera formed the first of his scientific intrigues.

After attending State Normal School, Gasser received two degrees in science at the University of Wisconsin, a bachelor's degree in zoology in 1910 and a master's in anatomy in 1911. However, Gasser's future interests were determined by a physiology course in the University's newly organized medical school. The young lecturer who emphasized the new spirit of research in medicine was Joseph Erlanger, the man with whom Gasser would share the Nobel Prize thirty-three years later. Though Gasser rejected the medical career his father had chosen, he became intrigued by medicine as a scientific discipline. In 1915, he earned his medical degree from Johns Hopkins University, where he conducted research on blood coagulation in his spare time. After another year of research in Wisconsin, Gasser joined Erlanger at Washington University in St. Louis, in 1916.

Enters Field of Nerve Physiology

Earlier scientists had provided painstaking microscopic slides of neurons and general theories of nerve networks in the body. Gasser's contributions made it possible to trace pathways while keeping the nervous system intact. Physiologists knew that impulses (action potentials) travel along nerves to convey sensation and to stimulate muscles, and that these impulses could be recorded by electrical instruments. A hypothesis existed that impulses moved faster along thick fibers than they did thin ones. Gasser's dramatic new method involved stimulating a given region of nerves and then reading the transmitted signal as it reached its destination, much like a physician tests a patient's knee jerk response with a rubber mallet. His problem was in finding recording devices capable of measuring, in fractions of a second, impulses that were small in quantity and short in duration. The available devices were inadequate. The string galvanometer and the capillary electrometer were slow and insensitive. The cathode-ray oscillograph, although quick, was insensitive to small currents.

The first breakthrough for Gasser came with the same vacuum tube amplifier that made radio possible. The three-stage amplifier had been brought to St. Louis by H. Sidney Newcomer, one of Gasser's classmates at Hopkins, who had built the device with the help of friends at the Western Electric Company. Nerve impulses could now be recorded, though the instrument's inertia caused distortions in timing the impulses. Their report describing this apparatus and experiments on nerves in the diaphragm appeared in 1921. This article was less important for its new knowledge about nerves than for its description of how sensations could at last be signalized.

A new technology, again from Western Electric, allowed Gasser and Joseph Erlanger to conduct the pioneering studies that eventually led to their Nobel Prize. It had been believed for over a decade that, should a means be discovered to test the Braun tube, the nerve impulse might accurately be recorded. But the tube, invented in 1897, used a cold-cathode technology, wherein the emission of electrons from the cathode's electrode is triggered by an outside force—this proved to be its downfall. Western Electric had, on the other hand, developed an oscillograph tube fitted with a hot cathode. This permitted the instrument to operate at a low voltage, which made it more sensitive to the small currents of the nerve action potentials. The instrument could record both the time elapsed between impulses and the change in nerve reactions. Though the tube was a breakthrough for Gasser and Erlanger, they still had to devise auxiliary apparatus to coordinate their induction shocks with the action potentials that were displayed on the screen. This work was reported in 1922.

Using the cathode-ray oscilloscope, Gasser and Erlanger almost immediately made two discoveries about the unexpected complexity they found in nerve trunks. In one, they determined that the sequence of events of nerve impulse transmission consists of two parts. There is an initial, large, rapid deviation in electric potential, called the spike, which ascends then descends during the actual transmission. The spike is followed by a sequence of small, slow potential changes, called the after-potential, that first has a negative and then a positive deviation.

In their other discovery, Gasser and Erlanger found that the composite action potential of a nerve has a range of velocities. They eventually identified three distinct patterns based on the length of spikes and their after potentials, and classified the fibers into three main groups. The fastest and thickest are A fibers, the intermediate size are B fibers, while the thinnest and slowest are C fibers. Their findings thus confirmed the hypothesis that thick fibers conduct impulses faster than thin ones.

Erlanger and Gasser next showed how these three types of fibers are distributed over the incoming and outgoing fibers of the spinal cord, the sensory and motor roots. The perception of pain is carried by the thin, slow fibers, while muscle sense and touch and muscle movement are conducted by the fast fibers. Gasser subsequently explored the excitability of nerve fibers in relation to after-potentials. He also continued to refine the oscilloscope, first using X-ray film and eventually a camera to record the impulses.

Career Culminates as Director of the Rockefeller Institute

Gasser served as professor of pharmacology at Washington University from 1921 to 1931. During a two-year leave of absence between 1923 and 1925, he worked with **Archibald V. Hill** and **Henry Hallett Dale** in London, Walter Straub in Munich, and Louis Lapicque at the Sorbonne, on investigations involving muscle contractions and excitation of nerves. In 1931, Gasser became professor of physiology at Cornell University Medical College in New York City. In 1935, at age 47, Gasser became the second scientific director of the Rockefeller Institute for Medical Research, succeeding **Simon Flexner**. Gasser's medical training and his grasp of mathematical and physical sciences equipped him well to lead and to comprehend the expanding field of scientific medicine. His tenure bridged the economic depression of the 1930s, World War II, and the unsettling changes in the funding of scientific research after the war. Despite these trying times, Gasser, nevertheless, led the institute's transition from its original emphasis on pathology and infectious diseases to a broader biological approach to human diseases. From 1936 to 1957, he also served as editor of *The Journal of Experimental Medicine.*

During World War II, many Rockefeller Institute laboratories closed and their facilities and staff were organized to support war efforts. Gasser returned to work he had done on chemical warfare during the first world war, chairing a civilian committee on research development in that field. So it was a great surprise for Gasser when a cable arrived in 1944 from Stockholm, announcing that he had won a Nobel prize. He described in his autobiography that he was so dismayed by his long estrangement from work on nerve fibers that he "went into retreat to regain touch with the state of the subject through reading [my] own reprints." Gasser retired from the institute in 1953 and was succeeded by **Detlev W. Bronk**. With a change to emeritus status came the opportunity for Gasser to return to the laboratory. Instead of plunging into new areas of nerve physiology, he returned to unfinished work on differentiation of the thin C fibers. The introduction of electron microscopy helped him confirm many of his earlier findings. Gasser's scientific contributions were recognized by honorary degrees from twelve universities. He was elected to the National Academy of Sciences in 1934, the American Philosophical Society in 1937, and was a member of over twenty other scientific societies in the United States, Europe, and South America. He received the Kober Medal in 1954, from the American Association of Physicians.

Gasser was a tall, thin, fragile man, and lifelong bachelor, who suffered from migraine headaches. Rockefeller Professor Emeritus Maclyn McCarty told Carol Moberg in an interview that Gasser enjoyed entertaining scientific associates at home, regaling them with his technically-sophisticated hi-fidelity recording system, or his player piano. His hobbies included literature, theater, travel, and music. For twenty years he shared a summer cottage with the Bronk family on Cape Cod. Following a second stroke, Gasser died in New York Hospital on May 11, 1963.

SELECTED WRITINGS BY GASSER:

Books

(With Joseph Erlanger), *Electrical Signs of Nervous Activity,* University of Pennsylvania Press, 1937.

(Contributor) *Experimental Neurology,* supplement 1, 1964, pp. 1–38.

Periodicals

(With H. S. Newcomer), "Physiological Action Currents in the Phrenic Nerve. An Application of the Thermionic Vacuum Tube to Nerve Physiology," *American Journal of Physiology,* Volume 57, 1921, pp. 1–26.

(With Erlanger), "A Study of the Action Currents of Nerves with the Cathode-Ray Oscillograph," *American Journal of Physiology,* Volume 62, 1922, pp. 496–524.

(With Erlanger), "The Role Played by the Sizes of the Constituent Fibers of a Nerve Trunk in Determining the Form of its Action Potential Wave," *American Journal of Physiology,* Volume 80, 1927, pp. 522–47.

(With Erlanger), "The Ending of the Axon Action Potential and Its Relation to Other Events in Nerve Activity," *American Journal of Physiology,* Volume 94, 1930, pp. 247–77.

SOURCES:

Books

American Philosophical Yearbook, 1963, pp. 144–49.

Biographical Memoirs of Fellows of the Royal Society, Volume 10, Royal Society (London), 1964, pp. 74–82.

Other

Moberg, Carol, interview with Maclyn McCarty, August 4, 1993.
Moberg, interview with Merrill W. Chase, September 10, 1993.

—*Sketch by Carol Moberg*

Bill Gates
1955-
American software designer

Bill Gates

Bill Gates's supreme accomplishment was to design and develop innovative software for the personal computer that helped make PCs the universally popular machines they are today. Communicating with computers is a matter of "translating" a person's native language into the codes that a computer understands. The easier this translation is to make, the easier it is to work with the computer and the more accessible and widely used the computer becomes. Gate's gift for software design as well as his skills in business made Microsoft—the company he started up with a high school friend in Redmond, Washington—a multibillion-dollar empire.

William Henry Gates III was born October 28, 1955, in Seattle, Washington. He was the second child and only son of William Henry Gates Jr., a prominent Seattle attorney, and Mary Maxwell, a former school teacher. Although Gates's parents had in mind a legal career for their son, he developed an early interest in computer science and began studying computers in the seventh grade at Seattle's Lakeside School. At Lakeside, Gates became acquainted with Paul Allen, a teenager with a similar interest in technology who would eventually become his future business partner.

Gates's early experiences with computers included debugging (or eliminating errors from) programs for the Computer Center Corporation's PDP-10, helping computerize electric power grids for the Bonneville Power Administration, and—while still in high school—founding with Allen a firm named Traf-O-Data. Their small company earned them twenty thousand dollars in fees for analyzing local traffic patterns.

While working with the Computer Center's PDP-10, Gates was responsible for what was probably the first computer virus, which is a program that copies itself into other programs and ruins data. Discovering that the machine was hooked up to a national network of computers called Cybernet, Gates invaded the network and installed a program on the main computer that sent itself to the rest of the network's computers. Cybernet crashed. When Gates was found out, he was severely reprimanded and he kept away from computers for his entire junior year at Lakeside. Without the lure of computers, Gates made plans in 1970 for college and law school. In 1971, however, he was back helping Paul Allen write a class scheduling program for their school's computer.

The Article That Started It All

Gates entered Harvard University in 1973 and pursued his studies for the next year and a half. His life was to change, however, in January of 1975 when the magazine *Popular Electronics* carried a cover story on a three hundred-fifty dollar microcomputer, the Altair, made by a firm called MITS in New Mexico. When Allen excitedly showed him the story, Gates knew where he wanted to be: at the forefront of computer software design.

Gates and Allen first wrote a BASIC interpreter for the Altair computer, "BASIC" being a simple, interactive computer language designed in the 1960s and "interpreter," a program that executes a source program by reading it one line at a time and performing operations immediately. MITS, which encouraged and helped them, finally challenged them to bring their software in for a demonstration. Because Gates and Allen did not own an Altair (nor had they seen the 8080 microprocessing chip that was the heart of the machine), Gates had to write and test his BASIC interpreter on a simulator program which acted like the 8080. To the credit of Gates's and Allen's genius, their BASIC ran the first time it was tested at MITS.

Gates dropped out of Harvard in 1975, ending his academic life and beginning his career in earnest as a software designer and entrepreneur. At this time, he and Allen cofounded Microsoft. They wrote programs for the early Apple and Commodore machines and expanded BASIC to run on microcomputers other than the Altair. Gates's big opportunity arrived in 1980 when he was approached by IBM to help with their personal computer project, code named Project Chess. Eventually asked to design the operating system for the new machine, Gates developed the Microsoft Disk Operating System, or MS-DOS as it is popularly known. Not only did he sell IBM on the new operating system, but he also convinced the computer giant to shed the veil of secrecy surrounding the specifications of its PC so that others could write software for the machine. The result was a proliferation of licenses for MS-DOS as software developers quickly moved to become compatible with IBM. Over two million copies of MS-DOS were sold by 1984. Because IBM's PC architecture was opened up by Gates, MS-DOS and its related applications can run on almost any IBM compatible PC. By the early 1990s, Microsoft had sold more than one hundred million copies of MS-DOS, making the operating system the all-time leader in software sales. For his achievements in science and technology, Gates was presented the Howard Vollum Award in 1984 by Reed College in Portland, Oregon.

In 1987 Gates entered the world of computer-driven multimedia when he began promoting CD-ROM technology. CD-ROM is an optical storage medium easily connected to a PC, and a CD-ROM disc has an incredibly large capacity that can store encyclopedias, feature films, and complex interactive games. Gates hoped to expand his business by combining PCs with the information reservoirs provided by CD-ROM and was soon marketing a number of multimedia products.

Gates's competitive drive and fierce desire to win has made him a powerful force in business but has also consumed much of his personal life. In the six years between 1978 and 1984 he took a total of only two weeks vacation. In 1985 a popular magazine included him on their list of most eligible bachelors. His status did not change until New Year's Day, 1994, when he married Melinda French, a Microsoft manager, on the Hawaiian island of Lanai. The ceremony was held on the island's Challenge golf course and Gates kept it private by buying out the unused rooms at the local hotel and by hiring all the helicopters in the area to keep photographers from using them. His fortune at the time of the wedding was estimated at close to seven billion dollars.

In *Hard Drive,* James Wallace and Jim Erickson quote Gates as saying, "I can do anything if I put my mind to it." His ambition has made him the head of a robust, innovative software firm and, by some accounts, the richest man in America.

SOURCES:

Periodicals

"The Future of Microsoft," *Economist,* Volume 327, May 22, 1993, pp. 25–27.

New York Times, January 3, 1994.

New Yorker, January 10, 1994, pp. 48–61.

Books

Encyclopedia of Computer Science, Van Nostrand Reinhold, 1993, p. 519.

Ichbiah, David, and Susan L. Knepper, *The Making of Microsoft,* Prima, 1991.

Manes, Stephen, and Paul Andrews, *Gates,* Doubleday, 1993.

Slater, Robert, *Portraits in Silicon,* MIT Press, 1987.

Wallace, James, and Jim Erickson, *Hard Drive,* Wiley, 1992.

—Sketch by Frank Hertle

Sylvester James Gates, Jr.
1950-
American theoretical particle physicist

Sylvester James Gates, Jr., is a physicist working at the very edge of present scientific knowledge about the possible structure of the universe. Utilizing quantum field theories and newly-discovered supersymmetrical or "superstring" theories, Gates creates and experiments with esoteric mathematical models in the hopes of building a real model that will explain all of the diversity and complexity of our universe. As a young, African American physicist of enormous achievement, he has already published over one hundred research papers, contributed to several books, served as university department head, and obtained a six million dollar grant from NASA to establish the Center for the Study of Terrestrial and Extraterrestrial Atmospheres at Howard University.

Gates was born in Tampa, Florida, on December 15, 1950, to Charlie (Engels) and Sylvester J. Gates, who retired as a sergeant-major after twenty-four years in the United States Army. The oldest of four children (two brothers and one sister), Gates knew early on that he wanted to do something in a scientific field. While attending high school in Orlando, Florida, Gates had his first encounter with physics when he was in the eleventh grade, and knew immediately that it was the subject he wanted to pursue. In 1969, he won a National Merit Scholarship and attended the Massachusetts Institute of Technology (MIT) in Cambridge, Massachusetts. At MIT, Gates took a dual major—mathematics for practical reasons and physics because he loved it—and received two B.S. degrees upon graduation in 1973. Remaining at MIT for his graduate studies, Gates received a Ph.D. in physics on June 6, 1977. His graduate thesis was titled "Symmetry Principles in Selected Problems of Field Theory."

For the next five years, Gates continued his postdoctoral studies, first at Harvard University where he was a junior fellow, and then at the California Institute of Technology where he was a research fellow. His teaching career began at MIT in 1982, appointed to assistant professor of applied mathematics. In 1984 Gates joined the University of Maryland Department of Physics and Astronomy, becoming a full professor in 1988. While at Maryland, he was also affiliated with Howard University, serving as professor of physics and chair of the department of physics and astronomy from 1991 to 1993.

Gates, a theoretical particle physicist, seeks to discover the "unified field theory" that eluded the discoverer of special relativity, **Albert Einstein**. The goal of a unified field theory is to reduce all of the diversity and complexity in the universe to a few simple building blocks and their interactions. Recent theoretical breakthroughs called "superstring theories," which tell us that electrons, quarks, and all other particles like photons (particles of light beams) are intimately related, hold out a hope that such a unified theory may be discovered.

Much of the actual work Gates does is to create abstract mathematical models that involve what is happening when one considers the universe at incredibly small dimensions. At such extremely small sizes, the usual laws of everyday behavior—like gravity—do not apply. Thus Gates describes the actual research he carries out as "playing" with exotic mathematics, a task which he finds highly rewarding.

Among Gates's many honors and awards is the 21st Century Award from Howard University in 1992. He was elected president of the National Society of Black Physicists in 1993, and was chosen 1993 National Technical Achiever of the Year and 1993 Physicist of the Year by the National Technical Association. In April, 1994, he became the first recipient of the American Physical Society Prize for Visiting Minority Professor Lectureship. Gates serves as referee for eight physics journals, reviews proposals for the National Science Foundation and the Department of Energy, and has organized several conferences. A member of the American Physical Society and Sigma Xi, he is married, the father of twins, and enjoys bowling, horseback riding, running, and dancing.

SELECTED WRITINGS BY GATES:

Books

Superspace or 1001 Lessons in Supersymmetry, Benjamin-Cummings, 1983.

(Editor with C. R. Preitschopf and W. Siegel) *Proceedings of the Strings '88 Workshop,* World Scientific Publishing, 1989.

Periodicals

(With W. Siegel) "Taking the Particle Out of Particle Physics," *Quotient,* Volume 12, Number 4, 1986.

"Superstring Theory: To See the Entire Universe in the Pulsing of a String," *Washington Technology,* September 3, 1987.

SOURCES:

Gates, Sylvester J., Jr., interview with Leonard C. Bruno conducted January 31, 1994.

—Sketch by Leonard C. Bruno

Enrique Gaviola
1900-1989
Argentine physicist

Enrique Gaviola was the first of many distinguished native-born Argentine physicists, making contributions to physical chemistry, mathematical physics, and astrophysics, particularly spectroscopy. He was sometimes called the dean of Argentine physics, because he advocated advanced study in the physical sciences in Argentina and was the driving force behind the establishment of many research institutes in the country. He also directed the Astronomical Observatory of Córdoba.

One of ten children, Ramón Enrique Gaviola was born August 31, 1900, in Mendoza, Argentina. He attended school in Mendoza, graduating from the local secondary school, the colegio nacional, in 1916. He then went to study engineering at the University of La Plata near Buenos Aires (then the finest scientific university in Latin America—and one of the very best in the New World). There he fell under the spell of Richard Gans, the German professor of physics who twice turned down a professorship in Germany (Strasbourg in 1913; Munich in 1947) for one at La Plata. Gans encouraged Gaviola to study physics in Germany. In 1921 he took a diploma in civil engineering (delayed by upheavals in the so-called university reform movement) and returned to Mendoza, where he worked to earn money for his studies abroad.

Gaviola arrived at the University of Göttingen in 1922 with a letter of introduction from Gans to the experimental physicist Richard Pohl. Gaviola studied there for three semesters. Then he went to the University of Berlin, where he attended a physics colloquium frequented by **Max Planck**, **Albert Einstein**, and **Max von Laue**. One of his professors at Göttingen, **James Franck**, had written to Berlin experimental physicist Ernst Pringsheim about Gaviola, and Pringsheim invited Gaviola to work with him on a doctorate. Professor and student published several papers together on the problem of fluorescence. Gaviola returned to Argentina to spend four months in the army (his military obligation), received a scholarship for completing his doctorate, and in 1926 defended his dissertation in Berlin, under Pringsheim's direction, on extinction time in fluorescence.

Contributions to Spectroscopy

Upon receiving his doctorate, Gaviola obtained a fellowship from the National Research Council on a recommendation by Albert Einstein. He was the first Latin American scientist to receive such a fellowship. Gaviola went to Johns Hopkins University to investigate the Doppler effect as physicist Robert R. Wood's amanuensis. The Doppler effect is a shift in observed frequency of light or sound waves when the observer and source of the waves move away from or towards each other. Such shifts in the light spectra of stars enable astronomers to estimate the speeds at which stars move away from the earth. Ultimately, this research led to the theory that the universe is expanding steadily. Wood was notoriously difficult with students, but he and Gaviola worked well together, publishing two major papers on the quantum theory of mercury spectra. After a year at Johns Hopkins, Gaviola received a Carnegie fellowship to work with **Merle A. Tuve** and Lawrence Randolph Hafstad at the Department of Terrestrial Magnetism of the Carnegie Institution of Washington. The topic concerned Tuve's high-tension discharges produced by a Van de Graaf generator—one of the earliest particle accelerators in the United States.

Gaviola's credentials resulted in an appointment as professor of physical chemistry at La Plata in 1929. But the atmosphere there was not conducive to research. Gans had returned to Germany for a professorship of physics at the University of Königsberg, and his replacement, his former student Ramón G. Loyarte, had just been exposed as an incompetent experimentalist by a junior physicist colleague, Enrique Loedel Palumbo. Gaviola took a leave without pay and returned to Germany, where he published a philosophical critique of quantum theory—coming down firmly in favor of **Werner Karl Heisenberg** 's indeterminism. He looked for a permanent position in the United States and received an invitation from physicist **John Van Vleck** to teach engineering physics at the University of Wisconsin. In the end he took up university teaching posts in Buenos Aires and La Plata.

Gaviola returned to Argentina at the time of the military coup of General José Félix Uriburu, which ended two generations of representative democracy. At this time, and at personal risk, he began a crusade for university reform, hoping to bring Argentine academic life into line with what he had seen in the northern hemisphere. With the nominal restoration of democracy in 1932, Gaviola gave voice to socialist beliefs. He hoped that Argentina would not fall victim to fascism and that it would be able to transcend the limitations of the liberal democracies, which he believed had caused the bankruptcy of Argentina during the Great Depression.

Heads Córdoba Observatory

In 1935 Gaviola received a Guggenheim fellowship that allowed him to spend a year at the California Institute of Technology, studying physical chemistry with **Linus Pauling**. He used the fellowship, however, to retrain as an astrophysicist, in anticipation of directing the Córdoba Observatory upon the retirement of its director, the United States astronomer Charles Dillon Perrine. At Caltech, Gaviola worked with John Strong in pioneering a method of applying aluminum coating to large telescopic reflecting mirrors.

The conservative ecclesiastical hierarchy at Córdoba, which controlled the university, rather than appointing him director of the observatory, made Gaviola serve as an astrophysicist from 1937 to 1940, when he finally became director. Gaviola was joined at Córdoba by physicist Guide Beck, a refugee from Austria and France. Together they ran a colloquium that eventually led to the founding of the Argentine Physical Association in 1944.

Under the Bonapartist strongman Juan Domingo Perón, whose regime began with his participation in a military coup of 1943, Argentine academic life witnessed hundreds of summary dismissals. Because Perón had broad popular support (he was subsequently elected and reelected president), scientists and intellectuals opposed his policies at their peril. To protest high-handed political maneuvers, Gaviola resigned from his Córdoba directorship in 1947. Until the fall of Perón, Gaviola worked in the commercial firms of Cristalerías Rigolleau and General Electric in Buenos Aires. After Perón's leading physicist Ronald Richter fell from grace late in 1951 (he had been in charge of an enormous research complex at Bariloche, in the southern Andes, where he claimed to have developed controlled nuclear fusion), Gaviola successfully pressed for transforming Richter's laboratory into a national center for nuclear physics.

One year after the revolution that toppled Perón in 1955, Gaviola regained his directorship at the Córdoba Observatory, along with a chair in physics. He devoted himself to teaching there and at the universities of Tucumán, Buenos Aires, and San Juan, and in 1962 he was named a professor at the Instituto Balseiro of the Centro Atómico of Bariloche. A member of the National Academy of Sciences of Córdoba (Argentina's oldest scientific academy), he received a number of distinctions at the end of his career. Among these were the Ricardo Gans award of the Physics Institute of La Plata and an honorary doctorate from the National University of Cuyo through its affiliate, the Balseiro Institute. Gaviola died August 7, 1989, in Mendoza, and was survived by his second wife Elena.

SELECTED WRITINGS BY GAVIOLA:

Books

Reforma de la universidad argentina y brevario del reformista, [Buenos Aires], 1931.

SOURCES:

Books

Mariscotti, Mario, *El secreto atómico de Huemul: Crónica del origen de la energía atómica en la Argentina,* Sudamericana-Planeta, 1985, pp. 252–258.

Pyenson, Lewis, *Cultural Imperialism and Exact Sciences: German Expansion Overseas, 1900–1930,* Peter Lang, 1985, pp. 240–246.

Periodicals

"Dr Enrique Gaviola," *La Prensa* (Buenos Aires), August 8, 1989.

Bernaola, Omar, Véronica Grünfeld, and I. M. Falicov, "Enrique Gaviola," *Physics Today,* November 1990, pp. 105–106.

—Sketch by Lewis Pyenson

Helene Doris Gayle
1955-
American epidemiologist and pediatrician

Helene Doris Gayle is a specialist in the epidemiology of acquired immune deficiency syndrome (AIDS) and the human immunodeficiency virus (HIV) in children and teenagers. She is the coordinator of the AIDS Agency and chief of the HIV/AIDS Division at the U.S. Agency for International Development, Office of Health. In her position she has travelled to Africa and Asia to investigate the ways the disease affects different societies and to help coordinate international efforts to study it.

Born the third of five children on August 16, 1955, in Buffalo, New York. Her father, Jacob Sr., was an entrepreneur and her mother, Marietta, was a psychiatric social worker. Gayle was influenced by her parents from an early age, for her parents impressed upon their children the importance of making a contribution to the world. Gayle was also affected by growing up during the Civil Rights movement, and served as head of the black student union in her high school.

Gayle pursued a bachelor of arts degree in psychology in 1976 at Barnard University, followed by a medical degree from the University of Pennsylvania in 1981. Medical school opened the door for Gayle to the "social and political aspects of medicine," she told *Ebony* writer Renee D. Turner. After hearing a noted researcher speak on the efforts to eradicate the deadly smallpox virus, Gayle decided to seek a masters of public health, which she received from Johns Hopkins University in 1981. She then began a residency and internship in pediatrics at Children's Hospital Medical Center in Washington, D.C., where she worked for three years.

In 1984, Gayle was accepted to the epidemiology training program at the Centers for Disease Control and Prevention (CDC) in Atlanta, where she focused on the AIDS virus. She held various positions at the CDC, concentrating her efforts on the effect of AIDS on children, adolescents and their families, both in the United States and worldwide. Gayle has found that the U.S. black community, especially its women, is at high risk of contracting the fatal disease. In the late 1980s, black women made up 52 percent of the female AIDS population nationwide even though they only constituted 11 percent of the entire population. Gayle is an advocate for education as an important tool for the prevention of HIV/AIDS; as she told Turner, "Learning more about the spread of the disease also will provide some ammunition" in combating it. Gayle has traveled extensively studying the risk factors which contribute to the spread of HIV/AIDS in her position with the AIDS division for the Agency for International Development. The author of many articles and studies on HIV/AIDS risk factors, Gayle has received numerous awards, including the Henrietta and Jacob Lowenburg Prize, the Gordon Miller Award, and the U.S. Public Health Service achievement medal. She taught at various universities and is on the editorial board of the *Annual Review of Public Health.* Gayle is unmarried and has no children. As she told Turner, "I don't regret having placed a high priority on a career that enables me to make a contribution to mankind." Besides, she added, "we have no choice but to try to make an impact."

SELECTED WRITINGS BY GAYLE:

Periodicals

New England Journal of Medicine, Nov. 29, 1990.

SOURCES:

Books

Burgess, Marjorie, "Helene D. Gayle," *Contemporary Black Biography,* Volume 3, Gale, 1993, pp. 74–76.

Periodicals

Black Enterprise, October, 1988.
Turner, Renee D., "The Global AIDS Warrior," *Ebony,* November, 1991.

—*Sketch by Denise Adams Arnold*

Hans Geiger
1882-1945
German experimental physicist

Hans Geiger was a German nuclear physicist best known for his invention of the Geiger counter, a device used for counting atomic particles, and for his pioneering work in nuclear physics with Ernest Rutherford.

Johannes Wilhelm Geiger was born in Neustadt an-der-Haardt (now Neustadt an-der-Weinstrasse), Rhineland-Palatinate, Germany, on September 30, 1882. His father, Wilhelm Ludwig Geiger, was a professor of philology at the University of Erlangen from 1891 to 1920. The eldest of five children, two boys and three girls, Geiger was educated initially at Erlangen Gymnasium, from which he graduated in 1901. After completing his compulsory military service, he studied physics at the University of Munich, and at the University of Erlangen where his tutor was Professor Eilhard Wiedemann. He received a doctorate from the latter institution in 1906 for his thesis on electrical discharges through gases.

Joins Ernest Rutherford in Manchester

That same year, Geiger moved to Manchester University in England to join its esteemed physics department. At first he was an assistant to its head, Arthur Schuster, an expert on gas ionization. When Schuster departed in 1907, Geiger continued his research with Schuster's successor, **Ernest Rutherford,** and the young physicist Ernest Marsden. Rutherford was to have a profound influence on young Geiger, sparking his interest in nuclear physics. Their relationship, which began as partners on some of Geiger's most important experiments, was lifelong and is documented in a series of letters between them.

In addition to supervising the research students working at the lab, Geiger began a series of experiments with Rutherford on radioactive emissions, based on Rutherford's detection of the emission of alpha particles from radioactive substances. Together they began researching these alpha particles, discovering among other things that two alpha particles appeared to be released when uranium disintegrated. Since alpha particles can penetrate through thin walls of solids, Rutherford and Geiger presumed that they could move straight through atoms. Geiger designed the apparatus that they used to shoot streams of alpha particles through gold foil and onto a screen where they were observed as scintillations, or tiny flashes of light.

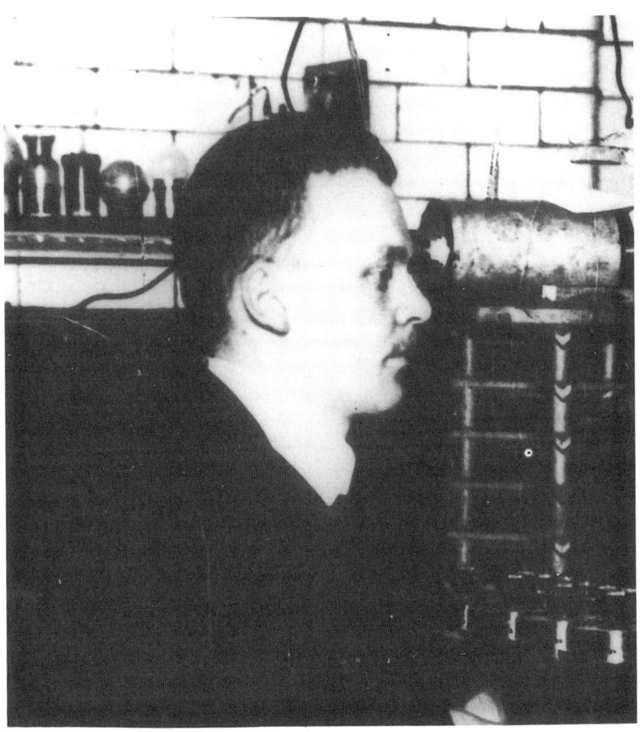

Hans Geiger

Manually counting the thousands of scintillations produced per minute was a laborious task. Geiger was reputedly something of a workaholic, who put in long hours recording the light flashes. David Wilson noted in *Rutherford: Simple Genius* that in a 1908 letter to his friend Henry A. Bumstead, Rutherford remarked, "Geiger is a good man and work[s] like a slave. . . . [He] is a demon at the work and could count at intervals for a whole night without disturbing his equanimity. I damned vigorously after two minutes and retired from the conflict." Geiger was challenged by the haphazardness of their methodology to invent a more precise technique. His solution was a primitive version of the "Geiger counter," the machine with which his name is most often associated. This prototype was essentially a highly sensitive electrical device designed to count alpha particle emissions.

Geiger's simple but ingenious measuring device enabled him and Rutherford to discern that alpha particles are, in fact, doubly charged nuclear particles, identical to the nucleus of helium atoms traveling at high velocity. The pair also established the basic unit of electrical charge when it is involved in electrical activity, which is equivalent to that carried by a single hydrogen atom. These results were published in two joint papers in 1908 entitled "An Electrical Method of Counting the Number of Alpha Particles" and "The Charge and Nature of the Alpha Particle."

In bombarding the gold with the alpha particles Geiger and Rutherford observed that the majority of the particles went straight through. However, they unexpectedly found that a few of the particles were deflected or scattered upon contact with the atoms in the gold, indicating that they had come into contact with a very powerful electrical field. Rutherford's description of the event as recorded by Wilson revealed its importance: "It was as though you had fired a fifteen-inch shell at a piece of tissue paper and it had bounced back and hit you." These observations were jointly published by Geiger and Marsden in an article entitled "On a Diffuse Reflection of the Alpha-Particles" for the *Proceedings of the Royal Society* in June of 1909.

Thirty years later Geiger recollected, "At first we could not understand this at all," Wilson noted. Geiger continued to study the scattering effect, publishing two more papers about it that year. The first, with Rutherford, was entitled "The Probability Variations in the Distribution of Alpha-Particles." The second, referring to his work with Marsden, dealt with "The Scattering of Alpha-Particles by Matter." Geiger's work with Rutherford and Marsden finally inspired Rutherford in 1910 to conclude that the atoms contained a positively charged core or nucleus which repelled the alpha particles. Wilson noted Geiger's recollection that "One day Rutherford, obviously in the best of spirits, came into my [laboratory] and told me that he now knew what the atom looked like and how to explain the large deflections of the alpha-particles. On the very same day, I began an experiment to test the relation expected by Rutherford between the number of scattered particles and the angle of scattering."

Geiger's results were accurate enough to persuade Rutherford to go public with his discovery in 1910. Nonetheless, Geiger and Marsden continued their experiments to test the theory for another year, completing them in June of 1912. Their results were published in German in Vienna in 1912 and in English in the *Philosophical Magazine* in April of 1913. Wilson noted that Dr. T. J. Trenn, a modern physics scholar, characterized Geiger's and Marsden's work of this period: "It was not the Geiger-Marsden scattering evidence, as such, that provided massive support for Rutherford's model of the atom. It was, rather, the constellation of evidence available gradually from the spring of 1913 and this, in turn, coupled with a growing conviction, tended to increase the significance or extrinsic value assigned to the Geiger-Marsden results beyond that which they intrinsically possessed in July 1912."

In 1912 Geiger gave his name to the Geiger-Nuttal law, which states that radioactive atoms with short half-lives emit alpha particles at high speed. He later revised it, and in 1928, a new theory by **George Gamow** and other physicists made it redundant. Also in 1912 Geiger returned to Germany to take up a post as director of the new Laboratory for Radioactivity at the Physikalisch-Technische Reichsanstalt in Berlin, where he invented an instrument for measuring not only alpha particles but beta rays and other types of radiation as well.

Geiger's research was broadened the following year with the arrival at the laboratory of **James Chadwick** and **Walter Bothe,** two distinguished nuclear physicists. With the latter, Geiger formed what would be a long and fruitful professional association, investigating various aspects of radioactive particles together. However, their work was interrupted by the outbreak of the First World War. Enlisted with the German troops, Geiger fought as an artillery officer opposite many of his old colleagues from Manchester including Marsden and **H. G. J. Moseley** from 1914 to 1918. The years spent crouching in trenches on the front lines left Geiger with painful rheumatism. With the war over, Geiger resumed his post at the Reichsanstalt, where he continued his work with Bothe. In 1920, Geiger married Elisabeth Heffter, with whom he had three sons.

Perfects the Geiger-Mueller Counter

Geiger moved from the Reichsanstalt in 1925 to become professor of physics at the University of Kiel. His responsibilities included teaching students and guiding a sizable research team. He also found time to develop, with Walther Mueller, the instrument with which his name is most often associated: the Geiger-Mueller counter, commonly referred to as the Geiger counter. Electrically detecting and counting alpha particles, the counter can locate a speeding particle within about one centimeter in space and to within a hundred-millionth second in time. It consists of a small metal container with an electrically insulated wire at its heart to which a potential of about 1000 volts is applied. In 1925, Geiger used his counter to confirm the Compton effect, that is, the scattering of X rays, which settled the existence of light quantum, or packets of energy.

Geiger left Kiel for the University of Tubingen in October of 1929 to serve as professor of physics and director of research at its physics institute. Installed at the Institute, Geiger worked tirelessly to increase the Geiger counter's speed and sensitivity. As a result of his efforts, he was able to discover simultaneous bursts of radiation called cosmic-ray showers, and concentrated on their study for the remainder of his career.

Geiger returned to Berlin in 1936 upon being offered the chair of physics at the Technische Hochschule. His upgrading of the counter and his work on cosmic rays continued. He was also busy leading a team of nuclear physicists researching artificial radioactivity and the by-products of nuclear fission (the splitting of the atom's nucleus). Also in 1936 Geiger took over editorship of the journal *Zeitschrift fur Physik,* a post he maintained until his death. It was at this time that Geiger also made a rare excursion into politics, prompted by the rise to power in Germany of Adolf Hitler's National Socialist Party. The Nazis sought to harness physics to their ends and engage the country's scientists in work that would benefit the Third Reich. Geiger and many other prominent physicists were appalled by the specter of political interference in their work by the Nazis. Together with **Werner Karl Heisenberg** and Max Wien, Geiger composed a position paper representing the views of most physicists, whether theoretical, experimental, or technical. As these men were politically conservative, their decision to oppose the National Socialists was taken seriously, and seventy-five of Germany's most notable physicists put their names to the Heisenberg-Wien-Geiger Memorandum. It was presented to the Reich Education Ministry in late 1936.

The document lamented the state of physics in Germany, claiming that there were too few up-and-coming physicists and that students were shying away from the subject because of attacks on theoretical physics in the newspapers by National Socialists. Theoretical and experimental physics went hand in hand, it continued, and attacks on either branch should cease. The Memorandum seemed to put a stop to attacks on theoretical physics, in the short term at least. It also illustrated how seriously Geiger and his associates took the threat to their work from the Nazis.

Geiger continued working at the Technische Hochschule through the war, although toward the latter part he was increasingly absent, confined to bed with rheumatism. In 1938 Geiger was awarded the Hughes Medal from the Royal Academy of Science and the Dudell Medal from the London Physics Society. He had only just started to show signs of improvement in his health when his home near Babelsberg was occupied in June of 1945. Suffering badly, Geiger was forced to flee and seek refuge in Potsdam, where he died on September 24, 1945.

SELECTED WRITINGS BY GEIGER:

Books

(With Walter Makower) *Practical Measurements in Radio-Activity,* [London], 1912.

Periodicals

(With Ernest Rutherford) "An Electrical Method of Counting the Number of Alpha Particles from Radioactive Substances," *The Proceedings of the Royal Society,* Volume 81, 1908, pp. 141–161.

(With Rutherford) "The Charge and Nature of the Alpha Particle," *The Proceedings of the Royal Society,* Volume 81, 1908, pp. 162–173.

(With Ernest Marsden) "On a Diffuse Reflection of the Alpha-Particles," *Proceedings of the Royal Society,* June, 1909.

(With Rutherford) "The Number of Alpha Particles emitted by Uranium and Thorium and by Uranium Minerals," *Philosophical Magazine,* October, 1910, p. 691–698.

SOURCES:

Books

Beyerchen, Alan D., *Scientists under Hitler: Politics and the Physics Community in the Third Reich,* Yale University Press, 1979.

Dictionary of Scientific Biography, Volume 5, Scribner, 1972, pp. 330–333.

Williams, Trevor I., *A Biographical Dictionary of Scientists,* John Wiley & Sons, 1982, p. 211.

Wilson, David, *Rutherford: Simple Genius,* MIT Press, 1983.

Periodicals

"Geiger and Proportional Counters," *Nucleonics,* December, 1947, pp. 69–75.

"Hughes Medal Awarded to Professor Hans Geiger," *Nature,* Volume 124, 1929, p. 893.

Krebs, A. T., "Hans Geiger: Fiftieth Anniversary of the Publication of His Doctoral Thesis, 23 July 1906," *Science,* Volume 124, 1956, p. 166.

"Memories of Rutherford in Manchester," *Nature,* Volume 141, 1938, p. 244.

—Sketch by Avril McDonald

Hilda Geiringer
1893-1973
Austrian-born American mathematician

Hilda Geiringer was an applied mathematician who made important contributions to the theory of plasticity of materials. She formulated the Geiringer equations for plane plastic deformations in 1930. She also pursued research in probability, statistics, genetics, and numerical methods. A refugee from Europe during World War II, Geiringer was among the European mathematicians who brought an emphasis on applied mathematics to the United States, where pure mathematics predominated. In the summer of 1942, she participated in the development of an applied mathematics program at Brown University, presenting a series of lectures on the geometric foundations of the mechanics of a rigid body. After the death of her husband, mathematician **Richard von Mises**, in 1953, Geiringer worked on the publication of new editions of his works as well as her own research.

Hilda Geiringer was born in Vienna, on September 28, 1893. She was the daughter of Ludwig, a textile manufacturer, and Martha Wertheimer Geiringer. She showed a talent and interest in mathematics at an early age. Her parents supported her studies in mathematics at the University of Vienna, where she received a Ph.D. in 1917 for her thesis on double trigonometric series. In 1919 and 1920 Geiringer assisted the editor of *Fortschritte der Mathematik* (Advances in Mathematics).

During the following year, Geiringer moved to Germany to work at the Institute of Applied Mathematics in Berlin, under Richard von Mises, a founder of mathematical aerodynamics and contributor to probability theory. This was the beginning of Geiringer's productive career in applied mathematics. She began to publish papers on probability and on the mathematical characterization of plasticity, the bending of material after deformation. In 1927 Geiringer became a lecturer at the University of Berlin.

Flight and Refuge

Geiringer, who was Jewish, was removed from the University in 1933; she moved to Belgium and then to Turkey. From 1934 to 1939 she was Professor of Mathematics at the University of Istanbul. There, she learned Turkish for her lectures. When war broke out in 1939, Geiringer fled to the United States, where she taught at Bryn Mawr from 1939 to 1944. During this period, Geiringer published papers on probability as well as notes for her lectures at Brown.

Geiringer had married Felix Pollaczek in 1921. They had one daughter, Magda, born in 1922, but they divorced in 1925. Geiringer took Magda with her to Istanbul and then to the United States. In 1943 Geiringer married Richard von Mises, who had also come to the United States via Turkey. He became a lecturer and then Professor of Aerodynamics and Applied Mathematics at Harvard. Geiringer became a United States citizen in 1945.

From Bryn Mawr, Geiringer went to Wheaton College in Norton, Massachusetts, where she became Chairman of the Mathematics Department. In the late forties, Geiringer wrote several papers on statistics applied to Mendelian genetics and two papers on numerical methods. In the early fifties she took up plasticity again in a more general form. After the death of von Mises, Geiringer worked at Harvard under a grant from the Office of Naval Research to complete his work. In 1957 she published a new edition of his book *Probability, Statistics, and Truth.* Her work with G.S.S. Ludwig and von Mises, *Mathematical Theory of Compressible Fluid Flow,* appeared in 1958. The new edition of von Mises' *Mathematical Theory of Probability and Statistics,* with Geiringer's complementary material, was published in 1964. Geiringer wrote papers and lectured on probability during this period and wrote an article entitled "The Mathematical Theory of the Inelastic Continuum" with A.F. Freudenthal for the *Encyclopedia of Physics.*

Geiringer retired from Wheaton in 1959, but continued her research work at Harvard. Wheaton gave her an honorary degree in 1960. Geiringer was made Professor Emeritus by the University of Berlin in 1956, and was honored by the University of Vienna on the fiftieth anniversary of her graduation. On March 22, 1973, during a visit with her younger brother, Karl, a noted musicologist, in Santa Barbara, Geiringer died of influenzal pneumonia.

SELECTED WRITINGS BY GEIRINGER:

Books

Mathematical Foundations of the Theory of Isotropic Plastic Bodies (title translated), Mémorial des Sciences Mathématiques, 1937.

Geometrical Foundations of Mechanics, Brown University, 1942.

SOURCES:

Books

Dictionary of Scientific Biography, Volume 9, Scribners, 1974, pp. 419–420.

Notable American Woman: The Modern Period, Harvard University Press, 1980, pp. 267–268.

Periodicals

Boston Sunday Globe, March 25, 1973.

New York Times, July 19, 1953, p. 25; March 24, 1973, p. 36.

Rees, Mina, "The Mathematical Sciences and World War II," *American Mathematical Monthly,* October, 1980, pp. 607–621.

—Sketch by Sally M. Moite

Margaret Joan Geller
1947-
American astronomer

Margaret Joan Geller, an astronomy professor at Harvard University and a senior scientist at the Smithsonian Astrophysical Observatory, helped discover a "Great Wall" of galaxies in space stretching at least 500 million light-years. The existence of this structure, the largest ever seen in the universe, presents a conundrum for theorists dealing with the early universe.

Geller was born in Ithaca, New York, on December 8, 1947, to Seymour Geller and Sarah Levine Geller. She received her bachelor's degree at the University of California at Berkeley in 1970, and was a National Science Foundation fellow from 1970 to 1973. Her M.A. followed at Princeton University in 1972, and her Ph.D. thesis, entitled "Bright Galaxies in Rich Clusters: A Statistical Model for Magnitude Distributions," was received at Princeton University in 1975. She was a fellow in theoretical physics at the Harvard-Smithsonian Center for Astrophysics from 1974 to 1976, and a research associate at the center from 1976 to 1980. She was a senior visiting fellow at the Institute for Astronomy in Cambridge, England, from 1978 to 1982, and an assistant professor at Harvard University from 1980 to 1983. Geller became an astrophysicist with the Smithsonian Astrophysical Observatory in 1983 and a professor of astronomy at Harvard University in 1988.

Since 1980 Geller has collaborated with astronomer John P. Huchra on a large-scale survey of galaxies, using redshifts to measure the galaxies' distance. (A redshift is a shift toward the red or longer-wavelength end of the visible spectrum that increases in proportion to distance.) Cosmologists have long predicted that galaxies are uniformly distributed in space, despite recent evidence of irregularities. Geller and Huchra hypothesized that three-dimensional mapping of galaxies beyond a certain brightness over a large-enough distance—500 million light-years—would confirm the predictions of uniformity. In January 1986 Huchra and Geller published their first results. But instead of the expected distribution, their "slice" of the cosmos (135 degrees wide by 6 degrees thick) showed sheets of galaxies appearing to line the walls of bubblelike empty spaces.

Discovers Largest Structure Known in Universe

Geller and Huchra's so-called Great Wall is a system of thousands of galaxies arranged across the universe—its full width was indeterminable because it fell off the edges of the survey map. The wall contains about five times the average density of galaxies; but "what's striking," Geller told M. Mitchell Waldrop of *Science Research News* in 1989, "is how incredibly *thin*[—fifteen million light-years—the bubble walls] are." Large structures such as the Great Wall pose a problem for astronomers—they are too large to have formed as a result of gravity since the big bang (a cosmic explosion that the universe was born out of and expanded from over time), unless a significant amount of clumpiness was present at the origin of the cosmos. This theory, however, is contradicted by the smoothness of the cosmic microwave background, or "echo" of the big bang. Dark matter, invisible elementary particles left over from the big bang and believed to constitute 90 percent of the mass of the universe, is another possible explanation. But even dark matter may not be capable of producing so large an object as the Great Wall. "There is something fundamentally missing from our understanding of the way things work," Geller told Waldrop. Between January 1986 and November 1989, Geller and Huchra published four maps (including the first), and in each found the same line of galaxies perpendicular to our line of sight. Geller and Huchra's survey will eventually plot about fifteen thousand galaxies.

Geller won a MacArthur fellowship—also known as a "genius award"—in 1990 for her research. She received the Newcomb-Cleveland Prize of the American Academy of Arts and Sciences that same year. In addition to galaxy distributions, Geller is interested in the origin and evolution of galaxies and X-ray astronomy. She is a member of the International Astronomical Union, the American Astronomical Society, and the American Association for the Advancement of Science.

SELECTED WRITINGS BY GELLER:

Books

(With A. C. Fabian and A. Szalay) *Large Scale Structures in the Universe,* Geneva Observatory, 1987.

Periodicals

(With Antonaldo Diaferio and Massimo Ramella) "Are Groups of Galaxies Viralized Systems?" *Astronomical Journal,* June 1, 1993, p. 2035.

(With Ann I. Zabludoff and John P. Huchra) "The Kinematics of Dense Clusters of Galaxies," *Astronomical Journal,* October 1, 1993, p. 1301.

SOURCES:

Periodicals

Bartusiak, Marcia, "Mapping the Universe," *Discover,* August, 1990, pp. 60–63.

Powell, Corey S., "Up against the Wall," *Scientific American,* February, 1990, pp. 18–19.

Waldrop, M. Mitchell, "Astronomers Go up against the Great Wall," *Science Research News,* November 17, 1989, p. 885.

—Sketch by Sebastian Thaler

Murray Gell-Mann
1929-
American physicist

Murray Gell-Mann, a particle physicist, helped to develop the Stanford model, which describes the behavior of subatomic particles and their forces. He contributed some unique ways of categorizing and naming elementary particles including strangeness, the eight-fold way, and the quark. Though a theoretical physicist, Gell-Mann has made many important suggestions to experimental physicists for detecting the particles that he predicted in theory. For his work in classifying these particles and their interactions, Gell-Mann was awarded the Nobel Prize for physics in 1969.

Murray Gell-Mann was born on September 15, 1929, in New York City. His father, Arthur Gell-Mann, was the proprietor of a language school and very learned in the areas of astronomy, archeology, and mathematics. Like his father Murray Gell-Mann had many varied interests including archeology, linguistics, and ornithology. In an interview for *Omni* magazine he said that when he asked his father about studying one of them for a career, his father replied, "You'll starve." So he accepted his father's alternative: physics. Gell-Mann's first experiences with the subject were not positive. He studied physics in a high school for the intellectually gifted, but found it dull. It was, he said in the *Omni* interview "the only course I'd ever done badly in." He found language, mathematics, and history more to his liking. Nevertheless, he entered Yale University at the age of fifteen and graduated in 1948 with a B.S. in physics. He then entered the Massachusetts Institute of Technology, and at twenty-one earned his Ph.D., again in physics.

Taming the Zoo

When Gell-Mann entered academia in 1951, particle accelerators were beginning to produce a variety of new subatomic particles. The number of particles grew to over 200, and came to be known as a "zoo." Nuclear physicists were troubled, because the

Murray Gell-Mann

sheer number of particles seemed to contradict the order and simplicity with which they preferred to view the universe. Moreover, these particles exhibited strange behavior, and did not decay at the rates expected. In 1953, while he was associate professor at the University of Chicago's Institute for Nuclear Studies, Gell-Mann published a paper explaining the unexpected behavior of these particles. Gell-Mann's principle, called *strangeness,* predicted numerous events in the decay of these particles; it also predicted the existence of a new particle called Xi zero. In 1959, scientists at the University of California found evidence for the existence of this particle in photographs of an accelerator experiment.

Gell-Mann's principle of strangeness described the electrical charge and spin of particles that resulted from collisions in large accelerators or atom smashers, particles that existed for only a few millionths of a second or less. With this principle, Gell-Mann classified particles by assigning appropriate strangeness numbers; he then formulated equations that represented the relationships between these particles and their interactions. The results of the equations were then compared to experimental results. With this system, Gell-Mann was able to predict which particles could be found experimentally and which could not, giving scientists a means of reducing the great variety of particles that confronted them.

Following the Eight-fold Way

In 1955 Gell-Mann became an associate professor of physics at the California Institute of Technology, and in the following year became full professor. During this time, Gell-Mann began to develop his notion of strangeness into a scheme for the orderly arrangement of newly-discovered subatomic particles. He assigned to the particles eight quantum numbers, representing their various characteristics. Gell-Mann facetiously named his system the "eight-fold way" after the Buddhist list of eight virtues for achieving enlightenment. With this system Gell-Mann formalized the patterns he saw among the particles' mass, charge, and spin.

Gell-Mann arranged the eight-fold way much like Dmitry Mendeleev had the periodic table, charting the known particles and leaving spaces for those he thought would be discovered later. In so doing, Gell-Mann predicted particles and their characteristics long before they were found through experimentation. Gell-Mann's subsequent recommendations for constructing larger, more powerful accelerators in order to find these predicted particles led to the discovery of the Eta particle in 1962, the Phi particle in 1963, and the Omega-minus particle in 1964. The Omega-minus particle turned out to have a mass of almost exactly the value that had been predicted for it in theory.

"Three Quarks for Muster Mark"

As Gell-Mann continued to examine subatomic particles, he began to see patterns in their characteristics and behavior; for example, he found that particles exhibited properties that were based on the number 3 and arrangements that formed triangles. Eventually, Gell-Mann suggested that the number 3 kept appearing because these particles were themselves composed of three sub-particles, which he proposed were the ultimate building blocks of matter.

Because of his interest in linguistics, Gell-Mann frequently played with words. In naming the new subparticles he initially had thought that the sound *kwork* seemed suitable. He decided on the spelling *quark* while reading the phrase in James Joyce's novel *Finnegan's Wake,* "three quarks for muster mark." Gell-Mann's playful naming of serious scientific concepts, however, did have a practical intent as well, for he felt that to continue the tradition of naming particles after Greek letters and roots was pretentious and that often these new terms quickly outgrew their validity. (Proton, from the Greek meaning "first," for example, is no longer considered the first particle in any sense, and atom, from the Greek "indivisible," has been subdivided several times since it was named.)

In keeping with his fondness for odd words, Gell-Mann named his three quarks *up, down,* and *strange.* With these curiously-named entities he was able to explain the make-up of the over 200 sub-atomic particles confronting physicists at the time. Then, in two separate 1974 antimatter experiments, a particle emerged that the three-quark theory could not account for. Scientists suggested the existence of a fourth quark. Eventually, physicists discovered evidence of two additional quarks. Consistent with Gell-Mann's whimsical scheme for naming particles, the three new quarks were dubbed *charm, beauty,* and *truth.* All six became known as the "flavors" of quarks.

Gell-Mann's research on quarks was wholly theoretical, entirely based on mathematical formulations; however, physicists at various particle accelerators observed experimental results that they could only account for if Gell-Mann's quark theory was valid. No quarks have been isolated from a nucleus—and in fact Gell-Mann himself said in an interview for *Omni* magazine, "I believe that the confinement is absolute"—but physicists in the 1970s found indirect evidence in the laboratory for the existence of quarks.

A Physicist's Mind at Work

Gell-Mann considered himself a theoretical physicist, and as such wrote equations based on measurable quantities that described particles and their interactions. Often he compared the results of his equations with experimental results in an attempt to predict new experimental figures. Gell-Mann felt that his brand of physics was fundamental to all other sciences in that their laws were ultimately based on the laws that elementary particles obey. In Theodore Berland's *The Scientific Life,* Gell-Mann said, "It's such a marvelous thing to contemplate a universe made up of all these absolutely identical—wherever you find them—particles."

Gell-Mann was interested in almost everything that confronted him, and his mind always seemed to have something simmering on the back burner. While he was in the middle of explaining another scientist's paper to a group in Princeton, he discovered an error in his work on the chalkboard; he stepped back from the board to sit down, and in that moment his theory of strangeness came to him. At first he felt that his strangeness principle was too silly to share with his colleagues; in 1953, however, he heard other physicists talking about a similar notion, which he felt was wrong, so he put his strangeness theory on paper and published it.

Gell-Mann had such faith in his scientific method that he felt it could apply to social contexts as well. For example, when he heard about the activities of the politically conservative John Birch Society, he researched the group; after learning of its viewpoints, Gell-Mann believed he could predict how this group would act in future circumstances, in much the same way that he predicted the future behavior of elementary particles.

A Man of Worldly Interests

Gell-Mann rose to prominence in the field of particle physics during the Cold War, drawing the U.S. military and the defense industries to seek out his expertise. Gell-Mann did some work for the Rand Corporation on antisubmarine and anti-ICBM projects, and served as a consultant to the Institute for Defense Analysis for issues like the detection of nuclear test detonations. In addition to his 1969 Nobel Prize, Gell-Mann has been honored with the American Physical Society's Heineman Prize, the United States Atomic Energy Commission's Ernest Orlando Lawrence Memorial Award for Physics, the Franklin Institute's Franklin Medal, and the National Academy of Sciences' John J. Carty Medal; Yale bestowed upon him an honorary degree in 1959.

As someone who is interested in almost everything, Gell-Mann has developed strong opinions about almost everything, as well. Regarding education, for example, with which he has had much contact, he feels that the traditional lecture approach is ineffective. He believes that the education system should model itself after the old practice of apprenticeship, where a young person would pair up with an older, experienced mentor. Gell-Mann feels that this approach to education would allow the teacher more time to discuss problems, answer questions, and inspire students.

When he isn't scratching equations on a chalkboard, Gell-Mann travels in search of adventure, seeking out the diversity of the world wherever he goes. Underneath this love of diversity is Gell-Mann's respect for the individual and his concern for nature; moreover, he feels that the lot of both man and nature could improve if, as he said in Berland's *The Scientific Life,* "there were fewer people and more wild animals."

SELECTED WRITINGS BY GELL-MANN:

Books

(With Y. Ne'eman) *The Eight-fold Way,* 1964.

(With K. Wilson) *Broken Scale Variance and the Light Cone,* 1971.

SOURCES:

Books

Berland, Theodore, *The Scientific Life,* Coward-McCann, 1962.

Periodicals

Horgan, John, "Profile: Murray Gell-Mann," *Scientific American,* March, 1992, pp. 30–32.

Schultz, Ron, "Interview: Murray Gell-Mann," *Omni,* May, 1985, p. 54.

—Sketch by Lawrence Souder

Albert Ghiorso
1915-
American nuclear chemist

Albert Ghiorso

Trained as an electrical engineer, Albert Ghiorso was drawn into nuclear physics through his work with the Manhattan Project, which built the first atomic bomb. This led to his participation over a period of thirty years in the discovery of twelve new elements—organizing and leading the effort for the last six—and in the development of the Heavy Ion Linear Accelerator and its successor, the SuperHILAC.

Ghiorso was born July 15, 1915, in Vallejo, California, one of the seven children of John and Mary Ghiorso. His father was a riveter. Ghiorso attended the University of California at Berkeley, where he received his B.S. degree in electrical engineering in 1937. He then went to work for a small electronics firm called Cyclotron Specialties Company in Moraga, California, where he designed and constructed various kinds of radio equipment. While with Cyclotron Specialties, Ghiorso engineered and built the first commercial Geiger-Mueller counters for measuring radiation and sold them to the radiation laboratory at Berkeley.

When the United States entered World War II, Ghiorso decided to seek a commission in the U.S. Navy and contacted **Glenn T. Seaborg**, whom he knew from the radiation laboratory at Berkeley, for a reference. Instead, Seaborg invited Ghiorso to join him at the wartime metallurgical laboratory at the University of Chicago. Only after Seaborg assembled his team could he reveal what their project was: to perform nuclear and chemical research on plutonium, as part of the Manhattan Project. Seaborg had discovered the new element in 1940, but the discovery had been kept secret. Furthermore, although plutonium had been detected by highly sensitive tracers, it had not yet actually been seen, and nothing was yet known about its properties. Drawing on his electrical engineering background, Ghiorso helped develop the methods and intricate instrumentation needed to separate plutonium from uranium and fission products. In the process, he learned nuclear physics and nuclear chemistry.

Participates in the Discovery of New Elements

In 1944, Seaborg decided to extend his work to a search for elements with a higher atomic number than plutonium. (Uranium, with an atomic number of 92, is the last naturally occurring element; elements from atomic number 93 and higher are synthetically produced and are called transuranium elements.) To do this, Seaborg chose two chemists, Ralph A. James and Leon O. Morgan, to master the difficult chemical separation techniques, and he asked Ghiorso to develop techniques to measure the alpha-particle energy needed to identify the elements. First, outside labs bombarded plutonium in cyclotrons and neutron reactors; the samples were then flown to Chicago, where the group examined the fractions for unusual alpha-particle radioactivity, using the measuring counter Ghiorso had developed called a mica-absorber. After a series of unsuccessful experiments, in July, 1944, they found a new alpha particle in a sample of irradiated plutonium. They had discovered the first transplutonium element—curium, element 96. They followed this with the discovery of element 95, americium, in October, 1944.

In 1946, Seaborg returned to the University of California at Berkeley, and Ghiorso—along with other members of the Chicago team—came with him.

This team established and equipped a very strong nuclear chemical division at the radiation laboratory. Meanwhile, nuclear reactors were producing large enough quantities of americium and curium to serve as target materials for the production of other transuranic elements. These target elements were extremely radioactive; any new elements had to be rapidly and very efficiently separated from them. This was a complicated technical problem, and to overcome it Ghiorso developed a forty-eight-channel pulse-height analyzer, along with a gridded ion chamber to detect alpha recoils. In December, 1949, he participated in the discovery of element 97, berkelium, and in February, 1950, he was part of the group that discovered element 98, californium; the separations for this last element had to be made even more quickly, as it had a half-life of only forty-five minutes.

In a speech at the Robert A. Welch Foundation Conference in October, 1990, Ghiorso recalled the discovery of the next two transuranic elements as the most dramatic in the series: "It was so unexpected, absolutely unexpected and out of the blue; within four days ... we had discovered element 99 ... and a few months later element 100.... [T]o leapfrog from uranium to fermium was pretty spectacular." The drama began in November, 1952, with the first large-scale thermonuclear explosion, which was set off in the South Pacific on Eniwetok Atoll. Fallout from the explosion revealed that the intense neutron flux had instantaneously created previously unknown heavy isotopes. Ghiorso calculated that it might be possible to find traces of neutron-heavy elements up to atomic number 100 in this nuclear debris. He convinced his colleagues at Berkeley to acquire and examine a filter paper from airplanes that had flown through the radiation cloud. Within a few days, he and Stanley G. Thompson had found element 99, einsteinium, using Ghiorso's forty-eight-channel analyzer. In January, 1953, Ghiorso and his colleagues chemically isolated element 100, fermium, from larger samples of fallout collected from the bombed island's coral. Scientists at the Argonne National Laboratory and the Los Alamos Scientific Laboratory also contributed to the discovery of elements 99 and 100.

New techniques were needed for the discovery of the next transuranic elements, because the half-lives of these were so short that the standard method of chemically separating transmuted atoms from the target material was ineffective. Ghiorso solved the problem by harnessing the recoil he had previously observed in cyclotrons and applying it to a very thin layer of target material. As the target material (in this case, einsteinium) was struck in the cyclotron by an ion beam, the newly transmuted atoms recoiled onto a catcher foil. These recoil atoms could then be recovered from the catcher foil rather than from the entire highly radioactive target. The mechanics of the process were unusual: the bombardment was done at the Berkeley cyclotron, and the extraction from the foil was performed in Ghiorso's Volkswagen as he sped up the hill to the laboratory, where the final chemistry and pulse analysis were performed. This method produced single atoms of element 101, mendelevium, discovered by Ghiorso and his colleagues in February, 1955.

Designs Heavy Ion Linear Accelerator

Discovery of the next elements required the acceleration of heavy ions, for which improvements to the existing linear accelerator were necessary. With his colleagues, Ghiorso designed the Heavy Ion Linear Accelerator (HILAC), which was in operation by October, 1957. The HILAC was the first accelerator ever to use magnetic strong focusing. Ghiorso and his fellow scientists combined the use of the HILAC with the devices they had developed to measure the alpha energies they were discovering. Although an international group working at the Nobel Institute in Sweden and a Soviet group both reported finding what they thought to be element 102 (nobelium), Ghiorso and his colleagues made the definitive discovery in 1958 using a double-recoil technique. They followed this with the identification of element 103 (lawrencium) in 1961, element 104 (rutherfordium) in 1969, element 105 (hahnium) in 1970, and element 106 in 1974. (A dispute by Russian experimenters about the discovery of element 106 delayed its naming until March, 1994.) In the course of the search for the transuranic elements, Ghiorso and his coworkers in 1964 invented a highly advanced double-ring synchrotron called the Omnitron that could accelerate all elements up to uranium to high energies. The Vietnam War blocked funding for the Omnitron, so Ghiorso instead improved the HILAC into the Super HILAC, capable of accelerating heavy ions to high energies. This was completed in 1971. Ghiorso then invented the Bevelac, which was able to accelerate heavy ions up to velocities close to the speed of light. The Bevelac became a valuable tool for research in high-energy physics, nuclear chemistry, biology, and medicine.

Ghiorso also was a direct participant and, in many instances, research leader in the discovery of approximately 150 isotopes, including many of the known isotopes in the heavy element range. He has also been deeply involved in attempts to find the hypothetical "island of stability" of superheavy elements, also called super transuranics; these are elements, as yet undiscovered, with atomic numbers around 114, and scientists believe they may have greater nuclear stability because of longer half-lives. To aid in this search, Ghiorso built a recoil separator, the Small Angle Separating System (SASSY) and its second-generation version, SASSY2, which provided a very effective means of looking for superheavy elements with extremely short half-lives—the half-lives of some of these elements are as short as a microsecond. After the discovery in the 1990s of two new isotopes of element 106 by a Russian team working with American counterparts, Ghiorso and his Berkeley colleagues began working on the possibility of creating superheavy elements of atomic numbers 110 through 114 from these isotopes.

Ghiorso was a senior scientist at the Lawrence Berkeley Laboratory from 1946 until 1982, and he was named director of Berkeley's HILAC in 1969. Although he officially retired in 1982, he has continued to work at the Berkeley lab as senior scientist emeritus. He received an honorary doctor of science degree from Gustavus Adolphus College in 1966, and in 1973 he received the American Chemical Society's Award for Nuclear Applications in Chemistry. He is a fellow of the American Physical Society and a member of the American Academy of Arts and Sciences, and has written numerous articles about his findings for scientific journals. He married Wilma Belt in 1942; they have a daughter and a son, who has worked with Ghiorso at the Lawrence Berkeley Laboratory as a technician.

SELECTED WRITINGS BY GHIORSO:

Periodicals

"The Search for New Elements," *Discovery,* November, 1961, p. 488.

"The Berkeley HILAC Heaviest Element Research Program," *Proceedings of the Robert A. Welch Foundation Conference on Chemical Research XIII: The Transuranium Elements-The Mendeleev Centennial,* Houston, Texas, November 17–19, 1969.

"A History of the Discovery of the Transplutonium Elements," *Actinides in Perspective,* edited by N. M. Edelstein, Pergamon Press, 1982.

"The Discovery of Elements 95–106," *Proceedings of the Robert A. Welch Foundation Conference on Chemical Research XXXIV: Fifty Years with Transuranium Elements,* Houston, Texas, October 22–23, 1990.

SOURCES:

Books

Groueff, Stéphane, *Manhattan Project: The Untold Story of the Making of the Atomic Bomb,* Little, Brown, 1967.

Hyde, Earl K., Synthetic Transuranium Elements, U.S. Atomic Energy Commission, 1964.

McGraw-Hill Modern Scientists and Engineers, McGraw, 1980.

Seaborg, Glenn T., *Man-Made Transuranium Elements,* Prentice-Hall, 1963.

Periodicals

Henahan, John F., "Albert Ghiorso, Element Builder," *Chemical and Engineering News,* January 18, 1971, pp. 26–30.

Other

Ghiorso, Albert, biographical sketches and curriculum vitae, furnished to Kathy Sammis, January, 1994.

Ghiorso, Albert, telephone interviews with Kathy Sammis conducted January, 1994.

—Sketch by Kathy Sammis

Riccardo Giacconi
1931-
Italian-born American astrophysicist

Riccardo Giacconi has been a stellar member of the world's astronomical community. He invented the space telescope, an instrument that enabled astrophysicists and astronomers to probe the mysteries of the "X-ray universe." His work in the field of X-ray astronomy brought detailed knowledge of previously undetectable X-ray phenomena, like black holes, white dwarfs, and X-ray stars. His career has followed a trajectory from Milan, Italy, to several prestigious space research institutions in the United States, and back to Europe in 1993 to become director of the European Southern Observatory at its headquarters in Garching, Germany.

Giacconi was born to Antonio and Elsa Giacconi in Genoa, Italy, on October 6, 1931. Educated at the University of Milan, Giacconi wrote his thesis on elementary particles. He taught at the University of Milan from 1954 to 1956, then came to the United States on a Fulbright grant to study at Indiana and Princeton universities. He became a naturalized citizen of the United States in 1967.

X-ray Astronomy in Its Infancy

At Princeton, Giacconi did experimental cosmic ray research, looking for proton interactions. However, with the invention of high-energy atom smashers, his work began to look obsolete. The powerful particle detectors could do in minutes what Giacconi's painstaking collection methods had taken two years to produce. Therefore, by 1959 he was looking for a new research direction. The new turn in his career came about through a meeting with Bruno Rossi, a scientist who had done pioneering work in cosmic-ray physics. Rossi had ties to American Science and Engineering (AS&E), a private company located near the Massachusetts Institute of Technology. AS&E did commercial and defense-related research and engineering, but they were also interested in doing "pure science." Rossi urged Giacconi to pursue X-ray astronomy research at AS&E, following which Giacconi instituted an X-ray astronomy program there. The program's immediate purpose was to improve existing X-ray collectors, counters, and detectors; its result was the design and launching of the first X-ray telescope.

At AS&E, early work on X-ray astronomy was conducted for the U.S. Army Air Force. Observation of X-ray activity on the moon met with some success, but it was former President John F. Kennedy's decision to test the country's nuclear weapons (in response to Soviet nuclear testing) that gave Giacconi and his colleagues an opportunity to measure electrons, X rays, and gamma rays in the atmosphere. In connection with the nuclear testing program, the AS&E team designed, built, and launched twenty-four rocket payloads and six satellite payloads in an eight-month period. These launchings had a 95 percent success rate, and propelled AS&E into its next phase of X-ray astronomy—searching for sources of cosmic X rays.

On June 18, 1962, a rocket launch began sending back data that at first seemed too good to be true. The data were signifying an X-ray source beyond the solar system. At first, fearing system malfunction or atmospheric interference, the group was skeptical, but after checking and rechecking, the results were deemed convincing. Two months later, Giacconi and several of his colleagues presented their findings at a symposium on X-ray analysis at Stanford University in California. The pioneering group named their X-ray source after the Scorpius constellation in which it was found. The field of X-ray astronomy now began a growth period, and by 1967 more than thirty X-ray sources were identified.

For the funds to study these sources, Giacconi and his group turned to the National Aeronautics and Space Administration (NASA), proposing a five-phase program. Phase 1 would continue the existing rocket program that searched for new X-ray sources; phase 2 proposed the opportunity to conduct an experiment on the fourth Orbiting Solar Observatory; phase 3 would build an "X-ray explorer" satellite, designed expressly for X-ray astronomy; phase 4 would build a medium-sized spacecraft to carry a focusing X-ray telescope; and phase 5 would build a much larger version of that X-ray telescope. NASA's approval of phase 1 was expected, but it was its approval of phase 4, the building of the space telescope satellite, that was met with great excitement. As a result of this decision, the *X-Ray Explorer,* was launched in Kenya, Africa, on December 12, 1970. Because the launch fell on Kenya's Independence Day, the *X-Ray Explorer* was renamed *Uhuru,* which means "freedom" in Swahili. In the years following, *Uhuru* provided Giacconi and his group much information about the nature of X-ray stars, gave evidence of the existence of black holes (invisible regions in space from which matter and energy cannot escape), and looked beyond the Galaxy to detect other active galaxies, a quasar (a celestial object that resembles a star), and clusters of galaxies. *Uhuru's* accomplishments also marked the end of small-satellite X-ray astronomy.

X-ray Telescope Observatory is Next Step

In 1973 Giacconi was invited to become associate director of the Harvard-Smithsonian Center for Astrophysics. He accepted the offer because he was looking to insulate his research group at AS&E from the increasingly commercial aspects of the company, and felt the Center for Astrophysics would provide the right intellectual atmosphere for their next project, the X-ray telescope observatory. In 1977 NASA launched its High Energy Astronomy Observatory satellite (HEAO–1), one of a series of three HEAO satellites. The three-and-a-half-ton satellite was designed to map the X-ray sky and provide scientists with details on individual X-ray sources. It also discovered a "superbubble" in the constellation Cygnus. This unusual feature is a cloud of gas stretching more than one thousand light-years and containing the energy of thousands of suns. Really an expanded *Uhuru,* the HEAO–1 was fifty times larger but only seven times more sensitive. It was apparent to Giacconi that a better detection approach was still needed. That was to be realized with HEAO–2. Because no single instrument could do the precise measurements and provide the clarity of images needed, the observatory would be built using a complex of a high-resolution imager, an imaging proportional counter, a solid-state spectrometer, and a focal-plane crystal spectrometer. Using both existing and new technology, Giacconi's group developed instrumentation on a level with the best optical and radio telescopes. The HEAO–2, now named *Einstein,* was successfully launched at Cape Canaveral (now Kennedy Space Center) on November 13, 1978, and remained in operation until April 26, 1981. During that time, it made more than five thousand X-ray observations, and brought X-ray astronomy into the mainstream by making its information widely available to the astronomical community.

Giacconi left the Center for Astrophysics in 1981 to become director of the Space Telescope Science Institute in Baltimore, Ohio. Here Giacconi led the team responsible for the design and launching of the Hubble Space Telescope. Shortly after the launch, it became apparent that there was a serious flaw in the Hubble telescope's mirror, causing it to transmit blurry images. The problem was later determined to be the fault of the optics manufacturer. However, Giacconi stated in the January 1991 issue of *Sky & Telescope:* "One should ask whether we are building this very sophisticated instrumentation with a methodology that is adequate. . . . Ultimately, the scientists *must* take on much more of the responsibility; they can't just wait for Daddy to prepare the instrument and then let them use it." In 1993 NASA launched a crew of astronauts on an extended repair mission for the purpose of correcting the Hubble telescope's vision.

Giacconi left the Space Telescope Science Institute in 1993 to become director of the European Southern Observatory. He was to oversee the construction of the $200 million Very Large Telescope (VLT) in northern Chile, a facility expected to be the world's premier astronomical observatory.

Numerous honors have been awarded to Giacconi, among them the Dannie Heineman Prize in Astrophysics, the American Astronomical Society's Henry Russel Lectureship, and the Wolf Prize. He has held membership in numerous professional societies and organizations and has published several books and many journal articles. He was married in 1957 to Mirella Manaira. They have two daughters.

SELECTED WRITINGS BY GIACCONI:

Books

The X-ray Universe, Harvard University Press, 1985.

Periodicals

"The *Einstein* X-ray Observatory," *Scientific American,* February, 1980.

"1962–1972 (Up through *Uhuru*)," *Journal of the Washington Academy of Science,* Volume 71, 1981.

SOURCES:

Periodicals

Aldhous, Peter, "European Observatory Catches U. S. Star," *Science,* Volume 256, June 19, 1992, p. 1622.

Physics Today, May, 1981, p. 93.

Sky & Telescope, January, 1991, p. 18.

—Sketch by Jane Stewart Cook

Ivar Giaever
1929-
Norwegian-born American physicist

Ivar Giaever carried out the work that was to lead to his most famous discovery, that of the phenomenon of tunneling in semiconductors at very low temperatures. He won a share of the 1973 Nobel Prize for physics with **Leo Esaki** and **Brian Josephson** for that research. Giaever's later research has been concerned with the applications of physics to biological problems.

Giaever was born in Bergen, Norway, on April 5, 1929. He was the second child of John A. Giaever, a pharmacist, and Gudrun M. Skaarud Giaever. After attending elementary school in Tolen, Sweden, he graduated from the Hamar Secondary School in 1946. He then worked at the Ranfoss Munitions plant. In 1948, Giaever enrolled at the Norwegian Institute of Technology, from which he received his bachelor of engineering degree in 1952. In that year, Giaever married the former Inger Skramstad. The Giaevers eventually had four children, John, Guri, Anne Kari, and Trine. He was then inducted into the Norwegian army, where he served his year of compulsory military service. After his discharge, he took a job as patent examiner at the Norwegian Patent Office.

In 1954, Giaever emigrated to Canada, where he worked briefly at an architectural firm. He then accepted a job as mechanical engineer at General Electric (GE)'s Advanced Engineering Program. Two years later, he moved to Schenectady, New York, where he worked as an applied mathematician. The move marked a critical turning point in Giaever's life as the work in which he became involved was more closely related to problems in theoretical physics than in applied technology. As a result, he decided to begin a doctoral program at the Rensselaer Polytechnic Institute in nearby Troy. He continued his studies part time while working full time at GE and was finally awarded his Ph.D. degree in theoretical physics in 1964, the same year he became a U.S. citizen. Giaever's research at GE eventually led to an important discovery about the phenomenon known as tunneling. According to classical physics, a particle cannot surmount a barrier unless it has some minimal amount of energy. For example, a charged particle cannot pass across an insulating layer if the resistance of the layer is greater than the electron's energy. Early in the development of quantum physics, however, it became apparent that this law—so obvious to the logical mind—may not necessarily be true. Quantum physics postulates that if an insulating film is thin enough, it is possible for an electron to "tunnel" through and cross the barrier.

Ivar Giaever

In his studies, Giaever applied the concept of tunneling to another recently developed concept, superconductivity, the tendency of a material to lose all resistance to the flow of an electrical current as it is cooled to very low temperatures. Although superconductivity had first been observed in 1911 by the Dutch physicist **Heike Kamerlingh Onnes**, a full explanation of the phenomenon had only been developed in 1957 by the American physicists **John Bardeen, Leon Cooper,** and **J. Robert Schrieffer**. According to their theory, named the BCS theory after the three men, the energy states of electrons in a metal change dramatically as the metal is cooled to temperatures close to absolute zero (–273.15 degrees celsius or –459.67 degrees fahrenheit), permitting superconductivity to occur.

It occurred to Giaever that this transition might result in changes in the conductivity of two semiconductors, one or both of which was maintained at near-absolute zero temperatures. In his studies, Giaever compared the conductivity in systems consisting of two semiconductors (1) when both are maintained at normal temperatures, (2) when one is at near-absolute zero temperatures and the other at normal temperatures, and (3) when both are at near-absolute zero temperatures. He found that in the last of these instances, a negative resistance developed. He was able to confirm many of the predictions of both quantum physics and of the BCS theory of superconductivity in his experiments.

Giaever's discovery has had significant impacts on both theoretical and applied physics. Within a very few years, for example, the Welsh physicist Brian Josephson predicted a number of new tunneling effects based on Giaever's findings. In addition, those findings have led to the development of precise methods for measuring very small electrical and magnetic effects in semiconductors. For this research, Giaever received a share of the 1973 Nobel Prize for Physics with Josephson and Leo Esaki.

Among his other awards have been the Oliver E. Buckley Prize of the American Physical Society in 1965 and the V. K. Zworkyn Award of the National Academy of Engineers in 1974. In recent years, Giaever has become more interested in the applications of physics to biological phenomena. In this connection, he received a Guggenheim Fellowship in 1970 to study biophysics at Cambridge University. After returning to GE's Research and Development Center in 1971, he then took up the study of the behavior of organic molecules on solid surfaces and the interaction of cells with surfaces. In 1975, he spent a sabbatical year in San Diego, where he was adjunct professor at the University of California at San Diego and visiting professor at the Salk Institute for Biological Studies at La Jolla.

In 1988, Giaever was appointed Institute Professor of Science at Rensselear Polytechnic Institute and Professor-at-Large at the University of Oslo. He is also president of Applied Biophysics, Inc., a small corporation developing applications of electric sensor devices.

SELECTED WRITINGS BY GIAEVER:

Periodicals

"Electron Tunneling between Two Superconductors," *Physical Review Letters,* Volume 5, 1960, p. 464.

(With M. D. Fiske) "Superconductive Tunneling," *Proceedings of the IEEE,* Volume 52, 1964, p. 1155.

"Electron Tunneling and Superconductivity," *Science,* Volume 183, 1974, pp. 1253–1258.

"Applications of Adsorbed Proteins at Solid and Liquid Substrates," *ACS Symposium Series,* Book 343, American Chemical Society, 1987.

SOURCES:

Books

A Biographical Encyclopedia of Scientists, Volume 1, Facts on File, 1981, pp. 311–312.

McGraw-Hill Modern Scientists and Engineers, Volume 1, McGraw-Hill, 1980, pp. 429–430.

Nobel Prize Winners, H. W. Wilson, 1987, pp. 372–374.

Weber, Robert L., *Pioneers of Science: Nobel Prize Winners in Physics,* American Institute of Physics, 1980, pp. 231–232.

Other

Giaever, Ivar, letter to David E. Newton, 1993.

—*Sketch by David E. Newton*

William F. Giauque

1895-1982

Canadian-born American chemist

William F. Giauque is best known for his research in two areas, thermodynamic studies at very low temperatures and the isotopic composition of oxygen. In order to carry out the first of these investigations, Giauque found it necessary to develop a new technique of cooling gases to temperatures close to absolute zero, a method known as adiabatic demagnetization. By using this system, Giauque was able to obtain temperatures within a few thousandths of a degree from absolute zero. For his research, Giauque was awarded the 1949 Nobel Prize in chemistry. His findings led to improvements in the production of gasoline, steel, rubber, and glass. His discovery of the previously unknown oxygen isotopes 17 and 18 resulted in the recalibration of atomic weight scales.

William Francis Giauque was born in Niagara Falls, Ontario, Canada, on May 12, 1895. His mother, Isabella Jane (Duncan) Giauque, and his father, William Tecumseh Sherman Giauque, were United States citizens. When Giauque was young, his family moved back to the United States where his father took a job with the Michigan Central Railroad as a station master. When the elder Giauque died in 1908, his family returned to Canada, where William enrolled in the Niagara Falls Collegiate and Vocational School.

At first, it seemed that Giauque would have to assume the responsibility of supporting his family. After completing his two-year course at the vocational school, he found a job at the Hooker Electro-Chemical Company in Niagara Falls, New York. But his mother was determined to convince him to pursue a college education, and her employer, chemist J. W. Beckman, influenced his decision to enroll at the University of California at Berkeley in 1916. Giauque subsequently received his bachelor of science in chemistry in 1920 and then entered graduate school at Berkeley. There he was exposed to some of the nation's greatest chemists, including **Gilbert Newton Lewis**, George E. Gibson (his thesis advisor), Joel Hildebrand, and G. E. K. Branch. Giauque's dissertation concerned the properties and behavior of materials at very low temperatures, a subject which remained the focus of his academic career.

Solves Problems in Low Temperature Research

The focus of Giauque's earliest research was the Third Law of Thermodynamics, first proposed by German physical chemist **Walther Nernst** in 1906. Nernst hypothesized that the entropy (the measure of randomness in a closed system) of a pure crystalline substance at absolute zero is zero. In order to test this hypothesis, it was necessary to find ways of cooling materials to temperatures as close to absolute zero as possible.

The "father" of low-temperature research of this kind had been the Dutch physicist **Heike Kamerlingh-Onnes**. During the first decade of the twentieth century, Kamerlingh-Onnes had developed methods for cooling gases by causing them to evaporate under reduced pressure. Using this method, he had obtained temperatures of about one degree kelvin (1 K). While other researchers had produced even lower temperatures to within a few tenths of a degree kelvin over the next two decades, Kamerlingh-Onnes' method seemed to reach its limit by the early 1920s.

In 1924 Giauque suggested a new technique for producing cooling; **Peter Debye** proposed the same procedure independently at about the same time. In this method, a weakly magnetic material is magnetized in such a way that all of its molecules line up in exactly the same direction. This material is then surrounded with liquid helium and demagnetized. During demagnetization, the material's molecules go from a highly ordered to a highly disordered state. The energy needed to bring about this change is removed from the liquid helium, causing its temperature to fall even further.

This method was beset with a number of practical problems, including the difficulty of measuring the very low temperatures produced. Giauque devoted nearly twenty years to refining the technique and obtaining results with it. Finally, in 1938, he was able to report having reduced the temperature of a sample of liquid helium to 0.004 K, by far the lowest temperature yet observed.

Entropy Studies Lead to a Chance Discovery

During the 1920s, Giauque was also working on the study of entropy in gases. As part of this work, he regularly examined the band spectra produced by such gases. In 1928, while working on this problem, Giauque made an unexpected find. He observed that the spectrum of normal atmospheric oxygen consists of one set of strong lines and two sets of very weak, barely visible lines. The conclusion he drew was that normal oxygen must consist of three isotopes, one (oxygen–16) that is abundant and two (oxygen–17 and oxygen–18) that are relatively rare.

Giauque's professional reputation continued to grow at Berkeley and throughout the world. He was promoted to assistant professor in 1927, associate professor in 1930, and full professor in 1934. At his retirement in 1962, he was named emeritus professor of chemistry. In addition to his 1949 Nobel Prize in chemistry, he was also recognized by a number of other awards, including the Chandler Foundation Medal in 1936, the Elliot Cresson Medal in 1937, and the American Chemical Society's Gibbs and Lewis Medals in 1951 and 1955, respectively.

Giauque was married to the former Muriel Frances Ashley, a physicist, on July 19, 1932. They had two sons, William Francis Ashley and Robert David Ashley. Giauque died at his home in Berkeley on March 28, 1982 as a result of a fall.

SELECTED WRITINGS BY GIAUQUE:

Books

Low Temperature, Chemical, and Magneto Thermodynamics: The Scientific Papers of William F. Giauque, Dover, 1969.

Periodicals

(With G. E. Gibson) "The Third Law of Thermodynamics," *Journal of the American Chemical Society,* Volume 45, 1923, pp. 93–104.

"Thermodynamics Treatment of Certain Magnetic Effects: A Proposed Method of Producing Temperatures Considerably Below 1^0 Absolute," *Journal of the American Chemical Society,* Volume 49, 1927, pp. 1864–1870.

(With H. L. Johnston) "An Isotope of Oxygen, Mass 17, in the Earth's Atmosphere," *Journal of the American Chemical Society,* Volume 51, 1929, pp. 3528–3534.

(With H. L. Johnston) "An Isotope of Oxygen, Mass 18," *Journal of the American Chemical Society,* Volume 51, 1929, pp. 1436–1441.

SOURCES:

Books

Gillispie, Charles Coulson, editor, *Dictionary of Scientific Biography,* Volume 17, Scribner, 1982, pp. 337–344.

McGraw-Hill Modern Scientists and Engineers, Volume 10, McGraw-Hill, 1980, pp. 430–431.

—*Sketch by David E. Newton*

William Francis Gibbs
1886-1967
American naval architect and marine engineer

William Francis Gibbs was an American naval architect best known as the designer of the S. S. *United States,* a passenger ship launched in 1952 that set a new speed record across the Atlantic, traveling at 35.05 knots (40.3 miles per hour) on average. Although intended for commercial use, Gibbs designed the ship to strict naval specifications, enabling it to be easily adapted to military use. Gibbs was a pioneer in safety design, and his ship not only incorporated the most sophisticated safety and comfort features of its time, including the use of fire-retardant materials, but was able to meet new levels of economy and efficiency. Gibbs's firm Gibbs & Cox, with its design of the Liberty ship, was responsible at one time for building over sixty percent of all the ships made in the United States—a formidable achievement for a man whose background was in neither engineering or architecture, but in law and economics.

William Francis Gibbs was born on August 24, 1886, in Philadelphia, Pennsylvania. His father, William Warren Gibbs, was a financier who at one time was a multimillionaire, but lost his fortune during the Rich Man's Panic of 1907. His mother was the former Frances Ayres Johnson. Johnson was a sickly child, a condition which kept him out of school for long stretches of time and allowed him to indulge his interest in ships and mathematical calculations. He studied at the Delancey School in Philadelphia, and determined to become an engineer. His plans were resisted by his father, however, who urged him to go into economics.

Gibbs enrolled in the economics program at Harvard in 1906. After getting his degree in 1910, he entered Columbia University's law school. By 1913, he had been awarded both an M.A. and LL.B. His education complete, Gibbs joined a law firm which specialized in real estate. His heart, however, was not in a legal career. In 1914, a tragic event occurred that unexpectedly changed the course of his life. A thousand lives were lost when the *Empress of Ireland,* a luxury passenger liner, went down after colliding with another vessel. The tragedy got Gibbs to thinking about designing safer ships. He determined to throw in the towel at the law firm in order to dedicate himself to shipbuilding.

Gibbs believed that properly designed bulkheads and simple compartmentalization could have averted the accident of the *Empress of Ireland.* He spent a year researching the shipbuilding business before establishing Gibbs Brothers Inc. (later Gibbs & Cox Inc.) with his brother Frederick, a company dedicated to supervising the reconditioning of various kinds of vessels. The company's first commission was a thousand-foot ship that reduced the time of the transatlantic crossing by 14 hours. The brothers' work interested Ralph Peters, president of the Long Island Railroad, and later American financier J. P. Morgan. The latter offered to pay the brothers a salary while William Gibbs perfected his design. The project never came to fruition, however, as World War I broke out.

The war presented new opportunities to the Gibbs' company. William Gibbs became chief designer at J. P. Morgan, and later, naval architect to the Shipping Control Board. When the war ended, Gibbs returned to New York where he got a job as chief of construction at the International Mercantile Marine Company. In 1922, he received a major commission when the U.S. Government contracted the Gibbs' firm to recondition the S.S. *Leviathan.* Their work on the vessel won high praise and many more contracts to build and recondition ships.

New Ship Designs Emphasize Safety

In 1924, Gibbs designed and oversaw building of the S.S. *Malolo,* the fastest liner of its time. The project showcased Gibbs's special safety features, such as watertight compartmentalization. It was this that saved it—and demonstrated its effectiveness—when the ship collided fiercely with another boat during its trials. By dividing the ship's hold into several watertight compartments, Gibbs's design prevented a leak in one compartment from spreading through the entire ship, thus making the vessel less likely to flood and sink. Gibbs's multiple compartment approach to building quickly gained acceptance and became standard practice.

Gibbs married socialite Vera Cravath Larkin, a past president of the New York Metropolitan Opera Guild, in 1927. In 1929, in partnership with the yacht maker Daniel Hargate Cox, Gibbs designed and constructed the world's largest pleasure craft, the *Savarona.* She was built for Mrs. Richard Cadwalader and incorporated such features as a public address system, gold-plated bathrooms, and mother-of-pearl inlaid bathrooms. In the early 1930s, the company also constructed the luxury ships *Santa Rosa, Santa Paula, Santa Elena,* and *Santa Lucia.*

From 1933 onwards, Gibbs was instrumental in the modernization of the U.S. Navy and in persuading it to adopt high-pressure and high-temperature steam turbines (rotary engines) for its fleet. His company was commissioned to design and build destroyers for the U.S. Navy. Gibbs developed high-pressure, high temperature steam turbine machinery used in building battleships, aircraft carriers, cruisers, and destroyers. The firm was enormously productive—it directed the preparation of working plans for almost seventy percent of all ships (excepting submarines and battleships) built in the United States during World War II. Between 5,000 and 6,000 of all ships constructed during the war were built to Gibbs's specifications.

This enormous output was made possible only by the adoption of Gibbs's special time-saving and efficiency techniques. It was Gibbs, as Controller of Shipbuilding, War Production Board, who directed the famous Liberty Ship program under which so much of the U.S. fleet was produced. Instead of a single shipyard constructing a vessel from start to finish, Gibbs divided operations into various stages that were carried out at a range of locations. By this and other time-saving devices, Gibbs was able to reduce production time for a Liberty-type boat from four years to four days and increase production for more complex ships by about 700 percent over pre-war rates. According to a 1942 report on Gibbs & Cox in *Time,* "Every day, Gibbs and Cox turn out 8,000 to 10,000 blueprints, twenty-six acres of blueprint a month. . . . Not a day goes by that the company does not contract for at least $100,000,000 worth of materials." By the mid–1940s, two thousand Liberty ships were in service, most in the U.S. Navy.

In 1937, Gibbs designed the S.S. *America,* the fastest and biggest merchant ship ever to be built in the United States. He also built the *Firefighter,* a fireboat for the City of New York. In 1942, he was appointed controller of shipbuilding with responsibility for the coordination "of the programs of the Army, the Navy, and the Maritime Commission." Later in the war, Gibbs served as chairman of the American-British-Canadian Combined Shipbuilding Committee on Standardization of Design of the Combined Chiefs of Staff. He was appointed special assistant to the director of the Office of War Mobilization and later, representative of the Office of War Mobilization on the Procurement Review Board of the Navy. In these capacities, Gibbs was instrumental in achieving new ways to streamline the U.S. Navy's fleet. For example, he reduced the variety of merchant ship types, which helped stimulate mass production.

When the war finished, Gibbs's firm continued accepting commissions for the U.S. Navy, as well as designing passenger ships. Gibbs returned to New York in September 1943, and continued his work there. Despite his success as a shipbuilder, Gibbs had a number of brushes with the law during his career. He was investigated by the seven Government agencies, including the FBI, when it became known that Gibbs & Cox had accepted an order from the Soviet Union to build a warship. In 1944, the House Naval Affairs Committee investigated Gibbs's firm on charges of profiteering; in both instances, however, the government found no wrongdoing and Gibbs was exonerated.

One year after the 1952 launch of the record-setting S.S. *United States,* Gibbs's illustrious career was recognized with his receipt of the Franklin Medal of the Franklin Institute of the State of Pennsylvania. He was elected to the National Academy of Sciences in 1949, and to the National Academy of Engineering in 1965. He was also a member of the Institute of Naval Architects, of the Society of Naval Architects and Marine Engineers, the Institute of Aeronautical Sciences, and the New York Bar. Gibbs died in New York City on September 7, 1967. He was remembered as a sharp-tongued, sardonic character who shunned the limelight. He once said of publicity that a man exposed to it "gets to thinking he is so goddamn bright that it just paralyzes him."

SOURCES:

Books

Biographical Encyclopedia of Scientists, Volume 1, Facts-on-File, 1981, pp. 313.

Chambers' Biographical Encyclopedia of Scientists, Facts-on-File, 1981.

Modern Scientists and Engineers, Volume 1, McGraw-Hill, 1980.

Periodicals

Saturday Evening Post, January 20, 1945, pp. 9–11; January 27, 1945, p. 20; February 3, 1945, pp. 217–220.

Time, September 28, 1942, pp. 20–22; September 20, 1943, p. 21.

—*Sketch by Avril McDonald*

Eloise R. Giblett
1921-
American hematologist and geneticist

Eloise R. Giblett is best known for her work in the study of blood and human genetics, particularly the discovery that an inadequate supply of two specific enzymes causes inherited deficiencies in the body's immune system. She also discovered a wide range of new inherited characteristics, so-called genetic markers, including blood groups and serum protein, and wrote a basic text on genetic markers.

Eloise Rosalie Giblett was born on January 17, 1921, in Tacoma, Washington, the daughter of William R. Giblett, a businessman, and Rose G. Giblett, a musician and homemaker. Under the influence of her mother, Giblett developed an early interest in music, taking lessons in voice and violin until graduation from Lewis and Clark High School in Spokane. With entrance to Mills College in Oakland, California, she found a new passion: science. After two years at Mills College, Giblett returned to her native Washington state to finish out her B.S. at the University of Washington in Seattle in 1942. The Second World War interrupted her studies for a time, and she served as a medical technician with the Waves. It was during this time that she developed a strong interest in medicine, and with the help of the G.I. Bill, was able to finish her formal education after the war, receiving an M.S. in microbiology from the University of Washington in 1947, and an M.D. from the University of Washington Medical School in 1951. She spent her internship and residency at the University of Washington and was a postdoctoral fellow at the same institution as well as in London from 1953 to 1955, specializing in hematology and human genetics.

Discovers Genetic Markers

Upon return to Seattle, Giblett accepted two positions: a full professorship in medicine at the University of Washington, and the associate directorship of the Puget Sound Blood Center. For the next thirty years Giblett worked tirelessly as a researcher, educator, and administrator. Perhaps her most notable achievement was the discovery in the mid–1970s that deficiencies of the enzymes adenosine deaminase and nucleoside phosphorylase—both vital in the purine cycle—cause inherited immunodeficiencies. These defects may be curable by gene therapy, and Giblett pointed the way for such research. Her discoveries of new genetic markers have also been important, especially her findings regarding polymorphisms—variant genetic forms in one population—in blood cell enzymes. Giblett also did important research in blood group antibodies, and authored over 200 papers and textbook chapters on various aspects of inherited characteristics, particularly those in human blood. In 1969 she published the book, *Genetic Markers in Human Blood,* and ten years later was named executive director of the Puget Sound Blood Center. Giblett has been widely recognized for her researches in immunohematology, receiving the Emily Cooley Award in 1975, the Karl Landsteiner Award in 1976, and the Philip Levine Award from the American Association of Clinical Pathologists in

1978. She is also a member of the National Academy of Sciences, 1980, and a fellow of the American Association for Advanced Science. In 1973 she was the president of the American Society of Human Genetics. Giblett never married, and since her retirement in 1987 she has returned to her first love—music—playing violin in five different chamber music ensembles in the Seattle area.

SELECTED WRITINGS BY GIBLETT:

Books

Genetic Markers in Human Blood, Blackwell Scientific, 1969.

Periodicals

"Immune Cell Function and Recycling of Purine," *New England Journal of Medicine,* December 9, 1976, pp. 1375–1376.

"Genetic Polymorphisms in Human Blood," *Annual Review of Genetics,* Volume 11, 1977, pp. 13–28.

"Adenosine Deaminase and Purine Nucleoside Phosphorylaee Deficiency: How They Were Discovered and What They Mean," *Ciba Foundation Symposium,* Volume 68, 1978, pp. 3–18.

"Blood Genetic Markers in Man," *Transplantation Proceedings,* December, 1979, pp. 1697–1700.

"Inherited Biochemical Defects in Lymphocytes Causing Immunodeficiency Disease," *Progress in Clinical and Biological Research,* Volume 58, 1981, pp. 123–134.

"ADA and PNP Deficiencies: How It All Began," *Annals of the New York Academy of Sciences,* Volume 451, 1985, pp. 1–8.

SOURCES:

Giblett, Eloise Rosalie, interview with J. Sydney Jones conducted January 3, 1994.

—*Sketch by J. Sydney Jones*

Walter Gilbert
1932-
American molecular biologist

Walter Gilbert is a molecular biologist who shared the 1980 Nobel Prize in chemistry for his discovery of how to sequence, or chemically describe, deoxyribonucleic acid (DNA) molecules.

Walter Gilbert

Gilbert also identified repressor molecules, which modify or repress the activity of certain genes, and collaborated with Noble laureate biologist **James Watson**'s in his efforts to isolate messenger ribonucleic acid (RNA). Later in his career, Gilbert helped form and was chief executive officer of the biotechnology firm Biogen, and became a moving force in the medical research project known as the human genome project.

Gilbert was born in Cambridge, Massachusetts on March 21, 1932. His father, Richard V. Gilbert, was an economist at Harvard University, and his mother, Emma Cohen Gilbert, was a child psychologist who provided her children's early education at home. In 1939 the family moved to Washington, D.C., where Gilbert initially performed poorly in school. He did, however, show a great deal of interest in science. He was fascinated by astronomy, and at age twelve he ground his own glass for telescopes; he also "nearly blew himself up brewing hydrogen in the pantry," writes Anthony Liversidge in *Omni.* As a senior at Sidwell Friends High School, he would go to the Library of Congress to expand his knowledge of nuclear physics.

In 1949, Gilbert entered Harvard University, where he majored in chemistry and physics, earning his B.A. *summa cum laude* in 1953. Gilbert remained at Harvard for a master's degree in physics, which he received in 1954. He went to Cambridge University for doctoral work in theoretical physics, studying under the physicist **Abdus Salam**. His doctoral dissertation focused on mathematical formulae that could predict the behavior of elementary particles in so-called "scattering" experiments. He received his Ph.D. in mathematics in 1957. Gilbert returned to Harvard as a National Science postdoctoral fellow in physics, and he gained an appointment as assistant professor in 1959.

Moves from Physics to Molecular Biology

While at Cambridge, Gilbert had met biologists **James Watson** and **Francis Crick**; just a few years before, these two men had established the structure of DNA and constructed a three-dimensional model of it. Their work had launched a new field of science called molecular biology, and when Watson moved to Harvard in 1960 he and Gilbert met again. Watson discussed with Gilbert his interest in isolating messenger RNA. This is the substance believed to be responsible for transmitting information from DNA to ribosomes, which are the cellular structures in which protein synthesis takes place. At Watson's invitation, Gilbert joined him and his colleagues to work on this project. This collaboration with Watson began Gilbert's move into molecular biology. He became convinced that his future lay in this field, and he made up for a lack of formal training in biochemistry through hard work. Within a few years he was publishing articles on molecular biology. He was made a tenured associate professor of biophysics at Harvard in 1964, and he became a full professor of biochemistry in 1968. In 1972, Harvard named him the American Cancer Society Professor of Molecular Biology.

In the middle of the 1960s, Gilbert began research on how genes are activated within cells. This was a problem that had been introduced by the French geneticists **Francois Jacob** and **Jacques Lucien Monod**; DNA should, in theory, encode proteins continually, and they wondered what kept the genes from being activated. If cells contain some sort of element that in effect represses some genes, this would explain in part how cells perform different functions even though each cell contains the same complement of genetic instructions. Gilbert set out to determine whether actual "repressor" substances exist within each cell.

Repressor Molecules and Sequencing DNA

Working with the *Escherichia coli* bacterium, Gilbert attempted to find what he called the lac repressor. *E. coli* manufactures the enzyme betagalactosidase when the milk sugar lactose is present, and he hypothesized that the gene responsible for producing the enzyme was repressed by a substance that would only detach itself from the DNA molecule in the presence of lactose. If this hypothesis could be proven, it would confirm the existence of repressors. In 1966, Gilbert and his colleagues added radioactive lactose-like molecules to a concentration of the bacteria as a means of tracing any potential lac repressor activity. As he had hoped, the lac repressor bonded with the radioactive material. By 1970, he was able to determine the precise region of DNA (called the lac operator) to which the repressor bonds in the absence of lactose.

The next phase of Gilbert's research focused on sequencing DNA. His aim was to identify and describe chemically any strand of DNA. Working with graduate student Allan Maxam, he began to sequence parts of the DNA strand. It was known that the molecules could be "broken" at specific chemical junctures by using certain chemical substances, and a colleague introduced Gilbert and Maxam to a procedure that broke DNA molecules into fragments that were easier to describe. After breaking radioactively labeled DNA into fragments, Gilbert and Maxam worked to separate them. They used a technique known as gel electrophoresis, in which an electric current causes the fragments to pass through a gel substance. Upon exposure to X-ray film, the fragments can be read and the chemical code of DNA can be identified. Working independently, the British scientist **Frederick Sanger** developed a similar sequencing technique. In recognition of both their contributions, Gilbert and Sanger were awarded half the 1980 Nobel Prize in chemistry. The other half went to the American biochemist **Paul Berg** for his work with recombinant DNA, more commonly referred to as "gene splicing."

From Researcher to Business Executive

With the breakthroughs that were being made by Gilbert, Sanger, Berg, and others, the concept of applying technological principles to biology came of age in the 1970s. The idea of being able to alter the genetic composition of a cell, for example, opened up such possibilities as curing or even eradicating many diseases. The possibilities in biotechnology intrigued not only scientists but the business community. Here was a concept that could be both revolutionary and lucrative—a company that held the patent to a definitive cure for cancer, for example, could become quite wealthy and powerful. Business leaders began to approach scientists, Gilbert among them. Most scientists were skeptical at first, but in 1978 Gilbert met with a group of venture capitalists who wanted to start a biotechnology firm. After receiving assurances that they would have considerable control over research and development, he and other scientists formed Biogen N.V., with Gilbert as the chairman of the scientific board of directors. Gilbert was so convinced of Biogen's potential that he left Harvard in 1981 to become the company's chief executive officer.

Despite widespread belief in the company's potential, Biogen had some difficult years in the beginning. After four years, it was still unprofitable and Gilbert had become increasingly disillusioned with business. He found the differences between the business world and the scientific community difficult to reconcile. The science of creating new products is vastly different from the business of bringing them to market. Scientists need to be patient because their breakthroughs might take years to obtain, but sound business practice dictates cutting one's losses when a project fails to produce after a reasonable time, and these differences led to conflicts with others at Biogen. Gilbert also found it time-consuming and expensive to run a company (although he personally profited from the venture), and in late 1984 he resigned his position at Biogen, while maintaining some involvement with the firm. In 1985, he was named H. H. Timken Professor of Science in Harvard's cellular and developmental biology department. In 1987 he became chairman of the department and Carl M. Loeb University Professor.

The Human Genome Project

Gilbert resumed his research, unhindered by the responsibilities of running a business. But he soon became interested in an undertaking that was bigger than Biogen: the human genome project. This project, wrote Robert Kanigel in the *New York Times Magazine,* "would reveal the precise biochemical makeup of the entire genetic material, or genome, of a human being. . . . It would grant insight into human biology previously held only by God." The plan was to create a map or library of human DNA. Such information would help researchers not only find cures for diseases but also identify potentially harmful gene mutations. Gilbert spoke out enthusiastically in favor of the genome project, and along with many others he encouraged Congress to support it with federal funds. Frustrated by the political process and believing that the project would be damaged by the bureaucracy federal participation would impose, he tried a different approach. In 1987 he announced plans to create his own company, which would sequence DNA, copyright the information, and sell it. Although he failed to get adequate backing for that project, he did win a two million dollar annual grant from the U.S. government to conduct his work at Harvard under the auspices of the National Institutes of Health.

In an interview with *Omni,* Gilbert has explained what he sees as some of the benefits of a complete genetic map of the human being: "The differences between people are what the genetic map [is] about. That knowledge will yield medicine tailored to the individual. One will first identify obvious genetic defects like cystic fibrosis. The next round of genetic mapping will show us clusters of genes for common diseases from arthritis to schizophrenia. We will be able to predict the side effects of those drugs and tailor the right dose to each person." Gilbert has estimated that the project would take at least ten to twenty years to complete.

Gilbert has also expressed concern as a researcher, arguing in favor of what he calls a "paradigm shift in biology." As scientific techniques are perfected, he contends, new scientists should be able to concentrate on new research, not repeating old research. Writing in *Nature,* he has noted that "in 1970, each of my graduate students had to make restriction enzymes in order to work with DNA molecules; by 1976 the enzymes were all purchased and today no graduate student knows how to make them." While it is important for scientists to understand what they are doing and why, he continues, "this is not the meaning of their education. Their doctorates should be testimonials that they [have] solved a novel problem, and in so doing [have] learned the general ability to find whatever new or old techniques were needed." As more and more of the technological problems of molecular biology are solved, he believes that biological research will begin with theoretical rather than experimental work.

In addition to the Nobel Prize, Gilbert shared with Sanger the Albert Lasker Basic Medical Research Award in 1979. He also won the Louisa Horwitz Gross Prize from Columbia University in 1979, and the Herbert A. Sober Memorial Award of the American Society of Biological Chemists in 1980. His memberships include the American Academy of Arts and Sciences, the National Academy of Sciences, and the British Royal Society.

Gilbert has been married to Celia Stone since 1953; the couple have a son and a daughter. Although his career has sometimes seemed almost as complex as the substances he studies, he is widely respected as a scientist. Younger scientists have called him "intimidating," but despite his successes he remains a committed teacher and researcher.

SELECTED WRITINGS BY GILBERT:

Periodicals

"Useful Proteins From Recombinant Bacteria," *Scientific American,* April, 1980.

"Towards a Paradigm Shift in Biology," *Nature,* January 10, 1991, p. 99.

SOURCES:

Books

Hall, Stephen S., *Invisible Frontiers,* Atlantic Monthly Press, 1987.

Periodicals

Gannes, Stuart, "Striking it Rich in Biotech," *Fortune,* November 9, 1987, pp. 131–142.

Kanigel, Robert, "The Genome Project," *New York Times Magazine,* December 13, 1987, p. 44.

Liversidge, Anthony, "Interview: Walter Gilbert," *Omni,* November, 1992, pp. 91–101.

—Sketch by George A. Milite

Frank Gilbreth
1868-1924
American engineer

Frank Gilbreth, best known for his work with construction workers on the efficiency of motion, developed many of the concepts and applications that are now part of modern management techniques. With **Lillian Gilbreth**, his wife and professional partner, he introduced the application of psychology to industrial management. He also developed intricate studies of motion that he adapted for use by injured soldiers and the physically disabled, as well as laborers. His work established that psychology and education are integral parts of successful management.

Frank Bunker Gilbreth was born in Fairfield, Maine on July 7, 1868, to John and Martha Bunker Gilbreth. The Gilbreth family came from a long line of New Englanders; they all lived in the same farming community, where Gilbreth's father ran a hardware business. His father died when Gilbreth was three, and his mother's passion for education led her to move the family twice in search of the best schools, first to Andover, Massachusetts, and then to Boston. Dissatisfied with the grade school Gilbreth attended, she took him home and tutored him herself. He eventually graduated from English High School in Boston in 1885. Gilbreth passed the entrance exams to the Massachusetts Institute of Technology, but he decided not to attend college and went straight into business.

Gilbreth began his career as a bricklayer's apprentice. An attentive observer, he learned by watching the movements of veteran bricklayers that each one used motion in a different way, some more economically than others. It was here that Gilbreth became committed to his lifelong goal—finding "the one best way" of mastering any task. Gilbreth quickly learned every trade in the contracting business. Before long he was laying stone, estimating costs, working railway construction, and supervising. Gilbreth went to night school to learn mechanical drawing; he advanced to foreman and then to superintendent without the typical three years of apprentice work.

In 1895, at the age of 27, Gilbreth started his own contracting firm. Bricklaying was then being replaced by the use of concrete, and he patented many inventions for the changing construction industry. Among his inventions was a concrete mixer that supplemented early gravity mixers and concrete conveyors. The slogan of his company was "Speed Work," and its goals were the elimination of waste, the conservation of ability, and the reduction of cost. When Gilbreth applied these ideas to the construction of the Lowell Laboratory, he made newspaper headlines with his short construction time. His projects included dams, canals, houses, factory buildings, industrial facilities, and the entire town of Woodland, Maine; he serviced clients all over the United States and eventually expanded his business to England.

Changes Focus to Industrial Management

In 1903, in Boston, Gilbreth met Lillian Moller, a teacher with a strong professional drive that matched his. They began a twenty-year partnership with their marriage on October 19, 1904. Lillian Gilbreth was the force behind the shift in Frank Gilbreth's career from construction to management. Together they became leaders in the new field of scientific industrial management—writing books and articles, lecturing and teaching, while raising twelve children. He and his wife applied their management techniques to the running of their large household; two of their children would later write humorous accounts of their family life, *Cheaper by the Dozen* and *Belles on Their Toes.*

In 1908, Gilbreth published *Field System,* his first book. The book contained the ideas of the men he employed: he had gathered information by asking his workers to record exactly what they did during the course of the day and what they would recommend for improvement. Written for laborers, the book was the first of its kind, documenting daily organizational and functional practices in construction. It was also the first in a series of similar books by Gilbreth, in which he would provide specific information on work tasks, even using photographic details to show the positions of a worker's feet during certain tasks.

As he integrated his work on the expediency of motion with his wife's concentration on the psychology of the individual, Gilbreth grew less involved in the construction industry. He and his wife began to join their efforts in pursuit of the link between psychology and management, and together they established the fundamental place of psychology and education in effective management. In 1913 the

Gilbreths started the Summer School of Scientific Management, which for four years was attended by academic and industry professionals from around the world. Contacts developed through the school gave Gilbreth an international consulting reputation.

Innovative Work for the Physically Challenged

The early months of World War I found Gilbreth in Germany, visiting industrial plants, teaching, testing, installing new machines, and establishing laboratories. As injured soldiers began returning to Germany, Gilbreth worked to improve surgical procedures, and he was the first to use motion-picture photography in the operating room for the education of surgeons. He also became an expert in the rehabilitation of injured soldiers. He visited hospitals throughout Europe, watching the motions of the injured soldiers, and developed ways to teach them to manage their daily activities. His paper on this subject, "Motion Study for the Handicapped," was written with his wife and presented at the Tenth Sagamore Sociological Conference in 1917. It included ideas such as a typewriter with all capital letters, eliminating the need for a shift key, which requires two-handed operation. But perhaps the most interesting aspect of Gilbreth's work during this period was the study of the seventeen fundamental motions used to perform physical tasks, such as search, find, select, grasp, and position. He created a visual chart, used to adapt jobs to injured soldiers, that illustrated each fundamental motion, thereby enabling the visual dissection of tasks and the substitution of motions from one task to another.

The increasing intensity of World War I slowed Gilbreth's work abroad, so he concentrated on building a consulting business that catered to the firms he felt most needed his expertise. He shunned companies that treated their employees poorly, believing that bad treatment of the consultant would follow. Gilbreth loathed companies that benefited from his time-saving methods to increase profits only to keep them from their employees, and contracted with companies that promised to increase wages as sales increased, among them Eastman Kodak, U.S. Rubber, and Pierce Arrow. When the United States entered the war, Gilbreth enlisted and received a commission in the Engineers Officers Reserve Corps. He reported to the War College in Washington to prepare educational films for soldier training, but a heart ailment ended his service shortly thereafter. The Gilbreth family bought a small house in Nantucket, Massachusetts, to facilitate his recovery, but from that time on he would carry heart medication with him at all times.

Gilbreth's consulting business thrived after the war. In 1920, the American Society of Mechanical Engineers instituted its Management Division, something Gilbreth had been working to establish for many years. He was now one of the most widely known American engineers in the United States and Europe, reaping financial rewards and many professional honors. He suggested the first international management congress in history to the American Society of Mechanical Engineers, and it was held in Prague in 1924. He died suddenly of a heart attack shortly afterwards, on June 14, 1924, while traveling from his home in Montclair, New Jersey, to New York City. He was posthumously honored with the Gantt Gold Medal in 1944 from the American Society of Engineers and the American Management Association. The honor was shared and received by his wife.

SELECTED WRITINGS BY GILBRETH:

Books

Field System, Myron C. Clark, 1908.
Concrete System, Engineering News, 1908.
Bricklaying System, Myron C. Clark, 1909.
Motion Study, Nostrand, 1911.
Primer of Scientific Management, Nostrand, 1914.
(With L. M. Gilbreth) *Fatigue Study: The Elimination of Humanity's Greatest Unnecessary Waste,* Sturgis and Walton, 1916.
(With L. M. Gilbreth) *Applied Motion Study,* Sturgis and Walton, 1917.

SOURCES:

Books

Carey, Ernestine G., and Frank B. Gilbreth, Jr., *Cheaper by the Dozen,* Crowell, 1948, expanded edition, 1963.
Carey, Ernestine G., and Frank B. Gilbreth, Jr., *Belles on Their Toes,* Crowell, 1950.
Gilbreth, Lillian M., *The Quest of the One Best Way: A Sketch of the Life of Frank Bunker Gilbreth,* Society of Industrial Engineers, 1926.
Spriegel, W. R. and C. E. Meyers, editors, *The Writings of the Gilbreths,* Richard D. Irwin, Inc., 1953.
Yost, Edna, *Frank and Lillian Gilbreth, Partners for Life,* Rutgers University Press, 1949.

—Sketch by David N. Ford

Lillian Gilbreth
1878-1972
American engineer

Lillian Gilbreth was one of the founders of modern industrial management. She brought psychology to the study of management in the early twentieth century and then brought them both to the forefront of the business world. She broke new ground with her book *The Psychology of Management,* which concerned the health of the industrial worker. An outstanding academician who developed new curricula for major universities throughout the United States, Gilbreth became widely known for making human relations an integral part of management theory and practice.

Gilbreth was born Lillian Evelyn Moller on May 24, 1878, in Oakland, California. She was the oldest of nine children of William and Annie Delger Moller, who ran a devout household of strong German influence. Her mother was the daughter of a prominent Oakland businessman, and her father was a dedicated husband who had sold his New York business to buy into a partnership in the hardware industry in California. Because of her mother's poor health, Gilbreth's public school education did not begin until she was nine, but she progressed quickly and was academically successful in high school. Her passions at the time were literature and music, which she studied with composer John Metcalfe. She was well traveled as a high school student, visiting New York, Boston, and Chicago with her father.

Although very proud of his daughter's talents, Gilbreth's father did not believe that women should attend college. She convinced him, however, to let her enter the University of California and live at home, continuing to care for her sisters. She studied modern languages and philosophy, and her goal was to teach English. Gilbreth was the first woman in the university's history to speak on commencement day in 1900, when she received her B.A. in literature. After graduation, Gilbreth entered Columbia University to pursue a master's degree in literature, but illness forced her to return home in her first year. She reentered the University of California, finished her master's degree in literature in 1902, and began work on a Ph.D.

In 1903, Gilbreth took a break from her studies to travel abroad. She stopped first in Boston, where she met **Frank Gilbreth**. Ten years her senior, he owned a construction business and was working on the development of motion-study techniques—methods to minimize wasted time and energy and increase productivity in industry. They corresponded through the mail for ten months after they met, and they were married on October 19, 1904. They would have twelve children, two of whom would later record their humorous memories of family life in the popular books *Cheaper by the Dozen* and *Belles on Their Toes.*

Lillian Gilbreth

Begins Work on Time-and-Motion Studies

Work was the focus of Frank Gilbreth's life. He wanted a complete partnership with his new wife and began to teach her about construction. He saw that her interest in the human aspects of industry complemented his ideas and he encouraged her to work with him. Their goals and their personalities influenced each other so strongly that both of their careers were redirected into new areas. The mental and physical health of workers was then largely neglected, and Lillian Gilbreth became increasingly interested in her husband's work as she recognized her potential contribution. Her doctoral studies shifted from literature to psychology.

Lillian Gilbreth's marriage began with several major responsibilities—her academic work, starting a large family, and becoming acquainted with the business world. She started as a systems manager in her husband's consulting business and was soon acknowledged as an expert in the study of worker fatigue and production. Her reputation was partially due to her precise measurements when collecting data. Among her contributions were the analysis of machinery and tools, the invention of new tools and the methods to simplify their use, and the standardization of tasks. Most importantly, her work led to a greater understanding of the importance of the welfare of individual in business operations. This was instrumental in broadening acceptance of her husband's work on increasing productivity.

In 1910, the Gilbreths moved their growing family to Providence, Rhode Island, where Lillian Gilbreth entered Brown University to continue her doctoral studies in psychology. She began writing about industrial management from a scientific and psychological perspective. A lecture she delivered at the Dartmouth College Conference on Scientific Management in 1911 on the relationship between management and psychology became the basis for her doctoral dissertation.

In 1913, Frank and Lillian Gilbreth started the Summer School of Scientific Management. The school trained professionals to teach new ideas about management, and it emphasized the study of motion and psychology. Tuition was free, admission was by invitation, and classes were well attended by professors and business people from the United States and abroad. The Gilbreths ran the summer school for four years. Lillian Gilbreth received her Ph.D. from Brown in 1915. Her dissertation had already been published as a book, *The Psychology of Management,* in 1914. She was the first theorist in industrial management to emphasize and document the importance of psychological considerations in management.

After Frank Gilbreth's death in 1924, Lillian Gilbreth moved her family to her home state of California, where she provided a new home and college educations for her children, maintained a consulting business, and continued teaching and researching on efficiency and health in industry. Gilbreth became a well respected businesswoman; Johnson & Johnson hired her consulting firm to train their employees, and Macy's in New York had her study the working conditions of their salespeople to investigate techniques to reduce fatigue. The Dennison Co. and Sears & Roebuck were also clients, among many others. She started a new school called Gilbreth Research Associates, which catered to retail interests and went international in 1926. But by 1929, several universities were modeling motion in their engineering schools, using laboratories complete with photographic devices and movement measurement tools. Convinced that her ideas would now be carried on, she closed Gilbreth Research Associates. That same year she traveled to Tokyo to speak at the First World Power Congress. Gilbreth was now lecturing at universities such as Stanford, Harvard, Yale, and the Massachusetts Institute of Technology. She joined the Purdue University faculty in 1935 as a professor of management, becoming the first woman professor in the engineering school.

When America entered World War II, Gilbreth consulted at the Arma Plant in Brooklyn, New York, which handled huge Navy contracts. The staff at the plant grew from a few hundred to eleven thousand men and women, and she managed the personnel restructuring and worker training for this enormous expansion. Especially notable was her development of an exercise program for the women; although white-haired and over sixty years old, she kept up with the younger women.

In 1948, Gilbreth began teaching at the Newark College of Engineering in New Jersey. She was the first woman professor in this school of engineering as well, and she stayed there for two years. She went on to teach in Formosa from 1953 to 1954 and at the University of Wisconsin in 1955. Gilbreth remained active professionally well into her eighties, speaking and writing on management issues. She also became a widely sought speaker on human relations problems in management. Gilbreth received over a dozen honorary degrees. She was the recipient of the Hoover Medal from the American Society of Civil Engineers in 1966, and other engineering and management professional organizations around the world bestowed many awards upon her for her pioneering work. She died in Phoenix, Arizona, on January 2, 1972.

SELECTED WRITINGS BY GILBRETH:

Books

The Psychology of Management, Sturgis and Walton, 1914.

(With Frank Gilbreth) *Fatigue Study: The Elimination of Humanity's Greatest Unnecessary Waste,* Sturgis and Walton, 1916.

(With Frank Gilbreth) *Applied Motion Study,* Sturgis and Walton, 1917.

The Quest of the One Best Way: A Sketch of the Life of Frank Bunker Gilbreth, Society of Industrial Engineers, 1926.

SOURCES:

Books

Carey, Ernestine G., and Frank B. Gilbreth, Jr., *Cheaper by the Dozen,* Crowell, 1948, expanded edition, 1963.

Carey, Ernestine G., and Frank B. Gilbreth, Jr., *Belles on Their Toes,* Crowell, 1950.

Haas, Violet B. and Carolyn C. Perrucci, editors, *Women in Scientific and Engineering Professions,* University of Michigan Press, 1984.

Spriegel, W. R. and C. E. Meyers, editors, *The Writings of the Gilbreths,* Richard D. Irwin, 1953.
Yost, Edna, *Frank and Lillian Gilbreth, Partners for Life,* Rutgers University Press, 1949.

Periodicals

"Lillian Moller Gilbreth: Remarkable First Lady of Engineering," *Society of Women Engineers Newsletter,* Volume 24, 1978.
Trescott, M. M., "A History of Women Engineers in the United States, 1850–1975: A Progress Report," in *Proceedings of the Society of Women Engineers 1979 National Convention,* New York Society of Women Engineers, 1979.

—*Sketch by David N. Ford*

Donald Glaser
1926-
American physicist

Donald Glaser

The work for which Donald Glaser is best known, his bubble chamber invention for tracking the movement of high-energy particles, is said to have begun over a glass of beer. In the early 1950s, while teaching physics at the University of Michigan, Glaser followed a hunch that bubbles rising from a glass of beer might provide a clue for detecting high-energy radiation. Although his first attempt to prove this hypothesis, using beer, soda water, and ginger ale, failed, he kept working. In 1953 he created a small bubble chamber filled with superheated ether that was successful in capturing the trail of bubbles left by nuclear particles as they passed through the liquid. The bubble chamber invention won Glaser the 1960 Nobel Prize in physics and was a vital step in understanding atomic function. It also enabled the discovery of new atomic particles, such as the rho and omega minus particles, at the same time advancing visualization of charged-particle interactions, and furthering the study of particle mass, lifetime, and decay modes.

Donald Arthur Glaser was born in Cleveland, Ohio, on September 21, 1926, to William and Lena Glaser. Glaser's parents had come to the United States from Russia. His father operated a wholesale sundries business in Cleveland and Glaser attended elementary and secondary schools there. As a child he was given violin and viola lessons. Later he studied composition at the Cleveland Institute of Music. An accomplished musician, he became a member of a local symphony orchestra at age sixteen. Glaser remained in Cleveland for his undergraduate education, entering Case Institute of Technology (now Case Western Reserve University) to study mathematics and physics. He completed his graduate course work at the California Institute of Technology (Caltech) and received his Ph.D. in 1950, a year after he accepted a position as instructor at the University of Michigan. He remained at Michigan until 1959, and was made full professor there in 1957 at the age of thirty-one. He left Michigan to accept a visiting professorship at the University of California at Berkeley. That position was made permanent, and Glaser was to remain at Berkeley for the rest of his career, except for brief periods away on fellowships.

Bubble Chamber Fills a Gap

Other physicists before Glaser had attempted to make nuclear particles visible. The 1927 Nobel Prize was given to **C. T. R. Wilson**, a British scientist, for his cloud chamber method. In 1950 **C. F. Powell** received that honor for an emulsion method. But both these methods, while effective for elementary particle study, became inadequate with the advent of high-energy particle acceleration machines, such as that built at Berkeley in the late 1950s. These accelerators had capacities one thousand times greater than those used for the cloud chamber and emulsion techniques.

Continuing to refine the bubble chamber method he had developed at the University of Michigan, Glaser next tried superheated liquids of higher density, such as liquid hydrogen and xenon gas. Experiments with these liquids provided glimpses of subatomic functions never before seen, and made possible the tracking of neutral as well as charged particles. As Glaser continued to refine his bubble chamber methods, information gathering increased a thousandfold. For example, in his first two years at Berkeley, Glaser was able to collect almost half a million tracking photographs. The machine that made this possible was Berkeley's new, two-million-dollar bubble chamber. Built by **Luis W. Alvarez**, the size of this bubble chamber was six feet long, quite a jump from the one-half- to one-inch bubble chambers Glaser had used earlier. The Berkeley bubble chamber was capable of measuring particle tracks at a rate of every fourteen seconds, shooting three photographs of each instance. *Science* magazine reported that the Nobel Prize Committee credited Glaser's bubble chamber invention with filling "the wide gap in range" left by the cloud chamber and the emulsion methods. **Kai M. Siegbahn**, speaking for the Royal Swedish Academy of Sciences, said: "Several other scientists also left important contributions to the practical shaping of different types of bubble chambers, but Glaser is the one who made the really fundamental contribution."

In the years after receiving the Nobel Prize, Glaser extended his knowledge of physics to the field of molecular biology. He studied microbiology at the University of Copenhagen in 1961, then returned to Berkeley, where he did research on bacterial evolution, regulation of cell growth, and the causes of cancer and genetic mutation. Using photo-analyzing equipment developed for the bubble chamber, Glaser was able to identify bacterial species through computer scanning. He was made professor of physics and molecular biology at Berkeley in 1964. Glaser retained his lifelong love of music, often playing with local chamber music groups. His other pastimes have included mountain climbing, tennis, and sailing. During his career, he has held membership in the American Physical Society and the National Academy of Sciences. In addition to the Nobel Prize in physics, he was awarded the Henry Russel Award of the University of Michigan in 1955, the Charles Vernon Boys Prize of the Physical Society in London in 1958, the American Physical Society Prize in 1959, the Gold Medal of the Case Institute of Technology in 1967, and the Alumni Distinguished Service Award from the California Institute of Technology, also in 1967. He married the former Ruth Louise Thompson in 1960. They had two children, a son, William, and a daughter, Louise.

SELECTED WRITINGS BY GLASER:

Periodicals

"Some Effects of Ionizing Radiation on the Formation of Bubbles in Liquids," *Physical Review,* Volume 87, August 15, 1952, p. 665.

"Progress Report on the Development of Bubble Chambers," *Nuovo cimento supplement,* Volume 11, 1953, pp. 361–68.

(With D. C. Rahm) "Characteristics of Bubble Chambers," *Physical Review,* Volume 97, January 15, 1955, pp. 474–79.

(With D. C. Rahm and C. Dodd) "Bubble Counting for the Determination of the Velocities of Charged Particles in Bubble Chambers," *Physical Review,* Volume 102, July 15, 1956, pp. 1653–58.

SOURCES:

Books

Nobel Prize Winners, H. W. Wilson, 1987, pp. 382–84.

Periodicals

Science, Volume 132, November 11, 1960, p. 1384.

Time, November 14, 1960, p. 89.

Wiskari, Werner, "Two U. S. Scientists Win Nobel Prizes," *New York Times,* November 4, 1960, pp. 1, 27.

—*Sketch by Jane Stewart Cook*

Sheldon Lee Glashow
1932-
American physicist

Sheldon Lee Glashow contributed to the independent work of **Steven Weinberg** and **Abdus Salam** to develop the electroweak theory, which shows how two fundamental forces—the weak and electromagnetic forces—can be viewed as separate manifestations of a single, more basic force, termed an electroweak force. Among his contributions to the Weinberg-Salam theory was his invention of the property of charm for elementary particles. For his research, he shared the 1979 Nobel Prize in physics with Weinberg and Salam.

Glashow was born in New York City on December 5, 1932. His parents, Lewis Gluchovski and Bella (Rubin) Gluchovski, had immigrated to New York from Bobruisk, Russia, to avoid anti-Semitic oppression by the Czarist government. Upon his arrival in the United States, the senior Gluchovski changed his name to Glashow and opened a plumbing business that would become very successful. The Glashows had two other sons, fourteen and eighteen years older than Sheldon; one became a dentist and the other had a career as a doctor.

Embarks on Career in Particle Physics

Glashow attended one of the nation's most prestigious high schools, the Bronx High School of Science. There he claims to have learned as much about physics from his classmates as he did from his instructors. Among those classmates were future fellow Nobel Laureate Weinberg and later Columbia physicist Gerald Feinberg. By the time Glashow had graduated from Bronx High in 1950, he had decided his career: he wanted to be a particle physicist.

In order to pursue this goal, Glashow enrolled at Cornell in the fall of 1950, choosing it in preference to the Massachusetts Institute of Technology and Princeton. Harvard had denied his application. He later told biographer Arthur Fisher in an interview for the book *A Passion To Know* that he was not very impressed with the faculty at Cornell. "I spent a good deal of time in the poolroom," he explained. "Most successful people in physics made it by going off by themselves and learning what they wanted to."

After receiving his bachelor's degree from Cornell in 1954, Glashow entered Harvard to do his graduate work. There, he studied under Nobel Laureate **Julian Schwinger**, who was to become a major influence in Glashow's life. His doctoral thesis, "The Vector Meson in Elementary Particle Decay," was a preliminary effort to combine two of the basic forces of nature, the weak and the electromagnetic forces.

Awarded Noble Prize for Electroweak Theory

Efforts to find ways of unifying the four basic forces of nature—the strong, weak, electromagnetic, and gravitational forces—go back to the turn of the century, especially to the work of **Albert Einstein**. These efforts are grounded in the belief among most physicists that these four fundamental forces are not actually distinct from each other, but are somehow four different manifestations of a single basic force.

One problem with this assumption is that the unification of forces is thought to be observable only at energies far greater than those encountered in everyday life. The belief is, for example, that the weak and electromagnetic forces actually merge into a single force only at the very high energies produced within particle accelerators. Higher unification may occur only at energies that once existed at the creation of the universe.

Development of unification theories has been, therefore, a highly complex, intricate theoretical exercise that may be testable initially only by checks of internal consistency and only later by experimental studies. In the 1960s, Weinberg and Salam devised such a theory, an explanation of the way in which the weak nuclear force and the electromagnetic force could be conceived of as manifestations of a single unified force, the electroweak force. That original theory, although very attractive, dealt only with one class of particles, the leptons (electrons and neutrinos).

Shortly after Weinberg and Salam announced their results, Glashow found a method for extending their theory to other elementary particles, such as mesons and baryons. In order to do so, he found it necessary to invent a new property for particles, a property he designated as "charm." In the decade following the formulation of the electroweak theory, experimental evidence supporting the theory gradually began to appear. In 1973, for example, researchers for the first time detected a previously unknown phenomenon known as "neutral currents" that had been predicted by the Salam-Weinberg theory. By 1979, support for the theory had become solid enough to justify the Nobel Prize committee's awarding the physics prize that year to the three researchers.

Since winning the Nobel Prize, Glashow has continued to work on unification theories. Now his goal is to find ways of incorporating the strong force into the electroweak force. He carries out that work at Harvard, where he has been on the faculty since 1966, and at Texas A & M University, where he accepted a joint appointment in 1983. Glashow was married to the former Joan Shirley Alexander in 1972. They have three sons, Jason David, Jordan, and Brian Lewis, and one daughter, Rebecca Lee. In addition to the Nobel Prize, Glashow was awarded the J. Robert Oppenheimer Memorial Medal in 1977, the George Ledlie Prize in 1978, and the Castiglione di Silica Prize in 1983.

SELECTED WRITINGS BY GLASHOW:

Periodicals

"Quarks with Color and Flavor," *Scientific American,* October, 1975, pp. 38–50.

"Toward a Unified Theory: Threads in a Tapestry," *Science,* Volume 210, 1980, pp. 1319–1323.

SOURCES:

Books

Fisher, Arthur, "The Charm of Physics," in *A Passion To Know,* edited by A. Hammond, Scribner, 1984, pp. 24–35.

Periodicals

Coleman, Sidney, "The 1979 Nobel Prize in Physics," *Science,* December 14, 1979, pp. 1290–1291.

"Nobel Prizes: To Glashow, Salam and Weinberg for Physics . . . ," *Physics Today,* December 1979, pp. 17–19.

"Nobels for Getting It Together in Physics," *New Scientist,* October 18, 1979, pp. 163–164.

—Sketch by David E. Newton

John H. Glenn, Jr.
1921-
American astronaut and senator

John H. Glenn, Jr., was the first American to orbit the earth. In the wake of this 1962 feat Glenn became a national hero on the order of trans-Atlantic aviator Charles A. Lindbergh—a status that helped carry him to a second career in the United States Senate.

John Herschel Glenn, Jr., was born on July 18, 1921, in Cambridge, Ohio, and grew up in nearby New Concord. He was the son of plumber John Herschel Glenn and the former Clara Sproat. Glenn's parents had two other children, both of whom died in infancy, and later they adopted his sister Jean. Glenn credits his parents with instilling his deep-rooted Presbyterian faith and the accompanying philosophy that everyone is given certain talents and a duty to use them to the fullest. In high school Glenn was a diligent student who earned top grades. He worked hard athletically as well, lettering in three sports. After high school Glenn entered Muskingum College in New Concord, majoring in chemistry. His high school sweetheart, Anna "Annie" Castor, enrolled as well.

Flies in World War II and Korea

After two and a half years of study, Glenn entered a local civilian pilot training program and learned to fly. He then left college to enter the Naval Aviation Cadet Program. In 1943 he was graduated and commissioned as a lieutenant in the Marine Corps. He married Annie before going on to advanced training and assignment to a combat unit. Glenn flew F4U Corsair fighter-bombers on fifty-nine missions in the Pacific theater during World War II.

When peace came, Glenn remained in the corps, serving as a fighter pilot and then as a flight instructor. He and Annie began their family, with John David arriving in 1945 and Carolyn Ann in 1947. In 1952 Major Glenn was sent to Korea. He flew primarily ground-attack missions in that war as well, repeatedly returning in aircraft riddled with bullet and shrapnel holes. Through an interservice exchange program, Glenn transferred to an Air Force squadron just before the end of the war. Flying the F–86 Sabre, Glenn downed three North Korean MiG fighters in nine days.

Following Korea, Glenn attended the Naval Test Pilot School, part of the Naval Test Center in Patuxent River, Maryland. After graduating as a test pilot, he spent two years as a project officer evaluating new aircraft. Glenn moved on to the Navy Bureau of Aeronautics in Washington, D.C., where he continued to oversee development of new fighters. These included the F8U Crusader, a plane Glenn made famous in 1957. In Project Bullet, a test Glenn conceived himself, he flew a Crusader coast to coast, making the first transcontinental supersonic flight in a record time of three hours and twenty-three minutes.

Selected for Astronaut Program

When Glenn learned of the upcoming astronaut program, he was captivated by the challenge of spaceflight. He immediately began to strengthen his qualifications, improving his physical condition, volunteering for centrifuge tests and other research projects, and pursuing courses at the University of Maryland. (Glenn did not actually receive a college degree until after he had flown in space, when Muskingum College awarded him a bachelor's degree in mathematics.) In April 1959, the newly promoted Lieutenant Colonel Glenn was selected as one of America's seven Mercury astronauts.

Glenn helped design the cockpit layout and instrumentation of the Mercury capsule. He became the unofficial spokesperson for the astronaut team, and it was a surprise to the country and to Glenn when fellow astronaut **Alan B. Shepard, Jr.**, a lieutenant commander with the U.S. Navy, was chosen to make the first U.S. spaceflight. Shepard and then Gus Grissom, an Air Force captain and astronaut, made suborbital flights, in which the Mercury craft was launched by a Redstone rocket. These efforts were eclipsed in the popular imagination by the Soviet Union's successful orbital manned flights, and the pressure was on the National Aeronautics and Space Administration (NASA) to match the Russian feat as soon as possible. Glenn was chosen to make the first orbital effort, officially known as Mercury-Atlas 6.

After several frustrating postponements caused by unsuitable weather and technical glitches, Glenn's capsule, *Friendship 7,* roared into orbit on February 20, 1962. The astronaut fed ground controllers a constant stream of observations and physiological reports, performing experiments such as pulling on an elastic cord to determine the effects of physical work in weightlessness. Tremendous publicity surrounded the flight, in contrast to the secretive Russian launches. Not publicized at the time, however, was a telemetry signal's indication that Glenn's heat shield, vital for safe reentry to the earth's atmosphere, might not be secured to the capsule. Glenn was directed to change the original plan of jettisoning his retro-rocket package after it had been used to slow the capsule; instead it would be kept in place, strapped over the heat shield, to keep the shield from coming loose.

Glenn was briefed on the problem. (He later argued that NASA policy should be to notify airborne astronauts as soon as any abnormality is detected.) Glenn left the retropack on and took manual control of his craft, guiding the capsule to a perfectly safe reentry after three orbits of the earth. It was later determined that the telemetry signal was false, but the incident solidified Glenn's view that spacecraft needed humans aboard who could respond to the unexpected.

Leaves NASA for Senate Run

Glenn was bathed in national attention. President John F. Kennedy pinned the NASA Distinguished Service Medal on his chest. He was invited to address a joint session of Congress, an honor normally reserved for top officials and visiting heads of state. Glenn told the assembly that the real benefits of space exploration were "probably not even known to man today. But exploration and the pursuit of knowledge have always paid dividends in the long run—usually far greater than anything expected at the outset."

Glenn received hundreds of thousands of letters, some of which he collected in a book, *Letters to John Glenn.* Glenn also became friends with President Kennedy and his brother, U.S. Attorney General Robert Kennedy. The president urged Glenn to cnter politics and, unknown to the astronaut, directed that Glenn's life not be risked by another spaceflight. Glenn worked on the preliminary designs for Project Apollo, which had the goal of putting a man on the moon, then left NASA and applied for military retirement to enter the Ohio Senate race in 1964. He withdrew from that contest after suffering a serious head injury in a bathroom fall.

Colonel Glenn retired from the Marines on January 1, 1965, with six Distinguished Flying Crosses and eighteen Air Medals, among other decorations. He had logged over 5,400 hours of flying time. Glenn's space exploit also garnered him numerous civilian honors, including induction into the Aviation Hall of Fame and the National Space Hall of Fame, and, in 1978, the award of the Congressional Space Medal of Honor. He was granted honorary doctorates in engineering by four universities.

After retiring from the military, Glenn went into business, first with the Royal Crown cola company and later with a management group that operated Holiday Inn hotels. His business ventures made Glenn a millionaire, but his political dreams remained foremost in his mind. In 1970 Glenn again declared his candidacy for the U.S. Senate. He narrowly lost in the Democratic primary to Howard Metzenbaum, who outspent and out-organized his less experienced rival. When another Senate seat opened in 1974, Glenn started earlier, ran harder, and won the election.

Despite being new to Washington politics, Glenn gained a reputation for hard work and effective legislating. His voting record marked him as generally liberal on both domestic and foreign policy. Glenn was considered for the vice presidency by presidential nominee Jimmy Carter, but Walter Mondale, a Minnesota senator, was chosen instead. In the Senate, Glenn became best known for his work against nuclear proliferation. He was willing to oppose President Carter on some issues, most notably the second Strategic Arms Limitation Talks (SALT II) arms accord, which Glenn considered unverifiable. He sought the Democratic presidential nomination in 1984; once again, however, Mondale grasped the prize Glenn sought, eliminating Glenn before the party's convention with a better-run campaign.

Glenn continued serving in the Senate, where he supported increased funding for education, space exploration, and basic scientific research. He was a strong advocate of a permanent research station in space. Outside the Senate, Glenn served on the National Space Society's Board of Governors, on Ohio's Democratic Party State Executive Committee, and as a Presbyterian elder, among many other commitments.

SELECTED WRITINGS BY GLENN:

Books

(Coauthor) *We Seven, by the Astronauts Themselves: M. Scott Carpenter, L. Gordon Cooper, John H. Glenn, Virgil I. Grissom, Walter M. Schirra, Alan B. Shepard, Donald K. Slayton,* Simon & Schuster, 1962.

(Compiler) *Letters to John Glenn: With Comments by J. H. Glenn, Jr.*, World Book Encyclopedia Science Service, 1964.

SOURCES:

Books

Pierce, Philip N., and Karl Schuon, *John H. Glenn: Astronaut,* Franklin Watts, 1962.

Van Riper, Frank, *Glenn: The Astronaut Who Would Be President,* Empire Books, 1983.

Wolfe, Tom, *The Right Stuff,* Farrar, Straus, 1979.

Periodicals

Crawford, Mark, "Glenn Asks Reagan to Halt Pakistan Aid Pending Review of Nuclear Programs," *Science,* March 18, 1987, p.1321.

—Sketch by Matthew A. Bille

Robert H. Goddard

Robert H. Goddard
1882-1945
American physicist and rocket pioneer

Robert H. Goddard was one of the foremost pioneers in the field of rocket research and the theory of space flight. Alone among the first generation of rocket and space pioneers, he not only contributed to space flight theory but also engaged over most of his adult life in the actual development of rockets. As a result, he is credited with launching the world's first liquid-propellant rocket. He developed and patented a large number of innovations in rocket technology that were later used in the much larger rockets and missiles employed by the Germans during World War II and, thereafter, by the United States' and Soviet Union's missile and space programs, among others. Paradoxically, Goddard's influence upon modern rocketry was not as great as it would have been had he been less a solitary inventor and more inclined to publish his findings in scientific journals and elsewhere.

Robert Hutchings Goddard was born on October 5, 1882, in Worcester, Massachusetts, to Nahum Danford Goddard, himself something of an inventor, and Fannie Louise Hoyt Goddard, the daughter of a machine knife manufacturer for whom her husband worked at the time of their marriage. Of modest means but old New England stock, Goddard's parents had a second son who died in infancy. Goddard himself was prone to illness and fell behind in school, compensating with self-education. Encouraged by his father in his early inclinations towards experimentation and invention, Goddard also heeded his father's advice to mind his own business and work for himself rather than someone else. Science fiction proved another early influence upon him, one that apparently led to a transforming experience he had in a cherry tree on October 19, 1899, when he imagined a device that might ascend to Mars. As he stated in an autobiographical memoir, the experience suddenly made life seem purposeful to him. Throughout the rest of his life, he recorded the date in his diary as "anniversary day," and he revisited the tree on that date whenever he was in Worcester.

Goddard received his early education in the Boston area, where his father had been working, and had not done well in algebra during his first year in high school. When the family moved back to Worcester in 1898 after his mother was diagnosed with tuberculosis, his experience in the cherry tree compelled him to excel in math and physics at South High School. Because of his own illnesses, Goddard did not graduate from South High until 1904, when he was 21. He went on to earn a bachelor's degree in general science, with a concentration in physics, from Worcester Polytechnic Institute in 1908, and a master's degree from Clark University in 1910. By 1909, he had already begun teaching physics at Worcester

Polytechnic and shortly after receiving his doctorate from Clark in 1911, he became an honorary fellow in physics there. Working as a research instructor in physics at Princeton University, Goddard fell dangerously ill in 1913 and, like his mother, was diagnosed with tuberculosis. Initially given only two weeks to live, he recovered sufficiently the following year to become a physics instructor at Clark, where he was promoted to assistant professor in 1915. Goddard would remain at Clark throughout much of his academic career, allowing for leaves of absence to pursue rocket research. Goddard eventually became head of Clark's physics department and director of the physical laboratories, obtaining the rank of full professor in 1934. On June 21, 1924, the confirmed bachelor married Esther Christine Kisk, the much younger secretary to the president of Clark. Although the couple had no children, they became devoted to one another and to Goddard's rocket research, in which Esther became very much a partner.

Begins Rocket Research

Although long interested in space travel and rocketry as a means thereto, Goddard apparently did not begin serious work on rocket development until early 1909, while a graduate student at Clark. He had, by 1914, obtained a patent for a two-stage powder rocket, followed by patents for a cartridge-loading rocket and a rocket that burned a mixture of gasoline and liquid nitrous oxide. While he was aware of the greater efficiencies of liquid propellants, Goddard found them hard to obtain, preferring instead, smokeless powder, which offered fewer experimental difficulties. Using a steel combustion chamber and a sleeker exhaust nozzle, named for Swedish engineer Carl de Laval, Goddard was able to achieve higher rates of energy efficiency and exhaust velocities than previous rockets had exhibited. He also developed a device that allowed him to fire a rocket in a vacuum, showing that it could operate in the upper atmosphere where air density was small and also demonstrating that it did not require a reaction against the air, as many knowledgeable people at the time supposed.

Until 1916, Goddard had conducted these experiments using the meager funds and facilities provided by Clark, as well as money from his own pocket. No longer able to support the research required to advance his theories, Goddard applied for funding to the Aero Club of America and the Smithsonian Institution. After several inquiries into his request, Goddard reported to the Smithsonian that he had developed a means of propelling meteorological recording devices to heights previously unattainable by sounding balloons, indicating that altitudes of 100–200 miles could be reached within a year's time. By January 1917, The Smithsonian had awarded Goddard a grant for $5,000. This proved to be the first of many grants from the Smithsonian, Clark University, the Carnegie Institution of Washington, Daniel Guggenheim, and especially the Guggenheim Foundation. Not counting military support during World Wars I and II, such grants totaled about $210,000—extremely generous funding for the pre-World War II period in America.

Before the Smithsonian funds could be put to use, America became embroiled in World War I. Supported by the U.S. Army, Goddard and a number of technicians developed both multiple-charge and single-charge recoilless rockets, the latter serving as a prototype for the bazooka which proved effective against tanks during World War II. While tests proved these weapons successful, the armistice intervened before they could be employed. Once World War I was over, Goddard's department head at Clark prodded him into publishing the results of his solid-propellant rocket researches in a paper entitled "A Method of Reaching Extreme Altitudes," which appeared in the *Smithsonian Miscellaneous Collections.* In it, he not only explained the experiments he had conducted, but laid the foundations for much of the early theory of modern rocketry. While devoted primarily to the solid propellants he had used in his research, the paper did mention the greater efficiencies of propellants such as hydrogen and oxygen used in their liquid states. The paper briefly discussed the use of stages (propulsion units coupled together to fire in sequence) in order to reach extreme altitudes, and included numerous calculations of such matters as the reduced resistance a rocket would face as it climbed higher and entered less dense portions of the earth's atmosphere.

The reaction to this paper was shaped by a Smithsonian press release emphasizing a point Goddard had not intended as the focus of the work. It suggested the possibility of using a rocket to send a small quantity of flash powder to the dark side of the moon, where, when ignited, it could be viewed from the earth through telescopes, thereby proving that extreme altitude had been reached. The press played up the idea of a moon rocket, and Goddard was embarrassed by the publicity. His inclination against publicizing his work until rockets were actually capable of reaching such altitudes was reinforced. Nevertheless, he persisted in his rocket development in his native Massachusetts for the next decade. Frustrated at the problems he encountered in using solid propellants, he switched to liquid propellants in 1921, though it was not until March 16, 1926—almost ten years after his initial proposal to the Smithsonian—that he launched the world's first liquid-propellant rocket from a hill in Auburn, Massachusetts. Since this was an important event in the history of rocketry, it is noteworthy that the hill, on his Aunt Effie's farm, had an Indian name meaning "a turning point or place." The small rocket only rose forty-one feet—far short of the altitudes he sought to reach—but it represented a significant beginning to the age of rocket flight, comparable, perhaps, to the **Wright** brothers' contributions to aviation.

Moves Rocket Research to New Mexico

From a number of standpoints, including its weather and its population density, Massachusetts was hardly an ideal location for launching noisy, fire-belching rockets. So, when Goddard received a generous $50,000 grant from philanthropist Daniel Guggenheim in mid–1930, he took a two-year leave of absence from Clark University and, with his wife and some technical assistants, rented a farmhouse near Roswell, New Mexico, where he proceeded with his rocket development. Loss of funding after 1932 interrupted his research there, but he returned to Roswell in 1934 to resume his testing. In the process, he invented and patented a large number of innovations, including a gyroscopically-controlled guidance system, and a method for cooling the combustion chamber that used a film of propellant streaming along the sides of the chamber. Parachutes were incorporated for recovery of the rocket and a number of instruments were devised for measuring the rocket's performance. Goddard also searched for ways to make a more lightweight, streamlined rocket casing. But he never succeeded in putting all of these components together to create a vehicle capable of reaching anything close to the 100–200 miles of altitude he had originally expected to achieve. The greatest height one of his rockets reached was estimated at 8,000 to 9,000 feet on March 26, 1937.

Turns to Defense-Related Research

In 1941, he discontinued his attempt to reach extreme altitudes and began work for the armed forces on defense-related rocket research as he had during World War I. In 1942, he moved his crew of assistants to the Naval Engineering Experimental Station in Annapolis, Maryland, where they worked on developing jet-assisted take-off devices for aircraft, pumps, and a variable-thrust rocket motor that became the basis for the one later used on the Bell X–2 rocket plane, the first aircraft in America to use a throttleable engine. This, like the bazooka, was a very important and tangible result of his research. His many patented inventions were also significant. In June 1960 the Army, Air Force, Navy, and National Aeronautics and Space Administration recognized their importance when they granted Mrs. Esther C. Goddard and the Guggenheim Foundation a settlement of $1,000,000 for the right to use many of Goddard's patents.

Despite his technical achievements, however, Goddard's career remained somewhat flawed by his failure to reach the extreme altitudes he sought, and by his secretive nature and consequent failure to communicate most of the details of his research to other scientists and engineers. In 1936, he did publish another paper entitled "Liquid-propellant Rocket Development." Here, Goddard devoted much more attention to liquid propulsion than he had in 1919, and while he did include pictures of some of his rockets and discussed some of their features, the brevity of his treatment (some seventeen pages in his published papers) made the work of limited utility to other scientists and engineers engaged in rocket development. While some of them were inspired by Goddard's example, for the most part they had to develop their own counterparts to his innovations without the benefit of a detailed knowledge of his pioneering inventions. This was notably the case with Frank J. Malina and his rocket team, at what would eventually become the Jet Propulsion Laboratory in southern California. This group developed solid-propellant rocket technology that was important for later missile technology. In relation to Goddard's endeavors, the Malina team succeeded on October 11, 1945, in launching a sounding rocket, named the WAC Corporal, to an altitude of some 230,000 feet—far higher than any of Goddard's rockets ever reached.

Despite this failing, Goddard was a remarkable figure in the history of rocket development. His persistence in pursuing his research, despite his tuberculosis, attests to his determination and perseverance. As it turned out, when he died on the morning of August 10, 1945, it was apparently not from tuberculosis, but throat cancer, which had been diagnosed only two months earlier. His importance is attested by the numerous memorials to his work. Of the many streets, buildings, and awards named in his honor, perhaps the most significant is NASA's Goddard Space Flight Center, dedicated on March 16, 1961—the 35th anniversary of the first flight of a liquid-propellant rocket. On that occasion, Mrs. Goddard accepted a Congressional Gold Medal presented posthumously to him. A little more than nine years later, Clark University named its new library after him. Since 1958, the National Space Club in Washington, DC, has awarded a Goddard Memorial Trophy for achievement in missiles, rocketry, and space flight. Finally, it might be noted that in 1960 Goddard was the ninth recipient of the Langley Gold Medal, awarded only sparingly since 1910 by the Smithsonian Institution for excellence in aviation.

SELECTED WRITINGS BY GODDARD:

Books

(Edited by Esther C. Goddard and G. Edward Pendray), *Rocket Development: Liquid-Fuel Rocket Research, 1929–1941,* Prentice-Hall, 1948.

The Papers of Robert H. Goddard, 3 volumes, McGraw-Hill, 1970.

SOURCES:

Books

Lehman, Milton, *Robert H. Goddard: Pioneer of Space Research,* Da Capo, 1988.
Stoiko, Michael, *Pioneers of Rocketry,* Hawthorn, 1974.
Winter, Frank H., *Rockets into Space,* Harvard University Press, 1990.

Periodicals

American Heritage, Volume 31, No. 4, June/July, 1980, pp. 25–32.
History of Rocketry and Astronautics, Volume 8, 1989, pp. 317–41.

—*Sketch by J. D. Hunley*

Kurt Friedrich Gödel

Kurt Friedrich Gödel
1906-1978
Austrian-born American mathematician

Kurt Friedrich Gödel was a mathematical logician who proved perhaps the most influential theorem of twentieth-century mathematics—the incompleteness theorem. Although he was not prolific in his published research and did not cultivate a group of students to carry on his work, his results have shaped the development of logic and affected mathematics and philosophy, as well as other disciplines. The philosophy of mathematics has been forced to grapple with the significance of Gödel's results ever since they were announced. His work was as epoch-making as that of **Albert Einstein**, even if the ramifications have not been as visible to the general public. Gregory H. Moore, in *Dictionary of Scientific Biography*, related that in May of 1972 mathematician Oskar Morgenstern wrote that Einstein himself said that "Gödel's papers were the most important ones on relativity theory since his own [Einstein's] original paper appeared."

Gödel was born in Brünn, Moravia (now Brno, Czech Republic), on April 28, 1906, the younger son of Rudolf Gödel, who worked for a textile factory in Brunn, and Marianne Handschuh. Gödel had an older brother, Rudolf, who would study medicine and become a radiologist. The Gödels were part of the German-speaking minority in Brünn, which subsequently became one of the larger cities in the Czech Republic. The family had no allegiance to the nationalist sentiments around them, and all of Gödel's educational experience was in German-speaking surroundings. He was baptized a Lutheran and took religion more to heart than the rest of his family.

Gödel began his education in September, 1912, when he enrolled in a Lutheran school in Brünn. In the fall of 1916 he became a student in a gymnasium, where he remained until 1924. At that point he entered the University of Vienna, planning to major in physics. In 1926, influenced by one of his teachers in number theory, he changed to mathematics; he did, however, retain an interest in physics, which he expressed in a number of unpublished papers later in life. He also continued his studies in philosophy and was associated with the Vienna Circle, a gathering of philosophers of science that had great influence on the English-speaking philosophical community. Gödel never was one, however, to follow a party line, and he went his own way philosophically. He felt that his independence of thought contributed to his ability to find new directions in mathematical logic.

Proves the Incompleteness Theorem

Gödel's father died in February of 1929, and shortly thereafter his mother and brother moved to

Vienna. Gödel completed the work for his dissertation in the summer of that year. He received his doctorate in February of 1930 for his proof of what became known as the completeness theorem. The problem that Gödel had considered was the following: Euclidean geometry served as an example of a kind of branch of mathematics where all the results were derived from a few initial assumptions, called axioms. However, it was hard to tell whether any particular list of axioms would be enough to prove all the true statements about the objects of geometry. Gödel showed in his dissertation that for a certain part of logic, a set of axioms could be found such that the consequences of the axioms would include all true statements of that part of logic. In other words, the collection of provable statements and the collection of true statements amounted to the same collection. This was a reassuring result for those who hoped to find a list of axioms that would work for all of mathematics.

In September of 1930, however, mathematical logic changed forever when Gödel announced his first incompleteness theorem. One of the great accomplishments of mathematical logic earlier in the century had been the work of two British mathematicians, **Alfred North Whitehead** and **Bertrand Russell**. Their three-volume work *Principia Mathematica* (Latin for "mathematical principles" and based on the title of a work by Isaac Newton), tried to derive all of mathematics from a collection of axioms. They examined some areas very thoroughly, and though few mathematicians bothered to read all the details, most were prepared to believe that Whitehead and Russell would be able to continue their project through the rest of mathematics.

Gödel's work was written up under the title "On Formally Undecidable Propositions of *Principia Mathematica* and Related Systems." In this paper, which was published in a German mathematical journal in 1931, Gödel introduced a new technique which enabled him to discuss arithmetic using arithmetic. He translated statements in logic into statements involving only numbers, and he did this by assigning numerical values to symbols of logic. It had long been known that there were problems involved in self-reference; any statement that discussed itself, such as the statement "This statement is false," presented logical difficulties in determining whether it was true or false. The assumption of those who hoped to produce an axiomatization of all of mathematics was that it would be possible to avoid such self-referring statements.

Gödel's method of proof enabled him to introduce the technique of self-reference into the very foundations of mathematics; he showed that there were statements which were indisputably true but could not be proved by axiomatization. In other words, the collection of provable statements would not include all the true statements. Although the importance of Gödel's work in this area was not immediately recognized, it did not take long before those seeking to axiomatize mathematics realized that his theorem put an immovable roadblock in their path. The proof was not obvious to those who were not used to thinking in the terms that he introduced, but the technique of Gödel numbering rapidly became an indispensable part of the logician's tool kit.

Of the schools of mathematical philosophy most active at the time Gödel introduced his incompleteness theorem, at least two have not since enjoyed the same reputation. Logicism was the belief that all mathematics could be reduced to logic and thereby put on a firm foundation. Formalism claimed that certainty could be achieved for mathematics by establishing theorems about completeness. In the aftermath of Gödel's work, it was even suggested that his theorem showed that man was more than a machine, since a machine could only establish what was provable, whereas man could understand what was true, which went beyond what was provable. Many logicians would dispute this, but no philosophy of mathematics is imaginable which does not take account of Gödel's work on incompleteness.

Moves to Princeton and Begins Work on Set Theory

Gödel was never a popular or successful teacher. His reserved personality led him to lecture more to the blackboard than to his audience. Fortunately, he was invited to join the Institute for Advanced Study at Princeton, which had opened in the fall of 1933, where he could work without teaching responsibilities. Despite the attractions of the working environment in Princeton, Gödel continued to return to Austria, and it was there that he lectured on his first major results in the new field to which he had turned attention, the theory of sets.

Set theory had been established as a branch of mathematics in the last half of the nineteenth century, although its development had been hindered by the discovery of a few paradoxes. As a result, many who studied the field felt it was important to produce an axiomatization that would prevent paradoxes from arising. The axiomatization which most mathematicians wanted was one which would capture the intuitions they had about the way sets behaved without necessarily committing them to points about which there was disagreement. Two of the statements about which there were disagreement were the axiom of choice and the continuum hypothesis. The axiom of choice said that for any family of sets there is always a function that picks one element out of each set; this was indisputable for finite collections of sets but was problematic when infinite collections of sets were introduced. The continuum hypothesis stated that, although it was known that there were more real (rational and irrational) numbers than whole numbers (integers), there were no infinite sets in size between the real numbers and the whole numbers.

Gödel's major contribution in set theory was the introduction of what are known as constructible sets. These objects formed a model for the standard axiomatization of set theory. As a result, if it could be shown that the axiom of choice and the continuum hypothesis applied to the constructible sets, then those disputed principles had to be at least consistent with the standard axiomatization. Gödel successfully demonstrated both results, but this still left open the question of whether the two statements could be proved from the standard axiomatization. One of the major accomplishments of set theory in the second half of the century was the demonstration by **Paul Cohen** that neither the axiom of choice nor the continuum hypothesis could be proved from the standard axiomatization.

Gödel had suffered a nervous breakdown in 1934 which aggravated an early tendency to avoid society. He married Adele Porkert Nimbursky, a nightclub dancer, on September 20, 1938. He had met his wife when he was twenty-one, but his father had objected to the match, based on the difference in their social standing and the fact she had been married before. After his marriage, his domestic situation was something of a comfort in the face of the deteriorating political situation in Austria, especially after the union of Austria and Germany in 1938, when Adolf Hitler was in power. When he returned to Vienna from the United States in June of 1939, he received a letter informing him that he was known to move in "Jewish-liberal" circles, not an attractive feature to the Nazi regime. When he was assaulted by fascist students that year, he rapidly applied for a visa to the United States. It was a sign of his stature in the profession that at a time when so many were seeking to escape from Europe, Gödel's request was promptly granted. He never returned to Europe after his hasty departure.

Gödel was appointed an ordinary member of the Institute for Advanced Study in Princeton, where he would remain for the rest of his life. His closest friends were Einstein and Oskar Morgenstern, and he took frequent walks in Einstein's company. Einstein and Gödel were of opposing temperaments, but they could talk about physics and each respected the other's work. Morgenstern was a mathematical economist and one of the founders of the branch of mathematics known as game theory. Gödel and his wife were content with this small social circle, remaining outside the glare of publicity which often fell on Einstein.

After his arrival in Princeton, Gödel started to turn his attention more to philosophy. His mathematical accomplishments guaranteed his philosophical speculations a hearing, even if they ran counter to the dominant currents of thought at the time. Perhaps the most popular philosophical school then was naturalism—the attempt to ground mathematics and its language in terms of observable objects and events of the everyday world. Gödel, however, was a Platonist and he believed that mathematics was not grounded in the observable world. In two influential published articles, one dealing with **Bertrand Russell** and the other with the continuum hypothesis, Gödel argued that mathematical intuition was a special faculty which needed to be explored in its own right. Although the bulk of mathematical philosophers have not followed him, they have been obliged to take his arguments into account.

Although Gödel moved away from mathematics in his later years, he contributed occasionally to the field. One of his last mathematical articles, published twenty years before his death, dealt with the attempt to formalize the approach to mathematical philosophy known as intuitionism. Gödel himself was not partial to that approach, but his work had wide influence among the intuitionists. American mathematician Paul Cohen was also careful to bring his work on the axiom of choice and the continuum hypothesis to him for his approval.

In his years at the Institute for Advanced Study, awards and distinctions began to accumulate. In 1950, Gödel addressed the International Congress of Mathematicians and the next year received an honorary degree from Yale; in 1951, he also received the Einstein award and delivered the Gibbs lecture to the American Mathematical Society. Harvard gave him an honorary degree in 1952 and in 1975 he received the National Medal of Science. That same year he was scheduled to receive an honorary degree from Princeton, but ill health kept him from the ceremony. By contrast, Gödel refused honors from Austria, at least as long as he lived; however, the University of Vienna gave him an honorary doctorate posthumously.

Gödel had a distrust of medicine that amounted in his later years to paranoia. In late December of 1977 he was hospitalized and he died on January 14, 1978 of malnutrition, brought on by his refusal to eat because of his fear of poisoning. His wife survived him by three years; they had no children. Gödel's heirs were the mathematical community to which he left his work and the challenge of understanding the effects of his results. The year after his death Douglas Hofstadter's book *Gödel, Escher, Bach* became a bestseller, illustrating Gödel's ideas in terms of art and music.

SELECTED WRITINGS BY GÖDEL:

Books

Collected Works, edited by Solomon Feferman and others, 4 volumes, Oxford University Press, 1986-.

SOURCES:

Books

Dawson, John W., Jr., *Logical Dilemmas,* A & K Peters, 1995.

Gillespie, Charles Coulson, editor, *Dictionary of Scientific Biography,* Volume 17, Scribner, 1990, pp. 348–357.

Hofstadter, Douglas R., *Gödel, Escher, Bach,* Basic Books, 1979

Nagel, Ernest, and J. R. Newman, *Gödel's Proof,* New York University Press, 1958.

Van Heijenoort, Jean, editor, *From Frege to Gödel,* Harvard University Press, 1967.

Yourgrau, Palle, *The Disappearance of Time,* Cambridge University Press, 1991.

Periodicals

Lucas, J. R., "Minds, Machines and Gödel," *Philosophy,* 1961, pp. 120–124.

—*Sketch by Thomas Drucker*

Maria Goeppert-Mayer

Maria Goeppert-Mayer
1906-1972
German American physicist

Maria Goeppert-Mayer was one of the inner circle of nuclear physicists who developed the atomic fission bomb at the secret laboratory at Los Alamos, New Mexico, during World War II. Through her theoretical research with nuclear physicists **Enrico Fermi** and **Edward Teller**, Goeppert-Mayer developed a model for the structure of atomic nuclei. In 1963, for her work on nuclear structure, she became the first woman awarded the Nobel Prize for theoretical physics, sharing the prize with **J. Hans D. Jensen**, a German physicist. The two scientists, who had reached the same conclusions independently, later collaborated on a book explaining their model.

An only child, Goeppert-Mayer was born Maria Göppert on July 28, 1906, in the German city of Kattowitz in Upper Silesia (now Katowice, Poland). When she was four, her father, Dr. Friedrich Göppert, was appointed professor of pediatrics at the University at Göttingen, Germany. Situated in an old medieval town, the university had historically been respected for its mathematics department, but was on its way to becoming the European center for yet another discipline—theoretical physics. Maria's mother, Maria Wolff Göppert, was a former teacher of piano and French who delighted in entertaining faculty members with lavish dinner parties and providing a home filled with flowers and music for her only daughter.

Dr. Göppert was a most progressive pediatrician for the times, as he started a well-baby clinic and believed that all children, male or female, should be adventuresome risk-takers. His philosophy on child rearing had a profound effect on his daughter, who idolized her father and treasured her long country walks with him, collecting fossils and learning the names of plants. Because the Göpperts came from several generations of university professors, it was unstated but expected that Maria would continue the family tradition.

When Maria was just eight, World War I interrupted the family's rather idyllic university life with harsh wartime deprivation. After the war, life was still hard because of postwar inflation and food shortages. Maria Göppert attended a small private school run by female suffragists to ready young girls for university studies. The school went bankrupt when Göppert had completed only two of the customary three years of preparatory school. Nonetheless, she took and passed her university entrance exam.

From Quantum Mechanics to the Bomb

The University of Göttingen that Göppert entered in 1924 was in the process of becoming a center for the study of quantum mechanics—the mathematical study of the behavior of atomic particles. Many well-known physicists visited Göttingen, including **Niels Bohr**, a Danish physicist who developed a model of the atom. Noted physicist **Max Born** joined the Göttingen faculty and became a close friend of Göppert's family. Göppert, now enrolled as a student, began attending Max Born's physics seminars and decided to study physics instead of mathematics, with an eye toward teaching. Her prospects of being taken seriously were slim: there was only one female professor at Göttingen, and she taught for "love," receiving no salary.

In 1927 Göppert's father died. She continued her study, determined to finish her doctorate in physics. She spent a semester in Cambridge, England, where she learned English and met **Ernest Rutherford**, the discoverer of the electron. Upon her return to Göttingen, her mother began taking student boarders into their grand house. One was an American physical chemistry student from California, Joseph E. Mayer, studying in Göttingen on a grant. Over the next several years, Maria and Joe became close, going hiking, skiing, swimming and playing tennis. When they married, in 1930, Maria adopted the hyphenated form of their names. (When they later moved to the United States, the spelling of her family name was anglicized to "Goeppert.") Soon after her marriage she completed her doctorate with a thesis entitled "On Elemental Processes with Two Quantum Jumps."

After Joseph Mayer finished his studies, the young scientists moved to the United States, where Mayer had been offered a job at Johns Hopkins University in Baltimore, Maryland. Goeppert-Mayer found it difficult to adjust. She was not considered eligible for an appointment at the same university as her husband, but rather was considered a volunteer associate, what her biographer Joan Dash calls a "fringe benefit" wife. She had a tiny office, little pay, and no significant official responsibilities. Nonetheless, her position did allow her to conduct research on energy transfer on solid surfaces with physicist Karl Herzfeld, and she collaborated with him and her husband on several papers. Later, she turned her attention to the quantum mechanical electronic levels of benzene and of some dyes. During summers she returned to Göttingen, where she wrote several papers with Max Born on beta ray decay—the emissions of high-speed electrons that are given off by radioactive nuclei.

These summers of physics research were cut off as Germany was again preparing for war. Max Born left Germany for the safety of England. Returning to the states, Goeppert-Mayer applied for her American citizenship and she and Joe started a family. They would have two children, Marianne and Peter. Soon she became friends with Edward Teller, a Hungarian refugee who would play a key role in the development of the hydrogen bomb.

When Joe unexpectedly lost his position at Johns Hopkins, he and Goeppert-Mayer left for Columbia University in New York. There they wrote a book together, *Statistical Mechanics,* which became a classic in the field. As Goeppert-Mayer had no teaching credentials to place on the title page, their friend **Harold Urey**, a Nobel Prize-winning chemist, arranged for her to give some lectures so that she could be listed as "lecturer in chemistry at Columbia."

In New York, Goeppert-Mayer made the acquaintance of Enrico Fermi, winner of the Nobel Prize for physics for his work on radioactivity. Fermi had recently emigrated from Italy and was at Columbia on a grant researching nuclear fission. Nuclear fission—splitting an atom in a way that released energy—had been discovered by German scientists **Otto Hahn**, **Fritz Strassmann**, and **Lise Meitner**. The German scientists had bombarded uranium nuclei with neutrons, resulting in the release of energy. Because Germany was building its arsenal for war, Fermi had joined other scientists in convincing the United States government that it must institute a nuclear program of its own so as not to be at Hitler's mercy should Germany develop a nuclear weapon. Goeppert-Mayer joined Fermi's team of researchers, although once again the arrangement was informal and without pay.

In 1941, the United States formally entered World War II. Goeppert-Mayer was offered her first real teaching job, a half-time position at Sarah Lawrence College in Bronxville, New York. A few months later she was invited by Harold Urey to join a research group he was assembling at Columbia University to separate uranium–235, which is capable of nuclear fission, from the more abundant isotope uranium–238, which is not. The group, which worked in secret, was given the code name SAM—Substitute Alloy Metals. The uranium was to be the fuel for a nuclear fission bomb.

Like many scientists, Goeppert-Mayer had mixed feelings about working on the development of an atomic bomb. (Her friend Max Born, for instance, had refused to work on the project.) She had to keep her work a secret from her husband, even though he himself was working on defense-related work, often in the Pacific. Moreover, while she loved her adopted country, she had many friends and relatives in Germany. To her relief, the war in Europe was over early in 1945, before the bomb was ready. However, at Los Alamos Laboratory in New Mexico the bomb was still being developed. At Edward Teller's request, Goeppert-Mayer made several visits to Los Alamos to meet with other physicists, including Niels Bohr and Enrico Fermi, who were working on uranium fission. In August of 1945 atomic bombs were dropped on the

Japanese cities of Hiroshima and Nagasaki with a destructive ferocity never before seen. According to biographer Joan Dash, by this time Goeppert-Mayer's ambivalence about the nuclear weapons program had turned to distaste, and she was glad she had played a relatively small part in the development of such a deadly weapon.

The "Madonna of the Onion" Wins the Nobel Prize

After the war, Goeppert-Mayer returned to teach at Sarah Lawrence. Then, in 1946, her husband was offered a full professorship at the University of Chicago's newly established Institute of Nuclear Studies, where Fermi, Teller, and Urey were also working. Goeppert-Mayer was offered an unpaid position as voluntary associate professor; the university had a rule, common at the time, against hiring both a husband and wife as professors. However, soon afterwards, Goeppert-Mayer was asked to become a senior physicist at the Argonne National Laboratory, where a nuclear reactor was under construction. It was the first time she had been offered a position and salary that put her on an even footing with her colleagues.

Again her association with Edward Teller was valuable. He asked her to work on his theory about the origin of the elements. They found that some elements, such as tin and lead, were more abundant than could be predicted by current theories. The same elements were also unusually stable. When Goeppert-Mayer charted the number of protons and neutrons in the nuclei of these elements, she noticed that the same few numbers recurred over and over again. Eventually she began to call these her "magic numbers." When Teller began focusing his attention on nuclear weapons and lost interest in the project, Goeppert-Mayer began discussing her ideas with Enrico Fermi.

Goeppert-Mayer had identified seven "magic numbers": 2, 8, 20, 28, 50, 82, and 126. Any element that had one of these numbers of protons or neutrons was very stable, and she wondered why. She began to think of a shell model for the nucleus, similar to the orbital model of electrons spinning around the nucleus. Perhaps the nucleus of an atom was something like an onion, with layers of protons and neutrons revolving around each other. Her "magic numbers" would represent the points at which the various layers, or "shells," would be complete. Goeppert-Mayer's likening of the nucleus to an onion led fellow physicist **Wolfgang Pauli** to dub her the "Madonna of the Onion." Further calculations suggested the presence of "spin-orbit coupling": the particles in the nucleus, she hypothesized, were both spinning on their axes and orbiting a central point—like spinning dancers, in her analogy, some moving clockwise and others counter-clockwise.

Goeppert-Mayer published her hypothesis in *Physical Review* in 1949. A month before her work appeared, a similar paper was published by J. Hans D. Jensen of Heidelberg, Germany. Goeppert-Mayer and Jensen began corresponding and eventually decided to write a book together. During the four years that it took to complete the book, Jensen stayed with the Goeppert-Mayers in Chicago. *Elementary Theory of Nuclear Shell Structure* gained widespread acceptance on both sides of the Atlantic for the theory they had discovered independently.

In 1959, Goeppert-Mayer and her husband were both offered positions at the University of California's new San Diego campus. Unfortunately, soon after settling into a new home in La Jolla, California, Goeppert-Mayer suffered a stroke which left an arm paralyzed. Some years earlier she had also lost the hearing in one ear. Slowed but not defeated, Goeppert-Mayer continued her work.

In November of 1963 Goeppert-Mayer received word that she and Jensen were to share the Nobel Prize for physics with **Eugene Paul Wigner**, a colleague studying quantum mechanics who had once been skeptical of her magic numbers. Goeppert-Mayer had finally been accepted as a serious scientist. According to biographer Olga Opfell, she would later comment that the work itself had been more exciting than winning the prize.

Goeppert-Mayer continued to teach and do research in San Diego, as well as grow orchids and give parties at her house in La Jolla. She enjoyed visits with her granddaughter, whose parents were daughter Marianne, an astronomer, and son-in-law Donat Wentzel, an astrophysicist. Her son Peter was now an assistant professor of economics, keeping up Goeppert-Mayer's family tradition of university teaching.

Goeppert-Mayer was made a member of the National Academy of Sciences and received several honorary doctorates. Her health, however, began to fail. A lifelong smoker debilitated by her stroke, she began to have heart problems. She had a pacemaker inserted in 1968. Late in 1971, Goeppert-Mayer suffered a heart attack that left her in a coma. She died on February 20, 1972.

SELECTED WRITINGS BY GOEPPERT-MAYER:

Books

(With Joseph E. Mayer) *Statistical Mechanics,* Wiley, 1940.

(With J. Hans D. Jensen) *Elementary Theory of Nuclear Shell Structure,* Wiley, 1955.

Periodicals

"Nuclear Configurations in the Spin-orbit Coupling Model: I. Empirical Evidence, and II. Theoretical Considerations," *Physical Review,* April, 1950.

Other

Goeppert-Mayer's papers are collected at Central University Library, University of California, San Diego.

SOURCES:

Books

Dash, Joan, *The Triumph of Discovery: Women Scientists Who Won the Nobel Prize,* Messner, 1991.

Opfell, Olga S., *The Lady Laureates: Women Who Have Won the Nobel Prize,* Scarecrow, 1978, pp. 194–208.

Sach, Robert G., *Maria Goeppert-Mayer, 1906–1972: A Biographical Memoir,* National Academy of Science of the United States, 1979.

—*Sketch by Barbara A. Branca*

George W. Goethals
1858-1928
American engineer

George W. Goethals is credited with leading the U.S. Army in constructing the Panama Canal (for which he received the thanks of Congress in 1915), although he was the third engineer to take on the task. From 1914 to 1916, Goethals served as the first governor of the Canal Zone; he rose to the military rank of major-general before retiring as a civil engineer. The Goethals Bridge between Staten Island and New Jersey was named for him.

George Washington Goethals was born in Brooklyn, New York, on June 29, 1858, the second of three children of Belgian immigrants John Goethals, a woodworker, and Marie Baron. Goethals studied at the College of the City of New York from 1873 to 1876. He later attended the U.S. Military Academy at West Point, from which he graduated in 1880. During the summer of 1883 he met a classmate's sister, Effie Rodman, whom he married in 1884; they had two sons. George Rodman Goethals would follow in his father's footsteps, graduating from West Point in 1904 and later serving in the U.S. Army in the Canal Zone. Thomas Rodman Goethals attended Harvard University and became a doctor.

President Roosevelt Appoints Goethals to Direct Building of Panama Canal

After two civilian chief engineers resigned from the Panama Canal project, President Theodore Roosevelt decided to choose a successor from the Army Corps of Engineers—in other words, someone who would have to stay until relieved of duty. Thus in 1907 Roosevelt appointed Goethals to direct the building of the Panama Canal. Although he was an Army engineer, Goethals arrived to take his post not in uniform, but dressed in a white civilian suit that became his signature. When Goethals arrived, work had begun on the landscape, and much effort had been directed toward eliminating yellow fever and malaria, but most of the digging still needed to be done.

In *The Truth about the Panama Canal,* Denison Kitchel noted that "the key to Goethals' success, aside from the great organizational ability and leadership he brought to the task, was probably the great amount of authority Roosevelt gave to him. He wore three hats at the same time, chairman of the commission, chief engineer of the project, and president of the railroad." Kitchel added that the Panama Canal project was the largest test of engineering skill, coordination, and endurance at the time of its completion. "The creation of Goethals' 'bridge of water' was a series of engineering triumphs in the various phases of the enterprise: dredging the approach channels, clearing the Chagres valley, building the massive earthen dam at Gatun, forming the record-size lake, building and installing the locks, developing the water, power and drainage systems, and finally, the most difficult of all, completing the cut through the Continental Divide." Goethals had to overcome problems with organization, supplies, disease, climate, and labor to complete the canal ahead of schedule in 1914. The workforce averaged 47,308 on the payroll from 1907 to 1914, with a high of 56,654 in 1913.

The completion of the Panama Canal was overshadowed, however, by the beginning of World War I. Global attention was centered on Europe when the S.S. *Ancon* made the first official transit of the canal on August 15, 1914. After completing the Panama Canal project, Goethals retired from the armed services and became governor of the Panama Canal through 1916. He returned to active duty in the U.S. Army from 1917 to 1919. His service during World War I resulted in several war decorations, including a distinguished service medal. After the war, Goethals again retired from the military, this time to a career as a civil engineer. He headed the consulting engineering firm of George W. Goethals and Co. from 1923 to 1928. The College of the City of New York awarded Goethals an honorary bachelor of science degree in 1922. Goethals also accepted honorary degrees from Harvard, Yale, Columbia, the University of Pennsylvania, Johns Hopkins, Chicago Polytechnic, Princeton, Rutgers, and Dartmouth. Goethals died of cancer in New York on January 21, 1928, and was buried at West Point. Goethals's family presented his decorations, medals, and honorary degrees to the U.S. Military Academy during alumni week of 1928.

SELECTED WRITINGS BY GOETHALS:

Books

Government of the Canal Zone, Princeton University Press, 1915.

The Panama Canal: An Engineering Treatise, Volumes I and II, McGraw, 1916.

Periodicals

National Geographic, April, 1909, pp. 334–55.

"The Panama Canal," *National Geographic,* February, 1911, pp. 148–211.

SOURCES:

Books

Bishop, Joseph Bucklin, and Farnham Bishop, *Goethals: Genius of the Panama Canal, A Biography,* Harper, 1930.

Kitchel, Denison, *The Truth about the Panama Canal,* Arlington House, 1978.

McCullough, David, *The Path between the Seas: The Creation of the Panama Canal, 1870–1914,* Simon & Schuster, 1977.

—Sketch by Melinda Jardon Thach

Thomas Gold
1920-
Austrian-born American astronomer

Astronomer Thomas Gold is no stranger to controversy. He continues to argue for a "steady-state" theory of the origin of the universe rather than the more popular big bang thesis. Gold

Thomas Gold

has also postulated a geological origin of petroleum rather than the traditional biological one. And though he has been overruled by the majority of the scientific community on both counts, Gold stands by his theories. He has made a significant—and unquestioned—contribution with his 1970s argument that pulsars, a new type of star first described by **Antony Hewish**, are rapidly rotating neutron stars whose slowdown can be measured on Earth.

Born in Vienna, Austria, on May 22, 1920, to businessman Max Gold and his wife Josephine, Thomas Gold was ten when the family left to live in Berlin, Germany. That move lasted only three years: the family was intensely opposed to Hitler, and Gold's father was Jewish; the family's next move was to England. From that base young Thomas attended boarding school in Switzerland until 1938; he then returned to England to attend Cambridge University, graduating there in 1942 and staying on to obtain his master's degree in 1945. It was at Cambridge that Gold's penchant for taking on the establishment first asserted itself. For his master's thesis he proposed that in human hearing the inner ear generates its own tone.

He was unprepared for the storm of ridicule his theory engendered—a reaction strong enough to dissuade him not to enter the field. But Gold hadn't finished with the subject; thirty-six years later, he related to *Omni* that he was the guest of honor at a conference of cochlea specialists who supported his theory from back in his Cambridge days (one family, studies found, actually emitted sound from their ears loud enough to be heard without instruments).

Studying How the Universe Began

Following his schooling, Gold served during World War II in the Admiralty's radar research unit alongside his Cambridge mates **Fred Hoyle** and **Hermann Bondi**, who, he said in an interview with Joan Oleck, were forever challenging him verbally on physics questions from cosmology, the branch of astronomy that deals with the origins of the universe. "I was very flighty; I had no plans for my career. I did what was interesting," Gold said. Intrigued by his older friends' interests, he drifted into cosmology as a profession, working as a lecturer in physics at Cambridge from 1948 to 1952. It was during this period that he married his first wife, Merle Tuberg Gold. Their union produced three children. Moving up in his profession, Gold then joined the Royal Greenwich Observatory as assistant to the astronomer royal for three years. But a change in management set Gold to looking for a new environment, and he chose the United States.

Moving to the United States in 1956, Gold spent a year at Harvard before taking a post at Cornell University where he remains today. He also became director of the Center for Radiophysics and Space Research in 1959. He became a U.S. citizen in the early sixties and married his second wife, Carvel Beyer Gold, in 1972. This second marriage made Gold a father for the fourth time.

The kind of controversy Gold stirred up with his hearing theory was repeated as he made a name for himself in his field. For many years the cosmological principle has stated that the universe is homogenous and therefore looks the same from whichever point one regards it. The cosmological principle is a theory of the structure of the universe springing from the work of **Edwin Hubble**, who promoted the idea that our Milky Way is but one of countless galaxies that are moving away from each other (with a velocity in proportion to the distance between them) in an expanding universe, an idea justified in the equations of **Albert Einstein**'s theory of relativity.

In 1948 Gold and Bondi published *The Steady-State Theory of the Expanding Universe,* postulating what they called "the perfect cosmological principle." This was an extension of the cosmological principle and held that if the universe looks the same viewed from any point, then this idea ought to hold *in time* as well as in space: the universe ought to seem the same at any time in the past or future. This theory precluded the notion that the galaxies were closer to each other in the past and will be farther from each other in the future.

Instead, Gold and Bondi's steady-state theory held new matter forms in the space between galaxies as they separate. By the time that separation has doubled, enough matter has formed to make up a new galaxy; thus, the density with which galaxies fill space remains unchanged. The overall picture has not changed and the total number of galaxies has not increased, the two scientists said, because the farther a galaxy recedes from a reference point, the faster it moves until it reaches the speed of light and moves out of our universe.

To reconcile this work with that of Hubble—which showed that the galaxies are receding and the universe expanding—Gold and Bondi introduced another startling idea: the continuous creation theory. This explained the creation of new matter from nothing by calculating that only one hydrogen atom per cubic kilometer of space would be required every ten years, an amount too small to be detected. This then would form new galaxies at a rate just sufficient to make up for the recession of the old ones.

Although these theories proved attractive to many researchers, American scientists **Arno Penzias** and **Robert Woodrow Wilson** discovered in the 1960s the existence of background radiation, which others had predicted would result from a big bang scenario. Maarten Schmidt added more substance to the big bang theory with his work on quasars, celestial objects that resemble stars but are far more distant, and which emit radiation and radio waves.

Rejected by the scientific community, Gold found far more support with his work on pulsars. When Hewish discovered this new type of star with its high-frequency radio signal, Gold proposed a structure capable of producing this effect: rapidly rotating neutron stars, celestial objects that result from the collapse of much larger stellar bodies. These stars would be small and dense enough to rotate with a period equivalent to the radio pulses, putting out a beam of energy picked up on earth as a series of pulses.

This theory gained credence once pulsars were detected in the Crab and Vela nebulae. Gold then went on to predict that pulsars should be slowing down by a small but measurable amount because of their loss of energy: subsequent measurements proved him to be right on target.

Begins Controversial Search for Fuel

In 1975 Gold began to publicly debate the long-held scientific belief that oil and gas reserves result from decomposing organic material. He argued instead that virtually inexhaustible quantities of methane were trapped inside the Earth when the planet was formed, and he set about to prove his theory.

Unable to raise money in the United States, Gold presented his ideas to Vattenfall, Sweden's government-owned electric utility. Noting the region surrounding Siljan Lake, 150 miles north of Stockholm, Gold pointed out how the lake had been created by a meteor and the surrounding granite fractured for miles beneath the surface by the blow. A huge amount of oil and gas must have migrated from the earth's mantle into these fractures.

The Vattenfall board was persuaded and promptly provided four million dollars of financing for the project; more funds came from a private institute in Chicago, and a Swedish entrepreneur formed a holding company to buy shares to make up the investment from outside Vattenfall required by the Swedish government. The stock took off.

But the project itself never did. In July, 1986, the drilling began, with repairs swallowing up the financial reserves. Drilling still managed to reach 6.7 kilometers, but still there was no oil. The project was abandoned, despite Gold's team's contention they had struck oil, or at least oily sludge. Critics countered that this was merely drilling fluid and contaminants from the drilling operation. In October, 1991, the drilling began again nearby, reaching 6.1 kilometers. Still no oil. Gold, however, still clings to his theory, and in fact the scientific community has shifted toward his side, impressed at the biological material found in the most unexpected places. "What we now believe is that microbiological life has penetrated into every possible place where there is a chemical energy source for them, and one of these is petroleum in conjunction with oxygen in the rocks," Gold explained to Joan Oleck.

SELECTED WRITINGS BY GOLD:

Books

The Nature of Time, Cornell University Press, 1967.

Periodicals

"Sweden's Siljan Ring Well Evaluated," *Oil and Gas Journal,* Volume 89, January 14, 1991, p. 76.

SOURCES:

Books

Terzian, Yervant, and Elizabeth Bilson, editors, *Cosmology and Astrophysics: Essays in Honor of Thomas Gold,* Cornell University Press, 1982.

Periodicals

Begley, Sharon, "Gushers At 30,000 Feet; Dig Deeper Says This Theorist, for the Black Gold," *Newsweek,* June 27, 1988, p. 53.

Fuhrman, Peter, "A Tulip Wilts in Stockholm," *Forbes,* April 4, 1988, p. 49.

Kerr, Richard A., "When A Radical Experiment Goes Bust," *Science,* Volume 247, March 9, 1990, p. 1177.

Liversidge, Anthony, "Heresy! Three Modern Galileos," *Omni,* June, 1993, p. 44.

Marbach, William D., "Has A Controversial Oil Theory Struck Proof—Or Struck Out?" *Business Week,* June 13, 1988, p. 60.

"The Origins of Oil and Gas: Eureka, Perhaps," *Economist,* June 25, 1988, p. 88.

Other

Gold, Thomas, interview conducted with Joan Oleck, January, 1994.

—Sketch by Joan Oleck

Adele Goldberg
1945-
American computer scientist

A computer scientist and computer corporate executive, Adele Goldberg is best known for her work with **Alan Kay** and others in developing the object-oriented computing language Smalltalk in the 1970s and 1980s. For this work she has won both the 1987 Software Systems Award from the Association for Computing Machinery and *PC Magazine's* 1990 Lifetime Achievement Award. Goldberg was born on July 7, 1945, in Cleveland, Ohio, and grew up in Chicago, Illinois. Her parents were Lillian and Morris Goldberg. She received her bachelor's degree in mathematics from the University of Michigan at Ann Arbor, her master's degree in information science from the University of Chicago, and her Ph.D. in information science in 1973 from the University of Chicago. Her doctoral dissertation, titled "Computer-Assisted Instruction: The Application of Theorem-Proving to Adaptive Response Analysis," was prepared at Stanford University while she was a visiting research associate there. She has two daughters, Rachel and Rebecca.

Improves Speed and Accessibility of Programming

Goldberg began working as a researcher for Xerox in 1973 at its famous think-tank, the Palo Alto

Adele Goldberg

Research Center (PARC) in California. One of her most important accomplishments at PARC was managing the System Concepts Laboratory, whose team developed Smalltalk–80, an object-oriented programming language (object-oriented programming languages contrast with procedure-oriented programming languages such as BASIC, FORTRAN, and COBOL).

When Smalltalk was designed, a set of programming tools and a user interface were also invented. The user interface was the first to use pictures that allowed programmers to interact with the computer; a mouse could be utilized to interact with overlapping windows on graphical display screens. These windows contained the tools, menus, or lists of items which programmers employed to send messages to the system. Systems designed for procedure-oriented languages had previously restricted their users to keyboards and to typing in commands on lines of the computer screen. Because of this kind of input system, the interfaces of procedure-oriented programs are often called "command-line interfaces." Many consider object-oriented programming interfaces to be easier for programmers to use.

Object-oriented programming is organized around several important ideas. One of these ideas is modularity. In object-oriented programs, users create autonomous "objects" or modules, each of which contains its own private memory and set of operations. These objects or modules can pass messages to each other requesting information as actions. The objects in object-oriented programming are often represented by an icon and they can look very simple; while appearing very simple on a graphical interface, however, the icon, object, or module can conceal a very complex structure of data and functions. An important virtue of these autonomous objects is that they can be readily customized, copied, and placed where a user wants them. A programmer, for example, may have to assemble relatively few objects to create a program, which can save a lot of time.

Object-oriented programming is organized around a second important idea: that objects correspond to the identifiable parts in a problem situation. For example, if a problem is composed of ten parts, then the programmer can develop ten objects corresponding to each part of the problem, and these objects can send messages to each other to solve the problem. The objects have several important benefits. One advantage is that each can be reused in other situations in which similar problems occur; for example, a company could have many production lines for manufacturing its products, and a program with ten modules could be developed for troubleshooting problems with one production line. If the company needed a troubleshooting program on a second production line, then a programmer would not have to reinvent ten modules to solve this problem. He or she could simply import the useful modules from the first production line, customize them to solve the problems specific to the second production line, and quickly put the program to work. Because the objects in this type of programming are reusable and customizable, and because the objects correspond to the identifiable parts of a problem situation, they can be transferred from one situation to another, saving time and money.

A third important concept behind object-oriented programming is the reusable interface. An interface is the common boundary between two entities; these entities might include people, computer screens, or programs inside a computer system. If an interface is reusable, then it does not have to be redesigned each time it is used in a different situation. Reusable interfaces in object-oriented programs allow data to be passed more easily between objects or modules inside a computer system; they allow data to be passed more easily between a user and the computer interface (examples would be windows and pull-down menus), and they allow data to be passed more easily across a variety of applications in different business environments. Because of the idea of the reusable interface, Smalltalk–80's interface is much more economical and accessible than procedure-oriented interfaces. The windows software interfaces that became so popular in the late 1980s were direct descendants of the innovations developed at PARC by Goldberg, **Alan Kay**, and others.

Cofounds Her Own Software Company

After spending fourteen years at Xerox's Palo Alto Research Center developing object-oriented programming, Goldberg wanted to be sure that Smalltalk got a wider audience. She worked out a technology exchange agreement with Xerox, and in 1988 she cofounded ParcPlace Systems, a company that sells development tools for Smalltalk-based applications. Goldberg served as president and chief executive officer of ParcPlace from March, 1988, to April, 1992. Since then she has served the company as chief strategist and chairman of the board. ParcPlace went public on February 1, 1994, and saw its opening stock offer rise six dollars a share before the day was over, a very strong showing. Its revenues in the early 1990s were estimated at over twenty million dollars a year.

Goldberg was president of the Association for Computing Machinery (ACM) from 1984 to 1986, and she won the 1987 ACM Software Systems Award with **Alan Kay** and Dan Ingalls. She served as ACM's national secretary, and as editor-in-chief of the ACM journal *Computing Surveys;* she has also been a member of several ACM boards. She was a member of the scientific advisory board for the German National Research Centers, and was a fellow of the ACM. She wrote a regular column for *Object* magazine called "Wishful Thinking." One of her most significant honors was *PC Magazine's* 1990 Lifetime Achievement Award.

Since 1990, Goldberg has concentrated on issues that help programmers become more effective in using object-oriented technology to solve their problems. She has written extensively and lectured worldwide on project management as well as on the analytical and design methods needed to implement and advance object-oriented technology. The object-oriented programs sold by ParcPlace will considerably improve the productivity of programmers, because they give programmers greater opportunities to reuse existing objects and because they let programmers construct graphical user interfaces and database applications with visual construction tools.

SELECTED WRITINGS BY GOLDBERG:

Books

(With David Robson) *Smalltalk-80: The Language and its Implementation,* Addison-Wesley, 1983, revised as *Smalltalk-80: The Language,* 1986.

Smalltalk-80: The Interactive Programming Environment, Addison-Wesley, 1984.

(With Alan Kay) "Personal Dynamic Media," *A History of Personal Workstations,* edited by Adele Goldberg, Addison-Wesley, 1988, pp. 254–263.

(With Kenneth S. Rubin) *Succeeding with Objects: Decision Frameworks for Project Management,* Addison-Wesley, 1995.

Periodicals

"Introducing the Smalltalk-80 System," *Byte,* August, 1981, pp. 14–26.

(With Kenneth S. Rubin) "Object Behavior Analysis," *Communications of the Association for Computing Machinery,* September, 1992, pp. 48–62.

SOURCES:

Books

Levy, Steven, *Insanely Great: The Life and Times of Macintosh, the Computer that Changed Everything,* Viking, 1994.

Periodicals

Garber, Joseph R., "Working Faster," *Forbes,* April 12, 1993, p. 110.

Ingalls, Daniel H. H., "Design Principles Behind Smalltalk," *Byte,* August, 1981, pp. 286–298.

Other

Goldberg, Adele, interview with Patrick Moore conducted February 7, 1994.

—Sketch by Patrick Moore

Peter Carl Goldmark
1906-1977
Hungarian-born American physicist and engineer

A world-renowned physicist and engineer, Peter Carl Goldmark is best remembered for his invention of the long-playing microgroove record (LP) and his contributions to the development of color television. He was a chief engineer at the Columbia Broadcasting System for over twenty years, and he became known as the father of educational medical imaging. For his work he was awarded numerous patents and honors, including the National Medal of Science presented by President Jimmy Carter in 1977.

Goldmark was born in Budapest, Hungary, on December 2, 1906, the eldest child of Alexander and Emmy Goldmark. His great-uncle Joseph Goldmark was a chemist and inventor who discovered red phosphorus, an ingredient in the manufacture of matches, and invented the percussion caps for rifles that were first used in the American Civil War. Goldmark showed an early interest in science, building a laboratory in the family bathroom and later a radio telegraph receiver. Fascinated by motion pictures and slide projection, he built a device for duplicating movies that once caught fire when its nitrate film overheated. His first patent was for a "knietaster"—a device that allowed drivers to activate the car horn with their knee, so they could keep both hands on the steering wheel. Goldmark was educated at universities in Berlin and Vienna. He studied with Heinrich Mache, a nuclear physicist, and received a Ph.D. in physics from the Physical Institute at the University of Vienna in 1931. Mache presented Goldmark's dissertation, "A New Method for Determining the Velocity of Ions," before the Academy of Science in Vienna.

Dissertation Topic Forms Basis for Color Television Research

The work Goldmark did for his Ph.D. served as a basis for his remarkable innovations in television. While an undergraduate student in Vienna, Goldmark and a friend assembled a television receiver with a screen the size of a postage stamp. It was on this set that Goldmark saw his first television image in 1926, part of an experimental broadcast by the newly formed British Broadcasting Company in London. In 1931, Goldmark was hired in England as a television engineer at Pye Radio, Ltd., in Cambridge. He served there as head of the television department until 1933, when he moved to the United States and began working as a consultant for a number of television and radio companies in New York City. He was hired in 1936 as chief engineer of the newly formed television research department at CBS.

In 1940, after witnessing the brilliant color fidelity of "Gone with the Wind," Goldmark decided that black-and-white television was inferior and he resolved to invent color television. The system he devised, called the "field sequential system" of color television, was first demonstrated in New York on August 29, 1940; the test involved pictures of flowers, red sails in the sunset, and a girl chasing a ball on a beach. The system worked by using a rapidly spinning three-color disk to film images, which were then transmitted and viewed through a similar disk. The Federal Communications Commission eventually decided the system was too cumbersome for final approval, because it could not be adapted to the existing technology for black-and-white television. Although it never achieved commercial acceptance, Goldmark's system was widely used for instructional purposes. In May 1949 at the University of Pennsylvania, the first surgical operation to be televised in color used the sequential field system, and after that date the field sequential system continued to be used for medical education. The FCC later adopted as the industry standard a method developed by RCA called electronic color television; the system used electrons which were fired at red, green, and blue phosphorescent spots on the TV screen. Goldmark actually contributed to this method by creating a photographic mass production method for etching the red, green, and blue phosphorescent spots on the glass screens.

Respect for Music Inspires Revolution in Recording

Goldmark's love of music proved to have a profound effect on his life. Another great-uncle, Karl Goldmark, is considered one of the greatest Hungarian composers, and music remained very important to Goldmark's family. In his autobiography, *Maverick Inventor: My Turbulent Years at CBS,* Goldmark relates how his family lived on the Danube in Budapest during the 1919 civil war in Hungary. Rebels would cruise the river shooting at open windows along the banks. The Goldmarks were engrossed in the performance of a string quartet when a warning shout came from the river, ordering them to close their blinds. Goldmark's mother ignored the warning and kept the quartet at work. Shortly afterwards, a shot was fired into the ceiling, but much to the surprise of even young Peter his mother ignored the shot and silently insisted the musicians finish the movement. Only upon its completion did she close the blinds. This dedication to music as it was written was the motivating force of at least one of Goldmark's most important inventions.

In the fall of 1943, Goldmark was listening with a friend to a recent 78-rpm recording of Vladimir Horowitz playing Brahms's second piano concerto. He was so disturbed by the interruptions to change disks in the middle of movements that he resolved to create a new medium. The first LP was recorded with Goldmark on cello, a CBS secretary on piano, and an engineer on violin. In 1948, he officially demonstrated a recording system that would hold enough information to fit the average length of a movement (about twenty minutes) while offering improved fidelity. Goldmark's invention was pressed on vinyl, and it spun at 33 1/3 rpm. Considered a revolution in recorded music, it was soon adopted as the industry standard. By 1972, the LP accounted for a third of overall revenue at CBS.

At CBS, also under Goldmark's scientific supervision, the linotron was invented. Considered his most complex device, the linotron is a high-speed system for photocomposition which can electronically produce high-quality composition at the rate of 1000 characters per second.

During World War II Goldmark applied his scientific skills to the Allied war effort. In 1942, working for the Office of Scientific Research and Development, he helped design a device for jamming German radar; this was first used in the Allied invasion of Africa. He also contributed to the construction of what he called an "electronic spook navy"—a series of radio signals used to create radar distractions during the Allied invasion on D-Day. He did other important work for the government in the 1960s. After overcoming a series of technical obstacles, he contributed to NASA's lunar exploration by devising a technique for transmitting back to Earth high-resolution photographs taken by the Lunar Orbiter.

In 1971, Goldmark left CBS to found the Goldmark Communications Corporation, a subsidiary of Warner Communications. His aim was to stop the flow of people into the cities by creating a communications system to bring urban conveniences like entertainment, business, and medical centers to rural inhabitants. Goldmark's dedication to education, not only of young people but of adults, inspired a number of his other innovations. One such innovation was Electronic Video Recording (EVR), whereby any filmed or videotaped program could be transferred to a thin-film optical tape and stored in a small cartridge. The EVR player was attached to the antenna terminals of a standard television, and this allowed for the first time the showing of prerecorded programming in the home or classroom.

Goldmark became a naturalized citizen of the United States in 1937. He was married in 1936 to Muriel Gainsborough. This marriage ended and he married Frances Trainer in 1939; they were divorced after having four children. He later married Diane Davis, with whom he had two children. Goldmark maintained his interest in music throughout his life and was an accomplished player of both the cello and the piano. He was an avid skier, tennis player, and swimmer. Goldmark was also a humanitarian and educator, serving as head of the Antipoverty Office in Stamford, Connecticut and as a visiting professor for medical electronics at the University of Pennsylvania Medical School. In 1967, he was honored with the National Urban Service Award for his efforts in the country's War on Poverty. Goldmark was killed in an automobile accident in Westchester County, New York on December 7, 1977. He was seventy-one years old.

SELECTED WRITINGS BY GOLDMARK:

Books

(With Lee Edson) *Maverick Inventor: My Turbulent Years at CBS,* Saturday Review Press, 1973.

SOURCES:

Books

Crouse, W. H., editor, *Modern Men of Science,* Volume 2, McGraw-Hill, 1968, pp. 187–89.

Greene, J. E., editor, *Modern Scientists and Engineers,* McGraw-Hill, 1980, pp. 443–445.

Rothe, A., editor, *Current Biography,* H. W. Wilson, 1950, pp. 177–179.

Periodicals

"Crash Kills Peter Goldmark," *New York Times,* December 8, 1977.

—Sketch by John Henry Dreyfus

Winifred Goldring
1888-1971
American paleontologist

Winifred Goldring pursued a career in paleontology at a time when it was difficult for a woman to advance and succeed as a scientist. She did both, becoming a respected figure in her profession. Goldring was associated with the New York State Museum for forty years, rising to the position of state paleontologist, a post she held for fifteen years. In 1949 she became the first woman to be elected president of the Paleontological Society. A year later, Goldring became a vice president of the Geological Society of America, an organization that had elected her as a fellow in 1921.

Goldring was born February 1, 1888, just outside of Albany in Kenwood, New York. She was one of seven daughters and one son born to Frederick Goldring, an orchid grower and operator of a floral business, and Mary Grey Goldring, a one-time school teacher. When she was two, the family moved to Slingerlands, New York, southeast of Albany, to a home that Winifred lived in, on and off, for nearly eighty-one years. She attended local schools, graduating as valedictorian of her class in 1905.

Much of Goldring's college education was concentrated at Wellesley College in Massachusetts, where she studied geology and geography, developing her interest in paleontology. She earned her B.A. in 1909 and her M.A. in 1912. She took additional graduate level courses at Harvard, Columbia, and Johns Hopkins universities. Goldring began her career as a geology instructor at Wellesley and at the

Teacher's School of Science in Boston from 1912 to 1914.

Focuses on New York Fossils and Geology

In 1915 Goldring began her long association with the New York State Museum when she was hired as an assistant paleontologist. In subsequent years she was promoted to associate paleontologist, paleobotantist, assistant state paleontologist, and provisional state paleontologist. In 1939 Goldring was named state paleontologist, a position she filled with distinction and considerable energy until her retirement in 1950.

At the museum, and as a paleontologist, Goldring was particularly interested in the fossils and geology of New York state, especially those of the Devonian period, which flourished 345 to 395 million years ago. While her duties at the state museum required her to do much administrative work, she still found time to contribute to museum displays and engage in paleontological research. She enjoyed the process of creating museum displays, and her creation of a Devonian fossil forest diorama at the New York museum drew nationwide acclaim. As a researcher and educator, Goldring produced more than forty papers and books for journals and the general public. These ranged from paleontology handbooks for laypersons to a detailed 670-page book on the crinoids, a sea urchin-like animal, of New York.

For her achievements, Goldring was awarded an honorary doctor of science degree from Russell Sage College and Smith College in 1937 and 1957, respectively. In addition, she was a member of the American Association for the Advancement of Science, the New York Academy of Sciences, and the American Geophysical Union. Goldring remained single throughout her life and died in Albany on January 30, 1971.

SELECTED WRITINGS BY GOLDRING:

Books

The Devonian Crinoids of the State of New York, New York State Museum, 1923.

Handbook of Paleontology for Beginners and Amateurs; Part 1, The Fossils, New York State Museum, 1929.

Handbook of Paleontology for Beginners and Amateurs, Part 2, The Formations, New York State Museum, 1931.

Geology of the Berne Quadrangle, New York State Museum, 1935.

Geology of the Coxsackie Quadrangle, New York State Museum, 1943.

SOURCES:

Books

Memorials, Volume 3, Geological Society of America, 1974, pp. 96–101.

—Sketch by Joel Schwarz

Richard B. Goldschmidt

1878-1958

German-born American zoologist and geneticist

Richard B. Goldschmidt was a distinguished zoologist, biologist, and geneticist. Using moths, Goldschmidt conducted experiments on X-chromosomes to study spontaneous mutation, physiological genetics, and sex determination. He believed that the overall pattern of chromosomes and the chemical configuration of the chromosome molecule determine heredity, rather than the qualities of individual genes that make up the chromosomes. Forced out of Germany by the Nazis, Goldschmidt continued his work in the United States, and in 1940 published his magnum opus *The Material Basis of Evolution.* In this work, Goldschmidt theorized that macroevolution, in which large mutations he called "hopeful monsters" were created, led to the formation of new species.

Richard Benedict Goldschmidt was born in Frankfurt am Main, Germany, on April 12, 1878, to Salomon and Emma Rosette Flürscheim Goldschmidt, both members of old German-Jewish families. His father owned and managed a business consisting of a coffeehouse, wine trade, and confectionery. Goldschmidt attended the Gymnasium in Frankfurt. His passion for the natural sciences began early, perhaps because of visits to Frankfurt's splendid Senckenberg Museum. Goldschmidt himself offered another explanation. He related in his autobiography, *In and out of the Ivory Tower* that "during my first school year our family was enlarged by a baby sister. A few weeks before this event took place in our home I had watched a stork flying by, carrying a frog in his long beak. Rosa, the nurse, did not fail to tell me that the bird was carrying a baby to some family." The biologist continued: "When we children were admitted for the first time to my mother's bedroom to see the newborn sister, I hardly glanced at the old brown cradle . . . but insisted upon seeing my mother's leg. I supposed she was lying in bed because the stork had bitten her! I guess this was the beginning of my career as a biologist."

Goldschmidt entered the University of Heidelberg in 1896 as a medical student. He passed his premedical examinations after two years, then gave up medicine for zoology. He attended the University of Munich, where the famous zoologist Richard von Hertwig was teaching. In 1902, Goldschmidt returned to Heidelberg, continued his studies under Otto Bütschli, another zoologist, and defended his doctoral thesis on the maturation, fertilization, and embryonic development of the worm *Polystomum integerrimum.* Compulsory Army training interrupted his research for one year, after which Goldschmidt returned to Munich as Hertwig's assistant. He married Else Kühnlein in 1906, and they had two children: Ruth Emma and Hans.

Goldschmidt Pioneers Popularization of Science

At Hertwig's instigation, Goldschmidt began to offer popular science lectures. In doing so, he learned how to make even obscure topics clear to a general audience. He and Hertwig both felt that the popularization of science was the duty of a scientist. Over the years, Goldschmidt took on more of Hertwig's responsibilities. He ran the laboratory and advised Hertwig's research students and doctoral candidates; he also founded and edited the *Journal of Cytology* in 1906, which became a leading journal in the field. But he became frustrated by the university bureaucracy, which regarded him as an "assistant" long after he had taken on almost all of Hertwig's work.

A new opportunity arose in 1913, when Theodor Boveri and Karl Erich Correns organized the Kaiser Wilhelm Institute for Biology in Berlin. Goldschmidt accepted the directorship of the genetics department, an appointment he would hold until 1935. During his early years at the Institute, Goldschmidt investigated the genetics of sex determination, particularly as it related to hybrids of the nun moth. In 1915, the geneticist coined the term "intersex" to describe individuals which contained both male and female characteristics and yet had the same X-chromosome pattern in all of their cells. (This was in contrast to gynandromorphs, whose X-chromosome patterns vary from cell to cell, thus causing different sexual characteristics.) To account for intersexuality, Goldschmidt proposed the existence of sex factors whose strength or weakness, rather than number, would determine the sexual characteristics of an organism.

While the Institute was being built, Goldschmidt visited Japan, taking advantage of a travelling fellowship provided by Club Autour du Monde. There he continued his study of nun moths and taught. As a guest of the Imperial University in Tokyo, he promoted the popularization of science both by giving general lectures and by writing a book on heredity, to be translated for a Japanese popular encyclopedia of science.

Goldschmidt had hoped to be in Germany before war broke out, but his return from Japan took longer than anticipated. When World War I began, he had reached Honolulu. He went to San Francisco, where he learned that because of the British blockade, he could not travel to Germany. After two months in the Zoology Department of the University of California, Goldschmidt travelled to Yale University. He remained there for several years, doing pioneer work in tissue culture. In 1915, his wife and children were allowed to leave Germany and join him.

World Wars Interrupt Career

In 1917, Goldschmidt was placed in an internment camp in Fort Oglethorpe, Georgia, together with other "suspect" individuals of German nationality or descent. Although the experience was unpleasant, and the separation from his family was distressing, Goldschmidt and the other internees made the best of their situation. They played football, created a symphony orchestra (in which Goldschmidt played violin), and organized a camp university. The classes ranged from bookkeeping to languages to science; Goldschmidt studied Spanish and Chinese, and taught a biology class that was attended by four hundred men.

When Goldschmidt was finally repatriated to Germany, he returned to the Kaiser Wilhelm Institute. He found that the government was actively involved in the promotion of science, and that the annual meetings of the Kaiser Wilhelm Society were, as he said in his autobiography, "first-class scientific and social events." He continued to teach, lecture, and travel, revived the *Journal of Cytology,* took over another periodical, *Centralblatt,* and edited several others. During the years before World War II, he published extensively. As early as 1916, Goldschmidt had proposed a physiological basis to heredity, in which one gene corresponded to one enzyme. This theory was one of the first to link genetics and biology, and marked the start of physiological genetics. He published his work on this theory in 1920 in *The Mechanism and Physiology of Sex Determination.*

Because of his interest in the popularization of science, Goldschmidt then suggested to a German publisher, Dr. Ferdinand Springer, a plan for a series of popular science books written by eminent scholars. Dr. Springer liked both the idea and the title, *Verstandliche Wissenschaft* (*Science Made Understandable*). Goldschmidt's own book opened the series, and sold 15,000 copies before the Nazis stopped its sale. It was a "non-Aryan" work, and the German promotion of science had begun to be replaced by political interference.

As Hitler's power increased, German universities declined quickly and academic freedom died. Non-Aryan professors and students disappeared, and young, fanatical party members were put in charge. Nazis, not scholars, were now appointed to every available professorship and chair, including the newly-created chairs of military science and race doctrine. By 1935, the Nazi regime had made it impossible for Jewish scientists to work. Goldschmidt and his family left Germany for Berkeley, California. He became a professor in the Department of Zoology at the University of California, and, in 1942, an American citizen.

Goldschmidt brought with him to California his research on spontaneous mutation. During his first year in Berkeley, he lacked a proper laboratory in which to continue his research, but used his time to write a comprehensive book on physiological genetics. *The Material Basis of Evolution* reviewed previous work in the field, then suggested Goldschmidt's own ideas about the nature of the gene. The scientist had revised his earlier idea of "one gene, one enzyme" in favor of the concept of the chromosome as a giant chemical "macromolecule."

Goldschmidt Articulates Theory of "Hopeful Monsters"

Goldschmidt's theories of evolution and mutation are perhaps best known because of his "hopeful monsters," an unfortunate phrase that sometimes distracted readers from the important theories behind his research and conclusions. His ideas differed from those of the neo-Darwinians: Goldschmidt had spent years studying the genetics of geographic variation, and did not believe that it was the source of true evolution. He recognized the existence of microevolution, the constant accumulation of small changes in populations; this accounted for the geographic variations he had studied for so long. He did not believe, however, that microevolution led to the development of new species from existing ones, a phenomenon known as "speciation." In Goldschmidt's view, there were "bridgeless gaps" between true species which could not reasonably be explained by microevolution. They could, however, be accounted for by large sudden jumps—macroevolution. Goldschmidt proposed a connection between these jumps and the creation of "hopeful monsters" to explain how rapid changes could occur in lineages of organisms.

Goldschmidt believed that even a small change in the chromosomal "macromolecule" might have a disproportionately large effect on the physical traits of a species, what is known as its "phenotype." The zoologist further proposed that such effects, called "macromutations," might take place through "controlling" genes, which would regulate the expression of the organism's genetic blueprint. From his early studies of the nun moth, through his later work with different geographic species of gypsy moths, Goldschmidt came to believe that these mutants (once known as "monsters") or macromutations could occur in a single generation, produced by alteration of the early embryonic process. Under changing environmental conditions, such macromutations might possess some selective advantage, such as color changes in nun moths. The word "hopeful" referred to this possible advantage, as well as to the "hope" that the advantage, whatever it might be, might prove sufficiently useful to become a new norm. It was also theoretically possible that a given mutation might appear in enough members of a given population that similar "monsters" might meet and reproduce—another "hope."

With his "hopeful monsters," or macromutations, Goldschmidt presented an argument for macroevolution as the source of new species. But many of his contemporaries, Neo-Darwinists who ascribed speciation to to microevolution, were critical of this theory. By 1950, however, Goldschmidt's views were more accepted and he was invited to give the main address at the 50th Jubilee meeting of the Genetics Society of America. Stephen Jay Gould summarized the reception of Goldschmidt's ideas of macroevolution in *Natural History:* "When I studied evolutionary biology . . . , official rebuke and derision focused on Richard Goldschmidt, a famous geneticist who, we were told, had gone astray. . . . I do, however, predict that during this decade Goldschmidt will be largely vindicated in the world of evolutionary biology."

Goldschmidt's work and abilities were widely recognized. He received many honorary degrees: an M.D. from the University of Kiel, Germany, and honorary doctorates from the Universities of Madrid and Berlin. He was the author of more than 250 articles, and of nearly 20 books, which were translated into many languages. He was a member of Leopoldina, belonged to numerous academies and professional societies in 12 different countries, and was elected to the U.S. National Academy of Sciences in 1947, when he was almost seventy years old. Goldschmidt loved music, played both violin and viola, and was a connoisseur and collector of oriental art. He died in Berkeley on April 24, 1958.

SELECTED WRITINGS BY GOLDSCHMIDT:

Books

Die Urtiere, Teubner, 1906.

Mechanismus und Physiologie der Geschlechtisbestimung, Borntraeger, 1920, translated as *The Mechanism and Physiology of Sex Determination,* 1923.

Einführung in die Vererbungswissenschaft, Julius Springer, 1920.

Die Lehre von der Vererbung, Julius Springer, 1927.
Die sexuellen Zwischenstufen, Julius Springer, 1931.
Ascaris, the Biologist's Story of Life, [New York], 1937.
Physiological Genetics, McGraw-Hill, 1938.
The Material Basis of Evolution, Yale University Press, 1940, 1982.
Understanding Heredity: An Introduction to Genetics, Wiley, 1952.
Theoretical Genetics, University of California Press, 1955.
Portraits from Memory: Recollections of a Zoologist, University of Washington Press, 1956, published as *The Golden Age of Zoology,* 1966.
In and out of the Ivory Tower; the Autobiography of Richard B. Goldschmidt, University of Washington Press, 1960.

Periodicals

"On Spontaneous Mutation," *Proceedings of the National Academy of Sciences,* Volume 30, 1944, pp. 297–299.
"An Empirical Evolutionary Generalization Viewed from the Standpoint of Phenogenetics," *American Naturalist,* Volume 80, 1946, pp. 305–317.
"New Facts on Dependent, Successive, and Conjugated Spontaneous Mutation," *Journal of Experimental Zoology,* Volume 104, 1947, pp. 197–222.
"Evolution as Viewed by One Geneticist," *American Scientist,* Volume 40, 1952, pp. 84–98.
"Different Philosophies of Genetics," *Science,* Volume 119, 1954, pp. 703-710.

SOURCES:

Books

Richard Goldschmidt, Controversial Geneticist and Creative Biologist: A Critical Review of His Contributions; with an introduction by Karl von Frisch; edited by Leonie K. Piternick Birkhauser, 1980.
Stern, Curt, "Richard Benedict Goldschmidt," in the National Academy of Sciences' *Biographical Memoirs,* Volume XXXIX, Columbia University Press, 1967, pp. 141–192.

Periodicals

Gould, Stephen Jay, "Return of the Hopeful Monster," *Natural History,* Number 86, June, 1977, pp. 22—.

—*Sketch by Jessica Jahiel*

Victor Goldschmidt
1888-1947
Swiss-born Norwegian geochemist, petrologist, and mineralogist

Victor Goldschmidt, called the founding father of modern geochemistry, helped lay the foundations for the field of crystal chemistry. He was a highly esteemed mineralogist, petrologist, and geochemist who devoted the bulk of his research to the study of the composition of the earth. During his many years as a professor and director of a mineralogical institute in Norway, he also investigated solutions to practical geochemical problems at the request of the Norwegian government.

Victor Moritz Goldschmidt was born on January 27, 1888, in Zurich, Switzerland, to Heinrich Jacob Goldschmidt, a distinguished professor of physical chemistry, and Amelie Kohne. His family left Switzerland in 1900 and moved to Norway, where his father took a post as professor of physical chemists at the University of Christiania (now Oslo). Goldschmidt's family obtained Norwegian citizenship in 1905, the same year he entered the university to study chemistry, geology, and mineralogy. There he studied under the noted geologist and petrologist Waldemar Brogger, becoming a lecturer in mineralogy and crystallography at the university in 1909.

Goldschmidt obtained his Ph.D. in 1911. His doctoral dissertation on contact metamorphic rocks, which was based on rock samples from southern Norway, is considered a classic in the field of geochemistry. It served as the starting point for an investigation of the chemical elements that Goldschmidt pursued for three decades. In 1914, he became a full professor and director of the University of Christiana's mineralogical institute. In 1917, the Norwegian government asked Goldschmidt to conduct an investigation of the country's mineral resources, as it needed alternatives to chemicals that had been imported prior to World War I and were now in short supply. The government appointed him Chair of the Government Commission for Raw Materials and head of the Raw Materials Laboratory.

This led Goldschmidt into a new area of research—the study of the proportions of chemical elements in the earth's crust. His work was facilitated by the newly developed science of X-ray crystallography, which allowed Goldschmidt and his colleagues to determine the crystal structures of 200 compounds made up of seventy-five elements. He also developed the first tables of atomic and ionic radii for many of the elements, and showed how the hardness of crystals is based on their structures, ionic charges, and the proximity of their atomic particles.

Appointed Professor at Gottingen

In 1929, Goldschmidt moved to Gottingen, Germany, to assume the position of full professor at the Faculty of Natural Sciences and director of its mineralogical institute. As part of his investigation of the apportionment of elements outside the earth and its atmosphere, he began studying meteorites to ascertain the amounts of elements they contained. He researched numerous substances, including germanium, gallium, scandium, beryllium, selenium, arsenic, chromium, nickel, and zinc, using materials from both the earth and meteorites to devise a model of the earth. In this model, elements were distributed in different parts of the earth based on their charges and sizes. Goldschmidt stayed at Gottingen until 1935, when Nazi anti-Semitism made it impossible for him to continue his work. Returning to Oslo, he resumed work at the university there and assembled data he had collected at Gottingen on the distribution of chemical elements in the earth and the cosmos. He also began studying ways to use Norwegian olivine rock for use in industry.

When World War II began, Goldschmidt had confrontations with the Nazis that resulted in his imprisonment on several occasions. He narrowly escaped internment in a concentration camp in 1943 when, after the Nazis arrested him, he was rescued by the Norwegian underground. They managed to secretly get him onto a boat to Sweden, where fellow scientists arranged for a flight to Scotland.

In Scotland, Goldschmidt worked at the Macaulay Institute for Soil Research in Aberdeen. Later during the war, he worked as a consultant to the Rothamsted Agricultural Experiment Station in England. As reported in *Chemists,* Goldschmidt carried with him a cyanide suicide pill for use in the event the Nazis invaded England. When a colleague asked him for one, he responded, "Cyanide is for chemists; you, being a professor of mechanical engineering, will have to use the rope."

After the war, Goldschmidt returned to Oslo and his job as professor and director of the geological museum. There he worked on a newly-equipped raw materials laboratory supplied by the Norwegian Department of Commerce. He continued his work until his death on March 20, 1947.

Goldschmidt was a member of the Royal Society and the Geological Society of London, the latter of which awarded him the Wollaston Medal in 1944. He was also an honorary member of the British Mineralogical Society, the Geological Society of Edinburgh, and the Chemical Society of London. He wrote over 200 papers as well as a treatise, *Geochemistry,* which was published posthumously in 1954. Although he never married, he had many friends among his colleagues and students, many of whom became notable geochemists and heads of university departments.

SELECTED WRITINGS BY GOLDSCHMIDT:

Books

Geochemistry, edited by Alex Muir, [London], 1954.

SOURCES:

Books

Abbott, David, editor, *The Biographical Dictionary of Scientists,* Peter Bedrick Books, 1983.

Gillespie, Charles Coulston, editor, *Dictionary of Scientific Biography,* Volume 5, Scribner's, 1976, pp. 456–58.

Periodicals

New York Times, March 27, 1947, p. 28.

Science, April 4, 1947, p. 358.

—Sketch by Donna Olshansky

Avram Goldstein
1919-
American pharmacologist and neurobiologist

Avram Goldstein is a pharmacologist and neuroscientist who is internationally renowned for his studies of addictive drugs. He developed the scientific strategy used to demonstrate the existence of opiate receptors in the brain, and he has conducted clinical research on the treatment of addiction to opiates. He invented a technique, known as FRAT, for the detection of opiates and other drugs of abuse in urine, which the United States government used to deal with the Vietnam heroin epidemic. He conducted clinical research on the role of endogenous opioids, called endorphins, in pain regulation and emotions in humans; he also discovered one of the three groups of endorphins, the dynorphins. Goldstein was born in New York City on July 3, 1919, the son of Israel and Bertha Markowitz Goldstein. He received his B.A.

from Harvard in 1940 and his M.D. from the same university in 1943. After his internship at Mount Sinai Hospital in New York, he served for two years in the U.S. Army Medical Corps. He married Dora Benedict, who was also a doctor, on August 29, 1947. They later had four children.

Goldstein returned to Harvard in 1947, and he was a member of the faculty in the department of pharmacology for the next eight years. In 1955, he accepted a position as both professor and chair of the department of pharmacology at Stanford University. It was while at Stanford that his interest in the biological basis of drug tolerance and dependence, which had begun in medical school, matured. His wife also contributed to this interest; she was a pharmacologist who conducted research of her own on adaptive enzymes in bacteria. During the 1950s, Goldstein studied the effects and discriminative cues of nicotine, and he carried out the first double-blind clinical studies on caffeine—what effects it had on mood, its psychomotor performance, the sleep disturbance it caused, and the symptoms of withdrawal.

Discovers Opioid Activity in Pituitary Extracts

From results of experiments he conducted in 1971, which demonstrated that specific components of opiates bind themselves to receptor sites in the brain of mice, Goldstein became convinced that there was a specific opiate receptor in humans. His research team began searching for a natural substance with the properties of morphine (a well-known opiate) which would combine with these receptors. His earliest notebooks regarding this search are dated June 1972. In 1975, Goldstein and his group were able to report the discovery of opioid activity, with typical morphine-like pharmacological properties, in pituitary gland extracts. There were actually two different pituitary peptides, one of which was beta-endorphin, a substance which scientists had been aware of before by a different name. The other was the first dynorphin discovered, the third kind of endogenous opioid peptides; in naming the substance, Goldstein used the Greek word "dyn-" to describe its superior power as compared to the typical endorphin substances. Dynorphins are now thought to play a part in pain regulation in the spinal cord. Goldstein also discovered through further research that dynorphin acts primarily upon a different receptor than morphine does, and that there are different types of opioid receptors.

Invents FRAT Technique

Goldstein also conducted research regarding morphine in urine during this period, and he developed the first instantaneous immunoassay technique, known as FRAT (Free Radical Assay Technique). He was acting at the time as scientific advisor to the SYVA Company, which developed FRAT and passed it on to the United States government; it was used in Vietnam to screen addicted soldiers in order to detoxify them before sending them home. The technique was later developed further, so that civilian clinics could take advantage of it to render treatment more effective by allowing immediate confrontation over relapses.

Goldstein was very concerned with the practical and social applications of the body of scientific knowledge he was helping to develop. He had organized the first major methadone program for heroin addicts in California, and in 1974 he founded the Addiction Research Foundation in Palo Alto. It was here that he and an associate of his named Barbara Judson embarked on a series of studies on the uses of methadone, levomethadone, levo-alpha-acetylmethadol (LAAM), and naltrexone in treating heroin addiction. These studies stretched over a period of ten years, while they tried to ascertain the best methods for urine testing and detoxification, how opiate dependence could be verified quickly and reliably, and how treatment should be carried out. They found that LAAM was superior to methadone treatment in heroin addicts.

Goldstein's career in the fields of research on opioids and drug dependence in general has been widely recognized. He is the author of several books, and he has published over 350 research papers. He received both the Nathan B. Eddy Award, and the Todd Sollmann Award in 1980; in 1980, he was also presented with the prestigious Franklin Medal—the highest award given by the American society for Pharmacology and Experimental Therapeutics. He served two terms as a member of the National Institute on Drug Abuse and was elected to the National Academy of Sciences. He continues to live in California as Addiction Research Foundation Professor Emeritus at Stanford University.

SELECTED WRITINGS BY GOLDSTEIN:

Books

Biostatistics: An Introductory Text, Macmillan, 1964.

Principles of Drug Action, Wiley, 1974.

Opioid Research: A Reward Pathway, Plenary Lecture, International Narcotics Research Conference, 1992.

Addiction: From Biology to Drug Policy, W. H. Freeman, 1993.

Periodicals

"Tolerance to Opioid Narcotics: I. Tolerance to the 'Running Fit' Caused by Levorphanol in the Mouse," *Journal of Pharmacology and Experimental Therapeutics,* Volume 169l, 1969, pp. 175–184.

"Heroin Addiction—Sequential Treatment Employing Pharmacologic Supports," *Archives of General Psychiatry,* Volume 33, 1976, p. 353.
"Heroin Maintenance—A Medical View. A Conversation between a Physician and a Politician," *Journal of Drug Issues,* Volume 9, 1979, pp. 341–347.
"Thrills in Response to Music and Other Stimuli," *Physiological Psychology,* Volume 8, 1980, pp. 126–129.
"Drug Policy—Striking the Right Balance," *Science,* Volume 249, 1990, pp. 1513–1521.

SOURCES:

Periodicals

"Powerful Peptide Binds to Opiate Receptors," *Bioscience,* February, 1980, p. 131.
"The 'Social Chemistry' of Pharmacological Discovery: The Dynorphin Story," *Social Pharmacology,* Volume 3, 1989, pp. 15–34.

Other

Goldstein, Avram, interview for *Notable Twentieth-Century Scientists* with Janet Kieffer Kelley conducted on September 10, 1993.

—Sketch by Janet Kieffer Kelley

Joseph L. Goldstein
1940-
American molecular geneticist and physician

Joseph L. Goldstein is a prominent scientist and physician who discovered the receptor molecule, a structure on cell surfaces that regulates cholesterol levels in blood. He and **Michael Brown** worked for fifteen years before finding the molecule, which shed some light on the correlation between blood cholesterol level and heart disease. The National Institutes of Health, in part because of Goldstein's and Brown's work, recommended the lowering of fat intake in the U.S. diet. Goldstein is Professor of Medicine and Genetics and chairman of the department of molecular genetics at the University of Texas Health Science Center at Dallas. Brown is director of the Center for Genetic Disease. Colleagues there humorously refer to them collectively as "Brownstein," as their work keeps them inseparable, and together they have received awards from the National Academy of Sciences, the American Chemical Society, the Roche Institute of Molecular Biology, the American Heart Association and the American Society for Human Genetics.

Joseph Leonard Goldstein, the only son of Isadore E. and Fannie (Albert) Goldstein, was born on April 18, 1940, in Sumter, South Carolina. His parents owned a clothing store in the eastern part of the state. He graduated from Washington & Lee University in 1962 with a B.S. degree in chemistry, and attended Southwestern Medical School of the University of Texas Health Science Center in Dallas. There, Donald Seldin, chairman of the Health Science Center's department of internal medicine, offered him a future faculty appointment, provided he would specialize in genetics and then return to Dallas to establish a division of medical genetics there. He received his M.D. degree in 1966.

Goldstein's internship and residency at Massachusetts General Hospital brought him to Michael Brown, who had arrived from the University of Pennsylvania, having also obtained his M.D. degree in 1966. The two served in the same internship and residency program, and both were interested in research. After finishing their training in 1968, they joined the National Institutes of Health (NIH) in Bethesda, Maryland.

Studies Efficiency of Molecular Biology Approach to Human Disease

At the NIH biochemical genetics laboratory, Goldstein studied under the leadership of **Marshall Warren Nirenberg**, who was awarded the 1968 Nobel Prize in physiology or medicine for unraveling the way in which the genetic code determines the structure of proteins. Here, he learned about the excitement and efficiency of biology on a molecular level. At the same time he worked under Dr. Donald S. Fredrickson, clinical director of the National Heart Institute, who was investigating people with hypercholesterolemia, or abnormally high cholesterol levels. In particular, Goldstein was interested in those patients with homozygous familial hypercholesterolemia. Familial hypercholesterolemia, identified as a genetically acquired disease by Carl Müller of Oslo, Norway, involved a genetic defect which caused a metabolic error resulting in high blood cholesterol levels and heart attacks. But it was Fredrickson and Avedis K. Khachadurian of the American University of Beirut, who identified two forms of the disease: a heterozygous form, involving a single defective gene found in one in 500 people; and a homozygous form, in which two defective genes are present and which strikes about one in a million. Blood cholesterol levels reach four to eight times the normal amount with symptoms of atherosclerosis, or hardening of the arteries, beginning in childhood. Nearly every sufferer from the homozygous form dies from a heart attack before the age of thirty.

In 1972 Goldstein left the National Institutes of Health for Seattle under a two-year NIH fellowship in medical genetics. During this time he worked with Arno G. Motulsky, an internationally recognized expert in the field of genetic aspects of heart disease, and devoted himself to a study investigating the frequency of various hereditary hyperlipidemias (diseases of high blood-fat levels) in a random sampling of heart attack survivors. The samples were taken from 885 patients (who survived three months or more) out of 1,166 coronary victims admitted in an eleven-month period to thirteen Seattle hospitals from 1970 to 1971. Studying 500 of those survivors and 2,520 members of their families revealed that thirty-one percent of the survivors had high blood-fat levels, either high cholesterol, high triglycerides, or a mixture of both. Eleven percent had an inherited combination of high cholesterol and high triglycerides. Goldstein and his associates defined this disease as familial combined hyperlipidemia. He knew that due to its complexity, combined hyperlipidemia would be an arduous area in which to begin research. Patients with homozygous hypercholesterolemia—having no normal genes at the area of the unknown defect—might be easier to study regarding gene functioning and cholesterol level.

Study of Cholesterol Leads to Discovery of Receptor Molecule Factor

Returning to the University of Texas Health Science Center in 1972 as head of the medical school's first division of medical genetics, and assistant professor in the department of internal medicine which was still directed by Donald Seldin, Goldstein addressed the task of identifying the fundamental genetic defect in familial hypercholesterolemia (FHC). Brown had joined the staff the previous year.

The idea of cell receptors was known, but it had never been studied in relationship to fat and cholesterol in the blood. Over ninety-three percent of the cholesterol in the human body is found inside cells. There, it participates in functions critical to cell development and cell membrane formation. Cholesterol also contributes to the essential production of sex hormones, corticosteroids and bile acids. The remaining seven percent is dangerous, however, if it is not absorbed into the cells as it courses through the circulatory system, and sticks instead to the walls of blood vessels disrupting the flow of blood to the heart and brain.

Dietary cholesterol, found only in animal foods, is not necessary to the human body since the body produces its own cholesterol in the liver. If no cholesterol is available in the bloodstream, individual cells will produce their own. The human liver excretes that cholesterol which is not used by cells or deposited on artery walls. Cholesterol is fat-soluble, but attaches itself to water-soluble proteins, or lipoproteins, manufactured in the liver, as a means of moving through the bloodstream. The lipoproteins most favored by cholesterol are low-density ones, called LDLs , which are composed of much more fat than protein. Thus, high levels of LDLs are equated with the threat of heart disease.

Goldstein and Brown started their study by observing tissue cultures of the human skin cells known as fibroblasts, harvested from six FHC homozygotes, sixteen FHC heterozygotes and forty normal people. The cultured fibroblasts, like other animal cells, need cholesterol for the formation of the cell membrane. During this process, Goldstein and Brown were able to follow the manner in which the cells obtained cholesterol, and identify the process of cholesterol extraction from the lipoproteins in the serum of the culture medium, specifically LDLs. This discovery was made in 1973 with their demonstration of the presence of receptor molecules on the cells, which function to adhere LDLs and carry them into the cell. Goldstein and Brown noted that each individual cell normally has 250,000 receptors that bind low-density lipoproteins, and further located LDL receptors on circulating human blood cells as well as cell membranes from assorted animal tissues.

The cells of individuals with the heterozygous form of FHC have forty to fifty percent of the LDL receptors that are typically present on normal cells. Cells of individuals with the homozygous form of FHC have no LDL receptors or a very small number. Cholesterol, manufactured by the liver and attached to LDLs, is passed into the blood, but is removed from the circulatory system rather slowly. Under normal circumstances an LDL molecule spends a day and a half in the bloodstream, but in FHC heterozygotes this length of time is extended to three days, and in FHC homozygotes to five days, providing increased opportunity for cholesterol to accumulate in the walls of the blood vessels.

Work Facilitates Understanding of Cholestyramine

Cholestyramine, a drug used to treat high cholesterol levels, had been synthesized over twenty years before Goldstein's and Brown's study, but had never been fully understood. Goldstein and Brown discovered that cholestyramine works by multiplying LDL receptors in the liver, which then converts cholesterol into bile acids and passes them into the intestines. However, in spite of this action, cholestyramine had only limited effect on levels of serum cholesterol. Goldstein and Brown determined the reason for this: The increased numbers of LDL receptors in the liver signaled the need for more cholesterol and the liver responded by increasing cholesterol production. This increase in cholesterol level then shut down the production of LDL receptors in the liver. These findings indicated the need for a drug to impede the liver's synthesis of cholesterol that could be administered in tandem with cholestyramine. In 1976 Akiro Endo, a Japanese scientist, isolated compactin, an anticholesterol enzyme, from penicillin mold, and in the same year Alfred W. Alberts of Merck, Sharp and Dohme research laboratories isolated a structurally similar enzyme, mevinolin, from a different mold. Goldstein and Brown combined mevinolin and cholestyramine in animal experiments with good results, and in 1987 the Food and Drug Administration approved mevinolin, now called lovastatin, for marketing. The FDA made the recommendation with the stipulation that the drug should be used only when diet and exercise proved inadequate in treating high cholesterol. Goldstein anticipated a lapse of five to ten years before use of the drug would affect the nation's coronary death rate.

Work with Receptor Molecule Leads to Nobel Prize

For revolutionizing scientific knowledge about the regulation of cholesterol metabolism and the treatment of diseases caused by abnormally elevated cholesterol levels in the blood, Goldstein and Brown received the 1985 Nobel Prize in physiology or medicine. Results of their work were already being seen by the time of they received the prize. Stormie Jones, an FHC homozygous girl who had suffered a heart attack at age six and endured two triple bypass operations, was given a liver transplant. The new liver produced LDL receptors, her cholesterol level decreased from 1,100 milligrams to 300 milligrams, and later treatment with lovastatin dropped her cholesterol level to a normal 180.

Goldstein's and Brown's research illuminating the activity of LDL receptors and their function in the management of cholesterol levels has had far-reaching effects. Not only has their work increased understanding of an important aspect of human physiology, but it has also had a practical impact on the prevention and treatment of heart disease.

SELECTED WRITINGS BY GOLDSTEIN:

Periodicals

(With M. S. Brown) "Familial Hypercholesterolemia: Identification of a Defect in the Regulation of 3-hydroxy-3 methylglutaryl Coenzyme A Reductase Activity Associated with Overproduction of Cholesterol," *Proceedings National Academy of Sciences USA,* Volume 70, 1973, pp. 2804–2808.

(With Brown) "Expression of the Familial Hypercholesterolemia Gene in Heterozygotes: Mechanism for a Dominant Disorder in Man," *Science,* Volume 185, 1974, pp. 61–63.

(With Brown and M. J. E. Harrod) "Homozygous Familial Hypercholesterolemia: Specificity of the Biochemical Defect in Cultured Cells and Feasibility of Prenatal Detection." *American Journal of Human Genetics,* Volume 26, 1974, pp. 199–206.

SOURCES:

Books

Myrant, N. B., *Cholesterol Metabolism, LDL, and the LDL Receptor,* Harcourt, 1990.

Periodicals

Chicago Tribune, October 15, 1985, p. 1.

Motulsky, A. G., "The 1985 Nobel Prize in Physiology or Medicine," *Science,* January 10, 1986, pp. 126–129.

New York Times, October 15, 1985, p. A1.

U.S. News, May 25, 1987, p. 64.

—Sketch by Janet Kieffer Kelley

Camillo Golgi
1843-1926
Italian histologist and pathologist

Camillo Golgi, a clinician, researcher, and teacher, is best known for his Nobel Prize-winning work on the central nervous system, including his development of the chromate of silver method for better defining cell structures and his discovery of a small organ within the cytoplasm of the nerve cell now known as Golgi's apparatus. After the parasite responsible for malaria was identified in 1880, Golgi's study and subsequent diagnosis methodology made it possible to determine the different forms of malaria and means by which to treat patients. Golgi was born on July 7, 1843, in Corteno (renamed Corteno Golgi in his honor), Brescia, Italy. Following in the footsteps of his father, Alessandro, a medical practitioner in the village of Cava-Maria, Golgi attended the University of Pavia as a medical student. There he studied under Eusebio Oehl, distinguished as the first scientist in Pavia to make a systematic study of cell structures using the microscope. Upon earning his medical degree in 1865, Golgi joined the Ospedale di San Matteo in Pavia while continuing to work at the university. During this period, he was introduced to the science of histology through close acquaintance Giulio Bizzozero, director of the Institute of General Pathology, a laboratory of experimental pathology. It later came under the direction of Golgi as the Institute of General Pathology and Histology, and was eventually named after him.

In 1868, Golgi came to work as an assistant in the Psychiatric Clinic of Cesare Lombroso. Because of differences in personalities, the relationship was short-lived, but under Lombroso's supervision, and perhaps guidance, Golgi's commitment to the study of the central nervous system was established. He was soon influenced, as were many other scientists of his time, by the work of the great German pathologist Rudolf Virchow, taking from Virchow's *Cellular Pathology* the idea that diseases entered the body through the cells. This combination of influences from Virchow and Lombroso, and his histological studies in Bizzozero's lab, began to form the foundation for Golgi's life's work.

Discovers Cell Staining Method

Golgi left the Ospedale di San Matteo in 1871 and taught a private course in clinical microscopy. For financial reasons, the following year he accepted a position as chief resident physician and surgeon in a small hospital for incurable patients in the town of Abbiategrasso. Now no longer able to access the labs of the university or Bizzozero's institute, Golgi satisfied his voracious appetite for research in a makeshift laboratory that consisted of a microscope and various kitchen utensils. It was in this setting that Golgi invented the chromate of silver method (*la reazione nera*) for staining cells, a method he would later apply to his work on the central nervous system.

Before Golgi's method, scientists were stymied by the elaborate and entangled network of nerve cells, or neurons. Even the most sophisticated microscopes of the time could not break through the dense jungle of neuron vines, and the use of organic dyes by such prominent physicians as Walther Flemming and **Robert Koch** met with limited success. Golgi used samples of thinly sliced nerve tissues previously hardened with a bichromate, either potassium or ammonium, and immersed them in a silver nitrate solution. Under the microscope, the neurons were etched in black against an almost transparent background. By controlling the time in which the samples were subjected to the bichromate, one could discern numerous cells or exacting details, such as neuron fibers, demonstrating the elaborate network of the nerve connections.

In 1873 and 1874, while still working in his small laboratory in Abbiategrasso, Golgi published the first of his observations using this staining method, sometimes referred to as Golgi's silver stain. He identified the two main types of nerve cells whose differences lie in the length of their axons, or the filaments by which nervous impulses are conducted away from the cell body. Golgi's Type I and Type II nerve cells contain long and short axons respectively, the long type extending beyond the nervous system, the short type remaining intricately fixed within the central nervous system.

Over the next several years the stain enabled him to describe the structure of the olfactory bulb and the large nerve cells on the granular layer of the cerebellum, now known as Golgi's apparatus, Golgi bodies, or Golgi complex. Of particular note is the publication in 1874 of the paper *Sulle alterazioni degli organi centrali nervosi in caso di corea gesticolatoria associata ad alienazione mentale.* In it, Golgi showed that the involuntary movements brought on by chorea are caused by lesions on the nerve cells, neuroglia and blood vessels within the cerebral cortex and the cerebellum. This was contrary to the popular belief that such symptoms were caused by functional disturbances in locomotory parts of the body.

Golgi's silver stain received a somewhat lukewarm reception by his colleagues, perhaps due to the fact that it was difficult to replicate precisely. It wasn't until the early 1880s that other scientists began using the method, broadening scientific knowledge of the nerve cell structure. Chief among these scientists was Spanish histologist **Santiago Ramón y Cajal,** who would share the 1906 Nobel Prize with Golgi in the field of physiology for defining the structure of the nervous system. When rumblings persisted among some researchers that Golgi's stain did not always work with other kinds of cells, Golgi revised the method using arsenius acid, which produced more consistent results.

While Cajal made ardent use of Golgi's staining method and shared a research interest in the histology of the central nervous system, the two disagreed on neuron relationships. Golgi believed that the fibers within the complex neuron networks gradually lost their individuality and tried to establish continuity. Cajal, on the other hand, believed that each nerve cell represented a separate entity and that gaps, or synapses, separated them. Golgi used his Nobel lecture to cast doubt on Cajal's "neuron theory," a theory later supported by **Charles Scott Sherrington**'s research in nerve physiology.

Works Toward Combating Malaria

In 1875, Golgi returned to the University of Pavia as a lecturer in histology. After accepting the position of chair of anatomy at the University of

Siena in 1879, he returned to Pavia a year later, where he became professor of histology and succeeded Bizzozero as chair of general pathology. A fervent author, often publishing up to eight papers a year, Golgi released his monumental work *Sulla fina anatomia degli organi centrali del sistemi nervosa* in 1885, a collection of papers previously published in installments in the journal *Rivista sperimentale di freniatria,* of which he would later become co-editor. The volume, reprinted in French and German, was illustrated with plates made from Golgi's original drawings.

Between 1885 and 1893, while continuing his work on the nervous system, Golgi began to concentrate his research in malaria. The parasite itself had been discovered by **Alphonse Laveran** in 1880, and its development cycle studied by Antonio Marchiafava and Angelo Celli, whose work Golgi followed closely. Using the research of Marchiafava and Celli as the basis for his own research, Golgi eventually and accurately defined several types of malarial infestations. In the quartan and tertian forms of malaria, Golgi was able to correlate, in 1886, the onset of periodic fever fits with the life cycle of the parasite. In the quartan variation, the peaking of the fever every 72 hours could be attributed to the simultaneous division of the parasites in the blood. In the tertian form, the cycle peaked every 48 hours.

Golgi also described the quotidian fever, which he believed was caused by a double infection of the tertian parasite; and the estivo-autumnal type of malaria, which he described as an altogether separate type of malaria. These observations made it possible to diagnose and inevitably treat the disease. He discovered that quinine, to varying degrees, was effective against the parasite at different stages of its development—those in the early stages were most affected. By determining the cycle and subjecting the patient to quinine several hours before the fits, the new generation of parasites could be effectively acted upon. W. G. Whaley notes in *The Golgi Apparatus* that had Golgi "not made significant enough contributions in other fields, his malaria work alone would have withstood the test of time."

Golgi Apparatus Contributes to Science of Cytology

Golgi's place in the early annals of cytology was secured in 1898 with his description of the internal reticular apparatus, more commonly recognized as the Golgi apparatus. It was Golgi's staining method which allowed him to give a more detailed account of the small organelle within the nerve cell's cytoplasm, the substance between the membrane of the cell and its nucleus. The Golgi apparatus appears as a fine network of interlaced threads shown by Golgi and his students to be a consistent component in a variety of cell tissues. Unlike earlier investigators, Golgi was also the first to notice that its character and position were variable. The credit for its initial discovery has been attributed to La Valette St. George, and earlier descriptions of certain components by Platner and Murray showed a definite relationship to the apparatus described by Golgi. Cajal even tried to lay claim to its discovery in 1923, suggesting he had noted its appearance some thirty years earlier while studying the muscle cells of insects, but did not believe he had discovered a new organelle.

Early on, the Golgi apparatus was the focus of many studies. But the structure fell out of vogue in the 1930s and 1940s, the victim of the mistaken belief that it was an apparition created by the same staining method used to make it visible. But advances in electron microscopy later verified its existence and revealed that the Golgi apparatus plays a role in the synthesis and secretion of proteins, as well as the formation of the cell surface.

Golgi married Donna Lina Aletti, Bizzozero's niece, and adopted his own nephew, Aldo Perroncito, who followed Golgi into medicine. Golgi remained in Pavia the rest of his life, and served his country as a member of both the Royal Senate and the Superior Council of Public Instruction and Sanitation. He remained active at the university, where he was president as well as dean of the faculty of medicine. In his seventies at the outset of World War I, Golgi opened the first Italian hospital that ministered principally to patients with lesions of the nervous system. He taught histology until his retirement in 1918, and continued publishing until shortly before his death. Golgi died in Pavia on January 21, 1926.

SELECTED WRITINGS BY GOLGI:

Books

Opera Omnia, Volumes 1–3, Ulrico Hoepli (Milan), 1903–29.

SOURCES:

Books

Chorobski, Jerzy, *Neurological Biographies and Addresses: Foundation Volume,* Oxford University Press, 1936, pp. 141–150.

Dictionary of Scientific Biography, Volume 3, Scribner's, 1981, pp. 459–461.

Nobel Prize Winners, H. W. Wilson, 1987, pp. 392–393.

Stevenson, Lloyd G., *Nobel Prize Winners in Medicine and Physiology, 1901–1950,* Henry Schuman, 1953, pp. 33–39.

Whaley, W. G., *The Golgi Apparatus,* Springer-Verlag, 1975.

Periodicals

Da Fano, C., "Camillo Golgi," *The Journal of Pathology and Bacteriology,* Volume 29, 1926, pp. 500–514.

—Sketch by John Spizzirri

Mary L. Good
1931-
American chemist

Mary L. Good

Mary L. Good is a highly regarded chemist whose multifaceted career has ranged from academia, to the industrial sector, to the national government, where she serves as undersecretary of technology in the Department of Commerce. Good is described by Jeffrey Trewhitt in *Chemical Week* as an unabashed proponent of industrial chemistry. She told Trewhitt that "we've . . . gotten ourselves into a trap. . . . The word 'chemical' has become a bad name, and yet, without chemicals the world doesn't move. We've got to develop a better perspective."

Mary Lowe Good was born on June 20, 1931, in Grapevine, Texas, the daughter of John W. and Winnie (Mercer) Lowe. In 1950, she received a bachelor of science degree from the University of Central Arkansas, with a major in chemistry and with minors in both physics and mathematics. She received her master of science degree from the University of Arkansas in 1953, with majors in inorganic chemistry and radiochemistry. She completed her doctorate at Arkansas in 1955.

In 1954, Good accepted a post as instructor of chemistry at Louisiana State University in Baton Rouge, where she became assistant professor in 1956. She moved to Louisiana State University in New Orleans as associate professor in 1958, and became full professor three years later. At various intervals over the next two decades, she also was affiliated with the medicinal chemistry commission at the National Institutes of Health, the Lawrence-Berkeley Laboratory at the University of California, the research office of the United States Air Force, and the Brookhaven and Oak Ridge National Laboratories. She received the Agnes Faye Morgan Research Award in 1969, the Garvan Medal in 1973, and the Herty Medal in 1975. From 1972 to 1980, she served on the American Chemical Society's board of trustees, chairing the board from 1978 to 1980.

Good was named Boyd Professor of Chemistry within the LSU system in 1974, and returned to Baton Rouge as Boyd Professor of Materials Science in 1979. Among her areas of expertise is catalysis, a process whereby a substance—which remains unchanged chemically at the end of the reaction—induces a modification (an especially an increase) in the rate of the chemical reaction. An important facet of her research is the chemistry of ruthenium, a rare platinum metal that is used as a catalyst in the synthesis of hydrocarbons.

Shifts to Corporate Research and Development

In 1980, Good left academia to serve as vice-president and director of research at Universal Oil Products (UOP)—an affiliate of the Allied Signal Corporation—in Des Plaines, Illinois. Two years later she was named Scientist of the Year by *Industrial Research & Development* magazine for "her work as a chemist, educator, lecturer, author, research administrator, and industry spokesperson." Good told Barbara H. Brown in *Industrial Research & Development* that "the greatest challenge in applied science today is to devise more efficient and effective ways to reduce the transition time from laboratory 'proof of principle' to the commercial marketplace." In 1985, Good was promoted to president of the engineered materials research division of Allied Signal in Des Plaines.

Here, she supervised research in the industrial application of catalysis and polymerization (the chemical process whereby molecules combine into larger molecules characterized by repeating structural units). In 1988, she became senior vice-president at Allied Signal in Morristown, New Jersey, supervising the corporation's entire research and development department, whose 1992 budget amounted to $821 million.

Good was appointed to the National Science Board in 1980. From 1980 to 1985, she directed the inorganic division of the International Union of Pure and Applied Chemistry. In 1983, she was awarded the American Institute of Chemistry's Gold Medal. She became president of the American Chemical Society, the second woman elected to this honor, in 1987. In a 1987 *Chemical & Engineering News* article entitled "ACS in a Changing Environment," Good observed: "The challenge for ACS and individual chemists is to gain the recognition that chemistry, the molecular science, is at the heart of this new technology thrust. The chemical databases built over many years by chemists are the heart of the molecular design programs being utilized so aggressively in the development of new drugs, high-performance materials, specialty chemicals, and biotechnology products."

Her stance on technological advances through chemistry has led Good to promote research such as the "materials-by-design" studies of the Energy Conversion and Utilization (ECUT) project within the Department of Energy. Trewhitt in *Chemical Week* quoted Good's testimony before a congressional panel in support of these studies: "['Materials-by-design'] will replace the current trial-and-error approach, in which one material after another is tested until the one having the desired properties is found. The new approach allows scientists to design the materials they want on a computer, and then use the computer-generated recipes to make materials in the lab." Good emphasized that the "materials-by-design" strategy would be particularly beneficial in the development of catalysts, thereby enhancing the global competitiveness of the American petrochemical industry and expanding its usage of non-petroleum fuel sources. As head of the ACS, Good also focused on attracting students—particularly women—to careers in the applied sciences.

In 1986, Good was reappointed to the National Science Board, which she chaired from 1988 to 1991. She received the Delmer S. Fahrney Medal of the Franklin Institute in 1988. Three years later she served on the President's Council of Advisers for Science and Technology, and was awarded an Industrial Research Institute Medal. In the same year, the American Chemical Society recognized her "outstanding public service" with their prestigious Charles Lathrop Parsons Award. In 1992, she received the National Science Foundation Distinguished Public Service Award, the American Association for the Advancement of Science Award, and the Albert Fox Demers Medal Award from the Rensselaer Polytechnic Institute. Good, whose publications include several monographs and more than one hundred articles in professional journals, has received many honorary degrees.

Moves to Department of Commerce

In May of 1993, President Bill Clinton nominated Good as undersecretary of technology in the Department of Commerce; she was confirmed for this post on August 5, 1993. As quoted in *Chemical & Engineering News,* Charles F. Larson, executive director of the Industrial Research Institute, endorsed Good's nomination: "She has the perfect combination of background and experience to be an effective leader in that position and to interact with industry on important issues, rather than on those that are important just to the government." As undersecretary of technology, Good heads the Technology Administration, the National Institute of Standards and Technology, and the National Technology Information Service. In *Physics Today,* Irwin Goodwin declared that Good's task is to "strengthen the nation's technology base through government-industry-academic partnerships of many kinds, encourage the introduction of advanced technology into small and medium-sized firms through extension services, and reduce the risks of private investments in new or more sophisticated technology."

Mary Lowe married Billy Jewel Good on May 17, 1952. A former physics professor and college dean, Billy Good is now a full-time artist. The Goods have two sons, Billy John and James Patrick, and four grandsons. *Chemical Week* notes that Mary Good, an admirer of Edinburgh and the novels of Sir Walter Scott, is "a Scottish history buff"; her other hobbies include fly-fishing.

SELECTED WRITINGS BY GOOD:

Books

Integrated Laboratory Sequence, Barnes and Noble, 1970.

(Editor) *Biotechnology and Materials Science: Chemistry for the Future,* American Chemical Society, 1988.

Periodicals

"A Policy Mechanism for Science," *Chemical & Engineering News,* June 24, 1985, p. 5.

"ACS in a Changing Environment—New Directions in 1987," *Chemical & Engineering News,* January 5, 1987, pp. 2–3.

SOURCES:

Periodicals

Brown, Barbara H., "Mary Lowe Good Fills Roles of Scientist, Industry Spokesperson," *Industrial Research & Development,* October, 1982, pp. 155–156.

"Good Receives ACS Award," *Chemecology,* May/June, 1991, p. 15.

Gray, Julie, "Eureka! (Woman Scientist-Turned-Executive, M. L. Good)," *Working Woman,* September, 1985, p. 57.

Holusha, John, "Allied Officer Nominated for Commerce Job," *New York Times,* May 25, 1993, p. D5.

Lepowski, Wil, "Chemist Gets Top Commerce Technology Job," *Chemical & Engineering News,* May 31, 1993, pp. 7–8.

Trewhitt, Jeffrey, "Going to Bat for the Chemical Industry," *Chemical Week,* September 24, 1986, pp. 57–58.

—Sketch by M. C. Nagel

Jane Goodall

Jane Goodall
1934-
English ethologist

Jane Goodall is known worldwide for her studies of the chimpanzees of the Gombe Stream Reserve in Tanzania, Africa. She is well respected within the scientific community for her ground-breaking field studies and is credited with the first recorded observation of chimps eating meat and using and making tools. Because of Goodall's discoveries, scientists have been forced to redefine the characteristics once considered as solely human traits. Goodall is now leading efforts to ensure that animals are treated humanely both in their wild habitats and in captivity.

Goodall was born in London, England, on April 3, 1934, to Mortimer Herbert Goodall, a businessperson and motor-racing enthusiast, and the former Margaret Myfanwe Joseph, who wrote novels under the name Vanne Morris Goodall. Along with her sister, Judy, Goodall was reared in London and Bournemouth, England. Her fascination with animal behavior began in early childhood. In her leisure time, she observed native birds and animals, making extensive notes and sketches, and read widely in the literature of zoology and ethology. From an early age, she dreamed of traveling to Africa to observe exotic animals in their natural habitats.

Meets Leakey in Africa

Goodall attended the Uplands private school, receiving her school certificate in 1950 and a higher certificate in 1952. At age eighteen she left school and found employment as a secretary at Oxford University. In her spare time, she worked at a London-based documentary film company to finance a long-anticipated trip to Africa. At the invitation of a childhood friend, she visited South Kinangop, Kenya. Through other friends, she soon met the famed anthropologist **Louis Leakey**, then curator of the Coryndon Museum in Nairobi. Leakey hired her as a secretary and invited her to participate in an anthropological dig at the now famous Olduvai Gorge, a site rich in fossilized prehistoric remains of early ancestors of humans. In addition, Goodall was sent to study the vervet monkey, which lives on an island in Lake Victoria.

Leakey believed that a long-term study of the behavior of higher primates would yield important evolutionary information. He had a particular interest in the chimpanzee, the second most intelligent primate. Few studies of chimpanzees had been successful; either the size of the safari frightened the chimps, producing unnatural behaviors, or the observers spent too little time in the field to gain comprehensive knowledge. Leakey believed that Goodall had the proper temperament to endure long-term isolation in the wild. At his prompting, she agreed to attempt such a study. Many experts objected to Leakey's selection of Goodall because she had no formal scientific education and lacked even a general college degree.

While Leakey searched for financial support for the proposed Gombe Reserve project, Goodall returned to England to work on an animal documentary for Granada Television. On July 16, 1960, accompanied by her mother and an African cook, she returned to Africa and established a camp on the shore of Lake Tanganyika in the Gombe Stream Reserve. Her first attempts to observe closely a group of chimpanzees failed; she could get no nearer than five hundred yards before the chimps fled. After finding another suitable group of chimpanzees to follow, she established a nonthreatening pattern of observation, appearing at the same time every morning on the high ground near a feeding area along the Kakaombe Stream valley. The chimpanzees soon tolerated her presence and, within a year, allowed her to move as close as thirty feet to their feeding area. After two years of seeing her every day, they showed no fear and often came to her in search of bananas.

Chimpanzee Research Yields Numerous Discoveries

Goodall used her newfound acceptance to establish what she termed the "banana club," a daily systematic feeding method she used to gain trust and to obtain a more thorough understanding of everyday chimpanzee behavior. Using this method, she became closely acquainted with more than half of the reserve's one hundred or more chimpanzees. She imitated their behaviors, spent time in the trees, and ate their foods. By remaining in almost constant contact with the chimps, she discovered a number of previously unobserved behaviors. She noted that chimps have a complex social system, complete with ritualized behaviors and primitive but discernible communication methods, including a primitive "language" system containing more than twenty individual sounds. She is credited with making the first recorded observations of chimpanzees eating meat and using and making tools. Tool making was previously thought to be an exclusively human trait, used, until her discovery, to distinguish man from animal. She also noted that chimpanzees throw stones as weapons, use touch and embraces to comfort one another, and develop long-term familial bonds. The male plays no active role in family life but is part of the group's social stratification. The chimpanzee "caste" system places the dominant males at the top. The lower castes often act obsequiously in their presence, trying to ingratiate themselves to avoid possible harm. The male's rank is often related to the intensity of his entrance performance at feedings and other gatherings.

Ethologists had long believed that chimps were exclusively vegetarian. Goodall witnessed chimps stalking, killing, and eating large insects, birds, and some bigger animals, including baby baboons and bushbacks (small antelopes). On one occasion, she recorded acts of cannibalism. In another instance, she observed chimps inserting blades of grass or leaves into termite hills to lure worker or soldier termites onto the blade. Sometimes, in true toolmaker fashion, they modified the grass to achieve a better fit. Then they used the grass as a long-handled spoon to eat the termites.

Finds Audience through Television and Books

In 1962 Baron Hugo van Lawick, a Dutch wildlife photographer, was sent to Africa by the National Geographic Society to film Goodall at work. The assignment ran longer than anticipated; Goodall and van Lawick were married on March 28, 1964. Their European honeymoon marked one of the rare occasions on which Goodall was absent from Gombe Stream. Her other trips abroad were necessary to fulfill residency requirements at Cambridge University, where she received a Ph.D. in ethology in 1965, becoming only the eighth person in the university's long history who was allowed to pursue a Ph.D. without first earning a baccalaureate degree. Her doctoral thesis, "Behavior of the Free-Ranging Chimpanzee," detailed her first five years of study at the Gombe Reserve.

Van Lawick's film, *Miss Goodall and the Wild Chimpanzees,* was first broadcast on American television on December 22, 1965. The film introduced the shy, attractive, unimposing yet determined Goodall to a wide audience. Goodall, van Lawick (along with their son, Hugo, born in 1967), and the chimpanzees soon became a staple of American and British public television. Through these programs, Goodall challenged scientists to redefine the long-held "differences" between humans and other primates.

Goodall's fieldwork led to the publication of numerous articles and five major books. She was known and respected first in scientific circles and, through the media, became a minor celebrity. *In the Shadow of Man,* her first major text, appeared in 1971. The book, essentially a field study of chimpanzees, effectively bridged the gap between scientific treatise and popular entertainment. Her vivid prose brought the chimps to life, although her tendency to attribute human behaviors and names to chimpanzees struck some critics being as manipulative. Her writings reveal an animal world of social drama, comedy, and tragedy where distinct and varied personalities interact and sometimes clash.

Advocates Ethical Treatment of Animals

From 1970 to 1975 Goodall held a visiting professorship in psychiatry at Stanford University. In

1973 she was appointed honorary visiting professor of Zoology at the University of Dar es Salaam in Tanzania, a position she still holds. Her marriage to van Lawick over, she wed Derek Bryceson, a former member of Parliament, in 1973. He has since died. Until recently, Goodall's life has revolved around Gombe Stream. But after attending a 1986 conference in Chicago that focused on the ethical treatment of chimpanzees, she began directing her energies more toward educating the public about the wild chimpanzee's endangered habitat and about the unethical treatment of chimpanzees that are used for scientific research.

To preserve the wild chimpanzee's environment, Goodall encourages African nations to develop nature-friendly tourism programs, a measure that makes wildlife into a profitable resource. She actively works with business and local governments to promote ecological responsibility. Her efforts on behalf of captive chimpanzees have taken her around the world on a number of lecture tours. She outlined her position strongly in her 1990 book *Through a Window:* "The more we learn of the true nature of nonhuman animals, especially those with complex brains and corresponding complex social behaviour, the more ethical concerns are raised regarding their use in the service of man—whether this be in entertainment, as 'pets,' for food, in research laboratories or any of the other uses to which we subject them. This concern is sharpened when the usage in question leads to intense physical or mental suffering—as is so often true with regard to vivisection."

Goodall's stance is that scientists must try harder to find alternatives to the use of animals in research. She has openly declared her opposition to militant animal rights groups who engage in violent or destructive demonstrations. Extremists on both sides of the issue, she believes, polarize thinking and make constructive dialogue nearly impossible. While she is reluctantly resigned to the continuation of animal research, she feels that young scientists must be educated to treat animals more compassionately. "By and large," she has written, "students are taught that it is ethically acceptable to perpetrate, in the name of science, what, from the point of view of animals, would certainly qualify as torture."

Goodall's efforts to educate people about the ethical treatment of animals extends to young children as well. Her 1989 book, *The Chimpanzee Family Book,* was written specifically for children, to convey a new, more humane view of wildlife. The book received the 1989 Unicef/Unesco Children's Book-of-the-Year award, and Goodall used the prize money to have the text translated into Swahili. It has been distributed throughout Tanzania, Uganda, and Burundi to educate children who live in or near areas populated by chimpanzees. A French version has also been distributed in Burundi and Congo.

In recognition of her achievements, Goodall has received numerous honors and awards, including the Gold Medal of Conservation from the San Diego Zoological Society in 1974, the J. Paul Getty Wildlife Conservation Prize in 1984, the Schweitzer Medal of the Animal Welfare Institute in 1987, the National Geographic Society Centennial Award in 1988, and the Kyoto Prize in Basic Sciences in 1990. Many of Goodall's endeavors are conducted under the auspices of the Jane Goodall Institute for Wildlife Research, Education, and Conservation, a nonprofit organization located in Ridgefield, Connecticut.

SELECTED WRITINGS BY GOODALL:

Books

(Under name Jane van Lawick-Goodall; with Hugo van Lawick) *Innocent Killers,* Collins, 1970.

(Under name Jane van Lawick-Goodall) *In the Shadow of Man,* with photographs by Hugo van Lawick, Houghton Mifflin, 1971.

(Under name Jane van Lawick-Goodall; with Hugo van Lawick) *Grub: The Bush Baby,* Houghton, 1972.

The Chimpanzees of Gombe: Patterns of Behavior, Harvard University Press, 1986.

My Life with Chimpanzees, Simon and Schuster, 1988.

The Chimpanzee Family Book, Picture Book Studio, 1989.

Jane Goodall's Animal World: Chimpanzees, Macmillan, 1989.

Through a Window: My Thirty Years with the Chimpanzees of Gombe, Houghton, 1990.

Periodicals

"Life and Death at Gombe," *National Geographic,* Volume 155, number 5, 1979, pp. 592–621.

"Mountain Warrior: Dian Fossey and Her Research on Mountain Gorillas," *Omni,* May, 1986, p. 132.

"A Plea for the Chimpanzee," *American Scientist,* Volume 75, number 6, 1987, pp. 574–577.

SOURCES:

Books

Green, Timothy, *The Restless Spirit: Profiles in Adventure,* Walker, 1970.

Montgomery, Sy, *Walking with the Great Apes: Jane Goodall, Dian Fossey, Biruté Galdikas,* Houghton Mifflin, 1991.

Periodicals

Smith, Wendy, "The Wildlife of Jane Goodall, *USAir,* February, 1991, pp. 42–47.

—*Sketch by Tom Crawford*

Samuel A. Goudsmit
1902-1978
Dutch-born American physicist

A prominent figure in American physics, Samuel A. Goudsmit was an authority on atomic energy and nuclear research, and was the co-discoverer of the electron spin. Goudsmit was educated in the Netherlands, where he received his Ph.D. in physics from the University of Leiden in 1927. While still a graduate student, Goudsmit, in collaboration with fellow physics student **George Uhlenbeck**, made the discovery for which he is most famous: electron spin. That discovery explained some important theoretical predictions by physicists **Wolfgang Pauli** and **Paul Dirac** as well as a number of anomalies in the existing atomic theory. Nobel Prize winner and physics professor **I. I. Rabi** was quoted by Daniel Lang in *New Yorker* as observing that the discovery "was a tremendous feat. Why those two men never received a Nobel Prize for it will always be a mystery to me." During World War II, Goudsmit led a group of physicists and military personnel in a search through war-torn Europe, in an attempt to locate German scientist **Werner Heisenberg** and determine what the Germans had accomplished in terms of their atomic bomb research. For this mission he received the Medal of Freedom and the Order of the British Empire.

Samuel Abraham Goudsmit was born in The Hague, Netherlands, on July 11, 1902. His father, Isaac Goudsmit, was a prosperous dealer in bathroom fixtures, and his mother, Marianne Gompers Goudsmit, was the owner of a fashionable hat store called Au Louvre. Young Samuel developed a passionate interest in the millinery business early in life. He was excited by the tales his mother told of life in Paris, and he loved the challenge of trying to predict six months in advance what kind of hats the women of The Hague would be wearing.

Goudsmit's first introduction to the sciences came when he was eleven years old and off-handedly picked up his older sister's physics textbook. He was intrigued by a discussion on spectroscopic phenomena—the theory that the elements of the earth and the stars are identical. Although interested, Goudsmit developed no particular on-going curiosity about science until, after graduation from high school in 1919, he was influenced by a physics teacher. At the University of Leiden, Goudsmit decided to major in physics—he had earned his best grades in science and mathematics—and found himself in a class taught by **Paul Ehrenfest**. Ehrenfest recognized in Goudsmit an inquiring intellect combined with an infallible intuition, and took a particular interest in helping his young student to develop those qualities. Goudsmit's moderate interest in physics soon became a passionate pursuit under the guidance of his new teacher. As a result of Ehrenfest's encouragement, Goudsmit published his first scientific paper in 1921 on the fine structure of atomic spectra.

That topic was one of immense importance in the 1920s. The quantum model of atomic structure proposed by **Niels Bohr** in 1913 had been an extraordinary breakthrough and solved many problems in the field of atomic theory. But a number of important questions remained. One of these concerned the nature of atomic spectra produced when atoms are placed within a magnetic field. In particular, the spectra produced in such instances always contain twice as many lines as were predicted by Bohr's theory. The answer to that puzzle came in 1925, shortly after Goudsmit met George Uhlenbeck, another of Ehrenfest's students. The two were assigned to spend the summer working together on the problem of double spectral lines. The match of the two young students turned out to be nearly ideal. According to Goudsmit's biographer, Stanley Goldberg, in *Dictionary of Scientific Biography,* "Goudsmit supplied the intuitions necessary to recognize and summarize regularities not immediately obvious in the data . . . [while] Uhlenbeck was more analytically oriented, more readily able to make connections between formal synthesis and traditional physical concepts."

The Discovery of Electron Spin

As a result of this collaboration, Goudsmit and Uhlenbeck realized that the problem of double lines could be solved by assuming that the electron spins on its axis as it travels around the atomic nucleus. The two possible directions of spin—clockwise and counter-clockwise—could then explain two different orientations of an electron in a magnetic field and, hence, two spectral lines that are very close together in all other respects. Scientists immediately recognized the significance of this bold hypothesis. Only a few months earlier, Pauli had proposed his "exclusion principle," according to which no two electrons in an atom can have exactly the same set of quantum numbers. A condition of that theory, however, was that a fourth quantum number was necessary to describe any given electron, a quantum number that could have the values of plus or minus one-half. Pauli made no guess as to what this quantum number might represent physically, but the Goudsmit-Uhlenbeck hypothesis immediately answered that question. The values of plus or minus one-half corresponded, they pointed out, to the two possible directions of electron spin. The discovery led to a fundamental change in the mathematical structure of quantum mechanics, as scientists recognized that spin is an integral property not only of electrons but also of protons and neutrons.

Goudsmit and Uhlenbeck no sooner announced their theory of electron spin before they were both offered appointments at the University of Michigan. For Goudsmit, the decision to leave the Netherlands was a difficult one. He hated leaving behind family, friends, Ehrenfest, and his other European colleagues. But he accepted the Michigan offer nonetheless. A few years later, Goudsmit referred to himself during an interview as a "has-been," he was quoted as saying by Daniel Lang in *New Yorker.* His remarks suggested that his greatest accomplishment was behind him, and he could look forward only to a rather mundane career in the future. "As a physicist's career goes . . . a scientist can do useful work all his life, but if he is to carry learning one big step forward, he usually does so before he is thirty. Youth has the quality of being radical, in the literal sense of the word—of going to the root. . . . Obviously, if one hits on something through this approach, it may well be outstanding. After a scientist passes his creative peak, it seems to me the most useful thing he can do is teach the status quo to youngsters." While he continued to remain active in research throughout the rest of his life, Goudsmit continued to teach—with one abrupt, but eventful interruption—until his death in 1978.

Top Secret Assignments

The interruption was World War II. At the outbreak of war, Goudsmit left the University of Michigan to conduct a secret research project at the Massachusetts Institute of Technology (MIT) to test the theory of radar. In 1944 General **Leslie R. Groves** asked the physicist to serve as part of a secret intelligence mission. The project—code-name "Alsos"—was an effort to find out what German scientists had been able to discover about nuclear weapons and atomic-bomb research during the war. Goudsmit was placed in charge of a group of about one hundred men, six of whom were scientists, sent to Europe to track down **Werner Karl Heisenberg,** head of the German atomic weapons project. Goudsmit's team successfully found Heisenberg near Munich at the end of the war in Europe. Later, Goudsmit wrote a popular book titled *Alsos* describing his experience.

Goudsmit's participation with the Alsos project engendered an important change in his outlook on the future. In a 1951 interview with *New Yorker* writer Daniel Lang, Goudsmit explained that he felt he could not simply go back to the routine of university life again, but needed to "take an active part in scientific developments in order to—yes, at the time I perhaps meant it literally—to help save the world." As a consequence, after a brief stay at Northwestern University (1946 to 1948), he accepted an appointment at the Brookhaven National Laboratory, where he was promoted to Chair of the physics department in 1950. During his years at Brookhaven, he became very active in the political aspects of scientific research, including the development of scientific policy, the funding of research, and the defense of science against the attacks of McCarthyism—the extreme governmental opposition to communism which swept the United States in the 1940s and 1950s.

In the two decades between 1952 and 1974, Goudsmit took on another important responsibility with the editorship of the American Physical Society's (APS) *Physical Review.* During his long term of office, Goudsmit oversaw the expansion of the journal from a single publication of about five thousand pages per year, to a group of five related journals with a combined size of more than twenty-five thousand pages per year. He also recommended the creation of—and then put into production—an important new journal, *Physical Review Letters,* in 1958. Goudsmit retired from his editorial work at APS in 1974 and accepted a position as distinguished visiting professor at the University of Nevada at Reno. His only teaching assignment there was a large general education course in "physics appreciation." He was found dead of a heart attack in Reno on December 4, 1978.

SELECTED WRITINGS BY GOUDSMIT:

Books

(With Linus Pauling) *The Structure of Line Spectra,* McGraw-Hill, 1930.

(With R. F. Bacher) *Atomic Energy States,* Greenwood Press, 1932.

Alsos, H. Schuman, 1947.

(With Robert Claiborne) *Time,* Time-Life, 1966.

Periodicals

(With G. E. Uhlenbeck) "Spinning Electrons and the Structure of Spectra," *Nature,* 1926, pp. 264–265.

"How Germany Lost the Race," *Bulletin of the Atomic Scientists,* 1946, pp. 4–5.

"It Might As Well Be Spin," *Physics Today,* June, 1956, pp. 40–43.

SOURCES:

Books

Holmes, Frederic L., *Dictionary of Scientific Biography,* Volume 17, Scribner's, 1982, pp. 362–368.

McGraw-Hill Modern Scientists and Engineers, Volume 1, McGraw-Hill, 1980, pp. 452–453.

Periodicals

Lang, Daniel, "A Farewell To String and Sealing Wax," *New Yorker,* November 7, 1953, p. 46; November 14, 1953, p. 47.

—*Sketch by David E. Newton*

Stephen Jay Gould
1941-
American evolutionary biologist

Stephen Jay Gould

A Harvard University professor of geology, biology, and the history of science, Stephen Jay Gould is a science celebrity. He is a prolific science writer, best known in the lay community for his essays in the journal *Natural History.* In the scientific community Gould is recognized as an international authority on Cerion, a small tropical snail, and as a theorist of evolution. He has been awarded literary and academic honors, including a National Book Award and a MacArthur Prize.

Develops Interest in Natural Selection

Born September 10, 1941, in New York City, Gould grew up in a lower-middle-class home in Queens with his younger brother Peter. His father, Leonard Gould, was a court stenographer in the Queens County Supreme Court. A self-taught man and a Marxist, the senior Gould was also an amateur naturalist. During a trip with his father to the American Museum of Natural History in Manhattan when he was five years old, Gould saw his first reconstruction of the dinosaur *Tyrannosaurus rex.* He recalls that on the day of that trip he made the decision to devote his life to studies of geological periods. At the age of eleven, Gould became interested in the ideas of **George Gaylord Simpson**, who convinced his fellow paleontologists to accept Charles Darwin's theory of evolution by natural selection in his book *Meaning of Evolution.* In an interview with Mary Murray in *Science News,* Gould said that he had two life-time heroes: "Joe DiMaggio is the first; I patterned my batting stance after him. George Gaylord Simpson is the second; I patterned my life after him." Disappointed with the treatment of evolution in his biology textbooks when he was still in high school, Gould also started to read Darwin.

After graduation, Gould attended the University of Colorado for the summer and then entered Antioch College, where he received his B.A. in 1963. Inspired by the collection of an Antioch professor, Gould began an investigation of fossil land snails in Bermuda when he enrolled for his doctoral studies at Columbia University. In 1966 he returned to Antioch to teach geology. Awarded his Ph.D. in paleontology from Columbia in 1967, Gould left Antioch to become assistant professor of geology at Harvard University, where he advanced to associate professor in 1971 and to full professor in 1973. He also became curator of invertebrate paleontology at Harvard's Museum of Comparative Zoology. While teaching biology and geology at Harvard, he expanded his study of land snails to the West Indies and other parts of the world.

Develops Punctuated Equilibrium Theory with Colleague

In the early 1970s Gould introduced his most noted contribution to evolutionary theory, the concept of punctuated equilibrium, which he developed with fellow paleontologist **Niles Eldredge**. The theory runs counter to a central postulate of Darwinian evolution commonly known as phyletic gradualism. Darwin assumed that adaptations in species are the result of a continuous process of gradual change. Eldredge and Gould theorized that evolution is not quite so orderly but is characterized by largely stable periods, punctuated by "moments" of massive change. During such periods of change species evolve abruptly and new adaptations appear in riotous profusion. Concerned with the revelatory power of oddities in nature, Gould proposed that unpredictable events alter the course of natural history. He found the imperfections of nature significant where other scientists disregarded their evolutionary impact. Phyletic gradualism has always been plagued by a lack of fossil evidence of transitional species; this dearth has been comprehended as gaps in the fossil record. The theory of punctuated equilibria explains those gaps as adaptational leaps in species rather than an unfortunate failure of paleontologists to find the evidence. Gould and Eldredge first published the theory in 1972, in a paper entitled "Punctuated Equilibria: an Alternative to Phyletic Gradualism," which appeared in *Models in Paleobiology.* Gould developed the theory in further papers, and his work was recognized in 1975 with the Schuchert Award, presented by the Paleontological Society for excellence in research by a paleontologist under forty years old.

Publishes Scientific Column Intended for Educated Non-scientists

In 1974, Gould began writing a monthly column entitled "This View of Life" in the magazine *Natural History.* Addressing an educated lay audience, Gould clarified evolution in ordinary terms without simplifying its concepts. "The problem is that in this country the notion of writing for the public got somehow assimilated in the notion of cheapening, simplifying, adulterating," Gould said in an interview with John Tierney in *Rolling Stone.* "There's no reason why it should." Esteemed for his insightful analogies, Gould is a master of establishing connections between dissimilar subjects. Seemingly arcane topics serve to illustrate central principles in evolutionary thought or in the history and philosophy of science. Gould communicates the excitement of scientific discovery in his essays and captures the attention of a large audience with his eloquence. In 1977 Gould published the first collection of his essays in book form under the title *Ever Since Darwin: Reflections in Natural History.*

During the early 1980s, Gould became an increasingly popular writer, whose appeal centered on making science accessible to lay readers as well as scholars. The peculiar wristbone of the panda became the occasion for *The Panda's Thumb,* which won the 1981 American Book Award in Science. Gould centered the work on an oddity of nature. The enlarged wristbone of the panda, which functions as a thumb, enables the animal to strip leaves from bamboo shoots. Although the mutation in the wrist may have been minor, the eventual result was significant genetic change, transforming the panda from a meat-eating bear like others in its species to a primarily herbivorous animal. Gould's *The Mismeasure of Man* won the National Book Critics Circle Award for Essays and Criticism in 1982. The book features an explanation of the misuse of intelligence testing to assign value to human beings and to promote cultural prejudice. Although Gould concedes that human intelligence has a specific location in the brain and can be measured by a standard number score, he argues that any efforts to label groups as possessing inherently inferior or superior intelligence represents a misuse of scientific data and a violation of the scientific process.

In 1981 Gould served as expert witness in a trial in Little Rock, Arkansas, which challenged a state law mandating the teaching of "creation science" in tandem with evolution. Gould attacked the Biblical literalism of his religious opponents, for example discounting their view that Noah's flood could account for fossil remains around the globe. Gould argued that the theories of creation science are belied by all available scientific evidence and therefore do not deserve scientific status. Creationism was recognized as a religion and not a science with the help of Gould's testimony. That same year, he received a prize fellows award from the MacArthur Foundation.

In July of 1982 Gould was diagnosed with mesothelioma, a particularly deadly form of cancer. Recovering from the illness and the treatment, he continued his work with a renewed sense of urgency. Gould further explored the misuse of standardized testing to label social groups rather than study the effects of social factors on intelligence first portrayed in *The Mismeasure of Man.* He started writing about an increasingly wide range of topics, including the black widow spider, the "Hottentot Venus" (referring to an African woman who was caged to be publicly displayed in nineteenth century Europe), and the disappearance of .400 hitters in baseball. He won popular recognition for these essays, collected in *The Flamingo's Smile* in 1985. He addressed issues such as the dangers of nuclear winter and of biological determinism and started publishing in other periodicals, including *The New York Review of Books, Discover,* and the British journal *Nature.* "In my youth, I was very much into this macho idea of science as rigid, hard, quantifiable," Gould told Natalie Angier during a 1993 interview for the *New York Times.* "Now I'm more interested in the beautiful and quirky contingencies that nature often takes." Gould's audience benefits from this shift in interests.

Winner of the Rhône-Poulenc Prize and a best-seller, *Wonderful Life: The Burgess Shale and the*

Nature of History was published in 1989. Located in Yoho National Park in western Canada, the Burgess Shale is a slab of exposed rock that reveals the remains of the world's most unusual fossil bed. Spawned by a catastrophic event half a billion years ago, the Burgess Shale unveils some of the strangest animal fossils in existence.

According to Gould, the Burgess fossils show the random aspects of the development of life and demonstrate that the evolution of living beings is neither orderly nor progressive. Averse to the idea that evolution connotes progress, Gould eschews the belief that life moves toward a perfected state. His recent writings stress this position most strongly.

Gould lives in a small Victorian house in Cambridge, Massachusetts, with his wife and two sons, Jesse and Ethan. On October 3, 1965, Gould married artist and writer Deborah Lee, whom he met while at Antioch College. She teaches at Groton, and together they lead a quiet, private family life. An accomplished baritone with an undying love for Gilbert and Sullivan operettas, Gould sings in the eminent amateur choral group the Boston Cecilia Society. Future projects include the composition of a major work to modify Charles Darwin's theory of evolution. "I could not dent the richness in a hundred lifetimes," Gould wrote in *The Flamingo's Smile,* "but I simply must have a look at a few more of those pretty pebbles."

SELECTED WRITINGS BY GOULD:

Books

An Evolutionary Microcosm: Pleistocene and Recent History of the Land Snail P. (Poecilozonites) in Bermuda, [Cambridge, MA], 1969.

(With Niles Eldredge) "Punctuated Equilibria: An Alternative to Phyletic Gradualism," *Models in Paleobiology,* edited by T. J. M. Schopf, Freeman, Cooper, 1972.

Ontogeny and Phylogeny, Belknap Press, 1977.

Ever Since Darwin: Reflections in Natural History, Norton, 1977.

The Panda's Thumb: More Reflections in Natural History, Norton, 1980.

(With Salvador Edward Juria and Sam Singer) *A View of Life,* Benjamin-Cummings, 1981.

The Mismeasure of Man, Norton, 1981.

Hen's Teeth and Horse's Toes: Further Reflections in Natural History, Norton, 1983.

The Flamingo's Smile: Reflections in Natural History, Norton, 1985.

(With Rosamund Wolff Purcell) *Illuminations: A Bestiary,* Norton, 1986.

Time's Arrow, Time's Cycle: Myth and Metaphor in the Discovery of Geological Time, Harvard University Press, 1987.

An Urchin in the Storm: Essays about Books and Ideas, Norton, 1987.

Wonderful Life: The Burgess Shale and the Nature of History, Norton, 1989.

Eight Little Piggies: Reflections in Natural History, Norton, 1993.

SOURCES:

Periodicals

Angier, Natalie, "An Evolving Celebrity," *New York Times,* February 11, 1993, p. C1.

Bethell, Tom, "Good as Gould," *American Spectator,* August, 1991, pp. 9–11.

Cosmopolitan, February, 1987, pp. 130–131.

Goode, Stephen, "A Giant Totters: Can Darwin Survive?," *Insight,* December 21, 1992, pp. 6–11, 32.

Green, Michelle, "Stephen Jay Gould," *People,* June 2, 1986, pp. 109–114.

Levy, Daniel, "Evolution, Extinction, and the Movies," *Time,* May 14, 1990, pp. 19–20.

Murray, Mary, "Paean to a Leader in Evolutionary Theory," *Science News,* August 23, 1986, p. 121.

Tierney, John, "Stephen Jay Gould," *Rolling Stone,* January 15, 1987, pp. 38–41, 58–61.

U.S. News and World Report, February 8, 1988, p. 64.

—*Sketch by Marjorie Burgess*

Meredith Charles Gourdine
1929-
American engineer and inventor

Meredith Charles Gourdine is a pioneer in electrogasdynamics (EGD) technology, an energy conversion process with many practical applications. The holder of over seventy patents, Gourdine is the president and CEO of Energy Innovations, a Houston-based firm devoted to overseeing and improving the many technological innovations Gourdine is responsible for. The practical applications of his research and development in energy conversion systems have affected the daily lives of people throughout the world.

One of four children, Gourdine was born in Newark, New Jersey, on September 26, 1929. Al-

Meredith Charles Gourdine

though his father had won a scholarship to Temple University, he decided not to go and worked instead at various maintenance jobs. Gourdine's mother was a teletype operator who was also interested in mathematics. In 1936 the family moved to Harlem, where Gourdine was inspired by a math teacher at his elementary school. Gourdine went on to attend the highly competitive Brooklyn Tech High School, where he combined schoolwork with swimming and track and excelled as a quarter-mile runner. He also worked long hours for a radio and telegraph company, which provided him with funds to finance his first semester of college at Cornell University. Entering Cornell in 1948, Gourdine soon distinguished himself as a student and was awarded with a scholarship.

At Cornell, Gourdine became interested in physics as a more practical application of mathematics, a discipline which he felt was too abstract. However, as a freshman, he was not allowed to take classes in engineering physics—considered the most demanding and selective course at the university—because his high school grades were not good enough. Gourdine worked hard during his first term to score high grades in chemistry, engineering, physics, and calculus and was later allowed to transfer from electrical engineering to engineering physics.

Gourdine balanced his studies at Cornell with a developing career as a star athlete. In 1952 he earned a place on the United States Olympic Track team and won a silver medal in the broad jump competition at Helsinki, Sweden, missing the gold by four centimeters. Graduating in 1953 with a bachelor's degree in engineering physics, Gourdine married June Cave, whom he met during his sophomore year (they would have four children together and later divorce). He then joined the Navy for two years as an ex-NROTC student, but found the work undemanding. Turning his attention back to math and physics, he applied for fellowships at Princeton and Cornell universities, as well as the California Institute of Technology.

Discovers Formula for Electrogasdynamics

Gourdine decided to go to CalTech on a Guggenheim Fellowship. During his graduate school years, he also received the Ramo-Woolridge Fellowship and developed the formula for electrogasdynamics (EGD) while working at Jet Propulsion Labs. Electrogasdynamics involves the interaction between an electrical field and charged particles suspended in gas, an event which produces high voltage electricity. The phenomenon of EGD had been known since the eighteenth century, but its uses were limited until Gourdine figured out how to employ the principle to produce enough electricity for practical applications in the modern world. Although Gourdine was put off by Jet Propulsion Lab's lack of interest in his research, he was not yet ready to take on the responsibility of his own company.

By 1960 Gourdine had earned his Ph.D. in engineering science, an interdisciplinary field based on a comprehensive understanding of all branches of physics. From 1960 to 1962 Gourdine was laboratory director of Plasmadyne Corporation, where he continued his research into magnetohydrodynamics (MHD), another conversion method that generates power through the interaction between magnetic fields and gases. However, again, he had no corporate support and moved on. After two more years, serving as chief scientist of Curtiss-Wright Corporation's Aero Division, Gourdine struck out on his own.

As the president and chairman of the board for Gourdine Systems, based in Livingston, New Jersey, Gourdine worked on patenting practical applications of EGD, MHD, and plasma physics (the study of electrically-charged, extremely hot gases). From 1964 to 1973, Gourdine invented or co-invented close to seventy patents. Knowing his own limitations, both personal and financial, Gourdine decided not to manufacture or sell his inventions. Instead, he licensed the patents to other companies.

One of Gourdine's inventions was the Electradyne Spray Gun, which used electrogasdynamics to atomize and electrify any kind of paint, allowing for the easy spray-painting of irregularly shaped objects, such as bicycles. He also invented Incineraid, a device to reduce air pollution emitted by apartment building incinerators. In 1970, Gourdine Systems became a publicly owned company and decided to do its own manufacturing and selling of products, although it soon fell prey to bad timing and poor business strategies. For example, Gourdine Systems spent more money marketing the spray gun than it made, and when incinerators were outlawed in New York City, Incineraid became unsalable.

Establishes New Company to Develop and License Technology

Despite these setbacks, Gourdine held fast to his goal to invent and license practical applications for the highly specialized technologies of EGD, MHD, and other direct energy conversion methods such as thermovoltaics (which involves the conversion of chemical and thermal energy into electricity). In 1974, Gourdine founded a new company, Energy Innovations, based in Houston, Texas.

In 1986 Gourdine lost his eyesight due to diabetic retinopathy. He first developed diabetes during his time in the Navy, with his eyesight gradually deteriorating over the years. This disability, however, did not prevent him from running Energy Innovations. Although Gourdine cannot read Braille (the diabetes has reduced sensation in his fingertips), he continues to produce new applications for his technologies and license them to other companies with the help of his son and second wife, Carolina. Known for his vigor and positive attitude, Gourdine practices yoga and meditation, swims, and enjoys spectator sports.

Gourdine's career as a researcher and inventor spans over thirty years and continues to grow. His many honors include election to the National Academy of Engineering and a citation for service as a member of the United States Army Science Board. He is a member of the Black Inventors Hall of Fame and in 1987 was honored for outstanding contributions as a scientist by North Carolina State University. Some of Gourdine's energy-saving and cost-efficient applications include a battery for electric cars, a system for clearing fog at airports, a method of extracting oil from oil shale, a procedure for repairing potholes by recovering rubber from old car tires and combining it with asphalt, and the means for producing better refrigerators and air conditioners.

SELECTED WRITINGS BY GOURDINE:

Periodicals

"Nuclear Power in Space," *Discovery,* 1963.

"Electrogasdynamic Power Generation," *AIAA Journal,* August, 1964, pp. 1423–1427.

"EGD and Precipitation," *Industrial & Engineering Chemistry,* December, 1967, pp. 26–29.

SOURCES:

Books

Van Sertima, Ivan, editor, *Blacks in Science: Ancient and Modern,* 1983, Transaction Books, pp. 226–227.

Periodicals

Ebony, August, 1972, p. 125.

Field, Alan M., "Father of Invention," *Houston Metropolitan,* February, 1991, pp. 43–45, 53–54.

Pierce, Ponchitta, "Science Pacemaker," *Ebony,* April, 1967, pp. 53–58.

—*Sketch by Geeta Kothari*

Dwight Gourneau
1945(?)-
American computer scientist

Dwight Gourneau's achievements as a computer engineer at International Business Machines (IBM) have made him a role model for other Native Americans seeking careers in science and technology. In addition to the technological developments he pioneered at IBM, Gourneau also served as an important liaison between the company and prospective Native American employees. Since retiring from IBM, he has continued to be a mentor to aspiring engineers, working for the American Indian Science and Engineering Society as a teacher and administrator. As a child, Gourneau lived on a productive 200-acre farm in Belcourt, North Dakota, where he was a member of the Turtle Mountain band of the Chippewas. One of seven children, he enjoyed an active childhood and youth and was motivated by the success of other members of his family. His father was a commercial gardener, farmer, trapper, and the chairman of their community; several of the family's older children had attended college and moved into various professions after graduating.

When his own turn for college came, however, Gourneau had a hard time adjusting to surroundings that were very different from his predominately Native American hometown. Attending the University of North Dakota in the early-1960s, he found himself part of a tiny minority of Native American students, and after a year he dropped out. Nevertheless, he knew the importance of learning a trade, so he took a job as an engineering draftsman. Enjoying the work, he was soon planning to renew his engineering studies. He took advantage of the U.S. Government's Relocation Program, which allowed him to move to San Jose, California, with his wife Darlene. There he resumed his studies and two years later received an associate's degree in science and electronic technology.

After graduating, he was hired by IBM, the giant electronics corporation, and began to work in the field of computers. His work over the years included designing chips, programming computers, and advanced work in areas such as systems architecture, microprogramming design, and the analysis of computer performance. With a versatility that would become his trademark, he later branched into the manufacturing end of the business and then into customer service, working to alleviate on-site computer problems. Though he was originally located at the company's San Jose office, he later transferred to Rochester, Minnesota, and completed an engineering degree from the University of Minnesota in 1972.

Technology and Tradition

As the years passed, Gourneau's identity as a Chippewa became an asset both for him and for IBM, which called on him to recruit other Native Americans into the company. He has also reported that his cultural identity allowed him to better manage the stresses of corporate life, and he worked with other Native Americans in Rochester to help create a larger sense of community. They founded the Native American Center of Northeast Minnesota, a nonprofit organization that sponsored a host of cultural activities that were open to people of all races and ethnicities.

Gourneau stayed with IBM for more than a quarter century. For one of his inventions he received the company's Outstanding Technical Achievements Award and another of his ideas became an integral part of information systems nationwide. He also continued his education through internal classes and outside programs, receiving a degree in physics at Winona State University and an M.S. in manufacturing systems engineering from the University of Wisconsin.

After retiring from IBM in 1992, Gourneau struck off in a new direction. Having long been affiliated with the American Indian Science and Engineering Society (AISES), Gourneau began teaching physics and engineering in the society's special program for high school-aged Native Americans at the California Institute of Technology. Later that year he became deputy director of AISES. In this capacity, and through service on a number of advisory committees, Gourneau has helped foster educational and economic development among Native American tribes throughout the country.

SOURCES:

Periodicals

Major, Michael Jay, "The Best of Both Worlds," in *Equal Employment Opportunity BiMonthly,* c. 1993.

—Sketch by Nicholas Pease

Govindjee
1932-
Indian-born American biologist

Govindjee is a plant biologist whose research has centered on photosynthesis and the role played by bicarbonate in the food production of plants and cyanobacteria. He has also studied the mechanism of what is known as the "oxygen clock," which leads to the oxidation of water in plants.

Govindjee was born October 24, 1932, in Allahabad, Uttar Pradesh, India, the youngest of four children. His father, Vishveshwar Prasad, had dropped the family surname Asthana because he objected to the tradition that names should reveal caste. Govindjee's mother, Savitri Devi, raised the children while his father worked first as a college arts teacher and then as a representative for Oxford University Press. Govindjee credits his early love of reading to having the latest books at home. His father, however, died when Govindjee was eleven; his mother was in poor health, and he was raised by his elder brother, Krishnaji, who was ten years his senior.

In 1948, Govindjee graduated from Colonoganj High School in Allahabad and went on to receive a certificate in physics from Kayastha Pathsahala Intermediate College in Allahabad. He completed his B.S. in 1952 and his M.S. in 1954, both at the University of Allahabad. For the next two years he worked as a lecturer in botany at the university.

His interest in plant biology had grown during his early studies. When he was nineteen, Govindjee had organized a dramatic seminar in which six students dressed in period costume as famous scientists. Govindjee had the role of the eighteenth-century physician, Jan Ingenhousz, who showed that photo-

Govindjee

synthesis takes place only in the presence of light. It was the research he did for this role that led him to read about photosynthesis, including the work of the leaders in the field at that time. While lecturing at Allahabad, he decided to do a doctorate in plant biology. Seeking a doctoral supervisor, he wrote to three of the most prominent scientists in plant biology: Nobel Laureate **Otto Warburg** in Germany, **Melvin Calvin** at Berkeley (who would go on to win a Nobel Prize in chemistry in 1961), and Robert Emerson at the University of Illinois at Urbana-Champaign. After receiving replies from the American scientists, he chose Emerson at Urbana.

Emerson arranged a fellowship for him in 1956, and a year later he arranged one for Govindjee's fiancee, Rajni Varma, who was also a biologist. The two were married in Urbana on October 24, 1957. Govindjee was in the midst of finishing his doctoral studies on February 4, 1959, when Emerson was killed in a plane crash at La Guardia Airport in New York City. "I thought it was the end of my research life," he later recalled in an interview with Marianne P. Fedunkiw. But Emerson's colleague, a physical chemist named Eugene Rabinowitch, took on both Govindjee and Rajni as students, and Govindjee completed his studies and received his Ph.D. in 1960. He remained at the university in Urbana, first as a postdoctoral fellow, then as assistant professor of botany. Appointed associate professor of botany and biophysics in 1965 and full professor in 1969, Govindjee became a distinguished lecturer at the School of Life Sciences in 1979.

Govindjee's most significant contribution to plant biology has been in deciphering the details of the molecular steps involved in the unique oxygen-evolving photosystem of plants and cyanobacteria. He has shown that light energy is converted into chemical energy very rapidly, oxidizing a special chlorophyll molecule and reducing a special pheophytin molecule. He has also described how bicarbonate (hydrated carbon dioxide), apart from its direct role in the production of carbohydrates during photosynthesis (the Calvin cycle), is required for the production of other key intermediates needed to run photosynthesis. One of the goals of his ongoing research, he told interviewer Marianne P. Fedunkiw, is "to provide a detailed molecular understanding . . . of how exactly bicarbonate functions at the level of specific amino acids, and how, if at all, it is involved in regulating photosynthesis *in vivo.*

During his career Govindjee has also been a visiting scientist at institutions in France, Germany, India, The Netherlands, Japan, Canada, and Switzerland. Other honors include being elected as a Fellow of the American Association for the Advancement of Science in 1976, and as a Fellow and Life Member of the National Academy of Science in India in 1979. He was president of the American Society for Photobiology in 1981. He is also a member of the American Society of Plant Physiologists and the Biophysical Society of America.

Govindjee became a U.S. citizen in 1972. He and his wife, a senior research scientist in biophysics at the University of Illinois at Urbana, have two children.

SELECTED WRITINGS BY GOVINDJEE:

Periodicals

(With R. Govindjee) "Primary Events in Photosynthesis," *Scientific American,* Volume 231, 1974, pp. 68–82.

(With D. J. Blubaugh) "The Molecular Mechanism of the Bicarbonate Effect at the Plastoquinone Reductase Site of Photosynthesis," *Photosynthesis Research,* Volume 19, 1988, pp. 85–128.

(With M. R. Wasielewski, D. G. Johnson, and M. Seibert) "Determination of the Primary Charge Separation Rate in Isolated Photosystem II Reaction Centers with 500 Femtosecond Time Resolution," *Proceedings of the National Academy of Sciences U.S.A.,* Volume 86, 1989, pp. 524–548.

(With W. Coleman) "How Does Photosynthesis Make Oxygen?" in *Scientific American,* Volume 262, 1990, pp. 50–58.

SOURCES:

Books

Salwi, D. H., *Our Scientists,* Children's Book Trust, 1986, pp. 133–135.

Other

Govindjee, interview with Marianne P. Fedunkiw conducted December 29, 1993.

—*Sketch by Marianne P. Fedunkiw*

Ragnar Arthur Granit
1900-1991
Finnish neurophysiologist

Ragnar Arthur Granit conducted important research in two distinct areas of neurophysiology —during the first part of his career he researched the physiology of vision while in the later years he studied muscle spindles and neural control over movement. Although he made significant contributions to both fields, it was for his investigations into the physiology of vision that Granit was best known. He clarified the process by which the retina of the eye first encodes information about form and color, then transmits it to the brain via the optic nerve.

Granit was born in Helsinki, Finland, on October 30, 1900, the eldest son of Arthur W. Granit, a government forester, and Albertina Helena Malmberg Granit. Soon after his birth, the family started a forest-products business in Helsinki. Since both his parents were of Swedish origin, Granit attended the Swedish Normal School there. In 1918, Granit fought in Finland's war for independence from the Soviet Union, for which he received the Finnish Cross of Freedom.

Conducts Research on the Physiology of Vision

The following year Granit entered the University of Helsinki with the intention of studying experimental psychology. However, he decided that a medical education would provide the best foundation for this field. So he went on to complete a master's degree in 1923 and then an M.D. in 1927. It was while completing his medical studies that Granit became interested in studying the nervous system, particularly the eye. The English physiologist **Edgar Douglas Adrian** had just made the first recordings of electrical impulses in single nerve fibers, and Granit realized that Adrian's technique could be used to provide useful information about the nervous system as well as the retina. Thus, in 1928 Granit traveled to Oxford University to work with Adrian and another English physiologist, **Charles Scott Sherrington**, and learn the techniques of neurophysiology. Soon thereafter, Granit accepted a fellowship in medical physics at the University of Pennsylvania. It was here, while working at the university's Johnson Foundation for Medical Physics, that Granit first met **Haldan Keffer Hartline**, who along with **George Wald** would eventually share the Nobel Prize with Granit.

In 1935 Granit returned to the University of Helsinki as a professor of physiology, but he also continued his research into neurophysics. At this time, it was still unclear whether light could inhibit, as well as elicit, impulses in the optic nerve. During the early 1930s, Granit produced the first experimental evidence of this inhibition, a finding that remains fundamental to visual physiology. In early work, Granit employed such indirect measures as the sensitivity reported by human subjects to flickering lights. He showed that illumination focused on the retina would suppress the response of adjacent regions. This served to enhance the perception of visual contrasts. Granit soon confirmed these findings using an electroretinogram, a graphic record of electrical activity in the retina, similar to the record of heart activity known as an electrocardiogram.

The 1939 invasion of Finland by the Soviet Union interrupted Granit's work. During the war Granit served as a physician on three Swedish-speaking islands, including Korpo in the Baltic Sea. After the war, he was offered positions at both Harvard University in the United States as well as the Karolinksa Institute in Stockholm. He chose the latter, where he directed the Nobel Institute for Neurophysiology until his retirement in 1967.

While working at the Nobel Institute, Granit and his colleagues became the first scientists to use microelectrodes, tiny electrical conductors, for sensory research. By using microelectrodes to study individual cells in the retina, Granit now demonstrated that certain cells, called modulators, are color-specific, while others, called dominators, respond to a broad range of the spectrum. Although subsequent research has modified his views, Granit's studies were the earliest serious effort to investigate color vision by electrophysiological methods.

Studies Muscle Spindles and Motor Control

Beginning in 1945, Granit shifted the focus of his research to the study of muscle spindles, sensory end organs that are sensitive to muscle tension. Ultimately, the structure of muscle spindles and their function in motor control became one of the best-studied areas in neurophysiology, and Granit was at the forefront of the field. Throughout this period of his career, Granit maintained a hands-on presence in the laboratory and continued to take part in experimental operations on animals there. The procedures he most enjoyed performing were the meticulous dissection of nerves and the careful preparation of nerve roots for electrode placement. His surgical skill was much admired by younger students.

Granit's dual contributions to neurophysiology were honored on numerous occasions. In addition to the Nobel he was awarded such prizes as the 1947 Jubilee Medal of the Swedish Society of Physicians, the 1957 Anders Retzius Gold Medal of the University of Utrecht, and the 1961 Jahre Prize of Oslo University. He was once president of the Royal Swedish Academy of Sciences, and a member of such learned societies as the American Academy of Arts and Sciences, the American National Academy of Sciences, and the Royal Society of London. Active even after his retirement, Granit was appointed a resident scholar at the Fogarty International Center in Bethesda, Maryland, during part of the 1970s. He also accepted a visiting professorship at St. Catherine's College in Oxford, England. In addition, he spent many leisure hours sailing on the Baltic Sea, and he enjoyed gardening. Granit had married Baroness Marguerite Emma "Daisy" Bruun on October 2, 1929, just before leaving for the Johnson Foundation fellowship in the United States. They had one son, Michael, who became a Stockholm architect. In a 1972 essay printed in the *Annual Review of Physiology,* Granit reflected on his lengthy life and career, contrasting a young person's drive for discovery with an older one's need for understanding. He noted, "this second variant of scientific endeavour does not always suit the impatient passion of the young, ruled by an ambition which craves immediate satisfaction, but a little later in life it provides feelings of assurance and satisfaction in one's work." When Granit died of a heart attack at his home in Stockholm on March 12, 1991, he had lived to see the scientific fruit of seeds first sown six decades before.

SELECTED WRITINGS BY GRANIT:

Books

Sensory Mechanisms of the Retina, Oxford University Press, 1947.

Charles Scott Sherrington: An Appraisal, Doubleday, 1967.

The Basis of Motor Control, Academic Press, 1970.

Receptors and Sensory Perception, Greenwood Press, 1975.

The Purposive Brain, Massachusetts Institute of Technology Press, 1980.

Periodicals

"Discovery and Understanding," *Annual Review of Physiology,* 1972, pp. 1–12.

SOURCES:

Periodicals

Crescitelli, Frederick, "The 1967 Nobel Prizes for Physiology or Medicine," *Vision Research,* Volume 8, 1968, pp. 333–37.

Eccles, John C., "Professor Ragnar Granit's Contributions in the Field of Motor Control," *American Journal of Physical Medicine,* Volume 47, 1968, pp. 3–7.

Ratliff, Floyd, "Nobel Prize: Three Named for Medicine, Physiology Award—Ragnar Granit," *Science,* October 27, 1967, pp. 469–71.

Szumski, Alfred J., "Professor Ragnar Granit's Laboratory: Personal Impressions," *American Journal of Physical Medicine,* Volume 47, 1968, pp. 8–9.

Other

Karolinska Institute, letter to Linda Wasmer Smith, dated January 12, 1994.

—Sketch by Linda Wasmer Smith

Evelyn Boyd Granville

1924-

American mathematician

Evelyn Boyd Granville earned her doctorate from Yale University in 1949; in that year she and **Marjorie Lee Browne** (at the University of Michigan) became the first African American women to receive doctoral degrees in mathematics; it would be more than a dozen years before another black woman would earn a Ph.D. in the field. Granville's career has included stints as an educator and involvement with the American space program during its formative years.

Granville was born in Washington, D.C., on May 1, 1924. Her father, William Boyd, worked as a custodian in their apartment building; he did not stay with the family, however, and Granville was raised by her mother, Julia Walker Boyd, and her mother's twin sister, Louise Walker, both of whom worked as

Evelyn Boyd Granville

examiners for the U.S. Bureau of Engraving and Printing. Granville and her sister Doris, who was a year and a half older, often spent portions of their summers at the farm of a family friend in Linden, Virginia.

Achievement Encouraged throughout Academic Career

The public schools of Washington, D.C., were racially segregated when Granville attended them. However, Dunbar High School (from which she graduated as valedictorian) maintained high academic standards. Several of its faculty held degrees from top colleges, and they encouraged the students to pursue ambitious goals. Granville's mathematics teachers included Ulysses Basset, a Yale graduate, and Mary Cromwell, a University of Pennsylvania graduate; Cromwell's sister, who held a doctorate from Yale, taught in Dunbar's English department.

With the encouragement of her family and teachers, Granville entered Smith College with a small partial scholarship from Phi Delta Kappa, a national sorority for black women. After her freshman year, she lived in a cooperative house at Smith, sharing chores rather than paying more expensive dormitory rates. During the summers, she returned to Washington to work at the National Bureau of Standards.

Granville majored in mathematics and physics, but was also fascinated by astronomy after taking a class from Marjorie Williams. She considered becoming an astronomer, but chose not to commit herself to living in the isolation of a major observatory, which was necessary for astronomers of that time. Though she had entered college intending to become a teacher, she began to consider industrial work in physics or mathematics. She graduated summa cum laude in 1945 and was elected to Phi Beta Kappa.

With help from a Smith College fellowship, Granville began graduate studies at Yale University, for which she also received financial assistance. She earned an M.A. in mathematics and physics in one year, and began working toward a doctorate at Yale. For the next two years she received a Julius Rosenwald Fellowship, which was awarded to help promising black Americans develop their research potential. The following year she received an Atomic Energy Commission Predoctoral Fellowship. Granville's doctoral work concentrated on functional analysis, and her dissertation was titled *On Laguerre Series in the Complex Domain.* Her advisor, Einar Hille, was a former president of the American Mathematical Society. Upon receiving her Ph.D. in mathematics in 1949, Granville was elected to the scientific honorary society Sigma Xi.

Granville then undertook a year of postdoctoral research at New York University's Institute of Mathematics and Science. Apparently because of housing discrimination, she was unable to find an apartment in New York, so she moved in with a friend of her mother. Despite attending segregated schools, Granville had not encountered discrimination based on race or gender in her professional preparation. Only years later would she learn that her 1950 application for a teaching position at a college in New York City was turned down for such a reason. A female adjunct faculty member eventually told biographer Patricia Kenschaft that the application was rejected because of Granville's race; however, a male mathematician reported that despite the faculty's support of the application, the dean rejected it because Granville was a woman.

In 1950, Granville accepted the position of associate professor at Fisk University, a noted black college in Nashville, Tennessee. She was a popular teacher, and at least two of her female students credited her with inspiring them to earn doctorates in mathematics in later years.

Begins Affiliation with Space Program

After two years of teaching, Granville went to work for the Diamond Ordnance Fuze Laboratories as an applied mathematician, a position she held for four years. From 1956 to 1960, she worked for IBM on the Project Vanguard and Project Mercury space programs, analyzing orbits and developing computer procedures. Her job included making "real-time" calculations during satellite launchings. "That was exciting, as I look back, to be a part of the space programs—a very small part—at the very beginning of U.S. involvement," Granville told Loretta Hall in a 1994 interview.

On a summer vacation to southern California, Granville met the Reverend Gamaliel Mansfield Collins, a minister in the community church. They were married in 1960, and made their home in Los Angeles. They had no children, although Collins's three children occasionally lived with them. In 1967, the marriage ended in divorce.

Upon moving to Los Angeles, Granville had taken a job at the Computation and Data Reduction Center of the U.S. Space Technology Laboratories, studying rocket trajectories and methods of orbit computation. In 1962, she became a research specialist at the North American Aviation Space and Information Systems Division, working on celestial mechanics, trajectory and orbit computation, numerical analysis, and digital computer techniques for the Apollo program. The following year she returned to IBM as a senior mathematician.

Return to Teaching Marked by Involvement with Children

Because of restructuring at IBM, numerous employees were transferred out of the Los Angeles area in 1967; Granville wanted to stay, however, so she applied for a teaching position at California State University in Los Angeles. She happily reentered the teaching profession, which she found enjoyable and rewarding. She was disappointed in the mathematics preparedness of her students, however, and she began working to improve mathematics education at all levels. She taught an elementary school supplemental mathematics program in 1968 and 1969 through the State of California Miller Mathematics Improvement Program. The following year she directed a mathematics enrichment program that provided after-school classes for kindergarten through fifth grade students, and she taught grades two through five herself. She was an educator at a National Science Foundation Institute for Secondary Teachers of Mathematics summer program at the University of Southern California in 1972. Along with colleague Jason Frand, Granville wrote *Theory and Application of Mathematics for Teachers* in 1975; a second edition was published in 1978, and the textbook was used at over fifty colleges.

In 1970, Granville married Edward V. Granville, a real estate broker. After her 1984 retirement from California State University in Los Angeles, they moved to a sixteen-acre farm in Texas, where they sold eggs produced by their eight hundred chickens.

From 1985 to 1988, Granville taught mathematics and computer science at Texas College in Tyler. In 1990, she accepted an appointment to the Sam A. Lindsey Chair at the University of Texas at Tyler, and in subsequent years continued teaching there as a visiting professor. Smith College awarded Granville an honorary doctorate in 1989, making her the first black woman mathematician to receive such an honor from an American institution.

Throughout her career Granville shared her energy with a variety of professional and service organizations and boards. Many of them, including the National Council of Teachers of Mathematics and the American Association of University Women, focused on education and mathematics. Others, such as the U.S. Civil Service Panel of Examiners of the Department of Commerce and the Psychology Examining Committee of the Board of Medical Examiners of the State of California, reflected broader civic interests.

When asked to summarize her major accomplishments, Granville told Hall, "First of all, showing that women can do mathematics." Then she added, "Being an African American woman, letting people know that we have brains too."

SELECTED WRITINGS BY GRANVILLE:

Books

(With Jason Frand) *Theory and Application of Mathematics for Teachers,* Wadsworth Publishing, 1975.

Other

On Laguerre Series in the Complex Domain (dissertation), Yale University, 1949.

SOURCES:

Books

Grinstein, Louise S., and Paul J. Campbell, editors, *Women of Mathematics,* Greenwood Press, 1987, pp. 57–61.

Hine, Darlene Clark, editor, *Black Women in America,* Volume 1, Carlson, 1993, pp. 498–499.

Women, Numbers and Dreams, U.S. Department of Education, 1982, pp. 99–106.

Periodicals

Kenschaft, Patricia C., "Black Women in Mathematics in the United States," *The American Mathematical Monthly,* October, 1981, pp. 592–604.

Other

Granville, Evelyn Boyd, interview with Loretta Hall conducted January 11, 1994.

—Sketch by Loretta Hall

Wilson Greatbatch
1919-
American biomedical engineer

Wilson Greatbatch is an engineer and entrepreneur whose invention of the implantable cardiac pacemaker, a heart regulating device, has saved the lives of millions of people. An inventor of wide-ranging interests and abilities, his more than 150 patents covered efforts ranging from improved pacemaker batteries to biomass energy production to genetic engineering.

Greatbatch was born September 6, 1919, in Buffalo, New York. He was the only child of Walter Plant Greatbatch, a construction worker born in England, and the former Charlotte Rectenwalt; he did, however, have a half-brother in England from his father's previous marriage. After attending high school in West Seneca, New York, Greatbatch worked as a radio installer and engineer and entered the Naval Reserve in 1938. Volunteering for active duty in 1940, Greatbatch spent World War II as a radioman in various assignments, including teaching, maintenance, and flying combat missions as a tail gunner in carrier-based dive bombers and torpedo planes. He continued his education while in the service, taking courses by one method or another from five different institutions. When Aviation Chief Radioman Greatbatch left the Navy in 1945, he married Eleanor Wright, a high school home economics teacher whom he had met before the war when she was a student at the State University of New York at Buffalo. Greatbatch then resumed his own education by entering Cornell University, where he earned a bachelor's degree in electrical engineering in 1950. His graduate work included more studies at Cornell, then a stint as an assistant professor at the University of Buffalo. There Greatbatch also obtained his master's degree in electrical engineering.

Conceives and Develops the Cardiac Pacemaker

While at Cornell, Greatbatch had worked at the university's animal behavior farm, where he learned about physiology and about the problems which can incapacitate the natural pacemaker that signals the heart to beat. He immediately began tinkering with ideas for an artificial pacemaker. Greatbatch kept those ideas in his head for years before making them a reality. In 1956, he assembled an oscillator which proved to be perfect for sending a pulse to the heart once every second. This discovery he later described as a complete accident, occasioned when he was working on an unrelated device and installed the wrong resistor. By 1958, other researchers had marketed artificial pacemakers, but they required power sources outside the body that greatly restricted the patient's freedom and comfort. Greatbatch was now working at Taber Instrument Corporation, where his work on medical instrumentation included building equipment used to monitor test animals on early space flights. Greatbatch realized that the perfection of the transistor made it possible to build an implantable pacemaker which would be entirely self-contained. Encouraged by two surgeons, William Chardack and Andrew Gage, Greatbatch left his job and built the first pacemaker in his barn after three weeks of work.

Looking back on the amateur nature of his pioneering medical research, Greatbatch told an interviewer in 1988 that if he had pursued the same do-it-yourself approach twenty years later, government regulators would have sent him to prison. Homemade or not, the prototype was successful. Greatbatch and his two physician associates continued to perfect the design until, two years later, they were ready to try it in human patients. Granted a patent on the Chardack-Greatbatch Implantable Cardiac Pacemaker, he formed his own company, Wilson Greatbatch Inc., to license it. Greatbatch credited Dr. Chardack with convincing his medical colleagues of the new pacemaker's value, resulting in over two million implantations in the next three decades. In 1963, Greatbatch became vice-president and technical director of a reorganized company, Mennen-Greatbatch Electronics. Two years later, he helped produce the next step forward, the "demand" pacemaker, which functioned only when the natural pacemaker faltered instead of working continuously.

After producing the pacemaker, Greatbatch broadened his interest to include the electrochemical functioning of the human body, a subject on which he published several professional papers. Greatbatch returned to work on the pacemaker in 1970 because he felt the batteries available, which often required replacement after two years, could be improved. He experimented with nuclear power sources, then with lithium-based batteries, which proved to be the breakthrough creating the much-desired "lifetime" battery and almost eliminating battery-replacement surgery. His new company, Wilson Greatbatch Ltd., immediately became the leader in manufacturing pacemaker batteries. Greatbatch was made a Fellow of the American College of Cardiology in 1974, one of only two non-physician engineers ever so honored. In 1984, the National Society of Professional Engineers recognized the pacemaker as one of modern engineering's ten greatest contributions to society. Two years later, Greatbatch was inducted into the National Inventors Hall of Fame.

Moves on to New Fields of Science

By this time, Greatbatch had already branched out into new ventures. In 1975, he launched a company to explore biomass energy based on a special strain of poplar trees. This wasn't economically successful, although he enjoyed the project. One sideline of this research found Greatbatch converting a pickup truck into a rather cranky form of transportation fueled entirely by wood alcohol. The genetic aspects of his biomass work launched Greatbatch in another new direction. In 1985, Greatbatch left his eldest son as chair of Wilson Greatbatch Ltd. and founded yet another corporation, Greatbatch Gen-Aid Ltd., to pursue his interest in genetic engineering. In addition to agricultural applications arising from his biomass research, Greatbatch sought to apply his largely self-taught expertise to creating genes which would defeat the "retroviruses" which cause acquired immunodeficiency syndrome (AIDS) and T-cell leukemia. Greatbatch was a great believer in trying to synthesize various fields of science and engineering and in bypassing step-by-step research in favor of attempting great leaps, accepting the high risk of failure. He once stated that an average inventor might succeed in one out of ten such endeavors, and counted himself lucky to have succeeded, by his own scorecard, in three out of ten major efforts. Greatbatch thought of himself primarily as an entrepreneur, someone who actually got new things produced. Being an inventor was a means to that end.

One of his most original inventions was the solar-electric canoe. Having developed an interest in solar energy, Greatbatch powered his one-of-a-kind craft with a solar-charged battery and tested it with a trip of 150 miles. During his long and busy career as a technological entrepreneur, Greatbatch also found time to pick up four honorary doctorates, teach at three universities, father five children, write over 100 articles, and lead a busy life of public service inspired by his Christian faith. He took an active role in the Gideon Society, and spoke at many colleges, churches, and schools on engineering, AIDS research, and other topics. The dual achievements of creating the implantable pacemaker and a greatly improved power source won Greatbatch the National Medal of Technology, presented in 1990 by United States President George Bush.

SELECTED WRITINGS BY GREATBATCH:

Books

Implantable Active Devices, Wilson Greatbatch Ltd., 1983.

"The First Successful Implantable Cardiac Pacemaker," in *New Medical Devices,* edited by Karen B. Ekelman, National Academy Press, 1988, pp. 24–29.

Periodicals

"Twenty-Five Years of Pacemaking," *PACE,* January-February, 1974, pp. 143–147.

"History of Implantable Devices," *IEEE Engineering in Medicine and Biology,* September, 1991, pp. 38–49.

SOURCES:

Books

Brown, Kenneth A., *Inventors at Work,* Tempus, 1988.

Periodicals

"National Science, Technology Medalists Named," *Science,* November 16, 1990, p. 904.

Other

Greatbatch, Eleanor W., interview with Matthew A. Bille, August 29, 1993.

Teare, Elaine P., Wilson Greatbatch Ltd., interview with Matthew A. Bille, August 16, 1993.

—Sketch by Matthew A. Bille

Crawford H. Greenewalt
1902-1993
American chemical engineer and ornithologist

Crawford H. Greenewalt was a chemical engineer and an executive who worked for the Du Pont Company for nearly fifty years. He was closely associated with the Manhattan Project during World War II, acting as the liaison between Du Pont and **Enrico Fermi** in Chicago and directing the construction of plutonium plants in Tennessee and Washington. He rose to the presidency of the company after the war and served as chair of the board from 1962 to 1968. Greenewalt was also an amateur ornithologist who made extensive studies of hummingbirds, now considered some of the finest in the field.

Greenewalt was born in Cummington, Massachusetts, on August 16, 1902, the only child of Frank Lindsay and Mary Hallock Greenewalt. He grew up, however, in Philadelphia, where his father was resident physician at Girard College. His mother, born in Beirut, Lebanon, of English descent, was an author and concert pianist who toured as a soloist with the Pittsburgh and Philadelphia symphony orchestras. The scientific and creative interests of his parents influenced Greenewalt; early in life, he studied the cello, and after graduating from the William Penn Charter School in 1918, he enrolled at the Massachusetts Institute of Technology (MIT), where he studied chemical engineering. He graduated from MIT in 1922, and he was hired that fall as a control chemist by Du Pont at their heavy chemicals laboratory in Philadelphia.

After 1922 Greenewalt climbed quickly through the company ranks. In 1924 he was promoted to the chemical department experimental station, a sort of chemical think-tank at the Du Pont headquarters in Wilmington, Delaware. In 1927, he was promoted to group leader of the experimental station, and in 1933 he rose to assistant director. In 1939, he was elected director of the company, and two years later he was elected to the board of directors. In 1942, he was chosen chemical director of the Grasselli Chemical Department, a division that produced acids, insecticides, and other agricultural and commercial chemicals.

Instrumental in Spurring Nuclear Research for Du Pont

During World War II, the company agreed to build a plutonium reactor for the United States government at Oak Ridge, Tennessee. Soon after, Du Pont was asked to design, build, and operate a similar plutonium manufacturing plant in Hanford, Washington; in 1943, Greenewalt was named technical director of this project. His first job was to assume the role of liaison between Du Pont and the group of scientists headed by Enrico Fermi in Chicago. Greenewalt was among those who witnessed the world's first sustained nuclear chain reaction in the squash courts at the University of Chicago. The nuclear physicists working on the project did not at first respect Greenewalt, primarily because he was a commercial chemical engineer. But he came to understand the physics of the project and won their respect; he was reportedly urged by Fermi to leave industry and devote himself to pure research.

One of Greenewalt's most notable contributions to the Manhattan Project was his decisive leadership in the planning and construction of the Hanford Plant, which manufactured the plutonium necessary for the bomb. It was his decision to bypass the pilot-plant stage and proceed directly to construction, and this greatly sped completion of the project. Once construction on the Hanford Plant had begun, Greenewalt worked constantly at the site on the Columbia River; he is reported to have worked eighteen hours a day alongside the 55,000 others laboring there. In 1945, with the Hanford operations well underway, he returned to Du Pont headquarters. In 1948, the federal government awarded Du Pont the contract for construction of the Savannah River Nuclear Plant, considered one of the largest construction projects ever undertaken. The 200,000-acre site on the border of South Carolina and Georgia is home to a plant that produced key atomic ingredients for the American nuclear arsenal until the late 1980s.

In 1946 Greenewalt was elected vice-president of Du Pont, and in 1948 he rose to president, a post which he held until 1962; he then served as chair of the board until 1967. During Greenewalt's tenure at Du Pont, the company experienced phenomenal growth while its sales more than doubled. He was instrumental in the chemical engineering and commercial manufacture of the nylon fiber synthesized by **Wallace Carothers**. He is credited with bringing the revolutionary material out of the laboratory and into production; at one point nylon constituted 30 percent of the company's sales. A number of other materials that irrevocably changed industrial and commercial markets around the world were designed and produced while Greenewalt was at Du Pont's helm, and these included Dacron fibers, as well as Orlon, and Lycra Spandex fibers, Mylar film, and Teflon resin.

Conducts Highly Regarded Studies of Hummingbirds

Greenewalt was as renowned for his amateur endeavors as for those of his professional career. He built a fully equipped machine shop at his home, where he designed and produced a number of original devices. His forays into ornithology were widely honored and considered some of the finest to date; these included detailed studies of the physiology of hummingbird song production. After 1959, he spent much time studying and photographing hummingbirds, traveling more that 100,000 miles in pursuit of them. He designed and sometimes constructed novel equipment, including high-speed cameras and stroboscopic lights for this purpose. He is credited with taking more photographs of the elusive species than any person before him, and many of the birds he photographed were captured on film for the first time.

Greenewalt provided insights into the hummingbirds' unique mechanisms of flight and the optics of their iridescent colors. He established that their bright coloration was the result not of pigments in the feathers but of the nature of their reflective properties. He showed that the glossy feathers exploited a phenomenon called "thin-film interference." Greenewalt provided high-magnification photographs and electron-micrographs of the feathers to substantiate his findings. He also explained how the structure of the birds' wings, being rigid at the shoulder and flexible at the elbow, enabled them to accomplish in-flight acrobatics and high-speed, level flight. He developed wind tunnel experiments in which he found their top speed to be about thirty miles per hour.

In 1926, Greenewalt married Margaretta Lammot du Pont, daughter of Irenree du Pont, who was a former president of the company. Greenewalt and his wife had three children. They were both dedicated musicians—he played the cello and clarinet and she the violin. He was chair of the Wilmington Medical Center's board of trustees and director of the Winterthur Museum near Wilmington. He was widely published and honored with numerous awards, including the William Proctor Prize for Scientific Achievement in 1957, the Medal for the Advancement of Research from the American Society of Metals in 1958, the John F. Lewis Prize of the American Philosophical Society in 1961 for a paper on hummingbirds, and the U.S. Camera Achievement Award for his photography of hummingbirds in 1967. In 1992, he received the Arthur A. Allen Award from the Cornell University Laboratory of Ornithology for independent research on hummingbirds. He died of a cerebral hemorrhage on September 27, 1993, at the age of ninety-one.

SELECTED WRITINGS BY GREENEWALT:

Books

The Uncommon Man, McGraw-Hill, 1959.
Hummingbirds, Doubleday, 1960.
Bird Song: Acoustics and Physiology, Smithsonian Institution, 1969.

SOURCES:

Books

Rothe, A., *Current Biography,* H. W. Wilson, 1949.
Sudnik, G. D., *Du Pont and the International Chemical Industry,* Twayne, 1984.

Periodicals

"Ex-Du Pont Chief Greenewalt Dead at 91," *The News Journal,* September 28, 1993, p. A1.
"Former Du Pont Chairman Greenewalt Dies," *Chemical and Engineering News,* October 11, 1993, pp. 39.

Other

Greenewalt, David, interview with John Henry Dreyfuss conducted on February 1, 1994.

—Sketch by John Henry Dreyfuss

Frederick Griffith
1879(?)-1941
English microbiologist

Frederick Griffith's work with streptococci and pneumococci bacteria gave him an important place in the history of biology. However, the impact of his work on the science of genetics was even more crucial, although it is not clear whether Griffith himself ever realized his contributions to this field. His classic experiments, published in a single seminal paper in 1928, showed that some strains of bacteria could appropriate the disease-causing characteristics of other strains. Although interesting enough for the light it shed on the virulence of certain organisms, what he called the "transforming principle" was also the first clear evidence linking DNA to heredity in cells.

The details of Griffith's life are not completely known, partly because he lived very quietly and reclusively and partly because the importance of his work was not appreciated until well after his death. He was born in 1879 (some sources say 1877 or 1881) in Hale, in Cheshire, England, and he attended Liverpool University. His one older brother, A. Stanley Griffith, was also a microbiologist. After his graduation from the University of Liverpool in 1901, the younger Griffith worked for the Liverpool Royal Infirmary, the Thompson Yates Laboratory, and the Royal Commission on Tuberculosis. In 1910 he began working for the government, in what would later be called the Ministry of Health, under the supervision of Arthur Eastwood. The facilities were primitive, but as a friend wrote of Griffith in *The Lancet:* "He could do more with a kerosene tin and a primus stove than most men could do with a palace."

Griffith researched many kinds of microorganisms, but his most important work dealt with pneumococcus, the bacteria that can cause pneumonia. All types of these bacteria can theoretically cause disease, but some types (such as Type III) cause disease more readily than others (such as Type II). When Griffith began his work, he knew that the difference in virulence was due to a polysaccharide coating, or capsule, on the Type III organisms which protected the bacteria from the host's immune system. The Type II pneumococcus lacked the "capsule" that protected Type III. Bacterial colonies with capsules are called (S) colonies, and ones without capsules are called (R) colonies. They look quite different and are easy to identify in culture.

Research on Bacteria is Precursor to Genetics

Griffith injected some mice with Type II pneumococcus alone and other mice with Type III pneumococcus that had been killed by heating. None of the mice developed pneumonia. When he injected mice with both live Type II and dead Type III pneumococcus, however, the mice not only developed pneumonia, but live Type III bacteria could be extracted from their blood. Somehow the Type II bacteria had made protective capsules for themselves, "transforming" themselves into Type III. They had apparently acquired the characteristics from the dead Type III bacteria.

After later researchers managed to obtain transformed bacteria in a test tube instead of a live animal, work in the area declined for awhile. It was not until 1944 that **Oswald Avery**, **Colin Munro MacLeod**, and **Maclyn McCarty** took up Griffith's experiments again and tried to explain his results. They extracted the active transforming principle from Type III (S) pneumococcus and showed preliminarily that it was DNA. In "Studies on the Chemical Nature of the Substance Inducing Transformation of Pneumococcal Types," they cautiously stated that if DNA actually proved to be the transforming principle, " . . . then nucleic acids of this type must be regarded not merely as structurally important but as functionally active in determining the biochemical activities and specific characteristics of pneumococcal cells."

DNA is a very long molecule, or polymer, made up of linked, individual units. There are only four of these units, or nucleotides, however, scrambled in varying order along the length of the DNA. Biochemists of the time knew about nucleic acids, but they were certain that it was protein that caused inheritance; they were not inclined to suspect much of a hereditary role for a molecule (DNA) that seemed too simple for such a complex activity. Finally, in 1952, other researchers used radioactive labeling to prove that DNA was indeed the hereditary material that Griffith had first observed transforming bacteria. Griffith's work may thus be seen as pivotal in beginning the science of molecular biology.

Little is known about Griffith's private life except that he enjoyed skiing, walking, and vacations at his country cottage in Sussex. In the first Griffith Memorial Lecture, given in 1966, W. Hayes said, "Fred Griffith has been described as a shy and reticent man, whose quiet kindly manner, and his devotion to his job, made him a lovable personality to those few who got to know him." He published very little, but what he did was of a very high quality, and Hayes believed that this " . . . must be ascribed to an innate humility and capacity for self-criticism, so that he offered to posterity only those products of his research which he judged to be new and important." Griffith and a longtime colleague at the Ministry of Health, the bacteriologist William M. Scott, were killed in 1941 during the bombing of London when a bomb blew up the building in which they worked.

SELECTED WRITINGS BY GRIFFITH:

Periodicals

"The Significance of Pneumococcal Types," *Journal of Hygiene,* Volume 27, 1928, pp. 113–59.

SOURCES:

Books

Collard, P., *The Development of Microbiology,* Cambridge University Press, 1976, pg. 97–109.

Gabriel, M., and S. Fogel, editors, *Great Experiments in Biology,* Prentice Hall, 1955, pp. 134–140.

Magner, L. N., *A History of the Life Sciences,* Marcel Dekker, 1979, pp. 452–453.

Sturtevant, A. H., *A History of Genetics,* Harper and Row, 1965, pp. 104–105.

Periodicals

Avery, O. T., C. M. Macleod, M. McCarty, "Studies on the Chemical Nature of the Substance Inducing Transformation of Pneumococcal Types. Induction of Transformation by a Deoxyribonucleic Acid Fraction Isolated from Pneumococcus Type III," *Journal of Experimental Medicine,* Volume 79, 1944, pp. 137–157.

"Frederick Griffith," obituary in *The Lancet,* May 3, 1941, pg. 588–589.

Hayes, W., "Genetic Transformation: a Retrospective Appreciation. (The First Griffith Memorial Lecture)," *Journal of Genetic Microbiology,* Volume 45, 1966, pp. 385–397.

—*Sketch by Gail B. C. Marsella*

François Auguste Victor Grignard
1871-1935
French organic chemist

Organic synthesis owes a major debt to François Auguste Victor Grignard, whose pioneering studies were a critical early step in the advancement of the field. When he entered the profession at the turn of the century, the task of combining different organic chemical species was a major hurdle in the synthesis of new compounds. Grignard developed a process that enabled chemists to join many types of organic chemical compounds. It was a method that could be used with a broad array of organic reactants; it was also inexpensive and simple to perform, and it resulted in high yields. These features resulted in its rapid adoption by organic chemists around the world. Grignard shared the 1912 Nobel Prize in chemistry with **Paul Sabatier**. Grignard was born in Cherbourg, France, on May 6, 1871. His mother was Marie Hébert Grignard; his father, Théophile Henri Grignard, was a sailmaker and foreman at the local marine arsenal. During his early education, Grignard's parents steered him towards a career as a teacher, and at age eighteen he won a scholarship to the École Normale Spéciale, whose graduates routinely became secondary school teachers. But the school closed after he had completed only two years there, and then, despite further work at the University of Lyons, Grignard failed the mathematics exams that were then required for licensing as a teacher.

In 1892, Grignard did a year of compulsory military service, and upon his return to Lyons a friend urged him to study chemistry. Grignard had long considered chemistry scientifically uninteresting, believing it consisted mainly of unrelated facts and observations, but he soon found himself interested and began to pursue a graduate degree. Philippe Barbier became his supervisor and convinced him to do his doctoral thesis on chemical synthesis.

Barbier had been investigating the general problem of using a metal to attach together two organic radicals—chemical groups that remain unchanged by a reaction. Species made by joining an organic radical with a metal atom are known as organometallic compounds, and while the creation of these compounds was well known at the time, there were serious limitations on their uses. Some were extremely reactive (such as organosodium and organopotassium), while others were very unreactive (such as organomercury). Zinc had been used, but only a few compounds could be prepared with it, and organozinc compounds had the unfortunate tendency of spontaneously igniting at room temperature. Barbier had experimented with using magnesium to join organic radicals, but he had obtained inconsistent results.

Discovers the Grignard Reagent

This was the problem Grignard pursued for his thesis. He knew that one of his first challenges would be to solve the same problem that plagued the organozinc researchers; he had to avoid having his organomagnesium compounds spontaneously erupt in flame. His research showed him that workers had overcome this hazard when dealing with organozinc species by performing the reaction in anhydrous ether.

Thus Grignard added magnesium shavings in ether to methyl iodide. This solution, later to be known as the Grignard reagent, would react with an aldehyde or ketone, which were both readily obtained types of organic compounds. With the addition of dilute acid, the resultant compound broke apart with the formation of water to produce an alcohol. The particular alcohol produced depended solely on the particular aldehyde or ketone used in the reaction. The yield—the amount of alcohol produced relative to the aldehyde or ketone reactant—was high, the process simple, and the reaction consistent. Moreover, as Grignard and others rapidly discovered, the reaction was extremely flexible. Many different reactants besides aldehydes and ketones could be used, and the types of compounds that could be produced were virtually limitless.

Grignard's complete thesis was published by the University of Lyons in 1901, and several articles describing the process and its applications rapidly appeared in major chemistry journals. In 1909 Grignard left Lyons to take up a post at the University of Nancy, where he was soon named professor. In 1910, he married Augustine Marie Boulant. The first of their two children, Roger, was born the following year.

In 1912, Grignard's colleagues formally recognized the importance of his early studies by awarding him the Nobel Prize. He shared the 1912 Nobel Prize in chemistry with Paul Sabatier, also a Frenchman, who had developed another important methodology in organic synthesis, catalytic hydrogenation. The joint prize was the cause of great national pride, and one French newspaper announced that this proved chemistry was not "a predominately German science."

Grignard remained at Nancy for nearly a decade, and his research continued to focus on organomagnesium compounds and their reactions with a wide array of other chemical species. During World War I, Grignard worked on methods for synthesizing toluene, an important solvent, and on the analysis of chemical warfare gases. After the war, he returned to the University at Lyons, where he had been chosen to succeed Barbier, who was retiring. He remained at Lyons for the rest of his life, continuing his studies of organic synthesis processes and expanding his work to include other fields.

Grignard wrote two volumes of what he planned to be a fifteen-volume work on organic chemistry, but he died unexpectedly on December 13, 1935. Two more volumes of this work were published posthumously, with editorial assistance from his son Roger, who had followed his father and chosen a career in organic chemistry. Grignard's legacy includes 170 publications and a host of honors and awards for his work, including honorary doctoral degrees from the universities of Louvain and Brussels, and the title of Commander of the Legion of Honor.

SELECTED WRITINGS BY GRIGNARD:

Periodicals

"Sur quelques nouvelles combinaisons organométalliques du magnésium et leur application des synthèses d'alcools et d'hydrocarbures," *Comptes rendus de l'Académie des sciences,* Volume 126, 1898, p. 1322.

"Sur les combinaisons organomagnésiennes mixtes et leur application à des synthèses d'acides, d'alcools, et d'hydrocarbures," *Annales de l'Université de Lyon,* Volume 6, 1901, pp. 1–116.

SOURCES:

Books

Gillispie, C. C., editor, *Dictionary of Scientific Biography,* Volume 5, Scribner, 1971, pp. 540–541. Magill, Frank N., editor, *The Nobel Prize Winners: Chemistry, 1901–1937,* Salem Press, 1991, pp. 165–174.

—*Sketch by Ethan E. Allen*

Carol Gross
1941-
American bacteriologist

Carol Gross is a bacteriologist who has specialized in studying the production of cell proteins in response to heat. She also has conducted research on the RNA (ribonucleic acid) polymerase enzyme that regulates various functions in both DNA and RNA. In addition to her research, she has been active as a professor and a member of professional scientific organizations.

Gross was born in Brooklyn, New York, on October 27, 1941, to Samuel Polinsky and the former Mollie Hausman. Her father was an attorney and her mother a school guidance counselor. Carol graduated from Cornell University in 1962 with a B.S. degree and received her master's degree from Brooklyn College in 1965. While at Brooklyn College she met and married her husband; the couple had two children, Steven (born in 1965) and Miriam (born in 1969). In 1968 Gross obtained her Ph.D. from the University of Oregon; her dissertation investigated the regulation of lactose production in the *E. coli* bacteria.

Immediately after graduation Gross began a postdoctoral fellowship at the university. In 1973 she became project associate at the University of Wisconsin, studying RNA. Having developed an interest in cancer, Gross in 1976 was hired as assistant scientist at the McArdle Laboratory for Cancer Research at the university, rising to associate scientist in 1979. Two years later she became an assistant professor at the university's department of bacteriology, and she became a full-time professor in 1988. In 1985 Gross obtained a visiting professorship at the department of biochemistry in Nanjing, China, lecturing on gene regulation and recombinant DNA. That same year she became a member of the scientific advisory committee of the Damon Runyon-Walter Winchell Cancer Research Fund.

Gross continued to do research, particularly in the field of bacteriology, and was appointed editor of the *Journal of Bacteriology* in 1990. That same year she joined the editorial board of *Genes and Development.* In 1992 she became a member of the American Academy of Arts and Sciences and the National Academy of Sciences, and the next year Gross left her post at the University of Wisconsin to become professor at the University of California in San Francisco in the department of stomatology (diseases of the mouth) and microbiology.

One of Gross's major interests is the response of cell proteins to intense heat. When cells are exposed to high temperatures, nearly all begin to produce large quantities of certain proteins, characterized by their ability to grow and thrive at ordinarily lethal temperatures. Gross is trying to find the function these proteins serve and the precise nature of how they operate. Another field of investigation for her is the structure and function of ribonucleic acid (RNA) polymerase, an enzyme that binds compounds in and transcribes DNA and thus regulates how DNA interacts with the cell.

FOR FURTHER READING:

Books

Pines, Maya, *Inside the Cell: New Frontiers of Medical Science,* U. S. Department of Health, Education, and Welfare, 1978.

Other

Gross, Carol, interview with Francis Rogers, January 20, 1994.

—*Sketch by Francis Rogers*

Alexander Grothendieck
1928-
French mathematician

Alexander Grothendieck has had an influence on the mathematics of the second half of the twentieth century well beyond the scale of his publications. Grothendieck started off as an especially prolific contributor to each of the areas to which he turned, including functional analysis, algebraic geometry, and category theory, only to move away from mathematics later in his career. As a result, he has had fewer students to carry on his research tradition than if he had followed a more orthodox path. Nevertheless, one of the chief activities of the mathematicians in several areas has been to recast their field in the terms introduced by Grothendieck.

Grothendieck's early years have been difficult to reconstruct, due to his reluctance to deal in ordinary reminiscences and his distrust of biographers. The generally accepted date and place of his birth are March 28, 1928, and Berlin, but the identity of his parents is less clear. At least one version that Grothendieck has given, as noted by Colin McLarty, indicates that his father was named Morris Shapiro and that he was sentenced to death for attempting to assassinate the Russian Czar in 1905. After Shapiro served a number of years in prison in Siberia, he was released by the Bolsheviks and went to Germany in 1922, about which time he met his future wife. Grothendieck was their first child and took his name from that of the governess who cared for him from 1929 to 1939. In the latter year, his mother took him to France, where he learned for the first time that he was Jewish by ancestry. His father died in the Auschwitz concentration camp and Grothendieck was saved thanks to the cooperation of Protestant and Catholic clergy in Le Chambon sur Lignon in southern France. His mother died in the 1960s.

The story becomes much clearer once Grothendieck entered the French higher education system after the war. He studied at the University of Montpellier and spent a year at the École Normale Supérieure, one of the leading traditional scientific universities in France. At this time France was undergoing a mathematical renaissance, thanks to the pedagogic efforts of the group known under the collective pseudonym of Nicolas Bourbaki. Among those who took part in the grand program of rewriting all of mathematics in the Bourbaki mode were Jean Dieudonné and Laurent Schwartz, both at the University of Nancy. Grothendieck went to work in the area of functional analysis with the two Bourbakists and rapidly produced material sufficient and appropriate for a thesis.

Grothendieck's first conspicuous success was in the area known as functional analysis. This mixed the traditional area of calculus with the more recent developments in topology, the field dealing in properties of geometric configurations, to be able to handle broad ranges of questions. The idea was to replace detailed and lengthy calculations with shorter and more insightful proofs. It is not surprising that such an area attracted Grothendieck, who did not feel that his greatest strength was in long, technical arguments. His contributions came in the area of reconsidering disciplines from new perspectives.

Categorizes the Mathematical World

Grothendieck's most lasting influence came from his work in the area to which he now moved, algebraic geometry. This field had been in existence for many years and could be traced back to French mathematician and philosopher René Descartes in the seventeenth century. The idea of merging algebra and geometry to enhance the study of both received a new impetus with the accelerated development of abstract algebra in the late nineteenth century. There was a flourishing Italian school of algebraic geometry in the first half of the twentieth century, but it was effectively wiped out by the World War II. American mathematician Oscar Zariski carried on the Italian tradition in the United States, although he felt that he had added a good deal of algebraic sophistication.

Grothendieck was supported during his early investigations into algebraic geometry by the French national center for scientific research. This allowed him plenty of opportunity for travel and he spent part of the 1950s in Brazil and part in Kansas. Perhaps the most fruitful environment he found was at Harvard, where Zariski had settled. As his Harvard colleagues noted, Grothendieck was obsessed by mathematics and worked for many hours at a stretch in an unheated study, emerging with 3000-page manuscripts. On the strength of his energy and imagination, Grothendieck was able to revolutionize mathematics with his research.

One of the chief elements in Grothendieck's approach to mathematics involved the relatively recent field of category theory. Set theory had become an accepted part of the foundations of mathematics, but category theory sought to add a new idea to the basic notions of set and membership—the idea of function. Functions had long been used in mathematics, but category theory built them into the basis of the mathematical universe. One way of looking at the change was that mathematicians began to realize that what was important about the objects of mathematics was how they were connected by functions, not their composition out of basic elements.

Before the work of Grothendieck, category theory had been an active area of research but with limited applications. Grothendieck combined the ideas of category theory with the traditional studies of algebraic geometry to raise the latter to a new level of abstraction. The innovations introduced by Zariski in the previous generation shrank by comparison. As Zariski was quoted in *The Unreal Life of Oscar Zariski,* "After Grothendieck's great generalization of the field . . . what I myself had called abstract turned out to be a very, very concrete brand of mathematics."

In 1959 Grothendieck took a position with the Institut des Hautes Études Scientifiques (IHES), recently established in Paris upon the model of the Institute for Advanced Studies in Princeton, New Jersey. There Grothendieck had the chance to lecture on a regular basis on his work in algebraic geometry and to attract mathematicians from all over the world. Not surprisingly, in 1966 he received the Fields Medal from the International Mathematics Congress, the highest award that the mathematical community can convey. Among the attractions of his work was its applicability to extending a variety of theorems that had originally been established in narrow contexts. Questions about number fields that had required immense amounts of computation to answer could be replaced by conceptually simpler questions about algebraic varieties, and the answers would have wide domains of applicability.

This golden age for algebraic geometry came to an end in 1970. Grothendieck had never been comfortable with playing the role of the "great man" and felt that the adulation of students was not good for him as a human being or as a mathematician. He also moved in a radical direction politically and hoped to be able to galvanize the mathematical community into political action. As a result, he left the IHES and taught at other French universities, particularly Montpellier, from which he retired in 1988. In the meantime, his ideas about category theory continued to supply the fuel for other areas of mathematics, including the foundations. The idea of a topos, a particular kind of category especially useful for analyzing logic, was introduced by Grothendieck for purposes of algebraic geometry. The continued fertility of topos theory adds to the fields indebted to Grothendieck's work during his contributions to algebraic geometric issues.

Grothendieck's memoir, *Récoltes et Semailles,* discusses at length his views on a number of subjects, most of which are unrelated to mathematics. More representative of his career in mathematics is the three-volume set of papers gathered for his sixtieth-birthday *festschrift* and published in 1990. The range of contributors includes many of the names of leaders of the mathematical community. His vision of mathematics has led not just to individual results but to a new sense of the powers of the subject.

SELECTED WRITINGS BY GROTHENDIECK:

Books

Récoltes et semailles, Université des Sciences et de Techniques de Languedoc, 1986.

Periodicals

"Sur quelques points d'algébre homologique," *Tohoku Journal of Mathematics,* 1957, pp. 119–221.

SOURCES:

Books

Cartier, P., et al., editors, *The Grothendieck Festschrift,* Birkhäuser, 1990.

Dieudonné, Jean, *A History of Algebraic and Differential Topology,* Birkhäuser, 1989.

Parikh, Carol, *The Unreal Life of Oscar Zariski,* Academic Press, 1991.

Periodicals

McLarty, Colin, "Category Theory in Real Time," *Philosophia Mathematica,* 1994, pp. 36–44.

Other

McLarty, Colin, notes for upcoming biography of Grothendieck.

—*Sketch by Thomas Drucker*

Leslie Richard Groves
1896-1970
American civil engineer

No discussion of the Manhattan Project, the American program during World War II to create the atomic bomb, would be complete without recognizing General Leslie Richard Groves's role in bringing the project to a successful conclusion. Not only did Groves administer the Manhattan Project, he played a preeminent role in selecting as targets the cities of Hiroshima and Nagasaki. For his role in ushering in the atomic age, President Richard M. Nixon presented Groves with the Atomic Pioneers Award in 1970.

Groves was born in Albany, New York, on August 17, 1896. His father, who named his son Leslie after himself, had received training as a lawyer. Soon after the younger Leslie was born, however, the senior Groves became a Presbyterian minister and joined the Army as a chaplain. Because of his father's assignments to remote locations such as China, Cuba, and the Philippines, his mother was left to raise her three boys alone during much of Leslie's earliest years. Groves senior had a college degree and because of it, his son later remarked in an interview for Joseph J. Ermenc's book, *Atomic Bomb Scientists,* his main advantage in early life was that he had been brought up in "well educated circles."

From about the time Groves was in junior high school he wanted to attend the United States Military Academy at West Point. During the intervening years, Groves attended the University of Washington where he studied English, French, German, and mathematics for a year. He enjoyed riding horses in his spare time and even went so far as to avoid taking engineering courses (and the requisite lab work) because of his fondness for riding. Around this time Groves also acquired a life-long love for tennis, which he played both at the University of Washington and at the Massachusetts Institute of Technology, where he attended classes for two years before being accepted at West Point.

According to some accounts, Groves was disliked at West Point because his colleagues saw him as puritanical and arrogant, perceptions that would dog him throughout his career. Groves was a hard worker, however, and in 1918 he graduated fourth in his class with a commission as second lieutenant in the Army Corps of Engineers. To supplement the engineering courses at West Point, Groves was sent to the engineer school at Fort Humphreys (later Fort Belvoir). After World War I there was a glut of officers, particularly in Groves's field of engineering, so he (and most of his classmates) did not make captain until 1934 or 1935.

After two years at the engineer school at Fort Humphreys, the Army transferred Groves to Fort Worden on Puget Sound, where he met his future wife, Grace Wilson. They were married in February 1922. From there the young couple moved to the Presidio in San Francisco and then to Schofield Barracks in Honolulu, where under Groves's tutorship F Company won the post's highest rating in marksmanship. Later, after completing an assignment to open the silted-up harbor at Port Isabel, Texas, Groves's supervisor, according to biographer William Lawren, praised the lieutenant as the best officer he had ever had. Indeed, Groves was gaining a reputation for being a capable leader and a man who could be counted on to get things done. This reputation coexisted with widespread dislike of him and perceptions that he was a martinet.

The year 1929 found Lieutenant Groves in Nicaragua with the Corps of Engineers surveying an alternative route to the Panama Canal. His family, now including a daughter, Gwen, and his six-year-old son, Richard, followed in 1930 and took up residence in Granada, a town about fifty miles southeast of Managua. That year an earthquake demolished large sections of Managua, and Groves was called upon to restore the city's only water supply. The job was difficult and dangerous. As a tribute to Groves's successful work, Nicaragua's president, J. M. Moncada, awarded the army engineer the country's Legion of Merit.

From there Groves moved to the Army's Military Supply Division in Washington, DC, where he served the next four years planning and developing construction equipment. Still a first lieutenant during his final year in Washington, Groves became chief of the supply division of the Engineer Corps, a position that would later be filled by a brigadier general. This was followed in 1935, the year he made captain, by a brief tour at the Command and General Staff College. From there he gained two years' experience working on flood control as assistant to the division engineer in Kansas City. During the academic year of 1938–39 Groves attended the Army War College.

Advancement to captain and then major came as opportunities for responsibility increased in the expanding army. In response to Japanese depredations in Asia and war in Europe, President Franklin Delano Roosevelt ordered the building of military training bases around the country. Starting in 1940, Groves attended to the construction of these bases in his new role as assistant to the quartermaster general. During this period, Groves oversaw construction of the Pentagon.

The broad responsibilities assigned to Groves while in this position, his skill in administering a multimillion dollar budget, and his ability to crash through bureaucratic logjams provided invaluable experience for his most important mission. By now full colonel, Groves drew the attention of his superiors, Lieutenant General Brehon Somervell, chief of the Army Services of Supply, and his chief of staff, Major General W. D. Styer. They had been working with Dr. **Vannevar Bush**, chairman of the Office of Scientific Research and Development, an office created by Bush under Roosevelt's direction to coordinate civilian scientific research with military needs. Bush and others urged the United States to devote its scientific resources to making an atomic bomb. When it became clear that the Army would administer the Project, officially known as the Manhattan Engineer District (MED), Generals Somervell and Styer agreed that Colonel Groves would be the best qualified for the job.

Takes Charge of Manhattan Project

After meeting with Groves, Bush objected that the colonel's rudeness in dealing with people invited disaster. The generals prevailed, however, and Groves, now brigadier general, took full control of the Manhattan Project in September 1942. To many of the scientists who worked under him, Groves was an unfortunate choice. Some of these men, most of them with doctorates and professorships from leading universities, regarded Groves as hardly more than a boorish, stupid bureaucrat with no appreciation or understanding of science and scientists. Because of a personality conflict with physicist **Leo Szilard**, Groves tried unsuccessfully to get the FBI to intern him as an enemy alien. Szilard was a Jewish refugee from Hungary. According to biographer William Lawren, Kenneth Nichols, a colonel with a Ph.D. in experimental mechanics assigned to work under Groves, characterized him as "the biggest son of a bitch I ever met."

Despite his shortcomings, Groves could be an able administrator. Groves chose **Dr. J. Robert Oppenheimer**, a theoretical physicist from the University of California at Berkeley, to head the scientific team that would work on the Project. Scientists had objected to Oppenheimer because he lacked a background in experimental physics; security officials objected because they thought Oppenheimer was a crypto-Communist. Yet in retrospect he seemed to be the wisest choice. Indeed, to Groves, Oppenheimer was the only choice.

Dropping the atomic bomb on Hiroshima on August 6, 1945, brought a successful end to the Manhattan Project. Dropping a second bomb, on Nagasaki, brought an end to the war. By 1945 the Project had 600,000 employees and a budget of millions of dollars. Overseeing the Manhattan Project and bringing it to a successful conclusion was an immense accomplishment. **Dr. Glenn T. Seaborg**, a co-discoverer of plutonium and participant in the Project, was quoted in the *New York Times* as saying that Groves had "directed the most awesome project in the history of mankind."

After the war, Groves campaigned unsuccessfully against the Atomic Energy Commission and civilian control of nuclear energy. In 1947 he retired from the Army to become director of research for the Remington Rand Company. As vice-president for the company, Groves supervised the production of UNIVAC, one of the few computers commercially available in the early 1950s.

After he retired from Rand in 1961, Groves seemed to become less acerbic. He stopped playing tennis and took up golf, but his heart, burdened by the general's lifelong fight with obesity, finally gave out. On July 13, 1970, at the age of 73, Groves died in Walter Reed Army Hospital of heart failure. General Groves was buried with military honors at Arlington National Cemetery.

SELECTED WRITINGS BY GROVES:

Books

Now It Can Be Told: The Story of the Manhattan Project, Harper & Brothers, Publishers, 1962.

SOURCES:

Books

Cortada, James W., *Historical Dictionary of Data Processing: Biographies,* Greenwood Press, 1987, pp. 122–123.

Ermenc, Joseph J., *Atomic Bomb Scientists: Memoirs, 1939–1945,* Meckler, 1989.

Lawren, William, *The General and the Bomb: A Biography of General Leslie R. Groves, Director of the Manhattan Project,* Dodd, 1988.

Rhodes, Richard, *The Making of the Atomic Bomb,* Simon & Schuster, 1986.

Periodicals

"Gen. Groves of Manhattan Project Dies," *New York Times,* July 15, 1970, p. 1.

Goldberg, Stanley, "Groves Takes the Reins," *The Bulletin of the Atomic Scientists,* December, 1992, pp. 32–39.

Goldberg, Stanley, review of William Lawren's *General and the Bomb,* in *The Bulletin of the Atomic Scientists,* December, 1988, p. 44.

—Sketch by Karl Preuss

Charles-Edouard Guillaume
1861-1938
Swiss physicist

Charles-Edouard Guillaume was awarded the Nobel Prize in physics in 1920 for his work on metrology (the science of weights and measures) in general and his discovery of nickel-steel alloys in particular. During the course of his career, Guillaume made a number of contributions to the improvement of metrological (measuring) techniques, including a more precise determination of the volume of the liter. Perhaps his most important contribution, however, came as a by-product of his work in metrology. In 1896, he discovered an alloy of iron and nickel whose coefficient of thermal expansion is about half that of pure iron. The alloy, later named invar, became extremely valuable not only in the manufacturing of measuring devices, but also in a wide variety of other products.

Guillaume was born in Fleurier, Switzerland, on February 15, 1861. His grandfather, Charles Frederic Alexandre Guillaume, had left France for England during the French Revolution and had established a successful watchmaking business there. His son Edouard (Guillaume's father), later emigrated to Switzerland, where he established his own watchmaking business in Fleurier. Guillaume received his high school education at the Neuchâtel gymnasium. At the age of seventeen, he enrolled in the Zurich Polytechnic (later the Federal Institute of Technology). He rapidly developed an interest in physics, later claiming that François Arago's text, *Éloges académiques,* was particularly influential on his decision to pursue science as a career. Guillaume was awarded a Ph.D. in 1882 for his thesis on electrolytic capacitors.

Begins Long Career in Metrology

Guillaume spent his compulsory year of military service as an artillery officer, during which time he studied mechanics and ballistics. He was then offered a position with the newly created International Bureau of Weights and Measures in Sèvres, France, just outside Paris. He worked there over the next half century, becoming associate director of the bureau in 1902, director in 1905, and finally honorary director upon his retirement in 1936. Guillaume's earliest work at the bureau was in the establishment, duplication, and distribution of international standards. That work included the most fundamental metrological operations, such as calibrating thermometers and making precise copies of the standard meter for distribution to countries around the world.

It was the latter task that resulted in an accidental discovery for which Guillaume is perhaps best known. The standard meter bar kept at the bureau in Sèvres had been made of a platinum-iridium alloy to prevent corrosion and other changes. Making dozens of copies of this bar from such costly metals was, however, prohibitively expensive. As a result, Guillaume began to look for other materials from which to make duplicates of the standard meter bar.

Discovery of Invar Leads to Nobel Prize

One of the alloys Guillaume prepared consisted of about seven parts iron to three parts nickel. In working with this alloy, he found that it had an extremely low coefficient of expansion. He decided to undertake a systematic study of other iron-nickel alloys and eventually found one whose coefficient of expansion was zero. This alloy, containing about 36 percent nickel and 64 percent iron, was later named invar. The value of invar in metrology is obvious. Measuring devices made of the alloy will not change in size at all as a result of changes in temperature. But invar soon found applications in many other fields. For example, it became invaluable in clockmaking, as did a second alloy invented by Guillaume called elinvar. The watch part called the balance, if it contained one of these two alloys, eventually became known as a "Guillaume balance."

In addition to the Nobel Prize, Guillaume received a number of other honors during his lifetime, including selection as a grand officer of the Legion of Honor, election as president of the French Physical Society, and receipt of honorary degrees from the universities of Geneva, Neuchâtel, and Paris. Guillaume was married in 1888 to A. M. Taufflich; they had three children. Guillaume died at Sèvres on June 13, 1938.

SELECTED WRITINGS BY GUILLAUME:

Books

Traité pratique de thermométrie de précision, Gauthiers-Villans, 1889.

Les E'tats de la matiére, Societé Astronomique de France, 1908.

Periodicals

"Recherchés sur les aciers au nickel. Propiétés métrologiques," *Comptes rendus hebdomadaires des séances de l'académie des sciences,* Volume 124, 1897, p. 752.

"Les Anomalies des aciers au nickel et leurs applications," *Revue de métallurgie,* Volume 25, 1928, p. 35.

SOURCES:

Books

Dictionary of Scientific Biography, Volume 5, Scribner's, 1975, pp. 582–83.

Heathcote, Niels H. de V., *Nobel Prize Winners in Physics, 1901–1950,* Henry Schuman, 1953, pp. 173–79.

Weber, Robert L., *Pioneers of Science: Nobel Prize Winners in Physics,* American Institute of Physics, 1980, pp. 62–63.

A Biographical Dictionary of Scientists, Wiley, 1974, pp. 228–29.

Periodicals

"Dr. C.-E. Guillaume," *Nature,* August 20, 1938, pp. 322–23.

—Sketch by David E. Newton

Roger Guillemin
1924-
French-born American endocrinologist

Roger Guillemin is one of the founders of the field of neuroendocrinology, the study of the interaction between the central nervous system (such as the brain) and endocrine glands (such as the pituitary, thyroid, and pancreas). Guillemin focused his research on hormones produced by the brain, and their subsequent effect on body processes. He proved the correctness of a hypothesis first proposed by English anatomist Geoffrey W. Harris that the hypothalamus releases hormones to regulate the pituitary gland. For discoveries which led to an understanding of hypothalamic hormone productions of the brain, Guillemin and fellow endocrinologist **Andrew V. Schally** shared the 1977 Nobel prize for physiology or medicine with physicist **Rosalyn Sussman Yalow**. Guillemin and Schally were pioneers in isolating, identifying, and determining the chemical nature of such hormones as TRF (thyrotropin-releasing factor which regulates the thyroid gland), LRF (luteinizing-releasing factor which controls male and female reproductive functions), somatostatin (which regulates the production of growth hormones and insulin), and endorphins (which may be involved in the onset of mental illness). Guillemin's work led to scientific advances including an understanding of thyroid diseases, infertility, juvenile diabetes, and the physiology of the brain. According to Guillemin, the determination of the chemical structure of TRF marked an end to the pioneering era in neuroendocrinology and the beginning of a major new science.

Roger Charles Louis Guillemin was born on January 11, 1924, and raised in Dijon, France, the son of Raymond Guillemin, a machine toolmaker, and Blanche Rigollot Guillemin. He attended the University of Dijon where he received a Bachelor's degree in 1942, and then entered the University of Lyons medical school, graduating with a medical degree in 1949. However, Guillemin interrupted his studies during World War II in order to join the French underground during the Nazi occupation, becoming part of an operation helping refugees escape to Switzerland over the Jura Mountains. During and after the war Guillemin received three years of clinical training and briefly practiced medicine before joining a well-known Canadian physiologist, Hans Selye, as a research assistant. To work with Selye, Guillemin moved to the Institute of Experimental Medicine and Surgery at the University of Montreal in Canada. In 1950, he suffered a near-fatal attack of tubercular meningitis. After his recovery in 1951, Guillemin married Lucienne Jeanne Billard, who had been his nurse during his illness. They had six children, five daughters—Chantal, Claire, Helene, Elizabeth, and Cecile, and a son François.

Embarks on Career at Baylor University

Guillemin received his Ph.D. from the University of Montreal in 1953, and accepted an assistant professorship at Baylor University Medical School in Houston, Texas. His research involved endocrinology, the study of the hormones that circulate in the blood. The endocrine system is a hierarchical one in which hormones from the pituitary gland regulate other endocrine glands. It was thought that the head of the entire system was the hypothalamus, located at the base of the brain just above the pituitary gland. However, the way in which hypothalamic hormonal regulation occurred was unclear. The theory of regulation by nerve impulses was marred by the anatomical fact that there are few nerves that extend from the hypothalamus to the pituitary. Anatomist Geoffrey W. Harris theorized that hypothalamic regulation occurred by means of hormones, which are transported by the blood. Harris's experiments supported his hypothesis, proving altered pituitary function when the blood vessels were cut between the hypothalamus and the pituitary. The problem was that no one had yet been successful in isolating and identifying a hormone from the hypothalamus.

Begins Intense Research on Hypothalamic Hormones

Guillemin began an investigation to find the missing evidence, a task of extraordinary difficulty because very minute amounts of hypothalamic substances are involved. At Baylor, Guillemin worked together with Schally using a technique called mass spectroscopy and a new tool developed by physicists Solomon Berson and Rosalyn Sussman Yalow called radioimmunoassays (RIAs) which enabled scientists to isolate and identify the chemical structure of hormones. In the early 1960s Guillemin considered continuing his research in France, and obtained a concurrent appointment at both Baylor and the Collège de France in Paris. However, he left the Collège de France in 1963, and was appointed director of the Laboratory for Neuroendocrinology at Baylor University. By this time he and Schally had ended their scientific cooperation and had become fiercely competitive in a race to identify hypothalamic hormones.

Guillemin worked with sheep hypothalami which he obtained from slaughter houses. Obtaining the specimens was a large-scale, difficult operation. Only very minute amounts of substance existed in each sheep hypothalamus and it had to be extracted very soon after death. Guillemin and Roger Burgus, a chemist who worked with Guillemin, reported that their laboratory collected about five million hypothalamic fragments from sheep brains, which involved handling about five hundred tons of brain tissue. Finally in 1968, Guillemin and his coworkers isolated the hypothalamic hormone that effects the release of thyrotropin. The following year Guillemin, as well as Schally, who had been working independently, revealed the structure of TRF (a hypothalamic hormone which today is called thyrotropin-releasing hormone or TRH). When TRF is secreted by the hypothalamus, it causes the pituitary gland to secrete another hormone that in turn causes the thyroid gland to secrete its own hormones. Shortly thereafter Guillemin and his colleagues isolated and determined the chemical structure of GRH (growth-releasing-hormone), a hypothalamic hormone that causes the pituitary to release gonadotropin which in turn influences the release of hormones in the testicles or ovaries. This discovery led to advancements in the medical treatment of infertility.

In 1970 Guillemin moved to the Salk Institute in La Jolla, California. There he isolated a third hypothalamic hormone which he named somatostatin. This hormone acts by inhibiting the release of growth hormone from the pituitary gland. In 1977 Guillemin and Schally were awarded the Nobel Prize for their research on hypothalamic hormones. Guillemin wrote on the importance of their discoveries in an autobiography, published in *Pioneers in Neuroendocrinology II,* stating that: "I consider the isolation and characterization of TRF as the major event in modern neuroendocrinology, the inflection point that separated confusion and a great deal of doubt from real knowledge. Modern neuroendocrinology was born of that event. Isolations of LRF, somatostatin, and the recent endorphins were all extensions (as there will be still more, I am sure) of that major event—the isolation of TRF, a novel molecule in hypothalamic extracts, with hypophysiotropic activity, the first so characterized. . . . The event was the vindication of 14 years of hard work."

Guillemin soon turned his attention to another class of substances, known as neuropeptides. Produced by the hypothalamus and other parts of the brain, neuropeptides act at the synapses of the nerves (the area where the nerve impulse passes from one neuron or nerve cell to another). One group of neuropeptides, for example, called endorphins, seem to affect moods and the perception of pain. Guillemin's recent research includes neurochemistry of the brain and growth factors.

Guillemin is known as an urbane conversationalist who is interested in the arts and enjoys painting. He and his wife have a collection of contemporary French and American paintings, pre-Columbian art objects, and artifacts from around the world. Guillemin is also a connoisseur of fine food and wine.

SELECTED WRITINGS BY GUILLEMIN:

Books

"Pioneering in Neuroendocrinology 1952–1969," in *Pioneers in Neuroendocrinology,* Volume 2, edited by Joseph Meites, Bernard T. Donovan, and Samuel M. McCann, Plenum Press, 1978, pp. 220–239.

Periodicals

(With Burgus, Thomas F. Dunn, Dominic Desiderio, Darrell N. Ward, and Wylie Vale) "Characterization of Ovine Hypothalamic Hypophysiotropic TSH-Releasing Factor," *Nature,* Volume 226, April 25, 1970, pp. 321–25.

(With Roger Burgus), "The Hormones of the Hypothalamus," *Scientific American,* Volume 227, November, 1972, pp. 24–33, 134.

SOURCES:

Books

Wade, Nicholas, *The Nobel Duel: Two Scientists' 21-year Race to Win the World's Most Coveted Research Prize,* Doubleday, 1981.
Nobel Prize Winners, Wilson, 1987, pp. 399–401.

Periodicals

Chedd, Graham, "Nobel Prizes 1977: Medicine," *New Scientist,* Volume 76, October 20, 1977, pp. 144–145.
Meites, Joseph, "The 1977 Nobel Prize in Physiology or Medicine," *Science,* Volume 198, November 11, 1977, pp. 594–596.

—Sketch by Pamela O. Long

Allvar Gullstrand
1862-1930
Swedish ophthalmologist

Major contributions to our understanding of the human eye were made by Swedish ophthalmologist Allvar Gullstrand, particularly in the area of how the eye forms images. His mathematical approach to solving physiological problems had a great significance in the science of ophthalmology, and his discoveries won him the Nobel Prize for medicine or physiology in 1911. He also developed a number of devices, such as the slit lamp and the reflector ophthalmoscope, which became valuable tools in eye examinations and for the treatment of optical disorders. Gullstrand also served for many years as a member, and later as president, of the Nobel Committee responsible for awarding the prize for physics.

Gullstrand was born June 5th, 1862, in Landskrona, Sweden, to Pehr Alfred Gullstrand and Sophia Korsell Gullstrand. His father, the city physician, influenced his decision against a career in engineering, in favor of one in medicine. After studying at universities in Uppsala, Sweden, Stockholm, and Vienna, Gullstrand received his medical degree from Stockholm's Royal Caroline Institute in 1888. He earned his Ph.D. one year later through a dissertation on astigmatism, an eye defect involving faulty curvature of the optic lens. Utilizing his early training and natural aptitude in engineering, he formulated complex theories in optics, which considerably advanced knowledge in this field.

Increases Understanding of How the Eye Functions

During this time, Gullstrand began working as chief physician at the Stockholm Eye Clinic, and by 1892 he was both clinic director and lecturer at the Karolinska Institute. He left the University in 1894 to serve as a professor at the University of Uppsala, where his research in geometrical optics began to flourish. His studies in dioptrics of the eye, or the science of refracted light and its effect on the retina, helped clear up certain misconceptions regarding the way the eye functions. One such misunderstanding concerned the accommodation theory of optics, by which the eye adjusts its focus on objects near and far. In his *Handbook on Physiological Optics,* German biologist and physicist Hermann von Helmholtz postulated that the eyes react to the problems of focusing by altering the curvature of their lens. When the eye focused on a nearby object, the lens became more convex (curving-outward), while focusing on something farther away made the lens more concave (curving-inward). In his commentaries on the third edition of the *Handbook* (1908), which he reedited, Gullstrand demonstrated that Helmholtz's theory accounted for only two-thirds of the accommodation. The remaining one-third could be explained by what Gullstrand called "extracapsular accommodation," where the fibers behind the lens made the necessary adjustments. The concept of the human eye as an optical system was among Gullstrand's most important achievements.

Gullstrand was given an honorary degree from Uppsala University in 1907 for his advances in eye research. He invented two devices commonly used even today in eye examinations—the slit lamp and the ophthalmoscope (sometimes called the Gullstrand ophthalmoscope), in cooperation with the Zeiss Optical Works in Germany. The slit lamp, consisting of a light used in combination with a microscope, permits doctors to pinpoint the location of a foreign object or tumor in three dimensional space. The ophthalmoscope is a combined light and magnifying lens enabling doctors to look at the retina at the back of the eye, as well as the optic disk. Doctors use it in an inspection for eye defects, as well as arteriosclerosis and diabetes. Gullstrand also designed aspheric lenses for those patients whose lenses had been removed as a result of cataracts.

Earns Nobel Prize for Work in Optics

The Nobel Prize in medicine or physiology was awarded to Gullstrand in 1911 for his work on the refraction of light and formation of images in the eye. In his lecture to the Nobel Academy, Gullstrand noted that the laws concerning the formation of optical images had been completely unknown when he began studying the eye lens, and that much of what had been known at that time had since been proven false. A special chair in physical and physiological optics was established for him in 1914 at Uppsala, and he became a member of the Nobel Academy's Physics Committee, and later its president, serving until 1929. Gullstrand received honorary degrees from the University of Dublin and the University of Jena in Germany. He was also awarded the Björken Prize from the Uppsala Faculty of Medicine, the Swedish Medical Association's Centenary Gold Medal, and the Graefe Medal from the German Ophthalmological Society.

Gullstrand married the former Signe Christina Breitholtz in 1885. The couple had a daughter who died while still a young girl. After retiring from Uppsala University in 1927, Gullstrand died of a stroke on July 21st, 1930.

SELECTED WRITINGS BY GULLSTRAND:

Books

Allgemeine Theorie der monochromatischen Aberrationen und ihre nächsten Ergebnisse für die Ophthalmologie, Berling (Uppsala, Sweden), 1900.

Einführung in die Methoden der Dioptrik des Auges des Menschen, S. Hirzil (Leipzig, Germany), 1911.

Periodicals

"Objektive Differential-Diagnostik und photographische Abbildung von Augenmuskellahmungen," *Kungliga Svenska vetenskapsakademiens handlingar* 18, 1892.

SOURCES:

Morello, Robert, interview with Francis Rogers conducted October 4th, 1993.

—Sketch by Francis Rogers

Beno Gutenberg
1889-1960
German American seismologist

German-born seismologist Beno Gutenberg investigated and determined most of the currently accepted causes of microseismic disturbances, and he improved methods of epicenter and depth determinations. He worked with noted seismologist **Charles F. Richter** to derive more accurate travel time curves for earthquakes and to clarify the relationships among magnitude, intensity, energy and acceleration of vibrations in the earth. His research began in Germany and continued at the California Institute of Technology, where he held the position of director of the Seismological Laboratory from 1947 to 1958.

Born in Darmstadt, Germany, on June 4, 1889, Gutenberg was the son of Hermann Gutenberg and Pauline Hachenburger Gutenberg. He studied at the Realgymnasium and the Technische Hochschule in Darmstadt, completing course work in physics, chemistry and mathematics. While attending the University of Göttingen, his passion shifted from mathematics and physics to climatology. He also took courses with Emil Wiechert, a learned seismologist who taught Gutenberg practically everything then known in the field of seismology. Gutenberg decided to carry out his doctoral studies in the area of microseisms—weak, recurring vibrations of the earth's crust. He was awarded a doctoral degree in 1911.

From 1911 to 1918, Gutenberg worked as an assistant at the International Seismological Association in Strasbourg, except for a period of army service during World War I. In 1918 he became *Privatdozent* at the University of Frankfurt-am-Main, until he gained a professorship of geophysics in 1926. In that same year, Gutenberg's father died, and he took over the management of the family's soap manufacturing business. In 1930 Gutenberg accepted a position as professor at the California Institute of Technology, which gave him the opportunity to utilize the resources of the Seismological Laboratory of the affiliated Carnegie Institution.

Finds Evidence of Terrestrial Core

At the time Gutenberg began studying microseisms, the field baffled most seismologists. Through his research, Gutenberg identified numerous sources for these disturbances, and much of his work still stands. His most important research in microseismic disturbances provided important insights into the internal constitution of the earth. Investigations carried out in the 1930s on the travel time of waves enabled him to establish the existence of a solid terrestrial core which propagates waves more slowly than does the more viscous mantle, the region between core and crust containing molten matter. He calculated the core to lie at a depth of 2,900 kilometers, a calculation of such accuracy that it has yet to be improved upon.

Gutenberg employed recently perfected instruments to develop superior methods of epicenter detection and depth determination. In research performed jointly with Charles Richter, Gutenberg enhanced travel time curves for earthquakes, and was able to quantify the interrelations between magnitude, intensity, energy and acceleration of compressional waves disturbing the tranquility of the earth's interior. The two scientists also worked together to redetermine the epicenters, or origins, of all major earthquakes, establishing the patterns and geometry of major seismic disturbances. In addition, Gutenberg further developed Richter's magnitude scale, extending it to include deep-focus shocks.

Further Research on Earth's Interior

In 1947 Gutenberg was appointed Director of the Seismological Laboratory at the Carnegie Institution. Besides carrying out his administrative duties, he also continued his own research in seismology. Studying the variation in the amplitude of waves, Gutenberg found evidence that the earth has more superficial layers, through which waves travel relatively slowly. Further measurements of the focal depth of waves made possible a more precise determination of the location of these layers in the upper mantle, at a depth between one hundred and two hundred kilometers. This low-velocity channel later turned out to play an important role in plate tectonics (the movement of the earth's crust that is responsible for continental drift and causes volcanic activity and earthquakes).

Rather than confining his studies to the field of seismology, Gutenberg also maintained an interest in meteorology, a not uncommon secondary research focus for seismologists. His researches in the structure of the upper atmosphere led him to observe ring zones of silence surrounding profound air blasts. From this data he was able to deduce temperature patterns in the upper atmosphere.

Gutenberg retired from the directorship of the Seismological Laboratory in 1958, and died in Pasadena in 1960. Much of Gutenberg's work on earthquake travel times can be found in his 1939 publication, *Internal Constitution of the Earth.* Gutenberg's landmark work, "On Seismic Waves," published in four parts in the 1930s, elucidates his studies of the various phases of earthquake arrivals.

SELECTED WRITINGS BY GUTENBERG:

Books

(Editor and contributor) *Internal Constitution of the Earth,* Mc-Graw Hill, 1939.

(With Charles Francis Richter) *Seismicity of the Earth,* The Society, 1941.

The Physics of the Earth's Interior, International Geography Series, Volume 1, [New York], 1959.

Periodicals

(With C. F. Richter) "On Seismic Waves," *Beiträge zur Geophysik,* Volume 43, 1934, Volume 45, 1935, Volume 47, 1936, Volume 54, 1939.

SOURCES:

Periodicals

Jeffreys, H., "Beno Gutenberg," *Quarterly Journal of the Royal Astronomical Society,* Volume 1, 1960, pp. 239–42.

—Sketch by Karen Withem

Alan Guth
1947-
American physicist

In late 1979, while on sabbatical from Cornell University, Alan Guth made a theoretical discovery that changed the field of astrophysics. That discovery was the concept of an inflationary universe, a hypothesis that describes what happened in the first few moments after the creation of the universe. The inflationary hypothesis solved some of the critical problems that had long troubled cosmologists and suggested some exciting new directions for theoretical and experimental research. Guth's work was so impressive that he soon had a number of job offers to consider, one of which was from the Massachusetts Institute of Technology (MIT). Guth accepted the position in 1980 and has since become the institution's Jerrold Zacharias Professor of Physics.

Alan Harvey Guth was born in New Brunswick, New Jersey, on February 27, 1947, to Hyman and Elaine Cheiten Guth. He grew up in nearby Highland Park in a middle-class family. He has described his childhood as "uneventful," as cited in *Omni,* but one dominated by an interest in mathematics. Coupled with this intense interest in math was a penchant for drawing highly detailed structures of rocket ships, which he someday hoped to construct.

After graduating from high school, Guth entered MIT, where he earned both a bachelor's and master's degree in physics in 1969. He then stayed on at MIT to earn a doctorate in 1972. A year before leaving MIT, he also married Susan Tisch, with whom he had grown up in New Jersey. The Guths have two children, Lawrence David and Jennifer Lynn.

Guth's first academic appointment was at Princeton, where he was instructor of physics from 1971 to 1974. He then received an appointment as postdoctoral research associate at Columbia University, from 1974 to 1977, and then a similar position at Cornell, from 1977 to 1979. Nearing the end of his Cornell appointment, Guth found himself in a difficult position. Most Ph.D.'s would expect to have received a regular appointment within a few years of having earned their degree. Guth was now in his seventh postdoctoral year and knew, as he later said, that he was "nearing the end of the postdoctorate trail," as quoted in *Omni.* Fortunately, he was able to obtain an extension on his Cornell appointment by taking a one-year sabbatical at Stanford University's Linear Accelerator Center (SLAC). There he intended to carry out research on elementary particles while continuing to look for more permanent employment.

Discovers Inflationary Theory

It was at Stanford on December 6, 1979, that Guth's life changed radically. He was working on a problem that had long intrigued him: How the basic theories of particle physics could be applied to an understanding of the origins of the universe. One of the ironies of modern physics is the close association that exists between these two extreme levels of physics: the smallest and most fundamental units of which all objects consist, and the largest and most profound changes that have ever occurred (the "Big Bang," the theory that the universe was created billions of years ago in an explosion of a single point of energy density).

Guth had been attempting to find a way to apply Grand Unified Theory to the earliest events of cosmology. Grand Unified Theories (GUTs) are theoretical efforts to show how three of the four fundamental forces of nature—strong nuclear force, weak nuclear force, and electromagnetic force—are associated with each other. GUTs assume that at some point in the earliest history of the universe, these three forces were all equivalent to and indistinguishable from each other. Guth had come to a study of this problem more from his own background in particle physics than from much experience in cosmology, a subject about which, he claims, he knew relatively little.

In any case, the evening of December 6, 1979, was characterized by a sudden breakthrough. As Guth explained to interviewer and fellow physicist Gregory Benford in *Omni,* he worked on this solution for a time on the evening of the sixth, then raced to his SLAC office on his bicycle the next morning to complete the solution. He later told Benford that "I broke my personal [bicycling] record dashing to SLAC to whip out my notebook and continue these calculations."

The result of those calculations is a hypothesis now known as the inflationary theory. According to this theory, the universe began to expand much more rapidly than had previously been imagined during the first moments after the Big Bang, doubling in size about once every 10^{-35} second. The theory was an almost instantaneous success because it accounted for a number of features of the universe—such as its present even distribution of background cosmic radiation—that had thus far remained unexplained.

As news of the inflationary theory spread among scientists, the job offers that Guth had been seeking began to appear. He decided to accept one from his alma mater, MIT, where he rose from visiting associate professor in 1980, to Jerrold Zacharias Professor of Physics—a post he currently holds—in 1989. Between 1984 and 1990, Guth was also on the staff at the Harvard Smithsonian Center for Astrophysics.

SELECTED WRITINGS BY GUTH:

Books

(With Kerson Huang and Robert L. Jaffe) *Asymptotic Realms of Physics: Essays in Honor of Francis E. Low,* MIT Press, 1983.

(With Donald E. Osterbock and Peter H. Raven) *Origins and Extinctions,* Yale University Press, 1988.

SOURCES:

Periodicals

"Interview: Alan Guth," *Omni,* November, 1988, pp. 74–79, 94–99.

—*Sketch by David E. Newton*

Orlando A. Gutierrez
1928-
Cuban-born American engineer

In addition to his work in thermodynamics and aeroacoustics, Orlando A. Gutierrez did extensive work to promote Hispanic education and employment in the sciences. He has been leading the Society of Hispanic Professional Engineers (SHPE) as its national president since 1993. Having previously served as national treasurer of that organization as well as the manager of the National Aeronautics and Space Administration (NASA) Headquarters' Hispanic Employment and its Minority University programs, he successfully moved from the engineer's laboratory to the field of human resources.

Orlando Antonio Gutierrez was born in Havana, Cuba, on July 23, 1928. His parents were Antonio Maria Gutierrez, a newspaper manager, and Flora Maria Izaguirre Gutierrez. Gutierrez attended a private high school in Havana named Academia Baldor. As a young student, he was very interested in things technical and always wanted to be an engineer despite his mother's preference that he become a physician. His dream began to be realized when his parents agreed he could leave Cuba to attend college in the United States—there being no good engineering schools in his native country. Gutierrez left Cuba for the United States in August of 1945, having enrolled at Rensselaer Polytechnic Institute (RPI) in Troy, New York. Halfway through his schooling, in 1947, he married Helen LaBarge, with whom he went on to have five children—Peter, Antonio, Helenmary, Marco, and Alex. Two years after his marriage, Gutierrez received his B.S. in mechanical engineering and accepted his first job.

Gutierrez joined the IBM World Trade Corporation in 1949 and worked in both the United States and Cuba. In 1951 he accepted a position with the American Locomotive Company in Schenectady, New York, where he worked as a design and test engineer and then as a manager of its heat transfer laboratory. In 1961 Gutierrez joined NASA at its Lewis Research Center in Cleveland, Ohio. In his early years there, he did engineering research in heat transfer and other thermodynamics-related subjects aimed at building power plants for spacecraft. Later his research focused on aeroacoustics, with an emphasis on reducing noise from aircraft engines, and he worked on these jet acoustic studies as both a researcher and program manager.

During his later years at Lewis Research Center, Gutierrez also worked as manager of the center's Hispanic program, and in 1982 such human resource work became his career focus. Gutierrez left Lewis for a position as Hispanic Employment Program Manager at NASA Headquarters in Washington, D.C., where he continued his work of increasing Hispanic engineer representation throughout the entire agency. He worked in that area until 1990, when he became NASA's Minority University Program Manager. He retired from that position during November of 1992. From 1989 to 1992, Gutierrez also served as national treasurer for the Society of Hispanic Professional Engineers, during which time that organization's budget increased from $300,000 to over $1 million. In 1993 he became SHPE's national president.

Over the course of his engineering career, Gutierrez authored or coauthored over twenty-five papers and technical reports concerning heat transfer and aeroacoustics. He also coauthored a NASA special publication, *Forced-Flow Once-through Boilers: NASA Research,* published in 1975. Despite his expertise and love of engineering, Gutierrez found that he was equally involved and dedicated to the cause of improving the participation and status of Hispanics in engineering and science, and he finally chose to sacrifice his technical career to that cause. He has received a number of awards for his work, including the NASA Equal Opportunity Medal and Exceptional Service Medal and the Mexican American Engineering Society's most prestigious award, the "Medalla de Oro."

SELECTED WRITINGS BY GUTIERREZ:

Books

(With James R. Stone and Vernon H. Gray) *Forced-Flow Once-through Boilers: NASA Research,* Lewis Research Center, National Aeronautics and Space Administration, 1975.

SOURCES:

Gutierrez, Orlando A., interview with Leonard C. Bruno conducted March 29, 1994.

—*Sketch by Leonard C. Bruno*

A. J. Haagen-Smit
1900-1977
Dutch-born American chemist

In the mid–1940s, A. J. Haagen-Smit led investigations into the origins of smog. Through his research he discovered that smog is created by the oxidation of organic material in the air. Haagen-Smit spent a major part of his life challenging industry in an attempt to curtail air pollution caused by burning fuels. As a result of his constant battle, factories now use smoke stacks that filter carbon fumes, and the auto industry has incorporated components to reduce pollution-causing vapors from car and truck exhaust.

Arie J. Haagen-Smit was born in Utrecht, The Netherlands, on December 22, 1900, the son of Jan Willem Adrianus Haagen-Smit and Maria Geertruida van Maanen. His father was a chemist who maintained a large science library in the home. Haagen-Smit credited his interest in science and technology to the early enthusiasm of his father's discussions about his work, and the accessibility of his family's library. He attended the Rijks Hoogere Burger School and in 1922 graduated from the University of Utrecht with a major in organic chemistry. He acquired practical experience in organic chemistry while working summers in a local munitions plant and serving in the Dutch army chemical corps. By 1926 he had earned his M.A. degree, and in 1929 he completed his Ph.D. While studying for his doctorate, he identified the structure of a group of hydrocarbons, called terpenes, found in volatile oils, or those vaporizing rapidly.

Haagen-Smit remained at the university for another five years, first as a chief assistant in organic chemistry, then as a lecturer. His primary interest was the chemical composition of natural products. In particular, he investigated and published his findings on plant hormones called "auxins." He also isolated and synthesized substances obtained from plant species related to poison ivy. Haagen-Smit rapidly gained a reputation as a specialist in the chemistry of plant hormones, as well as distinction as a highly talented researcher.

In 1936, he was invited to lecture at Harvard University. The following year, he was named associate professor of chemistry at the California Institute of Technology, and in 1940 he was named professor of bio-organic chemistry in the division of biology.

A. J. Haagen-Smit

His work during the 1940s focused on an extensive examination of essential oils—the volatile liquids extracted from plants by various means. His work on these essential oils was of great importance to the food industry. As Haagen-Smit explained in the May, 1961 issue of *Engineering and Science,* "an exact knowledge of these lost flavors becomes of decisive importance in the reconstitution of foods so that they regain most of their original quality." Other industries also were enriched by Haagen-Smit's work. The paint industry, for example, benefited from his research on the oil turpentine.

Conducts Research on Smog

Following World War II, the residents of southern California experienced difficulty in breathing and a burning in the eyes when weather conditions caused fog and haze to blanket the region. Haagen-Smit was asked by several government agencies to try and find a solution. By using techniques originally developed in his work on essential oils, he determined that the phenomena called smog was the result of a chemical change in the atmosphere induced by an oxidation process. Specifically, he showed that the two principal ingredients of smog were the by-product of petroleum combustion in automobiles, and nitrogen oxide fumes being spewed into the air when fuels were burned by local industries. He deduced that since a by-product of oxidation is ozone, he could create smog in a laboratory by subjecting the gaseous ozone to gasoline fumes wafting out of a test tube. His experiment worked, and—according to *Current Biography*—Haagen-Smit told members of the National Municipal League, "It was luck. We hit the jackpot with the first nickel." Haagen-Smit developed an ozone test to measure smog intensity marking a major breakthrough in air pollution control.

Haagen-Smit became an outspoken advocate for establishing air pollution standards to promote clean air. He campaigned diligently to get industry to filter smoke stack fumes and was among the earliest to urge the automobile industry to develop hardware to filter exhaust vapors. He served as a consultant to the Los Angeles Air Pollution Control District, the United States Public Health Service, and the California Department of Public Health. From 1965, until his retirement in 1971, Haagen-Smit was the director of the Plant Environmental Laboratory at the California Institute of Technology. For his work in several fields of bio-chemistry he received many awards, including two by the American Chemical Society, of which he was a trustee: the Fritizche award in 1950, and the Tolman Award in 1964. He was also a recipient of the Smithsonian Medal, the $50,000 Alice Tyler Ecology Prize, and the Rhineland Award. In 1947, the Netherlands government conferred on him the Knight Order of Orange-Nassau. Haagen-Smit was elected a Fellow of the New York Academy of Sciences and the Royal Academy of Sciences of the Netherlands.

He married Petronella Francina Pennings in 1930, and before her death in 1933, they had a son, Jan Willem Adrianus. Maria Wilhelmina Bloemers became his second wife on June 10, 1935. Haagen-Smit died of cancer on March 17, 1977, in Pasadena, California. He was survived by his wife Maria and three daughters: Maria Van Pelt, Margaret Scott, and Joan Demers.

SELECTED WRITINGS BY HAAGEN-SMIT:

Periodicals

Engineering and Science, May, 1961.

SOURCES:

Books

Current Biography, H. W. Wilson, 1966.

Periodicals

New York Times, March 19, 1977.

—*Sketch by Benedict A. Leerburger*

Fritz Haber
1868-1934
German chemist

One the foremost chemists of his generation, Fritz Haber's legacy did not end with his considerable achievements of both theoretical and practical value in the fields of physical chemistry, organic chemistry, physics, and engineering. Perhaps of even greater importance were his tireless attempts to promote communication and understanding between scientific communities across the globe. The Kaiser Wilhelm Institute for Chemistry, under his direction, became famous in the years after World War I as a leading center of research whose seminars attracted scientists from all nations. In his most outstanding contribution to chemistry—for which he won the 1918 Nobel Prize in Chemistry—Haber found an inexpensive method for synthesizing large quantities of ammonia from its constituent elements nitrogen and hydrogen. A steady supply of ammonia made possible the industrial production of fertilizer and explosives.

Haber was born on December 9, 1868, in Breslau (now known as Wroclaw, Poland), the only child of first cousins Siegfried Haber and Paula Haber. Haber's mother died in childbirth. In 1877, his father, a prosperous importer of dyes and pigments, married Hedwig Hamburger, who bore him three daughters. Haber and his father had a distant relationship, but his stepmother treated him kindly. From a local grade school, Haber went to the St. Elizabeth Gymnasium (high school) in Breslau. There he developed an abiding love of literature, particularly the voluminous writings of Goethe, which inspired him to write verse. Haber also enjoyed acting, considering it as a profession early on before settling on chemistry.

After entering the University of Berlin in 1886 to study chemistry, Haber transferred after a semester to the University of Heidelberg. There, under the supervision of Robert Bunsen (who gave his name to the burner used in laboratories everywhere), Haber delved into physical chemistry, physics, and mathematics. Getting his Ph.D. in 1891, Haber tried working as an industrial laboratory chemist but found its rigid routines too intellectually confining. He decided instead to enter the Federal Institute of

Fritz Haber

Technology in Zurich, Switzerland, in order to learn about the most advanced chemical engineering techniques of his time, studying under Georg Lunge.

Haber then tried, without success, to work in his father's business, opting after six months to return to academia. In 1894, after a brief stint at the University of Jena, he took an assistant teaching position with Hans Bunte, professor of chemical technology at the Karlsruhe Technische Hochschule in Baden. Haber enjoyed Karlsruhe's emphasis on preparing its students for technical positions, stressing the connections between science and industry. His studies led him to investigate the breakdown at high temperatures of organic compounds known as hydrocarbons, an area pioneered by the French chemist Marcelin Berthelot. After correcting and systematizing Berthelot's findings, Haber's results, published in 1896 as a book entitled *Experimental Studies on the Decomposition and Combustion of Hydrocarbons,* led to his appointment that year as lecturer, a step below associate professor.

Haber married another chemist, Clara Immerwahr, in 1901. They had a son, Hermann, born in June, 1902. While a lecturer, Haber moved his experimental focus from organic chemistry to physical chemistry. Although he lacked a formal education in this area, with the help of a colleague, Hans Luggin, he began to research the effect of electrical currents on fuel cells and the loss of efficiency in steam engines through heat. Haber also devised electrical instruments to measure the loss of oxygen in burning organic compounds, outlining this subject in a book published in 1898, *Outline of Technical Electrochemistry on a Theoretical Basis,* which earned him a promotion to associate professor. Haber's exceptional abilities as a researcher, which included his precision as a mathematician and writer, induced a leading German science group to send him in 1902 to survey America's approach to chemistry in industry and education.

Investigates Synthesis of Ammonia

Haber published a third book, *Thermodynamics of Technical Gas Reactions,* in 1905. In the volume he applied thermodynamic theory on the behavior of gases to establish industrial requirements for creating reactions. His clear exposition gave him an international reputation as an expert in adapting science to technology. That same year, Haber began his groundbreaking work on the synthesis of ammonia. Europe's growing population had created a demand for an increase in agricultural production. Nitrates, used in industrial fertilizer, required ammonia for their manufacture. Thus, Haber's goal to find new ways to fabricate ammonia grew out of a very pressing need. Other scientists had been synthesizing ammonia from nitrogen and hydrogen but at temperatures of one thousand degrees centigrade, which were not practical for industrial production. Haber was able to get the same reaction but at manageable temperatures of three hundred degrees centigrade.

The chemist **Walther Nernst** had obtained the synthesis of ammonia with gases at very high pressures. He also had disputed Haber's results for his high-temperature reaction. Goaded by Nernst's skepticism, Haber executed high-pressure experiments and confirmed his earlier calculations. He then combined Nernst's technique with his own to greatly increase the efficiency of the process. To augment the yield even further, Haber found a superior catalyst for the reaction and redirected the heat it produced back into the system to save on the expenditure of energy.

The final step of bringing Haber's work into the factory fell to the engineer **Karl Bosch**, whose company, Badische Anilin- und Sodafabrik (BASF), had supported Haber's research. After Bosch solved some key problems such as designing containers that could withstand a corrosive process over a period of time, full-scale industrial output began in 1910. Today the Haber-Bosch process is an industry standard for the mass production of ammonia.

In 1912 Haber was appointed director of the newly formed Kaiser Wilhelm Institute for Physical Chemistry and Electrochemistry at Dahlheim, just outside of Berlin; **Richard Willstätter** and Ernst Beckmann joined as codirectors. With the outbreak of World War I in 1914, Haber volunteered his laboratory and his expertise to help Germany. At first, he developed alternate sources of antifreeze. Then, the German War Office consulted both Nernst and Haber about developing a chemical weapon that would drive the enemy out of their trenches in order to resume open warfare. In January, 1915, the German Army began production of a chlorine gas that Haber's team had invented. On April 11, 1915, in the first chemical offensive ever, five thousand cylinders of chlorine gas blanketed 3.5 miles of enemy territory near Ypres, Belgium, resulting in 150,000 deaths.

Haber hated the war but hoped that in developing the gases he would help to bring it to a speedy end by breaking the deadlock of trench warfare. His wife, however, denounced his work as a perversion of science. After a violent argument with Haber in 1915, she committed suicide. Haber was married again in 1917 to Charlotte Nathan, who bore him a son and a daughter. Their marriage ended in divorce in 1927.

Receives Controversial Nobel Prize

In 1916 Haber was appointed chief of the Chemical Warfare Service, overseeing every detail in that department. His process for developing nitrates from ammonia became incorporated into Germany's manufacture of explosives. Because of his duties as supervisor of chemical warfare, American, French, and British scientists vehemently contested his 1918 Nobel Prize in Chemistry. Although many of the Allied scientists had also contributed to the war effort, they charged that Haber was a war criminal for developing chemical weapons.

Since the 1918 prize had been reserved for until after the war ended, Haber accepted his Nobel Prize in November, 1919. Unquestionably, Haber had invented, in the words of the prize's presenter, A. G. Ekstrand of the Royal Swedish Academy of Sciences, "an exceedingly important means of improving the standards of agriculture and the well-being of mankind." Yet the controversy over his award, on top of Germany's defeat, his first wife's suicide, and his developing diabetes, depressed Haber greatly.

Nevertheless, Haber continued to turn his technical acumen to patriotic ends. In 1920, to help Germany pay off the onerous war reparations that the Versailles Treaty had imposed, Haber headed a doomed attempt to recover gold from seawater. Unfortunately, he had based his project on unverified nineteenth-century mineral analyses that had grossly overestimated the quantities for gold. It turned out after several abortive sea voyages that there was simply not enough gold present in seawater to make refining profitable. However, Haber did perfect a very precise method for measuring concentrations of gold.

Haber had much greater success as continuing director of the Kaiser Wilhelm Institute. His proven leadership ability attracted some of the best talent in the world to his laboratory in Karlsruhe and to the Institute, where in 1929 fully half of the members were foreigners from a dozen countries. In 1919 he began the Haber Colloquium, an ongoing seminar that during the postwar years brought together the best minds in chemistry and physics, among them **Niels Bohr**, **Peter Debye**, **Otto Meyerhof**, and **Otto Warburg**. Haber's sharp wit, critical intelligence and broad knowledge of science were greatly appreciated at the seminars. When he ceased attending regularly, they became markedly less popular. Haber traveled widely to foster greater cooperation between nations. As an example, he helped establish the Japan Institute in that nation to foster shared cultural interests with other countries. From 1929 to 1933 he occupied Germany's seat on the Union Internationale de Chimie.

When the Nazis came to power in 1933, the Kaiser Institute fell on hard times. After receiving a demand from the minister of art, science, and popular education to dismiss all Jewish workers at the institute, Haber—a Jew himself—resigned on April 30, 1933. He wrote in his letter of resignation that having always selected his collaborators on the basis of their intelligence and character, he could not conceive of having to change so successful a method.

Haber fled Germany for England, accepting the invitation of his colleague William J. Pope to work in Cambridge, where he stayed for four months. Chaim Weitzmann, a chemist who would become the first president of Israel, offered Haber the position of director in the physical chemistry department of the Daniel Sieff Research Institute at Rehovot, in what is now Israel. Despite ill health, Haber accepted and in January, 1934, after recovering from a heart attack, began the trip. Resting on the way in Basel, Switzerland, he died on January 29, 1934. His friend and colleague Willstätter gave the memorial speech at his funeral. On the first anniversary of his death, over five hundred men and women from cultural societies across Germany converged on the institute—despite Nazi attempts at intimidation—to pay homage to Haber.

SELECTED WRITINGS BY HABER:

Books

Grundriss der technischen Elektrochemie auf theoretischer Grundlage (title means, "Outline of Technical Electrochemistry on a Theoretical Basis"), R. Oldenbourg, 1898.

Thermodynamics of Technical Gas Reactions, Longmans, Green, 1908.

Practical Results of the Theoretical Development of Chemistry, Franklin Institute, 1924.

Periodicals

(With C. Liebermann) "Bidioxymethylenindigo," *Berichte der Deutschen chemischen Gesellschaft,* Volume 23, 1890, p. 1566.

"Über einige Derwate des Piperonals," *Berichte der Deutschen chemischen Gesellschaft,* Volume 24, 1891, p. 617.

"Über den textilen Flachdruck," *Zeitschrift für angewandte Chemie und Zentralblatt für technische Chemie,* Volume 15, 1902, pp. 1117–1183.

SOURCES:

Books

Dictionary of Scientific Biography, Volume 5, Scribner, 1972, pp. 620–623.

Farber, Eduard, *Nobel Prize Winners in Chemistry, 1901–1961,* Abelard-Schuman, 1953, revised 1963, pp. 71–75

Wasson, Tyler, editor, *Nobel Prize Winners,* H. W. Wilson, 1987, pp. 402–404.

—Sketch by Hovey Brock

Jacques Hadamard
1865-1963
French mathematician

Widely considered the preeminent French mathematician of the twentieth century, Jacques Hadamard has made an impact on many fields of mathematics. Although an analyst and a student of theoretical calculus by training, he has influenced topology, number theory, and even psychology. His work on defining functions won him the Grand Prix of the Académie des Sciences early in his career, and his proof of the prime number theorem solidified his importance in the mathematical world. He wrote several textbooks on a variety of mathematical subjects, including one which explained a mathematician's thought processes. Hadamard was first and foremost a teacher, however, and he used his position to help both students and colleagues alike see the connections between seemingly unrelated fields.

Born in Versailles on December 8, 1865, Jacques-Salomon Hadamard was the son of two teachers. His mother, Claude-Marie Picard, taught piano, while his father, Amédée, taught Latin at a prominent Paris high school. In 1884, at the age of eighteen, Hadamard began studying at the École Normale Supérieure. His first teaching job was at a high school in Paris, the Lycée Buffon, in 1890. When he was not teaching, he worked on his doctoral dissertation, and the research he did during this period led to his first breakthrough in mathematics.

Work on Taylor Series Wins Grand Prix

Hadamard's dissertation concerned determining the shape of a function and finding certain points on that function where division by zero was involved in the original equation. Such functions had previously been considered undefined and unsolvable, but Hadamard found a way to solve them using a set of fractions known as the Taylor series. Published in 1892, his work was so revolutionary that the French Académie des Sciences immediately awarded him its highest honor, the Grand Prix. This was also the year Hadamard married Louise-Anna Trenel, with whom he would have five children. In 1892 Hadamard also accepted a position as lecturer at the Faculté des Sciences of Bordeaux, where he continued his work. Although his accomplishments in defining functions had been important to the mathematical community at large, for Hadamard it was just another step toward a larger goal. He wanted to find a proof of the prime number theorem. For years, some of the world's best mathematicians had attempted to prove that the total number of primes could be defined and that individual primes could be determined by something other than the endless testing of possible factors. Many had discovered estimates and close guesses, but no one had achieved accurate results.

Hadamard used his work on the Taylor series as a guide, and he established that the number of primes below any given number could be determined by using complex numbers, also known as imaginary numbers. While his theory only works when the numbers used are sufficiently large, mathematicians generally only concern themselves with primes when such large numbers are involved. Later attempts to improve upon or generalize Hadamard's 1896 prime number theorem by such noted mathematicians as **S. I. Ramanujan** have failed.

Career Research Spans Many Topics

Following publication of the proof of the prime number theorem, Hadamard left Bordeaux for a lectureship at the Sorbonne in Paris. A return to the intellectual center of Paris also meant greater involvement with the mathematical community, in which Hadamard had earned a high place. While many mathematicians were content to specialize in a small area of mathematics, Hadamard saw the importance of finding connections between the various fields. He was openly critical of mathematicians who limited their work to their immediate subject. In 1902 he argued, for example, that the definitions **Vito Volterra** had offered for the calculus terms *continuity, derivative,* and *differential* were inadequate because they could not be generalized to other fields, especially the relatively new area of topology. Instead of merely criticizing Volterra, however, Hadamard applied himself to generalizing analysis so it would be more applicable to other fields. His creation and definition of the term *functional,* first put forth in 1903, is one result of this generalization. Though Hadamard had used standard analysis to come up with functionals, the application of the idea to topology was important to establishing the validity of that field.

Hadamard's work forming connections between topology and analysis was interrupted in 1904 by a debate over mathematical logic which raged through the mathematical community. Ernst Zermelo, a German mathematician, had proposed that given an infinite number of sets, it would be possible to select exactly one, definable item from each set. This proposal was called the axiom of choice. Zermelo argued that it was obvious and thus needed no proof, but many of the most prominent mathematicians of the time, including **Émile Borel**, **Jules Henri Poincaré**, and **Henri Lebesgue**, disputed it. As Morris Kline describes the controversy in *Mathematics: The Loss of Certainty:* "The nub of the criticism was that, unless a definite law specified which element was chosen from each set, no real choice had been made, so the new set was not really formed." Yet the axiom of choice was necessary to establish sections of abstract algebra, topology, and standard analysis. Hadamard supported Zermelo. He rejected the idea that the item taken from the set could necessarily be defined, yet he felt that any theory which allowed mathematics to progress should be accepted, with or without formal proof.

In 1908, Hadamard spoke at the Fourth International Congress of Mathematicians in Rome, where he met the famous German topologist L. E. J. Brouwer. They began a correspondence relating to the mathematical ideas of their time, and the exchange of letters was crucial to Brouwer. The German mathematician used Hadamard's ideas as a springboard to some of his most important topological discoveries. In 1909, Hadamard left the Sorbonne for a more prestigious appointment as professor at the École Centrale des Arts et Manufactures. He would remain there, teaching concurrently at the Collège de France after 1920, until his retirement at the age of seventy-one.

In 1912, Hadamard's friend and colleague Jules Henri Poincaré died. Poincaré, like Hadamard, had been involved in several different fields of mathematics, and his work had greatly influenced Hadamard's interest in generalization. Saddened by the loss of this great mathematician, Hadamard devoted a great deal of his research time after Poincaré's death to writing biographical works of his friend. Hadamard did his last piece of major research in the field of calculus in 1932, when he addressed a problem posed by the French mathematician A. L. Cauchy. But even after his retirement in 1937, Hadamard continued to ponder some of the questions that had concerned him throughout his career. The old controversy over the axiom of choice became the basis of a new book on the importance of accepting intuition for the sake of mathematical progress. He published *The Psychology of Invention in the Mathematical Field* in 1945, at the age of eighty, and it was widely considered an innovative attempt at understanding how mathematicians come up with their ideas. Some of the work on this book was done in the United States, where he was a visiting professor at Columbia University in New York in 1941. Unlike many European mathematicians, however, Hadamard did not stay in America. He returned home to France, living out the rest of his life quietly. He died in Paris on October 17, 1963, at the age of ninety-seven.

SELECTED WRITINGS BY HADAMARD:

Books

The Psychology of Invention in the Mathematical Field, Princeton University Press, 1945.

Oeuvres de Jacques Hadamard, four volumes, Centre National de la Récherche Scientifique, 1968.

SOURCES:

Books

Cajori, F., *A History of Mathematics,* Chelsea Publishing Company, 1980.

Kline, Morris, *Mathematical Thought from Ancient to Modern Times,* Oxford University Press, 1972.

Kline, Morris, *Mathematics: A Loss of Certainty,* Oxford University Press, 1980.

Phillips, Esther, editor, *Studies in the History of Mathematics,* Mathematical Association of America, 1987.

—Sketch by Karen Sands

Otto Hahn
1879-1968
German chemist

Otto Hahn is noted for his work on radioactive materials, which in 1938 led to his discovery, with physicist **Lise Meitner** and chemist **Fritz Strassmann**, of the process of nuclear fission. In recognition of their work, Hahn and Strassmann received the 1944 Nobel Prize in chemistry, and Hahn, Strassmann, and Meitner received the Fermi Award in 1966. Hahn was born in Frankfurt-am-Main on March 8, 1879, to Heinrich Hahn, a glazier, and Charlotte Giese Stutzmann Hahn. The Hahns' early years in Frankfurt were marked by poverty: according to R. Spence, writing in the *Biographical Memoirs of Fellows of the Royal Society,* the four Hahn boys—Otto, his two brothers and his half-brother from Charlotte's first marriage—"slept in an unheated attic bedroom and took their weekly bath in a tub on the landing." Gradually, Heinrich's business became more successful, and the family attained "middle-class respectability." Otto, who attended the Klinger Realschule, demonstrated some early interest in science, carrying out simple chemical experiments in the family laundry house. But other subjects seemed more important to him, and the honors he received upon graduation were for gymnastics, religious studies, and music. Hahn's parents had hoped that he would pursue a career in architecture, but when he entered the University of Marburg in 1897, it was a course in chemistry that he decided to pursue. He interrupted his studies at Marburg to spend one year at the University of Munich, but then returned to Marburg, where he was awarded his doctorate in organic chemistry in 1901.

Biographers—and Hahn himself—mention Hahn's devotion to non-academic pursuits in college, especially cigar smoking and beer drinking. He felt obligated to join one of the student societies that were ubiquitous in German universities and on one occasion even challenged another student to a duel. Hahn's membership in the Nibelungia Society apparently brought him considerable happiness until he resigned in the 1930s in opposition to Nazi policies adopted by the group.

Travels to England for Further Study and to Learn English

After graduation, Hahn enlisted in the infantry for one year and then returned as an instructor at Marburg. Soon thereafter, hoping to better his chances at a job in the German chemical industry, Hahn decided to spend a year in an English-speaking institution where he could polish his language skills while advancing his knowledge in chemistry. Through the efforts of a former teacher, Hahn was offered a research post with **Sir William Ramsay** in his laboratory at University College, London. Hahn left for England in September, 1904.

Otto Hahn

Ramsay's fame rests primarily on his discovery of the inert gases argon, neon, krypton, and xenon. In the early 1900s, however, he had become interested in a new topic, radioactivity. When Hahn arrived in London, it was a problem in radioactivity, therefore, to which Ramsay assigned him. In some ways that decision was a peculiar one, since nothing in Hahn's background in organic chemistry had prepared him for research on radioactive materials. Ramsay seemed to believe that Hahn's lack of background in radioactivity might be an advantage, since he could proceed with no preconceived notions as to what to expect. The problem he assigned the young German chemist was to extract radium from a 100-gram sample of barium carbonate. After familiarizing himself with this new field of research, Hahn completed Ramsay's assignment, obtaining a few milligrams of radium. He discovered, however, that the radioactivity of the sample was greater than expected and eventually isolated a second radioactive material from the impure radium. He called the new substance "radiothorium," later identified as an isotope of thorium that decays into thorium-x.

At the conclusion of this research, both Ramsay and Hahn were convinced that the latter's future lay in radioactivity, not organic chemistry. Thus, Ramsay obtained for Hahn an appointment at Emil Fischer's Chemical Institute at the University of Berlin, where he could pursue this new interest. In preparation for the Berlin post, however, Hahn decided to spend another year of study, this time with the world's foremost authority on radioactivity, **Ernest Rutherford,** at McGill. During Hahn's year at McGill (1905–1906) he discovered a second radioactive substance, radioactinium, now known to be an isotope of thorium that decays into actinium-x.

Begins Association with Lise Meitner

Hahn began work at the Chemical Institute in Berlin in the fall of 1907, was appointed a Privat dozent (university lecturer) a year later, and was promoted to professor of chemistry in 1910. One of the most significant events of this period was the arrival of Lise Meitner as a student at the Chemical Institute. Prejudice against women in the sciences was very strong at the time, and Meitner was not allowed to work in the same laboratories as male students. Fischer did, however, allow her to share a tiny makeshift laboratory with Hahn in a converted workshop. Hahn and Meitner worked well together, with the former's chemical approach to problems complementing Meitner's outlook as a physicist. Thus a collaboration began that was to last for three decades. During their work together at the Chemical Institute, Hahn and Meitner concentrated on a study of beta emitters and, in the process, discovered more new radioactive isotopes.

In 1912, Kaiser Wilhelm authorized the establishment of a new research institute to consist of several separate departments. Invited to head up the section on radioactivity in the new Institute for Chemistry at Berlin-Dahlem, Hahn asked Meitner to join him there. One of the advantages of the new setting—in addition to much more space—was that radioactive materials had never been used in the rooms before, so that Hahn and Meitner were able to detect far lower levels of radiation than they could in their former laboratories. This allowed them to discover weakly radioactive isotopes of potassium and rubidium that had not yet been observed.

During this period, Hahn met Edith Junghans, whose father was a member of the Stettin City Council. The two became engaged in November of 1912. They were married in Stettin in March, 1913, and eventually had one child, a son, Hanno, born in April of 1922.

Hahn's personal and professional life were soon to be disrupted by the onset of World War I. In July, 1914, he was called into the army. After serving with distinction in the infantry at the battlefront, he was ordered back to Berlin, where he was assigned to work with a poison gas research unit headed by Fritz Haber. For the next three years, Hahn shuttled back and forth between Berlin and the battlefronts, developing and testing new gases. He was horrified by the results he saw when gases were used in battle, but he had become convinced that such atrocities might bring the war to an early end and save lives, the same argument eventually made for the use of nuclear bombs—built on the principle of nuclear fission discovered by Hahn—at the end of World War II.

During his stays in Berlin, Hahn was able to spend some time in his own laboratory at the Institute for Chemistry. One of the projects that he and Meitner pursued during this period was a study of a new radioactive element that had previously been announced by Kasimir Fajans and Oswald Göhring in 1913, an element they had named "brevium." Hahn and Meitner found the element in the residues of pitchblende ore and showed its relationship to parent and daughter isotopes. The name they suggested for the element, "protoactinium" (now protactinium), eventually became preferred to that recommended by Fajans and Göhring.

By the 1930s, Hahn's fame had begun to spread. In 1933, he was invited to spend a year as visiting professor at Cornell University and to deliver the prestigious Baker Lectures there. His visit to the United States was cut short, however, by news of the Nazi uprisings taking place in Germany. He decided that it was best for him to return to Berlin, which he did in the summer of 1933.

One of the great ironies of the 1930s was that while political turmoil was sweeping through the world's greatest scientific nation, Germany, momentous scientific discoveries with profound historical significance were also being made there. Hahn returned to a Germany where many of the world's finest scientists were either being expelled from their university posts or were fleeing Hitler's wrath for the United Kingdom, the United States, or other destinations.

Turns to Research on Neutron Bombardment of Uranium

In the midst of the political chaos around him, Hahn turned his attention to an exciting new field of research: the neutron bombardment of uranium and thorium. Two important recent discoveries convinced Hahn that he needed to go beyond the now nearly exhausted field of radioactivity. The first of these was the discovery by **Irène Joliot-Curie** and her husband **Frédéric Joliot-Curie** that an element can be made radioactive by bombarding it with alpha particles. The second was the discovery of the neutron by **James Chadwick** in 1932. These two discoveries had been utilized in the early 1930s by **Enrico Fermi**, who saw that neutrons would be far more effective "bullets" for bombarding atomic nuclei than were alpha or beta particles. In a short period of time, Fermi had used this technique to convert dozens of stable elements to radioactive forms. He was especially interested in trying this technique on uranium, since the predicted result of that reaction would be an element with an atomic number one greater than uranium. Since that element had never been observed in nature, a successful result of this experiment would be the formation of the world's first synthetic element. When Fermi carried out this experiment, the results he obtained were ambiguous, and he could draw no firm conclusion as to what had happened as a result of bombarding uranium with neutrons.

It was this problem to which Hahn turned in 1934. To work with him and Meitner on the problem, Hahn selected another radiochemist who had joined the Institute in 1929, Fritz Strassmann. Over the next four years, Hahn, Meitner, and Strassmann analyzed the complex mixture of isotopes formed when uranium is bombarded with neutrons. At first, they worked on the assumption that Fermi's hypothesis was correct and that isotopes with atomic numbers from about 90 to about 94 would predominate in the mixture. After all, the only nuclear reactions with which scientists were then familiar were those in which the atomic numbers of products differed from those of the original material by only one or two. By 1938, however, Hahn was convinced that something very different was taking place in this reaction. The evidence from his chemical analyses had become overwhelming. The product that had originally seemed to be an isotope of radium was actually an isotope of barium, whose atomic number is 36 less than that of uranium. Hahn and Strassmann were not completely willing to accept the apparent meaning of these results, however. In their January 6, 1939, paper announcing their results, they noted that, as chemists, they felt certain that barium was one of the products of the reaction, but they admitted that as nuclear physicists they were not yet willing to accept the "big step" that this conclusion suggested.

The paper carried the names of Hahn and Strassmann only because their colleague Meitner had been forced to flee Germany as a result of the Nazi purge of Jewish scientists. From her new home in Sweden, however, Meitner stayed in contact with her colleagues in Berlin. When details of the forthcoming Hahn-Strassmann paper reached her, she continued to think about the problem. The solution came during a Christmas outing with her nephew **Otto Robert Frisch**. Meitner and Frisch finally realized that the Hahn-Strassmann results could only be explained by accepting that the uranium nucleus had been split into two large, roughly equal parts, a reaction to which Meitner gave the name *nuclear fission*. For his part in the discovery of nuclear fission, Hahn was awarded a share of the 1944 Nobel Prize in chemistry.

Loyalty to Germany Prevents His Leaving during the War

During World War II, Hahn remained in Germany. Although he had no love for the Nazi party, he felt a loyalty to his homeland. He was able to avoid working on the German atomic bomb project, however, and instead carried out research on fission fragments during the war. That research came to an end in March, 1944, after the Institute for Chemistry was destroyed in a series of bombing raids. Hahn and his wife soon moved to the southern German town of Tailfinger, where they were captured by an advance team of U.S. intelligence officers in April, 1945. The Hahns were sent to England, where they were held for almost a year.

On January 3, 1946, Hahn was permitted to return to Germany, where he became president of the Kaiser Wilhelm Society, then re-named the Max Planck Society. He devoted the next 15 years to the effort to rebuild the scientific community of his native land. In his later years, he was showered with honors and awards, including election to scientific societies in Berlin, Göttingen, Munich, Halle, Stockholm, Vienna, Madrid, Helsinki, Lisbon, Mainz, Rome, Copenhagen, and Boston. He also became active in the international movement to control nuclear weapons and helped draft the 1955 Mainau Declaration by Nobel laureates, warning of the dangers of misusing nuclear energy.

The last years of Hahn's life were filled with personal tragedy. He was shot in the back in 1951 by a disgruntled inventor and had scarcely recovered before his wife suffered a nervous breakdown. In 1960, his son Hanno and Hanno's wife were killed in an automobile accident in France, leaving their young son to Hahn's care. Distraught at the accident, Hahn's wife never recovered her health. In the spring of 1968, Hahn was seriously injured while getting out of a car. His health slowly deteriorated until he died on July 28. His wife also died two weeks later. He was buried in Stadtfriedhof, Göttingen, West Germany.

SELECTED WRITINGS BY HAHN:

Books

Applied Radiochemistry, Cornell University Press, 1936.

New Atoms, Progress, and Some Memories, Elsevier (Amsterdam), 1950.

Vom Radiothor zur Uranspaltung, Friedr. Vieweg u. Sohn (Braunschweig), 1962, edited translation by Willy Ley published as *Otto Hahn: A Scientific Autobiography,* MacGibbon and Kee, 1966.

Mein Leban, Bruckmann (Munich), 1968, translation by Ernst Kaiser and Eithne Wilkins published as *Otto Hahn: My Life,* Macdonald (London), 1970.

Periodicals

"Personal Reminiscences of a Radiochemist," *Journal of the Chemical Society,* (1956), pp. 3997–4003.

SOURCES:

Books

Biographical Memoirs of Fellows of the Royal Society, Volume 16, Royal Society (London), 1970, pp. 279–313.

Dictionary of Scientific Biography, Volume 6, Scribner's, 1975, pp. 14–17.

Frisch, O. R., and others, editors, *Trends in Atomic Physics: Essays Dedicated to Lise Meitner, Otto Hahn, Max von Laue on the Occasion of Their 80th Birthday,* Interscience (New York), 1959.

Graetzer, Hans G., and David L. Anderson, *The Discovery of Nuclear Fission,* Van Nostrand, 1971.

McGraw-Hill Modern Scientists and Engineers, Volume 2, McGraw-Hill, 1980, pp. 7–8.

Nobel Lectures in Chemistry, 1942–1962, [Amsterdam], 1964, pp. 67–68.

Shea, William R., editor, *Otto Hahn and the Rise of Nuclear Physics,* Kluwer Academic, 1983.

—Sketch by David E. Newton

John Burdon Sanderson Haldane
1892-1964
English-born Indian physiologist and geneticist

John Burdon Sanderson Haldane

John Burdon Sanderson Haldane was a child prodigy who enthusiastically embraced mathematics, physiology, biochemistry, and genetics as well as politics and writing. His notorious association with the Communist Party and his ability to write "popular" science for a mass audience contributed as much to his public fame as did his ground-breaking studies of respiratory physiology, natural selection, and genetics. Haldane's eclectic approach to science allowed him to apply his expertise in mathematics on a cross-disciplinary basis, conducting studies in enzymes, the genetic linkage between hemophilia and color blindness, and hereditary mutation in population genetics. His eccentricities included conducting dangerous experiments on himself and other colleagues and living the latter part of his life as an expatriate in India, eschewing conventional Western dress for Indian clothes.

Haldane was born on November 5, 1892, Guy Fawkes Day in his native England, a holiday named after a notorious English rebel. Haldane noted the irony in this birthday since he, too, would form a strong political opposition to the English government. Haldane's family history can be traced back to his aristocratic ancestors in mid-thirteenth century Scotland. His mother, Louise Kathleen Trotter, came from a well-to-do Scottish family. His father, John Scott Haldane, a renowned physiologist in his own right, profoundly influenced his son's life, cultivating Haldane's young precocity into a sharp, scientific intellect.

Haldane could read by his third birthday and learned German at age five. Beginning at age four, he would accompany his father on atmospheric field tests in the areas of industrial mining accidents and mine safety. These experiences led the young Haldane to develop an early excitement about the "life and death" implications of scientific work. By the age of eight he was helping in his father's lab by taking mathematical notes. His interest in genetics had been piqued by age nine when he heard a lecture on recently rediscovered work of Gregor Mendel, the monk who pioneered studies of genetic inheritance and genes. Later, as he embarked on his own scientific career, Haldane embraced his father's daring and unusual approach to experimentation. Haldane's father preferred to conduct human experiments, primarily on himself, believing that a subject that could also take notes with a cold dispassionate eye was much better than some animal tainted by fear. In the course of his career, Haldane, too, often placed himself in precarious physical conditions for the sake of his studies.

In 1903, Haldane led his classes in Latin, translation, arithmetic, and geometry in the Dragon School. According to Haldane biographer Ronald W. Clark, Haldane's teachers described him as being "in a class by himself." His scientific curiosity led him to study the prodigious offspring of his sister's pet guinea pigs to confirm the laws of inheritance set down by Mendel. He won a scholarship to Eton, where he was bullied early on by fellow class mates and developed an antagonistic relationship with the school, primarily based on religious differences. During his years at Eton, he preferred an eclectic approach to his studies, taking courses in physics, chemistry, mathematics, biology, and history. He could read German, French, Greek, and Latin and won the Russell Prize as the second best mathematics student in the school.

Some teachers complained about Haldane's refusal to focus on one discipline. But at Oxford, after contributing the mathematical expertise to a paper written for the *Journal of Physiology* by his father and C. G. Douglas, Haldane seemed destined for a scientific career. However, in his characteristic disregard for academic conventions, he switched from a scientific curriculum to the arts. As a result, he never obtained a scientific degree or any scientific certification at Oxford. But Haldane's ability to apply cross-disciplinary techniques, such as mathematics to genetics, allowed him to engage in significant scientific research.

Embarks on Scientific Career

At the outbreak of World War I, Haldane, who was 22 years old, became a commissioned officer in the Third (Special Reserve) Battalion of the Scottish Black Watch regiment. Haldane admitted a certain affinity for war and said that it was probably due to his Scottish ancestry. Noted for his bravado in the face of danger, he was wounded twice, once on the Western Front and once in Mesopotamia. In response to German chemical warfare, the military assigned Haldane to collaborate with his father and Douglas on developing gas masks. (Haldane had already assisted his father in military research in a British navy study on how to avoid decompression in deep sea divers.) Typical of both the elder and younger Haldane, the scientists exposed themselves to toxic gases to test their designs. This assignment led to Haldane's interest in the physiology of respiration. It also furthered his distrust of authority when his father received little credit for this work, which saved thousands of lives, because of political reasons and differences of opinion with the war office. After being wounded for the second time in Mesopotamia, he was sent to Bombay, India, to recover, a trip that inspired his life-long interest in India and its society. Although he despised the Hindu caste system, he would eventually become drawn to the Hindu philosophy of life and death.

After the war, Haldane took a fellowship at New College, Oxford, where he soon began to teach physiology. Because of his lack of a strict physiological education, Haldane had to learn as he went along, being tutored early on by his father so he would be a few weeks ahead of his students. Following up on his father's earlier studies on carbon dioxide in blood, Haldane soon began his studies of how carbon dioxide in the blood stream enables the muscles to regulate breathing under different conditions. In the course of these studies, he devised a potentially-fatal experiment in which he introduced hydrochloric acid into his blood stream by drinking a water-diluted solution of ammonium chloride, an experiment which led to the eventual discovery by others that some babies had an extreme alkalinity of the blood that could cause them to die.

Although Haldane scoffed at his self-experimentation techniques as being over-sensationalized by the press, he often put himself and others in life and death situations. During his investigations into the loss of 90 lives when the submarine Thetis sank shortly before World War II, for example, Haldane and his colleagues braved a sealed chamber to simulate the conditions of the sinking submarine, including oxygen deprivation. During the course of this experiment, they experienced severe headaches, vomiting, and temporary incapacitation. Haldane would continue this type of dangerous experimentation throughout World War II—even using his future second-wife, Helen Spurway—focusing on problems of escaping from submarines and other undersea endeavors.

Haldane popularized his daring exploits in his 1924 essay "On Being One's Own Rabbit." It was through this essay and others that appeared in general interest magazines, such as the *Atlantic Monthly* and *Harper's Magazine* in the United States, that Haldane became famous for writing brilliant and lively pieces explaining science to lay persons. His first popular science book, *Daedalus, or Science and the Future,* also appeared in 1924.

In 1921 Haldane accepted a readership in biochemistry at Cambridge, where he studied chromosomal linkage and enzymes. In that same year, his studies on crossbreeding produced Haldane's Law, which posits the absence of sex or sterility in offspring produced by crossbreeding, as in the case of a mule produced by crossbreeding a horse and a donkey. His mathematical expertise enabled him to prove that thermodynamic laws regulate enzyme reactions. He also devised elegant mathematics to calculate the rates of enzyme reactions. His book *Enzymes,* published in 1930 and based on his lectures, provided a comprehensive yet practical view of enzymes in action.

In the opinion of many of his contemporaries, Haldane's most important writings were the ten dissertations (later published as *The Causes of Evolution*) he penned on naturalist Charles Darwin's theory of natural selection (the idea that entire species, or particular members of a species, who are best adapted to their environment survive and breed). Highly esoteric in nature, *The Causes of Evolution* focused on the mathematics of natural selection, showing how Darwin's theory could work. Haldane adhered to a conservative theory of heredity focusing on natural selection and dominant and recessive genes. Many of his equations, however, were eventually proven valid, often many years later. One particular case involved the Peppered Moth. Due to industrial pollution's decimation of white lichen, which provided a natural camouflage for the light-colored moths, the species had developed a wing-darkening gene. Haldane showed that those moths who were darker due to this gene had a 50% greater likelihood of surviving. Scientific investigation confirmed this finding nearly thirty years later.

In 1933, Haldane became Professor of Genetics at University College, London, and, in 1937, chair of biometry. At University College, Haldane focused a good deal of his work on genetics and to applying mathematical models to the study of genetics. He began to study the position of specific genes on the human X chromosome (the larger of the two sex chromosomes in humans, making it the only practicable one to investigate at that time). The provisional map that he developed in 1935 revealed the chromosome position for genes responsible for color blindness, night blindness, and several skin diseases and certain eye abnormalities. This work led to a collaboration with Julia Bell that showed a genetic linkage between hemophilia and color blindness. He also published the first estimate of the genetic mutation rate in man in the journal *Nature* in 1936. This mathematical calculation revealed how many mutations would take place naturally in any number of generations. Two years later, in the *American Naturalist,* Haldane showed the effects of recurrent harmful mutations in a population.

On the recommendation of **Julian Huxley,** Haldane had also been appointed the part-time "genetics expert" at the John Innis Horticultural Institution in 1927. Over a ten-year period he contributed his mathematical expertise to the study of plant genetics, primarily on studies of the variation in flower color and of a genetic linkage theory in the ornamental plant, *Primula sinensis.* However, his relationship with the Institution ended on unfriendly terms in 1936, due as much to Haldane's own aggressiveness in seeking promotions and appointments within the Institution as to his lack of expertise in botany and botanical research methods.

The Antiestablishment Scientist

Although Haldane claimed not to take politics seriously, his low opinion of British Prime Minister Neville Chamberlain, whose government vacillated in its relationships with Adolf Hitler and Benito Mussolini prior to World War II, led him to take an active interest in an alternative form of government. He joined the Communist Party shortly after the outbreak of the Spanish Civil War and advised the Republican government on precautions against gas attacks and air raids. As a result, at the outbreak of World War II, he had much-needed expertise on air raid bombings. Haldane was also a regular contributor for many years to the London *Daily Worker,* serving as chairman of this Marxist publication's editorial board.

By 1948, he had privately given up on communism, primarily in response to the Communist Party's unwavering dedication to Russian scientist T. D. Lysenko, who had become a political pawn of the dictator Joseph Stalin. Lysenko's fraudulent and eventually discredited theories of inheritance said that cells can absorb environmental influences or acquired individual characteristics, which are then inherited by the next generation. This theory was used to bolster Marxist arguments as to the effects of environment on the behavior of human beings.

Haldane's relationship with the British establishment, however, remained strained. In 1957, he and his second wife, Helen Spurway, emigrated to India. (Haldane and his first wife, Charlote Franken, a reporter, divorced in 1945.) Although Haldane reinforced the popular notion that he was leaving due to irreconcilable differences with England because of the Anglo-French aggression at the Suez Canal, he had been contemplating emigration for years. During a six-week lecture tour in India in 1952, Haldane had renewed his old love for the country. He admired Indian leaders Mahatma Gandhi and Jawaharlal Nehru and saw India as a place that offered better opportunities for biometric research. He would spend the remainder of his life there, gaining an appointment as director of the well-equipped Genetics and Biometry Laboratory in Orissa.

In 1961, Haldane became a naturalized Indian citizen. As his biographer Clark notes, Haldane often wore Indian clothes and once joked that "One of my reasons for settling in India was to avoid wearing socks." Haldane's irreverence for authority, politics, and many social conventions remained with him to the end. Dying of cancer, Haldane wrote a poem called "Cancer's a Funny Thing" for London's *New Statesman.* Typical of Haldane's life, this poem brought mixed reactions from readers, who both complained of his audacity and admired his courage. In an obituary filmed ten months prior to his death from cancer on December 1, 1964, Haldane said "what matters, in my opinion, is what I have done, good or evil, and not what people think of me." During his career, Haldane received the French Legion of Honor, 1937, the Darwin Medal of the Royal Society of London, 1953, the Darwin-Wallace Commemorative Medal from the Linnean Society, 1958, the Kimber Medal of the National Academy of Sciences, 1961, and the Feltrinelli Prize of the Accademia dei Lincei, 1961. He had also been given honorary degrees from the University of Groeningen, Oxford University, the University of Paris, and the University of Edinburgh. True to his belief in the utility of science, Haldane, a pioneer of interdisciplinary research, left instructions to have his body immediately refrigerated after death so it could be used for medical research.

SELECTED WRITINGS BY HALDANE:

Books

Daedalus, or Science and the Future, Dutton, 1924.

Possible Worlds and Other Essays, Chatto & Windus, 1927.

Enzymes, Longmans, Green, 1930.

The Causes of Evolution, Harper, 1932.

Periodicals

"The Origin of Life," *Rationalist Annual,* 1929, pp. 3–10.

"The Genetics of Primula Sinensis: Segregation and Interaction of Factors in the Diploid," *Journal of Genetics,* Volume 27, 1933, pp. 1–44.

"A Provisional Map of a Human Chromosome," *Nature,* Volume 137, 1935, p. 397.

"The Linkage between the Genes for Colour-Blindness and Haemophilia in Man," *Proceedings of the Royal Society,* Volume 123B, 1937, pp. 119–150.

SOURCES:

Books

Biographical Dictionary of Scientists, Peter Bedrick Books, 1984, pp. 56–57.

Biographical Memoirs of Fellows of the Royal Society, Volume 12, Royal Society (London), 1966, pp. 219–249.

Clark, Ronald W., *JBS: The Life and Work of JBS Haldane,* Coward-McCann, 1968.

Concise Dictionary of Scientific Biography, Scribner, 1981, p. 308.

The Great Scientists, Grolier Educational Corporation, 1989, pp. 186–191.

—Sketch by David Petechuk

George Ellery Hale
1868-1938
American astrophysicist

George Ellery Hale was an American astronomer and astrophysicist who pioneered spectroscopic research and the development and use of large telescopes. He is widely considered to be the father of modern solar observational astronomy, and is best known for his discovery in 1908 of the presence of magnetic fields in sunspots. Hale invented new instruments for studying solar and stellar spectra, including the spectroheliograph and the spectrohelioscope, and also founded three of the United States' leading observatories, at Yerkes, Mt. Wilson, and Palomar; the latter two were renamed the Hale Observatories in 1969.

Hale was born on June 29, 1868, in Chicago, Illinois. His father, William Ellery Hale, was a wealthy businessman who manufactured hydraulic elevators; his mother, Mary Scranton Browne, was the daughter of a Congregational minister who later became a doctor. Hale inherited from his mother an intense love of literature. As a child he read *Don Quixote,* the *Iliad,* Jules Verne's *From the Moon to the Earth,* and the poetry of Shelley and Keats. Hale was a sickly and overwrought child, subject to frequent bouts of illness; his delicate constitution troubled him throughout his life. As an adult he was overanxious and unable to relax, and suffered three nervous breakdowns.

Hale began his education at Oakland Public School, and later attended Adam Academy and the Chicago Manual Training School, where he was instructed in shopwork. His inventiveness manifested itself early, and was encouraged by his parents. As a boy, he tinkered in his self-constructed tool shop and laboratory, conducting simple experiments and building himself a telescope and other instruments. A neighbor and amateur astronomer, **Sherburne W. Burnham**, sparked his interest in astronomy, and particularly in spectroscopy, the study of solar and other spectra using a spectroscope. Burnham interested Hale in a secondhand Clark telescope that had come on the market, and Hale persuaded his father to buy it. The views it afforded of the moon and other planets further excited Hale's interest in astronomy and strengthened his resolve to make it his life's work. In 1884, at the age of sixteen, he succeeded in photographing the solar spectrum using a prism spectroscope purchased for him by his father. In 1886, Hale entered the Massachusetts Institute of Technology to study physics, chemistry, and mathematics. He found college less stimulating than his own experiments and found an outlet for his unsatiated intellectual energy in the independent study of spectroscopy and astronomy. Hale also volunteered as an assistant at the Harvard College Observatory, and, with money given by his father, set about building his own solar observatory at Kenwood, behind his house.

First to Photograph Solar Prominences in Daylight

Hale made his first scientific breakthrough in 1889, when he hit on an idea for an invention that would permit him to photograph solar prominences in full daylight. Solar prominences are flames or masses of incandescent vapor, composed usually of helium and hydrogen, that extend beyond the sun's disk. They are usually of enormous height and brilliant red in color. Although they vary in appearance, they are usually manifested in an arch or bridge shape, and are found near sunspots and flares. They can remain inactive for months before entering a dynamic stage. During this period, they change shape, sometimes obtaining heights equivalent to the diameter of the sun. They are visible during a solar eclipse or with the aid of a spectroscope. Unsuccessful attempts had previously been made to photograph the prominences; Hale's idea was to use an instrument of his own invention that he called a spectroheliograph. It relied on the light of one spectral line, selected by a slit, to photograph by continuously scanning either the whole or part of the sun. In his senior thesis, he outlined the results he obtained at the Harvard Observatory using this apparatus. Hale also published his first paper, entitled "The New Astronomy," in 1889. It appeared in the July issue of the *Beacon,* a photography journal.

Hale and his fiancee, Evelina Conklin of Brooklyn, New York, married on June 5, 1890, the day after Hale graduated from MIT. They had two children, Margaret and Bill. During their honeymoon, the newlyweds visited the Lick Observatory on Mount Hamilton, near San Jose, California, where Hale viewed the thirty-six-inch Lick telescope, then the largest in the world. Shortly afterward, Hale became the director of the Kenwood Observatory and persuaded his father to buy him a new twelve-inch refracting telescope. He used it to continue his experiments with the spectroheliograph, and succeeded in photographing the bright calcium clouds (flocculi) and the prominences around the sun's limbs for the first time.

The following year, Hale visited Europe and met many of that continent's leading astronomers and astrophysicists. They received him warmly. Upon his return, he founded the journal *Astronomy and Astrophysics* with William Payne, editor of the *Sidereal Messenger.* Hale became associate professor of astrophysics at the newly established University of Chicago in 1892. Later that year, hearing of the availability of two forty-inch lenses, he persuaded the traction magnate Charles T. Yerkes to sponsor a new observatory that would house a refracting telescope revolutionary in its focal length and light-gathering power. The vision and organizational ability demonstrated by Hale in this and later instances did much to advance astronomical research.

Hale traveled to Germany in 1893 while plans for the new observatory were being fine-tuned. At the University of Berlin, he worked with some of Germany's finest physicists, including **Max Planck**, **Hermann von Helmholtz**, and **Heinrich Rubens**. Although Hale's intention was to work towards a doctorate, this plan was later abandoned and Hale never received his Ph.D. On route back to the U.S., he tried but failed to photograph the solar corona from Mt. Etna.

In 1895, with James Keeler as coeditor, Hale founded a second publication, the *Astrophysical Journal,* whose editorial board was composed of the world's leading astrophysicists. It quickly established itself as the leading journal in its field. The following year, Hale persuaded his father to provide the disk for a sixty-inch reflecting telescope that would enable him to photograph the spectra of stars on so large a scale that their chemical makeup, the temperature and pressure in their atmospheres, and their motions could be investigated.

The Yerkes observatory opened in 1897. Hale staffed it with a small but highly talented and dedicated team of scientists, many of whom went on to become famous in their own right. They carried out spectroscopic, photographic, bolometric, and other types of optical experiments. Hale devoted himself to continued observation of sunspot spectra and the design of the Rumford spectroheliograph that he planned to attach to the forty-inch telescope. Hale used these tools to attain insight into the complete circulatory processes of the sun. He also investigated the stars, especially the low-temperature, red stars known as Secchi's fourth type, which he was the first to photograph.

Besides being a tireless researcher, Hale devoted much of his energy to institutional work and strengthening ties between astrophysicists around the world. In 1899, he helped found and became the first vice president of the American Astronomical and Astrophysical Society (the name was changed to the American Astronomical Society in 1914). Upon election to the National Academy of Sciences in 1902, he threw himself into reforming that body. In 1904, Hale helped to establish a committee to organize the International Union for Cooperation in Solar Research, under the auspices of the Academy, and went on to become its president.

With the Yerkes observatory up and running, Hale was anxious to apply his organizational powers to the establishment of a second observatory that would house his hoped-for sixty-inch telescope. He obtained $150,000 from the Carnegie Institute of Washington as seed money to found the Mt. Wilson Solar Observatory in Pasadena, California, in 1904. Hale was its director from 1904 to 1923. It was from Mt. Wilson that Hale, using a Snow telescope of his own design, took the first photographs of a sunspot spectrum in 1905. Sunspots are visible spots on the sun's disk, presumed to be of the nature of cyclonic storms in the sun's atmosphere. On analysis, Hale's spectroscopic results revealed that sunspots are colder than other regions of the solar disk, rather than hotter as was previously assumed.

In 1906, Hale became a trustee of the little-known Throop Polytechnic School in Pasadena. He used his position to transform it into a first-rate technological college. Hale was passionately interested in Pasadena's future and wished to see the town invigorated by the establishment there of a world-class research center. His ambition was realized when the Los Angeles transport giant Henry Huntington agreed to finance such a center. For his work on behalf of Pasadena, Hale was given the city's highest accolade, the Noble Medal.

Discovers Magnetic Fields in Sunspots

In 1908, Hale began construction of a sixty-foot tower telescope with a thirty-foot spectrograph in an underground dugout at Mt. Wilson. Using photographic plates sensitive to red light, he was able to detect hydrogen flocculi near sunspots. He was alerted to the possibility of there being powerful magnetic fields within sunspots and shortly afterwards was able to prove his hypothesis. Hale found that the magnetic fields in sunspots indirectly act as thermal shields and maintain sunspots' temperatures below that of the surrounding photospheres. Shortly afterwards, Hale achieved another breakthrough when he announced his fundamental polarity law. This states that twenty-two- to twenty-three-year intervals occur between the successive appearances in high latitudes of sunspots of the same magnetic polarity.

Having finally obtained his sixty-inch reflecting telescope, then the world's largest, Hale hoped to achieve an understanding of the nature of stellar evolution. He also turned his attention to the question of whether the sun itself might be a magnet. By 1912, work was completed on the construction of a 150-foot solar tower telescope with a seventy-five-foot vertical spectrograph. Hale used it to measure the sun's magnetic field. He found that the sun has a dipole magnetic field of about twenty gausses. A gauss is equal to the intensity produced by a magnetic pole of unit strength at a distance of one centimeter. Later measurements taken by other astrophysicists gave the field to be about four gausses. None of the results were conclusive, however. In fact, it was not until 1952 that the first accurate readings of the sun's magnetic field were obtained by two American astrophysicists. They gave it as a polar field of about two gausses, with a polarity opposite to that of the earth. The astrophysicist Robert Howard said during a speech at the Hale Centennial Symposium at Dallas, Texas, in 1968, "It is clear to us now that magnetic fields hold the key to the phenomenon called solar activity, and it is a tribute to the genius of Hale that he recognized at such an early stage the great importance of these elusive magnetic fields."

During World War I, Hale was an emissary from the National Academy to President Woodrow Wilson, offering its services. The result was the establishment of the National Research Council in 1916, with Hale as its chairman. Its purpose was to stimulate research in the sciences and in the application of the sciences to socially useful fields, such as medicine, agriculture, and engineering, for both peaceful and defensive purposes. In 1918 Hale, inspired by the success of the National Research Council in promoting cooperation between scientists and other professionals nationally, proposed establishing a similar body on an international scale. Thus was born the International Research Council, which eventually replaced the International Association of Academies in 1919. Until the war ended, though, only scientists from allied countries were allowed membership. By 1931, when it was renamed the International Council of Scientific Unions, forty countries had joined the council, and in 1932, Hale became its president.

Meanwhile, in his scientific work, by 1917 Hale was ready to begin using a new one-hundred-inch telescope, which had been built with the support of the Carnegie Foundation and a Los Angeles businessman named John D. Hooker. It was used by two members of Hale's team to measure the diameter of the huge red star Betelgeuse, which was found to be three hundred million miles. In 1923, **Edwin Hubble** used it to identify a Cepheid variable in a spiral nebula and prove that nebulae are external galaxies of dimensions similar to earth. Without the hundred-inch, such a breakthrough would have been impossible.

In 1923, troubled by continued ill health, Hale retired his directorship of Mt. Wilson, and turned his attention to the building of another observatory, the Hale Solar Laboratory, at Pasadena. There, he invented and built the world's first spectrohelioscope, a spectroscope with an oscillating slit, for use in the study of solar phenomena. The following year, he had the satisfaction of seeing his long-held dream of reinvigorating the National Academy of Sciences come to fruition. With a grant of $5 million from the Carnegie Corporation, a permanent scientific headquarters for the Academy was opened in Washington. Hale's work on behalf of the Academy went a long way towards revitalizing that institution.

Launches Plan to Build World's Biggest Telescope

In retirement, Hale was as busy as he had been at any time in his career. In 1928, he launched an ambitious plan to build a two-hundred-inch telescope. He was once again able to persuade wealthy investors to contribute to his visionary plans. The International Educational Board of the Rockefeller Foundation donated $6 million to the California Institute of Technology to build the telescope, in cooperation with the Mt. Wilson observatory. The completed instrument was set up atop Palomar Mountain in southern California. Unfortunately, Hale did not live to see it completed, although it was named the Hale telescope in his honor. He died on February 21, 1938, in Pasadena. Sir James Jeans remembered him thus: "Nature had not only endowed him with those qualities that make for success in science—a powerful and acute intellect, a reflective mind, imagination, patience, and perseverance—but also in ample measure with qualities that make for successes in other walks of life—a capacity for forming rapid judgments of men, of situations, and of plans of action; a habit of looking to the future, and thinking always in terms of improvements and extensions; a driving power which was given no rest until it had brought his plans and schemes to fruition; eagerness, enthusiasm, and above all a sympathetic personality of great charm."

SELECTED WRITINGS BY HALE:

Periodicals

"The New Astronomy," *Beacon,* July, 1889.

"Photography of the Solar Prominences," *Technology Quarterly,* Volume 3, 1890, pp. 310–316.

"The Astrophysical Journal," *Astronomy and Astro-Physics,* Volume 11, 1892, pp. 17–22.

"The Yerkes Observatory of the University of Chicago," *Astronomy and Astro-Physics,* Volume 11, 1892, pp. 741.

"The Spectroheliograph," *Astronomy and Astro-Physics,* Volume 12, 1893, pp. 241–257.

(With F. Ellerman) "The Rumford Spectroheliograph of the Yerkes Observatory," *Publications of the Yerkes Observatory of the University of Chicago,* Volume 3, 1903, pp. 1–26.

"Cooperation in Solar Research," *Astrophysical Journal,* Volume 20, 1940, pp. 306–312.

"A Plea for the Imaginative Element in Technical Education," *Technology Review,* Volume 9, number 4, 1907, pp. 467–481.

"Solar Vortices," *Astrophysical Journal,* Volume 28, 1908, pp. 100–116.

"Preliminary Results of an Attempt to Detect the Magnetic Field of the Sun," *Astrophysical Journal,* Volume 38, 1913, pp. 27–98.

SOURCES:

Books

Aller, Lawrence H., *Atoms, Stars, and Nebulae,* Cambridge University Press, 1943.

Dorschner, J., C. Friedmann, S. Marx, and W. Pfau, *Astronomy: A Popular History,* Almark Publishing, 1975.

Hearnshaw, J. B., *The Analysis of Starlight: 150 Years of Astronomical Spectroscopy,* Cambridge University Press, 1986.

Williams, Henry Smith, *The Great Astronomers,* Simon & Schuster, 1930, p. 419.

Wright, Helen, *Explorer of the Universe,* Dutton, 1966.

Wright, Helen, *The Legacy of George Ellery Hale,* MIT Press, 1972.

—*Sketch by Avril McDonald*

Lloyd Augustus Hall
1894-1971
American chemist

Chemist Lloyd Augustus Hall is best known for his work in the field of food technology, where he developed processes to cure and preserve meat, prevent rancidity in fats, and sterilize spices. In 1939, he cofounded the Institute of Food Technologists, establishing a new branch of industrial chemistry. Hall was born in Elgin, Illinois, on June 20, 1894. His father, Augustus Hall, was a Baptist minister and son of the first pastor of the Quinn Chapel A.M.E. Church, the first African American church in Chicago. Hall's mother, Isabel, was a high-school graduate whose mother had fled to Illinois via the Underground Railroad at the age of sixteen.

Hall became interested in chemistry while attending the East Side High School in Aurora, Illinois, where he was active in extracurricular activities such as debate, track, football, and baseball. He was one of five African Americans attending the school during his four years there. By the time he graduated among the top ten in his class, he'd been offered scholarships to four Illinois universities.

Hall chose to attend Northwestern University, working his way through school while he studied chemistry. During this time, he met Carroll L. Griffith, a fellow chemistry student, who would later play a part in his career. Hall graduated in 1916 with a bachelor of science degree in chemistry and continued his studies in graduate classes at the University of Chicago.

During World War I, Hall served as a lieutenant in the Ordnance Department, inspecting explosives at a plant in Wisconsin. However, he was subjected to such prejudice and discriminatory behavior that he asked to be transferred. The discrimination was also apparent in the civilian world: at one point, he was hired over the telephone by the Western Electric Company. When he arrived for work, he was told there was none.

In 1916, however, he was able to find a position in the Chicago Department of Health Laboratories. Within a year, he was made senior chemist. For the next six years, he worked at several industrial laboratories. In 1921, he was made chief chemist at Boyer Chemical Laboratory in Chicago. By then, he'd become interested in the developing field of food chemistry, and in 1922, he became president and chemical director of the Chemical Products Corporation, a consulting laboratory in Chicago.

In 1924, one of Hall's clients, Griffith Laboratories (his old lab partner at Northwestern had been Carroll L. Griffith) offered him a space where he could work for them while continuing his consulting practice. By 1925, Hall had become chief chemist and director of research at Griffith; in 1929, he gave up his consulting practice and devoted himself full-time to Griffith until 1959.

Develops "Flash-Drying" Method

When Hall started at Griffith, current meat curing and preservation methods were highly unsatisfactory. It was known that sodium chloride preserved meat, while chemicals containing nitrogen—nitrates and nitrites—were used for curing. However, not much was known about how these chemicals worked, and food could not be preserved for an extended period of time.

In experiments, Hall discovered that nitrite and nitrate penetrated the meat more quickly than the sodium chloride, causing it to disintegrate before it had a chance to be preserved. The problem was to get the salt to penetrate the meat first, thereby preserving it before it was cured. Hall solved this through "flash-drying"—a quick method of evaporating a solution of all three salts, so that crystals of sodium chloride enclosing the nitrite and nitrate were formed. Thus, when the crystals dissolved, the sodium chloride would penetrate the meat first.

Discovers How to Sterilize Spices

Hall's next accomplishment was in the area of spices. Although meat could now be preserved and cured effectively, the natural spices that were used to enhance and preserve it often contained contaminants. Spices such as allspice, cloves, cinnamon, and paprika as well as dried vegetable products like onion powder contained yeasts, molds, and bacteria. Hall's task was to find a way to sterilize the spices and dried vegetables without destroying their original flavor and appearance. Heating the foods above 240°F would sterilize them, but it would also destroy their taste and color. Hall discovered that ethylene oxide, a gas used to kill insects, would also kill the germs in the spices. He used a vacuum chamber to remove the moisture from the spices so that the gas could permeate and sterilize them when introduced into the chamber. The times and temperatures varied according to the type of bacteria, mold, or yeast to be destroyed.

The ability to sterilize spices had a major impact on the meat industry. The process also became popular in the hospital supplies industry and was used to sterilize bandages, dressings, and sutures. In fact, a number of industries in the United States benefited enormously from Hall's invention.

Researches Effects of Antioxidants on Fats

In his work at Griffith, Hall also discovered the use of antioxidants in preventing rancidity in foods containing fats and oils. Rancidity is caused by oxidation when constituents in the fats react with oxygen. By experimenting with various antioxidants, Hall found that certain chemicals in crude vegetable oil worked as antioxidants. Using some of these combined with salt, he produced an antioxidant salt mixture that protected foods containing fats and oils from spoiling.

During his thirty-five years at Griffith, Hall worked in several areas of food chemistry including seasoning, spice extracts, and enzymes. In 1951, Hall and an associate developed a way to reduce the time for curing bacon from between six and fifteen days to a few hours. The quality of the bacon was also improved, both in appearance and stability. He was also very interested in vitamins and the development of yeast foods. By 1959, Hall held over 105 patents in the United States and abroad and had published numerous papers on food technology. Hall served on various committees during his time at Griffith. During World War II, he was a member of the Committee on Food Research of the Scientific Advisory Board of the War Department's Quartermaster Corps; in that position he advised the military on the preservation of food supplies from 1943 to 1948. In 1944, he joined the Illinois State Food Commission of the State Department of Agriculture, serving until 1949.

As a further sign of the establishment of food chemistry as a field of science, the Institute of Food Technologists was founded in 1939. Hall was a charter member; he edited its magazine, *The Vitalizer,* and served on its executive board for four years. In 1954, Hall became chairman of the Chicago chapter of the American Institute of Chemists. The following year, he was elected a member of its national board of directors, becoming the first African American man to hold that position in the Institute's thirty-two-year history.

Upon his retirement from Griffith in 1959, Hall continued to serve as a consultant to various state and federal organizations. He also continued to work, and in 1961, he spent six months in Indonesia, advising the Food and Agricultural Organization of the United Nations. From 1962 to 1964, he was a member of the American Food for Peace Council, an appointment made by President John F. Kennedy. After retiring, Hall and his wife, Myrrhene, moved to California to benefit her health. Hall lived in Altadena, where he remained active in community affairs, until his death on January 2, 1971.

SOURCES:

Books

Carwell, Hattie, *Blacks in Science: Astrophysicist to Zoologist,* Exposition Press, 1977, pp. 27–28.

Haber, Louis, *Black Pioneers of Science and Invention,* Harcourt, 1970, pp. 102–111.

Miles, Wyndham D., editor, *American Chemists and Chemical Engineers,* American Chemical Society, 1976, pp. 193–194.

Sammons, Vivian Ovelton, *Blacks in Science and Medicine,* Hemisphere Publishing, 1990, pp. 109–110.

Periodicals

Drew, Charles Richard, "Negro Scholars in Scientific Research," *Journal of Negro History,* Volume 35, 1950, pp. 135–189.

—Sketch by Geeta Kothari

Viktor Hamburger
1900-
German-born American embryologist and neurobiologist

Often referred to as the founding father of developmental neurobiology, Viktor Hamburger is known for his work on the development of the nervous system in chick embryos and for defining and classifying the different stages in embryological development. He was elected to the National Academy of Sciences in 1953 for developing techniques of microneurosurgery; he was also honored for research which led to the discovery that developing nerve cells are dependent on the limbs to which they are connected. In 1989 he was awarded the National Medal of Science, and he is now the Edward Mallinckrodt Distinguished University Professor Emeritus of Biology at Washington University in St. Louis.

The first of three sons, Hamburger was born on July 9, 1900 to Max and Else Hamburger in the small town of Landeshut, Silesia, which was then an eastern province of Germany but is now part of Poland. His family was wealthy; his father owned a textile factory, and he provided housing for his workers and a nursery school for their children. Hamburger's mother nurtured his enthusiasm for the outdoors by frequently taking him to the countryside. Landeshut was near mountains and alpine streams, meadows, and forests; Hamburger was fascinated by the plant and animal life around him and one of his earliest desires was to be a naturalist. At six years old, he was collecting assorted plants and fossils from quarries. At that time, he also had an aquarium in which he observed frog and salamander eggs develop into tadpoles and larvae and then metamorphose. Hamburger was educated at home by a private teacher until the age of nine, when he entered a gymnasium, graduating in 1918.

Hamburger studied zoology at several universities before settling on the University of Freiburg. He studied at the University of Breslau from 1918 to 1919, Heidelberg from 1919 to 1920, and then Munich from 1921 to 1922. In an interview with the

Viktor Hamburger

St. Louis Post-Dispatch, he recalled that he ended up at Freiburg almost by chance: "I was more attracted by the Black Forest and the skiing and hiking. I grew up in the mountains, and I found the land around Heidelberg too flat." It was here, however, that Hamburger met **Hans Spemann**—a Nobel laureate and the leading German experimental embryologist. Spemann had discovered what he called the "organizer" in amphibian embryos: a portion of an embryo, when transplanted to another region in the embryo, grows an extra embryo around the transplanted piece; this piece of tissue has the organizing power to induce embryonic growth.

Under Spemann, Hamburger began experiments on the development of the nervous system in amphibian embryos, mostly in those of frogs and salamanders collected from local brooks and ponds. Spemann taught Hamburger to perform techniques for microsurgery which he had developed. Within two years of beginning work on the embryonic nervous system, Hamburger published a paper which refuted another scientist's earlier hypothesis, and earned him his doctorate in zoology in 1925. Hamburger continued his work in Freiburg, researching young nerve cells and the muscles they supply with nerves, until 1932, when he won a one-year Rockefeller Foundation fellowship. He left Germany for what he thought would be only a year and travelled to the University of Chicago to work with avian embryologist **Frank Rattray Lillie**.

Hamburger experienced culture shock in the United States. He said to the *St. Louis Post-Dispatch:* "I had moved from a small medieval town to Chicago, which was a wild city and still is. . . . But the campus was kind of an island of academic peace." In a letter to *NTCS* contributor Denise Adams Arnold, Hamburger also recalled that he appreciated the "non-philosophical, mechanist-materialistic positivist mental set" of his new colleagues and their "unassuming modesty and camaraderie . . . including very famous ones, in contrast to the feeling of superiority" he felt most German intellectuals had. Hamburger brought to Chicago his exacting technique of microsurgery, modified for chick embryos. Until this time amphibians had been the worldwide standard object of study for embryology in laboratories; Hamburger's work in Chicago created new avenues for examining the embryos of complex organisms closer to those of mammals. His work with chick transplantations revealed that the limbs of chick embryos grow even after being transplanted.

Hamburger, who is Jewish, expected to return to Germany in 1933, but he was notified by German colleagues that he should not return because of the political climate. He stayed at the University of Chicago as an instructor for two more years before accepting an appointment as an assistant professor of zoology at Washington University. By 1941, he was appointed professor and chairman of that department, a position he would retain until 1966.

Classifies Embryo Development by Stages

At Washington University, Hamburger continued his work on embryos, and with H. L. Hamilton he described and classified the stages of development of the chick embryo. Hamburger was particularly interested in the relationship between the limbs of an embryo and its nervous system. Just after World War II, he read an article on this subject by the Italian neurobiologist **Rita Levi-Montalcini**; she had repeated an experiment he had done and was disputing his conclusions. "It turned out Rita was right as usual," Hamburger is quoted as saying in the *Washington University Magazine.* He invited her to work with him in St. Louis.

Once they began working together, Hamburger and Levi-Montalcini found that when the embryonic limb was removed, the motor nerve cells that were to supply the limb with nerves failed to develop. The growth of the nerve cells was dependent on messages from the limb, also called the target. The questions the two scientists now faced were how and why these two components were interdependent. Hamburger theorized that there was some kind of communication between the limb and the spinal cord which triggered the production of motor neurons, but his conclusions were based on the principles of embryonic organization which he had learned in Spemann's laboratory. However, by painstakingly counting cells, Levi-Montalcini found that the development of nerve cells proceeded normally for a short time after the limb was removed. They were generated even without the limb, but they could not stay alive without instructions from it. The limb was somehow responsible for maintaining the life of the nerve cells. Levi-Montalcini identified a chemical substance produced in the peripheral target, called nerve growth factor (NGF), which sustained the nerve cells. For this discovery, she was awarded the Nobel Prize with biochemist **Stanley Cohen** in 1986, despite the fact that Hamburger did most of the writing of joint papers in 1951 and 1953 and "had considerable conceptual input," as Hamburger said in a letter to Arnold.

Work Conflicts with Psychological Research

As the work done by Levi-Montalcini and Cohen revealed more of the extraordinary properties of NGF, Hamburger withdrew from the project, feeling that he could not contribute more since the work had moved into the biochemical realm. In the late 1950s, Hamburger's research turned toward embryonic behavior. Psychologists had been arguing for some time about the source of behavior, some contending that it is learned, others that it is inherited. Hamburger made a little window in an egg—"like a window display in a department store," he told the *Washington University Magazine*—and he observed every movement of the embryos. He found that their movement was "generated autonomously in the nervous system" and was independent of outside stimuli, dispelling the notion set forth by behaviorists like B. F. Skinner. This study not only placed Hamburger in the center of disputes with the psychologists whose research he had called into question, but it also occasionally made him the target of personal attacks.

Hamburger has been described as one of the "supreme biologists of our time," and Stanley Cohen has said of him in the *Washington University Magazine:* "I learned from Viktor how an embryologist thinks. He is the epitome of a classical embryologist." Hamburger sees himself as one of a dying breed, however, with experimental embryology being effectively replaced by molecular biology. He retired in 1983 and has written a book on Hans Spemann, which is what he calls "the only authentic history of this scientific era which is now closed."

Hamburger married Martha Fricke in 1927. She died in 1966, leaving him with two daughters. He now has several grandchildren and great-grandchildren. An unpretentious man, Hamburger loves art, a trait he acquired from his father. Cohen considers him "a member of a vanishing breed who are not only scientists but have very broad cultural interests and a world view. Whether it is in history or art, Viktor is an extraordinarily well-rounded person and most kind."

SELECTED WRITINGS BY HAMBURGER:

Books

A Manual of Experimental Embryology, University of Chicago Press, 1942.

(With Benjamin H. Willier) *Analysis of Development,* Saunders Publishing, 1955.

(With W. Maxwell Cowan) *Studies in Developmental Neurobiology: Essays in Honor of Viktor Hamburger,* Oxford University Press, 1981.

The Heritage of Experimental Embryology: Hans Spemann and the Organizer, Oxford University Press, 1988.

Periodicals

(With Michael Locke) "The Emergence of Order in Developing Systems," *Developmental Biology,* supplement 2, 27th Symposium of the Society for Developmental Biology, 1968.

"The Developmental History of the Motor Neuron," *Neuroscience Research Program Bulletin,* Volume 15, supplement, MIT Press, 1977.

(With Stanley Cohen and Jose Regino Perez-Polo) "Special Issue on Growth and Trophic Factors," *Journal of Neuroscience Research,* Volume 8, Number 2/3, 1982.

SOURCES:

Periodicals

Fitzpatrick, Tony, "Hamburger Receives National Medal of Science," *Washington Record,* October 26, 1989, pp. 1–3.

Freeman, Karen, "Honor for a Pioneer," *St. Louis Post-Dispatch,* November 7, 1989.

Tucci, Linda, "A Man for All Seasons," *Washington University Magazine,* Volume 57, Number 2, 1987, pp. 12–19.

Other

Hamburger, Viktor, letter to Denise Adams Arnold, September 30, 1993.

—*Sketch by Denise Adams Arnold*

Alice Hamilton
1869-1970
American pathologist

Alice Hamilton was a pioneer in correcting the medical problems caused by industrialization, awakening the country in the early twentieth century to the dangers of industrial poisons and hazardous working conditions. Through her untiring efforts, toxic substances in the lead, mining, painting, pottery, and rayon industries were exposed and legislation passed to protect workers. She was also a champion of worker's compensation laws, and was instrumental in bringing about this type of legislation in the state of Illinois. A medical doctor and researcher, she was the first woman of faculty status at Harvard University, and was a consultant on governmental commissions, both domestic and foreign.

Alice Hamilton was born on February 27, 1869, in New York City, the second of five children born to Montgomery Hamilton, a wholesale grocer, and Gertrude (Pond) Hamilton. Alice Hamilton grew up in secure material surroundings. Her mother encouraged the children to follow their minds and inclinations, and this approach proved beneficial. Her sister, Edith, later became a noted Greek scholar and the editor of well-known books on Greek myths and literature. Alice was educated at home and for a few years at a private school.

Hamilton's decision to pursue a career in medicine came, in part, because it was one of the few professional fields open to women of her day. She earned a medical degree from the University of Michigan in 1893, without having completed an undergraduate degree and taking surprisingly few science courses. Realizing that she wanted to pursue research rather than medical practice, Hamilton went on to do further studies both in the United States and abroad: from 1895–1896 at Leipzig and Munich; 1896–1897 at Johns Hopkins; and 1902 in Paris at the Pasteur Institute. In 1897 she accepted a post as professor of pathology at the Women's Medical College at Northwestern University in Chicago, and when it closed in 1902, she became a professor of pathology at the Memorial Institute for Infectious Diseases, a position which she held until 1909.

Hull House Residency Leads to Industrial Concerns

In Chicago Hamilton became a resident of Hull House, the pioneering settlement designed to give care and advice to the poor of Chicago. Here, under the influence of Jane Addams, the founder of Hull House, Hamilton saw the effects of poverty up close.

Alice Hamilton

Investigating a typhoid epidemic in Chicago, she was instrumental in reorganizing the city's health department and in drawing attention to the role flies played in spreading the epidemic. After reading *Dangerous Trades* by Sir Thomas Oliver, Hamilton began her life-long mission to treat the excesses of industrialization. Unlike other countries such as Germany and England, the United States had no industrial safety laws at the time. During her time at Hull House, Hamilton investigated the steel industry and others for occupationally-caused lead poisoning.

In 1910 Hamilton was chosen by the governor of Illinois to head up his Commission on Occupational Diseases, and her research and investigation into the dangers of lead and phosphorous paved the way to the state's first worker's compensation laws. In 1911 she took up similar, non-salaried, duties for the federal government, becoming an investigator of industrial poisons for the fledgling Department of Labor. During World War I, Hamilton investigated the high explosives industry, discovering that nitrous fumes were responsible for a great number of supposedly natural deaths.

In 1919 she became the first female faculty member of Harvard University as assistant professor of industrial medicine, but was denied access to the male bastion of the Harvard Club and to participation in graduation ceremonies. Hamilton kept up her international contacts, serving as the only woman delegate on the League of Nations Health Commission to the U.S.S.R. in 1924, as well as acting as a consultant to the International Labor Office in Geneva, Switzerland. In 1925, she published her *Industrial Poisons in the United States,* the first text on the subject, and became one of the few worldwide authorities in the area of industrial toxins. At this same time, she was also instrumental in influencing the surgeon general to investigate the dangerous effects of tetraethyl lead and radium.

Hamilton retired from Harvard in 1935, but not from active public life. She became a consultant in the U.S. Labor Department's Division of Labor Standards and from 1937–1938 conducted an investigation of the viscose rayon industry. Hamilton demonstrated the toxicity involved in rayon processes, and these findings that led to Pennsylvania's first compensation law for occupational diseases. In her later years, Hamilton, who never married, wrote an autobiography and continued to be active politically, advancing causes of social justice and pacifism. She died of a stroke at her home in Hadlyme, Connecticut, in 1970. Hamilton was 101 at the time of her death, and had been the recipient of honorary degrees from around the world for her work in revealing the dangers of industrial poisons.

SELECTED WRITINGS BY HAMILTON:

Books

Industrial Poisons in the United States, Macmillan, 1925.

Industrial Toxicology, Harper & Brothers, 1934.

Exploring the Dangerous Trades: the Autobiography of Alice Hamilton, M.D., Little, Brown, 1943.

SOURCES:

Books

American Women Writers, Ungar, 1980, pp. 226–227.

Current Biography: Who's News and Why 1946, H. W. Wilson Company, 1946, pp. 234–236.

Noble, Iris, *Contemporary Women Scientists of America,* Julian Messner, 1988, pp. 13–14.

Notable American Women: the Modern Period, Harvard University Press, 1980, pp. 303–306.

Sicherman, Barbara, *Alice Hamilton, a Life in Letters,* Harvard University Press, 1984.

—Sketch by J. Sydney Jones

Hidesaburo Hanafusa
1929-
Japanese virologist and molecular oncologist

Hidesaburo Hanafusa is a prominent researcher in the genetics of cancerous viruses. As explained by Fulvio Bardossi and Judith N. Schwartz in a *Research Profile* distributed by the Rockefeller University, Hanafusa "has used his training as a biochemist, combined with new insights and new technologies from molecular biology and genetics, to observe, isolate, control, and explain the events that occur and the elements that interact when virus meets cell." Hanafusa's early work with the Rous sarcoma virus (RSV), a virus that causes cancer in birds, has laid the foundation for a new hypothesis on how cancer may be caused by damaged genes—so-called "oncogenes"—within an organism's own cells. The oncogene theory proposes that genes have the potential to cause a normal cell to become cancerous. Hanafusa's current investigations at the Rockefeller University in New York City focuses on oncogenes and explores how they induce cellular transformation from a normal to a cancerous state.

Hanafusa was born on December 1, 1929 in Nishinomiya, Japan. He is the son of Kamehachi and Tomi Hanafusa. He majored in biochemistry, and received his bachelor's degree in 1953, and his doctorate in 1960, both from Osaka University. On May 11, 1958, Hanafusa married Teruko Inoue, a fellow student at Osaka who has become one of his principal scientific colleagues. The couple have one daughter, Kei. In 1961, Hanafusa left his homeland in Japan and accepted a position in the laboratory of Harry Rubin, a pioneer in tumor virus research at the University of California in Berkeley.

Carries on Cancer Research First Begun by Peyton Rous

When Nobel Prize-winning pathologist **Peyton Rous** made the pioneering discovery in 1910 that a virus causes cancer in chickens, the basic mechanisms of cancer were as yet poorly understood. A half century later, Hanafusa continued the research into the causes of viral cancer. Hanafusa's initial project with Rubin at the University of California produced a major discovery. While trying to isolate pure RSV, the researchers found that the virus could transform normal cells into cancerous ones. Interestingly, however, the virus could not replicate itself without a protein from a helper virus. This virus became a tool for future experiments. By changing the properties and activities of the altered RSV, Hanafusa could analyze key reactions that are responsible for bringing

Hidesaburo Hanafusa

about a cancerous state. Hanafusa pursued these studies as a visiting scientist at the College de France in Paris from 1964 to 1966 and then as head of a laboratory of viral oncology at the Public Health Research Institute in New York City.

In 1973 Hanafusa became professor of viral oncology at the Rockefeller University. In a new set of experiments, he injected chickens with RSV that had been altered to remove most of the genetic information specifically responsible for tumor formation. To his surprise, the chickens developed tumors anyway. On examination, he found the viruses had reacquired the missing tumor gene—the oncogene—from the chicken cell's own genetic information. These experiments showed that inappropriate activation of normal cellular genes causes tumors. Since then, more than twenty such oncogenes have been identified as being responsible for various kinds of cancers.

The Ongoing Endeavor to Understand Cancer

While exploring the nature of the RSV sarcoma gene (an oncogene), Hanafusa learned that the RSV mutants which he had isolated were temperature sensitive. This proved to be an important clue that the substance produced was a protein. Subsequent speculations presume that oncogenes may have an important role in normal cell life—to manufacture a protein required by the cell. It is only when the protein is overproduced that cancer occurs. Hanafusa later learned that the RSV sarcoma gene induces the protein tyrosine kinase, which can, by itself, trigger a cell division. Further investigations by Hanafusa have explored the role of this protein in the cell's signaling apparatus, a complicated sequence of intracellular communication known as phosphorylation. Hanafusa found that when infected with RSV, many cellular proteins become phosphorylated on tyrosine, and this process is associated with changes in cell growth.

In 1988, Hanafusa identified a novel oncogene, *crk,* in an avian sarcoma virus. Although it has no known catalytic function, its overproduction induces tyrosine phosphorylation of some cellular proteins and causes cancer. This finding has contributed to a surge of interest in the interaction between the phosphotyrosine-containing proteins and peptide domains in the cell's signaling network.

For his contributions in cancer virus studies, Hanafusa received the Howard Taylor Ricketts Award in 1981, the Albert Lasker Basic Medical Research Award in 1982, the Asahi Press Prize in 1984, and the Alfred P. Sloan, Jr. Prize in 1993. He was elected a Foreign Associate of the National Academy of Sciences in 1985.

SELECTED WRITINGS BY HANAFUSA:

Periodicals

(With wife, T. Hanafusa, and H. Rubin) "The Defectiveness of Rous Sarcoma Virus," *Proceedings of the National Academy of Sciences,* Volume 49, 1963, pp. 572–580.

"Cellular Origin of Transforming Genes of RNA Tumor Viruses," in *The Harvey Lectures, 1979–1980,* 1981, Academic Press, pp. 255–275.

(With R. Jove) "Cell Transformation by the Viral *src* Oncogene," *Annual Review of Cell Biology,* Volume 3, 1987, pp. 31–56.

(With L-H. Wang) "Avian Sarcoma Viruses," *Virus Research,* Volume 9, 1988, pp. 159–203.

Other

A bibliography of Dr. Hanafusa's over two hundred publications is available from the Laboratory of Molecular Oncology, Rockefeller University, New York NY 10021-6399.

SOURCES:

Periodicals

Research Profiles, Number 10, Rockefeller University, Fall, 1982, pp. 1–6.

—*Sketch by Carol L. Moberg*

Marc R. Hannah
1956-
American computer scientist

Marc R. Hannah has achieved rapid success in the field of computer science. Since the early 1980s, Hannah's work—which has helped advance the technology of the military, health care, and motion pictures—and the prosperous company he helped found, Silicon Graphics, have become a permanent part of American culture and are familiar to countless people worldwide.

Hannah, a native Chicagoan, was born on October 13, 1956. His father, Hubert, an accountant, and his mother, Edith, a teacher, both encouraged him to strive academically; and he excelled as a student. While in high school at the Kenwood Academy, he took a computer-science course that kindled his interest in this relatively new field. Inspired, too, by the example of an older brother, he earned high grades that would qualify him for a Bell Laboratories-sponsored scholarship to engineering school.

In planning his future, Hannah believed that a science doctorate was strictly for those in research as opposed to the more practical career he sought, so he decided to only pursue a Master's degree. But during his interview with Bell Labs representatives, he learned that many Ph.D. holders were doing applied research. He reset his sights on the more advanced goal of earning a doctorate. He entered the Illinois Institute of Technology and received his Bachelor of Science in Electrical Engineering in 1977, and then went on to Stanford University for a Ph.D., awarded in 1985.

While at Stanford, he met James Clark, an engineering professor who impelled him toward a fateful decision. Clark was a pioneer in computer graphics, having invented a special chip called the Geometry Engine. This was the heart of an imaging process that could rotate an onscreen object from top to bottom and front to back simultaneously, presenting the image in three dimensions instead of two. Hannah redesigned the chip to operate five times faster, an advance that impressed Clark enough to invite Hannah to join him in founding a computer-graphics company. The deal was soon struck, and in 1981 Silicon Graphics—Hannah's life work from that time on—was born.

The firm grew quickly, garnering customers such as Boeing Aircraft, Bayerische Motoren Werke (BMW), and Levi Strauss & Co. It went public in 1986 and became a half-billion-dollar enterprise by the early 1990s, constantly expanding its applications; Silicon Graphics' technology has been used to enhance many devices, such as military flight simulators and medical CAT scans. Among the most lucrative areas for this technology, and certainly the one best-known, is that of video and film animation. The special effects made possible by three-dimensional imaging in films such as *Star Wars, Terminator II,* and *Jurassic Park*—pictures that have become cinematic classics—have thrilled millions.

Hannah, now vice president and chief scientist of the company's Entry Systems Division, maintains several professional affiliations including memberships in the Association for Computing Machinery, the Institute of Electrical and Electronics Engineers, the National Technical Association, and the Northern California Council of Black Professional Engineers. He also sits on the Illinois Institute of Technology's Board of Trustees and the Board of Overseers of the Illinois Institute of Technology's School of Design.

In an interview with contributor Nicholas Pease, Hannah spoke about his work. Looking back on his career in a field long underrepresented by African American scientists, Hannah echoes his mother's counsel in saying a good education is the key to success. For the future his main ambition is to extend his company's products into the consumer marketplace, in the form of interactive television and video games. Hannah never expects his own name to become a household word, but should his efforts succeed, that of Silicon Graphics' will.

SOURCES:

Periodicals

"African Americans in the Computer Industry," *Journal of the NTA,* fall, 1991.

"Dr. Marc Hannah: Computer Graphics Architect," *Journal of the NTA,* April, 1987, p. 37.

Other

Hannah, Marc R., interview with Nicholas Pease conducted February, 7, 1994.

—*Sketch by Nicholas Pease*

James Hansen
1941-
American climatologist

The questions and subsequent debate over the existence and implications of "global warming," a topic of much concern in the 1990s, were sparked by the research of James Hansen. Hansen predicted in

1988 that the "greenhouse effect," caused by gases including carbon dioxide, ozone, methane, and chlorofluorocarbons (CFCs) which trap the sun's heat like the glass plates of a greenhouse, would have serious implications, warming the earth enough to cause widespread droughts, fires, and floods. Environmentalists have embraced Hansen's theory and used it to support their plea to curb emissions of greenhouse gases. Yet government officials and even some of Hansen's fellow scientists have denounced his conclusions. Five years after Hansen publicly called for immediate action to prevent the disastrous effects of global warming, many are still debating whether global warming exists at all, and if so whether its implications are as dire as Hansen says.

Hansen developed his theory from a climate model, a computer program designed to predict climate changes. His model is based on the facts that greenhouse gases trap heat in the earth's atmosphere and that the levels of these gases have been rising since the start of the Industrial Revolution. The idea that the gases keep the climate's temperature about 50° F warmer than it would be otherwise is generally undisputed. It is also agreed that levels of greenhouse gases have increased in the past century: carbon dioxide has risen about twenty-five percent and methane has doubled. What Hansen's detractors do dispute is the role of other factors affecting the climate. These include the oceans, which absorb heat and act as a buffer against temperature changes, and clouds, which also temper global warming. These variables have led many scientists to conclude that Hansen's model cannot accurately predict future global temperature.

Inspired by Discoverer of Van Allen Belts

Hansen, a soft-spoken Midwesterner and self-described "quiet and shy scientist," according to interviewer Karen Wright in the *New York Times Sunday Magazine,* is an unlikely spokesman for a subject of such heated debate. He hails from the small farm town of Charter Oak, Iowa, where his mother, Gladys Hansen, worked as a waitress and his father, James Ivan Hansen, as a sharecropper, then later a bartender. He was born March 29, 1941, one of seven children. In high school Hansen was an unexceptional student. Mathematics and physics particularly appealed to him, so he chose them as his major at the University of Iowa. There he met **James Van Allen**, who discovered the radiation belts encircling the earth. Hansen was inspired by the famous astronomer, who assisted Hansen in gaining a postdoctoral fellowship at the Goddard Institute, of which he is now director. Hansen graduated with highest distinction from the University of Iowa in 1963 with a bachelor's degree in physics and mathematics, returning for a master's in astronomy, completed in 1965, and a doctorate in physics two years later.

At Van Allen's suggestion, Hansen chose the atmosphere of Venus as his dissertation topic. That research and Van Allen's recommendation in 1967 helped Hansen secure a coveted position at NASA's Goddard Institute for Space Studies in Manhattan from 1967 to 1969. Hansen left the Goddard Institute for a year-long postdoctoral fellowship at the Leiden Observatory in the Netherlands, returning to New York to become a research associate at Columbia University from 1969 to 1972. He then returned to the Goddard Institute and in 1981 became its director.

Hansen was still primarily interested in the atmosphere of Venus when Harvard researcher Yuk Ling Yung asked for his help in studying the earth's greenhouse gases in 1975. It was already known that carbon dioxide and CFCs trapped heat in the earth's atmosphere; in 1976 the two published a paper in *Science* magazine showing that methane, nitrous oxide and other gases also contributed to the greenhouse effect. As he learned more about his home planet, Hansen's interest in Venus waned. In 1978, he resigned as the principal investigator of NASA's Venus experiment to devote his time to building a model of the earth's climate.

In 1981, Hansen committed what he calls his original sin. He published a paper in *Science* magazine which was reported on the front page of the *New York Times.* The paper said that contrary to popular belief, the world was not growing colder, but warmer. He went on to predict that if the global warming continued into the twenty-first century, it would cause more droughts, fires, and a rising sea level. Hansen testified before Congress in 1982, 1986, and 1987, despite the polemic nature of his subject which has been blamed for numerous budget cuts affecting Hansen's research. Hansen told contributor Cynthia Washam in an interview, "It's certainly something I didn't bargain for. I think the scientific controversy is interesting in the sense that over the next decade we will see the extent to which our predictions are accurate."

While the administration scolded Hansen, the environmental community lauded him. The National Wildlife Federation in 1989 honored him with its Conservation Achievement Award. In the same year he earned the Glenn Seaborg Award of the International Platform Association for alerting the world to the significance of the greenhouse effect. In 1991, the University of Iowa chose Hansen for its Alumni Achievement Award. The honor that has given Hansen the most pride came in 1992, when he was elected a fellow of the American Geophysical Union, an honor bestowed upon only one in one thousand members.

Suggests Conservation May be Tempering Global Warming

By 1990, Hansen's predictions on global warming appeared to be on target. That year was the warmest on the meteorological record. He forecast then that the trend would continue through the next two years, but ash injected into the atmosphere by the 1991 eruption of Mount Pinatubo put the warming trend on ice. By 1993, however, global warming appeared to be making a comeback. Hansen predicted that by 1994, the global temperature would be back up to its pre-eruption level. Yet in spite of his dire predictions, Hansen has grown more optimistic about the future. In the early 1990s, CFC levels declined due to manufacturers' switch to less harmful chemicals. The rate of methane growth has also decreased, Hansen said, although he is not sure why. Carbon dioxide emissions have remained level for several years. "The growth rates of greenhouse gases are significantly less than five years ago," he told Washam. "There are reasons for optimism." Meanwhile Hansen continues to refine his climate model and expects to unveil a more accurate one in 1994.

When he's not working, Hansen does his own small part to save the planet, planting and nurturing trees at his home in New Jersey. Hansen also enjoys pitching for the Goddard Institute's softball team and reads literary classics for relaxation. He has been married since 1971 to Holland native Anniek (Dekkers) Hansen and has two children, Erik and Christine. In 1993, Hansen ventured into a new arena when he established a summer science program for underprivileged high school and college students. Although teaching high school students will be new for Hansen, he has taught at the college level since 1978, when he was appointed an adjunct associate professor at Columbia University. In 1985, he attained his current position of adjunct professor. "I was very fortunate to get into a university and research environment created by Professor Van Allen and now I'm trying to create that environment and opportunity for young people [in New York City]," he told Washam. "It's become obvious that there are deficiencies [in science curricula]," he continued. "We'll teach students how scientific research is done."

SELECTED WRITINGS BY HANSEN:

Books

(With others) "The Greenhouse Effect: Projections of Global Climate Change," *Effects of Changes in Stratospheric Ozone and Global Climate,* Volume 1, edited by J. Titus, Environmental Protection Agency/United Nations Environment Programme, 1986, pp. 199–218.

(With others) "Evidence for Future Warming: How Large and When," *The Greenhouse Effect, Climate Change, and U.S. Forests,* edited by W. E. Shands and J. S. Hoffman, Conservation Foundation (Washington, DC), 1987.

(Contributor with others) *Prediction of Near-Term Climate Evolution: What Can We Tell Decision-Makers Now?,* Government Institutes, Inc., 1988, pp. 35–47.

"Greenhouse Effect," *Yearbook of Science and Technology,* McGraw-Hill, 1993.

Periodicals

(With others) "Greenhouse Effects Due to Manmade Perturbations of Trace Gases," *Science,* Volume 194, 1976, pp. 685–690.

(With others) "Climate Impact of Increasing Atmospheric CO2," *Science,* Volume 213, 1981, pp. 957–966.

(With others) "Global Mean Sea Level: Indicator of Climate Change?," *Science,* Volume 219, 1983, pp. 997.

(With others) "Climate Effects of Atmospheric Carbon Dioxide," *Science,* Volume 220, 1983, pp. 874–875.

(With others) "On Predicting Calamities," *Climatic Change,* Volume 5, 1983, pp. 201–204.

"Global Sea Level Trends," *Nature,* Volume 313, 1985, pp. 349–350.

(With others) "The Ice-Core Record: Climate Sensitivity and Future Greenhouse," *Nature,* Volume 347, 1990, pp. 139–145.

(With others) "How Sensitive Is the World's Climate?," *National Geographic Research and Exploration,* Volume 9, 1993, pp. 142–158.

SOURCES:

Books

Gore, Al, *Earth in the Balance,* Houghton, 1992.

Periodicals

Davis, Bob, "Scientist Who Exposed Global Warming Proposes Satellites for Climate Research," *Wall Street Journal,* July 24, 1990, p. B3.

Kerr, Richard A., "Hansen vs. the World on the Greenhouse Threat," *Science,* June 2, 1989.

McKibben, Bill, "James Hansen, Getting Warmer," *Outside,* May, 1993, p. 117.

Science News, December 2, 1989, p. 367.

Wright, Karen, "Heating the Global Warming Debate," *New York Times Sunday Magazine,* Feb. 3, 1991.

Other

Hansen, James E., interview with Cynthia Washam conducted November 9, 1993.

—*Sketch by Cynthia Washam*

Arthur Harden
1865-1940
English chemist

Arthur Harden's groundbreaking work in the field of alcoholic fermentation has led to a greater understanding of metabolic processes, including the formation of lactic acid in muscles and the ossification of tissue. Apart from his discoveries in biochemistry, he distinguished himself as a Nobel laureate, professor, and contributor of scholarship to the field.

Born on October 12, 1865, Harden was the third of nine children—and the only son—of Manchester businessman Albert Tyas Harden and Eliza MacAlister Harden. His family's puritanical leanings and nonconformist attitude toward social conventions, such as the celebration of Christmas and interest in the theatre, remained an influence throughout Harden's life. Despite his austere upbringing, however, he was an accomplished skater and avid gardener, as well as a great fan of Charles Dickens and Victorian literature in general. He attended private school beginning at age seven, and then studied at Tattersall College between 1876 and 1881 in Staffordshire, reaching the age of sixteen at the time that he left there. His undergraduate studies at Owen College of the University of Manchester under the instruction of Henry Roscoe culminated in a degree with first class honors in chemistry in 1885. A year later he was awarded the Dalton scholarship and started graduate studies at the University of Erlangen under the tutelage of **Ernst Otto Fischer**. After completing his Ph.D. in 1888 by writing his dissertation on properties and purification of β-nitroso-a-naphthylamine, he returned to Owens where he served as junior and then senior lecturer under Roscoe's successor, H. B. Dixon.

Harden was more interested in teaching and writing than research. He was intrigued with the history of chemistry, and taught an honors class in that subject. Among the most prodigious writings he had done up until 1896 were several papers that had resulted from studying John Dalton 's notebooks with Roscoe in a joint research project. Their 1896 book, *A New View of the Origin of Dalton's Atomic Theory,* represented an area of interest which fascinated Harden for many years. (Dalton theorized his atomic principles by observing the diffusion of gases.) Harden then collaborated with F. C. Garrett on *Practical Organic Chemistry,* published in 1897, and revised and edited Roscoe's *Treatise on Inorganic Chemistry,* admirably supplementing his teaching salary of 200 or less a year.

After unsuccessfully applying for jobs as a private school principal and as an inspector, Harden was appointed professor of biochemistry in 1897 at the British Institute of Preventative Medicine (renamed a year later to the Jenner Institute and, in 1903, the Lister Institute), where Roscoe was treasurer. While the institute staff taught students pursuing careers as public health officers, testing water for city officials and otherwise doing little scientific research, Harden was hired at Roscoe's suggestion to teach chemistry and bacteriology. As medical schools began to offer the same subjects, Harden's classes were phased out and the head of the bacteriology department, recommended he consider research. Fermentation, or the breakdown of sugar by bacteria, became Harden's objective as he set upon discovering a chemical means of distinguishing various fermentation patterns in the bacteria *Escherichia coli.* Harden was able to show that the ratio of alcohol to acetic acid, two of the compounds formed during bacterial fermentation, was a useful guide in determining which variety of the bacterium was involved in a given fermentation process.

Expands Buchner's Studies on Enzymes

The year Harden arrived at the institute, **Eduard Buchner** had released his revolutionary research on fermentation. Buchner had discovered that fermentation could take place in the absence of living yeast cells, yielding an enzyme he named zymase. Although the reaction took longer than it would have had live cells been present, it produced the familiar end products of fermentation, carbon dioxide and alcohol. Buchner's experiment was the first evidence of the existence of enzymes. Like many others in the scientific community, Harden began to build on Buchner's work. He showed that fermentation could occur because zymase acted on glycogen (a sugar) that had been within the cells themselves. Assisted by William Young, Harden made significant discoveries about the role of phosphate in fermentation over the next decade.

In 1904, Harden put a semipermeable membrane bag full of yeast extract into pure water. Harden knew that the molecules, densely packed inside the bag, would move through the membrane into the water because of the lower density of yeast outside of the bag. He also knew that the membrane would allow only molecules of a given size to pass through—a process called dialysis. Zymase stopped breaking down the sugar inside the bag while reintroducing water from outside the bag which contained the small molecules that had diffused out through the membrane. When Harden boiled the yeast extract, it failed to cause fermentation at all, indicating that zymase actually consisted of two parts. Because zymase lost its activity after dialysis, he decided that the larger part remained trapped inside the bag; this, together with its loss of effectiveness led Harden to conclude that the larger part was probably a protein, the smaller part (having not perished during boiling), a nonprotein.

Pursuing the matter further, Harden and Young added boiled yeast juice to an ongoing fermentation and measured the amount of carbon dioxide released. Although all active agents should have been destroyed by the boiling, the addition sped up the process. They discovered the boiled juice contained a phosphate substance called cozymase. Harden's work showed that three factors are necessary for fermentation to occur: the ferment, the enzyme, and a coenzyme. By attending to the entire fermentation process—not only the end products as had been the previous practice—he laid the important groundwork for further understanding of metabolic processes, such as ossification.

In 1911, Harden was among the founders of the Biochemical Society, and the following year named coeditor of the *Biochemical Journal.* Although Harden left the institute in 1912 for a professorship in biochemistry at the University of London, his association with the institute was not over. He became acting director when the head of the institute went off to war in 1914. For the duration, his research focused on nutrition, particularly on the diseases beriberi and scurvy, while much of his free time was spent digging trenches with the Volunteer Reserve.

Harden married Georgina Sydney Bridge, of Christchurch, New Zealand, in 1900; they had no children. She died in 1928, a year before Harden and **Hans von Euler-Chelpin** received the Nobel Prize in chemistry for work in fermentation. In 1909 he was named a fellow of the Royal Society, being awarded its Davy Medal in 1935, and the following year he was knighted. He received honorary degrees from the universities of Manchester, Liverpool, and Athens, and was named an honorary member of the Institute of Brewing and a member of the Kasierlich Leopold Deutsche Akademie der Naturforsche, Halle.

A year after winning the Nobel Prize Harden retired from teaching, although he stayed on as editor of the *Biochemical Journal* until 1937. His garden at Bourne End remained one of his great joys until he died at home on June 17, 1940, of a progressive disease.

SELECTED WRITINGS BY HARDEN:

Books

(With Henry Roscoe) *A New View of the Origin of Dalton's Atomic Theory,* Macmillan, 1896.

(With F. C. Garrett) *Practical Organic Chemistry,* Longmans, 1897.

Alcoholic Fermentation, Longmans, 1911, revised editions, 1914, 1923, 1932.

Periodicals

"The Composition of Some Ancient Iron and a Bronze Found at Thebes," *Transactions of the Manchester Literary and Philosophical Society,* Volume 41, 1897, numbers 1–3.

(With William Young) "The Alcoholic Ferment of Yeast Juice," *Proceedings of the Royal Society,* Volume 77B, 1907, 405–420.

SOURCES:

Books

Chen, Victor, "Sir Arthur Harden, 1929," *The Nobel Prize Winners: Chemistry,* edited by Frank Magill, Volume 1: *1901–1937,* Salem Press (Pasadena, CA), 1990, pp. 310–317.

Farber, Eduard, *Nobel Prize Winners in Chemistry, 1901–1961,* Abelard-Schumann (New York City), 1963, pp. 111–112.

Periodicals

Smedley-Maclean, Ida, "Arthur Harden, (1865–1940)," *Biochemical Journal,* Volume 35, 1941, pp. 1071–1081.

—Sketch by F. C. Nicholson

Alister C. Hardy
1896-1985
English zoologist

Alister C. Hardy was a zoologist who made many contributions to marine biology and oceanography, but he is best known for his efforts to reconcile evolutionary theory with religion and belief in a supreme power. Hardy was convinced that religious experience had a biological origin which was possible to study scientifically, and he became the founding director of the Religious Experience Research Unit at Manchester College, Oxford.

Hardy was born outside the industrial city of Nottingham, England, on February 10, 1896, to Richard and Elizabeth Clavering Hardy. His father was an architect who appreciated the beauty of nature and encouraged Hardy to observe and treasure the world around him. At an early age, Hardy had his own assortment of insects gathered from the adjoining woods and fields, and when his father explained that the living room mantelpiece was made of fossiliferous marble—containing the remains of tiny animals that lived in the sea millions of years ago—Hardy decided to learn more about the ocean. He suffered from an eye disorder that affected his vision in one eye, and he was excused from the mandatory sports activities at Oundle School in Northamptonshire. He was allowed to go on country walks instead, while his classmates engaged in athletics. Hardy soon developed a talent for sketching, and he both drew and painted watercolors of the flora and fauna he observed.

The skills which Hardy had developed at drawing and observing nature were used by the British War Office during World War I. He enlisted in 1915 and served with the Royal Engineers as an assistant camouflage officer, flying over enemy territory searching for concealed gun emplacements as well as working with British coastal defenses. In 1918 he was discharged with the rank of captain and enrolled at Exeter College, Oxford, where he studied zoology. Awarded two prestigious fellowships as an undergraduate, Hardy became the Christopher Welch Biological Research Scholar, and was also named Oxford Biological Scholar at Stazione Zoologica in Naples, Italy. Graduating in 1921, he would receive his D.Sc. from Oxford in 1938.

In 1921, Hardy became assistant naturalist with the Fisheries Laboratory in Lowestoft, Suffolk, studying the feeding habit of herring. This work led to his invention of a continuous plankton recorder which measured the amount of the basic food available to herring in the North Sea. He applied for a scientific position on the research ship *Discovery,* and the quality of his work at Lowestoft was sufficient to earn Hardy the job as chief zoologist in 1924. Sailing with this ship until 1928, he studied and wrote about Antarctic marine life. Hardy's reports established him as one of his country's leading marine biologists; his extensive journals were published four decades later under the title *Great Waters.*

Upon his return to England in 1928, Hardy was named professor of zoology and oceanography at University College, Hull. He left Hull in 1942 and moved to the University of Aberdeen in Scotland as Regius Professor of Natural History. In 1946, he returned to Oxford as Linacre Professor of Zoology and Comparative Anatomy. In the 1960s, Hardy began to question publicly the widely held belief that humans evolved from apes on the African savannah. He observed that the only mammals which have both skin without hair or fur and a layer of fat beneath their skin are aquatic—whales, walruses, or hippopotamuses, for example. Hardy also suggested that primates might have begun walking on two feet while wading, to keep their heads above water. The theory was almost entirely ignored, and it has only recently begun to interest scientists who have grown frustrated with certain problems posed by the savannah theory.

Throughout his life, Hardy considered science and religion an inseparable union. He strongly believed that religious experience could be measured and explained on a biological level. Although a convinced Darwinist, he held that just as there is a natural evolution among species, there is also a natural religious awareness in humankind that evolves along similar paths and is essential to human survival. In 1963, Hardy returned to Aberdeen University as Gifford Lecturer, and he used this position to promulgate his views about the relationship between science and spiritual experience. During this period he published two books based on these beliefs: *The Living Stream: Evolution and Man* and *The Divine Flame: An Essay Toward a Natural History of Religion.* In 1969, Hardy founded the Religious Experience Research Unit (now known as the Alister Hardy Research Center) at Oxford's Manchester College. The group collected thousands of personal accounts and attempted to examine them the way a scientist evaluates collected data. They organized various religious experiences into twelve main categories. Many of his colleagues were skeptical, and *Time* magazine quoted an observation by Philip Toynbee, who wrote that Hardy was "trying to catch an angel in his butterfly net." He was careful to differentiate religious experience from a psychical experience such as extrasensory perception, though he accepted the existence of psychical experience. As a member of London's council of the Society for Psychical Research, he attempted to correlate biological and psychical studies. He was also a fellow of the Royal Society and the Zoological Society.

For his work as a marine biologist and scholar, Alister Hardy was knighted in 1957. In 1968, he also received the Pierre Lecomte du Nouy Prize for his book, *The Living Stream,* and in 1985 he was awarded the Templeton Prize for Progress in Religion. Hardy was married to Sylvia Lucy Garstang in 1927, and the couple had a son and a daughter together. Hardy died in Oxford at the age of eight-nine on May 23, 1985.

SELECTED WRITINGS BY HARDY:

Books

The Open Sea, Houghton, Volume 1: *The World of Plankton,* 1956, Volume 2: *Fish and Fisheries,* 1959.

The Living Stream: Evolution and Man, Harper, 1965.

The Divine Flame: An Essay Toward a Natural History of Religion, Collins, 1966.

Great Waters, Collins, 1967.

(With Robert Harvie and Arthur Koestler) *The Challenge of Chance,* Hutchinson, 1973.

The Biology of God, Taplinger, 1975.

Periodicals

"Biology and Psychical Research," *Proceedings of the Society of Psychical Research,* Volume 50, 1953, p. 183.

SOURCES:

Periodicals

Morgan, Elaine, "The Water Baby," *New Statesman and Society,* Volume 5, December, 1992, pp. 29–30.

Time, March 11, 1985, p. 65. *Times Literary Supplement,* June 8, 1967.

—Sketch by Benedict A. Leerburger

Godfrey Harold Hardy
1877-1947
English mathematician

Godfrey Harold Hardy was one of the foremost mathematicians in England during the early part of the twentieth century. He was primarily a pure mathematician, specializing in branches of mathematics that study the behavior of numbers (such as number theory and analysis). He also made important contributions to areas of applied mathematics, and is known for formulating the Hardy-Weinberg law of population genetics. He taught at both Cambridge and Oxford and published over three hundred-fifty research papers, either alone or in collaboration with other mathematicians—most notably John Edensor Littlewood and **S. I. Ramanujan**.

Born on February 7, 1877, in Cranleigh, England, Hardy was the elder of two children of Isaac and Sophia Hall Hardy. Both his parents came from poor families and were unable to afford university education for themselves, but they were people with a taste for intellectual and cultural pursuits and had made a place for themselves as schoolteachers. Hardy's father was the geography and drawing master at Cranleigh School, where he also gave singing lessons, edited the school magazine, and played soccer. His mother taught piano lessons there and helped run a boarding house for the younger students. They took great pains to educate their children well, and both Hardy and his sister Gertrude inherited their parent's love for education and the intellect. A gifted student, Hardy displayed a special talent and interest for mathematics from a very young age. When he was just two, he was writing down numbers into the millions, a common sign of future numerical ability. Rather than attend regular classes in mathematics, he was coached by a private tutor, and he completed sixth form at Cranleigh when he was only thirteen—about five years younger than the usual age—ranking second in class. He then won a prestigious scholarship to attend Winchester College, a private secondary school where he spent six years before graduating in 1896, winning another scholarship to attend Trinity College at Cambridge University.

Follows the Road to Mathematics

Hardy initially chose to attend Cambridge rather than Oxford because of its standing in mathematics, and Trinity College was the premier institution for the subject in England. During his first years at Cambridge, however, he very nearly gave up mathematics altogether, in disgust over the examination system then in existence. Mathematics students had to take the Tripos examination, which consisted of eight days of solving problems. Hardy disliked the system because, rather than gauging the ability and insight of the student, he believed it tested endurance and the ability to memorize formulae and equations. Special private coaches trained students for Tripos, while lecturers at the universities pursued their own mathematical research. Hardy considered Tripos an utter waste of time, and he tried to change his course of study to history. What kept him in the field was his professor, A. E. H. Love, who recognized Hardy's affinity for pure mathematics and recommended that he read a book by the French mathematician Camille Jordan.

Entitled *Cours d'analyse de l'Ecole Polytechnique,* Jordan's book kept Hardy in mathematics, and he persevered through Tripos, putting real mathematics aside for two years. In his autobiographical book, *A Mathematician's Apology,* Hardy wrote of his career after reading Jordan's book: "From that time onwards I was in my way a real mathematician, with sound mathematical ambitions and a genuine passion for mathematics." Despite his acute distaste for Tripos, Hardy ranked fourth in the first examination in 1898, and he scored the highest points in the second part of the examinations two years later. Upon his graduation in 1899, he was named a fellow of Trinity College at Cambridge.

As a fellow, Hardy was finally free to devote his time to pure mathematics, and he did so with great enthusiasm and fervor. Over the next ten years he produced several papers on number series that established his reputation as an analyst, and in 1908 he published a book, *A Course of Pure Mathematics.* This was the first mathematical textbook in the English language to explain rigorously the fundamental concepts of the subject. Until then, books and teachers had merely provided these formulae and moved on to using them in various practical applications. Continuing his interest in mathematical education, Hardy joined a panel and tried to reform Tripos as the first step—he hoped—to abolishing it altogether. Although this latter goal proved futile (Tripos is still in existence nearly a century later), the panel did succeed in eliminating the worst features of the system.

Also in 1908, Hardy made his only contribution to applied mathematics in the form of a letter to the American journal *Science*. Mendelian genetics being the subject of much debate at that time, an article that recently appeared in *The Proceedings of the Royal Society of Medicine* had disputed some of Mendel's theories of inheritance of various traits. In his letter, Hardy used simple algebraic principles to prove the error in the article, and he set down an equation that predicted the patterns of inheritance. In the same year, a German physician named **Wilhelm Weinberg** devised a similar mathematical method for prediction, and the principle was named the Hardy-Weinberg law in honor of them both. Widely used in the study of the genetic transmission of blood groups and rare diseases, this law appears today as a fundamental principle of population genetics.

Despite what many saw as his productivity during the years between 1900 and 1910, Hardy himself felt that he did not do too much of value, and he said so in *A Mathematician's Apology:* "I wrote a great deal during the next ten years but very little of any importance; there are not more than four or five papers I can still remember with some satisfaction." He believed that his best work came later, out of his associations with John Edensor Littlewood and S. I Ramanujan.

Cultivates Productive Partnerships

Hardy began his collaboration with the mathematician J. E. Littlewood in 1911. The partnership, which lasted for over thirty-five years and resulted in the publication of over one hundred papers, was described by C. P. Snow in his foreword to Hardy's *A Mathematician's Apology* as "the most famous collaboration in the history of mathematics. There has been nothing like it in any science or in any other field of creative activity." Some eight years younger than Hardy, Littlewood was a brilliant mathematician who had already made a name for himself in the mathematical community.

Not much is known about exactly how the two men worked together. At the height of their combined productivity, from 1920 to 1931, they were not even at the same university. Hardy had moved to Oxford by then, while Littlewood remained in Cambridge. According to Snow, Hardy always maintained that Littlewood was the better, more powerful mathematician, although at meetings and conferences it was always Hardy who presented the papers. Indeed, Littlewood seldom attended these meetings, and other mathematicians were known to have joked that they doubted whether he even existed.

Hardy's second collaboration began in 1913 with a letter from India. The writer of the letter, Srinivasa Iyengar Ramanujan, was then an unknown clerk in Madras, who had received no formal education or training in mathematics but who claimed to have made some original discoveries while working on his own. After a single paragraph of introduction, Ramanujan plunged into his mathematics, providing page after page (the letter was over ten pages long) of theorems and results written out neatly by hand. Hardy's first instinct was to disregard the letter as a crank, filled as it was with wild claims and bizarre theorems without offering any proofs to support them. Indeed, two other Cambridge mathematicians had done just that, having received similar letters from Ramanujan earlier.

But something about the letter, perhaps its very strangeness, also intrigued Hardy, and he decided it was worth a closer look. He invited Littlewood to join him. After three hours of perusing the papers, the two men decided that the work was that of a genius. Hardy then wrote back to Ramanujan asking for proofs for some of his results, but untrained as he was Ramanujan did not or could not furnish these. In fact, when he wrote again it was to present Hardy with even more results and theorems. To Hardy, who had reintroduced the concept of rigor in proof to England, Ramanujan's intuitive reasoning and unorthodox methods were very frustrating. He invited Ramanujan to England, where from 1914 to 1919 the two men worked together and published many important papers. Hardy personally trained Ramanujan in modern mathematics and analysis; as he did in his collaboration with Littlewood, he also wrote most of the papers and presented the talks. Ramanujan himself returned to India and died in 1920, having contracted tuberculosis in England, but Hardy continued to promote his work long after his death.

Leaves Cambridge for Oxford and then Returns

Meanwhile, Hardy was growing disenchanted with life at Cambridge, and controversies surrounding World War I had much to do with this. In his foreword to *A Mathematician's Apology,* Snow describes the years from 1914 to 1918 as the "dark years" for Hardy. Most of his friends were away at the war. His work with Littlewood was also suffering, as the latter had gone away to serve as a second lieutenant in the army. In 1916, **Bertrand Russell**, the noted philosopher, mathematician, and pacifist, was dismissed from his lectureship at Trinity for his antiwar activities. Hardy was a close personal friend of Russell's; outraged at this dismissal, he fought bitterly with many of his mathematical colleagues. In 1918, the university dismissed yet another person for their antiwar views, this time a librarian, upsetting Hardy even more, and he actively opposed the firing. Snow writes in *A Mathematician's Apology* that "it was the work of Ramanujan which was Hardy's solace during the bitter college quarrels."

Adding to his discontent was the fact that his duties at Cambridge were becoming increasingly administrative, leaving him little time for research. In 1919, he moved to Oxford University as Savilian Professor of Geometry at New College. Here, he reached the pinnacle of his career, setting up a flourishing research school and enjoying the best years of his collaboration with Littlewood. His flamboyance, radical antiwar views, and outspokenness were appreciated at Oxford. Hardy had an exceptional gift for working well with other people, and besides Ramanujan and Littlewood he collaborated with many other leading mathematicians of the day. He also spent one year as an exchange professor at Princeton University. In 1931, he returned to Cambridge as Sadleirian Professor of Pure Mathematics. He retired in 1942, after which he continued to live in his rooms at Trinity. Shortly before his death in 1947, the Royal Society awarded him their highest honor, the Copley Medal.

There was nothing in life Hardy cared about more than mathematics, but he did have other interests. During his early years at Cambridge, he was part of several social groups, including a secret intellectual society known as the Apostles. This society met weekly to discuss and debate philosophical issues, and over the years it boasted some brilliant minds among its membership. During Hardy's time the philosophers Bertrand Russell and G. E. Moore were members, and it was through this association that many of his closest friendships were fostered.

Hardy was intensely fond of sports, particularly cricket. He followed cricket matches and scores with great attention. Hardy was not above bringing his passion for cricket into the classroom, describing the quality of mathematical work he considered exceptionally good to be in the "Bradman" or "Hobbs" class. As both men were cricketeers, not mathematicians, such references were apt to confuse unsuspecting students. To the end of his days he remained passionately interested in cricket, and when he died he was listening to his sister read to him from a book on the history of Cambridge University cricket.

Hardy was also a talented writer. He was often called upon to write obituaries of famous mathematicians. In addition to numerous mathematical texts, he also wrote *Bertrand Russell and Trinity,* a recounting of the wartime controversy, and *A Mathematician's Apology,* a treatise describing his love for the subject. In this book he offered a justification for his choice of career: "I have never done anything 'useful'.... Judged by all practical standards the value of my mathematical life is nil." But he adds, "The case for my life is this: that I have added something more to knowledge, and helped others to add more."

SELECTED WRITINGS BY HARDY:

Books

A Course of Pure Mathematics, Cambridge University Press, 1908.

(Editor) *Collected Papers of Srinivasa Ramanujan,* Cambridge University Press, 1927.

A Mathematician's Apology, Cambridge University Press, 1940.

Bertrand Russell and Trinity (reprint), Cambridge University Press, 1970.

Periodicals

"Obituary, S. Ramanujan," in *Nature,* Volume 105, June 17, 1920, pp. 495–495.

SOURCES:

Books

Kanigel, Robert, *The Man Who Knew Infinity,* Macmillan, 1991.

Snow, C. P., foreword to *A Mathematician's Apology,* Cambridge University Press, 1940.

—Sketch by Neeraja Sankaran

Harriet Hardy
1905-1993
American pathologist

Harriet Hardy intended to be a simple general practitioner, but fortuitous events changed that plan. Through the investigation of a respiratory illness that was common among factory workers in two towns in Massachusetts, she discovered the often-fatal respiratory disease berylliosis—a discovery that led to her becoming one of the world's foremost authorities in the field of occupational medicine. In the course of her long career she battled against numerous diseases caused by dangerous substances to which workers are exposed, including silicosis and asbestosis.

Born on September 23, 1905 in Arlington, Massachusetts, Harriet Louise Hardy set her course early on for a career in medicine. In 1928 she graduated from Wellesley College, and four years later earned her M.D. from Cornell University. After interning and spending her residency at Philadelphia General Hospital, she started her practice at Northfield Seminary in Massachusetts as a school doctor. This simple practice, however, did not last long, and by 1939 she had accepted a post as college doctor and director of health education at Cambridge's Radcliffe College. It was here, while researching the fields of women's health and fitness, that Hardy's interests expanded to include industrial diseases.

Focusses on Occupational Medicine

In the early 1940s, Hardy began a collaboration with Joseph Aubt to study the effects of lead poisoning. Like **Alice Hamilton** and other pioneering pathologists of the time, Hardy began to recognize the dangers inherent in the modern factory, with workers coming into contact with all manner of toxic substances. There soon came word of a strange respiratory disease among the workers in the Sylvania and General Electric fluorescent lamp factories in nearby Lynn and Salem, Massachusetts. The sufferers all complained of shortness of breath, coughing, and loss of weight; in some cases, the disease was fatal. Hardy and her colleagues were initially baffled as to the cause of the disease, but it occurred to Hardy that the disease had to be occupationally related. Referring to research from Europe and Russia, Hardy finally found the connection to beryllium; a light metal used in the manufacture of fluorescent lamps, beryllium dust or vapor could be easily inhaled by factory workers. Hardy showed that this outbreak was indeed berylliosis, a condition whose symptoms sometimes are not manifested for up to 20 years after exposure to beryllium dust. Hardy subsequently became an expert in beryllium poisoning, writing papers which educated and alerted the medical community to its dangers. She also established a registry of berylliosis cases at the Massachusetts General Hospital (where she had been on staff since 1940); this registry later served as a model for the tracking of other occupation-related disorders.

Establishes Occupational Medicine Clinic

Hardy went on to establish a clinic of occupational medicine at Massachusetts General Hospital in 1947, directing it for the next 24 years. She continued to explore the disease-producing properties of work-related substances, and in 1954 she was among the first scientists to identify a link between asbestos and cancer. Hardy was also concerned with the effects of radiation on the human body; she worked with the Atomic Energy Commission in Los Alamos, New Mexico, to study radiation poisoning, making a number of suggestions toward better working conditions in nuclear power plants. In 1949 she teamed up with Alice Hamilton to write the second edition of *Industrial Toxicology,* which has become a standard text on the subject. Other areas of Hardy's research and investigation included mercury poisoning and treatments for lead poisoning. She also researched the harmful effects of benzene, and as a result of her findings the highest permissible concentration of the hydrocarbon used in industry was reduced by fifty per cent.

In 1955 she was named Woman of the Year by the American Medical Women's Association. An outspoken and forceful critic for change, Hardy was appointed clinical professor at Harvard Medical School in 1971, and during the course of her long career authored over 100 scientific articles. She died of an immune system cancer, lymphoma, on October 13, 1993 at Massachusetts General Hospital.

SELECTED WRITINGS BY HARDY:

Books

(With Alice Hamilton) *Industrial Toxicology,* P. B. Hoeber, 1949.

SOURCES:

Periodicals

Harvard Medical School Focus, October 21, 1993, p. 9.

Journal of the American Medical Women's Association, November, 1955, p. 402.

New York Times, October 15, 1993, p. B10.

—*Sketch by J. Sydney Jones*

E'lise F. Harmon
1909-1985
American engineer

An engineer who was a pioneer in micro-miniaturization of printed circuitry components, E'lise F. Harmon was responsible for one innovation which allowed American planes to fly above 15,000 feet for the first time during World War II. She worked variously as a high school and college teacher, and as an engineer with the National Bureau of Standards, the Naval Research Laboratory, Aerovox Corporation, and finally her own firm, Harmon Technical Consultants, before her death in 1985.

Harmon was born in Texas on September 3, 1909. After obtaining a B.S. degree in chemistry, she taught at several high schools and a junior college in her native state. During this time, she also educated the employees of several firms in chemistry and physics. Tiring of her teaching career, Harmon began working part-time, first for Davies Fruit Company and later for Pan American Airways, while she furthered her studies. She earned an M.S. degree in biology from the University of Texas, and she performed graduate studies in engineering at George Washington University and in chemistry at the University of Maryland.

From 1938 to 1942, Harmon served as a consultant to Standard Oil Company, performing tests and analyses on crude oil. She continued teaching oil field employees during evenings. The turning point of her career, as she described it in the *Society of Women Engineers Newsletter,* occurred in 1942 when she accepted a position with the Army Ordnance in St. Louis, Missouri. "I got the feel of engineering and worked with engineering instruments and blueprints," Harmon said. "I was crazy about it."

Wartime Innovation Leads to Higher Altitude Flights

During World War II, Harmon improved the performance of carbon brushes which were part of aircraft generators. The brushes on American planes would disintegrate at altitudes above 15,000 feet, which meant the technologically advanced German aircraft could climb much higher. Harmon developed a method of extending the life of these brushes under high altitudes—a significant contribution to the war effort.

Harmon joined the Aircraft and Electrical Division of the Naval Research Laboratory in 1945, where in addition to her continued innovations on high altitude carbon brushes, she investigated the effect of fungus growth and oxidation on electrical equipment needed for various geographical locations. She also tested the chemical characteristics of various materials to learn how they would perform as sliding contacts in electrical equipment under stressful flight conditions.

In 1948, Harmon accepted a position with the National Bureau of Standards Ordnance Division. There she studied the application of printed circuitry to military equipment. Harmon then joined the staff of Aerovox Corporation, where she remained throughout the 1950s, developing a new methodology to produce printed circuitry for both military and commercial use. Harmon is said to have been inspired by a cosmetic display in a drug store which featured a picture of a woman's face, with the lips printed on a raised surface. She contacted the printer who created the display and adapted his technique for printing resistors on circuits at varying depths. This method has widespread applications within contemporary electronic circuitry. One of her innovations in printed circuitry resulted in a patent, which is for a hot die stamp method used to infuse silver conductors on polymerized materials.

Harmon joined American Bosch Arma Corporation as senior engineer of computer development for one year in New York before being named staff chief engineer, senior technical specialist at Autonetics in Anaheim (later North American Rockwell Division). She remained there until 1969.

She directed Harmon Technical Consultants until her death in 1985. She was a member of the American Chemical Society, the Texas Academy of Sciences, and the Institute of Radio Engineers. Harmon was honored in 1956 with the Society of Women Engineers Achievement Award "in recognition of her significant contributions to the area of component and circuit miniaturization."

SOURCES:

Books

Society of Women Engineers Achievement Awards, 1993 edition.

Periodicals

"E'lise Harmon Receives Award," *Society of Women Engineers Newsletter,* June, 1956, p. 3.

—Sketch by Karen Withem

Cyril Harris
1917-
American physicist and acoustical engineer

Cyril Harris made major contributions to the understanding and application of acoustics. His integration of research and its application to architectural design made him an expert in the design of auditoriums and concert halls. Harris designed superior acoustics for many famous buildings, including the John F. Kennedy Center for the Performing Arts in Washington, D.C. He wrote or edited over seventy publications on vibration and acoustical design, several of which have become standard texts in the industry. Some of his publications have been translated into Chinese, Japanese, French, Spanish, and Rumanian editions. Harris has been honored with awards from the science, engineering, and architecture professions.

Cyril Manton Harris was born to Bernard O. and Ida Moss Harris in Detroit, Michigan, on June 20, 1917. He earned his Bachelor of Arts degree in mathematics from the University of California at Los Angeles in 1938 and his Master of Arts in physics from the same school two years later. In 1941 Harris began working as a researcher for the Carnegie Institute of Technology in Washington, D.C., moving that same year to New England to work at the Massachusetts Institute of Technology (MIT). At MIT, Harris joined the war research staff of the National Defense Council and became a teaching fellow. He also pursued doctoral studies while at MIT—his dissertation addressed the measurement of acoustics within rooms, a subject that would be a focus of his research for many years. In the years preceding World War I, Harris contributed to the country's defense efforts by working on the development of the proximity fuse, which detonated explosives when its sensor detected a target. And throughout the war, he applied his knowledge of acoustics to advance several types of sound-activated underwater mines.

Harris completed his graduate studies at MIT in 1945 earning his Ph.D. in physics. Following his graduation, Harris was employed at the Bell Telephone Laboratories as a research engineer, and he worked there for six years. During this time Harris worked primarily on the development of transducers for changing energy from one form to another, such as electricity into sound. He also researched a device for synthesizing human speech, for which he was awarded a patent. On July 12, 1949, while still a research engineer at Bell, Harris married Ann Schakne. They had two children, a son, Nicholas Bennet, and a daughter, Katherine Anne.

Work Establishes International Standards

In 1951 Harris was appointed a consultant to the United States Office of Naval Research, housed in the United States Embassy in London, England. While in Europe, he was also visiting Fulbright lecturer at the Technical University of Delft in the Netherlands during the 1951–52 academic year. A year later he became a member of the faculty of Columbia University in New York City, where he opened a research laboratory. This provided him with the means to study both the physical and architectural aspects of acoustics. Harris measured the rate of speed and absorption of sound as it travels through air in relation to temperature, humidity, and pressure. His work became the basis for defining international standards for the absorption of sound in air inside auditoriums, and as a factor in assessing noise radiation produced by aircraft. His knowledge contributed significantly to the development of equipment for acoustical analysis, effective noise control methods, and the evaluation of musical instruments.

Harris's interests expanded to include the impact of room shape and size on the listening experience of those inside the room. Harris was aware that people like some reverberation (the reflection of sound by physical boundaries surrounding a space after the source has stopped making the sound), but he also found out that too much reverberation can distort sound. Room reverberation can be measured by reverberation time. That is, how long it takes sound to soften to 1/1000th its original strength. However, room reverberation times can vary with different types of sound and with differing room sizes. Harris evaluated empirical data on people's preferences in a very important study which determined the reverberation times produced by different room sizes for different sound types. He used the results of his research in his work as a design consultant for several renowned auditoriums and concert halls, among them, the National Academy of Sciences Auditorium in Washington, D.C., and the Avery Fisher Hall at Lincoln Center in New York City, which was built in 1976. He also consulted on the acoustical design of concert halls outside the United States such as the National Center for the Performing Arts in Bombay, India.

While at Columbia, Harris held joint positions as professor of electrical engineering and architecture. He taught courses in both fields, as well as at the law school. In 1974 Harris became the chair of the Architectural Technology Division in the Graduate School of Architecture and Planning at Columbia University. During his tenure there, Harris also served in several acoustical, physics, and electrical engineering professional organizations. Additionally, he worked with the Noise Control Group of the National Research Council. Among the many honors Harris received, was the Franklin Medal from the Franklin Institute in 1977 and the American Institute of Architects medal in 1980. Harris contributed significantly to the understanding and use of acoustics in building design. His application of knowledge resulting from studies of reverberation and acoustical design auditoriums set architectural standards in auditoriums and concert halls.

SELECTED WRITINGS BY HARRIS:

Books

(Editor) *Historic Architecture Sourcebook,* McGraw-Hill, 1977.
(With Vern O. Knudsen) *Acoustical Designing in Architecture,* American Institute of Physics, 1978.
(With C. E. Crede) *Shock and Vibration Handbook,* McGraw-Hill, 1988.
(Editor) *Handbook of Acoustical Measurements and Noise Control,* McGraw-Hill, 1991.

SOURCES:

Books

Encyclopedia of Science and Technology, McGraw-Hill, 1982.
Greene, Jay E., editor, *Modern Scientists and Engineers,* McGraw-Hill, 1980.

—*Sketch by David N. Ford*

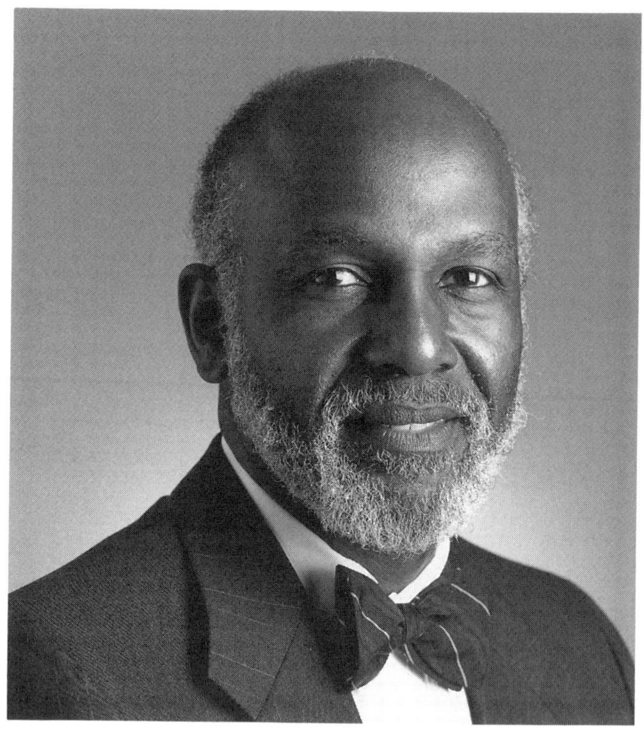
Wesley L. Harris

Wesley L. Harris
1941-
American aerospace engineer

As an engineer and an administrator for the National Aeronautics and Space Administration (NASA), Wesley L. Harris has participated in or directed a broad range of research initiatives that advanced aircraft, helicopter, and spaceflight technology. As an educator, he has increased opportunities for minority students and strengthened engineering education programs at three major universities.

Born in Richmond, Virginia, on October 29, 1941, Wesley Leroy Harris was one of three children of tobacco factory workers William and Rosa Minor Harris. Rosa Harris encouraged her children to educate themselves and learn all they could. For young Wes, that meant pursuing his fascination with airplanes. He not only read about them but built models of all types. When his elementary school held a writing contest on students' career ambitions, fourth-grader Harris won with his essay on his dream of becoming a test pilot.

Harris attended Armstrong High School in Richmond, where he found math and physics the most rewarding subjects. He also played football for a demanding coach, an experience he credited with teaching him that hard work and never giving up were the keys to success in any endeavor. Harris's imagination was sparked when the Soviet Union orbited *Sputnik I,* the first artificial satellite, in 1957, and his interest in aviation and space guided his life even more strongly from then on.

In 1960 Harris graduated from high school and went on to attend the University of Virginia. At the time only certain programs were open to black students, and Harris was not allowed to pursue his original idea of majoring in physics; he enrolled instead in aerospace engineering. He also married in that year. Despite the strain of having a family and being one of only a handful of African Americans at the school, Harris's determination made him a success. As a senior, he won an award from the American Institute of Aeronautics and Astronautics (AIAA) for his research on the turbulent flow of air over wing surfaces. Another honor was being chosen to introduce Dr. Martin Luther King, Jr., when the civil rights leader made a speech at the campus. In 1964 he received his bachelor's degree with honors.

On the advice of his professors, Harris moved on to Princeton University with the goal of earning a doctorate in engineering and becoming a professor himself. He earned a master's in aerospace engineering in 1966 and a Ph.D. in 1968 before returning to the University of Virginia as the school's first black engineering professor. He also became the first African American faculty member to receive tenure there. In addition to teaching, Harris performed research on aerodynamic noise analysis, hypersonic airflow, and short-takeoff-and-landing airplane technology. Harris eventually moved on to teach at two other universities. First came a year of teaching physics at Southern University in Louisiana. Then he moved to the Massachusetts Institute of Technology (MIT), where he stayed from 1972 to 1979. There he taught aeronautics, astronautics, and ocean engineering. He also started MIT's Office of Minority Education, charged with encouraging minority students in their studies. Harris's efforts won him MIT's 1979 Irwin Sizer Award, given for the most significant improvement to education at the school.

In 1979 Harris took his first position with the National Aeronautics and Space Administration. At NASA's Washington headquarters he served as manager of computational methods in the Office of Aeronautics and Space Technology. He also served as a program manager in the Fluid and Thermal Physics Office. There he performed groundbreaking research in using computers to model airflow, a field known as computational fluid dynamics. He returned to MIT in 1980 and taught until 1985, when he accepted the position of dean of the school of engineering at the University of Connecticut.

Harris's achievements in five years at Connecticut were many. He established an institute for environmental research and began partnerships between the school and area aerospace companies, such as United Technologies and Pratt & Whitney. He greatly boosted the recruiting and enrollment of minority students. Harris, whose early marriage had ended in divorce, married again in 1985. He had a total of seven children.

Among the areas Harris investigated during his academic career were shock wave patterns in gas mixtures, new techniques for analyzing aerodynamic noise, and hypersonic airflow. His study of the broadband noises created by helicopter rotors was of special interest to the U.S. Defense Department. Defense engineers used his discoveries to design quieter military helicopters, and Harris considered these studies and the several papers he produced on the subject to be his most significant achievement as an engineer.

In 1990 Harris was appointed vice president of the University of Tennessee Space Institute, where he steered the school through a reputation-threatening plagiarism scandal. He also reshaped its research program, focusing on space propulsion, energy conversion, laser applications, environmental studies, and applied mathematics. In the course of Harris's career in academia, he published more than one hundred technical papers.

In 1992 Harris was named a fellow of the AIAA for his research and education achievements, and he was also appointed the Herbert S. and Jane Gregory Distinguished Lecturer at the college of engineering of the University of Florida. That same year, Harris returned to NASA. He was drawn by new NASA administrator Daniel Goldin's call for NASA to put a new emphasis on aeronautics and lead a new age of American aviation progress.

Joins NASA in New Post

As NASA's first associate administrator for aeronautics, Harris supervised the Langley, Lewis, and Ames Research Centers and the Ames-Dryden Flight Research Facility and oversaw the agency's $1.6 billion aeronautics research budget. Programs under his direction included efforts to design an advanced supersonic transport, the runway-to-orbit national aerospace plane, and work on new supercomputers to improve modeling of aerodynamic forces and design better aircraft. Engineers employed under Harris also pursued work on improving the structure, engines, and instrumentation of airliners, testing new sensors to detect dangerous wind shear, and modernizing air traffic control.

While at NASA, Harris also served on the U.S. Army Science Board. This continued his long tradition of participating in advisory groups, including the National Research Council's Commission on Engineering and Technical Systems, the Board on Engineering Education, the Air Force Studies Board, the Committee on Aeronautical Technologies, and the National Science Foundation's Engineering Advisory Committee.

SOURCES:

Anderson, Priscilla, NASA Aeronautics Public Affairs office, interview with Matthew A. Bille, February 18, 1994.

"Dr. Wesley L. Harris" (biographical data sheet), NASA Public Affairs Office, December, 1993.

"The First 'A': NASA Aeronautics Research" (booklet), NASA Public Affairs Office, undated.

"Wes Harris: In Love with the Sky" (biographical sketch), NASA Public Affairs Office, undated.

—Sketch by Matthew A. Bille

Haldan Keffer Hartline
1903-1983
American physiologist and biophysicist

Haldan Keffer Hartline was a renowned physiologist who spent almost half a century investigating the process of vision. An early fascination with the metabolism of nerve cells led him to study the workings of the eye, especially the retinal mechanisms involved in vision and the electrical activity occurring in the individual cells of the retina and optic nerve. His comparative studies of the retinas of arthropods, mollusks, and vertebrates—representing each of the three major phyla having well-developed eyes—established principles of retinal physiology, thus providing the foundations for further investigations into the neurophysiology of vision and leading to an enhanced understanding of the wider realm of sense perception. For his work on analyzing the chemical and physiological retinal mechanisms of vision, he shared the 1967 Nobel Prize in physiology or medicine.

Hartline was born on December 22, 1903, in Bloomsburg, Pennsylvania, to Daniel Schollenberger Hartline and Harriet Franklin Hartline. He attended college at Lafayette College in Easton, Pennsylvania, graduating with a B.S. in 1923. He went on to study retinal electrophysiology as a graduate student at Johns Hopkins University, obtaining his M.D. in 1927. Hartline spent the next two years at Johns Hopkins University as a National Research Council fellow in medical sciences.

Between 1929 and 1931, Hartline was a Johnson Traveling Research Scholar from the University of Pennsylvania to the universities of Leipzig and Munich. He travelled extensively in Germany during those years before returning to the United States, where he joined the Eldridge Reeves Johnson Research Foundation for Medical Physics as an assistant professor of biophysics at the University of Pennsylvania. Hartline married Mary Elizabeth Kraus on April 11, 1936. They had three sons: Daniel Keffer, Peter Haldan, and Frederick Flanders.

Records Single Nerve Fiber Activity

From the early days of his career, Hartline was fascinated by the metabolism of nerve cells, and he eventually focused his attention on the workings of individual cells in the retina of the eye. During the late 1920s and early 1930s, Hartline used recently-developed methods of fiber isolation to record the activity of single nerve fibers in the retina. He began by experimenting with *Limulus Polyphemus,* the horseshoe crab. He chose this primitive creature because it possessed a feature that was ideal for his research: a compound eye with a long optic nerve and large individual photoreceptors. It seemed to Hartline that working with the horseshoe crab might allow him to record the electrical behavior of single nerve fibers. He succeeded in 1932, while working at the Eldridge Reeves Johnson Foundation. Hartline and Columbia University psychophysiologist Clarence H. Graham managed to isolate single nerve fibers from the optic nerve, placed electrodes on those single fibers, stimulated them with light, and recorded the nerve impulses that occurred. This was the first record of the activity of a single optic nerve fiber, and it proved to Hartline and Graham that their theories had been correct: information is relayed through individual optic nerve fibers by a series of uniform nerve impulses.

Hartline moved into another field of vision in 1938, when he began to study the vertebrate eye, using microdissection techniques to record the activity of individual fibers in the optic nerve of frogs. While recording the nerve impulses from the single nerve fibers lying behind the rods and cones of the eye, he found that the fibers making up the nerve did not all behave in the same way. Some were stimulated by steady light, others were stimulated by the light when it first hit the retina, and still others were stimulated only as the light was shut off. Hartline demonstrated that visual information begins to be differentiated in the retina and in the receptors themselves, as soon as the stimulation occurs, before the information can be conducted more deeply into the central nervous system. This research afforded new insights into the working of the retina. It also provided a new understanding of how the mechanisms of vision were integrated with, and how they affected, the nervous system as a whole. For this discovery, Hartline was awarded the Howard Crosby Warren Medal of the Society of Experimental Psychologists in 1948.

Hartline continued his teaching and research at the University of Pennsylvania, becoming professor of biophysics and chair of the department at Johns Hopkins in 1949. In 1953, Hartline joined the faculty of Rockefeller University in New York as professor of neurophysiology. There, Hartline began investigating the phenomenon of inhibition in the retina of the compound eye, using the horseshoe crab as a subject once again. He and his colleague, Floyd Ratliff, demonstrated the electrical response of nerve fibers and cells to light hitting the retina, and the mechanism by which this response allows the eye to differentiate shapes. He found that the receptor cells in the eye are interconnected in such a way that when one is stimulated, others nearby are depressed, thus sharpening the contrast in light patterns. In the 1960s, Hartline extended these studies to the dynamics of the receptors and their interactions, with a view to understanding visual phenomena such as motion detection. Hartline's findings eventually led to the development of a set of mathematical equations expressing the interrelationship of the receptor units of the compound eye; this information has been key to understanding brightness and contrast in the retinal image.

Work on Retinal Cells Leads to Nobel Prize

For his work on electrical activity on the cellular level within the eye, Hartline shared the 1967 Nobel prize in physiology or medicine with the American biologist **George Wald** and the Swedish neurophysiologist **Ragnar Granit**. This was not the only award received by Hartline during this period; he also received the A. A. Michelson Award of Case Institute, 1964, and the Lighthouse Award in 1969. In addition to the Nobel Prize and the other awards and honors received during his lifetime, Hartline was also presented with a number of honorary degrees. He was awarded doctorates from Lafayette College in 1959, the University of Pennsylvania in 1971, Rockefeller University in 1976, the University of Maryland in 1978, and Syracuse University in 1979; an LL.D. from Johns Hopkins University in 1971; and an M.D. from the University of Freiburg in 1971.

Hartline was a member of many important scientific organizations, many of them elective. He was elected to the National Academy of Sciences in 1948, and to the American Academy of Arts and Sciences in 1957. Hartline also held memberships in the American Philosophical Society and the Biophysics Society, and in 1966 was elected a foreign member of the Royal Society, London. The Optical Society of America made him an honorary member, as did the Physiology Society (U.K.). He was a member of Phi Beta Kappa and of Sigma Xi.

Hartline's death on March 17, 1983, in Fallston, Maryland, did not mean the end of the association of the name "Hartline" with scientific research. Richard Hartline, born in Reading, Pennsylvania, on July 21, 1932, studied biochemistry and organic chemistry. Peter Haldan Hartline, born in Philadelphia, Pennsylvania, on January 26, 1942, chose to specialize in neurophysiology and animal behavior, and—like his father—elected to conduct research on eyes.

SELECTED WRITINGS BY HARTLINE:

Books

Studies on Excitation and Inhibition in the Retina: A Collection of Papers from the Laboratory of H. Keffer Hartline, compiled by Floyd Ratliff, Chapman and Hall (London), 1974.

SOURCES:

Periodicals

"Hartline is Elected Optical Society Honorary Member," *Physics Today,* April 1980.

New York Times, March 19, 1983, p. 28.

—Sketch by Jessica Jahiel

Odd Hassel
1897-1981
Norwegian physical chemist

Through twenty-five years of painstaking work, Norwegian physical chemist Odd Hassel confirmed the long-suspected three-dimensional nature of organic molecules, and his work in this field, called conformational analysis, altered the perception of chemistry. He received the Nobel Prize for chemistry in 1969, which he shared with the English chemist **Derek H. R. Barton**. Although other Norwegians had won the prize before him, Hassel's win was a special source of pride for his countrymen, for he was the first winner whose work had been carried out almost entirely in Norway.

One of a set of twins, Odd Hassel was born May 17, 1897, in Kristiana (now Oslo), Norway. His father Ernst was a gynecologist. His mother, Mathilde Klaveness Hassel, raised her four sons and one daughter alone after her husband died when Odd was eight years old. While his brothers, including his twin Lars, entered law and civil engineering, Hassel chose a different route. He had disliked school except for mathematics and science. The interest he developed in chemistry during high school evolved into his major area of study at the University of Oslo, which he entered in 1915.

Hassel toured France and Italy for a year after his graduation in 1920, a common practice at the time. In 1922 he worked at K. Fajans's laboratory in Munich where he discovered adsorption indicators, organic dyes used in the analysis of silver and halide ions for greater accuracy. He returned to school to study at the University of Berlin, a center for chemistry and physics, where he was recommended for and received a Rockefeller scholarship. He earned his doctorate in 1924.

While in Berlin, Hassel worked at the Kaiser Wilhelm Institute, and learned the technique known as X-ray crystallography. In this method of analysis the atomic structure of a substance can be determined by striking a pure crystal of the substance with X rays. After passing through the crystal, the rays are bent, or diffracted; the pattern of this diffraction is captured on photographic film and, when analyzed, reveals the arrangement of the atoms within the substance.

Doughnuts, Boats, and Chairs

In 1925 Hassel returned to the University of Oslo as an instructor, and a year later was named associate professor of physical chemistry. In 1930 he began to investigate the three-dimensional structure of molecules, particularly ring-shaped carbon molecules. Many important organic molecules, including several carbohydrates and steroids, are built on a ring-shaped base. Although it was widely believed that all the carbon atoms in these molecules were arranged in one plane (rather like a doughnut lying on a plate), the possibility that they were actually three-dimensional had been proposed in 1885. Molecules having six or more carbon atoms, reasoned German chemist **Johann Friedrich Wilhelm Adolf von Baeyer**, would be under too much strain to lie flat; in 1890 chemist Ulrich Sachse suggested two configurations of cyclohexane (a six atom carbon ring). One, the boat form, was represented as four atoms framing the "sides" laying in the same plane with the remaining atoms in the plane above them, like the bow and stern of a canoe. The second, or chair configuration, resembled a reclining shape having four atoms in the central plane, with one end atom above, and one below. In the absence of more conclusive experiments, however, most scientists maintained that cyclohexane resembled a doughnut on a plate.

Hassel's work was to correct that view. His primary investigations used the X-ray crystallography technique he had learned in Berlin; the drawback however, was that the technique could be used only with solids. A technique called dipole measurement, the analysis of positive and negative charges in a molecule, was also used. But electron diffraction proved to be the best method to investigate the structure of molecules because it could be used with gases and free molecules. By 1938 Hassel's laboratory was able to afford an electron diffraction unit, and he devoted the next five years to studying cyclohexane. Not only did he confirm that the boat and chair forms did indeed exist as predicted nearly fifty years before, Hassel also discovered that the molecules oscillated between the boat and chair forms at an enormous rate, with the latter form occurring predominantly. His investigations made it possible to predict the chemical properties of many organic substances whose base was cyclohexane. He also determined that the hydrogen atoms bonded to the carbon atoms either perpendicular to the four-atom plane (axial) or parallel (equatorial). These observations further deepened the behavioral chemistry of cyclohexanes and their related compounds—substituted cyclohexanes.

Continues His Work in Concentration Camp

Hassel continued his work on cyclohexane even after Germany invaded Norway in 1940. He refused to publish his papers in German scientific journals, which limited the dissemination of his ideas. Some of his most important research was first reported in small Norwegian-language journals not circulated outside of Norway. In 1943, the Germans shut down the University of Oslo. Hassel, along with the other faculty members and scholars, was sent to a concentration camp at Grini, near Oslo. During his two years of imprisonment Hassel carried on his work, teaching physical chemistry without the consent of his captors. Despite his shy, reticent nature, he enlisted other scientists to work with him, including Per Andersen, and Ragnar Frisch, who remained a good friend and later received the Nobel Prize for economics the same year Hassel received one for chemistry. They were freed from Grini in November of 1944.

During the 1950s Hassel turned his attention to the physical structure of charge-transfer compounds. In such a compound, one part "donates" an electron to the other part, which "accepts" it. Because many of these compounds were too unstable to study in gaseous form, Hassel studied the solid forms with X-ray crystallography. He concluded that many of the theories about how these molecules worked were incorrect, and devised a new, simple set of rules that would inform the arrangement and size of the molecular bonds.

Hassel retired from the University of Oslo in 1964, but continued to research and publish until 1971. In the course of his career he published over 250 scientific papers, as well as *Kristallchemie* (1934), the first modern review of work in crystal chemistry. It was quickly translated into English, as *Crystal Chemistry,* and Russian. The book became a standard reference work for crystallographers and chemists throughout the field. From 1947 to 1957 Hassel was also the Norwegian editor of *Acta Chimica Scandinavica.* During his long career Hassel received numerous honors for his contributions to science. Apart from being honored with the Fridtjof Nansen Award in 1946, the Gunnerus Medal from the Royal Norwegian Academy of Sciences was awarded him in 1964, as well as the Guldber and Waage's Law of Mass Action Memorial from the Norwegian Chemical Society, of which he was an honorary fellow. In addition, he was a fellow of both the Royal Norwegian, and Royal Swedish Academies of Sciences, and Royal Danish Academy of Science. An honorary fellow of the British Chemical Society besides, Hassel received honorary degrees from the University of Copenhagen (1950) and the University of Stockholm (1960). He was made a knight of the Order of Saint Olav. In 1969, he shared the Nobel Prize for Chemistry with Derek Barton "for their contributions to the development of the concept of conformation and its application in chemistry." Speaking of the award to the *New York Times,* Hassel commented, "I had been among the chemistry candidates before, but did not expect to get the prize now. It was indeed very pleasing." He had doubts about going to Stockholm to accept the prize, however, saying, "I detest public appearances and have to think it over thoroughly." Hassel rarely attended international conferences and never married. "He prefers molecules," noted one of his students. After his twin brother died in 1980, Hassel reportedly lost his "zest for life." On May 15, 1981, Hassel died in Oslo, just two days before his eighty-fourth birthday.

SELECTED WRITINGS BY HASSEL:

Books

Kristallchemie, [Dresden], 1934, translation by R. C. Evans published as *Crystal Chemistry,* 1935.

SOURCES:

Books

Magill, Frank, editor, *The Nobel Prize Winners: Chemistry,* Volume 3: *1969–1989,* Salem Press, 1990.

Periodicals

New York Times, October 31, 1969, p. 20.
Science, November 7, 1969, pp. 718–720.

—*Sketch by F.C. Nicholson*

Herbert A. Hauptman
1917-
American mathematician and biophysicist

Herbert A. Hauptman has spent most of his adult life in and around the laboratory. In the early 1950s, he and his fellow New Yorker and former classmate, **Jerome Karle**, developed a mathematical system, usually referred to as the "direct method," for the interpretation of data on atomic structure collected through X-ray crystallography. The system, however, did not come into general use until the 1960s, and it was only in 1985 that Hauptman and Karle were jointly awarded the Nobel Prize in chemistry for their accomplishment.

Herbert Aaron Hauptman was born in New York City on February 14, 1917, the son of Israel Hauptman, an Austrian immigrant who worked as a printer, and Leah (Rosenfeld) Hauptman. He grew up in the Bronx and graduated from Townsend Harris High School. At the City College of New York, he majored in mathematics and received a Bachelor of Science degree in 1937. Karle, his later collaborator, also graduated from City College the same year. Hauptman went on to complete a master's degree in mathematics at Columbia University in 1939. He married Edith Citrynell, a schoolteacher, on November 10, 1940; they eventually had two daughters, Barbara and Carol. Hauptman worked for two years as a statistician in the United States Bureau of the Census before serving in the United States Army Air Force from 1942 to 1947. After his period of service ended, Hauptman went to work as a physicist and mathematician at the Naval Research Laboratory in Washington, remaining there until 1970. While working at the laboratory, he enrolled in the doctoral program in mathematics at the University of Maryland and received his Ph.D. in 1955.

At the Naval Research Laboratory, Hauptman renewed his acquaintance with Karle, who had come to the laboratory in 1946. The two men soon began to work together on the problem of determining molecular structures through the methodology of X-ray crystallography. Most of the work which later led to their joint Nobel Prize was done between 1950 and 1956. A brief monograph, *Solution of the Phase Problem, 1. The Centrosymmetric Crystal,* was published in 1953 that revealed many of the results of their studies.

Development of the Direct Method

The German physicist **Max von Laue** had discovered as far back as 1912 that it was possible to determine the arrangement of atoms within a crystal by studying the patterns formed on a photographic plate by X rays passed through a crystal. Since that time X-ray crystallography had become a standard tool for chemists, physicists, biologists, and other scientists concerned with determining the atomic structure of substances. X-ray crystallography, for example, had made possible the discovery of the double-helical structure of deoxyribonucleic acid (DNA) by molecular biologists **Francis Crick**, **James Watson**, and others in the 1950s. The problem with the technique was that interpreting the patterns on the photographic plates was a very difficult, laborious, and time-consuming task. The accurate determination of the atomic structure of a single substance could require one or more years of work based upon indirect inferences which often amounted to educated guesswork. The greatest difficulty arose from the fact that while photographic film could record the intensity of the X-ray dots that formed the patterns, it could not record the phases (the minute deviations from straight lines) of the X rays themselves.

The great achievement of Hauptman and Karle was to develop a very complex series of mathematical formulas, relying heavily on probability theory, which made it possible to correctly infer the phases from the data which was recorded on the photographic film. Their new mathematical system came to be known as the determination of molecular structure by "direct method." They demonstrated the workability of their new technique in 1954 by calculating by hand, in collaboration with researchers at the United States Geological Survey, the atomic structure of the mineral colemanite.

Hauptman and Karle's system met with a good deal of skepticism and resistance from the specialists in X-ray crystallography in the 1950s and was largely ignored for about ten years. This was partly due to the fact that most crystallographers of the time lacked the mathematical knowledge and sophistication to make use of the new technique. It also stemmed from the fact that the necessary mathematical calculations themselves were a laborious process. It was the introduction of computers and the development of special programs to deal with the Hauptman-Karle method in the 1960s that finally led to its widespread acceptance and use. The work that originally required months or years to complete could now be done in a matter of hours or, at most, days. By the mid 1980s the atomic structures of approximately 40,000 substances had been determined through use of the direct method, as compared to only some 4,000 determined by other methods in all the years prior to about 1970, and some 4,000 to 5,000 new structures were being determined each year.

Hauptman left the Naval Research Laboratory in 1970 to become head of the biophysics laboratory at the Medical Foundation of Buffalo, a small but highly regarded organization specializing in research on endocrinology. He also became professor of biophysical science at the State University of New York at Buffalo. Hauptman served as executive vice president and research director of the Medical Foundation from 1972 to 1985 and president from 1985 onwards. There he worked to perfect the direct method and to extend its use to the study of very large atomic structures. On June 2, 1993, the weekly scientific periodical *Inside R & D* announced that Hauptman, then aged seventy-six, had developed a new computer software package, called "Shake-and-Bake," which could "routinely solve structures of up to 300 or 400 atoms" in a few hours or days. In recognition of his skill and knowledge, Hauptman has received numerous awards, including the 1985 Nobel Prize in chemistry shared with Karle, the Award in Pure Sciences from the Research Society of America in 1959, and also with Karle, the A. L. Patterson Memorial Award of the American Crystallography Association in 1984.

SELECTED WRITINGS BY HAUPTMAN:

Books

(With Jerome Karle) *Solution of the Phase Problem, 1. The Centrosymmetric Crystal,* American Crystallographic Association, 1953.

Crystal Structure Determination: The Role of the Cosine Seminvariants, Plenum Press, 1972.

SOURCES:

Books

Nobel Prize Winners, H. W. Wilson, 1987, pp. 418–20.

The Nobel Prize Winners: Chemistry, Volume 3, Salem Press, 1990, pp. 1113–18.

Periodicals

Inside R & D, June 2, 1993, p. 9.

New York Times, October 17, 1985, pp. 1, B12; October 18, 1985, p. B3; October 20, 1985, p. 47.

Physics Today, December, 1985, pp. 20–21.

Science, January 24, 1986, pp. 362–64.

Scientific American, December, 1985, p. 78.

Time, October 28, 1985, p. 86.

—*Sketch by John E. Little*

Felix Hausdorff
1868-1942
German mathematician

Felix Hausdorff was a mathematician who contributed to the subject of topology, a field of geometry which studies the shapes of objects. His greatest contributions were the assertions that geometric spaces could be regarded as sets of points and sets of relationships among those points. These proposals have come to be called Hausdorff's Topological Spaces and Hausdorff's Neighborhood Axioms. His work had an impact on set theory, the study of relationships between sets of similar items.

Hausdorff was born on November 8, 1868, in the German city of Breslau, which is now Wroclaw, Poland. His father, Louis Hausdorff, was a successful dry goods merchant; his mother was Johanna Tietz Hausdorff. The family moved to Leipzig, Germany, in 1871. The young Hausdorff attended public school until the age of 10, when he enrolled at the Nicolai Gymnasium; he graduated in 1887. After studying astronomy and mathematics in Freiburg and Berlin, Hausdorff earned his Ph.D. in 1891 in Leipzig. His dissertation explored the theory of astronomic refraction, and his first four published papers dealt with topics in optics and astronomy.

In 1891, Hausdorff volunteered to serve in Infantry Regiment 106 in Leipzig. He achieved the rank of vice-sergeant before removing himself from consideration for further promotion in 1894. He was Jewish, and no acknowledged Jews had been commissioned as officers in the German military for nearly 15 years. In 1896, following his father's death, Hausdorff succeeded him as a partner in the publishing firm Hausdorff and Company, which produced the leading trade magazine for spinning, weaving, and dyeing. That same year, he was accepted as a lecturer at Leipzig University.

The Literary Hausdorff

Hausdorff had a lively interest in the fine arts and in philosophy. He was an accomplished pianist, and would have devoted his advanced studies to music except for the objections of his father. Throughout his life, his closest friends were musicians and artists, as well as several prominent mathematicians (including **Pavel S. Aleksandrov**). He developed a lifelong interest in the philosophy of Friedrich Nietzsche, carefully examining the philosopher's ideas, sometimes agreeing with them and sometimes not. He associated with other followers of Nietzsche, and even corresponded with the philosopher's sister.

In 1897, the first of Hausdorff's four full-length literary works was published. He wrote these books under the pseudonym Dr. Paul Mongré so that he could express himself freely without jeopardizing his university position. The first book, *Sant' Ilario: Thoughts from the Landscape of Zarathustra,* was primarily a collection of aphorisms relating to Nietzsche's *Thus Spoke Zarathustra.* It was published by the same company that had published Nietzsche's book, and was even produced with a similar cover.

The second book written under the name Mongré, *Chaos in Cosmic Choice,* dealt with metaphysical relationships between space and time. Hausdorff presented the same concepts in "The Space Problem," his inaugural lecture upon being appointed as an associate professor at Leipzig University in 1903. He had worked as a lecturer at Leipzig since 1896, but his promotion was opposed by a fourth of the faculty on the grounds that Hausdorff was of the "faith of Moses."

Mongré's third major literary work was *Ecstasies,* a volume of sonnets and poems published in 1900. He also wrote *The Doctor's Honor,* a satirical play that was successfully produced in Hamburg and Berlin; the work is an attack on the resurgence of the duel as a means of defending one's honor, a practice that accompanied the movement to establish an intellectual and political elitism in society.

The Mathematical Hausdorff

In 1897, Hausdorff began publishing papers on topics in mathematics, including non-Euclidean geometry, complex numbers, and probability. He became interested in **Georg Cantor**'s work on set theory —the study of the relationships between groups of similar items, such as numbers or letters—and during the summer semester of 1901 taught what may have been the first course on set theory to be presented in Germany. Also about this time, **David Hilbert** was publishing work applying set theory to geometry; his work may have been the inspiration for Hausdorff's greatest mathematical accomplishment.

In 1910, Hausdorff accepted a position as associate professor at the University of Bonn. Although he had written one or two technical articles per year for two decades, he published nothing from 1910 until 1914. He moved to Greifswald in 1913 to become a professor at the university there. The following year, he published his monumental *Grundzüge der Mengenlehre* (Basic Features of Set Theory). The *Grundzüge* was a comprehensive text dealing with set theory and point set topology (the idea that geometric shapes can be thought of as sets of points). Although the book was written for students at the advanced undergraduate level, Hausdorff noted in the preface that the volume also offered new ideas and methods to his professional colleagues. By organizing point set theory with just the right choice of axioms, he so thoroughly revised the related existing work that his book became the foundation on which modern topology has been developed.

In 1919, Hausdorff introduced another revolutionary concept. He generalized the notion of dimension (e.g., a two-dimensional triangle or a three-dimensional cube) to include the possibility of objects with fractal dimensions. (Fractals are geometric forms which, when examined from whatever distance, exhibit the same general shape.) The study of fractals has applications to such diverse areas as weather forecasting and the fracturing of glass or metal.

As Hausdorff noted in his preface to the *Grundzüge,* "in an area where simply nothing is obvious, conclusions frequently paradoxical, [and] the plausible wrong, there is hardly a remedy besides a consistent deduction to save oneself and the reader from deceptions." Indeed, one of his talents was that of clear exposition. A review of the *Grundzüge* appearing in the *Bulletin of the American Mathematical Society* praised its "happy choice and arrangement of subject matter, the careful diction, the smooth, vigorous and concise literary style, and the adaptable notation; above all . . . the highly pleasing unifications and generalizations and the harmonious weaving of numerous original results into the texture of the whole."

In 1921 Hausdorff returned to the University of Bonn, where he worked as a professor for the rest of his career. He was respected as the most capable mathematician in Bonn and as a professor whose lectures were well reasoned and clearly delivered. He taught until 1935, when he reached the mandatory retirement age of 67. He continued to publish mathematical papers until 1938.

The Personal Hausdorff

In 1899, Hausdorff married Charlotte Goldschmidt, the daughter of a doctor. His only child, a daughter named Lenore (usually called Nora), was born the following year. Although Charlotte came from a Jewish family, she had been baptized a Protestant Christian in 1896 and Lenore was similarly baptized. The members of the Hausdorff family held an enduring devotion for one another. Though Hausdorff was high-strung, he loved to listen to beautiful music with friends who were so close to him that they could share the experience without need of words. He maintained a congenial but reserved demeanor with acquaintances and was prone to depression; yet, he enjoyed dining with friends, and in their company he could relax, have some wine, and be quite jovial. When the family moved to Bonn in 1921, they bought a lovely home on a quiet street (which would be renamed Hausdorffstraβe in 1949). Hausdorff's normal routine was to spend the evenings enjoying the company of family or guests; taking advantage of the quiet nighttime hours, he would then work quite late in his study, enjoying strong tea and stout cigars. He would sleep until late in the morning and then go to the university.

Although he had been a member of the German Democratic Party for three years following the end of World War I, Hausdorff did not participate actively in politics. He believed in freedom and individual rights. In his 1904 essay "God's Shadow," written under the Mongré pseudonym, Hausdorff had warned against the "blonde beast" and the mysticism of racial purity. In 1921, he inscribed a copy of his book *Sant' Ilario* as a birthday gift to his friend Theodor Posner with a newly-written poem bemoaning the failure of the intelligentsia in the Weimar Republic and the decreasing political wisdom of the populace.

The anti-Semitism that had blocked his promotion in the infantry and threatened to prevent his promotion at Leipzig University continued to plague Hausdorff throughout his lifetime. For instance, a young professor whose 1926 appointment Hausdorff had supported became openly anti-Semitic in 1933, repudiating any former contacts with Jews and refusing to join the rest of the faculty in attending seminars given by Jewish mathematicians. Some of Hausdorff's Jewish friends emigrated to escape the persecution; others whose emigration was thwarted committed suicide.

Suicide was a topic addressed by Nietzsche; consequently, it had been a subject for reflection by Hausdorff. Zarathustra advocated "voluntary death" as a consummation of life for the noble man. "Death and Return," an 1899 essay by Mongré, treated the subject in the form of a letter to a fictitious depressed friend. In it, the author advises that "this final remedy really helps, that it does not [merely] plunge one into a futile expense for morphine or revolver cartridges."

The infamous November pogrom of 1938, in which government-fostered attacks resulted in the arrest of 20,000 Jews and 25 million marks' worth of damage to hundreds of Jewish homes, shops, and synagogues, occurred the day after Hausdorff's seventieth birthday. Charlotte Hausdorff and her sister, Edith Pappenheim (who had come to live with them a few months earlier), tried to bolster Hausdorff's spirits. After this pogrom, Hausdorff was required to adopt the additional first name Israel, and his wife the name Sara. He continued to work on his mathematics, but no longer published his results; instead, he put them into storage. Another ugly incident from this period happened in late 1941 when Hausdorff took his wife to the university dental clinic. As she was being treated, a senior staff doctor rushed toward her, ripped the napkin from her neck, and said, "Get out, get out. When Jews are sick, they should hang themselves."

In mid-January of 1942, the Hausdorffs received notification to report to an internment camp located at a former monastery; this would probably be followed by deportation to a concentration camp. After organizing their affairs and leaving property disposal and cremation instructions with trusted friends, Hausdorff, his wife, and her sister committed suicide on January 26, 1942. That evening, each of them took an overdose of the sedative barbital and sat down to read. Hausdorff died with his glasses on, holding a copy of the novel *Renate* by Theodor Storm.

On January 25, 1980, a memorial plaque honoring Hausdorff was placed at the entrance of the Mathematical Institute at the University of Bonn. From January 24 to February 28, 1992, an exhibition of photographs and personal, literary, and mathematical documents was held at the University of Bonn, commemorating the fiftieth anniversary of Hausdorff's death.

SELECTED WRITINGS BY HAUSDORFF:

Books

Grundzüge der Mengenlehre, Chelsea Publishing, 1965.

Set Theory, 2nd edition, Chelsea Publishing, 1978.

SOURCES:

Books

Boyer, Carl B., *A History of Mathematics,* Wiley, 1991, pp. 620–622.

Gillispie, Charles Coulston, editor, *Dictionary of Scientific Biography,* Volume VI, Scribner's, 1974, pp. 176–177.

Periodicals

Chowdhury, M. R., "Hausdorff," *Mathematical Intelligencer,* winter, 1990, pp. 4–5.

Shields, Allen, "Felix Hausdorff: *Grundzüge der Mengenlehre,* " *Mathematical Intelligencer,* winter, 1989, pp. 6–9.

Other

Brieskorn, Dr. Egbert, letters to Loretta Hall, 1993–94.

Felix Hausdorff—Paul Mongré—1868–1942 (in German), catalog for the 1992 memorial colloquium and exhibition, University of Bonn, 1992.

—Sketch by Loretta Hall

Stephen Hawking
1942-
English theoretical physicist

Stephen Hawking has been called the most brilliant theoretical physicist since **Albert Einstein**. His work concentrates on the puzzling cosmic bodies called black holes and extends to such specialized

Stephen Hawking

fields as particle physics, supersymmetry, and quantum gravity. The origin and fate of the universe are a central concern of Hawking's work. Though few people are able to understand these abstruse subjects, Hawking has gained a worldwide following, not only among other scientists, but among a great many laypeople. As an author and lecturer, he has become so famous as to approach rock-star celebrity.

Stephen William Hawking was born on January 8, 1942, in Oxford, England. He often refers to the fact that his birth date coincided with the 300th anniversary of Galileo Galilei 's death. Hawking was the eldest child of an intellectual and accomplished family. His father, Frank Hawking, was a physician and research biologist who specialized in tropical diseases; his mother, Isobel, the daughter of a Glasgow physician and a well-read, lively woman, was active for many years in Britain's Liberal Party. After Stephen's birth, the Hawkings had two daughters, Mary and Philippa, and adopted a boy, Edward.

Stephen Hawking's earliest years were spent in Highgate, a London suburb. In 1950, when he was eight, the family moved to St. Albans, a cathedral town some twenty miles northwest of London. Two years later, his family enrolled him in St. Albans School, a private institution affiliated with the cathedral. As Michael White and John Gribbin describe the young schoolboy in *Stephen Hawking: A Life in Science,* "He was eccentric and awkward, skinny and puny. His school uniform always looked a mess and, according to friends, he jabbered rather than talked clearly, having inherited a slight lisp from his father." Young Hawking's abilities made little impact on his teachers or fellow students. But he already knew he wanted to be a scientist, and by the time he reached his middle teens, he had decided to pursue physics or mathematics.

Awarded Oxford Scholarship

Gangly and unathletic, Hawking formed close friendships with a small group of other precocious boys at school. Intrigued by subjects that focused on measurable quantities and objective reasoning, Hawking began to show increasing skill at mathematics, and soon he was outdistancing his peers with high grades while spending very little time on homework. In 1958 Hawking and his pals built a primitive computer that actually worked. In the spring of 1959, Hawking won an open scholarship in natural sciences to University College, Oxford—his father's old college—and in October he enrolled there. It was at Oxford that his unusual abilities began to become more obvious. Hawking's ease at handling difficult problems made it seem to others that he didn't need to study. In *Stephen Hawking's Universe,* John Boslough wrote, "He took an independent and freewheeling approach to studies although his tutor, Dr. Robert Berman, recalls that he and other dons were aware that Hawking had a first-rate mind, completely different from his contemporaries."

Pioneers Studies in Black Holes

In 1962, after receiving a first-class honors degree from Oxford, Hawking set off for Cambridge University to begin studying for a Ph.D. in cosmology. Now he was beginning to deal with some of the themes that would preoccupy him throughout his life. One of these was the poorly understood question of black holes. As scientists were later to realize, a black hole is a cosmic body that by its very nature can never be seen. One type of black hole is thought to be the remnant of a collapsed star, which possesses such intense gravity that nothing can escape from it, not even light. Hawkings was also intrigued by "space-time singularities," those phenomena in the physical universe or moments in its history where physics seems to break down. In attempting to understand a black hole and the space-time singularity at its center, Hawking made pioneering studies, using formulas developed more than half a century earlier by Einstein.

Hawking received his Ph.D. in 1965 and obtained a fellowship in theoretical physics at Gonville and Caius College, Cambridge. He continued his work on black holes, frequently collaborating with **Roger Penrose**, a mathematician a decade his senior, who like Hawking was deeply interested in theories of space-time. Though still in his twenties, Hawking was beginning to acquire a reputation, and he would often attend conferences where he shocked people by questioning the findings of eminent scientists much older than himself.

In 1968, Hawking joined the staff of the Institute of Astronomy in Cambridge. He and Penrose began using complex mathematics to apply the laws of thermodynamics to black holes. He continued to travel to America, the Soviet Union, and other countries, and in 1973, he published a highly technical book, *The Large Scale Structure of Space-Time,* written with G. F. R. Ellis. Not long afterward, Hawking made a startling discovery: whereas virtually all previous thinking assumed that black holes could not emit anything, Hawking theorized that under certain conditions they could emit subatomic particles. These particles became known as Hawking Radiation.

Receives Albert Einstein Award

Early in 1974, at the unusually young age of 32, Hawking was named a fellow of the Royal Society. Soon afterward, he spent a year as Fairchild Distinguished Scholar at the California Institute of Technology in Pasadena. On returning to England, he continued to work toward a theory of the origin of the universe. In this endeavor, he made progress toward linking the theory of relativity, which deals with gravity, with quantum mechanics, which deals with minuscule events inside the atom. Such a theoretical linkage, long sought by researchers, is called the Grand Unification Theory, or GUT. In 1978, Hawking received the Albert Einstein Award of the Lewis and Rose Strauss Memorial Fund, the most prestigious award in theoretical physics. The following year he coedited a book with Werner Israel, called *General Relativity: An Einstein Centenary Survey.* In 1979, Hawking was named Lucasian Professor of Mathematics at Cambridge—a position held three centuries earlier by Sir Isaac Newton. In the 1980s, his work was beginning to lead him to question the big bang theory, which most other scientists were accepting as the probable origin of the universe. Hawking now asked whether there really had ever been a beginning to space-time (a big bang), or whether one state of affairs (one universe, to put it loosely) simply gave birth to another without beginning or end. Hawking suggested that new universes might be born frequently through little-understood anomalies in space-time. He also investigated string theory and exploding black holes, and showed mathematically that numerous miniature black holes may have formed early in the history of our universe.

Publishes Popular Book on the Cosmos

In 1988, Hawking's *A Brief History of Time: From the Big Bang to Black Holes* was published.

Intended for a general audience, it leapt onto best-seller lists in both America and Britain and remained there for several years. In that book, Hawking explained in simple language the evolution of his own thinking about the cosmos. Major articles followed in *Time, Popular Science,* and other magazines; films and television programs featured Hawking. He received honorary degrees from many institutions, including the University of Chicago, Princeton University, and the University of Notre Dame. His numerous awards included the Eddington Medal of the Royal Astronomical Society, in 1975; the Pius XI Gold Medal, in 1975; the Maxwell Medal of the Institute of Physics, in 1976; the Franklin Medal of the Franklin Institute, in 1981; the Gold Medal of the Royal Society, in 1985; the Paul Dirac Medal and Prize, in 1987; and the Britannica Award, in 1989.

In 1965, Hawking married Jane Wilde, and they had two sons and a daughter. The couple separated in 1990. Hawking suffers from amyotrophic lateral sclerosis, also called Lou Gehrig's disease, which confines him to a wheelchair and requires him to use a computer and voice synthesizer to speak.

SELECTED WRITINGS BY HAWKING:

Books

(With G. F. R. Ellis) *The Large Scale Structure of Space-Time,* Cambridge University Press, 1973.

(Editor with Werner Israel) *General Relativity: An Einstein Centenary Survey,* Cambridge University Press, 1979.

Is the End in Sight for Theoretical Physics?: An Inaugural Lecture, Cambridge University Press, 1980.

(Editor with M. Rocek) *Superspace and Supergravity: Proceedings of the Nuffield Workshop, Cambridge, June 16-July 12, 1980,* Cambridge University Press, 1981.

(Editor with G. W. Gibbons and S. T. C. Siklos) *The Very Early Universe: Proceedings of the Nuffield Workshop, Cambridge 21 June to 9 July 1982,* Cambridge University Press, 1983.

(Editor with G. W. Gibbons and P. K. Townsend) *Supersymmetry and Its Applications: Superstrings, Anomalies, and Supergravity: Proceedings of a Workshop Supported by the Ralph Smith and Nuffield Foundations, Cambridge, 23 June to 14 July 1985,* Cambridge University Press, 1986.

(Editor with Werner Israel) *Three Hundred Years of Gravitation,* Cambridge University Press, 1987.

A Brief History of Time: From the Big Bang to Black Holes, Bantam, 1988.

(Editor with G. W. Gibbons and T. Vachaspati) *The Formation and Evolution of Cosmic Strings: Proceedings of a Workshop Supported by the SERC and Held in Cambridge, 3–7 July, 1989,* Cambridge University Press, 1990.

Black Holes and Baby Universes and Other Essays, Bantam, 1993.

Periodicals

"A Brief History of a Brief History," *Popular Science,* August, 1989, pp. 70–72.

SOURCES:

Books

Boslough, John, *Stephen Hawking's Universe,* Quill/William Morrow, 1985.

White, Michael, and John Gribbin, *Stephen Hawking: A Life in Science,* Plume/Penguin, 1992.

Periodicals

Adler, Jerry, with Gerald C. Lubenow and Maggie Malone, "Reading God's Mind," *Newsweek,* June 13, 1988, pp. 56–59.

Begley, Sharon, with Jennifer Foote, "Why Past Is Past," *Newsweek,* December 28, 1992, pp. 52–53.

"A Brief History," *The New Yorker,* April 18, 1988, pp. 30–31.

Jaroff, Leon, "Roaming the Cosmos," *Time,* February 8, 1988, pp. 58–60.

Organ, Troy, "Dignifying Humanity: the Humor of Stephen W. Hawking," *The Humanist,* July/August, 1989, pp. 29–30, 50.

Raymond, Chet, "Stephen Hawking and the Mind of God," *Commonweal,* April 6, 1990, pp. 218–220.

Sampson, Russ, "Two Hours with Stephen Hawking," *Astronomy,* March, 1993, pp. 13–16.

—*Sketch by Wallace Mack White*

W. Lincoln Hawkins
1911-1992
American chemical engineer

A longtime employee of Bell Laboratories, W. Lincoln Hawkins was a chemical engineer whose work helped make universal telephone service possible. Until the late 1940s telephone cables were insulated with a lead coating, which was very expensive; this coating was also too heavy for use in the multi-cable conduits which would be required if most homes were to have telephones. It was clear to many that plastics could be a cheaper and lighter insulating alternative, but every plastic then in existence broke down rapidly when exposed to the elements. Hawkins, working at Bell Laboratories, helped to solve the problem by co-inventing a plastic coating that withstood heat and cold and had a life span of many decades.

Hawkins was always a tinkerer. Born Walter Lincoln Hawkins on March 21, 1911, in Washington D.C., he was the son of William Langston Hawkins, a lawyer for the Census Bureau, and Maude Johnson Hawkins, a science teacher. As a child, he was fascinated with how things worked, and he made spring-driven model boats to sail on Washington's Reflecting Pool. He also constructed a simple radio to listen to baseball games. "I always loved building things," he told Kim E. Pearson in a 1983 interview for *The Crisis.* "When I was about eleven years old, a friend and I tried to build a perpetual motion machine. We didn't know anything about thermodynamics—we had no idea that it couldn't be done." Hawkins's parents hoped their son would pursue a career in medicine, but it was engineering that captured his imagination. He attended Dunbar High School in Washington, a segregated public school renowned for its science and engineering programs—the faculty consisted primarily of African Americans with doctoral degrees who could not get a job elsewhere because of their race. One of his teachers had a new car every year, and when Hawkins learned it was partial compensation for the man's patent on a component of the car's self-starter, he realized that tinkering could actually earn a person a living.

After graduation from Dunbar High School, Hawkins and one other African American student attended the well-known engineering school in Troy, New York, Rensselaer Polytechnic Institute. They were the only black students in the school. The next year they were followed by two more African American students from Dunbar. While nearly two out of three students dropped out of Rensselaer, Hawkins and the three other black students completed their studies in four years. But the Depression awaited Hawkins upon graduation in 1932, so he continued his studies, and by 1934 he had earned a master's degree in chemistry at Howard University in Washington. Following this, he taught for a time in a trade school and then was convinced by a counselor at Howard University to apply for a fellowship in chemistry at McGill University in Canada. He won the fellowship and completed his Ph.D. in chemistry at McGill in 1938. That same year he won a National Research Council Fellowship in alkaloid chemistry and he accepted a position at Columbia University, where he would remain until 1942. During his time at Columbia he met Lilyan Varina Bobo, whom he married on August 19, 1939. They would have two sons.

Becomes First African American at Bell Laboratories

In 1942 Hawkins joined Bell Laboratories in Murray Hills, New Jersey, the first African American scientist to be hired there. Hawkins would stay at Bell for the next thirty-four years, researching and inventing new materials and products for the preservation and recycling of plastics; he completed his career as assistant director of the Chemical Research Laboratory. "I had a ball," Hawkins told Pearson, describing his years of service at the research lab. "There's a world of excitement there that's like nowhere else." Of the 18 domestic and 129 foreign patents Hawkins himself held, by far the most important was that to replace the lead insulation of telephone cables with a new weather-resistant plastic coating. Working together with Vincent Lanza in the late 1940s, he developed additives to create a new polymer that could resist both thermal degradation and the effects of oxidation and last up to seventy years in the elements. "Hawkins's work is arguably one of the major achievements which made universal telephone service economical," a colleague at Bell Laboratories told John Burgess of the *Washington Post.*

But engineering was only part of Hawkins's long and distinguished career. Retiring at age sixty-five, he remained a consultant to Bell on the education and employment of minorities. He also became research director for the Plastics Institute of America in Hoboken, New Jersey, from 1976 to 1983, and he worked privately as a materials consultant. In addition, he often spoke to minority youth about the importance of education. In 1981, he became the first chairman of the American Chemical Society's Project SEED, a campaign to promote science careers to minority students around the country. Hawkins worked for many years with the National Action Council for Minorities in Engineering (NACME), a committee set up by several major companies to get minorities into the field. He was also a member and chair of the board of trustees of Montclair State College in New Jersey. This second career in counseling was as successful as his first in engineering, and the kids listened to him as if he were a member of their own family. Robert Stephens of Montclair State College told Burgess of the *Washington Post* that the students said to themselves: "This guy is my uncle, this guy is my grandfather, but this guy is also somebody important."

Hawkins was widely honored for his pioneering work in polymers, winning the Honor Scroll of the American Institute of Chemistry in 1970, the Percy

Julian Award from the National Organization of Black Chemists and Chemical Engineers in 1977, and the International Medal of the Society of Plastics Engineering in 1984. But by far his most important honor was the 1992 National Medal of Technology, awarded to him not only for his work in chemical engineering, but also for his labors in attempting to bring minorities into the sciences.

Hawkins remained vital and active through his eighth decade. He and his wife traveled around the world and then moved to San Marcos, California, to be near one of their sons. On August 20, 1992, Hawkins died of heart failure at the age of eighty-one. Shortly after his death, an undergraduate research fellowship was established in his name by the National Action Council for Minorities in Engineering.

SELECTED WRITINGS BY HAWKINS:

Books

Polymer Degradation and Stabilization, Springer Verlag, 1984.

SOURCES:

Books

Sammons, Vivian Ovelton, *Blacks in Science and Medicine,* Hemisphere Publishing Corporation, 1990, pp. 114–115.

Periodicals

Burgess, John, "High Honors for a Telephone Pioneer," *Washington Post,* June 24, 1992, pp. F1-F2.

"Honoring a Pioneering Leader in Science," *About . . . Time,* March, 1993, p. 9.

Lambert, Bruce, "W. Lincoln Hawkins, 81, a Chemist and Inventor," *New York Times,* August 23, 1992, p. L46.

Pearson, Kim E., "Pioneering Black Bell Labs Engineer Still at Work at 71," *The Crisis,* April, 1983, pp. 192–193.

"W. Lincoln Hawkins Honored by President Bush," *American Chemical Society Chemunity News,* September, 1992, p. 3.

—*Sketch by J. Sydney Jones*

Walter Haworth
1883-1950
English chemist

Walter Haworth's earliest research was influenced by his contact with William Perkin at the University of Manchester and involved a study of terpenes, a class of hydrocarbons often found in plants. The work for which he is best known, however, involves his studies of various carbohydrates, including a number of important monosaccharides, disaccharides, and polysaccharides. Among his finest achievements was the determination of the molecular structure for glucose, perhaps the most important of all monosaccharides. The method he used for designating the formula of glucose and those of other carbohydrates is well known today to any student of organic chemistry as the Haworth formula. The 1937 Nobel Prize in chemistry was awarded to Haworth in recognition not only of his work on carbohydrates but also for his elucidation of the structure of vitamin C and the first artificial synthesis of this important compound.

Walter Norman Haworth was born in Chorley, Lancashire, England, on March 19, 1883. He was the fourth child and second son of Thomas and Hannah Haworth. Thomas Haworth, whose family enjoyed a distinguished reputation in business, was the manager of a linoleum factory and took it for granted that his son would follow him into that business. And, indeed, after completing school at the age of fourteen, young Haworth did take a job at the linoleum factory. He soon decided, however, that he had no interest in making his career in that kind of work. Instead, he had become fascinated with the chemical applications he saw all around him and had decided that he wanted a career in that field.

Becomes Interested in Terpenes

That road was made all the more difficult, however, when Haworth's parents withheld their approval and support for any additional education for their son. It was only through great personal effort and the aid of a private tutor that he was finally able in 1903 to pass the entrance examination at Manchester University. There he studied chemistry under the department chairperson, William Perkin, Jr., and became particularly interested in Perkin's own specialty, the chemistry of terpenes. Haworth received his degree in 1906, earning first-class honors in chemistry, and then stayed on at Manchester to work as Perkin's assistant.

In 1909 Haworth left Manchester to spend a year at the University of Göttingen studying with future

(1910) Nobel Prize winner **Otto Wallach**, an expert on terpenes. In only one year, Haworth had earned his Ph.D. and was on his way back to Manchester. One year later, he had qualified for his second doctorate, a D.Sc. in organic chemistry. Over the next fifteen years, Haworth held posts at three institutions. He was senior demonstrator at the Imperial College of Science and Technology in London from 1911 to 1912, lecturer at United College in the University of St. Andrews from 1912 to 1920, and professor of organic chemistry at Armstrong (later King's) College in the University of Durham from 1920 to 1925. In the latter year he was appointed Mason Professor of Chemistry at the University of Birmingham, a post he held until his retirement in 1948.

Begins Work in Carbohydrate Chemistry

The most important period for Haworth in his pre-Birmingham days was his tenure at St. Andrews. It was there that he was introduced to the new field of carbohydrate chemistry by Thomas Purdie and James Colquhoun Irvine, two of England's foremost authorities in the field. In the early 1910s, scientists knew a fair amount about the chemical composition of the carbohydrates, but relatively little about their molecular structure. It was to the question of molecular structure that Haworth soon turned his attention at St. Andrews, and before long, he had abandoned his work on terpenes.

World War I interrupted Haworth's new line of research, however. For the duration of the war, the chemical laboratories at St. Andrews (like other such facilities) were completely given over to the manufacture of chemicals with military importance. At the war's conclusion, however, Haworth returned to his work on carbohydrates. The first stages of that research were devoted to the monosaccharides, the simplest of the carbohydrates. Haworth developed a method by which he could determine the sequence of linkages within a molecule and was able to elucidate the detailed formulas for many compounds. Among the most important of these was glucose, which Haworth showed in 1926 to exist as a six-membered ring consisting of five carbon atoms and one oxygen atom. The convention he used to represent the glucose structure, showing the three-dimensional orientation of its components, has since become known as a Haworth formula or Haworth projection.

In his later work at Birmingham, Haworth took on more and more complex structures, eventually finding formulas for lactose and sucrose, two important disaccharides. He also took on yet another challenge—the determination of the structure for hexuronic acid. Hexuronic acid had been discovered in 1932 by **Albert Szent-Györgyi** in extracts taken from the adrenal gland, in cabbages, and in oranges. Szent-Györgyi suspected that his hexuronic acid might be identical to vitamin C, the antiscurvy agent, that had also been discovered recently.

In his own research, Haworth was able to elucidate the structure of this compound and then to synthesize it in his laboratory. That accomplishment was historic since it was the first time that a vitamin had been produced synthetically. Because of the compound's antiscurvy properties, Haworth suggested that it be renamed ascorbic acid ("not-scurvy" acid), a name by which it is now universally known. For his work both with carbohydrates and with vitamin C, Haworth was awarded a share of the 1937 Nobel Prize in chemistry with **Paul Karrer**.

Haworth's health failed him in 1938, but three years later he had recovered sufficiently to return to his research and other commitments. Included among those other commitments were a number of political and professional responsibilities. He served as chairperson of the British Chemical Panel for Atomic Energy during World War II. He also became dean of the faculty at Birmingham from 1943 to 1946 and served as president of the British Chemical Society from 1944 to 1946. At the same time, he continued an active program of research, concentrating on the most complex of all carbohydrates, the polysaccharides.

Haworth was married to Violet Chilton Dobbie in 1922. The couple had two sons. Haworth died at his home in Birmingham of a heart attack on March 19, 1950, his birthday. In addition to the Nobel Prize, he had been awarded the Longstaff Medal of the British Chemical Society in 1933, the Davy Medal in 1934, and the Royal Medal of the Royal Society in 1942. He was made a fellow of the Royal Society in 1928 and was knighted in 1948.

SELECTED WRITINGS BY HAWORTH:

Books

The Constitution of Sugars, Longmans, Green, 1929.

Periodicals

"The Constitution of Some Carbohydrates," *Chemische Berichte,* Volume 65A, 1932, pp. 43–65.

"The Structure, Function, and Synthesis of Polysaccharides," *Proceedings of the Royal Society,* Volume 186A, 1946, pp. 1–19.

"Carbohydrate Components of Biologically Active Materials," *Journal of the Chemical Society,* 1947, pp. 582–589.

SOURCES:

Books

Dictionary of Scientific Biography, Volume 6, Scribner's, 1975, pp. 184–186.

Legg, L. G. Wickham, and E. T. Williams, *Dictionary of National Biography: 1941–1950,* Oxford, 1959, pp. 368–369.

Periodicals

Hirst, E. L., "Walter Norman Haworth," *Journal of the Chemical Society,* 1951, pp. 2790–2806.

—*Sketch by David E. Newton*

Elizabeth D. Hay
1927-
American embryologist

Elizabeth D. Hay has made substantial contributions to the field of cytology, having been among the first to use electron microscopy to study the origin and ultrastructure of the regeneration of cells. Her research focus has now shifted to the study of cell migration and embryonic tissue transformations, and she is chairman of the department of anatomy at Harvard Medical School.

Elizabeth Dexter Hay was born in St. Augustine, Florida, on April 2, 1927, to Isaac Morris and Lucille (Lynn) Hay. After earning her B.A. at Smith College in 1948, she attended medical school at Johns Hopkins University and received her M.D. in 1952. After taking an internal medicine internship at Johns Hopkins Hospital for a year, she became an instructor in anatomy in 1953 at the Johns Hopkins University Medical School. Having become an assistant professor there in 1956, she accepted a similar position in 1957 at the Cornell University Medical School in New York. She moved on to the Harvard Medical School in 1960 and in 1964 became the Louise Foote Pfeiffer associate professor of embryology. She attained her current position as Louise Foote Pfeiffer professor of embryology in 1969. In 1975 she accepted the position of chairman of Harvard's department of anatomy and cellular biology.

Hay's early research interests at Harvard were in the field of amphibian limb regeneration, and it was in this field that she made substantial contributions to the field of cytology (the study of the structure and functions of cells). It was in her studies of the regeneration of cells and tissues that she made some of the first electron micrograph autoradiographs. This technique creates a photographic record for study of a biological specimen which is produced by its exposure to radiation that has been injected or absorbed. Her later research focused on embryonic tissue transformations. In these studies, she has attempted to discover at the cellular level the mechanism that causes the transformation of normal cells into tumors; this work could eventually provide insights into the causes of abnormal wound healing, congenital abnormalities such as cleft palate, and the underlying mechanisms that trigger the production and spread of cancer cells.

Hay is a member of a number of professional organizations, including the National Academy of Sciences, the American Association of Anatomists, the International Society of Developmental Biologists, and the American Society of Cell Biologists. Her accomplishments have been recognized with the Distinguished Achievement Award of the New York Hospital-Cornell Medical Center Alumni Council in 1985, the Alcon Award for Vision Research in 1988, the E. B. Wilson Award in 1989, and the Henry Gray Award in 1992. Hay is the author or editor of several texts in her field and served as editor-in-chief of the *Developmental Biology Journal* from 1971 to 1975. She also has chaired or served on several national advisory boards and councils.

SELECTED WRITINGS BY HAY:

Books

Regeneration, Holt, 1966.

(Editor) *Macromolecules Regulating Growth and Development,* Academic Press, 1974.

(Editor) *Cell Biology of Extracellular Matrix,* 2nd edition, Plenum Press, 1991.

SOURCES:

Periodicals

Holloway, Marguerite, "A Lab of Her Own," *Scientific American,* November, 1993, pp. 94–103.

—*Sketch by Leonard C. Bruno*

Elizabeth Lee Hazen
1885-1975
American microbiologist and mycologist

Elizabeth Lee Hazen was the codiscoverer of the antifungal antibiotic named nystatin which proved effective against a wide range of yeast infections of the intestine, skin, and mucous membranes.

Having begun life as an orphan on a poor Mississippi farm, she overcame considerable adversity to obtain a Ph.D. from Columbia and work for the New York State Department of Health. For her discovery, she received several major awards, and at the time of her death, she had channeled over thirteen million dollars in royalties to support further scientific work.

Hazen was born in Rich, Coahoma County, Mississippi, on August 24, 1885. The middle of three children, she was orphaned before she was four years old. Her cotton-farmer father, William Edgar Hazen, and her mother, Maggie Harper Hazen, both died before they were thirty. Hazen's younger brother died soon after, and she and her sister, Annis, were eventually taken in by their uncle and aunt, Robert Henry and Laura Hazen. Although Robert Hazen had not been to college, he was determined to obtain the best education for both his daughters and his nieces. Hazen attended public schools and entered the Mississippi Industrial Institute and College at Columbus, where she received her B.S. in 1910.

It was at college that her interest in science flourished, and after teaching high school in Jackson, Mississippi, for six years and taking summer classes at the University of Tennessee and the University of Virginia, she eventually began graduate study in the Department of Biology at New York's Columbia University. In 1917 she received her M.S., but further education was delayed when she volunteered to work in the U.S. Army laboratories during World War I. After the war, she took a job in the laboratory of a West Virginia hospital and did not return to Columbia until 1923. In 1927 she received her Ph.D. in microbiology at the age of forty-two; she was one of only a handful of women to obtain such an advanced degree in the medical sciences.

During the next four years, Hazen was an instructor at Columbia's College of Physicians and Surgeons, and in 1931 she joined the New York State Department of Health, Division of Laboratories and Research. Until the early 1940s, she concentrated on infectious diseases and demonstrated a keen scientific detective ability, having tracked down the sources of an outbreak of anthrax as well as the cause of the first case in the United States of *Clostridium botulinum,* a type of food poisoning found in improperly preserved foods. Her work during World War II led her to concentrate on fungal (called mycotic) infections that afflict humans, and she returned to Columbia University's Mycology Laboratory, having been encouraged by the recent discovery by **Alexander Fleming** of the antibacterial antibiotic called penicillin.

Hazen began to look systematically for an antifungal agent that might exist in nature, and collaborated at the New York State Department of Health's Division of Laboratories with the organic chemist, **Rachel Fuller Brown**, who worked at the State's Central Laboratory. Hazen collected and assayed soil samples and sent them to Brown for testing. In 1948 they discovered in the soil of a Virginia farm belonging to Hazen's friends a new antibiotic they first called fungicidin. By 1950 it had been renamed nystatin and was announced by the National Academy of Science.

Once the patent rights were settled and commercial production of this new drug had begun, the two scientists decided to have the funds from its sale distributed equally between two funds that would support related scientific research. In 1958 Hazen accepted an associate professorship at Albany Medical College. Two years later she retired and became a full-time guest investigator in the Columbia University Mycology Laboratory. In 1973 she moved to a Seattle nursing home where her ill sister was living, since her own health was failing, and she died there of acute cardiac arrhythmia on June 24, 1975. She had never married.

Among the many awards she received during her lifetime, one was especially noteworthy; a month before she died, she and Brown became the first women to receive the Chemical Pioneer Award given by the American Institute of Chemists. The Institute changed its bylaws to recognize Hazen who was a microbiologist and not a chemist. Hazen also shared the 1955 Squibb Award in Chemotherapy with Brown and received the Distinguished Service Award from the New York State Department of Health in 1968. Hazen's friends knew her as a warm, out-going person who shunned the spotlight. She always let Brown present their joint papers, and regularly avoided the press. Her friends knew well that the passion of her life was her work.

SELECTED WRITINGS BY HAZEN:

Books

Laboratory Identification of Pathogenic Fungi Simplified, Thomas, 1955.

SOURCES:

Books

Baldwin, Richard S., *The Fungus Fighters: Two Women Scientists and Their Discovery,* Cornell University Press, 1981.

Periodicals

Bacon, W. Stevenson, "Elizabeth Lee Hazen: 1885–1975," *Mycologia,* September-October, 1976, pp. 961–969.

—Sketch by Leonard C. Bruno

Bernadine Healy
1944-
American cardiologist

Bernadine Healy is a cardiologist and health administrator who was the first woman to head the National Institutes of Health (NIH) from 1991 to 1993. Known for her outspokenness, innovative policymaking, and sometimes controversial leadership in medical and research institutions, Healy has been particularly effective in addressing medical policy and research pertaining to women. She spent the early part of her career at Johns Hopkins University where she rose to full professor on the medical school faculty while also undertaking significant administrative responsibilities. She served as deputy science advisor to President Ronald Reagan from 1984–1985. In 1985 she was appointed Head of the Research Institute of the Cleveland Clinic Foundation where she remained until her appointment as director of the NIH in 1991. Healy was also president of the American Heart Association from 1988–1989 and has served on numerous national advisory committees. Her awards include two American Heart Association special awards for service and the 1992 Dana Foundation's Distinguished Achievement Award for her work on promoting research on the health problems of women.

The second of Michael J. and Violet (McGrath) Healy's four daughters, Bernadine Patricia Healy was born August 2, 1944, in New York City and grew up in Long Island City, Queens, New York. Her parents, second generation Irish-Americans, operated a small perfume business from the basement of their home. Healy attended Hunter College High School, a prestigious public school in Manhattan and graduated first in her class. At Vassar College she majored in chemistry and minored in philosophy, graduating summa cum laude in 1965. One of ten women in a class of 120 at Harvard Medical School, she received her M.D. cum laude in 1970.

Healy completed her internship and residency at Johns Hopkins Hospital in Baltimore and spent two years at the National Heart, Lung, and Blood Institute at NIH before returning to Johns Hopkins and working her way up the academic ranks to professor of medicine. During these years, she also served as director of the coronary care unit (1977–1984) and assistant dean for post-doctoral programs and faculty development (1979–1984). From there, Healy served the Reagan Administration as deputy director of the White House Office of Science and Technology Policy. President George Bush nominated her for director of NIH in September 1990 and she was later confirmed by the U.S. Senate. Her tenure with NIH ended when incoming President Clinton appointed a

Bernadine Healy

new director in 1993. Healy has been married to cardiologist Floyd D. Loop since 1985. With Loop she has a daughter, Marie McGrath Loop; her other daughter, Bartlett Ann Bulkley, is from her previous marriage to surgeon George Bulkley, whom she divorced in 1981.

Despite her various administrative posts, Healy has treated patients during much of her career. Her research has led to a deeper understanding of the pathology and treatment of heart attacks, especially in women. Her colleagues at Johns Hopkins described her as someone who often challenged conventional wisdom and created new directions in research. In addition, unlike many scientists and physicians, Healy viewed management positions as important and challenging. As she told Erik Eckholm of the *New York Times,* "I guess I tended to see those administrative issues, often seen as dreary work burdens, in terms of their broader policy implications." Healy demonstrated her administrative talents during her five-year directorship at the research institute of the Cleveland Clinic Foundation where research funding rose from eight million to thirty-six million dollars. Her responsibilities at the clinic, in addition to being a staff member of the cardiology department, involved directing the research of nine departments, including cancer, immunology, molecular biology, and cardiology.

Healy has manifested her talent and interest in shaping research policy through her many appointments to federal advisory panels, editorial boards of scientific journals, and other decision-making bodies. As the president of the American Heart Association she initiated pioneering research into women's heart disease and demonstrated that medical progress depends on the public and medical community's perception that there is a problem to be solved. Previously, heart disease was perceived as a male affliction despite the fact that it kills more women than men. Medical practitioners for years treated women's heart disease far less aggressively than men's, and most research on coronary heart disease (like most other medical research) used male subjects either predominantly or exclusively. Healy has set out to "convince both the lay and medical sectors that coronary heart disease is also a woman's disease, not a man's disease in disguise," she wrote in *New England Journal of Medicine.*

Directs NIH with Vigor

At the time that Healy was appointed director of the National Institutes of Health in 1991, the agency included thirteen research institutes, sixteen thousand employees, a research budget of over nine billion dollars, and was a world leader in bio-medical research. Yet when Healy assumed control, the agency was beset with problems, its effectiveness was in decline, and it had been without a permanent director for twenty months. Scientists were leaving in record numbers because of non-competitive salaries, politicization of scientific agendas (a prime example was the ban on fetal-tissue research because the Republican administration believed it encouraged abortion), and congressional investigations into alleged cases of scientific misconduct. The agency had been accused of sexism and racism in hiring and promotion. Low morale and bureaucratization added to the institute's problematic image. Healy brought an aggressive and visible management style to the NIH. Her appointment was viewed positively by many because of her outstanding experience in dealing with science policy issues. In addition, because she had been a member of a panel that advised continuation of fetal-tissue research, her appointment was also seen as a move away from politicized science. She also held a series of "town meetings" with NIH scientists to pinpoint problems and form committees to make recommendations concerning NIH research priorities. Furthermore, she initiated a large scale study of the effects of vitamin supplementation, hormone replacement therapy, and dietary modification on women between the ages of forty-five and seventy-nine. She established a policy whereby the NIH would fund only those clinical trials that included both men and women when the condition being studied affected both genders.

Healy's policy decisions at times proved controversial. For example, Healy charged the NIH Office of Scientific Integrity (OSI), whose job it was to investigate ethical matters, with improper conduct, including leaking confidential information and failing to protect the rights of scientists being investigated. In response, the head of OSI accused Healy of mishandling a scientific misconduct case at the Cleveland Clinic Foundation. The allegations led to a hearing in 1991 in which Healy vigorously defended herself, as well as the changes that she had implemented at OSI.

Another controversy involved gene patenting. Despite the objections of Nobel laureate **James Watson,** head of NIH's human genome project, Healy approved patent applications for 347 genes. She believed that patenting genes would promote, not hinder, the ability to access information about them and also spark much-needed international debate on the subject. A third controversy strained her relationship with the Congressional Caucus for Women's Issues. Healy lobbied against provisions in a congressional bill concerning the NIH that would make the inclusion of women and minorities in clinical studies a legal requirement, arguing that it represented "micro-management" of NIH. Attempting to negotiate a political compromise on another issue, she lobbied against overturning the Bush administration's ban on fetal tissue research, despite her previous support for such research.

Healy has described herself as a life-long Republican and a feminist. She credits her father's belief in the importance of education for girls as the reason for her enrollment in an academically competitive high school—an unorthodox move for a Catholic girl during that era. In both medical school at Harvard and during her career at Johns Hopkins she was forced to deal with incidents of sexism. Among her achievements at mid-career point is her success in pointing out and undermining the subtle but pervasive bias against women in medical research. Healy continues to provoke both criticism and praise for the vocal stances and decisive actions that have defined her career.

SELECTED WRITINGS BY HEALY:

Periodicals

The New England Journal of Medicine, July 25, 1991, pp. 274–275.

SOURCES:

Books

Current Biography Yearbook, 1992, H. W. Wilson, 1992, pp. 254–258.

Newsmakers: The People Behind Today's Headlines, Gale, 1993, pp. 35–36.

Periodicals

Chronicle of Higher Education, April 8, 1992, pp. A28–29.
New York Times, November 3, 1992, p. B2 (L).
New York Times Biographical Service, December 1991, pp. 1285–1287.
Science, February 1, 1991, pp. 508–511; August 30, 1991, p. 963; September 6, 1991, pp. 1087–1089.
Washington Post, July 14, 1993, pp. A1 ff.
Working Woman, September 1992, pp. 61–63 ff.

—*Sketch by Pamela O. Long*

Henry Jay Heimlich
1920-
American surgeon and inventor

Henry Jay Heimlich has achieved wide recognition for the Heimlich maneuver, a lifesaving squeeze that has replaced the backslap as a remedy for choking and is responsible for the saving of thousands of lives. Among his other innovations are a surgical procedure for replacing a damaged esophagus by using a flap from the patient's stomach, a simple emergency chest drainage device for victims of chest wounds, and a long-lasting portable oxygen tank to enhance mobility for victims of chronic lung disease. His publications include a home guidebook to emergency medicine, and he is a frequent and popular lecturer on medical topics. His public visibility, which began with his development of the Heimlich maneuver, has been heightened by his television appearances and an award-winning television series in which a cartoon Dr. Heimlich teaches first aid to children. He has also produced instructional videos. Heimlich directs the Heimlich Research Institute in Cincinnati, Ohio, where a staff of volunteers aids him in a range of activities, including work on malariotherapy and promotion of Computers for Peace, an international program aimed at preventing war.

Heimlich was born in Wilmington, Delaware, on February 3, 1920, to Philip and Mary Epstein Heimlich. The elder Heimlich was a prison social worker, and as a child Henry accompanied his father on visits to all of New York State's prisons. Heimlich received a bachelor's degree in 1941 from Cornell University, and an M.D. degree in 1943 from Cornell's medical school. His internship at Boston City Hospital was interrupted in 1944 by his entry into the U.S. Navy. During World War II he served as a surgeon in the Gobi Desert of Inner Mongolia, as part of America's program to forge alliances with the Chinese Nationalists. After the war Heimlich spent four years as a surgical resident at the Veterans Administration Hospital in the Bronx (1946–47), Mount Sinai (1947–48) and Bellevue (1948–49) hospitals in New York City, and Triboro Hospital in Jamaica (1949–50). In 1950 he became attending surgeon at Montefiore Hospital in New York City, where he remained through 1969, acting also as assistant clinical professor of surgery at New York Medical College. Heimlich served on the board of the National Cancer Foundation from 1960 to 1970, and was president for five of those years. In the mid-1960s he was also president of Cancer Care, and in 1965 was a member of the President's Commission on Heart Disease, Cancer, and Stroke.

Early Innovations

Heimlich's first medical innovation, devised in 1950, was a procedure for gastric tube esophagoplasty, constructing a new esophagus from a section of the patient's stomach. Having first proposed the idea to the chief of surgery at Montefiore to no effect, Heimlich negotiated a small grant and laboratory space at New York Medical College, and tried the procedure on dogs. Although interest in the procedure lagged in the United States, Heimlich's work came to the attention of a surgeon in Bucharest, Romania, who had been performing a similar procedure on humans. Heimlich conferred with the Romanian surgeon and tried the operation on U.S. patients in 1956. It has since become a standard surgical practice.

Heimlich's emergency chest drainage device for use with victims of chest injury was inspired by his World War II experiences. Heimlich's small unit used a flutter valve from a "Bronx cheer" noisemaker to prevent backflow of fluids. He tested it successfully with a hospital patient who was also hooked up to the conventional electrical suction device. The Heimlich chest drainage valve was widely used in Vietnam and is common in emergency facilities.

Devises the Heimlich Maneuver

In 1969 Heimlich became director of surgery at the Jewish Hospital of Cincinnati, Ohio. At about that time he began thinking about a treatment for choking, which was the sixth most common cause of accidental deaths in the United States, responsible for about four thousand deaths annually. Heimlich was aware that a hard slap on the back meant to aid a choking victim could easily lodge an obstruction more firmly. As a chest surgeon, Heimlich was also aware of the reserve volume of air that stays in the lungs after exhalation, and he reasoned that this reserve could be used to help expel an object. He tested his ideas on laboratory dogs. He closed off the upper end of an endotracheal tube and put it down the throat of an anesthetized dog; when he compressed the air in the dog's chest, the tube was forced out of the dog's airway. Heimlich found the best results were obtained by a subdiaphragmatic thrust, pushing up suddenly on the soft tissue under the diaphragm. When the technique is applied to humans, a rescuer stands behind the choking victim, wraps his arms around the victim's waist, makes a fist with one hand (thumb side in) and grasps it with the other hand, then gives a quick upward thrust. If a choking victim is lying unconscious, the diaphragm may be compressed by the heel of the rescuer's hand.

In 1974 Heimlich published his study in *Emergency Medicine.* He also brought the article to the attention of the press, and references to it began to appear in newspapers nationwide. A week later, the *Seattle Times* reported that a seventy-year-old restaurateur had saved the life of his neighbor's wife using Heimlich's technique. Many similar stories followed, including cases of children successfully performing the maneuver, and Heimlich was thrust into the national limelight. Heimlich has also defined the symptoms of choking—inability to speak or breathe, pallor followed by bluish skin color, and finally, loss of consciousness and collapse. He has publicized the fact that choking is often mistaken for a heart attack—the so-called café coronary. In 1975 the Heimlich maneuver was endorsed by the emergency medical services division of the American Medical Association. It was later recommended by the American Red Cross and the American Heart Association, who in addition advised its use with drowning victims. Deaths from choking declined dramatically following widespread publicity about the Heimlich maneuver, and in 1984 Heimlich was recognized with the Albert Lasker Public Service Award.

Heimlich Institute Established

In 1977 Heimlich became professor of advanced clinical sciences at Xavier University in Cincinnati. There he established the Heimlich Institute to continue work on innovations such as a portable oxygen system, the Micro-Trach. He is the founder and president of the Dysphagia Foundation, and has developed techniques for teaching stroke victims how to swallow. With the philosophy that elimination of war will promote the well-being of the largest number of people, Heimlich has developed Computers for Peace, a program that uses computer projections to show that the benefits of trade among hostile nations are so great it is against the self-interest of nations to go to war.

In 1985 he received a research grant from the Fannie L. Rippel Foundation to study the effects of malariotherapy, a new treatment against cancer. Heat was known to kill cancer cells, and Heimlich reasoned that the fevers of malaria may be useful in the treatment of cancer. When a cancer patient is deliberately infected with malaria, the resulting fever combats the cancer cells. Once the cancer is under control, drugs can be used to eradicate the malaria organism. The idea is not new; a similar procedure was used in the 1920s against syphilis. Heimlich has also advocated malariotherapy for treatment of Lyme disease, which like syphilis, is caused by a spirochete and has similar clinical manifestations.

Heimlich's projects are diverse, some are deceptively simple, and many have been controversial. "You're not being original if all your peers agree with what you're doing," he told an *Omni* interviewer in 1983. Heimlich is the author of many scientific and popular articles, and has used television to increase his audience. "I can do more toward saving lives in three minutes on television than I could do all my life in the operating room," he told *Omni.* Heimlich's television series for children, "Dr. Henry's Emergency Lessons for People," won an Emmy Award in 1980. Also in 1980, Heimlich published *Dr. Heimlich's Home Guide to Emergency Medical Situations,* and was named as one of the top ten speakers in the country by the International Platform Association. In 1984 he was honored by the Chinese ministry of health for his World War II service.

He married Jane Murray, daughter of dance studio personalities Arthur and Katherine Murray, on June 3, 1951; they have four children: Philip, Peter, and Janet and Elizabeth (twins).

SELECTED WRITINGS BY HEIMLICH:

Books

(With Lawrence Galton) *Dr. Heimlich's Home Guide to Emergency Medical Situations,* Simon & Schuster, 1980.

Periodicals

"How to Survive a Café Coronary," *Saturday Evening Post,* May-June, 1982, pp. 66–69.

Other

Dr. Heimlich's Home First Aid Video, directed by Ron Whichard and Ken Lisbeth, MCA, 1988.

SOURCES:

Books

Current Biography Yearbook, H. W. Wilson, 1986, pp. 215–218.

Periodicals

King, Michael L., "Dr. Heimlich Can Fix Choking Fast; Here's What Else He Treats," *Wall Street Journal,* April 30, 1982, pp. 1, 22.

McKay, Robert, "The Amazing Dr. Henry Heimlich," *Saturday Evening Post,* November, 1986, pp. 42–45.

McKay, Robert, "Dr. Heimlich: The Man behind the Maneuver," *Saturday Evening Post,* December, 1986, pp. 30–34, 72, 85.

Starr, Douglas, "Henry J. Heimlich," *Omni,* June, 1983, pp. 81–82, 130–134.

—Sketch by Jill Carpenter

Ernst Heinkel
1888-1958
German aeronautical engineer

Dr. Ernst Heinkel was a gifted airplane designer who pioneered many of the technologies now common in aircraft design. His He–176 was the world's first rocket-powered aircraft and his He–178 was the world's first jet aircraft. Despite his prodigious gifts, Heinkel had little regard for the moral consequences of his actions. During World War II, he built many of former German chancellor and leader Adolf Hitler's best aircraft, including the famous He–111 light bomber. After the war, he was tried as a war criminal by the Nuremberg War Crimes Tribunal.

Heinkel was born in 1888 in the Swabian village of Grunbach, the son of a coppersmith. He completed secondary school in Schorndorf, and attended Technical High School in Stuttgart. In 1908 Heinkel witnessed a Zeppelin dirigible explode into flames near a landing field in Stuttgart. This incident sparked his interest in "heavier-than-air" aircraft, a technology still in its infancy. In 1909 he visited the International Flying Expedition in Frankfurt, and saw first hand the advances that were being made in places like France and Belgium. Germany's poor showing in the event prompted him to design and build his first biplane, which was completed in 1911.

Designs Fighter Aircraft

During World War I, Heinkel was the chief aircraft designer for the Hansa Brandenburg Flugzeugwerke. His W–12 seaplane allowed the Kaiser's Luftwaffe to maintain complete air superiority over the North Sea. The W–12's successor was the W–20, one of the only practical monoplanes to see service in the war. After World War I, Germany was forbidden from maintaining an air force, and Heinkel returned to his native Swabia and opened an electrical components factory, settling down to an unexciting life in the country. He was easily convinced to break the Allied-imposed armaments laws, however, by Friedrich Christiansen, who had twenty-one confirmed kills flying Heinkel's seaplanes during the war. Heinkel was persuaded by Christiansen to move to Travenmude where, with Japanese and American connivance, he designed a collapsible seaplane for use on submarines. The resulting airplane, the U–1, could be assembled in thirty-three seconds, had a top speed of 87 miles per hour, and could climb to 3,300 feet in six minutes. Both the Japanese and American Navies, in defiance of the Treaty of Versailles, were Heinkel's customers.

Throughout the 1920s Heinkel designed aircraft for the reborn, though highly secret and illegal, Luftwaffe. In 1925, while working for the Japanese navy, he designed the first airplane catapult. Mounted on the deck of the battleship Nagato, the catapult was used to launch Heinkel's He–26. Heinkel bought the engines for his airplane from the British-owned company Napier-Lion. By 1939, Heinkel had designed and built the world's fastest airplane. On March 30, 1939, the Heinkel He–100 broke the existing world speed record by more than 30 miles per hour with a top speed of 464 miles an hour. However, the Luftwaffe general staff had already decided on the Messerschmitt 109 as the standard Luftwaffe fighter plane. Heinkel sold the aircraft, along with its plans and a license to build it, to the Russians.

In collaboration with **Wernher von Braun**, who would later design the Saturn V rocket, Heinkel designed the He–176, the world's first rocket plane and the precursor of the V–2 rocket. A few weeks after the test flight of the He–176, Heinkel unveiled the He–178, the world's first jet aircraft. Convinced, however, that the war would be over in a few years, the Luftwaffe General Staff refused to fund development of Heinkel's new aircraft—a decision they would pay dearly for in 1944 and 1945. Heinkel fell out of favor with the Luftwaffe after he harshly criticized the General Staff for refusing to fund his jet airplane program and for forcing him to sell his best airplane to the Russians. He had the satisfaction, however, of seeing his plane perform admirably against his rival Willy Messerschmitt's ME 109.

Tried For War Crimes

After the war, Heinkel was arrested as a war criminal. He originally was charged as a major offender for the use of slave labor in his factories. With the beginning of the cold war, and the subsequent rise of the importance of West Germany to

NATO, the Allies lost interest in trying Nazi industrialists. The charges against Heinkel were eventually reduced to "Nazi Follower," and he was fined 2000 marks for his activities. An appeals court threw this conviction out in 1948. Later, with his son Ernst, Heinkel once again returned to Swabia where he manufactured bicycles, motor scooters, and midget automobiles. He died on January 30, 1958. At the time he was reportedly working on the design for a new aircraft.

SELECTED WRITINGS BY HEINKEL:

Books

Stormy Life, [New York], 1956.

SOURCES:

Books

Bekker, Cajus, *The Luftwaffe War Diaries,* [Garden City, New York], 1968.

Killen, John, *A History of the Luftwaffe,* [Garden City], 1968.

Mason, Herbert M., *The Rise of the Luftwaffe, Forging the Secret German Air Weapon 1918–1940,* [New York], 1973.

—Sketch by Jeff Ranier

Werner Karl Heisenberg
1901-1976
German physicist

Werner Karl Heisenberg is best known for his discovery of the uncertainty principle, for which he was awarded the 1932 Nobel Prize in physics. The uncertainty principle states that it is impossible to specify precisely both the position and momentum of a particle at the same time. The enunciation of that principle contributed to the understanding of a number of problems in atomic physics. It was also to have a profound effect on a far more general level, in that it essentially invalidated the long-held and fundamental scientific thesis of cause and effect. One of Heisenberg's first great accomplishments was the development of a new approach for solving problems of atomic structure, matrix mechanics.

Werner Karl Heisenberg

Heisenberg was born in Würzburg, Germany, on December 5, 1901. His father, August Heisenberg, taught Greek philology at the University of Würzburg and ancient languages at the Altes Gymnasium (secondary school) of the same city. His mother, Annie Wecklein, was the daughter of the headmaster of Münich's Maximilian Gymnasium. Werner entered elementary school at Würzburg, but at the age of nine he moved with his parents and his elder brother to Münich, where his father had accepted an appointment as professor of Greek philology at the University.

In Münich, Heisenberg enrolled in the Maximilian Gymnasium, where his grandfather was headmaster. His education was interrupted, however, in the summer of 1918, when he was called to assist the faltering wartime effort by harvesting crops on a Bavarian farm. Shortly thereafter, he returned to Münich and served as a messenger for the democratic socialist forces that managed after bitter street fighting to oust a communist-oriented government that had briefly taken control of the Bavarian state. He also became involved with a number of youth groups that had organized in an effort to build a new society out of the wreckage left in the wake of World War I. Eventually he was elected leader of a group associated with the Bund Deutscher Neupfadfinder (New Boy Scouts), which, according to David C. Cassidy writing in the *Dictionary of Scientific Biography,* "strove for a renewal of supposedly decadent German personal and social life through the direct experience of nature and the uplifting beauties of Romantic poetry, music, and thought." Already a gifted pianist, Heisenberg would maintain his interest in music throughout his life; later, after his marriage, the whole Heisenberg family often assembled for an evening of chamber music.

Earns Education in Physics at Münich, Göttingen, and Copenhagen

After the war, Heisenberg completed his studies at the Gymnasium and, in 1920, decided to enter the University of Münich. He hoped to pursue a degree in mathematics, a subject in which he had long been interested and for which he had shown great talent; while still a student at the gymnasium he had taught himself calculus and had written a paper on number theory. Heisenberg changed his mind, however, when Münich's professor of mathematics, Ferdinand von Lindemann, refused to accept him as a student in an advanced seminar. On his father's advice, Heisenberg then applied for his second choice, physics. He requested an interview with **Arnold Sommerfeld,** then a professor of theoretical physics at Münich, who agreed to admit Heisenberg to his seminar.

As Sommerfeld's student, Heisenberg not only became rapidly involved in the most fundamental problems in theoretical physics, but also became acquainted with a group of scientists—including the physicists **Max Born, Niels Bohr, Wolfgang Pauli** and **Enrico Fermi**—whose work would dominate the field of atomic physics for years to come. At Münich, Heisenberg immediately began investigating some of the problems related to refinements of the Bohr model of the atom. In 1913, Bohr had employed the new concept of quantum physics to develop a model of the atom that explained much empirical data with amazing accuracy. However, a number of problems remained with the Bohr model. For one thing, no theoretical basis existed for the concept of quantized orbitals professed by Bohr. Also, inadequacies in the model's predictive ability suggested that some essential points were still missing from the Bohr theory. One of the earliest improvements on the Bohr model had been suggested by Sommerfeld himself when, in 1916, he hypothesized the existence of elliptical orbitals for electrons.

The topic to which Heisenberg first addressed his attention was the Zeeman effect, the splitting of spectral lines, a phenomenon for which no explanation had yet been suggested. In a series of papers, two written with Sommerfeld, Heisenberg developed an explanation for the Zeeman effect. His approach required an abandonment of some fundamental principles in both classical physics and quantum mechanics. But the hypothesis was attractive, nonetheless, and, as Cassidy points out, was "the first indication of the radical changes required for solving the quantum riddle." Heisenberg obtained his Ph.D. in 1923, although not without some difficulty. As he was primarily interested in theoretical physics, he had spent little time on laboratory experimentation. During his oral examinations for the doctoral degree, he was unable to answer questions put to him on instrumental matters by Wilhelm Wien, a professor of experimental physics, who consequently recommended that Heisenberg not be passed. Largely as a result of Sommerfeld's negotiation, however, Wien was overruled and Heisenberg received his degree.

The Zeeman papers brought Heisenberg's name to the attention of physicists throughout Europe. Thus, when Sommerfeld spent a year as visiting professor at the University of Wisconsin in 1922–1923, he made arrangements for Heisenberg to spend that year studying under Born at Göttingen. Born was so impressed with his new student's work that he recommended Heisenberg for a teaching position. This decision was quite remarkable since Heisenberg was only 22 at the time and had just taken his Ph.D. Heisenberg remained in Göttingen until 1926, with the exception of a semester back in Munich and another spent working under Bohr in Copenhagen in the fall of 1924.

Develops the Theory of Matrix Mechanics

One of the life-long medical problems with which Heisenberg had to deal was hay fever. He eventually became accustomed to leaving the inhospitable climate of Bavaria whenever a serious attack occurred and traveling to the less pollen-dense island of Heligoland. One such trip in June, 1925, was to have profound significance for theoretical physics. With weeks of free time on his hands, Heisenberg devised a new approach to the problem of the Zeeman effect in particular and of atomic theory in general. Physicists had devoted too much effort, he said, to devising pictorial models that might have some physical reality. A better approach, he suggested, would be to work strictly with experimental data and to determine the mathematical implications of that data.

In order to pursue this approach, Heisenberg devised a system that came to be known as matrix mechanics. Although, as he later learned, the mathematics of this technique was already familiar to professional mathematicians, its application to the problems of atomic physics was entirely new. After his return from Heligoland, he collaborated with Born and Born's assistant, Pascual Jordan, to publish a refined version of the theory of matrix mechanics. The paper marked a turning point in physics. As biographers Nevil Mott and Rudolf Peierls wrote in the *Biographical Memoirs of Fellows of the Royal Society,* "It is fair to regard this paper as the start of a new era in atomic physics, since any look at the physics literature of the next two or three years clearly shows the intensity and success of the work stimulated by this paper."

Matrix mechanics did prove to be very fruitful in the development of atomic theory. Still, many physicists were somewhat uneasy with the mathematical abstraction of the approach because it didn't provide them with physical models to which to relate. When Austrian physicist **Erwin Schrödinger** devised his wave mechanics about a year later, many physicists switched their allegiance to his more physically-based approach. The conflict between the two theories was resolved fairly soon, however, when Schrödinger showed that matrix mechanics and wave mechanics are mathematically identical.

The Heisenberg-Born-Jordan paper was published in November, 1925, and six months later Heisenberg left Göttingen to become Bohr's assistant in Copenhagen. The almost daily contact between the two great physicists was to lead to one of the most productive periods in Heisenberg's life, including his enunciation of the principle for which he is best known, the uncertainty principle.

Works on the Uncertainty Principle

Heisenberg turned his attention to uncertainty in February, 1927. He was involved in a study of the fundamental quantum properties of an electron in its orbit around the nucleus. At one point in that analysis, he imagined using a gamma ray microscope to study an electron's motion. It occurred to him that the very act of measuring an electron's properties by shining gamma rays on it would disturb the electron in its orbit; the act of observing the electron, therefore, altered its behavior, and objectivity was lost. Out of this realization, he developed a fundamental principle of physics that is now familiar to most high school students of the subject. According to the uncertainty principle, one can measure the position of a particle *or* its momentum with as much precision as desired. However, the more precise one of these measurements becomes, the less precise the other will be, such that the product of their inaccuracies (to use Heisenberg's original term) must always be less than Planck's constant (the unvarying ratio of the frequency of radiation to its quanta of energy). The principle was quickly and widely accepted by most, though not all, physicists, who soon acknowledged the concept as a fundamental law of nature. For the development of the uncertainty principle, as well as his other contributions to theoretical physics, Heisenberg was awarded the Nobel Prize for physics in 1932.

In 1927, Heisenberg was offered chairs at the universities of Leipzig and Zürich. He chose the former and, upon assuming the post of professor theoretical physics in October of that year, became the youngest full professor in Germany. His duties at Leipzig, unlike those of modern professors, were extensive, including a full schedule of teaching and administrative responsibilities. Not surprisingly, his scientific output diminished somewhat as a result of these competing demands for his time and energy. Nonetheless, he continued to pursue research interests in a number of directions, including ferromagnetism, quantum electrodynamics, cosmic radiation, and nuclear physics. Perhaps his best-known contribution in this period occurred after English physicist **James Chadwick** discovered the neutron in 1932. Heisenberg proposed a model of the nucleus that consisted of protons and neutrons rather than protons and electrons, as favored by some physicists. This theory did not originate with Heisenberg, however.

The last half of Heisenberg's life was complicated by the political turmoil taking place in Germany and around the world in the years surrounding World War II. With the rise of National Socialism in the early 1930s, the vast majority of German scientists fled the country to take up residence in the United Kingdom, the United States, and other free nations. Heisenberg, like his colleague **Otto Hahn,** was one of the few world-class scientists who determined to remain behind and protect, as well as he could, Germany's scientific traditions and institutions.

At first, Heisenberg and his colleagues resisted German leader Adolf Hitler's efforts to "purify" and nationalize German science, but the forces they faced were too great. Soon Nazi students were in command of universities, including that of Leipzig, ensuring that non-Aryan and "politically unacceptable" faculty members were weeded out. Heisenberg's position was especially tenuous since the Nazis regarded theoretical physics (as opposed to experimental physics) as a suspect, "Jewish" science. In 1935, an invitation from Münich for Heisenberg to succeed his former teacher Sommerfeld was met with violent opposition from German political leaders and professional colleagues, one of whom branded Heisenberg a "white Jew." Any hope that Heisenberg may have had of accepting the Münich offer was dashed and, for a time, even his personal safety was at risk.

At the beginning of World War II, the Nazi government recognized Heisenberg's value and made him director of the German atomic bomb project. For the next five and a half years, all of his efforts were devoted to this project. Questions have since been raised as to the morality of Heisenberg's decision. The fact remains that he chose to stay in his native country and devote his abilities to its war effort.

When the war came to an end in 1945, Heisenberg and his bomb research team were captured in a remote region of southern Germany, where they had been sent to be safe from Allied bomb attacks. After a six-month internment in England, Heisenberg was allowed to return to Göttingen, where he re-established the Kaiser Wilhelm Institute for Physics and renamed it the Max Planck Institute in honor of his colleague and friend, the originator of quantum theory.

Devotes Time to Administration, Politics, and Research

In the postwar years, Heisenberg worked diligently to restore German science to its former high standing. He was largely responsible for the creation of the Deutscher Forschungsrat (German Research Council), of which he became president. In this role, he came to represent West Germany in many international organizations and at many international meetings. His continuing administrative and political responsibilities did not deter Heisenberg from his research interests, however. In the postwar years, he became particularly interested in the search for a unified field theory, which would link all physical fields, such as gravitation and electromagnetism. He also pursued his interest in more general topics, such as the relationship between physical theory and philosophy.

Heisenberg retired in 1970, although he continued to write on a variety of topics. His health began to fail in 1973, and two years later he became seriously ill. He died on February 1, 1976, in Münich. He was survived by his wife, the former Elisabeth Schumacher, whom he had married in 1937. He also left seven children, four daughters and three sons.

SELECTED WRITINGS BY HEISENBERG:

Books

Die physikalischen Prinzipien der Quantentheorie, [Leipzig], 1930, translation by Carl Eckart and Frank C. Hoyt published as *Physical Principles of the Quantum Theory,* University of Chicago Press, 1930.

Wandlungen in den Grundlagen der Naturwissenschaft, [Leipzig], 1935.

Die Physik der Atomkerne, [Brunswick], 1943, translation published as *Nuclear Physics,* Philosophical Library, 1953.

Philosophic Problems of Nuclear Science, Faber, 1952.

Das Naturbild der heutigen Physik, [Hamburg], 1955.

Physics and Philosophy: The Revolution in Modern Science, Harper, 1958.

Introduction to the Unified Field Theory of Elementary Particles, [New York], 1966.

Das Naturgesetz und die Strucktur der Materie, [Stuttgart], 1967.

Schritte über Grenzen: Gesammelte Reden und Aufsatze, [Münich], 1971.

Werner Heisenberg: Gesammelte Werke/Collected Works, edited by Walter Blum, Hans-Peter Durr, and Helmet Rechenberg, 9 volumes, Springer-Verlag and Piper-Verlag, 1984—.

SOURCES:

Books

Beyerchen, Alan D., *Scientists under Hitler: Politics and the Physics Community in the Third Reich,* Yale University Press, 1977.

Biographical Memoirs of Fellows of the Royal Society, Volume 23, Royal Society (London), 1977, pp. 212–251.

Cassidy, David, and Martha Baker, *Werner Heisenberg: A Bibliography of His Writings,* University of California-Berkeley, 1984.

Dictionary of Scientific Biography, Volume 17, Scribner, 1982, pp. 394–403.

Heisenberg, Elisabeth, *Das politische Leben eines Unpolitischen: Erinnerungen an Werner Heisenberg,* [Munich], 1980, translation by S. Cappellari and C. Morris published as *Inner Exile: Recollections of a Life with Werner Heisenberg,* Birkhauser, 1984.

Jungk, Robert, *Heller als tausend Sonnen: Das Schicksal der Atomforscher,* [Bern], 1956, translation by James Cleugh published as *Brighter than a Thousand Suns: A Personal History of the Atomic Scientists,* Harcourt, 1958.

Weber, Robert L., *Pioneers of Science: Nobel Prize Winners in Physics,* American Institute of Physics, 1980, pp. 95–96.

Periodicals

Goudsmit, Samuel, "Werner Heisenberg (1901–1976)," *Year Book of the American Philosophical Society for 1976,* [Philadelphia], 1977, pp. 74–80.

—*Sketch by David E. Newton*

Philip Showalter Hench
1896-1965
American pathologist

Philip Showalter Hench, an American clinical pathologist, performed groundbreaking research in rheumatoid arthritis. His clinical tests of adrenal compound E, which Hench named cortisone, and of

ACTH, which produces cortisone naturally by stimulating the adrenal cortex, offered the first hope for patients suffering from rheumatoid arthritis. Hench and his colleague, biochemist **Edward C. Kendall**, gained immediate worldwide attention when they filmed the miraculous recovery of arthritis patients—some of whom could barely walk—as they climbed stairs and even jogged in place. Although prolonged clinical trials showed that neither cortisone or ACTH was a viable long-term therapy for arthritis due to side effects such as high blood pressure and high glucose levels, Hench's efforts opened new vistas in medical research, particularly in the study of both hormones and rheumatoid arthritis. A meticulous researcher who methodically collected his clinical data before publishing his results, Hench shared the 1950 Nobel Prize in physiology or medicine with Kendall "for their discoveries relating to the hormones of the adrenal cortex, their structure and biological effects." (Chemist **Tadeus Reichstein** also received a share of the prize for his independent work with the adrenal cortex and its hormones.)

Hench was born in Pittsburgh, Pennsylvania, on February 28, 1896. The son of Jacob Bixler Hench, a classical scholar and school administrator, and Clara John Showalter, Hench attended a private high school, Shadyside Academy, and then enrolled at the University of Pittsburgh in 1916. His education looked as though it would be interrupted when he enlisted in the U.S. Army Medical Corps. But Hench was transferred to the reserves so he could return to his studies, and he enrolled in Lafayette College in Easton, Pennsylvania. He received his B.A. from Lafayette in 1916 and enrolled at the University of Pittsburgh School of Medicine, where he received his M.D. in 1920.

After completing his internship at St. Francis Hospital in Pittsburgh, Hench became a fellow in medicine at the Mayo Foundation of the University of Minnesota. The bright young physician and scientist would spend his entire career at the Mayo Clinic, where, in 1926, he cofounded the Department of Rheumatic Disease, which was the first training program in rheumatology in the United States. Hench spent the 1927–28 academic year on sabbatical studying research medicine with Ludwig Aschoff, a leading rheumatic fever investigator, at Freiburg University. He also studied with clinician Freidrich von Müller in Munich. Hench completed his formal education in 1931 when he received a master of science degree in internal medicine from the University of Minnesota.

A physician first, Hench's research was clinically based. He began studying rheumatoid arthritis in 1923. Unlike osteoarthritis, a degenerative joint disease common in later life, rheumatoid arthritis is a chronic inflammatory disease of the joints often contracted at the relatively young age of 30 to 35. In advanced stages, rheumatoid arthritis could cause deformity due to bone and surrounding muscle atrophy. In 1929, Hench took note of a patient who had suffered from severe arthritis for more than four years. The patient had entered the Mayo Clinic suffering from jaundice, a disease caused by excess bilirubin, a liver product, in the bloodstream. Amazingly, the man's arthritis had abated and remained dormant for several weeks after his recovery from jaundice. Carefully collecting data, Hench waited until he had authenticated nine similar cases, among them patients who experienced remissions from painful fibrositis and sciatica, two other inflammatory conditions, before publishing his data in 1933.

Hench was convinced that these cases held a vital clue to a therapy for arthritis and set out to induce jaundice artificially. Hench's initial experiments used infusion or ingestion of bile to emulate jaundice's production of excess bile in the blood or the liver. Although these experiments failed, Hench's attention was soon drawn to another group of patients, women whose arthritis vanished during pregnancy. He also observed that some arthritic patients went into less complete remission after surgical operations, anesthesia, or severe fasting. Looking for a common physiological denominator, Hench, who enjoyed reading Sir Arthur Conan Doyle's novels of Sherlock Holmes, had a prime suspect—glandular hormones. Furthermore, the fact that both jaundice and pregnancy caused remission in almost the exact same manner led Hench to believe that his missing compound was not bilirubin or a female-only sex hormone.

Collaboration with Kendall Leads to Treatment for Arthritis

Fortunately, the Mayo Foundation's own Edward C. Kendall was a world renowned chemist in the field of steroids, a specific group of hormones. Kendall had isolated six steroids from the adrenal cortex, the outer part of the endocrine glands located atop the kidneys, which he alphabetized compound A through F. Hench's first try with compound A was a failure. Both Hench and Kendall then decided to try compound E. But at that time, in 1941, compound E was extremely difficult to synthesize and, as a result, costly. With both high (300 degrees Fahrenheit) and low (-100 degrees Fahrenheit) temperatures needed to produce compound E, the delicate work took time and attention and the slightest mistake could result in a useless compound. It wasn't until more than two years after World War II that scientists from the pharmaceutical firm Merck & Co. had developed a process that could produce enough compound E for Hench to attempt his experiment. Still, the compound was expensive to produce. Hench recalled in an interview for an article in the *Saturday Evening Post* that he and his colleagues "almost went into shock" when a $1,000 bottle of compound E was dropped on a marble floor.

Hench's results with compound E were miraculous. The first patient, a 29-year-old woman, experienced total remission of symptoms after three injections over three days. Hench's results were quickly confirmed by five other researchers across the country. Hench and his colleagues received instant public notoriety as a result of their studies both with compound E, which Hench named cortisone, and with adrenocorticotropic hormone (ACTH), a hormone produced by the pituitary gland which spurs the body's natural production of cortisone through the adrenal cortex.

Unfortunately, Hench's miraculous "cure" for arthritis turned out to be short lived. Without the use of cortisone or ACTH, rheumatic symptoms returned; and long-term use of cortisone or ACTH causes several side effects, including high blood glucose and high blood pressure, as well as obesity associated with adrenal or pituitary gland tumors. Much to Hench's credit, he maintained his scientific cautiousness throughout the heady early days of the discovery, quickly recognizing the harmful side effects and outlining future directions in research of these hormones. Nevertheless, the studies of Hench and Kendall, along with those of Tadeus Reichstein, opened entirely new avenues of medical research; as a result, the three scientists were awarded the Nobel Prize for medicine or physiology in 1950.

Hench retired from the Mayo Foundation in 1957. In addition to the Nobel Prize, he was a recipient of the numerous awards, including the prestigious Lasker Award, which he also shared with Kendall. Hench married Mary Genevieve Kahler in 1927, and the couple had two sons, Philip Kahler and John Bixler, and two daughters, Mary Showalter and Susan Kahler. His hobbies included photography, tennis, opera, and Sherlock Holmes novels. He died from pneumonia on March 30, 1965, while vacationing with his wife in Ocho Rios, Jamaica. To honor him, Hench's alma mater, the University of Pittsburgh, presents the annual Hench Award to a distinguished university alumnus.

SELECTED WRITINGS BY HENCH:

Periodicals

"The Systemic Nature of Chronic Infectious Arthritis," *Atlantic Medical Journal,* Volume 28, 1925, pp. 425–36.

"The Effect of a Hormone of the Adrenal Cortex (17-Hydroxy-11-Dehydrocorticosterone: Compound E) and of Pituitary Adrenocorticotrophic Hormone on Rheumatoid Arthritis," *Annals of the Rheumatic Diseases,* Volume 8, 1949, pp. 90–96.

SOURCES:

Books

Nobel Laureates in Medicine or Physiology: A Biographical Dictionary, Garland, 1990, pp. 231–235.

The Nobel Prize Winners: Physiology or Medicine, Salem Press, 1991, pp. 627–633.

Periodicals

Spencer, Steven M., "Victims of Arthritis Take Hope!," *Saturday Evening Post,* July 23, 1949, pp. 28–29; 71–74.

—Sketch by David Petechuk

Cornelius Langston Henderson
1888(?)-1976
American civil engineer

Cornelius Langston Henderson spent his entire engineering career with the Canadian Bridge Company in Walkerville, Ontario. Among many other projects, he helped design several of the structures that connect Canada and the United States, particularly the Ambassador Bridge over the Detroit River and the Detroit-Windsor tunnel underneath the river.

Henderson was born on December 11, 1888, (one source says 1887), in Detroit, Michigan, but as a young child moved to Atlanta, Georgia, where his father received an appointment as president of Morris Brown College. Henderson attended school there until he entered Payne University in Alabama. After graduation from Payne in 1906, Henderson returned to Michigan, partly to escape the racial segregation in the South. He graduated with a B.S. in civil engineering from the University of Michigan in 1911, only the second African American in the history of the school to do so. He turned down a teaching position with Tuskeegee Institute in favor of an entry level job offer with the Canadian Bridge Company, which would later become a Canadian subsidiary of U.S. Steel. After four years in drafting, he started up the corporate ladder, eventually reaching the position of structural steel designer. Bridge-building is always a cooperative effort; Henderson contributed design ideas to many bridges in Canada, the British West Indies, and several other countries, including the United States.

Each bridge consists of three basic parts: the substructure, which anchors the bridge to the ground; the superstructure, which rests on the substructure and actually spans the space to be crossed; and the deck, or roadway, upon which traffic moves. Several different designs are possible, but all bridges must be designed to hold a certain load across particular geological structures, even under stress. Tunnels present particular design challenges. The Detroit-Windsor tunnel, for example, one of the structures on which Henderson worked, was partly built above ground in cylindrical sections, and then the sections were sunk below the level of the Detroit River, into a trench cut to receive them. The sections were welded together, waterproofed, and finally covered over to form the underwater part of the tunnel. This section was then connected to the tunnel entry and exit points that had been dug underground in Detroit and Windsor. It was a remarkable engineering feat for the time, completed in 1930.

Henderson belonged to the Engineering Society of Detroit and was president of the National Technical Association before his retirement in 1958. He played the violin in his spare time. He had one son, Cornelius Langston Henderson, Jr., who was also a civil engineer.

SOURCES:

Books

Schodek, Daniel L. *Landmarks in American Civil Engineering,* 1987, MIT Press, pp. 186–187.

Young, Herman A. and Young, Barbara H., *Scientists in the Black Perspective,* 1974, Lincoln Foundation, pp. 130–131.

—Sketch by Gail B. C. Marsella

John Edward Henry
1932-
American entomologist

John Edward Henry has devoted his career to developing biological methods to control grasshoppers and prevent the crop devastation they can cause. "No accurate count has ever been taken, but certainly thousands of people have starved to death because these insects destroyed their only food supply," he told *Agricultural Record.* His work has helped to control grasshoppers and related insects in West Africa, Argentina, China and Indonesia, as well as North America.

Henry was born in Ponsford, Minnesota. He graduated from high school in Bemidji, Minnesota, and continued his education at San Jose State University in California, from which he graduated in 1959 with B.A. in entomology. Henry was awarded a research fellowship by the University of Idaho and earned an M.S. in entomology there in 1961. He received his Ph.D. from Montana State University in 1969. Henry's study of grasshoppers began in 1961 when he was hired as an entomologist by the U.S. Department of Agriculture at their research station in Bozeman, Montana.

He began his research studying grasshopper parasites—protozoa and viruses that under certain conditions cause plagues that can decimate a grasshopper population. He focused his attention on a study of the protozoan *Nosema locustae,* which is found in grasshoppers native to the United States. This protozoan can kill up to ninety percent of the grasshoppers in an area. Sick female grasshoppers pass the microscopic parasite on to their offspring while other grasshoppers become infected by eating the corpses. It can kill fifty to sixty percent of the grasshoppers in three to four weeks. Henry was able to infect fifty-eight species of grasshoppers with *Nosema locustae,* including the most agriculturally destructive species. He used the Great Plains to demonstrate his grasshopper-control methods to the Department of Agriculture's Animal and Plant Health Inspection Service. He also showed that *Nosema* does not infect beneficial insect species, and his work resulted in the first commercial use of a microbe to control grasshopper infestation.

In addition to harnessing microbes for grasshopper control, Henry discovered that wheat bran could serve as low-cost bait in which to plant the *Nosema.* He also developed a method for producing and storing large amounts of *Nosema* when they are in the spore stage, a method which is now used commercially. Today *Nosema locustae* is used in environmentally sensitive areas where chemicals cannot be used. Its chief defect is that it is slow-acting, and Henry has begun to search for a faster-acting biological weapon against grasshoppers.

In 1965 Henry discovered a virus in Montana which attacks grasshoppers. Viruses have distinct advantages over protozoa as a means of grasshopper control because they attack the grasshoppers more swiftly. Over the years Henry has been able to identify seven naturally occurring viruses in the United States and Africa that attack grasshoppers.

Since the 1980s, Henry has been working with the United States Agency for International Development, as well as the Food and Agriculture Organization of the United Nations, on developing biological means of insect control for use around the world. In 1988, after a locust invasion destroyed food crops in several African countries, he began work on that continent. Representatives of African nations had turned to Henry and his biocontrol methods because chemical pesticides that had been used to kill the locusts had killed beneficial insects and polluted the human food supply. Henry continues his work on the project, and fungi are being tested in Mali as well as Madagascar and Cape Verde.

Henry was promoted to research entomologist with the United States Department of Agriculture in Bozeman in 1964. He was later named a senior scientist, and he retired in 1987. He became an adjunct professor of entomology at Montana State University in Bozeman that year, a position he still holds. Henry became a council member of the Society for Invertebrate Pathology's division of microsporida in 1970. He served as vice-chairman of the society from 1974 to 1976 and chairman from 1976 to 1978. He was the North American representative to the Pan American Acridological Society from 1977 to 1979 and chairman of the society's Triennial Congress in 1979. Henry served as the society's president in 1981 and 1985. He chaired the annual meeting of the Society for Invertebrate Pathology in 1981 and was a trustee of the Society for Invertebrate Pathology in 1982 and 1984.

SELECTED WRITINGS BY HENRY:

Periodicals

(With M. C. Wilson, F. A. Oma, and J. L. Fowler) "Pathogenic Micro-organisms Isolated from the West African Grasshoppers (Orthoptera: Acrididae)," *Tropical Pest Management,* Volume 31, 1985, pp. 192–195.

(With D. A. Streett) "A Comparison of Spore Polypeptides in Microsporidia from a Grasshopper Control Program," *Journal of Protozoa,* Volume 32, 1985, pp. 363–364.

(With D. L. Johnson) "Low Rates of Insecticides and Nosema Locustae (Microsporidia: Nosematidae) on Baits Applied to Roadsides for Grasshopper (Orthoptera: Acrididae) Control," *Journal of Economic Entomology,* Volume 80, 1987, pp. 685–689.

SOURCES:

Periodicals

Ellis, Dianne, "Four From Mali," *Montana State University Staff Bulletin,* November 20, 1992.

Senft, Dennis, "Tiny Parasite Taking on Grasshopper," *Agricultural Research,* July, 1989, pp. 12–14.

—Sketch by Margo Nash

Warren Elliott Henry
1909-
American physicist

Warren Elliott Henry was among the most highly regarded African American physicists in the field of missile research in the post-World War II era. A specialist in cryogenics, electronics, and magnetism, he worked at the U.S. Naval Research Laboratory for twelve years before moving to the Lockheed Missiles and Space Company in 1960 and then to Howard University in 1969. During his career, he produced over one hundred publications and collaborated with more than twenty Nobel Prize laureates. Much of the work he did forty years ago has become important to the new interest in the connection between magnetism and superconductivity.

Henry was born in Evergreen, Alabama, on February 18, 1909. His parents, Nelson Henry and Mattye (McDaniel) Henry, were public school teachers, and were extremely supportive of their seven children, the oldest of whom was Warren. His parents took education very seriously and would allow their children to stay up past their normal bedtime only if they were reading or studying. When Henry was in the eleventh grade, his school was forced to close in February of the school year. His parents immediately borrowed railroad fare for him to attend another school in Greenville, Alabama. Henry later worked his way through college and received his B.S. from the Tuskegee Institute in 1931. That year he was appointed principal at the Escambia County Training School in Atmore, Alabama. He remained in this position until 1934 when he took a position as instructor of physics at both Spelman and Morehouse Colleges in Atlanta, Georgia. In 1936, Henry returned to school and earned his M.S. degree from Atlanta University the following year. After returning to Tuskegee as an instructor in chemistry in 1936, he reentered graduate school at the University of Chicago and received his Ph.D. in physics in 1941. In 1943, he left Tuskegee as an instructor in chemistry, physics, and radio and became a staff member at the radiation laboratories of the Massachusetts Institute of Technology in Cambridge. He remained there until 1946 when he returned to teaching at the University of Chicago. A year later he was named the acting head of the physics department at Morehouse College.

In 1948 Henry left teaching and accepted a position as a supervisory physicist at the Naval Research Laboratory (NRL) in Washington, D.C. He then entered the private sector in 1960 when he joined the Lockheed Missiles and Space Company as a senior staff scientist and engineer. Before he returned to teaching in 1968 at Howard University in Washington, D.C., Henry had established an impressive record in research specializing in magnetism, cryogenics (the science of refrigeration at very low temperatures), and solid state physics. The results of his work at both NRL and Lockheed have been used in space technology, oceanography projects, and cryogenic and electronic programs. At Howard, Henry was a professor of physics until his retirement in 1977; he also served as department chairman for one year. Henry was named professor emeritus in 1980 and since then has served Howard as Student Research Coordinator in the MARC Honors Undergraduate Research Training Program.

Henry has lectured in his field in France, Germany, Japan, and the U.S.S.R. He is also the designer of the Henry Elevator Lift, a device that allows for the precise mechanical placement of materials for study. A fellow of the American Physical Society, he has always been intensely interested in minorities in the sciences and served as chairman of that society's committee on minorities in physics. He is also a fellow of the American Association for the Advancement of Science and a member of the American Association of Physics Teachers, the Federation of American Scientists, the Scientific Research Society of America, the American Chemical Society, the Institute of Radio Engineers, Sigma Xi, and the Washington Philosophical Society. A winner of the Carver Award, he was also named a Presidential Associate of Tuskegee Institute. He is married to Jeanne Sally (Pearlson) and has one daughter, Eva Ruth.

SOURCES:

Books

Maclin, A. P., T. L. Gill, and W. W. Zachary, editors, "Magnetic Phenomena: The Warren E. Henry Symposium on Magnetism," *Lecture Notes in Physics,* Springer-Verlag, 1989.

Sammons, Vivian O., *Blacks in Science and Medicine,* Hemisphere Publishing Co., 1990, p. 117.

—Sketch by Leonard C. Bruno

Dudley R. Herschbach
1932-
American physical chemist

Dudley R. Herschbach was a student from a nonscholarly background who, with the aid of fine teachers and university scholarships, developed an aptitude for scientific subjects into a distinguished career as a researcher and theorist. He was a pioneer in the field of molecular reaction dynamics —the study of the motions of atoms during chemical reactions. He was responsible for developing an experimental method called the molecular beam technique, which is used to examine the collision of molecules during the course of a reaction. Herschbach has also advanced the theoretical understanding of basic chemical processes, and for his contributions to this field, he shared with **Yuan T. Lee** and **John C. Polanyi** the 1986 Nobel Prize in chemistry.

The first of six children, Dudley Robert Herschbach was born in San Jose, California, on June 18, 1932, to Robert and Dorothy Beer Herschbach. His father was at that time a building contractor and later a rabbit breeder. Herschbach grew up in a rural area a few miles outside San Jose and engaged in farm activities such as feeding livestock, milking cows, and picking plums, apricots, and walnuts. Although Herschbach was often involved in outdoor activities, he was also an enthusiastic reader and he developed an early interest in science, especially astronomy. He took all the science and mathematics courses available at Campbell High School; he also became a star football player there and was offered athletic scholarships at several institutions. However, he chose an academic scholarship from Stanford University. He did play football during his freshman year but abandoned the sport when the coach tried to forbid him from taking lab courses during the season. He concentrated on his rapidly developing scientific interests, earning a B.S. in mathematics in 1954 and a M.S. in chemistry in 1955.

Herschbach continued his graduate study at Harvard University. Working under E. Bright Wilson, he decided to specialize in the dynamics of chemical reactions. He did his doctoral research on the microwave spectra of molecules in methanol, and he received his Ph.D. in chemical physics in 1958. While at Harvard, he was a member of the institution's prestigious Society of Fellows. Herschbach began his teaching and research career at the University of California at Berkeley; he became an assistant professor of chemistry in 1959 and an associate professor in 1961. He returned to Harvard as professor of chemistry in 1963. In 1976 he was named the Frank B. Baird, Jr. Professor of Science.

Research in Chemical Reaction Dynamics

In the 1950s, the knowledge chemists had about the basic process of chemical reactions was not much advanced since the beginning of the century. Chemists mixed together specified quantities of substances under controlled conditions of temperature and pressure, and then they examined and measured the resulting products and the energy released or consumed during the reaction. In their measurements and examinations, what they observed was the combined products and energies of millions of individual molecules interacting in the substances. What actually took place among individual molecules during a reaction was not really clear. Herschbach's experiments provided the first real evidence of the details of a chemical reaction at the level of individual molecules.

It was his idea to borrow a technique from nuclear and particle physics; in this technique, directed beams of molecules were fired crosswise at each other and the resulting altered molecular products could be collected and studied as individual molecules or atomic particles. Herschbach had constructed a fairly simple apparatus at Berkeley, which heated substances into gaseous form and then directed beams of the molecules at each other at a ninety-degree angle in a vacuum. The molecules reacted at the crossing point and the altered molecules landed on a tungsten (later a platinum) filament through which an electric current was flowing. The dynamics of the reaction could then be studied by measuring the variation in the electric current caused by the altered molecules.

After returning to Harvard in 1963, Herschbach continued his work with a similar apparatus. However, his progress was hampered by the fact that these experiments were limited to reactions involving alkali metals and alkali halides, since these were the only kinds of molecules which the tungsten or platinum filaments could detect. The critical breakthrough in the study of the reactions of more complex molecules came in 1967 with the arrival of Taiwanese-born Yuan T. Lee. A postdoctoral fellow at Harvard, Lee designed and supervised the building of a very sophisticated machine which greatly improved the components of the earlier apparatus. He replaced the filaments with a mass spectrometer, which could detect and measure the reaction products of almost any kind of molecule. After Lee left for the University of Chicago in 1968, Herschbach continued to study increasingly complex chemical reactions at Harvard. He was particularly noted for his ability to devise theories which explained very complex molecular events in clear and relatively simple terms. His work and that of Lee and others transformed the entire field of chemistry, and for their achievements they shared with John C. Polanyi the Nobel Prize in chemistry in 1986.

Herschbach's success has been primarily due to his scientific talent. However, a portion of it has certainly stemmed from his warm and generous relationships with many colleagues and students. Progress in modern science is usually the result of a team effort, a fact of which Herschbach was well aware. In accepting the Nobel Prize, he referred to the speech he gave as a 'tour through a family album," and in an appendix to that address he listed the names of fifty-one graduate students and thirty-five postdoctoral fellows who had worked with him from 1962 to 1986. In the body of the address, he discussed the specific contributions of many of them, most notably Lee, and he also mentioned the assistance of many others, including the name of one staff member of the machine shop of the Harvard chemistry department. Unlike many famous scientists, he is also a popular teacher of both undergraduate and graduate students.

Herschbach married Georgene Botyos in 1964. She was then a graduate student in chemistry at Harvard; they had two daughters before she finished her Ph.D. in 1968. He and his wife served for five years as co-masters of Currier House, one of the Harvard residential colleges for undergraduates. In an autobiographical piece for *Les Prix Nobel 1986,* Herschbach recounted with relish how they were once summoned to a student's room to meet a seal in a bathtub. He now lives with his family in Lincoln, Massachusetts.

SELECTED WRITINGS BY HERSCHBACH:

Periodicals

"Dudley R. Herschbach" (autobiographical sketch), *Les Prix Nobel 1986,* pp. 113–116.

"Molecular Dynamics of Elementary Chemical Reactions: Nobel Lecture," *Les Prix Nobel 1986,* 1986, pp. 117–165.

SOURCES:

Books

Magill, Frank N., editor, *The Nobel Prize Winners: Chemistry,* Salem Press, 1990, Volume 3, pp. 1135–1141.

Wasson, Tyler, editor, *Nobel Prize Winners,* H. W. Wilson, 1987, pp. 438–440.

Periodicals

New York Times, October 14, 1986, p. B19.

Scientific American, December, 1986, p. 86.

Time, October 27, 1986, p. 67.

Waldrop, M. Mitchell, "The 1986 Nobel Prize in Chemistry," *Science,* November 7, 1986, pp. 673–674.

—Sketch by John E. Little

Alfred Day Hershey
1908-
American microbiologist

By seeking to understand the reproduction of viruses, the simplest form of life, Alfred Day Hershey made important discoveries about the nature of deoxyribonucleic acid (DNA) and laid the groundwork for modern molecular genetics. Highly regarded as an experimental scientist, Hershey is perhaps best known for the 1952 "blender experiment " that he and Martha Chase conducted to demonstrate that DNA, not protein, was the genetic material of life. This discovery stimulated further research into DNA, including the discovery by **James Watson** and **Francis Crick** of the double-helix structure of DNA the following year. Hershey's work with bacteriophages, the viruses that prey on bacteria, was often carried out in loose collaboration with other scientists working with bacteriophages. Hershey shared the Nobel Prize in Physiology or Medicine in 1969 with **Max Delbrück** and **Salvador Edward Luria**. The Nobel Committee praised the three scientists for their contributions to molecular biology. Their basic research into viruses also helped others develop vaccines against viral diseases such as polio.

Hershey was born on December 4, 1908, in Owosso, Michigan, to Robert Day Hershey and Alma Wilbur Hershey. His father worked for an auto manufacturer. Alfred attended public schools in Owosso and nearby Lansing. He received his B.S. in bacteriology from Michigan State College (now Michigan State University) in 1930 and his Ph.D. in chemistry from the same school in 1934. As a graduate student, Hershey's interest in bacteriology and the biochemistry of life was already evident. His doctoral dissertation was on the chemistry of *Brucella,* the bacteria responsible for brucellosis, also known as undulant fever. Undulant fever is transmitted to humans from cattle and causes recurrent fevers and joint pain. After receiving his Ph.D., Hershey took a position as a research assistant in the Department of Bacteriology at the Washington University School of Medicine in St. Louis. There he worked with Jacques Jacob Bronfenbrenner, one of the pioneers in bacteriophage research in the United States. During the

Alfred Day Hershey

sixteen years he spent teaching and conducting research at Washington University, from 1934 to 1950, Hershey was promoted to instructor (1936), assistant professor (1938), and associate professor (1942).

Bacteriophages—known simply as phages—had been discovered in 1915, only nineteen years before Hershey began his career. Phages are viruses that reproduce by preying on bacteria, first attacking and then dissolving them. For scientists who study bacteria, phages are a source of irritation because they can destroy bacterial cultures. But other scientists are fascinated by this tiny organism. Perhaps the smallest living thing, phages consist of little more than the protein and DNA (the molecule of heredity) found in a cellular nucleus. Remarkably efficient, however, phages reproduce by conquering bacteria and subverting them to the phage particles' own needs. This type of reproduction is known as replication. Little was known about the particulars of this process when Hershey was a young scientist.

By studying viral replication, scientists hoped to learn more about the viral diseases that attack humans, like mumps, the common cold, German measles, and polio. But the study of bacteriophages also promised findings with implications that reached far beyond disease cures into the realm of understanding life itself. If Hershey and other researchers could determine how phages replicated, they stood to learn how higher organisms—including humans—passed genetic information from generation to generation.

Exposing the Secret Life of Viruses

Hershey's study of phages soon yielded several discoveries that furthered an understanding of genetic inheritance and change. In 1945 he showed that phages were capable of spontaneous mutation. Faced with a bacterial culture known to be resistant to phage attack, most, but not all, phages would die. By mutating, some phages survived to attack the bacteria and replicate. This finding was significant because it showed that mutations did not occur gradually, as one school of scientific thought believed, but rather occurred immediately and spontaneously in viruses. It also helped explain why viral attack is so difficult to prevent. In 1946 Hershey made another discovery that changed what scientists thought about viruses. He showed that if different strains of phages infected the same bacterial cell, they could combine or exchange genetic material. This is similar to what occurs when higher forms of life sexually reproduce, of course. But it was the first time viruses were shown to combine genetic material. Hershey called this phenomenon genetic recombination.

Hershey was not the only scientist who saw the potential in working with bacteriophages. Two other influential scientists were also pursuing the same line of investigation. Max Delbrück, a physicist, had been studying phages in the United States since he fled Nazi Germany in 1937. Studying genetic recombination independently of Hershey, he reached the same results that Hershey did in the same year. Similarly, Salvador Edward Luria, a biologist and physician who immigrated to the United States from Italy in 1940, had independently confirmed Hershey's work on spontaneous mutation in 1945. Although the three men never worked side by side in the same laboratory, they were collaborators nonetheless. Through conversation and correspondence, they shared results and encouraged each other in their phage research. Indeed, these three scientists formed the core of the self-declared "phage group," a loose-knit clique of scientists who encouraged research on particular strains of bacteriophage. By avoiding competition and duplication, the group hoped to advance phage research that much faster.

The "Blender Experiment"

In 1950 Hershey accepted a position as a staff scientist in the department of genetics (now the Genetics Research Unit) of the Carnegie Institute at Cold Spring Harbor, New York. It was at Cold Spring Harbor that Hershey conducted his most influential experiment. Hershey wished to prove conclusively that the genetic material in phages was DNA. Analysis with an electron microscope had showed that phages consist only of DNA surrounded by a protein shell. Other scientists' experiments had revealed that during replication some part of the parental phages was being transferred to their offspring. The task before Hershey was to show that it was the phage DNA that was passed on to succeeding generations and that gave the signal for replication and growth.

Although Hershey was not alone in having reached the belief that DNA was the stuff of life, many scientists were unconvinced. They doubted that DNA had the complexity needed to carry the blueprint for life and believed instead that the genetic code resided in protein, a far more elaborate molecule. Furthermore, no one had yet demonstrated the technical skill needed to design an experiment that would answer the question once and for all.

With Martha Chase, Hershey found a way to determine what role each of the phage components played in replication. In experiments done in 1951 and 1952, Hershey used radioactive phosphorus to tag the DNA and radioactive sulfur to tag the protein. (The DNA contains no sulfur and the protein contains no phosphorus.) Hershey and Chase then allowed the marked phage particles to infect a bacterial culture and to begin the process of replication. This process was interrupted when the scientists spun the culture at a high speed in a Waring blender.

In this manner, Hershey and Chase learned that the shearing action of the blender separated the phage protein from the bacterial cells. Apparently while the phage DNA entered the bacterium and forced it to start replicating phage particles, the phage protein remained outside, attached to the cell wall. The researchers surmised that the phage particle attached itself to the outside of a bacterium by its protein "tail" and literally injected its nucleic acid into the cell. DNA, and not protein, was responsible for communicating the genetic information needed to produce the next generation of phage.

Clearly DNA seemed to hold the key to heredity for all forms of life, not just viruses. Yet while the blender experiment answered one question about DNA, it also raised a host of other questions. Now scientists wanted to know more about the action of DNA. How did DNA operate? How did it replicate itself? How did it direct the production of proteins? What was its chemical structure? Until that last question was answered, scientists could only speculate about answers to the others. Hershey's achievement spurred other scientists into DNA research.

In 1953, a year after Hershey's blender experiment, the structure of DNA was determined in Cambridge, England, by James Dewey Watson and Francis Harry Compton Crick. Watson, who was only twenty-five years old when the structure was announced, had worked with Luria at the University of Indiana. For their discovery of DNA's double-helix structure, Watson and Crick received the Nobel Prize in 1962.

Career Honored with a Belated Nobel Prize

Hershey, Delbrück, and Luria also received a Nobel Prize for their contributions to molecular biology, but not until 1969. This seeming delay in recognition for their accomplishments prompted the *New York Times* to ask in an October 20, 1969, editorial: "Delbrück, Hershey and Luria richly deserve their awards, but why did they have to wait so long for this recognition? Every person associated with molecular biology knows that these are the grand pioneers of the field, the giants on whom others—some of whom received the Nobel Prize years ago—depended for their own great achievements." Yet other scientists observed that the blender experiment merely offered experimental proof of a theoretical belief that was already widely held. After the blender experiment, Hershey continued investigating the structure of phage DNA. Although human DNA winds double-stranded like a spiral staircase, Hershey found that some phage DNA is single-stranded and some is circular. In 1962 Hershey was named director of the Genetics Research Unit at Cold Spring Harbor. He retired in 1974.

Hershey was "known to his colleagues as a very quiet, withdrawn sort of man who avoids crowds and noise and most hectic social activities," according to the report of the 1969 Nobel Prize in the October 17, 1969, *New York Times.* His hobbies were woodworking, reading, gardening, and sailing. He married Harriet Davidson, a former research assistant, on November 15, 1945. She later became an editor of the *Cold Spring Harbor Symposia on Quantitative Biology.* She and Hershey had one child, a son named Peter Manning. Born on August 7, 1956, Peter was twelve years old when Hershey won the Nobel Prize.

In addition to the Nobel Prize, Hershey received the Albert Lasker Award of the American Public Health Association (1958) and the Kimber Genetics Award of the National Academy of Sciences (1965) for his discoveries concerning the genetic structure and replication processes of viruses. He was elected to the National Academy of Sciences in 1958.

SELECTED WRITINGS BY HERSHEY:

Periodicals

"Reproduction of Bacteriophage," *International Review of Cytology,* Volume 1, 1952, pp. 119–134.

"Nuclear Acid Economy in Bacteria Infected with Bacteriophage T2. 2. Phage Precursor Nucleic Acid," *Journal of General Physiology,* Volume 37, 1953, pp. 1–23.

"Upper Limit to the Protein Content of the Germinal Substance of Bacteriophage T2," *Viruses,* Volume 1, 1955, pp. 108–127.

SOURCES:

Books

Fox, Daniel M., editor, *Nobel Laureates in Medicine or Physiology: A Biographical Dictionary,* Garland, 1990.

Magner, Lois N., *History of the Life Sciences,* Dekker, 1979.

McGraw-Hill Modern Scientists and Engineers, McGraw-Hill, 1980.

Wasson, Tyler, editor, *Nobel Prize Winners,* H. W. Wilson, 1987.

Periodicals

New York Times, October 17, 1969, p. 24; October 20, 1969, p. 46.

Science, October 24, 1969, p. 479–481.

"Three Americans Share Nobel Prize for Medicine for Work on Bacteriophage," *Chemical and Engineering News,* October 27, 1969, p. 16.

Time, October 24, 1969, p. 84.

—*Sketch by Liz Marshall*

Gustav Hertz
1887-1975
German physicist

Gustav Hertz's greatest fame came early in his career as the result of his collaboration with **James Franck** , a colleague at the University of Berlin. Hertz and Franck studied the energy changes that take place when an electron strikes an atom. Their results provided important confirmation of the Bohr theory of the atom, a theory announced only shortly before Hertz and Franck conducted their experiments. In recognition of their work, the Nobel Prize in physics was awarded jointly to Hertz and Franck in 1925.

Hertz was born in Hamburg, Germany, on July 22, 1887. His mother was Auguste Arning, and his father was Gustav Hertz, an attorney. Hertz was the nephew of the famous Heinrich Rudolf Hertz, who carried out a number of important studies on electromagnetic waves in the 1880s, and for whom the unit of frequency is now named.

Hertz received his secondary education at the Johanneum Realgymnasium in Hamburg. Between 1906 and 1911, he studied mathematics and physics at the universities of Göttingen, Munich, and Berlin. He eventually decided to concentrate on a career in experimental physics. In 1911, he earned a Ph.D. from the University of Berlin for his study of the infrared absorption spectrum of carbon dioxide.

A position as research assistant at the physical institute of the University of Berlin was offered to Hertz in 1913. When he began work at the institute, Hertz met Franck, and the two decided to collaborate on their research. The first project they undertook involved a study of the emission of electrons from a metal surface when bombarded by a stream of electrons. This type of research can be traced to studies of the photoelectric effect, the emission of electrons from a metal surface that has been exposed to light energy. In 1902, the German physicist **Philipp E. A. von Lenard** carried out some experiments on this effect. Three years later, **Albert Einstein** provided a theoretical explanation of Lenard's results and of the photoelectric effect in general. Hertz and Franck attempted to determine the properties of electrons emitted from a metal surface bombarded by electrons rather than by light.

In their experiment, Hertz and Franck accelerated electrons from a hot tungsten wire by means of a positively charged metal gauze placed a few centimeters from the wire. The electrons were forced to pass through an atmosphere of mercury vapor. A second positively charged wire gauze was then arranged so as to detect electrons that had collided with mercury atoms and lost energy. The experiment consisted of gradually increasing the charge on the metal gauze and tracking the loss of energy for electrons reaching the detector screen. Hertz and Franck found that this loss of energy was negligible until the potential difference reached 4.9 volts. At that point, the electron current reaching the detector dropped nearly to zero.

For some months, Hertz and Franck were not able to interpret their results. They thought that 4.9 volts might represent the ionization potential of mercury, the energy needed to remove a single electron from a mercury atom. In fact, the correct explanation for their results was already available in **Niels Bohr**'s recently announced quantum model of the atom. Hertz and Franck eventually realized that the 4.9 volt result they observed corresponded to the transition between the first two electron energy levels (K to L) in the mercury atom. In fact, that numerical value precisely matched the energy difference that Bohr had predicted in his theory. As such, the Hertz-Franck results provided one of the first pieces of experimental confirmation for Bohr's revolutionary new theory. In recognition of this achievement, Hertz and Franck were jointly awarded the 1925 Nobel Prize in physics.

Less than a year after completing his momentous experiments, Hertz was inducted into the German army. He was seriously wounded at the battle front in 1915 and spent more than a year in recuperation. After the war, he returned to Berlin, where he worked for three years as an unsalaried lecturer (privatdozent). He married Ellen Dihlmann in 1919, with whom he had two sons, Hellmuth and Johannes. In 1943, two years after Dihlmann died, Hertz was married a second time, to Charlotte Jollasse.

In 1920, Hertz accepted an offer of employment at the Philips Incandescent Lamp Works in Eindhoven, Netherlands. Philips was one of the first corporations to maintain a basic research laboratory. After five years at Philips, Hertz returned to Germany in October of 1925 as professor of physics and director of the physical institute at the University of Halle. He remained there for three years before returning once more to Berlin. There, he became professor of physics at the Charlottenburg Technical University.

With the rise of National Socialism (the Nazi party), Hertz faced yet another career change. Unwilling to sign an oath of loyalty to the new government, he was forced to resign his post at the Technical University. Surprisingly, he was offered and accepted a job with the Siemens and Halske Company in Berlin in 1934. He remained in that job until the end of World War II, at which time he moved to the Soviet Union. He told friends that he hoped to be able to make a contribution to Soviet physics. That hope was not realized, however, since he and his German colleagues were assigned to a segregated community in Sukhumi on the Black Sea, where they worked on atomic energy, radar, and supersonics projects in isolation from Soviet scientists. At the conclusion of his ten-year commitment to the Soviet government, Hertz returned to East Germany, where he became director of the physics institute at Karl Marx University in Leipzig. He retired from that position in 1961 and returned to Berlin, where he died on October 30, 1975.

SELECTED WRITINGS BY HERTZ:

Books

Lehrbuch der Kernphysik, 3 volumes, B. G. Teubuer, 1958–62.

Periodicals

"Collisions between Electrons and Molecules of Mercury Vapor and the Ionizing Voltage for the Same," *Vehr. Deut. Physik. Geo,* Volume 16, pp. 457–67.

(With J. Franck) "Impacts between Gas Molecules and Slowly Moving Electrons," *Ber. Physike. Geog.,* 1913, pp. 373–91.

SOURCES:

Books

A Biographical Encyclopedia of Scientists, Volume 1, Facts on File, 1981, pp. 370–71.

Heathcote, Niels H. de V., *Nobel Prize Winners in Physics, 1901–1950,* Henry Schuman, 1953, pp. 229–48.

Nobel Prize Winners, H. W. Wilson, 1987, pp. 442–44.

Weber, Robert L., *Pioneers of Science: Nobel Prize Winners in Physics,* American Institute of Physics, 1980, pp. 78–79.

—*Sketch by David E. Newton*

Ejnar Hertzsprung
1873-1967
Danish astronomer

Danish astronomer Ejnar Hertzsprung was a pioneer in stellar spectroscopy and photometry whose career spanned more than six decades. He is best remembered for discovering the relationship between the brightness and the temperature of stars, and for representing this information graphically in what is now known as the Hertzsprung-Russell diagram, one of the most important tools used by astronomers to study stars' characteristics. Among his other achievements were the formulation of the concept of absolute brightness among stars, and the identification of red giant and red dwarf stars. Hertzsprung also made the first measurement of an inter-galactic distance. These achievements rank him among the greatest astronomers of the twentieth century.

Born in Frederiksberg, Denmark, on October 8, 1873, Ejnar Hertzsprung was the son of Henrietta (Frost) and Severin Hertzsprung, who held a graduate degree in astronomy from the University of Copenhagen. However, the need to support a family forced Severin Hertzsprung to pursue a career in government rather than science; after working for the Danish government's Department of Finances he became director of the state life insurance company. He instilled in his son the love of science, mathematics, and astronomy. Ejnar chose to become a chemical engineer after his interest in chemistry was sparked by the writings of Danish chemist Julius Thomsen.

After graduating from Frederiksberg Polytechnic in 1898, Ejnar went to St. Petersburg, where he worked as a chemical engineer. He left Russia for Germany in 1901, when he went to Leipzig to study photochemistry with **Wilhelm Ostwald**. Around this time, he developed an interest in astronomy so he abandoned engineering for the profession for which his father had trained but was never able to pursue. In 1902, Hertzsprung returned to Denmark as an astronomer at the observatory of the University of Copenhagen and the Urania Observatory in Frederiksberg, which belonged to Victor Nielsen, a noted amateur astronomer. Hertzsprung realized how important photography would be in the study of astronomy, and applied what he had learned in Ostwald's lab to his work at the observatories.

Studies the Relation between Star Luminosity and Color

Since the mid–1800s, astronomers had been able to classify stars on the basis of light spectra. These spectra were determined by using a prism to separate the light from a star into its component colors. Soon after they began using spectroscopy, astronomers realized that only a few basic types of stars existed. Using photographic techniques and data compiled by such astronomers as Edward Pickering, **Annie Jump Cannon**, and **Antonia Maury** to classify stars on the basis of their spectra, Hertzsprung set out to discover what could account for the differences in stellar spectra. One of his first accomplishments was to establish the concept of "absolute magnitude"—the brightness of a star at the distance of ten parsecs, or 32.6 light years—as the standard for measuring the brightness of stars. He then discovered the relationship between a star's color (and thus, its temperature) and its brightness, recognizing that the bluer the star, the brighter it was. He also found that some stars did not fit this pattern, particularly some very luminous red stars, which he called "giants." In addition, Hertzsprung determined that stars could be divided into two major groups, based on their luminosity: the giants, with great luminosity, and the dwarfs, or dimmer stars. He observed that giant stars were far fewer in number than dwarf stars.

In 1905 Hertzsprung published many of these findings in "On the Radiation of the Stars" ("Zur Strahlung der Sterne"), which appeared not in an astronomical journal but in *Zeitschrift für wissenschaftliche Photographie,* a publication dedicated to photochemistry and photophysics. In 1906, Hertzsprung created the first diagram plotting the relation between a star's brightness and its temperature, but it was not published. A second paper, with a title identical to the first but surveying a different group of stars, appeared in 1907. Because the articles were published in a photographic journal, Hertzsprung's work did not become known to the astronomical community until **Henry Norris Russell**, an American astronomer, presented similar discoveries to the Royal Astronomical Society in 1913. Because the men came to similar conclusions while working from different sets of data, the landmark diagram that grew from their findings shares both names.

The Hertzsprung-Russell (H-R) diagram is a graph that plots stars' temperatures versus their absolute magnitudes. Most stars' measurements fall into an area of the graph called the "main sequence"—a curve that runs diagonally from the upper left to the lower right of the graph. Exceptions, such as blue giant stars and red dwarf stars, fall outside of the main sequence on the graph. A common use of the Hertzsprung-Russell diagram today is to illustrate stellar evolution. It is thought that most stars begin their lives as main sequence stars. As a stars burns, it swells and grows into a red giant. As the star gets older, it may evolve into a brown dwarf, black hole, or supernova; such bodies lie outside the main sequence on the H-R diagram. H-R diagrams also reveal important information about the sizes, masses, and distances of stars. According to K. Aa Strand in the *Dictionary of Scientific Biography,* the H-R diagram "remains the cornerstone of all astronomical research related to the formation and evolution of stars."

Hertzsprung's work attracted the attention of Germany's leading astronomer, Karl Schwarzschild, the director of the Göttingen Observatory. Largely through his influence, Hertzsprung was named a lecturer in astrophysics at Göttingen University in 1909. When Schwarzschild moved on to the Potsdam Astrophysical Observatory, Hertzsprung followed. Hertzsprung went on to the Leiden Observatory in the Netherlands, first as an observer, in 1919. He remained there for twenty-five years, retiring as director in 1944. He taught at the University of Leiden from 1920 to 1945; while at Leiden, Hertzsprung published a catalog of the mean color equivalents of almost 750 stars.

Calculates First Inter-Galactic Distance

Another of Hertzsprung's most significant accomplishments was the development of a method to determine the distances of stars from the earth. In the 1800s such distances were calculated using a method called annual parallax, but this method was accurate only for stars within one hundred light-years of the earth. In 1912, however, an important step was taken toward the calculation of greater cosmic distances. While studying the Cepheid variable stars (a class of pulsating stars characterized by regularly varying luminosity), **Henrietta Leavitt** discovered a relationship between the mean brightness of these variable stars and their periods, or rates, of variation. The Cepheids that were the subjects of Leavitt's study were located in neighboring galaxies called the Magellanic Clouds. Hertzsprung first reasoned that the Cepheids could all be considered to be the same distance from the earth. Comparing the brightness of Cepheid stars in our own Milky Way galaxy, whose distance from the earth he was able to determine, to the brightness of Cepheids in the Magellanic Clouds, Hertzsprung estimated the Small Magellanic Cloud to be 10,000 parsecs (32,600 light years) away from the earth. This method of distance determination, according to Strand, "became the basis for all measurements of very large distances in our galactic system, as well as in the expanding universe of the galaxies." Hertzsprung's measurement, although accurate in its method, held an error: he did not account for the light absorption by a galaxy, so his measurement is about one-fifth of the distance accepted today. But the calculation was the first measurement of inter-galactic distance, and for this achievement, the Royal Astronomical Society awarded him its Gold Medal in 1929.

Hertzsprung was well noted for his exacting standards, not only of others, but of himself. In one instance, he was attempting to verify the relation between light-curve shape and period while at Harvard in 1926. To make such a verification, the usual method would have been to take between a hundred and two hundred plate "estimates," or studies. Hertzsprung made between 384 and 1,056 estimates on each of the stars he was studying. Such thoroughness paid off in discoveries that a less-determined observer might have missed. During his stay in South Africa (1923–1925), he took many plates of the Eta Carinae region to study variable stars. Within three hours one night he took five plates. On the first two plates, he noted a faint star that on the third plate showed the first stellar flare to be observed reliably.

In his later work, Hertzsprung turned his attention to variable stars, like Polaris, and to double (binary) stars, which orbit each other. Through painstaking work, he was able to determine the positions of double stars with an unprecedented margin of error of just a few thousandths of a minute of an arc. Among his other achievements were the introduction of greatly improved photographic methods for determining stellar color and magnitude, and the use of measurements of star motion to determine the configurations of star clusters.

Over the course of his long career Hertzsprung, a modest man, received numerous accolades. Besides the Gold Medal of the Royal Astronomical Society, he received the Bruce Medal of the Astronomical Society of the Pacific in 1937. He received honorary doctorates from the University of Utretch in 1923, the University of Copenhagen (1946) and the University of Paris (1949). He was a member of the Danish Academy, the Dutch Academy, the Royal Astronomy Society, the American Astronomy Society, and the American Academy of Arts and Sciences.

Retirement was by no means an end to Hertzsprung's research. He continued to measure double stars and compiled a general catalog of such measures until after the age of ninety. After spending the last six months of his life in a hospital, Ejnar Hertzsprung died on October 21, 1967, in Roskilde, Denmark. In his obituary in *Sky and Telescope,* Axel V. Nielsen of the Ole Roemer Observatory wrote: "In his later years, Hertzsprung would tell visiting astronomers and would write in letters: 'You may be sure that if a theoretical step forward is not made today, it will be made tomorrow; but every day fine conditions for making certain observations are present, and similar conditions may not return for a long time, or never.' These sound words are the last message of a great astronomer to the astronomical world."

SELECTED WRITINGS BY HERTZSPRUNG:

Periodicals

"Zur Strahlung der Sterne," *Zeitschrift für wissenschaftliche Photographie,* Volume 3, 1905, pp. 429–422.

"Zur Strahlung der Sterne," *Zeitschrift für wissenschaftliche Photographie,* Volume 5, 1907, pp. 86–107.

"On the Relation Between Mass and Absolute Brightness of Components of Double Stars," *Bulletin of the Astronomical Institutes of the Netherlands,* Volume 2, 1923, pp. 15–18.

"The Pleiades," *Monthly Notices of the Royal Astronomical Society,* Volume 89, 1929, pp. 660–678.

SOURCES:

Books

Dictionary of Scientific Biography, Volume 6, Scribner's, 1972, pp. 350–353.

Periodicals

DeVorkin, David H., "Steps Toward the Hertzsprung-Russell Diagram," *Physics Today,* March, 1978, pp. 32–39.

"Ejnar Hertzsprung's 90th Birthday," *Sky and Telescope,* October, 1963, p. 199.

Nielsen, Axel V., "Ejnar Hertzsprung: Measurer of Stars," *Sky and Telescope,* January, 1968, pp. 4–6.

Strand, Aa. K., "Ejnar Hertzsprung and the Leiden Observatory," *Popular Astronomy,* Volume 55, August, 1947, pp. 361–364.

—*Sketch by F. C. Nicholson*

Gerhard Herzberg
1904-
German-born Canadian physical chemist

Gerhard Herzberg is known as the founding father of molecular spectroscopy, the science that observes the interaction of energy with matter to obtain information on the identity and structure of molecules. For his "contributions to the knowledge of the electronic structure and geometry of molecules, especially free radicals" Herzberg became the first Canadian to be honored by the Nobel Prize in chemistry in 1971. Herzberg also did pioneering work in other scientific fields, including astrophysics, and in association with the National Research Council of Canada, he founded the nation's premier molecular spectroscopy laboratory in 1948.

Herzberg was born December 25, 1904, to Albin and Ella (Biber) Herzberg. Raised and schooled in Hamburg, Germany, Herzberg graduated from the Darmstadt Institute of Technology with a B.S. in engineering in 1927. In 1928 he completed his Ph.D. with a thesis on the interaction of electromagnetic radiation with matter. Herzberg also studied at the University of Gottingen and the University of Bristol in England, before returning to Darmstadt in 1930 as an instructor.

Move to Canada

In 1935 Herzberg was forced to flee Germany as a result of Hitler's anti-Jewish policies. He subsequently obtained a position as Carnegie guest professor at the University of Saskatchewan, in Canada. Although the school lacked the resources and equipment Herzberg needed for his studies, the atmosphere was welcoming and supportive, and he accomplished a substantial amount of research while also publishing two books. While at Saskatchewan, Herzberg helped establish a graduate laboratory specializing in spectroscopy studies and obtained funding to improve the school's research facilities. Beginning in 1945, Herzberg spent three years as a professor at the Yerkes Observatory of the University of Chicago and then moved back to Canada to set up a spectroscopic research laboratory in Ottawa for the National Research Council. This laboratory was commended by the Swedish Royal Academy of Science, the Nobel Prize awarding institution, as "the foremost center for molecular spectroscopy in the world." Herzberg remained with the Canadian National Research Council for the remainder of his career becoming the first Distinguished Research Scientist of that organization. He became a naturalized Canadian citizen in 1945.

Herzberg's Contributions to Molecular Spectroscopy

Although Herzberg considered himself a physicist, his research in molecular spectroscopy had special significance to chemistry. His research was of great importance as it developed a method of analyzing molecular structure by measuring light transmited and absorbed by molecules. To do this, Herzberg used the spectroscope, a tool that enabled him to separate a molecule's radiant energy into different parts in the same way light is separated when passed through a prism. When molecules or atoms were passed through a spectroscope, the energy radiating from them separated into distinct lines or spectra, allowing an accurate analysis of their structure. At the time Herzberg began his experiments, spectroscopy, or the study of molecular structure, was a primitive science. Very little was known about atomic spectra when he began his analysis, and Herzberg made major contributions to the field by analyzing complicated spectra obtained from molecules, particularly diatomic molecules such as nitrogen, oxygen, and hydrogen. While still in Germany, for example, he and a colleague, Werner Heitler, showed that the nitrogen molecule's complex spectrum was much more significant than contemporary scientific belief acknowledged; the particles then believed to comprise nitrogen's nucleus could not account for the intensity of some of the spectral bands. The neutrons responsible for the inconsistency were discovered by the English physicist **James Chadwick** some time later.

Herzberg also discovered several molecular species in outer space and the upper atmosphere while at the Yerkes Observatory. He found elemental hydrogen in some planetary atmospheres. He also discovered new bands, now called Herzberg Bands, in the oxygen spectrum. Spectroscopy, however, allowed him to do much more throughout his career than just identify molecules. He accurately measured the electron energy levels in several species, using a combination of quantum mechanical theory and spectroscopy. By developing new experimental procedures, he was able to study short-lived molecules, or free radicals, that appear only briefly during chemical reactions. These chemical intermediates are difficult to study because they do not last long enough to apply other types of tests. Two important examples of his success in this area are the spectra of the methylene radical, CH_2, and the methyl radical, CH_3.

An Avid Researcher and Promoter of Science

Herzberg was also a voluminous writer throughout his career, publishing several hundred papers and many definitive books in the area of molecular and atomic spectra. He wrote in the introduction to his 1971 book, *The Spectra and Structure of Simple Free Radicals: An Introduction to Molecular Spectroscopy,* "My original plan, forty years ago, was to write a small book on [molecular spectroscopy] of no more than 200 pages. I was unable to prevent this original plan from leading to a three-volume work of over 2000 pages." Herzberg made a clear the distinction between scientific research and technological research. He believed that the former concentrated on finding out more about nature while the latter focused on the applications of science to society. In Herzberg's opinion, it was scientific research that was the true vocation of the scientist, and not technological research, which he believed to be the concern of politicians. He also championed the right of the scientist to work freely, without political or bureaucratic restrictions. Herzberg was awarded many honors in addition to the 1971 Nobel Prize in chemistry, including the Willard Gibbs Medal and the Linus Pauling Medal from the American Chemical Society, the Gold Medal of the Canadian Association of Physicists, and the Royal Medal of the Royal Society of London.

Herzberg married Luise H. Oettinger in 1929; the couple had two children, Paul and Agnes, both of whom chose teaching as their profession. Luise died in 1971 and Herzberg married Monika Tenthoff a year later. Herzberg's hobbies include music and mountain-climbing.

SELECTED WRITINGS BY HERZBERG:

Books

Molecular Spectra and Molecular Structure, Volume 1: *Spectra of Diatomic Molecules,* Prentice-Hall, 1939, Volume 2: *Infrared and Raman Spectra of Polyatomic Molecules,* Van Nostrand, 1945, Volume 3: *Electronic Spectra and Electronic Structure of Polygamic Molecules,* Van Nostrand, 1966.

The Spectra and Structure of Simple Free Radicals: An Introduction to Molecular Spectroscopy, Cornell University Press, 1971.

SOURCES:

Periodicals

Douglas, A. E. "Nobel Prize for Chemistry: Herzberg and Molecular Spectroscopy" *Science,* Volume 174, November 12, 1971, pg. 672.

—*Sketch by Gail B.C. Marsella*

Caroline L. Herzenberg
1932-
American physicist

Caroline L. Herzenberg's contribution to science goes beyond research and discovery in the traditional sense. She is probably best known for her work in underscoring the importance of women in science. As president of the Association for Women in Science (1988–90), she launched an effort to collect biographical information about women who have made contributions to the sciences. Her book *Women Scientists from Antiquity to the Present* (1986) is one of the most comprehensive listings of women in science available and contains a wealth of biographical information.

Caroline Stuart Littlejohn was born in East Orange, New Jersey, on March 25, 1932, the daughter of Charles Frederick and Caroline Dorothea (Schulze) Littlejohn. She attended the Massachusetts Institute of Technology, receiving her bachelor of science degree in 1953. She then went on to the University of Chicago, where she received her master's degree in 1955 and her Ph.D. in 1958.

Herzenberg remained at the University of Chicago as a research assistant but went to the Argonne National Laboratory in Argonne, Illinois, a year later. In 1961 she became assistant professor of physics at the Illinois Institute of Technology in Chicago. She held that position until 1967, when she became a research physicist at IIT's Research Institute. The Research Center named her senior physicist in 1970. During this same time, Herzenberg served as principal investigator of NASA's Apollo Returned Lunar Sample Analysis Program, working to investigate the composition of materials from the moon.

From 1972 to 1974 Herzenberg was a visiting associate professor of physics at the University of Illinois Medical Center in Chicago, and from 1975 to 1976 she was a lecturer at California State University at Fresno. After these years as an academic researcher and teacher, she returned to the Argonne National Laboratory as a physicist, where she remains. In 1991, she briefly returned to academia for a stint as distinguished visiting professor of physics at the State University of New York at Plattsburgh. During her long career, Herzenberg has contributed to journals in fields as varied as fluids engineering, crystallography, geophysics, and the physics of solids and planetary interiors.

She has been active in several professional science associations. In addition to her involvement with AWIS (where, besides taking on the presidency, she served as secretary from 1982 to 1986), she is a fellow of the American Physical Society. She also served as secretary/treasurer of APS' Forum on Physics and Society and as chair of the APS Committee on the Status of Women in Physics.

Herzenberg's compilations of information about women scientists and her efforts in publicizing women's role in the sciences since ancient times are invaluable research tools for students of history, science, and women's studies. She has written numerous articles on the role of women in the sciences, and her book *Women Scientists from Antiquity to the Present*provides bibliographical information for more than 2500 women. "Could you identify a woman scientist who lived before the time of Marie Curie?" she asks in the introduction. "Most people could not," she replies, "and neither could many scientists or engineers." Yet, she notes, women have been active in science for at least 6000 years. Currently, she and physicist Ruth Hege Howes are pursuing a major research effort to study the contributions of women scientists to the Manhattan Project during World War II and develop a better understanding of their role in developing the atomic bomb.

Married to Leonardo Herzenberg since 1961, Herzenberg is the mother of two daughters. She is past president of the Freeport, Illinois, chapter of NOW and was a candidate for alderman there in 1975. She became the first woman scientist to be inducted into the Chicago Women's Hall of Fame in 1989.

SELECTED WRITINGS BY HERZENBERG:

Books

Women Scientists from Antiquity to the Present: An Index, Locust Hill Press, 1986.

(With Ruth Hege Howes) "Women in Weapons Development: The Manhattan Project" in *Women and the Use of Military Force,* edited by Ruth Hege Howes and Michael R. Stevenson, Lynne Rienner, 1993, pp. 95–110.

Periodicals

(With Susan V. Meschel and James A. Altena) "Women Scientists and Physicians of Antiquity and the Middle Ages," *Journal of Chemical Education,* February, 1991, pp. 101–105.

(With Ruth Hege Howes) "Women of the Manhattan Project," *Technology Review,* November-December, 1993, pp. 32–40.

—Sketch by George A. Milite

Harry Hammond Hess
1906-1969
American geologist

Harry Hammond Hess spent much of his career studying what the ocean floor was made of and where it came from. He was a renowned geologist whose interests and influence ranged from oceanography to space science. One of his most important contributions to science was the concept of seafloor spreading, which became a cornerstone in the acceptance of the continental drift theory during the 1960s. As an officer in the United States Naval Reserve, he was able to combine military service with scientific investigation; in his later years, he became an important figure in NASA, helping direct the science of lunar exploration.

Hess was born in New York City on May 24, 1906, to Julian S. Hess, a member of the New York Stock Exchange, and Elizabeth Engel Hess. He attended Asbury Park High School in New Jersey before entering Yale University in 1923. At Yale he intended to study electrical engineering, but changed his mind and graduated in 1927 with a B.S. degree in geology. Hess then spent two years in northern Rhodesia (now Zambia) as an exploration geologist. Returning to the United States, Hess received his doctorate from Princeton University in 1932. He taught at Rutgers University for a year, conducted research at the Geophysical Laboratory at the Carnegie Institute of Washington, then finally returned to Princeton in 1934. He would remain at Princeton for essentially the rest of his career, serving as chair of the university's geology department from 1950 to 1966.

Annette Burns, daughter of a botany professor at the University of Vermont became Hess's wife in 1934. She was a source of strong support for Hess throughout his life, and accompanied him to conferences and scientific meetings. They had two sons, George and Frank.

Combines Admiralty and Oceanography

As a professor at Princeton, Hess continued his work on mountain ranges and island arcs, which are arc-shaped chains of islands that usually contain active volcanoes. By 1937 he had developed a unifying hypothesis that tied together the creation of island arcs with the presence of gravity anomalies and magnetic belts of serpentine (a rock which is formed by the crystallization of magma).

Hess's geological research was halted during World War II because he was a reserve officer in the Navy. He was initially assigned to duty in New York City, where he was responsible for estimating the positions of enemy submarines in the North Atlantic. Hess was then assigned to active sea duty and eventually became commander of an attack transport ship. This vessel carried equipment for sounding the ocean floor, and Hess took full advantage of it. He mapped a large part of the Pacific Ocean, discovering in the process the underwater flat-topped seamounts that he named guyots, in honor of A. H. Guyot, the first professor of geology at Princeton. The origin of guyots was puzzling, for they were flat on top as if they had been eroded off at the ocean surface, yet were two kilometers below sea level. As commander of the *U.S.S. Cape Johnson,* Hess also participated in four major combat landings, including the one at Iwo Jima. Remaining a reserve officer after the war, Hess was called on for advice in such emergencies as the Cuban missile crisis in October, 1962. By the time of his death he had achieved the rank of rear admiral.

After the war ended, Hess continued to study guyots as well as midocean ridges, which run down the centers of the Atlantic and Pacific oceans like an underwater backbone. He also continued his mineralogic studies on the family of pyroxenes, an important group of rock-forming minerals. In 1955, he proposed that the boundary between the crust and the mantle of the earth is due to a change in the chemical composition of rocks.

During the 1950s, Hess became an influential backer of the ill-fated "Project Mohole," which proposed to drill a hole through the shallow oceanic crust into the earth's mantle for scientific sampling. In 1961, an experimental hole was bored through 11,600 feet of water, six hundred feet of sediments, and forty-four feet of basalt. President John F. Kennedy telegraphed his congratulations to the National Science Foundation; John Steinbeck wrote an article for *Life*magazine about it. Despite amassing twenty-five million dollars in federal funding, Project Mohole foundered in 1966 under rising costs and political intriguing. It did, however, become an important steppingstone for the Deep Sea Drilling Project, successfully begun in the late 1960s.

Hess accepted visiting professorships at South Africa's Capetown University from 1949 to 1950 and at Cambridge University in 1965. Otherwise, he remained at Princeton until his death. He received numerous awards and honors, both at home and abroad, and was a major figure in the American Miscellaneous Society, a loosely-gathered group of scientists from different fields who liked to discuss "miscellaneous" ideas, such as Project Mohole.

From 1962 until his death, Hess chaired the Space Science Board that advised NASA on its lunar exploration program. He lived long enough to see the first person walk on the moon in July, 1969. One month later, while attending a space science conference in Woods Hole, Massachusetts, Hess died even as he was consulting a doctor about chest pains that he was experiencing.

The "Seafloor Spreading" Hypothesis

Hess made a major contribution to the continental drift theory, which viewed continental and oceanic positions as the result of the break up of a single 'supercontinent' (a theory first proposed by **Alfred Wegener** in 1912). Suggesting a mechanism by which continents could move away from each other without tearing up a rigid seafloor, Hess managed to unite several disparate elements: the youth of the ocean floor, the origin of midocean ridges, and the presence of island arcs and deep sea trenches surrounding the Pacific.

Hess's hypothesis gave geologists their first clue that drifting continents are carried passively on the spreading seafloor. In 1963, Fred Vine and Drummond Matthews at Cambridge University proposed a corollary to Hess's hypothesis: if the seafloor is created at the midocean ridges and spreads outward—and if the earth's magnetic field reverses polarity every few thousands of years—then the seafloor should be made of magnetized strips running parallel to the midocean ridges, alternating between normal and reverse polarity. Their idea, proposed independently by Lawrence Morley of the Geological Survey of Canada, was confirmed a few years later when scientists found the underwater bands of differently-magnetized rocks.

This oceanographic data established that continental drift does in fact, occur. Over the next couple of years, geologists eventually accepted the new and revolutionary idea. Although certain details of Hess's seafloor spreading hypothesis have become outdated, its central idea—that seafloor is created at ridges and destroyed under continents—has become an important foundation of modern earth science.

SELECTED WRITINGS BY HESS:

Books

"History of Ocean Basins," *Petrologic Studies: A Volume in Honor of A. F. Buddington,* edited by A. E. J. Engel and others, [New York], 1962.

(With Fred Vine) "Seafloor Spreading," *The Sea,* Volume 4, Part 2, edited by Arthur E. Maxwell and others, [New York], 1970.

Periodicals

"The ASMOC Hole to the Earth's Mantle," *Transactions of the American Geophysical Union,* Volume 40, 1959, pp. 340–345.

SOURCES:

Books

James, Harold L., "Harry Hammond Hess," *Biographical Memoirs,* Volume 43, Columbia University Press, 1973, pp. 109–128.

Frankel, Henry, "Hess's Development of His Seafloor Spreading Hypothesis," *Scientific Discovery: Case Studies,* edited by Thomas Nickles, 1980, [Boston], pp. 345–366.

—Sketch by Alexandra Witze

Victor Hess
1883-1964
Austrian physicist

Victor Hess shared the 1936 Nobel Prize for physics with **Carl D. Anderson** for his research involving the study of radiation of an unknown source and nature that appears to be present everywhere on the earth's surface. Through a series of ingenious experiments carried out in 1911 and 1912, Hess was able to show that this radiation originates from somewhere outside the Earth's atmosphere, although not from the sun. The radiation, at first called Hess radiation in his honor, was later renamed cosmic radiation by **Robert A. Millikan**.

Victor Francis Franz Hess was born at Schloss Waldstein, Austria, on June 24, 1883. His father was Vinzens Hess, chief forester to the prince of Oettinger-Wallerstein, and his mother was Serafine Edle von Grossbauer-Waldstätt. Hess received his secondary education at the Humanistisches Gymnasium in Graz, graduating in 1901. He then entered the University of Graz, where he was awarded his Ph.D. in physics summa cum laude in 1906.

Hess originally planned to conduct his postdoctoral studies in optics at the University of Berlin. When his intended mentor there, Paul Drude, committed suicide, however, he changed his plans. By 1910, Hess had become a research assistant at the University of Vienna's Institute for Radium Research, a position he held until 1920. At the Institute, Hess first became involved in the research that was to win him a Nobel Prize twenty-five years later.

Balloon Studies Demonstrate Source of Radiation

For many years, scientists had been puzzled by the fact that even the most carefully insulated electroscopes gradually lost their electric charge. It was obvious that some form of radiation was penetrating the best kinds of protection that scientists could devise for their instruments. Debate centered on the question of the source of that radiation. The most popular explanation was that it came from the earth itself. In order to test that hypothesis, in 1911, Theodor Wulf undertook measurements of the radiation at the base of the Eiffel Tower in Paris and at its top, 320 meters high. Wulf found that the intensity of radiation was significantly greater at the top of the tower, raising serious doubts about the earth-origin hypothesis.

In the same year, Hess devised an experiment to extend Wulf's research. He designed new instruments that could withstand changes in pressure and temperature thousands of meters above the earth's surface. He then arranged with the Austrian Air Club to make a series of balloon ascensions in order to measure radiation levels at very high altitudes. He eventually carried out ten ascensions, two in 1911, seven in 1912, and one in 1913.

The results of these studies were conclusive. Hess found that radiation levels were many times greater at altitudes of a few thousand meters than they were at the earth's surface. The source of the radiation was clearly located somewhere outside the earth's atmosphere. To test the suggestion that source might be the sun, Hess conducted one of his ascensions on April 12, 1912, during a solar eclipse. He found no significant change in radiation levels, indicating that the sun was not a source of the radiation. Hess's findings made relatively little impact on the scientific community, however, until more sophisticated devices for atmospheric studies were developed in the 1920s.

Hess Flees Europe for the United States

Hess left his post in Vienna in 1920 in order to accept a position as associate professor of experimental physics at the University of Graz. He remained at Graz until 1931, when he became professor of experimental physics and head of the institute for radiation research at the University of Innsbruck. He returned to Graz in 1937 but was at his post there for only a few months before being fired by the new Nazi government. Having been warned that they were scheduled to be sent to a concentration camp, the Hess family escaped to Switzerland and then traveled on to the United States. There, he was offered an appointment as professor of physics at Fordham University, a position he held until his retirement in 1956.

Following World War II, Hess became particularly interested in problems of radioactive fallout from nuclear weapons testing. In one series of experiments, he measured the level of fallout at the top of the Empire State Building, finding that bomb tests had significantly added to the natural background level of radiation. In 1947, Hess and William T. McNiff described a method they had developed for the detection of low levels of radiation in the human body.

Hess was married to Mary Berta Waermer Breisky on September 6, 1920. After his wife died in 1955, Hess married Elizabeth Hoencke on December 13, 1955. Hess had no children from either marriage. He died in Mount Vernon, New York, on December 17, 1964. In addition to the 1936 Nobel Prize for physics, Hess was honored with the Lieben Prize of the Austrian Academy of Sciences in 1919, the Ernst Abbé Prize of the Carl Zeiss Foundation in 1932, and honorary degrees from the University of Vienna, Loyola University in Chicago, Loyola University in New Orleans, and Fordham University.

SELECTED WRITINGS BY HESS:

Books

The Electrical Conductivity of the Atmosphere and Its Causes, Constable, 1928.

(With H. Benndorf) *Luft Elektrizität,* Brunswick, 1928.

(With Jakob Eugster) *Die Weltstrahlung und Ihre Biologische Wirkung,* Fuessli, 1940.

Periodicals

"The Cosmic Ray Observatory in the Hafelekar (2300 Meters)," *Terrestrial Magnetism and Atmospheric Electricity,* Volume 37, number 3, 1932, pp. 399–405.

"The Discovery of Cosmic Radiation," *Thought,* 1940, pp. 1–12.

SOURCES:

Books

Current Biography 1963, H. W. Wilson, 1963, pp. 180–82.

Dictionary of Scientific Biography, Scribner's, 1970–90.

Heathcote, Niels H. de V., *Nobel Prize Winners in Physics, 1901–1950,* Henry Schuman, 1953, pp. 339–45.

Wasson, Tyler, editor, *Nobel Prize Winners,* H. W. Wilson, 1987, pp. 445–47.

Weber, Robert L., *Pioneers of Science: Nobel Prize Winners in Physics,* American Institute of Physics, 1980, pp. 104–05.

Williams, Trevor, editor, *A Biographical Dictionary of Scientists,* Wiley, 1974, pp. 255–56.

Periodicals

Wilson, J. G., "Prof. V. F. Hess," *Nature,* July 24, 1964, p. 352.

—Sketch by David E. Newton

Walter Rudolf Hess
1881-1973
Swiss physiologist

Walter Rudolf Hess won the Nobel Prize for Physiology or Medicine in 1949, for his work in analyzing the function of the diencephalon, part of the interbrain, and its role in coordinating the body's internal organs. Introduced to the natural world by his father while still a very young child, Hess later wrote in an autobiographical sketch in *A Dozen Doctors:* "As time went on, I became aware of the significance of the ecological setting . . . of the specific interrelationship between flora and fauna. . . . More and more it became clear that functional manifestations, such as the germination of a seed or the rapid sprouting of a shoot from a willow, were more apt to capture my mind than purely morphological features." This emphasis on function and relationships carried over into much of Hess's work, particularly his investigations into the biological basis of emotions and the workings of the circulatory and respiratory systems. Despite the interference of two world wars, he designed many elegant experiments for studying physiological processes in living organisms.

Hess was born in the Swiss town of Frauenfeld to Clemens and Gertrud (Fischer Saxon) Hess on March 17, 1881. From his father, a physics teacher, he inherited a strong interest in science, and from his mother an energetic, good humored personality. After finishing high school, Hess began his college career, changing universities frequently and taking every opportunity to travel. He eventually received a medical degree from the University of Zurich in 1905, and took a hospital residency under the famous surgeon Dr. Konrad Brunner.

While working for Brunner, Hess designed an improved blood viscometer (to measure blood's thickness and consistency) and began thinking about research in earnest. He took a second residency in Zurich and specialized in ophthalmology (the physiology and diseases of the eye) under the mistaken impression that the discipline would allow him time to continue his circulatory system investigations. He indeed developed a successful ophthalmology practice with a good income, but it took up all of his time. In 1912 Hess gave up his practice and moved to the Institute of Physiology in Zurich, where he was given considerable freedom of action. Eventually he was named chair of the Physiology department, and began traveling to conferences and meetings throughout Europe. The stresses inherent in administrative work (which included a severe fire at the Institute, and the design and construction of a mountaintop research facility) and World War I cut into his research time again, but he still managed to publish two important monographs, *The Regulation of the Circulatory System* in 1930, and *The Regulation of Respiration* in 1931.

Brain Research Leads to Nobel Prize

Hess brought an unusual variety of tools and skills to his research. He had learned the basic principles of physics from his father, he knew a great deal about optics and hand-eye coordination from his days as an ophthalmologist, and he was a skilled surgeon. These all proved useful when he began conducting brain research on experimental animals. Hess's work on the circulatory and respiratory systems had included investigations of their interrelationship with other parts of animal physiology, including how blood flow and breathing were affected by the nervous system. Gradually this led to research on the areas of the brain responsible for regulating internal organs.

Of particular interest to Hess was the diencephalon, which is located under the cerebellum and is thus very difficult to access without damaging the rest of the brain. Hess designed very small electrodes and a mechanical guidance system that could implant the electrodes in experimental animals (cats) with the least possible disruption of their normal behavior. He also designed a method of delivering electrical stimulus pulses swiftly and accurately. On at least one occasion there was a public outcry about the use of animals for experimentation. Hess was instrumental in convincing the activists that, if properly regulated and humanely conducted, animal experiments were important for human welfare.

Using the electrodes to stimulate different areas of the brain, Hess observed the results on other areas of bodily function, such as blood pressure, respiration, and body temperature. He recorded his observations not only on paper, but also on film, and maintained meticulous records of dissections and cell studies. He also compared the results of electrical stimulation with behaviors resulting from naturally occurring brain lesions. He found that the diencephalon, and particularly the hypothalamus, controlled many of the body's responses, such as fear and hunger, and he was able to map out some of these responses in detail. Partly due to the isolation imposed by World War II, and partly because his papers were written entirely in German, the outside world knew little of his work until he had accumulated about 25 years worth of experiments. This may have been fortunate, because, as he wrote in his sketch, "The vast number of experiments turned out to be decisive; for generalization concerning symptoms, syndromes, and localizations could be supported only by such a large body of data."

In 1949, Hess won a share of the 1949 Nobel Prize for Physiology or Medicine; Portuguese neurosurgeon **Antonio Egas Moniz** shared the award for his work on white brain matter. The presenter said in his speech that Hess's results demonstrate "that in the midbrain we have higher centers of autonomic functions which coordinate these with reactions of the skeletal musculature adapted to the individual functions. . . . Through his research, Hess has brilliantly answered a number of difficult questions regarding the localization of body functions in the brain." Other recognitions the physiologist received included Switzerland's Marcel Benorst Prize in 1933 and the German Society for Circulation Research's Ludwig Medal in 1938.

Hess married the former Louise Sandmeyer in 1908; the couple had two children, Rudolf and Gertrud. When not working or traveling, Hess relaxed at his country house in southern Switzerland, where he cultivated grapes, tended his garden, and absorbed the pleasantries of Italian culture. He retired in 1951, although he continued his work and was instrumental in the establishment of an institute for brain research. He died in Locarno, Switzerland on August 12, 1973.

SELECTED WRITINGS BY HESS:

Books

The Functional Organization of the Diencephalon, Grune & Stratton, 1957.

"From Medical Practice to Theoretical Medicine" (autobiographical sketch), in *A Dozen Doctors,* edited by D. J. Ingle, University of Chicago Press, 1963.

The Biology of Mind, University of Chicago Press, 1964.

Biological Order and Brain Organization: Selected Works of W.R. Hess, Springer-Verlag, 1981.

SOURCES:

Books

"Hess, Walter R.," in *Nobel Prize Winners: An H. W. Wilson Biographical Dictionary,* Wilson, 1987, pg. 447.

—Sketch by Gail B. C. Marsella

Georg von Hevesy
1885-1966
Hungarian Swedish radiochemist

Georg von Hevesy developed radioactive tracer analysis, a method widely used in chemistry and medicine. For this accomplishment, which had far-reaching consequences in physiology, biochemistry, and mineralogy, he was awarded the Nobel Prize in chemistry in 1943. Hevesy was also the co-discoverer of the element hafnium.

Georg Charles von Hevesy was born in Budapest, Hungary, on August 1, 1885, to Louis Bisicz and his wife, the former Baroness Eugenie Schosberger. The family, who was given a title by Emperor Franz Joseph I in 1895, first changed their name to Hevesy-Bisicz and then simplified it to Hevesy; Hevesy always used the "von" in German correspondence and publications. (Many sources refer to him as "de Hevesy," while his first name often appears as "George" or "György.") Both sides of the family were well-to-do; facing no financial obstacles, Hevesy moved smoothly through the Piarist Gymnasium in Budapest, then studied physics and chemistry at the University of Budapest, and finally earned his doctorate at the University of Freiburg in 1908 with a thesis on the chemical behavior of sodium hydroxide in fused sodium metal.

Hevesy received his degree and became an assistant at the Eidgenössische Technische Hochschule in Zürich, commencing a career in which he knew or worked with nearly every major scientist of the first half of the twentieth century. He was acquainted with **Albert Einstein**, for example, in Zürich, where he continued his work with fused salts. After two years he moved on to work with **Fritz Haber** at the Technische Hochschule in Karlsruhe, but he realized that he lacked the research techniques for the electron-emission studies that Haber had set for him. Hevesy suggested that he join **Ernest Rutherford**'s group at the University of Manchester in England, and Haber agreed. He received an honorary research fellowship and left in 1911.

Develops Radioactive Tracer Analysis

At Manchester Hevesy worked with, among others, **Neils Bohr**, **Frederick Soddy**, **Henry Moseley**, and **Hans Geiger**. His first project was the chemistry of the radioactive decay products of actinium, and the effort yielded the finding that successive alpha decay products differ in chemical valence in steps of two. This provided support for the proposal Soddy had recently put forward concerning the existence of alpha-decay—the ejection of an alpha particle, or helium nucleus, from the radioactive nucleus. It was here, however, that Hevesy began the research which was to occupy him for the rest of his life, and it was Rutherford who set him on the road to it. The Austrian government had given Rutherford a hundred kilos of radioactive lead whose activity was known to be that of "radium-D," a decay product of radium. Hevesy was assigned the task of separating the radium-D from "all that lead." Over many months, he tried every chemical separation he knew, with a uniform lack of success. We now know that radium-D is the radioactive isotope lead–210; it is, in other words, a form of lead with the same number of protons and electrons, and hence the same chemistry, as any other lead, but with a different number of neutrons in its nucleus. Separation of isotopes can be done only by painstaking physical methods, and chemical separation is impossible.

Having failed in the separation study, Hevesy then acted on the principle of the popular saying, "If life hands you lemons, make lemonade." Since he could not separate it, he decided to use radium-D to trace the course of lead in chemical processes. Working with Friedrich Paneth at the Vienna Institute of Radium Research in 1913, he was able to conduct precise solubility studies of lead salts by mixing an insignificant mass of radium-D with a regular lead salt, then determining the amount dissolved not by the usual tedious gravimetric methods, but by simple measurement of the proportion of radioactivity found in solution. He was also able to demonstrate lead exchange between solid and solution, and the migration of lead atoms in the metal. He and Paneth showed that the electrochemical properties of radium-D were identical with those of lead, thereby adding to the growing evidence of the existence of isotopes.

In 1913 Hevesy returned to Hungary, where he served for a time as a lecturer at the University of Budapest before joining the Austro-Hungarian army during World War I. His post during the war was as technical supervisor at the state electrochemical copper plant, and he was able to continue his research on a limited basis. After the war he became a full professor at Budapest, continuing his lead tracer work, but the political situation in Hungary was disintegrating rapidly, and in 1920 he accepted an invitation to join Bohr's Institute for Theoretical Physics at the University of Copenhagen.

Participates in the Discovery of Hafnium

His first project there, carried out with **Johannes Brønsted**, was an attempt at isotopic separation by fractional distillation. They had limited success with metallic mercury, but obtained fairly pure isotopic samples of chlorine, whose two stable isotopes differ by about six percent in mass. Hevesy wished to learn X-ray spectroscopy, and in 1923 he turned for help to physicist Dirk Coster. The two of them set about finding element seventy-two, which Bohr's recent revision of the periodic table suggested should be a transition metal corresponding to zirconium. They found the anticipated spectral lines in extracts of zirconium ores, and were able to isolate and characterize the new element as its fluoride. They named it "hafnium" after the Latin name for Copenhagen.

In 1923 Hevesy also returned to his work with radioactive lead tracers, and for the first time he ventured into biology to study the uptake of lead in bean seedlings. This work was published in 1924, the year in which Hevesy married Pia Riis, who would bear him three daughters and a son. Two years later, he moved his new family to the University of Freiburg, where he developed X-ray fluorescence as an analytical tool, while expanding the university's X-ray spectroscopy program. As an administrator, however, Hevesy came into increasing contact with the new Nazi regime, and this caused him to return to Copenhagen in 1934.

Heavy water (water in which some of the hydrogen atoms are the heavier isotope hydrogen–2, or deuterium) had just become available, and in Copenhagen Hevesy was pleased to have this first non-toxic isotope available to study animal and human physiology. He and his colleagues quickly demonstrated the rapid exchange of internal and external water in goldfish, and measured the average turnover time of a water molecule in the human body (about thirteen days) and the approximate number of water molecules in the body (10^{27}).

In 1934, **Irène** and **Frédéric Joliot-Curie** succeeded in producing artificial radioisotopes by alpha particle bombardment. Hevesy seized the possibilities of this development by making radioactive phosphorus–32 from sulfur–32, a very large advance for the study of physiology. Here was an element central to all animal physiology, and a means of following its intake, circulation, exchange, and excretion. A number of discoveries followed from the use of this tracer, including the dynamic exchange of serum and bone phosphate and the synthesis and distribution of DNA and RNA. Today, these discoveries form the foundation of our understanding of body chemistry.

Phosphorus was only the first element that Hevesy used or introduced into use as a radioactive tracer. Others included calcium–45, potassium–42, sodium–24, chlorine–38, and carbon–14. There is little of physiological importance that lies outside this list except nitrogen, oxygen, and sulfur, and it is clear just how fundamental his contributions to science have been. It was in recognition of these accomplishments that Hevesy was awarded the Nobel Prize in chemistry in 1943. Announced in 1944 and overshadowed by the closing battles of World War II, the award received little public notice.

At the time he received the Nobel Prize, Hevesy had moved again. He had left Copenhagen in 1943, moving away from the Nazis for a second time, and settled in Stockholm. He worked at the Institute for Organic Chemistry there for the remainder of his life, becoming a Swedish citizen in 1945. Much of his later research focused on physiology and medicine, particularly the study of cancer. He published over four hundred books and papers in the course of his career and received many awards and honors, including honorary doctorates from nearly a dozen universities and honorary memberships in many scientific societies. He was also a foreign member of the Royal Society. In addition to the Nobel Prize, he received the Cannizzaro Prize in 1929 from the Academy of Sciences in Rome, the Copley Medal of the Royal Society in 1950, and the Faraday Medal in 1959. He also received the Atoms for Peace Award in 1959. Hevesy died at a clinic in Freiburg on July 5, 1966, after a long illness.

SELECTED WRITINGS BY HEVESY:

Books

(With Friedrich Paneth) *Manual of Radioactivity,* Oxford University Press, 1926.
Das Element Hafnium, Springer, 1927.
Chemical Analysis by X-Rays, McGraw-Hill, 1932.
Radioactive Indicators: Their Application in Biochemistry, Animal Physiology, and Pathology, Interscience, 1948.
Adventures in Radioisotope Research, 2 volumes, Pergamon, 1962.
Selected Papers of George Hevesy, Pergamon, 1967.

Periodicals

"A Scientific Career," *Perspectives in Biology and Medicine,* Volume 1, 1958.

SOURCES:

Books

Biographical Memoirs of Fellows of the Royal Society, Volume 13, Royal Society (London), 1967, pp. 124–166.
Dictionary of Scientific Biography, Volume 12, Scribner's, 1972, pp. 365–367.
James, Laylin K., editor, *Nobel Laureates in Chemistry: 1901–1992,* American Chemical Society, 1993, pp. 266–271.
Levi, H., *George de Hevesy: Life and Work,* A. Hilger, 1985.
Magill, Frank N., editor, *The Nobel Prize Winners: Chemistry,* Volume 2, Salem Press, 1990, pp. 451–458.

Periodicals

Mel'nikov, Volume P., "Some Details in the Prehistory of the Discovery of Element 72," *Centaurus,* Volume 26, 1983, pp. 317–322.
Spence, R., "George Charles de Hevesy," *Chemistry in Britain,* Volume 3, 1967, pp. 527–532.

—Sketch by Robert M. Hawthorne, Jr.

Antony Hewish
1924-
English astrophysicist

Antony Hewish is an English astrophysicist who won international prominence for his 1967 discovery, along with **Jocelyn Susan Bell Burnell**, of pulsars, or "pulsating stars." In recognition of his contribution to the advancement of the field, Hewish shared with fellow astronomer **Martin Ryle** the 1974 Nobel Prize for physics. It was the first time that the Nobel Prize was given for an achievement in astrophysics.

Hewish was born on May 11, 1924, in Fowey, Cambridge, the youngest of three sons born to Ernest William Hewish and Frances Grace Lanyon (Pinch) Hewish. Ernest Hewish was a banker, but from an early age, Antony decided not to follow in his father's footsteps. Instead, he wished to pursue a career in science. At King's College in Taunton, where he was sent in 1935 at the age of eleven, Hewish displayed a penchant for physics. In 1942, he entered Cambridge University, where he began studying for his B.A. He had been there only a year when the onset of World War II temporarily suspended his education. From 1943 to 1946, Hewish, like many physicists of his generation, worked for the British Government at the Royal Aircraft Establishment in Farnborough. He helped to design airborne radar counter-measure devices at the government's Telecommunications Research Establishment, which was based in Malvern. It was there that he met Martin Ryle, the English astrophysicist who became his closest colleague and with whom he would later share the Nobel Prize.

Hewish returned to Cambridge in 1946 to complete his degree. Upon graduating two years later, he accepted Ryle's invitation to join the latter's research team based at Cambridge's world famous Cavendish

Physical Laboratory. At the laboratory, Hewish was able to pursue his doctoral degree surrounded by some of the most well regarded scholars in the field of physics. It was at the Laboratory that Hewish first realized his interest in radiation—a pursuit that later led to his research into pulsars.

Researches Twinkling in Radio Stars

Hewish was interested in the emerging field of radio astronomy, which deals with electromagnetic radiations of wave frequencies received from outside the earth's atmosphere. Radio astronomy enables physicists to study the cosmos at the distant edge of the universe as well as to examine the properties of highly condensed matter in neutron stars, which are hypothetical, dense celestial objects that are thought to result from the collapse of much larger stellar objects. For many years, Hewish investigated the twinkling of radio stars—cosmic radio sources of very small dimensions and relatively high radiation. He followed the trail for many years without achieving any significant breakthrough. During that time he also married Marjorie Richards, and the couple eventually had one son and one daughter. By 1954, as Hewish recalled in a lecture that was published in *Science* in 1975, the astrophysicist had theorized "that, if radio sources were of small enough angular size, they would illuminate the solar atmosphere with sufficient coherence to produce interference patterns at the earth which would be detectable as a very rapid fluctuation of intensity." Hewish's idea did not advance any further, however, since all the known sources were, at least, one hundred times too big to cause the predicted effect.

In the early 1960s, Hewish assumed the post of lecturer in physics at Cambridge University, and in 1962, he also became a visiting professor at Yale University. Two years later, he achieved his first decisive breakthrough when he finally determined the cause of the twinkling in radio stars—otherwise known as interplanetary scintillations. Hewish studied radio waves that emanated from quasars (a term that is short for quasi stellar radio source), and used as his guide his knowledge of diffraction—the modification light undergoes when passed through or reflected by a surface. Hewish was able to show that when radio waves from a source with a small diameter, like quasars, travel through a collection of charged particles, called plasma clouds, the waves are diffracted. With the help of two team members, Hewish was able to observe other quasars and confirm the scintillation effect.

Hewish knew that interplanetary scintillations could be observed from any direction in space, and he used this knowledge to explore other astronomical occurrences. One phenomenon he studied was the solar corona, or the colored circle often seen around the sun, which is sometimes caused by diffraction produced by suspended droplets or particles of dust. He also mapped the solar wind (the plasma ejected from the sun's surface) outside the plane of the ecliptic, the great circle of the celestial sphere that is the apparent path of the sun among the stars as seen from the sun; this is an area spacecraft have not yet explored. He was also able to measure the angular diameter of distant radio sources. In the 1975 *Science* article, Hewish claimed: "The first really unusual source to be uncovered by this method turned up in 1965 when, with my student Okoye, I was studying radio emission from the Crab Nebula. We found a prominent scintillating component within the nebula which was far too small to be explained by conventional synchrotron radiation, and we suggested that this might be the remains of the original star which had exploded and which still showed activity in the form of the flare-type radio emission. This source later turned out to be none other than the famous Crab Nebula pulsar."

Chances upon Pulsars

Hewish's groundbreaking work with interplanetary scintillations laid the foundation for his next discovery—that of pulsars, which are essentially pulsating radio waves characterized by a short interval between pulses and a uniform rate of repetition. In 1967, following two years of intense work, he finished building an enormous, high-resolution radio telescope that was sensitive to weak radio sources and which consisted of more than two thousand dipole antennae spread over four-and-a-half acres. He decided upon a wavelength of 3.7 meters, based on the fact that signals caused by plasma are most observable at long wavelengths. With this apparatus, Hewish and his team of research students at Cavendish began to study more than one thousand radio galaxies.

In August of 1967, after more than a month of round-the-clock observations which involved surveying the entire available sky at one-week intervals (necessary so that every source could be examined at a variety of solar elongations, or distances), graduate student Jocelyn Susan Bell Burnell unexpectedly noticed, at a time when normal radio scintillations were not obvious, an unusually regular, though weak, signal issuing from halfway between the stars Vega and Altair. At first, Hewish thought the scintillations might be emanating from a man-made source, such as electrical machinery or space probes. But his measurements revealed that the scintillations were radiating from far beyond the solar system, though within the boundaries of the Milky Way galaxy. He then thought that they might be coming from a flare star, akin to the M-type dwarf stars (a star of small mass and size, and sometimes low luminosity) one of his colleagues was studying. Hewish was still pondering the source when the signals disappeared, only to reappear a few days later, and thereafter to reappear sporadically. By October, Hewish had decided that the scintillations were being caused by some unknown source. The Cavendish team began using a recorder with a faster response time to examine the nature of the fluctuating signals, but their investigations were stymied by the fact that the intensity of the scintillations were too weak to be detected by their equipment.

In late November, the team ascertained that the signals followed a regular pattern of pulses at intervals slightly greater than one second. "I could not believe that any natural source would radiate in this fashion," Hewish revealed in his 1974 lecture. He had no doubt that he had stumbled onto something new and unknown. It crossed the minds of some of the team members that perhaps the pulses were being transmitted by alien beings, or "little green men," as they termed them. Believing that if the press was notified of the team's investigation, journalists and reporters would descend en masse upon the observatory, Hewish kept the work quiet rather than divulging his findings in a scientific journal, as is the normal custom.

The team initiated observations using even higher resolutions. At the beginning of December, the intensity of the source of the scintillations increased greatly, and the pulses became clearly visible. Through study of the records, Hewish realized that the variations in the pulses initially recorded had been the result of random fluctuations in the source's intensity. Hewish began to record the pulses daily in mid-December, at which time he detected a pattern: At one certain frequency, the duration of each pulse was approximately 16 milliseconds. It became evident even to Hewish that the pulses could be caused by an extraterrestrial and stellar source: "We had to face the possibility that the signals were, indeed, generated on a planet circulating some distant star, and that they were artificial," he admitted in his 1974 lecture.

On February 24, 1968, Hewish, along with his colleagues at the observatory, finally published a paper in the journal *Nature* detailing their findings; they described the phenomena as "pulsating stars," or "pulsars," and indicated that the parameters of the pulsars were only roughly known. The paper presented the essential facts the team knew at that point and proposed that pulsars were generated from some type of condensed star—either vibrating neutron stars or white dwarf stars. The announcement sent a buzz of excitement through the astrophysics community: Many physicists requested advance information on the location and periodicities of the pulsars; at the same time, allegations arose about whether or not Hewish had deliberately withheld information, as he did not divulge data about the discoveries as soon as they were made. Hewish, however, would not release any further information on the pulsars until he had conducted additional research.

Quickly, a race ensued to discover the exact source of pulsars. "Radio telescopes all over the world turned toward the first pulsars and information flooded in at a phenomenal rate," Hewish recalled in his lecture. By the end of 1968, approximately one hundred reports detailing pulsar observations or interpretations had been published. Most of the papers overlooked Hewish's theory of a neutron star source and looked for an explanation in either white dwarf stars or various configurations of the binary system—a system in which two stars revolve around one another due to mutual gravitation. Working independently, however, both **Thomas Gold** of Cornell University and Franco Pacini proposed that pulses are caused by beams of radiation that pour out from spinning neutron stars, which measure several kilometers across and contain a mass greater than that of the sun. Gold also predicted that, because of the massiveness of neutron stars, their rotations should slow with time, and, consequently, the intervals between pulses should increase in time. Gold's hypothesis was soon substantiated when the short-period Crab Pulsar was discovered and when a slowdown in the pulsar's period was later detected. Other research revealed that pulsars emit pulses of light as well as of radio. In April of 1968, Hewish released his second paper on the pulsars, and in it he elaborated on the findings of the first paper.

Becomes First Astrophysicist to Win Nobel Prize for Physics

In 1969 Hewish assumed the post of reader at Cambridge, and since 1971, he has served as a professor of radio astronomy at the university; he also has continued his work in radio astronomy. His greatest distinction has been the receipt of the 1974 Nobel Prize for physics, which he shared with his colleague Ryle, for the decisive role both scientists played in radio astronomy research and for the role Hewish played in the discovery of pulsars. This marked the first time the Nobel Prize had been bestowed upon an astrophysicist. Less than ten years after Hewish's award-winning discovery, more than 130 pulsars had been detected, and Gold's theory had gained general acceptance.

SELECTED WRITINGS BY HEWISH:

Periodicals

(With J. S. Bell, J. D. H. Pilkington, P. F. Scott, and R. A. Collins) *Nature,* Volume 217, 1968, p. 709.

"Pulsars and High Density Physics" (lecture delivered on December 12, 1974, in Stockholm, Sweden), *Science,* Volume 188, 1975, p. 1079.

SOURCES:

Books

Manchester, R. N., and J. H. Taylor, *Pulsars,* W. H. Freeman, 1977.

Smith, F., *Pulsars,* Cambridge University Press, 1977.

Weber, Robert L., *Pioneers of Science: Nobel Prize Winners in Physics,* Institute of Physics, 1980.

—*Sketch by Avril McDonald*

William Hewlett
1913-
American electrical engineer

William Hewlett

In 1938, William Hewlett and his college friend **David Packard** invested 538 dollars to build their company's first "plant" in a garage in Palo Alto, starting what was to become a multi-billion dollar organization. Since its inception, Hewlett-Packard (HP) Company, characterized by a management style which has been widely imitated, has become a leading manufacturer of information systems and products used in medical, scientific, educational, business, and engineering applications.

Hewlett was born May 20, 1913, in Ann Arbor, Michigan, to Albion and Louise Reddington Hewlett. His father was teaching medicine at the University of Michigan, but in 1916 he moved the family to California, where he had accepted a position at Stanford University Medical School. Hewlett grew up in Palo Alto and went to Stanford for his undergraduate work, receiving his B.A. in 1934. He did not think much of his academic talents and even believed he had been accepted at Stanford only because of his father's position.

It was while at Stanford that Hewlett began his friendship with David Packard. During their undergraduate days, Hewlett and Packard acquired a mentor, Stanford professor **Frederick Terman**, who advised them to gain experience and knowledge before starting their own business, something they had discussed. They both went east after graduation—Packard to work for General Electric, and Hewlett to continue his studies at the Massachusetts Institute of Technology. Hewlett received his master's degree in electrical engineering from MIT in 1936. He returned to Stanford where Professor Terman helped Hewlett get a contract to construct an electroencephalograph—a device for recording brain waves. When Packard opted to leave General Electric and return to California in 1938, Terman arranged a research fellowship for him at Stanford and encouraged Hewlett and Packard to open their own business.

Co-founds Electronics Company

The garage behind Packard's house became their business address. Their first inventions—including a device for automatically flushing urinals, a shock machine for losing weight, a harmonica tuner, and a foul indicator for bowling alleys—did not do well. They had more success with a resistance capacitance audio oscillator based on a design from Hewlett's graduate school thesis. The device produced variable and stable signals in the low frequency needed for measurements in acoustics, medicine, oil exploration, seismology, oceanography, and many other fields involving low frequencies. A big break came when Walt Disney became interested in using them in the movie industry. Hewlett and Packard sold eight oscillators to Disney, who used them in the production of *Fantasia.* The year was 1939, and they had made one of their first major commercial sales.

Hewlett also received his engineering degree from Stanford in 1939. By the end of that year, Hewlett and Packard had made profits of over 1500 dollars. They moved to larger quarters in late 1939 and built their first building in 1941. In 1957 they moved into the Stanford Industrial Park. The proximity to the university gave HP access to both Stanford's research and its graduates. During the early years, Hewlett and Packard swept the floors, kept the books, and took the inventory themselves.

Hewlett and Packard decided from the beginning to specialize in electronic measurement and test instruments, and the company did well, with sales of 100,000 dollars by 1941. In 1941, Hewlett was called to serve in the Armed Forces. He was absent from HP until the end of the war, serving in the Army on the staff of the Chief Signal Officer and then as head of the electronics section of the New Development Division of the War Department's Special Staff. Hewlett was discharged in 1945 and returned home. In 1947, HP was incorporated, and Hewlett was made vice president. The company had become a one-million-dollar enterprise with 111 employees. But the end of the war also meant an end to lucrative defense contracts. A reduction in demand for products caused HP to scale back operations, and a number of employees left, primarily women returning to the home sphere after the war. Distressed by these disruptions, Hewlett and Packard resolved never to again become so dependent on government contracts. They struggled to develop a wide range of products for a broader market. By 1950, HP was had bolstered their product line and had 146 employees and revenues of two million dollars.

Develops Influential Management Style

HP was one of the first companies to make use of semiconductors, and their growth attracted an increasing number of new electronics businesses to Silicon Valley. The company influenced industry there in a number of ways, but perhaps most important was the management style fostered by Hewlett and Packard, which encouraged a corporate philosophy committed to people. This commitment involved a respect for the individual and expressed itself in management processes that included communications and teamwork. Managers made a point of being available to their employees and offering them help as soon as it was needed. In their book *In Search of Excellence,* Tom Peters and Robert Waterman, Jr. quote Hewlett on his philosophy; he describes it as "a spirit, a point of view. There is the feeling that everyone is part of a team, and that team is HP. . . . It is an idea based on the individual. It exists because people have seen that it works, and they believe that this feeling makes HP what it is." Hewlett considered the management of HP to be his greatest accomplishment there.

Part of the approach taken by the management at HP was maintaining the feeling of a small company. This was realized by splitting divisions when they reached a certain size. When a division exceeded 2,000 people and/or 100,000,000 dollars in business, it tended to become shackled by bureaucratic procedures that stifled innovation and growth. These divisions were divided into two or three new ones; the splits were made along product lines and people were put into new plants. In this way, size guidelines were reestablished, and the company was positioned for future growth. This approach has been described by *Forbes* contributor Julie Pita as creating a "confederation of independent businesses," and it remains one of HP's strongest features.

HP grew rapidly during the 1950s. By 1959, their product line had grown to 380. Hewlett was made executive vice president of HP in 1957 and president in 1964. In 1953, HP began the development of solid-state components, and in 1966 the company announced its first computer, the instrumentation computer. In 1968 HP introduced the HP 9100 calculator, the first of its type to be as small as a typewriter. Hewlett was pleased with the new machine, but he challenged its inventors to go one step further; he asked them to make a calculator that would fit in his pocket. The resulting product, the HP–35, was introduced in 1972 and called the "electronic slide rule." Prior to the introduction of this calculator, HP had marketed its computers to scientific and engineering specialists rather than to the general public. Hewlett changed this strategy for the HP–35. The device turned out to be the company's first real consumer product, and it proved to be a tremendous success. The HP–65 programmable calculator soon became extremely popular with students, scientists, and engineers.

Despite his innovations, Hewlett's business philosophy can be termed conservative. HP did not go public for twenty years. As Hewlett said in a 1987 interview in *Electronic News,* this gave them a free hand in running the business. When they did offer shares to the public, Hewlett said that one of their reasons was "to give the employees a share in the company." Hewlett went on to say that "one of the first things we did was to give stock to key employees. We set up stock option plans so that we had a chance to get them on board."

Remains Involved in HP During Retirement

In conformance with the plan for management succession at HP, Hewlett resigned the presidency in 1977 and retired as CEO in 1978. The everyday operation of the company was turned over to its new CEO, John Young. Hewlett served as chair of the company's executive committee from 1977 until 1983, then as vice-chair of the board of directors until 1987. He was named director emeritus in 1987. By that time, HP had become a company with annual sales of eight billion dollars. Packard had also taken on a different role at the company, serving as chair of the board from 1972 to 1993.

Even though Hewlett had stepped down in 1978, he and Packard still retained a strong interest in the company. This was made very clear to the business community in 1990, when the two men, each nearly 80, reasserted themselves in HP's operations. At that time, HP stock had dropped steeply and the company had become overly bureaucratic and overly centralized. Hewlett and Packard used their influence to reduce the number of committees, which had bloated the company's overhead and weakened the power of individual managers. They also allowed the medical division more freedom in choosing payment policies, and gave Lewis Platt, the head of the Computer Systems Group, free rein in building an inexpensive engineering workstation. Platt's project was a great success, and he eventually took over as president and CEO. By 1992 the company posted a profit while its chief competitors, IBM and DEC, were both in the red.

In addition to his work at HP, Hewlett has been active in the electronics industry and in the community at large. He served on the board of directors of the Institute of Electrical and Electronic Engineers (IEEE) from 1950 to 1957, and in 1954 he was named president. He helped form the American Electronics Association (formerly the Western Electronic Manufacturers Association), and in 1985 he was awarded the nation's highest scientific honor, the National Medal of Science.

His interests in medicine led him to serve first as board president and then as director of the Palo Alto-Stanford Hospital Center (now the Stanford Medical Center) from 1956 to 1962. He has also served as a director of the Kaiser Foundation Hospital and Health Plan (1972–1978) and of the Drug Abuse Council in Washington, D.C. (1972–1974). Hewlett's strong belief in education made him a trustee of Mills College in Oakland, California (1958–1968) and of Stanford University (1963–1974). In 1969 and 1970, he served on the Commission of White House Fellows. He has been a fellow of the American Academy of Arts and Sciences since 1970.

Hewlett holds patents on a number of resistance-capacitance oscillators and other electronic devices. In 1992, he received the National Inventors Hall of Fame Award. Other awards include the Corporate Leadership Award from MIT in 1970; the Henry Heald Award in 1984; the World Affairs Council Award in 1987; the Degree of Uncommon Man from Stanford in 1987; the National Business Hall of Fame Laureate Award in 1988; and the Silicon Valley Engineering Hall of Fame Award in 1991. Additionally, Hewlett holds eleven honorary degrees from American colleges and universities. Hewlett married Flora Lamson in 1939. The couple had five children, but Flora died in 1971. In 1978, Hewlett married his second wife, Rosemary Bradford. His outside interests have always reflected his love of nature and include botany, fishing, skiing, and mountain climbing.

SOURCES:

Books

Ingham, John N., and Lynne B. Feldman, *Contemporary American Business Leaders,* Greenwood Press, 1990, pp. 233–241.

Kanter, Rosabeth Moss, *The Change Masters,* Simon & Schuster, 1983.

Peters, Thomas J., and Robert H. Waterman, *In Search of Excellence,* Warner Books, 1982.

Periodicals

Nee, Eric, "William Hewlett: The Long Shadow of a Director Emeritus," *Electronic News,* March 7, 1987, pp. 4, 6.

Pitta, Julie, "It Had to Be Done and We Did It," *Forbes,* April 26, 1993, pp. 148–152.

Other

William R. Hewlett, press release from Hewlett-Packard Corporation.

—Sketch by Frank Hertle

Corneille Jean-François Heymans
1892-1968
Belgian physiologist and pharmacologist

Corneille Jean François Heymans, a Belgian scientist, conducted research in the field of respiratory and cardiovascular systems that produced new knowledge about the way breathing is regulated. His work won him the Nobel Prize for physiology and medicine in 1938.

Born in Ghent, Belgium on March 28, 1892, Heymans was the eldest of six sons of Jan-Frans Heymans, a noted pharmacologist who founded the J. F. Heymans Institute of Pharmacology and Therapeutics at the University of Ghent. As a youngster, Heymans watched the construction of the institute laboratory and helped his father take care of the animals that were used there. He and his father were to become a scientific team of considerable reputation—one of the few father-son scientific teams in history.

Heymans' career was delayed by four years of service as a field artillery officer in the Belgian Army during World War I. His performance won him the Belgian War Cross and the Order of the Crown of Leopold, among other decorations for valor.

After the war, Heymans received his medical degree from the University of Ghent in 1920. His father was his principal teacher and later would become his primary co-researcher in the experiments that ultimately led to the Nobel Prize in 1938. Had his father not died in 1932, he most likely would have shared the award with his son.

The year following his graduation from the university, Heymans married Berthe May, an ophthalmologist. The young couple studied abroad for several years, permitting Heymans to establish valuable contacts with some of the leading scientists of the day in his field, among them Eugène Gley at the Collège de France, Maurice Arthus at the University of Lausanne in Switzerland, **Ernest H. Starling** at University College in London, and Carl Wiggers at Western Reserve University's medical school in Cleveland, Ohio.

Succeeds His Father at University of Ghent

Heymans returned to the University of Ghent in 1922 to become a lecturer in pharmacodynamics, the study of the action of drugs in the body. He succeeded his father as professor of pharmacology and director of the Institute in 1930, but father and son continued to collaborate on many projects, including respiratory experiments that revealed previously unknown facts about how breathing is regulated in human beings and animals.

At that time, it had been well known for half a century that changes in blood pressure were associated with changes in the rate and the depth of breathing. The mechanism enforcing these changes in respiration was not known. It was believed, however, that alterations of breathing rates were the result of the direct action of blood pressure on the brain's respiratory center, the medulla. It was assumed that the medulla was able to detect changes in the blood circulating through it and regulate the rate of breathing accordingly.

Another scientist, Heinrich E. Hering, however, had noted a reflex action in the carotid artery (two major arteries on each side of the neck) that appeared to influence the heart beat. Through a series of experiments originally intended to refute Hering's contention, Heymans instead demonstrated that that the reflex in the artery also exerted control over breathing.

The effort to determine this fact involved what became known as the "isolated head" technique. The head of an anesthetized dog, attached to its body only by the vagus aortic nerves, was kept alive by the shared circulation of blood of a second anesthetized dog. The Heymans found that when they induced hypertension (increased blood pressure) in the isolated body of the first dog its medullary respiratory center was stimulated or inhibited appropriately. But when the aortic nerves were severed, all respiratory response to changes in the blood pressure ceased. This experiment enabled the Heymans team to demonstrate conclusively that the aortic nerves were the reflex mechanism's sole sensory pathway.

The experiment thus disproved the classical theory of the blood's direct action on the brain and provided the evidence for an alternative explanation. The Heymans later determined the sites at which changes in the blood were detected. They discovered that the reflex in the carotid artery contains pressure-sensitive areas, or presso-receptors, that can detect even slight changes in blood pressure. They also found small structures on the inside walls of the carotid artery and the aorta. These chemoreceptors responded to changes in the chemical composition of the blood. By making clear why certain drugs affected respiration and circulation, Heymans' discovery opened the way for improvements in the treatment of many diseases.

Known as a Gifted Teacher

Heymans' colleagues appreciated the thoroughness and accuracy of his work, which he documented in over eight hundred articles and papers published during his career. Heymans also won great recognition as a gifted teacher. Unlike most professors of his time, who tended to remain aloof from their students, Heymans regarded his students as fellow professionals and followed their work closely. Keeping track of their careers after they had left the university, he further inspired and encouraged their individual progress by sending them new data, providing help and support as they needed it.

Many scientific honors came to him. In addition to the Nobel Prize, he was awarded the Alvarenga Prize of the (Belgian) Académie Royale de Medécine, the Prix Quinquennal de Medécine of the Belgian government, the Pius XI Prize of the Pontificia Academia Scientiarum and the Monthyon Prize of the Institut de France. Heymans held sixteen honorary degrees and belonged to more than forty scientific and medical societies.

Throughout his career, he traveled widely both as a lecturer and a tourist. He lectured at several major American universities, including Harvard and the University of Chicago. He was fluent in many languages and conducted seminars in Montevideo, Chile, to help organize scientific exchange programs between that country and his own. He visited India on behalf of the World Health organization.

During World War II, he helped organize relief efforts to provide food for Belgian children. In so doing, he made several trips to Berlin to obtain the cooperation of German officials in getting Red Cross food shipments into Belgium. This evoked criticism from some Belgians who viewed his activities as collaboration with the enemy, but Heymans maintained that his actions were necessary to obtain vital assistance for his country.

Heymans and his wife had four children: Marie-Henriette, Pierre, Joan and Berthe. In 1963, upon his retirement from the Heymans Institute, he was designated professor emeritus. He continued to visit the institute several times a week until his death following a stroke in Knokke, Belgium on July 18, 1968.

SELECTED WRITINGS BY HEYMANS:

Books

Le Sinus Carotidien et la Zone Homologue Cardio-Aortique, G. Doin (Paris), 1933.

Introduction to the Regulation of Blood Pressure and Heart Rate, Charles C. Thomas, 1950.

(With Eric Neil) *Reflexogenic Areas of the Cardiovascular System,* Little, Brown, 1958.

(With Bjorn Folkow), "Vasomotor Control and Regulation of Blood Pressure," in *Circulation of the Blood, Men and Ideas,* edited by Alfred P. Fishman and Dickenson W. Richards, Oxford University Press, 1964, pp. 407–87.

SOURCES:

Books

Magill, Frank N., editor, *The Nobel Prize Winners: Physiology and Medicine,* Volume 1: *1968–1988,* Salem Press, 1991.

Weber, Robert L., *Pioneers of Science,* 2nd edition, Adam Hilger, 1988.

Periodicals

"Corneille Heymans, A Collective Biography," *Archives Internationales de Pharmacodynamie et de Thérapie,* Supplement, Volume 202, 1973, pp. 9–307.

Schmidt, Carl F. "Professor Corneille Heymans, Nobel Laureate in Physiology and Medicine for 1938," *Scientific Monthly,* Volume 49, 1939, pp. 576–79.

—Sketch by Tom K. Phares

Jaroslav Heyrovský
1890-1967
Czechoslovakian physical chemist

Jaroslav Heyrovský dedicated his life to the study and improvement of a technique to analyze chemical solutions. His work led to his invention of the polarograph, a piece of scientific equipment used to quickly and efficiently determine the composition of a solution. For this, he was awarded the Nobel Prize in chemistry in 1959. Throughout his long career, Heyrovský collaborated with many other scientists to develop his methods. He also made valuable contributions to scientific publications in his home country, gaining international recognition for the work being done by Czech scientists.

Heyrovský was born in Prague, Austria-Hungary (now the Czech Republic) on December 20, 1890, to Leopold, a professor of Roman law at Charles University in Prague, and Klára (Hanl) Heyrovský. It was during his years at the gymnasium (high school) in Prague that Heyrovský developed a deep interest in mathematics and physics. By the time he entered the Charles University in 1909, his father had become rector of the college. Heyrovský studied physics, chemistry, and mathematics at Charles, becoming influenced by physicists František Záviška and Bohumil Kučera. He also studied with chemist Bohumil Brauner, an association that led him in 1910 to University College in London, where he received his bachelor of science degree in 1913.

Frederick G. Donnan had succeeded **William Ramsay** at University College and stimulated Heyrovský's interest in electrochemistry, which became the subject of his doctoral studies. He was detained in Prague, however, during a visit home at the onset of World War I. Although poor health had exempted him for military service, he was assigned to a military hospital as a chemist and radiologist between 1914 and 1918. Continuing his research despite the war, he presented his doctoral thesis on the electroaffinity of aluminum in the fall of 1918 to Charles University. In 1919 he became an assistant professor of chemistry there, and in 1920, was appointed lecturer.

Heyrovský published articles from his thesis and these earned him a second doctorate from University College in 1921. By 1922, he was appointed associate professor and head of the chemistry department at Charles University, and in 1924, he was named extraordinary professor and director of a new establishment, the Institute of Physical Chemistry at Charles. He held the position of full professor from 1926 until 1950, when he was named director of the

Polarographic Institute of Czechoslovak Academy of Sciences.

Develops Lab Instrument for Quicker Research

Among his many associates and collaborators, Masuzo Shikata was instrumental in helping Heyrovský develop the polarograph. They published a description of the instrument they had designed, detailing how it automatically records the analysis of chemical solutions without altering them. This was one of the earliest laboratory instruments to help automate research. The two researchers had devised a method that reduced the process from over an hour to fifteen or twenty minutes. His work in this area is considered to have greatly aided the study of electrode processes, applications of which are useful in medicine and industry as well as in the research of biochemical reactions and the study of electrochemical processes of organic and inorganic compounds. In later work, Heyrovský was able to reduce the recording time of the process to fractions of seconds with great accuracy.

A Rockefeller Fellowship made it possible for Heyrovský to lecture at the University of Paris in 1926. The successful presentation of his work led to lectures on the polarographic process in the United States, notably at Berkeley in 1933 under a Carnegie visiting professorship. In 1934 he addressed the Mendeleev centenary in Leningrad. This worldwide recognition was aided, according to Heyrovský, by the help of Wilhelm Böttger in 1936. Böttger was the editor of an important chemical journal and invited Heyrovský to contribute an account on polarography for the second volume of his compendium on analytical methods in physical chemistry. During the 1940s, accounts of his discoveries were published in English and in German.

During World War II, Heyrovský's research continued in the midst of Nazi-occupied Czechoslovakia. While Czechs were removed from their teaching positions and replaced by Germans, Heyrovský's replacement was of mixed German-Czech parentage, and unsympathetic to Nazism. Heyrovský was permitted to carry on his work, and by the end of the war, he had completed important writing and begun new investigations.

Stresses the Importance of National Science Journals

Heyrovský believed that it was vital to Czech scientific culture that a journal be published in his native language. He was helped by the Royal Bohemian Society of Sciences to found a chemical journal for papers that had been written in French or English. Heyrovský accepted responsibility for translations of the English papers, while his associate, Emil Votoček, handled the French papers. The publication, *Collection of Czechoslovak Chemical Communications,* became internationally recognized. Heyrovsky also prepared a number of bibliographies on polarography with the help of a number of notable associates, including his wife, Marie Heyrovská.

Czech society was grateful for the work that Heyrovský did to reflect how the country's scientific community had matured. Specifically, he had created many Czech scientific terms in the belief that language was a critical tool in the development of research. In recognition, the Polarographic Institute of the Czechoslovak Academy of Sciences (founded as the Polarographic Institute at Charles University in 1950), was named the J. Heyrovský Institute of Polarography in 1964. Additionally, he was awarded the Czech State Prize in 1951 and the Order of the Czechoslovak Republic in 1955.

When Heyrovský received the Nobel Prize in chemistry in 1959, he revealed the intensity of his work. He had spent the better part of forty years working on polarography, sacrificing his spare time to work evenings and weekends on his projects. His dedication to his field and long hours of work did not totally preclude his pursuit of his interests in music, literature, and sports. He played the piano and he was a lover of opera. He has been noted for his good sense of humor and has been described as a generous host and an aficionado of good food and wine.

Heyrovsky married Marie Kořánova in 1926. They had a daughter, Jitka, who became a biochemist and a son, Michael, who followed his father to the Institute of Polarography. Heyrovsky died in Prague on March 27, 1967, at the age of seventy-six.

SELECTED WRITINGS BY HEYROVSKÝ:

Books

A Polarographic Study of the Electrokinetic Phenomena of Adsorption, Electroreduction and Overpotential Displayed at the Dropping Mercury Cathode, Hermann, 1934.

Polarographie: Theoretische Grundlagen, Praktische Ausfuhrung und Anwendungen der Elektrolyse mit der Tropfenden Quecksilberelektrode, Springer, 1941.

Bibliography of Publications Dealing with the Polarographic Method, 5 volumes, Nakladatelství Československé akademie véd, 1960–1964.

(With Jaroslav Kuta) *Principles of Polarography,* [Prague-London], 1965.

Periodicals

"The Electroaffinity of Aluminum," *Journal of the Chemical Society (Transactions),* Volume 117, 1920, number 1, pp. 11–36; number 2, pp. 1013–1025.

"Electrolysis with a Dropping Mercury Cathode," *Philosophical Magazine,* Volume 44, 1923, pp. 303–314.
"Oszillographische Polarographie," *Zeitschrift für physikalische Chemie,* Volume 193, 1944, pp. 77–96.
"The Development of Polarographic Analysis," *Analyst,* Volume 81, 1956, p. 189.

SOURCES:

Books

Gillispie, Charles Coulson, editor, *Dictionary of Scientific Biography,* Scribner, 1970, pp. 370–376.

—*Sketch by Jordan Richman*

Beatrice Hicks
1919-1979
American engineer

Beatrice Hicks built a distinguished career in the field of engineering at a time when women engineers were a rarity. She co-founded and served as the first president of the Society of Women Engineers (SWE), and held the presidency of the Newark Controls Co. from 1955 until her death in 1979. Hicks received the SWE's Achievement Award, its highest honor, in 1963, and was the first woman awarded an honorary doctorate of engineering by the Rensselaer Polytechnic Institute.

Hicks was born January 2, 1919, in Orange, New Jersey, to William and Florence (Neben) Hicks. She decided to become an engineer at age thirteen when her father, an engineer and founder of the Newark Controls Co. in Bloomfield, New Jersey, took her to the Empire State Building and the George Washington Bridge and explained that the structures had been designed by engineers. She received a bachelor of science degree in chemical engineering from Newark College of Engineering in 1939 and studied electrical engineering from 1939 to 1943.

Despite her engineering degree, when Hicks joined the staff of Western Electric in 1942, she was hired as a technician. However, her supervisor successfully lobbied for a salary increase and the title of engineer for her; she remained at Western Electric for three years.

Named Vice President of Engineering Firm

In 1945, Hicks joined her father's firm, Newark Controls Co., as chief engineer, and a year later added the role of vice president to her responsibilities. She also decided to further her education, earning a master of science degree in physics from Stevens Institute of Technology in 1949, the year after her marriage to engineer Rodney Chipp. In 1955, Hicks became president of Newark Controls. Hicks' work at Newark Controls focused on the effects of the environment on pressure switches, and she invented the gas density switch, an integral part of systems using artificial atmospheres.

Hicks co-founded the Society of Women Engineers (SWE) and was elected its first president in 1950. She remained active in the SWE throughout her career, serving as a board member from 1952 to 1953 and as a trustee from 1960 to 1964. She also served as director of the First International Conference of Women Engineers and Scientists, organized by the SWE and held in New York in 1964. *Mademoiselle* magazine named Hicks its 1952 "Woman of the Year in Business." She was a U.S. delegate to the Tenth International Management Congress in Sao Paulo, Brazil, in 1954, and to the Eleventh International Management Congress in Paris three years later, and was selected with her husband to participate in Project Ambassador, a goodwill and fact-finding tour of South America sponsored by the National Society of Professional Engineers in 1959. Hicks received the SWE's highest honor, the Achievement Award, in 1963, "in recognition of her significant contributions to the theoretical study and analysis of sensing devises under extreme environmental conditions, and her substantial achievements in international technical understanding, professional guidance, and engineering education." In 1965 Hicks became the first woman named an honorary doctor of engineering by Rensselaer Polytechnic Institute.

SOURCES:

Periodicals

"Beatrice Hicks, Society's First President, Dies," *Society of Women Engineers Newsletter,* November/December, 1979, p. 5.

—*Sketch by Karen Withem*

David Hilbert
1862-1943
German mathematician

David Hilbert

By the end of his career, David Hilbert was the best known mathematician in the world, as well as the most influential. His contributions did not merely affect but decisively altered the directions taken in many fields. In some ways, however, his career ended in disappointment; he had inherited one of the great mathematical centers for research and teaching, but from his retirement he had to watch its glory disappear under the ideological onslaught from the Nazi government. Nevertheless, the heritage of the contributions he made to mathematics, as well as the students he trained, has outlasted the disruptions of World War II.

Hilbert was born in Wehlau, near Königsberg, on January 23, 1862. His family was staunchly Protestant, although Hilbert himself was later to leave the church in which he was baptized. Otto Hilbert, his father, was a lawyer of social standing in the society around Königsberg, and his mother's family name was Erdtmann. The name "David" ran in the family—a fact Hilbert had subsequently to verify to the Nazi regime, which suspected that anyone with the name was of Jewish ancestry. Hilbert's early education was in Königsberg, which he would always consider his spiritual home.

In 1880, Hilbert entered the University of Königsberg, where he received his Ph.D. in 1885. By the next year he had become a privatdozent, and by 1892 Hilbert had been appointed to the equivalent of an assistant professorship at Königsberg, rising in the ranks to a professorship the next year. In 1895 he took a chair at Göttingen, where he remained until his retirement. As this rapid progress attests, Hilbert knew enough about academic politics to advance through the complexities of the German system. In this he had the guidance of a mathematician with great political skills, named Felix Klein, who had devoted much of his life to building the University of Göttingen into the world's mathematical center.

Researches Invariants and Contributes to Number Theory

Hilbert made his mathematical reputation on the strength of his research into invariant theory. The notion of an invariant had been created in the nineteenth century as an expression of something that remains the same under various sorts of transformations. As a simple instance, if all the coefficients in an equation are doubled, the solutions of the equation remain the same. A good deal of work had been done in classifying invariants and in trying to prove what sorts of invariants existed. The results were massive calculations, and books on invariant theory were made up of pages completely filled with symbols. Hilbert rendered most of that work obsolete by taking a path that did not require explicit calculation. Those who had been practicing invariant theory were taken aback by Hilbert's effrontery, and one of them described Hilbert's approach as "not mathematics, but theology." Invariant theory quickly disappeared from the center of mathematical interest, as Hilbert's work required some time to be absorbed. Only much later was the field reopened, as invariant theorists at last were ready to proceed from his calculations.

Perhaps the mathematician closest to Hilbert was **Hermann Minkowski**, two years younger than Hilbert but well-known at an even earlier age. At first, Hilbert's family did not approve of their friendship because Minkowski was the son of a Jewish rag merchant. Hilbert nonetheless kept in close contact with Minkowski, who had won a prize from the French Academy while still in his teens. Hilbert eventually managed to bring Minkowski to Göttingen.

In 1893 the German Mathematical Association appointed Hilbert and Minkowski to summarize the current state of the theory of numbers. Number theory was the oldest branch of mathematics, as it dealt with the properties of whole numbers. Much new work had been done by Karl Friedrich Gauss, and throughout the second half of the nineteenth century further progress had been made. The accessibility of the statement of problems in number theory made them attractive as an object of investigation, although the work of Leopold Kronecker, perhaps the biggest influence on Hilbert, was already well beyond what the nonmathematician could easily follow. Minkowski withdrew from the project, and in 1897 Hilbert submitted a report called *Der Zahlbericht* ("Number Report"). His work advanced the subject to a more technical level, one which has been maintained throughout the twentieth century. Many of the results included still bear Hilbert's name, a tribute to the longevity of his influence.

Poses Problems for the New Century

The next direction in which Hilbert pursued his research was somewhat unexpected. After all his work in algebra, he began to look at the foundations of geometry. Euclid had already laid the foundations more than two thousand years before, but detailed examination of some of Euclid's proofs revealed gaps in his presentation; he had made assumptions that were neither explicit nor justified by what had been proven earlier. In addition to problems posed by these gaps, another source for a new approach to geometry was the discovery during the nineteenth century of non-euclidean geometries. These shared some axioms or assumptions with Euclid's system, but differed in other respects. For example, in Euclidean geometry the sum of the angles of a triangle was equal to 180 degrees, while in non-euclidean geometries the sum could be greater or less. One of the reasons that it had taken so long to develop non-euclidean geometries was a general disagreement over what was true about geometrical objects. Hilbert felt that the only way to make progress was to be entirely explicit about each proof and not to trust to unspoken assumptions.

The safest way to avoid these assumptions was to regard the terms of the subject as defined only by the axioms in which they were used. Mathematicians might think they know what a "line" means and may be tempted to use this mental image in trying to prove a fact about lines. But that mental image could easily add something to the notion of line beyond what is given in the axioms. Taken in this way, the axioms can be considered as a kind of definition for the terms used in them. As Hilbert noted, the question of which theorems followed from which axioms had to be unchanged if all the technical terms of the subject (like point, line, or plane) were replaced by words from some other area. It was the form of the axiom that mattered, not what the objects were. This brought Hilbert into conflict with Gottlob Frege, one of the founders of mathematical logic. The controversy between Hilbert and Frege involved issues about the philosophy of mathematics that remained central to the field for much of the twentieth century. In general, it can be claimed that Hilbert's perspective has been more helpful in enabling mathematicians to pursue the foundations of geometry.

One of the highlights of Hilbert's career came in 1900, when he was invited to address the International Congress of Mathematicians in Paris. His talk consisted of the statement of twenty-three problems, which he offered to the twentieth century to solve. Although not all of the problems have proved to be of the same importance, by posing them Hilbert created an agenda that has been followed by many distinguished mathematicians. The first problem dealt with the question of how many real numbers there were, compared to the number of whole numbers. It was not resolved until 1963, when it was shown that the answer depends on which axioms are selected as the basis for the theory of sets. Hilbert's seventh problem dealt with the irrationality of certain real numbers, an area to which Hilbert himself had contributed. A number is rational if it is the ratio of two whole numbers, irrational if can't be so expressed, and transcendental if it is not the solution of a polynomial equation with whole number coefficients. Although Hilbert was not the first to prove that the numbers e and pi (the base of natural logarithms and the ratio of the circumference of a circle to its diameter, respectively) were transcendental, he had simplified the proofs considerably. A. O. Gelfond solved his seventh problem, by establishing that a whole class of numbers was transcendental. Hilbert's tenth problem, on the solubility of certain equations, required much progress in mathematical logic before it could be solved. Entire books and conferences have been devoted to the state of the solutions to Hilbert's problems.

In addition to the study of the foundations of geometry, Hilbert turned to mathematical analysis and left a decisive imprint on this field as well. The previous generation of mathematicians had found defects in one of the standard principles from earlier in the century. Hilbert showed that the principle could be preserved, and he proceeded from there to make great progress in the study of integral equations. Hilbert has been credited with the creation of functional analysis, and although there was more foundational work to be done after him, his brief involvement in the area had once again altered it irrevocably.

In the fall of 1910, the second Bolyai Prize was awarded to Hilbert as a confirmation of his mathematical stature. The best-known images of him come from the period surrounding World War I. His distinctive appearance, from Panama hat to bearded chin, and his sharp voice set the tone for mathematics in Germany and the world. During the war he refused to sign the "Declaration to the Cultural World," which claimed that Germany was innocent of alleged war crimes. He was also willing to put mathematics before nationality, and he included an obituary for a French mathematician in the journal *Mathematische*

Annalen (the showpiece of German mathematics) during the war. These acts made him unpopular with German nationalists. In the same way, he also took pleasure in fighting the academic establishment over the rights of **Amalie Emmy Noether**, who was both a woman and a Jew. Of the sixty-nine students who wrote their theses under Hilbert (an enormous number for any time), there were several women.

After a brief dalliance with theoretical physics (an area Hilbert felt too important to leave to the physicists but to which he made few lasting contributions), Hilbert returned to questions of the philosophy of mathematics that had arisen earlier during his work on geometry. He was eager to pursue a program that could result in the establishment of secure foundations for mathematics. While he was willing to grant some importance to finite mathematics, he felt that the infinite required special treatment. In his account, called formalism, he set out to prove the consistency of mathematics. This enterprise put him in conflict with the other philosophies of mathematics most frequently advocated. He gave expression to his views most notably in an address "On the Infinite" in 1925; he was challenged by many, including **L. E. J. Brouwer** and **Hermann Weyl**, but it was the incompleteness theorem of the young Austrian mathematician **Kurt Gödel** which threatened the entire program Hilbert was pursuing. Certain narrow interpretations of formalism were put to rest by Gödel's work, and some of Hilbert's views were included among these. On the other hand, Hilbert's account of the foundations of mathematics changed during his career, and a good part of the work he did in the area has survived within post-Gödel logic under the heading of proof theory.

Hilbert married Kathe Jerosch in 1892. While he was willing to be casual with regard to his appearance, his wife helped prevent at least some of his sartorial excesses. She also proved a source of strength to Hilbert in his disappointments, one of which was their only son Franz, who never lived up to his father's expectations and probably suffered from a mental disorder. The last years of Hilbert's life were also darkened by the advent of National Socialism and its dire effects on Germany's intellectual community. Hilbert was proud of receiving honorary citizenship from Königsberg in 1930, the year of his retirement from Göttingen, but nothing could assuage his grief over the sequence of losses that the university suffered from the departure of many of its leading minds. Hilbert turned seventy-one in 1933, the year the Nazis came to power, and it was too late for him to look for a new home. Many of his students had found academic homes abroad, and nothing could rebuild the university in the face of racial laws and hatred of the intellect. It is a measure of the state of German mathematics and the atmosphere in Göttingen that at Hilbert's death on February 14, 1943, no more than a dozen people attended his funeral.

SELECTED WRITINGS BY HILBERT:

Books

The Foundations of Geometry, Open Court Press, 1902.

Gesammelte Abhandlungen, 3 volumes, Springer-Verlag, 1932–1935.

SOURCES:

Books

Gillespie, C. C., editor, *Dictionary of Scientific Biography,* Volume 6, Scribner, 1970–1978, pp. 388–395.

Mathematical Developments Arising from the Hilbert Problems, American Mathematical Society, 1979.

Reid, Constance, *Hilbert,* Springer-Verlag, 1970.

Tiles, Mary, *Mathematics and the Image of Reason,* Routledge, 1991.

—*Sketch by Thomas Drucker*

Archibald V. Hill
1886-1977
English physiologist

The 1922 Nobel Prize for physiology or medicine recognized Archibald Hill for his discoveries relating to heat production and oxygen use in muscles. Prior to this distinction Hill was knighted for his military work during World War I and elected a member into the Royal Society, both in 1918. He represented Cambridge University in Parliament during World War II and also served on the War Cabinet Scientific Advisory Committee. It was only after the war, and his retirement in 1952, that Hill returned to research into the physiology of the muscles.

Sir Archibald Vivian Hill was born in Bristol, England, on September 26, 1886 into a family that had been in the lumber business for five generations. Hill's mother, Ada Priscilla Rumney Hill, single-handedly raised him and his younger sister, Muriel, after their father, Jonathan Hill, deserted the family when Hill was three. Until Hill was seven, his mother educated him at home, but when the family moved to nearby Weston-super-Mare, Hill was placed in a preparatory school of modest size. In 1899 the family moved to Tiverton, Devonshire, where Hill received the training he would need to enter college. At Blundell's School, he demonstrated exceptional abilities in mathematics, joined the debating team, and ran long-distance. Hill's sister Muriel later became a biochemist.

Changes Emphasis from Mathematics to Physiology

In 1905 Hill received a scholarship to study mathematics at Trinity College, Cambridge. There he completed a three-year course in two years, but found that even though he performed well in his chosen subject, he lacked sufficient interest or motivation to develop further as a mathematician. His tutor, Walter Morley Fletcher (1873–1933), who was a physiologist, had been working with **Frederick Gowland Hopkins** researching the chemistry of frog muscle physiology. Fletcher and Hopkins had discovered the importance of lactic acid in muscle contraction. Fletcher advised Hill to change from mathematics to physiology, even though Hill had finished third in his class in mathematics. Fletcher correctly believed that Hill's scientific curiosity was stronger than his urge to become a mathematician.

Hill graduated from Trinity College with a medical degree in 1907 but remained there for the next seven years doing research until war broke out in 1914. In 1909, he completed his examinations in natural science with honors and began research at the Cambridge Physiological Laboratory. The director of the laboratory, J. N. Langley, suggested that Hill expand the work of Fletcher and Hopkins on the chemistry of muscle contraction by the production of heat in the process of muscle contraction. Using a thermocouple recorder, which is a measuring device that records minute changes in heat temperatures, Hill was able to establish the basic procedures in this early work for his later discoveries which were to eventually earn him a Nobel Prize in physiology or medicine.

In 1911, after receiving a fellowship from Trinity College the year before, Hill visited Germany where his techniques for measuring heat changes in muscles produced by contraction were significantly improved. Two German scientists, Karl Burker and Friedrich Paschen, showed him how to improve his use of the thermocouple and galvanometer, instruments that allowed him to measure minute changes in electric current with greater degrees of accuracy.

In the three years following his trip to Germany, Hill continued at Cambridge, observing heat quantities produced by muscular contractions and recording those chemical changes taking place in the muscle, enabling it to do mechanical work. By 1913, Hill was able to demonstrate that when the muscle starts to contract, a small amount of heat is produced, while after the initial phase of the contraction, more heat develops, though at a slower rate and in much greater measure. He also showed at this time that molecular oxygen is used after the contraction takes place rather than at the time of the contraction itself.

The discovery that molecular oxygen is not required in the initial phase was demonstrated by placing muscle fibers in an atmosphere that excluded oxygen and instead used pure nitrogen. The production of heat at the onset—despite the absence of oxygen—indicated that oxygen was not necessary for the initiation of the contraction. However, the recovery phase did not take place, suggesting an energy exchange as a critical factor in heat being generated during the post contraction phase.

Hill's discoveries of how heat production and oxygen function in muscle tissue opened the way for a clearer understanding of the earlier work of Fletcher's and Hopkin's experiments. They had shown the formation of lactic acid in frog muscle during the contraction process, and observed its elimination when oxygen was present. Hill believed that the initial heat he noted was produced by a lactic acid formation from a precursor substance. The heat generated in the recovery phase signified the removal of lactic acid through oxidation.

Hill's muscle research was interrupted by World War I. He served first as a captain, then became a major in the Cambridgeshire Regiment. He was also commissioned by the government to develop a program for the improvement of anti-aircraft ordinance. After the war, Hill returned to Cambridge to continue his work on muscle physiology. In 1920 he accepted an appointment to the Brackenbury Chair of Physiology at Manchester University. There he challenged the accepted view of heat production in one phase only, or at the time of contraction, establishing the two phases of heat production in muscle contraction from his work with frogs' thigh muscles.

In order to develop further his findings relating to oxidation and muscle contraction, Hill did research with **Otto Meyerhof**, a German-American biochemist. Meyerhof had been studying the physiology of muscle contraction through chemical rather than mechanical dynamics and had been able to identify glycogen as the precursor of lactic acid. Hill theorized that since the heat produced by the two phases of muscular contraction was not enough to eliminate all the lactic acid, it probably changed back to its precursor. Meyerhof demonstrated that the energy levels created by the oxidation of the lactic acid were enough to reconvert it back to glycogen. The agreement of their work thus assured the validity of their research.

Hill and Meyerhof Awarded 1922 Nobel Prize

For their cooperative work in muscle physiology, Hill and Meyerhof shared the 1922 Nobel Prize for physiology or medicine. In his Nobel speech, Hill emphasized the need for continuing research in the area of muscle physiology. He reminded the audience of the complexity of the subject, of the different approaches to experimentation, and of the need for improved instruments with which to perform meaningful study and research.

In 1923, Hill received an appointment to University College, London, and became Foulerton Research Professor of the Royal Society. He continued his work in muscle physiology, but this time he turned his attention to the role of lactic acid build-up in human muscles. He found that with moderate exercise there is enough oxygen to remove the excess lactic acid, but with heavy exercise there is an excess amount of lactic acid build-up due to what he called an *oxygen debt.* This debt can be made up by deep breathing or allowing enough time at rest to allow for the absorption of the lactic acid surplus.

In the thirties, with the rise of Hitler in Germany, Hill voiced his protest against the anti-Semitic policies of the Nazis against Jewish scientists, as well as anti-Nazi scientists. He helped form groups to assist researchers escaping Nazi oppression. In World War II he again performed vital services on behalf of his country's military objectives, as he had done in World War I. Two major accomplishments of this period include his coordination of efforts to gain military cooperation with Canada and the United States, and a report he composed as a visitor to India recommending the restructuring and reorganization of the country's scientific and industrial resources. At the war's close, Hill reorganized his laboratory and recruited a staff for research at University College. He retired in 1952 but continued his scientific investigations in the area of muscle physiology.

Hill married Margaret Neville Keynes in 1913. She was a social worker and the sister of John Maynard Keynes, a well-known English economist. They had two sons, David and Maurice, and two daughters, Mary and Janet. On June 3, 1977 Hill died of a viral infection followed by complications.

SELECTED WRITINGS BY HILL:

Books

Muscular Activity, Williams and Wilkins, 1926.

Living Machinery, Harcourt Brace, 1927.

Muscular Movement in Man, McGraw-Hill, 1927.

Trails and Trials in Physiology, Williams and Wilkins, 1965.

First and Last Experiments in Muscle Mechanics, Cambridge, 1970.

SOURCES:

Books

Abbott, David, Editor, *The Biographical Dictionary of Scientists: Biologists,* Peter Bedrick Books, 1984, pp. 61–62.

Biographical Memoirs of the Fellows of the Royal Society, Volume 24, Royal Society (London), 1978, pp. 71–149.

—*Sketch by Jordan P. Richman*

Henry A. Hill
1915-1979
American chemist

Henry A. Hill was an expert on polymers, with a particular interest in resins, rubber, and plastics. Conscious of the limited opportunities for African Americans in the sciences in the 1940s and 1950s, Hill turned adversity to advantage and held a number of management positions in the chemical industry before starting his own company, Riverside Research Laboratory. Hill was frequently sought out by his colleagues for a range of consulting and advisory positions. He was responsible for developing guidelines for employers in the chemical industry, and was appointed by President Lyndon Johnson to the National Commission on Product Safety. In 1977 Hill served as president of the American Chemical Society.

Henry Aaron Hill was born May 30, 1915, in the small river town of St. Joseph, Missouri. His undergraduate education was completed at Johnson C. Smith University, a liberal arts school in North Carolina. Hill received a B.S. in chemistry in 1936. He then spent a year in graduate school at the University of Chicago, but went on to earn a Ph.D. in organic chemistry from the Massachusetts Institute of Technology (MIT) in 1942. At MIT Hill came briefly but memorably under the influence of James Flack Norris, who impressed Hill by being more interested in Hill's abilities as a chemist than in his heritage. Hill was later instrumental in establishing the American Chemical Society's Norris award.

Following his formal schooling, Hill held jobs involving several different research concerns, beginning as head of chemistry research at Atlantic Research Associates in Massachusetts from 1942 to 1943. In 1943 he was made a research director. In 1945 Hill was promoted to vice president in charge of research at what was now the National Atlantic Research Company. While moving quickly up the ranks, Hill spent his research time developing water-based paints, rubber adhesives, and synthetic rubber, among other projects. It was also there that Hill began to conceive of operating his own research laboratory.

Hill then spent six years, from 1946 to 1952, as group leader at the Dewey & Almy Chemical Company, working on polymer research. (Polymers are large molecules consisting of similar or identical small molecules or monomers linked together. Examples of naturally occurring polymers are proteins and silk; polymers synthesized in the laboratory include plastics and synthetic fibers.) Hill's experience led him to the collaborative development of National Polychemicals Inc., in Wilmington, Massachusetts, where he spent the next nine years beginning in 1952, the first four as assistant manager, and the last five as a vice president. This corporation was a manufacturer of chemical intermediaries used for polymers, and grew to have annual sales in 1971 of over ten million dollars. The company's success was largely credited to Hill's personal research contributions.

In 1961 Hill realized his ambition of operating his own research facility, establishing Riverside Research Laboratory. The mission of the corporation would be to provide research and development, as well as consulting, in the area of organic chemistry. Hill had a particular interest in resin, rubber, and plastics. By 1964 the company had moved to more spacious accommodations, where it would remain for the remainder of Hill's life. Hill eventually became known as an authority in polymer chemistry on fabric flammability.

Hill was active in the professional aspects of his field. In 1968 he served as chair of the committee on professional relations of the American Chemical Society. This committee produced widely used personnel guidelines for employers of chemists and chemical engineers. In 1968 Hill was appointed by President Lyndon Johnson to the National Commission on Product Safety, a position that galvanized Hill's interest in product liability and product safety. Hill was a fellow of both the American Association for the Advancement of Science and the American Institute of Chemists. He was a member of the American Chemical Society for thirty-eight years, served on its board of directors from 1971 to 1978, and was elected president in 1977. He was chair of the compliance committee of the National Motor Vehicle Safety Advisory Council, and a member of the Information Council on Fabric Flammability. He was married in 1943, and had one child.

Whatever obstacles Hill may have faced in his career owing to racial discrimination, his talent and persistence served him well in a highly competitive industry. In 1971 he was quoted in *Chemistry* as saying, "My successes have hinged upon a scratch below the surface, a little extra persistence." Hill died of a heart attack on March 17, 1979.

SOURCES:

Books

Young, Herman, and Barbara Young, *Scientists in the Black Perspective,* Lincoln Foundation, 1979.

Periodicals

"Henry Hill Dead of Heart Attack at 63," *Chemical and Engineering News,* March 26, 1979, pp. 6–7.

Massie, Samuel P., "Henry A. Hill: The Second Mile," *Chemistry,* January, 1971, p. 11.

—Sketch by Kimberlyn McGrail

Cyril N. Hinshelwood
1897-1967
English chemist and biochemist

Cyril N. Hinshelwood was not only a scientific thinker of the highest order but a great teacher who influenced a generation of chemists emerging from Oxford University in the decades before, during, and after World War II. His interests led him into the fields of physics, chemistry, biology, and even the philosophy of science, where he speculated on the nature of the scientific process. Hinshelwood's most notable achievement in a wide-ranging career took place in chemical kinetics, the study of the conditions under which chemical reactions occur. Specifically, he unraveled the daunting complexities of the reaction that produces water. In recognition of this work, Hinshelwood shared the 1956 Nobel Prize in chemistry with **Nikolay N. Semenov**, whose ideas he had used in his explanation.

An only child, Cyril Norman Hinshelwood was born on June 19, 1897, in London, England, to Norman MacMillan Hinshelwood, an accountant, and Ethel Smith Hinshelwood. The family moved to Canada, but because of Hinshelwood's health, he and his mother moved back to England in 1904. His father died soon afterward. Although he received a scholarship to Balliol College at Oxford in 1916, Hinshelwood delayed accepting it to work at the

Queensferry Explosive Supply Factory during World War I. Promoted to assistant chief chemist in 1918, his work on solid explosives sparked a lifelong interest in chemical kinetics.

Hinshelwood entered Oxford in 1919, becoming a fellow of Balliol in 1920 and a fellow and tutor of Trinity College, Cambridge, in 1921. During the 1920s he began to apply kinetic theory, the study of bodies in motion, to the chemical reactions that occurred in gases. In 1927 he began to investigate the interaction of hydrogen and oxygen. At certain pressure thresholds, the reaction became explosive. Following Semenov's conclusions about his experiments with phosphorus and oxygen, Hinshelwood applied the theory of the branching chain reaction, which posits that the products of the reaction assist in spreading the reaction so rapidly that an explosion results. The reaction of hydrogen and oxygen is so basic to chemistry that Hinshelwood's findings opened up several avenues of research in both organic and inorganic chemistry.

By the late 1930s Hinshelwood had shifted the focus of his research to decipher the mechanisms of bacterial growth with the tools of chemical kinetics. For the rest of his career, he elucidated key processes such as environmental adaptation and cell regulation by breaking them down into discrete chemical reactions. Although his views were met with initial skepticism among biologists, they are now widely accepted principles in biochemistry. After decades of work as a professor, scientist, and college administrator, Hinshelwood retired from his chair at Oxford in 1964 and moved to London. However, as a senior research fellow at London's Imperial College, he continued his study of bacterial growth, while also serving as a trustee of the British Museum and chair of the Queen Elizabeth College in London.

Hinshelwood died in London on October 9, 1967. Devoted to his mother until she died in 1959, he was a lifelong bachelor. Well read in the classics and literature, he was a member of the Dante Society and president of the Classical Association at Oxford. He was also president of the Modern Language Association, and knew eight foreign languages. As recreational pursuits, Hinshelwood dabbled in oil painting, appreciated classical music, and collected Chinese porcelain and Persian rugs.

A member of the Royal Academy, Hinshelwood was knighted in 1948. Apart from the Nobel Prize, he won the 1942 Davy Medal, the 1947 Royal Medal, and the 1962 Copley Medal of the Royal Society. He also held numerous honorary degrees from various universities.

SELECTED WRITINGS BY HINSHELWOOD:

Books

The Kinetics of Chemical Change in Gaseous Systems, second edition, Clarendon, 1929.

The Structure of Physical Chemistry, Clarendon, 1951.

The Chemical Kinetics of the Bacterial Cell, Clarendon, 1952.

SOURCES:

Books

Farber, Eduard, *Nobel Prize Winners in Chemistry, 1901–1961,* Abelard-Schuman, 1953, Revised 1963, pp. 263–274.

—Sketch by Hovey Brock

William Augustus Hinton
1883-1959
American medical researcher

William Augustus Hinton was the first black professor at Harvard Medical School, where he taught preventative medicine and hygiene, as well as bacteriology and immunology. He earned an international reputation as a medical researcher with his work on the detection and treatment of syphilis and other sexually transmitted diseases. He was integral in developing two common diagnostic procedures for syphilis, the Hinton test and the Davies-Hinton test.

Hinton was born on December 15, 1883, in Chicago, Illinois. His parents were Augustus Hinton and Maria Clark, both former slaves. Hinton grew up in Kansas and became the youngest student to ever graduate from Kansas City High School. After high school, he studied at the University of Kansas, completing the three-year premed program in two years. Hinton did some additional undergraduate work at Harvard University and received his B.S. there in 1905.

After graduation, Hinton spent some time working in a law office, but, as he reported in *Twenty-fifth Anniversary Report—Harvard Class of 1905,* he "discovered that legal appetite can't always be cultivated." Instead of pursuing work in law, Hinton turned to education, teaching science at Waldo University in Tennessee from 1905 to 1906 and at State School in Langston, Oklahoma, from 1906 to 1909. It was during this time—in Langston—that Hinton met and married Ada Hawes, a teacher, in 1909. They subsequently had two daughters, Ann and Jane.

William Augustus Hinton

In 1909, Hinton entered Harvard Medical School. Though offered a scholarship reserved for African American students, Hinton instead chose to compete for a scholarship offered to all students. He won the Wigglesworth scholarship two years in a row. By skipping the second year of school and finishing the Harvard medical program in only three years, Hinton received his M.D. in 1912.

After graduating, Hinton's first job was as a serologist at the Wassermann Laboratory of the Harvard Medical School. By 1915, he was named the director of the lab, which at the time had become the official lab for the Massachusetts State Department of Public Health. In 1916, Hinton also became chief of the laboratory department at the Boston Dispensary. One of his accomplishments there was developing a program to train women as lab technicians, a profession that at the time was not generally open to women.

From the start of his career until his retirement, his attention was directed toward "syphilis and the laboratory tests used in connection with its diagnosis and treatment," Hinton reported in *Fiftieth Anniversary Report—Harvard Class of 1905.* In 1927, Hinton developed a test—subsequently known as the Hinton test—to diagnose syphilis. Because it was easier, less expensive, and more accurate than previously used tests, the Hinton test was adopted as standard procedure for diagnosing syphilis. Later, with Dr. J. A. V. Davies, Hinton developed another diagnostic test for syphilis, know as the Davies-Hinton test.

Hinton began teaching at Harvard Medical School in 1923, as assistant lecturer in preventive medicine and hygiene. He continued teaching for 27 years. Hinton wrote one book during his career—*Syphilis and Its Treatment,* published in 1936. At the time, the book was considered controversial. In *Fiftieth Anniversary Report—Harvard Class of 1905,* Hinton wrote that the book contained "specific ways in which laboratory tests for syphilis should be used correctly." Though the book had "little support" at first, by 1955 Hinton noted that "except where new and superior drugs have replaced those then in use, most of it has been recognized." The *Harvard Medical Alumni Bulletin* of July 1959, in fact, described the book as "widely acclaimed." In an interview with the *Boston Daily Globe* in 1952, Hinton told reporter Frances Burns that he considered the book his most important contribution because it summed up both his research and the experience he gained through patients in clinics who had syphilis. "I had learned that race was not the determining factor but that it was, rather, the socioeconomic condition of the patient," he told Burns. "It is a disease of the underprivileged."

In addition to his work as a researcher, Hinton was a special consultant to the U.S. Public Health Service and, beginning in 1936, chief of the labs of the Boston Floating Hospital. He also taught at both Tufts University and Simmons College. In 1940, Hinton lost a leg in a car accident. This disability, however, did not keep him from teaching. In fact, in 1949, Harvard appointed Hinton clinical professor of bacteriology and immunology. He was the school's first black professor. Hinton retired one year later, in 1950. According to the *Boston Daily Globe,* however, he continued to teach without a salary. Hinton retired from the Massachusetts Department of Public Health Wassermann Laboratory in 1953.

At home, Hinton's hobbies were gardening and making furniture. He died at the age of 75 on August 8, 1959, in Canton, Massachusetts.

SELECTED WRITINGS BY HINTON:

Books

Syphilis and Its Treatment, Macmillan, 1936.

SOURCES:

Books

Fiftieth Anniversary Report—Harvard Class of 1905, Harvard University Printing Office, 1955, pp. 247–248.

Twenty-fifth Anniversary Report—Harvard Class of 1905, Harvard University Printing Office, 1930, p. 304.

Periodicals

Boston Daily Globe, September 15, 1952.
Boston Herald, June 30, 1949.
Boston Sunday Globe, August 9, 1959.
Boston Transcript, January 25, 1916.
Harvard Medical Alumni Bulletin, July 1959.

—*Sketch by Devera Pine*

George H. Hitchings
1905-
American pharmacologist

George H. Hitchings is among the most prolific of modern pharmaceutical scientists. He worked at Burroughs Wellcome Company, a British pharmaceutical company with research facilities in the United States, for more than thirty years before his retirement in 1975. Hitchings produced many important pharmaceuticals for treating diseases such as cancer, gout, and malaria, and for preventing rejection of transplanted organs. His contributions were based on the premise that an understanding of what makes diseased cells different from normal cells makes it possible to exploit those differences to destroy cancer cells or foreign invaders such as bacteria or viruses with drugs. For his work in finding treatments for serious diseases, Hitchings and his long-time Burroughs Wellcome collaborator Gertrude Elion shared the 1988 Nobel Prize in physiology or medicine with British pharmaceutical scientist Sir **James Black**. It was the first time since 1957 that pharmaceutical scientists had been awarded the prize.

George Herbert Hitchings was born to George Herbert Hitchings, Sr., a naval architect, and Lillian H. Belle Hitchings on April 18, 1905, in Hoquiam, Washington, on the Olympic Peninsula. His father's death when he was twelve and his admiration for Louis Pasteur, a preeminent scientist-philanthropist who became his role model, aimed Hitchings toward a career in medicine. As the salutatorian of his high school class, Hitchings gave an address to the graduating class on the germ theory and Pasteur's life.

Hitchings attended the University of Washington, where he received a bachelor's degree in chemistry in 1927 and a master's degree in chemistry in 1928. He also showed a fondness for many scholarly subjects, studying the arts and history in college. He began his career in scientific research at an early age. "The Chemistry of the Waters of Argyle Lagoon," the first of his more than three hundred scientific publications, appeared in the publications of the Puget Sound Biological Station in 1928, when he had just entered graduate school. He continued his graduate work in biological chemistry at Harvard College, where he received his Ph.D. in 1933. Hitchings' doctoral dissertation concerned the metabolism of nucleic acids, the chemicals that make up DNA, the carrier of genetic information. Hitchings did his work on nucleic acids before **James Watson** and **Francis Crick** discovered the structure of DNA, and at that time no one was interested in nucleic acids. Hitchings couldn't find a job. Finally, after working for nine years as a teaching fellow at Harvard (1933–39) and Western Reserve University (1939–42), he was hired by Burroughs Wellcome in 1942 and resumed his work on nucleic acids. He became vice president of research in 1967 and held the position until 1975, when he became scientist emeritus.

Pioneers Rational Drug Design

Until Hitchings and the pharmacologist **Gertrude Elion** came along, drug researchers sought new drugs by modifying natural products. The two pioneered a method that has come to be known as "rational" drug design. They reasoned that if they understood the differences between normal and diseased or infected cells, these differences could serve as a entry point to selectively kill diseased tissue without harming surrounding normal tissue. They implemented these ideas by investigating the chemical pathways of nucleic acid synthesis, which is crucial to cell metabolism. Hitchings synthesized chemicals similar in structure to natural nucleic acids, the purines and pyrimidines. These related compounds interfered with DNA synthesis. Because cancer cells divide quickly, the compounds are particularly disruptive to them, killing them as they try to divide. This form of chemotherapy is just one instance of the rational drug design that helped Hitchings accumulate eighty-five patents over his thirty-year career.

One compound in particular, 6-mercaptopurine (6MP), a purine analog synthesized in 1951, proved to be particularly effective. Working with scientists at Sloan-Kettering Institute, Hitchings and Elion perfected the drug, which was used to combat childhood leukemia. 6MP and thioguanine, also produced by Hitchings and Elion, are still used to treat acute leukemias.

In 1959 Hitchings discovered that 6MP inhibited production of antibodies in rabbits. A less toxic form called azathioprine, marketed under the trade name Imuran, was developed in 1957 to control rejection of transplanted organs and treat autoimmune diseases.

In the nearly nine thousand kidney transplants performed each year, Imuran remains the drug most commonly used to prevent organ rejection. 6MP is broken down in the body by xanthine oxydase, the same enzyme that converts purines into uric acid, the cause of the painful joint disease gout. Further investigation of purine analogs led to the development of allopurinol in the 1960s. It blocks uric acid production by competing for xanthine oxydase, an enzyme that converts purines to uric acid. Hitchings was also active in the development of other drugs, including pyrimethamine, which is used to treat malaria, and trimethoprim, which is used to treat urinary tract infections and other bacterial infections.

Philanthropy has always been a part of Hitchings' life, and he has said that when he was baptized his father dedicated his life to the service of mankind. He served as president of the Burroughs Wellcome fund, a charitable organization, from 1971 to 1990, and continues to serve as its director. In addition, he has served as director of a dozen local chapters of philanthropic organizations.

Hitchings married Beverly Reimer in 1933. The couple had two children, Laramie Ruth and Thomas Eldridge. Beverly died in 1985. In 1989, Hitchings was remarried to Joyce Shaver.

Besides the Nobel Prize, Hitchings has received numerous awards, including the Gregor Mendel Medal from the Czechoslovakian Academy of Science in 1968 and the Albert Schweitzer International Prize for Medicine in 1989. He has been awarded eleven honorary degrees and has been a member of the National Academy of Sciences in 1977. In addition, he has traveled widely, lecturing in Africa, Asia, Europe and South America.

SELECTED WRITINGS BY HITCHINGS:

Books

"Rational Design of Anticancer Drugs: Here, Imminent or Illusive?" *The Development of Target-Oriented Anticancer Drugs,* edited by Y.-C. Cheng, Raven Press, 1983, pp. 227–238.

Periodicals

"Relevance of Basic Research to Pharmaceutical Invention," *Trends in Pharmacological Science,* July, 1980, pp. 167–168.

SOURCES:

Periodicals

Hunter, Sara, "The Man who Made Immunosuppressive Drugs a Clinical Reality," *Modern Medicine,* July 1, 1975, pp. 90–104.

"Tales of Patience and Triumph," *Time,* October 31, 1988, p. 71.

Other

Hitchings, George, H., interview with Karyn Hede George conducted November 2, 1989.

—Sketch by Karyn Hede George

Gladys Lounsbury Hobby
1910-1993
American microbiologist and bacteriologist

Gladys Lounsbury Hobby was one of less than a handful of women who were part of the extensive network which brought penicillin from the laboratory to the clinic. Discovered by Sir **Alexander Fleming** in 1928, penicillin was one of the first antibiotics, medicines that could combat infections. In her book *Penicillin: Meeting the Challenge,* Hobby detailed the efforts in the early 1940s to discover a way to manufacture large amounts of penicillin, which would greatly aid in the treating of war wounded. In addition to her work as a microbiologist, Hobby wrote many articles and was also a teacher.

Hobby was born November 19, 1910, in New York City. She received her bachelor of arts degree from Vassar College in 1931; she then attended Columbia University, receiving her master's degree in 1932 and her doctorate in bacteriology three years later. From 1934 to 1943, she worked on perfecting penicillin specifically for several infectious diseases as part of a research team at the Columbia Medical School, while also being professionally involved at Presbyterian Hospital in New York City. In 1944, Hobby went to work for Pfizer Pharmaceuticals in New York, where she researched streptomycin and other antibiotics, discovering how antimicrobial drugs worked. In 1959, Hobby became chief of research at the Veteran's Administration Hospital in East Orange, New Jersey, where she worked on chronic infectious diseases. Before retiring in 1977, she was assistant research clinical professor in public health at Cornell Medical College.

Retirement for Hobby meant continuing her work. Hobby became a freelance science writer and a consultant. It was during this time that she penned her book, *Penicillin: Meeting the Challenge,* about the drug's odyssey from the laboratory to the hands of the clinician. Hobby, having taken meticulous notes, detailed each researcher's contribution to producing a

Gladys Lounsbury Hobby

safe penicillin on a large scale basis. She also authored more than 200 articles and was the founder and editor of the journal *Antimicrobial Agents and Chemotherapy*.

Hobby was a member of several professional organizations, including the American Association for the Advancement of Science, the American Academy of Microbiology, and the American Society of Microbiology. Hobby died suddenly of a heart attack on July 4, 1993, at her home in a retirement community in Pennsylvania.

SELECTED WRITINGS BY HOBBY:

Books

Penicillin: Meeting the Challenge, Yale University Press, 1985.

SOURCES:

Periodicals

Saxon, Wolfgang, "Gladys Hobby, 82, Pioneer in Bringing Penicillin to Public," *New York Times,* July 9, 1993.

—Sketch by Denise Adams Arnold

Alan Lloyd Hodgkin
1914-
English biophysicist

Alan Lloyd Hodgkin is best known for his work in defining the electrical and chemical characteristics of nerve impulses. Along with **Andrew F. Huxley** he performed experiments on the nerve fibers of squid and described the nerve impulses with a series of mathematical equations. For their research in this area, which resulted in the ionic theory of nerve impulses, the two men shared the 1963 Nobel Prize in physiology or medicine with **John C. Eccles**.

Hodgkin was born on February 5, 1914, in Banbury, Oxfordshire, England, to George L. and Mary Wilson Hodgkin. Hodgkin's father died in Baghdad during World War I, only a few years after his birth. Hodgkin was educated at the Downs School in Malvern and the Gresham School in Holt. In 1932, he entered Trinity College, Cambridge, where he first became interested in physiology. Hodgkin became a fellow at Trinity in 1936, serving as lecturer and later as assistant director of research at the physiological laboratory.

Hodgkin began studying the electrical properties of the nerve fibers in the shore crab while at Cambridge. He spent a year at the Rockefeller Institute in New York City between 1937 and 1938, and while there he met scientists who had developed new methods for studying nerve fibers. Hodgkin brought these ideas back to Cambridge, where with Andrew Huxley he devised an experiment to test an hypothesis about nerve impulses first proposed by German physiologist Julius Bernstein.

Establishes Relationship Between Resting and Acting Potentials

Bernstein had hypothesized that nerve cells possess a resting or unstimulated potential and an action or stimulated potential. During the resting potential, he believed, the nerve cell membrane had an unequal distribution of positively and negatively charged ions, with more negative ones on the inside. During resting potential, the membrane was permeable to the positively charged ions, but the negatively charged ions could not permeate the cell membrane. When the cell was stimulated, Bernstein argued, the membrane "gates" were temporarily opened, allowing ions to pass in both directions. By using the nerve cells of the shore crab, Hodgkin was able to establish that the resting potential was due to an outward movement of potassium ions; during the action potential the cell membrane's gates allowed in the more concentrated sodium ions. He also discovered that the action potential was usually much larger than the resting potential.

Some of the researchers Hodgkin had met in the United States were working with squid, whose nerve fibers are larger than those of most organisms. Hodgkin and Huxley were able to develop a method to study these fibers using microelectrodes, and they were able to confirm the results of their earlier experiment. Their progress, however, came to a halt during World War II, when Hodgkin worked on radar systems for aircraft for the Air Ministry. Hodgkin and Huxley were back in Cambridge in 1945, and they formed a small research group to pursue their pre-war investigations into nerve fibers.

In 1951, Hodgkin and his colleagues published the results of their research. They found that the membrane is permeable only to specific ions during the resting potential, because of the differing concentrations of potassium and sodium. The concentration of the positively charged sodium ions is greater on the outside of the membrane and the concentration of negative potassium ions higher on the inside during resting potential. During the action potential, the negative and positive ions travel through the membrane, so that the interior charge becomes positive and the exterior negative. This is followed by an equilibrium charge, then a return to the resting potential charge state. All this happens in milliseconds.

The work done by Hodgkin and Huxley which was most responsible for bringing them to the attention of the Nobel Prize committee was the development of a series of mathematical formulae they published in 1952. The purpose of these equations was to synthesize the experimental information then available about the electrical and chemical nature of nerve transmissions. Their goal was to analyze and predict each stage in the passage of the nerve cell membrane from resting to action potential. They were awarded the 1963 Nobel Prize in physiology or medicine, which they shared with John C. Eccles, an Australian who advanced the British team's findings by showing what happens to nerve impulses transmitted across the synapses, or intersections, between nerve cells.

Hodgkin was appointed Foulerton Research Professor of the Royal Society in 1952, and was awarded the Royal Medal in 1958. He was John Humphrey Plummer Professor of Biophysics at Cambridge from 1970 to 1981, president of the Marine Biological Association from 1966 to 1976, and a master of Trinity College.

Hodgkin has been married since 1944 to Marion Rous, the daughter of American Nobel Laureate **Peyton Rous**. The couple met during Hodgkin's year at the Rockefeller Institute in New York. They have four children.

SELECTED WRITINGS BY HODGKIN:

Books

Conduction of the Nervous Impulse, C. C. Thomas, 1963.

(With others) *The Pursuit of Nature,* Cambridge University Press, 1976.

Chance and Design: Reminiscences of Science in Peace and War, Cambridge University Press, 1992.

SOURCES:

Books

Parker, Sybil, editor, *Modern Scientists and Engineers,* Volume 2, McGraw-Hill, 1980, p. 72.

Periodicals

"Nobel Prize: 1963 Award Honors Three for Research on Nerve Function," *Science,* October 25, 1963, pp. 468–470.

Wiskari, Werner, "Three Win Nobel Prize for Nerve Studies," *New York Times,* October 18, 1963, p. 1.

—Sketch by Denise Adams Arnold

Dorothy Crowfoot Hodgkin
1910-1994
English chemist and crystallographer

Dorothy Crowfoot Hodgkin employed the technique of X-ray crystallography to determine the molecular structures of several large biochemical molecules. When she received the 1964 Nobel Prize in chemistry for her accomplishments, the committee cited her contribution to the determination of the structure of both penicillin and vitamin B_{12}.

Hodgkin was born in Egypt on May 12, 1910 to John and Grace (Hood) Crowfoot. She was the first of four daughters. Her mother, although not formally educated beyond finishing school, was an expert on Coptic textiles, and an excellent amateur botanist and nature artist. Hodgkin's father, a British archaeologist and scholar, worked for the Ministry of Education in Cairo at the time of her birth, and her family life was always characterized by world travel. When World War I broke out, Hodgkin and two younger sisters

Dorothy Crowfoot Hodgkin

were sent to England for safety, where they were raised for a few years by a nanny and their paternal grandmother. Because of the war, their mother was unable to return to them until 1918, and at that time brought their new baby sister with her. Hodgkin's parents moved around the globe as her father's government career unfolded, and she saw them when they returned to Britain for only a few months every year. Occasionally during her youth she travelled to visit them in such far-flung places as Khartoum in the Sudan, and Palestine.

Hodgkin's interest in chemistry and crystals began early in her youth, and she was encouraged both by her parents as well as by their scientific acquaintances. While still a child, Hodgkin was influenced by a book that described how to grow crystals of alum and copper sulfate and on X rays and crystals. Her parents then introduced her to the soil chemist A. F. Joseph and his colleagues, who gave her a tour of their laboratory and showed her how to pan for gold. Joseph later gave her a box of reagents and minerals which allowed her to set up a home laboratory. Hodgkin was initially educated at home and in a succession of small private schools, but at age eleven began attending the Sir John Leman School in Beccles, England, from which she graduated in 1928. After a period of intensive tutoring to prepare her for the entrance examinations, Hodgkin entered Somerville College for women at Oxford University. Her aunt, Dorothy Hood, paid the tuition to Oxford, and helped to support her financially. For a time, Hodgkin considered specializing in archaeology, but eventually settled on chemistry and crystallography.

Crystallography was a fledgling science at the time Hodgkin began, a combination of mathematics, physics, and chemistry. **Max von Laue**, **William Henry Bragg** and **William Lawrence Bragg** had essentially invented it in the early decades of the century (they had won Nobel Prizes in 1914 and 1915, respectively) when they discovered that the atoms in a crystal deflected X rays. The deflected X rays interacted or interfered with each other. If they *constructively* interfered with each other, a bright spot could be captured on photographic film. If they *destructively* interfered with each other, the brightness was cancelled. The pattern of the X-ray spots—*diffraction pattern*—bore a mathematical relationship to the positions of individual atoms in the crystal. Thus, by shining X rays through a crystal, capturing the pattern on film, and doing mathematical calculations on the distances and relative positions of the spots, the molecular structure of almost any crystalline material could theoretically be worked out. The more complicated the structure, however, the more elaborate and arduous the calculations. Techniques for the practical application of crystallography were few, and organic chemists accustomed to chemical methods of determining structure regarded it as a black art.

After she graduated from Oxford in 1932, Hodgkin's old friend A. F. Joseph steered her toward Cambridge University and the crystallographic work of J. D. Bernal. Bernal already had a reputation in the field, and researchers from many countries sent him crystals for analysis. Hodgkin's first job was as Bernal's assistant. Under his guidance, with the wealth of materials in his laboratory, the young student began demonstrating her particular talent for X-ray studies of large molecules such as sterols and vitamins. In 1934, Bernal took the first X-ray photograph of a protein crystal, pepsin, and Hodgkin did the subsequent analysis to obtain information about its molecular weight and structure. Proteins are much larger and more complicated than other biological molecules because they are polymers—long chains of repeating units—and they exercise their biochemical functions by folding over on themselves and assuming specific three-dimensional shapes. This was not well understood at the time, however, so Hodgkin's results began a new era; crystallography could establish not only the structural layout of atoms in a molecule, even a huge one, but also the overall molecular shape which contributed to biological activity.

Research and Recognition at Oxford

In 1934, Hodgkin returned to Oxford as a teacher at Somerville College, continuing her doctoral work on sterols at the same time. (She obtained her doctorate in 1937). It was a difficult decision to move from Cambridge, but she needed the income and jobs were scarce. Somerville's crystallography and laboratory facilities were extremely primitive; one of the features of her lab at Oxford was a rickety circular staircase that she needed to climb several times a day to reach the only window with sufficient light for her polarizing microscope. This was made all the more difficult because Hodgkin suffered most of her adult life from a severe case of rheumatoid arthritis, which didn't respond well to treatment and badly crippled her hands and feet. Additionally, Oxford officially barred her from research meetings of the faculty chemistry club because she was a woman, a far cry from the intellectual comradery and support she had encountered in Bernal's laboratory. Fortunately, her talent and quiet perseverance quickly won over first the students and then the faculty members at Oxford. Sir **Robert Robinson** helped her get the money to buy better equipment, and the Rockefeller Foundation awarded her a series of small grants. She was asked to speak at the students' chemistry club meetings, which faculty members also began to attend. Graduate students began to sign on to do research with her as their advisor.

An early success for Hodgkin at Oxford was the elucidation of cholesterol iodide's molecular structure, which no less a luminary than W. H. Bragg singled out for praise. During World War II, Hodgkin and her graduate student Barbara Low worked out the structure of penicillin, from some of the first crystals ever made of the vital new drug. Penicillin is not a particularly large molecule, but it has an unusual ring structure, at least four different forms, and crystallizes in different ways, making it a difficult crystallographic problem. Fortunately they were able to use one of the first IBM analog computers to help with the calculations.

In 1948, Hodgkin began work on the structure of vitamin B–12 the deficiency of which causes pernicious anemia. She obtained crystals of the material from Dr. Lester Smith of the Glaxo drug company, and worked with a graduate student, Jenny Glusker, an American team of crystallographers led by Kenneth Trueblood, and later with John White of Princeton University. Trueblood had access to state of the art computer equipment at the University of California at Los Angeles, and they sent results back and forth by mail and telegraph. Hodgkin and White were theoretically affiliated with competing pharmaceutical firms, but they ended up jointly publishing the structure of B–12 in 1957; it turned out to be a porphyrin, a type of molecule related to chlorophyll, but with a single atom of cobalt at the center.

Increasing Recognition Culminates in Nobel Prize and Order of Merit

After the war, Hodgkin helped form the International Union of Crystallography, causing Western governments some consternation in the process because she insisted on including crystallographers from behind the Iron Curtain. Always interested in the cause of world peace, Hodgkin signed on with several organizations that admitted Communist party members. Recognition of Hodgkin's work began to increase markedly, however, and whenever she had trouble getting an entry visa to the U.S. because of her affiliation with peace organizations, plenty of scientist friends were available to write letters on her behalf. A restriction on her U.S. visa was finally lifted in 1990 after the Soviet Union disbanded.

In 1947, she was inducted into the Royal Society, Britain's premiere scientific organization. Professor Hinshelwood assisted her efforts to get a dual university/college appointment with a better salary, and her chronic money problems were alleviated. Hodgkin still had to wait until 1957 for a full professorship, however, and it was not until 1958 that she was assigned an actual chemistry laboratory at Oxford. In 1960 she obtained the Wolfson Research Professorship, an endowed chair financed by the Royal Society, and in 1964 received the Nobel Prize in chemistry. One year later, she was awarded Britain's Order of Merit, only the second woman since Florence Nightingale to achieve that honor.

Hodgkin still wasn't done with her research, however. In 1969, after decades of work and waiting for computer technology to catch up with the complexity of the problem, she solved the structure of insulin. She employed some sophisticated techniques in the process, such as substituting atoms in the insulin molecule, and then comparing the altered crystal structure to the original. Protein crystallography was still an evolving field; in 1977 she said, in an interview with Peter Farago in the *Journal of Chemical Education,* "In the larger molecular structure, such as that of insulin, the way the peptide chains are folded within the molecule and interact with one another in the crystal is very suggestive in relation to the reactions of the molecules. We can often see that individual side chains have more than one conformation in the crystal, interacting with different positions of solvent molecules around them. We can begin to trace the movements of the atoms within the crystals."

In 1937, Dorothy Crowfoot married Thomas Hodgkin, the cousin of an old friend and teacher, Margery Fry, at Somerville College. He was an African Studies scholar and teacher, and, because of his travels and jobs in different parts of the world, they maintained separate residences until 1945 when he finally obtained a position teaching at Oxford. Despite this unusual arrangement, their marriage was a happy and successful one. Although initially worried that her work with X rays might jeopardize their ability to have children, the Hodgkins produced three: Luke, born in 1938, Elizabeth, born in 1941, and Toby, born in 1946. The children all took up their parents scholarly, nomadic habits, and at the time of the Nobel Ceremony travelled to Stockholm from as far away as New Delhi and Zambia. Although Hodgkin officially retired in 1977, she continued to travel widely and expanded her lifelong activities on behalf of world peace, working with the Pugwash Conferences on Science and World Affairs. Hodgkin died of a stroke on July 29, 1994, in Shipston-on-Stour, England.

SELECTED WRITINGS BY HODGKIN:

Periodicals

"The X-Ray Analysis of Complicated Molecules," *Science,* Volume 150, November 19, 1965, pp. 979–88.

SOURCES:

Books

McGrayne, Sharon B., *Nobel Prize Women in Science,* Carol Publishing Group, 1993.

Opfell, Olga S., *The Lady Laureates,* Scarecrow Press, 1986.

Periodicals

Journal of Chemical Education, Volume 54, 1977, p. 214.

Nature, May 24, 1984, p.309.

New Scientist, May 23, 1992, p. 36.

—Sketch by Gail B. C. Marsella

Roald Hoffmann
1937-
Polish-born American chemist

Roald Hoffmann

Roald Hoffmann is a theoretical chemist who has straddled the traditional boundary between organic and inorganic chemistry. He has emphasized the role of aesthetics in science and the inherent beauty of chemical systems, and he values clarity and simplicity in the formulation of theories about chemistry. He is best known for constructing a method of predicting the course of chemical reactions that is based on the symmetry of electron orbitals. Called the Woodward-Hoffmann rules, he developed them in collaboration with **Robert B. Woodward** at Harvard, and these rules have enabled chemists to predict reactions without using complicated mathematical equations. The achievement has been widely recognized as the most important conceptual advance in organic chemistry since World War II, and for this Hoffmann shared the 1981 Nobel Prize in chemistry with **Kenichi Fukui**.

Hoffmann was born Roald Safran on July 18, 1937, in Zloczów, Poland on the eve of World War II. His father was Hillel Safran, a civil engineer; his mother, Clara Rosen, was a schoolteacher. In 1941 German troops occupied Zloczów, and the family was sent first to a Jewish ghetto and then interred at a labor camp. Safran managed to arrange for his wife and son to escape the camp, and the two were hidden by a Ukrainian teacher in the dark, cramped attic of a schoolhouse, where Hoffmann began his education under the tutelage of his mother. Hoffmann's father made plans to follow them, but his escape was discovered by the Nazis and he was executed. Hoffmann and his mother were able to remain undetected until 1944, when the Red Army liberated Zloczów, which later became part of the Soviet Ukraine. The two moved to Kraków, Poland, where his mother met and married Paul Hoffmann, whose spouse had also been killed in the war. They lived in several camps for displaced persons in Austria and Germany. In an autobiographical passage in *Chemistry Imagined,* Hoffmann remembers learning German, which was by then his fourth language, and being fascinated by the biographies of **George Washington Carver** and **Marie Curie**. The Hoffmanns were able to emigrate to the United States in 1949, and they settled in New York City.

Hoffmann learned English and attended public schools in Brooklyn, including Stuyvesant High School, which specialized in science. He told *Scientific American* that as a child he "showed neither precocity nor early interest in chemistry." His mother wanted him to become a doctor, and he enrolled at Columbia University with this in mind. Taking an extra-heavy course load, Hoffmann exhibited a wide range of interests, including mathematics, French, and even art history, which nearly lured him away from science. He spent most of his summers studying the chemistry of cement and hydrocarbons at the National Bureau of Standards, and it was here his interest in chemistry really began. In 1958, after only three years, he graduated summa cum laude in chemistry, and then entered the doctoral program at Harvard University.

In 1959 Hoffmann was awarded a summer fellowship to attend a program in quantum chemistry at the University of Uppsala in Sweden. That same year he attended a summer symposium on quantum physics in Sweden and met Eva Börjesson. He married her in 1960, and the couple now has two children. He studied at Moscow University in the Soviet Union. After returning from Moscow in 1960, he began his doctoral work, studying under **William Nunn Lipscomb, Jr.** Hoffmann researched theoretical chemistry for his Ph.D. He examined questions relating to the electronic structure of certain organic molecules. He used computer programs to determine the electronic structure of boron hydrides and other polyhedral molecules and also to predict what shape these molecules would assume after a reaction. Hoffmann's work advanced the application of what is called the Hückel method, which is used to calculate the number of electrons in orbit around a molecule.

Develops Theory of Orbital Symmetry

Hoffmann received his Ph.D. in chemical physics in 1962, and he remained at Harvard on a three-year fellowship from the Society of Fellows. This fellowship offered Hoffmann the time to shift the focus of his research away from purely theoretical to applied theoretical chemistry. In 1964 he began working with organic chemist Robert B. Woodward, who had observed an unusual and unexpected reaction during an attempt to synthesize vitamin B_{12}. Hoffmann left Harvard in 1965 to accept a position as associate professor at Cornell University, but he continued his collaboration with Woodward.

The reaction Woodward had observed was one of a class which is now called pericyclic reactions, whose course was very difficult to predict. Hoffmann and Woodward initially began to formulate their rules in an effort to identify the conditions that would produce certain results, and one of the difficulties they faced in this effort was the complexity of predicting how energy was released during these reactions. The release of energy during a reaction is determined by changes in the motion of electrons known as orbitals. What Hoffmann discovered was that the course of the reaction depended on the symmetry of these orbitals. Hoffmann and Woodward examined how orbital symmetry determined different reactions, and using quantum mechanics they were able to develop a mathematical procedure to predict these symmetries and thus whether certain combinations of chemicals would result in reactions.

The result of their work was a clear and relatively simple method of prediction that was based on diagrams; it was now possible to calculate the course of a reaction, as the *New York Times* observed, by "jotting pictures on the back of an envelope." Andrew Streitwieser, Jr. wrote in *Science:* "The results of orbital symmetry correlation diagrams lend themselves to alternative formulations that are frequently easier to apply." The Woodward-Hoffmann rules are now widely used, and they have had important practical applications in medical and industrial research. When Hoffmann was awarded the Nobel Prize in chemistry in 1981, Woodward had already died, but Hoffmann mentioned him frequently in his Nobel lecture and believed they would have shared the prize had he lived.

Pursues Research in Inorganic Chemistry

During the course of his work with Woodward, Hoffmann became convinced that similarities in the structure and function of electrons bridged many of the traditional divisions in chemistry, particularly the distinction between organic and inorganic chemistry. Following the formulation and publication of their rules, Hoffmann began conducting research to show that their method of predicting orbital symmetry could be applied to inorganic as well as organic compounds. Hoffmann and others working in his laboratory made detailed examinations of both inorganic and organometallic molecules—organic compounds which include metal. They were able to establish the unity of structure and function which he originally suspected, and his work has increased the ability of chemists to predict the course of inorganic reactions. The American Chemical Society presented Hoffmann with the Arthur C. Cope Award in Organic

Chemistry in 1973, and the society named him as the recipient of their Inorganic Chemistry Award in 1982. He is the first American chemist to be honored in both disciplines.

Hoffmann has long been interested in the similarities between art and the creative process he believes is required in science. Inspired by memories of his undergraduate work with the literary critic Mark Van Doren at Columbia, and moved by the experience of reading the poems of Wallace Stevens, Hoffmann began writing poetry at the age of forty. He continues to work with a group of poets at Cornell, and he has published two volumes of his poems. He writes about science and the beauty of nature, as well as his childhood experiences during and after World War II. He has also written a book with artist Vivian Torrence on the relationship between chemistry and art.

Hoffmann was made a full professor at Cornell in 1968, and in 1974 he was named the John A. Newman Professor of Physical Science at that university. In addition to the Nobel Prize and his awards in organic and inorganic chemistry, Hoffmann received the Pauling Award in 1974, the Nichols Medal in 1981, and the Priestly Medal in 1990. He is a member of the National Academy of Sciences and a foreign member of the Royal Society in London.

SELECTED WRITINGS BY HOFFMANN:

Books

(With Robert B. Woodward) *Conservation of Orbital Symmetry,* Verlag Chemie, 1970.

Gaps and Verges, University of Central Florida Press, 1991.

(With Vivian Torrence) *Chemistry Imagined,* Smithsonian Institute Press, 1993.

Periodicals

(With Robert B. Woodward) "Orbital Symmetries and Endo-exo Relationships in Concerted Cycloaddition Reactions," *Journal of the American Chemical Society,* Volume 87, 1965, pp. 4388–4389.

(With T. A. Albright and D. L. Thorn) "Theoretical Aspects of the Coordination of Molecules to Transition Metal Centers," *Pure Applied Chemistry,* Volume 50, 1978, pp.1–9.

"Theory and Practice," *American Scientist,* Volume 80, July-August, 1992.

"How Should Chemists Think?" *Scientific American,* Volume 268, February, 1993, pp. 66–73.

SOURCES:

Books

McGraw-Hill Modern Scientists and Engineers, McGraw-Hill, 1980.

Magill, Frank, editor, *Nobel Prize Winners: Chemistry,* Salem Press, 1990.

Periodicals

Russell Ruthen, "Profile: Modest Maverick," *Scientific American,* July, 1990, pp. 33–35.

A. Streitwieser, Jr., "The 1981 Nobel Prize in Chemistry," *Science,* November, 1981, pp. 627–629.

—Sketch by David Petechuk

Robert Hofstadter
1915-1990
American physicist

A noted physicist and researcher, Robert Hofstadter was best known for his research on the nucleus of the atom. During his several years of experimentation, Hofstadter discovered that protons and neutrons were complex components of the atom, and not as straightforward in design as previously conjectured. Hofstadter went on to expand on this discovery, and over the years he provided increasingly precise measurements of the components of an atom. For his contributions to the study of the atom, Hofstadter was awarded a share of the 1961 Nobel Prize in physics.

Born in New York City on February 5, 1915, Hofstadter was the third of four children born to Louis Hofstadter, a salesman, and Henrietta Koenigsberg. After attending public schools in New York City, Hofstadter entered the City College of New York (now the City University of New York), where he majored in physics, graduating with a B.S. in 1935. His degree was awarded magna cum laude and was accompanied by the Kenyon Prize, given for exceptional achievement in physics and mathematics. Hofstadter went on to receive both his M.A. and Ph.D. degrees from Princeton University in 1938, where he stayed on for postdoctoral work. Supported by a Proctor fellowship, Hofstadter studied photoconductivity in crystals. At the conclusion of his postdoctoral work, he took a position as instructor in physics at the University of Pennsylvania in 1939. He became

Harrison Research Fellow at Pennsylvania before moving to the City College of New York, where he also became an instructor in physics.

Invents the Sodium Iodide-Thallium Scintillator

With the onset of World War II, Hofstadter took a job as research physicist at the National Bureau of Standards (NBS) in Washington, DC. There, he worked with American physicist **James Van Allen** on the development of the proximity fuse, a device used to detonate a bomb when it has approached but not yet struck its target. After a year at NBS, Hofstadter moved to Norden Laboratories in New York City, where the famous Norden bombsight had been developed.

At the war's conclusion, however, Hofstadter returned to Princeton as assistant professor of physics. There, he became interested in problems of radiation detection. As studies of radioactivity for both theoretical and practical purposes began to expand, the need for detection devices increased. In 1948, Hofstadter invented a device with a wide range of detection applications, the sodium iodide-thallium (NaI-Tl) scintillator. When radiation passes through the NaI-Tl scintillator, it causes the emission of light. The intensity of the light emitted provides a measure of the energy carried by the original radiation. Hofstadter's device is still used in particle accelerators today.

Hofstadter left Princeton in 1950 to accept an appointment as associate professor of physics at Stanford University. Four years later, he was promoted to full professor and then, in 1971, he was appointed Max H. Stein Professor of Physics. At his retirement in 1985, he was made emeritus professor of physics.

Begins Studies of the Atomic Nucleus

It was while working at Stanford University that Hofstadter became interested in studies of the atomic nucleus. One way that scientists learn about matter is simply to look at it. The light waves reflected off matter provide information about the gross structure of a material. But the use of light rays to observe matter is limited by the wavelength of visible light. Objects that are smaller than the wavelengths of visible light (such as an atom) do not reflect light, making it impossible to "see" them in the traditional sense.

Radiation with wavelengths smaller than that of light can, however, be used to see very small objects. X rays, gamma rays, and high-speed electrons are other forms of radiation that can be used to probe the submicroscopic structure of matter. When Hofstadter arrived at Stanford, he found that the university's linear accelerator (linac) was an excellent source of high-energy electrons that could be used to study the nucleus and its nucleons, the particles of which the nucleus is composed. He devoted a major part of his thirty-five years at Stanford to this kind of research.

In his earliest studies with the linac, Hofstadter bombarded a variety of atomic nuclei with electron beams and found that they all had similar structures. They differed in size, but all had a nearly uniform density. In the mid–1950s, Hofstadter turned to a study of the individual protons and neutrons of which nuclei are composed. He made the remarkable discovery that these particles are not solid, indivisible particles, but have detailed structure. By directing beams of very high energy electrons at gold, lead, tantalum, and beryllium targets, Hofstadter was able to obtain information about the structure of the nucleus (and later about the structure of protons and neutrons) from the way in which the electron beams were diffracted.

Hofstadter found that each proton or neutron consists of a dense, positively-charged core surrounded by two shells of mesonic material. In the proton, the outer shell is also positively charged, making the particle as a whole, positive. In the neutron, on the other hand, one of the outer shells is negatively charged, making the particle as a whole, neutral. In recognition of this discovery, Hofstadter received the 1961 Nobel Prize in physics, as well as a number of other honors and awards, including City College of New York's Townsend Harris Medal in 1962, the Roentgen Medal in 1985, Italy's Cultural Foundation Prize in 1986, the National Science Medal in 1986, and honorary doctorates from institutions, including the University of Padua, Carleton University, and the University of Clermont-Ferrand.

Hofstadter married Nancy Givan on May 9, 1942; they had three children, Douglas Richard, Laura James, and Mary Hinda. Hofstadter died of heart disease on November 17, 1990, in Stanford, California.

SELECTED WRITINGS BY HOFSTADTER:

Books

(With Robert C. Herman) *High-Energy Electron Scattering Tables,* Stanford University Press, 1960.

Editor, *Nuclear and Nucleon Structure,* Stanford University Press, 1963.

(Editor with L. I. Schiff) *Nucleon Structure: Proceedings,* Stanford University Press, 1964.

Periodicals

(Editor with B. Hahn and D. G. Ravenhall) "High-Energy Electron Scattering and the Charge Distributions of Selected Nuclei," *Physical Review,* Volume 101, 1956, pp. 1131–42.

SOURCES:

Books

Weber, Robert L., *Pioneers of Science: Nobel Prize Winners in Physics,* American Institute of Physics, 1980, pp. 182–83.

—Sketch by David E. Newton

Helen Sawyer Hogg

1905-1993

American-born Canadian astronomer

Helen Sawyer Hogg was the foremost person in Canada in the twentieth century to make astronomy popular. In addition to writing an astronomy column in the *Toronto Star* for thirty years, she located variable stars in globular clusters and cataloged them, using her data to determine the stars' distance. Hogg was the first to use the seventy-two-inch telescope at the Dominion Astrophysical Observatory in British Columbia to take extensive photographs; previously the telescope had been used only for obtaining stellar spectra. She taught science at the University of Toronto for four decades, and was the first woman to become president of the Royal Canadian Institute. In 1989, the observatory at the National Museum of Science and Technology in Ottawa was dedicated in her name.

Born in Lowell, Massachusetts, on August 1, 1905, to Edward Everett Sawyer, a former vice president of the Union National Bank in Lowell, and Carrie Myra (Sprague) Sawyer, Helen Battles Sawyer attended the Charles W. Morey School in Lowell and Lowell High School. In 1925, after witnessing a total eclipse of the sun, she decided on a career in astronomy. Sawyer received her bachelor's degree from Mount Holyoke College in 1926, and a master's degree from Radcliffe College in 1928. She continued at Radcliffe for her Ph.D. under the supervision of **Harlow Shapley**, and was the first of his students at Harvard to work on variable stars in globular clusters. Globular clusters are huge conglomerations of densely concentrated stars that exist in the outer halo of the Milky Way galaxy.

Began Independent Study of Stars

On September 6, 1930, Sawyer married Frank Scott Hogg, Harvard's first astronomy Ph.D., in Cambridge. The following year she moved with Hogg to Victoria, British Columbia, where he had accepted a post at the Dominion Astrophysical Observatory. Barred from holding a position in the observatory herself, ostensibly because Frank Hogg already had an appointment there, Helen instead began to assist her husband, initially at no salary. In 1929, **Edwin Powell Hubble** proposed the theory of the expanding universe and set off a flurry of efforts to measure the distance of galaxies beyond the Milky Way using spectrographic images of stars, which is the process of dispersing radiation into a spectrum and then photographing or mapping the spectrum. Hogg's approach was innovative but complementary; she used the observatory's seventy-two-inch telescope to take actual photographs of variable stars, or stars which change brightness in generally regular intervals. She concentrated on stars in globular clusters within our own galaxy, cataloging the cyclical changes in their brightness as an aid to determining their distance and evolution. The process was a tedious one, requiring hours of careful focusing and a makeshift arrangement for exchanging photographic plates. So determined was Helen to continue with her career that she brought her first child to the observatory with her in a basket.

In 1935 the Hoggs moved to Ontario, where Helen was able to obtain an assistantship at the David Dunlap Observatory of the University of Toronto. She was a research associate at the observatory from 1936 until her death, and held a concurrent position at the university in the department of astronomy, moving gradually up through the academic ranks. She was promoted to professor in 1957, and become professor emeritus in 1976. At the Dunlap Observatory, Hogg continued her work with variable stars, and she gained a reputation as a world authority on the subject of the night sky. A longtime co-worker, Christine Clement, told the *Toronto Star,* "The sky could be almost completely overcast, but Helen could look at a hole in the clouds and know what we could observe through it." Hogg took several brief sabbaticals (for the academic year 1940–41 she was professor and acting chair of the department of astronomy at Mount Holyoke College, and in 1955–56 she was program director for astronomy for the National Science Foundation in the United States), but she made her professional life in Toronto.

Wrote for Academics and Laypeople

Hogg contributed over a hundred articles to scientific journals, and was the author of *The Stars Belong to Everyone,* published in 1976. From 1951 to 1981 she contributed the weekly column "The Stars" to the *Toronto Star* and delighted her readers with explanations of phenomena such as the blue moon. She was the recipient of numerous awards and honors, including honorary degrees from Mount Holyoke College, the Universities of Waterloo and

Toronto, McMaster University, and St. Mary's University. In 1950 she won the Cannon Prize of the American Astronomical Society, and in 1967 the Centennial Medal of Canada and the Rittenhouse Medal. In 1976 she was named a Companion of the Order of Canada, a privilege shared by few. Asteroid number 2917, which orbits between Jupiter and Mars, bears her name.

Hogg was a member of the International Astronomical Society and a fellow of the Royal Society of Canada. She was president of the American Association of Variable Star Observers from 1939 to 1941. She also had to her credit a list of firsts: she was the first woman president of the physical sciences section of the Royal Society of Canada, a post she held in 1960 and 1961; the first female president of the Royal Canadian Institute, from 1964 to 1965; one of the first two women to serve on the board of directors of the Bell Telephone Company of Canada, from 1968 to 1978; and the founding president of the Canadian Astronomical Society, 1971 to 1972.

Frank Hogg died in 1951, leaving Helen and their three children, Sarah Longley, David Edward, and James Scott. On November 28, 1985, at the age of eighty, Hogg married Francis E. L. Priestley; he died in 1988. In 1989, the Helen Sawyer Hogg Observatory of the National Museum of Science and Technology in Ottawa was dedicated, and in June of 1992, the University of Toronto named its telescope in the Andes Mountains in Chile after her. Hogg enjoyed stamp collecting, knitting, gardening, and photography. She was active late into her life, and only days before her death had been interviewed for an educational video aimed at encouraging young women to seek careers in science. Hogg died of a heart attack on January 28, 1993.

SELECTED WRITINGS BY HOGG:

Books

Man and His World: The Noranda Lectures, University of Toronto Press, 1968.

Out of Old Books (collection of journal articles), David Dunlap Observatory, 1974.

The Stars Belong to Everyone: How to Enjoy Astronomy, Doubleday, 1976.

Periodicals

(With Christine M. Clement and Andrew Yee) "The Long-Term Behavior of the Population II Cepheid V1 in the Globular Cluster Messier 12," *Astronomical Journal,* November 1, 1988, p. 1642.

"Memories of the Plaskett Era of the Dominion Astrophysical Observatory, 1931–1934," *Journal of the Royal Astronomical Society of Canada,* December 1, 1988, p. 328.

(With Steve Butterworth and Amelia Wehlau) "Observations of Variable Stars in the Globular Cluster M80," *The Astronomical Journal,* April 1, 1990, p. 1159.

SOURCES:

Books

Jarrell, Richard A., *The Cold Light of Dawn: A History of Canadian Astronomy,* University of Toronto Press, p. 120.

Kass-Simon, G., and P. Farnes, editors, *Women of Science,* Indiana University Press, 1990, pp. 105–106.

Periodicals

Barnes, Alan, "Helen Hogg, 87, Was Pioneering Woman Astronomer," *Toronto Star,* January 29, 1993, p. A25.

Dickinson, Terence, "Canada's Best-Known Astronomer Was at the Forefront of Discovery," *Toronto Star,* February 7, 1993, p. B7.

Pearce, Joseph, "Some Recollections of the Observatory," *Journal of the Royal Astronomical Society of Canada,* Volume 62, p. 296.

—Sketch by Sebastian Thaler

Robert William Holley
1922-
American biochemist

Robert Holley is best known for his isolation and characterization of transfer ribonucleic acid (tRNA). Essentially, tRNA "translates" the genetic instructions within cells by first "reading" genes, the fundamental units of heredity, and then creating proteins—the building blocks of the body—from amino acids. Holley, along with **Har Gobind Khorana** and **Marshall Warren Nirenberg**, was awarded the 1968 Nobel Prize in medicine or physiology for determining the sequence of tRNA. But Holley's work on tRNA was only the beginning of a distinguished scientific career. Subsequently, he has investigated the molecular factors that control growth and multiplica-

Robert William Holley

tion of cells. His work in this area has had profound impact on understanding the processes that lead to cancer.

Robert William Holley was born in Urbana, Illinois on January 28, 1922. His parents, Charles Elmer Holley and Viola Esther (Wolfe) Holley, were both teachers. As well as Robert, they had three other sons—Charles E., Jr., Frank, and George. Holley grew up in Illinois, California, and Idaho, and early developed a life-long love of the outdoors and fascination with living things. The latter years of his childhood were spent in Urbana, where he attended high school and, in 1938, enrolled at the University of Illinois. He majored in chemistry, and was the photographer for the school's yearbook.

After obtaining his B.A. in 1942, Holley took up graduate studies in organic chemistry at Cornell University. He served in various positions at both the university and the medical college for the next several years. In 1945 he married Ann Lenore Dworkin, a chemist and high school mathematics teacher. They have one son, Frederick.

During the mid–1940s Holley participated as a civilian in war research for the United States Office of Research and Development. He was a member of the team of researchers that first succeeded in making penicillin, synthetically. Supported by a fellowship from the National Research Council, he completed his doctorate in organic chemistry at Cornell University in 1947 and did a year of postdoctoral work at Washington State College (now University) in Pullman before returning east. In 1948, he became assistant professor at the New York State Agricultural Experiment Station, a branch of Cornell, in Geneva. He became associate professor in 1950 and full professor in 1964.

Focuses Research on Mechanisms of Protein Synthesis

During a sabbatical on a Guggenheim Memorial Fellowship at the California Institute of Technology in 1955–1956, Holley started to investigate protein synthesis. In the wake of **James Watson**'s and **Francis Crick**'s discovery that DNA contained the information of heredity, Holley targeted the chemistry of nucleic acids, which carry and transmit genetic information. His course may have been inspired, at least in part, by Crick's suggestion that "adaptor molecules" of some sort must be involved in the translation of genetic information into proteins. Towards the end of his year away from Cornell, Holley began to look specifically at the structure of transfer RNA, the start of a nine-year effort to unlock its secrets.

Back at Cornell in 1957, Holley was appointed research chemist at the United States Plant, Soil, and Nutrition Laboratory, where he continued his studies on tRNA. Heading up a research team, he meticulously planned and carried out a painstaking series of experiments. He and his colleagues spent three years developing a technique to isolate and partially purify different classes of tRNAs from yeast. Finally they succeeded in isolating a pure sample of alanine transfer RNA. The next five years were devoted to elucidating the sequence and structure of this particular transfer RNA.

To appreciate the profound impact of Holley's work on research into the biochemistry of life, it is useful to review some fundamental concepts. Cells carry the instructions for all of their necessary tasks in their chromosomes. Chromosomes within a cell are made up of very long molecules called deoxyribonucleic acid, or DNA. Genes, the basic units of heredity for all living things, are small sections of the long strands of DNA. Genes themselves are made up of a series of units called nucleotides. Nucleotides are molecules composed of a particular sugar (either ribose or deoxyribose), a phosphate group (one phosphorous atom combined with three oxygen atoms), and one of five specific bases. These bases—guanine, adenine, cytosine, thymine, and uracil—thus distinguish the nucleotides from one another. They are, in essence, the alphabet from which all of our genetic instructions are composed.

Cells and bodies, however, are built not of genes but of proteins. Proteins are the structural elements of cells, providing form and stability. Equally important, certain proteins, called enzymes, mediate critical biochemical reactions, allowing the formation and breakdown of innumerable chemicals that cells use during growth, functioning, and division. Proteins are sequences of amino acids. The amino acids are a group of about twenty different molecules that share certain chemical characteristics (e.g., the presence of an amine group).

Holley's work centered on the question of how sequences of nucleotides in DNA specify sequences of amino acids in proteins. It had been known that DNA did not directly create protein, but copied itself instead (in a complementary, or negative sense) into strands of RNA. But it was not known how these long strands of RNA, called messenger RNA or mRNA, functioned in the creation of proteins. Holley believed that the much smaller tRNA molecules played a key role. He knew that a triplet of bases, or codon, specifies each of the twenty amino acids. Examining the sequence of bases within alanine tRNA (which specifies creation of the amino acid alanine), he found an anti-codon for alanine. This anti-codon would be able to bond chemically with an alanine codon on an mRNA strand.

By studying the molecular sequence of alanine tRNA, Holley and his students were able to determine its structure and then to deduce how it functioned. A tRNA anti-codon would bind to its matching codon along a strand of mRNA. The corresponding amino acid, held at the opposite end of the tRNA, would then be positioned to link up in series with the amino acid specified by the adjacent codon on the mRNA. In this manner, the series of nucleotides in a molecule of DNA would be translated into a series of amino acids that would make up a protein.

For his illumination of this vital process, Holley won a share of the 1968 Nobel Prize for physiology or medicine. He was also honored with the prestigious Albert Lasker Award for Basic Medical Research in 1965.

Redirects Research on Cell Growth and Replication Factors

From 1966 to 1967 Holley was on sabbatical at the Salk Institute for Biological Studies and the Scripps Clinic and Research Foundation in La Jolla, California. The following year he joined the Salk Institute as a resident fellow. Like his earlier sabbatical, Holley's move proved pivotal for his research, as he launched an investigation of the molecular factors that regulate growth and multiplication of cells. Rooted somewhat in his previous work on how the protein molecules underlying cell growth are formed, the new investigations had quite different interpretations and implications.

The control of cell growth and division is critical to normal functioning. Cancerous growths are characterized by uncontrolled cell division. Normally, a balance of stimulatory and inhibitory molecular factors keeps cellular multiplication at the proper rate; the number of new cells produced roughly equals the number of cells that wear out and die. Rapid cell proliferation might be caused by over-production of the stimulatory factors, excessive cell sensitivity to the stimulatory factors, a lack of the inhibitory factors, or some combination of these causes.

Holley examined the roles of hormones, blood-born chemicals—usually proteins—that are released by various tissues and organs and that interact with one another. Hormones can either stimulate or inhibit cell proliferation, or even, as Holley would later show, do both.

Holley discovered that the concentration of two types of hormones, known as peptide and steroid hormones, in a solution with dividing cells would determine the rate of cell division and ultimately, cell density. Further, he found that types of cells prone to develop into tumors responded dramatically to these growth factors, dividing rapidly in response to very low hormone levels. Subsequent experiments demonstrated that peptide and steroid hormones could act synergistically: several of these growth factors together in solution would produce a greater growth rate than the sum effects of each individually. Holley also found that different types of cells responded differently to particular hormones, and that their responses could change with the cells' population density. At low densities, cells take up and utilize growth factors more efficiently than they do under conditions of high density. Cellular receptors for certain growth-promoting hormones increased under conditions of low cell density, whereas receptors for certain other hormones increased as cell density increased.

Holley also studied the effects of non-hormonal factors, such as certain sugars and amino acids, on cell proliferation. He found that while cell growth patterns were quite insensitive to the levels of many amino acids, they were strongly regulated by others, notably glutamine.

Looking at the other side of the coin, Holley and his collaborators also identified growth inhibitors. Some of these compounds suppress cell growth by blocking DNA replication. Holley discovered that, in addition to blocking DNA activity, growth inhibitors stimulated production of specific proteins whose functions were unknown. Growth factors, too, were found to have an associated protein synthesis in addition to stimulating DNA activity. Interestingly, Holley noted that while growth and inhibitory factors canceled out each others' effects on DNA replication, they had no effect on each others' secondary production of hormones. With particular factors that increase both cell size and rate of cell division, Holley had noted similar effects. Adding a growth inhibitor would stop the cells from dividing, but not stop the individual cells from growing larger.

As he and his co-workers had done with tRNA, Holley's team eventually sequenced certain of the growth factors. These are considerably larger molecules than tRNA, but the techniques of molecular biology had improved so much over the years that these sequences were obtained much more readily. Holley identified the sequence of amino acids of a growth-inhibiting factor for a specific type of monkey cell. The sequence turned out to be identical to that for the human growth factor (TGF-beta 2).

Holley's work during the later phase of his career has shed new light on the factors that control how cells grow, differentiate, and divide. His research has striking implications for the development of drugs to suppress tumor growth and for understanding the fundamental causes of cancer. This entire field of investigation continues to be active, as new techniques and technologies allow researchers to ask questions of increasing sophistication. As an American Cancer Society research professor of molecular biology at the Salk Institute for Biological Studies, Holley has been in the forefront of the ongoing struggle to learn about and to control unchecked cell growth.

SELECTED WRITINGS BY HOLLEY:

Periodicals

"An Alanine-Dependent, Ribonuclease-Inhibited Conversion of AMP to ATP, and Its Possible Relationship to Protein Synthesis," *Journal of the American Chemical Society,* Volume 79, 1957, pp. 658–662.

(With J. Apgar, G. Everett, J. Madison, S. Merrill, and A. Zamir) "Chemistry of Amino Acid-Specific Ribonucleic Acids," *Cold Spring Harbor Symposia on Qualitative Biology,* Volume 28, 1963, pp. 117–121.

(With P. Bohlen and others) "Purification of Kidney Epithelial Cell Growth Inhibitors," *Proceedings of the National Academy of Sciences, U.S.A.,* Volume 77, 1980, pp. 5989–5992.

SOURCES:

Books

Judson, H. F., *Eighth Day of Creation,* Simon and Schuster, 1979.

Magill, F. N., editor, *The Nobel Prize Winners: Physiology or Medicine,* Volume 2: *1944–1969,* Salem Press, 1991, pp. 1007–1017.

—Sketch by Ethan E. Allen

Arthur Holmes
1890-1965
English geologist

Arthur Holmes was a leader in the field of geology and stood at the center of some of the most volatile controversies of his day. His work ranged across geophysics, petrology, and geochronology, though he is best known for his *Principles of Geology,* which was first published in 1944. It is still considered a standard text in the field.

Holmes was born in Hebburn-on-Tyne, England, on January 14, 1890, the son of David and Emily Dickinson Holmes. His father was a cabinet maker and his mother a teacher; both his parents were descended from Northumberland farmers, and Holmes took great pride in his ancestry. He attended Gateshead High School, where one of his physics teachers encouraged him to read William Thomson Kelvin's *Addresses,* which introduced him to the dispute between Lord Kelvin and geologists. Kelvin, a mathematician and physicist, had asserted that the earth had cooled from a molten state, but this theory only allowed the earth to be forty million years old, a figure far too small to satisfy geological evidence. Holmes' interest in the earth sciences was further stimulated by the newly translated *The Face of the Earth* by E. Seuss.

In 1907, Holmes received a scholarship to Imperial College in London to study physics. He earned his B.S. in physics and mathematics in 1909, but his interests went beyond these fields; during his college years he had also spent much time under the watchful eye of the geologist **Robert Strutt** (later the fourth Lord Raleigh). Holmes graduated as an Associate of the Royal College of Science in 1910. He did his postgraduate work with Strutt and this brought him back to the controversy over Kelvin; he and Strutt were primarily concerned with the application of radioactivity to geology. Following **Ernest Rutherford**'s contention that radioactive materials may well possess a self-contained "time log" of their existence, Strutt had begun work on the helium ages of minerals. Helium is an end product of decay in uranium, and by comparing the amounts of helium to uranium in minerals, he was able to determine the mineral's age. Holmes developed a ratio for helium and uranium, and in his first paper in 1911 he applied this ratio to geological time. His conclusion put the minimum age of the earth at 1600 million years.

In 1911, Holmes accompanied an expedition to Mozambique. He gathered valuable field work experience and expanded his interest in geochronology, the study of rock origins, and petrography, the description and classification of rocks. While in the field he contracted malaria, the effects of which would make him unfit for active service during World War I. Holmes returned to Imperial College in 1912 to teach geology, and in 1913 he published *The Age of the Earth,* which is now mostly of historical interest. He also made several controversial contributions to the field of petrology. He produced two texts which are still of relevance today: 1920's *The Nomenclature of Petrology,* which is a summary of the origins and significance of rock names, and 1921's *Petrographic Methods and Calculations,* which provides a listing of many standard procedures.

Holmes left Imperial College in 1920 to work for the Yomah Oil Company in Burma as chief geologist. The decision was largely a financial one, but the exploration for oil was unsuccessful and he returned to England in 1924 in search of employment. It was a difficult time to be a geologist, because of a downturn in the oil economy, but Holmes had a lucky break. Durham University was in the midst of creating of a number of science departments, and Irvine Masson invited Holmes to build a new geology department. He was joined in this endeavor by William Hopkins, and the two of them made a policy of never admitting more than three graduate students a year, thus enabling them to provide virtually private teaching, while also pursuing their own research.

Refines Idea of Continental Drift

Once settled at Durham, Holmes began to study the movement of the earth. In 1929, he proposed to the Geological Society of Glasgow a modification to **Alfred L. Wegener**'s continental drift hypothesis. One of the early objections to this theory were questions about how such large masses of rock could ever be moved. Holmes brought forward the concept of subcrustal convection currents as the principle cause of earth movements. There was much resistance to this theory, but Holmes pressed his ideas home; he argued that at the point of impact between an oceanic plate and a continent, the lighter rocks of the continent resist being submerged, while the heavier oceanic rocks are forced back down to the mantle. Holmes was able to enjoy a later revival of his theory with new evidence from the field of palaeomagnetics, the study of the magnetization a rock acquires at the time of its formation. The seemingly snug fit of the opposing Atlantic continents also supported his arguments.

Throughout this period, Holmes remained involved in petrology, and he participated in various controversies about the subject. K. H. Rosenbush and A. Harker had argued that igneous rocks were originally liquid magma, forced to the surface while still in their liquid state, but Holmes became increasingly dissatisfied with this theory. In 1931, he began a collaboration with the Geological Survey of Uganda which lead to his rejection of the concept of the magmatic origin of rocks. The discovery of the previously unknown mineral kalsilite led Holmes to the possibility of solid-state metasomatism —the alteration of preexisting rocks through intense heat and the addition of new materials.

In 1942, Holmes left Durham to accept the position of Regius Chair of Geology at Edinburgh. This was the same year he was elected to the Royal Society. Perhaps the most significant event of his Durham years had occurred outside his laboratory, while he stood watch for German incendiary bombs. It was there Holmes conceived of and began writing his *Principles of Physical Geology,* which was published soon after his arrival at Edinburgh. It has been lauded for its clarity and simplicity in dealing with the sometimes confusing, jargon-laden field of geology, and it remains his most important work.

Holmes received the Wollaston Medal from the Geological Society of London and the Penrose Medal from the Geological Society of America, both in 1956. In 1964, he received the Vetlesen Prize "for scientific achievement in a clearer understanding of the Earth, its history or its relation to the universe."

Holmes had married Margaret Howe in 1914, and they had one son. His first wife died in 1938, and in 1939 he married Dr. Doris Livesey Reynolds, a noted petrologist who had come to Durham in 1933. Holmes died in London on September 9, 1965.

SELECTED WRITINGS BY HOLMES:

Books

The Age of the Earth, Harper, 1913.

The Nomenclature of Petrology, Murby, 1920.

Petrographic Methods and Calculations, Murby, 1921.

Principles of Physical Geology, Nelson, 1944.

SOURCES:

Books

Biographical Memoirs of Fellows of the Royal Society, Volume 12, Royal Society (London), 1966.

Gillespie, Charles, editor, *Dictionary of Scientific Biography,* Volume 6, Scribner's, 1972.

Green, Jay, editor, *McGraw-Hill Modern Scientists and Engineers,* Volume II, McGraw-Hill, 1980.

—Sketch by Chris McGrail

Frederick Gowland Hopkins
1861-1947
English biochemist

Frederick Gowland Hopkins is considered the founder of British biochemistry. A pioneer in the study and application of what he called accessory food factors and what we call vitamins, he made important contributions to the study of uric acid, isolated tryptophan (a necessary component in nutrition), and developed the concept of essential amino acids. He also did pioneering work on cell metabolism, elucidating the role of enzymatic activity in oxidation processes. With the assistance of physiologist Walter M. Fletcher, he explained the relationship between lactic acid and muscle contraction. He became a member of the Royal Society in 1905, serving as its president in 1931. He was knighted in 1925 and received the Copley Medal of the Royal Society in 1926. For his contributions in the field of nutrition, he was awarded the 1929 Nobel Prize in physiology or medicine, sharing the award with the Dutch chemist **Christiaan Eijkman**. He was presented with the highest distinction of civil service, the Order of Merit, in 1935. In addition, many honorary degrees were bestowed on him by universities worldwide.

Frederick Gowland Hopkins

Education and Early Career

Hopkins was born in Eastbourne, Sussex, England, on June 20, 1861, to Frederick Hopkins and Elizabeth Gowland Hopkins. The poet Gerard Manley Hopkins was his second cousin. His father died soon after his birth and he was taken by his mother to live with her family in London. He was a solitary and scholarly boy, given to reading Charles Dickens and writing poetry, although he showed no particular aptitude for any subject in school except chemistry. According to the *Dictionary of Scientific Biography,* he was captivated by what he saw through the microscope, saying that "the powers of the microscope thus revealed to me were something very *important*—the most important thing I had as yet come up against." But his scientific education was delayed when his uncle secured a position for him in the insurance business. The seventeen-year-old Hopkins stuck it out for six months before leaving. He did publish his first paper while working for the insurance company, on the vapor ejected by the bombardier beetle. Although entomology remained an interest throughout his life, Hopkins said that his work on the beetle had made him realize that his true vocation was biochemistry. A small inheritance enabled him to study chemistry at the Royal School of Mines and London's University College, where he received a B.Sc. in 1890. An exemplary performance on his final chemistry examination led to a position as an assistant to Thomas Stevenson, an expert in forensic medicine at Guy's Hospital, who also served as medical jurist to the Home Office. As assistant to Stevenson, Hopkins used his analytical skills to help secure the convictions of several notorious murderers.

Despite these achievements, Hopkins was aware that he needed more education. He entered Guy's Hospital to study medicine in 1890, earning his M.B. in 1894. He remained at Guy's to teach for four years after receiving his degree. In 1898, at the age of thirty-seven, he was invited to Cambridge to undertake the triple duties of teacher, tutor, and developer of the chemical physiology department. The demands of that heavy workload caused Hopkins to suffer a temporary breakdown in 1910. Even with that workload and his subsequent ill health, Hopkins managed to publish more than thirty papers. Trinity College made him a fellow and elected him to a praelectorship in biochemistry. His appointment at Trinity, when he was nearly fifty years old, allowed him to give full attention to research and the advancement of biochemistry within the university.

Establishes Biochemistry Department at Cambridge

Hopkins became the first professor of biochemistry at Cambridge in 1914. He established an open admissions policy for his department and attracted biochemists from many nations, including some who had escaped from dire political situations. A great teacher as well as a brilliant and unassuming researcher, Hopkins was known for encouraging his students to pursue their own line of work and often handed over to them promising new research in which he had made a breakthrough. Any credit or distinction resulting from pursuit of that new work went to his students, not Hopkins. This generosity, coupled with his faith that biochemistry could provide important answers to biological questions, was largely responsible for the widespread development of biochemical thought and experimentation. At the time of his death, approximately seventy-five of his former students held professorial positions in universities throughout the world.

Makes Important Discoveries

One of his earliest contributions to biochemistry, made while he was still at Guy's Hospital and used for many years, was the method he developed to detect the presence of uric acid in urine. His work on uric acid led him to the study of proteins, the presence of which in the diet affects uric acid excretion. Hopkins first developed methods to isolate and crystallize proteins. He isolated the amino acid tryptophan and determined its structure. He also studied the effect of bacteria on tryptophan, laying the foundation of bacterial biochemistry. Hopkins showed that tryptophan is essential in the diet, since proteins lacking the substance are nutritionally inadequate. He also studied the role of the amino acids arginine and histidine in nutrition, which led to the theory that the presence of different amino acids determines the nutritional quality of proteins.

Hopkins, however, was not satisfied that an adequate diet depended upon the presence of essential amino acids alone. He suspected that additional substances, which he called accessory food factors, also played an essential role in nutrition. Experiments with rats that were fed a synthetic diet of milk proteins, carbohydrates, fats and salts showed that such a diet caused a decline in growth in the animals. When milk was added to the diet, even in small quantities, the rats once again underwent normal growth. This preliminary work enabled Hopkins to isolate what are now called vitamins A and D. His observations led him to conclude that such diseases as rachitis (popularly called rickets, and caused by a vitamin D deficiency) and scurvy occurred when food lacked certain vitamins. Although it had been known for a long time that scurvy, a common shipboard ailment, could be prevented or cured by supplementing one's diet with lemons, Hopkins' work on isolating vitamin C was the first to explain this experiential finding scientifically.

In 1912 Hopkins published the work for which he is probably best known, "Feeding Experiments Illustrating the Importance of Accessory Food Factors in Normal Dietaries." During World War I, Hopkins continued his work on the nutritional value of vitamins. His efforts were especially valuable in a time of food shortages and rationing. He agreed to study the nutritional value of margarine and found that it was, as suspected, inferior to butter because it lacked the vitamins A and D. As a result of his work, vitamin-enriched margarine was introduced in 1926. Hopkins' nutritional theories were contested by colleagues until about 1920 but have been considered indisputable since then.

Although Hopkins won the 1929 Nobel Prize in medicine and physiology (shared with Christiaan Eijkman) for his work in nutrition, he was primarily interested in the biochemistry of the cell. The originality and vision of his research in this area set the standard for those who followed him. His study with Fletcher of the connection between lactic acid and muscle contraction was one of the central achievements of his work on the biochemistry of the cell. Hopkins had long studied how cells obtain energy from a complex metabolic process of oxidation and reduction reactions. He showed that oxygen depletion causes an accumulation of lactic acid in the muscle. The research techniques developed by Hopkins and Fletcher to study muscle stimulation were later used by others to study other aspects of muscle metabolism. Their work paved the way for the later discovery by **Archibald Vivian Hill** and **Otto Meyerhof** that a carbohydrate metabolic cycle supplies the energy used for muscle contraction. The discovery that alcohol fermentation under the influence of yeast is a process analogous to the formation of lactic acid in the muscle is also due to Hopkins's ground-breaking work. Hopkins' work on muscle metabolism led to an understanding of the importance of enzymes as catalysts to oxidation. He isolated glutathione, which plays an important role as an oxygen carrier in cells, and several oxidizing enzymes. Hopkins and his assistant, E. J. Morgan, made further contributions to this field in the late thirties.

Hopkins married Jessie Ann Stevens in 1898. They had three children. A gentle eccentric who struggled with feelings of insecurity about his worth as a scientist throughout his life, he considered himself an "intellectual amateur," despite his achievements and the honors bestowed on him by his peers. Hopkins died at Cambridge on May 16, 1947.

SELECTED WRITINGS BY HOPKINS:

Books

Hopkins and Biochemistry (includes selection of his addresses, excerpts from his publications, and bibliography of his work), edited by Joseph Needham and Ernest Baldwin, Heffer, 1949.

SOURCES:

Books

Baldwin, Ernest, *Gowland Hopkins,* [London], 1961.

Gillispie, Charles Coulson, editor, *Dictionary of Scientific Biography,* Volume 6, Scribner, 1972.

—Sketch by Jane Stewart Cook

Grace Hopper
1906-1992
American computer scientist

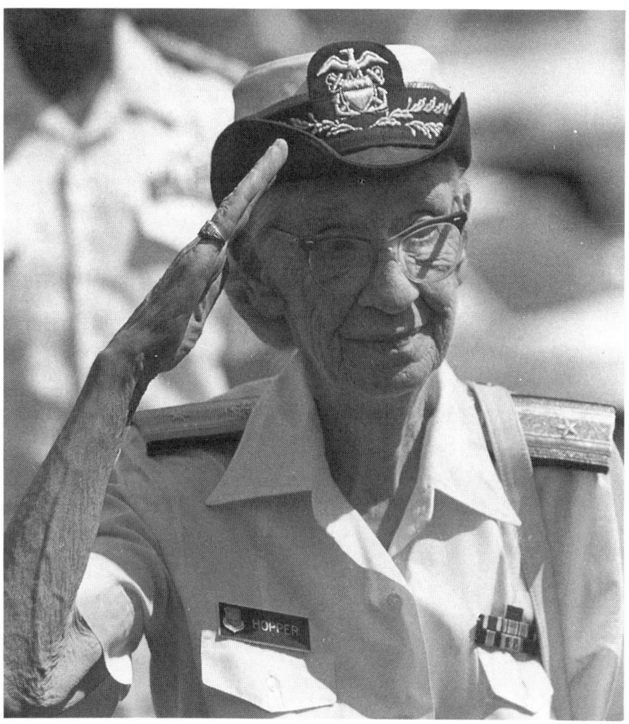

Grace Hopper

Grace Hopper, who rose through Navy ranks to become a rear admiral at age eighty-two, is best known for her contribution to the design and development of the COBOL programming language for business applications. Her professional life spanned the growth of modern computer science, from her work as a young Navy lieutenant programming an early calculating machine to her creation of sophisticated software for microcomputers. She was an influential force and a legendary figure in the development of programming languages. In 1991, President George Bush presented her with the National Medal of Technology "for her pioneering accomplishments" in the field of data processing.

Admiral Hopper was born Grace Brewster Murray on December 9, 1906, in New York City. She was the first child of Marry Campbell Van Horne Murray and Walter Fletcher Murray. Encouraged by her parents to develop her natural mechanical abilities, she disassembled and examined gadgets around the home, and she excelled at mathematics in school. Her grandfather had been a senior civil engineer for New York City who inspired her strong interest in geometry and mathematics.

At Vassar College, Hopper indulged her mathematical interests, and also took courses in physics and engineering. She graduated in 1928, then attended Yale, where she received a master's degree in 1930 and a doctorate in 1934. These were rare achievements, especially for a woman. As Robert Slater points out in *Portraits in Silicon,* U.S. doctorates in mathematics numbered only 1,279 between 1862 and 1934. Despite bleak prospects for female mathematicians in teaching beyond the high school level, Vassar College hired her first as an instructor, then as a professor of mathematics. Hopper taught at Vassar until the beginning of World War II. She lived with her husband, Vincent Foster Hopper, whom she had married in 1930. They were divorced in 1945 and had no children.

Begins Computer Work in Navy

In 1943, Hopper joined the U.S. Naval Reserve, attending midshipman's school and obtaining a commission as a lieutenant in 1944. She was immediately assigned to the Bureau of Ships Computation Project at Harvard. The project, directed by **Howard Aiken**, was her first introduction to Aiken's task, which was to devise a machine that would assist the Navy in making rapid, difficult computations for such projects as laying a mine field. In other words, Aiken was in the process of building and programming America's first programmable digital computer—the Mark I.

For Hopper, the experience was both disconcerting and instructive. Without any background in computing, she was handed a code book and asked to begin computations. With the help of two ensigns assigned to the project and a sudden plunge into the works of computer pioneer Charles Babbage, Hopper began a crash course on the current state of computation by way of what Aiken called "a computing engine."

The Mark I was the first digital computer to be programmed sequentially. Thus, Hopper experienced first-hand the complexities and frustration that have always been the hallmark of the programming field. The exacting code of machine language could be easily misread or incorrectly written. To reduce the number of programming errors, Hopper and her colleagues collected programs that were free of error and generated a catalogue of subroutines that could be used to develop new programs. By this time, the Mark II had been built. Aiken's team used the two computers side by side, effectively achieving an early instance of multiprocessing.

By the end of the war, Hopper had become enamored of Navy life, but her age —a mere forty years—precluded a transfer from the WAVES into the regular Navy. She remained in the Navy Reserves and stayed on at the Harvard Computational Laboratory as a research fellow, where she continued her work on the Mark computer series. The problem of computer errors continued to plague the Mark team. One day, noticing that the computer had failed, Hopper and her colleagues discovered a moth in a faulty relay. The insect was removed and fixed to the page of a logbook as the "first actual bug found." The words "bug" and "debugging," now familiar terms in computer vocabulary, are attributed to Hopper. In 1949, she left Harvard to take up the position of senior mathematician in a start-up company, the Eckert-Mauchly Computer Corporation. Begun in 1946 by **J. Presper Eckert** and **John Mauchly**, the company had by 1949 developed the Binary Automatic Computer, or BINAC, and was in the process of introducing the first Universal Automatic Computer, or UNIVAC. The Eckert-Mauchly UNIVAC, which recorded information on high-speed magnetic tape rather than on punched cards, was an immediate success. The company was later bought by Sperry Corporation. Hopper stayed with the organization and in 1952 became the systems engineer and director of automatic programming for the UNIVAC Division of Sperry, a post she held until 1964.

Hopper's association with UNIVAC resulted in several important advances in the field of programming. Still aware of the constant problems caused by programming errors, Hopper developed an innovative program that would translate the programmer's language into machine language. This first compiler, called "A-O," allowed the programmer to write in a higher-level symbolic language, without having to worry about the tedious binary language of endless numbers that were needed to communicate with the machine itself.

One of the challenges Hopper had to meet in her work on the compiler was that of how to achieve "forward jumps" in a program that had yet to be written. In *Grace Hopper, Navy Admiral and Computer Pioneer,* Charlene Billings explains that Hopper used a strategy from her schooldays—the forward pass in basketball. Forbidden under the rules for women's basketball to dribble more than once, one teammate would routinely pass the basketball down the court to another, then run down the court herself and be in a position to receive the ball and make the basket. Hopper defined what she called a "neutral corner" as a little segment at the end of the computer memory which allowed her a safe space in which to "jump forward" from a given routine, and flag the operation with a message. As each routine was run, it scouted for messages and jumped back and forth, essentially running in a single pass.

During the early 1950s, Hopper began to write articles and deliver papers on her programming innovations. Her first publication, "A Manual of Operation for the Automatic Sequence Controlled Calculator," detailed her initial work on Mark I. "The Education of a Computer," offered in 1952 at a conference of the Association of Computing Machinery, outlined many ideas on software. An article appearing in a 1953 issue of *Computers and Automation,* "Compiling Routines," laid out principles of compiling. In addition to numerous articles and papers, Hopper published a book on computing entitled *Understanding Computers,* with Steven Mandrell.

The Development of COBOL

Having demonstrated that computers are programmable and capable not only of doing arithmetic, but manipulating symbols as well, Hopper worked steadily to improve the design and effectiveness of programming languages. In 1957, she and her staff at UNIVAC created Flow-matic, the first program using English language words. Flow-matic was later incorporated into COBOL, and, according to Jean E. Sammet, constituted Hopper's most direct and vital contribution to COBOL.

The story of COBOL's development illustrated Hopper's wide-reaching influence in the field of programming. IBM had developed FORTRAN, the densely mathematical programming language best suited to scientists. But no comparable language existed for business, despite the clear advantages that computers offered in the area of information processing.

By 1959, it was obvious that a standard programming language was necessary for the business community. Flow-matic was an obvious prototype for a business programming language. At that time, however, IBM and Honeywell were developing their own competing programs. Without cooperative effort, the possibility of a standard language to be used throughout the business world was slim. Hopper, who campaigned for standardization of computers and programming throughout her life, arguing that the lack of standardization created vast inefficiency and waste, was disturbed by this prospect.

The problem was how to achieve a common business language without running afoul of anti-trust laws. In April 1959, a small group of academics and representatives of the computer industry, Hopper among them, met to discuss a standard programming language specifically tailored for the business community. They proposed contacting the Defense Department, which contracted heavily with the business industry, to coordinate a plan, and in May a larger group met with Charles Phillips. The result was the formation of several committees charged with overseeing the design and development of the language that would eventually be known as COBOL—an acronym for "Common Business Oriented Language." Hopper served as a technical advisor to the Executive Committee.

The unique and far-ranging aspects of COBOL included its readability and its portability. Whereas IBM's FORTRAN used a highly condensed, mathematical code, COBOL used common English language words. COBOL was written for use on different computers and intended to be independent of any one computer company. Hopper championed the use of COBOL in her own work at Sperry, bringing to fruition a COBOL compiler concurrently with RCA in what was dubbed the "Computer Translating Race." Both companies successfully demonstrated their compilers in late 1960.

Hopper was elected a fellow of the Institute of Electrical and Electronics Engineers (IEEE) in 1962 and of the American Association for the Advancement of Science (AAAS) in 1963. She was awarded the Society of Women Engineers Achievement Award in 1964. She continued her work with Sperry, and in 1964 was appointed staff scientist of systems programming, in the UNIVAC Division.

Returns to Navy Life

While at Sperry, Hopper remained active in the Navy Reserves, retiring with great reluctance in 1966. But only seven months later, she was asked to direct the standardization of high level languages in the Navy. She returned to active duty in 1967 and was exempted from mandatory retirement at age of sixty-two. She served in the Navy until age seventy-one.

Although she continued to work at Sperry Corporation until 1971, her activities with the Navy brought her increasing recognition as a spokesperson for the usefulness of computers. In 1969, she was named "Man of the Year" by the Data Processing Management Association. In the next two decades, she would garner numerous awards and honorary degrees, including election as a fellow of the Association of Computer Programmers and Analysts (1972), election to membership in the National Academy of Engineering (1973), election as a distinguished fellow of the British Computer Society (1973), the Navy Meritorious Service Medal (1980), induction into the Engineering and Science Hall of Fame (1984) and the Navy Distinguished Service Medal (1986). She lectured widely and took on vested interests in the computer industry, pushing for greater standardization and compatibility in programming and hardware.

Hopper's years with the Navy brought steady promotions. She became captain on the retired list of the Naval Reserve in 1973 and commodore in 1983. In 1985 she earned the rank of rear admiral before retiring in 1986. But her professional life did not end there. She became a senior consultant for the Digital Equipment Corporation immediately after leaving the Navy and worked there until her death, on January 1, 1992. In its obituary, the *New York Times* noted that "[l]ike another Navy figure, Admiral Rickover, Admiral Hopper was known for her combative personality and her unorthodox approach." Unlike many of her colleagues in the early days of computers, Hopper believed in making computers and programming languages increasingly available and accessible to nonspecialists.

SELECTED WRITINGS BY HOPPER:

Books

"A Manual of Operation for the Automatic Sequence Controlled Calculator," in *Annals of the Harvard Computation Laboratory,* Volume 1, Harvard University Press, 1946.

(With Steven Mandrell) *Understanding Computers,* West Publishing, 1984.

Periodicals

(With John W. Mauchly) "Influence of Programming Techniques on the Design of Computers," *Proc. IRE,* Volume 41, October, 1953.

"The Education of a Computer," *Annals of the History of Computing,* Volume 9, 1988.

SOURCES:

Books

Billings, Charlene W., *Grace Hopper, Navy Admiral and Computer Pioneer,* Enslow, 1989.

Slater, Robert, *Portraits in Silicon,* MIT Press, 1987.

Periodicals

New York Times, January 3, 1992.

Sammet, Jean E., "Farewell to Grace Hopper—End of an Era!" *Communications of the AMC*, April, 1992.

—Sketch by Katherine Williams

Michael Hastings Horn
1942-
American marine biologist

Michael Hastings Horn, a marine biologist and ichthyologist (a scientist who studies fish), has contributed broadly to the understanding of plant-fish interactions. Horn is also one of the premiere investigators into pelagic fish, or fish living in the middle depths and surface waters of the sea. However, as Horn told Sharon Suer in an interview, he feels that his greatest contribution is in the area of conservation.

Horn was born November 14, 1942, in Tahlequah, Oklahoma, to Tom and Mary Garrison Horn, both teachers. Receiving his bachelors of science degree in biology from Northeastern (Oklahoma) State College in 1963, Horn then acquired a masters of science degree in zoology from the University of Oklahoma. Four years later, in 1969, Horn attained a Ph.D in biology from Harvard University.

Horn spent two years doing postdoctoral work, at both the prestigious Woods Hole Oceanography Institute under a biology fellowship and the British Museum of Natural History under a NATO fellowship in science. He studied fish-plant interactions in coastal seas and tropical rain forests, fish-plant interactions of coastal, harbor and bay-estuarine fishes, and fish ecology and digestive physiology.

Following two years of postdoctoral fellowship, Horn began teaching at California State University at Fullerton in 1970. He served first as an assistant professor, then as an associate professor of zoology, and finally as a full professor of biology. In 1986, Horn spent a year as a visiting research scientist at Dunstaff Nage Marine Research Laboratory in Oban, Scotland. Throughout this period, he was a member of the American Society of Ichthyology and Herpetology. From 1985 to 1992, Horn was the editor of the *Ichthyology Book Review* and also served on its board of governors; beginning in 1994, he is a member of the editorial board.

Interesting his students in conservation remains an important objective to Horn, and he is instrumental in promoting teaching careers that focus on conservation. He teaches such classes as conservation biology and wildlife conservation, and is an active member of the Society for Conservational Biology. Horn's impact on and dedication to his students is reflected in the numerous awards he has received, such as the 1990 Lynne K. McVeigh Award for Exceptional Service to Students, bestowed by the school of natural science and mathematics at California State University, Fullerton.

One of the activities of which Horn is proudest is his work fostering the education of American Indian students. Having some Native American ancestry himself, he is a member of the American Indian Science and Engineering Society, the American Indian and Alaskan Natives Professors Association, and the Society for the Advancement of Chicanos and Native Americans in Science.

A member of approximately twenty professional organizations, Horn has been the recipient of seven academic awards and honors, and has received a combined total of nearly three-quarters of a million dollars in grants and contracts. His writings number over one hundred various manuscripts, including published abstracts, technical reports, book and film reviews, and popular press articles. Horn has also given over seventy presentations at regional, national, and international conferences and symposia.

Keeping in step with his professional leanings, Horn likes activities involving nature, such as hiking, camping, and outdoor photography, and also enjoys music. Horn is divorced with no children. As of 1994, he continues to teach biology at California State University at Fullerton.

SELECTED WRITINGS BY HORN:

Books

"The Amount of Space Available for Marine and Freshwater Fishes," *Readings in Ichthyology*, edited by M. S. Love and G. M. Cailliet, Goodyear Publishing, 1979.

SOURCES:

Books

American Men and Women of Science, 1992–1993, 18th Edition, Bowker, 1992.

Other

Horn, Michael H., interview with Sharon F. Suer conducted on January 24, 1994.

—Sketch by Sharon F. Suer

Dorothy Millicent Horstmann
1911-
American virologist

Dorothy Millicent Horstmann played a significant yet often unacknowledged role in the development of the polio vaccine. In the late 1940s and early 1950s, before polio immunizations were considered feasible, she conducted groundbreaking animal studies which proved that the polio virus reaches the nervous system through the bloodstream. In 1952, while working at the Yale School of Medicine, she set up an experiment to determine whether polio first appeared in the blood before moving on to the brain. She fed monkeys and chimpanzees small quantities of polio virus, then examined the blood for traces of it. The animals did not immediately develop symptoms of polio, yet small traces of virus were observable in their blood. Many of the animals later developed paralysis, one of polio's debilitating symptoms.

Horstmann was born July 2, 1911, in Spokane, Washington, to Henry and Anna (Humold) Horstmann. She received her B.A. in 1936 and her M.D. in 1940 from the University of California. After holding an internship at the San Francisco City and County Hospital from 1939 to 1940, she did her medical residency at Vanderbilt University. In 1942, she began her long affiliation with the Yale University School of Medicine. In 1945, Horstmann was appointed associate professor of medicine at Yale; from 1947 to 1948, she held a National Institutes of Health postdoctoral research fellowship there. In 1961, Horstmann rose to professor of epidemiology and pediatrics, and in 1969 she was named John Rodman Paul Professor of Epidemiology and Pediatrics. Since 1982, she has held the titles of emeritus professor and senior research scientist at Yale. Horstmann was led to her experiments by the work of William McDowell Hammon, who showed that injections of gamma globulin, an antibody-rich serum extracted from plasma, could produce temporary immunity to polio. From this lead, Horstmann hypothesized that the polio virus first travelled through the bloodstream before finally settling in the nervous system. The discoveries she made during her experiments with monkeys and chimpanzees were initially dismissed by some virologists as inconclusive, because in most patients who had developed polio, no virus had been found in their blood. It was subsequently established, however, that by the time the symptoms of polio became clinically evident, the virus had already left the bloodstream and established itself in the nervous system. Horstmann's work and the parallel studies of David Bodian at Johns Hopkins University proved that polio is an intestinal infection which can enter the nervous system through the bloodstream.

Throughout the 1950s and 1960s, Horstmann participated in field trials to establish the effectiveness and safety of polio vaccines. During her distinguished career, Horstmann also studied maternal rubella and the rubella syndrome in infants. She holds four honorary doctorates and has received numerous honors and awards, including the James D. Bruce Award of the American College of Physicians, 1975, Denmark's Thorvold Madsen Award, 1977, and the Maxwell Finland Award of the Infectious Diseases Society of America, 1978. She is a member of the National Academy of Sciences, the American Society of Clinical Investigations, the American College of Physicians, and the Royal Society of Medicine.

SELECTED WRITINGS BY HORSTMANN:

Books

Report on a Visit to the U.S.S.R., Poland, and Czechoslovakia to View Work on Live Poliovirus Vaccine, Yale University Press, 1960.

Periodicals

"Controlling Rubella: Problems and Perspectives," *Annals of Internal Medicine,* Volume 83, September, 1975.

SOURCES:

Books

Klein, Aaron E., *Trial by Fury: The Polio Vaccine Controversy,* Scribner, 1972.

Smith, Jane S., *Patenting the Sun: Polio and the Salk Vaccine,* Morrow, 1990.

Other

"Leaders in American Medicine: Dorothy M. Horstmann, M.D." (videocassette), The National Audiovisual Center, 1979.

—*Sketch by Tom Crawford*

Eugene Houdry
1892-1962
French-born American chemist

Eugene Houdry was trained as a mechanical engineer in France and spent the first thirty-eight years of his life in that country. There he worked in his father's steel plant and ultimately became interested in the development of catalysts for use in a variety of industrial processes. In 1930 Houdry came to the United States and refined a process for the conversion of crude oil products to high-quality gasoline that he had first begun in France. Some observers credit the Houdry process of catalytic cracking with providing the Allies with a decisive technological edge that allowed them to win World War II. Later in life Houdry turned his attention to the development of catalysts that would reduce the amount of pollution produced by internal combustion engines.

Eugene Jules Houdry was born in Domont, France, near Paris, on April 18, 1892. His parents were the former Emilie Thais Julie Lemaire and Jules Houdry, owner of a successful steel manufacturing plant. As a young man, Houdry decided to continue his father's business and so entered the Ecole des Arts et Métiers in Paris to major in mechanical engineering. He graduated in 1911, earning a gold medal from the French government for receiving the best grades in his class.

After graduation Houdry entered his father's company as an engineer and became a junior partner. With the onset of World War I, he was drafted into the French Army, where he eventually became a lieutenant in the tank corps. During the battle of Juvincourt in 1917, he was severely wounded while directing the repair of damaged tanks. For his courageous actions, he was later awarded the Croix de Guerre.

Becomes Interested in Motor Fuels

Houdry's service in the tank corps was to have unanticipated long-term consequences for his own career and on the petroleum industry. His experience working with tanks encouraged a fascination with auto racing that in turn led to an interest in improving the quality of motor fuels. Although he returned to the steel manufacturing business at the end of World War I, he spent more and more time on his hobby—auto racing—and on research into automotive fuels.

In 1922 that research received an impetus from the French government. Faced with one of its recurring fuel shortages, the government asked Houdry to work on methods for converting fossil fuels such as bituminous coal and lignite, which France had in abundance, to a synthetic form of petroleum. By 1925 Houdry had accomplished that goal. His success was moderated, however, by the fact that the method he developed could not compete economically with products obtained from natural petroleum. Although his work was a failure in one respect, Houdry had become convinced while working on the project that research on fuels was his real passion. He gave up his job at the steel factory to devote his full time to research. His first objective was to find a way of converting crude oil to a high-quality gasoline.

Originally the term *gasoline* referred to one of the products obtained during the fractional distillation (purifying process) of petroleum. With the development of automobiles, this petroleum fraction became increasingly in demand. As internal combustion engines were improved, however, the "straight-run" gasoline obtained directly from fractional distillation proved to be a less and less satisfactory fuel. Chemists realized that modifications would have to be found that would increase the octane number (a measure of the efficiency of a fuel) of the gasoline obtained from petroleum.

The first widely successful method developed was called cracking. During the cracking process, crude petroleum is heated to high temperatures, causing large, saturated hydrocarbons (hydrogen-and-carbon-containing compounds containing single bonds) with low octane numbers to break apart into smaller, unsaturated hydrocarbons with higher octane numbers. Gasoline obtained by means of this "thermal" (for "heat") cracking process has octane numbers of about 72, about twenty points higher than the octane number of straight-run gasoline.

Develops the Process of Catalytic Cracking

By 1927 Houdry had found that the efficiency of the thermal cracking process could be improved by the use of a catalyst. A catalyst is any material that changes the rate of a chemical reaction without undergoing any permanent change itself. The first catalysts used by Houdry were claylike materials made of silica and alumina. The "catalytically cracked" gasoline produced by the Houdry process had octane numbers of about 88. Later developments in the process raised that value to 100 or more.

Houdry tried to find an oil company in France that would finance the construction of a pilot plant utilizing the new catalytic process. He was without success, however, until 1930, when a U.S. firm, the Vacuum Oil Company, offered to finance continuation of his research. Houdry moved to the United States and formed the Houdry Process Corporation, one-third of which was owned by Vacuum Oil, one-third by the Sun Oil Company, and one-third by Houdry. By 1936 the first plant using Houdry's process had opened at Paulsboro, New Jersey, producing two thousand barrels a day of high-octane gasoline. Although other methods of improving the octane number in gasoline have since been developed, catalytic cracking has become a fundamentally important process in the petroleum industry. During World War II, for example, an estimated 90 percent of the high-quality fuel needed by airplanes was produced by the Houdry process.

Houdry became an American citizen in 1942, but never abandoned his native land. During World War II, he formed France Forever, an organization whose purpose it was to obtain support in the United States government for the Free French forces fighting under General Charles de Gaulle. Toward the end of World War II, Houdry turned his attention to a new problem, the release of carcinogenic materials in the exhaust gases from automobiles and industrial processes. He had become convinced that these pollutants were a major cause of lung cancer. Just a month before his death, Houdry was awarded a patent for a catalytic convertor for automobile exhaust systems of the type that is now standard on all U.S. automobiles.

Mr. Catalysis, as Houdry was often called, was married to Genevieve Marie Quilleret on July 1, 1922. The couple had two sons. Houdry died in Upper Darby, Pennsylvania, on July 18, 1962. Among the honors he received during his career were the Potts Medal of the Franklin Institute in 1948, the Perkin Medal of the Society of the Chemical Industry in 1959, and the Award in Industrial and Engineering Chemistry of the American Chemical Society in 1962.

SELECTED WRITINGS BY HOUDRY:

Periodicals

Oil and Gas Journal, Volume 37, 1938.

SOURCES:

Periodicals

"Eugene Houdry, Catalytic Cracking and World War II Aviation Gasoline," *Journal of Chemical Education,* August, 1984, pp. 655–656.

"Eugene J. Houdry," *Chemical and Engineering News,* November 8, 1948.

"Eugene J. Houdry," *Chemical and Engineering News,* July 30, 1962, p. 130.

"Houdry—Round-the-Clock Researcher," *Chemical and Engineering News,* January 12, 1959, pp. 76–77.

"Man of the Month: Eugene J. Houdry," *Chemical and Engineering News,* October, 1953.

—*Sketch by David E. Newton*

Godfrey Hounsfield
1919-
English biomedical engineer

Sir Godfrey Hounsfield pioneered a great leap forward in medical diagnosis: computerized axial tomography, popularly known as the "CAT scan." Ushering in a new and sometimes controversial era of medical technology, Hounsfield's device allowed a doctor to look inside a patient's body and examine a three-dimensional image far more detailed than a conventional X ray. The importance of this advance was recognized in 1979, the year Hounsfield received the Nobel Prize for physiology or medicine.

Godfrey Newbold Hounsfield was born August 28, 1919, in Newark, England, the youngest of five children of a steel-industry engineer turned farmer. Hounsfield's technical interests began when, to prevent boredom, he began figuring out how the machinery on his father's farm worked. From there he moved on to exploring electronics, and by his teens was building his own radio sets. He graduated from London's City and Guilds College in 1938 after studying radio communication. When World War II erupted, Hounsfield volunteered for the Royal Air Force, where he studied and later lectured on the new and vital technology of radar at the RAF's Cranwell Radar School. After the war he resumed his education, and received a degree in electrical and mechanical engineering from Faraday House Electrical Engineering College in 1951. Upon graduation, Hounsfield joined Thorn EMI (Electrical and Musical Industries) Ltd., an employer he has remained with his entire professional life.

At Thorn EMI, Hounsfield worked on improving radar systems and then on computers. In 1959, a design team led by Hounsfield finished production of Britain's first large all-transistor computer, the EMIDEC 1100. Hounsfield moved on to work on high-capacity computer memory devices, and was granted a British patent in 1967 titled "Magnetic Films for Information Storage."

Conceives the CAT Scanner during a Stroll

Hounsfield's work in this period included the problem of enabling computers to recognize patterns, thus allowing them to "read" letters and numbers. In 1967, during a long walk through the British countryside, Hounsfield's knowledge of computers, pattern recognition, and radar technology all came together in his mind. He envisioned a medical diagnostic system in which an X-ray machine would image thin "slices" through the patient's body and a computer would process the slices into an accurate representation which would display the tissues, organs, and other structures in much greater detail than a single X ray could produce. Computers available in 1967 were not sophisticated enough to make such a machine practical, but Hounsfield continued to refine his idea and began working on a prototype scanner. He enlisted two radiologists, James Ambrose and Louis Kreel, who assisted him with their practical knowledge of radiology and also provided tissue samples and test animals for scans. The project attracted support from the British Department of Health and Social Services, and in 1971 a test machine was installed at Atkinson Morely's Hospital in Wimbledon. It was highly successful, and the first production model followed a year later. These original scanners were designed for imaging the brain, and were hailed by neurosurgeons as a great advance. Before the CAT scanner, doctors wanting a detailed brain X ray had to help their equipment see through the skull by such dangerous techniques as pumping chemicals or air into the brain. As head of EMI's Medical Systems section, Hounsfield continued to improve the device, working to lower the radiation exposure required, sharpen the images produced, and develop larger models which could image any part of the body, not just the head. This "whole body scanner" went on the market in 1975.

CAT scanners generated some resistance because of their expense: even the earliest models cost over $300,000, and improved versions several times as much. Despite this, the machines were so useful they quickly became standard equipment at larger hospitals around the world. Hounsfield argued that, properly used, the scanners actually reduced medical costs by eliminating exploratory surgery and other invasive diagnostic procedures. The scanner won Hounsfield and his company more than thirty awards, including the MacRobert Award, Britain's highest honor for engineering. In 1979, Hounsfield's collection of scientific tributes was topped off with the Nobel Prize. That year's Nobel was shared with **Allan M. Cormack,** an American nuclear physicist who had separately developed the equations involved in reconstructing an image via computer. A surprising feature of the selection was that neither man had a degree in medicine or biology, or a doctorate in any field. Asked what he would do with the large monetary award which came with the Nobel selection, Hounsfield replied he wanted to build a laboratory in his home. In an interview with Robert Walgate of the British journal *Nature* after the Nobel announcement, Hounsfield commented, "I've always searched for original ideas; I am absolutely opposed to doing something someone else has done."

Hounsfield moved on to positions as chief staff scientist and then senior staff scientist for Thorn EMI. He continued to improve the CAT scanner, working to develop a version which could take an accurate "snapshot" of the heart between beats. He has also contributed to the next step in diagnostic technology, nuclear magnetic resonance imaging. In 1986, he became a consultant to Thorn EMI's Central Research Laboratories in Middlesex, near his longtime home in Twickenham.

SELECTED WRITINGS BY HOUNSFIELD:

Periodicals

(With P. H. Brown) "Computerized Transverse Axial Scanning (Tomography)," *British Journal of Radiology,* 1973, p. 1016.

SOURCES:

Books

Current Biography Yearbook, H. W. Wilson, 1980, pp. 153–155.

Engineers and Inventors, Harper, 1986, pp. 85–86.

Periodicals

Di Chiro, Giovanni, with Rodney A. Brooks, "The 1979 Nobel Prize in Physiology or Medicine," *Science,* November 30, 1979, pp. 1060–1062.

"Nobel Prizes," *Physics Today,* December, 1979, pp. 17–20.

"Nobel Prizes: Emphasis on Applications," *Science News,* October 20, 1979, p. 261.

"Scanning for a Nobel Prize," *New Scientist,* October 18, 1979, pp. 64–165.

Seligmann, Jean, "The Year of the CAT," *Newsweek,* October 22, 1979, pp. 75–76.

"Triumph of the Odd Couple," *Time,* October 22, 1979, p. 80.

Walgate, Robert, "35th Prize for Inventor of EMI X-ray Scanner," *Nature,* October 18, 1979, pp. 512–513.

—Sketch by Matthew A. Bille

Bernardo Houssay
1887-1971
Argentine physiologist

Bernardo Houssay studied nearly every aspect of human physiology, but is best known for his discovery of the role of the pituitary gland in the metabolism of carbohydrates, an accomplishment for

Bernardo Houssay

which he was awarded the 1947 Nobel Prize for Physiology. He led a highly productive life, authoring or coauthoring more than 600 scientific papers and books. Houssay taught at the University of Buenos Aires for twenty-five years before losing his position for political reasons. He then helped to establish the independent Institute of Biology and Experimental Medicine, a research facility that soon became a primary focus of scientific studies in Latin America.

Bernardo Alberto Houssay was born in Buenos Aires, Argentina, on April 10, 1887; his parents had emigrated from France before his birth. His father was Albert Houssay, a lawyer who also taught literature at the National College of Buenos Aires, and his mother was the former Clara Laffont. Juan T. Lewis, writing in *Perspectives in Biology,* describes how Houssay early on began to practice a way of life that was "distinguished by concentration of purpose, hard work and the avoiding of loss of time and energy in frivolous pursuits." As evidence of these attitudes, young Bernardo promised his father at the age of thirteen that he would henceforth assume all responsibility for his own personal financial expenses.

Houssay completed his secondary education at the Colegio Británico at the age of fourteen. Three years later he earned his degree in pharmaceutical chemistry from the University of Buenos Aires, receiving the highest honors in his class. He then enrolled in the school of medicine at the university and was granted his M.D. at the age of twenty-three. Houssay's medical studies took somewhat longer to complete than might have been expected, given his previous academic record, because he simultaneously worked as a hospital pharmacist in order to help pay for his expenses.

Having completed his studies, Houssay was appointed provisional professor, and, in 1912, full professor of physiology at the university's school of veterinary science. In 1913, he became chief physician at Alvear Hospital as well as a laboratory director in the newly created National Public Health Laboratories. Houssay's 1919 return to the university as chair of physiology marked the beginning of his greatest impact in the field. It was at the university that he established and became director of the Institute of Physiology, a research center that was to attain worldwide distinction. At its peak, the Institute was home to 135 graduate students from every part of the world, extending Houssay's influence far beyond the borders of Argentina. In 1920 Houssay married María Angélica Catán, a chemist. All three of their children, Alberto Bernardo, Héctor Emilio José, and Raúl Horacio, earned medical degrees.

In spite of his many administrative responsibilities, Houssay continued to be very active in research throughout his life. He was intensely interested in every aspect of physiology, from the cardiovascular to the respiratory to the gastrointestinal systems. But his major accomplishments resulted from his studies of the endocrine system, studies that dated to research begun while he was still a medical student. That research received an important impetus in 1921 when Canadians Frederick Banting and Charles Best and Scottish physiologist John Macleod discovered the role of insulin in the development of diabetes.

Discovery Rewarded with Nobel Prize

From 1923 to 1937, Houssay studied the interaction between the pancreas and insulin, on the one hand, and the pituitary gland (then called the hypophysis) and its secretions, on the other. One of his first major discoveries was the role of the anterior lobe of the pituitary gland in the metabolism of carbohydrates. A more important discovery was that the oxidation of sugars in the body depends not simply on the presence or absence of insulin, but on a complex interaction between insulin and other hormones, such as prolactin and somatotropin, produced in the pituitary gland. For his unraveling of this process, Houssay received a share of the 1947 Nobel Prize for Physiology.

The political turmoil that swept Argentina in the 1940s altered Houssay's career. During the uprisings of 1943, he signed a petition calling for the democratization of the Argentine government. As a result, he was dismissed from his post at the university. Two years later, the dismissal was voided, and Houssay returned to the university. He was there only briefly, however, before he was asked to retire, which he did in 1946. In the meantime, he and some colleagues had founded the independent Institute of Biology and Experimental Medicine in order to continue with their research. Even when Houssay was yet again reinstated to his old post at the university in 1955, he continued to serve as director of the Institute.

Houssay was a major leader of Argentine science for many years. He founded, assisted in the establishment of, or served as head of nearly every major scientific organization in the country between 1920 and 1970. He was honored not only by his own nation, but by scientific societies all over the world. He was given honorary doctorates by more than twenty-five universities and was elected to membership in scientific societies in Great Britain, Germany, France, Italy, Spain, and the United States. Houssay died in Buenos Aires on September 21, 1971.

SELECTED WRITINGS BY HOUSSAY:

Books

La acción fisiológica de los extractos hipofisarios, [Buenos Aires], 1918.

(With A. Sordelli) *Tiroides e immunidad, estudio crítico y experimental,* [Buenos Aires], 1924.

Functions of the Pituitary Gland, [Boston], 1936.

(With others) *Fisiología humana,* El Ateneo (Buenos Aires), 1946; translated by Juan T. Lewis and Olive T. Lewis as *Human Physiology,* McGraw-Hill, 1951.

"The Role of the Hypophysis in Carbohydrate Metabolism and in Diabetes," in *Nobel Lectures in Physiology or Medicine, 1942–1962,* Elsevier, 1964, pp. 210–217.

SOURCES:

Books

Lewis, J. T., "Bernardo Alberto Houssay," *Perspectives in Biology,* Elsevier, 1963, pp. vii-xiv.

Nobel Lectures in Physiology or Medicine, 1942–1962, Elsevier, 1964, pp. 218–219.

—Sketch by David E. Newton

Fred Hoyle
1915-
English astronomer and mathematician

A prolific and talented author in both science fact and fiction, Fred Hoyle is best known for publicizing the controversial steady state theory of the creation of the universe. Hoyle also helped develop radar and advance the understanding of the nuclear processes that power the stars. He has taught at both Cambridge and Cornell universities, received numerous awards and honors, and was knighted in 1972.

Born on June 24, 1915, at Bingley, Yorkshire, England, Hoyle is the son of Benjamin Hoyle and Mabel (Picard) Hoyle. He attended Bingley Grammar School and went on to Emmanuel College at Cambridge, where he studied mathematics and astronomy, receiving his Master of Arts degree in 1939. On December 28, 1939, Hoyle married Barbara Clark and the couple eventually had two children; Geoffrey, who like his father became a writer, and Elizabeth Jeanne.

During World War II, Hoyle served in the Admiralty at London where he helped the British Navy develop radar (radio detection and ranging) technology. The Royal Air Force's victory in the Battle of Britain has been credited to the navy's improvement of radar during this period. After the war, numerous radar dishes were acquired by fledgling radio astronomers and converted into radio telescopes. These amateurs' discoveries in the 1960s ultimately helped to refute the theories Hoyle developed in the 1940s and 1950s.

The Secret Life of Stars

During the early 1940s, Hoyle focused his attention on an issue that arose through the work of physicist **Hans Bethe**: energy production in stars. In 1938 Bethe had suggested a sequence of nuclear reactions that fuel the stars: Four hydrogen atoms were fused into a single atom of helium, resulting in a minute amount of mass being converted into energy. While this process of nuclear fusion was consistent with the predicted amounts of stellar energy observed, Bethe's theory did not account for the production of elements heavier than helium—heavy elements that exist within other stars and that are also abundant on earth.

Hoyle expanded Bethe's findings. Elaborating on gravitational, electrical and nuclear fields, he determined what would happen to elements at ever increasing temperatures. He theorized that when a star has nearly exhausted its supply of hydrogen,

Fred Hoyle

nuclear fusion halts, and the outward radiation pressure generated by the fusion reaction also comes to a halt. Without this outward flow, the star begins to collapse because of gravitation. This causes the core of the star to heat up and reach a temperature great enough to fuse helium into carbon. The collapse of the star is then halted by the outward pressure of this new fusion radiation, and the star becomes stable. Hoyle's investigation into the nature of the carbon atom had the added benefit of helping scientists understand the origin of the atoms within the human body.

As the fusion cycle of stellar evolution continues, oxygen, magnesium, sulfur and heavier elements build up until the element iron is formed. At this point, no more fusion reactions can occur, and the star collapses catastrophically, becoming a white dwarf (a star dimmer than the sun but much more dense). During this implosion, the star's outer layers ignite to become a supernova (an explosion whose luminosity is many times greater than the sun). The supernova explosion creates elements heavier than iron which are then hurtled into space by the explosion's force. It was from stellar debris such as this, Hoyle hypothesized, that the second generation stars with the heavier elements were formed.

Hoyle further proposed that the sun was once part of a binary (double) star system whose companion became a supernova eons ago. The resulting heavy elements it ejected into space became the material from which the planets were formed. Hoyle's remarkable theory of stellar evolution appeared to be correct; it agreed with scientists' observations and accounts for the heavy elements in the solar system. However, whether the sun had a companion star or not is still disputed; some believe a passing star was the culprit.

The "Big Bang" Controversy Explodes

Following the war, Hoyle returned to Cambridge and became a professor of astronomy and mathematics. The pivotal point in his career came in 1948 when nuclear physicist **George Gamow,** building upon a theory first suggested by Georges Lemaître, a Jesuit priest and astonomer, and supported by the telescopic observations of the astronomer **Edwin Powell Hubble**, published what became known as the big bang theory of the creation of the universe. The big bang theory states that billions of years ago there was an enormous explosion in which all the matter of the universe was created. Galaxies formed and evolved from this matter and are still moving away from each other at tremendous velocities as a result of the explosion.

The concept that the universe had a specific beginning—and the implication that it will have an end—was abhorred by many scientists and laymen. Consequently, **Thomas Gold** and **Hermann Bondi,** an astronomer and mathematician respectively, proposed the steady state theory that theorized that the universe was perpetual, an idea that appeared to agree with scientific observation. Through the steady state theory, Gold and Bondi conceived of a universe in which matter was created continuously. As galaxies drift apart, new matter appears in the void and evolves into new galaxies. Since the universe seemed homogeneous (the same) regardless from which direction it was observed, or how far away (i.e. how far back in time) it was observed, Gold and Bondi suggested the cosmos was the same every "where" and every "when." That is, the physical state of the universe remains the same in the past, the present, and the future. The steady state concept had several virtues, not the least of which was avoiding the troublesome issue of the beginning and end of creation. It was simple, symmetrical and attracted as many adherents as did Gamow's big bang theory. Hoyle became one of steady state's most influential and talented supporters.

Gold and Bondi had not based their concept on general field theory, but instead on an intuitive physical principle. To rectify this, Hoyle delved into the complex equations of **Albert Einstein**, modified them, and produced a mathematical model that supported the steady state theory, thereby giving it both respectability and plausibility. He became the official spokesperson for the theory and produced many books, some extremely technical, others geared for popular consumption, that publicized steady state cosmology.

The greatest objection to the steady state theory concerned the issue of the continual creation of new matter forming from nothing—an idea that seemed to violate the laws of nature. Hoyle claimed it was easier to accept the idea of matter being created slowly and continuously over the eons than believing that all matter in the universe was created in a single instant from a single blast. For the next fifteen years, proponents of each side interpreted new astronomical discoveries in ways that supported the theory to which each adhered.

In 1952, however, astronomer **Walter Baade** demonstrated that the accepted cosmological "yardstick" of measurement was seriously flawed. This "yardstick" was derived from the relationship between the brightness and the rate of pulsation of certain stars called Cepheid variable stars. According to Baade's findings, such stars were much farther away than had been previously calculated. This meant that the universe was much older, had been evolving longer, and was more than two times larger than had been believed. If the steady state theory were to hold up, astronomers surveying space would expect to see "old" galaxies created billions of years ago and containing aging stars, as well as "new," recently created galaxies containing lighter elements and new stars. Yet observed galaxies appeared to be similar in age, supporting the big bang theory. Proving that matter is continuously created was more complicated than it seemed for the steady state theorists. Since space is so vast and the amount of matter that needs to be created at a given moment for the theory to be proven was so small, scientists were not able to detect the instantaneous creation of matter.

The debate between the factions continued. Hoyle acknowledged in his 1962 book *Astronomy* that there are "cosmological theories in which the universe had a finite and 'explosive' origin," but he manages to discuss them without once using the contentious phrase "big bang"; an ironic point since the term "big bang" is attributed to Hoyle. A decade earlier, Gamow's book *The Creation of the Universe* remarked that "Astronomical observations" concerning the brightness of the Milky Way stars in relation to the brightness of neighboring stars suggest "that the theory of [Bondi, Gold and Hoyle] may not correspond to reality." In order to maintain the relevance of his work, Hoyle made several modifications to the steady state theory throughout the 1950s and 1960s.

The Scales Tip

The 1963 discovery of quasars by Maartin Schmidt created an awkward complication for the steady state theory. Quasars, distant objects brighter than and emitting more energy than stars, did not fit into the steady state explanation of the universe. This tipped the balance toward the big bang theory, which had no trouble embracing these "quasi-stellar" objects. In the following year, **Arno Penzias** and **Robert W. Wilson** discovered background microwave radiation in outer space by using radio telescopes. Claiming they had discovered the "remnants" of the big bang explosion with their telescopes, which had evolved from Hoyle's work on radar during World War II, Penzias and Wilson sealed the fate of the steady state theory which was now abandoned in favor of the big bang theory. Subsequently, Hoyle found working with radio astronomers at Cambridge University increasingly difficult. When his proposed grant for a computer was rejected by the Science Research Council in 1972, Hoyle left the university in favor of working elsewhere. Since then he has not had a permanent academic position, preferring to work as a visiting professor at various institutions, including the University of Manchester in England and the University of Cardiff in Wales.

Still More Controversy

Hoyle stirred up controversy again in 1981 when he proposed that one-celled life could be found in interstellar dust or comets and life on earth may have originated from a close encounter with a comet. He also suggested that the abrupt appearance of global epidemics could be caused by space-borne contaminants, a suggestion not taken seriously by most scientists. In 1985 Hoyle ignited yet another controversy when he claimed that the British Museum's fossil of Archaeopteryx was a fake, but he had not been alone in that contention.

A prodigious amount of information has flowed from Hoyle's pen during his career. With his talent for simplifying complex theories for general audiences, he has produced technical treatises, textbooks, popular science fiction stories, an opera libretto, even a radio and a television play. The radio play, *Rockets in Ursa Major,* and the television play, *A for Andromeda,* were both written in collaboration with his son, Geoffrey, in 1962. His research on the development of stars and their age, including giants and white dwarfs, helped establish some of cosmology's major theories.

During his career, Hoyle was widely recognized for his achievements with many honors. In 1956 he became a member of the staff at Mount Wilson and Palomar observatories. In 1957 he was elected to the Royal Society of London; the following year he became Plumian Professor of Astronomy and Experimental Philosophy at Cambridge, and in 1962 he became the director of the Institute of Theoretical Astronomy. Following his departure from Cambridge in 1972, he became professor-at-large at Cornell University. He was honored by his country when he was knighted in 1972.

SELECTED WRITINGS BY HOYLE:

Books

Some Recent Researches in Solar Physics, Cambridge University Press, 1949.

The Nature of the Universe, Harper, 1951, revised edition, 1960.

(With John Elliot) *A for Andromeda,* Harper, 1962.

Astronomy, Doubleday, 1962.

Galaxies, Nuclei, and Quasars, Harper, 1965.

(With Geoffrey Hoyle) *Rockets in Ursa Major* (science fiction novel), Harper, 1969.

From Stonehenge to Modern Cosmology, W. H. Freeman, 1972.

Astronomy and Cosmology, W. H. Freeman, 1975.

(With G. Hoyle) *The Incandescent Ones* (science fiction novel), Harper, 1977.

Steady-State Cosmology Re-Visited, Longwood, 1980.

The Quasar Controversy Resolved, Longwood, 1981.

The Planet of Death (science fiction novel; illustrated by Martin Aitchison), Ladybird, 1982.

The Intelligent Universe: A New View of Creation and Evolution, Holt, 1984.

Living Comets, Longwood, 1985.

The Small World of Fred Hoyle (autobiography), Joseph, 1986.

(With Chandra Wickramasinghe) *Archaeopteryx, the Primordial Bird: A Case of Fossil Forgery,* Longwood, 1987.

SOURCES:

Books

Abell, George, David Morrison, and Sidney Wolfe, *Exploration of the Universe, 6th Edition,* Saunders College Press, 1991.

Academic American Encyclopedia, Grolier Electronic Publishing, 1991.

Briggs, Asa, *Dictionary of Twentieth Century World Biography,* Oxford University Press, 1992.

Devine, Elizabeth, *Thinkers of the Twentieth Century,* Gale, 1987.

Gamow, George, *The Creation of the Universe,* Bantam, 1952.

Magill, Frank N., *Great Events from History II, Science and Technology Series, Volume 1–5,* Salem Press, 1991, pp. 825–829; 1309–1313; 1320–1324; 1539–1544.

Magnusson, Magnus, *Cambridge Biographical Dictionary,* Cambridge University Press, 1990.

McGraw-Hill Modern Men of Science, Volume II, McGraw-Hill, 1968.

Vernoff, Edward and Rima Shore, *International Dictionary of 20th Century Biography,* New American Library, 1987.

—*Sketch by Raymond E. Bullock*

Aleš Hrdlička
1869-1943
Czechoslovakian-born American physical anthropologist

Aleš Hrdlička is remembered for amassing one of the United States' most important collections of human skeletal remains and for his somewhat controversial theories about the nature of human intelligence and the origins of human habitation in North America. Hrdlička was born on March 29, 1869, in Humpolec (in what was then Bohemia) to Maxmilian Hrdlička and his wife Karolina. Aleš Hrdlička's father was a cabinetmaker, as was his maternal grandfather. The family moved to the United States in 1882; a Jesuit priest who had been his Latin and Greek tutor gave young Aleš a recommendation to an American college at which he could pursue a business degree. When Aleš and his parents arrived in New York, however, Aleš's father discovered that the college was in the midwest, farther away than he had realized, and, in addition, Aleš would have to learn English before he could attend. Remaining in New York, Aleš began working in a tobacco factory to earn money to finance his education; an attack of typhoid fever led him, through the influence of his physician, to pursue a medical career, which began at the Eclectic Medical College of New York. This was followed by an advanced degree from the New York Homeopathic Medical College, and a position at the State Homeopathic Hospital for the Insane in Middletown, New York.

It was through his case studies of mentally ill patients that Hrdlička began amassing data that he would later use in his anthropological research. One of his earliest publications was of the measurements of the skulls of 1,000 patients classified according to the nature of their illness. A pioneer in the area of anthropometry, or the comparative measurement of the human body, he eventually collected data on 40,000 individuals. In the pursuit of his career, he traveled to Paris to study. His need for comparative data on a "normal" population led him to Mexico, where he made his first trip in 1898 with anthropologist Karl Sofus Lumholz to study the native Indian populations of the Tarahumare, the Huichols, and the Tepehuanes; until 1902 and again between 1905 and 1910, he made numerous expeditions to Mexico and the southwestern United States as well as Florida and Egypt under the auspices of the Hyde Expeditions for the American Museum of Natural History in New York. In addition, he conducted studies of tuberculosis among Native American groups. In 1903 he was appointed assistant curator at the National Museum of the Smithsonian Institution in Washington, D.C., and he began to organize its division of physical anthropology; he became curator in 1910, remaining until his retirement in 1942.

Hrdlička's research resulted in extensive travel throughout the world. A series of lectures delivered in Peking in 1920 led to substantial research in Asia, and he followed this with excursions to Europe, Australia, and South Africa. As was common at the time, Hrdlička believed that the site of the origin of humankind was Europe rather than either Asia, which was becoming the focus of attention after the discovery of early fossilized human remains there, or Africa, which is where most scientists now feel the first humans evolved. Although Hrdlička initially encouraged investigation of the Piltdown remains (apparent evidence that humans originated in Europe that was later proved to be a hoax), he was one of the first anthropologists to question their authenticity. He also was a proponent of the so-called Neanderthal phase theory, which held that the Neanderthals, an early form of prehistoric humans in Europe, represented a stage in the direct evolutionary sequence that culminated in modern humans rather than a separate species that was to die out, as is now generally believed. In fact, he maintained that all humans through their history belonged to a single species.

The origins of humans in North America was one of his principal research areas. Much of Hrdlička's research was carried out in the Aleutian Islands, where he sought evidence of the first migrations of humans onto the continent. Noting physical similarities between certain Asian peoples and Native American groups, he tried to find an explanation by studying patterns of migration as revealed by the human remains found in Siberia and Alaska. One of the first to classify Native American peoples as related to the so-called Mongoloid peoples of Asia, he held to the theory that human populations first entered this continent from Asia across a land bridge that formerly connected Siberia and Alaska. Hrdlička believed that this migration occurred relatively recently, perhaps as late as 4,000 or 5,000 years ago. When other scientists postulated an earlier date, Hrdlička steadfastly maintained his view. Yet evidence began accumulating that contradicted Hrdlička's firmly held opinion. In 1926 in Folsom, New Mexico, archaeologists found flint stones that were apparently spear points made by humans; although no human remains were found, these so-called Folsom points were found in conjunction with fossilized bison bones. Some of the weapons appeared to have been used in the killing of the bison, providing evidence that humans had lived in the area far earlier than had been thought. In 1931 the fossilized remains of a fifteen-year-old human female were found in Minnesota; the remains were believed by their discoverer to be approximately 20,000 years old. A site in Colorado containing more Folsom points was geologically dated at 25,000 years. Despite this growing evidence that humans had lived on the North American continent as early as 15,000 or even 20,000 years ago, Hrdlička held to his conviction that human habitation first occurred there much more recently; he was willing to concede that humans arrived in North America no more than 7,000, or possibly 10,000, years ago.

One of Hrdlička's Aleutian finds was a skull of a human that had a cranial capacity of 2,005 cubic centimeters (compared to 1,450 cc for an average modern human), making it one of the largest human crania ever found in the Western Hemisphere. This discovery tied in with Hrdlička's research into the changes that had taken place over time in the cranial capacity of humans and his study of the divergence of human skull morphology, especially as it related to intelligence. Hrdlička's theory that some persons undergo an increase in skull size that corresponds to increased intellectual development, the so-called big heads theory, was ridiculed in some quarters; this controversial idea, along with his refusal to accept the evidence of the antiquity of humans in North America, did some damage to his reputation in his later years.

Hrdlička was associate editor of the *American Naturalist* from 1901 to 1908, and he was the founder, in 1918, and later editor of the *American Journal of Physical Anthropology.* He also served as the secretary general of the 19th International Congress of Americanists in 1915. He was the founder, in 1928, of the American Association of Physical Anthropology, and he served as its president from 1929 until 1932. He also supported anthropological work conducted by universities in his native Czechoslovakia, where he was especially closely associated with Charles University in Prague. Hrdlička married the former Marie S. Dieudonnée, a medical student, in 1896; she died in 1918. He remarried in 1920. In his later years he served as an associate in anthropology at the Smithsonian Institution. He died in Washington, D.C., on September 5, 1943.

SELECTED WRITINGS BY HRDLIČKA:

Books

Skeletal Remains Suggesting or Attributed to Early Man in North America, Government Printing Office, 1907.

Early Man in South America, Government Printing Office, 1912.
Physical Anthropology: Its Scope and Aims, Its History and Present Status in the United States, Wistar Institute of Anatomy and Biology, 1919.
Anthropometry, Wistar Institute of Anatomy and Biology, 1920.
Old Americans, Williams and Wilkins, 1925.
Skeletal Remains of Early Man, Smithsonian Institution, 1930.
Practical Anthropometry, Wistar Institute of Anatomy and Biology, 1939.

SOURCES:

Periodicals

"Horatius at the Bridge," *Time,* February 19, 1940, pp. 48–49.

—Sketch by Michael Sims

Alice Shih-hou Huang
1939-
Chinese-born American microbiologist

Alice Shih-hou Huang's discovery of reverse transcriptase, an enzyme that allows viruses to convert their genetic material into deoxyribonucleic acid (DNA)—the molecular basis of heredity, led to a major breakthrough in understanding how viruses function. Searching for clues on how to prevent viruses from replicating, Huang also isolated a rabies-like virus that produced mutant strains which interfered with viral growth.

The youngest of four children, Huang was born in Kiangsi, China, on March 22, 1939. Her father, the Right Reverend Quentin K. Y. Huang, was the second Chinese bishop ordained by the Anglican Episcopal Ministry in China. Her mother, Grace Betty Soong Huang, undertook a career of her own by entering nursing school at the age of forty-five. In 1949, when China became communist, the Huangs sent their children to the United States for a more stable life and greater opportunities.

Huang was ten years old when she and her siblings arrived in the United States. She studied at an Episcopalian boarding school for girls in Burlington, New Jersey, and at the National Cathedral School in Washington, DC, and became a United States citizen her senior year in high school. While in China, Huang had seen many people suffering from illness and decided to become a doctor. She attended Wellesley College in Massachusetts from 1957 to 1959, and subsequently enrolled in a special program at the Johns Hopkins University School of Medicine, where she earned her B.A. in 1961 and her M.A. in 1963. While at Johns Hopkins, she chose to pursue medicine not as a doctor, but as a scientist. She published several papers on viruses, including the herpes simplex viruses, and earned her Ph.D. from Johns Hopkins in 1966. That same year Huang served as a visiting assistant professor at the National Taiwan University. In 1967 Huang worked as a post-doctoral fellow with **David Baltimore** at the Salk Institute for Biological Studies in San Diego, California. At the time, scientists knew little about how viruses replicated. "It was as if they disappeared into a big black box and out would come thousands of copies of that same virus," Huang told Miyoko Chu in an interview. When asked if she found the work daunting, she replied: "When you don't know something, you don't know the extent of your lack of knowledge. We were just enjoying ourselves, discovering new things every day." Huang and Baltimore married in 1968; they have one daughter.

Huang and Baltimore took their work to the Massachusetts Institute of Technology in 1968. At the time scientists understood that the genetic material DNA in cells was converted into ribonucleic acid (RNA, nucleic acids associated with the control of chemical activities within cells), and then into proteins. But one of the viruses Huang studied had an enzyme that did something different—it made RNA from RNA. The work led to Baltimore's research on tumor viruses and his discovery of the enzyme called reverse transcriptase, which threw the usual process in reverse by converting RNA to DNA. Baltimore and American oncologist **Howard Temin**, who had independently discovered reverse transcriptase, were awarded the Nobel Prize in medicine in 1975 for their work on tumor viruses.

Huang became assistant professor of microbiology and molecular genetics at Harvard Medical School in 1971, was promoted to associate professor in 1973, and to full professor in 1979. She also served as an associate at the Boston City Hospital from 1971–73 and director of the infectious diseases laboratory at the Children's Hospital in Boston from 1979–89. Huang studied a rabies-like virus that produced mutant strains which interfered with further growth of the viral infection. She sought to understand where the mutants came from and how they affected the viral population, knowledge she hoped could be applied to halt the spread of viral infections in humans. For this research, Huang was awarded the Eli Lilly Award in Microbiology and Immunology in

1977. In 1987 she was appointed trustee of the University of Massachusetts. The following year Huang became president of the American Society for Microbiology, the first Asian American to head a national scientific society in the United States. She is also a member of the American Association for the Advancement of Science, the American Society for Biochemistry and Molecular Biology, and the Academia Sinica in Taiwan. Huang remained at Harvard until 1991, when she was appointed Dean for Science at New York University.

Though Huang sees her role in administration at New York University as important and necessary, her first love remains basic research. "Information and knowledge give me a sense of exhilaration," she told Chu. "Sometimes I can transmit this to a student when they do an experiment and get a nice clean result and can make a conclusion. I tell the student, "You and I are the only people in the world who know this!'" Huang has numerous research publications to her credit, and has served on the editorial boards of *Intervirology, Journal of Virology, Reviews of Infectious Diseases, Microbial Pathogenesis,* and *Journal of Women's Health.* She became a trustee of Johns Hopkins University in 1992, and joined the council of the Johns Hopkins-Nanjing University Center for Chinese and American Studies in 1993. In addition to her duties as university administrator, scientist, and mother, Huang is an avid reader of mystery novels, and enjoys sailing and snorkeling in her spare time.

SELECTED WRITINGS BY HUANG:

Books

(With E. L. Palma) "Defective Interfering Particles as Antiviral Agents," *Perspectives in Virology IX,* edited by M. Pollard, Academic Press, 1975, pp. 77–90.

(With D. Baltimore) "Defective Interfering Animal Viruses," *Comprehensive Virology,* Volume 10, edited by H. Fraenkel-Conrat and R. R. Wagner, Plenum, 1977, pp. 73–116.

"Virology," *Highlights in Microbiology,* edited by R. L. Moon and D. D. Whitt, American Society for Microbiology, 1981, pp. 32–33.

"Modulation of Viral Diseases by Defective Interfering Particles," *RNA Genetics: Variability of RNA Genomes,* edited by E. Domingo and others, CRC Press, 1988, pp. 195–208.

Periodicals

(With D. Baltimore) "Defective Viral Particles and Viral Disease Processes," *Nature,* Volume 226, 1970, pp. 325–327.

(With others) "Status of Women Microbiologists," *Science,* Volume 183, 1974, pp. 488–494.

"Science Education Shouldn't be Restricted to Narrow Boxes," *Scientist,* August 31, 1992.

(With John M. Coffin) "How Does Variation Count?" *Nature,* Volume 359, 1992, pp. 107–108.

SOURCES:

Periodicals

Miller, Susan Katz, "Asian-Americans Bump Against Glass Ceilings," *Science,* Volume 258, 1992, pp. 1224–1228.

Other

Huang, Alice Shih-hou, interview with Miyoko Chu conducted January 20, 1994.

—*Sketch by Miyoko Chu*

Philip G. Hubbard
1921-
American electrical engineer

Philip G. Hubbard is a well-respected researcher in fluid dynamics (the study of the motion of matter in gas, liquid, plastic, or plasma state) who pioneered methods of measuring and analyzing turbulence in fluid flow. He was born Philip Gamaliel Hubbard in Macon, Missouri, on March 4, 1921, to Philip Alexander Hubbard, a semi-skilled craftsman and Rosa Belle Guy, a teacher. Both parents were believed to be direct descendants of free slaves. Tragically, just eighteen days after the birth of young Hubbard his fifty-one-year-old father succumbed to pneumonia. While his mother continued teaching, the job of caring for the baby fell to his grandparents, Molly and Richard Wallace.

In 1925 Rosa Belle, her three sons from a previous marriage and young Hubbard moved to Iowa so the four boys could enroll in unsegregated schools. In an interview with Roger Jaffe, Hubbard noted he was usually the only non-white student and was accepted on an equal basis in school; outside of school things were very different and the races were highly unequal.

Hubbard Begins Association with the University of Iowa

Philip Hubbard entered the University of Iowa in 1940, graduated in 1943 with a degree in chemical

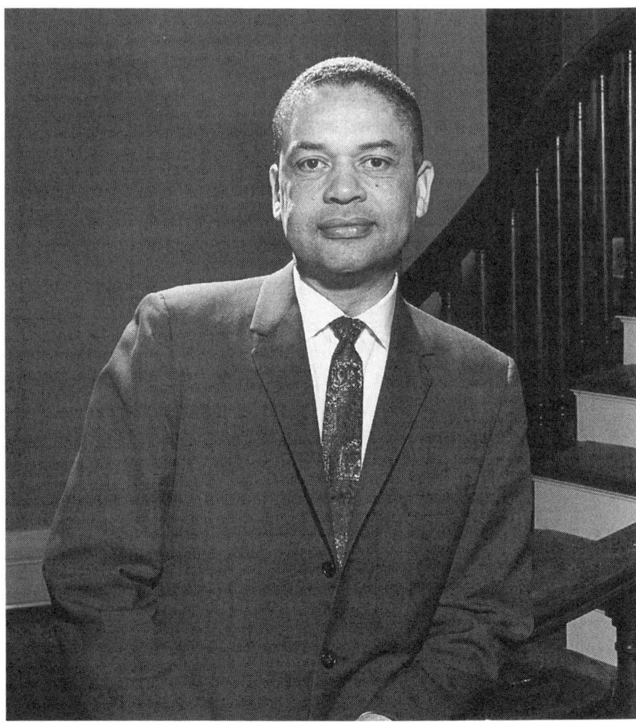

Philip G. Hubbard

engineering and married Wynonna Marie Griffin. Hubbard and his wife had five children, four boys and one girl. After serving two years in the army he received another bachelor's degree in electrical engineering in 1946; he was offered a full-time position at the university as a research engineer and later as the head of the instrumentation division. He received his master's degree in mechanics and hydraulics in 1949; his Ph.D. was awarded in 1954 in the same field.

The Hot Wire Anemometer

Hubbard's electrical engineering degree gave him the necessary background to investigate fluid measurement instrumentation and would later prove invaluable in his research of fluid flow. At the time there was a need to measure turbulence in a fluid flow. In a water distribution system for a city, for example, many miles of pipes are required. If certain types of pipeline cause less turbulence and fewer interruptions of the smooth fluid flow than others, those pipes are better suited for the job since they are more efficient. Industry needed a way to measure this kind of turbulence.

Hubbard developed the hot wire anemometer, a device that has a length of very thin wire that is heated with an electric current and placed in the fluid. Measuring the rate at which heat is dissipated from the wire leads to the measurement of fluid turbulence. The wire is only 50 microns in diameter—about one-seventh the thickness of a human hair. The small wire allows the device to respond very quickly so fluid turbulence can be measured as it happens.

The instrument became so popular with industry that while in the university environment, Hubbard could not make enough to satisfy the demand. He formed the Hubbard Instrument Company in 1951 to manufacture and market hot wire anemometers and related measuring devices while retaining his position at the University of Iowa.

Hubbard's Focus on Education

Hubbard joined the teaching faculty of the University as an assistant professor of mechanics and hydraulics in 1954, became an associate professor in 1956, and then a professor in 1959. This made Hubbard the first African American tenured professor at the University of Iowa. In 1966 Hubbard was appointed the dean of academic affairs, a position he held until his retirement. During his tenure as dean, he also held the positions of vice provost, vice president of student services, and the director of the "Opportunity at Iowa" program. Even after his retirement in 1991, Hubbard remains active in the university community. He sits on numerous boards for various academic and educational organizations and has three awards in his name given to deserving students at the university each year.

SELECTED WRITINGS BY HUBBARD:

Books

(Contributor) *Advanced Mechanics of Fluids,* edited by Hunter Rouse, John Wiley, 1959.

'Whence Come Megatrends?," *Megatrends in Hydraulic Engineering,* Colorado State University Press, 1986.

Periodicals

(With S. Ling) "The Hot-Film Anemometer: A New Device for Fluid Mechanics Research," *Journal of Applied Sciences,* September 1956.

Other

Hubbard, Philip G., letter and personal information provided to Roger Jaffe, January, 1994.

Hubbard, Philip G., interview with Roger Jaffe conducted January 20, 1994.

—*Sketch by Roger Jaffe*

M. King Hubbert
1903-1989
American geologist and geophysicist

A highly regarded geologist and geophysicist, M. King Hubbert redirected the course of petroleum exploration by mathematically calculating the arbitrary patterns of oil and gas entrapment beneath the earth's crust. The seismic shock of the scientific community over this discovery, however, was nothing compared to Hubbert's prediction in 1948—correct, as it turned out—that the production of crude oil worldwide was not without limits and that the supply within the United States would actually peak about 1971, leading to foreign dependence. For this pronouncement Hubbert became an "energy expert," constantly quoted by the *New York Times* and other major media outlets during the 1970s. Hubbert's accomplishments were lauded in 1981 when he received the highest honor in the earth sciences—the Vetlesen Prize, geology's equivalent of the Nobel.

Born in 1903, the son of William Bee and Cora (Lee) Hubbert, Marion King Hubbert grew up on a farm in San Saba County, Texas, attending a tiny rural school in between growing seasons. Dissatisfied with the level of education he received at a nearby junior college, Hubbert applied and was admitted to the University of Chicago. With little money to live on, he travelled there the hard way, sleeping in haystacks, working his way north by harvesting wheat and replacing railroad ties for Union Pacific. Arriving in Chicago in 1924, he enrolled in school, choosing a major in geology and physics in order to fulfill his first academic love, mathematics. Although still a young man, Hubbert was already showing the "crusty" personality that would be ascribed to him the rest of his life. "He turned out to be something of an iconoclast," fellow geologist F. J. Pettijohn remarked in a memorial to Hubbert published by the Geological Society of America. "King neither needed nor accepted advice and supervision. He was a very independent individual—a student of nobody."

After a stint with Amerada Petroleum Corporation, Hubbert returned to Chicago to work as a teaching assistant. It was at this point that Hubbert first attracted the attention of the scientific community with his paper on isostasy, which is a theory that accounts for the differences of the pull of gravity toward the center of the earth depending on the site where it's measured. "His paper said that most 1930s ideas on isostasy were confused," explained Dr. David Doan, a close friend and colleague who delivered Hubbert's memoriam. "He showed mathematically that the ideas of isostasy really needed rethinking." By redefining isostasy as a force of equilibrium that allowed the earth's crust to be both weak and strong, he created a platform upon which to construct his forthcoming theories.

Accepting a job as an instructor of geophysics at Columbia University in 1931, Hubbert became the center of controversy within the department by lobbying to change the geology curriculum, which he believed should incorporate comprehensive physics, math and geophysics. "They thought he was kind of a troublemaker and they finally parted by mutual consent," Doan informed in an interview. Academic politics were of little concern to Hubbert, however. He was too busy working on his 1937 paper which applied continuum mechanics to the geometric scale models that are so vital in the geologic field. Hubbert's paper suggested that immediate observation and direct measurement were of less use than prescriptive empiricism—a finding that ironically validated his cause celebre: namely, that geology students needed more calculus and physics education. His recommendation took root when his scale modeling paper was accepted by the University of Chicago as his Ph.D. dissertation. The next year Hubbert married Miriam Berry, a Kentucky-born staffer at a New York pharmaceutical company.

Looks Beneath the Earth's Surface

While at Columbia, Hubbert initiated a reinvestigation of the findings of nineteenth century geologist Henry Darcy. Expanding on Darcy's work, Hubbert published *Theory of Ground Water Motion* in 1940, a paper which included the field equations for the movement of water and other fluids through the permeable subterranean passages of the earth. Introducing the concept of gravitational potential, Hubbert showed mathematically that fluids are not constrained to flow only from higher to lower pressure. This discovery, which was criticized by both hydrologists and petroleum engineers, was defended by Hubbert in a series of strong rebuttals.

Hubbert left Columbia in 1941 and spent two years working with the United States Board of Economic Warfare during World War II, then, in 1943, he joined Shell Development in Houston. A paper published in 1945, *The Strength of the Earth,* not only updated his own scale-model findings but secured his position as a general consultant with Shell.

Finally relieved of administrative duties, Hubbert improved on his ground water motion findings and presented his results in *Entrapment of Petroleum Under Hydrodynamic Conditions*—a "blockbuster," according to Doan. In this project Hubbert showed the basis for differential migration of oil and gas under the earth's surface, and the unexpected inclination of gas-oil-water interfaces. In short, oil and gas flow through cracks and pores in rocks and do not remain in static, subterranean pools as had been previously thought. This theory of movement beneath the earth's crust changed the course of petroleum exploration.

Correctly Predicts Limits to Resources

Hubbert went on to make other contributions to geological science. He revealed how to pump water under high pressure down a hole so as to split the rock and improve permeability, resulting in a better flow of oil and gas up the well bore. He also warned that the supply of crude oil in the United States would peak in 1971, although it was not until the Arab oil embargo of 1973 that his message was taken seriously and conservation policies implemented. Hubbert's work won him election to the National Academy of Sciences in 1955 and the American Academy of Arts and Sciences in 1956. He was later awarded the Rockefeller Public Service Award in 1977 and the prestigious Vetlesen Prize in 1981. Hubbert's accomplishments established him as an "energy expert" for the media—"somewhat to his annoyance," Doan wrote in the memorial. "He regarded himself as an analytical expert."

Subject to mandatory retirement in 1964, Hubbert went to work for the United States Geological Survey for the next decade and also served as a professor of geology and geophysics at Stanford University. During those years he never gave up his efforts to bring about unification of learning in the physical sciences. He also strove to encourage pure scholarship in geology, which he believed the funding crunch discouraged. A man who loved Mozart and Beethoven but who was not above laughing at a caricature of himself—or launching into a very public chorus of *Yes, We Have No Bananas* on at least one occasion—Hubbert never lost his edge nor his crustiness, and was widely respected by his peers. Said C. Barry Raleigh, director of the Lamont Doherty Geological Survey, at the Vetlesen honors in 1981: "Being outspokenly correct when the conventional wisdom would have it otherwise may not win popularity contests, but the vitality and intellectual integrity of men such as King Hubbert are rare and precious qualities." Hubbert died October 11, 1989, of a suspected embolism.

SELECTED WRITINGS BY HUBBERT:

Books

Theory of Ground-Water Motion, University of Chicago Press, 1940.

Periodicals

"Isostasy: A Critical Review," *Journal of Geology* Volume 38, pp. 673–695, 1930.

"Theory of Scale Models As Applied to the Study of Geological Structures," *Geological Society of America Bulletin* Volume 48, pp. 1459–1520, 1937.

"The Theory of Ground-Water Motion," *Journal of Geology* Volume 48, pp. 785–844, 1940.

"Strength of the Earth," *American Association of Petroleum Geologists Bulletin* Volume 29, pp. 1630–1653, 1945.

"Entrapment of Petroleum Under Hydrodynamic Conditions," *American Association of Petroleum Geologists Bulletin* Volume 37, pp. 1954–2026, 1953.

(With David G. Willis) "Mechanics of Hydraulic Fracturing," *American Institute of Mining and Metallurgical Engineers Transactions* Volume 210, pp. 153–166, 1956.

(With William W. Rubey) "Mechanics of Fluid-Filled Porous Solids and Its Application to Overthrust Faulting," *Geological Society of America Bulletin*, Volume 70, pp. 115–166, 1959.

SOURCES:

Books

Doan, David, "Memorial to M. King Hubbert," *Geological Society of America Memorials,* Volume 24, Geological Society of America, 1994.

Other

Doan, David, interview with Joan Oleck conducted September 3, 1993.

—Sketch by Joan Oleck

Edwin Hubble
1889-1953
American astronomer

Edwin Hubble was an American astronomer whose impact on science has been compared to pioneering scientists such as the English physicist Isaac Newton and the Italian astronomer Galileo. Hubble helped to change our perception of the universe in two very important ways. In an era when the Milky Way was perceived as the extent of the entire universe, Hubble confirmed the existence of other galaxies through his observations from the

Edwin Hubble

Mount Wilson Observatory in Pasadena, California. Furthermore, with the help of other astronomers of his time, Hubble showed that this newly discovered universe was expanding and developed a mathematical concept to quantify this expansion now known as Hubble's law.

Edwin Powell Hubble was born on November 20, 1889 in Marshfield, Missouri to John P. Hubble, an agent in a fire insurance firm, and Virginia Lee James Hubble, a descendant of the American colonist Miles Standish. The third of seven children, Hubble spent his early childhood in Missouri, entering grade school in 1895. In 1898, John Hubble transferred to the Chicago office of his firm, and the Hubble family moved first to Evanston and then to Wheaton, both Chicago suburbs.

Hubble attended Wheaton High School, excelling in both sports and academics. He graduated in 1906 at the age of sixteen, two years earlier than most students. For his efforts, he received an academic scholarship to the University of Chicago, where he studied mathematics, physics, chemistry, and astronomy. In the summer, Hubble tutored and worked to earn money for his college expenses. In his junior year he received a scholarship in physics, and by his senior year he was working as a laboratory assistant to physicist **Robert A. Millikan**. Hubble graduated in 1910 with a B.S. in mathematics and astronomy. In addition to his academic career, the six foot, two inch Hubble was an amateur heavyweight boxer. According to one unconfirmed story, sports promoters urged him to become a professional boxer and fight against heavyweight champion Jack Johnson, an offer Hubble declined.

In 1910, Hubble was awarded a Rhodes Scholarship, following which he went to attend Queen's College at the University of Oxford in England. There he studied jurisprudence, completing the two-year course in 1912. He began working on a bachelor's degree in law during his third year, but renounced it for Spanish instead. He also continued his athletic endeavors, excelling in the high jump, broad jump, shot put and running. In 1913, Hubble returned to the United States and began practicing law in Louisville, Kentucky, where his family was now living. Bored with his law career within a year, Hubble returned to the University of Chicago in 1914 to work towards his doctorate in astronomy.

The Turn to Astronomy

At the time Hubble attended the University of Chicago, Yerkes was a waning institution that did not actually offer formal courses in astronomy. However, working under the supervision of Edwin B. Frost, the observatory's director, Hubble made regular observations on Yerkes' telescope and studied on his own. It is believed that Hubble's work at this time was influenced by a lecture he attended at Northwestern University. At the presentation, Lowell Observatory astronomer, **Vesto M. Slipher** presented evidence that spiral nebulae (in that era, the term nebulae was used to describe anything not obviously identifiable as a star) had high radial velocities—the velocities with which objects appear to be moving toward or away from us in the direct line of sight. Slipher found spiral nebulae that were moving at much higher velocities than stars generally moved—evidence that the nebulae might not be part of the Milky Way.

During his term at Yerkes, Hubble also met astronomer **George Ellery Hale**, founder of the Yerkes Observatory and then the director of the Mount Wilson Observatory in Pasadena, California. Hale had heard of Hubble, and in 1916 invited him to join the Mount Wilson Staff once he received his doctorate. However, Hubble's acceptance of this offer was delayed by World War I, which he joined in 1917. Hubble attained the rank of major, and after his discharge in 1919, he finally began work at Mount Wilson. The observatory had two telescopes, a 60-inch reflector and a newly operational 100-inch telescope, the largest in the world at that time. It was here that Hubble began the major portion of his life's work.

Discoveries at Mount Wilson

Hubble's first notable achievement at Mount Wilson was the confirmation of the existence of galaxies outside the Milky Way. From observations made in October 1923, Hubble was able to identify a type of variable star known as a Cepheid in the Andromeda nebula (known today as the Andromeda galaxy). By using information about the relationship between brightness, luminosity (how much light a star radiates), and the distances of Cepheid stars in our galaxy, Hubble was able to estimate the distance to the Cepheid in the Andromeda nebula to be about one million light years. Hubble also discovered other Cepheids, as well as other objects, and calculated the distances to them. Since scientists knew that the maximum diameter of the Milky Way was only 100,000 light years, Hubble's figures established the existence of galaxies outside our own. Eventually, he determined the distances to nine galaxies. Consistent with scientific terminology of his time, Hubble called these "extragalactic nebulae." The results of Hubble's work were publicly announced at the December 1924 meeting of the American Astronomical Society, settling one of the great scientific debates of that era.

Also in 1924, Hubble married Grace Burke Leib. His personal interests included dry-fly fishing (his favorite fishing haunts were in the Rocky Mountains and in England) and collecting antique books about the history of science. He served as a member of the Board of Trustees of the Huntington Library in San Marino, California from 1938 until he died in 1953.

Hubble's work at Mount Wilson was interrupted during World War II, when he served as chief of exterior ballistics and director of the supersonic wind tunnel at the Ballistics Research Laboratory at Aberdeen Proving Ground in Maryland. He worked at Aberdeen from 1942 to 1946 and received a Medal of Merit for his efforts.

Returning to Mount Wilson after the war, Hubble continued his observations of galaxies. In 1925 he introduced a system for classifying them at a meeting of the International Astronomical Union; according to this system, galaxies were either "regular" or "irregular." In addition, regular galaxies were either spiral or elliptical, and each of these classes could be further subdivided. The system used to classify galaxies today is still based on Hubble's structure.

In 1927 Hubble was elected a member of the National Academy of Sciences, but another great achievement was yet to come. By combining his own work on the distances of galaxies with the work of American astronomers Vesto M. Slipher and **Milton L. Humason**, Hubble proposed a relationship between the high radial velocities of galaxies and distance. He systematically looked at a number of galaxies and found that except for a few nearby, all of the others were moving away from us at high speed. He discovered a correlation between this velocity and distance, and the result was a mathematical concept now known as Hubble's law. Simply put, Hubble's law states that the more distant a galaxy is from us, the faster it's moving away from us. Although Hubble didn't actually discover that the universe is expanding, he put the theory together in a coherent way. Today, the expanding universe is part of the big-bang theory of the creation of the universe.

Besides his pioneering work in astronomy, Hubble helped develop the Mount Palomar Observatory in California, as well as the Hale 200-inch telescope. Hubble has been described as an accomplished speaker; in fact, many of his lectures, including several honorary lecture series at Yale and Oxford universities, were published as books, such as *The Realm of the Nebulae.* For his contributions to astronomy, Hubble received many awards, including that of honorary fellow of Queen's College, Oxford. The Hubble Space Telescope, launched by NASA in 1990, is named after him. Hubble's final contribution to astronomy was a photographic guide to the classification of galaxies, which he was in the process of working on when he died. *The Hubble Atlas of Galaxies* was finished by **Allan R. Sandage**, who had worked with him. Hubble suffered from heart disease in the last years of his life, but continued to work at Mount Wilson and Palomar. He died of a cerebral thrombosis (a type of stroke) on September 28, 1953.

SELECTED WRITINGS BY HUBBLE:

Books

Red Shifts in the Spectra of Nebulae, Oxford University Press, 1934.

The Realm of Nebulae, Oxford University Press, 1936.

The Observational Approach to Cosmology, Oxford University Press, 1937.

Periodicals

"Explorations in Space: The Cosmological Program for the Palomar Telescopes," *Proceedings of the American Philosophical Society,* Volume 95, 1951, pp. 461–70.

"The Law of Red-Shifts," *Monthly Notices of the Royal Astronomical Society,* Volume 113, 1953, pp. 658–66.

SOURCES:

Books

Biographical Memoirs, The National Academy of Sciences, Columbia University Press, 1970, pp. 175–214.

Dictionary of Scientific Biography, Scribner, 1972, pp. 528–33.

Hawking, Stephen W., *A Brief History of Time* Bantam, 1988.

Periodicals

"A Man Named Hubble," *U.S. News & World Report,* March 26, 1990, p. 61.

Osterbrock, Donald E., Ronald S. Brashear, and Joel A. Gwinn, "Edwin Hubble and the Expanding Universe," *Scientific American,* July 1993, p. 84.

Osterbrock, Brashear, and Gwinn, "Self-Made Cosmologist: The Education of Edwin Hubble," in *Evolution of the Universe of Galaxies: Edwin Hubble Centennial Symposium,* Astronomical Society of the Pacific, 1990, pp. 1–18.

Smith, Robert W., "Edwin P. Hubble and the Transformation of Cosmology," *Physics Today,* April 1990, p. 52.

—Sketch by Devera Pine

David H. Hubel
1926-
Canadian-born American neurobiologist

David H. Hubel (pronounced hyü-ble) is a neurobiologist whose research into the relationships between the eye and the brain began at the Walter Reed Army Institute of Research. He later joined the research team at Johns Hopkins led by Stephen Kuffler, a neurophysiologist of vision. In Kuffler's laboratory, Hubel worked with **Torsten Wiesel**; their teamwork lasted over twenty years and led in 1981 to their sharing the Nobel Prize in physiology or medicine. The prize was awarded to them because they had discovered what role neurons played in the visual system and how the arrangement of cells operated in the visual process.

Born February 27, 1926, in Windsor, Ontario, of American parents, Elsie M. Hunter Hubel and Jesse H. Hubel, David Hunter Hubel grew up in Montreal. From his father, who was a chemical engineer, Hubel developed an interest in science, especially chemistry and electronics. In one particularly memorable childhood chemistry experiment, Hubel told an *Omni* magazine interviewer, he investigated the "percussive properties" of potassium chlorate and sugar by setting off a small brass cannon in the street outside his home. The local police quickly discouraged further experiments in that line. Hubel displayed musical as well as scientific talent during childhood, and playing flute duets remains one of his favorite forms of enjoyment.

From 1932 to 1944, Hubel attended the Strathcona Academy in Outremont, Ontario. He began his college studies at McGill University in 1944. Although he received his B.S. with honors in mathematics and physics, he decided to enter McGill University Medical School in 1947—a decision which he appears to have made almost on the spur of the moment, since he had not taken any college course in biology. He also worked summers at the Montreal Neurological Institute, where he began his studies of the nervous system. He received his medical degree in 1951 and spent the next four years studying clinical neurology, first at the Montreal Neurological Institute and then at Johns Hopkins University in Baltimore, Maryland.

Encouraged to Pursue Independent Research

In 1955, Hubel was drafted into the United States Army, which sent him to the Neurophysiology Division of the Walter Reed Army Institute of Research in Washington, D.C. At Walter Reed, Hubel discovered a stimulating group of physiologists who encouraged him to do original research for the first time in his life. Determined to study sleep, he developed a device, known as a tungsten microelectrode, to record the electrical impulses of nerve cells. He used this device on cats to measure the activity of nerve cells in sleep. He described these experiments in his *Omni* interview: "I had concocted one electrode strong enough to penetrate the membranes over the cortex. It was a stiff tungsten wire a little thicker than a hair. It was so sharp that it went in without doing any damage, so far as we knew. It was attached to a bunch of amplifiers and finally to loudspeakers. When a cell fired, you heard it as a brief pop or click. If it fired fast, it sounded like a machine gun."

During his research on sleep, Hubel became more interested in the reactions of his subjects to the firing responses recorded by the microelectrodes during waking states. He had placed the microelectrodes in the visual cortex area of the brain for his sleep experiments, and he began to realize that it was possible to understand how the brain operates in the visual process. In reading the work of other scientists on this subject, Hubel discovered the research papers of Stephen Kuffler, who was then a leading figure in the neurophysiology of vision. In the *Omni* interview, Hubel credits Kuffler with being "the first person to study optic nerve fibers in a mammal to find the important things that they were doing that the rods and cones in the retina don't do."

Joins Kuffler and Meets Wiesel

After his army service ended in 1958, Hubel went to Johns Hopkins University where he did further research on the surface of the brain, the gray matter of the cerebral cortex, in the laboratory of Vernon Mountcastle. But shortly afterwards he moved to the Wilmer Institute, also at Johns Hopkins, and joined Stephen Kuffler's research team. There he met Torsten Wiesel, and under the direction of Kuffler the two of them began to make discoveries about the relationship of the retina to the visual cortex as part of the general physiology of the brain.

In 1959, Hubel and Wiesel, along with the rest of Kuffler's research team, followed Kuffler to the Harvard Medical School in Boston. By 1964, Harvard had formed a new department of neurobiology, naming Kuffler as its chairman. Hubel became chairman of this department in 1967, and in 1968 he was named the George Packer Berry Professor of Physiology.

Pursues Research on the Relationship Between the Eye and the Brain

Much of the work done by Hubel and Wiesel, using microelectrodes and electronic equipment, centered around a section of the visual cortex in the brain known as area 17. The cells in this section of the visual cortex form several thin layers that are arranged in columns running through the cortex. Hubel and Weisel discovered that certain cells of area 17 in the brain respond to the stimulation of specific retinal cells in the eye. In particular, they found that cells in the cortex are specialized to respond to different types of stimulation. There are types of cortical cells that respond to light spots and others that respond specifically to the different angles of a tilted line. They discovered that some respond only to definite directions of movement, while others respond only to definite colors.

Hubel and Wiesel's research has made the visual cortex the most mapped-out section of the brain, and it has deepened the scientific understanding of how the visual system works. In addition, their work has led to practical ophthalmological applications for the treatment of congenital cataracts, as well as a condition occurring in childhood known as strabismus, where one eye is unable to focus with the other because of a muscle imbalance. Hubel and Wiesel discovered that at birth the visual cortex begins to develop its structures from the stimulation of the newborn's retina. The development of the brain is shaped by the activity of the eye, and the sooner childhood eye disorders are corrected, therefore, the better the chances of avoiding serious visual impairments in the future. Before their research, the customary medical practice had been to delay operating on these conditions, but today doctors recognize the importance of the early removal of cataracts and the prompt treatment of strabismus.

For their work on how the retinal image is read and interpreted by the cells of the visual cortex, Hubel and Wiesel shared the first half of the 1981 Nobel Prize for physiology or medicine. For his work on split-brain physiology, **Roger W. Sperry** won the second half.

Hubel has been married to Shirley Ruth Izzard Hubel since 1953, and they have three sons.

SELECTED WRITINGS BY HUBEL:

Books

Eye, Brain, and Vision, Scientific American Library, 1988.

Periodicals

(With T.N. Wiesel) "Receptive Fields of Single Neurones in the Cat's Striate Cortex," *Journal of Physiology,* Volume 148, 1959, pp. 574–591.

(With T.N. Wiesel) "Receptive Fields, Binocular Interaction and Functional Architecture in the Cat's Visual Cortex," *Journal of Physiology,* Volume 160, 1962, pp. 106–154.

(With T.N. Wiesel) "Brain Mechanism of Vision," *Scientific American,* September, 1979.

"Exploration of the Primary Visual Cortex," *Nature,* Volume 299, 1982, pp. 515–524.

SOURCES:

Books

Nobel Prize Winners, H. W. Wilson, 1987, pp. 484–486.

Periodicals

Harvard Magazine, November, 1984.

Science, October 30, 1981, pp. 518–520.

Stewart, Doug, "Interview: David Hubel," *Omni,* February, 1990, pp. 74–110.

—Sketch by Jordan P. Richman

Robert Huber
1937-
German biochemist

The study of photosynthesis—the ability of plants, algae, and bacteria to translate sunlight into energy to build various chemical compounds—has long intrigued scientists, yet it is only since the 1950s that this process has begun to be understood in any detail. The analytic work of Robert Huber has played a significant role in the development of this understanding, and his most important achievement was matching the structure of a photosynthesizing protein complex to its function. Huber's work in X-ray diffraction enabled him and a co-worker to map the atomic structure of a bacterial photosynthetic reaction center—the basic unit or heart of the photosynthetic process. Such a description has helped advance not only photosynthesis research, but also various medical investigations. For his work in "unraveling the full details of how [such a] protein is built up, revealing the structure of the molecule atom by atom," the Nobel committee awarded Huber and two other German co-researchers the 1988 Nobel Prize in chemistry.

Robert Huber was born on February 20, 1937 in Munich, Germany to Sebastian and Helen Kebinger Huber. His father was a bank clerk and the family had a hard time during World War II and the years following. In 1947 Huber entered the Humanistisches Karls-Gymnasium in Munich, a school with an emphasis on humanistic studies. In an autobiographical piece for *Les Prix Nobel,* Huber remembers the teaching of Latin and Greek as being "intense," but it was here he developed an interest in chemistry. Few chemistry classes were available, so he taught himself "by reading all the textbooks I could get." In 1956 he graduated from the gymnasium and entered the Technische Hochschule of Munich—later renamed the Technical University—to study chemistry. He graduated in 1960, and he married Christa Essig that same year. Various stipends and grants helped Huber and his growing family—they would have four children—through the years he spent as a graduate student in the crystallography laboratory of W. Hoppe.

Develops X-ray Crystallography Techniques

As a graduate student, Huber worked with a number of prominent chemists, including Walter Hieber in the field of inorganic chemistry, **Ernst Fischer** who studied organometallic chemistry, and F. Weygand in organic chemistry. But it was crystallography that won Huber's interest. Though his thesis work for his 1963 doctorate was done on the crystal structure of a diazo compound, it was crystallographic studies on the insect metamorphosis hormone ecdysone that set him on the path of X-ray crystallography. Working with Hoppeat both the Technical University and at the Physiological-Chemical Institute of the University of Munich, Huber was able to determine the molecular weight and steroid nature of ecdysone. He employed X-ray diffraction techniques (where an X-ray beam is shot at a crystallized substance) to determine the atomic structure of ecdysone by analyzing how the beam was dispersed by the crystal. Huber was so impressed by the results he attained that he decided to concentrate on crystallographic research.

After determining the structure of several organic compounds and developing some improvements in existing X-ray crystallography methods, in 1967 Huber and H. Formanek set out to elucidate the structure of erythrocruorin, an insect protein. Their results showed a marked similarity between erythrocruorin and mammalian proteins. Their work also suggested for the first time that there might be a universal globin fold—the globin fold being the manner in which the chain of amino acids constituting the protein folds upon itself, endowing the protein with a shape specific to its function. In 1968, Huber became a lecturer at the Technical University, and three years later he accepted a position as a director at the prestigious Max Planck Institute for Biochemistry at Martinsried near Munich. He maintained his affiliation with the Technical University as well, becoming a full professor there in 1976.

Throughout the 1970s, Huber and his co-workers refined and perfected the techniques of X-ray crystallography, elucidating the structures of various proteins in collaboration with both foreign and domestic laboratories. His work in enzyme inhibitors and immunoglobulins has been of particular interest to researchers developing technologies for drug and protein design. Huber's laboratory at Martinsried became internationally recognized for the high quality of its work, and for Huber's delight in undertaking projects others thought impossible.

Wins Nobel Prize for Work on Photosynthesis

In 1982 a fellow researcher at Martinsried named **Hartmut Michel** came to Huber with a monumental task: to elucidate the atomic structure of the protein complex that powers photosynthesis in the purple bacteria, *Rhodopseudomonas viridis.* Michel had managed to isolate and crystallize a protein complex known as a membrane-bound protein, which is situated on the outer membrane of the bacterium. These proteins, made up of a tangle of four protein subunits and molecules of chlorophyll, help transport energy across the walls of cells. Yet they had been extremely difficult to isolate, because of their intermediary position on the membrane wall. Many believed these proteins were impossible to isolate, but by 1982 Michel had grown crystals of this protein complex, which functions as a photosynthesis reaction center. The reaction center is the place where electrons—released by a photon-excited chlorophyll molecule—create an electrical charge difference that produces the energy to power the synthesis of chemical compounds such as sugar, carbohydrates, and other nutrients.

Huber agreed to take on the task of developing a structural analysis of the proteins Michel had crystallized. Working with German biochemist **Johann Deisenhofer** at Martinsried and several other biochemists, his team used their improved X-ray crystallographic techniques to determine the exact atomic structure of the reaction center. By 1985 they had mapped over 10,000 separate atoms, and their structural analysis confirmed predictions as to the path that electrons follow in the reaction center. Though there are significant differences in the process of photosynthesis in green plants and in bacteria, the three-dimensional atomic model that Deisenhofer and Huber developed has proved to be of immense importance in further photosynthesis research in general. It has also been vital in research into the part that membrane-bound proteins may play in diseases such as cancer and diabetes. The work of the three main researchers in this project—Huber, Michel and Deisenhofer—was recognized by a joint award of the Nobel Prize for chemistry in 1988.

Huber has also been instrumental in developing computer models, such as FILME, PROTEIN, FRODO, and MADNESS to help in determining atomic structures through X-ray crystallography. Besides the Nobel Prize, Huber's work has been recognized by the E. K. Frey Medal from the German Society for Surgery in 1972, and the Otto Warburg Medal from the German Society for Biological Chemistry in 1977. He has received the Emil von Behring Medal from the University of Marburg in 1982, and the Keilin Medal from the London Biochemical Society and the Richard Kuhn Medal from the Society of German Chemists, both in 1987, as well as the Sir Hans Krebs Medal in 1992. He has also received numerous honorary doctorates and memberships in foreign chemical and biochemical societies.

SELECTED WRITINGS BY HUBER:

Periodicals

(With J. Deisenhofer, O. Epp, K. Miki, and H. Michel) "X-ray Structure of a Membrane Protein Complex," *Journal of Molecular Biology,* Volume 180, 1984, pp. 385–98.

(With Deisenhofer, Epp, Miki, and Michel) "Structure of the Protein Subunits in the Photosynthetic Reaction Center of *Rhodopseudomonas viridis* at 3 Angstrom Resolution," *Nature,* Volume 318, 1985, pp. 618–24.

"Structural Basis for Antigen-Antibody Recognition," *Science,* Volume 233, 1986, pp. 702–03.

SOURCES:

Books

Les Prix Nobel 1988, Almqvist & Wiksell, 1988, pp. 183–231.

Nobel Prize Winners Supplement 1987–1991, H. W. Wilson, 1992, pp. 91–93.

Periodicals

Hall, Nina, and MacKenzie, Debora, "A Whiff of Cordite over Chemistry Prize," *New Scientist,* October 29, 1988, pp. 31–32.

Horgan, John, "Chemistry: Germans Win for Illuminating an Engine of Photosynthesis," *Scientific American,* December, 1988, p. 33.

Levi, Barbara Goss, "Nobel Chemists Shed Light on Key Structure in Photosynthesis," *Physics Today,* February, 1989, pp. 17–18.

Lewin, Roger, "Membrane Protein Holds Photosynthesis Secrets," *Science,* November 4, 1988, pp. 672–73.

Lindley, David, and Maxine Clarke, "1988 Nobel Prizes Announced for Physics and for Chemistry," *Nature,* Volume 335, October 27, 1988, pp. 752–53.

—Sketch by J. Sydney Jones

Charles B. Huggins
1901-
Canadian American surgeon

Charles B. Huggins was awarded the Nobel Prize for physiology or medicine in 1966 for his discovery in the 1930s of the role played by hormones in the onset and growth of prostate and breast cancer. This breakthrough led Huggins to make a number of important medical advances, including the subsequent development of hormone therapy, the first non-radioactive, non-toxic chemical treatment for cancer. In other studies, Huggins found that cancer cells are not necessarily self-reliant and self-perpetuating and that some cancers actually depend on normal hormone levels to develop and grow. He then developed a blood test to measure two particular enzymes to determine the extent of the cancer and the effect of hormone therapy. In addition, Huggins discovered the compensatory action of adrenal glands after hormone therapy and performed the first surgical removal of the adrenal glands to combat cancer regrowth. He also developed cortisone replacement therapy to compensate for the loss of normal adrenal gland function.

Charles Brenton Huggins, the oldest of two sons, was born on September 22, 1901, in Halifax, Nova Scotia, to pharmacist Charles Edward and Bessie Marie (Spencer) Huggins. He earned his B.A. from Acadia University, Wolfville, Nova Scotia, in 1920, graduating in a class of twenty-five students. That same year, he moved to the United States to attend Harvard Medical School, graduating in four years with both an M.A. and M.D. He did his internship at the University of Michigan Hospital and was appointed instructor in surgery at the University's Medical School in 1926. The following year he became instructor of surgery on the original faculty of the University of Chicago Medical School, and in that same year, he married Margaret Wellman. The couple had a son, Charles Edward, and daughter, Emily Wellman. Huggins was promoted to assistant professor in 1929, then to associate professor in 1933, the year he became an American citizen, and he attained the rank of full professor of surgery in 1936. In 1946, he spent a brief period with the Johns Hopkins University as professor of urological surgery and director of the department of urology. He was director of the University of Chicago's Ben May Laboratory for Cancer Research from 1951 to 1969 and continued his research at the university until 1972, when he returned to Acadia University to become chancellor. He retired from the post in 1979 and moved to Chicago.

Research on Urinary Tract Leads to Prostate Studies

Huggins' initial specialty was urology, but his interest in cancer was actually sparked in 1930, when he met German Nobel Prize-winning cancer researcher **Otto Warburg**. Upon his return to the University of Chicago in the early 1930s, Huggins and his colleagues experimented with changing normal connective tissue elements into bone, using cells from the male urinary tract and bladder. His interest soon turned to the male urogenital system, particularly the role played by chemicals and hormones in the prostate gland, the male accessory reproductive gland located at the base of the urethra. He and his colleagues developed what Paul Talalay and Guy Williams-Ashman in *Science* called "an ingenious surgical procedure . . . [which] isolated the prostate gland of dogs from the urinary tract." This procedure, introduced in 1939, allowed the analysis and measurement of secretions of the gland which form much of the ejaculatory fluid. The research was at times frustrated by the formation of prostate tumors in some of the dogs, the only animal other than man known to develop cancer of the prostate. Higgins, however, saw the the obstacle as an opportunity. He turned his energy to studying the development and growth of prostate cancer, a painful and often fatal disease prevalent in men over the age of fifty that causes obstruction of the urinary tract and, if left untreated, metastasizes (spreads) to the bone and liver.

Huggins discovered high levels of testosterone, a male sex hormone, in secretions from a cancerous prostate. He also discovered that reducing male hormone secretions by either orchiectomy (castration) or estrogen (a female hormone) therapy, or both, drastically reduced testosterone levels and inhibited the growth of advanced metastatic prostate cancer. In his first human trials, four out of twenty-one patients treated with this method survived for twelve years. He also developed a blood test to measure acid phosphatase, which is secreted by the prostate, and alkaline phosphatase, which is secreted by bone-forming cells in bone tissue, both of which showed increased levels in patients with metastasized prostate cancer. Using these measurements, he could determine the extent of the cancer and the effect of the hormone treatments.

Huggins found that although the level of androgens (male sex hormones) dropped drastically after orchiectomy, in some cases they rose again, often to a level higher than before the surgery. Investigations led him to believe that the adrenal glands were producing androgens of their own, apparently compensating for the lowered levels induced by the hormone therapy. These androgens, too, encouraged the growth of the cancer. In 1944, he performed the first bilateral adrenalectomy, (removal of the two adrenal glands located above the kidneys), producing some positive results, even before cortisone was readily available for replacement therapy. In 1953, Huggins reported that, when used in combination, adrenalectomy and cortisone replacement had a beneficial effect on fifty percent of patients suffering from either prostate or breast cancer, but had no effect on other types of cancer. This was a radical treatment, however, and used only as a last resort.

Focuses on Breast Cancer

In the 1950s, Huggins left the clinical environment to return to the laboratory. While delivering the tenth Macewen Memorial Lecture at the University of Glasgow in 1958 he referred to breast cancer as "one of the noblest of the problems of medicine." In his lecture, entitled *Frontiers of Mammary Cancer,* he said, "Cancer of the breast in the United States has the highest prevalence rate of any form of neoplastic disease in either sex . . . Commonly, the disease advances with dreadful speed and ferocity." Huggins and two students, D. M. Bergenstal and Thomas Dao, developed a treatment for cancer that entailed removal of both ovaries and both adrenal glands. Combined with cortisone replacement therapy, the treatment brought about improvement in thirty to forty percent of the patients with advanced breast cancer, sometimes with quite definite and prolonged improvement.

Breast cancer research was being hampered, however, because of the long delay between stimulation and growth of artificially-induced mammary tumors in animals. In 1956, Huggins discovered that a single dose of 7,12-dimethylbens(a)anthracene (DMBA) would quickly induce mammary tumors in certain types of female rats and that many of these tumors were, like some in humans, hormone dependent and responded to regulation of the hormonal environment. Huggins' rat tumors soon became the focus of experiments in laboratories all over the world.

In the mid-1960s, a major scientific controversy developed around whether birth control pills encourage cancer of the breast and other reproductive organs. Huggins, who by that time had spent more than thirty years researching the relationship between hormones and cancer, studied data collected from thousands of women taking birth control pills. He believed that "the pill" did not encourage such cancers in women. Some specialists later came to believe some evidence indicating that the pill may even discourage the growth of some types of cancer.

For his research on hormones and cancer, Huggins shared the 1966 Nobel Prize with **Peyton Rous**, who was honored for his work fifty-five years earlier on viral causes of cancer. Only one person previously had been awarded the Nobel for cancer research—**Johannes Fibiger** in 1926 for developing a method of growing artificial tumors. Colleagues agreed that both Huggins and Rous should have received the award many years earlier. In addition to the Nobel Prize, Huggins was awarded one of the highest honors to be bestowed by American medicine, the Lasker Clinical Research Award, in 1963. He was also the first recipient of the Charles L. Mayer Award in cancer research from the National Academy of Sciences in 1943. Huggins also was awarded two gold medals for research from the American Medical Association, the Order of Merit from Germany, and the Order of the Sun from Peru. He was made honorary fellow of the Royal College of Surgeons in both Edinburgh and London, and is the recipient of numerous honorary degrees.

A devoted family man, a lover of the music of Bach and Mozart, and a self-admitted workaholic, Huggins is said to have a wry wit. He lives with his wife in Chicago.

SELECTED WRITINGS BY HUGGINS:

Books

Frontiers of Mammary Cancer, Jackson, 1961.

The Scientific Contributions of the Ben May Laboratory for Cancer Research, University of Chicago, 1961.

Experimental Leukemia and Mammary Cancer: Induction, Prevention, Cure, University of Chicago Press, 1979.

SOURCES:

Books

Current Biography, H.W. Wilson, 1965, pp. 205–208.

Nobel Prize Winners: An H. W. Wilson Biographical Dictionary, H. W. Wilson, 1987, pp. 486–488.

The Nobel Prize Winners—Physiology or Medicine, Salem Press, 1991, pp. 967–972.

Periodicals

New York Times, October 16, 1966.

Talalay, Paul, and Guy Williams-Ashman, "1966 Nobel Laureates in Medicine or Physiology," *Science,* October 21, 1966, pp. 362–364.

—Sketch by David Petechuk

Russell A. Hulse
1950-
American astrophysicist

In 1974 two astrophysicists, **Joseph H. Taylor, Jr.** and his graduate student Russell A. Hulse, using the three-hundred-meter-diameter radio telescope at Arecibo, Puerto Rico, discovered a double star system (two stars orbiting around a common axis), known as a binary pulsar. Unlike others, this pulsar was in a binary system in which one component releases rapid pulses of radio energy. Pulsars, which are rarely more than thirteen kilometers wide yet are as massive as the sun, are extremely dense stars composed mostly of neutrons rather than whole atoms. Their gravitational pull is so enormous that a person standing on the surface would weigh several hundred billion pounds.

Russell A. Hulse

Ever since **Albert Einstein** published his revolutionary general theory of relativity in 1915, scientists have sought to verify Einstein's theoretical postulate through various astronomical observations. When Taylor and Hulse measured variations in their pulsar's "pulse rate," about six one-hundredths of a second between pulses, the only way these variations could be explained was in terms of a Doppler shift due to the pulse rate's orbital motion of an unseen companion star. Detailed timing measurements of these pulses over twenty years helped confirm Einstein's relativity theory. For their discovery Taylor and Hulse were awarded the Nobel Prize in physics in 1993.

Russell Alan Hulse was born on November 28, 1950, in New York City. His parents, Alan Hulse and the former Betty Joan Wedemeyer, encouraged his interest and understanding of the world around him. As a boy, Hulse enjoyed working with chemistry and mechanical engineering construction sets as well as biology dissection kits. He also delved into butterfly collecting and electronics. As he recalled in a biographical note written for the Nobel Foundation, his intense interest in science created some problems with his early teachers, who had a hard time dealing with his fascination with the sciences. In 1963 he was admitted to the prestigious Bronx High School of Science, a facility devoted to the encouragement of scientific values. While in high school, Hulse enjoyed summers spent at his parents' retreat in the Catskill mountains, where he experimented with various electronic gadgets salvaged from old television parts and surplus military equipment. One summer he constructed his own radio telescope.

Following graduation in 1966, he was admitted to Cooper Union. He received his bachelor's degree in physics in 1970 and started graduate school at the University of Massachusetts at Amherst the same year. "When I was approached by Joe Taylor . . . to see if I was interested in doing a pulsar search for my thesis, it did not take too long for me to agree," he remembered in his Nobel acceptance lecture. "Such a project combined physics, radio astronomy, and computers—a perfect combination of three different subjects all of which I found particularly interesting."

Intermittently from December 1973 until January 1975, Hulse used the Arecibo telescope, the world's largest single-element radio telescope, to search the skies for the weak radio signals emitted by pulsars. With a detailed computer program of his own design, he was able to detect some fifty pulsars, forty of which had never been identified. When analyzing data from a pulsar first detected on July 2, 1974, he noticed an unexpected variation in the pulsar's period. "My reaction, of course, was not 'Eureka—it's a discovery' but instead a rather annoyed "Nuts—what's wrong now?" he recalled in his Nobel lecture. After days of checking and reviewing data, Hulse realized that he had discovered a binary pulsar.

In 1975 Hulse received his Ph.D. in physics and accepted a post-doctoral appointment at the National Astronomy Observatory in Charlottesville, Virginia, where he continued his work in radio astronomy. Although he enjoyed the challenge of astronomy, he had serious concerns about "the lack of long-term career prospects in astronomy," as he noted in his Nobel biography. Thus in 1977, when he noticed an advertisement in *Physics Today* for a physicist working with controlled fusion at the Princeton University Plasma Physics Laboratory (PPPL), he applied for the job. For more than a decade, Hulse has conducted research on hydrogen fusion at PPPL. In 1994 he was involved in computer modeling of impurity ions and electron transport in the high-temperature plasmas of the controlled thermonuclear fusion devices, as well as working on advanced computer software. Hulse is a member of the American Physical Society and the American Astronomical Society.

SELECTED WRITINGS BY HULSE:

Periodicals

(With Joseph H. Taylor) "A Deep Sample of New Pulsars and Their Spatial Extent in the Galaxy," *Astrophysical Journal Letters,* July 15, 1974.

(With Joseph H. Taylor) "Discovery of a Pulsar in a Binary System," *Astro-physical Journal Letters,* October 15, 1975.

Other

"The Discovery of the Binary Pulsar" (lecture), Nobel Foundation, 1994.
"Russell Alan Hulse" (biographical sketch), Nobel Foundation, 1994.

SOURCES:

Periodicals

The New York Times, October 12, 1993, p. B9.

—*Sketch by Benedict A. Leerburger*

Milton L. Humason
1891-1972
American astronomer

Although he did not even have a high-school diploma, Milton L. Humason rose from the post of janitor at the Mount Wilson Observatory to become a self-taught astronomer, highly valued for the accuracy of his observations. He worked closely with **Edwin Hubble**, and it was his careful observations of distant galaxies which ultimately provided support for Hubble's theory that the universe was expanding.

Milton Lasell Humason was born on August 19, 1891, at Dodge Center, Minnesota. He was fourteen years old when his parents took him to a summer camp at Mount Wilson near Pasadena, California. He went home for only a few days at the end of the summer and managed to convince his parents to allow him to return to Mount Wilson for a year. He never went back to school, thus becoming, according to Nicholas U. Mayall in *Mercury,* "one of astronomy's most notable dropouts." Between the years 1908 and 1910, Humason was a mule driver for the packtrains delivering building materials to the Mount Wilson Observatory for telescope support facilities, cottages, and observer's quarters. In 1910, he became engaged to Helen Dowd, daughter of the electrical engineer for the observatory.

Humason was married in 1911, and he left the observatory for the next six years. In 1917, with the support of his father-in-law, he sought and received a job as an observatory janitor, hoping the position would yield an interesting future. He was promoted a year later to relief night assistant. During his work assisting astronomers Hugo Benioff and **Harlow Shapley**, Humason learned how to take photographic plates, a skill that would become a key to his later work. Both these astronomers recognized Humason's skill and recommended that he be appointed assistant astronomer. He was given this post and he held it until 1954, when he became astronomer at Mount Wilson and Palomar Observatories. He was appointed secretary of both observatories in 1948, undertaking administrative tasks in addition to research.

In his most important work, Humason collaborated with other astronomers in using spectra to study the stars—spreading out the light from the stars into bands of color with a prism or diffraction grating. In 1928, he launched a program of photographing the spectra of distant galaxies at the request of Edwin Hubble. Hubble earlier had established that the cloudy masses of distant stars known as nebulae were actually galaxies. He had theorized that the universe was expanding, and he and Humason used a spectral phenomenon known as "red shifts" to test this theory. The spectra of certain bright stars in these distant galaxies shifted toward the red or longer wavelengths of light; this shift was an instance of the Doppler effect (a change in frequency which occurs when the source of the waves and the observer are getting closer or farther apart) and it indicated not only that these stars were in motion but that they were moving away from Earth. Because the light from the stars had also taken so many years to reach Earth, red shifts could be used to measure the motion of stars over time. Hubble wanted Humason to help him test his theory by establishing that the most distant galaxies showed the largest red shifts.

Humason used the 100-inch telescope at Mount Wilson to photograph distant and extremely faint galaxies. Sometimes it took him ten nights or more to obtain a spectrum using the equipment then available. As **Allan R. Sandage**, a colleague of Humason's, noted in *Scientific American:* "The history of the red-shift program in those years is a story of extreme skill and patience at the telescope and of steady improvement in instrumentation." In 1951, after the completion of the 200-inch Hale telescope at Palomar Observatory, Humason resumed the red-shift studies. After Hubble's death in 1953, Humason asked Sandage to help continue the work. Humason published his results with Sandage and Mayall in a paper entitled "Redshifts and Magnitudes of Extragalactic Nebulae," which filled most of the *Astronomical Journal* in April of 1956. The paper gave the velocities of more than 800 galaxies, most of them measured by Humason. The farthest, faintest galaxies measured were moving faster in proportion to the closer galaxies, indicating that the universe a billion years ago was expanding more rapidly than it was now.

While gazing toward galaxies, Humason also studied faint blue stars and supernova, stars that explode and fade. He discovered Comet 1961e, which was noted for a number of unusual characteristics. He was awarded an honorary doctor of philosophy degree by the University of Lund in Sweden in 1950. He retired in 1957, his reputation that of a meticulous and skilled observer. As Mayall wrote in *Mercury:* "In retrospect, I cannot think of many of his peers who would have had the patience, determination, and selflessness that he maintained for thirty years." Humason died at his home near Mendocino, California, on June 18, 1972.

SELECTED WRITINGS BY HUMASON:

Periodicals

(With Allan R. Sandage, and Nicholas U. Mayall) "Redshifts and Magnitudes of Extragalactic Nebulae," *Astronomical Journal,* April, 1956.

SOURCES:

Books

The Biographical Dictionary of Scientists: Astronomers, edited by David Abbot, Peter Bedrick Books, 1984, pp. 80–81.

Overbye, Dennis, *Lonely Hearts of the Cosmos: The Scientific Quest for the Secret of the Universe,* HarperCollins, 1991.

Periodicals

Mayall, Nicholas U., "Milton L. Humason, Some Personal Recollections," *Mercury,* January-February, 1973, pp. 3–8.

"Observer of Galaxies," *Sky and Telescope,* August 1972, pp. 71, 87.

Sandage, Allan R., "The Red-Shift," *Scientific American,* September, 1956, pp. 170–182.

—Sketch by Julie Anderson

Jerome C. Hunsaker
1886-1984
American aeronautical engineer

Jerome C. Hunsaker was an internationally known pioneer in aeronautical research and engineering during the first half of the twentieth century. He made enormous contributions to the development of flight systems, including the establishment of the scientific and mathematical basis for flight and the creation of the aeronautical engineering program at the Massachusetts Institute of Technology (MIT). His interest in the field of aerodynamics fired the enthusiasm of more than a generation of later engineers involved in aviation research.

Early Life

Born on August 26, 1886, in Creston, Iowa, to Walter J. and Alma Clarke Hunsaker, Jerome Clarke Hunsaker was educated in the public schools of Detroit and Saginaw in Michigan, where his father published newspapers. A fine student and a good athlete, Hunsaker was admitted to the U.S. Naval Academy at Annapolis in 1904, and graduated at the head of his class in 1908. Even as a boy he had become enthralled with the exploits of the Wright Brothers, Samuel Pierpoint Langley, and other aviators, and while at the academy he researched questions related to the problems of flight.

Creates an Aeronautical Engineering Curriculum

When Hunsaker completed his schooling as a Midshipman and was commissioned, he obtained an appointment to MIT where he would later pursue graduate training and set up a technical program to study the development of aircraft as a naval weapon. While at MIT, Hunsaker obtained his M.S. in 1912 and was also awarded the institute's first doctorate in aeronautical engineering in 1916. It was also during these years that Hunsaker organized and taught the first American course in aeronautical engineering. Based on the success of this course, Hunsaker founded MIT's internationally known Department of Aeronautical Engineering which he headed between 1939 and 1952. Hunsaker realized the uniqueness of this program, and he once commented that "In the beginning it was not possible to teach the principles of aeronautical engineering because none of us knew them. The principles had to be discovered, which meant that we had to investigate the difficulties of the past, collect a lot of facts, and then, after finding the meaning of the facts, determine the engineering principles of flight." Among those Hunsaker taught during this period was **Donald W. Douglas**, another

Annapolis Midshipman who had been sent to MIT to study aeronautical engineering, and with whom Hunsaker worked to develop the first effective U.S. wind tunnel to study aerodynamics. Douglas went on, in 1920, to establish the Douglas Aircraft Corporation, a major supplier of aircraft and equipment to the navy.

Something of a Naval Career

Notwithstanding his contributions to research and education, Hunsaker's appointment to MIT was in fact a naval commission. In 1916, therefore, he was called to serve in Washington as head of the Aircraft Division of the Navy Bureau of Construction and Repair. During the war he had responsibility for the design, development, and manufacturing of all naval aircraft, including airplanes, seaplanes, and airships. By the end of the war, Hunsaker had overseen the construction of more than 1,000 flying boats. Hunsaker also encouraged Douglas's efforts through the 1920s. Douglas had formed his own aircraft manufacturing company in southern California, and as head of the Navy's aircraft production program, Hunsaker purchased ninety-six DT–1 torpedo bombers from him. This was the beginning of a long partnership between the Douglas Aircraft Company and the United States Navy. As head of the navy's production program, Hunsaker also helped develop lighter-than-air craft, and he sponsored the construction of numerous nonrigid airships for submarine patrol. He was largely responsible for the development of the *U.S.S. Shenandoah,* the Navy's first lighter-than-air vessel, a rigid airship that was intended for aerial observation and strategic bombardment. Hunsaker had become interested in airships during the first World War, where Germany used Zeppelin airships as an effective bombing force. Although Zeppelins made huge targets and the hydrogen that kept them aloft was highly flammable as it could be ignited with machine gun fire, their high cruising had ensured their safety from fighter attacks until the closing months of the war. The *Shenandoah,* contracted for in 1919 and delivered in the summer of 1923, would provide a similar capability for the U.S. Navy. Also, since it was inflated with helium, it would not ignite in the same way as hydrogen. Hunsaker was thrilled when the *Shenandoah* made its maiden flight on September 4, 1923, flying round trip between the Navy's lighter-than-air facility at Lakehurst, New Jersey, and St. Louis, Missouri, in less than two days. Unfortunately, the airship was lost in a tragic accident in Ohio on September 3, 1925, in which thirteen men died. For his services during the First World War, Hunsaker was awarded the Navy Cross. Included in his other honors were the Presidential Medal for Merit awarded to him after World War II and the Wright Brothers Memorial Trophy for his outstanding public service to aviation.

Back to MIT

In 1926, after attaining the rank of commander, Hunsaker resigned his naval commission, and for the next few years he worked with several private corporations, including Bell Telephone Laboratories and the Goodyear Zeppelin Company. In 1933, however, Hunsaker returned to MIT as head of the Department of Mechanical Engineering. He was also in charge of the aeronautical engineering program, and when the Department of Aeronautical Engineering was formed in 1939 he became its chair. In this capacity he helped to train more than two generations of aeronautical engineers. And although he retired in 1952, Hunsaker stayed at MIT as a lecturer until 1957 when he attained emeritus status.

Hunsaker died at the age of 98 on September 10, 1984, in Boston, Massachusetts. His wife, Alice P. Avery, had died in 1966, and he was survived by his son, Jerome C. Hunsaker, Jr., and two daughters, Sarah P. Swope and Alice M. Bird.

SELECTED WRITINGS BY HUNSAKER:

Books

Engineering Applications of Fluid Dynamics, with B.G. Rightmire, 1947.

Aeronautics at the Mid-Century, 1952.

SOURCES:

Books

Collier, Basil, *The Airship: A History,* Putnam, 1974.

Cunningham, Frank, *Sky Master: The Story of Donald Douglas and the Douglas Aircraft Company,* Dorrance, 1943.

Ingham, John N., *Biographical Dictionary of American Business Leaders,* Greenwood Press, 1983.

Rae, John B., *Climb to Greatness: The American Aircraft Industry, 1920–1960,* MIT Press, 1968.

Periodicals

Bassler, Robert E., "Jerome C. Hunsaker: The Early Days of Naval Aviation," *Shipmate,* March, 1983, pp. 20–22.

Tillman, Barrett, "Douglas Aircraft: Armorer of Naval Aviation," *Journal of the West,* January 30, 1991, pp. 58–68.

—*Sketch by Roger D. Launius*

G. Evelyn Hutchinson
1903-1991
English-born American ecologist

In a 1943 essay for the *American Scientist,* G. Evelyn Hutchinson wrote that "the most practical lasting benefit science can now offer is to teach man how to avoid destruction of his own environment." The Yale professor of ecology lived by his words, and at the time of his death in 1991 he had long been instrumental in the development of the science of ecology. Although he had no breakthrough discoveries to his name, Hutchinson's years of researching, teaching, and writing about the living world launched the careers of dozens of followers and earned him a reputation as one of the United States' foremost scientists.

Born January 30, 1903, in Cambridge, England, George Evelyn Hutchinson was the son of Arthur Hutchinson, a professor of mineralogy at Cambridge University, and Evaline Demeny Shipley Hutchinson, an ardent feminist. He demonstrated an early interest in flora and fauna and a basic understanding of the scientific method. In 1918, at the age of fifteen, he wrote a letter to the *Entomological Record and Journal of Variation* about a grasshopper he had seen swimming in a pond. He described an experiment he performed on the insect and included it for taxonomic identification.

In 1924, Hutchinson earned his bachelor's degree in zoology from Emmanuel College at Cambridge University, where he was a founding member of the Biological Tea Club. He then served as an international education fellow at the Stazione Zoologica in Naples from 1925 until 1926, when he was hired as a senior lecturer at the University of Witwatersrand in Johannesburg, South Africa. He was apparently fired from this position two years later by administrators who never imagined that in 1977 the university would honor the ecologist by establishing a research laboratory in his name.

Hutchinson earned his master's degree from Emmanuel College *in absentia* in 1928 and applied to Yale University for a fellowship so he could pursue a doctoral degree. He was instead appointed to the faculty as a zoology instructor. He was promoted to assistant professor in 1931 and became an associate professor in 1941, the year he obtained his United States citizenship. He was made a full professor of zoology in 1945, and between 1947 and 1965 he served as director of graduate studies in zoology. Hutchinson never did receive his doctoral degree, though he amassed an impressive collection of honorary degrees during his lifetime.

Hutchinson was best known for his interest in limnology, the science of freshwater lakes and ponds. He spent most of his life writing the four-volume *Treatise on Limnology,* which he completed just months before his death. The research that led to the first volume—covering geography, physics and chemistry—earned him a Guggenheim Fellowship in 1957. The second volume, published in 1967, covered biology and plankton. The third volume, on water plants, was published in 1975, and the fourth volume, about invertebrates, appeared posthumously in 1993.

Founds Hutchinson School of Ecology

The *Treatise on Limnology* was among the nine books, nearly 150 research papers, and many opinion columns which Hutchinson penned. He was an influential writer whose scientific papers inspired many students to specialize in ecology. Hutchinson's greatest contribution to the science of ecology was his broad approach, which became known as the "Hutchinson school." His work encompassed disciplines as varied as biochemistry, geology, zoology, and botany. He pioneered the concept of biogeochemistry, which examines the exchange of chemicals between organisms and the environment. His studies in biogeochemistry focused on how phosphates and nitrates move from the earth to plants, then animals, and then back to the earth in a continuous cycle. His holistic approach influenced later environmentalists when they began to consider the global scope of environmental problems.

In 1957, Hutchinson published an article entitled "Concluding Remarks," considered his most inspiring and intriguing work, as part of the Cold Spring Harbor Symposia on Quantitative Biology. Here, he introduced and described the ecological niche, a concept which was been the source of much research and debate ever since. The article was one of only three in the field of ecology chosen for the 1991 collection *Classics in Theoretical Biology.*

Hutchinson won numerous major awards for his work in ecology. In 1950, he was elected to the National Academy of Science. Five years later, he earned the Leidy Medal from the Philadelphia Academy of Natural Sciences. He was awarded the Naumann Medal from the International Association of Theoretical and Applied Limnology in 1959. This is a global award, granted only once every three years, which Hutchinson earned for his contributions to the study of lakes in the first volume of his treatise. In 1962, the Ecological Society of America chose him for its Eminent Ecologist Award.

Hutchinson's research often took him out of the country. In 1932, he joined a Yale expedition to Tibet, where he amassed a vast collection of organisms from high-altitude lakes. He wrote many scientific articles about his work in North India, and the trip also inspired his 1936 travel book, *The Clear Mirror.* Other research projects drew Hutchinson to Italy, where in the sediment of Lago di Monterosi, a lake north of Rome, he found evidence of the first case of artificial eutrophication, dating from around 180 B.C.

Recognized for His Literary Talent

Hutchinson was devoted to the arts and humanities, and he counted several musicians, artists, and writers among his friends. The most prominent of his artistic friends was English author Rebecca West. He served as her literary executor, compiling a bibliography of her work which was published in 1957. He was also the curator of a collection of her papers at Yale's Beinecke Library. Hutchinson's writing reflected his diverse interests. Along with his scientific works and his travel book, he also wrote an autobiography and three books of essays, *The Itinerant Ivory Tower* (1953), *The Enchanted Voyage and Other Studies* (1962), and *The Ecological Theatre and the Evolutionary Play* (1965). For twelve years, beginning in 1943, Hutchinson wrote a regular column titled "Marginalia" for the *American Scientist.* His thoughtful columns examined the impact on society of scientific issues of the day.

Hutchinson's skill at writing, as well as his literary interests, was recognized by Yale's literary society, the Elizabethan Club, which twice elected him president. He was also a member of the Connecticut Academy of Arts and Sciences and served as its president in 1946.

Recognized as an Effective Teacher

While Hutchinson built his reputation on his research and writing, he also was considered an excellent teacher. His teaching career began with a wide range of courses including beginning biology, entomology, and vertebrate embryology. He later added limnology and other graduate courses to his areas of expertise. He was personable as well as innovative, giving his students illustrated note sheets, for example, so they could concentrate on his lectures without worrying about taking their own notes. Leading oceanographer Linsley Pond was among the students whose careers were changed by Hutchinson's teaching. Pond enrolled in Yale's doctoral program with the intention of becoming an experimental embryologist. But after one week in Hutchinson's limnology class, he had decided to do his dissertation research on a pond.

Hutchinson loved Yale. He particularly cherished his fellowship in the residential Saybrook College. He was also very active in several professional associations, including the American Academy of Arts and Sciences, the American Philosophical Society and the National Academy of Sciences. He served as president of the American Society of Limnology and Oceanography in 1947, the American Society of Naturalists in 1958 and the International Association for Theoretical and Applied Limnology from 1962 until 1968.

Continues Writing and Research in Long Retirement

Hutchinson retired from Yale as professor emeritus in 1971, but continued his writing and research for 20 more years, until just months before his death. He produced several books during this time, including the third volume of his treatise, as well as a textbook titled *An Introduction to Population Ecology* (1978), and memoirs of his early years, *The Kindly Fruits of the Earth* (1979).

He also occasionally returned to his musings on science and society, writing about several topical issues in 1983 for the *American Scientist.* Here, he examined the question of nuclear disarmament, speculating that "it may well be that total nuclear disarmament would remove a significant deterrent to all war." In the same article, he also philosophized on differences in behavior between the sexes: "On the whole, it would seem that in our present state of evolution, the less aggressive, more feminine traits are likely to be of greater value to us, though always endangered by more aggressive, less useful tendencies. Any such sexual difference, small as it may be, is something on which perhaps we can build."

Career Honored with the Tyler Award

Several of Hutchinson's most prestigious honors, including the Tyler Award, came during his retirement. Hutchinson earned the $50,000 award, often called the Nobel Prize for conservation, in 1974. That same year, the National Academy of Sciences gave him the Frederick Garner Cottrell Award for Environmental Quality. He was awarded the Franklin Medal from the Franklin Institute in 1979, the Daniel Giraud Elliot Medal from the National Academy of Sciences in 1984, and the Kyoto Prize in Basic Science from Japan in 1986. Having once rejected a National Medal of Science because it would have been bestowed on him by President Richard Nixon, he was awarded the medal posthumously by President George Bush in 1991.

Hutchinson's first marriage, to Grace Evelyn Pickford, ended in divorce in 1933. During the six weeks residence the state of Nevada then required to grant divorces, he studied the lakes near Reno and wrote a major paper on freshwater ecology in arid climates. Later that year, Hutchinson married Margaret Seal, who died in 1983 from Alzheimer's disease. Hutchinson cared for her at home during her illness. In 1985, he married Anne Twitty Goldsby, whose care enabled him to travel extensively and continue working in spite of his failing health. When she died unexpectedly in December 1990, the ailing widower returned to his British homeland. He died in London on May 17, 1991, and was buried in Cambridge.

SELECTED WRITINGS BY HUTCHINSON:

Books

The Clear Mirror, Cambridge University Press, 1937.

The Itinerant Ivory Tower, Yale University Press, 1952.

A Treatise on Limnology, Wiley, Volume 1, 1957, Volume 2, 1967, Volume 3, 1979, Volume 4, 1993.

A Preliminary List of the Writings of Rebecca West, Yale University Library, 1957.

The Enchanted Voyage and Other Studies, Yale University Press, 1962.

The Ecological Theater and the Evolutionary Play, Yale University Press, 1965.

An Introduction to Population Ecology, Yale University Press, 1978.

The Kindly Fruits of the Earth, Yale University Press, 1979.

Periodicals

"A Swimming Grasshopper," *Entomological Record and Journal of Variation,* Volume 30, 1918, p. 138.

"Lanula: An Account of the History and Development of the Lago di Monterosi, Latlum, Italy," *Transactions of the American Philosophical Society,* Volume 64, 1970, part 4.

"Marginalia," *American Scientist,* Volume 31, 1943, p. 270.

"Marginalia," *American Scientist,* November-December, 1983, pp. 639–644.

"Concluding Remarks," *Bulletin of Mathematical Biology,* Volume 53, 1991, pp. 193–213.

SOURCES:

Periodicals

Edmondson, Y. H., editor, "G. Evelyn Hutchinson Celebratory Issue," *Limnology and Oceanography,* Volume 16, 1971, pp. 167–477.

Edmondson, W. T., "Resolution of Respect," *Bulletin of the Ecological Society of America,* Volume 72, 1991, pp. 212–216.

Times (London), June 4, 1991, p. 16.

—*Sketch by Cynthia Washam*

Andrew Fielding Huxley
1917-
English physiologist

Andrew Fielding Huxley is an English physiologist whose research on nerve impulse transmission earned him the 1963 Nobel Prize for medicine and physiology, which he shared with his colleague **Alan Lloyd Hodgkin** and the Australian physiologist **John Carew Eccles**. Huxley and Hodgkin confirmed scientists' earlier discovery that nerve impulse transmission involves a momentary change in the nerve fiber's membrane, affecting the ability of particles to pass through it.

Huxley was born in London, England, on November 22, 1917, to a prominent and successful family. His grandfather was the nineteenth-century biologist Thomas Henry Huxley. **Julian Sorel Huxley**, also a noted biologist, was Andrew's half-brother, as was the author Aldous Huxley. Andrew's father, Leonard, was also a writer. His mother was Rosalind (Bruce) Huxley. Huxley was educated at Trinity College, Cambridge, where he received his B.A. in 1938 and his M.A. in 1941. He began studying the physical sciences but switched to physiology in his last year.

In 1939, Huxley joined Alan Hodgkin at the Plymouth Marine Biological Laboratory to study the transmission of nerve impulses. There, Huxley and Hodgkin attempted to verify the work of other scientists, including Julius Bernstein, **Joseph Erlanger**, and **Herbert Spencer Gasser**. These scientists had hypothesized that a nerve impulse produces an electrical current between the active and resting regions of a nerve, and that this impulse causes a fleeting change in the permeability of the nerve fiber membrane. Hodgkin and Huxley went about their research by experimenting on squid, which have giant axons, or nerve fibers, and therefore were known to be particularly useful in studying nerve systems. They inserted a small electrode into the squid's axon, and connected it to a system that would measure the electrical currents produced when the nerve was stimulated.

Huxley's work was interrupted during World War II, when he spent two years doing operational research for the Anti-Aircraft Command and later worked for the Admiralty. In 1946, he returned to his alma mater, serving in a variety of positions—fellow, assistant director of research, director of studies, and reader in experimental biophysics—while he carried out and perfected his research with Hodgkin. He was married to Jocelyn Richenda Gammell Pease in 1947; they had five daughters and one son.

In the course of their research, Huxley and Hodgkin were surprised to learn that, contrary to earlier hypotheses, the outer layer of a nerve fiber is not equally permeable to all ions (charged particles). While a resting cell has low sodium- and high potassium-permeability, Huxley and Hodgkin found that, during excitation, sodium ions flood into the axon, which instantaneously changes from a negative to a positive charge. It is this sudden change that constitutes a nerve impulse. The sodium ions then continue to flow through the membrane until the axon is so highly charged that the sodium becomes electrically repelled. The stream of sodium then stops, which causes the membrane to become permeable once again to potassium ions.

The Nobel and Knighthood

Huxley and Hodgkin first announced their findings in 1951 and published a series of highly regarded papers in 1952. In 1955, Huxley was named to the Royal Society, and in 1960 he became the Jodrell Professor of Physiology at University College, London, where, according to Ronald Clark's history of the Huxley family, *The Huxleys,* he occupied the desk of his grandfather, T. H. Huxley. He remained professor at University College until 1983. In 1974 he was knighted.

When he received the Nobel Prize in 1963, Huxley described the often laborious research and computations involved in his work. While crediting those scientists whose findings he built upon, he also allowed that there was much more work to be done in this field. One of the many applications of the methods and findings of Huxley and Hodgkin was discovered by John Carew Eccles, who shared the Nobel Prize with the two Englishmen. Eccles studied motor neurons in the spinal cord and synapses using microelectrodes similar to those used by Huxley and Hodgkin. Huxley himself devoted much of his later research to studying muscle contraction. His findings have increased the understanding of diseases of the nervous system, as well as similar ionic mechanisms in the kidney and heart.

SELECTED WRITINGS BY HUXLEY:

Books

Reflections on Muscle, Princeton University Press, 1980.

Periodicals

(With Alan Lloyd Hodgkin) "Properties of Nerve Axons, I. Movement of Sodium and Potassium Ions During Nervous Activity," *Cold Spring Harbor Symposia on Quantitative Biology,* Volume 17, 1952, pp. 43–52.

SOURCES:

Books

Clark, Ronald W., *The Huxleys,* McGraw-Hill, 1968.

Sourkes, Theodore L., *Nobel Prize Winners in Medicine and Physiology, 1901–1965,* Abelard-Schuman (London), 1966, pp. 407–420.

Periodicals

"Nobel Prize: 1963 Award Honors Three for Research on Nerve Functioning," *Science,* October 25, 1963, pp. 468–470.

—Sketch by Dorothy Barnhouse

Julian Huxley
1887-1975
English zoologist

Julian Huxley was one of the best known scientists of the twentieth century. He had a talent for making technical topics understandable, which he used both to explain and popularize science. Huxley wrote dozens of scientific and popular books, lectured the world over, and participated in regular radio broadcasts. His areas of interest ranged from evolution and bird behavior to religion and human overpopulation. Huxley made several major contributions to the development of science, including making field observation an accepted and respected scientific method. He also did substantial work on evolution and how an organism develops from egg to adult. In addition to academic positions, his career included appointments as secretary of the Zoological Society of London and the first director-general of the United Nations Educational, Scientific and Cultural Organization.

Julian Sorell Huxley was born in London on June 22, 1887 to Leonard Huxley, who was a biographer, and Julia Arnold Huxley, who founded the Prior's Field School for Girls. Huxley was the oldest of five children; his brother Aldous would become a famous novelist, and his half-brother, **Andrew Fielding Huxley** went on to win a Nobel Prize in physiology or medicine. As a child, Huxley displayed a strong interest in the natural world, spending many hours reading and watching birds in rural England. It was perhaps his grandfather, Thomas H. Huxley, who had the greatest influence on the boy's future choice of a

Julian Huxley

career. T.H. Huxley was a well-known biologist and an early defender of Darwin's theory of evolution.

Huxley's education began in 1900 as a King's Scholar at Eton College, a secondary school where he gained a love for zoology. He decided then to make biology his career, and in 1906 he was admitted to Balliol College, Oxford. The study of biology at that time involved a great deal of literature in German, and Huxley prepared for his course work at Oxford by spending a few months in Germany to learn the language. Once at Oxford, he found he had a talent for poetry, and he won the Newdigate Prize in poetry at the college. In 1909 he earned a "first" in the final examinations, the highest degree, with a specialization in zoology. Huxley then accepted a scholarship from Oxford to spend a year studying at the biological station in Naples. Here, he did research on sponges and their ability to reform into miniature sponges once they had been divided into individual cells by being pressed through fine cheesecloth.

Finds Patterns in Bird Behaviors

Huxley returned to Balliol College and accepted a position as lecturer in zoology. At that time, he also began conducting field studies of birds. He examined the courtship behavior of redshanks, noting that the male followed a set pattern of movements and displays directed at the female, and then published what would become the first of many papers on the courtship behavior of birds. In his autobiography, *Memories,* Huxley wrote: "I am not a little proud that I used the word 'formalized' for some of the male's actions, for we now know that much courtship behavior is indeed stereotyped in a special formalism, and much prouder of having made field natural history scientifically respectable." In addition to his lecturing and field studies, Huxley began writing the first of his books, *The Individual in the Animal Kingdom,* while at Balliol. Huxley was one of very few biologists conducting field work during this period, and his work helped establish the importance of observations made outside the laboratory.

In 1912, Huxley left Europe for the United States. He spent the next four years at the Rice Institute in Houston, Texas, advancing through the position of research associate to full professor. While working to create a biology department at the institute, he continued his studies of bird behavior, using great crested grebes as his subjects. He discovered that both males and females had the plumage patterns and colors previously associated only with the sexual display of males and that both sexes used the same display behaviors. In most species the male does the majority, and often all, of the courting rituals, but in the courtship of great crested grebes Huxley found that males and females played equal roles.

When World War I began, Huxley returned to England and joined the British army, eventually attaining the rank of staff lieutenant in the intelligence unit. In 1919, after the war, he married Marie Juliette Baillot, a governess from Switzerland. The couple eventually had two children, Anthony and Francis.

Brings Science to the Public

In England, Huxley returned to Oxford, this time to New College, where as a fellow and senior demonstrator in zoology he resumed his scientific research. He had heard about experiments demonstrating that a diet of thyroid glands could bring about the early metamorphosis of tadpoles into frogs. He did similar experiments with the axolotl, a salamander-like amphibian that normally remains in a tadpole stage throughout its life. His experiment worked. The axolotls became large, dry-skinned, air-breathing creatures. Following the publication of his results, the popular press picked up on his work and sensationalized his findings; it was widely claimed that Huxley had discovered the "elixir of life." Fearing for his scientific credibility, he wrote a rebuttal with an accurate explanation of his results. This was his first attempt at the kind of popular writing about science that would bring him national and world renown.

While at Oxford, Huxley organized and participated in a polar expedition to Spitsbergen, a Norwegian island near the North Pole. He also published *Essays of a Biologist,* where he wrote: "In broadest terms, the biological phase of evolution stems from the new invention of self-reproducing matter; the human phase from that of self-reproducing mind." Huxley left Oxford in 1925 to become a professor of zoology at King's College, London. Here, he began considering the problems of human overpopulation. His interest in this issue led to articles, speeches, and support for family planning, as well as the Lasker Award from the Planned Parenthood Federation.

Popularity as a Writer Increases

His writing career took a leap in 1926 with the publication of his *Essays in Popular Science,* which was followed by an invitation from H.G. Wells to work on the book *The Science of Life.* Wells envisioned *The Science of Life* as an encyclopedia covering a wide range of science topics including anatomy, physiology, habitat selection, evolution, reproduction, disease, and behavior. Huxley accepted the challenge, resigning as professor at King's and remaining only as an honorary lecturer, so he would have the time to complete the research and writing required for this extensive project.

During this period, Huxley also served as Fullerian Professor of Physiology at the Royal Institution. His views on religion and science became well known in 1927 with the publication of his controversial *Religion Without Revelation.* Huxley was a humanist, favoring human interests instead of beliefs in the supernatural. He wrote: "Religion in the light of science is seen not as a divine revelation, but as a function of human nature. . . . It is no more and no less a function of human nature than fighting or falling in love, than law or literature." He believed that humans had evolved to the point that we could control our own fate.

In 1929, Huxley visited East Africa to study and provide advice on native education. The trip had an strong impact on him, and he wrote *Africa View* upon his return, an account of the trip and the region's prospects for the future. In this book, he also argued for the importance of wildlife reserves, arguments which helped provide the impetus to establish national parks in East Africa.

The following years were very active for Huxley both as a scientist and a writer. He wrote numerous books including *Ants* (1929), the four-volume *Introduction to Science* (1931–1935), and *Bird-Watching and Bird Behavior* (1930). He also published *Problems of Relative Growth* in 1932, a technical work for specialists in the field which discussed his research into differences in growth rates. In the same year, Huxley also completed *A Scientist Among the Soviets,* a book based on his trip to Russia, and a book of verse titled *The Captive Shrew.* In 1934, he published the classic *Elements of Experimental Embryology* with Gavin R. de Beer. The book, which dealt with the nature of embryonic development and the conditions affecting it, gave a significant boost to this expanding field. He prepared an Oscar-winning film in 1934, *The Private Life of the Gannets,* with R.M. Lockley. The film was based on Huxley's studies of a huge breeding colony of seabirds called gannets. He served as general supervisor of biological films for Great Britain Instructional Ltd. through 1936.

Begins Work in Radio and Television

In 1935, Huxley left King's College to become secretary of the Zoological Society of London; a year later he published *At the Zoo,* but his plans for the zoo were curtailed with the advent of World War II. During the war, he joined the Brains Trust program on BBC radio as a regular panelist who would answer questions from the public. In *Memories,* Huxley says he felt the public would have quickly tired of the program except "the combination of an argumentative philosopher with an equally argumentative biologist, and an endearing buffoon as foil to the two intellectuals, proved irresistible." The third member of the panel was a seafarer who had traveled extensively.

Huxley, who had become a fellow of the Royal Society in 1938, continued his writing with the comprehensive *Evolution, the Modern Synthesis* in 1942. The book covers natural selection, adaption, genetics, and evolutionary progress. In the same year he wrote the booklet *Reconstruction and Peace,* under the pseudonym Balbus, in which he discussed the problems he believed the world would face after the war.

In 1944, Huxley traveled to West Africa to review and make recommendations on higher education. Two years later, he had an opportunity to gain further ground for science when he accepted a two-year post as director-general of the newly created United Nations Educational, Scientific and Cultural Organization, UNESCO. Huxley was primarily responsible for the fact that the word "Scientific" was included in UNESCO's title and that science shared importance with the educational and cultural sides of the organization. He guided the organization with the 1947 publication *UNESCO: Its Purpose and Its Philosophy.* In a memorial article published in *Nature* soon after Huxley's death, René Maheu wrote: "In matters concerning the preservation of nature and its ecological balances, the proper management of the resources of the biosphere, the quantitative and qualitative implications of population growth, and the problems of human settlements, the views and the programs that Julian Huxley recommended to UNESCO were a quarter of a century ahead of the ideas of the time."

Huxley remained busy writing and lecturing after his term ended at UNESCO, and in 1953 he published *Evolution in Action,* in which he wrote of individual fulfillment: "It is true that one aspect of fulfillment lies in working for others, but another aspect consists in his enjoyments and the free exercise of his capacities. . . . Each time you enjoy a sunset or a symphony, each time you understand an interesting fact or idea, each time you find satisfaction in making something, or in disciplined activity like sport, evolution has brought another of its possibilities to fruition." In the 1950s, he also published *Kingdom of the Beasts, The Wonderful World of Life,* and *Biological Aspects of Cancer,* among other scientific and popular books. In 1953, UNESCO honored Huxley with its Kalinga Prize for his substantial popular scientific writing. Later in the 1950s, he also received the Darwin Medal of the Royal Society for his work on evolution. He was knighted in 1958.

Advocates Scientific Humanism

Throughout this period of his life, Huxley continued his interest in humanism. In *The Huxleys,* biographer Ronald E. Clark explains that "the exposition and advocacy of scientific humanism . . . was by the 1950s becoming one of the most important of Julian's activities." In 1960, at the age of 74, Huxley's attentions again turned to Africa, where he acted as adviser for UNESCO, traveling to eastern Africa to review wildlife conservation practices. His writing and lecturing through the decade spanned a wide variety of topics, including courtship behaviors and sexual selection, evolution, and population control.

In 1973, Huxley had a stroke, and he died two years later at the age of 87. In *Nature,* Nobel Prize-winning scientist **Peter Medawar** wrote: "Certainly nobody since has made contributions of comparable magnitude to fields so diverse. . . . I do not know and cannot imagine any scale of evaluation of scientific merit along which Huxley would not stand out as one of the foremost biologists of the 20th century."

SELECTED WRITINGS BY HUXLEY:

Books

Essays of a Biologist, Knopf, 1923, 3rd edition, 1926.

Africa View, Harper, 1931.

Scientific Research and Social Needs, Watts & Co., 1934, published as *Science and Social Needs,* Harper, 1935.

(With H. G. Wells) *How Animals Behave,* Cassell, 1937.

Animal Language, Country Life Ltd., 1938, new edition, Grosset, 1964.

Evolution: The Modern Synthesis, Allen & Unwin, 1942, Harper, 1943, 3rd edition, Hafner, 1974.

Evolution in Action, Harper, 1953.

Religion Without Revelation, Harper, 1957.

The Story of Evolution: The Wonderful World of Life, Rathbone Books, 1958, published as *The Wonderful World of Life: The Story of Evolution,* Doubleday, 1958, 2nd edition published as *The Wonderful World of Evolution,* Macdonald, 1969.

The Human Crisis, University of Washington Press, 1963.

Man in the Modern World: An Eminent Scientist Looks at Life Today, New American Library, 1964.

The Future of Man: Evolutionary Aspects, Ethical Culture Publications, 1966.

Memories, Volume 1, Allen & Unwin, 1970, Harper, 1971, Volume 2, Harper, 1973.

SOURCES:

Books

Biographical Memoirs of Fellows of the Royal Society, Volume 22, Royal Society (London), 1976.

Clark, Ronald W., *The Huxleys,* McGraw-Hill, 1968.

Julian Huxley, United Nations Educational, Scientific and Cultural Organization, 1978.

Periodicals

Maheu, Rene, Peter Medawar, and others, "Huxley Remembered," *Nature,* March 6, 1975, pp. 2–5.

—*Sketch by Leslie Mertz*

Ida H. Hyde
1857-1945
American physiologist

The opportunities of generations of women scientists and academics have been enlarged and enhanced by the pioneering work of Ida H. Hyde, a physiologist of respected stature and the first woman to win a doctorate at Germany's Heidelberg University. Hyde's research in vertebrate and invertebrate circulatory, respiratory, and nervous systems was only outdone by her untiring efforts at securing scholarships and placement for worthy women scientists.

Ida Henrietta Hyde personally knew the difficulties a woman faced in the late-nineteenth century. She was born in Davenport, Iowa, on September 8, 1857, one of four children of German immigrant parents. Her father, Meyer Heidenheimer, was a merchant, and her mother was Babette Loewenthal Heidenheimer. Upon their arrival in the United States, they adopted the name Hyde. Education at the time was something reserved for men, and at age sixteen Hyde was apprenticed to a millinery establishment, where she remained for the next seven years. But she always retained a dream of studying and attended evening classes at the Chicago Athenaeum. Finally Hyde quit her job and entered the University of Illinois in 1881, but she had only enough money for one year of study. Already she was leaning toward natural history, the study of plants and animals.

There followed another seven-year stint of work, this time teaching in the Chicago public schools, before she could return to college. She enrolled at Cornell University in 1888, earning her B.S. in premedicine in 1891. From there she went on to two years of graduate study at Bryn Mawr, studying with the well known physiologist **Jacques Loeb**. During the summers she studied and worked at the marine laboratory at Woods Hole in Massachusetts. Hyde's research project toward a graduate degree was on jellyfish development, and she was invited to Germany's University of Strassburg to continue her work. She won a fellowship from the Association of Collegiate Alumnae—the American Association of University Women, as it was later known—enabling her to accept the invitation.

Takes Degree from Heidelberg

More hurdles faced Hyde in Germany, however, for Strassburg would not let a woman earn a doctorate, even though research she submitted was considered sufficient for the degree by her professor. She had to transfer to the University of Heidelberg, where, still facing prejudice against women in academia, she finally received her Ph.D. in physiology. Before returning to the United States in 1896, Hyde visited two other European research facilities. She spent some time at the Naples Zoological Station, a European equivalent of Woods Hole, where she researched the physiology of salivary glands. Briefly, she also conducted research at the University of Berne, Switzerland.

Once back in America she was instrumental in setting up a visiting research position for women at the Naples laboratory. From 1896 to 1897, while a research fellow at Radcliffe College, Hyde became the first woman to do research at the Harvard Medical School, and in 1898 she accepted a position at the University of Kansas as an assistant professor in physiology. She became a noted educator as well as researcher, writing both a basic text in physiology (*Outlines of Experimental Physiology,* 1905) and a laboratory manual (*Laboratory Outlines of Physiology,* 1910). She contributed scores of articles to journals on topics from embryonic development to the microtechniques for individual cell study. Her achievements were honored in 1902 by her election to the American Physiological Society as the first woman member. In 1905 she became a full professor of physiology in the newly-created physiology department at the University of Kansas, researched marine physiology at Woods Hole for several summers, and completed most of the requirements for a medical degree through summer study from 1908 to 1912 at Rush Medical College in Chicago.

Hyde retired from the University of Kansas in 1920, but not from active involvement in both scientific and social pursuits. During 1922 and 1923, she worked once again at Heidelberg, researching the effects of radium, and she donated $25,000 to fund the Ida H. Hyde Woman's International Fellowship through the American Association of University Women. Always a champion of women's rights, Hyde set an example by her life and works for others to follow. On August 22, 1945, at the age of eighty-eight, she died of a cerebral hemorrhage in Berkeley, California, where she had spent the final years of her life.

SELECTED WRITINGS BY HYDE:

Books

Outlines of Experimental Physiology, University of Kansas, 1905.

Laboratory Outlines of Physiology, University of Kansas, 1914.

Periodicals

"The Effect of Distention of the Ventricle on the Flow of Blood Through the Walls of the Heart," *American Journal of Physiology,* Volume 1, 1898, pp. 215–224.

"A Study of the Respiratory and Cardiac Activities and Blood Pressure in the Skate Following Intravenous Injection of Salt Solutions," *University of Kansas Science Bulletin,* Volume 5, number 4, 1911, pp. 27–63.

"The Development of a Tunicate without Nerves," *University of Kansas Science Bulletin,* Volume 9, number 15, 1915, pp. 175–179.

"Before Women Were Human Beings," *Journal of the American Association of University Women,* June, 1938, pp. 226–236.

SOURCES:

Books

American Women 1935–1940: A Composite Biographical Dictionary, Volume 1, Gale, 1981, p. 444.

Notable American Women 1607–1950, Volume 2, Harvard University Press, 1971, pp. 247–249.

Ogilvie, Marilyn Bailey, *Women in Science, Antiquity through the Nineteenth Century,* MIT Press, 1986, pp. 103–104.

Read, Phyllis J. and Witlieb, Bernard L., *The Book of Women's Firsts,* Random House, 1992, p. 224.

Women in the Scientific Search: An American Bio-Bibliography, Scarecrow Press, 1985, pp. 268–270.

Periodicals

"Ida H. Hyde, Pioneer," *Journal of the American Association of University Women,* fall, 1945, p. 42.

Sloan, Jan Butin, "The Founding of the Naples Table Association for Promoting Scientific Research by Women, 1897," *Signs: Journal of Women in Culture and Society,* autumn, 1978, pp. 208–216.

—Sketch by J. Sydney Jones

Libbie Henrietta Hyman
1888-1969
American invertebrate zoologist

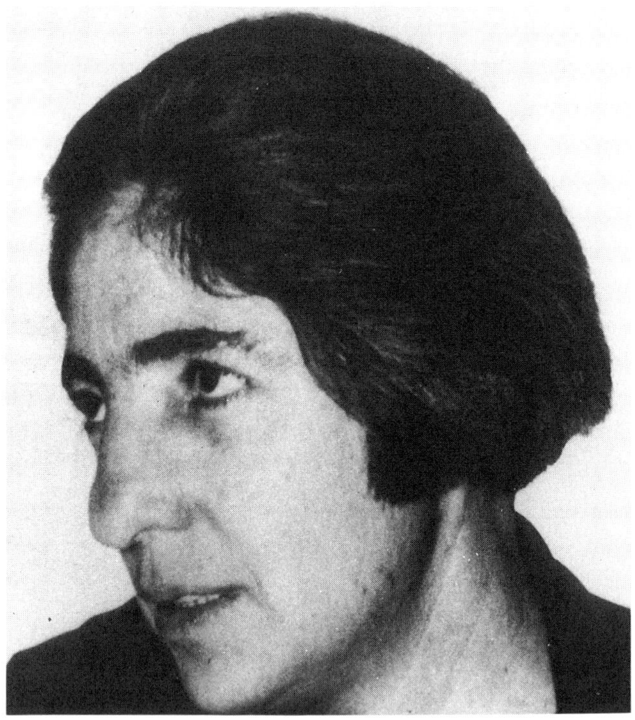

Libbie Henrietta Hyman

Libbie Henrietta Hyman earned an international reputation for her monumental six-volume work on the classification of invertebrates. Although she considered her invertebrate treatise essentially a "compilation" of the literature, others have called it a remarkable synthetic work. Compiled by one independent woman with enormous knowledge of the field and a great facility for translating European languages, it represents a textbook of the invertebrate animal kingdom that whole academies might have attempted. Hyman's treatise consists of judicious analysis and integration of previously scattered information; it has had a lasting influence on scientific thinking about a number of invertebrate animal groups, and the only works that can be compared with hers are of composite authorship. Hyman also influenced the teaching of zoology classes nationwide with the publication of her laboratory manuals.

Hyman was born on December 6, 1888 in Des Moines, Iowa, the third of four children and the only daughter. Her parents were Jewish immigrants; her father, Joseph Hyman, came to the United States from Konin, Poland, at age fourteen, and her mother, Sabina Neumann, was born in Stettin, Germany. Hyman's childhood and youth were spent in Fort Dodge, Iowa, where her father kept an unsuccessful clothing store. Her home life was strict and without affection. Her father, twenty years older than her mother, worried about his declining fortunes and ignored his children, although he did have scholarly inclinations, keeping volumes of Dickens and Shakespeare, which Hyman read. In her brief autobiography, Hyman remembered her mother as being "thoroughly infiltrated with the European worship of the male sex." Her mother required her to do "endless housework" caring for her brothers, whom Hyman believed were "brought up in idleness and irresponsibility."

From an early age, Hyman demonstrated an interest in nature. She learned the scientific names of flowers from a high-school botany book that belonged to her brothers, and she made collections of butterflies and moths. She remembered being initially puzzled by classification, until she suddenly realized that the flowers of a common cheeseweed were the same as the flowers of a hollyhock. In 1905, she graduated from Fort Dodge High School. She was class valedictorian but had failed to attract the attention of her science teachers. Although she passed the state examination for teaching in the country schools, she was too young to be appointed to a teaching position and so returned to high school during 1906 for advanced studies in science and German. When these classes ended, she took a factory job, pasting labels on oatmeal cereal boxes.

Attends the University of Chicago

On her way home from the factory one fall afternoon, she met Mary Crawford, a Radcliffe graduate and high school language teacher who was "shocked" to learn what she was doing. Crawford arranged for Hyman to attend the University of Chicago with scholarship money that was available to top students. "To the best of my recollection," Hyman said, "it had never occurred to me to go to college. I scarcely understood the purpose of college." At the university, she began a course in botany, but was discouraged by anti-semitic harassment from a laboratory assistant. Instead, she majored in zoology and graduated in 1910 with a B.S. degree. Professor **Charles Manning Child**, from whom she had taken a course during her senior year, encouraged her to enter the graduate program. As Child's graduate assistant, she directed laboratory work for courses in elementary zoology and comparative vertebrate anatomy.

Hyman was not free from family responsibilities, however. Her father had died in 1907; her possessive mother moved to Chicago with her brothers, and Hyman was again required to keep house for them and endure their continuing disapproval of her career.

Hyman received her Ph.D. in 1915, when she was twenty-six years old, for a dissertation entitled, "An Analysis of the Process of Regeneration in Certain Microdrilous Oligochaetes." She then accepted an appointment as Child's research assistant, a position she held until he neared retirement. Her work in Child's laboratory consisted of conducting physiological experiments on lower invertebrates, including hydras and flatworms. It was during this time that Hyman realized that many of these common animals were misidentified because they had not been carefully studied taxonomically. She became a taxonomic specialist in these invertebrate groups. Hyman's interest in invertebrates had a strong aesthetic component; she confessed a deep fondness for "the soft delicate ones, the jellyfishes and corals and the beautiful microscopic organisms."

During her time as a laboratory assistant, helping Child direct his classes, Hyman had felt that a better student guide book was needed, and now she wrote one. *A Laboratory Manual for Elementary Zoology* was published in 1919 by the University of Chicago Press. The first printing quickly sold out, and in 1929 she wrote an expanded edition. She also published, in 1922, *A Laboratory Manual for Comparative Vertebrate Anatomy,* which also enjoyed brisk sales. The second edition of this manual was published in 1942 as *Comparative Vertebrate Anatomy.* She was never excited about vertebrates, however, and she refused to consider a third edition. (The third edition was published in 1979, the work of eleven contributors.)

Laboratory Manuals Assure Financial Independence

By 1930, Hyman had realized she could live on the royalties from the sale of her laboratory manuals, and she resigned her position in the zoology department, leaving Chicago in 1931 to tour western Europe for fifteen months. She never again worked for wages. When she returned from her travels, she settled near the American Museum of Natural History in New York City, where she lived modestly, close to the museum's "magnificent" library, determined to devote all of her time to writing a treatise on the invertebrates. In 1937, she was made an honorary research associate of the museum. Although unsalaried, she was given an office, where she placed food and water at the window for pigeons. The first volume of *The Invertebrates* appeared in 1940.

Hyman had always wanted to live in the country and indulge her interest in gardening. In 1941, she bought a house in Millwood, Westchester County, about thirty-five miles north of Times Square. She commuted to her work at the museum until 1952, when she sold the house and returned to New York City. Although she said that gardening and commuting had taken time away from her treatise, during those years of residence in the country she completed the second and third volumes, which were both published in 1951. At the museum, Hyman spent most of her time in the library. She read, made notes, digested information, composed in her head, and typed the first and only draft of her books on her manual typewriter. She also taught herself drawing, and her books contain her own illustrations. She apparently never had a secretary or an assistant. The fourth volume of the treatise was published in 1955, and the fifth in 1959.

Hyman loved music and regularly attended performances of the Metropolitan Opera and the New York Philharmonic. Her physical appearance had been altered by a bungled sinus operation in 1916, and to many she presented a brusque and formidable exterior, but she was not a recluse. She carried on a lively correspondence with scientists who sent her specimens or consulted her. She encouraged young scientists and contributed to charitable causes. She acquired a small, but valuable art collection, and made summer collecting trips to marine laboratories.

Receives Awards and Honors

Hyman's recognition began with publication of her first invertebrate volume. The University of

Chicago awarded her an honorary doctor of science degree in 1941, and honorary degrees followed from other colleges. She received the Daniel Giraud Elliot Medal of the National Academy of Sciences in 1951, the Gold Medal of the Linnaean Society of London in 1960, and the American Museum presented her with its Gold Medal for Distinguished Achievement in Science in April 1969, a few months before she died.

Hyman served as president of the Society of Systematic Zoology in 1959, and she edited the society's journal, *Systematic Zoology,* from 1959–1963. She was vice president of the American Society of Zoologists in 1953 and a member of the National Academy of Sciences, as well as Phi Beta Kappa, Sigma Xi, the American Microscopical Society, the American Society of Naturalists, the Marine Biological Laboratory of Woods Hole, the American Society of Limnology and Oceanography, and the Society of Protozoologists. In addition to her books, she published 135 scientific papers between 1916 and 1966. Her early papers represent contributions to Child's physiological projects; her taxonomic and anatomical papers began to appear in 1925.

In the last decade of Hyman's life, her health was poor and her work on invertebrates had become more difficult. In 1967, at the age of seventy-eight and suffering from Parkinson's disease, she published the sixth volume of her treatise. She announced in its preface that this would be the last volume of *The Invertebrates* from her hands, although McGraw-Hill intended to continue the series with different authors. "I now retire from the field," Hyman wrote, "satisfied that I have accomplished my original purpose—to stimulate the study of invertebrates." She died on August 3, 1969.

SELECTED WRITINGS BY HYMAN:

Books

A Laboratory Manual for Elementary Zoology, University of Chicago Press, 1919.

A Laboratory Manual for Comparative Vertebrate Anatomy, University of Chicago Press, 1922.

The Invertebrates, Volume I, Protozoa through Ctenophora, McGraw-Hill, 1940.

The Invertebrates, Volume II, Platyhelminthes and Rhynchocoela, McGraw-Hill, 1951.

The Invertebrates, Volume III, Acanthocephala, Aschelminthes, and Entoprocta, McGraw-Hill, 1951.

The Invertebrates, Volume IV, Echinodermata, McGraw-Hill, 1955.

The Invertebrates, Volume V, Smaller Coelomate Groups, McGraw-Hill, 1959.

The Invertebrates, Volume VI, Mollusca I, McGraw-Hill, 1967.

SOURCES:

Books

Hyman, Libbie H., and G. Evelyn Hutchinson, "Libbie Henrietta Hyman: December 6, 1888-August 3, 1969," *Biographical Memoirs,* National Academy of Sciences, Volume 60, 1991, pp. 103–14.

Rossiter, Margaret W., *Women Scientists in America: Struggles and Strategies to 1940,* Johns Hopkins University Press, 1982, pp. 210–11, 294, 373, 374.

Sicherman, Barbara, and Carol Hurd Green, editors, *Notable American Women: The Modern Period,* Belknap Press of Harvard University Press, 1980, pp. 365–67.

Stunkard, Horace W., "In Memoriam: Libbie Henrietta Hyman, 1888–1969," in Riser, Nathan W., and M. Patricia Morse, editors, *Biology of the Turbellaria,* McGraw-Hill, 1974, pp. 9–13.

Periodicals

Winston, Judith E., "Great Invertebrate Zoologists: Libbie Henrietta Hyman (1888–1969)," *American Society of Zoologists, Division of Invertebrate Zoologists Newsletter,* fall, 1991.

—Sketch by Jill Carpenter

Elmer Samuel Imes
1883-1941
American physicist

Elmer Samuel Imes was the second African American to receive a Ph.D. in physics. (The first was Edward Bouchet, who graduated from Yale in 1876.) He became internationally known for his research on the infra-red spectra and became head of the department of physics at Fisk University. An inspiring teacher knowledgeable in many fields, Imes also taught for many years in schools run by the American Missionary Association.

Imes was born in Memphis, Tennessee, on October 12, 1883. His parents, Benjamin A. and Elizabeth W. Imes, were missionaries, and his father was a graduate of Oberlin College and Theological Seminary. The elder Imes was among the pioneers in educational and church work in the southern field of the American Missionary Association. There were also two other sons in the family, Albert L. and William L. Imes. Before the younger Imes began his graduate studies in physics he, too, taught for several years in the American Missionary schools, mainly in Albany, Georgia, at the Albany Normal School. Imes received his B.A. in 1903 and his M.A. in 1910 from Fisk University in Nashville, Tennessee. He was later accepted in the doctoral physics program at the University of Michigan, where he was a fellow from 1916 to 1918. When he received his Ph.D. in physics from that university in 1918 with a dissertation entitled "Measurements on the Near Infra-red Absorption of Some Diatomic Cases," he had the distinction of being only the second African American to receive a Ph.D. in physics.

Imes worked in New York City as a research and consulting engineer and physicist both before and after earning his Ph.D., and in 1922 he took a position as a research physicist at the Federal Engineer's Development Corporation. In 1924 he moved to the Burrows Magnetic Equipment Corporation, and in 1927 he took a position as research engineer with E. A. Everett Railway Signal Supplies. Imes remained in the private sector until 1930, when he returned to teaching as professor and head of the department of physics at Fisk University. He was to remain in that position until his death in 1941, creating a well run and highly successful department.

A member of the Physical Society and the Society of Testing Materials, Imes was known for his appreciation of literature and music. A former student, W. F. G. Swann, remembered him as a considerate and sensitive man who brought "to any discussion an atmosphere of philosophic soundness and levelheaded practicalness." Imes died on September 11, 1941, at Memorial Hospital in New York.

SOURCES:

Books

Sammons, Vivian, *Blacks in Science and Medicine,* Hemisphere Publishing, 1990, p. 127.

Periodicals

New York Times, September 12, 1941, p. 22.

Swann, W. F. G., "Elmer Samuel Imes," *Science,* December 26, 1941, pp. 600–601.

—Sketch by Leonard C. Bruno

Abram F. Ioffe
1880-1960
Russian physicist

Abram F. Ioffe (the name is also transliterated as Joffé) was among the most influential Russian scientists of this century. His interest and contributions extended from highly theoretical and philosophical aspects of science to everyday applications in technology and agriculture. He also engaged in organizational work on the national and international levels, and he helped modernize scientific research and establish several teaching and research institutions in Russia. Ioffe's most lasting and momentous legacies are the contributions he made to the understanding of the mechanical and electrical properties of crystals and the characteristics of semiconductors, areas in which he and his students conducted pioneering work.

Abram Fedorovich Ioffe, the oldest of five children, was born on October 29, 1880 (some sources say

October 30, 1880), in the small Ukrainian town of Romny. The descendent of a family of Jewish artisans and craftsmen, he was the son of Fedor Vasil'evich and Rahel Abramovna Ioffe, née Veinstein. His father had only a limited formal commercial education and held a position as bookkeeper in the local bank. But both parents were much interested in intellectual pursuits and undoubtedly greatly influenced and encouraged Abram Fedorovich, who showed early signs of extraordinary intelligence; at the age of three, he could read, and a year later, he could write. After having finished high school in his hometown, he went to St. Petersburg to study at the Technical Institute, where he graduated in 1902, as a technical engineer.

His interest in physics prompted him to go to Germany, where he worked and studied in Munich under the direction of physicist **Wilhelm Röntgen**, the discoverer of X rays and the first Nobel laureate in physics. Röntgen was impressed with the skill and abilities of his new student. Initially the question arose whether Ioffe could be admitted as a doctoral candidate, because he lacked a proper *Gymnasium* education. But his certificate in technical engineering was ultimately accepted as an equivalent degree. In 1905, he obtained his first doctorate, a Ph.D. summa cum laude. An abbreviated version of his dissertation on the mechanical properties of crystals was published in the prestigious *Annalen der Physik.*

Although Röntgen expected his talented student to return to Munich after the summer vacation of 1906, Ioffe decided to stay in Russia. In the fall of that year, he obtained a position as laboratory assistant at the Polytechnical Institute in St. Petersburg. In order to satisfy his intense interest in physics and to further his career, Ioffe pursued his studies at the University of St. Petersburg. He earned a master's degree with distinction, thereby winning a prize from the Russian Academy of Sciences. He subsequently became a professor at the Polytechnical Institute, with which he remained associated for the next thirty-five years. His doctoral dissertation at the University of Petrograd in 1915, was based on further research on the characteristics of crystals.

In 1916, Ioffe started a physics seminar at the Polytechnical Institute that was to become influential in the development of theoretical and applied physics in Russia. He was among the first Russian scientists to accept and disseminate the new ideas of quantum mechanics and relativity. Ioffe's and his students' extensive and advanced research on the conductivity of crystals and the dielectric (nonconductive) strength of isolators led to some discoveries that are basic to modern physical concepts, particularly to an understanding of dielectric phenomena, the electrical sustaining capacity of a substance or material used as an insulator.

After the first world war and the Russian Revolution, Ioffe helped establish the Röntgenological and Radiological Institute and became the director of its physical-technical section. His lifelong interest in the practical applications of physics led to his involvement in the establishment and operation of a laboratory, which eventually became the Physico-Technical Institute, to which Ioffe served as director until 1950. He also was active in the establishment of several small industrial laboratories throughout the country. Agrophysics, a subject seemingly removed from his theoretical and technical research, also captivated his interest. Besides his other duties, he became the first director of the Institute of Physical Agriculture (Agrofizicheskii Nauchno-Issledoval'skii Institut) that he helped found in 1931.

During World War II, the Physico-Technical Institute, which in 1939 had become part of the Academy of Sciences, was evacuated to Kazan. Only a small staff remained in Leningrad during the long siege of the city. In both places, research on immediate technical military problems continued under difficult circumstances. Among other projects, major efforts were made to develop more effective armor plates and to find methods to demagnetize ships to protect them from magnetic mines.

After the war, Ioffe concentrated on the study of semiconductors, whose scientific importance and industrial potential he had early recognized. Realizing the greater efficiency of semiconductors over metals in thermoelectric devices, he envisioned their widespread use for heating or cooling purposes or, conversely, as small electric generators, where other power sources were not practical or available. In the early 1950's, he became director of the Academy's Semiconductor Institute (Institut Poluprovodniko), a post that he held until his death.

Through his frequent and sometimes prolonged visits to foreign countries, his attendance at various conferences, and his extensive writings, Ioffe became internationally well known and respected among his colleagues. Early in the 1920s, he had returned to Germany to acquire scientific literature and equipment. Subsequently, he went to England where he met with **William Henry** and **William Lawrence Bragg**, **Ernest Rutherford**, and other famous physicists of the time. From 1927 to 1928, he visited the United States. While there, he received an honorary doctorate from the University of California, Berkeley.

Ioffe received many other honors in his country and abroad. In 1920, he was elected an ordinary member of the Russian Academy of Sciences (after 1925, Akademiia Nauk SSSR) and was one of its vice presidents from 1926 to 1929, and again, from 1942 to 1945. From 1945 to 1952, he was also a member of the Academy's Presidium. In 1929, Ioffe became an honorary member of the American Academy of Arts and Sciences. A year earlier, he had been elected a corresponding member of the German Academy of Sciences in Berlin, but resigned in November 1938, in protest against the Nazi regime and its excesses. His membership was reinstated on March 14, 1956. A member of several other academies, including the venerable Accademia Nazionale dei Lincei in Rome, the Göttinger Akademie, and the National Academy of Sciences of India, Ioffe participated in many national and international scientific meetings, among them several Solvay Congresses. For many years, he was a member of the Solvay Committee. In 1957, he served as vice president of the International Union for Pure and Applied Physics.

Ioffe was not immune to political intrigue and controversy. Over the years, he had differences with colleagues who objected to his views on modern physics. At one point, he complained that some of his Russian friends' criticism of the theory of relativity and quantum mechanics bore a macabre resemblance to those of their nationalistic counterparts in the Germany of the time. In 1950, Ioffe was forced to give up the directorship of the Physico-Technical Institute, with which he had been associated for three decades. The official emphasis in the U.S.S.R. was then on nuclear physics, to the detriment of other research, including that on semiconductors.

Ioffe was the author of numerous papers, textbooks, and monographs on subjects that range from theoretical, historical, and philosophical concepts, to the practical applications of science in everyday life. Most of the works are in Russian, but some, particularly his early substantial articles, are in German, a language of which he had an excellent command. Later works appeared also in English. His *Physics of Crystals* was published by the United States in 1928. The first Russian edition of this book was apparently published a year later. For several years, he was the editor of the *Zhurnal Eksperimental'noi i Teoreticheskoi Fiziki* and, for the last two years of his life, he was chief editor of *Fizika Tverdogo Tela.* He was also on the editorial boards of other journals. Because Ioffe believed in the importance of divulging scientific ideas as widely as possible, some of his writings are accessible to the general reader. An article on thermoelectricity, a subject that, as already noted, Ioffe believed to have great practical potential, was published in the November, 1958 issue of the *Scientific American.* Ioffe's writings contain interesting reminiscences of the famous scientists and other personalities whom he had met over the years. A short autobiography appeared in 1933.

His long time friend, Janos Plesch, the personal physician of Einstein, described Ioffe as kind, cordial, loyal, and modest, endowed with an incisive mind, who tended to find simple solutions to complicated problems. Far from living only for his science, Ioffe had, according to Plesch, wide ranging interests. In spite of all his duties, he never seemed hurried or fatigued and always knew how to make the best of things. He organized his activities with care and had little patience with time-consuming formalities and superfluous paper work.

In all his research, he observed high ethical standards. According to Ioffe's obituary in *Nature,* written by **Nikolai N. Semenov** and V. N. Kondratiev, Ioffe claimed "authorship only in investigations that were carried out with his own hands," not those that were done merely under his guidance by his students. Though reserved and not much given to jesting, Ioffe was courteous and friendly to everybody he met. Not a smoker himself, he disliked smoking in others. He read widely and enjoyed walking, playing tennis, and attending the theater and concerts. He loved to talk, but did not care to write letters.

Ioffe was married twice. In 1908, he married Vera Andreevna Kravcova, a dentist. Their daughter, Valentina Ambramovna, was born in 1910. After his divorce, Ioffe was married, in the 1930's, to Anna Vasil'evna Echeistora, a young physicist whom he had met at a scientific congress. Ioffe died in Leningrad on October 14, 1960. Obituaries appeared in periodicals in many countries, including the *New York Times* and *Nature.* After his death, the institute that he had helped found and under whose directorship it had long remained, was renamed the Leningradski Fiziko-Tekhnicheskii Institut imeni A. F. Ioffe.

SELECTED WRITINGS BY IOFFE:

Books

The Physics of Crystals, McGraw-Hill, 1928.
Physics of Conductors, Academic Press, 1960.
Fundamentals of Agrophysics, Israel Program of Scientific Translations, 1966.

Periodicals

"The Revival of Thermoelectricity," *Scientific American,* November, 1958, pp. 31–37.

SOURCES:

Books

Kant, Horst, *Abram Fedorovi Ioffe; Vater der sowjetischen Physik,* Teubner, 1989.
Nernst, Walter, "Wahlvorschlag für Abram Fedorovich Joffe," in *Physiker über Physiker,* Volume 1, Akademie Verlag, 1975, pp. 248–49.

Periodicals

Semenov, N. N. and Volume N. Kondratiev, "Academician A. F. Joffé," *Nature,* May 27, 1961, pp. 761–63.

—*Sketch by Eliseo Fernandez*

Alick Isaacs
1921-1967
Scottish-born English virologist and biologist

In 1957 Alick Isaacs and Swiss virologist Jean Lindenmann published a paper describing the existence of a protein which interfered with viral infection. It seemed this protein, named interferon by Isaacs, inhibited secondary cellular infection, meaning infection in the cell with one virus prevented infection by a second. Studies on interferon and its actions occupied Isaacs for the rest of his life, and earned him election as Fellow of the Royal Society of London in 1966.

Isaacs was born July 17, 1921, in Glasgow, Scotland. He was the eldest of four children of Louis and Rosine (Lion) Isaacs. Isaacs's paternal grandparents were immigrants from Lithuania. His paternal grandfather was a peddler, which Louis carried on, though with more success. Isaacs' maternal grandparents had settled in England earlier, and were more wealthy. His maternal grandfather was a leather merchant.

Isaacs was sent to local public school, but also received training in Judaism through Hebrew School and private tutors. He developed an interest in chess and music which he retained throughout his life. Isaacs graduated from Glasgow University in 1944 from the faculty of medicine. During school he won several awards, including first prizes in clinical surgery and dermatology, but did not develop a real inclination for the clinical side of medicine. From 1945 to 1947 he was McCann research scholar in the Department of Bacteriology, still at Glasgow University. His work there produced a simple test which could be used to differentiate two types of bacteria. In part because of this early success, Isaacs won a 1947 Medical Research Council Studentship to Sheffield University for one year, during which time he began his work with the influenza virus.

In 1948 Isaacs was awarded a Rockefeller Travelling fellowship which took him to the Walter and Eliza Hall Institute in Melbourne, Australia. At the end of a year, the Medical Research Council provided him with a grant which allowed for a second year of research. His work was still centered on influenza, with particular interest drawn to the different types of viruses causing flu and the response of the body to the viruses—virus variation and virus interference.

Isaacs had become engaged while at Sheffield, so when his stay in Australia was extended, his fiancee, Susanna Gordon Foss, sailed to meet him. They were married in the town hall in 1949. The daughter of a musician, Susanna Isaacs began her career as a pediatrician, and eventually became a well-known child psychiatrist. The Isaacs had two sons (twins) and a daughter. In 1950 Isaacs returned to London to take on the position of Director of the World Influenza Centre at the National Institute for Medical Research. Work at the facility included serologic identification of influenza strains, and pin-point identification of the origin of epidemics. His influenza work finally earned him an M.D. from Glasgow University in 1954 as well as the Bellahouston Gold Medal.

Studies Lead to Discovery of Interferon

Isaacs always found time to continue his studies of virus interference, and his persistence paid off with the discovery of interferon in 1957. It was during 1957 that Isaacs wrote two papers described by Dr. Michael Stoker, chairperson of a 1967 symposium on interferon dedicated to Isaacs, as the "supreme event in his scientific life." Isaacs, in these articles, describes the viruses involved as "interfering" and "challenging." One virus, the "interferer," exists in the cell. The presence of this virus, through the production of interferon, a protein, limits the infective ability of the "challenging" virus. This may not seem like a major discovery, but Isaacs also found that the "interfering" virus could be inactivated itself. This means that a dead, non-disease-causing virus, injected into a cell, has the potential, as Isaacs saw it, to prevent a real infection by a live virus. Viewed in this way, the implications for vaccine or immunotherapy are great, if one knows which viruses interfere with live viruses, and under what circumstances they are effective.

The announcement of interferon in 1957 was not met with unanimous approval. Many scientists were skeptical of the importance, or even existence, of such a substance, and Isaacs was thought by some to have misinterpreted his lab results. This reception did not deter Isaacs, who continued to study and attempted to expand knowledge related to interferon. His further work tried to explain interferon's role in defense against viruses and to ascertain its specific mechanism of action. Isaacs found a link between the efficacy of interferon and the virulence of the challenging virus, with interferon losing impact when up against more virulent viruses. He also hypothesized some role for interferon in carcinogenesis, though he was never able to explain either of these occurrences fully during his lifetime.

In 1961 Isaacs was appointed as head of the Virology Division at the National Institute for Medical Research, but soon after his health began to decline. In 1962 he received an honorary degree from Catholic University of Louvain in Belgium. In 1964 he suffered a subarachnoid hemorrhage, which was inoperable. Although his health improved in time, he never recovered fully. Soon after, he gave up his post as division head, becoming head of the Lab for Research on Interferon. Isaacs was elected Fellow of the Royal Society of London in 1966 due to his work with interferon, but unfortunately did not survive long after. He had a recurrence of intracranial hemorrhaging in 1967, which was fatal in two days. Isaacs died on January 26, 1967, in London, England.

Work with interferon has continued in many laboratories worldwide. Understanding of interferon has been expanded dramatically, although far-reaching medical implications of it have yet to be determined. It has been used, with some success, in the treatment of cancer. With the publication of more than one hundred scientific papers, Isaacs laid the groundwork for a field of medical study which has yet to be exhausted.

SELECTED WRITINGS BY ISAACS:

Periodicals

Isaacs, A., and J. Lindenmann, "Virus interference. I. The interferon," *Proceedings of the Royal Society of London,* September 12, 1957, pp. 258–267.

Isaacs, A., J. Lindenmann, and R. C. Valentine, "Virus interference. II. Some properties of interferon," *Proceedings of the Royal Society of London,* September 12, 1957, pp. 268–273.

SOURCES:

Books

Biographical Memoirs of the Fellows of the Royal Society, Volume 13, Royal Society (London), 1967, pp. 204–221.

Daintith, J., S. Mitchell, and E. Tootill, editors, *A Biographical Encyclopedia of Scientists, Volume I,* Facts on File, 1981, pp. 411–412.

Wolstenhoulme, G. E. W., and M. O'Connor, editors, *Interferon: Ciba Foundation Symposium Dedicated to Alick Isaacs, F.R.S.,* J. & A. Churchill Ltd., 1968.

Periodicals

Stuart-Harris, C. H., "Dr. Alick Isaacs" (obituary), *Nature,* February 11, 1967, p. 555.

—Sketch by Kimberlyn McGrail

Keiichi Itakura
1942-
Japanese-born American molecular biologist

Keiichi Itakura and his colleagues were the first to synthesize genes for peptides, compounds formed from linkage between certain amino acid groups. This enables scientists to develop such medically important hormones as insulin and somatostatin in the laboratory rather than from living matter, allowing for the production of these substances in greater quantities.

Itakura was born on February 18, 1942, in Tokyo, Japan, to Tsuneo Itakura and Nobuko Orimoto Itakura. Graduating from Tokyo Pharmaceutical College in 1965, he obtained a Ph.D. in organic chemistry from the college in 1970. Following graduation, Itakura chose to embark on a fellowship in deoxyribonucleic acid (DNA) synthesis, rather than peptide synthesis (DNA is a substance found in the cell nucleus which determines heredity at the molecular level). Itakura commented in an interview with Francis Rogers that he found the field of DNA "more fundamental, exciting, and challenging." Another factor in his decision was news of the discovery of a synthesized gene of t-RNA (transfer ribonucleic acid, which is similar to DNA) by Indian chemist **Gobind Khorana**. Because of his desire to live in Canada, Itakura wound up working with Dr. S. Narang at the National Council of Canada in Ottawa. In 1974 he became a senior research fellow at the California Institute of Technology.

The next year Itakura became an associate research scientist at the City of Hope National Medical Center in Los Angeles, California, where he continued his studies into DNA. In 1976, Itakura—along with a number of colleagues—was able to artificially create a gene for the peptide somatostatin, a substance that inhibits the secretion of certain hormones and is useful in the treatment of such diseases as acromegaly, diabetes, and pancreatitis. Somatostatin was selected because of its low toxicity and because it is easier to handle in the lab. Utilizing the bacteria *E. coli,* the scientists were able to synthesize and clone a somatostatin gene. This discovery enabled scientists to

Keiichi Itakura

develop medically important peptides such as insulin and various growth hormones inexpensively and ten times faster than previous methods. In addition, the new method also allows medical researchers to direct DNA sequencing and create mutations of various genes more effectively.

Because of his part in developing synthetic peptides, Itakura was given the David Rumbough Scientific Award in 1979 from the Juvenile Diabetes Foundation. The next year he was promoted to senior research scientist and director of the molecule genetics department at the City of Hope, and in 1989 became director of its genetics laboratory.

Itakura credits Professor Ishiwata of Tokyo Pharmaceutical College with allowing him latitude to do his own research while a student there. In the interview with Rogers, Itakura commented that unlike other Japanese "old professors," Ishiwata gave his students considerable freedom in the realm of experimentation. "Instead of directing my research, he would just point out what was wrong with my experiments and thinking when I made mistakes," Itakura said.

Itakura has been married since 1970 to the former Yasuko Shimada; the couple have a son, Noby, and a daughter, Yuko. A member of the New York Academy of Sciences since 1991, Itakura supplements his intensive intellectual work with athletic pursuits such as tennis, running, soccer, and skiing.

SELECTED WRITINGS BY ITAKURA:

Periodicals

(With Roberto Crea, Tadaaki Hirose, and Arthur Riggs) "Expression in Escherichia coli of a Chemically Synthesized Gene for the Hormone Somatostatin," *Science,* December, 1977, pp. 1056–1063.

(With Arthur Riggs) "Chemical DNA Synthesis and Recombinant DNA Studies," *Science,* September, 1980, pp. 1401–1405.

SOURCES:

Books

Judson, Horace, *The Eighth Day of Creation: The Making of a Revolution In Biology,* Simon & Schuster, 1979.

Lampton, Christopher, *DNA Fingerprinting,* Franklin Watts, 1991.

Other

Itakura, Keiichi, interview letter sent to Francis Rogers, January 14, 1994.

—*Sketch by Francis Rogers*

F. Kenneth Iverson
1925-
American metallurgist

Francis Kenneth Iverson is a metallurgist and businessman who devised ways to manufacture basic steel products more efficiently and for less cost by using small steel mills. At a time when it seemed that the death knell for the American steel industry had sounded in the late 1970s and early 1980s, Iverson proved that a "mini-mill" could be a viable entity in this country, either with or without union workers, and be competitive with the foreign steel industry.

Iverson was born to Norris Byron and Pearl Irene Kelsey Iverson on September 18, 1925, in Downer's Grove, Illinois. His father was an electrical engineer who worked for the Western Electric Corporation, while his mother had been a school teacher before having children. Iverson graduated from high school in 1943 and immediately entered the Navy's V12 program, a special war-time program designed to accelerate capable students through college in order to commission and deploy them into the field as fast as possible. Iverson matriculated at Northwestern University, but spent only a couple of semesters there before the Navy transferred him to Cornell University, where he earned his bachelor of science in aeronautical engineering in two and one half years. Upon graduation in the spring of 1945, Iverson entered the Navy as a lieutenant junior grade and was sent to Johnson Atoll in the South Pacific. World War II ended three months later, and Iverson returned to graduate school at Purdue University. In 1947 he received a master's degree in mechanical engineering, with a minor concentration in metallurgy. Iverson explains his dual studies this way: "I wanted to study something completely empirical, and that was metallurgy. At that time, there was no link between metallurgy and physics. A lot of things about steel were unexplained then, and they still aren't explained today. . . . There is an art to making steel."

Begins Metallurgical Career

After graduate school, Iverson was an assistant chief research physicist for the International Harvester Manufacturing Research Center in Chicago. His job involved operating an electron microscope that photographed metals at the molecular level and using other analytical means to garner new knowledge about the mechanical properties of metals. These were duly published in professional periodicals. In 1952, Iverson took a job as the chief engineer for the Illium Corporation, a foundry located in Freeport, Illinois. When Illium received a contract to make tubes used in extruding pork sausage casings, they found that the nozzles were to be made of an exotic metal alloy difficult to work with and store. Illium needed a special casting machine for the task but could not afford anything expensive. Iverson designed and built one for a mere $6,000. When the machine was dry-casted, it flew across the floor, terrifying other workers. Iverson pressed on with an actual pouring of hot metal into the casting machine and it worked perfectly. But when the board of directors came to watch this much-touted machine, the device exploded. Afterward, Iverson went to the board with a proposal that they build a state-of-the-art foundry. Put off by the board, Iverson left Illium.

Iverson next worked for Cannon Muskegon Corporation, a maker of exotic cobalt, nickel and iron alloys. From 1954 to 1960, he held the positions of sales manager and chief metallurgist. In 1960, Iverson moved on, taking a job with Coast Metals of Little Ferry, New Jersey. Although he was only at Coast Metals until 1962, it was through this job that Iverson met David Thomas, the president and chairman of the Nuclear Corporation of America. One of Thomas' interests was buying other companies. At one point, he became interested in purchasing Vulcraft Corporation of Florence, South Carolina. Iverson checked the company out for Thomas, advising him that it was a good buy.

Moves into the Fore of the Steel Business

After Thomas purchased Vulcraft, he hired Iverson as its general manager in 1962. By 1965, Nuclear Corporation of America was headed for bankruptcy and Thomas left the company, leaving the board of directors to search for a new president. In the meantime, Sam Siegel, who was Nuclear's long-time accountant, quit. On the 30th of July, Siegel sent the board of directors this telegram: "I would consider continuing with Nuclear if the following occurred: (1) Ken Iverson is given an employment contract as president of Nuclear." Because of this recommendation, Iverson became Nuclear's president with the express task of staving off the impending bankruptcy. He immediately sold off some of the firm's unprofitable businesses. Profitable businesses, including Vulcraft, were expanded.

Vulcraft's primary business was making steel joists for use in the construction of buildings. To do this, they needed steel bars. When the price of steel bars rose so high as to threaten the company's profitability, Iverson determined that the best course would be to make the bars in-house. So in 1968, Nuclear began construction of a little steel mill in Darlington, South Carolina. Instead of milling the steel from iron ore, which was the traditional and very expensive method, an electric arc furnace was used to melt scrap metal. The mill eventually became profitable, making steel bars not only for Vulcraft, but for clients up and down the East Coast as well. By 1975 Nuclear Corporation, now renamed Nucor, had constructed three other successful mini-mills.

Iverson's mini-mills were not the first in the country. But his were significant in that they pioneered the manufacture of basic steel products. They were also the first to be able to do continuous casting. However, Iverson never patented any of his processes, telling Susan E. Kolmer that "Process patents are not worth the paper they're written on." Nucor had its industrial secrets, but chose not to use any other means to protect itself.

In 1987, Iverson took the mini-mill idea one step further. In Crawfordsville, Indiana, he broke ground for a revolutionary new mill that would produce sheet metal out of scrap. The steel industry said it could not be done; that the result would be "distressed metal," worthless stuff. But Iverson applied state-of-the-art German technology to produce a thin slab of steel instead of the traditional thick slab which required extensive rolling. Thus, the required forming process was drastically reduced, making the process cost efficient enough to be profitable. After ten months of operation, the Crawfordsville plant turned a profit and was manufacturing sheet steel of first quality. It was estimated that the Crawfordsville plant was at least six times as labor efficient as a modern Japanese factory, using only 0.66 man-hour labor per ton of steel made. Later, a second sheet metal plant was opened in Hickman, Arkansas. Then, in 1994, both of these plants were doubled in size to greatly increase their outputs. Indeed, by 1993, Nucor was the fourth largest steel maker in the United States.

In the summer of 1994, Nucor built a plant in the nation of Trinidad. Using iron ore imported from Brazil, and mostly local labor, the Trinidad plant (chosen because of the local abundant supply of natural gas) manufactured iron carbide, a sand-like, semi-processed material. The iron carbide was shipped to Nucor plants in the United States where it could be melted into steel.

Iverson's innovations in steel manufacturing have made him a popular speaker with business and civic groups. He was honored as the Best Chief Executive Officer in the Steel Industry in 1993 by the *Wall Street Transcript.* He twice received the National Medal of Technology, in 1991 and 1992. Iverson married the former Martha Virginia Miller on October 24, 1945, and has two children, Claudia and Marc Miller.

SELECTED WRITINGS BY IVERSON:

Periodicals

Iverson, F. Kenneth, *Changing the Rules of the Game,* Planning Review, September 1, 1993, p. 9.

SOURCES:

Books

Preston, Richard, *American Steel,* Prentice Hall, 1991.

Periodicals

Konrad, W. and M. Schroeder, "Nucor: Rolling Right into Steel's Big Time," *Business Week,* November 19, 1990, p. 76.

Other

Iverson, F. Kenneth, interview with Susan E. Kolmer conducted February 21, 1994.

—Sketch by Susan E. Kolmer

Shirley Ann Jackson
1946-
American physicist

Shirley Ann Jackson is a theoretical physicist who has spent her career researching and teaching about particle physics—the branch of physics which uses theories and mathematics to predict the existence of subatomic particles and the forces that bind them together. She was the first African American woman to receive a Ph.D. from the Massachusetts Institute of Technology (MIT), and she spent many years conducting research at AT & T Bell Laboratories. She was named professor of physics at Rutgers University in 1991 and is the recipient of many honors, scholarships, and grants.

Jackson was born on August 5, 1946, in Washington, DC. Her parents, Beatrice and George Jackson, strongly valued education and encouraged her in school. Her father spurred on her interest in science by helping her with projects for her science classes. At Roosevelt High School, Jackson attended accelerated programs in both math and science, and she graduated in 1964 as valedictorian. Jackson began classes at MIT that same year, one of fewer than twenty African American students and the only one studying theoretical physics. While a student she did volunteer work at Boston City Hospital and tutored students at the Roxbury YMCA. She earned her bachelors degree in 1968, writing her thesis on solid-state physics, a subject then in the forefront of theoretical physics.

Although accepted at Brown, Harvard, and the University of Chicago, Jackson decided to stay at MIT for her doctoral work, because she wanted to encourage more African American students to attend the institution. She worked on elementary particle theory for her Ph.D., which she completed in 1973. Her research was directed by James Young, the first African American tenured full professor in MIT's physics department. Jackson's thesis, "The Study of a Multiperipheral Model with Continued Cross-Channel Unitarity," was subsequently published in the *Annals of Physics* in 1975.

Jackson's area of interest in physics is the study of the subatomic particles found within atoms, the tiny units of which all matter is made. Subatomic particles, which are usually very unstable and short-lived, can be studied in several ways. One method is using a particle accelerator, a device in which nuclei are accelerated to high speeds and then collided with a target to separate them into subatomic particles. Another way of studying them is by detecting their movements using certain kinds of nonconducting solids. When some solids are exposed to high-energy particles, the crystal lattice structure of the atoms is distorted, and this phenomenon leaves marks or tracks that can be seen with an electron microscope. Photographs of the tracks are then enhanced, and by examining these photographs physicists like Jackson can make predictions about what kinds of particles have caused the marks.

As a postdoctoral student of subatomic particles during the 1970s, Jackson studied and conducted research at a number of prestigious physics laboratories in both the United States and Europe. Her first position was as research associate at the Fermi National Accelerator Laboratory in Batavia, Illinois (known as Fermilab) where she studied hadrons—medium to large subatomic particles which include baryons and mesons. In 1974 she became visiting scientist at the accelerator lab at the European Center for Nuclear Research (CERN) in Switzerland. There she explored theories of strongly interacting elementary particles. In 1976 and 1977, she both lectured in physics at the Stanford Linear Accelerator Center and became a visiting scientist at the Aspen Center for Physics.

Jackson joined the Theoretical Physics Research Department at AT & T Bell Laboratories in 1976. The research projects at this facility are designed to examine the properties of various materials in an effort to discover useful applications. In 1978, Jackson became part of the Scattering and Low Energy Physics Research Department, then in 1988 she moved to the Solid State and Quantum Physics Research Department. At Bell Labs, Jackson explored theories of charge density waves and the reactions of neutrinos, one type of subatomic particle. In her research, Jackson has made contributions to the knowledge of such areas as charged density waves in layered compounds, polaronic aspects of electrons in the surface of liquid helium films, and optical and electronic properties of semiconductor strained-layer superlattices. On these topics and others she has prepared or collaborated on over 100 scientific articles.

Jackson has received many scholarships, including the Martin Marietta Aircraft Company Scholarship and Fellowship, the Prince Hall Masons Scholarship, the National Science Foundation Traineeship, and a Ford Foundation Advanced Study Fellowship. She has been elected to the American Physical Society and selected a CIBA-GEIGY Exceptional Black Scientist. In 1985, Governor Thomas Kean appointed her to the New Jersey Commission on Science and Technology. Then in the early 1990s, Governor James Florio awarded her the Thomas Alva Edison Science Award for her contributions to physics and for the promotion of science. Jackson is an active voice in numerous committees of the National Academy of Sciences, the American Association for the Advancement of Science, and the National Science Foundation, where her aim has been to actively promote women in science.

Jackson is very involved in university life at Rutgers University, where in addition to being professor of physics she is also on the board of trustees. She is a lifetime member of the MIT Board of Trustees and was formerly a trustee of Lincoln University. She is also involved in civic organizations that promote community resources and developing enterprises. She is married and has one son.

SELECTED WRITINGS BY JACKSON:

Books

(With R. People) "Structurally Induced States from Strain and Confinement," in *Semiconductors and Semimetals,* Academic Press, 1990.

Periodicals

(With P. A. Lee and T. M. Rice) "Amplitude Modulation of Discommensurations in Charge Density Wave Structures," *Bulletin of the American Physical Society,* Volume 22, 1977, p. 280.

(With P. M. Platzman) "The Polaronic State of Two Dimensional Electrons on the Surface of Liquid Helium," *Surface Science,* Volume 142, 1984, p. 125.

(With F. M. Peeters) "Frequency Dependent Response of an Electron on a Liquid Helium Film," *Physical Review,* Volume B31, 1985, p. 7098.

SOURCES:

Books

Carwell, Hattie, *Blacks in Science: Astrophysicist to Zoologist,* Exposition Press, 1977, p. 60.

Notable Black American Women, Gale, 1992, pp. 565–566.

Blacks in Science and Medicine, Hemisphere, 1990, p. 130.

—Sketch by Barbara A. Branca

François Jacob
1920-
French biologist

François Jacob made several major contributions to the field of genetics through successful collaborations with other scientists at the famous Pasteur Institute in France. His most noted work involved the formulation of the Jacob-Monod operon model, which helps explain how genes are regulated. Jacob also studied messenger ribonucleic acid (mRNA), which serves as an intermediary between the deoxyribonucleic acid (DNA), which carries the genetic code, and the ribosomes, where proteins are synthesized. He also demonstrated that bacteria follow the same general rules of natural selection and evolution as higher organisms. In recognition of their work in genetic control and viruses, Jacob and two other scientists at the Pasteur Institute, **Jacques Lucien Monod** and **André Lwoff**, shared the 1965 Nobel Prize for Physiology or Medicine.

Jacob was born on June 17, 1920, in Nancy, France, to Simon Jacob, a merchant, and the former Thérèse Franck. Jacob attended school at the Lycée Carnot in Paris before beginning his college education. He began his studies toward a medical degree at the University of Paris (Sorbonne), but was forced to cut his education short when the German Army invaded France during World War II in 1940. He escaped on one of the last boats to England and joined the Free French forces in London, serving as an officer and fighting with the Allies in northern Africa. During the war, Jacob was seriously wounded. His injuries impaired his hands and put an abrupt end to his hopes of becoming a surgeon. For his service to his country, he received the Croix de Guerre and the Companion of the Liberation, two of France's highest military honors.

Despite this physical setback, Jacob continued his education at the University of Paris. In his autobiography, *The Statue Within,* Jacob said he got the idea for his thesis from his place of work, the National Penicillin Center, where a minor antibiotic called tyrothricin was manufactured and commercialized. For his thesis, Jacob manufactured and evaluated the drug. Nearing thirty years old, he earned his

François Jacob

M.D. degree in 1947, the same year he married Lysiane "Lise" Bloch, a pianist. They would eventually have four children: Pierre, Odile, Laurent and Henri.

With his professional future unsure, Jacob continued to work for a while at the National Penicillin Center. The tide turned when he and his wife had dinner with her cousins, including Herbert Marcovich, a biologist working in a genetics lab. Jacob recalled, "As Herbert spoke, I felt an excitement rising like a storm. If a man of my generation could still go into research without making himself ridiculous, then why not I?" He decided to become a biologist the next day.

Begins Career as Biologist in "The Attic"

Jacob joined the Pasteur Institute in 1950 as an assistant to André Lwoff. Lwoff's laboratory location and its cramped quarters earned it the name of "the attic." The year 1950 was an exciting one in Lwoff's lab. Lwoff had been working with lysogenic bacteria, which are destroyed (lysed) when attacked by bacteria-infecting virus particles called bacteriophages. The bacteriophages invade the bacterial cell, then multiply within it, eventually bursting the cell and releasing new bacteriophages. According to Lwoff's research, the bacteriophage first exists in the bacterial cell in a non-infectious phase called the prophage. He could stimulate the prophage to begin producing infective virus by adding ultraviolet light. These new findings helped to give Jacob the background he would need for his future research.

Jacob continued his education at the University of Paris during his first years at the Pasteur Institute, earning his bachelor of science in 1951 and studying toward his doctor of science degree, which he received in 1954. For his doctoral dissertation, Jacob reviewed the ability of certain radiations or chemical compounds to induce the prophage, and proposed possible mechanisms of immunity.

Once on staff in the lab, Jacob soon formed what would become a very fruitful collaboration with Élie Wollman, also stationed in Lwoff's laboratory. In the summer of 1954 he and Wollman discovered what they termed erotic induction in the bacteria *Escherichia coli.* They later changed the name of the phenomenon to zygotic induction. In zygotic induction, the chromosome of a male bacterial cell carrying a prophage could be transferred to a female cell which was not carrying the prophage, but not vice versa. Zygotic induction showed that both the expression of the prophage and immunity was blocked in the latter instance by a variable present in the cytoplasm which surrounds the cell's nucleus.

In another experiment, he and Wollman mated male and female bacterial cells, separating them before they could complete conjugation. This also clipped the chromosome as it was moving from the male to the female. They found that the female accepted the chromosome bit by bit, in a certain order and at a constant speed, rather similar to sucking up a piece of spaghetti. Their study became known as the "spaghetti experiment," much to Wollman's annoyance.

In the book *Phage and the Origins of Molecular Biology,* Wollman explained that by following different genetic markers in the male, they could determine each gene's time of entry into the zygote and correctly infer its position on the DNA. Jacob and Wollman also used an electron microscope to photograph the conjugating bacteria and time the transmission of the genes. "With Élie Wollman, we had developed a tool that made possible genetic analysis of any function, any "system," Jacob said in his autobiography. The two scientists also discovered and defined episomes, genetic strains which automatically replicate as part of the development of chromosomes.

Jacob and Wollman also demonstrated that bacteria could mutate and adapt in response to drugs or bacteriophages. Evolution and natural selection worked in bacteria as well as in higher life forms. Jacob and Wollman summarized their research in the July, 1956, issue of *Scientific American:* "There is little doubt that the basic features of genetic recombination must be similar whether they occur in bacteria or in man. It would be rather surprising if the study of sexual reproduction in bacteria did not lead to deeper understanding of the process of genetic recombination, which is so vital to the survival and evolution of higher organisms."

In 1956 Jacob accepted the title of laboratory director at the Pasteur Institute. Within two years Jacob began to work with Jacques Monod, who had left Lwoff's lab several years earlier to direct the department of cellular biochemistry at the Pasteur Institute. Arthur Pardée also often joined in the research. Jacob and Monod studied how an intestinal enzyme called galactosidase is activated to digest lactose, or milk sugar. Galactosidase is an inducible enzyme, that is, it is not formed unless a certain substrate—in this case lactose—is present. Inducible enzymes differ from constitutive enzymes which are continuously produced, whether or not the inducer is present. By pairing a normal inducible male bacteria with a constitutive female, they showed that inducible enzyme processes take precedence over constitutive enzyme synthesis. In the experiments conducted by Jacob and Monod, the inducer, lactose, served to inhibit the gene that was regulating the synthesis of galactosidase.

Afterward, Jacob realized that his work with Monod and his earlier work with Wollman on zygotic induction were related. In *The Statue Within,* he said, "In both cases, a gene governs the formation of a cytoplasmic product, of a repressor blocking the expression of other genes and so preventing either the synthesis of the galactosidase or the multiplication of the virus." Their chore then was to determine the location of the repressor, which appeared to be on the DNA.

Discovers mRNA, Genetic Control Mechanism

By the end of the decade, Jacob and Monod had discovered messenger RNA, one of the three types of ribonucleic acid. (The other two are ribosomal RNA and transfer RNA.) Each type of RNA has a specific function. MRNA is the mediator between the DNA and ribosomes, passing along information about the correct sequence of amino acids needed to make up proteins. While their work continued, Jacob accepted a position as head of the Department of Cell Genetics at the Pasteur Institute.

In 1961 they explained the results of their research involving the mRNA and the now-famous Jacob-Monod operon model in the paper, "Genetic Regulatory Mechanisms in the Synthesis of Proteins," which appeared in the *Journal of Molecular Biology.* Molecular biologist Gunther S. Stent in *Science* described the paper "one of the monuments in the literature of molecular biology."

According to the Jacob-Monod operon model, a set of structural genes on the DNA carry the code that the messenger RNA delivers to the ribosomes, which make proteins. Each set of structural genes has its own operator gene lying next to it. This operator gene is the switch that turns on or turns off its set of structural genes, and thus the oversees the synthesis of their proteins. Jacob and Monod called each grouping of an operator and its structural genes an operon. Besides the operator gene, a regulator gene is located on the same chromosome as the structural genes. In an inducible system, like the lactose operon (or lac operon as it is called), this regulator gene codes for a repressor protein. The repressor protein does one of two things. When no lactose is present, the repressor protein attaches to the operator and inactivates it, in turn, halting structural gene activity and protein synthesis. When lactose is present, however, the repressor protein binds to the regulator gene instead of the operator. By doing so, it frees up the operator and permits protein synthesis to occur. With a system such as this, a cell can adapt to changing environmental conditions, and produce the proteins it needs when it needs them.

A year after publication of this paper, Jacob won the Charles Leopold Mayer Prize of the French Academy of Sciences. In 1964, Collège de France also recognized his accomplishments by establishing a special chair in his honor. His greatest honor, however, came in 1965 when he, Lwoff, and Monod shared the Nobel Prize for Physiology or Medicine. The award recognized their contributions "to our knowledge of the fundamental processes in living matter which form the bases for such phenomena as adaptation, reproduction and evolution."

During his career, Jacob wrote numerous scientific publications, including the books *The Logic of Life: A History of Hereditary* and *The Possible and the Actual.* The latter, published in 1982, delves into the theory of evolution and the line that he believes must be drawn between the use of evolution as a scientific theory and as a myth.

Throughout his autobiography, *The Statue Within,* Jacob notes his drive to continually look ahead. He writes, "I am bored with what has been done, and excited only by what is to do. Were I to frame a prayer, I would ask to be granted not so much the 'strength' as the 'desire' to do."

SELECTED WRITINGS BY JACOB:

Books

La Bacteries lysogenes et la notion de provirus, Masson, 1954.

(With Élie Wollman) *La Sexualité des bacteries,* Masson, 1959, translation published as *Sexuality and the Genetics of Bacteria,* Academic Press, 1961.

(With Wollman) *Viruses and Genes,* Freeman, 1961.

La Logique du vivant: Une Histoire de l'heredité, Gallimard, 1970, translation by Betty E. Spillman published as *The Logic of Life: A History of Heredity,* Pantheon, 1973, published in England as *The Logic of Living Systems,* Allen Lane, 1974.

The Possible and the Actual, Pantheon, 1982.

The Statue Within, Basic Books, 1988.

Periodicals

"Sexuality in Bacteria," *Scientific American,* July, 1956, pp. 109–119.

SOURCES:

Books

Cairns, John, Gunther S. Stent, and James D. Watson, editors, *Phage and the Origins of Molecular Biology,* Cold Spring Harbor Laboratory of Quantitative Biology, 1966.

Lwoff, André and Agnes Ullmann, editors, *Origins of Molecular Biology,* Academic Press, 1979.

Periodicals

Stent, Gunther, "1965 Nobel Laureates in Medicine or Physiology," *Science,* October 22, 1965, pp. 462–464.

—*Sketch by Leslie Mertz*

Karl Jansky
1905-1950
American radio engineer

One of the ways modern astronomers study the universe is by tracing light waves through telescopes; another is by studying radio waves. The man who discovered the existence of these extraterrestrial radio waves and thus founded radio astronomy was Karl Jansky. Employed as an engineer in Bell Laboratories, New Jersey, Jansky was assigned the job of reducing static noise on transatlantic radio transmissions, and it was while inquiring into the origin of this static that he made his discovery. Jansky was very modest about what he had done. In a letter he wrote to British physicist **Edward Appleton**, later quoted in *The Invisible Universe Revealed* by Gerrit L. Verschuur, Jansky said: "If there is any credit due to me, it is probably for a stubborn curiosity that demanded an explanation for the unknown interference and led me to the long series of recordings necessary for the determination of the actual direction of arrival."

The third of six children, Karl Guthe Jansky was born on October 22, 1905 in Norman, Oklahoma, while that region was still a territory. His father, Cyril Jansky, was a college professor who taught electrical engineering and eventually became the head of the School of Applied Science at the University of Wisconsin. Jansky was named after Karl Guthe, a German-born physicist under whom his father had studied at the University of Michigan. Jansky attended the University of Wisconsin, where he played on the ice hockey team. He hoped to join the Reserve Officer's Training Program there but was diagnosed with a chronic kidney condition called Bright's disease; Jansky suffered from it all his life. He wrote his senior thesis on vacuum tubes, and he earned his B.S. in physics in June 1927. He stayed on at the University of Wisconsin for another year and supported himself by teaching while studying to complete the course work for his master's degree. He did not, however, write a thesis, and it would be years before he actually earned the degree.

After leaving the University of Wisconsin, Jansky applied for work at the Bell Communications Laboratories. The company was reluctant to hire him because of possible complications from Bright's disease. But Jansky's older bother, who was a professor of electrical engineering at the University of Minnesota, knew many Bell personnel. He intervened on behalf of his younger brother and secured the job for Jansky. Fearful of the stress he might suffer if he worked at their headquarters in New York City, the company assigned Jansky to work at its facilities in New Jersey.

Works on Transatlantic Radio Communication

Although transatlantic radio communication was possible in the early 1930s, it was very expensive and poor in quality. It cost seventy-five dollars to talk for three minutes from New York to London, and the transmissions, which occurred not through cables but through radio waves, were routinely interrupted by static. There were clicking, banging, crackling, and hissing noises that sometimes obliterated the conversation. At Bell, Harald Friis assigned Jansky the job of determining what was causing the static. This was in the summer of 1931, and the first step Jansky took to resolve the problem was to design a new antenna. He built a directional antenna that was capable of receiving a much wider range of wavelengths than conventional antennas of the time. He also developed a receiver that generated as little static as possible, to minimize its interference with his efforts to measure static from outside sources. Lastly, Jansky developed an averaging device for recording the variations in static. The antenna and the rest of the equipment were installed in Holmdel, New Jersey, a rural area where there would be very little interference from man-made radio signals.

The antenna that Jansky assembled at Holmdel was mounted on wheels and moved on a turntable. This allowed it to scan the sky in all directions once every twenty minutes; it could also be pointed at different heights above the horizon. Known as Jansky's "merry-go-round," the antenna is believed to have been the largest of its type at the time. It operated at 20 MHz or 14.6 meters. He categorized the static into three different types: local thunderstorms, distant thunderstorms, and steady static. Jansky was able to establish that thunderstorms were the source of clicks and bangs. But he observed of the last type of static, as quoted in *Mission Communications: The Story of Bell Laboratories,* that it was "a very steady hiss type static, the origin of which is not yet known."

Establishes the Origin of Hiss-Type Static

Jansky recorded the intensity of the hiss-type static, and he observed that it peaked when the antenna was pointed at a certain part of the sky. At first, Jansky thought that the point of peak intensity followed the sun, and he initially assumed that the static was solar generated. However, as he continued to make his observations, he saw that the peaks were moving further and further from the sun. Indeed, he observed that the peak intensities occurred every twenty-three hours and fifty-six minutes. This was perhaps the first time that Jansky truly considered the idea that this static could have an extraterrestrial origin.

Jansky knew little about astronomy, but after consulting some colleagues who did, he learned that while the Earth takes twenty-four hours to rotate once on its axis in relation to the sun, its rotation with respect to the stars is four minutes shorter. Known as a sidereal day, this phenomenon was precisely what Jansky had observed: peak intensities in static readings that occurred at intervals of twenty-three hours and fifty-six minutes. Although the existence of radio waves other than those generated by people on Earth had never even been considered as a possibility, Jansky did not doubt his findings. He had made a discovery that was entirely new, and he had done it by accident. He was also fortunate in another respect. His investigations were conducted at a time when the eleven-year cycle of solar activity was at a minimum, which rendered the ionosphere transparent to 20 MHz wavelengths at night. If this had not been the case, solar flares would have drowned out the weak hisses from space, and Jansky would never have been able to measure them.

Jansky had observed that the static was most intense when his antenna was aimed at the center of the Milky Way, the galaxy in which the Earth is located. His measurements indicated a direction of 18 hours right ascension and –10 degrees declination. Such a location put the peak static emissions in the constellation of Sagittarius. These observations led Jansky to form two hypotheses concerning the origin of the static: either radio sources are distributed much as the stars are in the galaxy, or the radio emissions come from stars like our own sun. Since Jansky never did pick up such emissions from the sun (weaker types were found by others), he rejected the second theory; his investigations during a partial solar eclipse in 1932 also seemed to support his belief that the sun was not emitting radio waves. The first hypothesis was supported by the fact that radio emissions were most intense from the center of the Milky Way, which contains the densest clusters of stars. Jansky also reasoned that the emissions from space would be found all along the electromagnetic spectrum, a hypothesis confirmed by later researchers.

It was in December, 1932, that Jansky realized the extraterrestrial nature of the static he was studying, and he issued his first report on the subject that same month in a paper titled "Directional Studies of Atmospherics at High Frequencies." He presented it to the Institute of Radio Engineers, but no one made much of his discovery. Indeed, Jansky's boss, Harald Friis, cautioned him against proposing that static came from extraterrestrial sources in case he should be proved wrong. In April, 1933, Jansky presented a second paper on these radio signals at a meeting of the International Scientific Radio Union in Washington, D.C. On May 5, 1933, Bell Laboratories issued a press release on the subject, and the next day the *New York Times* headlined his work as "New Radio Waves Traced to the Center of the Milky Way." On May 15, NBC's Blue Network broadcast a sample of Jansky's "star noise" to the nation. It was described by reporters as "sounding like steam escaping from a radiator." Jansky presented his second paper again at the annual convention of the Institute of Radio Engineers (IRE) in June, 1933, and it was published the following October.

While researching "star noise," Jansky worked on other projects. He designed a new receiver that could automatically change bandwidths, as well as studied the general effects of bandwidth on an incoming signal. When Bell realized that nothing could be done about the hiss-type static that Jansky was studying, they assigned him to a different project. Jansky wrote to his father in January, 1934, as quoted in the *Invisible Universe Revealed:* "I'm not working on the interstellar waves anymore. Friis has seen fit to make me work on the problems of and methods of measuring noise in general. A fundamental and necessary work, but not near as interesting as interstellar waves, nor will it bring near as much publicity. I'm going to do a little theoretical research of my own at home on the interstellar waves, however." Although Jansky presented his findings to astronomers, they largely ignored the implications of his work. One reason was that they did not believe the Milky Way could possibly be such a giant and intensive radio source. Resources were also scarce during the Great Depression of the 1930s, and there was little money for equipment to pursue this discovery. But the primary reason Jansky's work was neglected was that astronomy was then an optical venture. No one had any idea what to do with radio measurements. Jansky was, however, able to use his papers on "star noise" as a thesis for his master's degree. The University of Wisconsin awarded him this degree on June 16, 1936.

Jansky made other contributions to the understanding of radio communications while he worked at Bell. He became adept at detecting the direction of arrival of short-wave transmissions from all over the globe, which led to a better understanding of the effects of radio propagation. The information Jansky gained helped refine the design of both transmitting and receiving antennas. He also conducted research on noise reduction in receivers and other circuits. The outbreak of World War II made it even more difficult for Jansky to pursue his research on "star noise." Still working for Bell Laboratories, he was assigned to a classified project which concerned the development of direction finders for German U-boats or submarines. Jansky also worked on identifying particular transmitters by their "signatures," and his contributions led the military to issue him an Army-Navy citation. After the war, Jansky designed and developed frequency amplifiers which met the requirements of wide bandwidth and low noise.

Disappointed by the fact that he never had the time to investigate extraterrestrial radio waves further, Jansky applied for a teaching position at Iowa State University. He hoped that he would be able to use their facilities to further his research, but he was not hired. In 1948, the IRE made Jansky a fellow, but by this time Bright's disease was causing him to suffer from hypertension and heart problems. Although he tried to ward off the effects of his disease with specialized diets and health care, a massive stroke killed him on February 14, 1950. He was only forty-four years old. He left behind his wife, Alice, to whom he had been married since August 3, 1929, and two children who were still teenagers.

Although never recognized for his contributions to radio astronomy during his lifetime, Jansky's work was honored twenty-three years later. In 1973, the General Assembly of the International Astronomer's Union adopted the jansky as a unit of measurement. Defined as 10 to the –26 watts per meter squared hertz, the jansky measures intensity of radio waves.

SELECTED WRITINGS BY JANSKY:

Periodicals

"Directional Studies of Atmospherics at High Frequencies," *Proceedings of the IRE,* December, 1932, pp. 1920–32.

"Electrical Disturbances Apparently of Extraterrestrial Origin," *Proceedings of the IRE,* October, 1933, pp. 1387–98.

"Electrical Phenomena That Apparently Are of Interstellar Origin," *Popular Astronomy,* Volume 41, 1933, pp. 549–55.

SOURCES:

Books

Jastrow, Robert, and Malcolm H. Thompson, *Astronomy: Fundamentals and Frontiers,* Wiley, 1972.

Kellerman, K., and B. Sheets, editors, *Serendipitous Discoveries in Radio Astronomy,* National Radio Astronomy Observatory, 1983.

Mabon, Prescott C., *Mission Communications: The Story of Bell Laboratories,* Bell Telephone Laboratories, 1975.

Pawsey, J. L., and R. N. Bracewell, *Radio Astronomy,* Oxford University Press, 1955.

Struve, Otto, and Velta Zebergs, *Astronomy of the 20th Century,* Macmillan, 1962.

Verschuur, Gerrit L., *The Invisible Universe,* Springer-Verlag, 1974.

Verschuur, Gerrit L., *The Invisible Universe Revealed,* English Universities Press, 1987.

—Sketch by Susan E. Kolmer

Dan Janzen
1939-
American conservationist, ecologist, and biologist

Dan Janzen is one of the world's leading spokespeople for the preservation of our tropical rain forests. In 1989, he was highly influential in the founding of Costa Rica's National Biodiversity Institute in order to conduct experiments, identify and sort, and maintain on a permanent basis that country's estimated half-million species of plants and animals. Called the "dean of tropical biologists" by Pulitzer Prize-winning Harvard biologist **Edward O. Wilson**, as quoted in *Smithsonian,* Janzen was awarded the Crafoord Prize—biology's equivalent of the Nobel Prize—from the Royal Swedish Academy of Sciences in 1984. He received this award, according to *Smithsonian,* for "imaginative and stimulating studies on coevolution which have inspired many researchers to [continue] work in this field." Coevolution involves two species evolving a dependence upon one another for survival.

Daniel Janzen was born in Milwaukee, Wisconsin, on January 18, 1939. His father, Daniel Janzen, Sr., was the director of the U.S. Fish and Wildlife Service and a strong influence during his son's formative years. Dan Janzen grew up in northern Minnesota, and his early years were spent hunting and fishing in the North Woods, alone or with his father. By the age of nine, Janzen was familiar with the science of collecting and had already assembled an impressive assortment of moths from the Minnesota environs. While many of his teenage peers might have been involved with sports, Janzen spent his time alone in the woods or fields observing nature and collecting specimens. At the age of fifteen he undertook his first serious scientific-collection trip: an expedition to Mexico to collect butterflies.

Although his first love was the out-of-doors, Janzen enrolled at the University of Minnesota as an engineering major. He married while in college and, to support his wife and young child, ran a trap line catching and selling fur-bearing animals. He also used his experience as a hunter to put meat on his family's table. "I caught all the meat we ate in the last two years" of college, Janzen told *Smithsonian* magazine. While at Minnesota Janzen happened to walk one day into the school's zoology hall, which featured a wide variety of mounted birds and drawers of preserved specimens. For the first time he realized that insect collecting could be more than a hobby. He recounted in *Smithsonian,* "Until then I was an engineering major. It hadn't occurred to me that you could make a living studying insects."

Visits the Rain Forest

Janzen graduated from the University of Minnesota in 1961 and left immediately for the University of California, Berkeley, to study entomology. Within four years he acquired both his masters degree and a doctorate in entomology from Berkeley. While studying in California, however, an event occurred that was to alter the course of his career: Janzen was invited by the National Science Foundation to attend a biology seminar in Costa Rica. There he had his first encounter with a tropical rain forest replete with untold species of birds, animals, and plant life, as well as insects he had never before seen.

Yet, as excited as he was to experience the dense forest teeming with life, Janzen was shocked to learn that rain forests were being destroyed by humans at an alarming rate. (By the 1990s, the world's great rain forests would be destroyed at the frightening rate of an acre a second.) Janzen commented in *Smithsonian* magazine in 1986 that eighty percent of the foods we eat each week—including corn, eggs, orange juice, and sugar—originate in the tropics. "Costa Rica had four times the tropical forest then [in the 1960s] than it has today," he recalled. "It was fantastic, as if what had existed in Mexico 6,000 years ago had survived intact." Janzen estimated in *Smithsonian* that all of our tropical forests, except for the land that we've preserved in parks, would be destroyed in thirty years.

Janzen's immediate response to this new information was to create a highly influential eight-week field course in tropical biology in Costa Rica, administered by the Organization for Tropical Studies, a consortium of forty institutions from the U.S. and Costa Rica. Although he taught it only until the early 1970s, the course was later taught by others according to his original design. After receiving his Ph.D. from Berkeley in 1965, Janzen accepted a position as assistant professor of biology at the University of Kansas. He remained at Kansas for three years before moving to the University of Chicago and becoming an associate professor. In 1972 he was offered an associate professorship at the University of Michigan, where he advanced to full professor status. Janzen left Michigan in 1976, when he was hired by the University of Pennsylvania as a professor of biology, a position he still retains.

Works to Establish Tropical Refuge

Since 1965 Janzen has been researching the interactions between tropical plants and animals in the sprawling Guanacaste Conservation Area of Costa Rica. He established his headquarters in Santa Rosa, a tiny jungle town on the lush slopes of a volcano overlooking the Nicaraguan border. Janzen splits his time equally between his students at the University of Pennsylvania and his work in Santa Rosa, where he also serves as advisor to the Costa Rican government. He often works with his second wife, Winnie Hallwachs, collecting and cataloging tropical fauna. Janzen is the author of more than 300 papers on the subject of tropical biology, and was editor of and chief contributor to the 816-page volume, *Costa Rican Natural History.* For his work on tropical plants, he received the Gleason Award in 1975 from the American Botanical Society.

Janzen is dedicated to raising enough money among governments and conservation groups to create a 270-square-mile refuge to be named the Guanacaste National Park. To this end Janzen donated half of his $100,000 Crafoord Prize to the new park's endowment and donated the remainder of the prize to energize the town of Santa Rosa. According to Thomas Lovejoy, U.S. executive vice president of the World Wildlife Fund, as quoted in *Smithsonian,* Janzen is "probably one of the best articulators we have of the value of tropical conservation." As Janzen tours the world, raising money to endow his dream project, his basic message, as stated in *Smithsonian,* is always the same: "If we let the tropics go under we will have committed the greatest criminal act that life on Earth ever could or will sustain."

SELECTED WRITINGS BY JANZEN:

Books

(Editor with Thomas B. Reed) Swedish Academy of Engineering staff, *Gengas: The Swedish Classic on Wood Powered Vehicles,* 2nd edition, translated by Maria Geuther, Tipi Workshop Books, 1982.

(Editor and contributor) *Costa Rican Natural History,* University of Chicago Press, 1983.

SOURCES:

Periodicals

Lessem, Don, "From Bugs to Boas, Dan Janzen Bags the Rich Coast's Life (Costa Rica)," *Smithsonian,* December, 1986, p. 110.

Moseley, Bill, "Daniel Janzen: Restoration Ecologist," *Omni,* April, 1993, pp. 73–74, 76–77, 94–95.

—*Sketch by Benedict A. Leerburger*

Robert K. Jarvik
1946-
American physician, biomedical engineer, and inventor

Physician Robert K. Jarvik is designer and biomedical engineer of the first artificial heart used as a permanent implant in a human being. The device, named Jarvik-7, was implanted in Barney Clark on December 2, 1982, at the University of Utah Medical Center. Mr. Clark lived 112 days with the artificial heart. Jarvik has also performed research on other artificial organs and is author of more than 60 technical articles. He holds a number of patents on medical devices and has received numerous awards, including two citations of "Inventor of the Year"—from Intellectual Property Owners in 1982 and from National Inventors Hall of Fame in 1983. Jarvik also holds honorary doctorates from Syracuse University and Hahnemann University, presented in 1983 and 1985 respectively.

Robert Koffler Jarvik was born May 11, 1946, in Midland, Michigan, son of physician Norman Eugene Jarvik and Edythe Koffler Jarvik, and was raised in Stamford, Connecticut. As a teenager, Jarvik was a tinkerer and inventor. He watched his father in surgery and before he graduated from high school had invented an automatic stapler for use during surgery, which would replace the process of manually sewing up living body parts. He entered Syracuse University in 1964 and took courses in mechanical drawing and architecture, but his father's heart disease prompted him to change his course of study. Jarvik began premedical course work and graduated in 1968 with a bachelor's degree in zoology. His immediate plans were stalled when mediocre grades prevented him from acceptance into an American medical school. As an alternative, he attended medical school at the University of Bologna in Italy. After two years he returned to the United States to pursue a degree in occupational biomechanics at New York University, receiving an M.A. in 1971.

Shortly following graduation, Jarvik was hired as an assistant design engineer at the University of Utah by **Willem Kolff,** a leading expert in the development of artificial organs. Dr. Kolff had been working on inventing an artificial heart since the mid–1950s. In 1967 he had been appointed head of a new division at the University of Utah, which became known as the Institute of Biomedical Engineering. Its primary project was to develop an artificial heart.

Jarvik's achievements in biomedical engineering are closely tied to his employment at the institute, as it was headed by a world expert on man-made organs who had been working on developing an artificial heart for more than fifteen years, and had the full institutional support of the University of Utah, an essential condition for such a large-scale and complex medical project. Jarvik's inventive genius soon solved several problems associated with the devices. By the early 1980s, Jarvik developed an artificial heart that could be implanted in a human being. While working at the institute, Jarvik received his M.D. from the University of Utah in 1976.

The artificial heart program at the Utah institute aimed to re-create the lower two chambers or ventricles of the heart, which comprise the pumping portion of the organ. Creating the pump with a suitable power-source was the major obstacle facing the project. The ideal solution was considered a single unit containing both the pump and the power source that would be completely encased in the recipient's body. Before Jarvik arrived, Kolff had worked hard to create an electrical power source and, after failing at that, a nuclear one. When this strategy also failed, Kolff decided to concentrate on the pump and to rely on power from compressed air from a machine outside the body connected by tubes to the artificial heart. Scientifically, the decision was sound, as it divided a complex problem into two simpler parts. In practicality, however, it meant that recipients of the artificial heart would be permanently attached by tubes to a machine.

Develops the Jarvik–7 Artificial Heart

When Jarvik arrived at the institute, he immediately began working on the "Kwann-Gett heart," which was designed in 1971 by a member of Kolff's team, Clifford S. Kwann-Gett. This device used a rubber diaphragm as the pumping element that forced blood in and out of the artificial heart. The diaphragm represented an improvement in that it lowered the possibility of mechanical failure. However, it also caused blood to clot on its surface, which could cause death. Jarvik's improved version, called the "Jarvik–3," was shaped to better fit the anatomy of the experimental animals. In addition, the rubber of the diaphragm had been replaced by three highly flexible layers of a smooth polyurethane called 'biomer,' which eliminated the clotting problem. By the mid–1970s, Jarvik was working on a version intended for the human body. The plastic and aluminum device would replace the lower pumping chambers, known as the ventricles, and would be attached to the two upper chambers of the heart known as the atria, which receive blood from the veins. Such a device, called the "Jarvik–7," was implanted into Barney Clark on December 2, 1982.

Clark was a 61-year-old retired dentist suffering from cardiomyopathy, a degenerative disease of the heart muscles. He was a terminally ill man who believed that the experimental surgery would give him hope and would also contribute to the progress of medical science. In a seven and a half hour operation performed by surgeon William C. DeVries with assistance from Jarvik, Clark's ventricles were replaced by the Jarvik–7 which was driven by an outside air-compressor connected to the artificial heart by tubes. The surgery received world-wide publicity. Shortly after the operation, Clark suffered from disabling brain seizures. He died less than four months later. The artificial heart itself (except for a malfunctioning valve, which was replaced) functioned throughout, and was still pumping when Clark died of multiple organ failure. The surgery performed on Clark has provoked debate concerning various issues of medical ethics.

Ventures into Manufacturing Artificial Organs

In 1976, Jarvik became a vice-president of Symbion, Inc., (originally known as Kolff Associates) an artificial organs research firm founded by Dr. Kolff. Jarvik was an aggressive officer of the company, and was appointed president in 1981. Seeking venture capital, Jarvik arranged a deal with an outside investment firm in which Kolff was to be deliberately excluded from direct management of the company. The move became the source of friction between Kolff and Jarvik, but has since been resolved. Under Jarvik's direction, the company branched out to include development and manufacturing of other organs, including an artificial ear.

After Barney Clark's surgery, a number of other modified Jarvik hearts were implanted but none of the recipients lived more than 620 days. The Jarvik–7 was also frequently and more successfully used as a temporary measure for patients awaiting a natural heart transplant. After Jarvik's own departure from the University of Utah and Symbion in 1987, the Jarvik–7 artificial heart did not fare well. Federal funding for the Jarvik project stopped in 1988, and artificial heart implantation was restricted to temporary implantation only. In 1990, the Food and Drug Administration (FDA) withdrew approval for the experimental use of the Jarvik–7, citing Symbion's poor quality control in the manufacturing process and inadequate service of equipment.

In 1987, Jarvik moved to New York City where he became president of his own company, Jarvik Research, Inc. In the same year, he married Marilyn vos Savant, a writer who is reported by the *Guinness Book of World Records* to have the highest IQ score in the world and whose writings include a well-known column in *Parade* magazine. Jarvik had been previously married to journalist Elaine Levin, with whom he had two children, Tyler and Kate. Jarvik continued artificial heart research, concentrating on the Jarvik 2000, described by Julie Baumgard in *New York* as a "rotary hydrodynamic axial-flow pump" in which "the valves have been eliminated and the whole device miniaturized." Based on principles quite different from the Jarvik–7, both the pump and its power source would be implanted entirely inside the heart. In an article in *After Barney Clark,* contributor Renée C. Fox described Jarvik as the "boyishly glamorous culture hero of bioengineering in whom the values of the 1960s and of the 1980s seem to be joined." Jarvik's interests are skiing, weight-lifting, poetry, art, sculpting, and physics.

SELECTED WRITINGS BY JARVIK:

Periodicals

"The Total Artificial Heart," *Scientific American,* January, 1981, pp. 74–80 and 170.

SOURCES:

Books

After Barney Clark: Reflections on the Utah Artificial Heart Program, edited by Margery W. Shaw, University of Texas Press, 1984.

Berger, Melvin, *The Artificial Heart,* F. Watts, 1987.

Contemporary Newsmakers, 1985 Cumulation, Gale, 1986, pp. 183–185.

Current Biography Yearbook, 1985, H. W. Wilson, 1985, pp. 201–204.

Periodicals

Altman, Lawrence K., "U.S. Halts the Use of Jarvik Heart," *New York Times,* January 12, 1990, p. A20.

Baumgold, Julie, "In the Kingdom of the Brain: How Love Changed the Smartest Couple in New York," *New York,* February 6, 1989, pp. 36–43.

McMurran, Kristin, "There's Nothing Artificial about the Way Robert Jarvik's Heart Beats for his Brainy Bride-to-Be," *People Weekly,* July 27, 1987, pp. 47–50.

—Sketch by Pamela O. Long

Robert S. Jason
1901-1984
American physician and pathologist

Robert S. Jason was the first African American to earn a Ph.D. in pathology. Jason had a medical degree as well and served as head of the department of pathology at Howard University and later as dean of its college of medicine. During his last years at Howard, he was coordinator for design and planning of its new University Hospital. In recognition of his many contributions to the university, the department of pathology at Howard's College of Medicine established in 1967 the Robert S. Jason Award in Pathology.

Robert Stewart Jason was born in Santurce, Puerto Rico on November 29, 1901. He was the son of Reverend Howard Talbot Jason, a Presbyterian missionary who was originally from Maryland, and his missionary wife, Lena B. (Wright) Jason. After attending local schools in Corozal, Puerto Rico and graduating from the Polytechnic Institute of San German, Puerto Rico, Jason entered Lincoln University in Pennsylvania and received his B.A. degree in 1924. He then attended the Howard University College of Medicine in Washington, D.C., and was awarded his M.D. degree in 1928. From the local schools of Puerto Rico through college and medical school, Jason was regularly ranked first in his class. In 1929 he completed his internship at Freedman's Hospital in Washington, D.C., and chose to continue his studies at the University of Chicago, where he was awarded his Ph.D. in pathology in 1932.

During that time, Jason joined the medical faculty at Howard's College of Medicine as an assistant professor of pathology. In 1934 he became associate professor and acting head of the department of pathology, and, by 1937, he was the department head and a full professor as well. He then served as vice dean of the college of medicine from 1946 to 1953, and as dean from 1955 to 1965. In that year he took on a new position as coordinator for the design and planning stages of a new facility to replace Howard's old Freedman's Hospital. He retired as professor emeritus in 1970 and lived in San Diego, California, before moving to New York City in 1979. As a pathologist, he was concerned with the structural and functional changes in cells, tissues, and organs caused by disease, and he focused specifically during his research career on the pathology of syphilis and tuberculosis. As department head and dean, he ran an extremely efficient operation, and these same skills were used to plan and organize Howard's new hospital.

Besides research, teaching, and administration, Jason held many professional appointments. He was a consultant in pathology to the National Institutes of Health from 1955 to 1970, consultant to the Veterans Administration Hospital from 1960 to 1970, member of the International Committee on Health of the Agency for International Development, and member of the National Advisory Council on Education for the Health Professions from 1964 to 1968. Jason also received several honors and awards during his long career. Besides two honorary doctorates and several awards from Howard University, he received the Professional Achievement Award given by the University of Chicago Alumni Association in 1970 and the Distinguished Service Award of the National Medical Association in 1969. Jason considered the most significant honor he received to be Howard University's College of Medicine naming an award after him in 1967. According to the *Journal of the*

National Medical Association, "it is presented to a graduating student chosen on the basis of distinguished scholastic achievements, demonstrated interest in fundamental aspects of disease, integrity, self-discipline, and compassion, attributes common to the recipient and Dr. Robert S. Jason."

Jason was a volunteer with the American Cancer Society as well as a member of the American Medical Association, the American Association of Pathologists and Bacteriologists, and the International Academy of Pathologists. He was also a fellow of the College of American Pathologists and belonged to Alpha Omega Alpha (a national medical honor society), Alpha Phi Alpha Fraternity, and the Alpha Pi Boule of Sigma Pi Phi Fraternity.

Jason died of Alzheimer's disease at his home in New York City on April 6, 1984. He was survived by his wife, the former Elizabeth Gaddis, a daughter, Mrs. Jean Elizabeth Wright, a son, Robert S. Jason, Jr. M.D., and one brother and four sisters.

SELECTED WRITINGS BY JASON:

Periodicals:

"Howard University and the College of Medicine," *New Physician,* Volume 8, 1959, pp. 61–70.

"Opportunities, Obligations and Challenges We Cannot Refuse," *Journal of the National Medical Association,* Volume 61, 1969, pp. 417–21.

SOURCES:

Books

Sammons, Vivian O., *Blacks in Science and Medicine,* Hemisphere Publishing, 1990, p. 131.

Periodicals

"Dr. Robert Stewart Jason Awarded Distinguished Service Medal for 1969," *Journal of the National Medical Association,* Volume 62, January, 1970, pp. 60–61.

"Jason and Harden to New Posts at Howard," *Journal of the National Medical Association,* Volume 58, March, 1966, pp. 131–32.

Obituary, *Washington Post,* Saturday, April 14, 1984, p. B4.

"Robert Stewart Jason, S.R., M.D., Ph.D., D.Sc.: 1901–1984," *Journal of the National Medical Association,* Volume 76, September, 1984, pp. 934–35.

—*Sketch by Leonard C. Bruno*

Harold Jeffreys
1891-1989
English astronomer and geophysicist

Sir Harold Jeffreys enjoyed an illustrious scientific career that spanned more than four decades and brought to the world important work in such fields as geophysics, astronomy, mathematics, and meteorology. His *Earth: Its Origin, History, and Physical Constitution* is a classic in its field, and the *Seismological Tables* Jeffreys computed with Keith Edward Bullen became a long-standing resource in understanding earthquakes. Although Jeffreys pushed the limits of statistics in his research and was often criticized by colleagues for his unusual methods, he was honored with many awards and distinctions, including the knighthood in 1953 and the Guy Medal from the Royal Statistical Society in 1963.

The son of Robert and Elizabeth Jeffreys, Harold Jeffreys was born in Fatfield, Durham County, England, on April 22, 1891. Jeffreys's curiosity for the natural world developed early. "My interest in astronomy was acquired through the works of Sir Robert Ball and G. F. Chambers," Jeffreys told *Contemporary Authors (CA).* "I was a keen naturalist from the age of nine." Jeffreys pursued undergraduate degrees in science, studying physics, mathematics, chemistry, and geology. He earned a bachelor of science degree in 1910 and a master of science degree in 1913 from the University of Durham and a bachelor of arts degree with honors from St. John's College, Cambridge University, also in 1913. "My main interest became geophysics, and here the work of Sir [English astronomer] George Darwin was my inspiration," Jeffreys explained to *CA.* "Although he was alive when I reached Cambridge, I did not meet him." Four years later Jeffreys was awarded a doctorate from the University of Durham and a master of arts degree from St. John's College.

Although he was already a fellow at St. John's College, from 1917 to 1922 Jeffreys worked as a professional assistant in the Meteorological Office. He returned solidly to academia in 1922 with his post of university lecturer in mathematics at Cambridge University, a position he held for ten years. For the next fourteen years, Jeffreys was a reader in geophysics at Cambridge. In 1946 he was elected to the chair of Plumian Professor of Astronomy and Experimental Philosophy at Cambridge, from which he retired in 1958.

Explores the World in Landmark Publication

Early in his career, Jeffreys produced the seminal work *The Earth,* a study of the structure and formation of the planet. At intervals throughout his career, Jeffreys revised and updated this work. Its sixth and final edition appeared in 1961 and was reprinted in 1976. In *The Earth* Jeffreys investigated, among other subjects, the theory of continental drift, which states that the planet's major land masses move slowly due to the presence of a viscous layer deep within the Earth. Jeffreys opposed the theory throughout his life. The book also presented material on the effects of the tides, particularly the Earth's nutation, that is the planet's wobbling on its axis like a top due to the combined gravitational forces of the sun and moon. In the realm of meteorology, Jeffreys investigated monsoons and air currents.

While it was commonly believed that the surfaces of the outer planets of the solar system were extremely hot, Jeffreys thought otherwise in the early 1920s. Flying in the face of then-current scientific opinion, Jeffreys proposed that the temperatures of the surface of these outer planets are frigid on the basis of his mathematical calculations. Direct observations by other scientists eventually proved Jeffreys to be correct.

Jeffreys was also able to calculate the hardness of the Earth's core after studying the effects of the tides. In 1926 he was the first to maintain that the center of the Earth is composed of molten rock. Later, drawing on the work of scientist James Dean, Jeffreys estimated the age of the solar system at several thousand million years. He also formulated models of Neptune, Uranus, Saturn, and Jupiter that showed the internal formations of these planets.

Jeffreys and Bullen Contribute to the Field of Seismology

During the 1930s and 1940s Jeffreys and Keith Edward Bullen calculated and compiled their *Seismological Tables.* The "JB Tables," as they became commonly known, provided the travel times of earthquake waves and thus allowed scientists to determine the epicenter of an earthquake and the distance of an observer from it. These have been key measurement tools at the International Seismological Centre.

On September 6, 1940, Jeffreys married Bertha Swirles, a mathematician and fellow at Girton College, Cambridge. Together they produced *Methods of Mathematical Physics,* one of several works on mathematics Jeffreys published during his career. In his other mathematical works, Jeffreys delved into statistical probability theory, Cartesian tensors, operational calculus, and asymptotic approximations.

During his long and illustrious career, Jeffreys earned many prestigious awards, among them the Victoria Medal from the Royal Geological Society, the Bowie Medal from the American Geophysical Union, and the Vetlesen Prize from the Royal Astronomical Society. He was awarded honorary degrees at several colleges, including Trinity College in Dublin, Ireland, and Southern Methodist University; in 1962 the Royal Astronomical Society founded a university chair in his name. A volume of essays on statistics was published in Jeffreys's honor in 1980, a fitting tribute to a man who used statistics in creative and daring ways.

SELECTED WRITINGS BY JEFFREYS:

Books

The Earth: Its Origin, History, and Physical Constitution, Cambridge University Press, 1924, sixth edition, 1961; reprinted, 1976.

Operational Methods in Mathematical Physics, Cambridge University Press, 1927, second edition, 1931.

The Future of the Earth, Norton, 1929.

Cartesian Tensors, Cambridge University Press, 1931; reprinted, 1971.

Scientific Inference, Cambridge University Press, 1931, third edition, 1973.

Earthquakes and Mountains, Methuen, 1935, second edition, 1950.

Theory of Probability, Oxford University Press, 1939, third edition, 1961.

(With Keith Edward Bullen) *Seismological Tables,* International Seismological Association, 1940, second edition, 1958.

(With wife Bertha Jeffreys) *Methods of Mathematical Physics,* Cambridge University Press, 1946, third edition, 1956.

Asymptotic Approximations, Oxford University Press, 1962.

(With B. Jeffreys) *Collected Papers on Geophysics and Other Sciences,* six volumes, Gordon & Breach, 1971–77.

SOURCES:

Books

Biographical Encyclopedia of Scientists, Volume 1, Facts on File, 1981, p. 416.

Contemporary Authors, Volume 109, Gale, 1983, pp. 229–30; Volume 128, Gale, 1990, p. 210.

Daintith, John, Sara Mitchell, and Elizabeth Tootill, editors, *A McGraw-Hill Encyclopedia of World Biography,* Volume 5, 1973, pp. 553–54.

McGraw-Hill Modern Men of Science, Volume 1, McGraw-Hill, 1966, pp. 255–57.

McGraw-Hill Modern Scientists and Engineers, Volume 2, McGraw-Hill, 1980.

Periodicals

Times (London), March 23, 1989.

—*Sketch by Jeanne M. Lesinski*

Zay Jeffries
1888-1965
American metallurgist

Zay Jeffries is widely regarded as one of the prominent metallurgists of the first half of the twentieth century. He spent six years as a teacher at the Case School of Applied Science in Cleveland, Ohio, and worked many years as a consultant to a number of industrial firms, including the General Electric Company and the Aluminum Company of America. Jeffries made contributions in both the theoretical and applied fields of metallurgy. His slip-interference theory of metal hardening guided a large portion of the experimental research carried out in metallurgy for many years, and his early studies of grain size in metals with the properties of tungsten were breakthroughs in their fields.

Jeffries was born on April 22, 1888, on a farm near the small town of Willow Lake, in what was then the Dakota Territories (now the state of South Dakota). His biographer W. D. Mogerman suggests that the name Zay was an abbreviation for a given name of Isaiah, although Jeffries was universally known by the shortened version of the name. He was the seventh of eleven children, of whom ten survived, born to Johnston Jeffries and the former Florence Sutton. The Jeffries had met in Mattoon, Illinois, and were to spend much of their lives traveling around the upper Midwest, trying to scratch out a living and to find a climate amenable to Johnston's increasingly poor health.

Jeffries attended elementary school in Fort Pierre, South Dakota, where his family had moved in 1890. He then had to travel across the Missouri River to continue his education at the high school in Pierre, the new state's capital city. In 1906 Jeffries graduated from high school and enrolled at the South Dakota School of Mines in Rapid City. At the time, the facility was a modest struggling institution of eleven instructors and forty-four students. It had been established, according to Mogerman, "to help young men like Zay prepare for exploitation of the state's mining and metallurgic resources." It was in Rapid City that Jeffries first met Frances Schrader, who was to become his wife a few years later on December 27, 1911. The Jeffries later had two daughters, Elizabeth (always known as Betty) and Marion.

When Jeffries first arrived in Rapid City, he planned to become a geologist. He switched to metallurgy, however, partly because of the greater prospect of employment in that field and also due to the influence of Charles A. Fulton. It was in the field of mining engineering, therefore, that Jeffries received his bachelor of science degree in 1910. He was also valedictorian, class president, and quarterback of the football team in a graduating class of nine men.

Begins Teaching and Consulting in Cleveland

For several months Jeffries worked as an assayer in Deadwood and then as a mine superintendent in Custer. On June 1, 1911, however, he was offered a job as instructor in metallurgy and ore dressing at the Case School of Applied Science in Cleveland. He accepted the job and began work at Case the following fall. Jeffries's affiliation with Case lasted until he resigned in 1917.

By 1914 Jeffries had embarked on a new phase of his career, consulting. His first job was with the Electric Railway Improvement Company of Cleveland. The firm was having difficulties keeping its rails bonded. Jeffries's success with this problem quickly brought him a number of other consulting opportunities with businesses such as the Cleveland Steel Tool Company, the Lincoln Electric Company, the U.S. Tyler Company, and the National Lamp Works of the General Electric Company. Jeffries's work for General Electric involved a study of the tungsten wire then being developed for use in electric lamps. He was asked to find out if there was any way to overcome what appeared to be inherent problems in the use of tungsten in electric lightbulbs.

Jeffries undertook an exhaustive study of the metal that was summarized in a September 1918 paper on "The Metallurgy of Tungsten," read before the American Institute of Mining Engineers. In this work, Jeffries described the process of second recrystallization and discussed the effects of inclusions (foreign bodies enclosed in minerals) on metal strength. He also received permission to submit this paper as a doctoral thesis at Harvard University, from which he was granted a Ph.D. in 1918. The work on tungsten marked the beginning of an association with General Electric that was to last more than three decades.

Jeffries also conducted important experimental research on grain size in metals. Until the late 1910s, metallurgists had relatively little understanding of the way in which the crystalline structure of metals could be determined and how such information could be used in the preparation and treatment of metals. In a careful series of studies carried out at Case, Jeffries developed techniques for observing and measuring grain size and for predicting the ways in which crystalline structure would affect the properties of a metal. The results of this work were summarized in a 1916 paper in the *Transactions of the Faraday Society* under the title "Grain Size Measurements in Metals and Importance of Such Information."

Develops Slip-Interference Theory

The research on grain size led Jeffries in two different directions. First, he put the knowledge to practical use in the development of a number of new alloys, especially alloys of aluminum. In the 1920s, Jeffries and his colleague R. S. Archer were granted about a dozen patents for new alloys and for methods of treating alloys. Second, Jeffries's work on alloy development led him to devise a notion about the way in which metals harden, a theory called slip-interference theory of metal hardening. According to Cyril Stanley Smith in the *Dictionary of Scientific Biography,* it was "the first theory of metal hardening to be based realistically upon crystalline structure and was the immediate precursor of dislocation theory."

As the 1920s drew to a close, Jeffries had essentially given up his own research in favor of administrative responsibilities. By 1928 he had become consulting metallurgist for Alcoa (the Aluminum Company of America), a post he held until 1936. He had also retained his close ties with the General Electric Company and had become technical director of the company's lamp division. He also continued to consult with other corporations, such as the National Tube Company of the U.S. Steel Corporation. Jeffries had also become president of the Carboloy Company, a firm established to manufacture and sell the new carboloy alloy with great potential for use as a high-speed steel-cutting material.

During World War II, Jeffries was asked by **Arthur Holly Compton** to consult with him on some of the difficult metallurgical problems being encountered in the Manhattan Project's development of the first atomic bomb. Jeffries began that work in January of 1943 and then, eighteen months later, was asked by Compton to chair a committee on postwar work on nucleonics. Jeffries himself had coined the term *nucleon,* to refer to protons and neutrons, and the term *nucleonics,* to describe the practical applications of nuclear physics.

After a short illness in the late 1940s caused by a benign brain tumor, Jeffries decided to take early retirement from General Electric on December 31, 1949. Biographer Mogerman claims that Jeffries's retirement festivities "have probably never been equalled at General Electric since, and rarely anywhere else." December 17, 1949, was declared Zay Jeffries Day throughout the company's chemical department.

Retirement did not mean a retreat from work for Jeffries, however. He continued to consult and to participate in a variety of professional and governmental activities. In 1951 he was asked to be a member of the National Academy of Science's Metallurgical Advisory Board, later the Materials Advisory Board. Jeffries had also become a senior statesperson of the American metallurgical industry, writing and speaking frequently about the role of metals and nucleonics in the modern world. In 1964 he learned that he had prostate cancer and, a year later, on May 21, 1965, died of the disease in his home in Pittsfield, Massachusetts.

Of the numerous awards that Jeffries received were the James Douglas Medal of the Institute of Metals Division of the American Institute of Mining and Metallurgical Engineers in 1927, the Albert Sauveur Achievement Award in 1935, the Gold Medal of the American Society for Metals in 1943, the Francis J. Clamer Silver Medal of the Franklin Institute in 1945, and the Powder Metallurgy Medal of the Stevens Institute of Technology in 1945. Jeffries was elected to membership in the National Academy of Sciences in 1936.

SELECTED WRITINGS BY JEFFRIES:

Books

(With F. C. Frary and J. D. Edwards) *The Aluminum Industry,* two volumes, McGraw-Hill, 1930.

(With R. S. Archer) *The Science of Metals,* McGraw-Hill, 1942.

Periodicals

"Grain Size Measurements in Metals and Importance of Such Information," *Transactions of the Faraday Society,* Volume 12, part 1, 1916.

"Metallography of Tungsten," *Transactions of the American Institute of Mining and Metallurgical Engineers,* Volume 60, 1919, pp. 588–656.

"The Slip Interference Theory of the Hardening of Metals," *Chemical and Metallurgical Engineering,* Volume 24, 1921, pp. 1057–1067.

"The New Term 'Nucleonics,'" *Chemical and Engineering News,* Volume 24, 1946.

SOURCES:

Books

Dictionary of Scientific Biography, Volume 7, Scribner's, 1975, pp. 92–93.

Mogerman, W. D., *Zay Jeffries,* American Society of Metals, 1973.

—*Sketch by David E. Newton*

Mae C. Jemison
1956-
American physician and astronaut

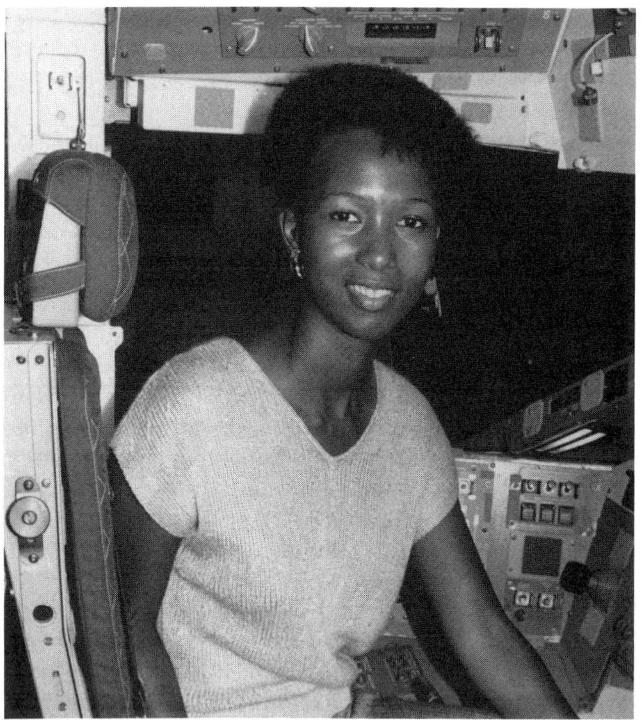

Mae C. Jemison

Mae C. Jemison had received two undergraduate degrees and a medical degree, had served two years as a Peace Corps medical officer in West Africa, and was selected to join the National Aeronautics and Space Administration's astronaut training program, all before her thirtieth birthday. Her eight-day space flight aboard the space shuttle *Endeavour* in 1992 established Jemison as the United States' first female African American space traveler.

Mae Carol Jemison was born on October 17, 1956, in Decatur, Alabama, the youngest child of Charlie Jemison, a roofer and carpenter, and Dorothy (Green) Jemison, an elementary school teacher. Her sister, Ada Jemison Bullock, became a child psychiatrist, and her brother, Charles Jemison, is a real estate broker. The family moved to Chicago, Illinois, when Jemison was three to take advantage of better educational opportunities there, and it is that city that she calls her hometown. Throughout her early school years, her parents were supportive and encouraging of her talents and abilities, and Jemison spent considerable time in her school library reading about all aspects of science, especially astronomy. During her time at Morgan Park High School, she became convinced she wanted to pursue a career in biomedical engineering, and when she graduated in 1973 as a consistent honor student, she entered Stanford University on a National Achievement Scholarship.

At Stanford, Jemison pursued a dual major and in 1977 received a B.S. in chemical engineering and a B.A. in African and Afro-American Studies. As she had been in high school, Jemison was very involved in extracurricular activities including dance and theater productions, and served as head of the Black Student Union. Upon graduation, she entered Cornell University Medical College to work toward a medical degree. During her years there, she found time to expand her horizons by visiting and studying in Cuba and Kenya and working at a Cambodian refugee camp in Thailand. When she obtained her M.D. in 1981, she interned at Los Angeles County/University of Southern California Medical Center and later worked as a general practitioner. For the next two and a half years, she was the area Peace Corps medical officer for Sierra Leone and Liberia where she also taught and did medical research. Following her return to the U.S. in 1985, she made a career change and decided to follow a dream she had nurtured for a long time. In October of that year she applied for admission to NASA's astronaut training program. The *Challenger* disaster of January 1986 delayed the selection process, but when she reapplied a year later, Jemison was one of the fifteen candidates chosen from a field of about two thousand.

Joins Eight-Day Endeavour Mission

When Jemison was chosen on June 4, 1987, she became the first African American woman ever admitted into the astronaut training program. After more than a year of training, she became an astronaut with the title of science-mission specialist, a job which would make her responsible for conducting crew-related scientific experiments on the space shuttle. On September 12, 1992, Jemison finally flew into space with six other astronauts aboard the *Endeavour* on mission STS–47. During her eight days in space, she conducted experiments on weightlessness and motion sickness on the crew and herself. Altogether, she spent slightly over 190 hours in space before returning to Earth on September 20. Following her historic flight, Jemison noted that society should recognize how much both women and members of other minority groups can contribute if given the opportunity.

In recognition of her accomplishments, Jemison received several honorary doctorates, the 1988 *Essence* Science and Technology Award, the *Ebony* Black Achievement Award in 1992, and a Montgomery Fellowship from Dartmouth College in 1993, and was named Gamma Sigma Gamma Woman of the Year in 1990. Also in 1992, an alternative public school in Detroit, Michigan—the Mae C. Jemison Academy—was named after her. Jemison is a member of the American Medical Association, the American Chemical Society, the American Association for the Advancement of Science, and served on the Board of Directors of the World Sickle Cell Foundation from 1990 to 1992. She is also an advisory committee member of the American Express Geography Competition and an honorary board member of the Center for the Prevention of Childhood Malnutrition. After leaving the astronaut corps in March 1993, she accepted a teaching fellowship at Dartmouth and also established the Jemison Group, a company that seeks to research, develop, and market advanced technologies.

SOURCES:

Books

Hawthorne, Douglas B., *Men and Women of Space,* Univelt, 1992, pp. 357–359.

Smith, Jessie Carney, editor, *Notable Black American Women,* Gale, 1992, pp. 571–573.

—Sketch by Leonard C. Bruno

J. Hans D. Jensen
1907-1973
German physicist

The German physicist J. Hans D. Jensen proposed the shell theory of nuclear structure. The nucleus was not just a random grouping of neutrons and protons, he concluded, but a structure of layers or shells, each filled with neutrons and protons spinning in their own orbits. Jensen's model of the nucleus won him the 1963 Nobel Prize in physics, which he shared with the physicist **Maria Goeppert-Mayer**, who had arrived at the same hypothesis independently, and with the physicist **Eugene Paul Wigner**, who was honored for unrelated research.

Johannes Hans Daniel Jensen was born in Hamburg, Germany, on June 25, 1907. His mother was Helene Ohm Jensen, and his father was Karl Jensen, a gardener. The youth's outstanding performance in school won him a scholarship to the Oberrealschule in Hamburg. After graduating in 1926, he attended the University of Hamburg, majoring in physical chemistry, mathematics, and philosophy. He received a doctorate in physics in 1932 and remained at the university as a scientific assistant. In 1936 he obtained an additional postgraduate degree and in 1937 became a lecturer at the university. In 1941, Jensen was appointed professor of theoretical physics at the Technical University of Hanover.

Jensen's first research applied quantum mechanics—the mathematical theory of the interaction between matter and radiation—to the study of crystals, whose atoms are arranged in a repetitive pattern. He also observed the properties of crystals under high pressure. Jensen was also interested in constructing a theoretical model of the atomic nucleus. Since the early 1930s, scientists had been seeking to construct a theoretical model of the atomic nucleus. **James Chadwick**'s discovery of the neutron in 1932 had demonstrated that the nucleus was composed of protons and neutrons. In 1933, German physicist Walter Elsasser suggested a model portraying protons and neutrons in some kind of orbit with their energy corresponding to the physical laws laid down by quantum theory (the theory of matter that describes behavior on the atomic level).

World War II temporarily halted the progress of Jensen's research. Jensen would later recall the isolation in which German physicists had to work during the war and the stifling effect this had on their research. His interest in constructing a model of the nucleus was renewed after the war when he read a paper on the subject by an American physicist, Maria Goeppert-Mayer. Jensen's frequent visits to **Niels Bohr**'s institute in Copenhagen after the war provided additional inspiration.

Develops Nuclear Shell Model

Jensen's early investigation of crystals evolved in 1947 to an examination of the recoil distribution of nuclear radiation in molecules and crystals. Jensen showed that rays or particles discharged by the nuclei of radioactive atoms are caught within a crystal in a backward movement similar to the recoil of a rifle. The importance of the recoil research was later borne out in a discovery by **Rudolf Mössbauer**, called the Mössbauer effect, which describes what happens when nuclei discharge gamma rays and the emission is thrust backward and absorbed within a crystal. In 1949, Jensen became professor of physics at the University of Heidelberg. That year he proposed a model of a nuclear structure of protons and neutrons grouped in onion-like layers of concentric shells. He suggested that the nucleons (protons and neutrons) spun on their own axis while they moved in an orbit within their shell and that certain patterns in the number of nucleons per shell made the nucleus more stable.

In the United States, Goeppert-Mayer, whose paper Jensen read after the war, had come up with the same shell model that he had. After Jensen submitted his hypothesis in a paper to the *Physical Review* in 1949, he learned that she had also submitted a paper with the same conclusions. Both papers were published. In 1955 Jensen and Goeppert-Mayer collaborated on a book titled *Elementary Theory of Nuclear Shell Structure.*

When the nuclear shell model was first announced in 1949, many physicists were skeptical because of its description of strong spin-orbit coupling, which was contrary at the time to notions about the motion of nucleons. Jensen discounted this skepticism when he wrote to Goeppert-Mayer that the most important battles had been won, since she had convinced **Enrico Fermi**, the Nobel Prize-winning physicist who aided the atomic bomb project, and he himself had convinced **Werner Heisenberg**, the Nobel Prize-winning physicist who developed the theory of quantum mechanics. In subsequent years, the nuclear shell model hypothesis was confirmed in the laboratory, and Jensen and Goeppert-Mayer were awarded the Nobel Prize in physics in 1963. In his acceptance speech, Jensen emphasized the need for communication among scientists internationally.

A Flourishing Career

Following his groundbreaking work on the structure of the nucleus, Jensen accepted a series of visiting professorships at academic institutions throughout the United States. In 1951 he taught at the University of Wisconsin; in 1952 at the Institute for Advanced Study in Princeton and the University of California at Berkeley; in 1953 he taught at Indiana University. In 1955, he was appointed dean of science at the University of Heidelberg, where despite his travels he maintained a permanent position. In 1956 he again visited the United States, this time teaching at the University of Minnesota. Jensen's last visiting professorship in the United States was at the University of California at La Jolla in 1961.

Throughout the 1950s, Jensen worked on radioactivity, significantly advancing the understanding of the phenomenon. He received an honorary degree from the Technical University of Hanover, and was named to the Heidelberg Academy of Science and the Max Plank Society. Starting in 1955, he served as coeditor of the journal *Zeitschrift für Physik* (Journal of Physics). In 1969 he was named professor emeritus at the University of Heidelberg. A life-long bachelor, Jensen resided in an apartment above the Institute for Theoretical Physics in Heidelberg. He found relaxation gardening in the institute garden and caring for his pet turtles. Jensen passed away on February 11, 1973.

SELECTED WRITINGS BY JENSEN:

Books

(With Maria Goeppert-Mayer) *Elementary Theory of Nuclear Shell Structure,* Wiley, 1955.

SOURCES:

Books

McGraw-Hill Modern Scientists and Engineers, 1980, pp. 505–07.

Periodicals

New York Times, November 6, 1963.
Newsweek, November 18, 1963, p. 78.
Science, November 15, 1963.

—*Sketch by Margo Nash*

Niels K. Jerne
1911-
English Danish immunologist

Considered both the founder of modern cellular immunology and its greatest theoretician, Niels K. Jerne won the 1984 Nobel Prize for medicine or physiology for his body of work that explained the function of the immune system, the body's defense mechanism against disease and infection. He is best known for three theories showing how antibodies—the substances which protect the body from foreign substances such as viruses and poisons—are produced, formed, and regulated by the immune system. His theories were initially met with skepticism, but they later became the cornerstones of immunological knowledge. By 1984, when he received the prize, colleagues agreed that he should have been recognized for his important contributions to the field much earlier than he was. Jerne's theories became the starting point from which other scientists, notably 1960 Nobel Prize winner **Frank MacFarlane Burnett**, furthered our understanding of how the body protects itself against disease.

Niels Kaj (sometimes transliterated Kai) Jerne was born on December 23, 1911, in London, England, to Danish parents Else Marie Lindberg and Hans Jessen Jerne. The family moved to the Netherlands at the beginning of World War I. Jerne earned his baccalaureate in Rotterdam in 1928 and studied physics for two years at the University of Leiden. Twelve years later he entered the University of Copenhagen to study medicine, receiving his doctorate in 1951 at the age of forty. From 1943 until 1956 he worked at the Danish State Serum Institute conducting research in immunology.

In 1955, Jerne traveled to the United States with noted molecular biologist **Max Delbrück** to become a research fellow at the California Institute of Technology at Pasadena. The two worked closely together, and it was not until his final two weeks at the Institute that Jerne completed work on his first major theory—on selective antibody formation. At this time, scientists believed that specific antibodies (molecules that defend the body from infection) do not exist until an antigen (any substance originating outside the body such as a virus, snake venom, or transplanted organs) is introduced and acts as a template from which cells in the immune system create the appropriate antibody to eliminate it. (Antigens and antibodies have surface patches, called combining sites, with distinct patterns. When an antibody and antigen with complementary combining sites meet, they become attached, fitting together like a lock and key.) Jerne's theory postulated instead that the immune system inherently contains all the specific antibodies it needs to fight specific antigens; the appropriate antibody, one of millions that are already present in the body, attaches to the antigen, thus neutralizing or destroying the antigen and its threat to the body.

Not until some months after developing his theory did Jerne share it with Delbrück, who sent it to the *Proceedings of the National Academy of Sciences* for publication. Jerne later noted that his theory probably would have been forgotten, except that it caught the attention of Burnett, leading him to the development in 1959 of his clonal selection theory, which built on Jerne's hypothesis to show how specific antibody-producing cells multiply to produce necessary quantities of an antigen's antibody. The following year Jerne left his research in immunology to became chief medical officer with the World Health Organization in Geneva, Switzerland, where he oversaw the departments of biological standards and immunology. From 1960 to 1962 he served on the faculty at the University of Geneva's biophysics department.

From 1962 to 1966 Jerne was professor of microbiology at the University of Pittsburgh in Pennsylvania. During this period he developed a method, now known as the Jerne plaque assay, to count antibody-producing cells by first mixing them with other cells containing antigen material, causing the cells to produce an antibody that combines with red blood cells. Once combined, the blood cells are then destroyed, leaving a substance called plaque surrounding the original antibody-producing cells, which can then be counted. Jerne became director of the Paul Ehrlich Institute, in Frankfurt, Germany, in 1966, and, in 1969, established the Basel Institute for Immunology in Switzerland, where he remained until taking emeritus status in 1980.

In 1971, Jerne unveiled his second major theory, which deals with how the immune system identifies and differentiates between self molecules (belonging to its host) and nonself molecules (invaders). Noting that the immune system is specific to each individual, immunologists had concluded that the body's self-tolerance cannot be inherited and is therefore learned. Jerne postulated that such immune system "learning" occurs in the thymus, an organ in the upper chest cavity where the cells that recognize and attack antigens multiply, while those that could attack the body's own cells are suppressed. Over time, mutations among cells that recognize antigens increase the number of different antibodies the body has at hand, thereby increasing the immune system's arsenal against disease.

Jerne introduced what is considered his most significant work in 1974—the network theory, wherein he proposed that the immune system is a dynamic self-regulating network that activates itself when necessary and shuts down when not needed. At that time, scientists knew that the immune system contains two types of immune system cells, or lymphocytes: B cells, which produce antibodies, and T cells, which function as "helpers" to the B cells by killing foreign cells, or by regulating the B cells either by suppressing or stimulating their antibody producing activity. Further, antibody molecules produced by the B cells also contain antigen-like components (idiotypes) which can attract another antibody (anti-idiotype), allowing one antibody to recognize another antibody as well as an antigen. Jerne's theory expanded on this knowledge, speculating that a delicate balance of lymphocytes and antibodies and their idiotypes and anti-idiotypes exists in the immune system until an antigen is introduced. The antigen, he believed, replaces the anti-idiotype attached to the antibody. The immune system then senses the displacement and, in an attempt to find the anti-idiotype a "mate," produces more of the original antibody. This chain-reaction strengthens the body's immunity to the invading antigen. Experiments later demonstrated that immunization with an anti-idiotype will stimulate the production of the required antibody. It may well be that because of Jerne's network theory, vaccinations of the future will administer antibodies rather than antigens to bring about immunity to disease.

Jerne retired to southern France with his wife, Ursula Alexandra Kohl, whom he married in 1964; the couple has two sons. Both a British and a Danish citizen, Jerne has received honorary degrees from American and European universities, is a foreign honorary member of the American Academy of Arts and Sciences, is a member of the Royal Danish Academy of Sciences, and has won, among other honors, the Marcel Benorst Prize in 1979 and the Paul Ehrlich Prize in 1982. A devoted scientist, Jerne had little interest in politics. He also disliked clocks and other technology. In his spare time, he enjoyed literature, music, and French wine. At a reception in Basel to celebrate his Nobel Prize, Jerne, as reported in the *New York Times,* joked: "It would have been nice if it had come earlier to convince my brothers and sisters that I am not the oddball they regarded me for a long time. I will enjoy the prize and enjoy life."

SELECTED WRITINGS BY JERNE:

Books

"The Natural Selection Theory of Antibody Formation: Ten Years Later," in *Phage and the Origins of Molecular Biology,* Cold Springs Harbor Laboratory of Quantitative Biology, 1966, pp. 301–312.

Periodicals

"The Natural Selection Theory of Antibody Formation," *Proceedings of the National Academy of Sciences, U.S.A.,* Volume 41, 1955, pp. 849–856.

"Antibodies and Learning," *The Neurosciences,* 1967, pp. 200–205.

"The Immune System," *Scientific American,* Volume 229, 1973, pp. 52–60.

(With others) "Plaque-Forming Cells: Method and Theory," *Transplantation Reviews,* Volume 18, 1974, pp. 130–191.

"Towards a Network Theory of the Immune System," *Annales d'Immunologique,* Volume C125, 1974, pp. 373–389.

SOURCES:

Books

Nobel Prize Winners, H. W. Wilson, 1987, pp. 509–511.

Nobel Prize Winners—Physiology or Medicine, Salem Press, 1991, pp. 1447–1454.

Periodicals

New York Times, October 16, 1984, p. C2.

"Nobel Prize for Inventors of Monoclonals," *New Scientist,* October 18, 1984, pp. 3–5.

Ur, Jonathon W., "The 1984 Nobel Prize in Medicine," *Science,* November 30, 1984, pp. 1025–1028.

—Sketch by David Petechuk

Frank Baldwin Jewett
1879-1949
American engineer

Frank Baldwin Jewett was an engineer and an industrial leader. He spent most of his professional years with the American Telephone and Telegraph Company (AT&T), rising early in his career to become one of its vice presidents. Under his direction, America's transcontinental telephone system was developed. When AT&T's research wing, the Bell Laboratories, was established in 1925, he became its first president. He also gave service to government and the military, advising the U.S. War Department on matters pertaining to electrical communication during World War I and presiding over the National Academy of Sciences during the critical years of World War II.

Jewett's parents, Stanley P. Jewett and Phebe C. Mead Jewett, originally from Ohio, settled in Pasadena, California, on a twenty-five-acre parcel of land given to them as a wedding present. Frank Baldwin Jewett, the elder of the couple's two children, was born there on September 5, 1879. At the time the area consisted of ranchers and farmers, and Jewett's childhood was filled with fishing, hunting, and working in the orchards. A childhood infection blinded him in one eye and impaired his vision in the other, but his disability never stood in the way of his ambition.

Jewett's father was a rancher as well as a train engineer. He had helped organize the Los Angeles and San Gabriel Valley Railroad, which later became the main line of the Santa Fe Railroad. Throughout his youth Jewett intended to make railroading his career as well. He received his high school education at the Throop Institute of Technology's prep school. In 1898 at the age of nineteen he received an A.B. degree from the Throop Institute, which later became the California Institute of Technology.

Frank Baldwin Jewett

In the late 1890s streetlights were installed in southern California. The new technology caught Jewett's interest. However, his plans to attend the Massachusetts Institute of Technology (MIT) to study engineering were aborted by the death of his mother. Instead, one of his professors from the Throop Institute urged him to study at the University of Chicago. Jewett received his doctorate in physics from the newly established university in 1902. While he was a student, he served as a research assistant to **Albert Michelson**, who in 1907 became the first American to win the Nobel Prize in physics. At the university, Jewett met and became engaged to Fannie Frisbie, a fellow graduate student in physics. They were married in 1905, and together they had three children: a daughter who died in infancy, and two sons, Harrison Leach and Frank Baldwin Jr.

Not long after Jewett had become an instructor of physics at MIT, a chance introduction to George A. Campbell of AT&T, the parent company of the Bell System, led to an invitation to join the company's research group. Although his acceptance of the position was delayed for a year because of his contractual obligations with the university, Jewett joined AT&T in 1904 and became involved in solving the problems inherent in building telephone transmission lines.

Spearheads Development of Transcontinental Telephone Communication

In 1904 the nation's telephone system was in its infancy. The longest distance over which a voice could be transmitted was from Boston to Chicago, and this transmission took place over a single open-wire circuit. Jewett started out at AT&T as a transmission engineer working under Campbell. His talent as a manager soon became apparent, and within two years he was made head of the electrical department in AT&T's Boston laboratory, succeeding Campbell.

In 1908 Jewett was given the task of completing a transcontinental phone line that would link New York City with San Francisco. The job was to be completed by 1915 in order for coast-to-coast phone calls to be featured at the Panama-Pacific Exposition, which was to be held in San Francisco. Operating out of a New York laboratory, he assembled some of the brightest young engineers of the day to work out the various obstacles to long-distance telephone communication. The technology his group of engineers developed enabled AT&T to build the cross-country line successfully. By opening day of the exposition, it was possible to carry on a conversation by phone over a distance of approximately three thousand miles.

Among the many technological challenges Jewett's engineers met was to create a high quality "repeater," a device to amplify the voice signal after it had been weakened by transmission across a line. The longer the line, the more amplification was needed. To solve this problem, Jewett hired H. D. Arnold, who developed a high-vacuum electronic tube. Arnold's vacuum tube allowed speech signals to be amplified without causing distortion. The vacuum tube proved so successful that it was used in communication devices such as radios and televisions well into the 1950s when it was replaced by transistor technology. Throughout his career Jewett was recognized for his clear grasp of technological issues and his ability to select the right individuals for the particular task at hand, and Arnold was a good example of this.

On the heels of the first successful transcontinental telephone communication came another achievement. On October 21, 1915, the first transatlantic telephone conversation took place between the U.S. Naval Radio Station in Arlington and the Eiffel Tower in Paris using radio telephony. Other landmark events followed over the next few years, including ship-to-shore communication in 1916 and airplane-to-ground communication in 1917. Radio broadcasting became possible two years later, and the first radio-broadcasting wire network was established by the Bell System in 1923.

Assumes Leadership of Bell Laboratories

Jewett rose rapidly through the administrative ranks at AT&T. By 1912, as his success with the transcontinental communication project was becoming apparent, he became the assistant chief engineer of the Western Electric Company, the manufacturing division of the Bell System. By 1922 he was its vice president and controlled all of the Bell System's development and research work. Under his direction, advances such as the introduction of machine switching on a large scale and development of high-speed submarine telegraph cables occurred. At the start of 1925 Jewett's engineering department was incorporated as Bell Telephone Laboratories, and he became its president. At the same time he was named a vice president of AT&T.

The advances in sound and speech transmission, and eventually television transmission, that occurred during the 1920s and 1930s were in large part associated with technological breakthroughs of Bell Laboratories' researchers and engineers. Work at Bell on waveguide transmission during the 1930s was vital to the development of radar. During Jewett's years as its president, from 1925 until 1940, Bell Laboratories grew to be the largest industrial research organization in the world. In 1940 he resigned the presidency to become chairman of its board of directors, a position he retained until his retirement in 1944.

Aids U.S. Government during War Years

In addition to providing leadership within AT&T, Jewett gave service to his country. When the United States entered World War I in 1917, the military was in need of help with electrical communication. The research departments of AT&T were consulted, and Jewett was commissioned as a major in the Signal Corps of the U.S. Army Reserves. Within the year he was promoted to lieutenant colonel in the Signal Corps of the U.S. Army. After the war he served on advisory boards for the navy and the State Department, providing expertise in submarine communication, radio telephony, and cables. In 1927 he became a lieutenant commander in the volunteer reserve of the navy. For his service in World War I, Jewett was awarded the Distinguished Service Medal from the army. In 1939 he was elected to direct the National Academy of Sciences. He served two consecutive four-year terms, presiding during the war years, a time during which the academy functioned as a top scientific advisory agency to the U.S. government. During World War II he also served as a member of the National Defense Research Committee.

Over the course of his career Jewett authored many papers on the topics of electrical engineering and physics. He presided over the American Institute of Electrical Engineers in 1923. Several honors were bestowed on him by the Japanese government, including the Fourth Order of the Rising Sun in 1923 and the Third Order of the Sacred Treasure in 1930. His engineering and research awards include the Edison Medal from the American Institute of Electrical Engineers in 1928, the Faraday Medal of the Institute of Electrical Engineers in London in 1935, the Franklin Medal in 1936, the John Fritz Gold Medal in 1938, and posthumously in 1950 both the Medal of the Industrial Research Society and the Hoover Medal. His personal hobbies included gardening and working in a small shop at his home in Short Hills, New Jersey. Jewett died at the age of seventy, on November 18, 1949, after emergency abdominal surgery.

SELECTED WRITINGS BY JEWETT:

Periodicals

(With B. Gherardi) "Progress in the Art of Communication," *Electrical World,* January 24, 1920, pp. 202–204.

"The Telephone Switchboard, Fifty Years of History," *Bell Telephone Quarterly,* July, 1928, pp. 149–165.

"What Science Achieved in 1929—Communication," *Popular Science,* January, 1930, p. 20.

"The Relationship of Research and Invention to Economic Conditions," *Journal of the Patent Office Society,* March, 1939, pp. 195–208.

SOURCES:

Periodicals

Buckley, Oliver E., "Biographical Memoir of Frank Baldwin Jewett," *National Academy of Sciences,* fall, 1950.

—Sketch by Leslie Reinherz

Steven Jobs
1955-
American electronics engineer

Steven Jobs was the founder, along with **Stephen Wozniak**, of Apple Computer, Inc., perhaps the most innovative force behind the personal computer revolution of the 1980s. Unlike large, established computer companies, Apple aimed from the beginning to bring computers into every household. Its watchword was "user-friendly," and this user-oriented philosophy is generally cited as a key to its phenomenal early success. Only six years after Jobs and Wozniak created the prototype for the Apple I,

Steven Jobs

the company they founded was listed on the Fortune 500.

Jobs himself was the business force behind Apple Computer, whereas Wozniak provided the engineering acumen. Jobs became a powerful presence at Apple during the late 1970s and early 1980s, heading up the Macintosh division until his departure in 1985. Widely recognized for his contributions to the computer field, Jobs, along with Wozniak, was presented with a National Medal of Science in 1985.

Develops Entrepreneurial Skills

Born February 24, 1955, Jobs was raised by his adoptive parents, Paul, a machinist at Spectra-Physics, and Clara, in California. Young Jobs's early interest in machines was inspired by his father's work. His early boredom with school was tempered by several positive experiences, including his first encounter with a desk-top computer, which took place during a school field-trip to a Hewlett-Packard plant in Palo Alto. A short time later, Jobs telephoned **William Hewlett** to ask for help constructing a school project. Hewlett agreed to provide the necessary parts; then he offered the high-school freshman a summer job.

That summer in 1968, Jobs met Stephen Wozniak, a college drop-out and electronics wizard five years his senior, at Hewlett-Packard. Wozniak had graduated from the high school Jobs attended, and, together, they began developing and peddling several electronics devices. Some of these—including a box that enabled the user to make free long-distance phone calls—bordered on the illegal. Jobs also repaired and sold stereos during his high school years, further developing his entrepreneurial skills. Yet he was clearly not headed for a conventional marketing career.

After graduating from Homestead High School in Los Altos and spending a year at Reed College, Jobs began experimenting with alternate lifestyles, including a flirtation with a Hare Krishna sect. Then, in 1974, he became a consultant for the video game company, Atari. He began to attend weekly meetings of the Homebrew Computer Club, one of the many user groups springing up in the Bay area. Wozniak, an original member of Homebrew, was working at Hewlett-Packard during the day and trying to construct a computer at night. With a twenty-five-dollar microprocessor and a few memory chips, Wozniak, encouraged by Jobs, devised a crude but relatively powerful circuit board—the original Apple I computer.

Apple Spearheads a Computer Revolution

Jobs began the arduous process of marketing and publicizing this computer, using contacts from the Homebrew club to sell the product. Scraping together investment capital and moving their small operation into his father's garage, Jobs began to prod Wozniak into developing a much more powerful computer, with a keyboard and video display. As the Apple II computer gained attention, Apple Computer, Inc., was born. Investors provided backing and seasoned executives started to join the fledgling company. Jobs created a sleek design for the Apple II, using a plastic casing and introducing the Apple logo—the image of an apple with a missing bite, playing on the word "byte," one of the central units of information in computer languages.

The Apple II was introduced in 1977, and, after further refinements, became the standard for personal computers. Three factors contributed to its success: first, it was an open system, allowing add-ons like modems and music synthesizers; second, models built after the summer of 1978 included a disk-drive developed and engineered by Wozniak; third, in the fall of 1979, two Apple devotees from the Massachusetts Institute of Technology (MIT) developed a spreadsheet program that ran only on Apple computers. The Apple II became an attractive prospect for American business. With the success of the Apple II, Jobs found himself as the majority shareholder in a multimillion dollar company. Apple went public in 1980, and Jobs's holdings at that time were valued at 165 million dollars. For the next two years, Apple led the market in personal computers. As the company grew, it continued to create a market that invited competition. International Business Machines (IBM) introduced its first personal computer in 1981, and within two years had garnered nearly one-third of the market.

Apple responded by introducing several models intended to compete with IBM, but the Apple II remained the company's best-selling model throughout the early 1980s. In 1979, Jobs launched a project designed to revolutionize the way people used computers. Apple developed the first computer model to use a mouse and called it the "Lisa" (Local Integrated Software Architecture). Intended to herald the new age of software, the Lisa provided a new way for users to interact with their computers. However, priced at $10,000, it was too expensive for the home market.

But the mouse technology developed for the Lisa spawned the Macintosh division—the ambitious unit of Apple headed by Jobs in the early 1980s. The new Macintosh computer, Jobs insisted, would set an industry standard. It was not IBM compatible. Its easy-to-use software and its point-and-click mouse brought wordprocessing, spreadsheet capability, and powerful graphics to the most computer-phobic user. Its use of icons and windows provided a strong alternative to the forbidding "C:\>" prompt used in IBM compatibles. Indeed, within a decade of its 1984 release, the operating system called WINDOWS, capable of being run on IBM compatible machines, borrowed many of the Macintosh hallmarks.

The success of Macintosh did little to calm the highly charged and uncertain atmosphere at Apple. The company was increasingly threatened by IBM's competition, and Apple II employees were angered that so much of the company's energies were being devoted to Jobs's Macintosh division. In 1985 Wozniak resigned, and Jobs was demoted by John Sculley, the former Pepsi-Cola Company president whom Jobs had brought into Apple in 1983. After some hesitation, Jobs left Apple to begin NeXT Company, an operation that would focus on educational computing. Jobs's departure brought more trouble, however, in the form of a lawsuit: Apple accused him of stealing the company's research and some of its key employees for his new endeavor.

Jobs managed to settle the matter out of court, and turned to the task of developing a new computer. The final product, aimed primarily at students and educators, sold poorly. Nevertheless, the NeXT workstation concept, with its high-level graphics and advanced technology, generated much interest among educators, and resulted in a 1989 Software Publishers Association Lifetime Achievement Award for Jobs.

In 1991, Jobs married Laurene Powell, and now has two children. Jobs continues to head NeXT, researching, developing, and marketing new computer technology. Using the prestige and influence he earned at Apple to advance computer technology, Jobs pushed the UNIX operating system, with its multiprocessing capabilities, as an alternative to both IBM's DOS and the Macintosh operating system. In 1993, NeXT announced the development of NextStep, for Intel Processors, a development platform designed to aid users in creating custom applications.

SOURCES:

Books

Butcher, Lee, *Accidental Millionaire: The Rise and Fall of Steve Jobs at Apple Computer,* Paragon House, 1988.

Rose, Frank, *West of Eden: The End of Innocence at Apple Computer,* Viking, 1989.

Slater, Robert, *Portraits in Silicon,* MIT Press, 1987.

Young, Jeffrey, *Steve Jobs,* Scott, Foresman, 1988.

Periodicals

Dalglish, Brenda, "The Wonder Boys Hit Middle Age," *Maclean's,* May 11, 1992, p. 36.

Daly, James, "Steve Jobs: Counterculture Hero," *Computerworld,* June 22, 1992.

Pitta, Julie, "Steve Jobs, Version 2.0," *Computerworld,* October 24, 1988, p. 45.

—Sketch by Katherine Williams

Wilhelm Ludvig Johannsen
1857-1927
Danish biologist

Wilhelm Ludvig Johannsen helped lay the foundation for the modern science of genetics. His studies with bean plants enabled him to distinguish between genotype (characteristics that can undergo natural selection) and phenotype (characteristics independent of natural selection.) He established a new vocabulary for studying heredity, including the word "gene," and was among the first biologists to apply rigorous statistical methods to research data. Although Johannsen was trained as a pharmacist, had no formal university degree, and pursued his research mostly as an accomplished amateur, he was eventually made a professor at the University of Copenhagen and was widely revered for his scientific contributions. Ojvind Winge reported in *Journal of Heredity* that Johannsen once wrote about his unusual intellectual background: "That training which ... [more formally educated] naturalists received has, partly due to its almost purely descriptive direction, provided them with blinkers which I, with all my scientific unsophistication, thank Heaven for that I lack, even though my glance is thereby more scattered, more shifting, and often too little concentrated in one direction—I am, and always will be, a free-lance in science." Some of Johanssen's ideas have been superseded, but the core of his work occupies the crossroads between old and new ways of thinking in the sciences of heredity and evolution.

Johannsen was born to Otto and Anna Ebbesen Johannsen in Copenhagen, Denmark, on February 3, 1857. His father, an army officer, was transferred to the city of Helsingoer when Johannsen was eleven years old. Johannsen later attributed his scientific interest to a combination of his mother's appreciation for the natural world, and his father's sense of order and discipline. Despite an excellent early education in Copenhagen, and a good performance on university entrance examinations some years later, Johannsen was financially unable to attend college full time. Instead, he was apprenticed to a pharmacist in 1872, and worked in that field both in Denmark and Germany (he spoke and wrote fluent German) for several years. During that time, he taught himself botany and chemistry, read widely in many fields, and continued a more formal education in pharmacy that culminated in high honors on a German pharmaceutical examination.

In 1881 he started work in the new Carlsberg Laboratory (financed by profits from the Carlsberg Breweries) as an assistant to the famous chemist Johann Kjeldahl. There he began doing actual research, particularly on plant metabolism. After 1887, he supported his own research with stipends and a small inheritance. In 1892 he left the Carlsberg Laboratory to take a post as lecturer, and finally, in 1903 he became professor of botany and plant physiology, at the Copenhagen Agricultural College. The University of Copenhagen hired him in 1905 as a professor of plant physiology (not without controversy, given Johannsen's lack of formal education in the field), and in 1917 he became rector of that university. He traveled frequently throughout his career, and became well known as a witty and interesting speaker.

Research on Plants Leads to Distinction between Genotype and Phenotype

Initially, Johannsen's research dealt with the anatomy and physiology of barley and wheat. He developed a new method for "waking" dormant plants in winter, and developed a large-grained barley that was also low enough in nitrogen to be useful in the beer making process. He gradually began studying inherited characteristics in bean plants, particularly the Princess bean. Normally, any single species shows some variation in each of its characteristics; individual organisms in the species will have one of the variations of each character. Natural selection operates because individual organisms possessing the most useful set of variations will be the most likely to survive and reproduce. The other variations continue to survive (although in fewer individuals) as long as they are not actively detrimental to the species. Beans are self-fertilized, so Johannsen was able to show, by careful breeding, that within each species there existed "pure lines" of individuals who possessed a single set of inheritable variations. Generation after generation, the inheritable characteristics of a pure line remained the same. (Variation of characteristics in a whole species therefore results from all the pure lines mixing together.) Johannsen showed that any observable difference in the individuals of a single pure line—different seed size, for example—was not inheritable and was entirely the result of environmental forces such as amount of light or water.

This work was important because the study of inheritance was in its infancy at the time, and very few genetic principles were even partially understood. Darwin's work on evolution as a result of natural selection was taken seriously, but some scientists suspected that some observable variations in characteristics were the result of heredity and some were the result of environment. They had only limited ability to differentiate the two, and were not at all certain whether environmental characteristics could be inherited or not. Johannsen brought the beginnings of order to this muddle by clearly showing with statistical analysis of his pure lines that internal variations were inherited and environmental variations were not; thus, a difference existed between genotype (the internal blueprint of the organism) and phenotype (how the organism looks, metabolizes, and behaves in its unique surroundings.)

Following the turn of the century, Johannsen recognized the importance of Austrian botanist Gregor Mendel's work with garden peas, which revealed characteristics of inheritance. As a result Johannsen began meshing Mendelian principles with his own ideas. He had more difficulty with the idea that genes were actual locations on the chromosome—he preferred a more mathematical and abstract view of them—and it was many years before he accepted the theory. After his work was finished on the pure lines, he gave up experimentation and spent the rest of his career writing, thinking, and critically analyzing the sciences.

SELECTED WRITINGS BY JOHANNSEN:

Books

Laerebog i plantefisiologi med henblik paa plantedyrkningen, [Copenhagen, Denmark], 1892.

Om arvelighed og variabilitet, [Copenhagen], 1896, enlarged as *Arvelighedslaerens elementer,* [Copenhagen], 1905, rewritten and enlarged as *Elemente der exakten Erblichkeitslehre,* [Jena, Germany], 1909, revised edition, 1926.

Das Aether-Verfahren beim Frühtreiben mit besonderer Berücksichtigung der Fliedertreiberei, [Jena], 1900.

Falske analogier, med henblik paa lighed, slaegtskab, arv, tradition of udvikling, [Copenhagen], 1914.

Arvelighed i historisk og experimental belysning, [Copenhagen], 1923.

SOURCES:

Books

Dictionary of Scientific Biography, Scribners, 1981, p. 113.

Sturtevant, A. H., *A History of Genetics,* Harper and Row, 1965.

Periodicals

Winge, Ojvind, "Wilhelm Johannsen: The Creator of the Terms Gene, Genotype, Phenotype, and Pure Line," in *Journal of Heredity,* Volume 49, 1958, p. 82–88.

—*Sketch by Gail B. C. Marsella*

Barbara Crawford Johnson
1925-
American engineer

Barbara Crawford Johnson

As an engineer in the aerospace industry, Barbara Crawford Johnson created the Entry Monitor System (EMS), the backup entry guidance system designed for the Apollo space missions. The EMS was a graphic display for the astronauts to use in the event of primary guidance failure. Graphic displays are now a part of the instrument panels on virtually all space- and aircraft, in addition to many automobiles.

In 1946 Johnson became the first woman to earn a bachelor of science degree in engineering from the University of Illinois at Champaign-Urbana. Her study was in general engineering with an emphasis in aeronautics. Upon graduation, she joined Rockwell International's Space Division in California, where she would become project leader for the Hound Dog air-to-ground weapon used by the B–52 bomber. In this capacity, she supervised, from concept through design, the configuration, performance, and stability analysis of the missile.

During the 1960s, Johnson served as Supervisor of Entry Trajectories at Rockwell, and it was during this period that she oversaw the conceptual design and performance evaluation of the EMS for the Apollo missions. "The whole idea that opened my world was the fact that we were working on a project to send a man to the Moon, to have him leave the Earth's gravitational field, and then bring him back alive," Johnson remarked. Johnson's innovations enabled the Apollo spacecraft to safely re-enter the Earth's atmosphere with the necessary precision. "Before the early 1960s, a spacecraft had never come from hypervelocity—a speed greater than that of the Earth's rotation," she said. If the Apollo had reentered the atmosphere too shallowly, overheating would have been a danger; if too deeply, the astronauts would have been subjected to unbearable gravitational forces.

In 1968, Johnson was appointed System Engineering Manager for the Apollo Program. She supervised system analysis in support of the lunar landing and exploration, the Apollo/Soyuz test program (for which she supervised a staff of over two hundred), and numerous ancillary projects and studies. She was named Manager of Mission Requirements and Integration for the Rockwell Space System Group in

1973, a position she maintained until her retirement in 1982. In this capacity she directed the mission, flight performance and trajectory design analyses of the Space Shuttle and Orbiter projects.

Johnson's honors include the American Astronautical Society's Dick Brower Award, the 1974 Achievement Award of the Society of Women Engineers (SWE), and a medallion from the National Aeronautics and Space Administration (NASA) for her role in the first landing on the Moon. She was also named a Fellow of the Institute for the Advancement of Engineering and received its Outstanding Engineer Merit Award, and was presented with the Distinguished Alumni Merit Award from the University of Illinois and the Mother's Association Medallion of Honor.

Johnson and her husband, Robert Johnson, also an engineer with Rockwell, live in San Pedro, California, and have one son, Eric. "When I was a kid, I loved looking at the stars, the planets," Johnson said. "I always thought there was life out there in other galaxies. I still do."

SOURCES:

Periodicals

"Achievement Award Winner," *Society of Women Engineers Newsletter,* September, 1974, p. 1.

Other

Johnson, Barbara Crawford, interview with Karen Withem conducted March 29, 1994.

—*Sketch by Karen Withem*

Clarence L. Johnson
1910-1990
American aeronautical engineer

Clarence L. Johnson designed some of America's most advanced airplanes. As an engineer for Lockheed Aircraft Corporation, Johnson served as flight test engineer, stress analyst, weight engineer, and performed countless aerodynamic tests with wind tunnels. During his tenure as chief research engineer Johnson created the Skunk Works, a division within Lockheed that designed advanced, secret military projects. It became associated with some of Lockheed's most impressive achievements in aviation.

Early Poverty

Johnson's father, Peter, left his native Sweden in 1882 to avoid military service and embarked for the United States. After settling in northern Michigan, he sent for his fiancée, Christine Anderson. They had nine children, of whom Clarence was the seventh; he was born February 27, 1910. Johnson's father eked out a living as a mason. His mother earned money by washing other people's laundry on her wash board and by scrubbing floors. Although they were poor, Johnson recalled happy memories of his childhood. Even in the dead of winter he liked to hike in the forests and explore nature.

Learning appealed to the young Johnson, and he received good grades. He would spend hours poring over Tom Swift adventure books admiring Swift's exploits as a builder, engineer, and designer. By watching his father, whom he described as a skilled craftsman, Johnson acquired an early appreciation of what human hands could accomplish. Johnson's interest in things mechanical seems to have been nurtured by these early influences. By the time he was twelve, Johnson had already developed a love for airplanes and had decided that he would one day build them. His parents and the local school principal supported this interest. The principal even invited Johnson to address the Lions Club on aviation.

Johnson acquired the nickname "Kelly" from an incident during his early years in school. As Johnson told the story in his autobiography, *Kelly: More Than My Share of It All,* a boy from the wealthy part of the village had tormented Johnson by calling him "Clara." To pay him back, Johnson jumped on the boy's leg from behind and broke it. Johnson's schoolmates were impressed and gave him "a good fighting Irish name" from the popular song "Kelly from the Emerald Isle."

In 1923, when Johnson was thirteen, his family moved to Flint, Michigan, where prospects for employment were more encouraging. The family's economic position improved and Johnson saved enough money by working to attend Flint Junior College, where he studied mathematics and physics. He did well, and in 1929 the University of Michigan in Ann Arbor accepted him to study aeronautical engineering. Johnson graduated with a bachelor's degree in 1932. He returned the following year for graduate work after having spent the summer searching in vain for a position as an aeronautical engineer. Although Lockheed Aircraft Corporation in Burbank, California, did not hire him then, the chief engineer suggested that Johnson get a master's degree and then apply for a position. The company had recently been purchased and was in a state of uncertainty.

Events went as planned and Lockheed hired Johnson in 1933. Johnson lost no time in telling his new employers that he disagreed with their design of the reorganized company's first aircraft, the Lockheed Electra. He said the airplane would be unstable. Hall L. Hibbard, Lockheed's chief engineer and a graduate of the Massachusetts Institute of Technology, had helped design the aircraft. He was uncertain of Johnson's argument but was willing to let the new employee have a chance.

Hibbard sent Johnson back to the University of Michigan to test a model of the aircraft in the university's wind tunnel, where Johnson had recently worked as a student. After many trials Johnson solved the problem of instability by adding a double vertical stabilizer to the tail. Lockheed included the idea in its early metal aircraft. It appeared as a three-tail design in Lockheed's famous Constellation, which remained in production until the mid-1950s.

As tensions grew in Europe during the late 1930s, the Army Air Corps sought development of a new fighter. Lockheed's P-38 was a response to this need. The new airplane set speed records of over 400 miles per hour and became one of the most versatile aircraft in the U.S. fighter fleet. Various models served as strafers, reconnaissance aircraft, rocket carriers, and ambulances. By 1945 some 10,000 of these airplanes had rolled off the assembly line.

Although the P-38 had impressive speed, its piston engine imposed limitations both on the airplane's speed and performance. Lockheed urged the Army Air Corps to consider letting it design a jet aircraft. The Air Corps rebuffed Lockheed's overtures and urged the company to correct existing bugs in the P-38. Developments with **Frank Whittle**'s jet engine in the United Kingdom in 1941, however, alerted the Air Corps to possibilities for jet aircraft in the United States.

Creates Skunk Works

Johnson promised to deliver a prototype jet aircraft in 180 days. The aircraft would be powered by a jet engine Whittle had designed in the United Kingdom. To make good on his promise, Johnson corralled a number of Lockheed engineers and workers and made work space from wooden shipping crates. Johnson and his crew cobbled together a rudimentary administration, including a purchasing department, so that their design and production efforts would not interfere with Lockheed's already overburdened main plant. The new administration and production facilities acquired the name "Skunk Works." Under Johnson's direction the Skunk Works created some of the most radical and most successful designs in aircraft.

Having established the Skunk Works, Johnson and his crew set about to create the first American operational jet fighter. The experimental version, the XP-80, first flew at Muroc Dry Lake (later Edwards Air Force Base) on January 8, 1944, at speeds over 500 miles per hour. Johnson had fulfilled his promise to deliver a jet airplane within 180 days. Production models did not come off the assembly line until 1948, however, when the plane was redesignated the F-80.

When the Korean conflict broke out in 1950, the F-80 Shooting Star performed well against the North Korean MiG-15. American pilots complained, however, that the MiGs could elude American fighters by ascending to higher altitudes. This demand for altitude and speed set Johnson again to designing new capabilities. The outcome was Lockheed's F-104 Starfighter, the "missile with a man in it." Designed as an interceptor-fighter, the F-104 was the first aircraft to hold speed and altitude records at the same time. In 1958, for example, an F-104 set a speed record of 1,404.19 miles per hour and (in a separate flight) an altitude record of 91,243 feet. In 1959 an F-104 set a new altitude record of 103,395.5 feet.

Johnson had also made his mark on non-fighter aircraft. Lockheed's Constellation, designed as a commercial airliner, saw service as a military transport during World War II. General Dwight D. Eisenhower flew in a Constellation named *Columbine I* when he was commander of the North American Treaty Organization (NATO). As president, he flew in another Constellation, named *Columbine II.*

Designs U-2 Spy Plane

The versatile military cargo airplane, the C-130 Hercules, also bore Johnson's imprint as did the high-flying reconnaissance airplane, the U-2. Francis Gary Powers was flying a U-2 when the Soviets shot him down on May 1, 1960, leading to a tense face-off between President Eisenhower and Soviet premier Nikita Khrushchev. As designer of the U-2 and other important military aircraft, and corporate vice president since 1956, Johnson was now an important figure in the Cold War calculations of parry and riposte. During this period Johnson slept with a pistol near his bed. After the Soviets released Powers from captivity in 1962, he worked for Johnson at the Skunk Works.

Johnson's last and most difficult project was in designing the SR-71, a high-altitude, long-range strategic reconnaissance airplane that repeatedly set speed and distance records. The Blackbird, as it was unofficially called, could reach speeds of over 2,200 miles per hour at an altitude of 80,000 feet. This airplane was the first to incorporate "stealth" technology to avoid (or lessen) radar detection.

Johnson retired with his wife, Althea, to their ranch near Santa Barbara, California. She had been the paymaster at Lockheed when Johnson first joined the company. After a four-year courtship they married in 1936. She died later in life, and Johnson married his secretary, Maryellen Elberta Meade. Together they enjoyed horseback riding and golf at their ranch, but she died only a year and a half after their marriage. Johnson married again shortly thereafter but died in Burbank of undisclosed causes on December 21, 1990, after a prolonged illness.

Johnson's many awards, most of them received after retirement, included honorary doctorates; the Medal of Freedom, presented in 1964 by President Lyndon B. Johnson; and the National Security Medal, presented by President Ronald Reagan in 1983.

SELECTED WRITINGS BY JOHNSON:

Books

Kelly: More Than My Share of It All, Smithsonian Institution Press, 1985.

SOURCES:

Books

"Johnson, Clarence L(eonard)," *Current Biography Yearbook,* 1968, H. W. Wilson, pp. 198–200.

Periodicals

"Clarence Johnson Is Dead at 80; A Top Aircraft Designer in U.S.," *New York Times,* December 22, 1990, p. 33.

"Kelly Johnson, Founder of 'Skunk Works,' Dies," *Aviation Week & Space Technology,* January 7, 1991, p. 32.

"Skunk Works," *Air Progress,* September, 1986, pp. 60–61.

—*Sketch by Karl Preuss*

John B. Johnson, Jr.
1908-1972
American physician and cardiologist

John B. Johnson, Jr. was one of the first African American physicians to assume a leadership position as department chairman of the Howard University Medical College. A pioneer in the diagnostic use of angiocardiography and cardiac catheterization, he also was one of two African American physicians appointed to Georgetown University Hospital's staff in 1954 as part of a successful effort to offer District of Columbia physicians equal opportunity.

John Beauregard Johnson, Jr., was born in Bessemer, Alabama, on April 29, 1908. He was the eldest of three sons of John B., Sr., a postman, and his wife Leona Duff Johnson. After completing high school at Tuskegee Institute, Alabama, he attended Oberlin College in Ohio, and earned a letter in track as well as his B.A. degree in 1931. From there, he went directly to medical school at Western Reserve University in Cleveland and earned his M.D. there in 1935. After serving his internship at Cleveland City Hospital, he went to Howard University in 1936 as a laboratory assistant in physiology and spent his entire career in that institution. The following year he joined the Department of Medicine as an assistant and became an instructor in 1938.

When Johnson first joined Howard, its Dean, Numa P. G. Adams, was beginning to search for well-trained young physicians to staff the medical school's full-time clinical faculty. Adams selected Johnson as a promising potential candidate for leadership in the medical school, and sent him to the University of Rochester in 1939 for two years of postgraduate study in internal medicine. Johnson was given a General Education Board Fellowship. Upon returning to Howard, Johnson became director of Clinical Laboratories in 1941 and was made acting chair of the Department of Medicine from 1944 to 1949. During those years, Johnson spent one year at the Columbia University Division of Bellevue Hospital in New York under another General Education Board fellowship. In 1954, Johnson and another African American physician, Dr. R. Frank Jones, were appointed to the staff of Georgetown University Hospital. This marked a major breakthrough in the long campaign to secure parity of opportunity for minority physicians in the District of Columbia. At Howard, Johnson ended his career as the director of its Division of Cardiology.

As a cardiologist, or specialist in the treatment of heart disease, Johnson was an early proponent of angiocardiography, which is a diagnostic procedure that X rays the heart and its vessels after an intravenous injection of dye has been administered. The resulting picture shows blockages and abnormalities in the circulatory system. He also pioneered the technique of cardiac catheterization, in which a catheter—a thin, flexible tube—is inserted into the heart itself through a major vein in the arm. Johnson employed this technique to obtain samples of blood in the heart, to discover its abnormalities, and to determine the pressure of the heart itself. In addition, the physician studied hypertension—high blood pressure—and its disproportionate effects on African Americans. Johnson excelled in his field and published 64 papers during his career. One of these was awarded a citation from the journal *Angiology Research* for the Outstanding Publication of 1966.

As an educator, Johnson was described as an excellent teacher with infectious energy and enthusiasm whose lectures were both dramatic and exciting, as well as an individual who drove himself hard. He served on the board of directors of the American Heart Association from 1958 to 1961, and was awarded the Distinguished Service Medal of the National Medical Association. Twice he received the Susan B. and Theodore Cummings Humanitarian Award of the American College of Cardiology, in 1964 and 1965. After his retirement, the Howard University College of Medicine voted unanimously to name a chair after him. Its incumbent has the title of John Beauregard Johnson Professor of Medicine. When Johnson died in Freedman's Hospital on December 16, 1972, after a cerebral hemorrhage, he was survived by his third wife, Audrey Ingram Johnson, a stepdaughter, Adrienne, and a daughter from his second marriage, Linda.

SELECTED WRITINGS BY JOHNSON:

Periodicals

"Observations of the Effect of Pyrogens in the Treatment of Patients with Hypertension," *Journal of the American Medical Association,* Volume 43, 1951, p. 300.

(With L. A. Anthopoulos and Mitchell Spellman) "Arteriovenous Fistula and Multiple Saccular Arterial Aneurysms of a Finger, Following Childhood Human Bite," *Angiology Research,* Volume 16, number 89, 1965.

(With Edward B. Cross) "Hearts Too Good to Die—Problems in Acute Myocardial Infarction," *Journal of the National Medical Association,* Volume 59, number 1, 1967.

SOURCES:

Books

Dictionary of American Medical Biography, Volume I, 1984, p. 397.

Periodicals

Cobb, W. Montague, "John Beauregard Johnson, M.D., D.Sc., F.A.C.P., 1908–1972," *Journal of the National Medical Association,* March, 1973, pp. 166–170.

"Dr. J. B. Johnson, Medical Professor Howard U., Dies," *Jet,* January 4, 1973, p. 17.

"Wide-Awake Patients Given Heart Surgery," *Evening Star* (Washington, D.C.), April 17, 1959.

—*Sketch by Leonard C. Bruno*

Joseph Lealand Johnson
1895-1991
American physiologist and physician

Joseph Lealand Johnson was the second African American to earn both a Ph.D. and an M.D. degree. Although his parents had been born into slavery in North Carolina, Johnson was able to secure an education and eventually became dean of the Howard University Medical School and chairman of its Department of Physiology. It was through his efforts that this department became a fully modernized place of research.

Johnson was born in Philadelphia, Pennsylvania, on January 14, 1895. His parents had moved there from North Carolina and eventually had fourteen children. Johnson was the youngest of the ten that survived infancy. His father was a laborer who died when Johnson was two, and his mother supported the family as a midwife. Although the ten-year-old Johnson was so interested in the law that he would regularly cut school to attend trials at City Hall, he took the advice of his high school principal and applied for a scholarship in agronomy at Pennsylvania State University. "I knew I first had to get to college if I wanted to study law," Johnson recalled later in an interview with Allen B. Weisse in *Conversations in Medicine,* "and this was the first step."

Upon admission, Johnson found himself to be the only black on the entire campus. His education was interrupted by World War I, and when Johnson discovered there were no officer training camps available to him as there were for his white classmates, he wrote directly to the Secretary of War. The Secretary responded that a special camp was being formed at Fort Des Moines, Iowa. Johnson joined up, was commissioned second lieutenant, and was assigned to the 350th Field Artillery at Fort Dix, New Jersey. After being honorably discharged in January, 1919, he returned to Penn State and received his B.S. degree in June of that year.

That autumn, Johnson began teaching at the Kansas Vocational and Industrial Institute in Topeka, Kansas, where he also was an assistant coach of the men's basketball team as well as coach of the women's basketball team. The next year he moved to Kansas

City to teach general science and zoology at Lincoln High School. It was while attending a summer education course at the University of Chicago that Johnson first became interested in medicine as a way of helping the people of his poor Kansas City neighborhood called West Bottoms. "I got the feeling that those people were not getting the medical care that they should have because they couldn't afford it," Johnson explained to Weisse. "The idea struck me that I would go away and prepare myself thoroughly in medicine, and then come back to Kansas City and serve the people in the West Bottoms." With the help of the Lincoln High School principal who secured the backing of a wealthy friend, Johnson was able to resign from teaching and to dedicate himself to medical school.

By 1931, Johnson had earned his combined M. D. and Ph.D. degree in medicine and physiology at the University of Chicago. He was offered a physiology professorship at Howard University in Washington, D.C., by Dr. Numa P. G. Adams who had just become the first black dean of its medical school. Johnson accepted the offer, and it was under his guidance and direction that Howard's physiology department was completely revamped, renovated, and redirected into a modern facility where meaningful research could take place. When Dr. Adams died suddenly in 1940, Johnson became acting dean of Howard's medical school. In 1947 he became dean and remained in that position until 1955 when he returned to full-time teaching and research in physiology. He retired in 1971.

Johnson was a member of the board of directors of the National Medical Association and a member of the Medico Chirurgical Society of the District of Columbia. He also held memberships in the AAAS, NAACP, AMA, Foundation for Tropical Medicine, International College of Surgeons, Walter Reed Society, American Physiology Society, and was a fellow of the New York Academy of Sciences. He was a member of the honorary medical society, Alpha Omega Alpha, and Alpha Phi Alpha fraternity. He also served as the 1960–61 Imhotep Conference Chairman. Johnson died of cancer in Silver Spring, Maryland, in 1991.

SOURCES:

Books

Weisse, Allen B., editor, *Conversations in Medicine,* New York University Press, 1984, pp. 231–254.

Periodicals

Jet, January 14, 1991, p. 18.

—Sketch by Leonard C. Bruno

Katherine Coleman Goble Johnson
1918-
American aerospace technologist

Trained as a mathematician and physicist, Katherine Coleman Goble Johnson was instrumental in the development of calculations for tracking the orbits of spacecraft and satellites. The combination of planetary motion and gravitational pull makes it essential for a spacecraft to leave the Earth's orbit and return at precisely the right time. Johnson's work with the National Aeronautics and Space Administration (NASA) provided the basis for more accurate navigation procedures for space missions. As a result of her contributions, she is one of twenty-four scientists included in a permanent collection at the Afro-American Historical and Cultural Museum in Philadelphia.

Katherine Coleman was born in White Sulphur Springs, West Virginia, on August 26, 1918. Because there were few educational opportunities for blacks in West Virginia, Coleman's father, a laborer, would move the family to the town of Institute (where West Virginia State College is located) each fall to begin school.

It was at West Virginia State College that Coleman received her bachelor of science degree *summa cum laude* in education in 1937. Her majors were mathematics and French. She went on to West Virginia University, where she did graduate work in math and physics. Soon after she married James Goble and took a job teaching math and French in Marion, Virginia. Later, after giving birth to three daughters, she moved her family to Newport News, Virginia, where she worked first as a substitute teacher, and later as a program director for the local USO.

In 1953, she went to work as a mathematician at NASA's Langley Research Center in Hampton, Virginia. Her first project was the B–17 bomber. She recalled in a 1976 interview that much of the calculation work that today would be done by computer had to be done by her project group by hand. The calculations determined interplanetary trajectories, and helped track navigational patterns and orbit paths. Among the projects on which she worked were astronaut **Alan B. Shepard, Jr.**'s first space mission, and the Earth Resources Satellite, which helps locate underground minerals. Later, she analyzed data that had been gathered during the lunar missions of the 1960s. Her work won her and her colleagues two NASA Group Achievement Awards in 1967 and 1970. She also won special achievement awards in 1970, 1980, and 1985. She retired in 1992.

After the death of Johnson's first husband, she married James A. Johnson, with whom she resides in Hampton. One of her daughters is a mathematician; the other two are teachers. This is hardly surprising, considering Johnson's firm belief in the importance of education—in particular, math. "The reason a lot of children don't like math," she explained in 1976, "is because their teachers don't like it or their parents don't like it." She has been active in introducing children to math, through such means as participation in a television documentary on math sponsored by the U.S. Department of Education. In addition to her interest in science, Johnson has also been active in civic affairs with local chapters of such organizations as the Girl Scouts and the YWCA and with her local Presbyterian church.

SOURCES:

Books

Sammons, Vivian Ovelton, *Blacks in Science and Medicine,* Hemisphere Publishing, 1990, p. 135.

Spradling, Mary Mace, editor, *In Black and White: A Guide to Magazine Articles, Newspaper Articles and Books Concerning More than 15,000 Black Individuals and Groups,* Gale, 1980, p. 514.

Other

Black Contributors to Science and Energy Technology, U.S. Department of Energy (DOE/OPA-0035), 1979.

NASA Langley Research Center, Office of External Affairs, Hampton, Virginia.

—*Sketch by George A. Milite*

Marvin M. Johnson
1928-
American petroleum chemist

Marvin M. Johnson has taken strong initiative in leading the petroleum industry into an era of increasingly stringent environmental rules. In 1977 at Phillips Petroleum's research center, he invented an improved process for re-refining used motor oil into fresh lubricant. This process turns used oil, a pollutant, into a valuable resource. He also has invented a method for preventing the fouling of catalysts used in refining heavy crudes, thus enhancing the value of these lower-quality feedstocks. In 1985 President Ronald Reagan presented him with the National Medal of Technology.

Marvin M. Johnson

Marvin Merrill Johnson was born on March 21, 1928, in Salt Lake City, Utah, the son of John Ivan and Hildur (Johnson) Johnson. His father, an insurance broker, was descended from early Mormon pioneers, which gave Johnson a strong attachment to that city. He was to stay in Salt Lake City through nearly the first three decades of his life, attending the University of Utah, from which he received a B.S. in 1950 and a Ph.D. in 1956, both in chemical engineering. He then joined the Phillips Petroleum Company in Bartlesville, Oklahoma, spending most of his career there and rising to the level of senior scientist.

Stretches Oil Reserves with New Process

When Johnson arrived at Phillips, the technology of oil refining was well established, reflecting the experience of decades. Nevertheless, Johnson proceeded to demonstrate that there still was plenty of room for innovation. An important topic for his research lay in the refining of heavy crudes, which are available from Alaska's North Slope. These form a major portion of America's domestic reserves, easing the country's reliance on imported oil. However, these crudes have posed problems at the refinery.

Refineries have depended upon catalytic cracking to boost yields of gasoline. In this process, components of crude oil having high molecular weight contact catalysts and break into hydrocarbons whose molecules are considerably smaller. About half of America's gasoline comes from this process, but its success depends on preventing the catalysts from fouling. This is not difficult with light crudes, which are of high quality. However, heavy crudes contain trace contaminants that include heavy metals, notably vanadium and nickel. These deposit on the catalysts and impair their ability to produce gasoline.

In 1972 Johnson found that it was possible to avoid this problem simply by adding small quantities of suitable compounds of antimony to the heavy crude feedstock. This solution was particularly beneficial because it required essentially no change in operating procedure and could be implemented at low cost. Yet it provided a substantial boost in the ability of existing refineries to process heavy crudes. This technique, called "metals passivation," first saw use in 1978 and went on to become an industry standard. Its appearance was timely, for it stretched America's oil reserves and helped to address the energy crisis.

Finds Bonanza in Used Motor Oil

Johnson's second major contribution addressed the reclamation of waste lubricants. Used motor oils are a significant source of pollution in the United States, with more than one billion gallons discarded annually. During the 1970s, attempts at reclamation achieved only limited success. The yields of reusable oil were no better than 50 to 75 percent, and these reclamation processes provided little environmental benefit because they produced substantial volumes of toxic waste. After 1980 a number of re-refining operations went out of business because they could not comply with Environmental Protection Agency regulations.

In 1977 Johnson introduced a new process that overcame these difficulties. He raised the yield to more than ninety percent while improving the quality, making re-refined oil as good as virgin lubricating oil and sometimes even better. Further, the process did not produce useless waste; rather, nearly all of its by-products had industrial value and could be sold. Johnson's invention thus stood as an important contribution to the technology of recycling, for he turned used oil from a noxious waste into a useful resource. In recognition of his contributions, President Ronald Reagan presented him with the National Medal of Technology at a White House ceremony in 1985.

In 1951 he married Marilyn Wite. They have four children: Mark, Jennifer, Lorelie, and Marianne. He has also been prolific as an inventor, with some 175 patents as of early 1994; he continues to pursue research at Phillips Petroleum. He is an active member in the Church of Jesus Christ of Latter-Day Saints and has served as president of the American Legion Baseball Committee. In addition, he is an avid gardener.

SOURCES:

Periodicals

"Inventor's Formula: Brains, Hard Work," *Phil-News,* November, 1990, p. 6.

"Marvin Johnson Presented National Medal of Technology," *R&D News* [Phillips Research Center], March, 1985.

—Sketch by T. A. Heppenheimer

Virginia E. Johnson
1925-
American psychologist and sex therapist

In collaboration with Dr. **William Howell Masters**, psychologist and sex therapist Virginia E. Johnson pioneered the study of human sexuality under laboratory conditions. She and Masters published the results of their study as a book entitled *Human Sexual Response* in 1966, causing an immediate sensation. As part of her work at the Reproductive Biology Research Foundation in St. Louis and later at the Masters and Johnson Institute, she counseled many clients and taught sex therapy to many professional practitioners.

Johnson was born Virginia Eshelman on February 11, 1925, in Springfield, Missouri, to Hershel Eshelman, a farmer, and Edna (Evans) Eshelman. The elder of two children, she began school in Palo Alto, California, where her family had moved in 1930. When they returned to Missouri three years later, she was ahead of her school peers and skipped several grades. She studied piano and voice, and read extensively. She entered Drury College in Springfield in 1941. After her freshman year, she was hired to work in the state insurance office, a job she held for four years. Her mother, a republican state committeewoman, introduced her to many elected officials, and Johnson often sang for them at meetings. These performances led to a job as a country music singer for radio station KWTO in Springfield, where her stage name was Virginia Gibson. She studied at the

University of Missouri and later at the Kansas City Conservatory of Music. In 1947, she became a business writer for the St. Louis *Daily Record.* She also worked briefly on the marketing staff of KMOX-TV, leaving that position in 1951.

In the early 1940s she married a Missouri politician, but the marriage lasted only two days. Her marriage to an attorney many years her senior also ended in divorce. On June 13, 1950, she married George V. Johnson, an engineering student and leader of a dance band. She sang with the band until the birth of her two children, Scott Forstall and Lisa Evans. In 1956, the Johnsons divorced.

Chosen by William Howell Masters as Research Associate

In 1956, contemplating a return to college for a degree in sociology, Johnson applied for a job at the Washington University employment office. William Howell Masters, associate professor of clinical obstetrics and gynecology, had requested an assistant to interview volunteers for a research project. He personally chose Johnson, who fitted the need for an outgoing, intelligent, mature woman who was preferably a mother. Johnson began work on January 2, 1957, as a research associate, but soon advanced to research instructor.

Gathering scientific data by means of electroencephalography, electrocardiography, and the use of color monitors, Masters and Johnson measured and analyzed 694 volunteers. They were careful to protect the privacy of their subjects, who were photographed in various modes of sexual stimulation. In addition to a description of the four stages of sexual arousal, other valuable information was gained from the photographs, including evidence of the failure of some contraceptives, the discovery of a vaginal secretion in some women that prevents conception, and the observation that sexual enjoyment need not decrease with age. In 1964, Masters and Johnson created the non-profit Reproductive Biology Research Foundation in St. Louis and began treating couples for sexual problems. Originally listed as a research associate, Johnson became assistant director of the Foundation in 1969 and co-director in 1973.

In 1966, Masters and Johnson released their book *Human Sexual Response,* in which they detailed the results of their studies. Although the book was written in dry, clinical terms and intended for medical professionals, its titillating subject matter made it front-page news and a runaway best seller, with over 300,000 volumes distributed by 1970. While some reviewers accused the team of dehumanizing and scientizing sex, overall professional and critical response was positive.

Develops Sex Therapy Institute

At Johnson's suggestion, the two researchers went on the lecture circuit to discuss their findings and appeared on such television programs as NBC's *Today* show and ABC's *Stage '67.* Their book and their public appearances heightened public interest in sex therapy, and a long list of clients developed. Couples referred to their clinic would spend two weeks in intensive therapy and have periodic follow-ups for five years. In a second book, *Human Sexual Inadequacy,* published in 1970, Masters and Johnson discuss the possibility that sex problems are more cultural than physiological or psychological. In 1975, they wrote *The Pleasure Bond: A New Look at Sexuality and Commitment,* which differs from previous volumes in that it was written for the average reader. This book describes total commitment and fidelity to the partner as the basis for an enduring sexual bond. To expand counseling, Masters and Johnson trained dual-sex therapy teams and conducted regular workshops for college teachers, marriage counselors, and other professionals.

After the release of this second book, Masters divorced his first wife and married Johnson on January 7, 1971, in Fayetteville, Arkansas. They continued their work at the Reproductive Biology Research Foundation, and in 1973 founded the Masters and Johnson Institute. Johnson was co-director of the institute, running the everyday business, and Masters concentrated on scientific work. Johnson, who never received a college degree, was widely recognized along with Masters for her contributions to human sexuality research. Together they received several awards, including the Sex Education and Therapists Award in 1978 and Biomedical Research Award of the World Sexology Association in 1979.

In 1981, the team sold their lab and moved to another location in St. Louis, where they had a staff of twenty-five and a long waiting list of clients. Their book *Homosexuality in Perspective,* released shortly before the move, documents their research on gay and lesbian sexual practice and homosexual sexual problems and their work with "gender-confused" individuals who sought a "cure" for their homosexuality. One of their most controversial conclusions from their ten-year study of eighty-four men and women was their conviction that homosexuality is primarily not physical, emotional, or genetic, but a learned behavior. Some reviewers hailed the team's claims of success in "converting" homosexuals. Others, however, observed that the handpicked individuals who participated in the study were not a representative sample; moreover, they challenged the team's assumption that heterosexual performance alone was an accurate indicator of a changed sexual preference.

The institute had many associates who assisted in research and writing. Robert Kolodny, an M.D.

interested in sexually transmitted diseases, coauthored the book *Crisis: Heterosexual Behavior in the Age of AIDS* with Masters and Johnson in 1988. The book, commented Stephen Fried in *Vanity Fair,* "was politically incorrect in the extreme": it predicted a large-scale outbreak of the virus in the heterosexual community and, in a chapter meant to document how little was known of the AIDS virus, suggested that it might be possible to catch it from a toilet seat. Several prominent members of the medical community questioned the study, and many accused the authors of sowing hysteria. Adverse publicity hurt the team, who were distressed because they felt the medical community had turned against them. The number of therapy clients at the institute declined.

The board of the institute was quietly dissolved and William Young, Johnson's son-in-law, became acting director. Johnson went into semi-retirement. On February 19, 1992, Young announced that after twenty-one years of marriage, Masters and Johnson were filing for divorce because of differences about goals relating to work and retirement. Following the divorce, Johnson took most of the institute's records with her and is continuing her work independently.

SELECTED WRITINGS BY JOHNSON:

Books

(With William Howell Masters) *Human Sexual Response,* Little, Brown, 1966.

(With William Howell Masters) *Human Sexual Inadequacy,* Little, Brown, 1970.

(With William Howell Masters) *The Pleasure Bond: A New Look at Sexuality and Commitment,* Little, Brown, 1975.

(With William Howell Masters) *Homosexuality in Perspective,* Little, Brown, 1979.

(With William Howell Masters and Robert Kolodny) *Masters and Johnson on Sex and Human Loving,* Little, Brown, 1986.

(With William Howell Masters and Robert Kolodny) *Crisis: Heterosexual Behavior in the Age of AIDS,* Grove, 1988.

SOURCES:

Books

Robinson, Paul. *The Modernization of Sex: Havelock Ellis, Albert Kinsey, William Masters, and Virginia Johnson,* Cornell University Press, 1988.

Periodicals

Duberman, Martin Bauml, review of *Homosexuality in Perspective, New Republic,* June 16, 1979, pp. 24–31.

Fried, Stephen, "The New Sexperts," *Vanity Fair,* December 1992, p. 132.

"Repairing the Conjugal Bed," *Time,* March 25, 1970.

—*Sketch by Evelyn B. Kelly*

Harold S. Johnston
1920-
American physical and atmospheric chemist

Harold S. Johnston has been recognized as one of the world's leading authorities in atmospheric chemistry. He was among the first to suggest that nitrogen oxides might damage the Earth's ozone layer. His research interests have been in the field of gas-phase chemical kinetics and photochemistry, and his expertise has been employed by many state and federal scientific advisory committees on air pollution, motor vehicle emissions, and stratospheric pollution.

Harold Sledge Johnston was born on October 11, 1920, in Woodstock, Georgia, to Smith L. and Florine Dial Johnston. He graduated with a chemistry degree from Emory University in 1941 and, later that year, entered the California Institute of Technology as a graduate student. During the early 1940s, he was a civilian meteorologist attached to a United States Army unit in California and Florida, after which time he returned to graduate studies and earned his Ph.D. in chemistry and physics in 1948, the same year he married Mary Ella Stay. The couple has four children: Shirley Louise, Linda Marie, David Finley, and Barbara Dial. Johnston was on the faculty of the chemistry department of Stanford University from 1947 to 1956 and of the California Institute of Technology from 1956 to 1957. He then became a professor of chemistry at the University of California, Berkeley, serving as dean of the College of Chemistry from 1966 to 1970.

Johnston's introduction to meteorology occurred when he was a civilian scientist working on a defense project in World War II. In 1941, Roscoe Dickinson, Johnston's research director at the California Institute of Technology, was overseeing a National Defense Research Council project, with which Johnston became involved. Dickinson's group tested the effects of poisonous volatile chemicals on charcoals that were to be used in gas masks. Later, they studied how gas clouds moved and dispersed under different condi-

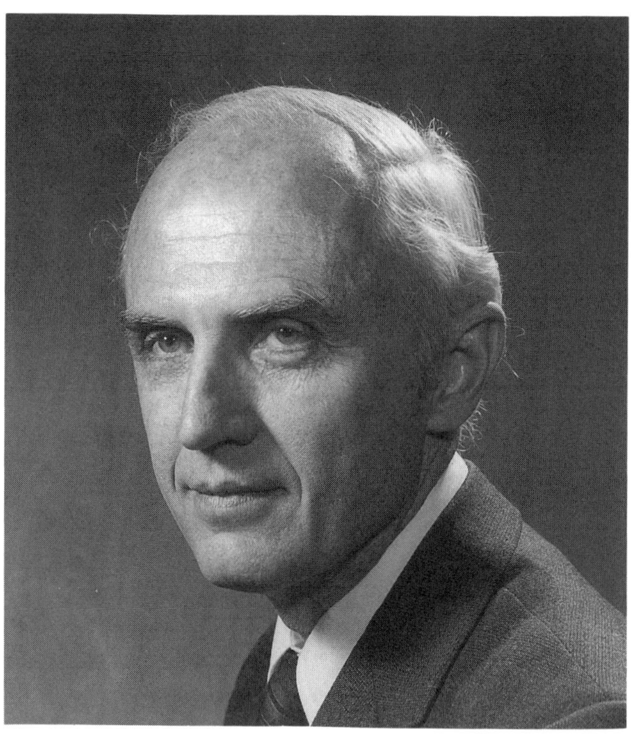

Harold S. Johnston

tions in order to appraise coastal areas that might be vulnerable to chemical attacks.

In 1943, Johnston moved with the Chemical Warfare Service to Bushnell, Florida, where he worked with, and eventually headed, the Dugway Proving Ground Mobile Field Unit of the U.S. Chemical Warfare Service. This unit carried out test explosions to assess how the dispersion of gas was affected by meterological changes. While he was there, Johnston and John Otvos developed an instrument to measure the concentration of various gases in the air.

Johnston applied his meteorology work to his Ph.D. studies, which he resumed in 1945. He wrote his thesis on the reaction between ozone, a naturally-occurring form of oxygen, and nitrogen dioxide, a pollutant formed during combustion. Later, during his tenure at Stanford, Johnston worked on a series of fast gas-phase chemical reactions. Using photo-electron multiplier tubes left over from the war, he pioneered a method of studying gas phase reactions that was a thousand times faster than existing techniques. Johnston then spent the years 1950 to 1956 researching high and low pressure limits of unimolecular reactions, and for the subsequent ten years, expanded his research to apply activated complex theory to elementary bimolecular reactions.

One of Johnston's most significant research efforts has been on the destruction of the ozone layer. This layer in the Earth's upper atmosphere protects people from the sun's ultraviolet rays. Chlorofluorocarbons (CFCs), gaseous compounds often used in aerosol cans, refrigerants, and air conditioning systems, deplete this ozone layer, resulting in increased amounts of harmful sun rays reaching the Earth's surface. The Environmental Protection Agency has imposed production cutbacks on these harmful chemicals. Much like CFCs, nitrogen oxides also damage the ozone layer. During the late 1960s, the federal government financed the design and construction of two prototype supersonic transport (SST) aircraft. An intense political debate over whether the program should be expanded to construct five hundred SSTs was waged. Although Congress was split almost evenly, both houses voted to terminate the SST program in March, 1971. Johnston's articles and testimony suggesting the negative effects SSTs could produce on the atmosphere led two senators to introduce the Stratosphere Protection Act of 1971, which established a research program concerned with the stratosphere. The resulting program, with which Johnston was affiliated, was called the Climatic Impact Assessment Program (CIAP) and began its work in the fall of 1971. Among other things, CIAP concluded that nitrogen oxides from stratospheric aircraft would further reduce ozone. CIAP recommended that aircraft engines be redesigned to reduced nitrogen oxide emissions.

Throughout his career, Johnston has served on many state and federal scientific advisory committees. In the 1960s, he was a panel member of the President's Science Advisory Board on Atmospheric Sciences and was on the National Academy of Sciences (NAS) Panel to the National Bureau of Standards. Johnston served on the California Statewide Air Pollution Research Center committee and the NAS Committee on Motor Vehicle Emissions during the early 1970s. He also served on the Federal Aviation Administration's High Altitude Pollution Program from 1978 to 1982 and the NAS Committee on Atmospheric Chemistry from 1989 to 1992. He has been an advisor to High Speed Civil Transport Studies for the National Aeronautics and Space Administration (NASA) since 1988.

Johnston is the author of the book *Gas Phase Reaction Rate Theory* and the author or coauthor of more than 160 technical articles. He is a member of the NAS, the American Academy of Arts and Sciences, the American Chemical Society, the American Physical Society, the American Geophysical Union, and the American Association for the Advancement of Science. Among Johnston's numerous awards are the 1983 Tyler Prize for Environmental Achievement, the 1993 NAS Award for Chemistry in Service to Society, and an honorary doctor of science degree from Emory University.

SELECTED WRITINGS BY JOHNSTON:

Books

Gas Phase Reaction Rate Theory, Ronald, 1966.

Periodicals

"Reduction of Stratospheric Ozone by Nitrogen Oxide Catalysts from Supersonic Transport Exhaust," *Science,* August 6, 1971, Volume 173, pp. 517–522.

"Pollution of the Stratosphere," *Annual Review of Physical Chemistry,* Volume 26, 1975, pp. 315–338.

"Human Effects on the Global Atmosphere," *Annual Review of Physical Chemistry,* Volume 35, 1984, pp. 481–505.

"Atmospheric Ozone," *Annual Review of Physical Chemistry,* Volume 43, 1992, pp. 1–32.

—Sketch by Philip Duhan Segal

Frédéric Joliot-Curie

Frédéric Joliot-Curie
1900-1958
French nuclear physicist

Frédéric Joliot-Curie was a French nuclear physicist who, together with his wife, **Irène Joliot-Curie**, discovered artificial radioactivity, for which they received the 1935 Nobel Prize in chemistry. Their efforts made nuclear fission and the subsequent development of both nuclear energy and the atomic bomb feasible. Joliot met his wife while working as an assistant at the Radium Institute at the University of Paris. Irène Curie was the daughter of **Marie** and **Pierre Curie**, the Nobel Prize laureates who discovered radium and founded the Radium Institute. Irène became Frédéric's lifelong research collaborator and they usually published their findings under the combined form of their last names, Joliot-Curie. After World War II, Frédéric Joliot-Curie brought France into the atomic age as director of France's atomic energy commission.

Jean-Frédéric Joliot was born on March 19, 1900, in Paris to Henri Joliot and Emilie Roederer. According to tradition, all the Joliot men were named Jean in honor of Jean Hus, a champion for spiritual freedom who had been burned at the stake in the fifteenth century. Henri Joliot came from a long line of liberal thinkers and had been part of the French Communard movement at the end of the Franco-Prussian War. He became a Parisian dry goods merchant and the family was settled into a middle-class life, yet Henri remained passionate about his leftist political concerns. He also had a great love of the outdoors and of music, combining the two by composing a number of calls for the hunting horn. His son Frédéric would someday be an avid outdoorsman despite his busy scientific career. Frédéric's mother Emilie was also from a liberal family and Frédéric was exposed to progressive social ideas at a young age. The social and political leanings of his parents had a profound influence on young Frédéric and he was an atheist and political leftist his entire life.

Joliot was educated at the Lycée Lakanal in a suburb of Paris, then at the École Primaire Supérieure Lavoisier in Paris. In 1920 he was admitted to the École Supérieure de Physique et de Chimie Industrielle of Paris, a preparatory school that turned out most of France's industrial engineers at the time. The director of the school, a brilliant physicist named **Paul Langevin**, recognized Joliot's interest and aptitude for scientific research and became Joliot's lifelong mentor.

After graduating at the head of his class, Joliot worked in industry for a short time. Following Langevin's advice, however, he took a position as research assistant at the Radium Institute in Paris under the guidance of Madame Marie Curie, a Nobel laureate in nuclear physics. Joliot held Marie and Pierre Curie in high esteem, going so far as to have pictures of them hanging on the wall of his makeshift home laboratory. Working at the Institute, he was instructed by Madame Curie to be initiated into the rudiments of studying radioactivity by Irène Curie, the couple's elder daughter. For as affable and charming as Frédéric was, Irène was serious and aloof. Yet the two shared their love of research as well as political and social leanings and were married in 1926. They both adopted their combined last names to preserve the scientific Curie lineage.

Research in Artificial Radioactivity Leads to Nobel Prize

Joliot-Curie began his research improving the Wilson chamber, a cloud chamber in which the charged particles of an atom can be detected as they leave a trail of water droplets in their wake. His engineering background made him a master at instrumentation and he redesigned the chamber so that the pressure could be lowered, making the tracks longer and more easily discernible. He also supervised the making of a camera that photographed what went on in the chamber. Further improvements allowed the energy of emissions to be measured using the amount of curvature shown by the tracks when placed in a magnetic field. Conducting experiments within the chamber had an elegance that Frédéric considered to be the most beautiful experience in the world.

In 1930, Joliot-Curie completed his doctoral thesis entitled *A Study of the Electrochemistry of Radioactive Elements,* thus beginning intensive research in the area of radioactivity. Later that same year, he and Irène became interested in the experiments of German physicists **Walther Bothe** and Hans Becker. The German pair had discovered that very strong radiation was emitted from some of the lighter elements when they were bombarded with alpha rays. An alpha ray is an energetic particle that resembles the nucleus of a helium atom and contains two positive charges. Such rays had only been discovered at the turn of the century as had the basic particles of the atom. Because of the readily available source of alpha rays—radium—stockpiled at the Radium Institute, Frédéric and Irène began doing research in which they bombarded nuclei of various elements with alpha particles.

In the course of experimentation, the Joliot-Curies had come very close to discovering two other subatomic particles, the neutron and the positron. But instead of investigating these anomalies, they focused their efforts on their alpha-particle research. As Joliot-Curie and his wife worked with radioactive polonium as a source of alpha rays they found that when an element such as aluminum is bombarded, some alpha particles are absorbed by the nuclei, transmuting the atoms to phosphorus. Aluminum usually has 13 protons in its nucleus, but when bombarded with alpha particles, which contain two positive charges each, the protons were added to the nucleus, forming a nucleus of phosphorus, the element that normally contains 15 protons. The phosphorus produced was different from naturally-occurring phosphorus because it gave off a strong radiation, as predicted by Bothe and Becker. It was a radioactive isotope produced artificially.

The Joliot-Curies' discovery of artificial radioactivity was announced to the Academy of Science in 1934 and won them the Nobel Prize for chemistry in 1935. (The prize was awarded in chemistry rather than physics because of their synthesis of new radioactive elements.) Sadly, though she had predicted the success and recognition of her daughter and son-in-law, Marie Curie died of leukemia the year before the award, a casualty of lifelong exposure to radiation.

In the latter part of the 1930s, experiments by Joliot-Curie showed that a nucleus of a radioactive element such as uranium could be divided into two smaller nuclei of comparable size with a release of energy emissions. It was predicted that this phenomenon, known as nuclear fission, could occur very quickly in a chain reaction and therefore needed to be controlled or moderated. This conclusion led other researchers such as **Otto Hahn** and **Enrico Fermi** to work on nuclear fission experiments which eventually led to the creation of the atomic bomb as well as atomic energy.

The Joliot-Curies enjoyed these productive years in the company of their two children, Helene (born in 1927), and Pierre (born in 1932). Because of Irène's often fragile health, the family spent as much time away from work in Paris as possible, swimming or sailing at the beach or hiking or skiing in the mountains. It was said that rather than carry around pictures of his family in his wallet, Frédéric Joliot-Curie carried instead a picture of a giant pike he had once caught on a fishing trip. He was a very sociable man, telling not only fish stories, but entertaining both colleagues and family with his wit and charm.

Nuclear Physics and Communist Politics Prove a Volatile Mix

By the time the Germans occupied Paris during World War II, Joliot-Curie, who was staunchly part of the French Resistance, continued to do research but kept a low profile. He wanted to prevent the Germans from gaining information about nuclear fission. In fact, he had a stockpile of heavy water, which was used as a moderator in nuclear fission experiments, sent out of the country so that the Germans could not gain possession of it. Inspired in part by the arrest of his friend and mentor, Paul Langevin, Joliot-Curie became more politically active. In 1942, when Langevin's son-in-law, Jacques Solomon, was tortured and shot by the Nazis for turning out a resistance newspaper, Joliot-Curie joined the Communist Party. Arrested twice and fearing for his safety and that of his family, Joliot-Curie went underground in Paris and sent Irène and their two children to Switzerland.

After World War II, Joliot-Curie was instrumental in convincing the government of Charles de Gaulle to establish an Atomic Energy Commission in France, modeled after the similar agency in the United States. After being appointed its Commissioner, Joliot-Curie oversaw the installation of a major nuclear research center. With the advent of the Cold War and tensions between the Soviet Union and the West, Joliot-Curie's membership in the Communist Party and his radical activism drew governmental concern over his reliability. He was relieved of his position as high commissioner of Atomic Energy.

Losing his position was a blow to Joliot-Curie both professionally and personally. He and his wife also began to suffer ill health from their lifelong exposure to radiation. Still dedicated to his leftist politics, he became president of the World Organization of the Partisans of Peace. In March of 1956, Irène finally succumbed to leukemia. Frédéric succeeded her as head of the Radium Institute and continued her efforts to build a new physics laboratory south of Paris. At 58, his liver badly damaged by exposure to radiation, Frédéric Joliot-Curie died following an operation made necessary by an internal hemorrhage.

SELECTED WRITINGS BY JOLIOT-CURIE:

Books

Textes Choisis, [Paris], 1959.
(With wife, Irène Joliot-Curie) *Oeuvres Scientifigues Completes,* [Paris], 1961.

Periodicals

(With Irène Joliot-Curie) "Sur la nature du rayonnement absorbable qui accompagne les rayons alpha du polonium," *Comptes rendus hebdomadaires des seances de l'Academie des sciences,* 1929, p. 1270.

SOURCES:

Books

de Broglie, Louis, *La vie et l'oeuvre de Frédéric Joliot,* [Paris], 1959.
Pflaum, Rosalynd, *Grand Obsession: Madame Curie and Her World,* Doubleday, 1989.

—Sketch by Barbara A. Branca

Irène Joliot-Curie
1897-1956
French chemist and physicist

Irène Joliot-Curie, elder daughter of famed scientists **Marie** and **Pierre Curie**, won a Nobel Prize in chemistry in 1935 for the discovery, with her husband **Frédéric Joliot-Curie**, of artificial radioactivity. She began her scientific career as a research assistant at the Radium Institute in Paris, an institute founded by her parents, and soon succeeded her mother as its research director. It was at the Institute where she met her husband and lifelong collaborator, Frédéric Joliot. They usually published their findings under the combined form of their last names, Joliot-Curie.

Born on September 12, 1897, in Paris to Nobel laureates Marie and Pierre Curie, Irène Curie had a rather extraordinary childhood, growing up in the company of brilliant scientists. Her mother, the former Marie Sklodowska and her father, Pierre Curie, had been married in 1895 and had become dedicated physicists, experimenting with radioactivity in their laboratory. Marie Curie was on the threshold of discovering radium when little Irène, or "my little Queen" as her mother called her, was only a few months old. As Irène grew into a precocious, yet shy child, she was very possessive of her mother who was often preoccupied with her experiments. If, after a long day at the laboratory, the little Queen greeted her exhausted mother with demands for fruit, Marie Curie would turn right around and walk to the market to get her daughter fruit. Upon her father Pierre Curie's untimely accidental death in 1908, Irène was then more influenced by her paternal grandfather, Eugene Curie. It was her grandfather who taught young Irène botany and natural history as they spent summers in the country. The elder Curie was also somewhat of a political radical and atheist, and it was he who helped shape Irène's leftist sentiment and disdain for organized religion.

Curie's education was quite remarkable. Marie Curie made sure Irène and her younger sister, Eve Denise (born in 1904), did their physical as well as mental exercises each day. The girls had a governess for a time, but because Madame Curie was not satisfied with the available schools, she organized a teaching cooperative in which children of the professors from Paris' famed Sorbonne came to the laboratory for their lessons. Madame Curie taught physics, and other of her famous colleagues taught math, chemistry, language and sculpture. Soon Irène became the star pupil as she excelled in physics and chemistry. After only two years, however, when Irène was 14, the cooperative folded and Irène enrolled in a private school, the College Sevigne, and soon earned her

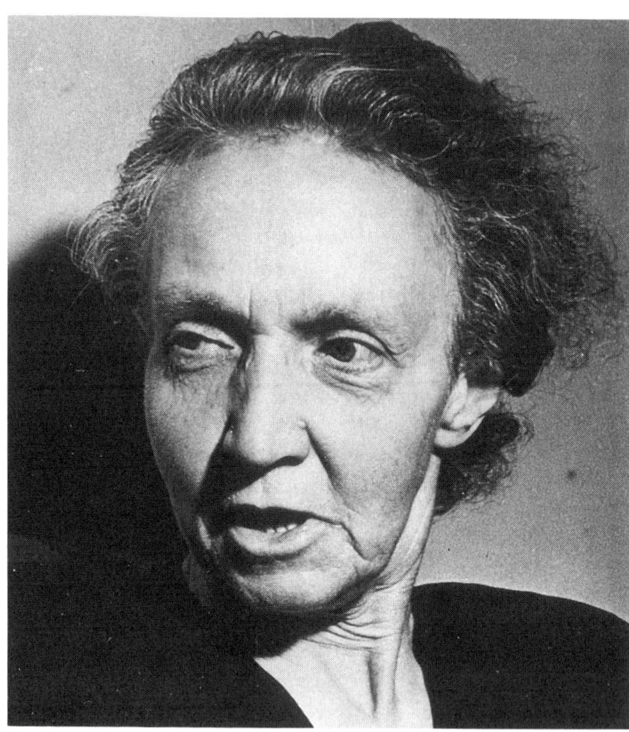

Irène Joliot-Curie

degree. Summers were spent at the beach or in the mountains, sometimes in the company of such notables as **Albert Einstein** and his son. Irène then enrolled at the Sorbonne to study for a diploma in nursing.

During World War I, Madame Curie went to the front where she used new X-ray equipment to treat soldiers. Irène soon trained to use the same equipment and worked with her mother and later on her own. Irène, who was shy and rather antisocial in nature, grew to be calm and steadfast in the face of danger. At age 21, she became her mother's assistant at the Radium Institute. She also became quite adept at using the Wilson cloud chamber, a device which makes otherwise invisible atomic particles visible by the trails of water droplets left in their wake.

Work on Artificial Radioactivity Leads to a Nobel Prize

In the early 1920s, after a jubilant tour of the United States with her mother and sister, Irène Curie began to make her mark in the laboratory. Working with Fernand Holweck, chief of staff at the Institute, she performed several experiments on radium resulting in her first paper in 1921. By 1925 she completed her doctoral thesis on the emission of alpha rays from polonium, an element that her parents had discovered. Many colleagues in the lab, including her future husband, thought her to be much like her father in her almost instinctive ability to use laboratory instruments. Frédéric was several years younger than Irène and untrained in the use of the equipment. When she was called upon to teach him about radioactivity, Irène started out in a rather brusque manner, but soon the two began taking long country walks. They married in 1926 and decided to use the combined name Joliot-Curie to honor her notable scientific heritage.

After their marriage, Irène and Frédéric Joliot-Curie began doing their research together, signing all their scientific papers jointly even after Irène was named chief of the laboratory in 1932. After reading about the experiments of German scientists **Walther Bothe** and Hans Becker, their attention focused on nuclear physics, a field yet in its infancy. Only at the turn of the century had scientists discovered that atoms contain a central core or nucleus made up of positively charged particles called protons. Outside the nucleus are negatively charged particles called electrons. Irène's parents had done their work on radioactivity, a phenomenon which occurs when the nuclei of certain elements release particles or emit energy. Some emissions are called alpha particles which are relatively large particles resembling the nucleus of a helium atom and thus contain two positive charges. In their Nobel Prize-winning work, the elder Curies had discovered that some elements, the radioactive elements, emit particles on a regular, predictable basis.

Irène Joliot-Curie had in her laboratory one of the largest supplies of radioactive materials in the world, namely polonium, a radioactive element discovered by her parents. The polonium emitted alpha particles which Irène and Frédéric used to bombard different elements. In 1933 they used alpha particles to bombard aluminum nuclei. What they produced was radioactive phosphorus. Aluminum usually has 13 protons in its nuclei, but when bombarded with alpha particles which contain two positive charges each, the protons were added to the nucleus, forming a nucleus of phosphorus, the element with 15 protons. The phosphorus produced is different from naturally-occurring phosphorus because it is radioactive and is known as a radioactive isotope.

The two researchers used their alpha bombardment technique on other elements, finding that when a nucleus of a particular element combined with an alpha particle, it would transform that element into another, radioactive element with a higher number of protons in its nucleus. What Irène and Frédéric Joliot-Curie had done was to create artificial radioactivity. They announced this breakthrough to the Academy of Sciences in January of 1934.

The Joliot-Curies' discovery was of great significance not only for its pure science, but for its many applications. Since the 1930s many more radioactive isotopes have been produced and used as radioactive trace elements in medical diagnoses as well as in countless experiments. The success of the technique encouraged other scientists to experiment with the releasing the power of the nucleus.

It was a bittersweet time for Irène Joliot-Curie. An overjoyed but ailing Marie Curie knew that her daughter was headed for great recognition but died in July of that year from leukemia caused by the many years of radiation exposure. Several months later the Joliot-Curies were informed of the Nobel Prize. Although they were nuclear physicists, the pair received an award in chemistry because of their discovery's impact in that area.

From Popular Nobel Laureate to Unpopular Political Activist

After winning the Nobel Prize, Irène and Frédéric were the recipients of many honorary degrees and named officers of the Legion of Honor. But all these accolades made little impact on Irène who preferred spending her free time reading poetry or swimming, sailing, skiing or hiking. As her children Helene and Pierre grew, she became more interested in social movements and politics. An atheist and political leftist, Irène also took up the cause of woman's suffrage. She served as undersecretary of state in Leon Blum's Popular Front government in 1936 and then was elected professor at the Sorbonne in 1937.

Continuing her work in physics during the late 1930s, Irène Joliot-Curie experimented with bombarding uranium nuclei with neutrons. With her collaborator Pavle Savitch, she showed that uranium could be broken down into other radioactive elements. Her seminal experiment paved the way for another physicist, **Otto Hahn**, to prove that uranium bombarded with neutrons can be made to split into two atoms of comparable mass. This phenomenon, named fission, is the foundation for the practical applications of nuclear energy—the generation of nuclear power and the atom bomb.

During the early part of World War II, Irène continued her research in Paris although her husband Frédéric had gone underground. They were both part of the French Resistance movement and by 1944, Irène and her children fled France for Switzerland. After the war she was appointed director of the Radium Institute and was also a commissioner for the French atomic energy project. She put in long days in the laboratory and continued to lecture and present papers on radioactivity although her health was slowly deteriorating. Her husband Frédéric, a member of the Communist Party since 1942, was removed from his post as head of the French Atomic Energy Commission in 1950. After that time, the two became outspoken on the use of nuclear energy for the cause of peace. Irène was a member of the World Peace Council and made several trips to the Soviet Union. It was the height of the Cold War and because of her politics, Irène was shunned by the American Chemical Society when she applied for membership in 1954. Her final contribution to physics came as she helped plan a large particle accelerator and laboratory at Orsay, south of Paris in 1955. Her health worsened and on March 17, 1956, Irène Joliot-Curie died as her mother had before her, of leukemia resulting from a lifetime of exposure to radiation.

SELECTED WRITINGS BY IRÈNE JOLIOT-CURIE:

Books

(With husband, Frédéric Joliot-Curie) *Oeuvres Scientifiques Completes,* [Paris], 1961.

Periodicals

(With P. Savic) "Sur les radioelements formes par l'uranium irradie par les neutrons," *Journal de physique et le radium,* Volume 8, 1937, p. 385.

SOURCES:

Books

Opfell, Olga S., *The Lady Laureates: Women Who Have Won the Nobel Prize,* Scarecrow, 1978.

Pflaum, Rosalynd, *Grand Obsession: Madame Curie and Her World,* Doubleday, 1989.

—*Sketch by Barbara A. Branca*

Fred Jones
1893-1961
American inventor

Fred Jones was a gifted inventor with an insatiable need to learn about the mechanical and scientific world. Jones was best known for inventing and patenting revolutionary techniques for mobile refrigeration, a discovery allowing for the safe and economical transport of refrigerated and frozen food. Although this was one of the few ideas he patented, Jones' many unpatented ideas also had a great impact on society.

Childhood Aptitude Leads to Career of Discovery

Frederick McKinley Jones was born on May 17, 1893, in Covington, Kentucky, just across the river from Cincinnati, Ohio. His father, John Jones, was a white Irish railroad worker; his mother was an African American woman who abandoned her son shortly after he was born and was never seen again. As a boy, Jones only spent four years in school. His father was constantly exasperated by Jones' method of learning how mechanical machinery worked—he always took things apart. The elder Jones would come home from work to find a clock in pieces one day and a carburetor the next. The boy was always able to put things back together in working order, however, and many times the item was improved.

At seven years of age, Jones' father sent him to live at the rectory of a local Catholic church to obtain an education. He never found a home there, as he rejected the discipline and expectations imposed by the priests. Jones always had a deep love and fascination for cars, so as a boy he learned about them at every opportunity. When he was eleven, he ran away from the rectory, crossed the river into Cincinnati and within days found a job at a garage. Although he was just hired to keep the place clean, it was not long before he was repairing cars with the rest of the mechanics. When he turned fourteen, the legal employment age, Jones was made a full-time mechanic and, just a year later, he became the shop foreman.

The next twenty years found Jones almost always employed throughout the Mid-West and the South, but racial barriers made life more difficult for him the further south he traveled. Jobs included working aboard a Mississippi River steamship in St. Louis, furnace repair and maintenance, farm machinery repair, and of course, automobile repair. In 1913 Jones moved to Hallock in the northwest corner of Minnesota, making the journey with a family that had befriended him and employed him to tend to their hotel boiler equipment. They had just purchased some land to start a farm and requested that Jones accompany them to help with the machinery.

Jones served his country during World War I and put his repair skills to good use. He could fix just about anything and the military recognized this talent. At first he was sent to an African American military unit, but as word of his abilities spread throughout the allied command, his services were soon requested by other divisions.

During his life, Jones invented many things that are commonplace today. The condenser microphone was one such device and it revolutionized the broadcast industry. Unfortunately, he never patented it and soon it was patented and manufactured by someone else. The mobile X-ray machine was developed by Jones in response to a challenge issued by the Hallock town doctor. This invention made it possible for the X-ray machine to come to the patient and removed the burden of transporting sick, elderly, and disabled patients to the radiology room. Like the condenser microphone, Jones never patented the X ray, and just a year later it was re-invented and patented by a German engineer. Jones also invented a device to read the soundtrack that was carried on the motion picture film—a process that had recently been introduced. State-of-the-art equipment to perform this function was available to movie theaters but it was very expensive and difficult to maintain. With his device Jones made the process affordable for even small-town theaters.

Invention Sparks the Birth of an Industry

Perhaps his most notable achievement was the development of a way to put refrigeration equipment on trucks capable of moving cargo over long distances. Until this time, food transport was done with ice and was not very efficient or cost-effective. Jones' work allowed for the shipment of refrigerated and frozen products across very long distances and gave birth to the frozen food industry.

When Jones patented this invention, the company he founded with his good friend and partner Joseph Numero and named Thermo-King quickly became a household name, and at the outbreak of World War II, Jones again served his country when mobile refrigeration equipment was badly needed on the front lines. Thermo-King's equipment was the best the military had ever seen. Now based in Minneapolis, Thermo-King is still a major player in the refrigeration industry.

Jones was married twice. His first marriage, to a Swedish woman from Hallock, lasted just a few years until he moved to Minneapolis. His 1946 marriage to his second wife, Lucille, lasted until his death in 1961.

Jones was the first African American to become a member of the American Society of Refrigeration Engineers. He was also the recipient of an honorary doctorate from Brown University. Although Jones never had any direct ownership of his patents and was not materially wealthy, he was always well cared for by those close to him. His genius, generosity, and willingness to help touched many people and society has a higher standard of living because of his inventive spirit and his investigations of how things work.

SOURCES:

Books

Ott, Virginia, and Gloria Swanson, *Man with a Million Ideas,* Lerner, 1977.

—Sketch by Roger Jaffe

Mary Ellen Jones
1922-
American biochemist

Mary Ellen Jones, a prominent biochemist and enzymologist, is known for isolating carbamyl phosphate, one of a number of molecules that are the building blocks of biosynthesis. By synthesizing this substance, Jones helped lay the groundwork for major advances in biochemistry, particularly in research on deoxyribonucleic acid (DNA) and ribonucleic acid (RNA). She has explored enzyme action, how the products of metabolism (metabolites) control enzyme activity, and metabolic pathways. The metabolic pathway is essential for cell division and differentiation, and studies of it are crucial to the understanding of the developing fetus and child, of cancer, and of some mutations in humans. Jones was recognized for her work by being named the first woman Kenan Professor at the University of North Carolina at Chapel Hill in 1980.

Mary Ellen Jones was born on December 25, 1922, in La Grange, Illinois, to Elmer Enold and Laura Anna (Klein) Jones. She earned her bachelor of science degree from the University of Chicago in 1944. She then went on to receive her Ph.D. in biochemistry at Yale University, where she was a U.S. Public Health Service Fellow in the department of physiological chemistry from 1950 to 1951.

Jones solidly established herself as an enzymologist during her postdoctoral studies with **Fritz Lipmann**, a 1953 Nobel Prize winner for physiology or medicine, who was then director of the Chemical Research Laboratory at Massachusetts General Hospital. In the 1950s he and a team of researchers discovered a group of molecules that were considered the building blocks of biosynthesis. It was during this time that Jones isolated cabamyl phosphate, one of the most important of these essential molecules. The synthesis of this molecule made important advances in biochemistry possible. Carbamyl phosphate is present in all life. Knowledge of it led to scientific understanding of two universally essential pathways of biosynthesis, the production of a chemical compound by a living organism.

Jones and Lipmann noticed that during certain biosynthetic reactions, the energy-releasing reaction was a splitting of adenosine triphosphate (ATP) that yielded a mononucleotide and inorganic pyrophosphate. The discovery suggested that DNA and RNA synthesis might occur with the liberation of inorganic pyrophosphate from ATP and other trinucleotides—a suggestion that was later proven true by the biochemist **Arthur Kornberg**. Jones remained in the Biochemical Research Laboratory at Massachusetts General Hospital until 1957 and served as a faculty member in the Department of Biochemistry at Brandeis University until 1966.

In 1966, Dr. Jones joined the University of North Carolina as an associate professor of biochemistry, was promoted to professor two years later, and in 1968 was appointed professor in the department of zoology. She left Chapel Hill in 1971 for the University of Southern California and was a professor of biochemistry there until 1978. She returned to the University of North Carolina as a professor and chair of the biochemistry department and was named a Kenan Professor in 1980.

Dr. Jones is the author of over ninety papers related to biochemistry and has received international recognition for her creative scientific research. She has been a member of the Institute of Medicine since 1981, was inducted into the National Academy of Sciences in 1984, and in 1986 served as president of the American Society of Biological Chemists and was named the North Carolina American Chemical Society distinguished chemist. She was awarded the Wilbur Lucius Cross Medal in 1982 by the graduate school at Yale University for her work as a "gifted investigator of the chemistry of life."

SELECTED WRITINGS BY JONES:

Books

(Editor, with Patricia A. Hoffee), *Purine and Pyrimidine Nucleotide Metabolism,* Academic Press, 1978.

Structural and Organization Aspects of Metabolic Regulation, John Wiley & Sons, 1990.

SOURCES:

Jones, Mary Ellen, correspondence with Janet Kieffer Kelley, March 6, 1994.

—*Sketch by Janet Kieffer Kelley*

Brian D. Josephson
1940-
English physicist

While still a graduate student, Brian D. Josephson made a discovery that was to earn him a share of the 1973 Nobel Prize for physics. That discovery concerned the flow of electrons across two superconducting materials separated by a thin nonconducting barrier. Josephson found that his own calculations predicted a far greater flow than would have been expected on the basis of traditional quantum mechanics. His predictions were experimentally confirmed shortly after his announcement of the effect.

Josephson was born in Cardiff, Wales, on January 4, 1940. His parents were Mimi and Abraham Josephson. After graduating from Cardiff High School, Josephson entered Trinity College, Cambridge. He earned his B.A. degree there in 1960 and his M.A. and Ph.D. in 1964. Between 1962 and 1969, he also held an appointment as junior research fellow at Trinity.

Studies Mössbauer and Tunneling Effects

Josephson's first research interest as a graduate student was the Mössbauer effect, the recoilless emission of gamma rays from a crystal. He found that very small temperature differences in emitter and detector in experiments using the Mössbauer effect could have significant effects on the outcome of those experiments. Researchers had not appreciated this point until Josephson published his calculations, and many had to repeat their work in order to take this effect into account.

In 1962, while still a graduate student, Josephson shifted his attention to the phenomenon of tunneling in superconducting materials. The model with which he worked consisted of a pair of metals maintained at temperatures close to absolute zero and separated by a thin layer of nonconducting material. According to traditional quantum theory, a small number of electrons should be able to "tunnel through" (pass across) the potential barrier represented by the nonconducting layer between the two conductors. To his great surprise, Josephson found that his own calculations predicted a much larger flow of current. In addition, he discovered that that current should be susceptible to an external magnetic field (i.e., very small changes in the magnetic field should result in large changes in electron flow).

Josephson was not able to detect these effects himself, but two colleagues, **Philip Warren Anderson** and J. M. Rowell, soon did so for DC currents, as did S. Shapiro for AC currents. A decade later, Josephson was awarded a share of the Nobel Prize in physics (with **Leo Esaki** and **Ivar Giaever**) for this discovery, which has had enormous practical significance. The currents Josephson studied are highly sensitive to very small magnetic fields, and they have found application in a variety of detecting devices as well as in basic research.

Except for a year at the University of Illinois as a visiting research professor (1965–66), Josephson has spent his entire academic career at Cambridge. He has held appointments there as assistant director of research (1967–72), reader in physics (1972–74), and professor of physics (1974-). After receiving his Ph.D., Josephson continued his research on superconductivity and critical phenomena. Then, in the late 1960s, he began to drift away from conventional physics. The problem, he told an *Omni* interviewer, was that "conventional physics didn't offer much opportunity to achieve [the] sort of breakthrough" in which he had become interested. That breakthrough involved a study of intelligence, language, and higher states of consciousness and the paranormal.

Interest Shifts to Studies of the Mind

Josephson was powerfully influenced by a theorem developed by theoretical physicist John Bell in 1965. According to Bell's theorem, any two objects obtained from a single large source will always exert an influence on each other, no matter how far apart they may become in the universe. To Josephson, this type of phenomenon created the possibility of interactions with which conventional physical laws are incapable of dealing.

An important turning point in Josephson's life occurred in 1971, when he heard a radio announcement for a lecture on transcendental meditation (TM). He attended the lecture, became an adherent of TM, and has since become a student also of the Maharishi Mahesh Yogi. As part of his daily routine (that may include walking, ice skating, photography, and astronomical studies), Josephson now also meditates for about two hours.

Josephson married Carol Anne Oliver in 1976. They have one daughter. Among his honors and awards are the 1969 New Scientist Award, the 1969 Research Corporation Award, the 1970 Fritz London Award, and the 1972 Hughes Medal of the Royal Society.

SELECTED WRITINGS BY JOSEPHSON:

Books

Consciousness and the Physical World, Pergamon, 1980.

Periodicals

"Potential Differences in the Mixed State of Type II Semiconductors," *Physical Letters,* Volume 16, 1965, pp. 242–243.

SOURCES:

Books

Nobel Prize Winners, H. W. Wilson, 1987, pp. 520–521.

The Omni Interviews, Ticknor & Fields, 1984, pp. 316–331.

Weber, Robert L., *Pioneers of Science: Nobel Prize Winners in Physics,* American Institute of Physics, 1980, pp. 233–234.

Periodicals

Langenberg, D. N., "The 1973 Nobel Prize for Physics," *Science,* November 16, 1973, pp. 702–4.

"Nobel Prize Shared by Esaki, Giaever, and Josephson," *Physics Today,* December, 1973, pp. 73ff.

—*Sketch by David E. Newton*

Percy Lavon Julian
1899-1975
American organic chemist

Percy Lavon Julian

Percy Lavon Julian is best known for discovering how to synthesize physostigmine, a chemical used to treat the eye disease glaucoma. He also developed an economical method for producing sterols, making it possible for many people with arthritis to afford cortisone. An African American who eventually grew frustrated with the discrimination he faced in academia, Julian turned to industry and worked at the Glidden Company in Chicago, Illinois, before starting his own business.

Julian was born in Montgomery, Alabama, on April 11, 1899, to James and Elizabeth Adams Julian. His father was a railway clerk and his mother a schoolteacher. His paternal grandfather was a former slave who had two fingers cut off his right hand for learning to write. Julian was one of six children, all of whom went to universities and graduated with higher degrees. Julian attended public school until the eighth grade, but, because there was only one public high school in Alabama that accepted African American students, he attended a private school called the State Normal School. He graduated at the top of his class in 1916 and was admitted to DePauw University in Greencastle, Indiana. His high school education had not been satisfactory, however, and for two years he had to take remedial classes in addition to a regular course load. He lived in the attic of a fraternity house during this time and earned money by waiting on tables downstairs. He also played in a jazz band and tended furnaces. Despite his heavy workload, Julian graduated in 1920 with a degree in chemistry; he was class valedictorian and a member of Phi Beta Kappa.

When Julian had decided to major in chemistry, his father had tried to persuade him to become a physician instead, feeling that Julian would not find many career opportunities in chemistry beyond teaching because of his ethnicity. His father's concerns proved well-founded. Although Julian wanted to go to graduate school, the head of his department was told that an African American would not find work in the field; Julian was denied fellowships by the same people who had been his role models.

Julian taught chemistry at Fisk University in Nashville, Tennessee, for the next two years. In 1922, he received the Austin Fellowship in chemistry at Harvard University, which enabled him to earn his master's degree in chemistry by 1923. However, afraid that white students from the American South would object to an African American teacher, Harvard did not offer Julian a teaching assistantship, despite his high grades. Julian took various research assistantships in order to continue to work toward his doctorate. He stayed at Harvard until 1926, studying biophysics and organic chemistry.

From 1926 to 1927, Julian taught at West Virginia State College, and in 1928 he went to Howard University in Washington, D.C., as associate professor and head of the Department of Chemistry. By this time, Julian had begun to follow the research that was being done at the University of Vienna by

Ernst Spath, who had developed methods for synthesizing nicotine and ephedrine. In 1929, Julian received a fellowship from the General Education Board and went to Vienna to study with Spath. While there, he became interested in the soya bean, which was then being used in Germany to manufacture certain drugs, including physostigmine and sex hormones. In 1931, he received his Ph.D. from the University of Vienna. When he returned to Howard, he resumed his teaching and was promoted to full professor.

Succeeds in Synthesizing Physostigmine

Working with two colleagues from Vienna who had come back to Howard with him, Julian began to investigate the structure and synthesis of physostigmine, which was used to treat glaucoma, an eye disease that eventually leads to blindness by slowly damaging the retina. In 1932, just as he and his colleagues began to see some results, a disagreement with the Howard administration forced Julian to leave. A former professor arranged for Julian to return to DePauw as a research fellow and teacher of organic chemistry. There he was able to identify the chemicals that lead to the formation of physostigmine. In 1934, he presented his findings to the American Chemical Society, challenging the work of **Robert Robinson**, the head of the chemistry department at Oxford University. By February, 1935, Julian had accomplished the first synthesis of physostigmine, proving his method and research correct.

Despite his successes, Julian continued to face discrimination; he was denied two positions, one at DePauw and one at the University of Minnesota, on the basis of his race. He decided to seek employment at an industrial laboratory and accepted a position as director of research and chief chemist at the Glidden Company in Chicago, becoming the first African American in United States history to direct a major industrial laboratory.

In 1936, a milk protein called casein was being used to coat paper. Because this was expensive, Julian's first task at Glidden was to extract the soya bean protein, which was cheaper but equally effective, for use in textiles, paints, and paper coating. The results of his work proved profitable for Glidden, and in one year the company went from a deficit of $35,000 to a profit of $135,000. Julian's experiments with soya protein also yielded a new product, "Aero Foam," which was used to extinguish oil and gas fires.

Develops Methods for Manufacturing Sex Hormones and Cortisone

One of Julian's most important achievements was the synthesis of sex hormones from sterols extracted from soya beans. Progesterone was used to prevent miscarriages, while testosterone was used to treat older men for diminishing sex drive. Both hormones were also important in the treatment of cancer. Traditionally, these hormones were made using cholesterol from the brains and spinal cords of cattle. German scientists had developed a process to extract sterols from the soya bean and convert them into hormones, but it was slow and very expensive. From watching how plaster of Paris puffed up into a porous, foamy mass after the addition of quicklime, Julian developed a method to convert the soya bean oil into a porous foam from which sterols could be easily extracted. He was able to synthesize progesterone and testosterone from the sterols, increasing the supply of these chemicals and reducing their cost.

Cortisone had recently been found to be effective in treating rheumatoid arthritis, but its method of production made it extremely expensive and beyond the reach of most patients: it took the bile of 14,600 oxen to produce enough cortisone to treat one patient for one year. Julian perfected an economical method for synthesizing cortexolone from soya beans. The difference between cortisone and cortexolone, which Julian called Substance S, was one oxygen atom; he devised a method to add this missing atom to cortexolone and the resulting synthetic cortisone was just as effective in the treatment of arthritis as the organic form.

In 1954, Julian left Glidden to open his own plant and company, Julian Laboratories Inc., in Chicago, and the Laboratorios Julian de Mexico in Mexico City, Mexico. He had found that using wild yams was more effective than soya beans in the production of Substance S, and within a few years Julian Laboratories had become of one of the world's leaders in the production of drugs using wild yams. In 1961, Julian sold his Oak Park plant to Smith, Kline, & French. He stayed on as president until 1964, when he founded the Julian Research Institute and Julian Associates Inc. in Franklin Park, Illinois.

In 1947, Julian received the National Association for the Advancement of Colored People's Spingarn Medal; in 1949, he was presented with the Distinguished Service Award from the Phi Beta Kappa Association for his work with Substance S and synthetic cortisone. In 1990, Julian was elected to the National Inventors Hall of Fame, along with agricultural chemist **George Washington Carver**. They were the first African Americans to be so honored since the institution was created in 1973.

Julian married Anna Johnson, who had a Ph.D. in sociology, on December 24, 1935. They had two children, a girl and a boy. Julian continued to investigate synthetic drugs and the chemistry of various substances until his death in 1975.

SELECTED WRITINGS BY JULIAN:

Periodicals

(With J. Pikl) "Studies in the Indole Series. V. The Complete Synthesis of Physostigmine (Eserine)," *Journal of American Chemistry Society,* Volume 57, 1935, p. 755.

(With J. Wayne Cole) "Process for the Recovering of Sterols," *Chemistry Abstracts,* Volume 36, 1942, p. 3692.

(With Cole, A. Magnani, and H. E. Conde) "Procedure for the Preparation of Progesterone," *Chemistry Abstracts,* Volume 42, 1948, p. 1710.

SOURCES:

Books

Current Biography, H. W. Wilson, 1947, pp. 29–31.

Haber, Louis, *Black Pioneers of Science and Invention,* Harcourt, 1970, pp. 86–101.

Toppin, Edgar Allen, *A Biographical History of Blacks in America since 1528,* McKay, 1971, pp. 341–343.

Periodicals

Cobb, W. Montague, "Percy Lavon Julian," *Journal of the National Medical Association,* March, 1971, pp. 143–147.

—*Sketch by Geeta Kothari*

Joseph M. Juran
1904-
Romanian-born American engineer

Joseph M. Juran has been one of the leaders in the field of quality management and he has had a broad influence on industry in the United States and Japan, as well as other countries. His career has spanned seven decades in a variety of professional roles including engineering manager, corporate executive, government administrator, university professor, labor arbitrator, lecturer, and author. Among his many honors was the Order of the Sacred Treasure by the Emperor of Japan in 1981, the highest decoration given to a non-Japanese citizen, for developing quality control in Japan and facilitating relations with the United States. Juran became a member of National Academy of Engineering in 1988, and in 1992 he was awarded the National Medal of Technology for "his lifetime work of providing the key principles and methods by which enterprises managed the quality of their products and processes, enhancing their ability to compete in the global marketplace."

Juran was born on December 24, 1904, in the small village of Braila, Romania, which was then part of the Austria-Hungarian Empire. His parents were Jacob and Gitel (Goldenberg) Juran; his father was a shoemaker in the nearby village of Gurahumora. In 1912, when Juran was eight, he emigrated with his family to Minneapolis, Minnesota. In "A Tale of the Twentieth Century," he wrote about his childhood: "We lived, eight of us, crowded into a so-called tar paper shack—a primitive little cabin in the woods." As a child, Juran earned money for the family and his college tuition by holding a number of jobs, including newsboy, shipping clerk, printer's devil, laborer, shoe salesman, bookkeeper, and the editor of a chess column for a small newspaper.

Juran became a naturalized American citizen in 1917. He entered the University of Minnesota and graduated in 1924 with a B.S. in electrical engineering. On June 5, 1926, at the age of twenty-two, he married Sadie Shapiro, his high-school sweetheart; they would have three sons and one daughter. Juran would later continue his education in the middle of his career, attending law school at Loyola University and receiving his law degree in 1936.

Develops Quality-Management Techniques

Shortly after completing his bachelor's degree, Juran sought a position with the Bell System at the Hawthorne Works of Western Electric Company in Illinois and was hired as an inspector for their manufacturing engineering unit. The Hawthorne Works of Western Electric played a unique and vital role in the manufacture of early telephone equipment for the nation. It was here that the famous "Hawthorne Experiments" were conducted by Elton Mayo, F. J. Roethlisberger, and Theodore Whitehead—experiments which were the forerunner to the theoretical movement known as human-factors engineering. While at the Hawthorne Works, Juran became involved in a program to increase quality in production. Concern was growing among management that inspector fatigue, human factors, and mechanical malfunctions were leading to defects in work. Since it was too costly and time consuming to inspect all items in every lot of equipment, ideas were being developed for new, cost-saving, quality-control tools. Juran took a statistics course during this period and was exposed to the idea of measuring quality mathematically.

Juran became one of a three-member team at Western Electric to run a statistical inspection department. It was the first such department in the history of volume line production in America. In "A Tale of the Twentieth Century," Juran wrote: "On this new job, I became closely involved with the premiere effort to apply statistical tools to quality control of manufacturing processes and became associated with the well-known practitioners on quality: George Edwards, Walter Shewhart, Harold Dodge and Harry Romig." Juran's work led to the development of several manufacturing innovations. One of these was sampling tables, where manufactured equipment was scrutinized for poor or inadequate construction. He also introduced various statistical concepts such as the creation of terminologies for sampling risk; the development of single, double, and continuous sampling plans; and the process-average concept. In the latter half of the twentieth century, these mathematical tools became rudimentary analytical procedures for industrial statisticians, and they have been the base for quantitative aspects of industrial manufacturing quality control.

During World War II, Juran worked for the United States government and served as an officer in the United States Signal Corps Reserve. He became an assistant administrator for the Office of Lend Lease Administration and worked as an assistant to the Foreign Economic Administration. "At the request of E. R. Stettinius, who was then the Lend Lease Administrator, I took six weeks leave of absence from Western Electric to go into the federal government. That six weeks stretched out to four years," Juran wrote. The Lend Lease Administration was set up to carry out the directives of the Lend Lease Act, passed by Congress in March of 1941. The act conferred upon President Roosevelt the power to lend or lease any equipment to any nation whose defense he considered essential to the protection of the United States. Approximately half the goods handled by Lend Lease were munitions and petroleum products, about one-fifth were industrial commodities, and the rest were food and services. Juran's work was primarily related to the industrial commodities being sent to Great Britain and the Soviet Union; about eighty percent of the total amount of materials lent or leased by America went to these two nations. Juran began to build an international network that would later take him around the world with his ideas on quality control.

After the war ended, Juran left Washington and went to New York, where he became the chair and a professor of the Department of Industrial Engineering at New York University. It was from this position that he became involved with the rebuilding of Japan. Bombing during World War II, including the dropping of the atomic bomb, had leveled the Japanese industrial sector. W. Edwards Deming, an American professor, was recruited in 1947 to conduct a statistical survey of surviving industrial facilities and equipment. Deming found there were virtually no heavy industrial materials or equipment left in the country. At the request of the Union of Japanese Scientists and Engineers—the official Japanese government body overseeing reconstruction of the industries—Deming began delivering lectures on quality control to Japanese workers, plant managers, and engineers. Juran became interested in this ongoing work and in 1950 he went to Japan to give his first set of lectures on the managerial aspects of quality control.

Quality Concepts Aid Industry

Juran's work led to the infusion of quality control throughout Japanese manufacturing. He mobilized workers, encouraging them to participate in the operational decision-making process. One example of his contributions was the work he did with the Quasar Corporation: originally there were 150 to 180 defects per one hundred television sets, and his ideas on quality brought this number down to under ten. In 1951, Juran published the *Quality Control Handbook,* which was updated numerous times over the years. Juran's quality concept was very structured and consisted of several universal steps he later called the Juran trilogy. This trilogy was taken from financial planning and relied on the concepts of planning, control, and improvement as a framework. Juran believed these concepts and principles were the basis for successful management in any area.

Juran left New York University in 1951, and he wrote in "A Tale of the Twentieth Century": "By 1952, I had concluded that I was too individualistic to be part of a big company so I embarked on a new career." The *Quality Control Handbook* had generated numerous invitations for lecturing and consulting. "There followed twenty-eight years of blissful free-lancing and consulting," Juran wrote. From 1952 to 1979, Juran wrote and rewrote numerous books and hundreds of papers. He developed training courses and lectures on quality control and conducted them widely in the United States and abroad. Collectively, his books, articles and training aids were translated into sixteen languages. Juran summarized this era of his life: "I made many friends amid inspiring cultural vistas. The land of opportunity turned out to be a bountiful reality." Numerous accolades followed Juran's work. He became an honorary member of Australian, Argentinean, British, and Philippine quality-control societies. He received several domestic and foreign medals.

In the late 1970s the American industrial sector began lagging behind in the quality production of light and heavy industrial and consumer goods. The manufacturing of high-technology goods in Japan was surpassing North America. In 1979, at the age of seventy-five, Juran created an institute under his name to produce training aids such as video cassettes, manuals, textbooks, and bound sets of notes for increasing quality in American industry. The Juran Institute assisted clients in designing, developing, and implementing quality-control concepts. In 1987, Juran stepped down as head of the institute and remained chairman emeritus.

In addition to the Order of the Sacred Treasure and the National Medal of Technology, Juran has also received the Wallace Clark Medal from the American Society of Mechanical Engineering in 1967 and the Gilbreth Award from the American Institute of Engineers in 1981. In 1988, the Stevens Institute of Technology awarded him an honorary doctorate for his outstanding contributions to the field of engineering. In 1992, he received three honorary doctorates—two in science from the University of Minnesota and the Rochester Institute of Technology, and one in law from the University of New Haven.

SELECTED WRITINGS BY JURAN:

Books

Quality Control Handbook, McGraw, 1951.

(With J. K. Louden) *The Corporate Director,* American Management Association, 1966.

Juran on Planning for Quality, The Free Press, 1988.

Juran on Quality by Design: the New Steps for Planning Quality Into Goods and Services, The Free Press, 1992.

Periodicals

"A Tale of the Twentieth Century," *Juran Report,* autumn, 1989, pp. 4-13.

SOURCES:

Books

Gabor, Andrea, *The Man Who Discovered Quality: How W. Edwards Deming Brought the Quality Revolution to America,* Penguin Books, 1990.

Schonberger, Richard J., *Japanese Manufacturing Techniques: Nine Hidden Lessons in Simplicity,* The Free Press, 1982.

—Sketch by Mary Raum

Ernest Everett Just
1883-1941
American zoologist and marine biologist

Ernest Everett Just was a zoologist who did groundbreaking work on the embryology of marine invertebrates. He conducted research on fertilization, as well as the development of eggs without fertilization—a process known as parthenogenesis—but his most important achievement was probably his discovery of the role the protoplasm plays in the development of a cell. An African American, Just conducted his research despite widespread discrimination, and he spent most of his career at Howard University when that institution was still little more than a college, with few graduate students and fewer facilities. In addition to his international reputation as a zoologist, Just was a dedicated teacher whose scientific successes inspired many younger men and women. In *Black Pioneers of Science and Invention,* Louis Haber calls him "Howard's vindication before the scientific world."

Just was born on August 14, 1883, in Charleston, South Carolina, to Charles and Mary Cooper Just. His father was a dock builder who died when Just was still a young boy, and his mother was a schoolteacher who supervised his education. After sending him to the Colored Normal, Industrial, Agricultural and Mechanical College in South Carolina, she enrolled him at a northern preparatory school called Kimball Union Academy, in Meriden, New Hampshire. Just did extremely well there, completing the four-year course in three years, while serving as editor of the school newspaper and president of the debating society.

He then entered Dartmouth College, which was only a few miles away from Kimball. Here, he found himself the only black in a freshman class of 288 students. Although he performed exceptionally well in Greek during his first year, he majored in biology the next year, and by the time he graduated with an B.A. degree in 1907, he had taken all the courses the college offered in that subject. He had even supplied studies and drawings on frog embryo formation for a zoology textbook being written by the head of the biology department, William Patten. In recognition of his superior performance as an undergraduate, he was elected to Phi Beta Kappa; he also received special honors in zoology and history, and he was the only student in his class to graduate *magna cum laude.* Upon graduation, he gained a teaching appointment at Howard University in Washington, D.C., first in the English department, and then as professor of zoology and physiology in its medical school.

Ernest Everett Just

Makes Start at Woods Hole Laboratory

Although he was now teaching Just had no higher degrees, and he began his graduate training in 1909 at the Marine Biological Laboratory (MBL) in Woods Hole, Massachusetts. This world-famous research institution gives scientists an opportunity to pursue their investigations during the summer months without the interruptions of teaching or other duties. Just's teaching load at Howard was very heavy, and for the next twenty years he would do most of his research here. He found Woods Hole an ideal place to study marine organisms, and he was often called upon for advice by other scientific investigators. In 1911, he became a research assistant to the director of the MBL, **Frank Rattray Lillie**, who was also head of the zoology department at the University of Chicago. Their research focused on the fertilization process in the sandworm *Nereis;* in 1912, Just published his first paper, describing the results of research which showed that when the fertilized egg of the *Nereis* undergoes its first cleavage division, the polar bodies determine the plane of development of the embryo, together with the point of entrance of the spermatozoon.

Just's research on fertilization won him the first Spingarn Medal awarded by the National Association for the Advancement of Colored People. Designed to honor men and women of African descent, it was presented to him in 1915 by the governor of New York State, Charles S. Whitman. In a letter quoted in the *Journal of the National Medical Association,* Just called the award "a new day in my life." The recognition encouraged him in his effort to pursue his research despite the obstacles presented to him by an effectively segregated society: "I have suddenly become a real human being, alive and anxious to work. I have a feeling that *anything* in the way of sacrifice is worthwhile; somebody appreciates my striving and learning." At the time of this award, Just had not yet yearned his doctorate. Lillie had arranged for him to enter the doctoral program at the University of Chicago, but his teaching duties delayed completion of his dissertation and the awarding of his Ph.D. until 1916.

Just spent twenty summers at Woods Hole, and as Lillie recalled in an obituary in *Science:* "He became more widely acquainted with embryological resources of the marine fauna than probably any other person." Lillie praised Just for "the very fine methods he had developed for work in this field," and it was these skills that enabled him to advance the study of parthenogenesis. This was a subject which had been pioneered by **Jacques Loeb**, who discovered that sea urchin eggs and frog eggs could be induced to develop without being fertilized by sperm; development could begin after pricking the eggs with a needle or subjecting them to certain kinds of salt-water solutions. Just conducted numerous experiments on invertebrate eggs, subjecting them to outside influences, such as various concentrations of seawater and butyric acid. On the basis of the results of his experiments, he came to question aspects of Loeb's procedures, as well as his theory explaining parthenogenesis.

As Just returned to Woods Hole year after year, he became established as a member of the Corporation of the Marine Biological Laboratory. He also served as an associate editor of the laboratory's *Biological Bulletin.* In addition, he became associate editor of the *Journal of Morphology, Physiological Zoology,* and the German journal, *Protoplasma.* In recognition of his professional qualifications, he was elected to membership in such scientific societies as the American Society of Naturalists, the American Ecological Society, the American Association for the Advancement of Science, and the American Society of Zoologists, of which he became vice president. In 1920, the philanthropist Julius Rosenwald supported Just's research work with an individual financial grant that was to continue for a number of years, culminating in an overall grant to Howard University in 1928 of 80,000 dollars. This enlarged Just's work in the zoology department and allowed him to travel to European centers of research.

Contributes to Knowledge of Cell Function

In 1939, Just published *The Biology of the Cell Surface,* which was the result of research he had done at Woods Hole in the 1920s and in Europe during the

1930s. Before Just completed his research on cell biology, it was widely believed that all the activities of the cell were controlled by the nucleus. Just established the important role played by the living substance that lay outside the nucleus in a cell, known as the protoplasm. He also emphasized the importance of the ectoplasm—the rigid, outer layer of the protoplasm. Drawing on two decades of observing the activity of the ectoplasm in the egg cells of marine animals undergoing the process of fertilization, he was able to demonstrate the important influence the ectoplasm exerts even before the nucleus of the sperm fuses with the nucleus of the egg. Just concluded that the combined influence the ectoplasm and the nucleus have on the protoplasm contributes to the actions of the gene in determining heredity. He further claimed that the factors influencing heredity are already present in the protoplasm and are then extracted from it by the genes.

Just was frequently consulted on selections to the National Academy of Sciences but he himself was never elected to this society, and during his career he became increasingly bitter about racial discrimination in the United States. The fellowships and research grants he won never lasted long enough to give him a sense of security, and despite his success in the laboratory he was never granted an appointment at a major research institution. Lillie wrote of him in *Science:* "An element of tragedy ran through all Just's scientific career due to the limitations imposed by being a Negro in America, to which he could make no lasting psychological adjustment despite earnest efforts on his part. . . . He felt this as a social stigma, and hence unjust to a scientist of his recognized standing." In 1929, Just left for Europe, and he returned there often for most of the rest of his life, in what Lillie described as "self-imposed exile." First invited by M. Hartmann to study at the Kaiser Wilhelm Institute for Biology in Berlin, Just also studied at the Sorbonne in Paris and the Stazione Zoologica in Naples. He died in the United States from cancer on October 27, 1941, at the age of fifty-eight. He was survived by his wife, Ethel Highwarden Just, and three children.

SELECTED WRITINGS BY JUST:

Books

The Biology of the Cell Surface, Blakiston's Sons & Co., 1939.

Basic Methods for Experiments on Eggs of Marine Animals, Blakiston's Sons & Co., 1940.

Periodicals

"The Relations of the First Cleavage Plane to the Entrance Point of the Sperm," *Biological Bulletin,* Volume 22, 1912, pp. 239–252.

"Fertilization-Reaction in Eggs of *Asterias rubens,*" *Anatomical Record,* Volume 78, 1940, p. 132.

SOURCES:

Books

Haber, Louis, *Black Pioneers of Science and Invention,* Harcourt, 1970, pp. 113–121.

Manning, Kenneth R., *Black Apollo of Science, The Life of Ernest Everett Just,* Oxford University Press, 1983.

Periodicals

Cobb, W. Montague, "Ernest Everett Just, 1883–1941," *Journal of the National Medical Association,* Volume 49, 1957, pp. 349–351.

Lillie, Frank R., "Ernest Everett Just," *Science,* Volume 95, February 2, 1942, pp. 10–11.

—Sketch by Maurice Bleifeld

Heike Kamerlingh Onnes
1853-1926
Dutch physicist

Heike Kamerlingh Onnes was a Dutch experimental physicist distinguished for his work in the field of low-temperature physics. He was the first scientist to succeed in liquefying helium, a breakthrough which yielded a previously unattainable degree of cold. This accomplishment won him the 1913 Nobel Prize for physics, in addition to numerous other awards. He is also credited with the discovery of superconductivity—that is, the complete disappearance of electrical resistance in various metals at temperatures approaching absolute zero.

Kamerlingh Onnes was born in Groningen, the Netherlands, on September 21, 1853. His father owned a tile factory, and both his parents were strict, imbuing Kamerlingh Onnes and his brothers with an understanding of the value of hard work and perseverance. He was initially educated at Groningen High School under J. M. van Bemmelan, and in 1870 he enrolled in the physics program at the University of Groningen. The following year he submitted an essay on vapor density and won first prize in a contest sponsored by the University of Utrecht. In October 1871, Kamerlingh Onnes transferred to the University of Heidelberg in Germany, where he was taught by the eminent German chemist Robert Wilhelm Bunsen. He was one of only two students allowed to work in the private laboratory of German physicist Gustav Robert Kirchhoff. In April 1873, he returned to the University of Groningen, where he spent the next five years studying for his doctorate.

In 1878, Kamerlingh Onnes moved to Delft Polytechnic where he became an assistant to the professor of physics there. In 1879 he travelled to Groningen to defend his thesis, entitled "New Proof of the Earth's Rotation." He was awarded his physics doctorate *magna cum laude.* At Delft Polytechnic, Kamerlingh Onnes composed a paper on the general theory of fluids from the perspective of kinetic theory. He soon realized though that such a general theory of the nature of fluids required accurate measurements of volume, pressure, and temperature over as wide a range of values as possible. To this end, he turned his attention to the problem of attaining and maintaining very low temperatures.

Becomes Head of Cryogenic Laboratory

In 1882, at the age of twenty-nine, Kamerlingh Onnes accepted Holland's first chair in experimental physics at Leiden University. He also became the director of the laboratory there, where he was able to pursue his interest in low-temperature physics, also known as cryogenics. A dedicated experimentalist, Kamerlingh Onnes declared in his inaugural address: "I should like to write 'through measuring is knowing' as a motto above each physics laboratory." He would spend the rest of his career at Leiden. During the next forty-two years, he established it as the undisputed world headquarters of low-temperature research.

When Kamerlingh Onnes began his pioneering work, cryogenic physics was a relatively unknown science. Before him, the liquefaction of gases at very low temperatures was considered an end in itself, but Kamerlingh Onnes was interested in low-temperature physics in order to gather experimental evidence about the atomic nature of matter. When he set out to cool gases such as oxygen, hydrogen, and helium to extremely low temperatures, there were three means at his disposal. A cooling effect due to the rapid evaporation of a liquid had been discovered in 1877 by the Swiss physicist R. P. Pictet. That same year, the French physicist L. P. Cailletet had achieved low temperatures when he was able to cool oxygen by the application of intense pressure. The final method was based on the 1850 discovery by J. P. Joules and W. Thomson (Lord Kelvin) that when a gas under pressure is released through very small openings, its temperature is lowered by an amount that depends on the nature of the gas. In Munich in 1895, Carl Linde constructed an apparatus that made use of the so-called Joule-Thomson effect; gas was put under pressure and repeatedly forced into a coil of tubes that also acted as a heat exchanger. This was known as the regenerative process. The amount of liquid gas produced by all of these means was, however, negligible.

In trying to achieve very low temperatures, Kamerlingh Onnes employed a combination of Pictet's and Linde's methods. His first objective was to liquefy oxygen—the creation of a bath of liquid oxygen being necessary for the liquefaction of other gases, particularly hydrogen. Kamerlingh Onnes vaporized oxygen, then liquefied it, and then forced it under pressure into a closed, circulating system. The system was bathed in gases that had achieved progressively lower temperatures than the circulating oxygen. This methodology proved successful and Kamerlingh

Onnes was able to produce about fourteen liters of liquid air an hour.

The production of liquid helium and liquid hydrogen proved more difficult than the production of liquid air. Kamerlingh Onnes theorized that if he could begin from a point of normal pressure and liquefy oxygen by the application of immense pressure, then it would be possible to liquefy hydrogen, starting with the temperature of liquid oxygen. In 1892, he was midway through this painstaking process when the Scottish chemist and physicist James Dewar succeeded in liquefying oxygen using a modified form of Pictet's cascade method. The process yielded about a pint of liquid oxygen.

Succeeds in Liquefying Helium

One practical advantage of Dewar's achievement was that Kamerlingh Onnes now had a source of cold with which to attempt to liquefy helium. He believed that if he started out from the freezing point of hydrogen—the lowest temperature to which it was possible to cool it—he could thereby liquefy helium using Linde's regenerative process. Kamerlingh Onnes constructed a system with a jacket of liquid hydrogen; the liquid hydrogen evaporated, which cooled the helium, and then the helium was forced under pressure through a small aperture which cooled it further, liquefying some of it. He then compressed the helium in a refrigerator, where it passed through an elaborate circuit surrounded by circuits of liquid hydrogen, which were themselves surrounded by liquid air, which were in turn surrounded by a flask in which warmed alcohol circulated.

In 1908, Kamerlingh Onnes finally succeeded in the long-elusive goal of liquefying helium. At first, he and his colleagues did not even notice what they had achieved: the liquid helium was colorless, and it was not until the circuit was almost full that they realized what had finally appeared before them. The accomplishment meant that a previously unattainable degree of cold was now at their disposal. Liquid helium was found to have a temperature of –268.8 degrees Celsius, only about four degrees above absolute zero —absolute zero being a hypothetical temperature characterized by a complete absence of heat and equivalent to about –273.15 degrees Celsius or –459.67 degrees Fahrenheit. Kamerlingh Onnes now set out to solidify the liquid helium in order to reach even lower temperatures, and in 1910, by boiling liquid helium under reduced pressure, he reached just over one degree above absolute zero.

Discovers Superconductivity at Low Temperatures

Kamerlingh Onnes used these temperatures to extend the range of his research into the properties of substances at low temperatures, and the results of these investigations were published regularly in English as "Communications from the Physical Laboratory at Leiden." In 1911, Kamerlingh Onnes made yet another breakthrough when he discovered the complete disappearance of electrical resistance in various metals at temperatures approaching absolute zero. The phenomenon of superconductivity is still not fully understood, although its implications are thought to be far-reaching. Kamerlingh Onnes also discovered that the superconductor effect can be negated without changing the temperature by the application of a magnetic field.

Kamerlingh Onnes and his team remained preoccupied with the challenge of crystallizing helium. Their experiments yielded some intriguing if baffling results. In 1911, they found that the density of liquid helium peaked at a temperature of 2.2 degrees Kelvin. When the various physical properties of liquid helium were measured, Kamerlingh Onnes discovered strange behavior in the helium in and around this temperature. Above 2.2 Kelvin it was violently agitated, but at or below this temperature it seemed to lose its dynamic qualities. Kamerlingh Onnes was unable to explain this phenomenon. This was because he was attempting to understand it in terms of the classical laws of physics, but the behavior of liquid helium at these temperatures, unbeknownst to him, obeys the laws of quantum mechanics. Kamerlingh Onnes simply did not have the tools at his disposal to account for his findings. In the end, he and his colleagues put them down to some fault in their methodology and published only "definite and reliable" values for temperatures above 2.2 Kelvin, the position of the inexplicable maximum of the density of liquid helium.

Although he had yet to achieve absolute zero, in 1913 Kamerlingh Onnes was awarded the Nobel Prize for physics for his investigations into the properties of matter at low temperatures leading to the discovery of liquid helium. By 1921, Kamerlingh Onnes came within a degree of reaching absolute zero, and for the next three years he relentlessly pursued his quest. In 1926, he came across further peculiarities in the behavior of helium at 2.2 degrees Kelvin. This time Kamerlingh Onnes did not dismiss his findings as due to technical faults but began to seriously consider the possibility that some kind of fundamental change in helium occurred at this temperature. Unfortunately, although he was on the right track, Kamerlingh Onnes did not live long enough to resolve the mystery. His successor at Leiden, W. H. Keesom, came to the conclusion that helium above and below 2.2 degrees Kelvin is in fact two separate liquids, differing in fundamental ways. Keesom also completed another aspect of Kamerlingh Onnes' work: he succeeded in obtaining solid helium by cooling the liquid to about –272 degrees Celsius under pressure.

Kamerlingh Onnes was widely recognized for his work in low-temperature physics, and he received a number of awards in addition to the Nobel Prize. In 1904, he received the first of many distinctions when he was created Chevalier of the Order of the Netherlands Lion. In that same year, which was the twenty-fifth anniversary of his doctorate, his students and colleagues at Leiden issued a *Gedenkboek,* a survey of the work carried out at the laboratory from 1882 to 1904. A second *Gedenkboek* was issued in 1922, commemorating Kamerlingh Onnes' forty-year tenure as professor of experimental physics at Leiden. In 1912, he was awarded the Royal Society of London's Rumford Medal, and four years later the society made him a foreign member. In 1923, he was elevated from Chevalier to Commander of the Netherlands Lion. Despite being known by his friends as "the gentleman of absolute zero," Kamerlingh Onnes died at Leiden on February 21, 1926, without ever having achieved it (German chemist **Walther Nernst** proved it was impossible to reach absolute zero in an experimental setting when he articulated the Third Law of Thermodynamics in 1905). That same year, he was posthumously elected a Corresponding Member of the Prussian Academy of Sciences in Berlin.

SELECTED WRITINGS BY KAMERLINGH ONNES:

Periodicals

"On the Cryogenic Laboratory at Leiden and on the Production of Very Low Temperatures," *Communications from the Physical Laboratory at the University of Leiden,* Volume 14, 1894.

"The Importance of Accurate Measurements at Very Low Temperatures," *Communications from the Physical Laboratory at the University of Leiden,* supplement 9, 1904.

"On the Lowest Temperature Yet Obtained," *Communications from the Physical Laboratory at the University of Leiden,* Volume 159, 1922.

SOURCES:

Books

Klein, Martin J., *Paul Ehrenfest: The Making of a Theoretical Physicist,* North-Holland Publishing Co., 1970.

Livanova, Anna Landau, *A Great Physicist and Teacher,* Pergamon Press, 1980.

—*Sketch by Avril McDonald*

Yuet Wai Kan
1936-
Hong Kong-born American geneticist

Yuet Wai Kan helped make possible the utilization of deoxyribonucleic acid (DNA) to analyze diseases—particularly hereditary anemias—and to both identify genetic disorders and differentiate individuals. The latter is of particular importance in the area of forensic medicine and criminal investigations. In addition, Kan also developed the first prenatal test for sickle-cell anemia.

Kan was born on June 11, 1936, in Hong Kong. His father was Kan Tong-Po and his mother Kan Lai-Wai. Receiving a B.S. from the University of Hong Kong Medical School in 1958, Kan served for two years as an intern at Hong Kong's Queen Mary Hospital. He then came to the United States, where he became a fellow in hematology at Peter Bent Brigham Hospital and an assistant in medicine at Harvard Medical School. After leaving these institutions in 1962, Kan served at a number of universities and hospitals, including the Massachusetts Institute of Technology, Pittsburgh's Presbyterian University, and Royal Victoria Hospital in Montreal. Kan has been married since 1964 to Alvera Kan, and the couple have two children, Susan, born in 1966, and Deborah, born in 1967.

In 1972 Kan became associate professor in the medical department at the University of California in San Francisco. That same year he was also appointed chief of hematology services at San Francisco General Hospital. While there Kan continued his research on blood diseases, particularly such hereditary anemias as sickle-cell and thalassemia. The latter two present a major public health problem in many parts of the world, including Africa, Southeast Asia, and the Mediterranean region.

Kan became an investigator at the Howard Hughes Medical Institute for the Study of Human Genetic Diseases in 1976, and the next year he joined the University of California's Department of Medicine and Laboratory Medicine. While researching gene mutations in 1978, Kan and his colleagues found the mutation responsible for sickle-cell anemia and thalassemia. Through this discovery they were able to devise a test that determines whether a person carries a gene for these diseases. Shortly thereafter, Kan also developed a prenatal test—the first of its kind—for sickle-cell anemia. These findings enabled him to win the Dameshek Award from the American Society of Hematology.

In the early 1980s Kan was the first scientist to describe DNA polymorphism, by which DNA can

Yuet Wai Kan

crystallize in different forms and sequences, depending on the genes in individuals (DNA, a substance found in cell nuclei, influences heredity on the molecular level). This has proved useful not only in the medical field, where it can be used to analyze genes and detect those which are diseased, but also in the legal field, where DNA analysis has been used in rape and murder cases to identify suspects and determine whether they have committed a particular crime.

The 1980s were a momentous period for Kan. In 1983 he was promoted to head the division of genetics and molecular hematology at his university. The next year he became a citizen of the United States and was given two major honors: the Allan Award from the American Society of Human Genetics (of which he is a member) for his discoveries regarding DNA, and the Gairdner Foundation International Award. Kan became chief of the division of molecular medicine and diagnostics at the University of California's Department of Laboratory Medicine in 1989, and a year later he became director of the Institute of Molecular Biology at the University of Hong Kong.

Kan has been a member of many international medical societies, such as the American Academy of Arts and Sciences, the British Royal Academy of Physicians, the Hong Kong College of Physicians, and the Third World Academy of Sciences. He has also held leadership positions in a number of organizations, including president of the American Society of Hematology, president of the Association of Chinese Geneticists in America, and section chairman of the National Academy of Sciences.

SELECTED WRITINGS BY KAN:

Periodicals

(With A. Cao, R. A. Filley, M. Furbetta, and M. S. Golbus) "Pre-Natal Diagnosis of Thalassaemia and Sickle-Cell Anemia: Experience With 24 Cases," *Lancet,* Volume I, 1977, pp. 269–271.

(With A. M. Dozy) "Polymorphism of DNA Sequence Adjacent to Human B-Globin Structural Gene: Relationship to Sickle Mutation," *Proceedings of the National Academy of Sciences USA,* Volume 75, 1978, pp. 5631-5635.

(With Dozy, J. C. Huang, and Y. F. Lau) "A Rapid Screening Test for Antenatal Sex Determination," *Lancet,* Volume I, 1984, pp. 14–16.

"New Application for DNA Polymorphism," *New England Journal of Medicine,* Volume 316, 1987, pp. 478–480.

SOURCES:

Books

Cerami, Anthony, and Washington, Elsie, *Sickle-Cell Anemia,* Third Press, 1974.

Lampton, Christopher, *DNA Fingerprinting,* Franklin Watts, 1991.

Other

Kan, Yuet Wai, interview with Francis Rogers conducted January 21, 1994.

—Sketch by Francis Rogers

Pyotr Kapitsa
1894-1984
Russian physicist

Pyotr Kapitsa was a Russian physicist who directed the Mond Laboratory in England and the Physical Problems Institute in the Soviet Union during the 1930s and 1940s. He performed important

Pyotr Kapitsa

research on high-density magnetic fields and high-energy plasma, but he is best known for his work on low-temperature physics, for which he shared the 1978 Nobel Prize in physics with **Arno Penzias** and **Robert W. Wilson**. Though many scientists believed that Kapitsa led the Soviet effort to develop an atomic bomb during World War II, Kapitsa, a longtime opponent of the Communist government, always denied the claim, and he is now generally not regarded as one of the bomb's designers.

Pyotr Leonidovich Kapitsa was born on July 8, 1894, in Kronstadt, an island near St. Petersburg, Russia. His father, Leonid Petrovich Kapitsa, was a lieutenant general in the engineers corps. His mother, Olga Ieronimovna Stebnitskaya, was an educator and a well-known folklorist. Kapitsa received his preparatory education in Kronstadt and then enrolled at the Polytechnic Institute of Petrograd. He married Nadeshda Tschernosvitova in 1916 and graduated in 1918 with a degree in electrical engineering. He became a lecturer at the institute, while developing a method of measuring magnetism with another student, **Nikolai N. Semenov** (who would one day win the Nobel Prize in chemistry). Their groundbreaking work was refined by **Otto Stern** in 1921, who himself won the Nobel Prize in physics in 1943.

Leaves Russia to Study in England

Kapitsa's research on magnetism at the Polytechnic Institute occurred in the midst of the collapse of czarist Russia and the turmoil of the Bolshevik Revolution. The country suffered widespread famine as a result of the civil unrest, and both his wife and their young child died. Kapitsa was repeatedly urged to study abroad, but his requests to do so were consistently refused by the new Communist government. Maxim Gorky, the Russian writer, interceded on his behalf, and in 1921 Kapitsa was allowed to leave for England where he worked with Nobel laureate **Ernest Rutherford** at Cambridge University's Cavendish Laboratory.

Rutherford initially balked at accepting Kapitsa, claiming that he had no room for another student. But Kapitsa was able to change Rutherford's mind with his innovative approach to research and his engineering background. His first experiments at the Cavendish Laboratory were on magnetic deflection of alpha- and beta-particles emitted by radioactive nuclei. He subsequently became involved in a study of high-density, temporary magnetic fields. Kapitsa developed an electric battery which discharged into a small copper magnetic coil, producing magnetic fields seven times stronger than any other previous mechanism had produced. These strong magnetic fields were the result of the short duration of the electric charges, which only lasted about 0.01 second each. This led Kapitsa to state that he was the world's highest paid physicist if his work were measured by the hour.

In 1923 Kapitsa received his doctorate from Cambridge University and won the James Clerk Maxwell fellowship, the first of his many awards. The following year he became the assistant director of magnetic research at Cavendish and shortly thereafter was made a fellow at Trinity College. Kapitsa seemed to feel at home in Cambridge and adopted many English habits—he rode a motor cycle, smoked a pipe, and wore tweeds.

In his work on high-density magnetic fields, Kapitsa devised ways of measuring how these fields affected the temperatures and properties of metals. It was this line of research that first interested him in the effects of temperature, and he began to work in low-temperature physics. Finding that the available supply of frigid liquefied gases was small, he invented his own apparatus for liquefying helium. The existing methods for liquefying helium, developed several decades earlier, produced only small quantities. Kapitsa developed a method which produced two liters an hour. His apparatus allowed the helium to expand rapidly, and the speed of the expansion caused it to cool before heat could be transferred into the helium chamber from the outside.

Kapitsa was elected a fellow of the Royal Society, the first foreigner to receive the honor in over two-hundred years, and in 1930 he became Messel Research Professor of the Royal Society. Rutherford, who considered Kapitsa his protégé, persuaded the society to build him a laboratory in which to study low-temperature physics. Endowed by German-born chemist and industrialist Ludwig Mond, the Mond Laboratory was custom-built for Kapitsa's experiments and opened in 1933. Kapitsa proved to be an industrious inventor and the new laboratory contained even more powerful magnets than he had developed earlier, as well as a cryogenics lab for low-temperature studies.

Remains in Russia After Detainment

By the time the Mond Laboratory opened, the Soviet government had repeatedly asked Kapitsa to return to his native country. He suggested he might if he was granted certain conditions, including the freedom to travel, but this was not acceptable to the government. In 1927 Kapitsa had married Anna Alekseevna Krylova, the daughter of a Soviet mathematician, and the couple frequently returned to the Soviet Union for personal and professional reasons. In 1934, however, at the end of his first year at the Mond Laboratory, Kapitsa and his wife left England for Russia, but once inside the country they were denied their exit visas. A series of confrontations between Kapitsa and authorities in Russia followed, while Rutherford and others in England were unable to contact him and their inquiries to the government went unanswered. His wife was finally allowed to return to England for their two sons, only if Kapitsa remained, and by 1936 he had come to an agreement with them about his future.

In 1935 the Soviet government announced the creation of a new research facility, the S.I. Vavilov Institute for Physical Problems. For nearly a year Kapitsa refused the directorship of the institute because the government would not meet his conditions. By 1936 the government had relented and he accepted the position—though he still was not allowed to travel. Rutherford was disappointed by this turn of events; he had expected Kapitsa to succeed him as head of the Cavendish Laboratory. But Kapitsa's new position made him the leading force in Russian physics, and Rutherford arranged for the sale of the cryogenics equipment from the Mond Laboratory to the Soviet government. Thus, Kapitsa was able to continue his low-temperature research in the new laboratory in Russia.

The fact that Kapitsa had resisted Soviet leader Joseph Stalin's offers for a year placed him in a strong bargaining position, and his abilities at negotiation served him well under a totalitarian government. He not only developed one the best physics staffs in the world, but he was able to acquire amenities for himself, such as custom-built living quarters that resembled a comfortable English cottage. He saw to it that the atmosphere of the new Physical Problems Institute was more western and informal, devoid of the usual Soviet bureaucracy.

Low-Temperature Studies Lead to Superfluidity

In 1937 after the equipment dismantled from the Mond Laboratory was reassembled at the Physical Problems Institute, Kapitsa went back to low-temperature research. He focused on the properties of helium II, liquid helium that exists at temperatures hovering right above absolute zero (0° Kelvin, or K). He measured the viscosity (thickness) of helium II when cooled below 2.17° K. He coined the term "superfluid" to describe the behavior of helium II, which conducts heat extremely rapidly. His papers on superfluidity, which were published in 1938 and again in 1942, are considered his most important contributions.

Kapitsa's research was continued by **Lev Davidovich Landau**, who was able to describe helium II in a way that was consistent with quantum mechanics. Landau, who was head of the theoretical section at the institute, would win the Nobel Prize for this work in 1962. During the 1930s, the sharp-tongued Landau was arrested and charged with anti-Soviet activity and was even accused of being a Nazi spy despite the fact that he was Jewish. Kapitsa went to the Kremlin and told the authorities he would resign if Landau were not released. With this bold move, Kapitsa again demonstrated his strength of conviction and character in the face of authoritarian rule. Landau was released.

During World War II, many western scientists believed Kapitsa was working on Russian development of the atomic bomb. However, it is known that he refused to cooperate with Lavrentii Beria—who was not only head of the Russian effort to develop an atomic bomb but also head of the secret police. The fact that Kapitsa was stripped of his directorship and placed under house arrest toward the end of the war corroborates his claim that he refused to participate in the making of the bomb. According to *Annual Obituaries,* "It was long rumored in Soviet scientific circles that Beria had wanted Kapitsa executed, but that Stalin refused." For the next decade he conducted experiments out of an improvised laboratory in his home. Kapitsa returned to the institute as director in 1955, two years after the death of Stalin. Kapitsa reportedly refused to have any KGB officers working at the institute and he regained the right to choose his own workers. As director, Kapitsa continued to conduct his own research as well as direct the research of others. In those postwar years he worked on the hydrodynamics of thin layers of fluid, the nature of ball lightning, and the standing waves produced by plasma.

The main focus of Kapitsa's research in the 1950s was high-power microwave radiation and plasma physics. Plasma, sometimes referred to as the fourth state of matter, is gas heated to temperatures so high that the molecules are stripped of their electrons and thus become electrified ions. Kapitsa found that a microwave generator can heat gas to an extremely high temperature—2,000,000° K—over a very short space. His staff sought a way to use microwave radiation to heat plasma for thermonuclear fusion reactions, which require such high temperatures.

Kapitsa's skill and dedication as a teacher, as well as his administrative abilities, were almost as important to physics as the contributions of his research itself. He continued to improve the facilities at the Physical Problems Institute and he worked with most of the leading physicists in the Soviet Union. He remained an outspoken critic of Soviet bureaucracy, as well as Soviet science. He never joined the Communist party and complained how the Soviet press was quick to cover scientific theories that agreed with Soviet dogma rather than those that demonstrated scientific validity. His English-style home, situated near the institute, was a gathering place for Soviet dissidents. He was friends with writers Aleksandr Solzhenitsyn and Andrei Sakharov, yet the government never placed him in the same category. He protested the pollution of Lake Baikal from nearby pulp mills, called for the abolition of the death penalty in Soviet Russia, and denounced the detainment of Soviet scientists.

In 1965 Kapitsa left the USSR for the first time in thirty-one years to receive the Niels Bohr International Gold Medal of the Danish Society and to lecture on high-energy physics. In 1966 he went back to England and toured his old laboratory, and several years later he and his wife visited the United States. In 1978, decades after his seminal work on helium II, he received the Nobel Prize in physics for his work in low-temperature physics. He shared the award with Americans Penzias and Wilson, who discovered cosmic microwave background radiation. In his later years Kapitsa was revered as a leader of Russian physics. He played chess, collected antique clocks, and watched his two sons become scientists. He died in Moscow at age eighty-nine on April 8, 1984.

SELECTED WRITINGS BY KAPITSA:

Books

High Power Microwave Electronics, 1962.
Collected Papers, 3 Volumes, 1964–67.
A Life for Science, 1965.
Experiment, Theory, Practice, 1966.
Problems of Physics, 1972.

SOURCES:

Books

Abbott, David, editor, *The Biographical Dictionary of Scientists: Physicists,* Peter Bedrick Books, New York, 1984, p. 90.
Annual Obituary: 1984, St. James Press, 1985, pp. 223–226.
Parry, Albert, *Peter Kapitsa on Life and Science,* 1968.
Wasson, Tyler, editor, *Nobel Prize Winners,* H.W. Wilson Co., 1987, pp. 527–530.

—*Sketch by Barbara A. Branca*

Isabella Karle
1921-
American chemist, crystallographer, and physicist

Isabella Karle is a renowned chemist and physicist who has worked at the Naval Research Laboratory in Washington, D.C., since 1946 and heads the X Ray Diffraction Group of that facility. In her research, she applied electron and X-ray diffraction to molecular structure problems in chemistry and biology. Along with her husband **Jerome Karle**, she developed procedures for gathering information about the structure of molecules from diffraction data. For her work, she has received numerous awards such as the Annual Achievement Award of the Society of Women Engineers in 1968, the Federal Woman's Award in 1973, and the Lifetime Achievement Award from Women in Science and Engineering in 1986. Her work has been described in the book *Women and Success.*

Isabella Lugoski Karle was born on December 2, 1921, in Detroit, Michigan. Her parents were Zygmunt A. Lugoski, a housepainter, and Elizabeth Graczyk, who was a seamstress. Both her parents were immigrants from Poland, and Karle spoke no English until she went to school. While still in high school, she decided upon a career in chemistry, even though her mother wanted her to be a lawyer or a teacher. She received her B.S. and M.S. degrees in physical chemistry from the University of Michigan in 1941 and 1942. Determined to continue her studies, Karle ran into serious financial problems since teaching assistant positions at the University of Michigan were reserved exclusively for male doctoral students. She managed to stay in school on an American Association of University Women fellowship, however, and

Isabella Karle

in 1943 also became a Rackham fellow. She received her Ph.D. in physical chemistry from the University of Michigan in 1944, at the age of twenty-two.

After receiving her doctorate, Karle worked at the University of Chicago on the Manhattan Project (the code name for the construction of the atomic bomb), synthesizing plutonium compounds. She then returned to the University of Michigan as a chemistry instructor for two years. In 1942 she had married Jerome Karle, then a chemistry student. In 1946 she and her husband joined the Naval Research Laboratory, where she worked as a physicist from 1946 to 1959. In 1959 she became head of the X-ray analysis section, a position she maintained through the 1990s.

Investigates Structure of Crystals

When Karle began her work at the Naval Research Laboratory, information about the structure of crystals was limited. Scientists had determined that crystals were solid units, in which atoms, ions, or molecules are arranged sometimes in repeating, sometimes in random patterns. These patterns or networks of fixed points in space have measurable distances between them. Although chemists had been able to investigate the structure of gas molecules by studying the diffraction of electron or X-ray beams by the gas molecules, it was believed that information about the occurrences of the patterns—or phases—was lost when crystalline substances scattered an X-ray beam. The Karles, working as a team, gathered phase information using a heavy-atom or salt derivative. The position of a heavy atom in the crystal could be located by scattered X-ray reflections, even though light atoms posed more serious problems. When a heavy atom could not be introduced into a crystal, its structure remained a mystery. In 1950 Jerome Karle, in collaboration with the chemist **Herbert A. Hauptman**, formulated a set of mathematical equations that would theoretically solve the problem of phases in light-atom crystals. It was Isabella Karle who solved the practical problems and designed and built the diffraction machine that photographed the diffracted images of crystalline structures.

While investigating structural formulas and the make-up of crystal structures using electron and X-ray diffraction, Karle made an important discovery. She found that only a few of the phase values—no more than three to five—are sufficient to evaluate the remaining values. She could then use symbols to represent these initial values and also numerical evaluations. This process for determining the location of atoms in a crystal was amenable to processing in high-speed computers. Eventually, it became possible to analyze complex biological molecules in a day or two that previously would have taken years to analyze. The rapid and direct method for solving crystal structure resounded through chemistry, biochemistry, biology, and medicine, and Karle herself has been active in resolving applications in a range of fields.

In addition to describing the structure of crystals and molecules, Karle also investigated the conformation of natural products and biologically active materials. After a crystallographer determines the chemical composition of rare and expensive chemicals, scientists can synthesize inexpensive substitutes that serve the same purpose. Karle headed a team that determined the structure of a chemical that repels worms, termites, and other pests and occurs naturally in a rare Panamanian wood. The team was then able to produce a synthetic chemical that mimics the natural chemical and is equally effective as a pest repellent. In another application, Karle studied frog venom. Using extremely minute quantities of purified potent toxins from tropical American frogs, the team headed by Karle established three-dimensional models, called stereoconfigurations, of many of the toxins and showed the chemical linkages of each of these poisons. The inexpensive substitutes of the toxins were of great importance in medicine. The venom has the effect of blocking nerve impulses and is useful to medical scientists studying nerve transmissions. Karle has also researched the effect of radiation on deoxyribonucleic acid (DNA), the carrier of genetic information. She demonstrated how the structural formulas of the configurations of amino acids and nucleic acids in DNA may be changed when exposed to radiation. Her research into structural analysis also established the arrangement of peptide bonds, or combinations of amino acids.

Karle has held several concurrent positions, such as member of the National Committee on Crystallography of the National Academy of Science and the National Research Council (1974–1977). She has long been a member of the American Crystallographic Society and served as its president in 1976. She was elected to the National Academy of Sciences in 1978. From 1982 to 1990 she worked with the Massachusetts Institute of Technology, and she has been a civilian consultant to the Atomic Energy Commission.

Karle has received numerous awards including the Superior Civilian Service Award of the Navy Department in 1965, the Hildebrand Award in 1970, and the Garvan Award of the American Chemical Society in 1976. She has received several honorary doctorates. Her most recent awards have been the Gregori Aminoff Prize from the Swedish Academy of Sciences in 1988 and the Bijvoet Medal from the University of Utrecht, the Netherlands, in 1990. She has written over 250 scientific articles.

Isabella and Jerome Karle have three daughters, Louise Isabella, Jean Marianne, and Madeline Diane. All three have become scientists like their parents. Jerome Karle, who is chief scientist at the Laboratory for Structure and Matter of the U.S. Naval Laboratory, received the Nobel Prize in chemistry in 1985 for developing a mathematical method for determining the three-dimensional structure of molecules.

SELECTED WRITINGS BY KARLE:

Periodicals

"Modular Design of Synthetic Protein Mimics," *Journal of the American Chemical Society,* Volume 112, December 5, 1990, pp. 9350–56.

SOURCES:

Books

Kundsin, Ruth, *Women and Success,* Morrow, 1974.

McGraw-Hill Modern Scientists and Engineers, McGraw-Hill (New York), 1980, pp. 147–48.

Noble, Iris, *Contemporary Women Scientists of America,* Meissner, 1979.

—Sketch by Evelyn B. Kelly

Jerome Karle
1918-
American physical chemist

Jerome Karle is a chemist whose research into the structure of atoms, molecules, glasses, crystals, and solid surfaces has greatly advanced the understanding of chemical composition. He is best known for his contributions to the use of X-ray crystallography in determining the structure of crystal molecules, which earned him the 1985 Nobel Prize in chemistry. It was awarded to him jointly with his colleague **Herbert A. Hauptman** for "their outstanding achievements in the development of direct methods for the determination of crystals." The direct method has greatly increased the accuracy of X-ray crystallography and been of great importance in ascertaining the structure of large molecules. Using the direct method, scientists can determine which parts of molecules are biologically active; this has, among other advances, enabled pharmaceutical companies to engineer artificial compounds with identical properties which can be used as medicinal drugs.

Karle was born in Brooklyn, New York, on June 18, 1918, to Louis Karfunkle, a businessman, and Sadie Kun, an amateur pianist. His mother hoped that her son would inherit some of the family's artistic talents and perhaps become a professional pianist, but Karle decided at an early age that his career would be in science. He attended Abraham Lincoln High School in Brooklyn from 1929 to 1933. Upon graduating, he enrolled in chemistry and biology at the City College of New York, taking extra classes in mathematics and physics. In 1937, he was awarded his B.S. degree and the First Caduceus Award for Excellence in the Natural Sciences. He then studied biology for a year at Harvard and received his M.A. in 1938. Karle worked as a laboratory assistant at the New York State Health Department in Albany from 1939 to 1940, with the intention of saving money to return to graduate school. One of his discoveries, a method of measuring the amount of fluorine in water, became a standard in the field.

In 1940, Karle enrolled as a Ph.D student in the chemistry department of the University of Michigan. Sitting at an adjoining desk on the first day of class was Isabella Lugoski, a fellow chemist whom he would marry in 1942; they would have three children and collaborate closely with each other in their research. At Michigan, Karle and Isabella, both of whom were interested in physical chemistry, studied under Lawrence O. Brockway. By the end of the summer of 1943, Karle had completed work on his doctoral thesis and went to work on the Manhattan Project at the University of Chicago.

Jerome Karle

Develops Direct Method for X-ray Crystallography

In 1944, having received his M.S. and Ph.D. for his work on gas electron diffraction, Karle and **Isabella Karle** returned to the University of Michigan. Karle joined the Naval Research Laboratory where he carried out some experiments on the structure of monolayers of long-chain hydrocarbon films; he also formulated a theory about electron diffraction patterns. In 1946, he and his wife joined the U.S. Naval Research Laboratory in Washington, D.C., where they worked together on developing a quantitative analysis of gas-electron diffraction.

The solution of a problem in gas-electron diffraction had, as Karle recalls in an autobiographical statement, "evident implications for crystal structure analysis." When Herbert A. Hauptman became affiliated with the laboratory, they moved to find ways to understand three-dimensional molecular structure using X-ray crystallography. But Karle has often insisted that it was his early collaboration with his wife that laid the groundwork for their Nobel Prize-winning work. With Hauptman, Karle developed the basic mathematics necessary to establishing a general method for solving all types of crystal structures. Later, after Hauptman left the laboratory, Karle and Isabella developed the general procedure of interpreting three-dimensional structures by means of X-ray crystallography.

X-ray crystallography uses the diffraction of X-ray beams to record the structure of a crystal; the crystal is exposed to the beams and a photographic plate captures the pattern of the X rays deflected by the atoms. When Karle, Hauptman, and Isabella Karle began their work, there was no accurate method for translating the pattern of dots the X rays left on the photographic plate into knowledge about the exact atomic structure of the crystal. Their pioneering direct method of interpreting the internal structure of crystal molecules relied on a mathematical formula for determining the phase of an X-ray beam as it traveled through a crystal—that is, the degree of displacement of the beam. From these mathematical calculations it was possible to construct an electron-density map depicting the precise position of each atom and hence, the molecule's structure. Ingenious though the direct method was, it was some time before it gained general acceptance. When it was introduced in a paper in 1953, many chemists were initially skeptical, partly because it relied on complex mathematics that few chemists understood. In time, however, its usefulness came to be widely recognized. In 1951, as their work on X-ray crystallography continued, Karle was made professor of chemistry at the University of Maryland, a position he held until 1970. Between 1954 and 1956, Karle was a member of the National Research Council. He would later serve on it again, from 1967 to 1987. In 1968, he was named to a specially created chair of science at the Naval Research Laboratory and became chief scientist of the Laboratory for the Structure of Matter. During the late 1960s, his collaborative work on the direct method was accorded wider acceptance in the scientific community as a result of practical demonstrations of its usefulness in analyzing large molecules given by Isabella Karle.

In the 1960s, Karle and his wife developed a method of crystal structure determination that encompassed the range of crystals, centrosymmetric as well as noncentrosymmetric. The "symbolic addition procedure," as it was known, built on their work of the 1950s. Karle also dedicated himself to theoretical and experimental analysis of gas-electron diffraction. Since the 1970s, Karle has been investigating macromolecular structure and the evaluation of triplet phase invariants to discover their potential usefulness.

While working at the Naval Research Laboratory, Karle also spent some time as a visiting lecturer of mathematics and physics in England, Italy, Canada, Poland, Brazil, Japan, and Germany. He served as president of the American Crystallographic Association in 1972, president of the International Union of Crystallography between 1981 and 1984, and chair of the Chemistry Section of the National Academy of Sciences between 1988 and 1991. He is a fellow of the American Physical Society and the American Mathematical Society, and a member of the American Chemical Society, the American Philosophical Society, the American Crystallographic Association, and the American Association for the Advancement of Science. He has been a member of the National Science Foundation and the Committee on Human Rights of the National Academy of Sciences. Karle is also a member of the Union of Concerned Scientists and a National Sponsor of the Committee of Concerned Scientists.

Karle has won the Distinguished Public Service Award of the United States Navy in 1968, the Hillebrand Award of the American Chemical Society in 1970, the A. L. Patterson Memorial Award of the American Crystallographic Association in 1984, and the first National Research Laboratory Lifetime Achievement Award in 1993. He has received honorary degrees from Georgetown University, the University of Maryland, City College of New York, and the University of Michigan. His greatest accolade came in 1985, when, more than forty years after he and his wife created the basic mathematical formulas upon which the direct formula is based, he and Herbert A. Hauptman were jointly awarded the 1985 Nobel Prize for chemistry. Of his wife's involvement with the project, he has said: "It is unfortunate that she was not included in the Nobel Prize."

SELECTED WRITINGS BY KARLE:

Books

(With Herbert A. Hauptman) *Solution of the Phase Problem I: The Centrosymmetric Crystal,* American Crystallographic Association, 1953.

SOURCES:

Books

Wasson, Tyler, editor, *Nobel Prize Winners,* H. W. Wilson, 1987.

Periodicals

Physics Today, December, 1985.

Science, Volume 231, January 24, 1986, pp. 362–364.

"Two Americans Share Nobel Prize in Chemistry," *New York Times,* October 17, 1985, p. A1.

Other

Karle, Jerome, autobiographical statement sent to Avril McDonald, February 17, 1994.

—*Sketch by Avril McDonald*

Samuel Karlin
1924-
Polish-born American mathematician

Samuel Karlin, an eminent mathematician, is known for his research in several areas of pure and applied mathematics. He has made important contributions particularly to the theory of total positivity, probability theory, statistics, and stochastic processes. His work on applications of his mathematical theories to game theory, economics, and biology—in the areas of theoretical population genetics and DNA structure—have made possible significant advances in these sciences. Karlin is also a renowned educator and an inspiration to others working in a variety of fields.

Karlin, the youngest of several children, was born on June 8, 1924, in Yonova, Poland, to Morris Karlin and Anna Rosenshine. At the age of two months, he arrived in Chicago, Illinois, with his family. Morris Karlin, who had been a Hebrew teacher in Poland, became a carpenter and painter in Chicago. During the depression, when he was just nine or ten years old, Karlin started working in a store to help out with the family finances. At age fifteen he taught Hebrew.

Although his father wanted him to become a religious scholar, Karlin followed a secular path in his education and received a scholarship to the Illinois Institute of Technology. During his last year at IIT, Karlin received encouragement from two eminent mathematicians—Herbert Busemann and George Mackey—to prepare for a career in mathematics. Busemann, a renowned mathematician who had had to leave Europe during the regime of German dictator Adolf Hitler, allowed Karlin to enroll in a graduate course he was teaching in advanced calculus. Karlin received a B.S. in mechanics from IIT in 1944. Busemann was instrumental in Karlin's going to Princeton University for an advanced degree in mathematics, a Ph.D., which was awarded to him in 1947. After a year of work as a research fellow at the California Institute of Technology (Caltech), Karlin started his teaching career in 1948, accepting a position as instructor at Caltech. He continued to serve in the mathematics department there until 1956.

Most of Karlin's early work focused on mathematical analysis and inventory theory. During his time at Princeton, Karlin had studied with **John von Neumann**, who just previously had published his book on game theory and its applications to economics, *Theory of Games and Economic Behavior.* When Karlin was at the California Institute of Technology, he worked to elaborate von Neumann's ideas. Karlin's own book on the subject, *Mathematical Methods and Theory in Games, Programming, and Mathematical Economics,* came out in 1959. Subsequent contributions to the social sciences were primarily in the areas of management science and operations research, the application of scientific, especially mathematical, methods and techniques to decision-making problems.

Develops Theory of Total Positivity

In 1956 Karlin was appointed professor of mathematics at Stanford University, where he was to remain into the 1990s. Karlin began work on the theory of total positivity, a concept in pure math that deals with variation. Karlin was instrumental in establishing the importance of total positivity and worked out many of its ramifications. Total positivity is of great usefulness to statistics and the theory of probability. It is a powerful tool in describing stochastic processes (processes involving random variables and governed by laws of probability). Karlin published widely on the subject of stochastic modeling and its application to a variety of scientific fields. Total positivity is also relevant in understanding chains of linked probabilities, or Markov processes. With regard to statistics, the theory is particularly useful in clarifying densities and distribution. Many of his results in this field appeared in the book *Tchebycheff Systems: With Applications in Analysis and Statistics.* Karlin published a comprehensive review of his work on total positivity in the 1968 book entitled *Total Positivity.*

Ventures in Biology

Karlin also became interested in mathematical biology and biometrics during the 1960s. He made significant contributions over the following decades particularly to the science of population genetics. He started out working on the problems involved in understanding the evolution of small populations and later also worked on the evolution of traits in populations with inbreeding and other restricted mating practices. In 1968 Karlin published *Equilibrium Behavior of Population Genetic Models with Non-random Mating.* Subsequently, he also made important contributions to the subject of combinatorics, the study of the arrangement of elements into sets. Karlin's primary research interest since the 1970s has been the study of patterns in strings of DNA (deoxyribonucleic acid, which contains the genetic information that determines heredity).

Karlin's role in unifying the sciences and other subject areas with mathematics and creating mathematical applications for a wide range of fields is illustrated over and over again by his research and his publications. He has also been an inspiring colleague and teacher, who has collaborated with numerous scientists from a wide range of disciplines. In 1992 the biology department of Stanford University honored Karlin by establishing the Karlin Prize in Mathematical Biology. This annual award gives recognition, with a stipend, to an exceptional graduate or undergraduate student working in mathematical biology. Karlin received the National Medal of Science in 1993, the highest American award in science. His books have been translated into Chinese, French, German, Hungarian, Japanese, Russian, and Spanish, and a number of his papers have appeared in foreign language books and journals. Karlin has also been personally involved on the international front, serving as an advisory dean of the mathematics department of the Weizmann Institute of Science in Israel from 1970 to 1977.

Karlin is married to Dorit Carmelli, a behavioral geneticist, and the two have collaborated on a number of scientific papers. They have two sons, Kenneth and Manuel, and a daughter, Anna. Kenneth is a nationally known research chemist. Karlin's leisure interests include tennis and concerts. He speaks French, German, and Hebrew fluently.

SELECTED WRITINGS BY KARLIN:

Books

Mathematical Methods and Theory in Games, Programming, and Economics, two volumes, Addison-Wesley, 1959; reprinted in one volume, Dover, 1992.

(With William J. Studden), *Tchebycheff Systems: With Applications in Analysis and Statistics,* Interscience, 1966.

(With H. M. Taylor) *A First Course in Stochastic Processes,* Academic Press, 1966, 2nd edition, 1975.

Equilibrium Behavior of Population Genetic Models with Non-random Mating, Gordon & Breach, 1968.

Total Positivity, Stanford University Press, 1968.

(With Taylor) *A Second Course in Stochastic Processes,* Academic Press, 1981.

(With Taylor) *An Introduction to Stochastic Modeling,* Academic Press, 1984.

(With Sabin Lessard) *Theoretical Studies on Sex Ratio Evolution,* Princeton University Press, 1986.

SOURCES:

Books

McGraw-Hill Modern Scientists and Engineers, McGraw, 1980, pp. 148–49.

Periodicals

Notices of the American Mathematical Society, January, 1990, pp. 20–23.

Other

Karlin, Samuel, interview with Jeanne Spriter James conducted September 24, 1993.

—*Sketch by Jeanne Spriter James*

Paul Karrer

1889-1971

Russian-born Swiss organic chemist

Paul Karrer's long and distinguished career in chemistry included the study of sugars and plant pigments, subjects that led him to the description and synthesis of vitamin A as well as several other vitamins. Karrer's work with vitamins helped to solve their chemical riddle, enabling physiologists to define the way in which the body utilizes them. In 1937 Karrer shared the Nobel Prize for Chemistry for research that incorporated the vitamins A and B.

Paul Karrer was born in Moscow, Russia, on April 21, 1889, the son of Julie Lerch Karrer and Paul Karrer, a Swiss dentist who was practicing in Russia. At three years of age Karrer and his family returned to Switzerland, initially to Zürich, but later settling in the canton, of Aargau, a region in the north of the country. Karrer was educated in schools in this canton, and it was while in secondary school that he began showing a passion for science. In 1908 he entered the University of Zürich, ultimately studying chemistry under **Alfred Werner**, whose work on the linkage of atoms in molecules won him the Nobel Prize in 1913. Karrer, after completing his doctoral dissertation on cobalt complexes in 1911 and earning his Ph.D., became Werner's lecture assistant. His attention soon turned to organic arsenical compounds, and Karrer's first paper on the subject, published in 1912, caught the eye of **Paul Ehrlich**, a renowned chemist in Germany whose work at the turn of the twentieth century had helped to explain the action of poisons and how to neutralize their effects by antitoxins. Ehrlich subsequently invited Karrer to join him as a research assistant in Frankfurt-am-Main at the Georg Speyer-Haus, a research institute.

Directs Chemical Research in Germany and Switzerland

Karrer remained in Germany until the beginning of World War I when he was called back to Switzerland for national service. While serving in an artillery unit, he met and married Helene Frölich, the daughter of the director of a psychiatric clinic. They would have three sons, but only two of them, Jurg and Heinz, survived infancy. In 1915 Ehrlich died in Frankfurt, and Karrer accepted the position of researcher and director of the chemical research division of the Georg Speyer-Haus, returning to war-time Germany. Karrer stayed in Germany for the next three years, and during this time he focused more closely on plant product chemistry. Then in 1918 he returned to the University of Zürich, first taking a position as associate professor of organic chemistry, and with Werner's death in 1919, becoming a full professor of chemistry as well as director of the Chemical Institute. Karrer would remain at the University of Zürich for the rest of his career, acting as rector from 1950 to 1953.

Karrer, of necessity, had to split his time between administration, teaching, and research. With the latter, he turned his attention to the spatial or steric configuration of atoms in molecules of amino acids, proteins, and peptides. But by the late–1920s he had shifted his focus to the pigmentation of plants, and more specifically, to the anthocyanins, the blue and red colors of berries and flowers. Though these substances had been isolated by another researcher, Karrer—by splitting their macromolecules with enzymes—helped to clearly describe their chemical make-up. More importantly, it was these researches in plant pigments that eventually led him to his work on carotene.

Vitamin Research Leads to Nobel

From anthocyanin, Karrer moved on to crocin, the yellow pigment of flowers such as the crocus. In connection with yellow pigments, Karrer tackled the structure of carotenoids, the orange-to-yellow pigments found in foods such as carrots and sweet potatoes. **Richard Kuhn**, a German chemist, had managed to isolate beta-carotene at about this time, and he and Karrer became something of rivals in explaining beta-carotene's chemical constitution. By 1930 Karrer had solved the structure of the carotene molecule. It was a logical progression from the study of plant pigments to that of vitamins, for Karrer learned that the body actually synthesizes vitamin A from carotene. Thus, he was soon on the track of the chemical make-up of vitamins themselves. By 1931 Karrer had become the first scientist to describe the structure of a vitamin, successfully demonstrating that vitamin A is very similar to one half of the symmetrical carotene molecule. Up until the time of his discovery, scientists had thought vitamins to be some peculiar state of matter, perhaps a colloid—a dispersed solution in suspension. But Karrer managed to show that vitamin A, in specific, is made up of atoms of hydrogen, carbon, and oxygen in a regular ring-like formation.

Karrer carried on his vitamin research over the next decade, ultimately synthesizing vitamin A in the laboratory. He then went on to research the chemical structure of several B vitamins, riboflavin being the first that he actually synthesized. In 1937, for his work on carotenoids and flavins, he shared the Nobel Prize for Chemistry with **Walter Haworth**, an Englishman who researched the make-up of carbohydrates and vitamin C. Karrer, however, was not one to rest on his laurels, and the very next year he synthesized vitamin E, and soon after, vitamin K.

From vitamin research, Karrer turned to an investigation of the enzyme nicotinamide adenine dinucleotide (NAD) which is involved with the energy system of cells. By 1942 he had contributed greatly to the understanding of both the NAD structure and function in cellular electron transfer. In his sixties, Karrer went back to earlier work, both in carotenes and in poisons—this time alkaloids. In the former, he successfully synthesized all the carotenoids, some forty different compounds. His work in alkaloids helped to determine the structure of curare, a resinous extract from certain South American trees used by indigenous peoples for poison arrows. Its medicinal uses include general anesthesia and reduction of muscle spasms.

Apart from his research, Karrer was a tireless administrator and teacher, directing over 200 dissertations in his academic career. He was also a prolific writer, with over 1,000 publications to his credit, including the 1928 organic chemistry textbook, *Lehrbuch der organischen Chemie.* Aside from the Nobel, Karrer won numerous awards and prizes, among them the Marcel Benoist Prize from Switzerland in 1923, the Cannizzaro Prize from Italy in 1935, and the Officier de la Legion d'Honneur from France in 1954. Despite fame, wealth, and offers from universities around the world, Karrer stayed on in Zürich until his retirement in 1959, eschewing luxuries such as a car. He died on June 18, 1971, after a short illness.

SELECTED WRITINGS BY KARRER:

Books

Lehrbuch der organischen Chemie, Thieme Verlag, 1928.

(With Ernst Jucker) *Die Carotenoids,* Birkhäuser, 1948.

Periodicals

(With K. Morf) "Vitamin A," *Helvetica Chimica Acta,* Volume 16, 1933, p. 625.

"Chemie der Vitamine A und C," *Chemical Reviews,* Volume 14, 1934, pp. 17–30.

SOURCES:

Books

Nobel Prize Winners, H. W. Wilson, 1987, pp. 533–534.

Farber, Eduard, *Nobel Prize Winners in Chemistry 1901–1961,* Abelard-Schuman, 1963, pp. 161–164.

Periodicals

"Paul Karrer," *Chemical & Engineering News,* Volume 33, 1955, p. 2820.

Wettstein, A., "Paul Karrer," *Helvetica Chimica Acta,* Volume 55, 1972, pp. 317–328.

—Sketch by J. Sydney Jones

Alfred Kastler
1902-1984
French physicist

Alfred Kastler developed methods for exciting atoms so that they would travel from one sublevel to another in very precise ways, emitting energy in the process. These techniques, called double resonance and optical pumping, later found application in a number of inventions, including the maser and the laser, which use the energy emitted by excited atoms. His research into methods of exciting and controlling this atomic process led Kastler to be awarded the 1966 Nobel Prize in physics.

Kastler was born in the Alsatian village of Guebwiller on May 3, 1902. The village was then a part of Germany, although it was to revert to French control at the end of World War I. His parents were Frederic and Anna (Frey) Kastler. He began his schooling in Guebwiller, but moved with his family to Colmar after World War I began. He studied at the Colmar Oberrealschule (high school), where he became especially interested in mathematics and science courses.

As part of the Versailles peace treaty at the end of World War I, Alsace was ceded to France, and the Oberrealschule became the Lycée Bartholdi. Kastler was not fluent in French; he decided to leave school to become a carpenter. An aunt insisted that he continue his education, however, and he graduated from the lycée a year later. He then traveled to Paris, where he was admitted to the prestigious École Normale Supérieure in spite of having failed the entrance examination. He was admitted under a special disposition offered to residents of the newly regained Alsace territory.

After graduating with a teaching certificate in 1926, Kastler held a series of teaching jobs at lycées in Mulhouse, Colmar, and Bordeaux. He then received an appointment in 1931 as research assistant at the University of Bordeaux, which permitted him to begin his graduate studies there. Five years later, he was awarded his degree of Docteur des Sciences Physiques for his dissertation on the excitation of mercury atoms.

Kastler's first job after receiving his doctorate was at Clermont-Ferrand University, where he was a lecturer in physics from 1936 to 1938. He then accepted an appointment as professor of physics at the University of Bordeaux, where he remained until 1941. Returning to Paris, he became director of the Hertzian spectroscopy group and assistant professor of physics at his alma mater, the École Normale Supérieure. There, he attained the rank of full professor in 1945. After retiring from the École Normale Supérieure in 1968, Kastler served as director of research at the National Center for Scientific Research, a post he held until 1972.

Studies Energy-Matter Interactions

As Kastler was beginning his graduate studies in the early 1930s, scientists were still trying to unravel the problems of the electronic structure of atoms. **Niels Bohr** had provided a broad, general theory for atomic structure in 1913, one in which electrons were allowed to occupy certain specific energy levels, but not the spaces between those energy levels. Later studies showed that Bohr's model lacked precision, that sub-orbitals existed within any given energy level. Electrons could occupy any one of these sub-levels, their position often being dependent upon the presence of external magnetic fields.

One technique used by scientists to study electron energy levels involved the addition of energy to an atom. By shining light on it, an electron in an atom would then absorb some of that energy and move to a higher energy level. After remaining briefly in that new energy level, the electron would reemit the absorbed energy and fall back to a lower energy level. The emitted energy, in the form of light, could then be studied in order to obtain information about the relative location of the energy levels.

Kastler made two important contributions to this line of research. The first is known as double resonance, because it involves the application of two types of external energy fields, a beam of light and a radiofrequency field. In the first step, energy from a light beam shined on a group of atoms causes some electrons to be excited and to move to a higher energy level. Those electrons distribute themselves unevenly, however, among the sub-levels within that higher energy level.

In the second step, the application of a radiofrequency field, electrons are forced from populated to unpopulated sub-levels. At this point, the excited electrons in all sub-levels emit their absorbed energy, fall back to lower energy states, and give off beams of light that can be analyzed. Kastler reported the results of these studies carried out with his former student and later collaborator, Jean Brossel, at a meeting of La Société Française de Physique on May 30, 1950.

Discovery Leads to Many Applications

A few months later, Kastler extended his work on double resonance methods to the development of another technique known as optical pumping. In optical pumping, polarized light is shined on a group of atoms. Electrons in one sub-level of the atoms absorb light and move to a higher energy level, while electrons in a second sub-level will not absorb light and remain in their ground state. When the excited electrons return to their original state, however, they distribute themselves between both ground sub-levels, absorbing and non-absorbing.

Because this technique is a way of getting electrons from an absorbing to a non-absorbing level, it is called optical pumping. In later years, optical pumping was used in the development of a variety of practical devices, including the maser and laser, the atomic clock, and the magnetometer. In recognition of his important role in these developments, Kastler was awarded the 1966 Nobel Prize in physics. His award brought rejoicing in France, where Kastler was called the "Grandfather of the Laser" by one national newspaper. It was the first Nobel Prize in physics awarded to a French citizen in thirty-seven years. Kastler married Élise Cosset on December 24, 1924. They had three children, Daniel, Claude-Yves, and Mireille. The two boys became teachers, and the daughter became a physician. After World War II, Kastler became increasingly active in the pacifist movement, opposing both the war in Vietnam and France's occupation of Algeria. He died in Bandol, France, on January 7, 1984.

SELECTED WRITINGS BY KASTLER:

Books

La Diffusion de la Lumiére par les Milieux Troubles, Hermann, 1952.

Cette Etrange Matiére, Stock, 1976.

SOURCES:

Books

Current Biography 1967, H. W. Wilson, 1967, pp. 216–18.

Nobel Prize Winners, H. W. Wilson, 1987, pp. 534–536.

Weber, Robert L., *Pioneers of Science: Nobel Prize Winners in Physics,* American Institute of Physics, 1980, pp. 207–209.

Periodicals

Pipkin, Francis J., "1966 Nobel Laureate in Physics: Alfred Kastler," *Science,* November 11, 1966, pp. 747–749.

—*Sketch by David E. Newton*

Robert W. Kates
1929-
American geographer

Robert W. Kates will never be accused of thinking small. The American geographer's goal is no less than to end world hunger. "I'm basically a scientist," he told contributor Cynthia Washam in an interview, "but in my work on hunger, I am an advocate. I think people have a responsibility to act on what they know." Through the late 1980s and early 1990s, Kates earned a reputation as one of the country's foremost authorities on world hunger. For six years starting in 1986, he directed the Alan Shawn Feinstein World Hunger Program at Brown University, the only major research program in the country dedicated to eradicating world hunger. He has also written extensively about hunger for both lay and professional publications. *Hunger in History: Food Shortage, Poverty, and Deprivation,* a book he coedited in 1990, is considered one of the most important of nineteen books he wrote or edited.

Even after retiring from his post at Brown in 1992, Kates continued fighting hunger as cochair of an international group of advocates, practitioners, and researchers called Overcoming Hunger in the 1990s. Kates was a cofounder of the organization in 1989. Overcoming Hunger's goals for the 1990s are to end famine deaths; cut extreme, chronic hunger by half; cut hunger in children by half; and virtually eliminate deficiencies of vitamin A and iodine.

Poor Childhood Influenced Career Choice

The geographer's concern for the hungry is rooted in his own impoverished childhood. Kates was born in Brooklyn, New York, on January 31, 1929, nine months before the stock market crashed. He never really knew his father, Simon, a salesman who died three months after his son's birth. His mother, Helen, stayed at home caring for Kates and his sister through the Great Depression. "It was a struggle for her," Kates said. "That certainly influenced my social conscience."

From the age of 12, Kates worked at odd jobs to help support his mother and sister. He delivered vegetables, worked in a shoe store, and later in a print shop. His high school grades were unimpressive, although he was one of only two students in his graduating class to win a college scholarship based on performance on a standardized test. Kates credits his success on the test to his diverse interests.

Kates began his college career at New York University, but love and economic necessity soon drew him away from academia to the working world. At age 18, he moved to his fiance's home city of Gary, Indiana, where he began working in a steel mill. He and Eleanor Hackman married a year later and soon started their family. The couple have three children, Jonathan, Katherine, and Barbara.

For 13 years, Kates supported his family as a steelworker in Gary's mills. He was still laboring in the mills in 1957, when he began studying geography at Indiana University in Gary. The following year, he was accepted into the master's program in geography at the University of Chicago, although he had not completed his bachelor's degree. There he earned his master's, and in 1962, his doctoral degree in geography. After earning his Ph.D., Kates returned with his family to the Northeast. He was hired in 1962 as an assistant professor at the Graduate School of Geography at Clark University in Worcester, Massachusetts. He taught at Clark until 1987, becoming a full professor in 1974.

Kates's interests are focused on man's use of natural resources and response to hazards. That broad view led him into several areas of research before he settled on world hunger. His early efforts centered on flooding. In 1965, he wrote two research papers on flooding and an article on the subject for *Climatology* magazine. In 1967, Kates took a three-year leave from Clark to direct the Bureau of Resource Assessment and Land Use Planning at the University of Dar es Salaam in Tanzania. After his return, he cowrote and coedited several books on drought, flooding, and the environment, which were published in the 1970s and 1980s.

Earned Prestigious MacArthur Prize Fellowship

Kates's research earned the kudos of several prestigious science organizations through the 1970s and 1980s. In 1975 he was elected to the National Academy of Sciences and in 1976 to the American Academy of Arts and Sciences. One of his most coveted awards came in 1981 when he received a five-year MacArthur Prize Fellowship.

Kates left Clark in 1986 to head the Alan Shawn Feinstein World Hunger Program at Brown University in Providence. During his six years at Brown, Kates was named a fellow of the American Association for the Advancement of Science in 1987 and received the prestigious National Medal of Science from United States President George Bush in 1991. Although he stepped down as program director in 1992, Kates has kept his links to Brown as an adjunct professor. He is also affiliated with Clark University as well as the College of the Atlantic near his home in Trenton, Maine.

Since his retirement from academia, Kates has embarked on several new projects. In 1993, he became the executive editor of *Environment* magazine. That same year he became president of the Association of American Geographers. His first book for lay readers is titled *The Jeremiah Experiment: Hope for a Sustainable World* and looks back on the doomsday forecasts of **Rachel Carson** and other post-World War II alarmists. "I think the Jeremiahs serve us well by alerting us to the problems," Kates said. "I don't always agree with their rhetoric. They usually underestimate the ability of technology."

As for his own pet cause, world hunger, Kates is cautiously optimistic. He pointed out that international relief agencies can stave off famines by bringing emergency food supplies to areas at risk. The famines in the 1990s have been caused primarily by leaders using hunger as a weapon against people. "We've almost licked famine," he said. "The only obstacle is war. Over the last 50 years, food production has outpaced population growth."

Kates devoted much of his time in 1993 to planning Overcoming Hunger in the 1990s's five-year anniversary meeting in Thailand scheduled for 1994. There, the members will take a close look at what they have achieved in five years and what must be done for them to reach their goals by the year 2000. After the meeting in 1994, Kates expects to put aside his hunger research of the last eight years and focus more on the environment. "I do a lot of future thinking," he said. "My central question is what ought to be the human use of the earth, and how can I tell others about it?"

SELECTED WRITINGS BY KATES:

Books

(Editor with Lucile F. Newman, William Crossgrove, Robley Matthews, and Sara Millman) *Hunger in History: Food Shortage, Poverty, and Deprivation,* Basil Blackwell, 1990.

(Editor with B.L. Turner II, William C. Clark, John F. Richards, Jessica T. Mathews, and William B. Meyer) *The Earth as Transformed by Human Action: Global and Regional Changes in the Biosphere Over the Past 300 Years,* Cambridge University Press, 1990.

Periodicals

"Where the Poor Live: Are the Assumptions Correct?," *Environment,* May, 1992, pp. 4–11, 25–28.

"Ending Deaths From Famine: The Opportunity in Somalia," *New England Journal of Medicine,* April 8, 1993, pp. 1055–1057.

SOURCES:

Periodicals

Little, Carl, "Faculty Associate Profile: Dr. Robert Kates, Renaissance Geographer," *COA News,* Fall, 1993, pp.7, 17.

Weisenthal, Debra Blake, "Hungry for Justice," *Vegetarian Times,* January, 1993, p. 20.

Other

Kates, Robert W., interview with Cynthia Washam conducted November 12, 1993.

—*Sketch by Cynthia Washam*

Tosio Kato
1917-
Japanese-born American mathematical physicist

Tosio Kato, whose career in mathematics ranged over more than forty years, made major contributions to the field of mathematical physics. A prolific writer, he produced hundreds of published articles during his career. His most important research, on perturbation theory, won him acclaim and awards in both his native country of Japan and in the United States, where he spent most of his career.

Kato was born on August 25, 1917, in Tochigiken, Japan, the son of Shoji and Shin (Sakamoto) Kato. He attended the University of Tokyo, where he received a bachelor's degree in 1941; he would receive a doctor of science degree from the university ten years later. In 1943, he began teaching at the University of Tokyo, and due to the stability this position provided he was able to marry Mizue Suzuki the following year.

Discovers Key Ideas behind Perturbation Theory

Even before his appointment to full professorship at the university, which he achieved upon receiving his doctorate in 1951, Kato had begun to publish the beginnings of his research in perturbation theory. Perturbation theory is the study of a system which deviates slightly from a less complex, ideal system. This is an important field of research because most systems that mathematicians and physicists study are not ideal. Kato examined only the perturbation theory which relates to linear operators (functions). The groundbreaking work in the field had been accomplished by John Rayleigh and **Erwin Schrödinger** in the 1920s.

Kato's contributions to perturbation theorywere threefold. First, he laid the mathematical foundation for the theory, applying ideas in modern analysis and function theory. Second, he established the selfadjointness of Schrödinger operators—in other words, he showed that Schrödinger operators are symmetric. This was significant because these operators are a fundamental tool of quantum physics and knowledge of their symmetry makes their manipulation much simpler. Finally, he began the study of the spectral properties of the operators, which describes the variety of simple effects which the operators can have when applied to specific elements of a given set. This is important as it allows the operators to be described in terms of many simple effects which can be combined into larger ones. The term *spectral* is related to the way in which a complicated operator splits into distinct effects, as light can be split into distinct colors.

The culmination of his work was his definitive book on the subject, *Perturbation Theory for Linear Operators,* which he began writing in Japan and completed in the United States, after accepting a professorship at the University of California at Berkeley in 1962. Although the book did not appear until 1966, his home country had already recognized him as a leading researcher in his field, presenting him with the Asahi Award in 1960.

In the United States, Kato continued his research into perturbation theory and used functional analysis to solve problems in hydrodynamics and evolution equations. Even though Kato was well known in the American mathematical community by his hundreds of published articles, acknowledgement of the importance of his work came late in the United States. It was not until 1980 that the American Mathematical Society and the Society for Industrial and Applied Mathematics jointly awarded him the Norbert Wiener Prize for applied mathematics. In Japan, Kato continued to receive recognition. On the occasion of his retirement from the University of California in 1989, the University of Tokyo held a conference in his honor. The conference, entitled "The International Conference on Functional Analysis in Honor of Professor Tosio Kato," paid homage to Kato's many contributions in the field of mathematical physics.

SELECTED WRITINGS BY KATO:

Books

Perturbation Theory for Linear Operators, Springer-Verlag, 1966.

A Short Introduction to Perturbation Theory for Linear Operators, Springer-Verlag, 1982.

Periodicals

"On the Convergence of the Perturbation Method, I, II," *Progressive Theories of Physics,* Volume 4, 1949, pp. 514–523.

SOURCES:

Books

Fujita, H., T. Ikebe, and S. T. Kuroda, editors, *Functional-Analytic Methods for Partial Differential Equations,* Springer-Verlag, 1980.

Periodicals

Notices of the American Mathematical Society, Volume 27, October 1980, pp. 528–529.

—Sketch by Karen Sands

Bernard Katz
1911-
German-born English physiologist

Renowned as a skilled experimentalist at a young age, Bernard Katz's research concerned the nature of nerve transmissions, especially those that cause the stimulation of muscles. He discovered the existence of tiny packages, or "quanta," of neurotransmitter molecules that are responsible for many neural phenomena. For this discovery, he was awarded a share of the 1970 Nobel Prize for Physiology or Medicine with biochemical pharmacologist **Julius Axelrod** and physiologist **Ulf von Euler**.

Katz was born in Leipzig, Germany, on March 26, 1911. His father was Max Katz and his mother, the former Eugenie Rabinowitz. He completed his high school education at Leipzig's Albert Gymnasium in 1929 and then embarked on a study of medicine at the University of Leipzig. In 1933, Katz was awarded the university's Siegfried Garten Prize for research in physiology. A year later he received his medical degree.

Katz's future prospects in Germany in 1934 were not promising. Adolf Hitler had been named chancellor of the German Reich a year earlier and had already begun his purge of Jewish intellectuals. Katz had no problem, therefore, in deciding that he had to leave his native land, and he was able to obtain a postdoctoral fellowship at the University of London. There he continued his physiological research under physiologist **Archibald Vivian Hill,** Nobel Prize winner in Physiology or Medicine in 1922 for his discovery of the thermodynamics of muscle activity.

As Katz was awarded his Ph.D. in physiology in 1938, the outbreak of war in Europe was imminent. He thought it wise to leave England for the relative safety of Australia where he became Beit Memorial Research Fellow at Sydney Hospital. In 1942, the war in the Pacific had also broke out, and Katz joined the Royal Australian Air Force, where he served as a radar officer. At the war's conclusion, he returned to London and joined the staff at University College, London. He was appointed assistant director of research in the Biophysics Research Unit and Henry Head Research Fellow in 1946. Four years later he became a Reader in Physiology and, in 1952, was chosen to be head of biophysics, a post he held until his retirement in 1978.

Katz first studied the nature of nerve transmissions in the early 1940s, in conjunction with physiologist **John C. Eccles** and neurophysiologist Stephen Kuffler. The problem on which this team worked was the mechanism by which neurons (nerve cells) stimulate muscle cells. At the time, it was still not clear whether this process was purely electrical or whether it involved a chemical component.

At University College in 1950, Katz began the work for which he was later awarded a Nobel Prize, the study of electrical and chemical changes at the end of a neuron. Some years earlier, physiologists and pharmacologists **Henry Hallett Dale** and **Otto Loewi** had demonstrated that neurons release the chemical acetylcholine at their terminal end. Acetylcholine eventually was recognized as the first of a group of chemical compounds known as neurotransmitters, a name that identifies their function of transmitting neural messages across the synapsis (the point at which a nervous impulse passes from one neuron to another or from a nerve to a muscle or other tissue) between cells. In the early 1950s, Katz made two important discoveries about the release of acetylcholine by neurons. First, he found that this release occurs continuously and spontaneously, even if the neuron is at rest, although at much lower levels than during excitation. Second, he discovered that acetylcholine is released in discrete particles that contain a few hundred or few thousand molecules of the chemical, but whose size is always some integral multiple of the smallest package observed. These "packets" of neurotransmitters are, then, similar to quanta of excitatory units. Some years later, these packets—now called vesicles—were actually observed within neurons by means of electron microscopy.

Working with a variety of associates, Katz continued to study the nature of nerve transmission within a neuron and between neurons. In 1967, for example, he and Ricardo Miledi found that the release of acetylcholine is mediated by a calcium ion. Two years later, he and his colleagues were able to show that the electrical potential at the terminal of an axon (the long tubular extension of the neuron cell body that transmits nerve impulses away from the cell body) can be precisely and quantitatively associated with the electrochemical potential of the number of acetylcholine molecules found within a vesicle. It was for these discoveries and his work on "the humoral transmitters in the nerve terminals and the mechanism for their storage, release, and inactivation" that he received a share of the 1970 Nobel Prize for Physiology or Medicine.

In addition to the Nobel Prize, Katz has been awarded the Baly Medal of the Royal College of Physicians and the Copley Medal of the Royal Society, both in 1967. He has also served as Herter Lecturer at Johns Hopkins University in 1958, Dunham Lecturer at Harvard in 1961, and Croonian Lecturer at the Royal Society, also in 1961. He was knighted by Queen Elizabeth II in 1969. Katz married the former Marguerite Penly in 1945. They have two sons.

SELECTED WRITINGS BY KATZ:

Books

Electrical Excitation of Nerve, Oxford University Press, 1939.

Nerve, Muscle, and Synapse, McGraw-Hill, 1966.

The Release of Neural Transmitter Substances, Liverpool University Press, 1969.

SOURCES:

Books

Nobel Prize Winners, H. W. Wilson, 1987, pp. 538–540.

—*Sketch by David E. Newton*

Donald L. Katz
1907-1989
American chemical engineer

Donald L. Katz was a distinguished chemical engineer as well as an expert in the field of petroleum technology and the underground storage of natural gas. He not only travelled the world as a consultant to many of the large petroleum companies but also spent more than fifty years of his life mentoring chemical engineers of the future. His many contributions were recognized in 1983 with the National Medal of Science.

Katz's main research interests were reservoir engineering, a discipline he established in 1936 that is concerned with the properties of crude oil and natural gas as well as sand, water and other underground substances; phase behavior, an area of reservoir engineering involving the classification of petroleum forms and the effects of production upon these; and hydrocarbon systems, the analytical study of the compounds of petroleum which determines their uses, from methane, ethane, propane, butane, to gasoline. Throughout his career Katz maintained a balance between university teaching and professional engineering practice, always seeking practical and socially beneficial engineering applications for his innovative research, while bringing real engineering problems into the classroom.

Donald LaVerne Katz, of German descent on both sides of his family, was born on August 1, 1907, in Jackson, Michigan, to Gottlieb and Lucy (Schnackenberg) Katz. His father died just eight years later. Although Katz's educational beginnings were humble he soon showed an aptitude for engineering, learning car mechanics, and plumbing at an early age. He developed an interest in the agricultural applications of chemistry and even found a seam of lime on the family farm, recognizing its potential as an alfalfa fertilizer. Katz was the only pupil in his grade throughout elementary school, where few children from his rural community expected to attend school beyond the eighth grade. However, Katz did go on to more structured academic environments and graduated from Jackson High School, where his principal noticed his academic excellence and encouraged him to enroll at the University of Michigan in Ann Arbor.

In order to attend the university Katz had to earn money for tuition, so he spent a year working at the Morrison Stamping Company in Jackson, then continued working part-time as a janitor in the civil engineer's office through his undergraduate years. In 1931 he received his bachelor of science degree in engineering from the University of Michigan. Staying on at Michigan as a graduate student, he earned a master's of science degree in 1932. Under the direction of George Granger Brown, Katz then completed his doctoral dissertation, *The Calculation of Vaporization of Petroleum Fractions,* in 1933, publishing it the same year. The day after receiving his Ph.D., Katz boarded a bus for Bartlesville, Oklahoma, to work as a research engineer for Phillips Petroleum Company. He remained in Bartlesville for three years.

Returns to University of Michigan

Katz returned to Ann Arbor in 1936 to accept a teaching position at the University of Michigan. It was an association that he would maintain and nurture even after his formal retirement from the university in 1977.

Between 1936 and 1966 Katz served as an associate professor and professor of chemical engineering, and acted as chairman of the Department of Chemical and Metallurgical Engineering from 1951 to 1962. During his tenure at the university, Katz would supervise more than fifty doctoral students. He also enjoyed a prolific writing career, publishing over 290 papers, including *The Movement of Water in Contact with Natural Gas, The Underground Storage of Fluids, Retrograde Condensation in Natural Gas Pipelines,* and *Compressed Air Storage.* Many of his papers resulted from collaborations with former students. Katz's most significant publication is 1959's *Handbook of Natural Gas Engineering* which established him as a world authority in this field. He became an innovator in the application of computers in engineering in the early 1950s with a three year nationwide project funded by the Ford Foundation. In 1966, Katz was appointed Distinguished Alfred Holmes White University Professor in chemical engineering at the University of Michigan, a distinction he continued to hold as an emeritus following his retirement in 1977.

While carrying out his duties at Michigan, Katz also served as a consultant for more than one hundred companies, including Phillips Petroleum, Oklahoma City Secondary Recovery Association, Michigan Consolidated Gas Company, Natural Gas Pipeline Company of America, Northern Indiana Public Service Company and the Northern Illinois Gas Company. He was a pioneer in researching the difficulties of engineering the underground storage of natural gas and the effectiveness of petroleum reservoirs. He directed research at the Wolverine Tube Company, a division of Calumet and Heela Company, Inc., and also spent time researching liquid metals. Katz's research in the area of heat transfer led in the 1950s to participation in projects at the Oak Ridge National Laboratory in Tennessee which explored the use of fan pipes in nuclear energy delivery; he also served on the advisory committee for chemical technology at Oak Ridge and contributed to the development of nuclear science, including work with graduate students on heat transfer in nuclear submarine power generation.

Consistent with his strong commitment to the national welfare, Katz served on a dozen public advisory committees during his career. In 1964 he was appointed chairman of the hazardous materials committee for the Merchant Marine Safety Office of the U.S. Coast Guard, a position he held for eight years. In this capacity Katz advised the Coast Guard on the safe transportation of petroleum products and other hazardous materials. In addition, Katz joined a Commerce Department committee on the elimination of lead from gasoline, and in 1975 he served on a prestigious subcommittee which recommended stack gas cleaning to reduce power plant sulphur emissions, which Katz was early to recognize as a cause of acid rain.

Katz was an active and respected member of numerous professional organizations, receiving a total of twenty-four honors and awards throughout his career. The Hanlon Award, presented to Katz by the Natural Gasoline Association of America in 1950, was one of the earliest and most prestigious awards he received. Additionally, he was given the John Franklin Carll Award by the Society of Petroleum Engineers and received the Founders Award from the American Institute of Chemical Engineers. Katz's accolades and honors continued with the establishment in 1971 of the Donald L. Katz Lectureship in Chemical Engineering at the University of Michigan. In recognition of Katz's service to the Coast Guard, Rear Admiral W. F. Rea III presented Katz with the Distinguished Public Service Award—the Coast Guard's highest civilian honor—upon his retirement from the hazardous materials committee in 1971. In May, 1983, Katz received the National Medal of Science from President Ronald Reagan for "solving many practical engineering problems by delving into a wide group of sciences and making their synergistic effects evident."

Katz married (Lila) Maxine Crull in September, 1932, and the couple had two children together, Marvin LaVerne and Linda Maxine. Katz enjoyed tracing his and Maxine's genealogy and wrote several books about both families. Maxine died in March, 1965, of cancer; Katz then married Elizabeth (Harwood) Correll of Ann Arbor in November, 1965. Betty, as she was called by family and friends, was a widow and active member of the community who had three sons: Richard, Steven and Jonathan. Katz died from cancer in 1989 at the age of eighty-one.

SELECTED WRITINGS BY KATZ:

Books

(With J. G. Knudsen) *Fluid Dynamics and Heat Transfer,* McGraw, 1958.

Handbook of Natural Gas Engineering, McGraw, 1959.

Engineering Concepts and Perspectives, Wiley, 1968.

Periodicals

"A Method of Estimating Oil and Gas Reserves," *Transactions of the Institution of Mining Engineers,* Volume 118, 1936, pp. 18–32.

(With K. H. Hackmuth) "Vaporization Equilibrium Constants in a Crude Oil, Natural Gas System," *Industrial and Engineering Chemistry,* Volume 29, 1937, pp. 1972–1977.

(With F. Kurata) "Retrograde Condensation," *Industrial and Engineering Chemistry,* Volume 32, 1940, pp. 817–827.

(With M. R. Tek) "Overview on Underground Storage of Natural Gas," *Journal of Petroleum Technology,* June, 1981, pp. 943–951.

"Overview of Phase Behavior in Oil and Gas Production," *Journal of Petroleum Technology,* June, 1983, pp. 1205–1214.

—Sketch by Amy M. Punke

Alan C. Kay
1940-
American computer scientist

Alan C. Kay has been called the father of the personal computer in acknowledgment of his many contributions to the field of personal computing. His concept of the Dynabook lap-top computer was the inspiration of Alto, a forerunner of the Apple and Macintosh computers. Kay also pioneered the use of icons and windows, and his invention of Smalltalk—a very high-level, object-oriented programming language—gave children and nonprogrammers a hitherto unprecedented degree of access to computing.

Kay was a founding member of the Xerox Palo Alto Research Center (PARC) in 1970, leaving ten years later to become chief scientist at Atari, Inc. He joined the Apple Computer Company in 1984 as an Apple Fellow, a title held by a select group of scientists chartered to explore technology for Apple's future. In 1987, he shared the ACM Software Systems Award with his former colleagues **Adele Goldberg** and Dan Ingalls.

Born in Springfield, Massachusetts, to Hector William Kay, a physiologist, and Kathrine Johnson Kay, an artist/musician, Kay grew up in Australia, Massachusetts, and New York, where he attended the Brooklyn Technical High School. After high school, Kay joined the Air Force, where he worked as a computer programmer. He received a bachelor's degree in mathematics and molecular biology from the University of Colorado at Boulder in 1966, and a Ph.D. in computer science from the University of Utah in 1969. Following a stint as an assistant professor at the University of Utah, Kay joined the Artificial Intelligence Project at Stanford University, where he served as a research associate and lecturer.

During his 10 years at Xerox PARC—especially during what has been called the golden years of PARC from 1971 to 1976 when Xerox granted an exceptional degree of freedom to a group of creative young computer scientists—Kay and his colleagues introduced many of the basic notions of personal computing. As principal scientist and head of the Learning Research Group, Kay was able to develop the idea, formed in the 1960s when he was a graduate student at the University of Utah, of a personal computer, about the size of a notebook, that would provide an individual with a tool for storing, manipulating and communicating information in many different forms.

The initial attempt to implement that vision occurred between 1967 and 1969, when Kay and Edward Cheadle designed a system called FLEX. It was the first personal computer to provide direct support for a programming language that included the use of graphics, as well as of simulation—the ability to dynamically model the interactions of objects and processes in a particular domain.

From Kay's point of view, however, FLEX was not sufficiently easy for non-programmers to use. That limitation led Kay and Cheadle to study the work of Seymour A. Papert, Wallace Feurzeig and others, who had developed a programming language called LOGO with children specifically in mind. Kay's subsequent work was strongly influenced by children, particularly by the way in which they learn and express themselves at different stages of development. In his attempt to capture in a programming language children's distinctive approaches to problem solving and understanding, Kay also drew on the psychological theories of Jean Piaget and of Jerome Bruner, who had distinguished specific phases in the intellectual growth of a child. Kay transposed the notion of developmental stages into that of successive levels of abstraction at which a user could represent a concept in a computer programming language.

At Xerox PARC, Kay and his colleagues integrated these ideas into an approach to personal computing that exploited a "multilane" interface between the user and the computer. Starting with a desktop unit with a removable disk memory of three million bytes (the equivalent of about 2,500 double-spaced pages of type), a high-resolution display and high-fidelity sound output, they added a variety of input devices. In addition to the standard keyboard, their experimental system had a mouse, a pencil-like pointer, a joystick, a microphone, a television camera, and an organ-like keyboard for entering music. The use of windows, a technique later to be widely used, provided the sense of multiple sheets of paper, allowing users to display information in a variety of ways simultaneously. Kay introduced the technique of overlapping windows by means of a mouse, and of temporarily collapsing a given window into a small rectangular box with a name or iconic identifier. It was the software, however, that provided the inspiration for the computer. Kay's high-level, interactive programming language called Smalltalk—whose design was influenced both by LOGO and by Simula, a language developed in the mid-1960s by Ole-Johan Dahl and Kristen Nygaard in Norway—was expressly created to allow novice computer users to write relatively advanced programs. Smalltalk is a so-called object-oriented language, in which the objects—called "activities"—replace the notions of data structures and procedures found in more traditional languages. The activities, which are grouped into families characterized by sets of "traits," or things that the activities can do, are the basis for every interaction in the system, all of which involve the exchange of messages between activities. Smalltalk was the first computer-programming language to be based wholly on the use of activities and messages.

Having worked with children throughout his career, Kay has devoted considerable attention to understanding the potential role computers can play in the learning process. In 1986, Kay and his colleague Ann Marion, in collaboration with the Open School: Center for Individualization, in Los Angeles, initiated a research project—the Apple Vivarium Program—aimed at discovering how computers can serve as "amplifiers for learning." They concluded that, as more powerful computers became increasingly prevalent and widely linked through networks, significant benefits for learning would arise. Through enhanced user interfaces, including virtual reality, students will be able to interact with, and experience, phenomena that are currently mere abstractions, such as the relativistic distortions of objects traveling near the speed of light. Multimedia, simulations and multiple windows will allow ideas to be presented in various formats and perspectives, as well as dynamically. Intelligent agents will assist learners by asking and answering questions and by bringing relevant information to their attention. Finally, networks will make accessible a vast, universal library, creating the potential for a transformation of culture as momentous as that of the Renaissance.

The role of musical interfaces in Kay's personal computers and the use of musical ideas and metaphors in his writings reflect the important position that music has occupied in Kay's life. In addition to having worked as a professional jazz musician, he has composed music, built a variety of musical instruments and maintained a professional membership—his only one—in the International Society of Organ Builders. For many years, he has traveled each summer to New Hampshire, where he plays chamber music at a music camp.

SELECTED WRITINGS BY KAY:

Periodicals

(With Adele Goldberg) "Personal Dynamic Media," *Computer,* March, 1977, pp. 31–41.

"Microelectronics and the Personal Computer," *Scientific American,* September, 1977, pp. 230–244.

"Computer Software," *Scientific American,* September, 1984, pp. 52–59.

"Computers, Networks and Education," *Scientific American,* September, 1991, pp. 138–148.

Other

"Doing with Images Makes Symbols: Communicating with Computers" (videocassette), Apple Computer, 1987.

SOURCES:

Periodicals

Davidson, Clive, "The Man Who Made Computers Personal," *New Scientist,* June 19, 1993, pp. 32–35.

—Sketch by Rowan L. Dordick

Arthur Keith
1866-1955
Scottish anatomist and physical anthropologist

A prominent anatomist and paleontologist during the late nineteenth and early twentieth centuries who may have been involved in the Piltdown hoax of 1912, Arthur Keith was born in Persley, Aberdeen, Scotland, on February 5, 1866, the fourth son of John Keith, a farmer, and Jessie Macpherson. He began his career as a physician, having received his bachelor of medicine degree in 1888 from the University of Aberdeen. While in Siam (Thailand) from 1889 to 1892, where he served as a physician to gold miners (many of whom were suffering from malaria), Keith took advantage of the opportunity to collect examples of the fauna for the botanical gardens at Kew, England, and also developed an interest in primate anatomy and the evolution of human racial types. After the failure of the mine, Keith returned to London, where he continued his studies of anatomy, specializing in primate musculature and receiving the Struthers prize in 1893. After receiving his M.D. in 1894, he became a lecturer in anatomy at London Hospital Medical School, where he remained until 1907. Keith wed Celia Gray in 1899, the same year he became head of the department of anatomy at the London Hospital.

During the early years of the twentieth century, Keith published several books, including two anatomy textbooks and a major monograph. During the remaining years of the decade, he specialized on malformations of the heart, and his work was of great significance to medical science, especially his description of the sinoatrial node, a tissue located in the right atrium that transmits the impulse that controls the beating of the heart.

Turning his attention to physical anthropology, Keith studied the development of early humans throughout Europe, North Africa, and at Mount Carmel, located in Israel. By the time he completed his research on Stone Age human remains in Palestine, he had become one of the leading authorities on human fossils, and he would be one of the teachers of English paleontologist and anthropologist **Louis Leakey**.

Begins Work in Human Evolution

Beginning in 1908, Keith served as the conservator of the Hunterian Museum of the Royal College of Surgeons in London, and was also a professor of physiology at the Royal Institution from 1918 to 1923. Although trained as an anatomist, Keith had long pursued an interest in human evolution, and this field became his major concentration. The study of human evolution at that time was primarily the search for the "missing link" between the early apes and modern man. The discovery of Neanderthal bones during the nineteenth century provided the first evidence of how ancient human origins actually were and scientifically challenged the belief, based on the calculations of Archbishop Ussher of Armagh, who grounded his work on biblical evidence, that humans were created in 4004 B.C., the date posited by many anti-evolutionists of the period. By the 1860s, fossil evidence had begun to sway some scientists' minds about the timetable of human origins, although there was no consensus about the age when humans developed; more than a hundred years later, there is still disagreement about the extent of human antiquity and the nature of the sequence in which this development took place.

It was at a time of fixed ideas and little physical evidence that Keith formulated his theories of human development, and his view changed as evidence accrued and research methods improved. He originally believed that the Neanderthals were the progenitors of modern humans and rejected the idea that earlier forms were related to humans. Taking large cranial capacity as the chief criterion for distinguishing humans from apes, he did not consider erect posture as significant, and therefore could eliminate the australopithecines (a genus of hominids, found in Africa, which had a semierect posture and a humanlike jaw structure but a small cranium) from consideration as early humans. In Keith's words, "the essential mark of man lies neither in his teeth nor in his postural adaptations, but in his brain," as Leakey quoted in his book *By the Evidence: Memoirs, 1932–1951.* Keith believed that humans had achieved bipedal locomotion much earlier than they had reached a modern cranial capacity—as early as the Pliocene, roughly five million years ago. He also held that there was a correlation between the ability to make tools and the ability to produce speech, that toolmaking was a step in the direction of the development of a larger brain capacity.

In the early part of his career, Keith subscribed to a linear view of human evolution, which held that humans had evolved in a series of progressive steps away from an original simian form. He believed that the earlier forms, pithecanthropus and the Neanderthals, were "the piers of a ruined bridge which once continuously connected the kingdom of man with the rest of the animal world," as Frank Spencer quoted in his study *Piltdown: A Scientific Forgery.* As further discoveries of early skeletal material were made throughout Europe, it became apparent that the remains of fully modern humans predated some Neanderthal remains. By 1912, the evidence was sufficient for Keith to make an abrupt change in his view: that there had been two parallel human forms, and that one had become extinct, possibly through the arrival of a more advanced form of human to the area. One of these bits of evidence was the so-called Piltdown man.

Many Europeans who accepted the possibility that human origins extended back to prehistoric times believed that humankind had originated in Europe. English paleontologists of the period thought that evidence would be found for the existence of prehistoric humans in England. This belief appeared to be justified by the announcement in late 1912 of the discovery, made by amateur paleontologist Charles Dawson and others, of fragments of a prehistoric human skull at Piltdown, England. The skull comprised what was apparently a humanlike brain case and a simianlike jaw. Although the discoverers conceded that the skull and the jaw probably did not come from the same individual, they proposed that they came from two examples of the same species, and they used fossils found nearby as evidence of the age of the fragments.

Interprets Piltdown Findings

Keith had reservations about the Piltdown jaw, which at that time was lacking its canine teeth. These teeth, which were crucial to the determination of the human nature of the jaw, were supposedly found, along with several other fragments, in 1913, the same year Keith was elected into the Royal Society. Keith's interpretation of the fragments was at odds in several respects with that of Dawson and others. The fragments as restored did not fit his predictions. Basing his conclusions on plaster casts of the fragments, he had predicted that the teeth would be similar to those of modern humans, but the newly found evidence was that the teeth were apelike. Keith also argued that the cranial capacity was similar to that of modern humans, assuming that, as in other early human skulls, the left and right sides would be almost equal, a view countered by several other scientists on the basis of the fragments. Later, Keith was willing to admit that the specialization of the hemispheres of the brain might have occurred early enough for the brain to have been asymmetrical and lowered his estimate of the cranial capacity of the Piltdown skull. He postulated a much earlier date for the fragments than did Dawson—the Pliocene rather than the Pleistocene, a little more than one and a half million years ago. He did not, however, question the authenticity of the fragments, and his presence at the 1912 public unveiling, given his stature in the scientific community, lent credence to the proceedings. In Keith's words, the discovery at Piltdown was "the most important [find] ever made in England, and of equal, if not of greater importance than any other yet made, either at home or abroad," as Spencer quoted.

Keith interpreted new findings in the light of his own theories, some of which were derived from the Piltdown evidence. For example, a skull found in 1924 in South Africa had originally been thought to be that of a prehistoric ape, but **Raymond A. Dart**, an anatomist at the University of the Witwatersrand, made the claim that the skull resembled a modern human's more than an ape's in the shape of its forehead, the position of the *foramen magnum* (the hole into which the spinal column enters the brain), the dentition (the development of teeth), and the shape of the jaw. Dart proposed assigning to the skull a new taxonomic label, *Australopithecus africanus,* a name that emphasized that this find pointed to an African origin of humankind.

Keith, who had been knighted in 1921, questioned Dart's interpretation, feeling that because the skull had come from an immature individual it was not possible to make a definitive identification. Also, he was not inclined to support evidence that suggested humans originated other than in Europe. Keith discounted Leakey's discoveries of early human remains in Kenya in 1932, concentrating instead on discoveries in Germany and England in 1935, which he used as additional data for refining his theories about the Piltdown man. As evidence began to pile up, however, Keith adjusted his position and admitted that the australopithecines of Africa were ancestral to modern humans, that modern forms were not as antiquated as he had supposed, and that he had overestimated the importance of the Piltdown remains.

In the decades after its discovery, numerous scientists had cast doubt on the authenticity of the Piltdown fragments, feeling that the apelike mandible could not have come from an individual with the cranial configuration of the rest of the skull. It was not until 1953 that, by means of analysis of the fluorine content of the fragments, the Piltdown man was proven to be a forgery, the combination of a human skull and an orangutan jawbone. There is still speculation about the identity of the forger, but Spencer has presented evidence that Keith himself conspired with Dawson to perpetrate the hoax in order to enhance his reputation by providing evidence for his own theories on the antiquity of humans, which had changed just at the time the Piltdown remains had been "discovered." Ronald Millar, in his book *The Piltdown Men,* has suggested that Keith's prestige had protected him from suspicion in the case.

For three years beginning in 1930, Keith was rector of the University of Aberdeen. He spent the last twenty-one years of his life as the master of a research institute founded by the Royal College and located in Downe, Kent, England. He also served as the honorary secretary of the Royal Institution, as the editor of the *Journal of Anatomy* from 1916 to 1936, and as president of the Royal Anthropological Institute, the Anatomical Society, and the British Association for the Advancement of Science. Keith died on January 7, 1955, in Downe, two years after the exposure of the Piltdown hoax.

SELECTED WRITINGS BY KEITH:

Books

Ancient Types of Men, [London], 1911.

Antiquity of Man, [London], 1915, second edition, two volumes, 1925.

A New Theory of Human Evolution, [London], 1927.

New Discoveries Relating to the Antiquity of Man, [London], 1931.

(With T. D. McCown) *The Stone Age of Mount Carmel: The Fossil Human Remains,* [Oxford], 1939.

An Autobiography, [London], 1950.

SOURCES:

Books

Biographical Memoirs of Fellows of the Royal Society, Volume 1, Royal Society (London), 1955, pp. 145–162.

Leakey, Louis, *By the Evidence: Memoirs, 1932–1951,* Harcourt, 1974.

Millar, Ronald, *The Piltdown Men,* St. Martin's, 1972.

Spencer, Frank, *Piltdown: A Scientific Forgery,* Oxford University Press, 1990.

Wiener, J. S, *The Piltdown Forgery,* Dover, 1980.

Periodicals

Brash, J. C., and A. J. E. Cave, "Sir Arthur Keith," *Journal of Anatomy,* Number 89, 1955, pp. 403–418.

—Sketch by Michael Sims

Frances Oldham Kelsey
1914-
Canadian-born American pharmacologist and physician

Frances Oldham Kelsey became nationally famous in 1962 when she prevented the sedative drug thalidomide from entering the United States. Thalidomide was found to have caused birth defects in 10,000 European children in the late 1950s and early 1960s. For preventing an American thalidomide tragedy, Kelsey was awarded the government's highest civilian award, the President's Distinguished Federal Civilian Service Award. Kelsey's vigilance led to the strengthening of investigational drug regulations, greater attention to the safety of drugs in pregnancy, and increased interest in research on teratology, the biological study of congenital deformities and abnormal development.

Kelsey was born in Cobble Hill, British Columbia, on July 24, 1914. In 1934, she received a bachelor's degree in science from McGill University in Montreal and attained a master's degree in science there in 1935. Kelsey received her professional degrees, a doctorate in pharmacology in 1938 and an M.D. in 1950, from the University of Chicago. She completed an internship at Sacred Heart Hospital in Yankton, South Dakota, in 1954 and was associate professor of pharmacology at the University of South Dakota from 1954 to 1957. She remained in South Dakota until 1960, and was in private practice there between 1957 and 1960. In 1955, Kelsey became a naturalized U.S. citizen. She had married F. Ellis Kelsey in 1943, and they had two children.

Studies Side Effects of Drugs on Children

Early in her career, Kelsey investigated the cause of 107 deaths, most of them in children, from a new sulfa drug. In the 1940s, she coauthored several papers with her husband on the metabolism of antimalarial drugs. In 1943, they published a study in the *Journal of Pharmacy and Experimental Therapy* about the effects of antimalarial drugs on the embryo. They found that the drug could be broken down by the liver of adult rabbits, but fetal livers could not break it down, and the drug could have deleterious effects. This research laid the groundwork for Kelsey's continuing interest in the safety of drugs during pregnancy.

Attains Pharmaceutical Regulatory Position

Kelsey's civil service career began in August, 1960, when she became a medical officer for the Food and Drug Administration (FDA). After one month on the job, Kelsey was asked to review what was expected to be a simple and routine marketing application for thalidomide. Thalidomide, a sleep inducer, had been developed in West Germany in the 1950s, and was widely marketed in Europe; belief in its safety was so widespread that the drug was available without prescription.

Kelsey soon became suspicious of the safety of thalidomide. In February, 1961, she read a letter from a doctor in the *British Medical Journal* suggesting an association between thalidomide and peripheral neuritis, a tingling sensation in the arms and legs of adult users. Kelsey promptly asked Richardson-Merrill, distributor of thalidomide, for additional animal study data and reports of all clinical trials of thalidomide to supplement the company's application for American approval. She later notified the company that she suspected thalidomide might have some effect on unborn children, although she did not yet suspect it as a cause of deformity. Throughout her review, Kelsey remained concerned that the company had failed to provide adequate data to demonstrate the safety of thalidomide.

In November, 1961, a German scientist alleged a strong association between use of the drug by pregnant women and an increase in deformed babies born in Germany. Finally, in December, 1961, the company acknowledged the German reports and requested that women of childbearing age discontinue its use. More than 10,000 cases of phocomelia, a condition causing underdevelopment or absence of arms and legs, in European children were eventually attributed to use of thalidomide. Seventeen cases of thalidomide embryopathy resulting from a then-legal experimental distribution of the drug were later documented in the United States.

Receives Top U.S. Award

On July 15, 1962, the *Washington Post* ran an article about Kelsey that began, "This is the story of how the skepticism and stubbornness of a government physician prevented what could have been an appalling American tragedy. . . ." A wave of publicity and acclaim swept the world. Only a month later, Congress voted to award a gold medal to Kelsey "in recognition of the distinguished service to mankind . . . by withholding, despite the great pressures brought to bear upon her, approval of the horror-drug thalidomide which has caused thousands of babies to be deformed." In October, 1962, with Kelsey present at the ceremony, President Kennedy signed a landmark drug law, the Kefauver-Harris Amendments. The law required drug manufacturers to register with the Food and Drug Administration proof that new drugs were both effective and safe, and provided for more rapid recall of new drugs deemed hazardous. In

1963, Kelsey became chief of the Investigational Drug Branch of the FDA, and in 1968 was appointed to her current position as director of the Office of Scientific Investigations.

SELECTED WRITINGS BY KELSEY:

Books

(With F. E. Kelsey and E. M. K. Geiling) *Essentials of Pharmacology,* Lippincott, 1947, 4th edition, 1960.

Periodicals

"Drug Embryopathy—the Thalidomide Story," *Maryland State Medical Journal,* December, 1963.

"Problems Raised for the FDA by the Occurrence of Thalidomide Embryopathy in Germany 1960–1961," *South Dakota Journal of Medicine and Pharmacy,* January, 1964.

"Drugs in Pregnancy," *Minnesota State Medical Association Journal,* February, 1965, pp. 175–180.

"Events After Thalidomide," *Journal of Dental Research,* Volume 46, 1967, pp. 1201–1205.

"Thalidomide Update: Regulatory Aspects," *Clinical Pharmacology and Therapeutics,* Volume 3, 1988, p. 3. "Good Clinical Practice in the U.S.: Impact of European Guidelines," *Drug Information Journal,* Volume 26, 1992, pp. 125–132.

SOURCES:

Books

Sjostrom, H., and R. Nilsson, *Thalidomide and the Power of the Drug Companies,* Penguin, 1972.

Periodicals

"Dr. Kelsey Will Receive a High Presidential Award," *New York Times,* August 12, 1962, p. 1.

"Drug Reform Bill is Signed at White House, With Dr. Kelsey Present," *New York Times,* October 11, 1962, p. 31.

Grigg, W., "The Thalidomide Tragedy—25 Years Ago," *FDA Consumer,* February, 1987, pp. 14–17.

Hunter, M., "Stiffer Drug Law Urged by Kennedy," *New York Times,* August 12, 1962, p. 1.

—*Sketch by Laura Newman*

John G. Kemeny
1926-1992
Hungarian-born American mathematician

John G. Kemeny, a mathematician and college president, pioneered "new math" and the use of computers in general education. As a teenager he worked with American mathematician **John von Neumann** on the United States Government's Manhattan Project and, as a graduate student, he was a research assistant for American physicist **Albert Einstein**. Working with **Thomas Eugene Kurtz**, a colleague at Dartmouth College, he coauthored the BASIC (Beginner's All-Purpose Symbolic Instruction Code) computer programming language. Though intended only for Dartmouth mathematics students, BASIC became the world's most well-known programming language.

John George Kemeny was born in Budapest, Hungary, on May 31, 1926, to Tibor and Lucy Kemeny. He lived in Budapest with his parents and sister until 1940, when his father, fearing an imminent German invasion, took his family to the United States. At the time, Kemeny spoke three languages, none of which were English. Nevertheless, when he graduated from high school in 1943, he led his class scholastically. He entered Princeton University, but his studies were interrupted in 1945, the year he became a naturalized American citizen, when he was drafted into the U.S. Army. Employed as a military computer (a person who did mathematical computations), he was assigned to the computing center of the theoretical division of the Manhattan Project in Los Alamos, New Mexico. His superior, von Neumann, was involved in calculating the blast characteristics of the atomic bomb in order to determine how to detonate it in the most effective way. After the war, Kemeny returned to Princeton, where he served as the president of the German Club and the Roundtable. He graduated at the top of his class in 1947. While pursuing his doctorate, which he received from Princeton in 1949, he worked as an assistant to the American mathematician **Alonzo Church** in mathematics research and to Einstein on the unified field theory. On November 5, 1950, Kemeny married Jean Alexander. They had two children, Jennifer and Robert.

Throughout his professional life, Kemeny was an enthusiastic educator. He joined the Princeton faculty as an instructor in mathematical logic immediately after earning his Ph.D. and was a teacher in one capacity or another for the rest of his life. He moved to Dartmouth College in 1953 and remained there until shortly before his death. As chair of the Dartmouth Department of Mathematics, Kemeny took steps to change the methods of education in math. He was a pioneer in doing away with courses based on drills and basic problem solving. He stressed the efficient use of reference materials, introduced first-year differential calculus, and developed Dartmouth's first doctoral program in mathematics.

Creates BASIC

With professor Thomas E. Kurtz, Kemeny developed a time-sharing scheme in the early 1960s to make computers available to Dartmouth students. Then, computers were large institutional machines, but they were becoming more common and it was clear that they had more uses than their original computational purpose. One of the problems with making computers available to students was that computers were only valuable to people who knew how to program them. At the time, it took months or years to learn how to program a computer in machine language, and the few higher-level languages available, such as FORTRAN, were not much better. A language that could be used by students was clearly needed.

To meet this need, Kemeny and Kurtz gradually developed BASIC. The first program written in BASIC ran on a time-shared GE 225 computer on May 1, 1964, at 4 A.M. (Computer time was valuable and had to be taken whenever available.) Since BASIC was initially developed for the use of Dartmouth students, and since the students had ready access to the authors in case of trouble, Kemeny and Kurtz were able to do a quick and thorough job of testing and modifying the language.

Neither Kemeny nor Kurtz intended BASIC for public use. It was meant for non-expert students, but was also designed so they could use it when they left the college. Never intending to profit from the invention, Kemeny and Kurtz put it in the public domain. Dartmouth copyrighted it but made it available at no cost.

BASIC had advantages over other available high-level languages. It was adaptable for general purposes and was easy for people with little computer or math background to learn. Because of this, it swiftly became the most popular programming language ever written. In 1965, General Electric adopted BASIC for its time-sharing system. The late 1960s and early 1970s saw a proliferation of computer time-sharing in education and BASIC was commonly the language of choice. When personal computers arrived, a host of BASIC versions were written by different developers, many of them inferior to the original and all violating the rules of structure that Kemeny and Kurtz had laid down. Disdainful of pretenders and alarmed at the effect the counterfeit languages were having on BASIC's industry reputation, Kemeny and Kurtz began work in 1983 on a new generation of BASIC, called True BASIC. They formed the company True BASIC, Inc., and began shipping copies on March, 1985. Through the company, Kemeny also developed other software packages for personal computers in high schools and colleges.

Presides over Dartmouth

Through his influence as a lecturer and officer of the Mathematical Association of America, Kemeny worked tirelessly to introduce "new math" in American public schools. In 1967, he resigned as chair of the Dartmouth Department of Mathematics to become Coordinator of Educational Plans and Development, in charge of revising the curriculum of the entire school. In 1970, he was elected president of the College. He placed as a condition on his accepting the presidency that he be allowed to continue teaching his classes in mathematics and philosophy.

Kemeny's political and ethical beliefs were always very close to the surface. He was deeply liberal and felt that Dartmouth should be reaching out to the community to a much greater degree than it did. In addition to making the College coeducational in 1972, he changed enrollment policies to ensure opportunities for minorities and poor students. He also involved himself with groups protesting the Vietnam War and other issues, suspending all academic activities at Dartmouth during the "strike week" that followed the shooting of students by National Guard troops at Kent State University.

Kemeny was popular with many students for his accessibility and his liberal policies. But many alumni, fond of Dartmouth's traditions, were shaken by Kemeny's turning the small men's school into a year-round coeducational university, in addition to his many smaller changes. When Kemeny did away with Dartmouth's Indian mascot, which he considered offensive, conservative alumni protested.

Kemeny's professional affiliations included memberships in the Association for Symbolic Logic, the American Philosophical Association, and the American Mathematical Society. He was also an associate editor of the *Journal of Mathematical Analysis and Applications.* In 1979, Kemeny was appointed by U.S. President Jimmy Carter to head the Federal commission that investigated the accident at the Three Mile Island nuclear power plant. The commission's report was highly critical of the nuclear power industry and its regulators. In 1981, he returned full-time to teaching, his first love, from which he retired in 1990. Kemeny died in Lebanon, New Hampshire, on December 26, 1992, at the age of 66.

SELECTED WRITINGS BY KEMENY:

Books

(With J. Laurie Snell and Gerald L. Thompson) *Introduction to Finite Mathematics,* Prentice-Hall, 1957.

A Philosopher Looks at Science, Van Nostrand, 1959.
Random Essays on Mathematics, Education, and Computers, Prentice-Hall, 1964.
Man and the Computer, Scribner, 1972.
(With Thomas E. Kurtz) *Back to BASIC: The History, Corruption, and Future of the Language,* Addison-Wesley, 1985.

Periodicals

"An Extremely Small Malfunction ... And Then Something Terrible Happened," *Dartmouth Alumni Magazine,* December, 1979, pp. 30–37.
"Saving American Democracy: The Lessons of Three Mile Island," *Technology Review,* June/July, 1980, p. 33.

SOURCES:

Books

Slater, Robert, *Portraits in Silicon,* MIT Press, 1987.

Periodicals

"True Basic," *Dartmouth Alumni Magazine,* May 1993, pp. 28–33.

—*Sketch by Joel Simon*

Edward C. Kendall
1886-1972
American biochemist

Edward C. Kendall is best remembered as a pioneer in the discovery and isolation of several important hormones. As a young scientist he isolated the hormone thyroxine from the thyroid glands of cattle; today, thyroxine is produced synthetically and used in the treatment of thyroid disorders. Later, he isolated six hormones produced by the adrenal cortex. One of these was cortisone, which proved to be a breakthrough in the treatment of rheumatoid arthritis. Kendall's work led to the 1950 Nobel Prize in medicine and physiology, which he shared with colleagues **Philip S. Hench** and **Tadeus Reichstein**.

Edward Calvin Kendall was born on March 8, 1886, in South Norwalk, Connecticut, the youngest of three children. His father, George Stanley Kendall, was a dentist, and his mother, Eva Frances (Abbott), was active with the Congregational Church. Kendall showed a curious nature early on, and when he entered Columbia University in 1904 he chose chemistry as his primary area of study. He earned his bachelor of science degree in 1908, his master's degree in 1909, and his Ph.D. in chemistry in 1910—all from Columbia.

Upon his graduation, he accepted a position with the pharmaceutical firm Parke, Davis, and Company in Detroit. He found the atmosphere stifling, however, because he had no opportunities for the kind of research he wanted to do. In his memoirs, *Cortisone: Memoirs of a Hormone Hunter,* he expressed his disdain for the rigid, controlled environment at Parke, Davis. As an example, he noted the company policy that all lab employees punch in and out on a time clock. "After working 18 hours a day for some weeks to finish my thesis," he recalled in his biography, "I could not accept the thought that my value to the company could be determined by the hours spent in the building."

Begins Groundbreaking Work on Thyroxine

After four months at Parke, Davis, Kendall left and returned to New York. He soon found a position at St. Luke's Hospital. It was at St. Luke's where Kendall began his work on isolating thyroxine. Nearly twenty years earlier, the German chemist Eugen Baumann had discovered high concentrations of iodine in the thyroid gland. Scientists were later able to obtain a protein called thyroglobulin; Kendall's aim was to isolate the active compound in this protein.

He was able to purify the protein, and early experiments with patients at St. Luke's proved successful. But while the physicians at St. Luke's were eager to find new ways to treat patients, their emphasis on actual research was not as strong as Kendall thought it should be. He left St. Luke's at the end of 1913 and headed west to the Mayo Clinic, where over the next four decades he did his most important work.

By the end of 1914, Kendall had isolated thyroxine. This breakthrough discovery eventually led to synthetic production of the substance, which in turn led to more effective treatment of thyroid disorders. For his work he was awarded the Chandler Prize by his alma mater in 1925. Kendall also isolated the peptide glutathione from yeast and determined its structure.

Now Kendall was ready to tackle the challenge of isolating hormones from the adrenal gland. During the 1930s he managed to isolate more than two dozen hormones, or corticoids (so called because they came from the cortex, or outer section, of the gland). The six most important hormones were each assigned a letter A through F. Compound E—cortisone—turned out to be the most significant of these.

Synthesizes Cortisone from Cattle Bile

Compound E was not easy to synthesize. Kendall worked for several years with a substance obtained from cattle bile and was finally successful in producing a small amount of the compound late in 1946. Kendall's research got a boost from the U.S. Government, which gave top medical priority to the investigation of cortisone during the Second World War. This was prompted in part by rumors (later proven untrue) that German scientists had been extracting adrenal gland extract from Argentine cattle and giving it to Nazi pilots to boost their strength (they were supposed to be able to fly planes at heights up to 40,000 feet). The U.S. Office of Scientific Research and Development (with which Kendall served as a civilian during the war) gave him support, and the pharmaceutical firm Merck and Company sent a scientist to help him complete the synthesis.

Research by Kendall's colleague Hench showed that cortisone might be useful in the treatment of rheumatoid arthritis. Actual experimentation with patients began in 1948, and the results were dramatic. Rheumatoid arthritis is a painful condition that causes severe pain and swelling in the joints; cortisone, though not a cure, was able to control the symptoms. It also controlled symptoms in some skin diseases and eye disorders. Reichstein, working independently of Kendall and Hench, also synthesized cortisone in Switzerland. It was for their work and research with cortisone that the three men were awarded the Nobel Prize. Kendall was also awarded several honorary degrees, including one from Columbia.

In 1951, Kendall accepted a position as visiting professor at Princeton University, where he remained for the rest of his life. Among his other awards were the American Public Health Association's Lasker Award and the American Medical Association's Scientific Achievement Award. He was a member of several organizations, and in addition to his book *Thyroxine* and his memoirs, he wrote articles for numerous scientific publications. He served as president of the American Society of Biological Chemists from 1925 to 1926 and the Endocrine Society from 1930 to 1931.

Kendall married Rebecca Kennedy in 1915 and had three sons and a daughter. All three of Kendall's sons died before their father passed away. Kendall himself died in Rahway, New Jersey, on May 4, 1972 and was buried in Rochester, Minnesota, home of the Mayo Clinic.

SELECTED WRITINGS BY KENDALL:

Books

Thyroxine, Chemical Catalog, 1929.
Cortisone: Memoirs of a Hormone Hunter, Macmillan, 1981.

SOURCES:

Books

Current Biography 1950, H. W. Wilson, 1950, pp. 292–294.
Nobel Prize Winners, H. W. Wilson, 1987, pp. 542–544.

Periodicals

New York Times, October 27, 1950, p. 1.

—*Sketch by George A. Milite*

Henry W. Kendall
1926-
American physicist

In awarding the 1990 Nobel Prize in physics to Henry W. Kendall, **Richard Taylor**, and **Jerome Friedman**, the Royal Swedish Academy of Sciences recognized the importance of the discovery of quarks. Building upon Nobel laureate **Ernest Rutherford**'s research into the structure of the atom, Kendall and his colleagues utilized the newly invented particle accelerator to explore the interior of protons and neutrons. Their results proposed that these components of atoms are composed of even smaller particles called quarks and that quarks are bound together by massless particles known as gluons.

Henry Way Kendall was born on December 9, 1926, in Boston, Massachusetts, the oldest of three children. His parents were Henry P. Kendall, a businessman, and Evelyn Way Kendall. Kendall completed his secondary education at the Deerfield Academy in western Massachusetts in 1945 and immediately entered the United States Merchant Marine Academy. He stayed at the academy one year before resigning in order to enroll at Amherst College in Amherst, Massachusetts.

Follows in Hofstadter's Footsteps at Stanford

Although he was interested in a wide variety of subjects, Kendall decided to major in mathematics and earned his bachelor of arts degree in 1950. He conducted his graduate work at the Massachusetts Institute of Technology and was awarded his Ph.D. in nuclear and atomic physics in 1954. After two years as a postdoctoral fellow at the Brookhaven National Laboratory on Long Island, Kendall was appointed a research associate in a group headed by **Robert Hofstadter** at Stanford University's High Energy Laboratory.

At Stanford Kendall met two other researchers, Richard Taylor and Jerome Friedman, with whom he collaborated over the next decade. Their first project was to follow up on research begun in the early 1950s by Hofstadter—research that had won Hofstadter the 1961 Nobel Prize in physics. Hofstadter's research involved the bombardment of various atomic nuclei with high energy electrons. By studying the way electrons were reflected, Hofstadter was able to determine the structure of the nuclei. He found that nuclei consist of a central core surrounded by two outer shells of particles called mesons.

The work begun by Kendall and his colleagues in 1956 was not expected to yield anything especially remarkable. They assumed that they might get a better look at the nucleus, but they would not obtain new qualitative results. This assumption proved true in their earliest experiments, but soon two new factors changed the situation. Kendall, Taylor, and Friedman had gained access to a new particle accelerator—the two-mile long, twenty billion electron volt linear accelerator (linac)—at Stanford. The Stanford linac gave the researchers a far more powerful electron-beam probe than Hofstadter had ever had.

Another factor that influenced their research was a suggestion by a Stanford colleague, James Bjorken, who proposed that the team study inelastic collisions as well as the elastic collisions on which the team had been concentrating. In an elastic collision, an incoming electron strikes an atomic nucleus and bounces off with no loss of energy. By focusing on this type of reaction, Kendall and his colleagues had improved the precision of Hofstadter's findings, but had made no new breakthroughs. In an inelastic collision, an incoming electron strikes a nucleus with enough force to blow it apart. Bjorken argued that inelastic collisions were really the best way to get a close look at the protons and neutrons that make up the nucleus.

Bjorken's Suggestion Leads to the Discovery of Quarks

Kendall and his associates redesigned their equipment to detect inelastic collisions and found that protons and neutrons are composed of tiny, apparently solid sub-particles. These sub-particles appeared to be the quarks that had been postulated a few years earlier by physicist **Murray Gell-Mann** as the fundamental particles of which matter is composed. The results of their studies were so revealing that the team was even able to identify other particles—later called gluons—that appear to hold quarks together within protons and neutrons.

When it was announced that the 1990 Nobel Prize in physics had been awarded to Kendall, Taylor, and Friedman, the decision was met with wide approval in the scientific community. **Burton Richter**, director of the Stanford Linear Accelerator Center, was quoted in *Science* as saying "the only question in my mind is, why did it take so long?"

Kendall was appointed assistant professor at MIT in 1961 and became a full professor of physics in 1967. During this decade, he commuted from coast to coast so that he could teach and conduct research at MIT as well as continue his long-term work on quarks at Stanford. Kendall has long been involved in efforts to engage scientists in the debate over how their discoveries and inventions should be used in society. He was a founding member of the Union for Concerned Scientists in 1969 and served as the organization's chairperson for many years. He has also been an active member and officer of the Arms Control Association and a member of the board of directors of *The Bulletin of the Atomic Scientists.*

SELECTED WRITINGS BY KENDALL:

Books

Energy Strategies, Union of Concerned Scientists, 1980.

Periodicals

"Observed Behavior of Highly Inelastic Electron-Proton Scattering," *Physical Review Letters,* Volume 23, 1969, p. 935.

SOURCES:

Periodicals

Sutton, Christine, "Nobel Trophy for the Hunters of the Quark," *New Scientist,* October 27, 1990, p. 14.

Waldrop, M. Mitchell, "Physics Nobel Honors the Discovery of Quarks," *Science,* October 26, 1990, pp. 508–509.

—Sketch by David E. Newton

John Kendrew
1917-
English physicist and biochemist

The decades following World War II saw an increase in using physical methods to solve biological problems, which led to a greatly increased knowledge of living systems. John Kendrew's contribution to this trend was formulating the first three-dimensional structure of the protein myoglobin by using X-ray crystallography. For this achievement he shared the 1962 Nobel Prize in chemistry with his colleague **Max Perutz**, who had done similar work with hemoglobin.

John Cowdery Kendrew was born in Oxford, England, on March 24, 1917, the only child of Wilfrid and Evelyn Sandberg Kendrew. His father was a lecturer in climatology, and his mother was an art historian; thus he was nurtured in an academic atmosphere. He attended the Dragon School in Oxford and finished his secondary schooling at Clifton College in Bristol. He matriculated at Trinity College, Cambridge, where he studied chemistry and graduated in 1939.

His academic career was interrupted by World War II, when he served with the Ministry of Aircraft Production. He worked for a time on radar, and then acted as scientific advisor to the Allied air commander in chief in Southeast Asia. While serving in Asia, Kendrew met physicist J. D. Bernal. Bernal was convinced that the intersection between biology and the physical sciences would soon be an important area of research, and this greatly influenced Kendrew's career path. On a side trip to California, Kendrew also met the American physical chemist **Linus Pauling**, whose protein work would later serve as a foundation for his own.

After the war Kendrew became a doctoral candidate at the Cavendish Laboratory at Cambridge where he met Perutz, who had once been a student of Bernal's. Together they worked under physicist **Lawrence Bragg**, who had helped establish the science of X-ray crystallography (a process that outlines a substance's atomic structure) in the early twentieth century. By 1947 Bragg had convinced the secretary of the medical research council that the government should finance the kind of work that Kendrew and Perutz were doing. A special unit for the study of the molecular structure of biological systems was founded for the two scientists, housed in an empty shed at Cambridge.

Research on Myoglobin Uses X-ray Methods

Kendrew's doctoral thesis dealt with the differences between fetal and adult sheep hemoglobin, a component of red blood cells that contains iron and assists with oxygen transport. The project gave him valuable experience in X-ray methods and a chance to work with proteins, which he came to regard as the most important class of biological molecules. After receiving his Ph.D. in 1949, Kendrew commenced research on the protein myoglobin. Myoglobin is the molecule that binds and transports oxygen in the muscles, and was readily available from whales. Perutz was already working on determining the structure of hemoglobin. At the time Kendrew started his research, little was known about myoglobin, except that it was a protein.

John Kendrew

The first problem Kendrew faced was to produce crystals of pure myoglobin. To do this, he planned to use X-ray crystallography, which required samples with regular crystal structures. The technique involved shining X rays through the crystal and observing on photographic paper the pattern of spots that leaves the crystal. The atoms in the crystal diffract the X rays through definite angles, concentrating them in patterns of bands or spots from which the scientist must calculate the kind of atomic arrangement that produced such a pattern.

Kendrew and his colleagues obtained their crystals and good X-ray pictures of them, but the pictures proved to be too complex to interpret. Fortunately, Perutz recalled a technique he had learned from Bernal in which a heavy metal atom bonded with a protein to serve as a marker so that the diffracted X rays could be sorted out. Kendrew, however, had to try a number of heavy metals before he could make interpretable pictures; in all he made well over ten-thousand images. When he finally had the laboratory data he wanted, he made his mathematical calculations of electron densities with a computer.

Even after Kendrew obtained his densities, a formidable problem remained. The densities had to be plotted for planar slices through the crystal at intervals of a few angstrom units (one ten-billionth of a meter), and the contours of electron density (like elevations on a topographical map) had to be determined. High density indicated an atom, and certain atoms (like nitrogen and oxygen) could be distinguished by the magnitude of their density. Since computers were not yet capable of these calculations, Kendrick's group had to do all the plotting by hand. They announced their findings in 1960, in the same issue of *Nature* in which Perutz published his preliminary findings on hemoglobin.

Clear Picture of Myoglobin Results in Nobel Prize

The myoglobin molecule proved to be a dense, lumpy structure. It had none of the beauty and regularity that molecular biologists **Francis Crick** and **James Watson** had found in their X-ray work on deoxyribonucleic acid (DNA), for which they received the Nobel Prize in medicine or physiology in 1962—the same year that Kendrew and Perutz were awarded the Nobel Prize in chemistry. One writer commented that the significance of Kendrew's work lay not in the new insights it provided, but in the fact that it could be done at all. Kendrew had risked analyzing a complex structure when many simpler ones had not yet been attempted, and he had succeeded.

Although Kendrew continued his work on the structure of myoglobin after receiving the Nobel Prize, he was increasingly drawn into administration and government advisory positions. The department Kendrew and Perutz created at Cambridge was now known as the Laboratory for Molecular Biology, and Kendrew acted as deputy chairman of the organization from its inception until 1974. The following year he established the European Molecular Biology Laboratory in Heidelberg, Germany, and served as its director until 1982. Earlier in his career he founded the *Journal of Molecular Biology* and acted as its editor-in-chief until 1987. From 1954 to 1968 he was a reader at the Davy-Faraday Laboratory of the Royal Institution, London, and from 1981 to 1987 he was president of St. John's College, Oxford. In addition, he has served as president of the International Organization of Pure and Applied Biophysics, and as both secretary general and president of the International Council of Scientific Unions.

Kendrew has been recognized for his achievements with many awards in addition to his Nobel Prize. He is an honorary fellow of Peterhouse, Cambridge, and St. John's, Oxford. He is also a fellow of the Royal Society, a foreign associate of the National Academy of Sciences in the United States, and a foreign honorary member of the American Academy of Arts and Sciences. He was knighted and given the Order of the British Empire in 1963. He is unmarried.

SELECTED WRITINGS BY KENDREW:

Books

The Thread of Life: An Introduction to Molecular Biology, Harvard University Press, 1966.

Periodicals

"The Three-Dimensional Structure of a Protein Molecule," *Scientific American,* Volume 205, 1961, pp. 96–110.

(With G. Bodo, H. M. Dintzis, R. G. Parrish, et al.) "A Three-Dimensional Model of the Myoglobin Molecule Obtained by X-Ray Analysis," *Nature,* Volume 181, 1961, pp. 662–666.

"Myoglobin and the Structure of Proteins (Nobel Address)," *Science,* Volume 139, 1963, pp. 1259–1266.

"How Molecular Biology Got Started," *Scientific American,* Volume 216, 1967, pp. 141–143.

SOURCES:

Books

Stryer, Lubert, *Biochemistry,* Freeman, 1988.

—*Sketch by Robert M. Hawthorne Jr.*

Charles Franklin Kettering
1876-1958
American engineer and inventor

Charles Franklin Kettering played a major role in the technological advances of the first half of the twentieth century. His research and inventions in the fields of electricity, power systems, and aircraft revolutionized entire industries. Kettering's genius was his ability to develop new technologies with practical applications. His curiosity expanded his research from industrial products into the domains of

Charles Franklin Kettering

plant life, refrigeration, education, and medicine. Kettering's success allowed him to become a generous philanthropist and avid proponent of educational reform in the latter portions of his life.

Kettering, the fourth of five children, was born to Jacob and Martha Hunter Kettering on August 29, 1876, near Loudonville, Ohio. His father ran the family farm and occasionally built barns. Kettering's mother was quiet and stern with an interest in music. Repeated eyesight problems and financial constraints forced Kettering to delay and interrupt his college education at Ohio State University. At one point, he worked in the fledgling telephone industry, whose undeveloped technology provided Kettering the freedom to develop innovative approaches to technological problems. His success stirred his interest in the possible uses of electricity and developed his abilities to spur those around him to assist him in his research.

Kettering developed a personal philosophy of scientific discovery and invention that was unusual in his day: he believed in trying to understand nature by simplifying engineering to fundamental characteristics and relationships. He combined this understanding with a conscious rejection of conventional wisdom and a liberal use of analogous reasoning. His experiments were designed and performed using a trial and error process, and produced slow, incremental, and typically productive results.

Innovates at National Cash Register

National Cash Register (NCR) hired Kettering in 1904 after he graduated from Ohio State University with an electrical engineering degree. His first assignment was to motorize NCR's manually-cranked cash registers. Kettering led a small team of inventors on a year-long journey through technological failures and corporate firings to produce an electric motor that could operate all of NCR's registers. Kettering's team endowed him with his lifelong nickname of "Boss Ket." In the summer of 1905, Kettering married Olive Williams. Their only child, Eugene, was born in 1908.

Kettering stayed at NCR for four years after the electric cash register motor project was completed. He developed a low-priced cash register powered by springs, a phone system linking clerks with the credit office within department stores, and the basis for a successful line of accounting machines.

Starts Delco

Kettering began discussing automobile engines with Edward Deeds, the vice president and general manager of NCR. By 1908, they had decided that reliable power required an ignition system with short, strong sparks instead of the continuous showers of weaker sparks then employed. In their spare time, they started experimenting with a new ignition system in Deeds's garage. In 1909, Kettering left NCR to concentrate on developing a new automobile ignition. Some of his former colleagues became so interested in his work that they volunteered to assist him in his efforts. When the prototype was successfully tested for the chief engineer of Cadillac, the car company's president, Henry Leland, ordered 5,000 ignition sets for his 1910 cars. Kettering and Deeds quickly formed a company, called Dayton Engineering Laboratories Company and known as Delco, to produce the ignitions. The prototype was far from ready for mass production and Kettering rushed to incorporate many refinements into the new ignition to make it ready for the 1910 Cadillacs.

Leland recognized Kettering's genius and assigned him to develop an electric starter to replace the crank used to start automobiles. Many other inventors, including the American **Thomas Alva Edison**, had tried unsuccessfully to develop a self-starter for the automobile. Kettering and his team discovered the correct electrical principle in their first day of experimenting. Their mechanism successfully started the Cadillac engine Leland had donated to the work in Deeds's garage, but the starter was too big to fit in a car. Kettering led marathon sessions to reduce the size of the starter in time for the 1912 line of Cadillacs. Kettering and Deed expanded Delco quickly to produce the self-starters and thereby help Leland and

Cadillac win an industry award for producing the first self-starting automobile.

Delco grew as Kettering improved the automobile components he had invented and experimented with new projects. One of his favorite projects during the early years of Delco was working on an electric lighting system for farms meant to replace kerosene lamps. Kettering had also been interested in the iceboxes used in most kitchens to keep food fresh and was considering how electricity might be used to keep ice frozen when he and Deeds sold Delco to United Motors in 1916.

Leads Research at General Motors

The American industrialist Alfred P. Sloan integrated United Motors with General Motors (GM) a few years after Kettering and Deeds sold Delco and convinced Kettering to lead research at GM from an isolated, well-funded research center near Dayton, Ohio. Kettering's first major opportunity as the head of research was to develop an automobile engine cooled by copper instead of water. He labored over the technology research and new car engine development. Three thousand vehicles were produced and sold in 1922, but the entire line was recalled and canceled because GM's chief engineers considered the engine too radical. By this time, Kettering had been promoted to vice president of GM and elected to the board of directors. The failure of the copper-cooled engine was a severe blow to Kettering; only Sloan's refusal to accept his resignation kept him at GM.

GM research under Kettering concentrated on technological improvements to existing systems that would benefit customers. Advancements were made in brake, gear, spring, and lighting systems, producing safer and more comfortable automobiles. Technological advancements in non-automotive systems were also discovered, such as the use of Freon in cooling systems to replace the toxic gas first used in refrigerators. Kettering strongly endorsed this customer-benefit approach to research and development.

Kettering directed the research to reduce the size of the diesel engine to fit trains and other, more portable uses. He was attracted to the diesel as a power source by its fuel economy and high power production. Kettering's desire to test smaller diesel engines under varied and demanding conditions inspired him to become a yachtsman, using his boats, the *Olive K* and *Olive K II,* as floating laboratories for his lightweight diesels. GM acquired two diesel engine manufacturers and presented their diesel engine at the Century of Progress in Chicago, Illinois, in 1933. The president of the Burlington Railroad was so impressed that he convinced Kettering to test GM's diesels in a lightweight passenger train. The successful non-stop run of the Pioneer Zephyr from Chicago to Denver, Colorado, on May 26, 1934, helped open the door to the next major improvement to the diesel engine. Kettering and GM's expertise allowed them to develop less-polluting diesel engines with increased power, economy, speed, and efficiency. Kettering passed the duty of designing further diesel improvements to his son, also a successful engine designer. GM produced the first diesel-powered freight locomotive in 1939.

One of Kettering's most widely used products is ethyl gasoline, which prevents car engines from knocking. Kettering started the ethyl research by borrowing a theory from his interest in photosynthesis in plants. Because the trailing arbutus plant stored sunlight in its red leaves, he reasoned that the color red could be an indicator of heat absorption. Kettering instructed his researcher to search for a color indicator of heat concentration and resulting knock during engine combustion. The subsequent research took over seven years and was interrupted by World War I, but in 1923 Ethyl Anti-Knock was launched. The next year, the top three finishers in the Indianapolis 500 auto race used the gasoline. In 1925, the new gasoline was withdrawn from the market due to health concerns, but it returned after two years of extensive testing by both federal and private agencies.

Applies Talents to Avocations

Kettering applied his talents for invention to his avocations as well as to his career. He became an avid pilot in the dawn of powered flight. Expanding his work for the government on an unmanned plane, Kettering developed the first practical retracting landing gear, new instrumentation, and improvements to wing structures. He also researched the ability of plants to produce energy with photosynthesis, wanting to find a way to mimic plants' use of solar energy in order to increase the food supply. This work, which started in his own greenhouse and later moved to Antioch College in Ohio, was driven by Kettering's belief that humans should become independent of plant life because of humanity's careless use of available resources.

Kettering's enormous success as a researcher and inventor made him a wealthy and well-known man. Throughout the latter portion of his life, Kettering used the rewards of his success to support numerous charitable causes and to promote his philosophies concerning education and innovation. In 1927, he founded the Charles Kettering Foundation for medical and photosynthesis research, and in 1945 he and Sloan founded the Sloan-Kettering Institute to research cancer in humans, built two years later in New York City as a state-of-the-art facility active in cancer research and treatment. Kettering supported wide-ranging educational reform to replace structured lessons with independent and cooperative learning and applied his leadership skills to support Antioch College for several decades. In 1952, the city of

Kettering, Ohio, named itself after its most famous resident.

In his later years, Kettering became very active as a speaker and advocate for the opportunities available through the use of innovative approaches and the need for continuous technological improvement. He stressed the need for industrial research laboratories and investment in technological advancement. Kettering was often honored for his achievements, including being elected the first president of the Thomas Alva Edison Foundation, winning the Horatio Alger Award in 1952 for personifying the American tradition of rising from rags to riches, and receiving almost forty honorary degrees. Although he retired as head of the GM Research Corporation in 1947, Kettering did not fully retire from research and development until after he turned 80. He remained active until he suffered a stroke while at a GM dinner. He died shortly thereafter on November 25, 1958, at his home near Dayton, Ohio.

SELECTED WRITINGS BY KETTERING:

Books

(With H. G. Bowen) *A Short History of Technology,* Thomas Alva Edison Foundation, 1952.

SOURCES:

Books

Boyd, T. A., *Professional Amateur: The Biography of Charles Franklin Kettering,* Dutton, 1957.
Boyd, T. A., editor, *Profit of Progress: The Speeches of Charles F. Kettering,* Dutton, 1961.
Lavin, S. A., *Kettering: Master Inventor,* Dodd Mead, 1960.
Leslie, Stuart W., *Boss Kettering: Wizard of General Motors,* Columbia University Press, 1983.
Zehnpfennig, Gladys, *Charles F. Kettering: Inventor and Idealist,* T. S. Desison & Co., 1962.

—*Sketch by David N. Ford*

Bernard Kettlewell
1907-1979
English geneticist and entomologist

Bernard Kettlewell is best known for his research on industrial melanism, or the effects of industrial pollution on pigmentation in insects, particularly moths and butterflies. He specialized in entomological fieldwork and made a significant contribution to the *Lepidoptera* collection at the British Museum of Natural History. Kettlewell's work on industrial melanism at Oxford in the 1950s was considered to be the first rigorous scientific study to confirm Charles Darwin's theory of natural selection.

Henry Bernard Davis Kettlewell was born in Howden, Yorkshire, on February 24, 1907, to Kate (Davis) and Henry Kettlewell, a member of the British Corn Exchange. He attended the prestigious Charterhouse public school from 1920 to 1924, spent a year studying in Paris, then enrolled at Caius College, Cambridge University, in 1926 to study medicine and zoology. He accepted appointments at several hospitals in England, including St. Bartholomew's in London and St. Luke's in Guildford, where he served for a short time as an anesthetist. After receiving his medical degree in 1935, Kettlewell established a general practice in the town of Cranleigh, Surrey. A year later he married Hazel Margaret Wiltshire, with whom he had two children. Kettlewell left his medical practice at the onset of World War II, when he was assigned to Woking War Hospital.

Following the war, the British government instituted the National Health Service program, which significantly changed the profession of medicine in England. Kettlewell left medicine at that time to pursue his lifelong hobby, entomological fieldwork, in a professional capacity. In 1949 he accepted a research appointment at the International Locust Control Center at Cape Town University in South Africa. While in Africa, Kettlewell pursued his passion for fieldwork by making scientific expeditions throughout the continent, including Mozambique, Zaire, the Knysna Forest, and the Kalahari Desert. He was awarded a Nuffield Research Fellowship at Oxford University and returned to England in 1952. Two years later he was appointed senior research officer in the zoology department at Oxford, where he was to perform his most celebrated experiments—those dealing with industrial melanism. Over a span of two decades, Kettlewell worked with a small research team in the laboratory of his good friend Edmund Brisco Ford to link the world of the field naturalist with that of professional biology.

Long before Kettlewell's research in England, animals indigenous to regions subject to industrial pollution were known to exhibit darker coloration as time passed. More than seventy species of moths, for example, had darkened in color since the onset of the Industrial Revolution in Britain. This phenomenon was often interpreted as evidence that the polluting chemicals themselves were darkening, or melanizing, the animals. Moreover, those scientists who suspected that the melanization was actually a result of natural selection could not demonstrate a mechanism by which the animals were being selected.

Kettlewell's work was significant because he discovered, and captured on film, the process of selection at work in the peppered moth, *Biston betularia.* The peppered moths—and all moths subject to industrial melanization—were active at night, resting motionless on tree trunks during the day. In nonindustrial regions, the peppered moth was usually white with black spots and was well camouflaged against the pale, lichen-covered surfaces of most tree trunks. In industrial areas, Kettlewell found that the soot from the factories killed the lichens and darkened the tree trunks. In this environment, the light-colored moth was no longer protected by its coloration and was subject to bird predation. The dark form of the peppered moth, quite rare before industrialization, became the new beneficiary of camouflage and flourished with its selective advantage. Kettlewell concluded that in polluted areas, twice as many black moths as pale moths survived, and that in unpolluted areas, the opposite was true. He strengthened his case by producing film footage of birds eating the conspicuous moths.

In his later research, Kettlewell developed more sophisticated experiments concerning the evolution of dominance in inherited characteristics and the creation of new species. The centerpiece of his work remained *Lepidoptera,* moths and butterflies, and he was one of the primary contributors of specimens to the British Museum of Natural History's Rothschild-Cockayne-Kettlewell collection. In addition to this contribution to evolutionary biology, Kettlewell's research also led to several advancements in the methods of entomology. For example, Kettlewell developed new techniques for radioactive labelling of insects for purposes of identification, through which he was once able to demonstrate that a moth captured in his yard had migrated from North Africa by determining that it had flown through a French nuclear test site.

Kettlewell's research was particularly embraced in the Communist Bloc, and he received the Soviet Union's Darwin Medal in 1959, as well as Czechoslovakia's Mendel Medal in 1965. He retired in 1974 and was awarded an honorary degree from Oxford University the following year. Renowned for his ability to turn enthusiasm for field research into progress in evolutionary science, Kettlewell was praised in *Antenna* by geneticist Cyril A. Clarke as "by far the best field-worker cum scientist of his generation." Kettlewell died in 1979.

SELECTED WRITINGS BY KETTLEWELL:

Books

The Evolution of Melanism: The Study of a Recurring Necessity, Clarendon Press, 1973.

Periodicals

"Selection Experiments on Industrial Melanism in the Lepidoptera," *Heredity,* Volume 9, 1955, pp. 323–342.

"Darwin's Missing Evidence," *Scientific American,* March, 1959, pp. 48–53.

SOURCES:

Books

Dictionary of Scientific Biography, Volume 17, Scribner, 1981, pp. 469–471.

Ford, E. B., *Ecological Genetics,* Methuen, 1964.

Periodicals

Clark, Cyril A., "Henry Bernard Davis Kettlewell, 1907–1979," *Antenna,* Volume 3, No. 4, 1979, p. 125.

Ford, E. B., "H. B. D. Kettlewell," *Nature,* September 13, 1979, p. 166.

—*Sketch by G. Scott Crawford*

Har Gobind Khorana
1922-
Indian-born American biochemist

Har Gobind Khorana is considered a major contributor to the science of genetics. In addition to developing a relatively inexpensive method of synthesizing acetyl coenzyme A, a complex molecule used in biochemical research, he succeeded in cracking the genetic code of yeast by synthesizing parts of a nucleic acid molecule—an achievement for which he shared the Nobel Prize for physiology or medicine. Khorana went on to do other significant work,

Har Gobind Khorana

including the synthesis of the first completely artificial gene.

Khorana was born around January 9, 1922 in the small village of Raipur, India (now a part of West Pakistan), the youngest of five children of Ganpat Rai Khorana, a tax collector for the British colonial government, and Krishna (Devi) Khorana. His family, although poor, was one of the few literate families in his village. He received his early education under a tree in outdoor classes conducted by the village teacher, and went on to attend high school in Multan, Punjab (India). He later studied chemistry on a government scholarship at the Punjab University in Lahore, graduating with honors in 1943 and receiving a Masters of Science with honors in 1945.

After obtaining his M.S., Khorana went to the University of Liverpool on a Government of India Fellowship to study organic chemistry; there he earned a Ph.D. in 1948 for his research on the structure of the bacterial pigment violacein. From England, Khorana went to Zurich, Switzerland as a postdoctoral fellow to study certain alkaloids (organic bases) under the tutelage of **Vladimir Prelog**, and after a brief visit to India in 1949, returned to England. From 1950 to 1952, Khorana worked at Cambridge University under Sir **Alexander Todd**, who later received the Nobel Prize for his work with nucleic acids (large molecules in the nucleus of the cell). While working with Todd, Khorana, too, became interested in the biochemistry of nucleic acids.

Achieves International Recognition

In 1952, Khorana took a position as director of the British Columbia Research Council's Organic Chemistry Section, located at the University of British Columbia in Vancouver. There he made his first contribution to the field of biochemistry when he and a colleague, John G. Moffat, announced in 1959 that they had developed a process for synthesizing acetyl coenzyme A, an essential molecule in the biochemical processing of proteins, fats and carbohydrates within the human body. A complex structure, this coenzyme had previously been available only by an astronomically expensive method of isolating the compound from yeast. Moffat and Khorana were able to synthesize acetyl coenzyme A relatively cheaply, thereby making it widely available for research. This work gave Khorana international recognition within the scientific community.

In 1960, Khorana moved to the University of Wisconsin in Madison to accept a position as co-director of the Institute for Enzyme Research. He became a professor of biochemistry in 1962, and in 1964 was named to the Conrad A. Elvelijem Professorship of the life sciences. Khorana then began focusing his research on genetics—specifically, on the biochemistry of nucleic acids, the biosynthesis of enzymes, and on deciphering the genetic code.

At the time Khorana began his research in genetics, scientists already knew much about genes and how they determine heredity. They had discovered that genes are located on chromosomes in the cell nucleus, and that genes are made of deoxyribonucleic acid (DNA), a nucleic acid which controls the biochemical processes of the cell and governs an organism's inherited traits. DNA's double-helix shape resembles a spiral staircase with regularly spaced steps, with each step consisting of a pair of chemical compounds called nucleotides. The four different types of nucleotides are arranged on the staircase in a pattern of heredity-carrying code "words."

To decipher this code, scientists needed to learn how those words were translated into a second "alphabet" consisting of 20 types of amino acids, the building blocks of protein. Part of this translation had been accomplished prior to Khorana's work. The DNA in the nucleus of a cell causes another nucleic acid called messenger ribonucleic acid (mRNA) to be produced; the messenger RNA then attaches itself to ribosomes, where the cell's proteins are produced. Another type of RNA, called transfer RNA, transports loose amino acids to the ribosomes, where messenger RNA uses them to construct proteins.

Scientists knew that the code word on each transfer RNA molecule indicated the kind of amino acid it would deliver, and instructed it to take it only to a complimentary messenger RNA. They had also figured out that there were 64 possible combinations of nucleotides, each with its own signal. What they did not know was which nucleotide word called for which amino acid.

In 1961, Dr. **Marshall Warren Nirenberg** of the National Institutes of Health successfully decoded most of the messages in the nucleotides. Khorana carried Nirenberg's work even further, adding significant details. In 1964 he synthesized parts of the nucleic acid molecule, and later was able to duplicate each of the 64 possible genetic words in the DNA staircase. He was able to map out the exact order of the nucleotides, and showed that the code is always transmitted by three-letter words. He also learned that certain nucleotides order the cell to start or stop making proteins.

Khorana's research was based in part on work done separately by both Nirenberg and **Robert W. Holley** of Cornell University, who completed the first delineation of a complete nucleic acid molecule in 1966. For their contributions to deciphering the genetic code, these three scientists were awarded the 1968 Nobel Prize for Physiology or Medicine. At the presentation ceremony, the three were commended for having "written the most exciting chapter in modern biology."

Two years later, Khorana made another contribution to the field of genetics when he and his colleagues succeeded in synthesizing the first artificial DNA gene of yeast. Khorana announced his achievement in a characteristically modest way, by informing a small symposium of biochemists at the University of Wisconsin in June 1970. He also announced that he and most of his research team would move to the Massachusetts Institute of Technology in the fall. As he explained to a friend, "You stay intellectually alive longer if you change your environment every so often." Khorana joined MIT's faculty as the Alfred P. Sloan Professor of Biology and Chemistry.

Khorana's accomplishments in the laboratory include the artificial synthesis of another gene found in *Escherichia coli,* an intestinal bacteria known commonly as E. coli. Outside the laboratory, his professional activities include membership in several scientific societies, including the National Academy of Sciences and the American Academy of Arts and Sciences. He also served on the editorial board of the *Journal of the American Chemical Society* for many years, and published more than 200 articles on technical subjects in that journal and other professional publications.

Khorana has received numerous accolades in addition to the Nobel Prize, including the Lasker Award and the American Chemical Society award. He also was awarded an honorary doctorate by the University of Chicago, and he was named a fellow by Churchill College in Cambridge, England. Khorana also has been a visiting professor at Rockefeller University and Stanford University, and has given lectures at numerous scientific meetings.

Khorana married Esther Elizabeth Sibler in 1952. The couple has two daughters, Julia Elizabeth and Emily Anne, and one son, Dave Roy. Khorana became an American citizen in 1966. Extremely committed to his work, he seldom takes time off, and once went 12 years without taking a vacation. He takes daily long walks, carrying with him an index card to record any ideas that might come to him. He also enjoys going on hikes and listening to music.

SELECTED WRITINGS BY KHORANA:

Books

Some Recent Developments in the Chemistry of Phosphate Esters of Biological Interest, Wiley & Sons, 1961.

SOURCES:

Books

Current Biography Yearbook, H. W. Wilson, 1970, pp. 222–24.

Nobel Prize Winners, H. W. Wilson, 1987, pp. 546–48.

Periodicals

New York Times, October 17, 1968, p. 41.

Time, October 25, 1968, pp. 84–85.

Washington Post, June 8, 1970.

—*Sketch by Donna Olshansky*

Gurdev S. Khush
1935-
Indian plant geneticist

Gurdev S. Khush is a geneticist and plant breeder whose agricultural research has culminated in the development of over two hundred high-yielding varieties of rice. Large scale adoption of his improved-yield varieties played a major role in doubling world rice production between 1966 and 1990. Continuing with his research in agriculture, Khush holds the positions of principle plant breeder and head of the division of plant breeding, genetics, and biochemistry for the International Rice Research Institute (IRRI) in Manila, Philippines.

Khush was born on August 22, 1935, in Rurki, Punjab, India, to a family of subsistence farmers. With no electricity, roads, modern irrigation system, motorized farm equipment, or help from chemical fertilizers, he and his family struggled to produce food. Khush's childhood experience with primitive farming practices and his attendant poverty motivated him to choose a career in agriculture. A hard-working and able student, he graduated at the top of his class in 1951 and won a scholarship to the Government Agriculture College in Ludhiana, from which he received his B.Sc. with highest honors in 1955. Borrowing money for an airline ticket, he went to England to work for eighteen months in a factory, earning enough money to repay his airfare and buy another ticket, this time to the United States. In 1957, he entered graduate school at the University of California, Davis, receiving his Ph.D. in genetics in 1960. Khush obtained a research appointment at Davis that same year and began collaborating with geneticist Charles M. Rick on a project aimed at understanding the genetics of tomatoes. As an off-shoot of his work, he wrote a text called *Cytogenetics of Aneuploids,* now considered the authoritative reference work on the subject and used in many advanced genetics courses. In 1961, Khush married Harwant Kaur Grewal, with whom he has a son and three daughters.

In 1967, Khush accepted an invitation to join the research staff of IRRI, with which he has remained affiliated throughout his career, spearheading efforts to improve existing varieties of rice. Since beginning his involvement with the IRRI, Khush has succeeded in modifying various strains of rice, allowing them to grow more rapidly and respond more readily to chemical fertilizers. In addition, his work in genetics has led to the identification of genes that improve a plant's disease and insect resistance. Because of the improvements realized through Khush's agricultural research, his work is considered a cornerstone of the Green Revolution, a transformation in farming practices undertaken in recent decades that has dramatically increased world food production.

Khush has published over a hundred professional articles about agriculture and serves on the editorial boards of five international journals. He has received numerous awards for his contributions to the Green Revolution, including the Borlaug Award in 1977, the Japan Prize in 1987, the Fellows Award of the American Society of Agronomy in 1989, and the Emil M. Mrak Award from the University of California, Davis, in 1990. He received an honorary doctorate from Punjab Agricultural University in 1987.

SELECTED WRITINGS BY KHUSH:

Books

Cytogenetics of Aneuploids, Academic Press, 1973.

Periodicals

"Rice Breeding: Past, Present, and Future," *Journal of Genetics,* Volume 66, 1987, pp. 195–216.

—*Sketch by Leslie Reinherz*

Thomas M. Kilburn
1921-
English computer scientist

Thomas M. Kilburn was one of the leading contributors to the development of computers in Britain in the period following World War II. At Manchester University, where he spent most of his career, he played a key role in the development of the cathode-ray tube memory. (A cathode ray is the glowing beam that appears when an electrical discharge is passed through a gas under very low pressure in a tube.) Kilburn also was instrumental in developing one of the first stored-program computers, as well as in producing a series of other computers. In addition, he helped establish the institution's department of computer science.

Kilburn was born on August 11, 1921, in the Yorkshire town of Dewsbury, England, where his father had risen from a clerk to general secretary at a large woolen firm. Though neither of his parents had attended a university, both encouraged the young Kilburn to continue his studies at the graduate level. Kilburn's penchant for mathematics—a subject he studied almost exclusively between the ages of fourteen and eighteen at the local grammar school (the rough equivalent of an American public high school), gained him entrance to Cambridge University as an open scholar in 1939, just at the onset of World War II.

As a member of the air squadron at Cambridge, Kilburn hoped to serve as a pilot in the Royal Air Force after graduation; however, after receiving his B.A. in mathematics in 1942, he was recruited by C. P. Snow to work on a secret wartime project. Upon completion of several short courses on electricity, magnetism, and electronics, Kilburn was ordered to report to the Telecommunications Research Establishment (TRE) at Malvern, England, where he was assigned to a group headed by British electrical engineer **Frederic C. Williams**. Kilburn admits that he had no interest—and no experience—in radios or electronic equipment before his crash courses in the subject in the spring and summer of 1942. Yet he proved a fast learner. After about six months at TRE, as a result of the rapidity with which he constructed a large electronic circuit, Williams began to view him as a valuable addition to the group, whose mission, Kilburn discovered, was to supply circuitry for radar equipment as well as to diagnose equipment failures.

Helps to Develop Cathode-Ray Tube Memory

Kilburn completed his master's degree in mathematics at Cambridge in 1944. Two years later, in July of 1946, M. H. A. Newman, who had been the leader during World War II of the group that developed the Colossi code-breaking computers, set up the Royal Society Computing Machine Laboratory at the University of Manchester. In December, Williams was appointed as the university's Edwards Stocks Massey chair of Electro-Technics, and he, in turn, recruited Kilburn. Kilburn's introduction to digital computing had come in early 1945, when he first learned about the development of mercury-delay lines, one of the earliest forms of computer memory technologies. His first notable accomplishment, however, was his collaboration with Williams on another type of memory device—one that used an electron beam to store electric charges in very localized regions on the phosphor-coated inner surface of a cathode-ray tube (CRT). An early data storage system for electronic digital computers, the device was a significant development at the time since it allowed electronic computers to access data in memory randomly instead of serially, which made for much faster data retrieval. Though the device has come to be called a Williams tube, both men agreed it was a joint invention. Specifically, Williams came up with the idea of using a CRT as a digital memory, while Kilburn discovered a way of writing and reading data that led to its becoming a practical device. By the fall of 1947, Williams and Kilburn were able to store 2,048 digits on a single CRT, and Newman explained to them what sort of computer might be build around it. In December of 1947, Kilburn wrote a report describing the CRT memory and the hypothetical computer in which it would first be used.

Builds Stored-Program Computer

The ability of a computer to store and operate on both data and instructions (the program) in the same way and to modify its stored instructions during the course of a computation are the essential features of a stored-program computer. Both the origin of the concept and the designation of the machine that deserves the title of being the first stored-program computer are still the subject of historical debate. One of the stronger claimants to that title is a computer built at Manchester University, mainly by Kilburn, in large part to test the CRT memory. Known as the "baby machine"—because it was first of four versions of a machine called the Mark I—it became operational on June 21, 1948. Though it solved several small problems, including the calculation of the highest factor of an integer, the small size of its memory prevented it from being applied to realistic problems.

The Mark I was produced in February of 1951 by a firm called Ferranti Ltd., which was located near Manchester University and with which Williams and Kilburn had worked on radar during the war. Between the baby machine and the production Mark I, Kilburn and his collaborators produced two prototypes: the "improved machine" and the "large-scale machine." These prototype machines featured enlarged CRT memories, which were supplemented by magnetic drum storage. The improved machine contained an innovation—due to Kilburn, Newman, Williams, and Geoff C. Toothill, who had joined the department in 1947—that made use of a third CRT memory, which they called a B-tube because it complemented the A and C tubes used for the arithmetic and control registers. The B-tube provided an additional control register that made it possible to keep track of a program when it carried out a subroutine. They are now found in all computers and are known as index registers.

By 1953, Kilburn had completed both a Ph.D. and D.Sc. in computer research from Manchester University and had taken over from Williams the direction of the computer projects at the university. In addition, Kilburn continued the association with Ferranti, which led to a number of commercial computers, notably the "Greek" series of machines with such names as Mercury, Pegasus, and Orion. In 1956, a team headed by Kilburn started designing a powerful computer; by 1959 the computer had come to be called Atlas and was jointly developed with Ferranti. Atlas pioneered a number of hardware and software operating system concepts, including a virtual memory scheme, multiprogramming, and paging, and was one of, if not the most, powerful computers in the world on its inauguration in December of 1962. While Manchester University's role in computer innovation was overtaken at the end of the 1960s by advances being made elsewhere, primarily in the United States, an innovative computer called MU5, built by Kilburn and his team in the late 1960s and early 1970s, greatly influenced the development of the ICL 2900 series produced by International Computers Ltd.

Starts Computer Science Department

Kilburn was the first research student at Manchester University in what was called the Computer

Group, and he was named professor of computer engineering in the early 1960s, thus becoming the holder of the first formal academic position in computing in the United Kingdom. Four years later, the Computer Group evolved into a full-fledged computer science department—the first in the United Kingdom. Kilburn remained at the institution until 1981, when he became professor emeritus.

The recipient of numerous honors and awards, Kilburn was named a fellow of the Royal Society in 1965, and also received the organization's Royal Medal in 1978. He was named a foreign associate of the U.S. National Academy of Engineering in 1980, and was presented with the Computer Pioneer Award of the Institute of Electrical and Electronics Engineers (IEEE) Computer Society in 1981 and the Eckert-Mauchly Award of the Association for Computing Machinery (ACM)/IEEE Computer Society two years later. He has contributed papers on computer design to publications, including *Proceedings of the IEEE.*

SELECTED WRITINGS BY KILBURN:

Books

A Storage System for Use with Binary Digital Computing Machines, University of Manchester, 1947, reprinted, 1978.

Periodicals

(With F. C. Williams) "Electronic Digital Computers," 1948, reprinted in *Origins of Digital Computers: Selected Papers,* edited by Brian Randall, Spring-Verlag, 1982, pp. 415–416.

SOURCES:

Books

Goldstine, Herman H., *The Computer: From Pascal to von Neumann,* Princeton University Press, 1972.

Lavington, Simon, *Early British Computers: The Story of Vintage Computers and the People Who Built Them,* Digital Press, 1980.

Metropolis, N., J. Howlett, and Gian-Carlo Rota, editors, *A History of Computing in the Twentieth Century: A Collection of Essays,* Academic Press, 1980, pp. 433–443.

Randell, Brian, editor, *The Origins of Digital Computers: Selected Papers,* 3rd edition, Springer-Verlag, 1982.

Williams, Michael R., *A History of Computing Technology,* Prentice-Hall, 1985.

Periodicals

Bowker, Geof, and Richard Giordano, "Interview with Tom Kilburn," *IEEE Annals of the History of Computing,* Volume 15, 1993, pp. 17–32.

Campbell-Kelly, Martin, "Programming the Mark I: Early Programming Activity at the University of Manchester," *Annals of the History of Computing,* April, 1980, pp. 130–168.

Croarken, Mary, "The Beginnings of the Manchester Computer Phenomenon: People and Influences," *IEEE Annals of the History of Computing,* Volume 15, 1993, pp. 9–16.

—Sketch by Rowan L. Dordick

Jack St. Clair Kilby
1923-
American electrical engineer and inventor

Jack St. Clair Kilby is a pioneer in miniaturized electronics who holds more than sixty patents. He shares credit with **Robert Noyce** for inventing the integrated circuit chip while employed at Texas Instruments. Kilby also invented the hand-held calculator.

Kilby was born in Jefferson City, Missouri, on November 8, 1923. His father was an electrical engineer who became president of the Kansas Power Company when Kilby was four years old. The family moved to Salina, Kansas, where Kilby learned the intricacies of electricity during the summers when he accompanied his father on visits to company facilities throughout the western part of the state. His interest in electrical engineering was kindled in the winter of 1937 when his father used a ham radio to maintain contact with his power stations during a blizzard. Fascinated by radio, Kilby studied hard, soon gained his Federal Communications Commission license, and built his own radio using salvaged parts.

Throughout high school Kilby wanted to be an electrical engineer, and he planned to attend the Massachusetts Institute of Technology, the premier engineering school in the country. But he failed the entrance examination: the minimum passing grade was 500, and he scored 497. As crushing as the blow was, it created another problem—he had not applied to any other universities. He managed to enroll at his parents' alma mater, the University of Illinois.

Four months after the first semester began at the University of Illinois, the Japanese attacked Pearl Harbor. Kilby enlisted in the U.S Army Signal Corps and later served with the Office of Strategic Services (OSS). At the time, small groups of Allied soldiers were being airlifted into remote places to build resistance units. These soldiers were given backpack radios to communicate with their commanders. Although they represented the state of the art in radio technology, the radios were heavy and performed erratically; they had not been designed for jungle combat. In his attempt to remedy the situation, Kilby traveled to Calcutta for a truckload of black-market radio parts, and soon his unit was building smaller, more reliable radios for the troops. From this experience Kilby learned that if a machine does not quite meet certain needs, it can be rebuilt to do so.

After the war he returned to the University of Illinois and graduated in 1947 with a B.S. in electrical engineering. He then moved to Milwaukee, Wisconsin, where he took a job with an electronics company called Centralab. Kilby's early years with Centralab were spent finding ways to build electrical circuits in ever smaller and more efficient packages; he was particularly concerned with reducing manufacturing steps to improve profitability. For example, he used silk-screen techniques to build printed circuit boards, and he also perfected a way to print carbon resistors directly on a ceramic circuit base. While working at Centralab, he earned an M.S. in electrical engineering from the University of Wisconsin.

Begins Work on Transistors

In 1952 Bell Laboratories announced that it would sponsor seminars on its new transistors and issue production licenses. Eager to get into the transistor business, Centralab paid the fee and sent Kilby to the seminar. He had already been immersed in the field for several years, and his mind was soon occupied by the possibilities of a device that would eliminate vacuum tubes, which were large, hot, and consumed a great deal of power. He quickly learned, however, that transistorized circuits had limitations that prevented engineers from actually being able to build the circuits they designed. Although transistors were certainly an improvement over vacuum tubes, truly miniaturized circuits still could not be built because there were too many electrical connections too close together to be made by human workers. Kilby was determined to overcome this challenge, but to do so he needed more resources than were available to him at Centralab.

In 1958 Kilby went to work at a new company called Texas Instruments, which had already made a name for itself by reducing the price of once-expensive transistors and finding a place for them in the consumer market. In 1954 the company had been involved with manufacturing the first transistor pocket radio, which was enormously successful. Executives at Texas Instruments believed that the possibilities of electronic circuits were nearly endless. In May of 1954 company engineers perfected a process for making transistors out of silicon—an improvement which made them much less prone to fail when they got hot. In their research they discovered that several electrical components could be built from silicon, although at the time they were only interested in transistors.

When Kilby joined the company, Texas Instruments was already working on the problem of electrical connections in miniature circuits. In partnership with the U.S. Army, the company was trying to perfect a concept called the "micro-module"—a system of standardized components with built-in connections that could be snapped together to make instant circuits. Kilby considered this a bad idea; he believed they should concentrate on reducing the number of parts needed rather than making it easier to put the parts together. Though Kilby had little influence on the decisions being made, he did have the laboratory entirely to himself for a few weeks when most Texas Instruments employees were on vacation. He used this time to devise a better solution to the problem of electrical connections in miniature circuits.

Patents the Integrated Circuit

Kilby's solution to this problem has come to be called the "monolithic idea." He listed all the electrical components that could be built from silicon: transistors, diodes, resistors, and capacitors. He then conceived the idea of constructing a single device with all the needed parts that could be made of silicon and soldering it to a circuit board. He understood that if he could eliminate the wires between the parts, he could squeeze more parts into a smaller space, thus solving the obstacle of manufacturing complex transistor circuits. Thus, Kilby had conceived of the integrated circuit chip. His first chip, a "phase-shift oscillator," was half an inch long and narrower than a toothpick. He demonstrated it on September 12, 1958, to a group of company executives, and it worked perfectly. Several teams in different companies around the country were working on this problem simultaneously, and the competition to solve it first was fierce. Kilby's chip worked, but it was not a complete solution. Though he put all the components on a single chip, he had not connected them feasibly. His demonstrator chip connected all the parts with tiny gold wires, which were not practical in the long term. Responding to rumors that another company was about to patent a working chip, Texas Instruments applied for a patent for their chip on February 6, 1959, even though they had not yet devised a way to connect the parts.

Another engineer, Robert Noyce at Fairchild Electronics, had also been working on the problem. He applied for a patent on July 3, 1959, almost five months later than Kilby, but his working model achieved both integration and interconnection. Both inventors were eventually awarded patents: Noyce in May, 1962, and Kilby in June, 1964. This set the stage for a court fight between the two companies that was not settled until 1970, by which time integrated circuit chips had become a multi-billion dollar industry. In the summer of 1966 executives of the two companies had made an agreement to share ownership by granting production licenses to each other. Any other company that wanted to produce integrated circuits had to pay both Texas Instruments and Fairchild. As for Kilby, the scientific community informally agreed that both he and Noyce had invented the chip and that they both deserved credit.

Invents the Portable Calculator

The new chip was quickly adopted by the military, but there were no immediate consumer applications. Therefore, Texas Instruments directed Kilby to make a miniature calculator that could fit in a person's hand. At the time, calculators were the size of typewriters and cost over a thousand dollars. In 1971 Kilby and his team introduced the first handheld calculator, the Pocketronic. It weighed 2.5 pounds; it could add, subtract, multiply, and divide, and it cost 250 dollars. It was extremely successful and remained the single most popular application of the integrated circuit for years. The pocket calculator also illustrated the way production costs fell over the years. A decade after its introduction, Texas Instruments' pocket calculators were selling for under seven dollars.

Kilby left Texas Instruments in 1971 and began working as an independent consultant. From 1978 to 1984 he was Distinguished Professor of Electrical Engineering at Texas A&M University. He was awarded the National Medal of Science in 1969 and was inducted into the National Inventors Hall of Fame in 1982. He earned the National Academy of Engineering's Charles Stark Draper Prize along with Robert Noyce in 1989, the National Medal of Technology in 1990, and Japan's Kyoto Prize in 1993.

SELECTED WRITINGS BY KILBY:

Periodicals

"Invention of the Integrated Circuit," *IEEE Transactions on Electron Devices,* July, 1976.

"The Individual Inventor," *IEEE Transactions on Consumer Electronics,* February, 1979.

SOURCES:

Books

Reid, T. R., *The Chip,* Simon & Schuster, 1984.

Slater, Robert, *Portraits in Silicon,* MIT Press, 1987.

—Sketch by Joel Simon

Motoo Kimura
1924-
Japanese geneticist

Motoo Kimura has achieved international recognition for his numerous contributions to the fields of evolution and population genetics. He is considered the founder of the neutral theory of molecular evolution. According to this theory, evolutionary change and most of the variability within a species are caused at the molecular level by the random drift of mutant genes. By comparison, English naturalist Charles Darwin's theory of natural selection was based on the concept that evolution occurs at the species level, with those individuals best adapted to the environment most fit to survive. Kimura focused on the molecular changes that occur in the nucleotides of DNA and concluded that the resulting mutant genes are neutral and subject to random drift, or changes in gene frequencies due to pure chance. Kimura developed his theory quantitatively and thus, according to James F. Crow, writing in *Population Genetics and Molecular Evolution,* "laid a very strong foundation for a mathematical theory of evolution." At first these ideas were met with considerable skepticism by many other geneticists. With the accumulation of more evidence, however, they have gained more acceptance.

Kimura was born on November 13, 1924, in Okazaki, Japan, to Issaku Kimura and Kana Kaneiwa. After receiving his M.Sc. degree from Kyoto University in 1947, he served as an assistant at the university for the next two years. In 1949 he was appointed as a research member of the National Institute of Genetics in Mishima. He then came to the United States in 1953, where he was a graduate student at Iowa State College. In 1956 he received his Ph.D. from the University of Wisconsin, where he worked in the laboratory of James F. Crow. Shortly afterward he returned to the National Institute of Genetics and became the laboratory head, a position he was to hold until 1964. In that year he was

Motoo Kimura

appointed head of the department of population genetics, serving until 1988, when he became professor emeritus. Kimura married Hiroko Mino in 1957, and the couple had one son, Akio.

Advances Study of Population Genetics

During his career, Kimura established a mathematical approach to the field of population genetics. This branch of science deals with the distribution of genes in a population, where all individuals are considered to share the same gene pool. As the individuals interbreed, genes are exchanged, resulting in many recombinations and consequent variations among members. The significance of gene frequency in evolution of species was first recognized in 1908 by **Godfrey Harold Hardy** and **Wilhelm Weinberg** when they independently arrived at the same conclusion. Their findings, now summarized in the Hardy-Weinberg law, state that the gene pool of a population remains constant from generation to generation under the following conditions: the population is large and characterized by random matings, and there are no new factors such as mutations or migration. When these theoretical conditions are not present, gene frequencies change, leading to the emergence of new species.

Kimura used computer technology to calculate the genetic composition of populations and the gene frequencies to be expected under various conditions over hundreds of generations. He prepared mathematical equations to depict a variety of possible influences such as inbreeding, mutations, crossbreeding, selection, chromosomal aberrations, natural selection, and random drift. In so doing he was able for the first time to establish a mathematical basis for the entire process of change in the gene frequency of populations.

Over the years Kimura published more than one hundred research papers. He was elected to foreign membership in the U.S. National Academy of Sciences, l'Academie des Sciences of Toulouse, the Genetical Society of Great Britain, and the Royal Society of London. He has also served as visiting professor at the Universities of Wisconsin, Pavia (Italy), Princeton, and Stanford. Kimura has been honored with a number of Japanese awards, including a D.Sc. from Osaka University, the Genetics Society of Japan Prize, the Japan Academy Prize, the Japan Society of Human Genetics Prize, the Order of Culture National Medal from the Emperor, the Honorary Citizen of Okazaki award, and the Asaki Prize. Abroad he received additional awards from Oxford University, the French government, the U.S. Academy of Sciences, as well as the International Prize for Biology, honorary degrees from the universities of Chicago and Wisconsin, and the Darwin Medal of the Royal Society. In his spare time Kimura raises and hybridizes *Paphtopedilum,* lady's slipper orchids.

SELECTED WRITINGS BY KIMURA:

Books

(With James F. Crow) *Introduction to Population Genetics Theory,* Harper and Row, 1970.

The Natural Theory of Molecular Evolution, Cambridge University Press, 1983.

Periodicals

"Evolutionary Rate at the Molecular Level," *Nature,* Volume 217, 1968, pp. 624–626.

"How Genes Evolve: A Population Geneticist's View," *Annales de Génétique,* Volume 19, 1976, pp. 153–168.

"The Neutral Theory of Molecular Evolution," *Scientific American,* November 1979, pp. 98–124.

"The Neutral Theory of Molecular Evolution," *New Scientist,* Volume 107, number 1464, 1985, pp. 41–46.

"DNA and the Neutral Theory," *Philosophical Transactions of the Royal Society of London,* series B, Volume 312, 1986, pp. 343–354.

SOURCES:

Books

Crow, James F., "The Neutrality-Selection Controversy in the History of Evolution and Population Genetics," in *Population Genetics and Molecular Evolution,* edited by T. Ohta and K. Aski, Springer-Verlag, 1985, pp. 1–18.

Wright, Sewall, *Evolution and the Genetics of Population,* volumes 1–4, University of Chicago Press, 1978.

—*Sketch by Maurice Bleifeld*

Toichiro Kinoshita
1925-
Japanese-born American physicist

Toichiro Kinoshita's work has been concerned with the basic assumptions of quantum physics. Conducting a number of high-precision tests, he has attempted to reveal flaws in the theoretical framework of this field of study.

Born in Tokyo, Japan, on January 23, 1925, Kinoshita is the oldest child of Tsutomu and Fumi Kinoshita. His father Tsutomu was a high school teacher, giving Toichiro an early exposure to education. He earned his master's and doctoral degrees in physics from Tokyo University in 1947 and 1952, respectively, then immigrated to the United States where he has conducted much of his research.

This work has dealt with elementary particle physics, particularly as related to quantum electrodynamics. One of the quantum field theories, quantum electrodynamics attempts to explain the behavior of atoms and other electrically-charged particles when they interact with one another. This involves a study of the collisions that take place between electrons, positrons, and photons. The theory views the particles as having wave-like properties, an approach that is useful for predicting atomic energy levels.

Work in this field began in the late–1920s, when some of the basic assumptions about quantum mechanics were developed by **Paul Dirac**, **Werner Heisenberg**, and **Wolfgang Pauli**. These were later improved on by physicists **Richard P. Feynman**, **Julian Schwinger**, and **Sin-Itiro Tomonaga** in the 1940s. However, the early assumptions that were the basis of the theory stemmed from the technology and calculating power available early in the century. "My own involvement is to see if the starting point is really secure," Kinoshita told F. C. Nicholson during a telephone interview from his office in Japan, where he was conducting research. Physicists, he explained, believe that any theory will break down if examined closely enough. With the more powerful computers and more precise measurements of the late–20th century, Kinoshita is trying to make sure that fundamental beliefs of quantum physics really do fit the facts.

After coming to the U.S., Kinoshita joined the Institute for Advanced Study in Princeton, New Jersey, where he worked from 1952 to 1954. He then became a postdoctoral fellow at Columbia University, and in 1955 he joined the faculty of Cornell University as a research associate. He became an assistant professor at Cornell in 1958, associate professor in 1960, and full professor in 1963. In 1992 he was named the university's Goldwin Smith Professor of Theoretical Physics.

Kinoshita has been the recipient of numerous honors, including a Ford fellowship for 1963 and 1964, a Guggenheim memorial fellowship for 1973 and 1974, and the J. J. Sakurai Prize from the American Physical Society in 1990. He has also served on the many advisory panels and scientific committees and has published more than 120 articles in professional journals and conference proceedings. Having become a naturalized U.S. citizen in 1965, Kinoshita continues to work in both the United States and Japan. His wife Masako, who also trained as a physicist, is now a professional textile designer; they have three daughters.

SOURCES:

Kinoshita, Toichiro, interview with F. C. Nicholson conducted February 21, 1994.

—*Sketch by F. C. Nicholson*

Alfred Kinsey
1894-1956
American zoologist and sex researcher

Alfred Kinsey became a household name in the 1950s for his research on the sexual morès of American women and men. His two major texts, *Sexual Behavior in the Human Male* (1948) and *Sexual Behavior in the Human Female* (1953), broke new ground in the field of sex research and led to more open and honest investigations of sexual practices. Before he achieved international fame as a sex researcher, Kinsey had already established himself in the world of science as a leading zoologist and entomologist, becoming the world's foremost authority on the American gall wasp. Throughout his career, regardless of the subject, Kinsey remained inquisitive and scientifically high-minded.

Kinsey was born in Hoboken, New Jersey, on June 23, 1894. His father, Alfred, taught at the Stevens Institute of Technology, despite having only an eighth-grade education. His mother, Sarah Ann (Charles), the daughter of a carpenter, had completed only four years of schooling. Kinsey was a sickly child, plagued by rheumatic fever, rickets, and typhoid. His parents were strict and deeply religious, rejecting many of life's aesthetic pleasures. In spite of this puritanical upbringing, Kinsey acquired a life-long appreciation of music and poetry. Starting in the seventh grade, he began collecting botanical specimens. He undertook rigorous nature expeditions, which seemed to improve his poor health. He joined the Boy Scouts of America shortly after the organization was founded in 1910, earned the prestigious designation of Eagle Scout, and became a scout leader during high school. His early botanical studies were encouraged by his high school biology teacher, Natalie Roeth, with whom he would correspond throughout his life. During high school, inspired by Roeth, he wrote a paper entitled "What Do Birds Do When It Rains?"

After high school, Kinsey considered a career in the natural sciences, but his father wanted him to train as an engineer. He obligingly enrolled at the Stevens Institute and studied mechanical engineering for two years. His interest in engineering was limited, however, and, after reaching a compromise with his father, he enrolled as a junior at Bowdoin College in Brunswick, Maine, to study biology. During his two years at Bowdoin, he earned a reputation as a deadly serious student and a first-rate pianist. He received his B.S. from Bowdoin magna cum laude in 1916 and gave the commencement address at graduation.

Establishes Himself as America's Gall Wasp Expert

In 1916, Kinsey received a scholarship from Harvard University and began his postgraduate work at the Bussey Institution. He was immediately drawn to the study of gall wasps (American Cynipidae), a small, ant-sized insect which lays its eggs inside growths (or galls) in large plants. The gall wasp can stay in its pupal state for years, and its life-span is extremely short, often less than a few hours. During his time at the Bussey Institution, Kinsey wrote his first text, *Edible Wild Plants of Eastern North America,* which was not published until 1943, when survivalist concerns were stronger. After completing his graduate work, he embarked on a one-year Sheldon Traveling Fellowship, touring the southwestern U.S. in pursuit of gall wasps. In 1920, he accepted a teaching position in the department of zoology at Indiana University in Bloomington.

Kinsey, a well-respected teacher and lecturer, was an easily identifiable figure on Indiana University's campus due to his trademark bow tie, white shirt, and crew cut. He often took undergraduates outdoors for hands-on nature studies. In the summer of 1921, he married Clara Brachen McMillen, a Phi Beta Kappa chemistry scholar. In typical Kinsey fashion, the couple spent their honeymoon on a camping expedition in the White Mountains of New Hampshire. The Kinsey's four children were all born between 1922 and 1928.

During the late 1920s, Kinsey continued his entomological research, contributing numerous articles on the gall wasp to scientific journals. His high school textbook, *An Introduction to Biology,* appeared in 1926, to enthusiastic reviews. The next year a companion text, *Field and Laboratory Manual in Biology,* was published. Soon after the appearance of this text, Kinsey's oldest child, Donald, died, succumbing to complications from diabetes.

Abandons Gall Wasp Research and Turns to Human Subjects

Kinsey's first major text, *The Gall Wasp Genus Cynips: A Study in the Origin of the Species,* was published in 1930. In 1936, *The Origin of Higher Categories of Cynips,* appeared and bolstered Kinsey's reputation as the leading authority on the gall wasp and as one of the most original thinkers in the field of genetic theory. At this point, his firmly established career took an unusual twist. In the summer of 1938, Kinsey, then age 44, began teaching a noncredit marriage course for seniors at Indiana University. The course was the result of a petition sent to the Board of Trustees by a group of students the previous spring.

Before the course began, Kinsey, always the scientist, decided to study the subject of sex and marriage in detail. He read every known reference on the subject and was appalled by the inaccuracies and lack of scientific detail and honesty. The course he designed took a more biological approach. As part of the course, students were asked to complete detailed questionnaires, which constituted the first of Kinsey's case histories. Finding the questionnaires inappropriate and open to errors of interpretation, he began conducting face-to-face interviews, using a corner of his busy laboratory. By 1940, Kinsey's marriage course was opened to freshman and sophomores and grew so popular that enrollment soon reached 400 students per semester.

Around this time, Kinsey realized he needed a more general human sample in order to conduct meaningful research. He began to travel out of town to conduct interviews with additional subjects. At first, his trips were relegated to the weekends but, as his interest grew, his time away from the campus increased. Kinsey's growing involvement with sex research did not go unnoticed by his college's administration nor by the local clergy, the medical community, and, strangely enough, the University's department of sociology, all of whom wanted the course and Kinsey stopped. In 1940, he was called before Indiana University's president, Herman Wells, who demanded that Kinsey make a choice between his marriage course and sexual research. Kinsey resigned from the course. He then increased his number of out-of-town interviews and spent long hours interpreting data and training interviewers. David Halberstam, writing in *American Heritage,* reported that Mrs. Kinsey often said of her husband at this time, "I hardly see him at night any more since he took up sex."

During the 1940s, Kinsey embarked on a large-scale study of the sexual habits of men and women. Initially, his resources were limited, and he used his own money to hire staff and pay expenses. In 1943, he received a $23,000 grant from the Rockefeller Foundation, which enabled him to hire more staff and expand his efforts. Chief among his staff were colleagues W. B. Pomeroy, who also conducted thousands of sex interviews, Paul Gebhard, and Clyde Martin. The funding briefly legitimized his undertaking, which became known as the Institute for Sex Research of Indiana University.

Sex Books Create Political Turmoil

By 1948 Kinsey and his colleagues were ready to release their initial findings. He chose a well-established medical publications firm, W. B. Saunders of Philadelphia, to publish the book, attempting to stress the scientific nature of the text rather than its potentially more lurid aspects. To avoid possible financial retribution against Indiana University, the book was published while the Indiana legislature was in recess in December 1948. The 804 page book, *Sexual Behavior in the Human Male,* sold 185,000 copies in its first year in print and made the *New York Times* bestseller list. The book employed frank descriptions of biological functions and was nonjudgmental of its subject's activities. Kinsey reported his findings simply and directly, pointing out a number of falsely held assumptions. In particular, the book reported that extramarital and premarital sex were more prevalent than generally believed; that nearly all males, especially teenagers, masturbated and that masturbation did not cause mental illness; and that one in three men reported having at least one homosexual encounter in their lifetimes.

Early polls indicated that most Americans agreed with Kinsey's findings. The most vehement criticism came later from the expected sources: conservative and religious organizations. Most of these attacks were emotionally rather than scientifically based, but few of Kinsey's colleagues came to his defense. The growing criticism jeopardized Kinsey's relationship with the Rockefeller Foundation. One of his chief critics, Henry Pitney Van Dusen, head of the Union Theological Seminary, was a member of the Rockefeller Board. And the new head of the foundation, Dean Rusk—who would later serve as secretary of state during John F. Kennedy's presidential administration—was growing weary of the foundation's well-publicized relationship with the Institute for Sex Research. The final break with the Rockefeller Foundation would come after Kinsey and his colleagues published their next book, *Sexual Behavior in the Human Female.*

The second sex book, as Kinsey expected, caused an even greater uproar than the first. Some of the book's more controversial findings concerned the low rate of frigidity, high rates of premarital and extramarital sex, the rapidness of erotic response, and a detailed discussion of clitoral versus vaginal orgasm. The book soared up the best-seller charts, eventually reaching sales of 250,000 in the U.S. alone. Criticism was harsh, and Kinsey's methods and motives were once again questioned. Evangelist Billy Graham was quoted by Halberstam in *American Heritage* as stating: "It is impossible to estimate the damage this book will do to the already deteriorating morals of America."

In August 1954, the Rockefeller Foundation, under increasing political pressure, announced its decision to cease funding for Kinsey's Institute. The nonpolitical Kinsey was now branded a subversive and accused of furthering the Communist cause by undermining American morals. He responded to these attacks by working even more diligently. The Institute turned its focus to a large-scale study of sex offenders, and Kinsey seemed determined to carry on. But the incessant criticism and lack of support took their toll. He wrote a scathing letter to Rusk, excerpted in *American Heritage,* pointing out that, "to have fifteen years of accumulated data in this area fail to reach publication would constitute an indictment of the Institute, its sponsors, and all others who have contributed time and material resources to this work."

Kinsey searched in vain for new sources of funding. He was troubled by insomnia and began taking sleeping pills and other medications. In 1955, he traveled to England and Europe, where he lectured on various topics and studied local sexual morés.

Upon his return, he developed heart trouble and was hospitalized several times. In the spring of 1956, despite his poor health, he traveled to Chicago to conduct his final interviews, subjects 7,934 and 7,935. On August 25, 1956, at the age of 62, Kinsey died of pneumonia and heart complications.

SELECTED WRITINGS BY KINSEY:

Books

An Introduction to Biology, J.B. Lippincott Company, 1926.

The Gall Wasp Genus Cynips: A Study in the Origin of the Species, Indiana University Studies, 1930.

The Origin of Higher Categories in Cynips, Indiana University Publications, 1936.

(With W. B. Pomeroy and C. E. Martin) *Sexual Behavior in the Human Male,* W. B. Saunders Company, 1948.

(With Pomeroy and Martin) *Sexual Behavior in the Human Female,* W. B. Saunders Company, 1953.

Periodicals

"Life Histories of American Cynipidae," *Bulletin of the American Museum of Natural History,* Volume 42, 1920, pp. 357–402.

"The Economic Importance of Cynipidae," *Journal of Economic Entomology,* Volume 28, 1935, pp. 86–91.

"Homosexuality: Criteria for a Hormonal Explanation of the Homosexual," *Journal of Clinical Endocrinology,* Volume 1, 1941, pp. 424–28.

"Living with Music: Music and Love as Arts," *High Fidelity Magazine,* July 1956, pp. 27–28.

SOURCES:

Books

Christenson, C. V., *Kinsey: A Biography,* Indiana University Press, 1971.

Pomeroy, W. B., *Dr. Kinsey and the Institute for Sex Research,* Harper & Row, 1972.

Periodicals

Halberstam, David, "Discovering Sex," *American Heritage,* May/June, 1993, pp. 40–42.

—Sketch by Tom Crawford

Tadamitsu Kishimoto
1939-
Japanese immunologist

Tadamitsu Kishimoto's research into the human immune system led to the discovery of a protein involved in immune response mediation, interleukin–6 (IL–6). A messenger between cells, IL–6 has also been found to function in the liver, bone marrow, and endocrine and neural systems. More importantly, deregulated or abnormal production of IL–6 has also been found in cells affected by various cancers and benign tumors, suggesting that it is somehow involved in the development of such conditions and that its control may lead to their treatment.

Kishimoto was born in Osaka, Japan, on May 7, 1939. He graduated from the Osaka University School of Medicine with an M.D. in 1964, interned at Osaka University Hospital the following year, and received his Ph.D. from Osaka University in 1969. Except for short stints at Kyushu University, Johns Hopkins University in the United States from 1970 to 1973, and Kyoto University, most of Kishimoto's career has been spent at the School of Medicine at Osaka University, where he is a professor and chairperson of the Department of Medicine III.

Research on Immune System Leads to Discovery of Interleukin–6

The immune system has proven to be one of the most important areas of biochemical research in the last few decades, especially with the onset of Acquired Immunodeficiency Syndrome (AIDS). The functioning of T cells and B cells—two cell types that fight foreign substances in the body—has been a focal point of research worldwide. Since the discovery of helper T cells which affect the production of antibodies by B cells, the search has commenced to find the molecules that communicate between these two cells. Such mediating proteins are known as cytokines or interleukins, and it was on this field of research that Kishimoto decided to focus.

By 1986 several types of interleukins had been discovered. Kishimoto identified yet another type, interleukin–6, which mediates the helper function of T cells in B cell antibody production. Subsequent research showed that IL–6 functioned not only with B cells, but also in a myriad of other cells and systems from the hepatic to the hemopoietic (the system responsible for production of blood cells). Kishimoto and his colleagues were able to describe the structure and functioning of IL–6, which further enabled them to explain the ability of different cytokines to act on the same cell and produce similar effects. Target cells appear to have specific receptors on their surface with which the soluble molecules of cytokines interact. In addition, there is a signal transducing system which the cytokines employ in order to interact with the various cells, and this signal transducer appears to be non-specific, therefore allowing IL–6 to interact with a variety of different cells. The signalling system of IL–6 was shown, moreover, to be typical for most other cytokines.

Of particular importance in Kishimoto's research was the discovery of an abnormal production of IL–6 in rheumatoid arthritis, various cancers, and human immunodeficiency virus (HIV)-related diseases. This suggests that possible treatments for these conditions may involve suppression of IL–6 through its signalling pathway. It is clear that IL–6 is not only multifunctional, but that it creates both favorable and unfavorable effects in the human body.

Kishimoto is married and has been widely honored for his research in immunology. A foreign associate of the U.S. National Academy of Science, he has been awarded the Behring-Kitasato Prize in 1982, the Osaka Science Prize in 1983, the Asahi Prize in 1988, the Prize of the Japanese Medical Association in 1990, the Scientific Achievement Award from the International Association of Allergology and Clinical Immunology in 1991, the Imperial Prize from the Japan Academy, and the Sandoz Prize for Immunology, both in 1992. In addition to his membership in numerous professional societies, Kishimoto has been president of both the Japanese Society of Immunology and the International Society of Immunopharmacology, and is on the editorial board of over thirty journals.

SELECTED WRITINGS BY KISHIMOTO:

Periodicals

(With others) "Complementary DNA for a Novel Human Interleukin (BSF–2) That Induces B Lymphocytes to Produce Immunoglobulin," *Nature,* Volume 324, 1986, pp. 73–76.

(With others) "Molecular Structure of Human Lymphocyte Receptor for Immunoglobulin E," *Cell,* Volume 47, 1986, pp. 657–665.

(With T. Hirano) "Molecular Regulation of B Lymphocyte Response," *Annual Review of Immunology,* Volume 6, 1988, pp. 485–512.

(With others) "Autocrine Generation and Requirement of BSF–2/IL–6 for Human Multiple Myelomas," *Nature,* Volume 332, 1988, pp. 83–85.

(With others) "Cloning and Expression of Human Interleukin 6 (BSF–2/IFNb2) Receptor," *Science,* Volume 241, 1988, pp. 825–828.

"The Biology of Interleukin 6," *Blood,* Volume 74, 1989, pp. 1–10.

(With others) "Molecular Cloning and Expression of an IL–6 Signal Transducer, gp130," *Cell,* Volume 63, 1990, pp. 1149–1157.

(With Shizuo Akira and Tetsuya Taga) "Interleukin 6 and Its Receptor: A Paradigm for Cytokines," *Science,* Volume 258, 1992, pp. 593–597.

(With Akira and Taga) "Cytokine Signal Transduction," *Cell,* Volume 76, 1994, pp. 253–262.

SOURCES:

Kishimoto, Tadamitsu, interview with J. Sydney Jones conducted April 29, 1994.

—Sketch by J. Sydney Jones

George B. Kistiakowsky
1900-1982
Russian-born American chemist

George B. Kistiakowsky's career exemplifies the melding of pure and applied sciences. Trained as a chemist and working in the areas of molecular structures and mechanisms of chemical reactions, Kistiakowsky later became a key member of the Manhattan Project, which developed the world's first atomic bomb, and eventually served as President Dwight D. Eisenhower's special assistant on science and technology. In the realm of pure sciences, Kistiakowsky's contributions include both teaching and carrying out highly acclaimed research in such fields as spectroscopy, thermodynamics, and chemical kinetics. Toward the applied end of the science spectrum, Kistiakowsky developed chemical explosives and rocket propellants and contributed to the development of nuclear weapons. Moreover, he played a role in national science policy, arguing for a broader and more balanced approach to scientific research in the late 1950s and 1960s and later working on problems of nuclear arms control and disarmament.

George Bogdan Kistiakowsky was born on November 18, 1900, in Kiev, Ukraine. His parents, Mary Berenstam and Bogdan Kistiakowsky, were of Cossack background. His father was a professor of international law at the University of Kiev. Young George was sent to schools in both Kiev and Moscow. But this peaceful beginning was not to last. In 1918 Kistiakowsky joined the White Army to fight against the Bolsheviks. He served in the infantry and tank corps (even while suffering from typhus) until 1920, when he fled. After a brief internment in the Ottoman Empire, he made his way to Yugoslavia. There an uncle helped him pursue his education, enabling him to enroll in the University of Berlin in 1921.

Moves to United States

At Berlin, Kistiakowsky studied chemistry with Max Bodenstein, receiving his doctorate in 1925. He emigrated to the United States in 1928 to study at Princeton University with a fellowship in physical chemistry from the International Education Board. In that year, he married Hildegard Moebius and later had a daughter, Vera, with her. In 1928 Kistiakowsky became a staff member in Princeton's chemistry department.

In 1930 Kistiakowsky left Princeton and moved to Harvard as an assistant professor of chemistry. There, his career moved ahead rapidly. In 1933 he became an associate professor. Also in this year he became a naturalized United States citizen. He took on the Abbott and James Lawrence Professorship in Chemistry in 1938 as a full professor. During these years he established himself as both a highly regarded teacher and an original researcher. At that time, his most important research was in the fundamental mechanisms of chemical reactions.

In 1940 the United States Government recognized the need for a strong, central defense program. Kistiakowsky was asked to become a consultant for the National Defense Research Committee. He later became acting chair of the explosives section of this group. In 1942 he assumed the chair of the entire explosives division. In this role he organized the preparation, testing, and manufacture of both explosives and rocket propellants. His work covered the areas of performance and safety testing as well as explosive characteristics such as fragmentation and shock wave propagation.

One of Kistiakowsky's particular projects during this time was the development of the "Aunt Jemima" powder. This product was an explosive that looked like flour and could even be safely baked into breads and cookies without losing its efficacy as an explosive. The powder was sent to the Chinese in flour bags and was used against the Japanese occupying forces.

Involvement with Manhattan Project

From 1941 to 1943 Kistiakowsky worked with the Manhattan Project. His role in this coalition of military strategists and scientists was to manufacture the conventional explosives for detonating atomic bombs. This task made good use of Kistiakowsky's understanding of chemical kinetics and thermodynamics, as it demanded very precise control of explosive characteristics in order to achieve the required uniform and rapid compression of the nuclear core, which would result in the now typical atomic explosion. In July of 1945 a test explosion was carried out with Kistiakowsky's detonating device, and a month later the first atomic bomb was dropped on Nagasaki, Japan. The war years were a turbulent period in Kistiakowsky's personal life. He was divorced from Moebius in 1942. In 1945 he married Irma E. Shuler. (He was to divorce again in 1962, when he married his third wife, Elaine Mahoney.)

Early in 1946, Kistiakowsky returned to Harvard, where he was to serve as chair of the chemistry department from 1947 to 1950. He continued his research on shock waves, molecular spectroscopy, and the kinetics of chemical reactions. He also served on several university committees. Kistiakowsky's involvement with the government resumed in the early 1950s. From 1953 to 1958 he served as a member of the ballistic missiles advisory committee for the Department of Defense. In that capacity, he urged the rapid development of intercontinental ballistic missiles. He was also a member of the United States delegation at the Conference for Prevention of Surprise Attack in Geneva in 1958.

Kistiakowsky joined the President's Science Advisory Council in 1957. Two years later, he succeeded James R. Killian, Jr. as special assistant for science and technology to President Eisenhower. Over the next two years he had broad oversight roles in national science policy, helping coordinate research and development efforts among the various branches of government. He also argued passionately for an increased emphasis on science education.

Kistiakowsky published about two hundred scientific articles during his career along with two books: *Photochemical Processes* (1928) and *A Scientist at the White House* (1976). This self-described "poor Russian immigrant" received numerous awards and honors over the years. He was given honorary doctor of science degrees by Harvard (1955), William and Mary (1958), and Oxford (1959). Recognition from branches of the United States military includes the Army Ordnance Award, Navy Ordnance Award, and Exceptional Services Award from the Air Force. The American Chemical Society bestowed several awards on him, and he was given the President's Medal for Merit in 1946.

Kistiakowsky was a member of the National Academy of Sciences, American Academy of Arts and Sciences, American Chemical Society, American Philosophical Society, American Physical Society, and Sigma Xi. He was also a foreign member of the Royal Society of London and an honorary fellow of the Chemical Society of London. Kistiakowsky died in Cambridge, Massachusetts, on December 7, 1982.

SELECTED WRITINGS BY KISTIAKOWSKY:

Books

Photochemical Processes, Chemical Catalog Company, 1928.

A Scientist at the White House: The Private Diary of President Eisenhower's Special Assistant on Science and Technology, Harvard University Press, 1976.

SOURCES:

Books

Current Biography Yearbook, H. W. Wilson, 1960, pp. 219–20.

McGraw-Hill Modern Scientists and Engineers, Volume 2, McGraw-Hill, 1980, pp. 173–74.

—Sketch by Ethan E. Allen

Flemmie Pansy Kittrell
1904-1980
American nutritionist and educator

Flemmie Pansy Kittrell was an internationally-known nutritionist whose emphasis on child development and family welfare drew much-needed attention to the importance of the early home environment. During her more than forty years as an educator, she traveled abroad extensively, helping to improve home-life conditions in many developing nations. She was a founder of Howard University's school of human ecology and the recipient of several major awards which acknowledged her unique accomplishments. As the first African American woman to earn a Ph.D. in nutrition, she strove constantly to focus attention on the important role that women could play in the world and to push for their higher education.

Kittrell was born in Henderson, North Carolina, on Christmas Day, 1904. She was the youngest daughter of Alice (Mills) and James Lee Kittrell, both of whom were descended from African American and Cherokee forebears. Learning was of central importance to Kittrell's parents, and her father often read stories and poetry to her and her eight brothers and sisters. Her parents knew the importance of encouragement and the children frequently received praise for their perseverance and achievements.

After graduating from high school in North Carolina, Kittrell attended Hampton Institute in Virginia, receiving her Bachelor of Science degree in 1928. With the encouragement of her professors she enrolled at Cornell University, although there were not many black women during that era who became graduate students. In 1930 Kittrell received her M.A. from Cornell and in 1938, from the same institution, she accepted her Ph.D. in nutrition with honors.

Kittrell was offered her first job teaching home economics in 1928 by Bennett College in Greensboro, North Carolina, and it was to Bennett she returned after obtaining her Ph.D. She then became dean of women and the head of the home economics department at Hampton Institute in 1940, where she remained until 1944. In that year Kittrell accepted the personal offer of Howard University president Mordecai Johnson to preside over the home economics department at Howard University in Washington, D.C. At Howard, Kittrell developed a curriculum that broadened the common perception of home economics so that it included such fields as child development research.

In 1947 Kittrell embarked upon a lifetime of international activism, carrying out a nutritional survey of Liberia sponsored by the United States government. Her findings concerning "hidden hunger," a type of malnutrition which occurred in ninety percent of the African nation's population, led to important changes in Liberian agricultural and fishing industries. Kittrell then received a 1950 Fulbright award which led to her work with Baroda University in India, where she developed an educational plan for nutritional research. In 1953, Kittrell went back to India as a teacher of home economics classes and nutritional seminars. Then, in 1957, Kittrell headed a team which traveled to Japan and Hawaii to research activities in those countries related to the science of home economics. Between 1957 and 1961, Kittrell was the leader of three more tours, to West Africa, Central Africa, and Guinea.

During this period Kittrell remained at Howard University. In 1963, her fifteen-year struggle to obtain a building for the school of human ecology resulted in the dedication of a new facility. This innovative building attracted national attention as it provided a working example for the nation's Head Start program, which was just getting off the ground. Retiring from Howard University in 1972, Kittrell was named Emeritus Professor of Nutrition.

Kittrell's achievements were regularly recognized by awards and honors. For instance, she was chosen by Hampton University as its outstanding alumna for 1955. In 1961 she received the Scroll of Honor by the National Council of Negro Women in recognition of her special services. Cornell University gave her an achievement award in 1968 and the University of

North Carolina at Greensboro conferred on her an honorary degree in 1974. Also, a scholarship fund was founded in honor of Kittrell's career by the American Home Economics Association.

Kittrell continued to work despite her retirement from teaching in 1972. From 1974 to 1976 she was a Cornell Visiting Senior Fellow, and she served as a Moton Center Senior Research Fellow in 1977 and a Fulbright lecturer in India in 1978. Kittrell died unexpectedly of cardiac arrest on October 3, 1980, in Washington, D.C. During her life she had credited much of her success not only to her education, but also to the strength, love, and family unity she enjoyed in her parents' home, where learning was a very important aspect of family life.

SOURCES:

Books

Sammons, Vivian O., *Blacks in Science and Medicine,* Hemisphere Publishing, 1990, pp. 143–144.

Smith, Jesse Carney, editor, *Notable Black American Women,* Gale, 1992, pp. 636–638.

—*Sketch by Leonard C. Bruno*

Aaron Klug
1926-
Lithuanian-born South African and English molecular biologist

Aaron Klug made many breakthroughs that advanced the knowledge of the basic structures of molecular biology, but he is best known for his creation of the new technique of crystallographic electron microscopy which made possible not only his own scientific discoveries but those of many other scientists as well. For his development of this technique as well as for his contributions to scientific knowledge, he was awarded the Nobel Prize in chemistry in 1982. He was also knighted as Sir Aaron Klug by Queen Elizabeth II in 1988.

Klug was born on August 11, 1926, in Zelvas, Lithuania, the son of Lazar Klug, a cattle dealer, and Bella Silin Klug. When he was two years old, he and his parents emigrated to Durban, South Africa, where members of his mother's family were already established. He was educated in the Durban public schools and, while attending Durban High School from 1937 to 1941, he developed an interest in science. Klug became especially interested in microbiology through reading Paul De Kruif's well-known book, *Microbe Hunters,* first published in 1926. He entered the University of Witwatersrand in Johannesburg in 1942 to take the premedical curriculum but extended his courses to include additional chemistry, mathematics, and physics before graduating with a B.S. degree in 1945. He then attended the University of Cape Town on a scholarship to take a master's degree in physics. There he first learned the techniques of X-ray crystallography, a method of determining the arrangement of atoms within a crystal. This is accomplished by studying the patterns formed on a photographic plate after a beam of X rays is deflected by the crystal. This methodology was to be basic to much of his later research. He married Liebe Bobrow in 1948 and eventually became the father of two sons, Adam and David Klug.

In 1949 Klug and his wife moved to Cambridge, England, where he had received a fellowship to study at the Cavendish Laboratory of Cambridge University. He hoped to work in the research group examining biological materials under the direction of **Max Perutz** and **John Kendrew**. When he found that there were no positions available in that group, he decided to study the molecular structure of steel and wrote a thesis on the changes that occur when molten steel solidifies, for which he received his Ph.D. in 1952. Still wishing to use his training to study biological materials, Klug in 1953 obtained a fellowship to work at Birkbeck College in London. Here he came under the influence of **Rosalind Franklin**, a reticent scientist who had pioneered X-ray crystallographic analysis. This technique had made a vital contribution to the discovery of the double-helical structure of deoxyribonucleic acid (DNA), an accomplishment that had won a Nobel Prize for **Francis Crick** and **James Watson**. Franklin introduced Klug to the X-ray study of the structure of viruses, an undertaking that was to occupy him for several years. They worked together to determine the structural nature of the tobacco mosaic virus, which attacks tobacco plants. After Franklin's death in 1958, Klug became the director of the Virus Structure Research Group at Birkbeck College.

Esteemed Colleagues Spur Success

In 1962 Klug returned to Cambridge to accept a position at the Laboratory of Molecular Biology recently established by the British Medical Research Council. Here he found himself stimulated by a large group of distinguished scientists, including Francis Crick, Max Perutz, and John Kendrew, all three of whom won Nobel Prizes in 1962. Over the next thirty years Klug himself became an increasingly important part of the research team, becoming joint head of the division of structural studies in 1978 and director of the entire laboratory in 1986.

Klug's most important contribution to scientific research was the development over many years of a technique which came to be known as crystallographic electron microscopy. X-ray crystallography had proved adequate for many biological discoveries such as the double-helical structure of DNA. However, many complex biological molecular structures were simply not available in crystal form suitable for X-ray diffraction. The obvious alternative was the use of powerful electron microscopes which could magnify an object up to a million times and reproduce it on a photographic plate, or micrograph. But the problem with electron micrographs was that they presented an essentially two-dimensional picture of a three-dimensional object. The micrographs did, however, contain in a confused form much of the information necessary for a three-dimensional reconstruction of the object, especially if the object was examined from different angles in successive micrographs.

Klug's new idea was essentially to combine the techniques of the electron microscope and X-ray crystallography by doing X-ray diffractions of the electron micrographs themselves, just as one would do with a crystal. Then the researcher could gradually put together a three-dimensional reconstruction of the object under consideration, filtering out extraneous specks on the photographic plates that confused the picture. The process was a complex one that required, among other things, very sophisticated mathematical analysis in the course of the work. Armed with the new research technique, Klug and his colleagues were able to reveal the structures and modes of operation of many basic biological materials such as viruses, animal cell walls, subcellular particles, chromatin from the genetic material of the cell nucleus, and various proteins. His accomplishments were rewarded in 1982 when he received the Nobel Prize. He has also been awarded the H. P. Heineken Prize from the Royal Netherlands Academy of Arts and Sciences, Columbia University's Louisa Gross Horwitz Prize, and a host of honorary degrees.

SELECTED WRITINGS BY KLUG:

Periodicals

(With Roger D. Kornberg) "The Nucleosome," *Scientific American,* February 1981, pp. 52–64.

"Molecules on a Grand Scale," *New Scientist,* May 21, 1987, pp. 46–50.

SOURCES:

Books

The Nobel Prize Winners: Chemistry, Volume 3, Salem Press, 1990, pp. 1079–1086.

Nobel Prize Winners: An H. W. Wilson Biographical Dictionary, H. W. Wilson, 1987, pp. 560–562.

Periodicals

Caspar, D. L. D., and D. J. DeRosier, "The 1982 Nobel Prize in Chemistry," *Science,* November 12, 1982, pp. 653–655.

Chemical and Engineering News, October 25, 1982, pp. 4–5. Herman, Ros, "An Image of Molecular Biology," *New Scientist,* October 21, 1982, pp. 155–157.

New York Times, October 19, 1982, p. C6

Physics Today, January 1983, pp. 17–19.

—Sketch by John E. Little

Eleanora Bliss Knopf
1883-1974
American geologist

Eleanora Bliss Knopf was a geologist with the United States Geological Survey. She helped interpret the complex geological history of mountainous regions in Pennsylvania and New England. To help analyze the folding and structural changes in rock due to high temperatures and pressures, she sought the latest tools and techniques from scientists abroad, translating their works into English and introducing new approaches in the United States.

Knopf was born Eleanora Frances Bliss on July 15, 1883, in Rosemont, Pennsylvania. Her mother, Mary Anderson Bliss, studied languages and wrote poetry. Her father, General Tasker Howard Bliss, served as Chief of Staff of the United States Army during World War I. Bliss attended the Florence Baldwin School and entered Bryn Mawr College in 1900. She graduated in 1904 with an A.B. in chemistry and an A.M. in geology. Her mentor in geology was **Florence Bascom**, the first American woman to earn a Ph.D. in geology.

After graduating from Bryn Mawr, Bliss worked as an assistant curator in the geological museum there and as a demonstrator in the geology laboratory until 1909. Under Bascom's direction, Bliss and classmate Anna Isabel Jonas undertook a challenging dissertation on the geology of the Doe Run-Avondale district, just west of Bryn Mawr. Bliss was awarded her doctorate in 1912. That year, the United States Geological Survey (USGS) hired Bliss to continue working on the areas near the site where she had done the research for her dissertation. At the USGS she met geologist Adolph Knopf, a widower with three children; they married in 1920. The family moved to New Haven, Connecticut, where Adolph Knopf had been offered a teaching position at Yale University.

At that time, the faculty at Yale University did not hire women, and Knopf worked out of her husband's office and taught private courses. One of her former students, John Rodgers, described her in a memorial as a petite woman with a great deal of intellectual fortitude: "She never tolerated slipshod work or reasoning, and her criticisms were often the more devastating for being calmly and politely expressed." In addition to her teaching, Knopf continued to take USGS assignments, a practice she would continue until 1955. She actively sought new techniques to help her interpret the geologic faults and folds in the mountains along the border between New York and New England known as the Taconic region. She was one of the first geologists to use stereoptically viewed airplane photographs for field mapping. She also delved into the international geological literature, translating works from German. She introduced European techniques and approaches to the United States, including the use of laboratory work to study the deformation of rocks.

In 1951, Adolph Knopf took a new post at Stanford University in California. Eleanora Knopf worked as a research associate there, helping her husband to study a geological formation in the Rocky Mountains known as the Boulder batholith. She continued the work after his death in 1966; she herself died of arteriosclerosis in Menlo Park, California, on January 21, 1974.

SELECTED WRITINGS BY KNOPF:

Periodicals

(With Anna I. Jonas) "Stratigraphy of the Crystaline Schists of Pennsylvania and Maryland," *American Journal of Science,* Volume 5, 1923, pp. 40–62.

(With Louis M. Prindle) "Geology of the Taconic Quadrangle," *American Journal of Science,* Volume 24, 1932, pp. 257–302.

SOURCES:

Books

Sicherman, Barbara, and Carol Hurd Green, editors, *Notable American Women: The Modern Period,* Volume 6, The Belknap Press of Harvard University Press, 1980, pp. 401–403.

Periodicals

Rodgers, John, "Memorial to Eleanora Bliss Knopf, 1883–1974," *The Geological Society of America Memorials,* Volume 6, 1977, pp. 1–4.

—Sketch by Miyoko Chu

William Claire Knudsen
1925-
American geophysicist

William Claire Knudsen is a geophysicist who has made several advances in the understanding of the ionospheres of both Earth and Venus. In 1980, he was honored with the National Aeronautics and Space Administration Group Achievement Award for his role as principal investigator on the Pioneer Venus Orbiter mission. In the field of geophysics, he also made significant contributions to offshore oil exploration efforts throughout the world. Knudsen, a member of the American Geophysical Union, is widely published, and he has been awarded several patents for his work in various scientific fields.

Born in Provo, Utah on December 12, 1925, Knudsen was the second child of Nels and Julia (Brown) Knudsen. His parents were Mormons who raised their children with a strong focus on family and education. His father was a farmer and postman in Provo, but he was also a music teacher and he had degrees in music from both Brigham Young University and the Boston Conservatory. Knudsen himself remains a dedicated singer, and he has served as the choir director of his church on several occasions. Knudsen also studied the violin, playing in string quartets and orchestras throughout high school and college.

As a boy, Knudsen was fascinated by anything electrical and mechanical but particularly radios. He built a crystal radio receiver and later a more complex radio transmitter and receiver. At Provo High School, where he was valedictorian of his graduating class, he studied radio repair and cabinet and furniture making as well as physics and chemistry. During World War II, he served in the Army Signal Corps as a long-distance wire chief in the Philippines. He was responsible for maintaining both telephone and teletype communications between the U.S. Naval Base there, Clark Field Air Base, and military installations in Manila. After the war, Knudsen attended Brigham Young University. He had planned to study electrical engineering, but he became more interested in discovering the laws of nature than in applying them. He earned bachelor of science degrees in both physics and mathematics, graduating in 1950 with high honors. He then moved to the University of Wisconsin where he earned a master's degree in 1952 and a Ph.D. in physics in 1954, writing his dissertation on the properties of helium at very low temperatures.

Uses Sound Waves to Aid in Oil Exploration

After graduation, Knudsen moved to California and accepted a position as an oil-exploration physicist with the Standard Oil Company. At Standard, he researched sound-wave propagation in solids and liquids—work that contributed to successful seismic oil exploration both on land and at sea. He helped improve a particular technique for oil exploration at sea which employs an explosive charge; the charge is detonated beneath the surface and the seismic sound waves created are used to judge the nature of the geologic layers beneath the ocean floor. By measuring the time differential between the detonation and the return of echoes, oil explorers are able to determine the existence of potential oil reservoirs. Also at Standard, Knudsen worked on underground water hydrology and the effect of migrating water on oil accumulation from decaying organic matter underground. His research helped to explain the presence of the many large natural gas fields off the shore of Louisiana.

By 1962, Knudsen was bored at Standard Oil, and he realized that he needed to look elsewhere for scientific fulfillment. He accepted a position that year at Lockheed Palo Alto Research Labs, a division of Lockheed Missile and Space Company. With the launch of the Russian Sputnik in 1959, there was rapidly growing interest in planetary exploration throughout the world. In his first assignment at Lockheed, he further analyzed and interpreted data on the Earth's ionosphere that had been gathered by an instrument called a "retarding potential analyzer," flown aboard an early Lockheed satellite. The device had been designed and built by William Hanson of the University of Texas and would prove to be of great significance in Knudsen's career. Using Hanson's data, Knudsen developed computer programs that enabled him to obtain figures on ion concentration, temperature, and composition in the Earth's ionosphere.

Atmospheric Research Leads to Position with NASA

Knudsen built on his early work at Lockheed and was eventually able to provide great insights into the nature and behavior of planetary ionospheres. He wrote three major papers dealing with the formation and circulation of the ionospheres of Earth and Venus. His findings led to the recognition of a strong solar-cycle change in the thickness of the ionosphere on the day side of Venus and the consequent loss of ion flow from the day side to the night side. There had been neither recognition nor understanding of this phenomenon before his publications, and his papers led to a great deal of research on this subject throughout the world and eventually to a greatly increased understanding of geographical and time variations in the Earth's ionosphere over the polar regions. His theoretical work on planetary atmospheres grew to include the planet Mars as well as Venus and the evolution of helium in their atmospheres as a result of source and loss processes between the planet surfaces and atmospheres.

Knudsen worked as a staff scientist for Lockheed from 1962 to 1984. He was selected by NASA as the principal investigator for a retarding potential analyzer experiment on the Pioneer Venus Orbiter mission in 1973. From 1973 to its launch in 1978, he designed and built the most advanced retarding potential analyzer then in existence. The instrument, used for ionospheric research, flew on NASA's Pioneer Venus Orbiter and faithfully relayed data on the that planet's atmosphere for fourteen years until the craft descended into the lower atmosphere and was destroyed in 1992. Knudsen left Lockheed in 1984 to form his own corporation, Knudsen Geophysical Research. Primarily dedicated to research on planetary atmospheres, the corporation worked closely with NASA on the Pioneer Venus and other projects.

Raised in a strong Mormon tradition, Knudsen believes that by increasing his understanding of science, he is increasing his understanding of God. According to the Church of Jesus Christ of Latter Day Saints, "the glory of God is intelligence," and in keeping with this creed, Knudsen has spent his life trying to understand the universe, which he considers God's creation. Knudsen was married in 1948 to Ruth Crandall, also a Mormon, whom he met while an undergraduate at Brigham Young University; they have four children. His wife has also served as vice president and secretary of Knudsen Geophysical Research. Knudsen has been a High Priest in the Mormon church, a choir director, singer, instructor, and temple ordinance worker. In his leisure time he enjoys cabinet making and woodworking, but he has devoted much of his free time to his family and the upbringing of his children and fourteen grandchildren.

SELECTED WRITINGS BY KNUDSEN:

Periodicals

(With K. Spenner, K. L. Miller, and V. Novak) "Transport of Ionospheric 0^+Ions Across the Venus Terminator and Implications," *Journal of Geophysical Research,* Volume 85, 1980, p. 7803.

(With A. J. Kliore, and K. Spenner) "Median Density Altitude Profiles of the Major Ions in the Central Nightside Venus Ionosphere," *Journal of Geophysical Research,* Volume 92, 1987, p. 13,391.

"Solar Cycle Changes in the Morphology of the Venus Ionosphere," *Journal of Geophysical Research,* Volume 93, 1988, pp. 8576–8762.

"Venus Ionosphere from in situ Measurements" in *Venus and Mars: Atmospheres, Ionospheres and Solar Wind Interaction,* edited by J. G. Luhmann, M. Tatrallyay, and R. O. Pepin, American Geophysical Union, 1992.

Other

Knudsen, William Claire, interviews with John Henry Dreyfuss conducted in January, 1994.

—*Sketch by John Henry Dreyfuss*

Donald E. Knuth
1938-
American computer scientist

A California academic, Donald E. Knuth is considered by many the preeminent living scholar of computer science. His multivolume work *The Art of Computer Programming* is regarded as the bible of the subject. He has also revolutionized computer typesetting through the typography language TeX and the font-design system he invented, METAFONT.

Donald Ervin Knuth was born on January 10, 1938, in Milwaukee, Wisconsin, to Ervin Henry Knuth and Louise Marie Bohning. His father was a high-school bookkeeping teacher with a small printing business. As a child Knuth was fascinated by the patterns of numbers and words. When he was in the eighth grade, he entered a contest sponsored by a Milwaukee candy company. The purpose of the contest was to find how many words could be made from the letters in "Zeigler's Giant Bar," and Knuth won the contest handily, with a list of 4,500 words.

During his freshman year in high school, Knuth became obsessed with the patterns formed by algebraic functions. He developed a system that could find an equation for any pattern of connected straight lines. It would be difficult to imagine what his schoolmates made of this, but it turned out to have a practical application; Knuth later claimed that METAFONT, his system of computer-assisted typography, originated with his early interest in patterns and graphing. He graduated from Milwaukee Lutheran High School in 1956 holding that school's record for highest grade point average.

Discovers Computers in College

Knuth entered Case Institute of Technology that same year, torn between two loves—physics and music. He was a serious pianist and a developing composer. Although he chose to study physics, music remained a passion of his, and many years later he designed an organ with approximately one thousand pipes for the Bethany Lutheran Church in Menlo Park, California.

Knuth was a deeply insecure student when he was young; frightened by the prospect of failure, he worked ceaselessly to avoid it. For all his drive, however, Knuth showed a whimsical side. His first published article, which he wrote as a freshman in 1957, was entitled "The Potrzebie System of Weights and Measures"—a parody of the metric system that was published in *Mad* magazine. The article became a perennial favorite, and it has been reprinted twice, the last time as recently as 1991.

Knuth discovered computers in the summer following his first college year; he was drawing graphs for university statisticians, and he learned that the next room contained a new IBM 650. Soon Knuth was spending his nights at the console. The experience was seminal, and he later dedicated the first volume of *The Art of Computer Programming* "to the Type 650 computer once installed at Case Institute of Technology, in remembrance of many pleasant evenings."

Knuth abandoned physics at the end of his sophomore year to major in mathematics. He also became involved with the college basketball team in what was then an unusual capacity. Using the IBM 650, he developed a rating system that helped the team coaches assess the contributions of each player on the team, based on a range of factors broader than how many points they scored. In 1960, Case won the league championship, and the math wiz turned "computer nerd" found himself receiving attention from broadcast journalist Walter Cronkite and *Newsweek* magazine.

Upon his graduation from Case in 1960, Knuth was also awarded a master's degree by special vote of the faculty, an unprecedented event. He spent the following summer analyzing hardware and writing software at the Burroughs Corporation, a company that manufactured business machines and was beginning to become involved with computers. He then enrolled in the California Institute of Technology (Caltech) to study for his doctorate. The following year he married Nancy Jill Carter; the couple went on to have two children, John and Jennifer.

Starts Writing Treatise on Computer Programming

Knuth quickly made a name for himself both as a computer programmer and a writer, and in January 1962, while he was still a graduate student, the Addison-Wesley publishing company approached him to write a book on compiler programs. Computer literature at the time was in a state of extreme disorganization. Some of the documentation was inaccurate, and many new ideas were not widely available. A number of small journals published articles about programming and computer theory, but no objective effort had been made to summarize the state of the art. The computer industry needed a genuine computer expert who also knew how to write.

The Art of Computer Programming grew out of this need, and thus began one of the great works of Knuth's life. At first, he felt he had no great new insights to offer. But as he organized existing material and analyzed the methods and theories used by the programmers of his day, he began to fill in the gaps between various theories and develop a synthesis that could truly define computer programming. The single book his publishers requested grew into a seven-volume project, during which time he obtained his Ph.D. and began teaching math at Caltech. As of the early 1990s, three volumes had been published: *Fundamental Algorithms, Seminumerical Algorithms,* and *Sorting and Searching.* They have been reprinted many times and translated into numerous other languages. A fourth volume, *Combinatorial Algorithms,* was on the way. In 1974 Knuth was given the Alan M. Turing Award for the series by the Association of Computing Machinery, which said: "His series of books have done the most to transfer the whole set of erstwhile esoteric ideas into the standard practices of computer scientists of today."

In addition to these volumes, Knuth has written extensively on many other computer-related subjects. In particular, his five-volume work *Computers and Typesetting* put forth the results of his work on TeX and METAFONT, a new typography language and typeface-design system that revolutionized computer typography and the entire printing industry. Before METAFONT, designing all the characters in a new typeface was a task that could consume years; by computerizing the process, Knuth made sweeping changes in type style possible with simple keystrokes. A major contribution of TeX was the unprecedented flexibility it permitted in the spacing of text on a printed page.

Knuth's droll wit frequently comes through in his writing. In the index of volume one of *The Art of Computer Programming,* for instance, readers looking up *circular reasoning* will be directed to "See Reasoning, circular." Upon following the instruction, they will be told "See Circular reasoning." Knuth's 1974 book, *Surreal Numbers,* is actually a novella involving a numbering system invented by a friend and Harvard mathematician named John Conway. An excerpt reads, "And Conway said, 'Let the numbers be added to each other in this wise: The left set of the sum of two numbers shall be the sums of all left parts of each number with the other; and in like manner the right set shall be from the right parts, each according to his kind.' Conway proved that every number plus zero is unchanged, and he saw that addition was good. And the evening and the morning were the third day."

Knuth was on the staff of the California Institute of Technology as an assistant and associate professor of mathematics from 1963 to 1968, after which he left to become a full professor at Stanford. In 1990 Stanford created for him the position of Professor of the Art of Computer Programming. He retired in 1992 to concentrate on his books but still holds the title of professor emeritus.

Knuth's work has inspired hyperbolic comparisons. He has been compared to Euclid, whose work on geometry set the standard for centuries, for his work on *The Art of Computer Programming* and to Johannes Gutenberg, who invented movable type, for his work on computer typesetting. His numerous honors include more than a dozen honorary doctorates, national and international awards for mathematics and computing, and the National Medal of Science, which he received from U.S. President Jimmy Carter in 1979. Knuth synthesized the work of hundreds of scattered and isolated programmers into a complex and integrated whole, and perhaps more than anyone else he has defined computer science and given it an orderly basis.

SELECTED WRITINGS BY KNUTH:

Books

The Art of Computer Programming, Addison-Wesley, Volume 1: *Fundamental Algorithms,* 1968, Volume 2: *Seminumerical Algorithms,* 1969, Volume 3: *Sorting and Searching,* 1973.

Surreal Numbers, Addison-Wesley, 1974.

TeX and METAFONT: New Directions in Typesetting, American Mathematical Society/Digital Press, 1979.

Computers and Typesetting, five volumes, Addison-Wesley, 1986.

Literate Programming, Center for the Study of Language and Information, 1992.

SOURCES:

Books

Caddes, Carolyn, *Portraits of Success,* Tioga Press, 1986, pp. 78–79

Slater, Robert, *Portraits in Silicon,* MIT Press, 1987, pp. 341–51.

Periodicals

Discover, September, 1984, pp. 74–76, 78.
Peninsula, December, 1988, pp. 72–74.
"What's That about a Score Card? A Computer's the Thing," *Newsweek,* January 5, 1959, p. 63.

—*Sketch by Joel Simon*

Robert Koch
1843-1910
German bacteriologist

Robert Koch is considered to be one of the founders of the field of bacteriology. He pioneered principles and techniques in studying bacteria and discovered the specific agents that cause tuberculosis, cholera, and anthrax. For this he is also regarded as a founder of public health, aiding legislation and changing prevailing attitudes about hygiene to prevent the spread of various infectious diseases. For his work on tuberculosis, he was awarded the Nobel Prize in 1905.

Robert Heinrich Hermann Koch was born in a small town near Klausthal, Hanover, Germany, on December 11, 1843, to Hermann Koch, an administrator in the local mines, and Mathilde Julie Henriette Biewend, a daughter of a mine inspector. The Koch's had a total of thirteen children, two of whom died in infancy. Robert was the third son. Both parents were industrious and ambitious. Robert's father rose in the ranks of the mining industry, becoming the overseer of all the local mines. His mother passed her love of nature on to Robert who, at an early age, collected various plants and insects.

Before starting primary school in 1848, Robert taught himself to read and write. At the top of his class during his early school years, he had to repeat his final year. Nevertheless, he graduated in 1862 with good marks in the sciences and mathematics. A university education became available to Robert when his father was once again promoted and the family's finances improved. Robert decided to study natural sciences at Gottingen University, close to his home.

After two semesters, Koch transferred his field of study to medicine. He had dreams of becoming a physician on a ship. His father had traveled widely in Europe and passed a desire for travel on to his son. Although bacteriology was not taught then at the University, Koch would later credit his interest in that field to Jacob Henle, an anatomist who had published a theory of contagion in 1840. Many ideas about contagious diseases, particularly those of chemist and microbiologist Louis Pasteur, who was challenging the prevailing myth of spontaneous generation, were still being debated in universities in the 1860s.

During Koch's fifth semester at medical school, Henle recruited him to participate in a research project on the structure of uterine nerves. The resulting essay won first prize. It was dedicated to his father and bore the Latin motto, Nunquam Otiosus, or Never idle. During his sixth semester, he assisted Georg Meissner at the Physiological Institute. There he studied the secretion of succinic acid in animals fed only on fat. Koch decided to experiment on himself, eating a half pound of butter each day. After five days, however, he was so sick that he limited his study to animals. The findings of this study eventually became Koch's dissertation. In January 1866, he finished the final exams for medical school and graduated with highest distinction.

After finishing medical school, Koch held various positions; he worked as an assistant at a hospital in Hamburg, where he became familiar with cholera, and also as an assistant at a hospital for retarded children. In addition, he made several attempts to establish a private practice. In July, 1867, he married Emmy Adolfine Josephine Fraatz, a daughter of an official in his hometown. Their only child, Gertrude, was born in 1868. Koch finally succeeded in establishing a practice in the small town of Rakwitz where he settled with his family.

Begins Research on Anthrax

Shortly after moving to Rakwitz, the Franco-Prussian War broke out and Koch volunteered as a field hospital physician. In 1871, the citizens of Rakwitz petitioned Koch to return to their town. He responded, leaving the army to resume his practice, but he didn't stay long. He soon took the exams to qualify for district medical officer and in August 1872 was appointed to a vacant position at Wollstein, a small town near the Polish border.

It was here that Koch's ambitions were finally able to flourish. Though he continued to see patients, Koch converted part of his office into a laboratory. He obtained a microscope and observed, at close range, the diseases his patients confronted him with.

One such disease was anthrax, which is spread from animals to humans through contaminated wool, by eating uncooked meat, or by breathing in airborne spores emanating from contaminated products. Koch examined under the microscope the blood of infected sheep and saw specific microorganisms that confirmed a thesis put forth ten years earlier by biologist C. J. Davaine that anthrax was caused by a bacillus. But Koch was not content to simply verify the work of another. He attempted to culture, or grow, these bacilli in cattle blood so he could observe their life cycle, including their formation into spores and their germination. Koch performed scrupulous research both in vitro and in animals before showing his work to Ferdinand Cohn, a botanist at the University of Breslau. Cohn was impressed with the work and replicated the findings in his own laboratory. He published Koch's paper in 1876.

In 1877, Koch published another paper that elucidated the techniques he had used to isolate Bacillus anthracis. He had dry-fixed bacterial cultures onto glass slides, then stained the cultures with dyes to better observe them, and photographed them through the microscope.

It was only a matter of time that Koch's research eclipsed his practice. In 1880, he accepted an appointment as a government advisor with the Imperial Department of Health in Berlin. His task was to develop methods of isolating and cultivating disease-producing bacteria and to formulate strategies for preventing their spread. In 1881 he published a report advocating the importance of pure cultures in isolating disease-causing organisms and describing in detail how to obtain them. The methods and theory espoused in this paper are still considered fundamental to the field of modern bacteriology. Four basic criteria, now known as Koch's postulates, are essential for an organism to be identified as pathogenic, or disease-causing. First, the organism must be found in the tissues of animals with the disease and not in disease-free animals. Second, the organism must be isolated from the diseased animal and grown in a pure culture outside the body, or in vitro. Third, the cultured organism must be able to be transferred to a healthy animal, who will subsequently show signs of infection. And fourth, the organisms must be able to be isolated from the infected animal.

Isolates Causal Agent of Tuberculosis

While in Berlin, Koch became interested in tuberculosis, which he was convinced was infectious, and, therefore, caused by a bacterium. Several scientists had made similar claims but none had been verified. Many other scientists persisted in believing that tuberculosis was an inherited disease. In six months, Koch succeeded in isolating a bacillus from tissues of humans and animals infected with tuberculosis. In 1882, he published a paper declaring that this bacillus met his four conditions—that is, it was isolated from diseased animals, it was grown in a pure culture, it was transferred to a healthy animal who then developed the disease, and it was isolated from the animal infected by the cultured organism. When he presented his findings before the Physiological Society in Berlin on March 24, he held the audience spellbound, so logical and thorough was his delivery of this important finding. This day has come to be known as the day modern bacteriology was born.

In 1883, Koch's work on tuberculosis was interrupted by the Hygiene Exhibition in Berlin, which, as part of his duties with the health department, he helped organize. Later that year, he finally realized his dreams of travel when he was invited to head a delegation to Egypt where an outbreak of cholera had occurred. Louis Pasteur had hypothesized that cholera was caused by a microorganism; within three weeks, Koch had identified a comma-shaped organism in the intestines of people who had died of cholera. However, when testing this organism against his four postulates, he found that the disease did not spread when injected into other animals. Undeterred, Koch proceeded to India where cholera was also a growing problem. There, he succeeded in finding the same organism in the intestines of the victims of cholera, and although he was still unable to induce the disease in experimental animals, he did identify the bacillus when he examined, under the microscope, water from the ponds used for drinking water. He remained convinced that this bacillus was the cause of cholera and that the key to prevention lay in improving hygiene and sanitation.

Tuberculin Fails

Koch returned to Germany and from 1885–1890 was administrator and professor at Berlin University. He was highly praised for his work, though some high-ranking scientists and doctors continued to disagree with his conclusions. But Koch was an adept researcher, able to support each claim with his exacting methodology. In 1890, however, Koch faltered from his usual perfectionism and announced at the International Medical Congress in Berlin that he had found an inoculum that could prevent tuberculosis. He called this agent tuberculin. People flocked to Berlin in hopes of a cure and Koch was persuaded to keep the exact formulation of tuberculin a secret, in order to discourage imitations. Although optimistic reports had come out of the clinical trials Koch had set up, it soon became clear from autopsies that tuberculin was causing severe inflammation in many patients. In January 1891, under pressure from other scientists, Koch finally published the nature of the substance, but it was an uncharacteristically vague and misleading report which came under immediate criticism from his peers.

Koch left Berlin for a time after this incident to recover from the professional setback. He also suffered from a personal scandal during this time, divorcing his wife in 1893 and immediately marrying an actress, Hedwig Freiberg, thirty years his junior. But the German government continued to support him throughout this time. An Institute for Infectious Diseases was established and Koch was named director. With a team of researchers, he continued his work with tuberculin, attempting to determine the ideal dose at which the agent could be the safest and most effective. The discovery that tuberculin was a valuable diagnostic tool (causing a reaction in those infected but none in those not infected), rather than a cure, helped restore Koch's reputation. In 1892 there was a cholera outbreak in Hamburg. Thousands of people died. Koch advocated strict sanitary conditions and isolation of those found to be infected with the bacillus. Germany's senior hygienist, Max von Pettenkofer, was unconvinced that the bacillus alone could cause cholera. He sneered at Koch's ideas, going so far as to drink a freshly isolated culture. Several of his colleagues joined him in this demonstration. Two developed symptoms of cholera, Pettenkofer suffered from diarrhea, but no one died; Pettenkofer felt vindicated in his opposition to Koch. Nevertheless, Koch focused much of his energy on testing the water supply of Hamburg and Berlin and perfecting techniques for filtering drinking water to prevent the spread of the bacillus.

Awarded Nobel Prize

In the following years, he gave the directorship of the Institute over to one of his students so he could travel again. He went to India, New Guinea, Africa, and Italy, where he studied diseases such as the plague, malaria, rabies, and various unexplained fevers. In 1905, after returning to Berlin from Africa, he was awarded the Nobel Prize for physiology and medicine for his work on tuberculosis. Subsequently, many other honors were awarded him recognizing not only his work on tuberculosis, but his more recent research on tropical diseases, including the Prussian Order Pour le Merits in 1906 and the Robert Koch medal in 1908. The Robert Koch Medal was established to honor the greatest living physicians, and the Robert Koch Foundation, established with generous grants from the German government and from the American philanthropist, Andrew Carnegie, was founded to work toward the eradication of tuberculosis.

Meanwhile, Koch settled back into the Institute where he supervised clinical trials and production of new tuberculins. He attempted to answer, once and for all, the question of whether tuberculosis in cattle was the same disease as it was in humans. Between 1882 and 1901 he had changed his mind on this question, coming to believe that bovine tuberculosis was not a danger to humans, as he had previously thought. He espoused his beliefs at conferences in the United States and Britain during a time when many governments were attempting large-scale efforts to minimize the transmission of tuberculosis through meat and milk.

Koch did not live to see this question answered. On April 9, 1910, three days after lecturing on tuberculosis at the Berlin Academy of Sciences, he suffered a heart attack from which he never fully recovered. He died at Baeden Baeden on May 27 at the age of 67. He was honored after death by the naming of the Institute after him.

Koch's obituaries are full of admiration for his perseverance and his scrupulous scientific process. Yet underneath the praise there is an acceptance that these same qualities—so useful to science—produced in the man a stubborn arrogance and an inability to give credit to the work of others or to admit his own mistakes. His early work with tuberculin and his defense that bovine tuberculosis was not harmful to humans are examples of his mistakes. Nevertheless, his strong will proved to be remarkably productive for science. He never left laboratory findings in the laboratory. Rather, he insisted, albeit stubbornly at times, that what he found in the laboratory should make a difference in the world. In the first paper he wrote on tuberculosis, he stated his lifelong goal, which he clearly achieved: "I have undertaken my investigations in the interests of public health and I hope the greatest benefits will accrue therefrom."

SELECTED WRITINGS BY KOCH:

Books

Schwalbe, J., editor, *Gesammelte Werke von Robert Koch,* 2 volumes, [Leipzig], 1912.

Periodicals

"An Address on Bacteriological Research," *British Medical Journal,* 1890, pp. 380–383.

"The Etiology of Anthrax, Based on the Ontogeny of the Anthrax Bacillus," *Medical Classics,* 1937–1938, pp. 787–820.

SOURCES:

Books

Barlowe, C., *Robert Koch,* Heron Books, 1971.

Brock, Thomas D., *Robert Koch,* Springer-Verlag, 1988.

Dictionary of Scientific Biography, Volume 7, Scribners, 1973, pp. 420–435.

Metchnikoff, E., *The Founders of Modern Medicine: Pasteur, Koch, Lister,* [New York], 1939.

Periodicals

British Medical Journal, June 4, 1910, pp. 1384–1388.

Stewart, D. A., "The Robert Koch Anniversary—The Man and His Work," *Canadian Medical Association Journal,* Volume 26, April, 1932, pp. 475–478.

—Sketch by Dorothy Barnhouse

Theodor Kocher
1841-1917
Swiss surgeon

In 1870s Switzerland colloid goiter was a common ailment, usually marked by a huge glandular swelling on the front of the neck. In later years it would be understood that a simple iodine supplement to the diet could significantly reduce the disorder. But in the nineteenth century, surgical removal of the thyroid gland was the only known cure. However, in the absence of effective anesthetics and antisepsis, surgical attempts to remove a goiter meant almost certain death for the patient. This was the challenge faced by Swiss surgeon Theodor Kocher, who devoted his medical career to making thyroidectomy, or the removal of a thyroid gland, a relatively safe procedure by applying new notions of antisepsis. Kocher performed thousands of thyroidectomies in his career, and the post-operative research and data he collected helped amass new knowledge about the physiology of the thyroid gland and its related disorders. For his many contributions to medicine, and especially the treatment of goiter, Kocher received the Nobel Prize in medicine in 1909.

Emil Theodor Kocher was born August 25, 1841, the son of Jacob Alexander and Maria (Wermuth) Kocher, in Bern, Switzerland. His father was an engineer and his mother a descendant of the Moravian Brethren. She passed on to her son a deeply religious philosophy which would help him gain an empathetic understanding of his patients in years to come. Schooled in Berlin, Germany; London, England; Paris, France; and Vienna, Austria, Kocher received his M.D. from the University of Bern in 1869. That same year he married Marie Witschi-Courant—the couple would have three sons. Newly married and newly graduated from medical school, Kocher visited various European clinics, including one in Vienna, where he studied under the most famous European surgeon of the day, Theodor Billroth. In 1872 Kocher, who was only thirty-one years old at the time, was named professor of clinical surgery at Bern University, a post he would hold for the next forty-five years.

Kocher first gained recognition for developing a method for treating a dislocated shoulder, a technique now known by his name. Subsequently, he also created new methods or improvements in existing methods for operations upon the lungs, stomach, gall bladder, intestine, cranial nerves, and hernia. He also developed a special pair of surgical forceps, now known as "Kocher's forceps," instruments that were used for many years after his death. Despite his many successes and contributions that improved surgical procedures, Kocher was open to other suggestions and ideas. "It is an indication of his scientific objectivity that he was always ready to abandon any of his own techniques or gadgets in favor of improvements introduced by other surgeons," Theodore L. Sourkes has written in *Nobel Prize Winners in Medicine and Physiology.* The example Sourkes provides is Kocher's ready abandonment of his own style of operating hernia's in favor of another approach.

Kocher further contributed to medicine with his *Textbook of Operative Surgery* (the book was translated into several languages, including an English edition in 1895), his pioneering of ovariotomy and, especially, his application of the antiseptic techniques of the English researcher and doctor Joseph Lister.

Understanding the Thyroid Gland

Kocher himself credited his success with thyroidectomy operations in part to Lister's method of antisepsis. He said while receiving his Nobel Prize that it was because of Lister that one of the "most dangerous operations, the removal of the thyroid gland, so often appearing urgently necessary because of severe respiratory disturbances, could be performed without substantial danger." However, despite his mastery over the operation, Kocher himself considered the increased knowledge about the *physiological* function of the thyroid gland an even greater advancement in medical science. In 1883, at the congress of the German Surgical Society, Kocher reported that out of his first 100 thyroidectomies, 30 had resulted in a serious disorder. This ailment was apparently a result of the whole, rather than partial, removal of the goiter. The symptoms Kocher described were called operative myxedema, and were akin to naturally occurring myxedema. Patients suffering from myxedema usually reported weight gain, slowing of intellect and speech, hair loss, tongue thickening, and abnormal heart rates, as well as developing blood-related problems of anemia and altered white blood-cell counts. Kocher further related that myxedema symptoms were similar to problems experienced by patients suffering from sporadic cretinism and cachexia strumipriva, diseases that resulted in mental retardation and dwarfism. Because of Kocher's postulations, it was discovered that a lack of thyroid secretions was the cause of all these diseases. Kocher further pointed out that hypothyroidism can be traced not only to absence of the gland, whether congenital or surgical, but also to a goiter which has caused the gland to stop working. His descriptions of the thyroid disorder have clarified and brought together a series of medical observations on this subject over the years.

Kocher's observations also opened the way for future treatment of thyroid disorders. Although initial attempts to rectify the condition by administering thyroid hormone were not particularly successful, researchers recognized the importance of iodine, and in 1914 the effective part of the hormone, thyroxin, was isolated for effective treatment. Meanwhile, Kocher helped perfect surgical technique for thyroidectomy, and his surgical mortality rates dropped by a great margin over the years.

During his long surgical career Kocher performed more than 2,000 thyroidectomies. In time the need for the operation declined as iodine-deprived regions, like the "goiter belt" of the Great Lakes area in the United States and certain parts of Switzerland, incorporated supplements into their diets. Nevertheless, Kocher's contributions to combatting endemic goiter continue to be recognized in a world where nearly five percent of the population still continues to suffer this disorder.

Kocher died in Bern eight years after winning the Nobel. While placing a wreath on his tomb, American neurosurgeon Harvey Cushing said in a speech at the First International Neurological Congress in 1931, "From hard work and responsibility surgeons are prone to burn themselves out comparatively young, but Kocher had been blessed with an imperturbility of spirit or had cultivated these habits of self-control which enabled him to bear his professional labours, his years, and his honours with equal composure to the very end."

SELECTED WRITINGS BY KOCHER:

Books

Textbook of Operative Surgery, translated by H. J. Stikes, A & C Black, 1895.

SOURCES:

Books

Sourkes, Theodore L., *Nobel Prize Winners in Medicine and Physiology, 1901–65,* Abelard-Schuman, 1953, p. 57.

Talbot, John H., *A Biographical History of Medicine,* Grune & Stratton, 1970, p. 1012.

—Sketch by Joan Oleck

Kunihiko Kodaira
1915-
Japanese mathematician

The high reputation of Japanese mathematics owes a great deal to the work of the analyst Kunihiko Kodaira, both for his specific contributions and for his interest in education. Through his pioneering research in algebraic varieties, harmonic integrals, and complex manifolds, Kodaira became the first Japanese mathematician ever awarded the Fields Medal, as well as being frequently honored in his own country. He has provided the entire mathematical community with a legacy of research papers on a variety of subjects and textbooks for all ages.

Born March 16, 1915, in Tokyo to Gonichi and Ichi (Kanai) Kodaira, Kodaira grew up in Japan's biggest city and remained there when he began his university education in 1935. At the University of Tokyo, he maintained a wide variety of interests in various mathematical fields and published his first research paper, written in German, a year before he took his first undergraduate degree. His early influences were the works of M. H. Stone, **John von Neumann**, W. V. D. Hodge, **André Weil** and, most importantly, **Hermann Weyl**, whose work on Riemann surfaces was very well known. Kodaira was fascinated by algebraic geometry, in spite of his analytic bent, and he found the impetus for much of his work in the book *Algebraic Surfaces* by the Italian geometer O. Zariski. In 1938, Kodaira earned his undergraduate degree in mathematics; three years later, he earned a second in theoretical physics.

By the time Kodaira began his Ph.D. studies in 1941, World War II had isolated Japan from the rest of the world. Much of the work he did during this period was in ignorance of some of the most recent and important advances in his field, yet Kodaira still managed to solve some difficult problems. In fact, the major ideas that would form his doctoral thesis, his first important work, were present in a paper written in the depths of the war. The end of the war and peace with the Americans afforded Kodaira new opportunities to continue his research. In 1943, he married Sei Iyanaga; they have four children.

Advances Career in America

Kodaira worked on his dissertation while teaching at the University of Tokyo, where he had been appointed associate professor in 1944. His thesis covered the relation of harmonic fields to Riemann manifolds, a type of mathematical surface whose definition Kodaira would help establish. In mathematics something is defined as harmonic if, by examining only the boundary of the surface, the interior of that surface can be described. Kodaira wanted to use this idea to uncover the makeup of the Riemann manifold; his thesis was the beginning of this work.

He received his doctorate in 1949; during the same year his dissertation was published in an international mathematical journal, which Hermann Weyl read. Impressed with the article, Weyl became interested in the Japanese mathematician, and in 1949 he invited Kodaira to join him at Princeton's Institute for Advance Studies (IAS). Although Kodaira did not relish leaving his homeland, he was deeply honored by the invitation. Many of the world's top mathematicians were at the IAS, and Kodaira felt his best opportunities were there, so he made up his mind to bring his young family to the United States.

Through various collaborations with IAS mathematicians such as W. L. Chow, F. E. P. Hirzebruch, and especially D. C. Spencer, Kodaira continued his work on manifolds. He discovered that, by using a type of integral known as a harmonic integral, he could more completely define the Riemann manifolds, and he sought to generalize this knowledge. Complex manifolds, which are those involving complex numbers, form the basis of much of modern calculus; however, at the time, little was understood about their properties because many were not defined. Therefore, Kodaira's studies were critical to the advancement of the field of calculus. After a great deal of work on Riemann manifolds, he turned to another type of manifold called the Kählerian manifolds, where he would produce his most spectacular results.

Kodaira wanted to prove that the Kählerian manifolds, like the Riemann manifolds, were analytic in nature—in other words, that calculus could be used to solve or define them. He began to examine a small subset of the Kählerian manifolds known as the Hodge manifolds. Using a theorem he had created earlier, called the vanishing theorem, he successfully proved the existence of meromorphic functions, a type of analytic function, on the Hodge manifolds. These meromorphic functions could be solved using algebraic varieties, a set of points that satisfy certain polynomial equations, thus making the Hodge manifolds analytic. By extension, then, in a theorem Kodaira labelled the embedding theorem, he proved that if the Hodge manifolds were analytic, then all Kählerian manifolds were analytic as well.

Because each manifold is different and because they are so crucial to the theory of modern calculus, any theory or set of theories that can classify an entire group of them constitutes a major advance. For his work on algebraic varieties and Kählerian manifolds, Kodaira received the Fields Medal in 1954, which was presented to him in Amsterdam by Kodaira's friend and mentor, Hermann Weyl. Three years later, his native country followed with two of their most prestigious awards: the Japan Academy Prize and the Cultural Medal, given by the government of Japan.

Kodaira's research continued in the midst of all the attention he received. Between 1953 and 1960, he further examined complex manifolds with D. C. Spencer, using the idea of deformations to refine his definitions. A deformation is a function which twists or bends a surface without tearing it; this function is important for both theoretical and practical reasons. Theoretically, deformations are one of the fundamental ideas of topology; practically, they are applied in mechanical engineering to describe the bending of metals. Therefore, Kodaira was applying an extremely practical and concrete concept to a very abstract theory of surfaces.

Much in demand because of his high reputation, Kodaira spent the next several years as visiting professor at prestigious American universities. He remained at the IAS and Princeton until 1961, then spent a year at Harvard, and two years at Johns Hopkins; he taught at Stanford from 1965 to 1967. In 1967, he returned to Japan, accepting a position as full professor at the University of Tokyo.

Focuses on Education

Although Kodaira continued his research after his return to Japan, he became increasingly interested in the teaching of mathematics. In 1971, he collaborated with James Morrow on a textbook based on his research into complex manifolds, the first of several such works. In 1975, he took on additional teaching responsibilities at Gakushuin University in Tokyo. Also in that year, Kodaira's collected works appeared and he was granted emeritus status at the University of Tokyo. As an additional honor in a long list, he won the Fujihara Foundation of Science Prize for his theory of complex manifolds.

In the early 1980s, Kodaira joined a government-sponsored project to produce mathematics textbooks for students from grades seven to eleven. Kodaira produced the compulsory curriculum for grades seven through nine. These texts provided a weighty mathematics background with the intent of preparing Japanese students for any career. Kodaira's texts appeared in 1984 and were later published in translation in the United States in 1992 as an example of the high quality of foreign texts.

Just before his retirement from teaching in 1985, the Wolf Foundation of Israel awarded Kodaira their mathematics prize for his contributions to the field of complex manifolds. Even after retirement, Kodaira remained interested in mathematics, and he published another work which summarized his theory of complex manifolds in 1986.

SELECTED WRITINGS BY KODAIRA:

Books

(With James Morrow) *Complex Manifolds,* Holt, 1971.

Collected Works, 3 volumes, Princeton University Press, 1975.

Introduction to Complex Analysis, Cambridge University Press, 1978.

Complex Manifolds and Deformation of Complex Structures, Springer-Verlag, 1986.

Japanese Grade 7, 8, 9 Mathematics, 3 volumes, University of Chicago Mathematics Project, 1992.

SOURCES:

Books

Complex Analysis and Algebraic Geometry, edited by W. L. Baily and T. Shioda, Cambridge University Press, 1977.

Spencer, D. C., and S. Iyanaga, *Global Analysis: Papers in Honor of K. Kodaira,* Princeton University Press, 1969.

Periodicals

Weyl, H., "On the Work of Kunihiko Kodaira," paper presented at the 1954 International Congress of Mathematicians in Amsterdam.

—Sketch by Karen Sands

Georges Kohler
1946-
German immunologist

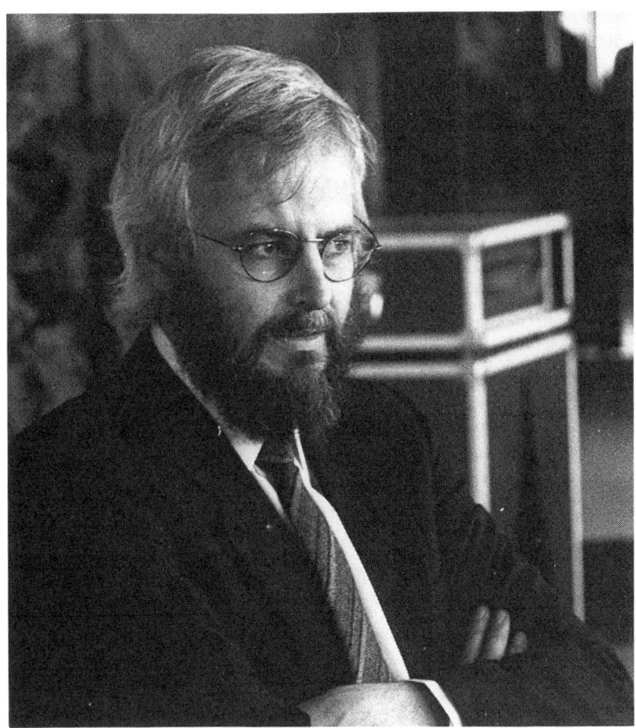

Georges Kohler

For decades, antibodies—substances manufactured by our plasma cells to help fight disease—were produced artificially by injecting animals with foreign macromolecules, then bleeding the animals and separating the antiserum in their blood. The technique was arduous and far from foolproof. But the discovery of the hybridoma technique by German immunologist Georges Kohler changed all that, making antibodies relatively easy to produce and dramatically facilitating research on many serious medical disorders such as the acquired immunodeficiency syndrome (AIDS) and cancer. For his work on what would come to be known as monoclonal antibodies, Kohler shared the 1984 Nobel Prize in medicine. He was only 38 years old at the time.

Born in Munich, in what was then West Germany, on April 17, 1946, Georges Jean Franz Kohler attended the University of Freiburg, where he obtained his Ph.D. in biology in 1974. From there he set off to Cambridge University in England, to work as a postdoctoral fellow for two years at the British Medical Research Council's laboratories. At Cambridge, Kohler worked under Dr. **César Milstein**, an Argentinean-born researcher with whom Kohler would eventually share the Nobel Prize. At the time, Milstein, who was Kohler's senior by nineteen years, was a distinguished immunologist, and he actively encouraged Kohler in his research interests. Eventually, it was while working in the Cambridge laboratory that Kohler discovered the hybridoma technique.

The Experiment in the Basement

Dubbed by the *New York Times* as the "guided missiles of biology," antibodies are produced by human plasma cells in response to any threatening and harmful bacterium, virus, or tumor cell. The body forms a specific antibody against each antigen; and César Milstein has told the *New York Times* that the potential number of different antigens may reach "well over a million." Therefore, for researchers working to combat diseases like cancer, an understanding of how antibodies could be harnessed for a possible cure was of great interest. And although scientists knew the benefits of producing antibodies, until Kohler and Milstein published their findings, there was no known technique for maintaining the long-term culture of antibody-forming plasma cells.

Kohler's interest in the subject had been aroused years earlier, when he had become intrigued by the work of Dr. Michael Potter of the National Cancer Institute in Bethesda, Maryland. In 1962 Potter had induced myelomas, or plasma-cell tumors in mice, and others had discovered how to keep those tumors growing indefinitely in culture. Potter showed that plasma tumor cells were both immortal and able to create an unlimited number of identical antibodies. The only drawback was that there seemed no way to make the cells produce a certain *type* of antibody. Because of this, Kohler wanted to initiate a cloning experiment that would fuse plasma cells able to produce the desired antibodies with the "immortal" myeloma cells. With Milstein's blessing, Kohler began his experiment.

"For seven weeks after he had made the hybrid cells," the *New York Times* reported in October, 1984, "Dr. Kohler refrained from testing the outcome of the experiment for fear of likely disappointment. At last, around Christmas 1974, he persuaded his wife," Claudia Kohler, "to come to the windowless basement where he worked to share his disappointment after the critical test." But disappointment turned to joy when Kohler discovered his test had been a success: Astoundingly, his hybrid cells were making pure antibodies against the test antigen. The result was dubbed "monoclonal antibodies." For his contribution to medical science, Kohler—who in 1977 had relocated to Switzerland to do research at the Basel Institute for Immunology—was awarded the Nobel in 1984. Said the blond-haired, bespectacled scientist when he found out about the honor: "My knees are still trembling."

Opening the Door of Immunology Wide

The implications of Kohler's discovery were immense, and as Milstein has told the *New York Times,* monoclonal antibodies have resulted in "a windfall of basic research." In the early 1980s Kohler's discovery had led scientists to identify various lymphocytes, or white blood cells. Among the kinds discovered were the T–4 lymphocytes, the cells destroyed by AIDS. Monoclonal antibodies have also improved tests for hepatitis B and streptococcal infections by providing guidance in selecting appropriate antibiotics, and they have aided in the research on thyroid disorders, lupus, rheumatoid arthritis, and inherited brain disorders. More significantly, Kohler's work has led to advances in research that can harness monoclonal antibodies into certain drugs and toxins that fight cancer, but would cause damage in their own right. Researchers are also using monoclonal antibodies to identify antigens specific to the surface of cancer cells so as to develop tests to detect the spread of cancerous cells in the body.

Despite the significance of the discovery, which has also resulted in vast amounts of research funds for many research laboratories, for Kohler and Milstein—who never patented their discovery—there has been little remuneration. In fact, during the years following the discovery until they won the Nobel Prize, Kohler received only a single honorary doctorate. Following the award, however, he and Milstein, together with Michael Potter, were named winners of the Lasker Medical Research Award.

In 1985 Kohler moved back to his hometown of Freiburg, Germany, to assume the directorship of the Max Planck Institute for Immune Biology—a position he has held ever since.

SELECTED WRITINGS BY KOHLER:

Periodicals

(With César Milstein) "Continuous Cultures of Fused Cells Secreting Antibody of Predefined Specificity," *Nature,* 256, 1975, p. 495.

(With H. Hengartner and M. J. Shulman) "Immunoglobulin Production by Lymphocyte Hybridomas," *European Journal of Immunology,* 8, 1978, p. 82.

"Immunoglobulin Chain Loss in Hybridoma Lines," *Proceedings of the National Academy of Sciences USA,* 77, 1980, p. 2197.

"The Technique of Hybridoma Production," *Immunological Methods,* 2, 1981, p. 285–90.

(With Osami Kanagawa, Barbara A. Vaupel, Shinyo Gayama, and Manfred Kopf) "Resistance of Mice Deficient in IL–4 to Retrovirus-Induced Immunodeficiency Syndrome," *Science,* Volume 262, October 8, 1993, p. 240–42.

SOURCES:

Periodicals

"A Discovery and Its Impact: Nine Years of Excitement," *New York Times,* October 16, 1984, section 3, p. 3.

"Five Named as Winners of Lasker Medical Research Awards," *New York Times,* November 15, 1984, section 1, p. 28.
New York Times, October 16, 1984, p. 1339.
"The 1984 Nobel Prize in Medicine," *Science,* November 30, 1984, p. 1025.
"Three Immunology Investigators Win Nobel Prize in Medicine," *New York Times,* October 16, 1984, section 1, p. 1.

—Sketch by Joan Oleck

Willem Johan Kolff
1911-
Dutch-born American physician and biomedical engineer

Willem Johan Kolff blended an aptitude for tinkering with a love for medicine and his patients to come up with some of the most vital artificial organs in the medical arsenal. He developed the first practical kidney dialysis machine as well as a heart-lung bypass machine that made open-heart surgery possible. He also helped to develop an artificial eye and ear, and his team at the Utah Medical Center developed and implanted in a human the first artificial heart. Widely known as the father of artificial organs, Kolff, along with his inventions, has saved the lives of countless people around the world and led the way to the creation of the field of biomedical engineering, or bionics.

Kolff was born in Leiden, the Netherlands, on February 14, 1911, the son of Adriana (de Jonge) and Jacob Kolff, a doctor who ran a tuberculosis sanatorium. Medicine was, therefore, an all but pre-determined course for the young Kolff, yet he had no desire to follow precisely his father's path nor to share in the frustrations inherent in treating an incurable disease. Instead, after graduating from medical school at the University of Leiden in 1938, Kolff accepted a teaching post at the University of Groningen. There he was influenced by a professor who introduced Kolff to the basic concepts of dialysis—the principle whereby a solution of a high concentration passes through a semipermeable membrane to a solution with a lower concentration. He was affected as well by patients who were dying of kidney failure. For Kolff, it was far too reminiscent of the sorrowful atmosphere of his father's sanatorium, and he was determined to take action.

Develops Practical Hemodialysis

The kidneys are vital organs in the body; among other duties, the pair of organs is responsible for eliminating liquid wastes from the body, filtering over four hundred gallons of blood daily. When the kidneys are not functioning correctly, uremia—a pathological condition caused by the accumulation of waste products normally removed in the urine—develops. The body swells, and if there is no intervention, death results. By the early twentieth century, doctors knew that they needed to create an external "kidney" to replace the function of damaged kidneys, realizing that the standard treatment of kidney failure—bleeding—was not effective. As early as 1913 in the United States, doctors had managed a crude blood dialysis, or blood filtering, of dogs using celloidin as the filtering membrane. A major problem that they could not overcome, however, was preventing the coagulation of the blood once it was outside the animal. During and just after World War I, a German doctor, Georg Haas, using a new anticoagulant, heparin, successfully managed the first human dialysis, but still there were problems: Haas's apparatus could not filter enough blood quickly enough, and the supply of the anticoagulant was minimal. Strangely, Haas left his researches half-completed, and the medical community all but forgot the possibilities of dialysis.

At Groningen, Kolff was able to capitalize on these ground-breaking achievements and completed his own dialysis research with a simple sausage packing made of cellophane. He discovered that when the sausage casing was filled with a liquid, such as blood, then agitated in saline solution, the casing made a perfect membrane for filtering wastes. Then in 1940, the Germans invaded Holland, and Kolff, visiting in The Hague, became involved in setting up one of Europe's first blood banks—one that is still functioning. With the German takeover of the country, Kolff, an outspoken anti-Nazi, left Groningen for the country town of Kampen, where he became the internist at the local hospital. There, in addition to carrying out his hospital duties and helping the resistance whenever possible, Kolff continued work on his dialysis machine. The anticoagulant heparin had become commercially available by that time, and he had amassed a large supply of sausage casing before leaving Groningen. To solve the problem of adequate blood supply he created large rotating drums, adopting an idea automotive magnate **Henry Ford** had used to design water pumps in his engines. Kolff's attempts with humans initially were unsuccessful, and it was not until just after the end of the war, in September of 1945, that he successfully treated a patient, saving the life, ironically, of a woman accused of German collaboration. But hemodialysis had proven to be practical, and the woman lived another seven years.

Continues Organ Designing in the United States

While still a medical student in 1937, Kolff had married Janke C. Huidekoper, and they already had four children, with another on the way, by 1950, when Kolff accepted a position in the United States at Ohio's Cleveland Clinic. Meanwhile, Kolff's dialysis machine was being improved upon by others around the world; it was not until the early 1970s, however, that the U.S. Congress decided that anyone needing the expensive service would receive federal support, thus ending the painful selection process that had been in use due to limited resources in kidney treatment centers. By then Kolff had moved on to other medical endeavors: he was intent on creating a heart-lung machine that could be used to keep bodily functions operating and thus enable open-heart surgery to take place. In the seventeen years he spent at the Cleveland Clinic Foundation as professor of clinical investigation, Kolff, working with C. P. Dubbelman, designed an artificial heart-lung device known as a pump-oxygenator. By 1961 another of Kolff's designs was in service: the intra-aortic balloon pump to be used in cases of circulation failure. In addition, his attention increasingly turned to designing and implanting an artificial heart. In December of 1957, Kolff and his Cleveland team removed the heart from a dog and replaced it with a pneumatic pump which kept the dog alive for ninety minutes, proving the viability of the artificial heart.

In 1967 Kolff moved from Cleveland to accept a position at the University of Utah as the head of both the Division of Artificial Organs and the Institute of Biomedical Engineering. As such, he led a team of surgeons, physicists, and cardiologists in designing an implantable artificial heart for humans. It was this team, using a heart designed by one of Kolff's students, **Robert K. Jarvik**, that implanted the first artificial heart in a human on December 2, 1982. The patient, Barney Clark, lived for 112 days, proving the viability of such a procedure. Although heart transplant is the preferred method, Kolff is quick to point out that there is an insufficient number of human hearts available to supply the needs of cardiac patients. Research thus continues into the improvement of the artificial heart. Kolff also designed an artificial ear and eye, though the latter, with its numerous devices necessary for operation, is far from a practical stage. Kolff also has gone on to develop a portable kidney dialysis machine, introducing, as early as 1975, the Wearable Artificial Kidney (or WAK), which allows for home dialysis.

When not in the lab, Kolff enjoys collecting paintings and sculptures, as well as gardening, bird-watching, and hiking in the Rocky Mountains. He is outspoken on social issues, including abortion rights and anti-nuclear policy. He became a naturalized U.S. citizen in 1956 and is the author of close to seven hundred articles and papers on the kidney, heart, and artificial organs. Recognized worldwide for his efforts in bionics, Kolff is the recipient of more than one hundred awards and honors, including the Landsteiner Silver Medal in 1942 from the Red Cross of the Netherlands, the Frances Amory Award in 1948 from the American Academy of Arts and Science, the Gairdner Prize in 1966, the Leo Harvey Prize in 1972, and the Japan Prize in 1986. He was named one of the one hundred most important Americans of the twentieth century by *Life* magazine in 1990. The medical tradition continues in the Kolff family: three of his children have become doctors, and a fourth is a hospital architect.

SELECTED WRITINGS BY KOLFF:

Books

(With others) *New Ways of Treating Uremia: The Artificial Kidney, Peritoneal Lavage, Intestinal Lavage,* Churchill, 1947.

Artificial Organs, Wiley, 1976.

Periodicals

(With others) "Use of Artificial Heart for Basic Cardiovascular Research," *Chest,* February, 1975, pp. 199–206.

(With others) "A Wearable Artificial Kidney: Functional Description of Hardware and Clinical Results," *Proceedings of the Clinical Dialysis and Transplant Forum,* November, 1975, pp. 65–71.

(With J. Lawson) "Perspectives for the Total Artificial Heart," *Transplantation Proceedings,* March, 1979, pp. 317–324.

(With others) "Intra-Aortic Balloon Pumping Device for Infants," *Clinical Cardiology,* October, 1979, pp. 348–353.

(With others) "Response of the Human Body to the First Permanent Implant of the Jarvik-7 Total Artificial Heart," *Transactions of the American Society for Artificial Internal Organs,* Volume 29, 1983, pp. 81–87.

SOURCES:

Books

Robinson, Donald, *The Miracle Finders: The Stories Behind the Most Important Breakthroughs of Modern Medicine,* McKay, 1976, pp. 68–73.

Periodicals

Adler, Jerry, and Jeff B. Copeland, "The Trio Who Did It," *Newsweek,* December 13, 1982, p. 73.

Weisse, Allen B., "Turning Bad Luck into Good: The Alchemy of Willem Kolff, the First Successful Artificial Kidney, and the Artificial Heart," *Hospital Practice,* February 28, 1992, pp. 108–128.

"Willem Kolff: The Physician-Mechanic Who Founded Bionics," *Life,* fall, 1990, p. 99.

Other

Kolff, Willem Johan, interview with J. Sydney Jones conducted January 5, 1994.

—*Sketch by J. Sydney Jones*

Andrey Nikolayevich Kolmogorov 1903-1987

Russian mathematician

Andrey Nikolayevich Kolmogorov, who made major contributions to almost all areas of mathematics, is considered one of the twentieth century's most eminent mathematicians. He is the founder of modern probability theory, describing its axiomatic foundations and developing many of its mathematical tools. Kolmogorov also helped make advances in many applied sciences, from physics to linguistics. A great teacher, he did much to keep the Soviet Union in the forefront of research in theoretical and applied mathematics and was responsible for reforms in mathematics education at the elementary and high-school level.

Kolmogorov was born in the town of Tambov in central Russia on April 25, 1903. In 1920, at the age of seventeen, he enrolled in Moscow University. By 1922, he had completed a study in the theory of operations on sets (published in 1928). In 1925, Kolmogorov received a doctoral degree from the department of physics and mathematics and became a research associate at Moscow University. At the age of twenty-eight, Kolmogorov was elected a full professor of mathematics and was appointed director of the university's Institute of Mathematics two years later, in 1933.

Describes Axiomatic Basis of Modern Probability Theory

While he was still a research associate, Kolmogorov published a paper, "General Theory of Measure and Probability Theory," in which he gave an axiomatic representation of some aspects of probability theory on the basis of measure theory. His work in this area, which a younger colleague once called the "New Testament" of mathematics, was fully described in the monograph *Grundbegriffe der Wahrscheinlichkeitsrechnung,* which was published in 1933. (The book was translated into English in 1950 under the title *Foundations of the Theory of Probability*). Kolmogorov's contribution to probability theory has been compared to Euclid's role in establishing the basis of geometry. He also made major contributions to the understanding of stochastic processes involving random variables and advanced the knowledge of chains of linked probabilities, to mention only a few of his advances in this field.

An appointment as Chair of Theory of Probability at Moscow University in 1937 served as official recognition of Kolmogorov's achievements in probability theory. Communication with the West was sporadic, however, and it was not until the late 1980s that Western mathematicians discovered that Kolmogorov had already determined the nature of many issues in probability theory they were still working to discover. In 1939, at the age of thirty-six, Kolmogorov became one of the youngest full members elected to the Academy of Sciences of the U.S.S.R. He was later appointed academician-secretary of the Academy's department of physical and mathematical sciences. These honors were in recognition not only of his work in probability theory but of his contributions to other areas of theoretical and applied mathematics. Kolmogorov did work in set theory, measure theory, integration theory, topology, functional analysis, constructive logic, differential equations, and the theory of approximation of functions. Among his many accomplishments in applied fields, Kolmogorov did essential work in biological statistics, econometrics, mathematical linguistics, and the theory of fluid turbulence besides other areas of mechanics. He helped develop a theorem, the Kolmogorov-Arnold-Moser (KAM) theorem, which is used to analyze stability in dynamic systems. Kolmogorov introduced the concept of entropy (a theoretical measure of unavailable energy in a thermodynamic system) as a measure of disorder. He also developed many applications of probability theory, creating a powerful technique for using probability to make observation-based predictions in the face of randomness and researching statistical inspection methods for mass production.

Kolmogorov was also actively interested in mathematical education in the U.S.S.R., working as the chairman of the Academy of Sciences Commission on Mathematical Education. He played a pivotal role in overhauling the teaching of mathematics during the 1960s, and his leadership in mathematics education for secondary schools and universities helped move the U.S.S.R. to the forefront of mathematics internationally during the following decades.

For his work, and among his many awards, Kolmogorov was named a Hero of Socialist Labor in 1963, and was awarded the State Prize in 1941 and the Lenin Prize in 1965. He was awarded the Order of the Red Banner and received the Order of Lenin six times. He received the Bolzano International Prize in 1963. Among his students were some of the Soviet Union's top mathematicians, including Lenin Prize laureates I. V. Arnold and Iu. A. Rozanov.

Kolmogorov remained an active member of the faculty and administration of Moscow University until his death, having served as Dean of the Department of Mechanics and Mathematics from 1954 to 1957. Kolmogorov died in Moscow on October 20, 1987, at the age of eighty-four.

SELECTED WRITINGS BY KOLMOGOROV:

Books

Foundations of the Theory of Probability, Chelsea Publishing, 1950.

(With S. V. Fomin) *Elements of the Theory of Functions and Functional Analysis,* Graylock Press, 1957.

(With Fomin) *Measure, Lebesgue Integrals and Hilbert Space,* Academic Press, 1961.

SOURCES:

Books

Boyer, C., and U. Merzbach, *A History of Mathematics,* John Wiley & Sons, 1989.

—Sketch by Maureen L. Tan

Izaak Maurits Kolthoff
1894-1993
Dutch-born American analytical chemist

Izaak Maurits Kolthoff, described by many as the father of modern chemistry, was a professor and department head at the University of Minnesota for thirty-five years. His research was at the forefront of major developments in the field of analytical chemistry, involving investigations of the reagents used in determining pH levels, crystalline precipitates, polarography and research on rubber and plastics. He also invented a method of synthesizing rubber, a discovery of immense value during World War II. The American Chemical Society's book *A History of Analytical Chemistry,* termed his contributions to the field of analytical chemistry as "monumental."

Kolthoff was born in Almelo, the Netherlands, on February 11, 1894, to Moses and Rosetta (Wysenbeek) Kolthoff. His chemistry career began informally in the kitchen of his home when he was fifteen. When his mother accidentally added sodium carbonate (soda) to a pot of chicken soup instead of sodium chloride (table salt), her son readily resolved the situation. He added hydrochloric acid to correct the pH level of the liquid until a strip of litmus paper turned pink. This treatment was effective, and the soup was saved.

Kolthoff received his formal training at the University of Utrecht in the Netherlands. Initially, he studied pharmacy, but later switched to analytical chemistry. After earning his Ph.D. in 1918, he taught at the University of Utrecht for nearly ten years. Kolthoff focused his research on the reagents used in determining pH, the acidity or alkalinity of a solution, and the significance of pH in bacteriology and industry, as well as in analytical chemistry. In 1927, after a lecture tour in the United States, he was offered a position at the University of Minnesota as professor and head of the analytical chemistry department. He later became a naturalized United States citizen.

Invents New Rubber Production Method

While at the University of Minnesota, Kolthoff researched the properties of crystalline precipitates, and also studied polarography, which is an electrochemical method of analysis that involves passing an electric current through the solution being investigated. During World War II, the American government asked him to turn his attention to researching a method of making synthetic rubber. Kolthoff and his associates succeeded in inventing a low-temperature method of producing high-quality synthetic rubber. Even after the war ended, most synthetic rubber was made by the Kolthoff method.

When government funding for rubber research ended in 1955, Kolthoff began research on improving the chemistry of rubber and plastics. He and his research team also analyzed acids and bases in non-water based reactions, and conducted studies involving the analysis of metal ions that were later used to help reduce water pollution.

Kolthoff became professor emeritus in 1962. He wrote or coauthored about 900 papers and books, including the standard work *Textbook of Quantitative Inorganic Analysis.* The recipient of numerous honors and awards, including the Polarographic Medal from the Polarographic Society of England, the Nichols

Medal from the American Chemical Society, and the first Kolthoff Gold Medal from the Academy of Pharmaceutical Science, he was also honored by the University of Minnesota, when a chemistry building there was named Kolthoff Hall in 1973. He received five honorary doctorates, was knighted by the government of the Netherlands, and was elected to the National Academy of Sciences in 1958.

Kolthoff's interests extended far beyond the laboratory and classroom. He enjoyed tennis and horseback riding in his spare time. He traveled to the Soviet Union on a least two occasions for scientific meetings, where, as he reported in an article for *Science,* he "was impressed by the large number of Chinese studying for advanced degrees at Moscow University." Remarking on the usefulness of educational and scientific links between countries, he regretted the United States policy of discouraging such contact. "This is too bad," he commented, "for scientific visitors like myself are in a unique position to establish much-needed relations with countries like China. From scientific contacts frequently come exchanges of opinion on other matters."

Domestically, Kolthoff devoted considerable time and effort in furthering his political beliefs. During World War II, he helped German scientists fleeing the Nazis to find jobs at the University of Minnesota. When he spoke out against McCarthyism during the 1950s, Senator Joseph McCarthy accused him of belonging to subversive groups, but never brought Kolthoff to testify before his Senate committee. In 1961 Kolthoff joined several colleagues in protesting nuclear weapons.

Kolthoff spent much of his time during his last years at the University of Minnesota library. He passed away on March 4, 1993, in St. Paul, Minnesota, at the age of 99; his *Star Tribune* obituary described him as an analytical chemist who helped to "revolutionize science in this century."

SELECTED WRITINGS BY KOLTHOFF:

Books

(With E. B. Sandhill) *Textbook of Quantitative Inorganic Analysis,* Wiley, 1936.

Acid Base Indicators, Macmillan, 1937.

Polarography, Wiley, 1952.

SOURCES:

Books

Laitinen, Herbert A. and Galen W. Furing, editors, *A History of Analytical Chemistry,* Division of Analytical Chemistry of the American Chemical Society, 1977, p. viii.

McGraw-Hill Modern Men of Science, McGraw-Hill, 1966, pp. 268–69.

Periodicals

"Chemistry Pioneer Izaak Kolthoff Dies," *Star Tribune,* March 6, 1993, p. 4B.

"Kolthoff Comments on Soviet Trip," *Science,* March 7, 1958, p. 512.

—Sketch by Donna Olshansky

Masakazu Konishi
1933-
Japanese-born American biologist

Masakazu Konishi is a biologist who has spent much of his professional career at the California Institute of Technology in Pasadena, studying the neurobiology of birds. Konishi's research work has resulted in a number of major findings. He proposed the template theory of song learning among songbirds. Later he developed a brain map of sound localization in the barn owl's brain, work that has become a model for studying animal sensory systems. Konishi also studied gender differences in the brains of songbirds and uncovered the phenomenon of biologically programmed death of nerve cells. Some of Konishi's research has long-term implications for understanding the origins of such human neurological disorders as Alzheimer's and Parkinson's disease.

Konishi, an only child, was born in Kyoto, Japan, on Feb. 17, 1933. His father, Shotaro, and mother, Hae, were both weavers. Because of post-World War II food shortages in Japan, he decided to study agriculture in junior high school. By the time he entered high school in Kyoto, however, he found that agriculture wasn't as interesting as animals and shifted to a more university-directed course of work that led him to study zoology at the university level. He earned a bachelor's and master's degree in zoology from Hokkaido University in Sapporo, Japan, in 1956 and 1958, respectively. In 1963 he completed his Ph.D. in zoology at the University of California, Berkeley, and went on to be a postdoctoral fellow in Germany at the University of Tubingen and at the Max Planck Institute in Munich.

Konishi began his academic teaching and research career as an assistant professor of biology at the University of Wisconsin in 1965; a year later he moved to Princeton University, becoming an associate professor there in 1970. In 1975, he began his long affiliation with California Institute of Technology as a professor of biology. Five years later, he was named Bing Professor of Behavioral Biology, a position he still holds.

Finds Songbirds Need a Tutor

While he was studying at Berkeley, Konishi entered the neurobiological debate over whether or not the central nervous system in birds requires auditory feedback in learning songs. He discovered that if a songbird is deafened before maturity and prior to learning its songs, it will develop abnormal songs. Using this information, Konishi developed the template theory, which explains how a younger bird learns from a tutor bird. He found that the memory of the tutor's songs act as a guide that a songbird uses to shape its own songs. This was the first example of a non-human animal requiring vocal feedback to develop vocalization.

At the California Institute of Technology, Konishi began exploring the neurophysiology of the barn owl's brain. Extensive work over two decades unraveled the "wiring" and showed that there are two audio pathways in the owl's brain. Konishi used another avian species, the Australian zebra finch, to study gender brain differences. The size and number of neurons are smaller in female zebra finches and prevailing theory was that male cells grew in the presence of the hormone testosterone while female cells remained the same when exposed to the hormone. Konishi used radioactive tracers and found that groups of brain cells related to song singing, a male characteristic, atrophy and die in female finches. In male finches, however, the same cells grow. This discovery, called programmed cell death, is believed responsible for the development of sex differences, and other researchers subsequently have found similar cellular behavior in mammals.

Konishi has published extensively and has been elected to the National Academy of Sciences. He also has been honored with a number of awards, including the Charles A. Dana Award for Pioneering Achievement in Health and the International Prize for Biology given by the Japan Society for the Promotion of Science.

SELECTED WRITINGS BY KONISHI:

Periodicals

With E. I. Knudsen, "A Neural Map of the Auditory Space in the Owl," *Science,* May 19, 1978.

With M. Gurney, "Hormone Induced Sexual Differentiation of Brain and Behavior in Zebra Finches, *Science,* 1980, pp. 1380–83.

With E. Akutagawa, "Neuronal Growth, Atrophy, and Death in a Sexually Dimorphic Song Nucleus in the Zebra Finch," *Nature,* 1985, pp. 145–47.

With S. T. Emlen, R. E. Ricklefs, and J. C. Wingfield, "Contributions of Bird Studies to Biology," *Science,* October 27, 1989, pp. 465–72.

With A. J. Doupe, "Song-Selective Auditory Circuits in the Vocal Control System of the Zebra Finch," *Proceedings of the National Academy of Sciences,* December 15, 1991, pp. 11339–43.

SOURCES:

Other

Interview conducted by Joel Schwarz for *Notable Twentieth-Century Scientists,* January 20, 1994.

—Sketch by Joel Schwarz

Arthur Kornberg
1918-
American biochemist

Arthur Kornberg discovered deoxyribonucleic acid (DNA) polymerase, a natural, chemical tool which scientists could use to make copies of DNA, the giant molecule that carries the genetic information of every living organism. The achievement won him the 1959 Nobel Prize in medicine or physiology (which he shared with **Severo Ochoa**). Since his discovery, laboratories around the world have used the enzyme to build and study DNA. This has led to a clearer understanding of the biochemical basis of genetics, as well as new strategies for treating cancer and hereditary diseases.

Kornberg was born in Brooklyn, New York, on March 3, 1918, to Joseph Kornberg and Lena Katz. An exceptional student, he graduated at age fifteen from Abraham Lincoln High School. Supported by a scholarship, he enrolled in the premedical program at City College of New York, majoring in biology and chemistry. He received his B.S. in 1937 and entered the University of Rochester School of Medicine. It was here that his interest in medical research blossomed and he became intrigued with the study of enzymes—the protein catalysts of chemical reactions.

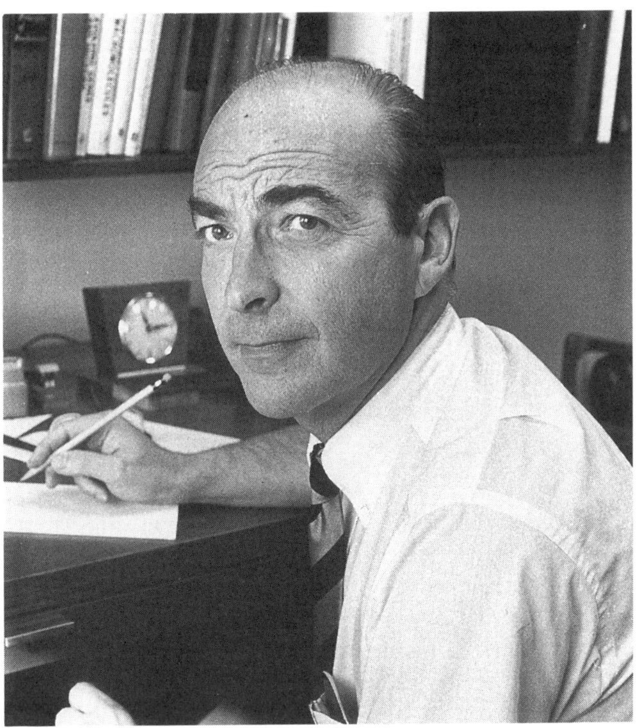

Arthur Kornberg

During his medical studies, Kornberg contracted hepatitis, a disease of the liver that commonly causes jaundice, a yellowing of the skin. The incident prompted him to write his first scientific paper, "The Occurrence of Jaundice in an Otherwise Normal Medical Student."

Researches Enzymes at the National Institutes of Health

Kornberg graduated from Rochester in 1941 and began his internship in the university's affiliated institution, Strong Memorial Hospital. At the outbreak of World War II in 1942, he was briefly commissioned a lieutenant junior grade in the United States Coast Guard and then transferred to the United States Public Health Service. From 1942 to 1945, Kornberg served in the nutrition section of the division of physiology at the National Institutes of Health (NIH) in Bethesda, Maryland. He then served as chief of the division's enzymes and metabolism section from 1947 to 1952.

During his years at NIH, Kornberg was able to take several leaves of absence. He honed his knowledge of enzyme production, as well as isolation and purification techniques, in the laboratories of Severo Ochoa at New York University School of Medicine in 1946, of **Carl Cori** and **Gerty Cori** at the Washington University School of Medicine in St. Louis in 1947, and of H. A. Barker at the University of California at Berkeley in 1951. Kornberg became an authority on the biochemistry of enzymes, including the production of coenzymes—the proteins that assist enzymes by transferring chemicals from one group of enzymes to another. While at NIH, he perfected techniques for synthesizing the coenzymes diphosphopyridine nucleotide (DPN) and flavin adenine dinucleotide—two enzymes involved in the production of the energy-rich molecules used by the body.

To synthesize coenzymes, Kornberg used a chemical reaction called a condensation reaction, in which phosphate is eliminated from the molecule used to form the enzymes. He later postulated that this reaction was similar to that by which the body synthesizes DNA. The topic of DNA synthesis was of intense interest among researchers at the time, and it closely paralleled his work with enzymes, since DNA controls the biosynthesis of enzymes in cells.

Receives Nobel Prize for His Work on DNA

In 1953, Kornberg became professor of microbiology and chief of the department of microbiology at Washington University School of Medicine in St. Louis. That year was a time of great excitement among researchers studying DNA; **Francis Crick** and **James Watson** at Cambridge University had just discovered the chemical structure of the DNA molecule. At Washington University, Kornberg's group built on the work of Watson and Crick, as well as techniques Ochoa had developed for synthesizing RNA—the decoded form of DNA that directs the production of proteins in cells. Their goal was to produce a giant molecule of artificial DNA.

The first major discovery they made was the chemical catalyst responsible for the synthesis of DNA. They discovered the enzyme in the common intestinal bacterium *Escherichia coli,* and Kornberg called it DNA polymerase. In 1957, Kornberg's group used this enzyme to synthesize DNA molecules. Although the molecules were biologically inactive, this was an important achievement; it proved that this enzyme does catalyze the production of new strands of DNA, and it explained how a single strand of DNA acts as a pattern for the formation of a new strand of nucleotides—the building blocks of DNA.

In 1959, Kornberg and Ochoa shared the Nobel Prize for their "discovery of the mechanisms in the biological synthesis of ribonucleic acid and deoxyribonucleic acid." The *New York Times* quoted Nobel Prize recipient **Hugo Theorell** as saying that Kornberg's research had "clarified many of the problems of regeneration and the continuity of life."

Continues His Work on Modeling DNA

In the same year he received the prize, Kornberg accepted an appointment as professor of biochemistry and chairman of the department of biochemistry at

Stanford University. He continued his research on DNA biosynthesis there with Mehran Goulian. The two researchers were determined to synthesize an artificial DNA that was biologically active, and they were convinced they could overcome the problems which had obstructed previous efforts.

The major problems Kornberg had encountered in his original attempt to synthesize DNA were twofold: the complexity of the DNA template he was working with, and the presence of contaminating enzymes called nucleases which damaged the growing strand of DNA. At Stanford, Kornberg's group succeeded in purifying DNA polymerase of contaminating enzymes, but the complexity of their DNA template remained an obstacle, until Robert L. Sinsheimer of the California Institute of Technology was able to direct them to a simpler one. He had been working with the genetic core of Phi X174, a virus that infects *Escherichia coli.*The DNA of Phi X174 is a single strand of nitrogenous bases in the form of a ring which, when broken, leaves the DNA without the ability to infect its host.

But if the dilemma of DNA complexity was solved, the solution raised yet another problem. The DNA ring in Phi X174 had to be broken in order to serve as a template. But when the artificial copy of the DNA was synthesized in the test tube, it had to be reformed into a ring in order to acquire infectivity. This next hurdle was overcome by Kornberg's laboratory and other researchers in 1966; they discovered an enzyme called *ligase,* which closes the ring of DNA. With their new knowledge, Kornberg's group added together the Phi X174 template, four nucleotide subunits of DNA, DNA polymerase, and ligase. The DNA polymerase used the template to build a strand of viral DNA consisting of 6,000 building blocks, and the ligase closed the ring of DNA. The Stanford team then isolated the artificial viral DNA, which represented the infectious, inner core of the virus, and added it to a culture of *Escherichia coli* cells. The DNA infected the cells, commandeering the cellular machinery that uses genes to make proteins. In only minutes, the infected cells had ceased their normal synthetic activity and begun making copies of Phi X174 DNA.

Kornberg and Goulian announced their success during a press conference on December 14, 1967, pointing out that the achievement would help in future studies of genetics, as well as in the search for cures to hereditary diseases and the control of viral infections. In addition, Kornberg noted that the work might help disclose the most basic processes of life itself. The Stanford researcher has continued to study DNA polymerase to further understanding of the structure of that enzyme and how it works.

Uses His Influence to Affect Government Policies

Kornberg has used his status as a Nobel Laureate on behalf of various causes. On April 21, 1975, he joined eleven speakers before the Health and Environment Subcommittee of the House Commerce Committee to testify against proposed budget cuts at NIH, including ceilings on salaries and the numbers of personnel. The witnesses also spoke out against the tendency of the federal government to direct NIH to pursue short-term projects at the expense of long-term, fundamental research. During his own testimony, Kornberg argued that NIH scientists and scientists trained or supported by NIH funding "had dominated the medical literature for twenty-five years." His efforts helped prevent NIH from being ravaged by budget cuts and overly influenced by politics.

Later that year, Kornberg also joined other Nobel Prize winners in support of **Andrei Sakharov**, the Soviet advocate of democratization and human rights who had been denied permission to travel to Sweden to accept the Nobel Prize in physics. Kornberg was among thirty-three Nobel Prize winners to send a cable to Soviet President Nikolai V. Podgorny, asking him to permit Sakharov to receive the prize.

Kornberg received the Paul-Lewis Laboratories Award in Enzyme Chemistry from the American Chemical Society, 1951, the Scientific Achievement Award of the American Medical Association, 1968, the Lucy Wortham James Award of the Society of Medical Oncology, 1968, the Borden Award in the Medical Sciences of the Association of American Medical Colleges, 1968, and the National Medal of Science, 1980. He is a member of the National Academy of Sciences, the American Academy of Arts and Sciences, the American Society of Biological Scientists, and a foreign member of the Royal Society of London. In addition, he is a member of the American Philosophical Society and, from 1965 to 1966, served as president of the American Society of Biological Chemists. Kornberg has been married to Sylvy Ruth Levy Kornberg since 1943. His wife, who is also a biochemist, has collaborated on much of his work. They have three sons.

SELECTED WRITINGS BY KORNBERG:

Books

Enzymatic Synthesis of DNA, Wiley, 1961.

DNA Replication, W. H. Freeman, 1980.

Periodicals

(With M. Goulian) "Enzymatic Synthesis of DNA. XXIII. Synthesis of Circular Replicative Form of Phage Phi X174 DNA." *Proceedings of the National Academy of Sciences,* Volume 58, 1967, pp. 1723–30.

(With M. Goulian and R. Sinsheimer) "Enzymatic Synthesis of DNA. XXIV. Synthesis of Infectious Phage Phi X 174 DNA." *Proceedings of the National Academy of Sciences,* Volume 58, 1967, pp. 2321–28.

SOURCES:

Books

Wasson, Tyler, editor, *Nobel Prize Winners,* H. W. Wilson, 1987, pp. 797–802.

—*Sketch by Marc Kusinitz*

Sergei Korolyov
1906-1966
Russian aerospace engineer

Sergei Korolyov was the engineer and organizer behind the Soviet Union's spectacular advances in military and civilian rocketry in the 1950s and 1960s. Walter McDougall, in his landmark history . . . *The Heavens and the Earth,* called Korolyov "the man who launched the Space Age." Working under a stifling blanket of official secrecy for much of his life, Korolyov was a driving force in the space race and the arms race.

Many dates and details of Korolyov's life are obscured by conflicting accounts, but he was apparently born Sergei Pavlovich Korolyov on December 30, 1906, in the town of Zhitomir in the Ukraine. Korolyov (spelled Korolev in many English-language works) had the fortune to be raised by well-educated parents who encouraged his studies. His father, Pavel Korolyov, was a teacher of literature. His mother, Mariya Nikolayevna, was a student who later earned her degree in languages. Pavel and Mariya's marriage failed, but Sergei later acquired a stepfather, Grigory Mikhailovich Balanin, an engineer who moved the family to the port city of Odessa. There he and his stepson joined a glider club, and Sergei's love of flight, apparent since the age of two, literally took wing. By 1924, Korolyov was not only flying gliders but designing them, and he was later to build the first aerobatic glider capable of performing loops.

Takes a Pioneering Role in Rocket Development

Korolyov attended the Kiev Polytechnical Institute and then the Moscow Higher Technical School. There his engineering thesis for the Department of Aerodynamics caught the attention of leading aircraft designer Andrei Tupolev. Korolyov went to work in Tupolev's design bureau after graduation, but his imagination had been captured by the works of his countrymen **Konstantin Tsiolkovsky** and Freidrich Tsander on the possibility of space exploration by rocket. In 1932, Korolyov became director of the Group for the Study of Rocket Propulsion Systems, known by its Russian initials as GIRD. Originally a private gathering of enthusiasts, GIRD soon attracted official funding for its rocket experiments. Those efforts included launching the first Russian liquid-fueled rocket in 1933 and adding rocket engines to conventionally-powered aircraft. Korolyov, who had earned his pilot's license in 1930, test-flew some of these hybrid aircraft himself. He became deputy director of GIRD's successor, a new military-sponsored agency called the Jet Scientific Research Institute (RNII). In 1934, Korolyov's book *Rocket Flight into the Stratosphere* was published by the Ministry of Defense. His RP–318–1 aircraft design was successfully flown in 1940 under rocket power alone. RNII experiments in ballistic wingless rockets also bore fruit, leading to the launch of the world's first two-stage rocket.

By this time, however, Korolyov was no longer in the RNII. In 1937, the Institute's head had been deemed a potential political enemy of Soviet leader Joseph Stalin. Korolyov and other members of RNII were tainted by their director's alleged treason and were sent en masse to the gulags. Korolyov was placed in the Tupolevskaya *shagara,* a work camp where he and other engineers were assembled to do the same tasks they'd been doing before being arrested. Korolyov languished in custody for at least seven years, most of which he spent designing rocket-powered takeoff assist systems for aircraft.

When the war ended, Korolyov was sent to study what remained of the V–2 works in Germany. Returning to Russia, he worked to improve on the V–2 design. While Korolyov remained at least nominally a prisoner, his talents could no longer be ignored, and he assumed increasing responsibilities in the growing Soviet rocket effort. He produced a V–2 copy, the R–1, which was launched in October, 1947. Korolyov followed this vehicle with the R–2, a "stretched" derivative that was capable of longer-range flights than the R–1. The R–2 was deployed as a missile and also used for suborbital research flights.

Builds the Soviet Space Program

After Joseph Stalin's death in 1953, Korolyov's alleged unreliability was forgotten. Korolyov joined the Communist party, knowing he needed all the political backing he could get to pursue his dream of space flight. He understood and accepted the fact that he could only build spaceships if the party and the military funded their development as weapons. When Nikita Khrushchev emerged as head of the Soviet state, Korolyov briefed him on the status of the top-secret rocket program. Khrushchev immediately realized the political value of success in space, and Korolyov made a second bargain, tailoring the space program to Khrushchev's politically-driven schedule in order to obtain the support he needed.

"When he expounded his ideas, you could see passion burning in his eyes," Khrushchev wrote of Korolyov in his book of memoirs *Khrushchev Remembers: The Last Testament.* "He had unlimited energy and determination, and he was a brilliant organizer." Under the secrecy which cloaked the USSR's military-directed space program, however, Korolyov was forbidden to communicate with anyone outside the USSR. His articles could appear only in officially-sanctioned Russian-language publications, and then only under pseudonyms. He held the title of Chief Designer, but his name was classified. Honors, such as the prestigious Lenin Prize he received in 1958, were also given in secret. His private life was accordingly concealed as well, although it is known that he married twice, divorcing Oxana Vincentini in 1946 after a union that produced one daughter and marrying Nina Kotenkova in 1947.

The private developments in Korolyov's life never slowed his pursuit of space flight. In 1957, he launched the R–7, the world's first Intercontinental Ballistic Missile (ICBM). This rocket's design illustrates Korolyov's ingenuity. Ordered to build a vehicle that could carry a primitive two-ton hydrogen warhead to the United States and constrained by the failure of Soviet metallurgists to concoct alloys needed for large rocket engines, Korolyov clustered twenty smaller engines, using a core vehicle plus four conical strap-on boosters. This approach, called "parallel staging," resulted in a squat, almost pyramid-shaped design. The cumbersome R–7 was never widely deployed as an ICBM, but it gained worldwide fame in another role. On October 4, 1957, Korolyov watched the R–7 launch Sputnik I, whose design Korolyov had also directed, into orbit. As the world's first man-made satellite, Sputnik's successful launch was recognized as an important landmark in the history of space flight. Korolyov later modified the R–7 into the Proton, which was still launching satellites in the 1990s.

Despite health problems dating to his gulag days and a 1960 heart attack, Korolyov continued to build a wide-ranging organization while still personally directing the design and launch of every Soviet space vehicle. Ordered to put a man into Earth orbit as soon as possible, Korolyov launched **Yuri Gagarin** aboard Vostok I on April 12, 1961, the first manned space flight in history. In August, 1962, Korolyov launched two Vostok capsules in two days, arranging the first rendezvous in space. Just over two years later, Voshkod I went into orbit with the first three-member crew. Officially Voshkod was an entirely new spacecraft, but in fact it was another Korolyov improvisation. Faced with an order to launch three men long before he had an appropriate spacecraft, Korolyov had managed to modify the one-man Vostok to accommodate two additional (very cramped) cosmonauts. Once again, Korolyov's ability produced a public relations triumph to reinforce Khrushchev's claims of Soviet space superiority.

Korolyov was also mounting an effort to beat the Americans to the moon. While resenting the political pressure on him, Korolyov admitted he found this challenge exciting. After Khrushchev was removed from power, however, Korolyov proposed that the USSR give up the moon race in favor of space station development.

On January 14, 1966, Korolyov entered a Moscow hospital for hemorrhoid surgery. The surgeon discovered colon cancer, which he attempted to remove without proper preparation. Korolyov died on the operating table. Only in announcing Korolyov's demise did the Soviets identify him as the man behind their space successes. Those successes included some Korolyov never lived to see, as probes designed under his leadership soft-landed on the moon and dropped into the atmosphere of Venus. The Soyuz spacecraft Korolyov designed did not fly until after his death, but it, too, went on to carry people and equipment into space for decades.

In death, Korolyov finally received some belated public recognition. He was given a state funeral, and his ashes were interred in the Kremlin Wall with those of the nation's heroes. The Soviet people learned for the first time that Korolyov was a member of the Presidium of the Soviet Academy of Sciences and had twice been made a Hero of Socialist Labor. An official biography and a film were soon released. These presented Korolyov's achievements, but ignored his long imprisonment. It was not until the post-Soviet era that the Russian people learned the whole story of the man who had brought spaceflight out of science fiction and made it a reality.

SELECTED WRITINGS BY KOROLYOV:

Books

Rocket Flight into the Stratosphere, USSR Ministry of Defense, 1934.

SOURCES:

Books

Khrushchev, Nikita, *Khrushchev Remembers: The Last Testament,* translated and edited by Strobe Talbott, Little, Brown and Co., 1974.

McDougall, Walter A., ... *The Heavens and the Earth,* Basic Books, 1985.
Oberg, James E., *Red Star in Orbit,* Random House, 1981.
Rauschenbach, B. V., "S. P. Korolyov and Soviet Rocket Technology," in *History of Rocketry and Astronautics* (Volume 9 of the AAS History Series), edited by Frederick I. Ordway, III, American Astronautical Society, 1989, pp. 283–290.
Riabchikov, Evgeny, *Russians in Space,* edited by Colonel General Nikolai P. Kamanin, translated by Guy Daniels, Doubleday & Co., 1971.
Stoiko, Michael, *Soviet Rocketry: Past, Present, and Future,* Holt, Rinehart and Winston, 1970.

—Sketch by Matthew A. Bille

Albrecht Kossel
1853-1927
German biochemist

Albrecht Kossel was one of the earliest scientists to apply the exact methods of organic chemistry to problems in the chemistry of living tissue. His investigations into the cell substance nuclein revealed that it contained both protein and nonprotein (nucleic acid) parts. His research into protein components led to the discovery of the amino acid histidine. For his work on cell chemistry and proteins, Kossel won the Nobel Prize for Physiology or Medicine in 1910.

Karl Martin Leonhard Albrecht Kossel was born on September 16, 1853, in Rostock, Germany. He was the eldest son of a merchant father, also named Albrecht Kossel, and Clara Jeppe Kossel. Botany was Kossel's first love, but his father saw no future in that, so in 1872 Kossel entered the University of Strasbourg to study medicine instead. While thcre, he came under the influence of Ernst Felix Immanuel Hoppe-Seyler, one of the forefathers of the then-emerging field of biochemistry. In 1877, Kossel passed the state medical exam and began working as an assistant at Hoppe-Seyler's institute of physical chemistry, also in Strasbourg. He received his doctor of medicine degree the following year.

Explores the Chemical Makeup of Nuclein

Kossel remained an assistant in Hoppe-Seyler's laboratory until 1881, when he qualified as a lecturer in physiological chemistry. Two years later, he was appointed director of the chemical division at the Berlin physiological institute by another leading German scientist, Emil Heinrich Du Bois-Reymond. From 1887 to 1895, Kossel was a professor at the University of Berlin.

Beginning in 1879 and continuing for many years, Kossel undertook what proved to be trailblazing research on the makeup of the cell substance nuclein. This substance had been discovered a decade before by another of Hoppe-Seyler's star pupils, Johann Frederick Miescher. However, nuclein was still a vague entity when Kossel first set about defining its composition.

Kossel soon determined that nuclein was made up of two parts, one protein and one not. Thus, the word nuclein was eventually replaced by the more specific term nucleoprotein, and the nonprotein portion came to be called nucleic acid. Nucleic acids differed from any other natural products that were known up to that point. When broken down, they produced carbohydrates and nitrogen-bearing compounds called purines and pyrimidines. Kossel further isolated two purines (adenine and guanine), as well as three pyrimidines (thymine, cytosine, and uracil). In addition, Kossel correctly concluded that the function of nuclein was somehow tied in to the formation of flesh tissue. His writings foreshadowed many important later developments, including modern investigations of nucleic acids as the storers and transmitters of genetic data.

Investigates the Composition of Proteins

In 1895, Kossel left Berlin for the University of Marburg, where he was a professor and director of the physiological institute. That same year, he began work that lasted for more than three decades as editor of the *Zeitschrift für physiologische Chemie,* a noted journal founded by Hoppe-Seyler that was for a time the only periodical in the world devoted exclusively to biochemistry. It was primarily in this journal that Kossel's own papers appeared. Then in 1901, Kossel moved again—this time to the University of Heidelberg, where he remained a professor and administrator until his retirement in 1924. Thereafter, he held the post of director of that city's institute for protein investigation.

Starting in the 1890s, Kossel's attention turned more and more to research on proteins. In particular, he studied the proteins in fish sperm cells, which proved simpler than those in other cells. He developed an elaborate theory to explain how complex ordinary proteins could be built from the simple bases present in spermatozoa. Unfortunately, his elegant explanation proved wrong. It was decades before anyone realized that the crucial compounds for this purpose are not the proteins but the nucleic acids, which are present in spermatozoa in their full complexity.

Given the technical limitations of his time, Kossel was remarkably successful at elucidating the makeup of proteins. He discovered histidine, an amino acid that is the chief component of protein. He also devised a method for comparing the amino acids in the sperm of different fish species. In the laboratory, Kossel was never satisfied with purely chemical findings; he always strove to understand the biological meaning of his discoveries. In this regard, he was a true pathfinder.

Based on such impressive achievements, Kossel received many honors in addition to the 1910 Nobel Prize. Notable among these were honorary degrees from universities in Cambridge, England; Edinburgh, Scotland; Dublin, Ireland; Ghent, Belgium; and Greifswald, Germany. He was also a member of various societies, including the Royal Society of Sciences in Sweden. Among Kossel's students over the years were several who achieved later prominence, including Phoebus Aaron Theodor Levene, who in 1909 became the first chemist to show that nucleic acids contain a sugar (ribose). Twenty years later, Levene demonstrated that other nucleic acids contain a different sugar (deoxyribose), thus defining the two types of nucleic acid: ribonucleic acid (RNA) and deoxyribonucleic acid (DNA).

Kossel married Luise Holtzmann in 1886. They had two children: a daughter, Gertrude, and a son, Walther. The latter, born in 1888, went on to become a distinguished physicist. Kossel died on July 5, 1927, in Heidelberg, Germany, after a brief illness. Upon his death, obituary notices were carried by such respected journals as *Nature, Science,* and the *Journal of the American Medical Association.*

SELECTED WRITINGS BY KOSSEL:

Books

The Protamines and Histones, Longmans, Green, 1928.

"The Chemical Composition of the Cell Nucleus," in *Nobel Lectures, Including Presentation Speeches and Laureates' Biographies: Physiology or Medicine, 1901–1921,* Elsevier, 1967, pp. 394–407.

SOURCES:

Periodicals

"Albrecht Kossel," *Journal of the American Medical Association,* August 13, 1927, pp. 524–25.

Kennaway, Ernest, "Some Recollections of Albrecht Kossel," *Annals of Science,* 1952, pp. 393–97.

Mathews, Albert P., "Professor Albrecht Kossel," *Science,* September 30, 1927, p. 293.

"Prof. Albrecht Kossel," *Nature,* August 13, 1927, p. 233.

—Sketch by Linda Wasmer Smith

Samuel L. Kountz
1930-1981
American transplant surgeon

Born in a small, poverty-stricken, all-black town in Arkansas, Samuel L. Kountz struggled to study medicine, and eventually became one of the most renowned kidney transplant surgeons in the world. During his career he developed techniques not only to preserve donated organs, but also to overcome tissue rejection, thus making kidney transplants more feasible.

Born Samuel Lee Kountz Jr. on October 20, 1930, in Lexa, Arkansas, he was the son of a Baptist minister and grandson of a woman born a slave. Lexa was so poor that it had no doctor to serve its population of under one hundred, and Kountz's father doubled as nurse to the sick. At an early age Samuel Kountz, with his grandmother's encouragement, determined to become a doctor. But educational opportunities were extremely limited in Lexa, and Kountz did not pass the entrance examination to Arkansas A & M College. He was so determined to attend, however, that he appealed to the college president and was given a chance, working his way through school as a waiter and graduating third in his class in 1952. He then won a scholarship to the University of Arkansas Medical School in Little Rock and was the first African American to be enrolled at that institution. In 1956 he earned an M.S. in biochemistry and, upon attaining his M.D. in 1958, Kountz interned at San Francisco General Hospital for two years, completing his extensive surgical residency at Stanford University School of Medicine in 1965.

Focuses on Renal Transplants

It was while interning in San Francisco that Kountz assisted on the first West Coast transplant of a kidney. Kidney transplant had come a long way by 1959, but the procedure still had some distance to go before it gained a degree of success. The first animal kidney transplant took place in 1902 in Austria; the first human transplant was performed by a Soviet surgeon in 1936. But only by 1959 had medicine begun to overcome the most difficult part of such an operation: rejection of the implanted organ by the immune system of the host body. Successful transplants between identical and fraternal twins had started in 1954, but it was only with the development of immunosuppressants such as azathioprine that transplants between non-siblings became a possibility. While interning at Stanford, Kountz began to study this rejection process and discovered that large amounts of the steroid methylprednisolone administered after the transplant operation helped to reverse the rejection of the new organ. He also teamed up with Folker O. Belzer to devise a technique for keeping organs healthy and functioning for up to sixty hours after they were cut out of donors. Additionally, he was responsible for setting up a system of organ donor cards through the National Kidney Foundation.

Most of all, however, Kountz was a master at surgery itself, transplanting more than a thousand kidneys over the course of his professional career. The American College of Cardiology honored him for his work in 1964 with an Outstanding Investigator Award, and his alma mater, the University of Arkansas, also paid him tribute in 1973 with an honorary doctor of law degree. Kountz was an associate professor of surgery at Stanford University from 1965 to 1967 and then transferred to the University of California at San Francisco, where he built one of the largest kidney transplant training and research centers in the nation. In 1972 he became full professor of surgery and department chair at the State University of New York, Downstate Medical Center in Brooklyn, as well as chief of surgery at Kings County Hospital Center. It became one of his goals after moving to New York to improve medical care in the African American community. On a teaching trip to South Africa in 1977, Kountz contracted an undiagnosed disease which caused brain damage and incapacitated him, ending his brilliant career. Married to Grace Yvonne Akin and the father of three children, Kountz died in Great Neck, New York, on December 23, 1981. He left behind a body of work including nearly two hundred articles and papers on kidney transplants and related topics, as well as scores of students he had trained and patients to whom he had given new life.

SELECTED WRITINGS BY KOUNTZ:

Periodicals

"The Effect of Bioscience and Technological Momentum on the Surgical Treatment of Chronic Illness," *Surgery,* June, 1975, pp. 735–740.

"Acute Effects of Stress on Renal Function in Healthy Donors. Preliminary Report," *New York State Journal of Medicine,* October, 1975, pp. 2138–2139.

(With others) "Vascular Complications in Human Renal Transplantation," *Surgery,* January, 1976, pp. 77–81.

(With K. M. Butt) "A New Vascular Access for Hemodialysis: The Arterial Jump Graft," *Surgery,* April, 1976, pp. 476–479.

(With others) "Renal Transplantation in Children," *Urologia Internationalis,* Volume 32, 1977, pp. 277–283.

(With others) "Effects of Intravenous Bolus Dosages of Methylprednisolone and Local Radiation on Renal Allograft Rejection and Patient Mortality," *Surgery, Gynecology and Obstetrics,* January, 1977, pp. 63–66.

(With others) "Organ Preservation and Tissue Banking," *Transplantation Proceedings,* March, 1977, pp. 1255–1256.

(With others) "Immunosuppression with Melengestrol," *Transplantation Proceedings,* June, 1977, pp. 447–453.

(With others) "The Impact of 1,000 Renal Transplants at One Center," *Annals of Surgery,* October, 1977, pp. 424–435.

SOURCES:

Books

Robinson, Donald, *The Miracle Finders,* David McKay, 1976, pp. 77–80.

Periodicals

"Dr. Samuel Kountz," *San Francisco Chronicle,* December 25, 1981, p. 42.

Journal of the National Medical Association, December, 1981, supplement, p. 1229.

Organ, Claude H., "The Black Surgeon in the Twentieth Century: A Tribute to Samuel L. Kountz, M.D.," *Journal of the National Medical Association,* September, 1978, pp. 683–684.

—Sketch by J. Sydney Jones

Edwin G. Krebs
1918-
American biochemist

In the 1950s Edwin G. Krebs and his longtime associate **Edmond Fischer** discovered reversible protein phosphorylation, a fundamental biological mechanism. Together Krebs and Fisher's work illuminates the basic processes that regulate many vital aspects of cell activity, such as protein synthesis, cell metabolism, and hormonal responses to stress. Medical application of their discoveries has helped in research on Alzheimer's disease, organ transplants, and certain kinds of cancer, and in 1992 the two scientists shared the Nobel Prize for Physiology or Medicine. In addition to his contributions in the field of biochemical research, Krebs has also been recognized for his teaching and administrative abilities.

Edwin Gerhard Krebs was born to William Carl Krebs and Louisa Helena Stegeman Krebs in Lansing, Iowa, on June 6, 1918. He was the third of four children. His father, a Presbyterian minister, died while Krebs was in his first year of high school. In order to keep Krebs's two older brothers enrolled at the University of Illinois in Urbana, Louisa Krebs moved the family from Greenville, where Edwin Krebs grew up, to the university town. There she rented a house big enough for her family, with extra rooms to rent out to students, keeping the family together and helping the children continue their education. She had been a teacher herself before her marriage.

In 1940, after completing his high-school and undergraduate work in Urbana, Krebs entered medical school at Washington University School of Medicine in St. Louis, Missouri. To Krebs's way of thinking, medicine had the advantage of being directly related to people. His general interest in science he attributed to concerns about economic security. At Washington University he received classical medical training and was also introduced to medical research. He had the opportunity to work under Arda A. Green, who was associated with **Carl Ferdinand Cori** and **Gerty T. Cori**. The Coris were a husband-and-wife team who had won the Nobel Prize in 1947 for research on carbohydrate metabolism and the enzyme phosphorylase. Krebs's later collaboration with Fischer at the University of Washington in Seattle had its beginning in the research conducted by the Coris.

After receiving his medical degree in 1943 and completing an eight-month residency in internal medicine at Barnes Hospital in St. Louis, Krebs became a medical officer in the navy, serving in that capacity until 1946. This was the only period in his career during which Krebs was a practicing physician. Due to the unavailability of a resident position, and on the advice of one of his professors, Krebs now began studying science. Because of his background in chemistry, Krebs chose to work in biochemistry and was accepted by the Coris as a postdoctoral fellow in their laboratory. For two years, while working for the Coris, Krebs studied the interaction of protamine (a basic protein) with rabbit muscle phosphorylase. This work seemed so rewarding to him that he decided to continue his efforts in the field of research, and when in 1948 he was invited by Hans Neurath to join the faculty in the department of biochemistry at the University of Washington, he jumped at the opportunity to become assistant professor.

Long Collaboration Leads to Nobel Prize

At this time Neurath's department greatly emphasized protein chemistry and enzymology (enzymes are proteins that act as catalysts in biochemical reactions). Work in the Coris' laboratory had established that the enzyme phosphorylase existed in active and inactive forms, but what controlled its activity was unknown. Combining his experience on mammalian skeletal muscle phosphorylase with Edmond Fischer's experience with potato phosphorylase after Fischer joined the department, Krebs and Fischer teamed up to uncover the molecular mechanism by which phosphorylase makes energy available to a contracting muscle. What they discovered was reversible protein phosphorylation. An enzyme called protein kinase takes phosphate from adenosine triphosphate (ATP), the supplier of energy to cells, and adds it to inactive phosphorylase, changing the shape of the phosphorylase and consequently switching it on. Another enzyme, called protein phosphatase, reverses this process by removing the phosphate from phosphorylase, thus deactivating it. Protein kinases are present in all cells.

Once it became evident that reversible protein phosphorylation was a general process, the impact of Krebs and Fischer's work was immeasurable. Their collaboration opened the field of biochemical research and paved the way to much of the work done in the area of biotechnology and genetic engineering. Protein phosphorylation has even been posited as the basis of learning and memory. Medical applications have included development of the drug cyclosporin, which blocks the body's immune response by interfering with phosphorylation to prevent rejection of transplants. As important as what happens when the process functions normally is what happens when it goes awry: protein kinases are involved in almost 50 percent of cancer-causing oncogenes.

Recognition for Krebs's work came through various awards besides the Nobel Prize. In 1988 Krebs and Fischer shared the Passano Award for their research, and Krebs was one of four scientists to share the Lasker Award for Basic Medical Research in 1989. He was co-recipient of the Robert A. Welch Award in Chemistry in 1991, followed by the Nobel Prize a year later. Besides concentrating his research on protein phosphorylation, Krebs has investigated signal transduction and carbohydrate metabolism.

Interest in Administration Leads to Appointment

In 1968 Krebs had left the University of Washington to accept the position of founding chairman of the department of biological chemistry at the University of California in Davis. When he returned to Washington in 1977 he became chairman of the department of pharmacology. In both positions he was able to assist in the recruitment of talented faculty, which Krebs considers critical to the continued development of the field of biochemistry. From 1977 until 1983, Krebs was associated with the Howard Hughes Medical Institute as well.

Krebs was married on March 10, 1945, to Virginia Deedy French, and they have three children, Sally, Robert, and Martha. As a young boy, Krebs loved to read historical novels about the Civil War and the settling of the West. He credits his wife for keeping him aware of the other aspects of living besides his work. The University of Washington dean of medicine, Philip Fialkow, commented in the *Daily,* a campus newspaper, that Krebs (along with Fischer) was "simply a joy to work with . . . [and] very considerate of students and the young faculty," giving credit to the contributions of others and accepting institutional responsibility when called on.

SELECTED WRITINGS BY KREBS:

Books

(Contributor) G. I. Drummond, editor, *Advances in Cyclic Nucleotide Research,* Raven Press, 1975, pp. 241–51.

Periodicals

(With Edmond H. Fischer) "The Phosphorylase *b* and *a* Converting Enzyme of Rabbit Skeletal Muscle," *Biochimica Biophysica Acta,* Volume 20, 1956, pp. 150–57.

(With Fischer and A. B. Kent) "The Muscle Phosphorylase *b* Kinase Reaction," *Journal of Biological Chemistry,* Volume 231, 1959, pp. 1698–1704.

Proceedings of the National Academy of Sciences, USA, 1988, pp. 7182–86; 1989, pp. 5257–61.

(With N. F. Zander, D. E. Cool, C. D. Diltz, and others) "Suppression of V-FMS-Induced Transformation by Overexpression of a Truncated T-Cell Protein Tyrosine Phosphatase," *Oncogene,* Volume 8, 1993, pp. 1175–82.

SOURCES:

Periodicals

Altman, Laurence K., "Americans Win Nobel for Clues to Cell Signals," *New York Times,* October 13, 1992, pp. B5, B9, C3.

Brown, Phyllida, "Protein Manipulators 'Stumble' on Nobel Prize," *New Scientist,* October 17, 1992, p. 7.

Chemical and Engineering News, June 10, 1991. p. 24; October 19, 1992, p. 6–7; October 23, 1992, pp. 542–43.

Liberal Arts and Sciences Newsletter, fall, 1992, p. 5.

Marx, Jean, "U.S. Researchers Gather a Bumper Crop of Laurels," *Science,* September 29, 1989. p. 1447.

Ogden, Karen, "UW Researchers Win Nobel Prize," *Daily* (University of Washington), October 13, 1992, pp. 1, 7.

Other

Krebs, Edwin G., unpublished autobiographical manuscript.

—*Sketch by Jordan Richman*

Hans Adolf Krebs
1900-1981
German-born English biochemist

Few students complete an introductory biology course without learning about the Krebs cycle, an indispensable step in the process our bodies perform to convert food into energy on which we subsist. Also known as the citric acid cycle or tricarboxylic acid cycle, the Krebs cycle derives its name from one of the most influential biochemists of our time. Born in the same year as the twentieth century, Hans Adolf Krebs spent the greater part of his eighty-one years engaged in research on intermediary metabolism. First rising to scientific prominence for his work on the ornithine cycle of urea synthesis, Krebs shared the Nobel Prize for physiology and medicine in 1953 for his discovery of the citric acid cycle. Over the course of his career, the German-born scientist published, oversaw, or supervised a total of more than 350 scientific publications. But the story of Krebs's life is more than a tally of scientific achievements; his biography can be seen as emblematic of biochemistry's path to recognition as its own discipline.

Hans Adolf Krebs

On August 25, 1900, Alma Davidson Krebs gave birth to her second child, a boy named Hans Adolf. The Krebs family—Hans, his parents, sister Elisabeth and brother Wolfgang—lived in Hildesheim, in Hanover, Germany. There his father Georg practiced medicine, specializing in surgery and diseases of the ear, nose, and throat. Hans developed a reputation as a loner at an early age. He enjoyed swimming, boating, and bicycling, but never excelled at athletic competitions. He also studied piano diligently, remaining close to his teacher throughout his university years. At the age of fifteen, the young Krebs decided he wanted to follow in his father's footsteps and become a physician. But World War I had broken out, and before he could begin his medical studies, he was drafted into the army upon turning eighteen in August of 1918. The following month he reported for service in a signal corps regiment in Hanover. He expected to serve for at least a year, but shortly after he started basic training the war ended. Krebs received a discharge from the army to commence his studies as soon as possible.

Begins Career in Research

Krebs chose the University of Göttingen, located near his parents' home. There, he enrolled in the basic science curriculum necessary for a student planning a medical career and studied anatomy, histology, embryology and botanical science. After a year at Göttingen, Krebs transferred to the University of Freiburg. At Freiburg, Krebs encountered two faculty members who enticed him further into the world of academic research: Franz Knoop, who lectured on physiological chemistry, and Wilhelm von Möllendorff, who worked on histological staining. Möllendorff gave Krebs his first research project, a comparative study of the staining effects of different dyes on muscle tissues. Impressed with Krebs's insight that the efficacy of the different dyes stemmed from how dispersed and dense they were rather than from their chemical properties, Möllendorff helped Krebs write and publish his first scientific paper. In 1921, Krebs switched universities again, transferring to the University of Munich, where he started clinical work under the tutelage of two renowned surgeons. In 1923, he completed his medical examinations with an overall mark of "very good," the best score possible. Inspired by his university studies, Krebs decided against joining his father's practice as he had once planned; instead, he planned to balance a clinical career in medicine with experimental work. But before he could turn his attention to research, he had one more hurdle to complete, a required clinical year, which he served at the Third Medical Clinic of the University of Berlin.

Krebs spent his free time at the Third Medical Clinic engaged in scientific investigations connected to his clinical duties. At the hospital, Krebs met Annelise Wittgenstein, a more experienced clinician. The two began investigating physical and chemical factors that played substantial roles in the distribution of substances between blood, tissue, and cerebrospinal fluid, research that they hoped might shed some light on how pharmaceuticals such as those used in the treatment of syphilis penetrate the nervous system. Although Krebs published three articles on this work, later in life he belittled these early, independent efforts. His year in Berlin convinced Krebs that better knowledge of research chemistry was essential to medical practice.

Accordingly, the twenty-five-year-old Krebs enrolled in a course offered by Berlin's Charité Hospital for doctors who wanted additional training in laboratory chemistry. One year later, through a mutual acquaintance, he was offered a paid research assistantship by **Otto Warburg**, one of the leading biochemists of the time. Although many others who worked with Warburg called him autocratic, under his tutelage Krebs developed many habits that would stand him in good stead as his own research progressed. Six days a week work began at Warburg's laboratory at eight in the morning and concluded at six in the evening, with only a brief break for lunch. Warburg worked as hard as the students. Describing his mentor in his autobiography, *Hans Krebs: Reminiscences and Reflections,* Krebs noted that Warburg worked in his laboratory until eight days before he died from a pulmonary embolism. At the end of his career, Krebs wrote a biography of his teacher, the subtitle of which described his perception of Warburg: "cell physiologist, biochemist, and eccentric."

Krebs's first job in Warburg's laboratory entailed familiarizing himself with the tissue slice and manometric (pressure measurement) techniques the older scientist had developed. Until that time biochemists had attempted to track chemical processes in whole organs, invariably experiencing difficulties controlling experimental conditions. Warburg's new technique, affording greater control, employed single layers of tissue suspended in solution and manometers (pressure gauges) to measure chemical reactions. In Warburg's lab, the tissue slice/manometric method was primarily used to measure rates of respiration and glycolysis, processes by which an organism delivers oxygen to tissue and converts carbohydrates to energy. Just as he did with all his assistants, Warburg assigned Krebs a problem related to his own research—the role of heavy metals in the oxidation of sugar. Once Krebs completed that project, he began researching the metabolism of human cancer tissue, again at Warburg's suggestion. While Warburg was jealous of his researchers' laboratory time, he was not stingy with bylines; during Krebs's four years in Warburg's lab, he amassed sixteen published papers. But Warburg had no room in his lab for a scientist interested in pursuing his own research. When Krebs proposed undertaking studies of intermediary metabolism that had little relevance for Warburg's work, the supervisor suggested Krebs switch jobs.

Unravels Secret of Urea Formation

Unfortunately for Krebs, the year was 1930. Times were hard in Germany, and research opportunities were few. He accepted a mainly clinical position at the Altona Municipal Hospital, which supported him while he searched for a more research-oriented post. Within the year he moved back to Freiburg, where he worked as an assistant to an expert on metabolic diseases with both clinical and research duties. In the well-equipped Freiburg laboratory, Krebs began to test whether the tissue slice technique and manometry he had mastered in Warburg's lab could shed light on complex synthetic metabolic processes. Improving on the master's methods, he began using saline solutions in which the concentrations of various ions matched their concentrations within the body, a technique which eventually was adopted in almost all biochemical, physiological, and pharmacological studies.

Working with a medical student named Kurt Henseleit, Krebs systematically investigated which substances most influenced the rate at which urea—the main solid component of mammalian urine—forms in liver slices. Krebs noticed that the rate of urea synthesis increased dramatically in the presence of ornithine, an amino acid present during urine production. Inverting the reaction, he speculated that the same ornithine produced in this synthesis underwent a cycle of conversion and synthesis, eventually to yield more ornithine and urea. Scientific recognition of his work followed almost immediately, and at the end of 1932—less than a year and a half after he began his research—Krebs found himself appointed as a *Privatdozent* at the University of Freiburg. He immediately embarked on the more ambitious project of identifying the intermediate steps in the metabolic breakdown of carbohydrates and fatty acids.

But Krebs was not to enjoy his new position in Germany for long. In the spring of 1933, along with many other German scientists, he found himself dismissed from his job as a result of Nazi purging. Although Krebs had officially and legally renounced the Jewish faith twelve years earlier at the urging of his patriotic father, who believed wholeheartedly in the assimilation of all German Jews, this legal declaration proved insufficiently strong for the Nazis. In June of 1933, he sailed for England to work in the biochemistry lab of Sir **Frederick Gowland Hopkins** of the Cambridge School of Biochemistry. Supported by a fellowship from the Rockefeller Foundation, Krebs resumed his research in the British laboratory. The following year, he augmented his research duties with the position of demonstrator in biochemistry. Laboratory space in Cambridge was cramped, however, and in 1935 Krebs was lured to the post of lecturer in the University of Sheffield's Department of Pharmacology by the prospect of more lab space, a semi-permanent appointment, and a salary almost double the one Cambridge was paying him.

Maps Out the Workings of the Krebs Citric Acid Cycle

His Sheffield laboratory established, Krebs returned to a problem that had long preoccupied him: how the body produced the essential amino acids that play such an important role in the metabolic process. By 1936, Krebs had begun to suspect that citric acid played an essential role in the oxidative metabolism by which the carbohydrate pyruvic acid is broken down so as to release energy. Together with his first Sheffield graduate student, William Arthur Johnson, Krebs observed a process akin to that in urea formation. The two researchers showed that even a small amount of citric acid could increase the oxygen absorption rate of living tissue. Because the amount of oxygen absorbed was greater than that needed to completely oxidize the citric acid, Krebs concluded that citric acid has a catalytic effect on the process of pyruvic acid conversion. He was also able to establish that the process is cyclical, citric acid being regenerated and replenished in a subsequent step. Although Krebs spent many more years refining the understanding of intermediary metabolism, these early results provided the key to the chemistry that sustains life processes. In June of 1937, he sent a letter to *Nature* reporting these preliminary findings. Within a week, the editor notified him that his paper could not be published without a delay. Undaunted, Krebs revised and expanded the paper and sent it to the new Dutch journal *Enzymologia,* which he knew would rapidly publicize this significant finding.

In 1938, Krebs married Margaret Fieldhouse, a teacher of domestic science in Sheffield. One year later, Margaret, who was thirteen years younger than Hans, gave birth to the first of the couple's three children. In the winter of the same year, the university named him lecturer in biochemistry and asked him to head their new department in the field. Married to an Englishwoman, Krebs became a naturalized Englishman in September, 1939, three days after World War II began.

The war affected Krebs's work minimally. He conducted experiments on vitamin deficiencies in conscientious objectors, while maintaining his own research on metabolic cycles. In 1944, the Medical Research Council asked him to head a new department of biological chemistry. Krebs refined his earlier discoveries throughout the war, particularly trying to determine how universal the Krebs cycle is among living organisms. He was ultimately able to establish that all organisms, even microorganisms, are sustained by the same chemical processes. These findings later prompted Krebs to speculate on the role of the metabolic cycle in evolution.

In 1953, Krebs received one of the ultimate recognitions for the scientific significance of his work—the Nobel Prize in physiology and medicine, which he shared with **Fritz Lipmann**, the discoverer of co-enzyme A. The following year, Oxford University offered him the Whitley professorship in biochemistry and the chair of its substantial department in that field. Once Krebs had ascertained that he could transfer his metabolic research unit to Oxford, he consented to the appointment. Throughout the next two decades Krebs continued research into intermediary metabolism. He established how fatty acids are drawn into the metabolic cycle and studied the regulatory mechanism of intermediary metabolism. Research at the end of his life was focused on establishing that the metabolic cycle is the most efficient mechanism by which an organism can convert food to energy. When Krebs reached Oxford's mandatory retirement age of sixty-seven, he refused to stop researching and made arrangements to move his research team to a laboratory established for him at the Radcliffe Hospital. On November 22, 1981, Krebs died at the age of eighty-one.

SELECTED WRITINGS BY KREBS:

Books

Otto Warburg: Cell Physiologist, Biochemist, and Eccentric (1883–1970), Clarendon Press, 1981.

(With Anne Martin) *Hans Krebs: Reminiscences and Reflections,* Clarendon Press, 1981.

Periodicals

(With W. A. Johnson) "The Role of Citric Acid in Intermediate Metabolism in Animal Tissues," *Enzymologia,* Number 4, 1937, p. 148.

"Excursion into the Borderland of Biochemistry and Philosophy," *Bulletin of the Johns Hopkins Hospital,* Number 95, 1954, p. 45.

"The Making of a Scientist," *Nature,* Number 215, 1967, p. 1244.

SOURCES:

Books

Holmes, Frederic Lawrence, *Hans Krebs: The Formation of a Scientific Life, 1900–1933,* Oxford University Press, 1991.

Periodicals

Holmes, Frederic Lawrence. "Lavoisier and Krebs: The Individual Scientist in the Near and Deeper Past," *Isis,* Volume 75, 1984, pp. 131–142.

New York Times, December 9, 1981.

—Sketch by Shari Rudavsky

Mathilde Krim
1926-
Italian-born American geneticist and philanthropist

Geneticist Mathilde Krim is best known as a cofounder of the American Foundation for AIDS Research (AmFAR). Krim first learned of acquired immunodeficiency syndrome (AIDS) while researching interferon at New York's Sloan-Kettering Cancer Center in 1980, when she heard about an unusual and fatal immune system breakdown of some of her colleagues' patients. In 1983 she founded the AIDS Medical Foundation, which was dedicated to providing funds for AIDS research and escalating public awareness of the disease. Her organization merged with a California-based group to form AmFAR in 1985, and in October, 1993, Krim received the prestigious John W. Gardner Leadership Award

Mathilde Krim

for her directorship of AmFAR. In acceptance she summarized her role in the fight against AIDS: "When the first cases of AIDS were reported, studied and first understood to be due to a transmissible infectious agent, there was a total vacuum of leadership committed to interpreting these facts for the public. I could see the real impending threat to the public health, which was obvious to any biologist. I was struck by the totally misguided stigma—obviously due to age-old prejudice and to ignorance of biological facts—that was being attached to the disease. I became, therefore, easily convinced that, both as a product of Judeo-Christian culture and as a biologist, I needed to call on widely shared values to foster human solidarity in the face of AIDS and that I had to explain the simple biological and historical facts necessary for the nature of the epidemic and its pattern of spread to be understood correctly."

Early Career in Genetics and Interferon Research

Krim was born Mathilde Galland in Como, Italy, on July 9, 1926. Her father was a Swiss zoologist; her mother was Czechoslovakian. Because of her international upbringing, Galland became fluent in several languages, including French, German, Italian, and later English and Hebrew. As a child her interest in science was inspired by her maternal grandfather, a school teacher. In 1932 her family moved to Switzerland to escape economic depression in Italy. She earned a B.S. in genetics from the University of Geneva in 1948 and completed her Ph.D. in 1953. While in graduate school, Galland was fascinated by the technology of the newly invented electron microscope. When asked to determine if the microscope was capable of viewing a gene, she examined the chromosomes of frogs' eggs in great detail. She eventually saw some "beautiful double threads," making her possibly the first person ever to view DNA.

Galland became involved in the Zionist movement at the conclusion of World War II, after viewing dramatic news footage of the liberation of Jewish prisoners from a Nazi concentration camp. She joined a local branch of the Irgun—a Zionist underground organization in southern France—and began cleaning guns and smuggling weapons. While engrossed in these pursuits she fell in love with a Bulgarian medical student, also a member of the Irgun. Against the wishes of her parents, she converted to Judaism, married, and moved to Israel. At the Weitzmann Institute of Science in Rehovot, Israel, she took a position as a junior scientist and later became a research associate. While she was there, her team pioneered a way to determine the sex of an unborn child through amniocentesis, a procedure that involves analyzing the fetal chromosomes found in the amniotic fluid surrounding a fetus.

In the 1950s Galland's personal life changed dramatically. She divorced her husband and gained custody of their only daughter, Daphne. In 1958 she remarried, this time to Arthur B. Krim, a New York attorney who was chairman of United Artists, former finance director of the Democratic party, and later founder of Orion Pictures. The Krims moved to New York City, where they moved in important social circles as a result of Arthur Krim's entertainment industry connections and political associations. However, after a while the glamour wore thin, and Krim joined a cancer research team in the virus research division at Cornell Medical College. At Cornell, Krim studied the protein interferon, an antiviral agent which she believed would gain widespread notice as useful in curing cancer. She continued working with interferon when she moved to New York's premiere clinic for cancer treatment, the Memorial Sloan-Kettering Cancer Center, and pushed for an interferon laboratory at Sloan-Kettering. Krim lobbied for the support of the National Institutes of Health as well as the National Cancer Institute for research into its effectiveness as a treatment for cancer. However, the cost of interferon treatment was considered prohibitive until the 1980s, when cloning techniques made it possible to produce greater amounts.

In the Laboratory and in the Public Eye Fighting AIDS

From 1981 to 1985 Krim worked on ways of treating leukemia with interferon. It was during this period that she became involved in AIDS research. AIDS is caused by the human immunodeficiency virus (HIV), which attacks the human immune system's defensive army of cells and inhibits their ability to eliminate foreign matter such as infectious bacteria from the body. Without such cells, the body is in a weakened state and is more likely to succumb to such opportunistic diseases as pneumonia, tuberculosis, and cancer. Krim initially worked on using interferon to treat Karposi's sarcoma, a type of cancer found in many persons with AIDS, but by 1983, it had become obvious that her role in the fight against AIDS would grow beyond the laboratory. Perceiving that public prejudice would be increased once it became widely known that AIDS was primarily affecting homosexual men, she felt that she should speak out and explain that infection was not a result of sexual orientation—that AIDS was caused by a virus.

While supporting AIDS research, Krim's personal crusade has been for AIDS prevention and treatment. She has strongly supported community testing of experimental drugs and has objected to the restriction of such drugs to control groups. Under Krim's direction, AmFAR has promoted the idea of community-based clinical research by offering financial support and technical assistance to groups of primary-care physicians practicing medicine in areas with a high population of persons with AIDS. By forming local, nonprofit clinical research centers, more clinical trials of experimental drugs could be conducted, upgrading the level of care to thousands of HIV patients.

Krim has also been a champion for AIDS education. She has promoted the use of condoms and of safe sexual practices to people worldwide. AmFAR has funded programs for AIDS education and prevention as well as needle exchanges to decrease the spread of AIDS and other infectious diseases among drug users. AmFAR has also lobbied the federal government for support and helped pass the Disabilities Act of 1990, which protects people with AIDS from discrimination. Krim's efforts have brought government officials, drug company executives, drug treatment experts, gay activists, and minority leaders together in the battle against AIDS. Through speaking engagements she is also alerting the country to another new health threat, multi-drug resistant tuberculosis (MDRTB), which is a serious problem in many cities along the Atlantic seaboard, especially among those who are HIV positive as well as the homeless, those in prison, and the poor. Under Krim's stewardship, AmFAR has provided over $65 million to more than 1,300 research teams. Most of the endowments are for small start-up or "seed" grants of $50,000 per year. Some of these have been grants in genetic research that may lead to the future use of gene therapy to treat AIDS.

Krim once told an interviewer for *The Advocate* that she views herself as "a hybrid"—part scientist and part activist. She has not been involved in laboratory research since the early 1980s but stays abreast of scientific developments so that she can make informed recommendations about how research money can best be spent. Known for her compassion and vision, Krim fears that AIDS not only kills people but harms our culture in that it suppresses our ability to "feel fulfillment and freedom." Although the government and other social and religious institutions have not responded quickly enough in her view, she believes that great strides have been made in managing the disease medically. Life expectancy for persons with AIDS has improved significantly from the mid-1980s into the 1990s, and she is optimistic that sufficient medical technology exists to allow people to live full and normal lives with the AIDS virus.

During her career, Krim has written or collaborated on over seventy scientific papers. A naturalized U.S. citizen, she has served on the boards of various philanthropic organizations and is the founding co-chairperson of AmFAR and current chairman of the board as well as a member of the organization's scientific advisory committee. In 1986 Krim became an associate research scientist at both St. Luke's Roosevelt Hospital Center and the College of Physicians and Surgeons at Columbia University in New York. For her extraordinary work against AIDS, Krim has received numerous awards, most notably the John W. Gardner Leadership Award and seven honorary doctorates.

SELECTED WRITINGS BY KRIM:

Books

Partners for the Cure, Reflection and Rededication: AIDS Research in the Second Decade, American Foundation for AIDS Research, 1993.

Periodicals

(With C. E. Metroka, S. Cunningham-Rundles, and others), "Generalized Lymphadenopathy in Homosexual Men: An Update of the New York Experience," *Annals of the New York Academy of Sciences: Acquired Immune Deficiency Syndrome,* Volume 437, 1984, pp. 400–11.

(With S. E. Krown, F. X. Real, and others) "Recombinant Leukocyte A Interferon in Karposi's Sarcoma," *Annals of the New York Academy of Sciences: Acquired Immune Deficiency Syndrome,* Volume 437, 1984, pp. 431–38.

SOURCES:

Books

Moritz, Charles, editor, *Current Biography Yearbook 1987,* H. W. Wilson, 1987, pp. 325–28.

Periodicals

Kraft, Ronald Mark, "Hetero Heroes: Mathilde Krim," *The Advocate,* November, 1993, pp. 68–70.

Robertson, Nan, "On the Front Lines," *Modern Maturity,* April-May, 1990, p. 72.

van Dam, Laura, "Fighting the Plague: An Interview with Mathilde Krim," *Technology Review,* July, 1992, p. 21.

—Sketch by Barbara A. Branca

August Krogh
1874-1949
Danish physiologist

August Krogh (pronounced Krawg) won the 1920 Nobel Prize for physiology or medicine for the discoveries he made concerning human respiration; he showed that most capillaries (the smallest blood vessels) of the body's organs and tissues are closed when they are at rest, but when there is activity and the need for oxygen increases, more capillaries will open. Krogh's explanations of respiration and capillary action were of major significance for the understanding of the physiology of the human pulmonary and circulatory systems. His research into respiration and circulation also had practical applications for the development of modern medical science.

Schack August Steenberg Krogh was born on November 15, 1874, in Grenaa, Jutland. His father was a brewer, shipbuilder, and a newspaper editor. His mother, Marie Drechmann Krogh, was of gypsy ancestry. Throughout his life Krogh was active in both zoology and human physiology, accomplishing his major discoveries in the physiology of respiration. In 1910 he was able to settle an important biological controversy by establishing that, in human lungs, the absorption of oxygen and the elimination of carbon dioxide takes place by diffusion rather than secretion. From his work on human respiration, Krogh went on to describe the operation of the capillary system and the mechanisms that regulate it.

Krogh's interest in various areas of science can be traced back to his childhood. His father, who had been trained as a naval architect, influenced Krogh's interest in ships and the sea; the young Krogh also spent time in his youth studying the insects he found in the fields near his home. When he was fourteen he left school to serve on a Danish patrol boat assigned to protect fisheries in Iceland. Instead of pursuing a naval career, however, Krogh decided to complete his education. His love for the sea, nonetheless, remained with him for the rest of his life.

Krogh returned to school at the Gymnasium at Aarhus, and then went on to the University of Copenhagen in 1893. He first entered Copenhagen with the intention of studying physics and medicine, but under the influence of zoologist William Sørensen, he changed to the study of zoology and physiology. Sørensen had advised Krogh to attend the lectures of Christian Bohr, an expert in circulatory and respiratory physiology. After attending Bohr's lectures at Copenhagen, Krogh began to work in Bohr's laboratory in 1897, and after receiving his master of science degree in 1899, he became Bohr's laboratory assistant.

Invents the Microtonometer

One of Krogh's earliest achievements was his invention of a microtonometer—an instrument that measures gas pressure in fluids—which he developed to help in his research with a marine organism named *Corethra.* As a student Krogh had done research on the larvae of *Corethra* to determine how its air bladders operated (he found that they worked like the diving tanks of submarines). Traveling in 1902 to Greenland, Krogh studied the amounts of oxygen and carbon dioxide dissolved in fresh and sea water. His research cast a new understanding on the role of the oceans in carbon dioxide regulation and at the same time he was able to improve his techniques for measuring gas pressures in fluids.

In 1903 Krogh received a Ph.D. in zoology from the University of Copenhagen, where, in his doctoral dissertation, he demonstrated the difference between the skin and lung respiration of the frog. Whereas the frog's skin respiration was constant and regular, Krogh found that the frog's lung respiration varied and was controlled by the autonomic system through the mechanism of the vagus nerve. Oxygen passed from the air sacs (alveoli) of the lung through a membrane to the capillaries and then to the blood stream where it formed carbon dioxide after it was used by the different tissues in the body. The process then reversed when the blood carried carbon dioxide to the alveoli of the lungs, where it was exhaled. Respiration would then vary according to the organism's need for oxygen.

Krogh was married in 1905 to Marie Jørgensen, a physiologist who also worked in Bohr's laboratory. (The couple would eventually have three daughters and one son, with the son and the youngest daughter becoming physiologists and the other two daughters trained in dental science.) In 1906 the first of Krogh's papers to receive international recognition, a work which showed that nitrogen is not involved in animal metabolism, was awarded the Seegen Prize from the Vienna Academy of Sciences. In 1907 Krogh received further international attention at Heidelberg, Germany, when he discussed his findings on the diffusion of pulmonary gases at the International Congress of Physiology.

In 1908 Krogh made another trip to Greenland with his wife to study the Eskimo's meat-eating dietary habits and the effects it had on their respiration and metabolism. He was also given an associate professorship of zoo physiology at the University of Copenhagen that year. Two years later Krogh and his wife were given a laboratory at Ny Vestergade for physiological research; the couple worked there together for a number of years. Krogh then became a full professor at Copenhagen in 1916.

Diffusion Theory Explains Oxygen Transfer to Blood

From 1908 to 1912 Krogh was engaged in research to resolve the question of how oxygen was transferred in the lungs to the blood. Bohr and **John Burdon Sanderson Haldane** (who was well-known for his own research into the mechanics of respiration), along with other scientists, believed that the lung acted as a gland in the alveolar transfer of oxygen to the blood; in other words, the lung secreted the oxygen. Krogh, in 1912, convincingly delivered the fatal blow to the secretion theory by first showing that in fishes there is no secretion of oxygen into the air sacs, and then by demonstrating that the amount of oxygen in the blood always equalled the amount that should be provided by his diffusion theory. The development of Krogh's microtonometer proved to be critical for verifying the results of these demonstrations.

Investigations into Capillaries Yields Nobel Prize

It was not until 1916, however, that Krogh accomplished the work that would, in 1920, earn him the Nobel Prize for physiology or medicine. He showed that muscle tension was always slightly lower than the tensions in the capillaries, even when the muscle was at work. Noting that there were few open capillaries when a muscle was at rest, Krogh demonstrated that as soon as the muscle became active many capillaries began to open up. He was also able to show that blood did not enter the capillaries through the pressure of the blood vessels but from the relaxed tonus (partial contraction) of the active muscle. The relaxation of the muscle allowed the field of capillaries to open and the blood to flow in, thus providing more oxygen to the muscle, organ, or tissue.

Krogh's discoveries relating to gas exchanges in the lung and to the operation of the capillary system helped to develop medical techniques for breathing through the trachea. His work also improved surgical methods for open heart surgery, such as the procedure for reducing body temperature to below normal levels to slow down the rate of gaseous exchange.

In 1922 Krogh became interested in insulin (which had been discovered by **Frederick G. Banting** and **John James Rickard Macleod** the year before), partly because his own wife had diabetes. Besides being active in insulin research, Krogh helped to promote manufacturing facilities in Denmark for its production. Krogh also maintained his interest in zoology, writing about insects and becoming particularly attentive to theories about the way honey bees communicate.

During World War II Krogh lived in Sweden, having been forced to flee Nazi-occupied Denmark because of his open opposition to Nazism. Krogh returned to Denmark in 1945, and died on September 13, 1949, in Copenhagen. His research in his last years was performed at the laboratories of the Carlsberg and Scandinavian Insulin Foundations.

SELECTED WRITINGS BY KROGH:

Books

Anatomy and Physiology of Capillaries, 1924, reprinted by Hafner, 1959.

Osmotic Regulations in Aquatic Animals, 1939, reprinted by Dover, 1965.

Comparative Physiology of Respiratory Mechanisms, 1941.

SOURCES:

Books

Hagedorn, H.C., "August Krogh," in *Meddelelser fra Akademiet for de Tekniske Videnskaber,* 1949, Volume 1, pp. 33–38.

Meddelelser fra Akademiet for de Tekniske Videnskaber (includes a complete catalog of Krogh's writings), 1949, Volume 1, pp. 39–50.

Rowntree, L. G., *Amid Masters of Twentieth Century Medicine,* [Chicago], 1958, pp. 171–174.

—Sketch by Jordan P. Richman

Doris Kuhlmann-Wilsdorf
1922-
German-born American metallurgist

Doris Kuhlmann-Wilsdorf is a metallurgist who is University Professor of Applied Science at the University of Virginia. She has received numerous awards and honors, served as consultant to top corporations as well as the National Institute for Standards and Technology, and has authored over 250 articles. She received the Society of Women Engineers Annual Achievement Award in 1989 "for foundational and preeminent contributions to our understanding of the mechanical behavior of solids."

Kuhlmann-Wilsdorf is a native of Bremen, Germany, where she was born on February 15, 1922. She served as an apprentice metallographer and materials tester from 1940 to 1942, prior to entering Göttingen University. There she completed her undergraduate and graduate studies in metallurgy, physics, mathematics and chemistry, earning a Ph.D. in 1947. She continued with her research on several postdoctoral assignments, first at Göttingen and later in England at the University of Bristol, where she studied under Nobel laureate **Nevill Francis Mott**. From 1950 to 1956, she was a lecturer in the department of physics at the University of Witwatersrand in Johannesburg, South Africa, where she earned a D.Sc. in 1954.

Kuhlmann-Wilsdorf came to the United States in 1957 to accept a position as associate professor with the department of metallurgical engineering at the University of Pennsylvania. In 1961 she achieved full professorship, and she continued her association with the University of Pennsylvania until 1963. In that year, she joined the faculty of the University of Virginia in Charlottesville, accepting a post as professor of engineering physics. She was named University Professor of Applied Science in 1966, the position she currently holds.

Kuhlmann-Wilsdorf's contributions include developing a model for surface deformation, which takes into account erosion as well as friction and wear. She has investigated the behavior and properties of various metals—for instance, studying why rolled aluminum sheets crinkle under pressure while other sheet metals break. Her most significant endeavor may be her design for electrical metal-fiber brushes; if followed by the modification of ship drives, this design could lead to widespread use of electric motors on Naval vessels. "This has been a gleam in the eye of the Navy for many years," Kuhlmann-Wilsdorf told contributor Karen Withem. The result of electric motors would be ships which are lighter, more maneuverable, and more efficient.

Her many honors include two Medals for Excellence in Research awarded by the South Eastern Section of the American Society for Engineering Education in 1965 and 1966. She received the Heyn Medal in 1988 from the German Society for Materials Science and the Ragnar Holm Scientific Achievement Award of the Institute of Electrical and Electronics Engineers in 1991. She was elected a Fellow of the American Physical Society in 1964, a member of the Society of the Sigma Xi in 1957, and a Fellow of the American Society for Metals International in 1989. She received the Americanism Medal from the Daughters of the American Revolution in 1966 and was plenary speaker at the centenary celebration of the Indian Association for the Cultivation of Science in Calcutta in 1977.

Kuhlmann-Wilsdorf has also served as consultant to the following agencies and corporations: General Motors Technical Center from 1960 to 1970; Chemstrand Research Laboratories from 1964 to 1966; the National Institute for Standards and Technology from 1981 to 1982; General Dynamics from 1985 to 1987; and Maxwell Laboratories from 1987 to 1989. She is a member of the American Association of University Professors, the Materials Research Society, and the South African Institute of Physics. In 1994, she was elected a member of the National Academy of Engineering. She received United States citizenship in 1950.

Kuhlmann-Wilsdorf believes the inclusion of women in the scientific fields to be essential. "We are 50 percent of the population. You are throwing away 50 percent of the talent if you say, 'Women can't do this' or 'Women can't do that,'" she told Withem. Based on her teaching experience, she believes that "innate in women is a particular dedication to duty and hard work and reliability."

SELECTED WRITINGS BY KUHLMANN-WILSDORF:

Periodicals

"On The Theory of Plastic Deformation," *Proceedings of the Physical Society,* Volume A64, 1951, pp. 140–155.

"A New Theory in Work-Hardening," *Transactions of the Metallic Society,* Volume 224, 1962, pp. 1047–1061.

SOURCES:

Books

Society of Women Engineers Achievement Awards, Society of Women Engineers, 1993.

Other

Kuhlmann-Wilsdorf, Doris, interview with Karen Withem conducted March 24, 1994.

—*Sketch by Karen Withem*

Richard Kuhn
1900-1967
Austrian German chemist

Richard Kuhn was a Nobel Prize-winning organic chemist who devoted much of his life to studying the synthesis of vitamins and carotenoids, the fat-soluble yellow pigments that are found in plants. He researched the chemistry of algae sex cells and optical stereochemistry, and spent a great deal of time understanding carbohydrates. He was determined to succeed in his work by uncovering the practical applications of substances in the fields of medicine and agriculture. Later in his career, Kuhn concentrated on studying how the body fights disease using organic compounds.

Kuhn was born in Vienna, Austria, on December 3, 1900, to Hofrat Richard Clemens, a hydraulics engineer, and Angelika (Rodler) Kuhn, an elementary school teacher. After spending almost ten years of his life at home under the educational guidance of his mother, Kuhn entered the Döbling Gymnasium, where he attended classes with future Nobel Prize-winning physicist **Wolfgang Pauli**. After graduating from the Gymnasium in 1917, he was drafted into the German (Austro-Hungarian) army and served until World War I ended in November of 1918.

Once Kuhn was discharged from the military, he entered the University of Vienna where a professor of medical chemistry, Ernst Ludwig, turned his interests towards chemistry. Just three semesters after entering the university, Kuhn transferred to the University of Munich, where he studied chemistry under noted scientist **Richard Willstätter**. Kuhn received his Ph.D. in 1922 for his thesis, "On the Specificity of Enzymes in Carbohydrate Metabolism." He worked briefly as Willstätter's assistant before leaving Munich in 1926 to join the Federal Institute of Technology at Zurich, a Swiss technological high school, where he spent three years as professor of general and analytical chemistry.

In 1929 Kuhn left Zurich and joined the University of Heidelberg's newly established Kaiser Wilhelm Institute for Medical Research (renamed the Max Planck Institute in 1950, with Kuhn's assistance) as both a professor of organic chemistry and director of the institute's chemistry department. Kuhn would turn down a number of other offers to spend the remainder of his career at the institute; he became its director in 1937.

Makes Advances in Research of Vitamin Production

Kuhn was particularly interested in how the chemistry of organic compounds was related to their function in biological systems. His early work concentrated on carotenoids. One such substance was carotene, the pigment found in carrots, whose chemical formula had been determined earlier by Willstätter at the University of Munich. After further research, Kuhn discovered that carotene was a precursor in the chemical production of vitamin A and that nature uses all kinds of chemical structures for biological actions. In addition, Kuhn and his colleagues discovered that carotenoids existed in numerous plants and animals and that vitamin A was an essential part of maintaining the body's mucous membranes.

At the time, Kuhn was just one of two scientists working with carotene; **Paul Karrer** at the University of Zurich was the other. The two men would remain fierce competitors throughout their careers. Through Kuhn's investigations, he found two distinct compounds in carotene: beta-carotene, which bends light, and alpha-carotene, which does not. Two years later Kuhn's work led to the discovery of a third form of carotene, called gamma-carotene. These compounds have exactly the same chemical formulas but different molecular structures; therefore, they are known as isomers.

In the 1930s, Kuhn's turned his attention to researching members of the water-soluble vitamin B group. Working with other scientists, he painstakingly isolated and crystallized a small amount of vitamin B2 (riboflavin) from skim milk. By determining the structure of riboflavin, Kuhn was able to clearly explain the chemical composition and to eventually synthesize this compound. He also demonstrated that B2 plays a primary role in respiratory enzyme action and provided the key to how vitamins function and what their applications are in living systems. For this work, Kuhn was offered the 1938 Nobel Prize. Then, in the late 1930s, Kuhn and three other co-workers determined both the chemical composition and molecular structure of adermin, now commonly referred to as vitamin B6, which acts against skin disease and helps to regulate the metabolism of the nervous system.

Forced to Reject Nobel Prize

Although Kuhn was to be awarded the Nobel Prize in 1938, he did not actually receive it until the late 1940s. Due to the political climate in Germany and the fact that a Nazi concentration camp prisoner, Carl von Ossietzky, was honored with the Nobel Peace Prize in 1934, Hitler instituted a policy forbidding German citizens from accepting the award. As a result, Kuhn was forced to turn down the award and was not properly honored until after the war ended in 1945. He received his medal and certificate in 1949 at a special ceremony in Stockholm for his work with carotenoids and vitamins.

The 1940s saw Kuhn expand his research to include carbohydrates. Kuhn researched alkaloid glycosides, which appear in potatoes and tomatoes, and tried to unlock their pigments and biological structures. He also returned to researching milk, from which he extracted carbohydrates using chromatography. In doing so, he greatly improved the use of chromatography, which is the chemical separation of mixtures into their original form. After becoming a professor of biochemistry at the Max Planck Institute in 1950, Kuhn focused much of his effort on the study of organic substances that are instrumental in the body's resistance to infection. His investigations into a variety of "resistance" factors effective against cholera and influenza uncovered the molecular interaction between an organism and its attacker. He also went on to identify pantothenic acid, an important ingredient in hemoglobin formation and the release of energy from carbohydrates, and para-aminobenzoic acid (PABA), a compound that proved useful in the synthesis of anesthetics.

Known to have an upbeat and outgoing personality, Kuhn enjoyed such activities as billiards, chess and tennis. He was also a skilled violinist who frequently played with a chamber ensemble for public enjoyment. Kuhn met his wife, Daisy Hartmann, while he was a professor and she a student at the Federal Institute of Technology at Zurich. They would marry in 1928; the couple had four daughters and two sons together.

In addition to winning the Nobel Prize, Kuhn was awarded the Pasteur, Paterno and Goethe Prizes for his work. He was a member of numerous national and international scientific societies and received honorary degrees from a variety of institutions including the Munich Technical University, the University of Vienna, and the University of St. Maria, Brazil. A charter senate member of the Max Planck Society for the Advancement of Science, he later served as vice-president. Kuhn became the editor of the chemical journal, *Annalen der Chemie,* in 1948, and served as president of the German Chemical Society. He published more than seven hundred scientific papers and received over fifty distinctions. Shortly before his death, the University of Heidelberg gave its first commemorative medal struck in honor of a scientist. Kuhn died July 31, 1967, at age sixty-six, in Heidelberg, Germany.

SELECTED WRITINGS BY KUHN:

Books

Kuhn, Richard, *Goethe ein Medizinische Biographie,* F. Enke, 1949.

SOURCES:

Books

The Biographical Dictionary of Scientists and Chemists, Peter Bedricks Books, 1983.

Dictionary of Scientific Biography, Volume 7, Scribner, 1973.

Farber, Eduard, *Nobel Prize Winners in Chemistry: 1901–1961,* Abelard-Schuman, 1961.

Periodicals

"Richard Kuhn, Biochemist, Dies; Was Denied Nobel Prize by Nazis," *The New York Times,* August 2, 1967.

—Sketch by Amy M. Punke

Gerard Peter Kuiper
1905-1973
Dutch-born American astronomer

Gerard Peter Kuiper was a highly admired planetary scientist whose theories of solar system formation and planetary features redefined man's knowledge of other worlds. An outstanding observer, Kuiper discovered moons of Uranus and Neptune, predicted what the surface of the Earth's moon would be like to walk on (long before Neil Armstrong proved him correct), and deduced the existence of frozen water in Mars' polar caps. The founder and long-time director of the Lunar and Planetary Laboratory at the University of Arizona, Kuiper played an instrumental role in the United States' early space program, helping pick the landing sites for the Apollo missions and serving as advisor on many projects.

Kuiper was born to Gerard and Anna (de Vries) Kuiper on December 7, 1905, in Harencarspel, the Netherlands. After graduating from the Gymnasium in Haarlem in 1924, Kuiper attended the University of Leiden and studied astronomy and physics, receiving his B.Sc. degree in 1927. From 1928 until 1933, Kuiper was an assistant observer at Leiden, accompanying members of the Dutch Solar Eclipse Expedition to Sumatra in 1929. In 1933, Kuiper received a Ph.D. in astronomy from Leiden with his thesis on binary stars (two stars which revolve around each other). That same year, Kuiper moved to America, serving as a fellow at the Lick Observatory of the University of California until 1935. After spending the following year as a lecturer in astronomy at Harvard University, Kuiper became assistant professor of practical astronomy at the Yerkes Observatory of the University of Chicago; he was promoted to associate professor in 1937 (the same year he became an American citizen) and remained at Yerkes until 1943.

In 1938 Kuiper discovered what was thought to be the largest star known at that time, with a diameter three thousand times that of the sun. Three years later, Kuiper studied systems where two stars revolve around each other about four times a day, showing a continuous change in brightness. These systems were shaped like dumbbells or peanuts, and to describe them, Kuiper coined the term "contact binary," which is still in use today. Kuiper served in 1944 as operations analyst for the Eighth Air Force in England, and that same year, he became the first to confirm the existence of an atmosphere around a moon of the outer planets, detecting telltale clues in the spectrum of Saturn's moon Titan that corresponded to methane.

Kuiper became a full professor at the Yerkes Observatory in 1943 and remained there until 1960. (He also directed the Yerkes and McDonald observatories from 1947 to 1949 and 1957 to 1960.) In 1948, Kuiper predicted (correctly) that carbon dioxide was a chief component of the atmosphere of Mars. More notably, that same year Kuiper discovered Uranus' fifth moon, Miranda, which was three hundred miles in diameter and 75,000 miles away from the planet. Also in 1948, Kuiper stated that the rings of Saturn were comprised of particles of ice (borne out by later observations), and he argued against the existence of higher life forms on Mars, citing that planet's low amount of oxygen and absence of protection from ultraviolet rays. In 1949, Kuiper discovered Neptune's second moon, Nereid. Only two hundred miles in diameter, it was at the time the faintest moon to be observed.

Proposes Model of Solar System Formation

Kuiper revealed his theory on the origin of the solar system in October, 1949, suggesting that the planets condensed out of a cloud of gas around the sun about three billion years ago. The cloud of gas collapsed into a pancake, which subsequently broke up (when its density reached a critical value) into "protoplanets," or baby planets. Kuiper proposed that the original mass of the gas cloud out of which the planets condensed was much greater than the current total mass of the planets—seventy times, in fact. In 1950, Kuiper became the first to measure Pluto's diameter reliably, employing the two hundred-inch telescope at Mount Palomar to arrive at 3,600 kilometers as the right value. Kuiper also suggested Pluto was once a moon of Neptune's.

In 1951, Kuiper suggested a possible source of comets which circle the sun relatively frequently; he proposed a flattened belt or ring of comets beyond Neptune's orbit, perhaps extending to distances of five hundred or one thousand times the distance from the Earth to the sun. (This so-called "Kuiper belt" should not be confused with the Oort cloud, another proposed comet source lying at huge distances from the sun.) The number of comets in the Kuiper belt was estimated to lie between one hundred million and one billion, and its total mass between one-hundredth and one-tenth of the Earth's. The Kuiper belt would have been a remnant of the flattened disk of matter that created the planets.

In September 1956, Mars came within 35,000,000 miles of the Earth—a once-in-fifteen-years occurrence. Kuiper took advantage of this event to show that the Martian polar icecaps were composed not of carbon dioxide, as had been previously supposed, but ice crystals spread very thinly over a maximum of four million square miles. In other planetary work, Kuiper discovered bands of methane on Uranus and Neptune (now called "Kuiper bands"), and he charted the poles and equator positions on Venus.

Kuiper moved in 1960 to the University of Arizona's Lunar and Planetary Laboratory. Visiting the White House in 1964, he showed moon pictures to President Lyndon Johnson, and that same year, told a Congressional hearing and national television audience: "I am willing to bet that if you walked on the moon it would be like crunchy snow." Kuiper based this prediction on photographs taken by Ranger spacecraft, whose crash-landings on the moon he directed. In later years, Kuiper was associated with the team that made the *Pioneer 10* probe's camera, which was responsible for sending back pictures of Jupiter.

On December 24, 1973, while Kuiper was in Mexico City looking at possible sites for a new observatory, he suffered a fatal heart attack. He was sixty-eight. Over the years he had been a member of the American Astronomical Society, the National Academy of Sciences, and the American Academy of Arts and Sciences. Kuiper married Sarah Parker Fuller on June 20, 1936, and had two children, Paul and Lucy.

Kuiper was among the first astronomers to realize that jet airplanes could serve well as high-altitude observatories. At the NASA Ames Research Center, Kuiper directed a group of flights using jet aircraft and took infrared spectra of the planet Venus. By examining the spectra (images broken down into various wavelengths of light), he observed water vapor in Venus' upper atmosphere. In January, 1974, a Lockheed C–141 jet aircraft was dedicated as the "Kuiper Airborne Observatory." It housed a permanent 90-cm telescope and was capable of making extended trips. The observatory has been the source of scientific papers on many facets of astronomy, from Supernova 1987a to Comet Halley. In March, 1977, the observatory helped detect the rings of Uranus, under the direction of James L. Elliott. Among other honors, Kuiper won the Janssen medal of the French Astronomical Society for his discoveries of Nereid and Miranda, and was named to the Order of Orange Nassau in the Netherlands. In addition, the International Astronomical Union named a crater on Mercury after him.

SELECTED WRITINGS BY KUIPER:

Books

(Editor) *The Atmospheres of the Earth and Planets,* University of Chicago Press, 1952.
(Editor) *The Solar System,* University of Chicago Press, 1953.
(Editor) *The Earth as a Planet,* University of Chicago Press, 1954.

SOURCES:

Books

Low, Frank J., "Airborne Observatories," *The Astronomy and Astrophysics Encyclopedia,* Van Nostrand Reinhold, 1992, pp. 492–493.

—*Sketch by Sebastian Thaler*

Igor Kurchatov
1903-1960
Russian physicist

In 1956, the government of the Union of Soviet Socialist Republics (U.S.S.R.) announced that Igor Kurchatov had been the leader of its nuclear sciences research project for well over a decade. Until that time, authorities in the West did not know who had been in charge of the development of the Soviet's first atomic bomb, first hydrogen bomb, and early nuclear power plants. Although at least three major works on Kurchatov's life are available in Russian, relatively little has been translated or published about him in English. A major biography by Igor N. Golovin, published in Russian in 1967, is still the primary source for much of what is known about Kurchatov's life. It is known that his early work dealt with electricity and magnetism, but his interests later shifted to nuclear physics. Although he was responsible for the Soviet research program on nuclear weapons during and after World War II, Kurchatov was apparently more interested in the development of peaceful applications of atomic energy. He became a member of the Communist Party in 1948 and two years later was elected to the Supreme Soviet.

Igor Vasilievich Kurchatov was born in Sim, Ufimskaya, Russia, on January 12, 1903, the son of Vasily Alekseevich Kurchatov, a land surveyor, and Maria Vasilievna Kurchatov, a school teacher. When Kurchatov was eight years old his family moved to Simbirsk (now Ulyanovsk) and then, a year later, to Simferopol, where Kurchatov attended the local high school, graduating in 1920. He then enrolled at the University of the Crimea with plans to major in mathematics. Over the next three years, however, his interests shifted to the sciences, and he eventually received his degree in physics in 1923. For two years after his graduation, Kurchatov continued his studies at the Baku Polytechnical Institute. He then accepted Abram F. Ioffe's invitation to join the Leningrad Physico-Technical Institute, of which Ioffe was director, as a research associate. Kurchatov moved to the Institute in 1925 and married in 1927.

Kurchatov's earliest research at Baku and Leningrad dealt with the electrical properties of dielectrics, materials that do not conduct direct electric current. His first important discovery came about during a study of the electrical and magnetic properties of Rochelle salt (sodium potassium tartrate; also known as Seignette's salt). With a colleague, P. P. Kobelko, Kurchatov found that the flow of electricity through this compound can produce a magnetic field somewhat similar to that produced in iron. Kurchatov and Kobeko named the phenomenon *seignetto-electricity,* although it is now known as ferroelectricity.

The 1930s were a period of great excitement in physics because many new discoveries about the atomic nucleus were being made. In response to these discoveries, Kurchatov abandoned his work on electricity to pursue the promising new field of nuclear physics. He began by repeating some of American physicist **Enrico Fermi**'s work on the bombardment of elements with neutrons and, in 1934, first observed nuclear fission during the bombardment of uranium. In the same year, he received his doctorate in physical and mathematical sciences. Among his major accomplishments during this period were his discoveries of the existence of nuclear isomers (compounds that have the same number of atoms but are structurally different), of the phenomenon of nuclear branching, and of the possibility of spontaneous fission in uranium. His primary research interest eventually became the theory of nuclear chain reactions. In 1938, Kurchatov was appointed director of the Nuclear Physics Institute in Leningrad, an institution later renamed the I. V. Kurchatov Institute of Atomic Energy in his honor.

Like their counterparts in the West, Soviet scientists were aware of the potential military applications of nuclear chain reactions. Relatively little was done in this area in the early years of World War II, however, because of the Soviet Union's desperate military situation. Kurchatov himself was assigned, in 1941, to work on methods for demagnetizing ships in order to protect them against floating magnetic mines. He was very successful in this work and was awarded the State Prize, First Degree, for his accomplishments. By 1942, the Soviet government had decided to move forward on the development of an atomic bomb, and Kurchatov was chosen to direct the project. Western scientists knew almost nothing about the Soviet effort but they assumed that the devastation caused by the war and a general lack of knowledge forestalled much of the project's success. They and the world were surprised, therefore, when the Soviets tested their first atomic device on August 29, 1949. The shock was even more profound when, on August 12, 1953, they also successfully tested the world's first fusion (hydrogen) bomb. Credit for the unexpected success of the Soviet nuclear endeavor was ascribed to Kurchatov.

During the late 1950s, Kurchatov became a prominent spokesperson for Soviet science throughout the world. He described his nation's efforts to develop nuclear power and other peaceful applications of atomic energy, both in his own country and in other Eastern Bloc nations. He also continued with his work on the development of particle accelerators, which he had first begun in the 1930s, with the construction of Europe's first cyclotron at Moscow's Radium Institute. Kurchatov died on February 7, 1960, in Moscow. In recognition of his life and work, Soviet scientists have suggested naming element number 104 *kurchatovium,* although no final decision has been made on this proposal.

SELECTED WRITINGS BY KURCHATOV:

Books

Segnetoelektriki (title means "Seignetto-electricity"), [Leningrad-Moscow], 1933.

Rasshcheplenie atomnogo yardra (Problemy sovremennoy fiziki) (title means "The Splitting of the Atomic Nucleus [Problems in Contemporary Physics]"), edited by Abram F. Ioffe, [Moscow-Leningrad], 1935.

SOURCES:

Books

Dictionary of Scientific Biography, Volume 7, Scribner, 1975, pp. 526–527.

Golovin, Igor N., *I. V. Kurchatov,* [Moscow], 1967.

Grinberg, A. P., and V. Ia. Frenkel', *Igor Vasil'evich Kurchatov Institute,* Nauka (Leningrad), 1984.

Vospominania ob Igore Vasilieviche Kurchatove (title means "Recollections about Igor Vasilievich Kurchatov"), edited by Anatolii Aleksandrov, Nauka (Moscow), 1988.

—Sketch by David E. Newton

Thomas Eugene Kurtz
1928-
American statistician and computer scientist

Thomas Eugene Kurtz, cofounder of True BASIC, Inc., was a professor of mathematics and computer science at Dartmouth College for thirty-seven years. During that time, he and **John G. Kemeny**, with whom he collaborated on many projects, designed and developed the Dartmouth Time Sharing System (DTSS) and the computer programming language, Beginner's All-purpose Symbolic Instruction Code, or BASIC. For those accomplishments, Kurtz and Kemeny received the first Pioneer's Day award from the American Federation of Information Processing Society in 1974.

Kurtz was born on February 22, 1928, in Oak Park, Illinois, to Oscar Christ Kurtz, who worked in various capacities at the International Lion's Club headquarters, and Helen Bell Kurtz. Interested in science from his youth, Kurtz entered Knox College in Galesburg, Illinois, with the intention of majoring in physics. He also took all of the mathematics courses available. Following the suggestion of an adviser to consider a career in statistics, which would allow him the opportunity to apply his mathematical

Thomas Eugene Kurtz

skills to many different scientific problems, Kurtz switched majors in his senior year and graduated in 1950 with a B.A. in mathematics.

Kurtz earned his graduate education at Princeton University, where his interest in computing was forged by Forman Acton, a professor of engineering. Acton made it possible for him to spend the summer of 1951 at the Institute of Numerical Analysis, a branch of the National Bureau of Standards located on the University of California at Los Angeles (UCLA) campus. There, in addition to attending lectures on computing, Kurtz interacted with a number of the early computer pioneers, many of whom frequented UCLA during the summer.

From 1952 to 1956, Kurtz served as a research assistant in the Analytical Research Group at Princeton, where he wrote programs to help solve classified research problems, such as those concerned with the effectiveness of air-to-air rocket salvos. The programs were run on an IBM Card Programmed Calculator, and occasionally his job involved tending the machine throughout the night, transferring cards from the output bin back to the input hopper.

Upon graduating from Princeton in 1956 with a Ph.D. in mathematical statistics, Kurtz was recruited by John G. Kemeny, who was chair of Dartmouth's mathematics department. Though Kemeny had previously taught at Princeton until 1953, and had even lived a short distance away from Kurtz at one point, the two scientists had not met before Kurtz was recruited. One of Kurtz's first assignments was as liaison to the New England Regional Computer Center, which had been established at the Massachusetts Institute of Technology (MIT) with funding from IBM and had the provision that educational institutions in the northeast could have access to its facilities. Kurtz spent August of 1956 at MIT, learning assembly language programming—the language that the machine understands—for the center's IBM 704, which was the first commercially available machine with a magnetic core memory.

Develops Dartmouth Time Sharing System

In 1959 Dartmouth finally purchased its own computer, an LGP–30, and Kurtz was appointed director of computing. Initially, the computer was used by just a small fraction of the Dartmouth student body and faculty, but Kurtz felt that all students should be able to use the computing facilities. One of the drawbacks to the widespread use of computers in the late 1950s was that users could not reserve time on a given machine, but had to submit their programs to be processed. The computer would run each request in the order it was received and then store the result. Such "batch processing" meant that users had to wait as much as a day or more to see their results, so that debugging a program could turn into a lengthy and frustrating process. "Time sharing," which allows many people to use a computer simultaneously by having the computer work on each person's problem for short periods of time, avoided the delay, but general-purpose time sharing systems were not available.

In February of 1964, Kurtz and Kemeny began developing a time sharing computer system with the General Electric Corporation. Completed in June, the Dartmouth Time Sharing System, one of the first general-purpose systems of its kind, was comprised in part of one GE–235, which served as the central processors, as well a GE Datanet–30, which handled communications with terminals all over campus. The goal of the project was to make access to computing as simple as checking out a book in the college library. It gave all Dartmouth students, as well as students from area colleges and schools, access to the computer whenever they wished, without the bureaucratic obstacles of forms, permission, and restricted hours. To ensure that this democratic approach worked in practice, the computer gave precedence to small jobs (typically student's programs) as opposed to large ones (typically those submitted by the faculty).

Develops BASIC Computer Programming Language

Having removed one of the primary barriers to computer use, Kurtz and Kemeny went on to simplify the user interface, so that a student could essentially learn enough to use the system in an hour or less. But writing programs in the computer languages then in use was a more challenging task. Though Kurtz initially tried to simplify certain existing languages, namely ALGOL and FORTRAN, Kurtz and Kemeny decided that a new, simplified programming language was needed. The resulting programming language was called Beginner's All-purpose Symbolic Instruction Code, or BASIC, and has become the most widely used language in the world. In 1983, Kurtz, Kemeny and several others formed True BASIC, Inc., with the intention of creating a personal computer version of BASIC for educational purposes.

Between stints as professor of mathematics and computing at Dartmouth, Kurtz served as director of the Kiewit Computation Center from 1966 to 1975, director of the Office of Academic Computing from 1975 to 1978, and vice-chair, 1979 to 1983, and chair, 1983 to 1988, of the Program in Computer and Information Science. Over the years, Kurtz served as principal investigator for various projects supported by the National Science Foundation to promote the use of computers in education. He also participated in many other activities related to the use of computing in teaching, including the Pierce Panel of the President's Scientific Advisory Committee.

From 1974 to 1984, Kurtz chaired a committee of the American National Standards Institute, devoted to developing a national standard for BASIC, which by then existed in many incompatible forms. He served from 1987 to 1994 as convener of an International Standards Organization working group, concerned with developing an international standard for BASIC. Kurtz received an honorary degree from Knox College in 1985, was recognized as a Computer Pioneer by the Institute of Electrical and Electronics Engineers (IEEE) in 1991, and was made a Fellow of the Association for Computer Machinery (ACM) in 1994.

SELECTED WRITINGS BY KURTZ:

Books

Basic Statistics, Prentice-Hall, 1963.

(With J. G. Kemeny) *Basic Programming* Wiley, 1967.

"BASIC," in *History of Programming Languages,* edited by Richard L. Wexelblat, Academic Press, 1981, pp. 515–49.

(With J. G. Kemeny) *Back to BASIC,* Addison-Wesley, 1985.

(With J. G. Kemeny and J. L. Snell) *Computing for a Course in Finite Mathematics,* Addison-Wesley, 1985.

(With J. G. Kemeny) *Structured BASIC Programming,* Wiley, 1987.

—Sketch by Rowan L. Dordick

Raymond Kurzweil
1948-
American inventor

Raymond Kurzweil is recognized as one of the leading inventors in the United States and an authority on artificial intelligence of the 1990s. He unveiled his ground-breaking invention, a reading machine that scans written text and turns it into synthesized speech, in 1976 when he was twenty-eight years old. The Kurzweil Reading Machine is considered the world's first consumer product that successfully incorporates artificial intelligence technology, and marks just one of many technological breakthroughs for Kurzweil in this field. In 1984, he produced a computer music keyboard that accurately reproduces the sounds of the grand piano and other orchestral instruments, and in 1987, he produced the first commercially marketed large vocabulary speech recognition technology. Kurzweil founded three companies to develop and market these products: Kurzweil Computer Products, Inc., Kurzweil Music Systems Inc., and Kurzweil Applied Intelligence, Inc.

Inventive at an Early Age

Precocious from an early age, Raymond C. Kurzweil has said that he knew he would be a scientist from the time he was about five years old. He was born on February 12, 1948, in Queens, New York, and was greatly influenced by a family of accomplished and independent thinkers. His father, Fredric, was a concert pianist and conductor who taught the young Kurzweil to play the piano. His mother, Hannah, was an artist, and one of his uncles was an inventor. Kurzweil built his own computer when he was twelve years old and soon thereafter wrote a statistical program that IBM later distributed to its customers. He won first prize in the International Science Fair in high school for developing an expert system that both analyzed the style of Mozart's compositions and composed new music in that style.

Kurzweil attended the Massachusetts Institute of Technology (MIT), where he majored in computer science and literature. Although he maintained top grades, he was known as "The Phantom" for being conspicuously absent from normal college activities while he worked on his own projects. In one of those projects, he developed a computer program that helped match high school students with appropriate colleges. By the time he completed his B.S. in 1970, the entrepreneur in Kurzweil was fully established as he sold the college matching program to Harcourt Brace Jovanovich for one hundred thousand dollars, plus royalties.

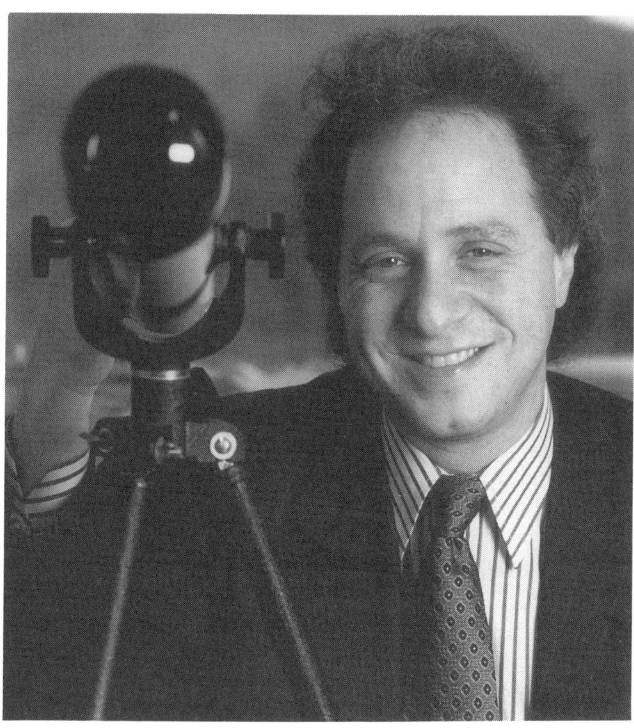

Raymond Kurzweil

At MIT, Kurzweil was influenced by such leaders in the artificial intelligence field as computer scientist **Marvin Minsky**, who founded MIT's Artificial Intelligence Laboratory. Determined to devote his energies to technology that would impact the lives of individuals, Kurzweil, soon after graduating, dedicated himself to the problem of pattern recognition, or the ability of a machine to distinguish one letter from another.

Artificial Intelligence Solves Pattern Recognition Problems

Pattern recognition technology did exist at the time, but it had limited capabilities. Kurzweil attempted to refine and expand the technology by applying principles of artificial intelligence to the problem. By the mid–1970s, he had formulated an approach for his omni-font optical character recognition program, in which any character in any typeface could be recognized and distinguished from others. Kurzweil decided to apply the technology to a practical purpose. He wanted to develop a machine that would convert the printed word into the spoken one.

But first, he had to define hundreds of pronunciation rules and thousands of explanations, and apply them to the words that were scanned into the computer from a book. Following this processing, the computer could assemble the information into discrete sets of "phonemes", or sounds, which could be articulated by a speech synthesizer to complete the process. In 1974, Kurzweil founded his first company—Kurzweil Computer Products, Inc.—to work on these problems. In quintessential entrepreneurial form, the company was underfunded, resources were scarce, and the young Kurzweil had to pawn his own possessions to keep it running. But within two years, he had developed the first print-to-speech reading machine, known as the Kurzweil Reading Machine; the system has been hailed as the most significant reading aid for the blind since Braille.

By this time Kurzweil had married Sonya Rosenwald, a psychologist, with whom he later had two children: Ethan and Amy. In the early 1980s Kurzweil sold Kurzweil Computer Products, Inc., to Xerox Imaging Systems for approximately six million dollars, and at the suggestion of blind musician Stevie Wonder (who had used one of the first Kurzweil Reading Machines), he then turned his energies to music. The result of his work was an electronic synthesizer that reproduced the rich sounds of orchestral instruments. The Kurzweil Music System makes use of artificial intelligence-based pattern recognition techniques to analyze and create sound models for musical instruments. The sound models can be stored in computer memory and used to re-create a desired sound at will.

Keenly interested in moving on to new problems, Kurzweil also sold the music system business, to Young Chang Akki Co., Ltd. In 1982, he founded Kurzweil Applied Intelligence, Inc., which is the largest speech recognition company in the world; he serves as both chair and co-chief executive officer of the organization. By the latter part of the 1980s, he had developed the first commercially marketed large vocabulary speech recognition technology; among the products in this area is the Kurzweil VoiceWriter, which can recognize approximately ten thousand words. Throughout his career, Kurzweil has received numerous awards and honors. He was named honorary chair for innovation for the White House Conference on Small Business by President Ronald Reagan in 1986. In 1988, he was named Inventor of the Year by MIT, the Boston Museum of Science, and the Boston Patent Law Association, and in 1990, he was voted Engineer of the Year by over one million readers of *Design News* magazine and received the publication's Technology Achievement Award. The Associated Services for the Blind presented Kurzweil with the Louis Braille Award in 1991, and he received the Massachusetts Quincentennial Award for Innovations and Discovery in 1992. Kurzweil also has received several honorary doctorates in science, engineering, music, and humane letters.

SELECTED WRITINGS BY RAYMOND KURZWEIL:

Books

The Age of Intelligent Machines, MIT Press, 1990.

The Ten Percent Solution for a Healthy Life: How to Eliminate Virtually All Risk of Heart Disease and Cancer, Crown, 1993.

Other

The Age of Intelligent Machines (documentary film), MIT Press, 1987.

SOURCES:

Books

Brown, Kenneth A., *Inventors at Work: Interviews with 16 Notable American Inventors,* foreword by James Burke, Tempus Books, 1988.

Gilder, George, *Microcosm: The Quantum Revolution in Economics and Technology,* Simon & Schuster, 1989.

Periodicals

Lipner, Maxine, "Raymond Kurzweil Invents His Own Success," *Compass Readings,* April, 1990, pp. 24–29.

Maloney, Lawrence D., "Technical Visionary," *Design News,* February 12, 1990, pp. 74–83.

Zeigler, Edward, "The Magic Machines of Ray Kurzweil," *Reader's Digest,* February, 1991, pp. 119–122.

—*Sketch by Olga K. Anderson*

Polycarp Kusch
1911-
German-born American physicist

Polycarp Kusch entered the field of physics along the newly established path of quantum electrodynamics. But like all great scientists, he left the known path to blaze a trail. His work helped to reshape the basic principles of atomic theory by demonstrating conclusively that the magnetic properties of the electron were not in agreement with existing theories. These studies of the so-called magnetic moment of the electron won for him the Nobel Prize in physics in 1955, which he shared with **Willis E. Lamb, Jr.**. The discovery also led to the development of an even more sophisticated theory of how light and matter interact, that is, the theory of quantum electrodynamics.

Kusch was born on January 26, 1911, in Blankenburg, Germany, to John Matthias Kusch, a Lutheran missionary, and his wife, Henrietta. He was named for Saint Polycarp, a second-century bishop and martyr, whose feast day is January 26. Polycarp's father brought the family to the United States in 1912, where they led a somewhat unsettled existence until John Kusch took a position with a book publisher in Cleveland, Ohio.

Young Polycarp, who became a naturalized citizen of the United States in 1923, attended public schools in Cleveland, and in 1927 matriculated at Cleveland's Case School of Applied Science (later renamed Case Western Reserve University), where he intended to study chemistry. He became a physics major instead, and received his B.S. in 1931. Polycarp was one of only a few in his school who majored in physics. Years later, Kusch told the *Columbia Alumni News,* "From the start I felt more adapted to physics than to something like engineering. To me engineering was a matter of cook books and heavy economic motivations." He continued his study of physics at the University of Illinois, where he held a graduate assistantship; he earned his M.Sc. degree in 1933 and his Ph.D. in 1936. While at the university, he met Edith Starr McRoberts, whom he married on August 12, 1935, and with whom he had three daughters, Kathryn, Judith, and Sara.

In 1937 Kusch became a research assistant to John T. Tate at the University of Minnesota. He became skilled at using mass spectroscopy, a technique that determines relative atomic masses by shooting electrically charged atoms and molecules through a magnetic field, where they are deflected with a force that depends on their mass. Through the support of Tate, Kusch received an appointment as an instructor at Columbia University in 1937 and went to work in the laboratory of **I. I. Rabi**. He had the fortune to participate in the first magnetic resonance absorption experiment, a type of spectroscopy with various applications in which atoms placed in a magnetic field and irradiated with electromagnetic energy in the radio wave region absorb part of the radiation. Different atoms absorb at different frequencies, which are monitored by a detector. The research garnered Rabi a Nobel Prize in 1944. Kusch stayed at Columbia until 1941, when he joined a team of researchers at the Westinghouse Laboratories in Bloomfield, Pennsylvania. There he contributed to the development of vacuum tubes, a critical component of radar that greatly assisted the U.S. defense effort during World War II. Kusch returned to Columbia in 1942 as a research associate until moving on to Bell Telephone Laboratories to work on vacuum tubes and microwave generators. Four years later, at the invitation of Rabi, Kusch accepted a position as associate professor of physics, and once again returned to New York. He was made a full professor in 1949 and served as chairman of the physics department from 1949 to 1952.

Lays Foundation for New Field in Physics

In 1947, while doing research in quantum mechanics (the branch of physics that deals with the behavior of matter at atomic and subatomic levels), Kusch completed his studies on the magnetic properties of electrons that won for him the Nobel Prize. Kusch and Henry Foley, his colleague at Columbia, changed the energy levels of atoms in a magnetic field by exposing them to high-frequency radio waves. Kusch and Foley observed the atoms, identifying those with electrons that had a specific magnetic abnormality that would make them easily identifiable. Through this magnetic and radio wave manipulation of atoms, the two researchers were able to observe minute variations in the magnetic characteristics of the electrons spinning around the atomic nuclei. Subsequent calculations based on this data demonstrated that earlier calculations by Nobel Prize winner **Paul Dirac** had underestimated the strength of the electron's magnetic charge by at least 0.125 percent.

The discovery led to the development of a set of scientific principles that formed the basis of a new field in physics. This new field, established by Dirac, **Werner K. Heisenberg**, and **Wolfgang Pauli**, is called quantum electrodynamics, the study of properties of electromagnetic radiation and its interaction with electrically charged matter, specifically, atoms and their electrons. The importance of quantum electrodynamics is immeasurable, in the sense that almost all phenomena readily perceived by the human senses are thought to be ultimately reducible to and understandable in terms of its laws.

Becomes Active in Administration and Public Policy

Kusch held the chair of the department of physics at Columbia again from 1960 to 1963. In May 1968 he was appointed to the executive committee of the faculty, which represented the faculty to the university during deliberations on the future of the university. In June 1968 the committee appointed a fact-finding commission headed by Archibald Cox to investigate the causes of a student uprising on campus that occurred during the restive school year and reflected changing attitudes of students to the role of universities in society, the responsibility of government to people, and the increasingly unpopular war in Vietnam.

Following the death of his first wife in 1959, Kusch married Betty Jane Pezzoni in 1960, with whom he would have two more daughters, Diana and Maria. Kusch was promoted to academic vice president and provost in 1969, a post he held until 1972.

While at Columbia, Kusch's meticulous work in the laboratory was reflected in his approach to teaching freshman and sophomore physics and graduate seminars. Rather than dispensing large amounts of scientific information, he preferred to give students a strong grounding in scientific technique in the context of a more limited amount of data. In fact, as a member of the Columbia College Committee on Instruction, he blocked institution of broad, undergraduate survey courses in the sciences, insisting that such a course of instruction would tempt instructors to make too many dogmatic statements. He preferred instead to offer analyses of selected scientific problems.

His knack for using science to solve problems was reflected in his prescient comments to the *New York Times Magazine* in 1962 concerning the role physics would play in the development of future technologies. Kusch ventured that advances in solid-state physics—the electric, magnetic, and other properties of solid substances—would expand beyond the simple transistor, computers, and tiny hearing aids. He predicted the development of wristwatch radio transmitters and receivers and television-telephones, two devices that by the early 1990s were being touted by scientists as inevitable. Kusch also predicted the current flurry of research into new materials such as metals and ceramics that have previously unattainable strength, as well as the appeal of superconducting materials that lose resistance to electrical flow at extremely low temperatures.

Kusch's interests ranged far from the laboratory, however, and included problems of overpopulation. In 1961, during the celebration of Columbia College's fiftieth annual Dean's Day reported in the *New York Times,* Kusch noted that "there is often a foolish, a pathetic or downright dangerous belief in the power of science to do anything at all. . . . No amount of scientific skill can find a way of feeding an indefinite expansion of the world's population." In 1966 he joined three other Nobel laureates testifying before a Senate Government Operations subcommittee on the need to curb the growth of the world's population in order to avoid starvation, social disruption, and the consequent interruption of scientific and intellectual progress. In 1972 Kusch accepted a professorship at the University of Texas, Dallas, where he was Eugene McDermott Professor from 1974 to 1980, and became Regental Professor Emeritus in 1982.

Kusch was elected to the National Academy of Sciences in 1956, and in 1959 Columbia University's Society of Older Graduates (graduates of Columbia College and the School of Engineering who received their degrees at least thirty years before) awarded Kusch its Great Teacher Award at the society's forty-ninth annual dinner meeting. According to the *New York Times,* the award citation read in part, "His search is not only for new knowledge but for those budding scientists from whom will come the important discoveries of a new generation." Columbia honored him again in 1961 by bestowing upon him the Alexander Hamilton Medal, presented annually by the Association of the Alumni of Columbia College to alumni or faculty members for "distinguished service in any field of human endeavor."

He received the Illinois Achievement award from the University of Illinois (1975) and was a fellow of both the Center for Advanced Study in Behavioral Sciences (1964–65), and the American Physical Society, a member of the American Association for the Advancement of Science, American Academy of Arts and Sciences, and the American Philosophical Society.

SELECTED WRITINGS BY KUSCH:

Periodicals

Kusch, P., and H. M. Foley, "The Magnetic Moment of the Electron," *Physical Review,* Volume 74, number 3, 1948, pp. 250–263.

"Hyperfine Structure by the Method of Atomic Beams: Properties of Nuclei and of the Electron," *Physics,* Volume 17, numbers 3–4, 1951, pp. 339–353.

"Analysis of the Band System of the Sodium Molecule," *Journal of Chemical Physics,* Volume 68, 1978.

SOURCES:

Books

Magill, Frank N., editor, *The Nobel Prize Winners: Physics,* Volume 2, *1938- 1967,* Salem Press, 1989, pp. 665–672.

Periodicals

Columbia Alumni News, January, 1952.

"Columbia Names Dr. Kusch, Nobel Physicist, as Vice President," *New York Times,* March 5, 1969, p. 1.

Cooley, Donald G. "Scientist's Show Goes on the Road," *New York Times Magazine,* February 16, 1958, p. 38.

"'Dark Age' Feared in Population Rise," *New York Times,* January 20, 1966, p. L21.

Galton, Lawrence, "Science Stands at Awesome Thresholds," *New York Times Magazine,* December 2, 1962, pp. 38–39, 90–94.

Pfeiffer, John, "The Basic Need for Basic Research," *New York Times Magazine,* November 24, 1967, pp. 23, 93–98.

WOLVERHAMPTON PUBLIC LIBRARIES

—Sketch by Marc Kusinitz

WOLVERHAMPTON
19 FEB 1996
REFERENCE LIBRARY